THE GREAT STAGE STARS

THE GREAT STAGE STARS

Distinguished theatrical careers of the past and present

SHERIDAN MORLEY

Facts On File Publications
New York, New York ● Oxford, England

First published in the United States by
Facts On File, Inc.
460 Park Avenue South
New York, New York 10016 in 1986
First published in the United Kingdom by
Angus & Robertson (UK) Ltd in 1986
First published in Australia by
Angus & Robertson Publishers in 1986

Library of Congress Cataloging-in-Publication Data
Morley, Sheridan, 1941-
   The great stage stars.

   1. Actors — Great Britain — Biography — Dictionaries.
   2. Actors — United States — Biography — Dictionaries.
   I. Title.
   PN2597.M64 1986 792'.028'0922 [B] 85-27548
   ISBN 0-8160-1401-9

Printed in Singapore

For Margaret,
whose book this really is.

• The Great Stage Stars •

Janet ACHURCH • Maude ADAMS • Max ADRIAN • Henry AINLEY

Meggie ALBANESI • Ira ALDRIDGE • George ALEXANDER

Edward ALLEYN • Sara ALLGOOD • Judith ANDERSON • Mary ANDERSON

Harry ANDREWS • George ARLISS • Yvonne ARNAUD • Oscar ASCHE

Peggy ASHCROFT • Adele ASTAIRE • Fred ASTAIRE • Robert ATKINS

Alan BADEL • Anne BANCROFT • Lady BANCROFT • Squire BANCROFT

Tallulah BANKHEAD • Jean-Louis BARRAULT • Ethel BARRYMORE

John BARRYMORE • Lionel BARRYMORE • Maurice BARRYMORE

Alan BATES • Barbara BEL GEDDES • Frank BENSON • Elisabeth BERGNER

Sarah BERNHARDT • Master BETTY • Claire BLOOM • Ray BOLGER

Edwin Thomas BOOTH • John Wilkes BOOTH • Junius Brutus BOOTH

Shirley BOOTH • Dion BOUCICAULT • Fanny BRICE

Richard BRIERS • Pamela BROWN • Yul BRYNNER

Richard BURTON • Douglas BYNG • Mrs Patrick CAMPBELL

Morris CARNOVSKY • Carol CHANNING • John CLEMENTS

Alec CLUNES • George M. COHAN • Constance COLLIER • Fay COMPTON

Gladys COOPER • Katharine CORNELL • Tom COURTENAY

Cicely COURTNEIDGE • Noel COWARD • Jane COWL • Lotta CRABTREE

Michael CRAWFORD • Hume CRONYN • Constance CUMMINGS

Cyril CUSACK • Jim DALE • Phyllis DARE • Zena DARE

Judi DENCH • Marlene DIETRICH • Alfred DRAKE • Ruth DRAPER

Georgie DREW • John DREW • Mrs John DREW • John DREW II

Gerald DU MAURIER • Eleonora DUSE • Jeanne EAGELS • Maxine ELLIOTT

• THE GREAT STAGE STARS •

Edith EVANS • Maurice EVANS • Albert FINNEY

Minnie MADDERN FISKE • Lynn FONTANNE

Johnston FORBES-ROBERTSON • David GARRICK • John GIELGUD

William GILLETTE • Hermione GINGOLD • Lillian GISH

Joyce GRENFELL • Alec GUINNESS • Lucien GUITRY • Sacha GUITRY

Uta HAGEN • Kay HAMMOND • Cedric HARDWICKE • Julie HARRIS

Rosemary HARRIS • Rex HARRISON • Charles HAWTREY • Helen HAYES

Eileen HERLIE • Wendy HILLER • Stanley HOLLOWAY • Michael HORDERN

Alan HOWARD • Bobby HOWES • Jack HULBERT • Henry IRVING

Glenda JACKSON • Derek JACOBI • Joseph JEFFERSON • Celia JOHNSON

James Earl JONES • Edmund KEAN • Charles KEMBLE • Elizabeth KEMBLE

Fanny KEMBLE • Frances KEMBLE • John Philip KEMBLE • Roger KEMBLE

Sally KEMBLE • Stephen KEMBLE • Madge KENDAL • Bert LAHR

Lillie LANGTRY • Angela LANSBURY • Charles LAUGHTON

Gertrude LAWRENCE • Wilfrid LAWSON • Evelyn LAYE

Eva LE GALLIENNE • Vivien LEIGH • Margaret LEIGHTON

Lotte LENYA • Beatrice LILLIE • Roger LIVESEY • Robert LORAINE

Alfred LUNT • Alec McCOWEN • Geraldine McEWAN • Ian McKELLEN

Siobhan McKENNA • Micheál MacLIAMMOIR • William Charles MACREADY

Fredric MARCH • Julia MARLOWE • Mary MARTIN • Raymond MASSEY

Jessie MATTHEWS • Ethel MERMAN • Bernard MILES

Helena MODJESKA • Robert MORLEY • Zero MOSTEL • Owen NARES

Anna NEAGLE • John NEVILLE • Ivor NOVELLO • Laurence OLIVIER

• THE GREAT STAGE STARS •

James O'NEILL • Peter O'TOOLE • Geraldine PAGE • Lilli PALMER

Joan PLOWRIGHT • Christopher PLUMMER • Eric PORTMAN

Robert PRESTON • Anthony QUAYLE • Denis QUILLEY • RACHEL

Michael REDGRAVE • Vanessa REDGRAVE • Ralph RICHARDSON

Diana RIGG • Adelaide RISTORI • Cyril RITCHARD • Brian RIX

Jason ROBARDS • Paul ROBESON • Flora ROBSON

Margaret RUTHERFORD • Paul SCOFIELD • Sarah SIDDONS

Donald SINDEN • Otis SKINNER • Maggie SMITH • E. H. SOTHERN

Robert SPEAIGHT • Kim STANLEY • Maureen STAPLETON

Tommy STEELE • Elaine STRITCH • Jessica TANDY

Laurette TAYLOR • Godfrey TEARLE • Marie TEMPEST

Ellaline TERRISS • Ellen TERRY • Sybil THORNDIKE

Herbert BEERBOHM TREE • Dorothy TUTIN • Peter USTINOV

Frederick VALK • Irene VANBRUGH • Gwen VERDON • Madame VESTRIS

David WARNER • Ethel WATERS • Orson WELLES • Emlyn WILLIAMS

Nicol WILLIAMSON • Peg WOFFINGTON • Donald WOLFIT

Irene WORTH • Charles WYNDHAM

LIST OF PLATES
In alphabetical order:

ACKNOWLEDGEMENTS

Photographs have been reproduced by permission of:

The Bettmann Archive, New York
The BBC Hulton Picture Library, London
The Kobal Collection, London
The Mansell Collection, London
Alastair Muir, London
The Board of Trustees of the Victoria and Albert Museum, London

INTRODUCTION

When, some twenty years ago now, I was a novice book reviewer faced with the daunting task of writing critically about an encyclopaedia of several hundred pages on a subject of which I knew all too little, an older and more cynical newspaper colleague told me simply to work out what the authors had been forced through lack of space to omit, and complain about that. It was advice which, if followed here, should give critics of this volume several happy paragraphs. Even an apparently simple and straightforward, indeed monosyllabic, title begs several questions: How Great? What Stage? What do I mean by Stars?

First, then, an explanation and a definition: this volume was conceived a decade ago by the then editorial director of Angus & Robertson as a companion to David Shipman's *The Great Movie Stars*. That was already running to two volumes, 450 entries and roughly 1000 pages, but I thought it might just be possible (given that the theatre has always been more selective than the cinema in bestowing stardom on its workers) to get the stage stars into one volume provided that certain rigid limitations were imposed. Most members of most audiences of most theatres in the world could name 200 of their own favourite stage stars, and those lists might only overlap by about 50 per cent. I knew, therefore, that the 200 to whom I was limited by the space at my disposal could not simply be critical favourites, nor even the 200 with whom I would most like to be shipwrecked on some desert island. Instead, they would have to pass a rigid test, devised after a lot of trial and error, which was this: could the candidate for inclusion create advance booking at a theatre box office before the first night, when appearing in a new and unknown play by a new and unknown author with an unknown supporting cast, and moreover could he or she do so without relying on fame acquired in the cinema or on television?

Once that basic rule had been devised, certain further limitations had to be imposed in order to keep the list down to a feasible length: if, for instance, the star had a distinguished stage record but had first or chiefly achieved fame in the cinema, then there would be no point in cataloguing his or her career here as it would already be found in Shipman. Then again, what about stars of the non-English-speaking theatre? These, I decided, should only be included if they had made a lasting impact in drama, musicals or comedies on the British, American or Australian stage. And 'drama, musicals or comedies' is another important qualification: this is not an encyclopaedia of opera, or ballet, or mime, or circuses: by 'stage' I mean what *Variety* has always meant by the more graphic description 'legit'. How about stars of the past? Again, they would only qualify if their fame genuinely lives on in critical or popular interest — had they, for instance, in the past twenty years been the subject of a new biography? And how about the stars of tomorrow? Rather than making a series of random guesses, since drama critics are not necessarily also qualified to be racing tipsters, I went for actors and actresses with an already proven track record, if only on a local level. An early King Lear or Hedda Gabler, even in less than ideal conditions, is usually some sort of indication of how a career is going to shape up.

I am by trade a critic, but I do not necessarily regard this as a critical volume: it is not a personal Top 200 but an attempt at pure information. Who opened when, where, in what and to what contemporary reaction? It may well be argued (as it often is of my drama books) that my concept of stardom is weighted towards the commercial rather than the academic or company theatre, to which I would reply simply that stardom is in fact a commercial concept. A great star may well emerge from a company theatre, as indeed many have over the last two decades, but a company theatre cannot sustain a star: he or she has then to be tested in the marketplace of Shaftesbury Avenue or Broadway. Nor do I see, in this context, any difference between the stardom of, say, Ralph Richardson and that of Ethel Merman . . . both were great blazing stars who fulfilled all the requirements for inclusion here, and then some.

And one last but hugely important acknowledgement: grateful as I am to my patient and wonderful editor Candida Hunt, this book would not have been remotely possible without the work done on it from the very beginning by my wife Margaret. Anything good here is hers; any mistakes are mine alone.

JANET ACHURCH

Bernard Shaw called her 'the only tragic actress of genius we now possess' and for several years his critical devotion to her was matched only by his equally strong loathing of Henry Irving. She repaid Shaw by playing both his Candida and his Cecily Waynflete in *Captain Brassbound's Conversion* at the Strand Theatre in 1900. However, her real fame rested on her being the very first English actress ever to play Ibsen.

Janet Achurch was born in Lancashire in 1864. A feminist before her time, she began her London career working with Genevieve Ward, and was at the Adelphi in *Harbour Lights* before joining Beerbohm Tree's company for three productions.

Then, in 1899, she was a triumphant Nora in *A Doll's House* and soon after that she formed her own company to tour Australia, India and America. Seven years later, still with her own company, she produced Ibsen's *Little Eyolf* at the Avenue Theatre, casting herself as Rita and Mrs Patrick Campbell (her successor in Shaw's affections) as the Rat Wife.

With her husband, the actor Charles Charrington, she then continued to tour, and theirs was the first British theatrical troupe ever to play Cairo. But her later career was marred by an addiction to morphia and cocaine and by constant domestic struggles in which she was not much helped by a financially inept husband. When she died, on 11 September 1916 aged only 52, she had already been off the stage for three years. Shaw took the view that his beloved Candida had allowed debts and drugs and carelessness to destroy her own great career; 'vice,' he once wrote, 'is a waste of life,' and certainly the later Achurch–Charrington years were closer to a Victorian melodrama of marital squalor than the brave feminism of Nora slamming her Doll's House door. But the *Times* obituary as usual said it all: 'Died: Mrs Charles Charrington, better known as Janet Achurch, whose wonderful performance in the first English production of *A Doll's House* was the talk of London for many a day.'

MAUDE ADAMS

Born in Salt Lake City on 11 November 1872, Maude Adams was one of the first great stars of the American stage, although her career began haltingly and came to an abrupt end after the death of her manager, Charles Frohman, who went down with the *Lusitania* in 1917. She began her stage life traditionally enough, being carried on as a baby by her mother, who was then leading lady of the Salt Lake City stock company. At the age of five she was already playing in San Francisco alongside an equally youthful David Belasco, and at 16 opposite E. H. Sothern.

In 1892 Frohman first engaged her to lead a company with John Drew. By that time she had, she said, been employed to 'dance, sing, and tumble about in farce for far longer than is necessary for the development of genius'. At first Frohman regarded her, in political terms, as 'a rather doubtful precinct with only about half the votes counted'. Yet she went on to become the first-ever American Peter Pan and to create most of

the major J. M. Barrie roles for Broadway. She was also a notable Portia, Rosalind and Joan of Arc, and scored another success in the Bernhardt role as *L'Aiglon*. Her early career was, in the words of Amy Leslie, 'a triumph of undoubted persistence', and another critic added: 'She is a bony young woman who tries very hard to use her feet and hands as if they were not hinged on wires . . . She is appealing, direct and a soothing artist whose keen mental digestion is one of the healthiest elements in her work.'

Following Frohman's tragic death at sea, Maude Adams retired from the stage and did not attempt a comeback until 1931, when she played Portia to Otis Skinner's Shylock, a performance so disastrous that it was thought wiser she should not open on Broadway. When she died, on 17 July 1953, she had been effectively retired from the stage for almost forty years but had been working as a professor of drama at Stephens College in Columbia, Missouri.

MAX
ADRIAN

'*A*n actor who could make the fantastic seem no more than everyday, with a voice like no other on the English stage — vestigially Irish and harshly attractive,' said the *Times*, but the really remarkable aspect of Max Adrian's career was the way he divided it almost equally between the major classics and starring appearances in intimate revue.

Adrian was born in Ireland on 1 November 1903. He was educated at the Portora Royal School in Enniskillen, half a century after another distinguished pupil of that establishment, Oscar Wilde. He made his stage début on the Isle of Man in August 1926, appearing in the chorus of *Katja the Dancer*. He then toured with *Lady Be Good* and *The Blue Train*, made his London début walking on in *The Squall* at the Globe in December 1927, and went on to work first with Tod Slaughter's company at Peterborough and then for two years in the Northampton Rep. In 1934 he opened on Broadway in a play called *College Sinners*, but despite a vast range of work in London and the provinces during the 1930s (he was Starkey in a 1937 Palladium *Peter Pan*), he did not really make his name until a remarkable nine-month season at the Westminster from September 1938, during which he played Pandarus in a modern-dress *Troilus and Cressida* and Bloomfield Bonnington in *The Doctor's Dilemma*.

He continued this distinguished classical work with Gielgud's company at the Haymarket during the war (Osric, Puck and Tattle), but then at the Lyric, Hammersmith, in 1947 began a series of revues (*Tuppence Coloured, Oranges and Lemons, Penny Plain, Airs on a Shoestring* and *Fresh Airs*) which established him in post-war eyes as a superlative — if eccentric — light comedian. The revues were united by his continuing presence, the contributions of — among many others — Flanders and Swann, and the direction of Adrian's close and constant friend, Laurier Lister. But with the decline in the fortunes of revue as a theatrical form in the mid-fifties, Adrian went back to America to appear as Pangloss in the Leonard Bernstein–Tyrone Guthrie *Candide*. He stayed there to work in summer stock for two or three years. When he returned to London, it was for a short-lived Noel Coward adaptation of a Feydeau farce, *Look After Lulu*.

There was, therefore, considerable surprise among those who had forgotten his extensive classical experience (including a splendidly camp Dauphin in Olivier's film of *Henry V*) when Peter

Hall invited him to join the newly born Royal Shakespeare Company at Stratford in 1960 to recreate his celebrated Pandarus (no longer in modern dress) and also to play Feste in *Twelfth Night* that season. He was to spend the next three years with the RSC in a vast range of highly impressive works (*The Duchess of Malfi, The Devils, The Hollow Crown*), and having launched the RSC at the Aldwych in one of their golden periods, he then pulled off a remarkable double by leaving them in 1963 to take part in the opening productions of the National Theatre Company at Chichester and the Old Vic. Here, for Olivier, he played the Inquisitor in *Saint Joan*, Serebryakov in *Uncle Vanya*, Balance in *The Recruiting Officer* and Brovik in *The Master Builder*. Two years later, he made the double into a treble. Having been in the inaugural seasons of the RSC at the Aldwych and the NT at the Vic, he was then invited to join the company that was to open the new Yvonne Arnaud Theatre at Guildford, where his friend Lister was to be the first artistic director.

At Guildford, close to where he and Lister then lived, he spent the seasons of 1965, 1966 and 1967; he also played a season there in 1969 but by now, despite failing health, his time was increasingly taken up with a highly successful one-man show about Shaw, *An Evening with GBS*, which he played not only in London and on Broadway, but also toured to Cyprus, the Far East, Africa, India and Australia as well as coast-to-coast across the United States. A less successful solo show about Gilbert and Sullivan followed in 1969, but it is the Shaw evening for which he will, I think, be best remembered. It was in the best traditions of Gielgud's Shakespeare solo and Emlyn Williams as Dickens; it took GBS from a young, red-bearded opera critic through half a century to a caustic old man remembering past glories. It was a remarkable tribute to Adrian's stagecraft and his recollections of his Irish ancestry. Late in his career he also became a favourite actor of the flamboyant director Ken Russell, for whom he made a superlative television appearance as Delius and later appeared to rather less effect in the films *The Boy Friend*, *The Music Lovers* and *The Devils*.

Adrian was essentially, as many critics noted, both a miniaturist and a caricaturist; his revue technique produced instant stage impressions, but they linger in the memory long after more intricate creations have faded. He was Peter Pan run to seed, an infinitely sinister Puck and a brilliant stage comedian. He died on 19 January 1973.

HENRY AINLEY

One of the great jobbing actors of the British theatre between the wars (though worth barely £3000 at his death), Henry Hinchcliffe Ainley was born in Leeds on 21 August 1879. He started out as a bank cashier in Sheffield and was a keen amateur actor in his spare time. Ainley met Sir George Alexander when the latter was on tour, and joined his company to walk on in *The Masqueraders* at Leeds. Later, he was to bridge the stylistic gap between the old actor–managers, such as Alexander, and the post-war realists.

He joined Benson's Shakespeare company and made his London début at the Lyceum in 1900 playing Gloucester in *Henry V*. The next three years he spent in Alexander's company at the St James's; but it was in New York that he got his first real break, playing leading roles opposite Maude Adams for Frohman in the 1903–04 season.

Returning to England, he became Lena Ashwell's leading man at the Savoy, and also worked for the Vedrenne–Barker management at the Royal Court. In December 1906 he replaced Gerald du Maurier as Raffles, in 1907 he was Orlando in an Oscar Asche production of *As You Like It*, and in 1908 he played the title role in Tree's production of *Faust* at His Majesty's.

Ainley then turned exclusively Shakespearian for a time. In 1909 he was a Stratford Shylock; a year later, in the Shakespeare Festival at His Majesty's, he played — within the space of two months — Cassius, Laertes, Bassanio and John of Gaunt. In 1911 he had one of his most popular successes at the Lyceum as Rudolf in *The Prisoner of Zenda*. He then did a memorable Leontes/Malvolio double at the Savoy and went into the long-running *Great Adventure*.

'Harry' Ainley served in the army in France and Italy during the First World War, and in 1919 took over the management of the St James's Theatre with Gilbert Miller. Here he played Mark Antony and the Hook/Darling double in a 1920 *Peter Pan* before parting company with Miller and doing a Prospero at the Aldwych and a long, modern-dress run in *If* with Gladys Cooper. Then came *The Dover Road* and another spell in management, this time at His Majesty's, where he again enjoyed long runs in the title roles of *Oliver Cromwell* and *Hassan*. By 1926 he was managing the New Theatre and a year later played Macbeth in a production by Sybil Thorndike in which she, of course, played his Lady.

Illness then kept Ainley away from the theatre until 1929, when he started an eighteen-month run as James Fraser in *The First Mrs Fraser* at the Haymarket, where he also found time to arrange and star in a Royal Command performance of *Hamlet*. In 1931 he created Dr Knox in *The Anatomist* and a year later the Archangel — again in a Bridie play, this one *Tobias and the Angel*. Further illness then forced his retirement, though he did return to the stage for a single performance of *Hassan* in 1938 and also did considerable pioneer work in radio drama for the BBC, notably as Jean Valjean in *Les Misérables* and in many of his famous stage roles.

His first film was made in 1915; his last was the Olivier–Bergner 1936 *As You Like It* in which he played the old Exiled Duke. He was also a memorable silent Prisoner of Zenda on screen. Twice married (to Suzanne Sheldon and Elaine Fearon) and twice divorced, he had two children, one of whom was the actor Richard Ainley.

'I blame nature,' wrote James Agate in his *Ego* when Ainley died (on 31 October 1945), 'for having given this near-great actor too much and not enough. For having lavished on him a form like Hamlet's father and a voice like a cathedral organ but then drawing back her hand and giving a man physically endowed to play tragedy, the instincts of a comedian. Only in the lower reaches did Ainley achieve anything that could be called greatness.'

MEGGIE ALBANESI

A tragically short-lived West End star, Meggie Albanesi was born in Kent on 8 October 1899, trained under Helen Hayes, and made her name in a range of work from Jill in *The Skin Game* through *Trelawney of the 'Wells'* to Mabel in *Loyalties*.

When her blazing light was abruptly extinguished on 9 December 1923, John Galsworthy wrote: 'She had a various and unique faculty — that of emotional truth. I never saw her (and I watched her through some sixty rehearsals) fumble, blur or falsify an emotional effect; but she had real devotion to her art, great quickness to seize shades of meaning, and a brain which she did not hesitate to use. She was not limited. She would have gone very far. Not often does Death so wastefully spill.'

Albanesi was the daughter of an Italian violin teacher at the Royal Academy of Music and his novelist wife Maria. She first studied the piano but then, at 17, went to RADA, where she won the Bancroft Gold Medal for her rendering of Lady Teazle. She then understudied in *Dear Brutus* before being discovered by Basil Dean and being given a leading role in, first, *The Skin Game* and then Clemence Dane's *A Bill of Divorcement* (1921). Dane later wrote of that first night: 'I can never forget the audience shouting, ''Meggie, we want Meggie,'' after the fashion of modern teenagers, and the critics standing in their places and waving their programmes.'

There followed a short-lived and emotionally catastrophic affair with the already-married Owen Nares, a Maugham melodrama (*East of Suez*), a film in Sweden with the great Victor Seastrom, and *Lilies of the Field*, all in a career which was to last rather less than six years.

Her last performance was never seen by the public; she was rehearsing the village girl in *A Magdalen's Husband* (again for Basil Dean) and got as far as the final runthrough before collapsing. She died a few days later in a Broadstairs nursing home following a severe haemorrhage which her mother attributed to 'peritonitis and constant overwork'. A more widespread belief was that her death had been the result of several ill-performed abortions, but in more romantic vein Agate wrote that 'too indomitable a spirit in too frail a body was the tragedy of this young actress', and Basil Dean added that 'she left the world at 25 having lived thousands of years'. A plaque to her memory in the foyer of the St Martin's Theatre announces that she was 'an artist who died in the service of the theatre'.

IRA ALDRIDGE

I ra Aldridge was the first of the great black American actors, although as he was willing to be neither a slave nor a minstrel his career had inevitably to play itself out abroad — first in England and later on tour throughout Europe. In 1863, four years before his death, he became a naturalized British subject.

Aldridge was born in 1804. During the 1820s he made an unsuccessful attempt to establish himself as an actor in Baltimore; later he found employment as a servant to Edmund Kean, who was then touring the United States. Kean brought him to London and encouraged his enthusiasm for the theatre. In 1826 Aldridge made his début at the Royalty Theatre as Othello, billed as 'the African Roscius'. Later, in Belfast, he again played Othello to the Iago of Kean's son Charles, and from there he went on to play both Lear and Macbeth, making good money as a leading actor and marrying a white woman. He toured increasingly frequently in later life, playing most often in Germany, where he would work in English with a German-speaking supporting cast.

GEORGE ALEXANDER

The son of a dry-goods agent, George Alexander Gibb Samson was born in Reading on 19 June 1858, was educated principally at the high school in Stirling, and at the age of 15 he started out as a clerk in the city. He was already a keen amateur actor, however, and soon quarrelled with his father about a career in the theatre. By the time he was 21 he was, despite his father, in repertory at the Theatre Royal, Nottingham, having dropped his last two names and become simply George Alexander.

For the next two years he toured the British provinces in minor roles, but by 1881 had landed himself a place in Irving's company at the Lyceum, where he was to remain (except for a brief engagement at the St James's) for the next six years. He learned a lot at the Lyceum, despite the fact that Irving initially regarded him as 'too much Piccadilly'. Once, when the company was touring America and Irving succumbed to a swollen leg in Boston, Alexander went on for him as Benedick in *Much Ado About Nothing*.

Back in London, he inherited many of the old William Terriss roles, including that of Faust; then, in 1889, he decided that the time had come to break with Irving and strike out on his own. He went first to the Adelphi, and then signed a brief lease on the old Avenue Theatre where he presented Fred Terry in a play called *Dr Bill*.

Having thus acquired a taste for actor-management, Alexander finally left the Lyceum in 1890 (though Irving promised he could always return if his own management failed) to take over the St James's Theatre, where he installed the then-revolutionary electric light, refurbished the auditorium and stayed for the next twenty-seven years to present (and often also to star in) no less than sixty-two full-length plays and nineteen one-acters. His major successes included Wilde's *Lady Windermere's Fan* and *The Importance of Being Earnest*, although he proved something less than a faithful friend to Oscar during and after the playwright's celebrated homosexuality trials.

Alexander also had considerable successes with Pinero (*His House in Order, The Second Mrs Tanqueray*) and with Anthony Hope (*The Prisoner of Zenda, Rupert of Hentzau*). His tenancy of the St James's was, true to his own character, efficient and enduring rather than spectacularly exciting, but for it he was in 1911 rewarded with a knighthood. He died of consumption four months before the end of the First World War, on 16 March 1918.

He was married to Florence Theleur, but there were no children. His theatrical 'family', the permanent St James's company and its guest stars, found Alexander somewhat humourless. Once, receiving a message from Sir George asking if she would mind not laughing when they were on stage together, Mrs Patrick Campbell is reported to have replied: 'Tell Sir George not to worry; I shan't laugh at him until I get home.'

EDWARD ALLEYN

This Elizabethan actor and manager was considered to be Burbage's only true rival; in fact, Edward Alleyn has found a greater claim to posterity in that he used his earnings from the theatre (and he was one of the very first British actors to make real money out of it) to endow the College of God's Gift at Dulwich, South London. His work lives on in more practical ways, too: Michael Croft's National Youth Theatre was formed while Croft was a teacher at Alleyn's school in the late 1950s.

Alleyn was the son-in-law (by a second marriage) of the poet John Donne and a one-time Master of the King's Bears. He was born on 1 September 1566 in London, and started out as an actor with the Earl of Worcester's Players in 1583. Nine years later he married into the Henslowe theatrical family, which gave him partial control over such theatres as the Rose and Fortune and the Paris Garden.

His best-known roles were all in the plays of Christopher Marlowe; he scored considerable successes as Tamburlaine, Dr Faustus and the Jew of Malta. As Burbage was to Shakespeare, so Alleyn was to Marlowe.

The theory that he founded Dulwich College in a fit of fear and remorse, after meeting the Devil nightly on stage in his role as Dr Faustus, has long

The dying Henry IV, played by Harry Andrews, hands over his
crown to Prince Hal, Richard Burton's first major classical role,
in a production of *Henry V* at the Shakespeare Memorial Theatre
(Stratford-on-Avon, August 1951)

Peggy Ashcroft as Lady Teazle in the Old Vic production of
Sheridan's comedy of manners *The School for Scandal*
(London, 1932)

since been disproved, but it is true that the college owes its existence to his theatrical success and his aptitude for marrying (twice) into reasonably wealthy families. More famous in his lifetime than Shakespeare himself, Alleyn was described by one French critic as having 'a pleasing voice, a good figure and a fine presence; he has raised the art of acting to a level hitherto unknown'. He died, aged 60, in Dulwich on 25 November 1626.

SARA ALLGOOD

The early career of this legendary Irish stage actress is also that of the Abbey Theatre. Born in Dublin on 31 October 1883 and trained by Frank Fay, Sara Allgood was with the Irish National Theatre Society early in 1904 and came with them to London, where she made her début that year as Cathleen in Synge's *Riders to the Sea*. For the next ten years she was to be seen at the Abbey as a founder member of that theatre company; her great roles there included the Widow Quin in *The Playboy of the Western World* (1907), Lavarcham in *Deirdre of the Sorrows* (1910) and the title role in *Cathleen ni Houlihan* (1913). She was also in at the start of the Liverpool Rep and of Miss Horniman's company at Manchester; for London she created Nannie Webster in Barrie's 1914 *The Little Minister*.

In 1916 she toured Australia in *Peg o' My Heart*, and by 1920 she was at the Lyric, Hammersmith, for Mrs O'Flaherty in *O'Flaherty VC*. She then revived her Widow Quin, and for London created both Juno Boyle in *Juno and the Paycock* and Bessie Burgess in *The Plough and the Stars*. She also played Mrs Henderson in the 1907 Court production of *The Shadow of a Gunman*.

Late in the 1920s she repeated all her O'Casey roles in New York, and spent the 1930s in London alternately reviving the O'Caseys and playing lovable old Irish ladies in a succession of less distinguished pieces. In 1929 she had started her film career in Hitchcock's *Blackmail*, and in 1940 she answered the call of Hollywood, where she spent the last decade of her life appearing in such films as *Lady Hamilton*, *How Green Was My Valley*, *Jane Eyre* and *The Spiral Staircase*. She took out American citizenship in 1945 and died there five years later, on 13 September 1950, a valued and respected character actress who, wrote one American paper in her obituary, had become 'Mother Ireland herself'. Brooks Atkinson added: 'Of all Junos, hers was the most overwhelmingly maternal.'

JUDITH ANDERSON

Probably still best known for her portrayal of the sinister and ultimately incinerated Mrs Danvers in Hitchcock's *Rebecca* (1940), Judith Anderson's career has, in fact, been primarily in the classic theatre, with a heavy emphasis on Greek tragedy and Shakespeare: she is to date the only woman to have played the title role in *Hamlet* at Carnegie Hall.

Judith Anderson was born Frances Margaret Anderson in Adelaide, South Australia, on 10 February 1898. Her first appearance on the stage was at the age of 17, at the Theatre Royal, Sydney, in *A Royal Divorce*. After a year spent touring Australia in *Monsieur Beaucaire* and *The Scarlet Pimpernel* she moved to America in 1918 and has lived there ever since. Her Broadway début was in a stock company at the old 14th Street Playhouse; then, in 1920, she toured the United States with William Gillette in *Dear Brutus*. Critics were already commenting on her 'unrestrained' stage style, as throughout the 1920s she graduated through a series of stock and regional companies until (after a brief return to her homeland in 1927) she succeeded Lynn Fontanne as Nina in O'Neill's *Strange Interlude* on Broadway in 1928.

Three years later she was Lavinia in O'Neill's *Mourning Becomes Electra*, and then, in 1936, Gertrude to Gielgud's Broadway Hamlet. In 1937 she made her London début at the Old Vic as Lady Macbeth, one of the two roles (the other being Medea, first played in 1947) which were to characterize her stage career; she also played Lady Macbeth on film to Maurice Evans' Macbeth in 1959. But much of the remainder of her film career consisted of going over the top in undistinguished screenplays, and for the stage she was, almost like a female Australian Wolfit, increasingly encouraged to tour as both New York and London grew disenchanted with her larger-than-life performances.

Nevertheless, her post-war work included a sinister Miss Madrigal (the role created in London by Peggy Ashcroft) in Enid Bagnold's *The Chalk Garden* (USA, 1956) and a 1960 appearance at the Edinburgh Festival as Arkadina in *The Seagull*, which marked the stage début of Tom Courtenay.

Back in America she took increasingly to recitals featuring scenes from her former Shakespearian and Greek triumphs, although when she played one of these 'evenings with' at her own native Adelaide Festival, the local press was somewhat less than ecstatic. In the Birthday Honours of 1960 she was made a Dame of the British Empire.

Her reputation seems likely to rest on her classical work, notably the Medea of which Rosamond Gilder wrote: 'It is pure evil, dark, dangerous, cruel, raging, ruthless. From beginning to end she maintains an almost incredible intensity, yet she varies her mood so constantly and moves with such skill through unexplored regions of pain and despair that she can hold her audience in suspense throughout the evening.'

MARY ANDERSON

Mary Anderson was an elegant and enchanting American stage actress who retired from the stage after her marriage in 1890 and settled in England, where she was to live for the next half-century. She was born in Sacramento, California, on 28 July 1859, educated at the Ursuline Convent in Louisville, Kentucky, and studied elocution under Vandenhoff. Her début was in the role of Juliet in an amateur production at Macauley's Theater in Louisville on 27 November 1875, which resulted in the offer of a professional contract there. Over the next three years she also appeared in New Orleans, Washington and San Francisco in a range of roles from Lady Macbeth to the Lady of Lyons. In this last role she made her New York début at the Fifth Avenue Theater on 12 November 1877; that same season she also played Lady Macbeth, Juliet and Meg Merrilees.

For the next five years she toured the United States and played frequent Broadway seasons in a variety of Shakespearian and Victorian melodrama productions. In 1883 she first came to London to play Parthenia in *Ingomar* at the Lyceum.

She returned to London in 1885 to play Rosalind at Stratford-on-Avon, and in 1887 (once more at the Lyceum) she became the first actress ever to double Hermione and Perdita in *The Winter's Tale*.

She made her farewell American appearance in those two roles in 1889, and then returned to England for marriage, to Antoine de Navarro, and retirement. In her last fifty years she did, however, make occasional appearances at charity matinées, principally for First World War fund-raising. She also wrote two autobiographies and co-authored (with Robert Hichens) the long-running drama, *The Garden of Allah*. W. S. Gilbert was one of her most devoted admirers and wrote his *Comedy and Tragedy* for her in 1884. She died in Broadway, Worcestershire, on 29 May 1940.

HARRY ANDREWS

A long and prolific career on the screen as a 'reliable' supporting actor (over fifty films, principally in military or espionage roles) has tended to obscure Harry Andrews' immensely distinguished stage career. He was born in Tonbridge, Kent, on 10 November 1911. He made his Broadway début in 1936 as Horatio to Gielgud's legendary Hamlet, and in more recent years has been both Henry IV and Othello at Stratford as well as Henry VIII at the Old Vic. He also played Menenius to Olivier's 1959 Coriolanus and in 1971 played the title role in Edward Bond's reworking of *Lear*, although this massive theatrical undertaking, at the Royal Court, was believed by many to be the last truly major stage role that Andrews' health would allow.

A craggy, lean and frequently bearded actor, the definitive Tolstoy in two television accounts of the novelist's life and times, on screen he has managed for several years to give the impression of being considerably greater than most of the parts he has been called upon to play, although few multinational wide-screen epics have been complete without him. Theatrically, his career has perhaps been less impressive, but it has given a similar impression of waste: a potentially great Hamlet who has always allowed himself to be cast as Horatio. Andrews was also a quintessential Enobarbus (most notably in the 1951 Olivier–Vivien Leigh production of *Antony and Cleopatra*), a part he has always listed alongside Bolingbroke as his favourite. 'Other actors,' wrote Kenneth Tynan in 1953, 'may be the heart, brain and fingertips of English Shakespearian acting: Harry Andrews is the indispensable backbone.' *See photograph opposite page 6.*

GEORGE ARLISS

A lthough now remembered primarily as a suavely villainous film actor — largely because his stage career ended with the 1920s — George Arliss in fact started out at the Elephant and Castle Theatre in London in September 1886. Born George Augustus Andrews on 10 April 1868, the son of a printer and publisher, he had grown up in London and was to have his first success at the Royalty in 1900, playing opposite Mrs Patrick Campbell in *The Second Mrs Tanqueray* and *The Notorious Mrs Ebbsmith*. He went with her and *Tanqueray* to New York, and stayed on Broadway for the next twenty-two years, working with Mrs Fiske and establishing himself in 1911 for the first time in what was to be his definitive stage (and later screen) role, that of Disraeli in Louis N. Parker's play.

His success there led to a series of biographical roles on Broadway (Paganini and Alexander Hamilton proved the longest lasting), and he then returned to London in 1923 to recreate another of his great Broadway successes: the Rajah of Rukh in *The Green Goddess*.

England did not detain him long, however, and by 1924 he was back on Broadway for a three-year run in *Old English* and then as Shylock. In common with many actors who followed him across the Atlantic, Arliss discovered that it was more profitable to be English in America than in England.

He remained a figure of considerable public and private distinction (Columbia University awarded him a doctorate as early as 1919, and in 1934 he was elected a Fellow of the Royal Society of Arts). He published an autobiography and a half-dozen plays, but it was in films that he truly came into his own. There were two screen *Disraelis* (1921 silent and 1930 sound), in addition to which he played Voltaire, Richelieu, Rothschild and Wellington. A monocle became his trademark; at his death in New York on 5 February 1946, his estate was valued at £136,000 — greater than that of any other British stage actors except Charles Wyndham and Squire Bancroft.

Y VONNE
A RNAUD

Yvonne Arnaud was the quintessential stage Frenchwoman, and for many years Guildford's most distinguished theatrical resident — hence the theatre there that still bears her name. Born in Bordeaux on 20 December 1895 and educated in Paris (where she was a child-prodigy pianist), she was working in London as early as 1911, when she made her début as Mathilde in *The Quaker Girl* at the Adelphi.

Like Maurice Chevalier in Hollywood, she rapidly discovered that her accent was her fortune and took care to preserve its heavy French intonations intact despite almost half a century of British residence.

She was a stylish light comedienne with a special line first in fluttery and then in semi-dowager eccentrics; she also continued to be a distinguished pianist, frequently incorporating her talent into her stage roles. In later years both Alan Melville (*Dear Charles*, 1952) and Robert Morley (*Six Months' Grace*, 1957) wrote for her, but initially her fame was made by a series of light comedies and musicals in the years around the First World War (*The Girl in the Taxi*, 1912; *Oh, Be Careful!*, 1915; *Kissing Time*, 1919; and *The Naughty Princess*, 1920).

Then she joined the Tom Walls team at the Aldwych for two classic farces (*Tons of Money*, 1922; and Ben Travers' *A Cuckoo in the Nest*, 1925) before playing Mrs Pepys in the London and Broadway premières of *And So To Bed*. During the 1930s she made occasional forays into Shakespeare and Shaw (Princess of France in *Henry V*, 1934; and *In Good King Charles's Golden Days*, Malvern, 1939) and made many films, principally of her stage vehicles, although also the screenplays, *Tomorrow We Live* and Lonsdale's *On Approval*. A talented comedienne with considerable technical knowledge of comic timing, Yvonne Arnaud found a place deep in theatregoers' affections by managing to give the constant impression of a French society hostess who had accidentally drifted on to the stage. Her marriage to an Englishman, Hugh McLellan, was long and happy and he was instrumental in the creation and running of the Arnaud Theatre. Yvonne Arnaud died in Surrey on 20 September 1958.

O SCAR
A SCHE

Oscar Asche is most famous now for having written, produced and starred in *Chu-Chin-Chow*, the legendary stage success at His Majesty's (which Asche was also managing at the time), where it played 2238 performances from 1916 to 1921 — to the horror of Tree, that theatre's previous manager, who was heard to describe it as 'more navel than millinery' on account of its bare-midriff costuming.

Asche was an eccentric and larger-than-life theatrical figure. The maker and spender of fortunes (he died leaving just £20, having spent most of the £200,000 *Chu-Chin-Chow* profits on a catastrophic sequel called *Cairo*), he was of Scandinavian parentage, though born in Geelong, Australia, on 26 January 1871, and at his father's suggestion studied for the stage in Norway before starting his career with Benson's company at the Lyceum. His first real success, in London and New York, was in the 1901 production of *Iris*, and a year later he joined Tree's company at the theatre that would one day be his own. In 1903 he appeared with Ellen Terry in a production of the remarkable economic disaster *The Vikings*, and a year later he started in management at the Adelphi, casting himself as Petruchio, Bottom, Claudius and Angelo in a six-month Shakespeare season.

He then took on his first tenancy of His Majesty's in 1907, playing the title role in *Attila the Hun* and Jaques in *As You Like It*, and also directing *Othello* and *The Taming of the Shrew*, which ran 1500 performances. In 1909 he returned to his native Australia, thereby pioneering the system of West End stars touring their best-known successes there. Back in England in 1911 he played Hajj in *Kismet*, the first in a long line of Eastern-promise roles that were to make his fortune. He toured that production to both Australia and South Africa, took a shortened version round variety halls in the North of England at the outbreak of war, played Shylock in Stratford's 1915 *The Merchant of Venice*, and then started his five-year stint as

Abu Hassan in *Chu-Chin-Chow*.

Asche still intermittently toured *Chu-Chin-Chow* as late as 1928, and nothing in his later life ever lived up to his success with it. He was a lavish spender in private as well as in public and for most of his later years he was occupied in trying to extricate himself from considerable debts with increasingly wild ventures. These included not only *Cairo* (which lost more money than any other show of its time) but also a historical pageant of his own devising, *The Good Old Days*, a modern-dress *Merry Wives of Windsor*, and another scenic extravaganza, *Eldorado*. In the 1930s he was reduced to replacing Baliol Holloway as Falstaff in

The Merry Wives and touring with his wife, actress Lily Brayton, in yet another Eastern saga of his own devising, entitled simply *Kong*.

His last notable job was playing the Emperor in a 1934 *Androcles and the Lion* at the Winter Garden, although he also wrote (with Dornford Yates) *Eastward Ho* and was director of the long-running *Maid of the Mountains*, which ran 1352 performances at Daly's while he himself was appearing nightly in *Chu-Chin-Chow*. His silent films included *Don Quixote* and *Scrooge*, and his publishing activities included a doubtful autobiography and a best-seller on the history of joss-sticks. He died in London on 23 March 1936.

PEGGY ASHCROFT

'*T*he best all-round actress on the English-speaking stage,' wrote J. B. Priestley in 1975, adding: 'Of all leading actresses she might be said to be the least "actressy" . . . She can think about other things, support various causes both political and cultural, and keep alive a circle of friends from many different walks of life. This means she can break into the open from the hot-house of the theatre; inside it she rises like an evening planet, but on the other side of the stage door she prefers to live the life of a sensible, middle-class professional woman.'

Peggy Ashcroft was born in Croydon on 22 December 1907. During her childhood there, where a theatre now carries her name, Peggy Ashcroft lost her father in the First World War and was brought up by her mother, a talented amateur actress. She was a pupil at Woodford School (with Diana Wynyard) and went on, like her mother before her, to study with Elsie Fogerty at her Central School of Speech Training in the Albert Hall. At 19 she was sent by Fogerty to Barry Jackson's Birmingham Rep, there to replace the ailing Muriel Hewitt as Margaret in *Dear Brutus* — also in that cast was a young Ralph Richardson. From there, clutching a London University Diploma in Drama, she went on to make her London début at three fringe theatres in 1927 before understudying Edith Evans as Millamant in *The Way of the World* at Wyndham's. Back at Birmingham she also played with a young Olivier in John Drinkwater's *Bird in Hand*.

The following year brought a lengthy provincial tour with Lilian Braithwaite and more fringe work in Hammersmith, Hampstead and

Kew, and then, in September 1929, she first began to make her name in the West End, playing Naomi, the innocent Cordelia-like daughter of Matheson Lang's *Jew Süss*. Paul Robeson saw that performance and offered her Desdemona to his *Othello* in a 1930 production which also featured Sybil Thorndike as Emilia and Ralph Richardson as Roderigo. Despite that casting it was not a great success, although John Gielgud noted that 'when Peggy came on in the Senate scene it was as if all the lights in the theatre had suddenly gone up. Later, in the Handkerchief scene, I shall never forget her touching gaiety as she darted about the stage, utterly innocent and light-hearted, trying to coax and charm Othello from his angry questioning.'

After that Shakespearian début she returned briefly to the modern theatre (notably as Judy in Maugham's *The Breadwinner*) before playing her first Juliet, in February 1932, as a guest player with the Oxford University Dramatic Society under the direction of Gielgud himself. Later that year, her twenty-fifth, she played during one remarkable nine-month Old Vic season not only Juliet but also Cleopatra, Rosalind, Portia, Perdita, Imogen, Kate Hardcastle, Lady Teazle and Mary Stuart, alternating between the Waterloo Road and Sadler's Wells, then also under the artistic control of Lilian Baylis.

In 1935 she repeated her Juliet for Gielgud, who was now alternating Romeo and Mercutio with Laurence Olivier at the New Theatre, and a year later at that theatre she was a memorable Nina in her husband Komisarjevsky's historic production of *The Seagull*. January 1937 saw her

Broadway début in Maxwell Anderson's *High Tor*, but by the autumn of that year she was back in Gielgud's company at the Queen's for Portia, Lady Teazle, Irina in *The Three Sisters* and the Queen to his Richard II, so taking her place at the head of a company which also included Michael Redgrave, Alec Guinness and Anthony Quayle. Agate was still writing of her 'youthful brilliance', although Charles Morgan for the *Times* was less happy to see her Lady Teazle in Guthrie's production as part of what appeared to be 'an elaborately stylized musical comedy'.

From the Queen's she went across to the Phoenix for a rather less successful repertory season there run by Michel St Denis (*Twelfth Night* and the Ackland–Bulgakov *White Guard*). She brought her pre-war career to a close with a dazzling Cecily Cardew in Gielgud's celebrated Haymarket revival of *The Importance of Being Earnest*, in which the *Times* compared her to 'a jewel changing colour with the light, now innocently olive-green, now an audacious pink'.

The war brought Clemence Dane's *Cousin Muriel*, in which Agate found 'Miss Ashcroft giving the performance of her career: this is acting of the highest possible intelligence and delicately graded sentiment. It is also extraordinarily graceful to watch'. She and Edith Evans (who had been Nurse to her Juliet and Lady Bracknell to her Cecily) began (on non-matinée days) their wartime poetry recitals; these continued as a feature of both their careers on stage, radio and record, long after hostilities ceased.

In 1940 she briefly replaced Jessica Tandy as Miranda to Gielgud's first Prospero at the Old Vic. The same year she married her third and last husband, Jeremy Hutchinson. She left the stage to have the first of their two children (her two earlier marriages had been childless) but returned in October 1942 for a Phoenix Theatre revival of *The Importance*. Then, in 1944 and still with Gielgud (though now at the Haymarket), she played Ophelia, Titania and the Duchess of Malfi before making her post-war début in the modern theatre as the drunken Evelyn Holt in Robert Morley's *Edward My Son*.

She recreated that role on Broadway in 1948 and then returned to London for another major success as the unloved and unlovely title character in *The Heiress*, a dramatization of Henry James' *Washington Square*, in which she was joined by Ralph Richardson as the domineering father and Donald Sinden as the faithless suitor. In 1950 she was at Stratford — surprisingly, for the very first time — playing Cordelia in *Lear* and Beatrice to Gielgud's Benedick, a *Much Ado* double-act that seemed to crown and typify their long Shakespearian partnership.

In 1951 she was Electra at the Old Vic and a year later returned to the modern theatre to play the suicidal Hester Collyer in Rattigan's *The Deep Blue Sea*, a role taken over for the infinitely less successful film version by Vivien Leigh.

The Ashcroft career on film, although it included appearances in such successes as Hitchcock's *The Thirty-nine Steps* (she was the sinister crofter's wife), *The Nun's Story* and James Ivory's *Hullabaloo Over Georgie and Bonnie's Pictures*, had curiously never echoed or paralleled the constant success she had had on stage for more than half a century until in 1985 she won an Oscar for her performance in David Lean's triumph, *A Passage to India*.

In 1953 she was back at Stratford for Portia and Cleopatra and a year later started a long London and European touring run of *Hedda Gabler*, a production by Peter Ashmore which she described as 'one of the tops' of her career. That started her on a chain of Ibsen productions (*Rosmersholm* in 1959, *Ghosts* in 1967), although along the way she also broke back into the modern theatre for Madrigal in Enid Bagnold's *The Chalk Garden* (1956, the first *Evening Standard* Best Actress Award). In the same year she was in the opening season of the English Stage Company at the Royal Court playing Shen Te in Brecht's *Good Woman of Setzuan*.

Two more Stratford seasons followed, in 1957 and 1960, during the second of which she played Kate to O'Toole's Petruchio. Peter Hall began to form his Royal Shakespeare Company in 1960, and she became a founder member of the RSC and the only one, apart from Hall himself, to remain an adviser as late as 1980. In these last twenty years, therefore, most of her major work has been with the RSC: *The Duchess of Malfi*, *The Hollow Crown*, Ranevsky in *The Cherry Orchard*, Emilia to Gielgud's catastrophic Othello, Queen Margaret in the epic *War of the Roses*, Beth in Pinter's *Landscape*, the Mother in Duras' *Days in the Trees*, Agnes in Albee's *A Delicate Balance*, Katherine in *Henry VIII* and Lidya in Arbuzov's *Old World*. Along the way, however, there have been one or two occasional and even surprising darts into the West End, most notably to play Lady Boothroyd opposite Ralph Richardson in William Douglas-Home's comedy of eccentric re-trenchment, *Lloyd George Knew My Father* (Savoy, 1972).

When Peter Hall first took over the National Theatre Company at the Old Vic, she joined briefly to play Winnie in *Happy Days* and Ella Rentheim in *John Gabriel Borkman* (with Richardson and Wendy Hiller, 1975), and then spoke a blessing in the words of Lilian Baylis on the night the National bade farewell to the Old Vic and moved across to its new building. Dame Peggy (the honour was bestowed in 1956, when she was 49; Sybil Thorndike was the only other actress to receive it at such an early age) did not go with them; instead she returned to her RSC home at the Aldwych for *Old World* (1976), and then increasingly turned to radio and television, notably in the ITV series 'Edward and Mrs Simpson' (1978) and in 'The Jewel in the Crown' (1984). She was to have made her return to the stage in the National Theatre's 1979 production of Simon Gray's *Close of Play*, but a cartilage operation prevented that. Later she did two more television plays, by Stephen Poliakoff and Dennis Potter, before at last returning to the stage — after a four-year absence — in the 1980 National Theatre production of Lillian Hellman's *Watch on the Rhine*, which opened at that year's Edinburgh Festival. 'I have,' she said in an interview shortly before the first night, 'missed the theatre terribly. It's where my life has been spent, where I am at home.'

See photograph opposite page 7.

Adele
AND
Fred Astaire

A dele and Fred Astaire were to become the most famous brother-and-sister act in the Broadway and London musical theatre of the 1920s; Adele retired from the stage in 1932 to marry Lord Cavendish, and Fred subsequently went on to movie fame.

Together, they were a remarkable stage double: Fred never did a show without his sister until her retirement, and there were many who thought that Hollywood never gave him a better partner, not even Ginger Rogers.

Born in Omaha, Nebraska, Adele Austerlitz (10 September 1898) and Frederick Austerlitz (10 May 1900) started out on the vaudeville circuit in 1907. In 1915 they were to be found together in Mary Pickford's film *Fanchon the Cricket*, and in 1917 they made their Broadway dancing début in *Over the Top*. Over the next fifteen years their major hits in London and New York included *Stop Flirting*, *Lady Be Good*, *Funny Face* and finally *The Band Wagon*. Arlene Croce wrote: 'Adele was a perfectly marvellous dancer with a large share of the idiosyncratic Astaire charm. With her long, slim legs, flashing smile and bold, dark eyes she was like a motto of the twenties; the daffodil dresses and face-framing hats might have been created for her, and in her cooey soprano was something vague, heartless and self-adoring, the very cuckoo-note of a heedless era. Indisputably she was the first soubrette of the American musical stage, and hers was the style that shaped the material that made Fred and Adele Astaire a starring attraction.'

They were a comedy act rather than a romantic duet, and of that act Adele was very much the star. In London, Agate wrote of Fred's 'sublimated Barriesque projection of the Little Fellow with the Knuckles in his Eyes ... Every woman in the place was urgent to take to her chinchilla'd bosom this waif with the sad eyes and the twinkling feet'.

But then Adele met and married Lord Cavendish; for Fred, Broadway was unthinkable without her. He had two possibilities: one was to work in London, where Jack Buchanan was already proving a formidable threat; the other was Hollywood, where the famous verdict on his first screen test read: 'Can't act. Slightly bald. Can dance a little.' The rest is, of course, screen history, but Fred was only ever to appear on stage again at the occasional benefit. As a stage act, the Astaires were a quintessential and characteristic part of the twenties and one that effectively started and ended with that decade.

ROBERT ATKINS

Robert Atkins was a Shakespearian actor–manager in charge of many summer seasons at the Open Air Theatre in Regent's Park, and has been the subject of more theatrical anecdotes than any of his contemporaries except, possibly, Donald Wolfit.

He was born in Dulwich, London, on 10 August 1886. After leaving school he became a pupil at Beerbohm Tree's Academy of Dramatic Art (later to become better known as RADA), and Tree himself then employed Atkins as an extra at His Majesty's. Atkins went on to work for Martin Harvey and (in America) Forbes-Robertson and Frank Benson, but it was Tree to whom he always referred as 'my old master'. From him, Atkins inherited the belief in Shakespeare as a calling — a profession almost in itself — as well as the more flamboyant traditions of the old thespian. Marginally more modest than Wolfit, Atkins did not trade in subtlety or innovation; his outdoor theatre was essentially a home for pageantry and 'the Bard', and his own oft-imitated tones were usually to be heard there in such roles as Bottom and Toby Belch, although later in life he took happily to the stage-managing Quince. Many believed, not surprisingly, that the best performance he ever gave was as the hammy old stock-company actor Telfer in *Trelawney of the 'Wells'*, a role he listed as a firm favourite.

A brisk, tough, no-nonsense manager of other actors, Atkins had a lugubrious sense of humour and survival which is still much quoted. His first real break came when Ben Greet hired him for the Old Vic Company in 1915, which then included Sybil Thorndike and her brother Russell. First World War service followed. When he was demobilized he wrote to Lilian Baylis, then in charge of the Old Vic, suggesting methods by which the production of Shakespeare might be modernized; these included the building of an apron stage and the masking of the footlights.

Between 1920 and 1923 Atkins staged at the Old Vic a complete cycle — the first of its kind — of all Shakespeare's plays except *Cymbeline*.

He then directed the first-ever London production of *Peer Gynt* (with Russell Thorndike in the title role) before moving to the Open Air Theatre in the 1930s. This was to occupy him, with varying degrees of success, for the next thirty years.

Constantly at the mercy of the fickle British weather, unable to pay high salaries, limited to short seasons and still more limited by the nature of open-air Shakespeare (there are only a certain number of ways in which *A Midsummer Night's Dream* can be produced and this was some years before the advent of Peter Brook), Atkins nevertheless soldiered on, attracting to the park such guest stars as Gladys Cooper and Anna Neagle and, more importantly, giving a start to a great many young actors in the days before subsidized companies. Box-office takings ranged from £16 on a wet night to £400 on an especially fine one.

In these years he would occasionally venture indoors, notably to direct *Lady Precious Stream* (1947) and for a Long John Silver at the Fortune (1948); he also did some guest-directing at Stratford in the 1940s and early 1950s. Undeterred by the withdrawal of an Arts Council grant, he staggered on at the Open Air Theatre until 1960, often reviving his Caliban and his Toby Belch. Finally, in 1960, he gave it up, although a year later he was back with the Old Vic company as Gluttony in *Dr Faustus*.

He received the CBE in the Birthday Honours of 1949 and was — somewhat more eccentrically — the holder of the Order of the Crown of Italy, which was bestowed on him in 1933 for directing a play about Napoleon. The author of the play was Benito Mussolini. He died in London on 10 February 1972.

ALAN
BADEL

'Films are for making money, television for making you famous — and the theatre is the place most properly for an actor to be,' Alan Badel once said.

He was born in Rusholme, near Manchester, on 11 September 1923, and educated at Burnage High School before entering the Royal Academy of Dramatic Art in 1939. There he was a Bancroft Gold Medallist. From RADA he went to the Repertory Theatre, Oxford, where he first appeared as George in *The Black Eye* in 1940. His first London appearance was at the Mercury Theatre on 18 August 1941, as Pierrot in *L'Enfant prodigue*. That same year he appeared in his first film, *The Young Mr Pitt*. In 1942 he played both Lennox and the Servant in *Macbeth* at the Piccadilly Theatre. War interrupted his stage work, and from 1942 to 1947 he served with the Parachute Regiment 6th Airborne Division. His wartime service left him with impaired hearing. During the war he did, however, manage to play Othello in Egypt with the Army Play Unit.

Now married to the actress Yvonne Owen, after the war he went to work with the Farnham Repertory Company, playing Morgan Evans in *The Corn is Green*. In July 1947 he played Stevie in *Peace In Our Time* at the Lyric Theatre, London, and in March 1948 played Sandman in *Frenzy* at the St Martin's, before touring. In a season at the Birmingham Repertory Company in 1949 Alan Badel played (among other parts) Everyman and Richard III. He went to the Memorial Theatre, Stratford-on-Avon, that Christmas to play Ratty in *Toad of Toad Hall* and remained for more serious roles the following season, playing Claudio in *Measure for Measure*, Octavius in *Julius Caesar*, Don John in *Much Ado About Nothing*, the Lord Chamberlain in *Henry VIII*, and the Fool in *King Lear*. The next Christmas he was at the Westminster Theatre playing the Prince in *Beauty and the Beast*. Spring took him back to Stratford, where for the 1951 season he played Poins and Justice Shallow in *Henry V Parts 1 and 2*, the Dauphin in *Henry V*, and Ariel in *The Tempest*. He was at the Old Vic for the winter, playing Quince in *A Midsummer Night's Dream* and François Villon in *The Other Heart*. The next season (1952–53) at the Old Vic he played Romeo. In September 1954 Alan Badel played Lovborg in *Hedda Gabler*, and in the spring of 1956 returned to Stratford to play Hamlet. Frank Granville-Barker said of it: 'Hamlet unhappily has only a few good things in a performance that generally lacks impetus. I could not feel any singleness of purpose behind the production gathering up the parts. Alan Badel's Hamlet, too, seems to lack force and cohesion. He sets out with admirable restraint, eschewing the temptation to rock the theatre with histrionic fireworks and there is every suggestion of intelligent study in his approach to the part. But each big moment seems to slip through his fingers — except the Closet Scene with the Queen, when we feel that the Prince is genuinely, desperately trying to love and reform his mother at the same time. This is most moving and revealing and we can see for a few moments the effect at which Alan Badel has aimed. But at other times he seems too cautious, suggesting uncertainty on his own part as well as on Hamlet's.' That season he also played in *Love's Labour's Lost* and *Measure for Measure*.

At the Arts Theatre, London, in October 1957 Alan Badel directed *The Public Prosecutor* and played Fouquier Tinville in it. Also at the Arts, in 1959, he played Stephen Dedalus in *Ulysses in Nighttown*, touring with it to Paris and Holland. At the Westminster in February 1960, Badel played Kreton in *Visit to a Small Planet*, under his own management. That same autumn he was playing Alex in *The Life of the Party* at the Lyric, Hammersmith. In April 1961 he played Hero in *The Rehearsal* at the Globe. He made his first New York appearance, at the Royale Theater in September 1963, as Hero. He opened as John Tanner in *Man and Superman* at the New Arts in November 1965, transferring to the Vaudeville in January. At the Oxford Playhouse in 1970 Alan Badel played Kean in September and Othello in October. He brought *Kean* to London to the Globe Theatre in January 1971.

Alan Badel returned to Richard III, his favourite part, in July 1976 at St George's Playhouse, Islington. The *Observer* reported: 'Alan Badel is the leader of the lost generation of English classicists who give St George's Playhouse its main reason for being ... His Richard is less a devil than a driven imp, rolling downstage to deliver his first speech as a deadpan joke on the audience and winning his way to the throne more by cheek than imposture ... His eyes are his tensest feature; they are hypnotically fixed as he waits to see how his victims will respond to his poison.' He died shortly before his sixtieth birthday, only a few months after the closing of *Richard III*; his daughter Sarah carries on the family acting tradition.

ANNE BANCROFT

Compared to her television and film work, Anne Bancroft's appearances on the stage have been infrequent — but they have also been stunning.

Anne Bancroft began life on 17 September 1931 as Anna Maria Luisa Italiano. Hollywood changed that. Her father was a dress-pattern maker and her mother a telephone operator. She had two sisters and a large, extended Italian family. After graduating from Christopher Columbus High School in the Bronx, New York, she studied for a year at the American Academy of Dramatic Art. Then came a time as a saleswoman and a receptionist before she headed West, where she made her film début in *Don't Bother to Knock* (1952). During the next five years she made eighteen highly forgettable appearances in movies. She explains: 'My early career was a comedy of errors. I was very young and eager to please, so I went along with the studio's idea of making me a glamour starlet ... Most of my acting consisted of being victimized by Indians, love-starved soldiers or wild animals... Off camera I posed for fan magazine pin-ups and went the whole Hollywood starlet route. It was ridiculous and ultimately damaging.' She also had a disastrous marriage to a man she describes as an 'Alan Ladd look-alike', which was dissolved in 1957. In 1964 she married the comedian Mel Brooks.

She made her Broadway début at the Booth Theater on 6 January 1958 as Gittel Mosca in *Two for the Seesaw* — a two-hander by William Gibson in which she co-starred with Henry Fonda. Brooks Atkinson reported that Anne Bancroft had been unknown but would not remain so. 'But if Miss Bancroft were not a glowing young lady without a mean bone in her body, the dialogue might sound more clever than honest. She is the animated half of the cast, making a vivid contrast with Mr Fonda's leisurely style: she explodes with gestures that are natural; she modulates the part with vocal inflections that are both funny and authentic and she creates a gallant character who rings true.' Anne Bancroft received the best actress Tony for this, her first stage role, as well as the *Variety* New York Drama Critics Award.

In October 1959 she opened at the Playhouse as Annie Sullivan in *The Miracle Worker*. For that performance she was again awarded a Tony, as well as the New York Drama Critics Award, the ANTA award and the New York Philanthropic League Award. She repeated the performance on film and won an Oscar.

At the Martin Beck Theater in March 1963 she played Mother Courage in Brecht's play. Kenneth Tynan was not altogether taken with her performance: 'As Mother Courage herself, a flinty peasant matriarch of the seventeenth century, Anne Bancroft is at once too young and too citified; although she ages effectively and ends up looking not unlike Helene Weigel in the Berliner Ensemble production. The difference has to do with emphasis. When Weigel says: "Curse the war!" she shrugs the line off as if it were a mournful cliché; Miss Bancroft yells it, clenching her fists. Similarly, instead of the immobile, soundless cry, head flung back, with which Weigel reacts to the death of her son, Miss Bancroft stumbles halfway across the stage, emitting strangled yelps. Now and then she is even willing to sob, because that is what customers demand.' But George Oppenheimer, not drawing comparisons with other actresses, thought: 'As played by Anne Bancroft she [Mother Courage] comes to life lustily and with complete conviction despite Miss Bancroft's youth ... [she] has become one of America's leading young players.'

Her next theatrical venture was as the Prioress in *The Devils* at the Broadway Theater in November 1965 with Jason Robards Jr. Howard Taubman found the production stunning, and Anne Bancroft 'particularly affecting as she recalls her childhood and its loneliness. A lost tenderness lights up her eyes. In her bursts of hysteria she communicates the hint of hollowness. Is the prioress play-acting or is she whipping herself into a frenzy so that she actually sees the orgiastic visions? One is never sure, and that is dramatically right'.

Anne Bancroft played Lillian Hellman's Regina Giddens in a revival of *The Little Foxes* at the Vivian Beaumont in October 1967, and in November 1968 at the same theatre she was Anne in *A Cry of Players*.

She has made many notable films since the first dreadful dozen and a half — *The Pumpkin Eater*, *The Graduate*, *The Turning Point* and her husband Mel Brooks' *To Be or Not To Be* among them — and in 1971 she received an Emmy as well as second prize at the Montreux Festival for her television special 'Annie, the Woman in the Life of a Man'.

THE BANCROFTS

*L*ady Bancroft was born Marie Effie Wilton in Doncaster on 12 January 1839 — practically in a trunk. Her father, much to the horror of his middle-class family who intended that he should enter the Church, became instead a travelling actor. From a very early age Marie was put on the stage, and when she could talk was coached by her mother. She was a great success from the very beginning. Her first recorded appearance, at the age of six, was at Norwich, playing the Emperor of Lilliput in the pantomime *Gulliver's Travels*. As a child she also played Fleance and the apparition of the crowned child in Macready's *Macbeth*, and Jo in *Bleak House*. She travelled incessantly until joining the Bristol Theatre Company, where she played in pantomime and also played Henri, the son of the title character in *Belphegor*. The lead was played by Charles Dillon, and when he became manager of the Lyceum in London he summoned Marie to repeat the role of Henri. She opened in London on 15 September 1856. That same season she was called upon to replace an ailing actress in a most taxing part, playing Perdita in William Brough's musical version of *The Winter's Tale*. The *Morning Post* reported: 'Miss Marie Wilton is a young (very young) lady quite new to us, but her natural and pathetic acting as the boy Henri showed her to possess powers of no ordinary character, which fully entitled her to the recalls she obtained. She appeared also as Perdita, the Royal Milkmaid, and made still further inroads into the favour of the audience ... She is a charming debutante, sings prettily, acts archly, dances gracefully and is withal a most bewitching presence.' (The words 'pathetic' and 'archly' evidently carried more favourable connotations in 1856 than they do now.)

The following year she moved on to the Haymarket to play Cupid in a musical extravaganza, and then to the Adelphi, where she found herself with little to do besides watch the great burlesque stars of the day. At the Strand she felt 'doomed to appear in a long line of burlesque boys' — this line included Little Fairy, Little Treasure, Little Savage, Little Sentinel, Little Devil, Little Don Giovanni — she was obviously expert at it and was soon the talk of London. Charles Dickens commented in a letter to a friend on her appearance as Pippo in *The Maid and the Magpie*: 'There is the strangest thing in it [the play] that ever I have seen on the stage — the boy Pippo, by Miss Wilton. While it is astonishingly impudent

(must be or it couldn't be done at all), it is so stupendously like a boy, and unlike a woman, that it is perfectly free from offence ... the girl's talent is unchallengeable. I call her the cleverest girl I have ever seen on the stage in my time and most singularly original.'

Marie Wilton continued to play a string of boys despite having very successfully performed Juliet in the balcony scene for a charity show. She wanted to play comedy and wrote to a number of managers in an effort to get out of burlesque — none would give her a chance. Her brother-in-law suggested lending her £1000 to lease her own theatre. At first she was daunted by the prospect, but after persuading the playwright Henry J. Byron to come into partnership with her she leased the Queen's Theatre in the unfashionable Tottenham Street. She completely redecorated it (to the extent of putting antimacassars on the backs of the velvet chairs), renamed it the Prince of Wales and opened in April 1865 in the comedy *A Winning Hazard* and also the burlesque *La Sonnambula*, having been persuaded that she must give the public what it expected — at least at first.

Squire Bancroft was hired to play a man-about-town in Byron's comedy. Marie Wilton married Bancroft in 1867; the following year they had a son, and ever after were known as 'the Bancrofts'.

Squire Bancroft was born on 14 May 1841. He was, throughout his life, inordinately proud that the future king was also born that year and that *Punch* magazine began publication in the very week of his birth. His unusual Christian name came from his paternal grandfather. Squire Bancroft had a comfortable, middle-class upbringing, being educated privately in England and France until his father's premature death made it essential that he earn his living. Having always been a stage-struck boy, at the age of 19 he wrote to every theatrical management he could think of requesting work and was taken on by the Theatre Royal, Birmingham. He made his first stage appearance there in January 1861, playing Lieutenant Manley in *St Mary's Eve*. Birmingham had thrice-weekly rep and Squire Bancroft played in, among other pieces, *The Bottle*, *The Lonely Man of the Ocean*, *Sweeney Todd* and *Thirty Years of a Gambler's Life*. He went to Cork Theatre during a summer's break and was mistakenly billed as Sydney Bancroft, a name that stuck to him for years. There he played Marcellus, Rosencrantz, the Second Player, a Priest, and Osric in *Hamlet*. He also worked in Devonport in a variety of roles, and in Dublin, where he acted with Charles Matthews and Charles Kean. He joined the rep at Liverpool, where he first met Marie Wilton who was doing a guest appearance. In all he spent four years and four months in the provinces, playing 346 parts, before opening in London, under Marie Wilton's management, on 15 April 1865 as Jack Crawley in *A Winning Hazard*.

After the departure of the playwright Byron from the partnership, Squire joined Marie in the management of the Prince of Wales. The Bancrofts brought many innovations to theatrical management, basing their work on a true company rather than the visiting star system, introducing realistic scenery, paying better wages, concentrating on providing comfort for the audience and allowing a single play to occupy an entire evening. Under their management the Prince of Wales became the leading house for comedy in England. Their greatest successes there were *The School for Scandal*, *London Assurance*, *The Rivals* and *Diplomacy*, and they introduced such playwrights as Robertson, Wilkie Collins, Tom Taylor and Pinero. William Archer summed up their success: 'The Bancrofts steered clear of the worst vices of actor-managership. Partly, no doubt, because they always formed a committee of two (a very different thing from an autocracy), they on many occasions showed a most commendable spirit of self-abnegation, and met with their reward in the increased esteem of all who know good acting when they see it, be the part small or great. Bancroft's Faulkland in *The Rivals* dwells in my memory as an altogether masterly performance, far more truly artistic than many a much-applauded piece of actor—manager bravura.'

The Prince of Wales Theatre became too small to house the enormous audiences the Bancrofts were attracting and they moved to the Haymarket, first overhauling the interior. When they opened in January 1880 with *Money* (Squire Bancroft played Sir Frederick Blount; Marie Bancroft played Lady Franklin) there was a near-riot because they had removed the 'pit' — being the very first management to replace the low-priced benches

with the more expensive stall seats. The Bancrofts remained successfully at the Haymarket for five years. They realized great profits; now financially secure, and having accomplished everything they had wished, they decided to retire while they were still ahead. They gave their last performance on 20 July 1885, in which they played selections from the plays most identified with them: *Money*, *London Assurance* and *Masks and Faces*.

Squire Bancroft reappeared on the stage on 28 September 1889 at the Lyceum, playing Abbé Latour in *The Dead Heart* with Sir Henry Irving — an opportunity he couldn't refuse; Marie joined him in 1893 playing Lady Henry Fairfax while he played Count Orloff in *Diplomacy* at the Garrick. After opening night, one of the critics reported: 'The cheering began as soon as her merry musical laugh was heard at the wings; it grew in volume directly she was seen ... The art of the actress was proved undimmed and her triumph was complete.' The couple were commanded by Queen Victoria to perform this piece at Balmoral in October of that year.

Marie Bancroft appeared twice more on the stage — at the Garrick in *Money* in 1894 and the following year at the Haymarket as Countess Olga in *Fedora*.

Squire Bancroft was knighted in 1897 and appeared subsequently only for charity functions. His readings of Dickens' *A Christmas Carol* raised substantial sums of money for hospitals. His last reading was given on 11 March 1913 at St James's Theatre, and his last stage appearance was at His Majesty's on 17 December, 1918, where he once more played Triplet in *Masks and Faces* in aid of the King George Pension Fund for actors. His last years were spent in advisory and administrative positions as President of RADA, President of the Green Room Club, member of the advisory board for the licensing of plays — and in writing his memoirs. Lady Bancroft died on 22 May 1921, and Sir Squire followed her on 19 April 1926.

TALLULAH BANKHEAD

Tallulah Bankhead lived at an enormous speed in a haze of tobacco, alcohol, Coca-Cola and cocaine. She revelled in an acid, self-deprecating wit, as though aware that there was always a Boswell within noting distance, and there usually was. She removed her clothes at every possible opportunity and delighted in shocking people. It seems that everyone connected with Broadway, Hollywood or the West End at the time has a favourite Tallulah anecdote. She revelled in all-night, or sometimes three-day, parties; her lovers have never been fully counted, although the one person she really loved was her father, who was a US Congressman and Speaker of the House of Representatives.

Tallulah Bankhead was born on 31 January 1903 in Huntsville, Alabama, and was named after her grandmother, who in turn had been given the Indian name for a waterfall found in the state. It was particularly appropriate for the young Tallulah — she spent most of her adult life being compared with Niagara.

As a teenager, newly blossomed into a beauty, she sent her photograph to a movie magazine in the hope of winning a part in a film. She did win, but the film came to nothing. She was, however, determined to become an actress, and she remained in New York, impoverished but surviving as a beautiful young girl could on parties and dinner invitations. She made an undistinguished New York début as Mary Sinclair in *The Squab Farm* on 13 March 1918 at the Bijou Theater. The following year she was equally undistinguished as Penelope Penn in *39 East* at the Broadhurst Theater. For the next two years she remained in work on Broadway, though not consistently. She still worried about earning enough to pay the rent. She played Hollie Livingston in *Nice People*, Phyllis Nolan in *Everyday* and Mary Hubbard in *Danger* (all 1921); Blanche Ingram in *Her Temporary Husband* and Rufus Rand in *The Exciters* (1922). Stardom continued to elude her until she crossed the Atlantic to London on borrowed money and talked herself into the part of Maxine in *The Dancers*, which opened at Wyndham's in February 1923. The reaction to her, especially by the young females who crowded the theatre balconies, was hysterical. She also became the darling of society, who found her flamboyant behaviour charmingly eccentric. Delighted by her rapturous reception, Tallulah worked in London for seven years, playing the title role in *Conchita*, Yvonne Taylor in *This Marriage*

and Anita Latter in *The Creaking Chair* (all 1924); Julia Sterroll in *Fallen Angels* and Iris Fenwick in *The Green Hat* (1925); Mary Denvers in *Scotch Mist*, Jerry Lamar in *The Gold Diggers* and Amy in *They Knew What They Wanted* (1926); Toni Lebrun in *The Garden of Eden* (1927); Daphne Manning in *Blackmail*, Polly Andrews in *Mud and Treacle* and Simon in *Her Cardboard Lover* (1928); Wanda Myro in *He's Mine* (1929); Marguerite in *The Lady of the Camellias* and Kitty Brown in *Let's Be Gay* (1930).

Her celebrity brought her Hollywood offers, and in 1931 she made three films for Paramount — *Tarnished Lady*, *My Sin* and *The Cheat* — followed in 1932 by *Thunder Below* and *The Devil and the Deep*, and *Faithless* which she made for MGM.

The following year she returned to New York trailing publicity and notoriety and remained very good box office. She played Mary Clay in *Forsaking All Others* at the Times Square Theater, opening in March 1933. Then, in 1934, she toured briefly in a variety show before playing Judith Traherne in *Dark Victory* at the Plymouth Theater. In 1935 she finally got to play Sadie Thompson in a revival of *Rain*. Tallulah had been after the part for years and pursued the author, Somerset Maugham, trying to convince him to let her play it in London. He refused, probably because he disliked being bullied and Tallulah could be most persistent. This part tested her more than any of her previous roles and she rose to the challenge. Brooks Atkinson, in the *New York Times* of 12 February 1935, had only slight reservations: 'Miss Bankhead is a dynamic actress of remarkable versatility with great powers of character description. In the first act she plunges into the part with the raffish, wobbly gusto of a gaudy strumpet. She has a savage attack for the climaxes. Being an actress of extraordinary range she has the proper equipment for every situation the play invents — fear, remorse, pathos, contempt and pity for the misery of the world. What leaves this commentator unwillingly reluctant about her Sadie is Miss Bankhead's failure to fuse all the details into the wholeness of a human characterization.'

After her enormous success with *Rain* Tallulah remained on Broadway, playing Monica Grey in *Something Gay* (1935), Miss Flood in *Reflected Glory* (1936), Cleopatra in *Antony and Cleopatra* (1937) and Judith Held in *I Am Different* (1938). In 1937 she married John Emory, an actor who happened to be a John Barrymore look-alike.

Marriage did not, however, lead Tallulah into a settled life — if anything the velocity increased. They divorced in 1941, and Tallulah never remarried.

In 1939 came the role that was to bring her enormous and unsparing critical acclaim, that of Regina Giddons in Lillian Hellman's *The Little Foxes*. Elliott Norton summed up her performance thus: 'She made Regina Giddons cold, calculating and calmly cruel, yet absolutely true and fascinating . . . Her laughter was a silver ripple on ice, the glint of a glacier. Her wrath, which came suddenly when one or another of her brothers tried to cross her, was the rumbling of thunder with flashes of lightning.'

Tallulah followed that triumph with a tour of *The Second Mrs Tanqueray* in 1940, and the next year played Mae Wilenskii in *Clash by Night* at the Belasco. She opened as Sabina in *The Skin of Our Teeth* at the Plymouth Theater in November 1943. Although Tallulah maintained that she did not understand a word of it, her performance was a triumph. *Newsweek* reported: 'As the French-farcical maid of the first act, the mincing bathing beauty of the second and the enthusiastic camp follower of the third, her perennial "other woman" is a superb comedy performance.' For this performance she received the Baxter Theater Award and the New York Drama Critics Award for best actress of the season.

It was after her triumph as Sabina that Tallulah Bankhead seemed to lose interest in acting and turned more to pure performing. She played Sophie Wind in *Foolish Notion* (1945), filmed *A Royal Scandal* for Fox and played the Queen in *The Eagle Has Two Heads* (1947). The last of these was primarily noteworthy because Tallulah managed to have Marlon Brando dismissed from the cast before the Broadway opening because she didn't like his attitude; nor did she think much of his acting ability. Brando opened in *A Streetcar Named Desire* that same season.

For a few years Tallulah toured the country as Amanda in *Private Lives*, but she was often a parody of herself, with the throaty, guttural drawl of 'Dahling' to everyone — taken up at first because she had trouble putting names and faces together. Her Amanda was usually terrible. As *Time* magazine pointed out: 'She lacks the stability and discipline to keep her gift under control over a long period. Her performances fluctuate more than most after the opening night. Says a friend: "The longer she plays in something the less you see of the play, the more you see of Tallulah!" She has turned *Private Lives* into a one-woman show — at once the triumph of a personality and the surrender of an actress.'

From 1950 to 1952 Tallulah called millions of listeners Dahling each week on 'The Big Show', which she recorded for NBC radio. It was a variety show in which she introduced famous guests, sang, joked, and performed sketches with them. She received the New York Newspaper Guild's Page One Award for 'putting new life back into Radio'. She tried to repeat her success on television in 1952 with 'All Star Revue' but failed. The next year she went back to Hollywood to film *Main Street to Broadway* for MGM, then opened as Dolores in *Dear Charles* at the Morosco (1954). In 1956 Tallulah at last appeared in a Tennessee Williams play (as Blanche Du Bois in a revival of *A Streetcar Named Desire*). For years Williams had been bringing his plays to her first, declaring that only she could breathe life into his women — that she was his model — but despite her less than model behaviour privately, she was shocked by his plays and refused to do them. She also put Williams on a lower social rung in the Southern ladder of gentility. She worked very hard on her performance as Blanche, struggling to overcome the mannerisms that had become her trade mark — the bourbon voice, the toss of the head — and to a great extent she succeeded. But unfortunately her audience had not come to see her acting. *Cue* magazine reported: 'Each passing reference to anything stronger than Coke brought forth gales of uproarious, pseudo-sophisticated laughter. These gay lads had come to see a travesty, and despite Miss Bankhead's sturdy refusal to commit one, they applauded as though by their actions they could call it into being.' Perhaps this was a natural reaction to the lady who took pride in saying that she had invented 'camp'. The *New York World-Telegram*, however, called Tallulah's Blanche, 'One of the most extraordinarily shattering performances of our time.'

Tallulah's next venture — a revue called *The Ziegfeld Follies* — closed on the road, and she took a shortened version of it, *Welcome Darlings*, to the Westport Country Playhouse in Connecticut for the summer. Her health deteriorated rapidly as she aged. She suffered from emphysema, and moreover her habitual drug-taking had wrecked her once-phenomenal memory for scripts. At first she had only to hear a part read twice and she knew it; but no more. In the last ten years of her life she played *Eugenia* (1957); Celia in *House on the Rocks* (1958 tour); Daisy Filberston in *Crazy October*, which closed on the road; *Here Today* (on the road 1962); and Mrs Goforth in *The Milk Train Doesn't Stop Here Anymore*, which ran for five disastrous performances at the Brooks Atkinson Theater in January 1964. Tallulah's stage career in both London and New York was at an end. There remained one film — a grotesque characterization in a horror called *Die! Die! My Darling!* — an appearance as a black spider woman on television's 'Batman' series and a few appearances on Merv Griffin's television chat show, on which she wheeled out the old personality even though she could barely walk and breathed only with great effort and the help of an oxygen cylinder. She came, she told Griffin, 'So everyone won't think I'm dead.' She in fact died a few months later, on 12 December 1968.

JEAN-LOUIS BARRAULT

'My only theory,' Jean-Louis Barrault has said, 'is to create a work which, as a member of the audience, I would like to see.' He was born on 8 September 1910 in Vesinet, a suburb of Paris. He had one older brother. His father was a chemist; both parents belonged to an amateur dramatic society, in which they played mainly in comedy. Barrault went to a private school when he was six — his parents separated at about that time, and his father died of typhus in 1918. Two years later his mother married an interior designer and painter and together they drifted into bohemianism, leaving Barrault's grandfather to look after the practical side of life. Jean-Louis Barrault greatly enjoyed school and excelled in almost everything. After his local school he was sent to the Collège Chaptal in Paris. At 18, having been told by his grandfather that he should earn his living, he became apprenticed to a bookkeeper, but left abruptly after three months of humiliation and boredom. He then went to work with his uncle in the flower market and studied painting at the Ecole du Louvre, but the flower market proved so time-consuming that there was no time for study. He returned to the Collège Chaptal as an usher, where he was given room and board but no salary. He felt unsuccessful at making a career as a painter and his love of the theatre turned into an obsession.

In 1931 Barrault wrote to Charles Dullin at the Théâtre de l'Atelier and was offered an audition. Barrault performed all the parts in the Narcisse and Neron scene from *Britannicus* and the scene with Chrysale from *Les Femmes savantes*. Dullin took him into the theatre school free. Barrault made his stage début on 8 September 1931 (his twenty-first birthday) at the Atelier, as one of the servants in *Volpone*; he experienced crippling stage fright, which was to plague him all his life.

Dullin opposed both the academicians of the Comédie-Française and the commercialism of the Boulevard. Also at the Atelier was Etienne Decroux, and Barrault became his disciple in the art of mime, discovering the complexity of his body. He dedicated himself completely to the theatre — even sleeping there. His next stage appearance was in Pirandello's *The Pleasure of Honesty*. He described it: 'The second act ends with the entry of the notary, followed by his three clerks. I was the third. At that moment the curtain fell. The public could see the first clerk, the legs of the second, never the third. I always arrived when the curtain was down. I took advantage of this to work at the art of make up ... every evening I would go in two hours before curtain up and transform myself into an old man, a chubby one, or a skeleton with masses of sticks, nose paste, wet white, etc.'

Barrault's military service was a nightmare; he was pleased to return to the Atelier, where in *Richard III* he played three parts as well as arranging the battle scenes. It was on 4 June 1935 that he produced, directed and acted in his first excursion into total theatre, inspired by William Faulkner's *As I Lay Dying*. He explained at the time: 'This kind of mime, I believe, has nothing to do with pantomime, education or aesthetics (or that disagreeable thing, the *tableau vivant*); it is an attempt to be purely animal. As a text this play does not exist. It exists if, and only if, a group of actors and a director work on a stage. It is theatre trying to purify itself.' The curtain rose on near-naked players, whom the audience greeted with laughter and derision. Sometimes there was more than twenty minutes silence on stage. After all, the written text would play only thirty minutes and the performance lasted for two hours. At the end of that time the audience was on its feet cheering, and critics were hailing a genius. There were only four public performances but the play marked the entry of Barrault into the theatrical life of Paris. It also resulted in his first film offer — *Les Beaux Jours*.

Jean-Louis Barrault left the Atelier and formed his own company — Le Grenier des Augustins. They identified with the surrealist movement and Trotskyists — improvised mime and recited poems in factories. In theatrical venues they performed *Un Homme comme les autres* and *Le Misanthrope*. Meanwhile, Barrault was becoming a cinema star, a matinée idol who set the style for romanticism. He made *Hélène* (his first meeting with Madeleine Renaud, the star), *Le Puritain* and *Drôle de drame*, among others, and used his cinema earnings to subsidize his theatrical experiments, a practice that was to continue throughout his career.

His next great excursion into total theatre was *Numance*, which ran for fifteen performances at the Théâtre Antoine, which he had hired for what was to be the Parisian theatrical 'event' of the season. His relationship with Madeleine Renaud grew during this period, as did his friendship with her husband, Charles Granval.

In September 1938 he took over the Atelier and produced Salacrou's *La Terre est ronde* and in March *Hamlet*, not by Shakespeare but by Jules Laforgue. This was followed by *La Faim* on which he had been working for years. When he had read the first act to Madeleine, her son called it *théâtre ta-ga-dag* ('ding-dong theatre') and the name stuck. In *La Faim*, Barrault explains that he was 'experimenting with many new resources: the play between actor and lighting (going up a staircase), simultaneous scenes, nonsense scenes — words that have no sense but whose sound plastically reproduces conversation and situation. Spoken text answered by a tune hummed with the mouth closed. Heartbeats, buzzings in the ears, "physiological" musical effects and, above all, a man and his double. Roger Blin was the double. I played the man Tangen. It was really a duet between us.'

After asking her ex-husband's permission, Barrault married Madeleine Renaud on 14 June 1940 as the Germans overran Paris. During the Occupation he joined the Comédie-Française, where for six years, he says, he learned craftsmanship — although he felt stifled. He made his début there on 11 November in *Le Cid*, which was not a success. He was, he concluded, too lightweight for the role of Roderique. He was, however, successful as Hamlet and directed a triumphant *Phèdre*. In 1942, rather unwillingly, he became a sociétaire and in 1943 began his association with the poet Claudel with his production of *Le Soulier de satin*. On Sunday 9 June 1946, at a matinée playing Moron in Molière's *La Princesse d'Elide*, he gave his last performance at the Comédie-Française and formed with his wife their own company at the Théâtre Marigny (Compagnie Madeleine Renaud–Jean-Louis Barrault). They opened on 17 October 1946 with *Hamlet*, followed on 24 October by *Les*

Fausses confidences and *Baptiste* (the complete mime play belonging to *Les Enfants du paradis*, which he had filmed in 1944) and in December presented *Les Nuits de la Collette*, establishing the company as they meant to go on, in repertory, for many reasons. 'Playing repertory is not only a source of artistic wealth, but a means of economic defence. To have at one's disposal a company capable of playing a whole repertoire, one must engage actors whose talents are diverse. These, by rubbing up against different styles day by day, add suppleness to their qualities and make progress ... Economically, there is no chance of making a fortune, because the breaking even and the profits of earlier productions are constantly invested in new ones. There is less risk of bankruptcy.'

In 1946 the company began the touring that was to be a major part of its activity, starting with a short season in Belgium, Holland and Switzerland.

Barrault had no single purpose for the company. He was never blinkered into one fashion or ideology. There were many goals, the major one being to create 'international theatre — French language section'. Other goals were to build a living theatre as varied and complex as life, to play both the classics and modern playwrights, to experiment and to incorporate different styles, ranging from vaudeville to tragedy, yet always using the same actors and stretching them. Particularly notable productions in the repertoire included Kafka's *The Trial*, in which Barrault played Joseph K, *Madame sans gêne* and *The Cherry Orchard*.

In 1947 the company had its first failure with *L'État de siège* by Albert Camus. It was especially disappointing for Barrault, as he had hoped for an intellectual and artistic union with Camus. What Molière was to the Comédie, he wanted Camus to be to the Compagnie. Barrault then returned to Claudel and produced *Partage de midi*, and it was the work of Claudel which provided him with the material for one of his most successful experiments. He wanted to 'go in search of a man through his whole work'. That desire resulted in *Connaissance de Claudel*, which the company played throughout the world. 'It was,' he says, 'easy to transport, needing only the presence of human beings to make it exist.'

Out of the forty-eight titles in the repertoire, twelve were classics and thirty-six modern. 'I like,' he said, 'a programme to make people think of a menu.' Le Petit Marigny, seating 250, was opened in January 1954 — in this intimacy Barrault could present both musicians and new playwrights such as Vauthier.

The company toured incessantly in the fifties — London, New York, Canada, South America,

Alan Bates (with Jenny Quayle) in *One for the Road*, written and
directed by Harold Pinter, and produced at the Lyric, Hammersmith
(London, March 1984)

Fay Compton was Ophelia to John Barrymore's Hamlet in this
historic production of Shakespeare's tragedy at the Haymarket Theatre
(London, February 1925)

Central America and the Iron Curtain countries. They went everywhere, from Anchorage through Bangkok, Tokyo, Athens, Venice and back again. They gave up the Marigny, spending two Paris seasons at the Théâtre Sarah Bernhardt. Then, in November 1958, they rented the Palais-Royal for a gigantic production of Offenbach's *La Vie parisienne* — the opening was 'one of the most sparkling evenings our company ever experienced'. They followed the operetta with *Le Soulier de satin* and Anouilh's *Le Petit Molière*.

André Malraux, Minister of State in de Gaulle's government, invited the company to create a national theatre — the Théâtre de France at the Odéon. Barrault had misgivings. For thirteen years the company had flourished on its own terms. To become the national theatre meant becoming institutionalized — but the Odéon was big and expensive to run so a subsidy was necessary. And it was an interesting challenge. The Théâtre de France opened with *Tête d'or* on 21 October 1959 and continued that season with *Le Petit Molière* and *Rhinocéros*. It was a difficult beginning. The

critics were suspicious of a national theatre and the audiences arrived with a 'show-me' attitude. But gradually the company prospered, performing the works of such distinguished contemporaries as Ionesco, Beckett, Genet and Marguerite Duras.

In 1968 it all came to an emotionally prolonged and violent end. The Odéon became a centre of the student revolution in May. The students called it a symbol of bourgeois culture and occupied the building for weeks, creating havoc and vandalizing it. In the midst of all the political manoeuvring which followed their final eviction by police on 14 June, Barrault was dismissed by the government. He had planned to stage *Rabelais* there. Not to be defeated, he rented the Elysée-Montmartre — a former wrestling arena with a glass roof and disastrous acoustics — and opened *Rabelais* there on 14 December 1968. Sir Laurence Olivier arrived and invited him to the National Theatre in London and he again began his tours. He has since been created a Chevalier de la Légion d'honneur and continues to lecture on the art of theatre and mime.

THE
BARRYMORES

The stardom of Ethel, John and Lionel Barrymore was just the culmination of the kudos which the public had been bestowing for generations on the great Drew acting family.

Mrs John Drew (Louisa Lane), grandmother of the spectacular triumvirate, was known and welcomed on stages across the breadth of America, and was especially noted for her performances of Mrs Malaprop in *The Rivals* and Lady Teazle in *The School for Scandal*. She also owned and managed a theatre in Philadelphia. In describing her, the drama critic T. Allston Brown wrote in 1896: 'In form, stature, mobility of countenance, and physique she is made to give the dramatic world assurance of an actress; while a lofty intellect, a passionate devotion to her art and a highly cultivated mind, have stamped the seal of excellence upon her brow.' It was she, pillar of the American stage, who both raised and guided the careers of her grandchildren. They lovingly, all their lives, referred to her as 'Darling Mum-Mum'. Her third husband, **John Drew**, was noted as the finest Irish comedian of a couple of generations. Two of their children, John and Georgiana, also became more than well known: **John Drew II** was referred to as 'the first

gentleman of the stage' and became a noted matinée idol, and **Georgie Drew** was an exquisite comedienne. Reviewing her performance in *The Senator* (1890) one critic wrote, 'Georgie Drew had been promising for several seasons to take the lead as a comedienne. Now she has taken it, handsome as a picture, brimming over with fun. An actress to the tip of her fingers, she captivated the audience at once and kept them in roars of laughter and applause.' She married **Maurice Barrymore**, also an actor as well as a playwright, and something of a playboy; he was particularly noted for his performances as Julian in *Diplomacy* and Orlando in *As You Like It*. He was described thus by the *New York Dramatic Mirror* in 1896: 'If ever a man was favored by nature to personate roles of the romantic order — that man is Maurice Barrymore. His face has been likened to that of a Greek god.'

The daughter of Georgie Drew and Maurice Barrymore, **Ethel Barrymore** was born in Philadelphia on 15 August 1879 and educated at a convent school, which she left briefly to accompany her tragically ill mother to California where it was thought she might recover. But Georgie Drew died there, and at the age of 13, Ethel picked up the threads of her life and returned East. Back at school, her main interest was in the piano and she longed to become a concert pianist, but money was short (as always in that family) so at nearly 15 she left school for good and joined her grandmother's theatrical company, which was touring in Canada. Ethel's first stage performance was as Julia in *The Rivals* in Montreal (May 1894). That tour ended disastrously without enough money even to pay the bills, and Ethel experienced her first moonlight flit as the company hurried out of town. She had to earn a living, so in New York Ethel began, rather unsuccessfully at first, to look for work on the stage. She has said, 'We became actors not because we wanted to go on the stage, but because it was the thing we could do best.' She was finally taken on by Charles Frohman as a tea-tray carrier in *The Bauble Shop*, which starred her uncle, John Drew. She graduated to the speaking part of Lady Kate Fennell when that production went on tour, and in Chicago a critic described her as 'an opalescent dream named Ethel Barrymore'. On that tour, in the company of her uncle she was introduced to the cream of society in each state — the society that would soon proclaim her a star and follow her every whim in fashion. But next Ethel had a one-line part in *The Imprudent Young Couple* and was the serving maid in *Rosemary*.

Still a teenager, she was taken by Frohman's company to London, where she played Miss Kitteridge in *Secret Service*. Her background, her youth, her beauty and her manner made her very popular with London society and she enjoyed their patronage greatly. In fact she stayed on after the play closed and joined Sir Henry Irving's company, for which she played in *The Bells* and *Peter the Great*. Irving's son Laurence was in love with her and Ethel became engaged to him for a time, but she broke the engagement. She was also engaged for a while to Gerald du Maurier. Other engagements were reported at this time on both sides of the Atlantic and she became well known in the gossip columns. None of this harmed her career, as the public turned out in great numbers to see this girl of whom they were continually reading. They went into the theatre out of curiosity, but they came out convinced of her talent. She acted with a naturalness that was new to the stage and the audiences responded to it. In New York for a small part in *Catherine* she received an ovation, and her Stella de Gex in *His Excellency, the Governor* on tour was a great success.

Ethel Barrymore was 21 when she got her first starring role. It was as Madame Trentoni in *Captain Jinks of the Horse Marines* and it was not an easy part. It required her to act both comedy and pathos, as well as to sing and dance.

Philadelphia did not care for it on its pre-Broadway run. A critic from that city reported: 'If the young lady who plays Madame Trentoni had possessed beauty, charm or talent, this play might have been a success.' However, when it opened at the Garrick Theater in New York on 4 February 1901, it *was* a spectacular success. After that Frohman starred her in a double bill — *Carrots*, in which she played a French boy, and *A Country Mouse*. With this she consolidated her stardom. 'Miss Barrymore,' a New York critic observed, 'as a star is no longer an experiment. Her success in the double bill has established her versatility.'

Each summer Ethel liked to hurry back to England, where she was always lavishly entertained. On her trip in 1903 she became engaged yet again, this time to Harry Graham, a writer and a captain in the Coldstream Guards. Again, she broke the engagement. In London in 1904 she played *Cynthia* at Wyndham's, but it was not well received. However, that same year back in New York, she had a new success, *Sunday*, in which she played a foundling of that name brought up by four miners. At the end of the second act she is supposed to be reading a letter from the miners to her English aunts when, coming to a very personal passage, she just stops. One of the aunts prompts her to go on, but according to the script Ethel is supposed just to run off stage. Ethel suggested that she should say something like, 'That's all there is. There isn't any more.' Frohman agreed, and that line became her trade mark, endlessly parodied by every mimic in the country. Ethel next did *A Doll's House* (1905), but a serious Ethel Barrymore was not what the public wanted and they were pleased to see her return with the smart drawing-room play *Her Sister* (1907), in which she wore the highest fashion, which was very much copied. During the tour of *Lady Frederick* (1909) Ethel once more became engaged; this time she went through with it and married Russell Colt on 14 March 1909. He was the son of a millionaire, although as it turned out he unfortunately did not have a way with money himself. Their son, Samuel Colt, was born in November. It was now that Charles Frohman, for whose theatrical management Ethel had always worked, said that her days in light plays were over. In Pinero's *Mid-Channel* (1910) she played Zoe Blundell, an unhappily married Englishwoman of 37. The critics agreed that she had 'triumphed over a gloomy play'. Always fascinated by repertory, in 1911 Ethel took out a tour which included *Alice-Sit-by-the-Fire*, *The Twelve-Pound Look*, *Mid-Channel* and *Trelawney of the 'Wells'*. Then she had two more children.

At the end of 1912 money was short once

again, so she took Barrie's dependable *The Twelve-Pound Look* on a vaudeville tour. But then she discovered the lucrative side of acting — films — and made more than fifteen of them before 1915, when she signed a contract with Metro for four films a year. That year she played, in a wheelchair, *The Shadow* on Broadway and both audience and critics were in tears. Ethel commissioned a play, *Our Mrs Chesney*, from Edna Ferber's short stories. *Camille*, *The Off Chance* and *Belinda* were staged in 1917.

It was on 6 October 1919 that she opened in one of her greatest hits, *Déclassé*, with which she toured after appearing briefly with her brother John in *Clair de Lune*, an unsuccessful play written by his then wife, society poetess Michael Strange. After nearly thirty years under Charles Frohman's management, in 1921 she left it and joined Arthur Hopkins, with whom both her brothers already worked. Under that management, on 26 September 1922 she opened *Rose Bernd* at the Longacre in New York. In this she played a peasant woman and got very mixed reviews — no one could quite take the patrician Miss Barrymore as a peasant. Following this, and at the age of 43, Ethel played Shakespeare's Juliet; the critics refrained from pointing out the mistake too loudly. However, at least the audiences were pleased to see her return to the trivial but witty drawing-room in *The Laughing Lady*, which was very successful. The critics were pleased when she performed Lady Teazle (her grandmother's standby) in *The School for Scandal* (1923). That same year she divorced her husband. Then she was back on tour yet again with *The Twelve-Pound Look*, following that with *A Royal Fandango* and a revival of *The Second Mrs Tanqueray*.

When she was 46 Ethel Barrymore had the courage, some would say audacity, to play Ophelia and a very low-key Portia. But it was in 1926 that she had her biggest hit of the twenties with W. Somerset Maugham's *The Constant Wife*. He said of her, 'There was always that extra way she put over a single word and she always exhibited a wonderful command over the audience.'

The Shuberts built a new Broadway theatre in 1928 and called it the Ethel Barrymore Theater. She inaugurated it on 17 December in *The Kingdom of God*, and the next year played *The Love Duel*. *Scarlet Sister Mary* (1930) included her children in the cast; she then went to Hollywood and made *Rasputin and the Empress* for MGM, with both her brothers in the cast. The publicity department reported a family feud, but it was largely mythical. It was, however, the last time all three siblings worked together in any medium.

The Depression years were very hard for Ethel Barrymore. She did summer shows, and vaudeville with the reliable *The Twelve-Pound Look*, although even that let her down when she took it to the London Palladium — it was a disaster with both the critics and the London audiences. While in England she visited her old friend Winston Churchill. He, too, was out of power, and they commiserated with each other. She performed back in the United States briefly with Eva Le Gallienne's company, did the occasional radio show, and revived *The Constant Wife* for a tour, but Broadway was no longer interested in her. The Internal Revenue Department was, however, constantly hounding her for back taxes. Not surprisingly, during these years she briefly took to the brandy bottle. In the summer of 1936 on a radio comedy show she announced her retirement from the stage and said she would thereafter train the young. But 1936 also brought a twenty-six-week radio series in which she chronologically revived her old roles, and by the following year she was able to settle with the taxmen. That year, too, she returned to the stage in the Theater Guild's production of *The Ghost of Yankee Doodle*, and the critics were once again beside themselves. Brooks Atkinson wrote: 'Miss Barrymore presides over the most attractive role with the patrician tossing of the head, the flashing eyes and the quiet grace of the celebrated Barrymore style.' They also raved over her next performance, that of a 101-year-old woman, Gran, in *Whiteoaks*. She was again a very old lady in *Farm of Three Echoes*. But disaster struck once more with *International Incident* which only ran fifteen performances. Even the legendary Ethel Barrymore could not keep the audiences coming.

Still, the best was yet to come: Miss Moffat, the Welsh school mistress, in *The Corn is Green*. 'Ethel Barrymore,' wrote John Mason Brown in the *New York Post*, 'gives the finest, most thoughtful and concentrated performance she has given in many years.' She was back on top with both critics and audiences. Describing her next Broadway role in *Embezzled Heaven*, Howard Barnes wrote, 'The queen of the theater's royal family has imbued the play with simplicity, eloquence and tremendous authority.' That was to be her last Broadway appearance. In 1944 she won an Oscar for being Cary Grant's mother in the film *None But the Lonely Heart*, and in 1945 moved to California for good. There she made three or four pictures a year, notably *Young at Heart*, *Pinkie* and *Portrait of Jennie*. She made guest appearances on television, which she found a very difficult medium, and was involved in the television series 'The Ethel Barrymore Theater'. Her last appearance before a live audience was on 29 January 1950, when for a theatre benefit night she performed a scene from, inevitably, *The Twelve-Pound Look*. Ethel Barrymore died in California on 18 June 1959, enquiring whether everyone was happy and assuring them that she was.

Hailed by all as the greatest Hamlet of his generation, **John Barrymore**, born in Philadelphia on 15 February 1882, never actually wanted to act. He wanted to draw; but by the age of 14 he was working in vaudeville with his father. When his grandmother, who looked after him, died he was sent to England, to King's College in Wimbledon where his father's brother-in-law was headmaster. As a teenager he was already enormously good-looking, and he began his drinking and romancing very early. He went to the Slade School of Art, where it was thought he had a talent for water-colours, and on returning to New York he began what he hoped would be a career by designing a poster for Charles Frohman's production of *If I Were King*. He produced illustrations for the *New York Journal* and did advertising drawings. In fact, *Cosmopolitan* magazine (January 1902) encouraged him by printing a critique from their arts writer: 'Mr Barrymore displays considerable power of thought and technique . . . his pictures give great promise for his future.'

John was, however, destined to go into the family business and Ethel got him a job in *Captain Jinks of the Horse Marines*. He then toured as Max in *Magda* (1903). In Cleveland a critic noted, 'He walked about the stage as if he had been all dressed up and forgotten.' That same year he made his New York début in *Glad of It*, in which he was seen by William Collier, a well-known comedian of the time, who hired John to play an absent-minded telegrapher in *The Dictator*. This ran for two years and toured Australia and England. During that time Collier taught him all there was to know about comedy and timing. Back in New York after the tour, John played Harlequin in *Pantaloon*, a curtain-raiser for Ethel's *Alice-Sit-by-the-Fire*. He got the lead in a play called *Toddles*, but it was not successful, and he then co-starred in *A Stubborn Cinderella*, which became one of the greatest hits in Chicago history. The critics there found him 'as fascinating as his father in his palmiest days'. This play brought him a measure of financial security but not Broadway stardom, as there it was unsuccessful. However, his next venture, *The Fortune Hunter* (1909) at the Gaiety Theater, was a massive success. John wrote in his book, *Confessions of an Actor*, 'It was goodbye to the irresponsibilities of youth. I had happened to be fairly good at them.' The next year he married

Kitty Harris, a New York socialite. He played in *Uncle Sam* (1911) on Broadway, but that same year *Princess Zim-Zim* did not make it to New York. It was during this period that he met the playwright Edward Sheldon, who was to be very influential in his career. John toured with *Half a Husband*, *The Affairs of Anatol* and *A Slice of Life*. *Believe Me, Xantippe* (1913) was followed by his first film, *An American Citizen*. In 1914 John signed a film contract with Famous Players, and during the next few years he made ten farces.

On Broadway in 1915 John Barrymore had his first serious success, as the downtrodden little bank clerk who forges a cheque which leads to his imprisonment, harassment and final suicide. For a man noted on stage, screen and personal life as a witty, worldly wise, extravagantly handsome, romantic figure was this character in Galsworthy's *Justice* really suitable? The *New York Times* reported: 'For Barrymore the first night of *Justice* was a milestone. By his simple, eloquent, deeply touching performance as young Falder, he arrested the attention of the city and gained overnight a prestige which is priceless in the theater, a prestige all his work in trivial entertainment would not give him. It is what the theater can bestow on those who serve it loyally. This comes now to a player whose years in the theater have been lackadaisical.'

In 1917 he toured with *Peter Ibbetson*, was divorced from Kitty Harris, made the film of *Raffles the Amateur Cracksman* (Gerald du Maurier's great English stage success) and began his liaison with Michael Strange, who was really called Blanche Delrichs but published poetry under (and preferred to be called by) her masculine pen-name. John appeared in Tolstoy's *Redemption* in 1918, and the following year with Lionel in *The Jest*. 'He was a splendid and exotic sight in *The Jest*. His long slim shanks were encased in mineral green, and he moved through the gore and passion of the play with the grace of a young sapling — a green flame against the burly shadow of the bully his brother had to play . . . in spite of the searching plaintiveness of his voice, it is on his brain and not his throat that Mr Barrymore relies,' wrote Gilbert W. Gabriel in *World's Work*. John did, however, work on his voice, having lessons with the well-known coach Mrs Carrington, and in 1920 approached Shakespeare as Richard III. Alexander Woollcott reported, 'Barrymore's first Shakespearian role marks a measurable advance in the gradual process of bringing his technical fluency abreast with his winged imagination and his real genius for the theater. The highest point has been reached in the rapid, unexpected ascent which began six years ago [with *Justice*], a rise which has been unparalleled in the theater of our time.'

John Barrymore did not, however, stay on that high. His life and career were filled with peaks and depressions. After four weeks as Richard III he suffered exhaustion and a breakdown, although that year he also managed to film *Dr Jekyll and Mr Hyde* and to marry Michael. Seven months after the wedding their daughter Diana Barrymore was born. She became noted for *Too Much, Too Soon*, the story of her tortured life.

Clair de Lune (1921), written by his wife, was not one of John Barrymore's peaks. It was a sort of dramatization of Victor Hugo's *The Man who Laughs*. John spent most of the play swathed in a cape and hood, and when he was not he had to perform herculean ballet movements (for which he trained with a Russian master). The stage was littered with dwarfs and the plot seemed rather vague. It was, however, the most eagerly awaited Broadway opening of the season, with a cast featuring all three Barrymores, and sets and costumes designed by John for the play written by his wife. Society would have killed for seats. One New York paper reported, 'All the world and his wife, and in a few remote cases someone else's wife, attended the opening.' But after the first night, 18 April 1921, most of the critics would have preferred to review the audience — the play was terrible.

John Barrymore had his greatest success yet to come. In November 1922 he opened as Hamlet on Broadway. His interpretation of the classic role was psychological; his was a very Freudian Prince of Denmark. He brought to the part his satiric wit, that gorgeous voice and a wonderful intelligence. His Hamlet was to become the touchstone for all others, so much so that when, years later, Ethel was called upon to give an Oscar to Laurence Olivier for his film performance of Hamlet, she could not keep a note of incredulity out of her voice in announcing his name. After all, her brother John *was* Hamlet. At least, so said all the critics in 1922. The *New York Times*: 'The atmosphere of historic happening surrounded John Barrymore's appearance last night as the Prince of Denmark; it was as unmistakable as it was indefinable. It sprang from the quality and intensity of the applause, from the hushed murmurs that swept the audience at the most unexpected moments, from the silent crowds that all evening swarmed about the entrance. It was nowhere — and everywhere. In all likelihood we have a great and lasting Hamlet.' Heywood Broun in *World*: 'John Barrymore is far and away the finest Hamlet we have ever seen.' Alexander Woollcott: '. . . an evening that will be memorable in the history of American theater.' John Barrymore played Hamlet for 101 performances in America. In

February 1925 he opened at the Haymarket, London, with it. This could have been regarded as bringing coal to Newcastle, but according to the foremost London drama critic, James Agate, John Barrymore's Hamlet was 'nearer to Shakespeare's whole creation than any I have ever seen. [He has] the purest diction, perfect enunciation and unexampled clarity. . . informed by intellectual capacity of a rare order and analytical power of extreme cogency.'

After a stormy relationship, John and Michael split up that year. The celebrity that *Hamlet* had brought him also brought an offer from Hollywood — a three-picture deal at $75,000 a picture. In June 1925 he moved permanently to Hollywood, and resumed an affair with Mary Astor that he had begun the year before while they were filming *Beau Brummel*. However, he soon took up with another actress, Dolores Costello.

At Warners, John Barrymore filmed *Don Juan*, *When a Man Loves*, and managed to introduce love interest into *Moby Dick*, which was retitled *The Sea Beast*. He then moved over to United Artists and made three more films. By 1928 he had another contract with Warners (for a million dollars) and he married Dolores. During his Hollywood years the moodiness to which he was subject increased; he was jealous, lonely, sulky, and terrified of going insane as his father had done. He drank harder and longer, with the result that his memory and health were ruined. He filmed his soliloquy from *Richard III* for the Warner Brothers' film *The Show of Shows*, so some of the expertise and power of his performance is encased in celluloid, but when the idea of filming *Hamlet* came up, neither his mind nor his body could handle it. He made many films notable for qualities beyond those displayed by his favoured left profile: *Grand Hotel* with Garbo, *A Bill of Divorcement*, introducing Katharine Hepburn, *Rasputin and the Empress* with Lionel and Ethel, *Topaze* and *Twentieth Century*, but by 1934 his dependence on alcohol had reached such a level that when deprived of it he resorted to drinking his wife's perfume. They were divorced in 1935. He did play Mercutio in the Leslie Howard–Norma Shearer *Romeo and Juliet*, but by the late thirties he was bankrupt, ill, married to Elaine Barrie Jacobs (another very stormy relationship) and making six films a year in an attempt to pay the bills.

In 1939 he returned to the stage in *My Dear Children*, in which he played an old actor and his wife played one of his daughters. It was directed by Otto Preminger and toured very successfully before Broadway, but for all the wrong reasons. John Barrymore had been in the news for years. His reckless lifestyle fascinated people and they turned up in droves at the theatres to see what would happen. Would he make the performance? Would he fall on his face? Would he make a fool of himself? And John usually managed to give them what they wanted. His performance did not, however, fool Brooks Atkinson when *My Dear Children* opened in New York in January 1940. He wrote: 'If Mr Barrymore were a ham, this trashy story, and his appearance in it, might be a pathetic ordeal for his old admirers. But he is a wit. He plays it with an alert sense of mischief. Although he has recklessly played the fool for a number of years, he is nobody's fool in *My Dear Children*, but a superbly gifted actor on a tired holiday.'

John Barrymore died slowly over the next two years. His slide could be noted in his films — *The Great Profile*, *The Invisible Woman*, *World Première* and *Playmates*. He had a weekly radio spot on Rudy Vallee's programme, and it was in the studios that he finally collapsed. He died on 29 May 1942, aged 60.

The eldest of the great Barrymore trio, **Lionel Barrymore** was born in Philadelphia on 28 April 1878. His first stage role was as Thomas the Coachman in a Kansas City tour of *The Rivals* when he was 16, but his main interest was in drawing and painting and he attended art school in New York for three years, interrupted by the occasional stage job to earn some money — and acting, after all, was the family business. These jobs included Sergeant Jones in *The Bachelor's Baby*, Max in *Magda* and Joey and Toby Crockett in *Oliver Twist*. By the time he was 21 he was already adept at playing character parts — on tour that year he played a man of 70 in *Arizona*.

Lionel made his New York début at the Republic Theater on 27 September 1900 in *Sag Harbour*, but unfortunately the character he played was his own age and he failed to impress the critics. That was followed by a part in *The Brixton Burglary* at the Herald Square Theater which ran for forty-eight performances. During this period he learned to play the piano and began composing music, an interest that was to stay with him all his life. But he needed to work, and Ethel interceded with the theatrical impresario, Charles Frohman, to get him some parts: Lieutenant Barker in *The Second Command* (1901), and an Italian organ-grinder in *The Mummy and the Humming Bird* (1902) which established him as a character actor. The *New York Daily Tribune* reported: 'The one vital character was the organ-grinder of young Lionel Barrymore. In his single short scene he exhibited a burst of genuine passion that was good to feel, for he made you feel it with him.'

When he was 26 he played a Boer army commandant in *The Best of Friends*, and became a smash hit as a famous fighter in *The Other Girl* when he was hailed as 'one of the greatest American character actors'. In June 1904 he married Doris Rankin and was in the double bill of *Pantaloon* and *Alice-Sit-by-the-Fire* with Ethel and John. But his heart was not in the theatre, and his wife encouraged him to concentrate on painting. It was, however, Ethel who provided the money. She shipped them both off to Paris with an allowance, and for three years Lionel studied painting. When Ethel had a family and responsibilities of her own, Lionel felt it was unfair that he and his family should also be dependants, and he returned with his wife and baby daughter to America and the theatre. He played Abdulla in *The Fires of Fate* (1909) and then spent more than a year touring in vaudeville. He made his film début in *Friends*, directed by D. W. Griffith, and wrote a screenplay, *The Tenderhearted*.

It was in films that Lionel spent most of his working life, first in New York and later in Hollywood. In 1915 he made eight films, but in 1917 he returned to the stage as Colonel Ibbetson, while his brother John played the title role, in *Peter Ibbetson*. The *New York Times* noted: 'Lionel Barrymore's arresting and ingenious playing of Colonel Ibbetson is an admirable thing.' Lionel really achieved his place as America's greatest character actor the following year, when as Milt Shanks in *The Copperhead* (1918) he took fifteen curtain calls. It remained his favourite part. He followed that with another success, playing the heavy in *The Jest* (1919). Alexander Woollcott, however, reported the disaster of Lionel's attempt at Macbeth (1921): 'The audience dispersed a little after midnight suffering chiefly from shock — shocked that Lionel Barrymore, while often good and occasionally very good, should never once have suffered greatness in all the length and breadth of the play.' But then the Scottish play has always been unlucky.

After seventeen years of marriage he divorced Doris, and within a year married the actress Irene Fenwick, to whom he remained devoted until her death in 1936. After she died the house he shared with her became a shrine in which he could not bear to live; he visited it occasionally, but her things remained untouched.

Lionel's films during the early twenties included: *Face in the Fog*, *Enemies of Women*, *Unseeing Eyes* and D. W. Griffith's *America*. With Irene in the cast, Lionel appeared in David Belasco's production of *Laugh, Clown, Laugh!* (1923), which was the Pagliacci story. This successfully ran for 133 performances. His next three plays, *The Piker*, *Taps* and *Man or Devil*, were badly received by both audiences and critics.

In 1925 Lionel Barrymore abandoned Broadway and followed his brother John to Hollywood. During his first year there he appeared in twelve feature films, then joined MGM and played mostly supporting roles. He was not worried about his casting as an actor as long as the roles paid the bills; his creative urges were still satisfied by music, painting and etching. When sound came, Lionel's career in films advanced, and he won an Oscar in 1931 for his performance as the drunken criminal lawyer in *A Free Soul*. He never returned to the theatre. Every Christmas for twenty years (with

only two omissions), from 1933 on, he played Scrooge in *A Christmas Carol* on radio — dressed for the part. In 1950 he was the narrator of *The California Story* on stage at the Hollywood Bowl, but he is best remembered for *Captains Courageous*, as Grandpa Vanderhof in *You Can't Take It With You*, *Down to the Sea in Ships* and all those 'Dr Kildare' films in which he played the old Dr Gillespie. He died of a heart attack on 16 November 1954.

See photograph of John Barrymore opposite page 23.

ALAN BATES

'*H*e is,' says the playwright Simon Gray, 'the most human actor of his generation.' From the age of 11 Alan Bates knew he wanted to be an actor, and in a very quiet way he has forged his career relentlessly and successfully. 'As an actor,' he says, 'I've never really been typed in a recognizable way; I want every part to cut across the previous one, so people won't know what to expect next. I don't go in for funny noses, though, or quirky walks to make the people I play look any different — they just are the way they're written and I play them like that. It's not for me to "take over" a character completely — it remains the creation of the author.'

Alan Arthur Bates was born on 17 February 1934 in Allestree, a village just outside Derby. He was the eldest of three boys and his father was an insurance salesman. At the Herbert Street Grammar School he played in the inevitable school plays and from there went to the Royal Academy of Dramatic Art, fitting in national service along the way. At RADA he won the Forbes-Robertson Award. In 1955 he joined Frank Dunlop's Midland Theatre Company in Coventry, where he stage-managed and made his professional début in *You and Your Wife*. Six months later he joined the English Stage Society at the Royal Court in London and gained a wealth of experience, playing Simon Fellowes in *The Mulberry Bush*, Hopkins in *The Crucible*, Cliff Lewis in *Look Back in Anger*, Stapleton in *Cards of Identity*, Mr Harcourt in *The Country Wife*, Monsieur le Crocheton in *The Apollo de Bellac* and Dr Brock in *Yes — and After* — all this in a period of two years. In 1956 he made his New York début at the Lyceum, playing Cliff again in *Look Back in Anger*. At this

point Bates was offered a seven-year film contract but he turned it down, preferring to maintain his artistic freedom. He opened at the Edinburgh Festival in 1959 as Edmund Tyrone in *Long Day's Journey into Night* and transferred with it to the Globe Theatre. The performance won him the Clarence Derwent Award.

As Mick in *The Caretaker* he opened at the Arts Theatre in April 1960, transferred to the Duchess and then went on to New York, again to the Lyceum.

The next few years were taken up with filming, playing Frank Rice in *The Entertainer* and making *Whistle Down the Wind*, *A Kind of Loving*, *Nothing But the Best* and *Zorba, the Greek*, among others.

In New York, at the Helen Hayes Theater, he played Richard Ford in *Poor Richard* in 1964 and the next year returned to London to the Saville, where he played Adam in *The Four Seasons*. A season at Stratford, Ontario, in 1967 provided him with the classic roles of Ford in *The Merry Wives of Windsor* and the title role in *Richard III*.

Back at the Royal Court in 1967, Bates played Andrew in David Storey's *In Celebration*, which was directed by Lindsay Anderson, a man he greatly respects. 'He taught me more than most,' Bates says. 'He showed me that acting wasn't to do with power games or insecurity or trying to prove anything. It's to do with knowing yourself, not hiding behind techniques or disguises.'

Alan Bates zealously guards his private life. He is married to Victoria Ward, a former model, and they have twin sons on whom Bates dotes. His main relaxation is driving, preferably a fast car.

In 1970 Bates tackled Hamlet, first at the

Playhouse, Nottingham, and later transferred to London to the Cambridge Theatre. Peter Roberts reported in *Plays and Players*: 'Alan Bates takes Hamlet's lines very fast and for the most part in a *sotto voce* delivery that can be wonderfully effective in a small theatre but which resulted in inaudibility in the vast reaches of the Cambridge ... I shall remember his Hamlet best for the brief moment of honeyed lyricism as he curses Ophelia in the Nunnery scene as though they were the most tender words of affection and love. I am sorry not to have got more from his performance because, as we have seen in the Storey play (*In Celebration*), Alan Bates has it in his nature to play tormented and self-divided characters with emotional truth and technical finesse.'

It was the following year, playing the messy, self-destructive middle-aged English teacher Butley in Simon Gray's play of the same name that Alan Bates won the *Evening Standard* Best Actor Award. It was a superb showcase for Bates' talents. Butley is witty and sad, appealing and repulsive, pitiable and terrifying all at once. John Russell Taylor summed it up: 'The play provides at the very least a superb set-piece for the actor playing Butley and Alan Bates seizes it with obvious relish.' *Butley* also ran in New York.

Pausing for a touch more of Shakespeare, Petruchio in *The Taming of the Shrew* at Stratford, in 1974 Bates returned once more to the Royal Court to play Allott in David Storey's *Life Class*. Then there was another Simon Gray play, *Otherwise Engaged*, which opened in July 1975 at the Queen's. According to B. A. Young: 'Much of the dialogue is in Simon Gray's well-observed professional manner, an ideal medium in which to conceal emotion. The part of his hero can't be an easy one to play, for it calls for glacial detachment throughout. I was not immediately moved by Alan Bates for Simon [the character] I think is not meant to move me: it is his several interlocutors who bear the emotional burden and it is through them that we feel our antipathy for this iceberg of self-regard. Mr Bates maintains his unvarying cool with superb imperturbability, handling his debonair conversation with great skill.' Alan Bates was named the stage actor of 1975 by the Variety Club for his performance.

Of his performance as Trigorin in *The Seagull*, originating at the Derby Playhouse but transferring to the Duke of York's in August 1976, Eric Shorter said: 'Mr Bates, bearded, dishevelled and extremely calm, points up ironically and sadly this tale of cruelly trivial people ... [Bates gives a] characteristically cool interpretation ...' In 1979, Alan Bates was back in a Simon Gray play again, this time a thriller, *Stage Struck*, at the Vaudeville Theatre. Since then he has been at the Chichester Festival Theatre, the Haymarket and in California with a revival of Osborne's *A Patriot for Me*, and at the Lyric, Hammersmith, in Pinter's *One for the Road*.

He has continued throughout his career to work in films, notably *Women in Love*, *The Shout*, *An Unmarried Woman*, *Far From the Madding Crowd* and *The Rose*. He was nominated for an Academy Award for his performance in the title role of *The Fixer*. He also works frequently on television, and while very happy that he is of a generation of actors who can work in all three media, he summed up his feelings about them thus: 'It [the stage] is the most rewarding medium of all. I love the cinema, but in film-making you are just an actor and the real fascination lies in putting the bits together. You tend to spend a lot of time lounging around, waiting for things to happen. With TV it's very much more concentrated — like a horribly demanding rep. I did a year of live TV and it was exhausting. The stage is very demanding too, but in a different sort of way and, to me, is much more exhilarating.'

See photograph opposite page 22.

BARBARA BEL GEDDES

It seems hard to believe that Miss Ellie of television's infamous *Dallas* was the original Maggie the Cat in Tennessee Williams' *Cat on a Hot Tin Roof*, but Barbara Bel Geddes has had a long and very distinguished Broadway career. She was born on 31 October 1922 into a theatrical family in New York City. Her father, Norman, was a designer, producer and theatre architect.

After graduating from Andebrook School in Tarrytown, New York, Barbara Bel Geddes went straight into summer stock; her first stage appearance was in a walk-on part in *The School for Scandal* at the Clinton Playhouse in Connecticut in July 1940. That season she also appeared in *Tonight at 8:30* and *The World We Make*, and she played Amy in *Little Women*.

Her New York début was at the Windsor Theater on 11 February 1941, playing Dottie Coburn in *Out of the Frying Pan*. After that she toured the military camps with a USO production of *Junior Miss*. She played Cynthia Brown in *Little Darling* (Biltmore, 1942) and Alice in *Nine Girls* (Longacre, 1943). Back in summer stock in Rhode Island during the summer of 1943, Barbara Bel Geddes played Ellen Murray in *Yes, My Darling Daughter* and the title role in *Claudia*. In January 1944 she married Carl Schreuer, an engineer (they subsequently had a daughter), and in March she opened at the Belasco Theater playing Wilhelmina in *Mrs January and Mr X*. In September 1945 she opened at the Fulton playing Genevra Langdon in *Deep Are the Roots*, a sensitive play about bigotry and prejudice in the South. Of her performance Lewis Nichols, writing in the *New York Times*, said: 'Barbara Bel Geddes, as the younger daughter, is giving a performance which she will find difficulty beating later on. She has grace and tenderness and an honesty which breathes life into the part.' She received the Clarence Derwent Award for the performance.

In 1947 Barbara Bel Geddes made her first film, *The Long Night*, and followed that with *I Remember Mama* and *Blood on the Moon* (both 1948), *Caught* (1949) and *Panic* (1950). In 1950 she returned to Broadway, opening at the Broadhurst in October in the role of Mordeen in *Burning Bright*. She then played Patty O'Neill in the comedy by F. Hugh Herbert, *The Moon is Blue*, at the Henry Miller Theater in 1951. Brooks Atkinson wrote: 'To say that it would not be funny if it were not acted so expertly is beside the point. For the only fact worth mentioning is that it is acted expertly ... As the amiable young lady, Miss Bel Geddes is radiantly beautiful — a fact that explains quite a lot about everything. But she also manages to act a coherent character, looking greatly puzzled by the behaviour of the helpless males, smiling enchantingly at the hopeful interludes in a cock-eyed manuscript and always waiting for the right moment to speak a line. Mr Herbert ought to regard her as a treasure. Everyone else inevitably does.'

That same year she was divorced and on 15 April married Windsor Lewis, a producer and director with whom she had a second daughter. He presented her in a series of plays at the Robin Hood Theater in Wilmington, Delaware. In the summer of 1952 she played in *Liliom*, *Born Yesterday* and *The Respectful Prostitute*. The following summer she did *Claudia*, *The Voice of the Turtle* and *The Winter Palace*.

In 1954 she toured summer theatres as Susan in *The Little Hut*, and returned to Broadway in November to play Rose Pemberton in *The Living Room* at the Henry Miller Theater. The next year she created Maggie, opening in *Cat on a Hot Tin Roof* at the Morosco on 24 March 1955. Brooks Atkinson in the *New York Times* continued to be impressed with her: 'The acting is magnificent. Barbara Bel Geddes [is] vital, lovely and frank as the young wife who cannot accept her husband's indifference.'

During the fifties Barbara Bel Geddes appeared often in television dramas (such as 'Studio One', 'Schlitz Playhouse' and 'Alfred Hitchcock Presents'), continued to make films (such as *Vertigo* and *The Five Pennies*) and also managed to work on Broadway as Mary in *The Sleeping Prince* (Coronet, 1956) and as Katherine Johnson in *Silent Night, Lonely Night* (Morosco, 1959). In March 1961 she opened at the Helen Hayes Theater in Jean Kerr's comedy, *Mary, Mary*. Howard Taubman said: 'Barbara Bel Geddes plays Mary with an agreeably light touch; her quirk of pausing for quick intakes of breath in the midst of phrases, whether a habit or not, seems felicitous here.'

She played Alice in *The Porcelain Year* at the Locust in Philadelphia in October 1965, and took over the role of Ellen Manville from Anne Jackson in *Luv* at the Booth in February 1966. In 1967 she played Jenny in *Everything in the Garden* at the Plymouth.

In 1971 Barbara Bel Geddes was operated on for cancer. After a full recovery she was back at the Plymouth in February 1973, playing Katy Cooper in *Finishing Touches*. She repeated the role at the Ahmanson in Los Angeles and then toured with it. She also toured (1975) in *Ah, Wilderness!*, and then came 'Dallas', from which she retired in 1984 due to illness.

FRANK BENSON

The distinguished drama critic J. C. Trewin describes Sir Frank Benson thus: 'Frank Benson looked like the noblest Roman of them all; he could have been a Greek in Periclean Athens; and he had a passionate loyalty to his own nation, and to the poet who was the nation's voice. As an actor–manager, he led the most astonishing company of young players — able again and again to renew its strength — that this land has known. As a man of business he was wholly unpractical, an idealist who could not read a balance sheet. To the end, even in years of ill-health and retirement enforced, he remained gallant and undefeated; still the visionary, still pondering upon some vast efflorescence of the folk arts, still Benson who could behave like Don Quixote, and speak with the voice of Shakespearian kings.'

Frank Benson was born on 8 November 1858 at Tunbridge Wells, Kent, into a wealthy, puritanical Quaker family. His father, previously a barrister, was a magistrate and landowner. Frank, one of six children, grew up in a large country house in Hampshire. His first school, which he attended at the age of nine, was Darch's Preparatory in Brighton. This was followed in 1871 by Winchester College, where he excelled himself in both sports and drama. He discovered Shakespeare there and was especially good in his reading of the women's parts.

After Winchester he entered New College, Oxford, where again he excelled in athletics and also discovered his true vocation — the stage. He produced, in Greek, the *Agamemnon* of Aeschylus, himself playing the part of Clytemnestra. The play was presented on 3 June 1880. Reviewing the production, Andrew Lang reported on Benson's performance: 'The tall, white figure, the waving arms, the face that expressed with equal skill horror, triumph, pity (when Iphigenia was named) and the fanatical conviction that right was wrong, are likely to dwell long in the memory of the audience.' Delighted with the play's reception, the students embarked on a mini-tour of Winchester, Eton and Harrow, and the following December gave three performances at St George's Hall in London that attracted all the leading professional actors of the day and succeeded in impressing them. Although now sure of his destiny, Benson also believed strongly in bodily fitness and proceeded to win the traditional three-mile race for Oxford against Cambridge.

In the summer of 1881 Benson staged *Romeo and Juliet* at the Imperial Theatre (already very run down) in London. He played Romeo as well as directing — his father footing the bill. He didn't much like his son's choice of career but supported him in every way he could. The production was pilloried in the press for its amateurishness but the profession still admired Benson's courage and style. He next produced the *Alcestis* of Euripides for Bradfield College.

Henry Irving had admired Benson as an undergraduate. Now that he had come down from Oxford and was living in London, Irving kept in contact. He invited Benson to play the part of Don Pedro in a private reading of *Much Ado About Nothing*, and he gave him his first job on the professional stage taking over the part of Paris in *Romeo and Juliet*. Benson made his London début in the role at the Lyceum on 2 September 1882.

Taking Irving's advice, Benson next joined the Shakespearian company of Charles Bernard and Miss Alleyn in Manchester; but he was disappointed in the parts he was given, which were minuscule, and to add insult to injury Bernard told him he was a terrible actor and advised him to leave the stage. Instead Benson joined another touring company, this one run by Walter Bentley. The company was in financial difficulties, and within a few months Bentley had fled, leaving behind his unpaid actors, his sets, costumes and lots of bills. Benson quickly got the necessary cash from his ever-helpful father and took over the company, beginning his management in Scotland on 7 May 1883. It was a disastrous tour but Benson, supported by weekly cheques from his father, was undaunted.

He opened his second tour, billing himself as F. R. Benson, from the Lyceum Theatre, London, in August 1883 at the Drill Hall, Ulverston. The company presented *Hamlet*, *The Merchant of Venice*, *The Lady of Lyons*, *The Corsican Brothers* and *The Rivals*, among others. Benson played the leading parts — after all, whose company was it? He had been impressed by the method of production pioneered by the company of George, Duke of Saxe-Meiningen. In these performances of Shakespeare everyone, even the crowds, were minutely rehearsed in a realistic presentation of historical plays. In these early years Benson always included on his programme, 'conducted in the Meiningen system'. The company toured the provinces for six years, sustained mainly by enthusiasm.

On 24 July 1886 Frank Benson married Constance Featherstonhaugh, an actress in his company. (They subsequently had two children.) That same year the company enjoyed its first of many seasons at the Stratford Festival. Benson pioneered the custom of playing Shakespeare's plays at his birthplace. Their first London season opened at the Globe Theatre on 19 December 1889 with *A Midsummer Night's Dream*. The production was a success but Benson, a believer in the repertory system, introduced *The Taming of the Shrew*, *Hamlet* and *Othello*, and playgoers felt that this was a sign that he had no faith in *Dream*. Also, unused to this system in London, the audiences stayed away in confusion over what play they might actually see if they ventured into the Globe. The critics generally found Benson's performances athletic, and Godfrey, Frank's younger brother, supplied the money which kept the season going.

Frank Benson and the Bensonians went on tour for another ten years, performing Shakespeare's plays in the provinces, now moving round on a regular schedule and warmly welcomed back each year to the Stratford Festival and such cities as Manchester, Birmingham, Liverpool and Inverness, as well as smaller towns. Benson constantly drew new young talent to himself and forged the early careers of performers such as Janet Achurch, Henry Ainley, Esmé Percy, Robert Morley and Basil Rathbone. He produced in his lifetime every Shakespearian play except *Titus Andronicus* and *Troilus and Cressida* — and at times had as many as four companies travelling the country under his banner.

The Benson company returned to London to the Lyceum, opening on 15 February 1900 with *Henry V*; London remained snobbish about this 'decent rep acting'. The *Times* reported: 'There is too much effort in his [Benson's] performance and he does not always keep to the words as closely as their beauty demands.' But it was Max Beerbohm's criticism in the *Saturday Review* that really hurt — condemning this veteran of seventeen years' Shakespearian experience to the status of well-meaning amateur and bringing up *ad infinitum* Benson's devotion to physical fitness. 'Art,' Beerbohm said, 'is a mysterious thing, in which cads and weaklings may often excel, and gentlemanly athletes may often fail. The old strollers lived a life of degradation, but it does not follow that their excess in alcohol and nicotine hurt them as mimes. The new strollers play cricket and other games, and are healthy and reputable fellows; but they do not necessarily act better for that ... Alertness, agility, grace, physical strength — all these good attributes are obvious in the mimes who were last week playing *Henry the Fifth* at the Lyceum ... Speech after speech was sent spinning

across the boundary, and one was constantly inclined to shout, "Well played, sir! Well played indeed." As a branch of university cricket, the whole performance was, indeed, beyond praise. But, as a form of acting, it was not impressive. Not one of the parts was played with any distinction.'

Henry V was followed by *A Midsummer Night's Dream*, a respectable *Hamlet* and a near-triumphant *Richard II*. The *Morning Post* critic said: 'It wants but one thing — an important thing certainly — to take its rank among the finest Shakespearian impersonations of the modern stage. The one thing needful is a tear ... but it is just this tear that is beyond Mr Benson's reach.'

The Bensonians went once more on the road, where they were appreciated. In December 1900 Frank Benson was back in London, sharing the Comedy Theatre with a German company. However, Queen Victoria died during the season; the theatres were closed and when they reopened the audiences did not return to the Comedy. The company nearly disbanded but, waiving salaries and accepting aid, they muddled through.

For the Stratford Festival Benson then planned the Historical Cycle — *King John*, *Richard II*, *Henry IV Part 2*, *Henry V*, *Henry VI Part 2* and *Richard III*. Then it was back on the road. The next year Benson officially started a travelling drama school.

Benson may not have been able to compete in London with Tree and Irving, but in the provinces and among those actors and actresses he had nurtured, he was not only 'Pa' he was also 'Sir'. Old Bensonians had annual dinners at which he spoke. He was respected in the profession and among the provincial theatregoers, and on 25 July 1910 Benson was given the Freedom of Stratford amid much acclaim.

In December 1910 he appeared in London at the St James's Theatre in *The Piper*, a disaster that virtually cost him his company. A syndicate moved in to control finances — and Benson no longer travelled under his own banner alone. Other people began to make the decisions for him.

In September 1913 Benson for the first time crossed the Atlantic and toured Canada and the United States. He triumphed in Canada, but in Chicago could do nothing right. The *Chicago Record-Herald* said Benson as Benedick was 'wrong in spirit and deplorable in execution. It was the performance of a fussy, superficial actor, and it meant nothing good'. Darby Foster, who was with Benson on the tour, explained: 'He just acted when he wanted to. I saw him give a mighty performance of Shylock to a meagre audience of miners, yet he could be appalling during the season at Los Angeles. None could control him in anything:

acting, money, production.'

When the First World War came Benson tried to enlist despite his age, but had to content himself with entertaining in war hospitals or addressing rallies or playing the ultra-patriotic *Henry V* — a part which came to be associated with him.

At the Drury Lane Theatre on 2 May 1916 he played the title role in *Julius Caesar* in celebration of Shakespeare's tercentenary. It was during an interval in the performance that the King, with a borrowed sword, knighted Frank Benson in the Royal Box — making him the only actor to be knighted within a theatre. The romance of the occasion overcame everyone. The *Times* reported that it was 'the creation of a knight by title of one who has been all his life a knight by nature vowed to the service of his Gloriana who is England'. Sir Frank Benson, now greeted everywhere by public acclaim, celebrated Shakespeare's tercentenary as if it were his own.

Benson's son Eric was killed in the war, and Sir Frank devoted himself to war work with the Red Cross. Driving a French ambulance, he rescued the wounded from a front-line attack and took them to a field hospital, and for his bravery under fire he was awarded the Croix de guerre.

When the Stratford Festival resumed after the war it was with a new director. Benson had been judged too old by the committee now in charge. After thirty years of Shakespeare it came as a cruel blow to Sir Frank. It was back to the provinces, with a season at Manchester in which Benson played Shylock, Caius, Petruchio, Hamlet, Richard III, and Antony in *Julius Caesar*. Neville Cardus, critic of the *Manchester Guardian*, said: 'His Richard III was a masterpiece of crooked, gargoyled irony, of inherited evil, evil attained by royal and satanic prerogative, with humour and relish added.'

In January 1920 he again tried London, opening at the St Martin's in *Pompey the Great*. Although he got a great personal ovation, the play was withdrawn after thirteen performances. He played Hamlet for a week after that but was judged too old. That summer it was back to Leeds and Manchester and on to the touring circuit, but many of the old theatres had been turned into cinemas and theatre audiences had dwindled. Touring was harder than ever. Sir Frank became absent-minded and even more mannered; his athleticism, however, defied his age.

He toured South Africa in 1921 and was greeted as the legend he had become. There, during the tour, he fell in love with a young actress in his company. Constance, who had stayed in England to run the drama school and the touring company, understood and on his return agreed to an amicable and unofficial separation. Sir Frank Benson continued touring until 1929. His London farewell performance was at the Winter Garden in December 1932, playing Dr Caius in *The Merry Wives of Windsor*. But he could not afford to retire, and in the spring of 1933 he was billed as guest artist on a tour playing Shylock, Caliban and Malvolio. He had just finished playing Shylock when, crossing the road, he was knocked down by a boy on a bicycle; he hit his head on a lamp-post and never acted again.

He lived then in a few rooms in London, virtually alone and able to exist only because of a meagre Civil List pension awarded him in recognition of his services to art. He became increasingly frail. Friends were moved to tears by the sight of his once-athletic body now shrunken and useless. Bronchial pneumonia set in, and he died on the evening of 31 December 1939. James Agate wrote: 'About Benson in his heyday I cannot and will not be dispassionate. He gave what, to a young playgoer, seemed tremendous things. The thwarted walk of Hamlet; the blood-crusted, wholly barbaric Macbeth; the patrician Coriolanus; the zoological, unsentimentalized Caliban ... He had four things most modern actors lack — presence, a profile befitting a Roman coin, voice, and virility to make you believe that Orlando overthrew more than his enemies.'

ELISABETH
BERGNER

She didn't care for Brecht or Shaw but very much liked O'Neill and Barrie. The real wonder is that she worked with all of them. Elisabeth Bergner was born in Vienna on 22 August 1900. She studied for the theatre at the Vienna Conservatory, and made her first professional appearance in Zurich with the City Theatre at the age of 19, playing Ophelia in Moissi's *Hamlet*. The following year she played Rosalind in *As You Like It* and repeated the performance in Vienna, Munich and Berlin. (Much later, in 1936, she made the film version, starring with Laurence Olivier.)

Elisabeth Bergner then stayed in Germany, appearing in the Berlin production of *The Wicked Mr Chu*. After that she worked with Max Reinhardt at the Deutches Theater playing a number of roles and establishing an international reputation. Among the parts she played were: Katharina in *The Taming of the Shrew*, the Queen in *Richard II*, Miss Julie, Nora in *A Doll's House*, Viola in *Twelfth Night* and Juliet in *Romeo and Juliet*. In 1924 she played St Joan, as well as Marguerite in *The Lady of the Camellias*. The following year she played in *The Circle of Chalk* and *He Wants to Have His Fun*. At the Koeniggraetzer Theater in Berlin in 1926 she played Mrs Cheyney in *The Last of Mrs Cheyney* and at the same theatre the next year appeared as Tessa in *The Constant Nymph*. Also in 1927 she played Portia in *The Merchant of Venice* at the Staettheater.

In 1928 Elisabeth Bergner toured Holland, Switzerland, Denmark, Sweden, Germany and Austria in *Hannele*, *Kaiser Karl's Geisel*, *Einsame Menschen*, *The Taming of the Shrew*, *Richard II*, *Queen Christina*, *The Circle*, *Miss Julie*, *Lanzelot and Sanderein*, *The Circle of Chalk*, *As You Like It*, *The Last of Mrs Cheyney*, *Saint Joan* and *Amphitryon 38*.

Back in Berlin in 1929, she played Nina Leeds in *Strange Interlude*. 'The authors that I have played,' she later said, 'have ripened me and made me grow in what they demanded of me. Let us take O'Neill. My first O'Neill experience was *Strange Interlude*. I fell in love with it and he asked me to age 18 to 70 — a whole life. This demand developed me.'

In 1930 and 1931 she was again working with Reinhardt, playing Juliet to Francis Lederer's Romeo, and again playing Alkemena in *Amphitryon 38*.

The next two years she spent working in films, establishing a relationship with the producer–director Paul Czinner, whom she married in 1933. That year Alexander Korda invited both of them to England to make *Catherine the Great*. 'He held out a hand when I needed it most,' she said. 'I remember the day I was having dinner with Emil Jannings and his wife in a hotel and Emil put his fingers to his lips. "Listen," he said, and through the wall we heard Goering and Goebbels and all those cardboard men talking. Such evil voices. So when Korda offered the film, I thought, good, I shall go to England and when we return it will all have blown over.' It was nearly twenty-five years before she again acted in Germany.

They settled in England and she made her stage début under C. B. Cochran's management at the Opera House in Manchester in November 1933, playing Gemma Jones in *Escape Me Never*. She opened in London in the same part in December and it was an immediate success. She took it to New York to the Shubert Theater in January 1935, making her American début. Brooks Atkinson reported in the *New York Times*: 'She is the stuff of which angels are fashioned behind the footlights ... Miss Bergner plays like a fiery particle in the theater's firmament. She is slight and small, with flaxen hair; she has little of the imposing personal beauty of the conventional star, and she employs none of the theater's aids to comeliness in make-up or costumery. But her acting has the insubstantiality of the breeze; it is light and spontaneous and gloriously free... She translates Gemma into an inspired creature who is half brat and half dryad. Sometimes she is only a gutter-snipe with common manners and an instinct for vulgar mockery. Sometimes she is pure spirit. It is impossible to tell what craft she has slipped into her characterization, for she dances through with incomparable buoyancy, as though it were a fresh improvization. No doubt Gemma Jones will be much the same character at tonight's performance. Bur those of us who were enkindled by its humour last evening and touched by its poignancy could swear that she had created it on the spur of the moment and could never recover the same impulses again.'

J. M. Barrie wrote *The Boy David* for her to play David. Miss Bergner had wanted to change her image — that of a fey gamin. She wanted, at 36 not surprisingly, to grow up. Barrie asked her if anything had impressed her and she told him of a picture she had seen in the Hague — a Rembrandt of David playing the harp for Saul. 'I cannot tell you,' she said later to Martin Esslin of the BBC, 'what took place at that moment, the shock he had when he heard this mentioned. I was frightened. Barrie took me to the lift and then grabbed me out again and whispered in my ear: "Goodbye David".' *The Boy David* opened in London at His Majesty's in December 1936 and was not a success. It was Barrie's last play and Miss Bergner thought it was its failure that killed him. However, when he died in 1937 he left £2000 in his will 'to my loved Elisabeth Bergner for the best performance ever given in any play of mine'.

In August 1938, at Malvern, she again played *Saint Joan* — her last appearance in England for ten years. There was an uproar in the press when she deserted England, her adopted country, for America during the war. She worked both in Hollywood, making such pictures as *Stolen Life* (1939), *Paris Calling* (1941) and *Escape Me Never* (1947), and on the stage in *The Two Mrs Carrolls* (Booth, 1943), *The Overtures* (directing at the Booth, 1945), *The Duchess of Malfi* (Ethel Barrymore Theater, 1946), *Miss Julie* (Forrest, Philadelphia, 1947), *The Cup of Trembling* (Music Box, 1948) and *Amphitryon 38* (1949).

Elisabeth Bergner toured Australia in 1950 in *The Two Mrs Carrolls* and in November returned to the English stage to the scene of her first triumph, the Opera House, Manchester, as Toinette in a version of Molière's comedy *Le Malade imaginaire*, called *The Gay Invalid*. She also played it in London at the Garrick in January 1951. The critics were less than enthusiastic but it must be remembered that they were still smarting from her 'desertion'. As the *Daily Telegraph* said cynically: 'Gallant entertainers worked throughout the blitz periods. ENSA concert parties defied alike danger and discomfort. But these things were not for Miss Bergner. Now, five years after the last bomb has fallen, she has elected to return.'

She also returned to Germany and Austria, touring in 1954 in Rattigan's *The Deep Blue Sea*, and in 1957 as Mary Tyrone in *Long Day's Journey Into Night*. At the Berlin Festival in October 1959 she played Mrs Patrick Campbell in *Dear Liar* and then toured it through Germany and Austria. At the Shubert, New Haven,

Connecticut, she played Nina Kacew in *First Love* in November 1961, and played again in *Dear Liar* at the Barbizon-Plaza, New York, in May 1963. She has twice received the Goldeneband at the International Film Festival, Berlin, and in 1963 she was awarded the Schiller Prize 'for outstanding contributions to the cultural life of Germany'. The next year, in September, she opened as Aurelia in *The Madwoman of Chaillot* in Düsseldorf and came to England in the role in 1967, playing at the Yvonne Arnaud Theatre, Guildford, and at the Oxford Playhouse. Ronald Bryden reported: 'It takes a few minutes to adjust to the fact that her Madwoman isn't the huge painted crone Matita Hunt created: a few more to get used to her accent — it must be a profound shyness indeed that still inhibits her English after thirty years. Then you forget both, caught up by the amazements of her voice and flawless, imperial technique ... Her technique's not showy — the gestures are sparse, a commanding forefinger, a swift glance to make sure that objects are still in their places, like a sparrow feeding on a tourist's wrists. Mostly she relies on her voice, floating it like a singer, spinning long phrases like steel threads around your attention. Its range is extraordinary, sinking from a high childish plaint to a deep purring growl. She winds it out with deliberate artifice, perfect control, from a fund of breath a Wagnerian soprano might envy.' And Eric Shorter: '[the part] is also a test, and Miss Bergner comes through it with engaging charm, confidence and — perhaps the key to the success of her performance — undoubted sincerity.'

At the Greenwich Theatre in October 1973 she played Mrs Orban in Mari Kuttna's translation of *Cat's Play* by Istvan Orkeny. In the *Guardian* Michael Billington exclaimed: 'Histrionic legends often turn out a trifle disappointing in reality. But not, emphatically not, Elisabeth Bergner.' And John Barber in the *Daily Telegraph*: 'That gleaming thin-lipped smile. The coy Peter Pan little figure. The gurgling laugh. The accent, cute as a dirndl. The conscious charm of those exclamatory gestures — flat palm on forehead, fingers splayed — she is just as we recall her in *Escape Me Never* and, as ever, a most accomplished performer.' Miss Bergner lives now in retirement in London.

SARAH BERNHARDT

Sarah Bernhardt was born Henriette Rosine Bernard in Paris on 23 October 1844, the illegitimate daughter of Judith Van Hard, a Jewish Dutch woman who had been a milliner but, on arrival in Paris, tired of that occupation and became a courtesan. She had no time for the child, who would have annoyed her gentleman callers, so Sarah was sent to the country with a nurse, where she was virtually ignored until her return, aged four. Her vivacious mother still had little time for this weak, tubercular child and Sarah was left to the servants until at eight it was decided to send her away to school. There she learned to read and write at last, and playing the Queen of the Fairies in a school production of *Clothilde*, she also learned the agonizing suffering caused by an attack of stage fright — a terror that remained with her all her life. When she was 10, Sarah was sent to the Convent of Grandchamps at Versailles, where she converted to Roman Catholicism and decided to be a nun. She continued in ill health through her teenage years and death became an obsession with her. She spent a great deal of time in the Paris morgue. Indeed, she pestered her mother into buying her a rosewood coffin, lined with white satin, in which she occasionally slept, 'to get used to it'. Sarah remained determined to be a nun, despite family objections, until she was taken to the Comédie-Française to see Racine's *Britannicus*. She became so involved in the action that she disturbed the rest of the audience by sobbing noisily until she was consoled by Alexandre Dumas, who said the girl was destined for the stage and bid her good night with a kiss and 'Bonsoir, petite étoile'.

It was the Duc de Morny, a friend of her mother, who arranged an audition for Sarah at the Conservatoire. Her mother thought Sarah far too skinny and much too eccentric-looking, with that tiny face topped by frizzled red hair, to be a successful actress.

Sarah, then 15, recited most unusually and naively La Fontaine's fable of *The Two Pigeons* for her audition and the jury was stunned by her performance. She spent the next two years at the Conservatoire and won second prize at the final declamation. Her professional stage début came in August 1862 in the part of Iphigénie, in the play of that name by Racine at the Comédie-Française. Of her performance a critic said, in *Le Temps*, merely that she 'carries herself well and pronounces with perfect precision. That is all that can be said about her at the moment'. That first season Sarah played

Henrietta in *Les Femmes savantes*, Hippolyte in *L'Etourdi* (both by Molière) and the title role in Scribe's *Valérie*, but none of the performances was particularly noteworthy. She was dismissed from the Comédie for fighting with a senior actress in a backstage fracas and, moreover, refusing to apologize. She was pleased by the masses of publicity she received, but it was hard to get another job, having been labelled difficult. Finally she secured one at the Gymnase, a Boulevard theatre. There was little for her to do except understudy parts, and to assuage her boredom it was during this period she began to take prominent lovers. After giving a terrible performance as Dumchinka, a Russian princess in an equally terrible play, *Un Mari qui lance sa femme*, Sarah was suicidal, but rather than kill herself she merely left Paris and threw herself into a social whirlwind, culminating in Brussels in an affair with Prince Henri de Ligne. Sarah returned pregnant to Paris, and after the birth of her only child, Maurice, being very much in need of money she got a job at Ponte-Saint-Martin Theatre, which specialized in melodrama and extravaganzas. There she had to content herself with walk-ons and understudies until she secured a contract with the Odéon, a theatre second only to the Comédie-Française. Her first performance there as Silvia in *Jeu de l'amour et du hasard* was not good. Dumas commented: 'She has the head of a virgin and the body of a broomstick.' Her Armande in Molière's *Les Femmes savantes* was not much better but her Cordelia in *King Lear* showed a great improvement. Sarah Bernhardt was finally getting into her stride, and as a boy, Zacharie, in Racine's *Athalie*, Sarcy wrote of her: 'She charmed her audience like a little Orpheus.' But it was in 1868 in a revival of Dumas' *Kean*, playing the female lead, Ann Damby, that Sarah scored her first personal triumph, by acting with simplicity and a stunning naturalness. The crowds cheered and threw flowers. At the stage door she was mobbed. For six years she remained the most popular actress at the Odéon, with an audience composed mainly of students, artists and left-wing *literati*. Her repertoire increased. Sarah had a startling memory. She learned a part by reading it four times, and even in old age she kept at least twenty-five parts word-perfect in her mind.

During the Franco-Prussian War, Sarah opened a field hospital, which she managed herself and in which she was the head nurse. After the war she returned to the Odéon in *Jean Marie*, but it was as the Queen in Victor Hugo's *Ruy Blas* in January 1872 that she established herself as a permanent star. She received a tumultuous ovation. Outside the theatre students unharnessed the horses from her carriage and pulled her home themselves, shouting: 'Make way for our Sarah!'

Having achieved such a level of stardom, Sarah's former misdemeanours were of course forgotten and she was re-engaged by the premier Parisian theatre, the Comédie-Française. She opened there in November 1872 in *Mille de Belle Isle*, and the directors watching her performance wondered if they had not made a mistake — it was a personal fiasco. But Sarah reclaimed her stardom a few nights later with a great performance as Junie in *Britannicus*, the very play that had so moved her on her first visit to the theatre.

Sarah, on at least friendly terms with every important artist in Paris, herself began to paint and sculpt with a degree of success. She held glittering salons with great success. She became the most painted, most talked about, most written about woman in Paris, and when she began an extravagant love affair with Jean Mounet-Sully the entire city swooned. He was not only exceedingly handsome but also an expert tragedian. Their names together on the billboard assured standing room only. In 1874 Sarah played the title role in Racine's *Phèdre* while her gorgeous lover played Hippolyte. Sir George Arthur wrote of 'the terrible mixture of triumph and self-loathing; and her grief and horror of herself were so poignant as to turn, for those of us who heard the agonized tones, horror for the sin into something like pity for the sinner.' Sarcey said, 'This is nature itself served by a marvellous intelligence, by a soul of fire, by the most melodious voice that ever enchanted human ears. This woman plays with her heart, with her entrails.' *Phèdre* became Bernhardt's masterpiece; she played it often over many years, terrified by it but always seeking to polish it to total perfection.

Sarah's outstanding role in 1877 was Dona Sol in Hugo's *Hernani*. In fact the author said it was the first time he had seen it properly acted. Her personal life continued to be frenetic. Sarah could not bear to be alone unless she was studying a part. She had the endearing habit of fainting if she was bored, even if she happened to be sitting at the dinner table. But she was never bored at her own parties: the guests were always amusing. The Prince of Wales was a frequent guest, as was Oscar Wilde, who wrote *Salomé* in French for her — and together they planned a production but it was banned.

Having completely and totally conquered Paris, in June 1879 Sarah Bernhardt crossed the Channel and opened for the first time in London, at the Gaiety Theatre. Matthew Arnold reported her 'a fugitive vision of delicate features under a shower of hair and a cloud of lace'. Both Society and Bohemia honoured her with parties. There was an exhibition of her paintings and sculpture at a Piccadilly art gallery under the patronage of the Prince of Wales. In London she collected three dogs, a parrot, a monkey, a cheetah, a wolf hound and seven chameleons to add to her menagerie.

On returning to Paris she quarrelled with the Comédie-Française over the part of Dona Clorinde in *L'Aventurière* and left them. She returned to London and the Gaiety Theatre with her own company. Sarah was now an actress–manager. There followed Brussels and then Copenhagen (where she received the Danish Order of Merit) before she returned to France and a triumphant provincial tour which included performances of *Frou-Frou* and *Adrienne Lecouvreur*.

Sarah Bernhardt then crossed the ocean and conquered America as completely as she had Europe. In 1880 she visited Boston, Montreal, Philadelphia, Chicago, New Orleans, Toledo . . . in all giving 157 performances in fifty-one cities. The favourite play of the tour, one that Bernhardt revived often, was *La Dame aux camélias* (which the Americans insisted on calling *Camille*).

On stage Bernhardt could now do little wrong. She was an astute judge of plays and audiences and her own performances — usually managing to include one of her elegant death scenes. But she fell in love with Jaques Damala, a notorious Don Juan eleven years younger than herself, and made the mistake of actually marrying him. He proved emotionally draining and very expensive — and although, back in Paris, she was enjoying an enormous success with her own theatre and her own company, when he left her abruptly she had to sell her jewels, carriages and horses and go immediately on another money-spinning tour to pay the debts he also left her. He occasionally returned to her, with his current mistress in tow and with more debts for her to pay off. She also, unwillingly, supported his drug addiction before she finally got him into a sanatorium and arranged for a legal separation.

In 1886 she toured again (all the Divine Sarah's tours were triumphant), this time all over South America. The next year she added Sardou's *La Tosca* to her repertoire. Clement Scott wrote of her performance: 'She looked superb, pale as death with distended eyes and the fierce glare of a Judith. Sarah Bernhardt, knife in hand, is the nearest thing to great tragedy that has ever been seen in modern times.'

At 45, a widow and a grandmother (a fact she joyously proclaimed), she played the 19-year-old

Sarah Bernhardt played the title role in Sardou's melodrama *Théodora*
(Paris, 1882)

As manager of the Winter Garden Theatre, Edwin Booth staged
this record-breaking production of *Hamlet*, in which he played the title role
(New York, 1865)

Jeanne d'Arc in the play by Jules Barnier, and did so convincingly. In 1891 she embarked on a grand world tour which took her through Europe, America (North and South), Russia and as far as Samoa. Although she had her own theatre in Paris she was now addicted to touring and did so at every opportunity. One London critic pointed out that Sarah Bernhardt was 'no longer an artist but an international institution'. Sarah even added *Hamlet* to her repertoire, playing the title role. There was a tradition of women seriously playing men in Paris but none such existed in London and audiences were rather surprised by it. The *Punch* critic playfully pointed out that all the production

needed for perfection was Henry Irving playing Ophelia. Finally, in 1914 Sarah was made a Chevalier of the Légion d'honneur. The following year she had a severely diseased leg amputated at the hip, yet it did not stop her performing. Finding a wooden leg unwieldy and refusing to resort to crutches, she designed a litter chair, finished in Louis XV style with gilt ornamentation, on which she was carried about; and she continued touring, balancing on one leg to acknowledge the ovations she received everywhere. When she lay dying, at the age of 79, she was murmuring: 'I wonder when my next tour will be.'
See photograph opposite page 38.

MASTER BETTY

*I*t is perhaps better to describe Master Betty in terms of a phenomenon than an actor; as a star he reigned supreme on the London stage for a season, forcing Sarah Siddons and Kemble to retire briefly when they realized that there was no advantage in trying to compete with this boy, who was both the result and the victim of an early example of the massive public and press attention more familiar in the latter part of this century.

Although he was born in Shrewsbury, England, on 13 September 1791, William Henry West Betty's earliest years were spent in Ireland and it was there is 1803, just a month short of his twelfth birthday, that he performed Osman in *Zara* — the venue was Belfast. He started out, and indeed continued, in the great tragic roles, organized and coached by his father and a friend of his father, William Hough. His father was by nature a squanderer, and in need of the cash which his son's celebrity could bring. It was Hough who trained the boy, controlled his performances and, perhaps more importantly, his publicity.

There is no doubt that Master Betty was beautiful. Portraits attest to this, especially Northcote's, which shows Betty dressed for the part of Norval in *Douglas*. He must have been clever to learn such immense roles, but could he possibly have overcome the essentially ludicrous idea of a boy playing the major acting roles in the company of adults?

The Belfast *News Letter* of 23 August 1803 reported: 'The young gentleman's person is handsome, his deportment majestic, and his voice bold and melodious; and the performance throughout, considering his age and its being his

first appearance, was truly astonishing. ... If his genius be rightly cultivated, under proper mentors, he bids fair to rival the first tragedian of the age and may not be unjustly styled the Minor Roscius.'

But 'his mentors', being more interested in the immediate than in cultivating for the future, took him on the road, changing 'Minor' to 'Young' Roscius in the publicity. They went to Waterford, Cork and Dublin in November 1803, causing a sensation at each performance. 'So wonderful a collection of natural powers never have been witnessed in so young a creature,' proclaimed the Dublin *Journal*.

Betty's sights were now set across the Irish Sea, London was where the action was — and they approached it by way of Glasgow, and Macready's Birmingham Theatre.

On 1 December 1804 Master Betty played Covent Garden. The public mobbed the theatre. Scenes of fainting and hysteria only increased the desire to see him. He played at both Covent Garden and Drury Lane during the four-month season, with both managers being eager to share in the spoils. They did not actually approve, seeing it for the fleeting fad it was, but no one was about to argue with all the profits. Both Sarah Siddons and Kemble retired for the season. They would have been trampled in the rush to see the divine youth. Tradition has it that the House of Commons adjourned so that Members of Parliament could attend Master Betty's performance of Hamlet. Society competed to fête him, money poured in (most of it — but not all — spent by his father), and Master Betty was adored, painted by the greatest artists and lauded by all.

But the overnight star so soon becomes yesterday's flavour, and the public, who had waited in their thousands outside the gates of his London house reading hourly bulletins on his health when he fell ill, soon tired of him. His Richard III was greeted with derision. The *Times* said: 'Nature has denied him the first and simplest materials of theatrical excellence; and art has not given him even the humblest compensation that art can give.' Still he spawned a number of imitators. It seemed that any prepubescent youth, male or female, who could remember lines was performing the classics. The craze died when London bored of it, but there was still money to be made in the provinces, which turned out to witness this now young man who was being hawked about, rather as a 'believe it or not' subject.

Betty continued his farewell performances until he was nearly 17 and then entered Christ's College, Cambridge. For a while after that he tried to settle down to the hunting, shooting, fishing life of a gentleman. He had property in Shrewsbury and enough money. He even became a cavalry captain in the North Shropshire Yeomanry. Although his father was by this time dead, Betty, perhaps trying to recapture those days when he was the most famous, most fêted person in London, returned to the stage, but he was barely successful, and then only as a curiosity. At 30 he was also unsuccessful in an attempt at suicide.

Finally, in 1824, he completely retired from the stage. He lived in the country in obscurity, where he devoted himself to good works and especially to theatrical charities. He lived until he was 82 (he died on 24 August 1874), so youthful celebrity could not have affected his constitution, and moreover his son became an actor — although he never even approached stardom.

CLAIRE BLOOM

'Claire Bloom is an actress of great subtlety and charm. To this she is able to add a virtue which is more rare and more important, provided the other two qualities are present. I mean sincerity. It was the utter sincerity of her acting in *Limelight* and in *Ring Round the Moon* which marked her as an actress of distinction. She seems to feel with intensity the part she plays and she allows one that always unforgettable pleasure of forgetting that she is acting.' So wrote a critic in *Plays and Players*.

Of Russian and German-Jewish descent, Patricia Claire Bloom was born in London on 15 February 1931. Her father was in advertising and her greatest memory of childhood was constantly moving house. They were living in Cardiff when, aged six, Claire saw Leslie Howard and Norma Shearer in the film of *Romeo and Juliet*. Her ambition to be a great actress was fired and within a week she had memorized the Balcony scene. The family went to live in America during the early war years and Claire returned to England with her mother in 1943 — her parents were by this time separated. She disliked school and spent her time reading and in the theatre. 'Acting to me,' she says, 'meant Shakespeare, classical theatre, the kind of work I saw at the Old Vic and wanted to emulate.' She won a scholarship to the Guildhall School of Music and Drama and studied privately under Eileen Thorndike before attending the Central School.

The Oxford Repertory Theatre in October 1946 was the scene of her first professional appearance. She played Private Jessie Killigrew in *It Depends What You Mean*, then Helen in *An Italian Straw Hat* and Jessie in *Pink String and Sealing Wax*. In London she walked on and understudied in the Helpmann production of *The White Devils*, which opened in March 1947 at the Duchess Theatre, and in June played in *He Who Gets Slapped*. At His Majesty's in September she played Erinna in *The Wanderer*.

Claire Bloom was only 17 when Robert Helpmann invited her to Stratford-on-Avon for a season at the Memorial Theatre. During the period April to September 1948 she appeared as Blanche in *King John*, Ophelia in *Hamlet* and Perdita in *The Winter's Tale*. In February 1949 she was back in London playing Daphne Randall in *The Damask Check* at the Lyric, Hammersmith, and moved to the Globe in May to play Alizon Eliot in *The Lady's Not For Burning* with Richard Burton. Then in Peter Brook's celebrated production of *Ring Round the Moon* at the Globe in January 1950, she played Isabelle, the ballerina.

She was barely 20 when Charlie Chaplin chose her and made her famous as the girl in his film *Limelight*, but at the time she said, 'I couldn't just be a film star. I'm much too ambitious for that.' And she returned to her beloved Shakespeare at the

Old Vic in 1952, playing a gravely lovely Jessica in *The Merchant of Venice* and her triumphant Juliet, of which the *Daily Telegraph* critic wrote: 'She gave a sweet new agony to the supreme love-drama in the language,' and Tynan said: 'The silly lamb became a real, scarred woman.' Ivor Brown wrote: 'Claire Bloom's Juliet turns from rapture to desperation with surprising strength. That she would bewitch us from the balcony was an easy guess: that she would so effectively deliver the ''serpent heart'' speech and so poignantly ''freeze up the heat of life'' in the potion scene was more remarkable because the less expected and so rarely achieved.' The Old Vic Company had had trouble attracting audiences before this production — not so after. At the Edinburgh Festival of September 1953, she played Ophelia in *Hamlet*, returning with it to the Old Vic Theatre and playing, as well, Helena in *All's Well That Ends Well* ('looking', according to Derek Granger, 'as silvery and mysterious as moonlight'); Viola in *Twelfth Night*; Virgilia in *Coriolanus*; and Miranda in *The Tempest*, a delightful and magical performance with John Neville as Ferdinand. At the Palace in July 1955, she appeared as Cordelia in *King Lear*, and back at the Old Vic in 1956 she again played Juliet before embarking with it on a tour of Canada and the United States. Her first stage appearance in New York was at the Winter Garden in October 1956 as Juliet, and then she played the Queen in *Richard II*.

In April 1958 at the Apollo in London she played the idealist killjoy Lucile to Vivien Leigh's practical Paola in Christopher Fry's translation of Jean Giraudoux's *Duel of Angels*. Peter Roberts reported that she 'discovers in Lucile a part which fits her as snugly as the proverbial glove. She appears to be maturing as an actress, having acquired that indefinable something which invests her performance with a new poise and authority.'

During the fifties Claire Bloom was also working in films, notably as Lady Anne in Olivier's *Richard III* and Alison in *Look Back in Anger*.

In January 1959, not pleased that the critics who had so praised her for her original Juliet were now beginning to criticize her for the very qualities they had once found so appealing, Claire Bloom went to New York, where she played the wife in *Rashomon* at the Music Box opposite Rod Steiger — the method actor who was the antithesis of her cool, prim Englishness. In September she married him and went to live in California, where she had her only child, Anna. The next nine years she refers to as her 'vagabond existence', travelling the world with Steiger as he made films, making films herself and only rarely appearing on the stage. She played Johanna in *Altona* at the Royal Court in

April 1961, transferring to the Saville in June. In Italy in 1963 she played Andromache in *The Trojan Women* at Spoleto. She came back to England in 1965 to Sasha in *Ivanov* at the Phoenix.

Of her films during that period her most notable performances were given in *The Spy Who Came In From the Cold* with Richard Burton and in Peter Hall's *Three Into Two Won't Go* in which she played an emotionally frigid housewife.

In 1969 she could bear the vagabond existence no longer. 'All I knew then,' she said, 'was that I wanted to live a different life.' She obtained a Mexican divorce from Rod Steiger and married an American producer, Hillard Elkins. She hoped to be asked to join the Royal Shakespeare Company or the National Theatre, but as the offers were not forthcoming she decided to make her own opportunities and carefully planned her re-emergence on the stage. In January 1971 she played Nora in *A Doll's House* and *Hedda Gabler* at the Playhouse, New York. Both productions were directed by Patrick Garland and both performances were acclaimed by the critics. At the Broadhurst Theater in New York in January 1972 she played Mary Queen of Scots in Robert Bolt's *Vivat! Vivat Regina!* It was in February 1973 that she brought *A Doll's House* to the Criterion in London. Helen Dawson said it was 'a performance of high theatrical intelligence; in retrospect you can see that from the beginning every bright-eyed, feverish, whimsical move had been laid to prepare for the climax; that every line had been charted and absorbed so that the growth of the character is at once inevitable and invisible'. It was in 1974 that she achieved universally magnificent reviews as Blanche Du Bois in *A Streetcar Named Desire* at the Piccadilly Theatre in London.

However, another Tennessee Williams play, *The Red Devil Battery Sign*, closed in Boston before reaching Broadway. In the same year Claire Bloom's second marriage failed. But she played Miss Giddons in *The Innocents* at the Morosco in New York in October 1976 and then, in London, Rebecca West in *Rosmersholm*. At the Chichester Festival Theatre she played Madame Ranevsky in *The Cherry Orchard* — only her second Chekhov.

Now living with the novelist Philip Roth, she finds she very much enjoys television work. She played Gertrude magnificently in Derek Jacobi's *Hamlet*, and for nearly eighteen months was involved in Granada Television's *Brideshead Revisited*, in which she played Lady Marchmain. Television, she says, suits her temperament and she likes the intimacy. But the theatre is still her ambition. 'I've never been in the mainstream,' she said. 'I've always had to do things for myself. So I'll go on doing it.'

RAY
BOLGER

Best remembered as the rubber-legged Scarecrow in the film of *The Wizard of Oz*, or for stopping the show on Broadway with 'Once in Love with Amy' in *Where's Charley?* for 792 performances, Ray Bolger spent nearly fifty years on stage and well into his seventies he danced for at least an hour a day 'to keep the joints from stiffening'.

Raymond Wallace Bolger was born in Dorchester, near Boston, Massachusetts, on 10 January 1904, the son of a house painter. When his father became ill and money was short Ray Bolger worked in the afternoons, first in a bank and then in an insurance company, but he was determined to finish his high school education, which he did in the mornings. When he was 15 he went to see Fred Stone on stage in Boston in *Jack o' Lantern*, which opened horizons beyond the books, and he determined to be an entertainer. The Jordan Hall, Boston, provided him with his first stage, for a dance recital when he was 18. The following year he made his first professional appearances, as a comedian and dancer in *One Hour From Broadway*, which distance he was literally, in Lykens, Pennsylvania. But in time he was three years from Broadway, and those years were spent touring the country in vaudeville, where he perfected his eccentric dancing style and learned so much about audiences. His Broadway début was in 1926 at the Imperial in *The Merry World*; then he went back to vaudeville at the Palace in Gus Edwards' *Ritz-Carleton Nights*, and spent two years with it on the Keith–Albee and Orpheum circuits. Bolger then went back to New York but mostly as a turn in revues. It was in 1936 that he introduced 'There's a Small Hotel' in *On Your Toes* at the Imperial. Hollywood and an MGM contract beckoned that year, but he remained a stage rather than a screen star. His style had more appeal in the flesh than on celluloid — with the notable exception of *The Wizard of Oz*, in which he was at first required to play the Tin Man. 'But I'm not tin — I'm fluid,' he remonstrated, and finally won. Coincidentally, his idol Fred Stone had originated the Scarecrow on stage.

Hollywood gave him time for reading — his magnificent library encompassed Rabelais, de Maupassant, Boccaccio and Balzac — together with all the dictionaries of the various languages. He never felt he spoke the language of his vaudeville companions.

As Sapiens in *By Jupiter* he was awarded the New York Newspaper Guild's Page One Award — but his next show in 1946 (after three films and a USO tour), *Three to Make Ready*, netted him two Donaldson Awards and a New York Drama Critics Award. However, Bolger's career had been waiting for *Where's Charley?* This musical, based on the evergreen comedy by Brandon Thomas, *Charley's Aunt*, was eagerly awaited on Broadway. The book was by George Abbott and words and music by Frank Loesser. It opened to a heavy advance at the box office — but the reviews were negative. All the critics liked Bolger but they thought he was deserving of better material. Rightly or wrongly, Bolger did not need better material. Sometimes dressed as the Oxford student, Charles Wykeham, sometimes as his own aunt, looking like a Victorian version of Whistler's mother, Bolger still managed to step, nay leap, in and out of character. 'Once in Love with Amy' always stopped the show, and encouraged by George Abbott, who was also the show's director, Bolger turned the encore into a vaudeville sing-along, and audiences loved it. The critics may have found the show unsophisticated but to those of us who were lucky enough to have been in the audience it was what theatre is all about. *Where's Charley?* won Bolger another Donaldson and, best of all, the Tony Award for 1949. When, after 792 performances, he was (not surprisingly) exhausted and had to leave the show, no one bothered to look for a replacement — there could be no such thing. They just closed the production. The touring company and a later revival without Bolger both failed. He repeated the role for Warner Brothers in 1952, but the film lacked the lustre and spontaneity of the stage production. It also, of course, lacked an audience to which Bolger could respond. And television could convey but a tiny proportion of the talent that sent audiences out of theatres convinced they too could dance, just like Bolger. However, in the fifties he did do two successful television series for ABC. Vaudeville being dead and long buried, Bolger turned to nightclub appearances and was on the opening bill of the Hotel Sahara, Las Vegas. His last Broadway appearance was in *Come Summer*, which ran for only seven performances.

THE
BOOTHS

*E*dwin Thomas Booth was born on a farm in Maryland on 13 November 1833 with a caul; to the hovering Negro servants the caul symbolized luck and mystical powers — a symbol that Booth himself took seriously in later years.

His father, Junius Booth, was the great touring actor, and although he was a quiet, withdrawn boy Edwin worshipped his swaggering parent. When he was 14, to impress his father he convinced the manager of the Holliday Street Theater in Baltimore to give him a small part in *The Spectre Bridegroom*. Edwin was not only sick but also very, very bad. He tried very hard to forget the experience, indeed never mentioning it in later years. He preferred to think that his stage début was made at the age of 16, on 10 September 1849, at the Boston Museum when he played Tressel (a small part inserted by Colley Cibber into his version of Shakespeare's play) to his father's *Richard III*. After that, as he was travelling with the tour anyway, partly as companion and partly as watchdog, he took on a variety of small parts and by 1850 he was generally advertised as supporting his father, playing the larger roles of Gratiano, Laertes, Macduff and Edgar.

Edwin played his first lead role in April 1851 when, at the National Theater, New York, his father suddenly announced he did not feel like acting and left the theatre. The manager, deciding that anything was better than giving the people their money back, let Edwin go on as *Richard III*. He stunned no one, although he was promising. After that he secured work on his own with a company in Baltimore, which was glad of the Booth name, but it specialized in farces, in which Edwin was clumsy. The next year, pleased to leave the farces behind, he again worked with his father, this time in California, which he thought to be the land of opportunity — a good place to strike out on his own. He stayed behind when his father left and made a living playing mining towns, where the audiences were not too demanding. It was only after his father's death that, despite the lingering shadow, he began to develop a style of his own. He played the classics in San Francisco and then toured Australia. But he returned to California in low spirits (a melancholia pursued him most of his life) and, as his father had, he turned to drink and a great number of women. Because of his unreliability he lost one job in California, and though he gained another his acting remained undistinguished. In 1856 he returned home, and began

playing the theatres his father had. In Richmond he played Romeo and was charmed by Mary Devlin, his Juliet; however, he had promised himself that he would never marry an actress and left her to continue his tour of the Southern states.

Edwin saw the advantages, especially monetary, of performing his father's famous roles. Of his rendering of Sir Giles Overreach in *A New Way to Pay Old Debts* the *Boston Transcript* reported in 1857: 'Quite a triumph. Young Booth's success was decided ... It brought back the most vivid recollections of the fire, the vigor, the strong intellectuality which characterized the acting of his lamented father.' But when Louisa May Alcott saw Edwin in Payne's play she commented: 'Saw young Booth in *Brutus* and like him better than his father.' Of his Hamlet, the *Transcript* said: 'We have seen actors play the part with more energy, dash more at effects ... but the beauty of Booth's Hamlet was its abstraction and intensity.'

After his season in Boston, Edwin went on a colossal binge, despite the worries and warnings of his manager, but he sobered up to play in New York. Booth saw himself as a hopeless drunkard and libertine, but he also knew that he was in love with Mary Devlin, and despite his vows never to marry an actress he did so in an Episcopal ceremony on 7 July 1860 and they rented an apartment in New York, settling into a season at the Winter Garden Theater. Then Edwin was asked to go to London and he was flattered. Although the Civil War had started and he felt guilty about not being involved, and even though Mary was pregnant and not very well, it was an opportunity he could not miss and together they sailed for Europe. He opened as Shylock on 30 September 1861 but it was not his best role and his performance was cool and lifeless. The audiences were sparse and unappreciative of it, and also of *A New Way to Pay Old Debts* and *Richard III*. Only his Richelieu brought a positive response. The reaction was much the same when he toured the provinces. He made little money and was as horrified by his reception as he was by the British attitude towards the Civil War: they were, emotionally at least, on the side of the Confederacy. Booth's daughter Edwina was born in London on 9 December 1861, under an American flag with which he had canopied Mary's bed.

Back in New York the following season Booth found that having played London conferred prestige, and the audiences were enthusiastic and full. His luck changed again, though, when Mary fell ill during a tour of Boston. She was advised to stay there and rest while Edwin returned to fulfil commitments in New York. He found himself plunged into deep gloom again and sought refuge in the bottle. His drinking began to show, but he was beyond caring. The *New York Herald* reported: 'Seldom have we seen Shakespeare so murdered as at the Winter Garden during the past two weeks. It would be better to disappoint the public by closing the theatre than to place Mr Booth upon the stage when he was really unfit to act.'

Having drunkenly ignored telegrams about his wife's condition, Booth suddenly, on 21 February 1863, made a dash to Boston to her bedside, but she was already dead when his train arrived. His wife's death had a profound effect on him. He turned to spiritualism and the occult and declared his intention to give up the stage. He sought mediums to put him in touch with Mary. But gradually he grew to a new responsibility. He began to feel he had a purpose in his life — a responsibility to his daughter and moreover, a responsibility to the stage. He became his own manager and ran the Winter Garden Theater himself for four years. It was there in 1865 that he mounted his record-breaking *Hamlet*, which ran for 100 performances. William Winter wrote: 'Edwin Booth's Hamlet was the simple, absolute realization of Shakespeare's haunted Prince ... It was dark, mysterious, afflicted, melancholy.' *Harper's* reported: 'Booth is altogether princely... His playing throughout has an exquisite tone, like an old picture.'

While he was playing in Boston, news of Lincoln's assassination by his brother, John Wilkes Booth, reached him. Edwin was in a state of shock and was besieged by angry mobs. The theatre was closed and he returned to New York where hate mail, which had been descending on all members of the acting profession, was particularly vicious towards him. His elder brother Junius was arrested as a possible conspirator, as was his brother-in-law, but Edwin was not, although he was kept constantly under surveillance.

In January 1866 Booth thought it safe to return to the stage. Much of the public was still witch-hunting. The *New York Herald* headlined his return: 'IS THE ASSASSINATION OF CAESAR TO BE PERFORMED? Will Booth appear as the assassin of Caesar? That would be, perhaps, the most suitable character.' Edwin had not wanted to return, to face an audience, but the entire family was in debt and they had but one trade — acting. He played Hamlet; as the curtain rose he waited on stage, preferring that to making an entrance, and he stood still, awaiting the audience's response. The cheering which greeted him moved him to tears.

The Winter Garden Theater was burned to the ground in March 1867 following a performance of *Brutus*, the climactic scene of which was a very realistic burning of Rome. A spark ignited the building, and the entire theatrical wardrobe of the Booths, father and son, perished in the blaze.

Determined to build his own theatre, no matter what the cost, Booth toured strenuously to raise money. The Booth Theater was opened on 3 February 1869, with Mary McVicker, Booth's new discovery, playing Juliet to his Romeo. He married this Juliet too, on 7 June 1869, but their life together was not to be happy. In July 1870 their son Edgar died within hours of his birth, and Mary never recovered from the loss.

In his professional life, however, and now at his own theatre, Booth was very successful, though he insisted upon such sumptuous productions that he never quite recovered his costs, and on 26 January 1874 Edwin had to give up the Booth Theater and file a petition of voluntary bankruptcy. His liabilities were estimated at about two hundred thousand dollars. The following year his father-in-law took over all his debts and Booth was discharged from bankruptcy, but it took him years to repay his father-in-law. Mary became ever more sullen and despondent; she was intensely jealous of Edwin's success, sometimes erupted into hysteria, and Booth's first wife was not allowed to be mentioned — ever.

He toured throughout the United States, earning money to repay his debt. In Chicago in 1879 there was an attempt on his life — a lunatic shot at him during a performance of *Richard II*. By this time he could call his earnings his own and he was bringing in a goodly sum. Edwin still managed to treat his now totally hysterical wife with tenderness and kindness.

Now financially secure, he decided to try England again. On 30 June 1880 he sailed with Edwina and his wife for England, opening in *Hamlet* in November. The critical response disappointed him. The *Daily News* called him 'cold and classical'. They were equally tepid about *Richelieu* and *Othello*. Finally, in February *King Lear* woke them up. 'Nothing finer of the kind has been known upon the English stage,' the *Era* proclaimed. That was more like what Booth had been expecting; but the season, though not a disaster, was far from being a triumph. However, Henry Irving saved the day by inviting Booth to play in *Othello* with him, indulging in the classic theatrical challenge of swapping the roles of the Moor and Iago back and forth. Ellen Terry was to play Desdemona. During rehearsals, Booth's wife got progressively worse: she was no longer even lucid and her lunatic shouts rang through the streets; she was also deteriorating physically. Booth was terrified that she would die just before the opening or in the early weeks and force his curtailment of the play. She did not. Both men were praised for their Iago, though neither satisfied the critics as Othello — and business boomed. By the time he sailed for New York on 18 June, Booth had at last had his London success. Amazingly, Mary survived the trip home; she died in New York on 15 November.

Booth returned to England for another season the following year and then went on to a European tour. In his later years he teamed up with Lawrence Barrett, whose ambition it was to be the second greatest actor in America. Booth was pleased to oblige him as he also did all the work, arranging the tours, booking the theatres, organizing casts and scenery.

Fairly wealthy now, Booth founded a club for actors in New York called the Players' Club, and bought for its headquarters a magnificent property on Gramercy Park where he himself lived on the third floor. It was there that he died on 7 June 1893 after a brain haemorrhage. He had retired from the stage two years earlier; he was only 58 years old but seemed a very old man indeed. At his death, flags on the theatres in New York were lowered to half mast.

John Wilkes Booth was the most attractive and the most vivacious member of the great acting family. He was born in Maryland on 10 May 1836. Even as a small child he was a charmer; he was adored and spoiled by his mother, who even managed to find excuses for the drunken fights in which he indulged when he was only 16 and for his later predilection for whores. At 17 he was taller than his brother Edwin, which was not difficult, but he was also exotically good-looking and voraciously ambitious. 'I must have fame,' he declared. He made his début at the St Charles Theater, Baltimore, as Richmond in *Richard III* in 1855. He was much too young to make anything of the part, and was more successful playing Horatio to his brother's Hamlet in Richmond, Virginia, two years later. He triumphed in 1860 as the evil Pescara in *The Apostate*, and when he played the part in Albany, New York, his performance was so like that of his father (which he had never seen) that spiritualists in the city met to discuss the possibility that it was indeed the spirit of Junius Booth on the stage. He was playing in Albany when the Civil War broke out, and was so vociferous in his praise of the South that he was told to keep quiet or leave town.

When the older brother Edwin went to England to tour John saw this as his chance to prove himself the greater actor, and starred in St Louis, Chicago and Baltimore, his posters proclaiming: 'I am myself alone.'

Sir Charles Wyndham described him: 'Seldom has the stage seen a more impressive, or a more handsome, or a more impassioned actor. Picture to yourself Adonis, with high forehead, ascetic face corrected by rather full lips, sweeping black hair, a figure of perfect youthful proportions, and the most wonderful black eyes in the world ... I was strongly attracted to him in the first place by his effective, thrilling presentation of Hamlet ... His Hamlet was insane, and his interpretation was fiery, convincing and artistic.'

On 18 March 1862 John Wilkes Booth made his début in New York City playing Richard III. The *New York Herald* reported: '...in the last act he created a veritable sensation. His face blackened and smeared with blood, he seemed Richard himself; and his combat with Richmond was a masterpiece. An audience packed and crammed beyond the usual limits of the theatre applauded him to the echo.' He had also, it was said, 'fire, dash and a touch of strangeness' in his acting.

At the Boston Museum, John broke all the records for that theatre playing Pescara in *The Apostate*. Many contemporaries reported that they never saw a better Romeo than his.

It was while he was playing in St Louis that he was arrested, for saying he wished that 'the whole damn government would go to hell'. After paying a fine and swearing allegiance to the Union he was released, but his allegiance was elsewhere. He was involved in a conspiracy to kidnap President Lincoln and exchange him for Confederate prisoners. There were two attempts at this bizarre plot but both ended in fiasco. When the war was over the kidnap plan became obsolete, but John's hatred and disgust at the treatment of the South deepened. As his sister tried to explain: 'His mind lost its balance between the fall of Richmond and the terrific end.'

At the bar next door to Ford's Theater in Washington, DC, on Good Friday, 14 April 1865, John Wilkes said to a fellow customer, who teased him about being a less successful actor than his brother Edwin, 'When I leave the stage I'll be the most famous man in America.' He made his final appearance as he limped across the stage of Ford's Theater after shooting and mortally wounding Abraham Lincoln. John Wilkes Booth himself died on 26 April in Virginia, shot while jumping from a blazing barn where he had been cornered.

Junius Brutus Booth, named after the Roman republican, was born in London on 1 May 1796 — the son of Richard Booth, a lawyer and grandson of a Jewish silversmith, John Booth. His father, always an ardent republican, was related to John

Wilkes, the parliamentary reformer, through his mother's family.

Junius, though given a good classical education by his father, was unruly and managed to sire two illegitimate children before he reached the age of 17. He became a clerk in his father's office but quickly bored of it and, joining a group of actors, wandered the countryside, sleeping by the side of the road and playing comedy, tragedy, farce and generally experimenting with audiences. In 1814 the troupe travelled to Amsterdam and Brussels, where Booth met Adelaide Delanny who came back to England with him. They married there on 8 May 1815.

Although physically unpromising (he was short, with stumpy legs, piercing black eyes and strangely pointed ears — he referred to himself as a satyr), Booth became very successful in the provinces and news of his acting spread to London. In 1817 he was invited to star at Covent Garden. He played Richard III in Colley Cibber's version. Kean, the star of the rival Drury Lane Theatre, considered the role of Richard III his private domain and took exception to this provincial upstart's performance of it, and more particularly to the enthusiastic reception it received. Kean then challenged Booth to play Iago to his own Othello. Kean, secure in his years of stage experience, pulled out all the stops and won.

At home, Booth seemed perfectly happy and settled. Although his daughter had died in infancy he had a son on whom he doted, called Richard. He was well established in the theatre and was now considered the heir apparent to Kean's crown. In 1820 he met Mary Ann Holmes, a Covent Garden flower-girl, fell in love with her and eventually, in May 1821, sailed with her to America — without informing Adelaide.

Booth's first appearance in the United States was as Richard III in Richmond, Virginia. Then, after Petersburg, he played it in New York where a critic for the *National Advocate* reported: 'In the conception of the character of the crooked back tyrant, Mr Booth seems to be perfect. He exhibited none of those stage tricks, which many who undertake the part substitute for their lack of judgement ... the burst of applause which proceeded from all parts of the house, even long before the actor had closed this scene, sufficiently demonstrated the preeminent extent of his powers.'

Booth settled into playing New York, Philadelphia and the Southern circuit. He also continued to support Adelaide and his son in England and to keep her ignorant of Mary Ann's existence, even though she eventually bore him nine children. Booth raised his second family on a large farm in Maryland. His father came from

England to manage the farm while he toured, but gradually gave up management for the bottle. Junius was also a victim of alcoholism, and moreover he was deeply mentally disturbed and at times deranged. The Booth children called his madness 'Father's calamity'. Once, after declaring to a Boston audience, 'I can't read! I'm a charity boy! Take me to a lunatic asylum!' he left the stage, and removing most of his clothes walked in his stockinged feet to Providence, Rhode Island, shaking his head and gesticulating wildly. Sometimes he played an entire performance on tiptoe for no reason. And sometimes he was just drunk.

In his later years it was not safe to let him tour alone. His older children took brief turns touring with him, but finally and most importantly the task fell to his son Edwin (who was to follow him onto the stage). Edwin tried very hard to keep his father sober and to get him promptly to theatres. Usually, Junius's powers were undiminished onstage. The drama critic for the *Spirit of the Times* reported in March 1848: 'Mr Booth has continued at the Park [Theater in New York City] since our last, drawing larger audiences, whom he gratified by his superior acting. During the week he presented himself in the character of Pescara in *The Apostate*, Sir Giles Overreach in *A New Way to Pay Old Debts*, *Lear*, and *Bertram*. In all these the greatness of his histrionic genius was fully developed and the heroes represented by him faithfully pictured ... He often performs the mere business of the stage in such a manner as to give it importance and as often accomplishes, by the mere excellence of his gesticulation and expression of face, effects that spirited dialogue and good reading by many actors of merit would not produce ... He is well known to every lover of drama and will be recalled to recollection whenever men whose fame exceeds their talent aspire to the highest places in art. The fast failing talent for the stage and the increasing rarity of genius on its boards ought to induce every man to see Booth ...'

Adelaide, informed by her son (who had visited) of Booth's other family, arrived in Maryland and tried to win Booth back by ranting and raving at him. She lived in Baltimore and often attacked him when, in his farmer guise, he sold his vegetables at market. Finally, in March 1851, she divorced him and he married Mary Ann.

The following year, Booth's son Junius Jr returned from California, where he had become a theatrical impresario, and convinced his father that he too should go West. Booth played the Jenny Lind Theater in San Francisco for two weeks to packed houses and then moved on to Sacramento, where the audiences were rather sparse. Booth, deciding that at 56 he was getting too old to make the effort of publicity to attract audiences, then sailed for home, stopping in New Orleans at the St Charles Theater to play six performances which netted him over a thousand dollars. He then took a steamer up the Mississippi River, headed for Cincinnati. Booth made the mistake of drinking river water and he picked up a virus. There was no doctor on board, and through vomiting and diarrhoea Booth quickly wasted away and died on the fifth day of the journey, just below Louisville, on 30 November 1852 at one o'clock in the afternoon.

See photograph of Edwin Booth opposite page 39.

SHIRLEY BOOTH

For her performance as the scatty but lovable and slightly know-it-all maid in the NBC television series 'Hazel' (1961), Shirley Booth won a total of twenty-eight awards, including the Emmy, as well as a loyal and enormous audience. But she was no stranger to awards, and theatre audiences had been marvelling at her talent for decades. Brooks Atkinson wrote of the 'depth and range' she had as the slovenly housewife in *Come Back, Little Sheba* and of her performance as the spinster schoolteacher in *The Time of the Cuckoo* as 'warm and gallant'. 'Distinguished' is the word most often used to describe a woman who is personally rather timid, according to her fellow actors.

Shirley Booth was born Thelma Booth Ford in New York City on 30 August 1907, the daughter of an IBM sales manager. She began her career in 1919 with the Poli Stock Company playing small roles in Hartford, Connecticut, and her New York début had to wait six years. It came in *Hell's Bells* (1926) followed closely by *Laff That Off* the next month. She played Mary Marshall in *High Gear* (1927) and Emily Rosen in *The War Song* (1928). In 1931 she worked in three plays as well as starring as Miss Duffy in the radio series 'Duffy's Tavern', which was compèred by her then husband Ed Gardner, from whom she was divorced in 1944. (She later married an investment counsellor, William H. Baker, who died in 1950.) Continuing to work constantly, she was seldom off the New York stage: *The Mask and the Face* (1933), *After Such Pleasures* and *Sunday Nights at Nine* (1934), *Three Men on a Horse* (1935), *Excursion* and *Too Many Heroes* (1937). In *The Philadelphia Story* (1939) she played Elizabeth Imrie, the wise-cracking photographer — the kind of female she brought to perfection as Ruth Sherwood in *My Sister Eileen* (1940). After *Tomorrow the World* (1943) she played in *Hollywood Pinafore* (1945).

No prizes for guessing the two Hollywood magpies on whom the character Louhedda Hopsons was based. 'She was,' as Brooks Atkinson points out, 'invariably cast as an expert character actress of sardonic heroines.' In 1946 she played Susan Pengilly in *Land's End* at the Playhouse, and then had a disaster with *Heartsong* which opened in Connecticut at the end of February and closed in Pennsylvania at the end of March. *The Men We Marry* (1948) was more successful but it was as Grace Woods in *Goodbye, My Fancy* (1948) that she got her first Tony for supporting Madeleine Carroll. She played Abby Quinn in *Love Me Long* (1949), and then the blowsy, slovenly but good-natured Lola in *Come Back, Little Sheba* (1950) won her another Tony and totally changed her image. Shirley Booth also transferred the part of Lola to the screen in 1952 — her first film — and she was given an Academy Award for the performance.

She followed her *Sheba* triumph with a musical, *A Tree Grows in Brooklyn*, in which she played Cissy (1951). It was then that the *New York Post* observed that Shirley Booth was 'one of the wonders of the American stage; a superb actress, a magnificent comedienne and an all-round performer of endless variety'. In 1952 she played Leona Samish in *The Time of the Cuckoo* and got yet another Tony. She declined to make the film of this. Katharine Hepburn did, and it was called *Summertime in Venice*. The ever-changeable Miss Booth went back to a musical in 1954, *By the Beautiful Sea*. She played Bunny Watson in *The Desk Set* (1955) and toured with it for two years, capturing the Sarah Siddons Award in Chicago. She has played Juno Boyle in *Juno* (1959), a musical version of *Juno and the Paycock*, *Nina* in summer stock (1959), Fanny in *A Second String* (1960) and Mother Maria in *Look to the Lilies* (1970), as well as in a revival of *Harvey* (1971).

DION BOUCICAULT

A good deal of mystery shrouds the beginnings of Dion Boucicault, but he was most probably born on 27 December 1820 in Dublin. His mother was Anna Maria Darley, two of whose brothers were playwrights, although unsuccessful ones. At the time of Dion's birth she was married to a wine merchant called Samuel Boursiquot, but it is understood that the boy's father was more likely to be the lodger, a lecturer at Trinity College, Dublin, called Dionysius Lardner, after whom the child was named. Dr Lardner became Dion's guardian and paid for his education, which took place in London, first at a variety of small private schools and then, when Dion was 13, at University College School followed by the Collegiate School in Middlesex. Here he had his first experience of acting (playing Rolla) in Sheridan's *Pizarro*, and also his first attempt at writing when he composed a sketch called *Napoleon's Old Guard*.

At 15 he decided on a career in the theatre, but he met with family opposition; it was not considered a respectable profession. He was apprenticed to Lardner in London as a civil engineer but he was determined to be an actor. At 17 he obtained by perseverance a job at the Theatre Royal, Cheltenham, using the name Lee Moreton. He first appeared on that stage on 2 April 1838, playing the Duke of Norfolk in an amateur production of *Richard III*, and got his first review in the Cheltenham *Looker-on*: 'The little which fell to the lot of the Duke of Norfolk to do was really well done, but, notwithstanding, the character was rendered ludicrous by the brogue of the representative.'

At the Theatre Royal, Gloucester, he played Richard III on 6 April and on the next night the lead in *Teddy the Tiler*, following on 18 and 20 April with Iago in *Othello*. Back in Cheltenham he played Sir Giles Overreach in *A New Way to Pay Old Debts* on 24 April. The *Cheltenham Journal* reported: 'Mr Lee Moreton convinced us by general correctness of his ideas of the parts and his originality in some particulars, that he has within him that which would, under judicious guidance, lead him on to the highest rank in the art ... Mr Moreton terminated his wonderful performance by one of the most striking scenes we ever witnessed: it was in all respects worthy of the elder Kean and stamped indelibly in our opinion the conviction that he may, if he chooses, contest the honour of succeeding that Prince of Actors with any one on the stage England now possesses.'

So effusive and unexpected was this critic's praise for the fledgling actor that Boucicault's biographer, Richard Fawkes, wonders if there were not a bit of bribery involved. Boucicault was certainly not above it. He was, however, very popular with local audiences and he had a prodigious capacity for learning parts. He next played the title role in *Rory O'More* and, on 8 May, Hamlet, following with Henry Fitzherbert in *The Handsome Husband* and Edward Mortimer in *The Iron Chest*.

Charles Hill had managed both the Gloucester and Cheltenham theatres, and when he moved to Brighton to take over the Theatre Royal there, Boucicault, still calling himself Lee Moreton, moved with him as his protégé and a permanent member of the company. He made his Brighton début as Sir Giles Overreach on 30 July and on 9 August played Tom Moore in *The Irish Lion*. The critics attacked him. They cared neither for his performance on stage nor for his extravagant and overbearing lifestyle off stage. Boucicault spent five months in Brighton and then moved back to Cheltenham, where he added Sir Benjamin Backbite in *The School for Scandal* and Sir Lucius O'Trigger in *The Rivals* to his repertoire before moving on to Bristol's Theatre Royal. There he made his début on 26 December 1838 as Mantalini in an adaptation of *Nicholas Nickleby*.

All this time, as well as occupying himself ostentatiously spending money he did not have, Boucicault was writing constantly. The first professional performance of one of his plays took place at Bristol on 18 February 1839. It was called *Lodgings to Let*; Boucicault himself played the male lead in this one-act farce. Encouraged by its reception in Bristol, he took the play to London, to the Haymarket, but it closed after only one night — being far too naive for the capital. Boucicault only managed to find minor roles for himself in London, and being voraciously ambitious he signed a contract for a season at the Theatre Royal, Hull, where he played in *The Irish Lion*, Trip in *The School for Scandal* and Osric in *Hamlet*. He adapted Harrison Ainsworth's novel, *Jack Sheppard*, into a full-length play for Hull's Christmas production and played the part of Jack himself. It was very successful, but some complained of the language and the manager shortened it from four to three acts without Boucicault's consent, which resulted in the first of the many rows with management that were to colour Boucicault's career. He left Hull in a fury.

After a time in Dublin licking his wounds, Boucicault went back to London and became a student at a new dramatic academy — despite his experience, he was still only 20.

Boucicault always had the capacity for spending money much faster than he could earn it. He had a very facile pen but not much luck in staging his plays until Charles Matthew (who with his wife Madame Vestris managed the extremely prestigious Theatre Royal in Covent Garden) told him that what he needed was not yet another farce but a good five-act modern comedy. Boucicault went home and wrote *London Assurance*. It opened in March 1841 and was an enormous success. Boucicault quickly became the flavour of the month and came out from behind his pseudonym. On the strength of his fame he proceeded to run up fantastic debts. His second play for Covent Garden, *The Irish Heiress*, did not match up to *London Assurance*; however, he was not yet 21 and mercifully for him was not yet responsible for his debts. He was not really very responsible for anything. He redeemed his growing reputation with his next play, *A Lover by Proxy*, and for the next eight years regularly wrote plays for Charles Matthew. There was a fashion at the time for straight translations of French successes, and with his facility for the language Boucicault found he could knock these off at amazing speed. Every shilling counted until, on 9 July 1845, he married a French widow a good deal older than he was and also a good deal richer. She died in March 1848 and there were rumours that he had pushed her off an Alp, but then Boucicault had a knack for making enemies, eager to think the worst of him, especially among members of the London press. Her money scarcely outlasted her, and by November Boucicault had declared bankruptcy.

He kept pointing out, loudly, that it was grossly unfair that a playwright only received a flat fee for his work while an actor got paid nightly for playing in it. His finances could stand the inequity no longer, and though he continually fought for an author's royalty, he could not wait and returned to the stage in his own play *The Vampire* in 1852. No less a critic than Queen Victoria reported to her diary: 'Mr Boucicault, who is very handsome and has a fine voice, acted very impressively. I can never forget his livid face and fixed look.' She even commissioned a watercolour of him to hang in Windsor Castle.

At this time he met Agnes Robertson, who became his second wife. After a rift with just about everybody in London they went together to America, where he became her manager. They eventually travelled the United States as a team, acting constantly, founding companies and

dissolving them, and producing six children. He never stopped writing plays but occasionally took a break from the stage itself. He made his American début in Boston on 22 September 1854, playing Sir Patrick O'Plenipo in *The Irish Artist*, and his New York début the following November as Sir Charles Coldstream in his own play *Used Up*.

In an effort to avoid constant touring, Boucicault founded a theatre company, which he based in New Orleans. It opened on 1 December 1855 but the venture failed after only three months and the Boucicaults once more took to the road, playing Charleston, Richmond, Washington and Philadelphia on the way back to New York. During this period he found the time to get a play copyright act passed by Congress.

After a few more years of impoverished touring Boucicault scored a financial success with a new play, *The Poor of New York*. (It was noted for its spectacular effects and continued life throughout the years as *The Poor of Liverpool* or *The Poor of London*.) Once more he tried to establish a theatre of his own, this time in Washington. That failed, so he tried in New York renaming the Metropolitan, which he had leased, the Winter Garden. This also ran into problems and the Boucicaults quit it. Success and temporary financial security did, however, come to him through his writing, particularly with *The Octoroon* and *The Colleen Bawn*.

In July 1860 he and Agnes and assorted children returned to England, opening *The Colleen Bawn* at the Adelphi in September 1860. It was an enormous success and they repeated it in Dublin in April. Boucicault was, however, soon typically involved in battles with theatre managers and once more decided to open his own. He acquired Astley's in Lambeth, south of the Thames, and renamed it the New Theatre Royal, Westminster. It opened in December 1862. He and his wife appeared first in Tom Taylor's *To Parents and Guardians* and then in his own *The Relief of Lucknow*. Although he called it Westminster, it fooled no one — it was on the unfashionable side of the river; in addition to this handicap the managers who disliked him mounted a campaign against his theatre which the newspapers were only too delighted to take up. By July, Boucicault was once again bankrupt. He sold personal property, mortgaged his successful plays and within six weeks he had paid off much of his debt and was discharged. So it was back to the life of a touring actor — at which he was very successful, always drawing large and appreciative audiences. Although by the time he was 45 he had written around 200 plays, it was as a fine comic actor that he was most appreciated.

In the autumn of 1872 he and Agnes returned

to New York for what was to be a short engagement at Booth's Theater. He was overwhelmed by the warmth of the American greeting. The *New York Tribune* reported: 'Time has treated him kindly. He is a better actor than he used to be, at least in this — that his method is quieter, more refined and more sharply intelligent; and it is absolutely precise.' In 1873 both Boucicaults became American citizens.

Always a ladies' man, Boucicault had many affairs, but Agnes usually managed to overlook them — until the actress Katherine Rogers came along, and Agnes left. Boucicault and Rogers toured the country together, but despite the rift in the marriage, at times of financial crisis Agnes rejoined him on the stage to their mutual advantage.

Boucicault spent the early 1880s constantly crossing and recrossing the Atlantic, but it was in America that he had the best reception. In 1885 he toured Australia with his own company, and managed to marry one of the actresses, Louise Thorndyke, in Sydney despite the fact that he was not divorced from Agnes. The novelty of the couple's appearance on the stage together (she was forty-four years his junior) brought in money for a while, but Boucicault, now in his late sixties, who had always been the best at gauging what an audience wanted and giving it to them, found himself an out-of-touch has-been. He was engaged to run a drama school in New York. He tried desperately to regain his rightful place in the theatre but bad health, a series of heart attacks and old age kept him from acting. His last two plays, *A Tale of a Coat* and *Lend Me Your Wife*, were not well received. He died, disheartened, on 18 September 1890.

FANNY BRICE

*T*here are not many stage stars about whom one can write a musical — and a smash-hit Broadway musical at that — but Fanny Brice was what Broadway thrived on. She was essentially New York. And so was *Funny Girl*. The musical was produced by Ray Stark, husband of Fanny's daughter Frances Arnstein, and many critics agreed that it was more authentic than most stage biographies, though it only covered part of the story.

Fannie Borach was born on 29 October 1891 on the poor lower east side of New York City. Her rise to fame epitomized the American dream. She began her career in 1904 at the age of 13, performing in amateur night contests — an ugly duckling with a remarkable talent not only for comic mimicry but also for belting out a ballad, she was soon performing in burlesque. Her first major New York performance was at the Columbia Burlesque House in 1910, in Max Speigel's *College Girl*, in which she introduced the Irving Berlin song, 'Sadie Salome', which told the story of a Jewish girl whose ambitions to become a shimmy dancer shocked her family. Flo Ziegfeld noticed her and she starred in his *Follies* of 1910 and nine successive *Follies*, introducing such songs as 'My Man', 'Rose of Washington Square', 'Second Hand Rose', 'I'm an Indian' and 'I Found a Million Dollar Baby in a Five and Ten Cent Store'.

In 1911 she married Frank White, but the marriage was annulled the following year and in 1918 she married the gambler Nicholas Arnstein. It was a rocky marriage and after nine years they were divorced. Her third husband, whom she married in 1929, was the producer Billy Rose. He produced her great musical success *Sweet and Low* in 1930. The *New York Post* reported: 'Fanny Brice is better known for her blackouts than for her bravuras. For years it was difficult to distinguish between Herr Ziegfeld's *Follies* and Fanny Brice. She was jocose and ribald and comically lyric in no less than fourteen of these festivals, until the suspicion grew that no Ziegfeld *Follies* was authentic unless the name of Fanny Brice was flung from the halyards.

'Fanny Brice is a person to whom that shockingly misused and misunderstood word "personality" can be tied without upsetting the purists. Hers is the method of the cartoonist. At her very best, in impersonations of young Jewish ladies in ecstasy or distress, she can tease the tear ducts with her rendition of a song swept with pathos. Here the dramatic urge juts out again. Witness her "My Man". And a thing to be remembered when laughing bits from other revues are cited for longevity is her burlesque of "The Swan Dance", hilarious exaggerations of the airy paces of Pavlova ... In addition to her cockney didoes Miss Brice finds time in her husband's frolics (*Sweet and Low*) to banter gaily with Mr

RICHARD • BRIERS

Jessel about their ill-fated adventures in celluloid, burlesque Muriel Kirkland in *Strictly Dishonorable*, do wrong by the Spaniards in a caprice with off-key castanets, sing a song called "Over Night" and render that old favorite "Rose of Washington Square" in the finale.'

In 1931 she appeared in the review *Crazy Quilt* and returned to Ziegfeld for the *Follies* of 1934 and 1936, in which she created the character of

Baby Snooks. As Baby Snooks, the angular Miss Brice dressed as a child and used a child's voice. It became her most famous characterization, first on stage, then on her own radio programme and finally in the very early days of television. She was divorced from Billy Rose in 1938 and remained unmarried for the rest of her life. Fanny Brice died in Hollywood on 29 May 1951.

RICHARD BRIERS

*B*est known perhaps, for his television work — 'Brothers-in-Law', 'Marriage Lines' and 'The Good Life' — Richard Briers has had a long and varied career on the stage; early on, Harold French noted: 'You've got one of the greatest gifts an actor can have — the audience likes you.'

Richard Briers was born in Croydon, Surrey, on 14 January 1934 and went to school in Wimbledon, where he was best known for pulling faces, doing funny walks and generally being the class clown until, aged 12, he played Macbeth and discovered a consuming passion for Shakespeare. He was later, however, asked to leave the Regent Street Polytechnic Amateur Theatrical Company. He was told that he spoke so fast no one could understand him — 'like a demented typewriter,' wrote one critic later. While in the RAF, an experience he rather enjoyed, he attended evening classes in drama and was accepted at the Royal Academy of Dramatic Art, where he won the Silver Medal. He then joined the Liverpool Repertory Company where he met Ann Davies, an actress. They were married within six months and it has been an enduring marriage.

In 1957 he toured in *Something About A Sailor* before appearing in rep at both Leatherhead and Coventry. In 1958 he was engaged by Sir John Clements to play Joseph Field in *Gilt and Gingerbread*, first on tour and then opening in London at the Duke of York's in April 1959. He regarded it as his breakthrough and still thinks of it as his favourite role. In 1960 he played Bill in *Special Providence* at St Martin's and that same year, at the Duke of York's, Christian Martin in *It's in the Bag*.

A double bill at the Arts in June 1960 gave him Bartholomeus II in *The Shepherd's Chameleon* and Detective in *Victims of Duty*. At the same theatre the following year he played

James Whinby in *The Form* and the Tramp in *A Slight Ache*, transferring with them to the Criterion. Also at the Criterion the next year he played David Madison in *Miss Pell is Missing*. At the Edinburgh Festival in 1964 Briers played Lieutenant William Hargreaves in *Hamp*, then toured that same year as Gerald Popkiss in *Rookery Nook*. Back in London, at the Queen's he opened in April 1965 as Roland Maule in a revival of *Present Laughter*. Hugh Leonard reported in *Plays and Players*: 'Not the least of this production's virtues was the performance of Richard Briers as the dreadful young playwright who arrives to berate Essendine and stays on in anything-but-mute adoration. Mr Briers' playwright was not dreadful at all: in fact he was irresistible ... his performance here sets the seal on a superb comic talent.'

Briers was well established by this time as the silly ass or jovial fool; audiences came to know what to expect from him and he didn't disappoint them. His sense of timing was always more than accurate and he had also learned to make his incredibly fast delivery comprehensible. At the Vaudeville in 1966 Briers played Mortimer Brewster in *Arsenic and Old Lace*, and at the Duke of York's in 1967 Greg in *Relatively Speaking*, Alan Ayckbourn's first London hit.

In 1968 Richard Briers tried extending his range, playing William Faulder in *Justice*, but he was soon back into comedy as Moon in Tom Stoppard's *The Real Inspector Hound*. Helen Dawson found that Briers played Moon, the stand-in critic, with 'sharp hopelessness and vindictiveness'. At the Prince of Wales in April 1969 he played Bois d'Enghien in *Cat Among the Pigeons* and then, in July 1970, played five parts in *The Two of Us*. It was in 1972, when he took over the part of Butley from Alan Bates, that he felt he had at last achieved his best role. The bitter-sweet character took him away from farce and allowed him to display the subtlety of which he was capable but which he had too seldom been asked to demonstrate. Perhaps slightly over-flushed with his success, Richard Briers then embarked on a tour with *Richard III*. As he describes it: 'We emptied theatres up and down the land — can you imagine the Grand Theatre, Leeds, with thirty people in for the matinée? I'd seen the film thirteen times and I think I must have sounded like a second understudy to Olivier.' Chastened by the experience, he hurried back to Alan Ayckbourn's *Absurd Person Singular* in July 1973, following that with another Ayckbourn in 1975, *Absent Friends*. Briers finds Ayckbourn 'curiously difficult: very economic, very disciplined, never a word too many, so you have to play him as tightly as he writes'. But playing economically and with discipline is Briers'

forte. As Noel Coward once told him: 'You're a great farceur because you never, ever hang about.' He never hangs about in a theatre either — six months is his maximum time in a play. Any longer, he says, and the words stop making sense to him. He is so expert at his craft that he makes it look easy — so easy, in fact, that even critics often neglect to praise him. That is Richard Briers, they say — and everyone knows what they mean. In 1979 he was at the Lyric playing in *Middle Age Spread*, and in 1980 he returned to the classics for a short Hammersmith season in *The Wild Duck*, followed by a 1981 revival for the West End of Shaw's *Arms and the Man*.

Several television series followed, and then he returned to the West End in Stanley Price's comedy of the recession, *Why Me?*

PAMELA BROWN

*P*amela Brown was born in London on 8 July 1917. She was educated at St Mary's Convent, Ascot, but ill health forced her to leave at 15; she trained for the stage at the Royal Academy of Dramatic Art. After the Academy she went immediately to the Festival Theatre, Stratford-on-Avon, in March 1936, where, at the age of 19, she played Juliet, Jessica in *The Merchant of Venice* and the Widow in *The Taming of the Shrew*, as well as Cressida in *Troilus and Cressida* — a performance that Audrey Williamson, writing about the season, singled out as being 'delicious, with a wanton lisp'.

She made her London début at the Little Theatre on 5 November 1936, playing Lady Blanche Hungerford in *The King and Mistress Shore*, and toured South Africa the following spring in *The Frog* and *The Amazing Dr Clitterhouse*. In June 1937 she played Hermia in *A Midsummer Night's Dream* at the Open Air Theatre and followed that in October with Moira Lethbridge in *Under Suspicion* at Richmond. It was soon afterwards that she joined the Oxford Rep Company for a season and met Christopher Fry, who was later to write for her one of her greatest successes. In the summer of 1938 she journeyed to Perranporth for a summer season in the company of Peter Bull and Robert Morley, playing a variety of parts, as they attempted to introduce American-style summer stock to Britain.

At the Gate Theatre in November 1938

Pamela Brown appeared as Fanny Brawne in *The Heart Was Not Burned*, and then, in January 1939, joined the Old Vic Company playing Bianca in *The Taming of the Shrew* and Constance Neville in *She Stoops to Conquer*. It was the latter part that first brought her to the attention of the critics, and they began to speak of her extraordinary intelligence in performance. The next summer she found herself back in Perranporth, and then she returned to the Playhouse at Oxford. During the 1940–41 season there she played a variety of roles: Juliet, Lady Teazle, Bella Manningham in *Gaslight*, Sadie Thompson in *Rain*, but it was as Hedda Gabler that she won acclaim and recognition. Subsequently she toured as Lorna Moon in *Golden Boy*, and then scored a great London success at the St Martin's in September 1942 playing the title part in *Claudia*.

In February 1944 Pamela Brown played Ophelia to Robert Helpmann's Hamlet at the New Theatre. It was thought generally that her portrayal was over-intelligent. ('Intelligent' was thereafter constantly used in connection with her performances, both as praise and as criticism.) Audrey Williamson said: 'Pamela Brown brought to Ophelia's madness a frantic pain and a cry that turned hell to harshness rather than to prettiness; it was a grim but vivid performance, though in the first scenes too intelligent and assured to suggest Ophelia's fatal inadequacy.'

Pamela Brown then played Madeleine at the

Lyric, Hammersmith, in June 1946 in a play of that name, and followed it at the same theatre with the part of Yolan in *Death of a Rat*, a play about a girl dying of tuberculosis and the scientific experiments involved in trying to save her. After this success she returned to the Old Vic Company at the Theatre Royal, Bristol, and opened at the New Theatre, London, in September 1946 as Goneril in a production that had Laurence Olivier as Lear, Margaret Leighton as Regan and Alec Guinness as the Fool. Of Pamela Brown's Goneril, Audrey Williamson said it was 'as bold in evil as her sister was soft and indolent. There is iron and fire in this daughter of Lear.' In October of that year she played the Orange Girl in *Cyrano de Bergerac*.

Pamela Brown made her New York début at the Royale Theater on 3 March 1947, playing the Hon. Gwendolen Fairfax in Gielgud's production of *The Importance of Being Earnest*. In the course of a rave review, Brooks Atkinson in the *New York Times* spoke of her 'icy condescension'. In May of that year she played Angelica in *Love For Love* at the same theatre.

Back in London, in June 1948 she scored an enormous success at the New, playing the murderess Janet Spence in *The Gioconda Smile*. Audrey Williamson reported: 'The final scene of strain and breakdown requires an actress of power and nervous sensibility; venom shot with anguish. Pamela Brown was remarkable here, and throughout played with a vivid yet subtle intelligence; this was a Hedda Gabler truly wronged by destiny and taking her revenge with a vicious hatred which was racked, in spite of herself, by torment.' Her greatest success was, however, to come the next year, when she opened at the Globe in May 1949 as the suspect-witch Jennet Jourdemayne in the play Christopher Fry had written especially for her, *The Lady's Not For Burning*. Together with John Gielgud she transferred the success across the Atlantic, opening at the Royale, New York, in November 1950. Brooks Atkinson reported: 'Pamela Brown gives a warm, rich and fluent performance that gleams with humorous coquetry.' She repeated it at the Gaiety, Washington, DC, in March 1951.

Back in London, in April 1952 she opened at the Duke of York's playing Connie May O'Leary in *The Mortimer Touch*, and at the Lyric, Hammersmith, in September 1952 played Marie Chassaigne in *The River Line*, transferring with the play to the Strand in October of that year.

Pamela Brown joined John Gielgud again for his season at the Lyric, Hammersmith, from February to May 1953. She played Mrs Millamant in *The Way of the World* — giving a performance of which Kenneth Tynan was scornful: 'Mr Gielgud, an impeccable Mirabell in plum velvet, has Pamela Brown begging for mercy almost before the battle is joined. This is, of course, a ghastly abdication on her part. Millamant must be the empress of her sex, and her words, whether tinkling like a fountain or cascading like Niagara, must always flow from a great height. From Miss Brown's mouth they do not flow at all, they leak, half apologetically, in dribs and drabs. Instead of saving up the revelation that she loves Mirabell, she lets us know it from the outset, thereby dethroning the empress and setting an ogling spinster in her place ... All I can offer by way of consolation is this: it is the kind of mistake only an actress of Miss Brown's intelligence could have made.'

However, he forgave all when he saw her next performance at that theatre, Aquilana in *Venice Preserv'd*: 'Pamela Brown, pop-eyed and imperious, has recaptured the fluent authority which in *The Way of the World* she seemed to have mislaid. The scene in which Aquilana caters to the masochistic whims of her decrepit senator, Antonio, was written as a scurrilous lampoon of the Earl of Shaftesbury. From this dunghill Miss Brown plucks a daisy of a performance, made up of boredom, contempt, and even a flicker of compassion.'

In December 1953 Pamela Brown opened at the Piccadilly as Rachel Gardiner in Wynyard Browne's *A Question of Fact* with Gladys Cooper and Paul Scofield. She played the wife of a schoolmaster who discovers that his father was a convicted murderer; Frith Banbury, the director, was congratulated by the critic Richard Buckle for casting her in the role, because 'it was very clever to choose an actress so odd and special as Pamela Brown ... we might have been irritated by an ordinary, nice, appealing little woman. She plays intelligently, and her bizarre personality removes any suspicion of conventional sweetness from the love scenes.'

At the Haymarket in April 1956 she succeeded Peggy Ashcroft in the role of Miss Madrigal in *The Chalk Garden*, and then in New York played Lady Fidget in *The Country Wife* (Adelphi, November 1957) and Lady Utterword in *Heartbreak House* (Billy Rose, October 1959). Her last stage appearance was at the Vaudeville Theatre, London, where she opened on 20 October 1960 as Margaret in *This Year, Next Year* — a play about two spinster sisters involved in a love-hate relationship. Brenda Bruce co-starred. The play closed after a run of only three and a half weeks. Bill Lester, writing in *Plays and Players*, explained: '... the play is too slight a piece to justify this array of acting talent. Some more dramatic clash is required to fend off the yawns.'

Pamela Brown made her first film, *One of Our Aircraft is Missing*, in 1942 and continued to appear sporadically in the medium until her retirement, turning up in *Lust For Life*, *Cleopatra*, *Becket* and *Lady Caroline Lamb*. Her most notable film success, however, was in the non-speaking role of Jane Shore in Olivier's *Richard III* (1955). As the *Times* said: '. . . a non-speaking part, but in her hands an eloquent symbol of clandestine love and conspiracy'.

Her television work was sparse but critically acclaimed. She played, among other works, in *Susan and God* (Celanese Theatre, ABC 1951),

The Violent Heart (Playhouse 90, CBS 1958) *John Gabriel Borkman* (ATV 1958), *The Gioconda Smile* (CBC 1960), *Hedda Gabler* (ATV) and *Victoria Regina* (Hallmark Hall of Fame, NBC 1961) for which she received an Emmy.

Pamela Brown was married briefly to the actor Peter Copley (the marriage was dissolved in 1953). At her death on 18 September 1975 the *Times* summed up her career: Pamela Brown was an actress who 'had contributed something distinctive to the theatre ever since the intelligence of her work and her remarkable, incandescent personality and striking good looks were first recognized during the early days of the Second World War.'

YUL BRYNNER

*E*very so often an actor's image becomes so entwined with a performance it is virtually impossible to separate one from the other. When that actor also refused to discuss his life, shrouded his past in mystery and looked continually inscrutable, then the merger was complete. Yul Brynner most probably *was* the King of Siam. Annas come and go (Gertrude Lawrence, Celeste Holm, Constance Carpenter, Deborah Kerr, Samantha Eggar, Virginia McKenna) but even though Herbert Lom played the part in London for years, Yul Brynner was the part.

Yul Brynner said at various times that he was Russian, Mongolian and a gypsy, and at other times he just smiled. The consensus seems to be that he was born on the island of Sakhalin, off the coast of Siberia, somewhere around 1915. It is also said he grew up in Paris and was a circus acrobat. It is certain that he and his guitar arrived in the United States in 1941 and that he joined Michael Chekhov's theatre company in Connecticut, where he made his stage début as Fabian in *Twelfth Night*. He was then a radio commentator for the USO War Information Department. In 1944 he was cast in *The House in Paris*, which did not make it to Broadway. Yul Brynner made his first Broadway appearance, fittingly enough (being rather a Chinese legend himself), in a musical based on a Chinese legend, called *Lute Song*, in which he played Mary Martin's husband. She tells the story in her autobiography: 'Somebody told us about him and we invited him out to the Connecticut house. He came with a guitar and sat on the floor, playing. We had seldom seen such an exciting man.

He created a special magic around himself and we knew we wanted him for *Lute Song*. When he moved on stage in that show he was grace itself, pure poetry. He seemed to float in and out of the beautiful panels designed by Bobby Jones. I can't remember whether he was bald then or not. I know he wore a black toupee to look more Oriental.'

In 1947 he opened in London in a gypsy musical called *Dark Eyes* which was vastly unmemorable and closed quickly.

He became a television actor and director in 1949 for CBS and made his first film playing the villain in *The Port of New York* that same year.

Rodgers and Hammerstein wanted first Noel Coward and then Rex Harrison for the part of the King in their new musical. They proved unavailable, so the composers–producers settled on Alfred Drake, who decided to play hard to get. Mary Martin recommended Brynner. Richard Rodgers described Brynner's audition: '. . . out he came with a bald head and sat cross-legged on the stage. He had a guitar and he hit the guitar one whack and gave out this unearthly yell and sang some heathenish sort of thing and Oscar and I looked at each other and said, "Well, that's it".'

The King and I opened at the St James Theater, New York, in March 1951, and ran for 1246 performances. Abe Laufe in his book *Broadway's Greatest Musicals* describes Brynner: '. . . he brilliantly portrayed the semibarbaric, headstrong, merciless and yet charming monarch. He walked, talked and spoke like a king, conveying equally well the man's fierceness and tenderness. He made the King's moments of ruthlessness, as in

Yul Brynner in his definitive role of the King of Siam (with
Virginia McKenna as Anna) in a stage revival of the Rodgers and
Hammerstein musical *The King and I* at the Palladium
(London, June 1979)

Mrs Patrick Campbell in the title role (with H. B. Irving as
Charles Wogan) in *The Princess Clementina* at the Queen's Theatre
(London, 1910)

his condemnation of Tuptim, believable; he made his moments of bewilderment understandable and by assuming a fierce scowl that melted into a smile when his youngest child appeared, he showed the King's capacity for affection.' For his Broadway performance Brynner received the Donaldson Award, and for his film performance in 1956 the Oscar.

The success of his King brought him a seven-year film contract. Many of his film performances were notable, probably most especially that of the black-garbed cowboy in *The Magnificent Seven*. He remained, throughout the years, one of the most highly paid film stars; he married three times and he became a Swiss citizen. In 1972 he made a television series, widely reshown, in which he again played the King of Siam. He revived the role on Broadway in 1977, toured with it and played it for a year at the Palladium in London, before returning to Broadway for a 'farewell' season in 1985. His King had mellowed over the years — most of the fierceness had gone, but it remains one of the theatre's most magnetic performances. He died in October 1985.

See photograph opposite.

RICHARD BURTON

Richard Burton, who has been referred to as 'the Frank Sinatra of Shakespeare', could occupy the headlines for months at a time and fill theatres with idolizing fans; yet most critics felt his promise was never fulfilled.

He was born Richard Walter Jenkins in Pontrhydyfen, South Wales, on 10 November 1925, the twelfth of thirteen children of a coal-miner and a former barmaid. His mother died in childbirth when Richard was two and he was raised by an elder sister and her coal-miner husband. He was a bright child and found books an escape from the poverty and boredom of his surroundings. Later in life he came to prefer drink and camaraderie as his escape. His first role, in a school play, was a minor one, Ambassador Mr Vanhattan in Shaw's *The Apple Cart*. His family could not afford to keep him in school beyond the age of 16, so for a while he worked as a salesman in the men's outfitting department of the local Co-op. Hating his work, he put his energies into the Youth Centre drama club, and by a miracle of luck, coincidence and timing he was readmitted to school as former teachers took up his cause — he was too promising a pupil to abandon. His main mentor, Philip Burton, became his guardian when he was 17 and Richard legally changed his name. His first professional appearance was at the Royal Court Theatre, Liverpool, twelve days after his eighteenth birthday. He played Glen in *Druid's Rest* as a member of Emlyn Williams' Welsh Company. The *New Statesman* reported: 'In a wretched part Richard Burton showed exceptional ability.'

This was wartime, and the Royal Air Force posted Burton as an officer cadet to Oxford to take the university Short Course. There, Nevill Coghill, a don who saw thousands of undergraduates acting, proclaimed this one to be a genius. While at Oxford, Burton played Angelo in *Measure for Measure* for the Oxford University Dramatic Society. The war was virtually over before Burton started in it. He spent two boring years waiting to be demobbed, and was pleased to leave the RAF to take up a contract with the theatrical producers, Tennent's, for which he was to receive £10 a week whether he worked or not.

In 1948 Burton got his first film role, again through the auspices of Emlyn Williams. He played a young Welshman in *The Last Days of Dolwyn* (London Films). Also on the film was a young Welsh actress, Sybil Williams, whom he married in 1949. From the very beginning of his career Burton divided himself between the theatre and films. In the theatre in those early days he played: Mr Hicks in *Castle Anna* (Lyric, Hammersmith, 1948), Richard in *The Lady's Not For Burning* (Globe, 1949), Cuthman in *The Boy with a Cart* (Lyric, Hammersmith, 1950), Teguus in *A Phoenix Too Frequent* (Brighton, 1950) and made his first appearance on Broadway in *The Lady's Not For Burning* at the Royale on 8 November 1950. During the same period he filmed *Now Barrabas Was a Robber* and *Waterfront*.

Richard Burton's first real test as a classical actor came in 1951, when he joined the Shakespeare Memorial Theatre at Stratford-on-Avon. That season he played Prince Hal in *Henry IV*, Henry V, and Ferdinand in *The Tempest*. It was as Prince Hal that he drew acclaim. Kenneth Tynan in the *Standard* said: 'Burton is a still brimming pool, running deep; at twenty-five he commands repose and can make silence garrulous.'

He received the Theatre World Award for Best Actor in 1951.

That autumn he went back to New York as the young musician in *Legend of Lovers*. The play was not a great success but the New York *Daily Mirror* referred to Burton as 'one of England's most gifted actors'. While playing the title role in *Montsarrat*, at the Lyric, Hammersmith, Burton made *The Woman With No Name* for Rank Films and *Green Grow the Rushes*, a disaster later released as *Brandy Ashore*. Then it was Hollywood, for *My Cousin Rachel*, *The Desert Rats* and the spectacular epic (the first in Cinemascope) *The Robe* — all for Fox. By the time he came back to England, to the Old Vic Company, he was trailing Hollywood's title, 'the newest gift to womanhood'. In the 1953–54 season Burton played Hamlet, Philip the bastard in *King John*, Toby Belch in *Twelfth Night*, Coriolanus, and Caliban in *The Tempest*. His Hamlet drew mixed reactions from the critics. W. A. Darlington said: 'This well graced and most promising actor gave us a Hamlet full of fire and passion and instinct with intelligence; yet not fully moving.' David Lewin spoke of Burton as 'a rugger-playing Hamlet — an uncomplicated prince determined to revenge the murder of his father. He plays the part with dash, attack and verve, not pausing to worry about psychology.' John Barber thought he looked like 'a film star with the sulks'.

Following his established pattern, Burton was soon back in Hollywood continuing to be a film star: *The Prince of Players* (1955), *The Rains of Ranchipur* (1955), *Alexander the Great* (1956).

Although many of his film roles are best forgotten, his stage appearances were always events, and when he returning to the Old Vic in 1956 it was as the smouldering, romantic idol whom Hollywood had made a household name. There were scenes of hysteria at the Old Vic as the teenagers mobbed the entrances and queued in the streets for glimpses of those burning eyes. He played Henry V, and this time the critics approved. The *Times* summed it up: 'Mr Burton's progress as an actor is such that already he is able to make good all the lacks of a few short years ago ... The whole performance — a most satisfying romantic one — is firmly under the control of the imagination.' And Kenneth Tynan said: 'Though it sometimes prefers rant to exuberance, this is an honest performance, true and watchful and ruthless.' Burton won the *Evening Standard* Best Actor Award in 1955. He followed the triumph with a spectacular *tour de force*. He and John Neville alternated the parts of Othello and Iago.

Except for his performance as Albert in *Time Remembered* in New York (Morosco, November 1957), instead of consolidating his claim as the leading contender to Olivier's crown Burton contented himself with making films and counting his money, for at this point he became a tax exile, fleeing the punitive British tax system and taking up residence in Switzerland. His only notable film during this period, one which gave him the opportunity to show his quality acting, was Osborne's *Look Back in Anger* (1959).

In 1960 he returned triumphant to the New York stage as King Arthur in the Lerner and Lowe musical, *Camelot*. Kenneth Tynan was also in New York to comment: 'Richard Burton of the furrowed face and accusing eyes makes a peerless king. His singing is bold rather than beautiful, but his stage presence has that intangible quality of weight, as distinct from bulk, by which actors always reveal themselves. This is a majestic performance.' For it Burton won the Tony Award. He also won the part of Antony in the Fox Cinemascope film of *Cleopatra* starring Elizabeth Taylor. During the protracted filming she left her husband, Burton left Sybil, and the whole affair was conducted in a whirlwind of international publicity. Their joint megastardom meant that they could command increasingly ludicrous salaries, counted in millions. It also meant that when Burton returned to the stage in 1964, everyone came to see his Hamlet. It was the theatrical event of the decade; crowds mobbed the stage door every night, audiences vied with each other to give the longest ovation, and all was duly reported by the eager press. The stage-door keeper at the Lunt-Fontanne Theater in New York said: 'Not even John Barrymore could draw crowds like this every night.' It became the most profitable Shakespearian stage production in New York history. It also broke the record for the greatest number of Hamlet performances on Broadway, notching up 136. The *New York Times* called Burton's Hamlet a 'performance of electrical power and sweeping vitality'. And *Time* magazine said the performance was 'a technical marvel'. It was the climax of Burton's stage career.

He continued to make successful films, the most notable of which was *The Spy Who Came In From the Cold*, but his theatrical activity was sparse. Briefly, in 1966 he played Dr Faustus to raise money for the OUDS; in 1976 he took over the part of the psychiatrist in *Equus* on Broadway. (He had been awarded the CBE in 1970.)

In the meantime he continued to make headlines and films. He divorced Miss Taylor, remarried her, divorced her again and then married Susan Hunt. He began an American tour in a revival of *Camelot* but was forced to leave it because of ill health. A catastrophic revival of

Private Lives on Broadway in 1983 briefly reunited him with Taylor, after which he filmed a nine-hour life of Wagner for television. He died suddenly in August 1984, having recently married for the fifth time.

See photograph opposite page 6.

DOUGLAS BYNG

Douglas Byng was born near Nottingham on 17 March 1893. His father was the managing director of Midland Counties District Bank and his mother a former schoolteacher. It was a large and very Victorian family. When he told his mother he wanted to be an actor she said: 'I hope, dear, you will never come to that.' He attended Waverley Prep School, Stanley House and Cliftonville but was good neither at academic work nor at sports. His chief preoccupation was sketching clothes and performing pantomimes on the top landing at his house or in a friend's stable. His only theatrical effort at school, however, was an end-of-term concert in which he played the part of a commercial traveller trying to sell 'The Disinfected Doormat'. To add a touch of reality he arranged for friends scattered through the audience to open vials of ammonia at the critical moment. The rest of the audience fled in tears.

When he was 16 Douglas Byng went to Plouen in Saxony, where his older brother owned a lace factory. There he studied music and the German language. Always interested in clothes and with a natural flair for designing, on his return to England he went to work for the costume designer Charles Alias in Soho Square.

In 1914 he answered an advertisement in *The Stage* for a 'light comedian for a concert party by the sea — 28-week resident season' and was engaged by Greville Hayes, who managed the Periodicals Concert Party. Dressed in a farmer's smock with a red spotted handkerchief and singing 'She's Fat and She's Beautiful' in a thick Somerset accent, he made his first appearance on stage at the Palacette, Hastings, on 7 July 1914. The local paper said simply: 'Mr Byng also proved a good comedian'.

His first theatre appearance was in a revival of the musical farce *The Girl in the Taxi*, playing, at the age of 21, Professor Charcot, a fortyish diplomat. He toured in it over 112 small towns. That, together with the second tour of *The Cinema Star*, occupied him through 1915 and 1916.

Douglas Byng did not fight in the First World War, having been classified as unfit because, he says, he was 'rather thin and weedy'. He was engaged as an understudy at the Gaiety Theatre in September 1916 and first appeared on the stage there in May 1917, when he played Mr Blissett in *Theodore and Co.* He then played in *Yes, Uncle* at the Prince of Wales in December 1917. Back touring in 1920, Douglas Byng played the juvenile lead, Christopher Deare, in *The Kiss Call*. At the Winter Garden in 1920 he was walking understudy in *A Night Out*, and for Christmas 1921 he played the Grand Vizier in *Aladdin* at the Palladium. From 1922 to 1924 he toured, playing twice nightly for 110 weeks in a revue called *Crystals*, and at Christmas 1924 he was at the New Oxford Theatre playing Eliza in *Dick Whittington and His Cat* — the first of his very popular pantomime dames. 'I have always been a snob about my dame characters,' Byng says. 'I refuse to be a cook or a nursemaid and insist on being Alderman Fitzwarren's housekeeper or governess to babes in the wood.'

In 1925 Byng was taken on by C. B. Cochran and opened at the London Pavilion on 25 April in *On with the Dance*, songs and sketches by Noel Coward. Byng played Grace Hubbard, an elderly lady in a Bloomsbury boarding house, and in another sketch, *Vicarage Garden Party*, he played an elderly clergyman. He remained with Cochran for five years, playing in *Still Dancing*, *Cochran's 1926 Revue*, *One Damn Thing After Another*, *This Year of Grace*, *Wake Up and Dream* and *Cochran's 1930 Revue*. During those five years he opened a nightclub off St Martin's Lane called the Kind Dragon. There, along with friends, he would entertain late at night, and it was here that he invented his female cabaret characters.

In 1931 he went to New York to appear in cabaret at the Club Lido, and the Americans were very impressed. One paper reported that his first appearance was 'without a doubt one of the most beautiful openings we have attended with the glamorous background of this newly decorated room'. The *New York Evening Journal* called him a 'well set up Englishman, very glamorous' and yet another 'a gifted fellow, an excellent comedian and more diverting than many a nightclub entertainer I can think of'. Douglas Byng loved New York, too.

He came back to London to appear in cabaret and was the first such artist to be hailed in neon lights in London, when his name shone over the entrance to Monseigneur Restaurant off Piccadilly Circus. In May 1932 he appeared at the Strand Theatre in *Duggy in Party* while continuing his late night cabaret, and in April 1933 was at the Comedy in *How D'You Do?*

Douglas Byng made his first appearance in variety at the Alhambra Theatre, Leicester Square, in a pantomime burlesque which he had originally written for Ivor Novello's birthday party. At the Comedy in 1934 he was in *Hi-Diddle-Diddle* and at the Vaudeville in September the next year in *Stop-Go!* In December 1935 he was again a pantomime dame — Wilhelmina Whackster in *Babes in the Wood* at the Prince of Wales in Birmingham. After that he toured in *A Magnum of Charlot*. Byng preferred Charlot's revues to Cochran's; Charlot, after all, had introduced the intimate revue to London and his were less structured. Besides, Byng could perform his own songs, which were and are a curious mixture of sophistication, schoolboy humour and *double entendre*.

In December 1936 he was once more the Dame in *Babes in the Wood* — this time at the Grand in Leeds. At the Comedy in London, he opened in November 1937 as Tony Brownlow in *Think of a Number*. It was at the Palace in July 1938 that Douglas Byng played his favourite role in a musical, that of Prince Zorpan in *Marzita*. He wrote all his own part as well as two numbers for himself to Emmerick Kalman's music. In the cabaret scene he appeared as a female violinist and sang, 'I'm the pest of Budapest that turned the Danube so blue'.

The next two Christmases he was again in *Babes in the Wood* — Edinburgh in 1938 and Manchester in 1939. For Christmas 1940 he was at Golders Green as Widow Twankey in *Aladdin*. For the next twenty years he was usually to be found each Christmas as the Dame somewhere in the country: Martha in *Humpty Dumpty* (Streatham Hill 1941), the Queen in *Sleeping Beauty* (Nottingham 1944 and Birmingham 1945), Dame in *Goody Two-Shoes* (Edinburgh 1947, Glasgow 1948, Newcastle-upon-Tyne 1949 and Liverpool 1950), Mrs Crusoe in his own version of *Robinson Crusoe* (Glasgow 1951, Edinburgh 1952, Liverpool

1953, Newcastle 1954 and Blackpool 1955), Widow Twankey in *Aladdin* (Wimbledon 1956), *Mother Goose* (Worthing 1957 and Bournemouth 1960).

Douglas Byng did not, however, abandon cabaret and revue; appearing in *Strike Up the Music* (1941), *Fine and Dandy* (1942), *Flying Colours* (1943), *The Shephard Show* (1946), *Sauce Piquant* (1950), *Bells of St Martin's* (1952). He also managed another trip to New York in 1948, where he appeared again in cabaret.

He opened as the Baron at the Palace in May 1947 in *The Bird Seller*, a musical which boasted an enormous orchestra conducted by Richard Tauber — but the show failed. *Oklahoma!* had opened two weeks previously and had changed the style of musicals.

At the New, Bromley, in July 1953 Douglas Byng played Soames in *Lady in Evidence* and at the Winter Garden in May 1956 he opened as Martin, the barrister, in the Feydeau farce *Hotel Paradiso*. Caryl Brahms reported that he played it 'with an elegance, style, panache that is one of the piece's many distinctions'. He recreated the role at the Henry Miller Theater in New York in April 1957.

In October 1959 he appeared in *The Love Doctor* at the Piccadilly with Ian Carmichael, but the show closed almost immediately, having been judged old-fashioned and corny by the critics. *Plays and Players* explained: '*The Love Doctor* was an unspectactular, unpretentious little musical comedy which would have given pleasure to thousands had it not been killed by the hypersensitive critics.' This time it was *West Side Story* that had altered the critical taste.

At the Phoenix in October 1963 he played General Kuititzky in *House of Cards* and toured the next year in *The Maid of the Mountains*. The film of *Hotel Paradiso* was made in 1965, and Douglas Byng again played Martin. He took over from Wilfrid Hyde-White in *Lady Windermere's Fan* at the Phoenix in January 1967 and toured the next year as Sir Jasper Fidget in *The Country Wife*. He was back in revue in Edinburgh as the guest star in *The Fols of 1968*, and in 1969 once more played Martin in *Hotel Paradiso*.

Living now in Brighton, Douglas Byng says: 'Actually I don't feel that I have ever really worked; everything I have done so far has also been my hobby.'

MRS
PATRICK
CAMPBELL

*T*he enigma of Mrs Patrick Campbell has never been fully explained. When young, she was the most beautiful actress on the stage, with a voice that, at her command, could produce tears or laughter in her audience. Everyone was in love with her — including the critics, who quite lost all sense of judgement when reviewing her performances. In old age she became fat and careless and her booming contralto was much mimicked. She was at one time considered on a par with Bernhardt, but her career collapsed; even in old age she could be the greatest actress on stage, but she could also be the worst in the course of a single evening. Her personality was as complicated. As John Gielgud explains: 'She could be wise and affectionate, and why she had to be so ill-behaved, sometimes even common and rude, it was difficult to tell. A kind of demon seized her and she could not resist being unkind to people, making cheap jokes at their expense. Yet she could also be witty, very ladylike and gracious.'

Beatrice Stella Tanner was born in London on 9 February 1865, one of six children of Luigia Romanini, the Italian daughter of a political exile, and John Tanner, whose father was heir to a wealthy Anglo-Indian family. But father spent money faster than he could make it and managed to dissipate two fortunes. Encouraged by her romantic mother, as a child Beatrice Stella became interested in music and poetry and spent most of her day dreaming. She attended school in Brighton and then in Hampstead. At the age of 15, to improve her French she was taken to Paris for a year by a spinster friend of the family. The following year she studied piano at the Guildhall School of Music and won a scholarship to study further in Germany, but she did not take it up. Instead she eloped with the handsome Patrick Campbell and within three years had two children.

Her first appearance on stage was with the Anomalies Dramatic Club, an amateur society. On 18 November 1866 she opened (for three nights only) as Marie Graham in *In His Power* at the Lower Norwood Institute. The *Stage* reported: 'The Anomalies are fortunate in counting Mrs Campbell as one of their members. It was this lady's first appearance on any stage on Thursday and her performance was therefore the more extraordinary. Mrs Campbell possesses a natural depth of pathos and yet a power and earnestness which, joined to a graceful, easy manner and

charming presence, render her a most valuable acquisition.' She went on with the Anomalies to play in *Blow for Blow*, *The Money Spinners* and *Palace of Truth*.

Patrick Campbell went to Australia and later travelled in Africa hoping to make his fortune, leaving Stella to cope. Although her family and friends were horrified, she decided to go onto the professional stage to earn her living and to support her children. She made her professional début at the Alexandra Theatre, Liverpool, on 22 October 1888 in *Bachelors*; the local press reported: 'The character of Mrs Lynne Loseby found a most vivacious representation in Miss Stella Campbell.' She herself recorded: 'When I came on to the stage my first feeling was that the audience was too far away for one to reach out to them, so I must, as it were, quickly gather them up to myself: and I think I may say that this has always been the instinctive principle of my acting.' She next played Rachel Denison in *Tares*, opening on 22 April 1889 with Mrs Bandmann-Palmer's touring company. There was a clash of personalities — already the famous Campbell temperament was asserting itself — and she left the company after six weeks, joining Ben Greet's Players, with whom she toured the country for two years playing Rosalind in *As You Like It*, Olivia in *Twelfth Night*, Helena in *A Midsummer Night's Dream*, the Princess in *Love's Labour's Lost* and Queen Eglamor in *Love-in-a-Mist*.

Mrs Patrick Campbell made her London début as Stella Maris in *A Buried Talent* at a single matinée, produced by Ben Greet at the Vaudeville on 5 June 1890. The *Daily Telegraph* pronounced her 'a graceful and accomplished artist, who, having gone through a valuable apprenticeship in the country, cannot be long before she is permanently settled in London at some house devoted to refined comedy.' She played Lady Teazle in February 1891 at an Adelphi matinée, and on 18 June 1891 Rosalind at the Shaftesbury, where she scored a huge success with a fashionable society audience, and was engaged by the producers, Messrs Gatti, for the new Adelphi melodrama, *The Trumpet Call*, which opened on 1 August. The *Daily Telegraph* noted: 'Actresses are made, not born and this performance shows that in Mrs Campbell we have the makings of a valuable melodramatic actress.'

She went on to the Adelphi, playing in *The*

Lights of Home, *The White Rose* and *The Black Domino*. Subject to delicate health, she often lost her voice and during the run of *Domino* she developed typhoid fever which kept her off the stage for six weeks. The producers blamed her for the show's lack of success.

Just when her fortunes seemed at their lowest ebb and she was wondering how she would support her children, George Alexander chose her to play Paula in Pinero's *The Second Mrs Tanqueray*. She opened at the St James's Theatre in May 1893 and found herself famous overnight. 'She played Paula Tanqueray with great beauty, witchery, wit, fun and pathos.' George Bernard Shaw went on to describe the following period of her life as 'the heyday of her Tanqueradiance'. She became the adored of fashionable society, and her portrait as Paula by Solomon J. Solomon was the most discussed work at the Royal Academy Exhibition.

Patrick Campbell returned in 1894, subject to bouts of malaria, and astounded and overawed by his wife's celebrity.

The Second Mrs Tanqueray closed on 23 April 1894, and five days later Mrs Pat opened as Dulcie Larondii, a barmaid in *The Masqueraders*, a part she loathed. She quarrelled constantly with George Alexander, who was not only her manager and director but also her leading man.

Mrs Patrick Campbell left the St James's and joined Beerbohm Tree at the Haymarket for the winter of 1894–95, playing Kate Cloud in *John-a-Dreams*.

Her next great role was Agnes Ebbsmith, an 'Ibsenish new woman', in Pinero's *The Notorious Mrs Ebbsmith*, which opened at the Garrick Theatre in March 1895. Max Beerbohm said: 'Despite its inconsistencies, the part of Mrs Ebbsmith is a fine one and Mrs Campbell invests it with all that quiet and haunting realism of which the secret is hers. Her glamour is as it has always been. Her art has become subtler, more potent.' And George Bernard Shaw: '. . . the play is bad. But one of its defects: to wit, the unreality of the chief female character who is fully as artificial as Mrs Tanqueray herself, has the lucky effect of setting Mrs Patrick Campbell free to do as she pleases in it, the result being an irresistible projection of the lady's personal genius, a projection which sweeps the play aside and imperiously becomes the play itself. Mrs Patrick Campbell, in fact, pulls her author through by playing him clean off the stage.'

At the Haymarket in May 1895 Mrs Patrick Campbell opened as Sardou's *Fédora*, one of the roles the great Bernhardt had made her own. It called for great histrionics and Mrs Campbell's untrained voice could not cope for long. She lost it eventually and the show closed.

In September 1895, at the Lyceum, she played Juliet to Forbes-Robertson's Romeo. Even GBS, who was totally bewitched by her, had to admit that she could not play Juliet — and, horror of horrors, she cut the difficult speeches. However, *Romeo and Juliet* ran for three months. This began her professional liaison with Forbes-Robertson. (Whether or not it was also a personal liaison was a matter for speculation.) She played the slave girl Militza in *For the Crown*, the great actress Magda in the play of that name, Lady Teazle in *The School for Scandal*, the Rat Wife in Ibsen's *Little Eyolf*, Lady Hamilton in *Nelson's Enchantress*, an 'original and unconventional' Ophelia in *Hamlet*, a 'charming' Lady Macbeth, and, at her own insistence, Mélisande in Maeterlinck's *Pelléas et Mélisande*. 'I knew Mélisande,' she said, 'as though she had been part of me before my eyes were open. I knew I could put the beauty of the written word into colour, shape and sound.' And all the critics agreed with her. The *Times* said: 'Her beautiful delivery of the words, the vague, dreamy manner in which she moves through the scenes and her exquisitely picturesque appearance — all make up an impersonation of rare physical grace, distinction and poetic charm.'

In 1899 she embarked on a provincial tour with Courtenay Thorpe as her leading man, and on 19 June 1899, dipping her toe into management, opened at the Kennington Theatre in Professor Gilbert Murray's *Carlyon Sahib*, an attack on Anglo-Indian imperialism. The *Times* said: 'The piece is to run at Kennington for a fortnight. But it can hardly be expected that so unreal a story, based on a motive which is so repugnant to the mind of Englishmen, will enjoy a long life.' She continued to be financed in her own management, and in September 1899 opened a joint season at the Prince of Wales with Forbes-Robertson in a Japanese play, *The Moonlight Blossom*, which turned out to be a fiasco. After trying to make up their losses by hurriedly introducing a one-act, *The Sacrament of Judas*, which had a marvellous part for him, they parted company. In November 1899 she introduced *The Canary* in which she dressed entirely in yellow and appeared with Gerald du Maurier.

Mrs Patrick Campbell took over the management of the Royalty Theatre on 28 January 1900 and ran it for two years. *The Canary* transferred there and she followed it with *Magda*, *The Fantasticks*, *Mr and Mrs Daventry*, *The Notorious Mrs Ebbsmith*, a Spanish play, *Mariana*, *The Second Mrs Tanqueray* (with which she also toured) and Bjornson's *Beyond Human Power*.

On 5 April 1900 Mrs Campbell's husband was killed in the Boer War. Although, despite everything, she still loved him dearly, she stayed away from the Royalty only for a week.

The management of the theatre did not make her rich. On the contrary, when it closed she was in debt — all the profits had gone into lavish sets and well-paid actors. But it did bring her even wider acclaim. She opened her first American tour on 7 January 1902 at the Chicago Opera House, and filled it. After that she played New York, and the receipts from these two cities paid off her debts.

For the next ten years she introduced no new parts of any importance into her repertoire. She played Dona Maria de Newborg in *A Queen's Romance* (Imperial, February 1904) and Theodosia Hemming in *Warp and Woof* (Vaudeville, June 1904). In July 1904 she played Mélisande (at the Vaudeville) once more, but this time her Pelléas was none other than Sarah Bernhardt — and they played in French. It was a great success. The following year they repeated it in a tour of the provinces. Again they were greeted with near rapture by all except one rather sour Dublin critic, who said: 'Mrs Campbell played Mélisande, Madame Bernhardt Pelléas; both are old enough to know better.'

Mrs Patrick Campbell toured America again in October 1904 playing, among other roles, Zoraya in Sardou's *La Sorcière*. In 1906, back in London, at the Criterion, she played the Countess Ellingham in *The Whirlwind* and also Margaretta Sinclair in *The Macleans of Bairness*. At Drury Lane that September she was Greeba in *The Bondman*. For seven matinées only at the Royal Court in March 1907 Mrs Campbell was an exquisite Hedda Gabler — a role that was to become a standby. She then toured America again, taking her daughter Stella to act with her. In New York in 1908 she was Electra and then Deirdre, and toured the provinces that year as Phyllis Mortimore in Pinero's *The Thunderbolt*.

On 19 January 1909 she opened at the Vaudeville as Olive in *Olive Latimer's Husband*, and in July at the Hicks Theatre as Fabia Sumner in *His Borrowed Plumes*. That September she was at His Majesty's playing Mieris in *False Gods* with Beerbohm Tree. The next year she was again touring America, opening as Fanny Armawry in *The Foolish Virgin* in New York, and in Chicago introducing *The Ambassador's Wife*, written by her son. She also performed in a playlet, *Expiation*, with which she did a vaudeville tour.

Back in England, she opened at the Haymarket again in March 1911 in *Lady Patricia*. *Punch* reported: 'Mrs Campbell was adorable and spoke every word of her part as if she really enjoyed it. It is no detraction from the merit of Mr Rudolph Besier's exquisitely humorous dialogue to say that

her personality was necessary to his triumph. Her recitation of jewelled verse in the presence of an embarrassed footman was a thing to be remembered always.'

She celebrated the Coronation by reciting Herbert Trench's prologue to the Ben Jonson masque *The Vision of Delight* at a gala performance at the same theatre. That autumn she toured the music halls in a playlet called *The Bridge*. Her son had married in 1909; in 1911 her daughter Stella married and went to live in East Africa. Mrs Patrick Campbell missed her greatly.

In December she returned to the St James's as a villainous heroine who poisons her husband in *Bella Donna*. She then was involved in a taxi accident which immobilized her for some months. Already a victim of bad health, she seemed to become accident-prone.

George Bernard Shaw asked her to play in his latest work. She kept putting him off, and in September 1913 opened in J. M. Barrie's *The Adored One* or *Leonora*. There was gossip about her relationship with Barrie; there was also, of course, gossip about her relationship with GBS — that they were in love with each other there was no doubt, but they actually seemed to be in love with each other's image rather than person. And it seems certain that their mutual adoration remained platonic. She finally consented to play Eliza Doolittle. Beerbohm Tree was to play Higgins and Philip Merivale, Pickering. Rehearsals were chaos. Tree and Campbell were constantly ordering each other out of the theatre, GBS was trying not only to keep the peace but also to maintain his play in one piece. Two days before the opening Mrs Patrick Campbell suddenly and secretly married George Cornwallis-West, who was ten years her junior and whose divorce from Lady Randolph Churchill had been made absolute that very morning. (Within a few years he abandoned Mrs Pat.)

Pygmalion opened at His Majesty's on 11 April 1914, and despite the fraught rehearsals it was a triumph — Mrs Pat's last triumph. She took it to New York in October and then toured the States with it. Philip Merivale played Higgins in America. (She revived the play at the Aldwych in 1920.)

In 1916 she revived *Bella Donna* at the St James's, and then played there in *The Law of the Sands*, an evening full of the mysterious Orient. Her next portrayal was that of a spiritualist medium in *The Thirteenth Chair*.

Her son was killed in action in France in January 1918. Mrs Pat played on. In June 1920 she played the writer Madame Sand without much success, and then devoted much of the next two years to writing her memoirs. In Blackpool in July 1922 she starred in a hopeless play called *Voodoo*; she continued to be a very bad chooser of plays, following it with the part of Adela Rivers in *The Adventurous Age* (1925), Countess Strong-i'-th'-Arm in *What Might Happen*, and the title role in *Madame Kurandi* (1926).

By this time her beauty had faded, her body turned to fat and her beautiful voice had become almost a caricature of its former glory. She refused to come to terms with any of it and still insisted upon centre stage, even when she could not be bothered to learn the lines. She played Adela Rivers in New York in February 1927; George Jean Nathan reported: 'Mrs Patrick Campbell is still a skilful comedienne, but what chance does mere skill at trivial comedy stand against the recollection of a once lovely woman become fat and yellow?'

But Mrs Pat battled on, leaving the bodies where they fell. For matinées only she played Mrs Alving in *Ghosts* at Wyndham's (March 1928), and then was Ella Rentheim in *John Gabriel Borkman* at the Q (October 1928).

In May 1929 she opened in her last London play, performing the role of Anastasia Rakonitz in *The Matriach*. James Agate said that the play was too weak 'to carry the full freight of Mrs Campbell's genius, personality, and, may one say, legend'. It ran for 227 performances.

In 1930 she toured the provinces in *Ghosts*. Mrs Patrick Campbell also had a lecture which she toured around both in England and in America called 'Beautiful Speech and the Art of Acting'. It generally became more of a recital than a lecture, with Mrs Pat quoting from some of her major parts.

In 1931 she went to America touring, and also playing in New York where she was the Countess Polaki in *The Sex Fable* (1931), Clytemnestra in *Electra* (1932) and Mrs MacDonald (a burlesque of herself by Ivor Novello) in *A Party* (1933). She went to Hollywood, where her sharp tongue was neither appreciated nor excused; she made a few unmemorable films as a character actress. In 1935 she retired to a log cabin on a mountain to work on further memoirs, which remain unpublished. She returned briefly to England to star in a play but left after a few rehearsals because she could not bear the separation from her Pekinese dog, Moonbeam, the last in a succession of small dogs with which Mrs Pat was obsessed. When asked by a reporter which was her favourite perfume she replied: 'The scent of a puppy dog's paw.'

Mrs Patrick Campbell spent her last years in France. She never returned to England because the quarantine regulations would mean six months' incarceration for her beloved. She lived simply — by necessity, for there was little money — and died of bronchial pneumonia on 9 April 1940, 'going down,' in the view of one old friend, 'like a battleship firing on her rescuers'.

Her biographer, Alan Dent, sums up her career thus: 'Mrs Campbell was never to acquire the application and the concentration of Duse or of Bernhardt or even Modjeska . . . she never found herself in Shakespeare . . . Mrs Campbell's most rewarding playwrights were Pinero and Maeterlinck, Ibsen and Shaw, Echegarat and Bjornson, Sudermann and Yeats. It is by no means a tawdry or even a humble list. But it does fall short of supreme classicism. The result is that she never became a truly supreme actress since she was never to attain the higher reaches of the actress's art. She never took that art quite seriously enough. She repeated a successful role without developing it. She was hardly ever wholly serious, absolutely dedicated.'

See photograph opposite page 55.

MORRIS CARNOVSKY

'*T*here was something of King Lear's grandeur in that leonine profile and those passionate eyes; there was a sense of Shylock's pride in the flare of his nostrils and a suggestion of Polonius in the slow cadence of his measured thoughts; and if you looked at the angles of his sculptured face you could see hints of Creon and Tchebeltykin and Schweyk. Even Falstaff peeked through in flashes of wit and in a vigorous appetite for the broiled trout polished off by a Napoleon for dessert.' This is how Morris Carnovsky, then aged 73, impressed Samuel Hirsch of the *Boston Herald Traveler* when they lunched together at the Ritz Carlton in March 1970. 'I began by adoring words,' Mr Carnovsky told him. 'I've always liked to learn words and as an actor I've learned how to use them for all their juiciness and malleability.'

Morris Carnovsky was born in St Louis, Missouri, on 5 September 1897. His father was a grocer. He went to Teatman High School in St Louis, where he first became interested in acting; he played the title role of Disraeli in a school production in June 1914. His university education was interrupted by the First World War, but he graduated Phi Beta Kappa from Washington University in 1920. He then went to Boston, Massachusetts, where he made his first appearance on the professional stage with the Henry Jewitt Players and then, in the same city, he worked with E. E. Clive's company.

On 20 December 1922 he made his first appearance on the New York stage at the Provincetown Theater, playing Reb Aaron in *The God of Vengeance*. That same year he married Florence Lasersahn (the marriage was dissolved ten years later). He joined the Theater Guild Acting Company in 1923 and for the next seven years worked exclusively with them at the Guild and the Martin Beck theatres playing a variety of roles: Commissioner of Police and the Magistrate in *The Failures*; La Hire and Brother Martin in Winifred Lenihan's *Saint Joan*; Philip Speed in *The Creaking Chair*; a General and a Priest in *Juarez and Maximilian*; the second Federal Man in *Ned McCobb's Daughter*; Alyosha in *The Brothers Karamazov*; Centuri and Aggazi in *Right You Are If You Say You Are*; Dr Schutzmacher in *The Doctor's Dilemma*; Kublai the Great Khan in *Marco Millions*; the Judge in *Volpone*; Beschyba in *Camel Through The Needle's Eye*. The parts were small but all the time Morris Carnovsky was studying and experimenting. He always looked upon acting as an art and dedicated himself totally. In 1929 he played the title role in Chekhov's *Uncle Vanya*, then Nicobar in *The Apple Cart*, Stephen Field in *Hotel Universe* and Francis Bacon in *Elizabeth the Queen*.

In 1931 Mr Carnovsky joined the Group Theater, founded that year by Cheryl Crawford, Harold Clurman and Lee Strasberg, who had been at the Theater Guild with him. The group was highly dedicated and extremely serious, concerned with theatre as art and not as a commercial enterprise. Except for his performances as Levering in *Both Your Houses* (March 1933) and Dr Lewis Golden in *Gentlewoman* (March 1934) for the Theater Guild, Morris Carnovsky worked exclusively with the Group until it disbanded ten years later. He played Robert Connelly in *The House of Connelly*, the Group's first offering. Brooks Atkinson, writing in the *New York Times*, was delighted by their arrival at the Martin Beck Theater: '...their group performance is too beautifully imagined and modulated to concentrate on personal achievements. There is not a gaudy, brittle or facile stroke in their acting. For once a

group performance is tremulous and pellucid, the expression of an ideal. Between Mr Green's prose poem and the Group Theater's performance it is not too much to hope that something fine and true has been started in the American theater.'

Morris Carnovsky next played Father Martinez in *Night Over Taos* (March 1932), Rufus Sonnenberg in *Success Story* (September 1932), Dr Levine in *Men in White* (September 1933), and Will Parrott in *Gold Eagle Guy* (November 1934). In February 1935 he played Jacob in *Awake and Sing*. Brooks Atkinson reported: 'The Group Theater actors play as if they felt at home inside Mr Odets' Bronx saga. As the lonely dreamy old man Morris Carnovsky plays with endearing gentleness; he is an actor of artistic eminence.' The week before, the Group had done another Odets play, the one-act *Waiting for Lefty*, in which Morris Carnovsky had played Fayette. Next he was Leo Gordon in *Paradise Lost* (December 1935), The Speaker in *The Case of Clyde Griffiths* (March 1936), Chief of Allied Command in *Johnny Johnson* (November 1936), and in November 1937 played Mr Bonaparte in Odets' *Golden Boy*. Brooks Atkinson continued to be impressed: 'Morris Carnovsky beautifully conveys the silent grief of the affectionate father who realizes that he is losing his boy.' It was in this role that Mr Carnovsky made his first and only appearance in London, at the St James's, opening for a season on 21 June 1938. On his return to New York he continued with the Group until its demise, playing Ben Stark in *Rocket to the Moon* (November 1938), Captain Joshua in *Thunder Rock* (November 1939) and finally Rosenberger in *Night Music* (November 1940).

In 1940 Morris Carnovsky began a ten-year association with the Actors' Laboratory in California where, over the years, he directed *Volpone*, *The Dragon*, *Monday's Heroes* and *Distant Isles*. During this time, he appeared in New York as John Adams in *Suzanne and the Elders* (Morosco, October 1940) and Mr Appopolous in *My Sister Eileen* (Biltmore, December 1940). In 1949 he married Phoebe Brand, also an actress, director and teacher (they subsequently had one son). Mr Carnovsky went on to play in *Cape Crown* (Cort, January 1942), Kulkov in *Counterattack* (Windsor, March 1943), Sam Blumenfield in *Joy to the World* (Plymouth, March 1948), Mayor Stockman in *An Enemy of the People* (Broadhurst, December 1950), Aaron Katz and the Presiding Angel in *The World of Shalom Aleichem* (Barbizon-Plaza, May 1953). He also appeared in this as Play of the Week for WNTA in 1961. In 1954 he was Tzaddik in *The Dybbuk* (Fourth Street Theater, October), Andrey in *The*

Three Sisters (Fourth Street Theater, February 1955), Priam in *Tiger at the Gates* (Plymouth, October 1955) and Probus in *The Lovers* (Martin Beck, May 1956).

It was in 1956 that Morris Carnovsky began a long and fruitful relationship with the American Shakespeare Festival of Stratford, Connecticut. Here he was to do his best work. Winters for the next years were spent in New York City; summers in Connecticut. The first season he played the Earl of Salisbury in *King John*; the Provost in *Measure for Measure* and Gremio in *The Taming of the Shrew*. He went with Gremio and the Provost to the Phoenix on Broadway in early 1957. For the 1957 season at Stratford he gave his first Shylock in *The Merchant of Venice* and played Antonio in *Much Ado About Nothing*. That winter he was at the Belasco playing Jacob Freidland in *Nude with Violin*. For the summer of 1958 he was Claudius in *Hamlet* and Peter Quince in *A Midsummer Night's Dream*, and then opened at the Morosco in December 1958 as Mr Sacher in *The Cold Wind and the Warm*. Kenneth Tynan, aiming a swipe at the Method style of acting, said: 'Morris Carnovsky, shrugging to the manner trained, performs wearily and well as Mr Behrman's fictional father, a rabbinical grocer.'

In 1959, at Stratford, he played Capulet in *Romeo and Juliet* and Dr Caius in *The Merry Wives of Windsor*, and in 1960 Feste in *Twelfth Night*, Prospero in *The Tempest* and Lepidus in *Antony and Cleopatra*. At the Longacre in January 1961 he opened as the Logician in *Rhinoceros*. For the summer of 1961 he gave Connecticut a miss and played Shylock at the Globe Theater in San Diego, California. At the Billy Rose Theater, back on Broadway in January 1962, he was Morris Siegel in *A Family Affair*. The following March he was in Chicago at the Goodman Theater playing Azdak in *The Caucasian Chalk Circle* and then in October embarked on a United States tour playing Mr Baker in *Come Blow Your Horn*. Back in Chicago in 1963 he did Shylock once more, and returning to Connecticut that summer he played *King Lear*. He took the King to Chicago in April 1964 and to Los Angeles in June.

In March 1965, at the Coconut Grove Playhouse, Miami, he played Max Faessler in *The Man with the Perfect Wife*. He then went to Brandeis University as a Professor of Drama and opened their Spingold Theater on 2 December 1965 playing Volpone. Alan Bunce, writing in the *Christian Science Monitor*, reported: 'Mr Carnovsky's throaty, growling delivery served him well in an engrossing and authoritative portrayal of Volpone, the rich old Levantine who feigns dire

infirmity to expose the avarice and hypocrisy of his legacy-hunting associates ... At times laughter rumbles irrepressibly in Mr Carnovsky's throat as he struggles to maintain a moribund appearance before those who impatiently await his demise.'

The following summer he brought his Lear back to Stratford, and Howard Taubman, writing in the *New York Times*, tried hard to explain the man's art: 'Two years ago Mr Carnovsky undertook Shakespeare's most challenging and most profound tragic role at the American Shakespeare Festival Theater here and achieved moments of greatness ... To one who has watched Mr Carnovsky cope with Lear in Connecticut, in California and again in Connecticut it is clear that he keeps searching for new ways to plumb the overwhelming tragedy's depths. In his latest try he has arrived at his most coherent and sustained realization. Surely and steadily Mr Carnovsky has moved toward a performance that reminds one of a secret of the greatest musicians — their capacity to manage a wealth of subtle inflections within a carefully controlled compass. Mr Carnovsky's current Lear is masterly in the delicacy and penetration of its nuances. Indeed it is more poignant than ever because it is so vulnerably and sadly human. But it is no less heroic than before, even if grandeur is not sought for in thunder. For its heroism is firmly rooted in an awareness and acceptance of the human condition ... Mr Carnovsky perseveres imaginatively and eloquently in his search for an ultimate Lear, knowing, as we do, that there is triumph in seeking.'

In the summer of 1967 at Stratford he played Creon in Jean Anouilh's *Antigone* and a totally triumphant Shylock in *The Merchant of Venice*. Elliott Norton reported in the *Boston Advertiser*: 'In a production of *The Merchant of Venice* which is often handsome but otherwise undistinguished, Morris Carnovsky is giving a heroic performance as Shylock: powerful, rich in understanding, proud to the very end and infinitely moving ... Although he excuses nothing Shylock does, he feels enormous sympathy for the man; for the abuse and contempt to which he is subjected and which drive him ultimately to something like bestiality. His Shylock is old, long since bitter, and when he has been pushed as far as he can go he turns monster — yet not quite. Mr Carnovsky is magnificent in all the great scenes. He is proud, plausible and for all his fawning, somehow dignified as he first meets the contemptuous Antonio. Tall, strong and handsome, he makes his man a heroic figure confronting pygmies. He is big in pride, colossal in control, awesome in the awful hatred he bears these tormentors, these men who seek to demean him ... At that final point, Shylock has been denied his revenge, stripped of everything, humiliated afresh and now ill, is staggering out of the courtroom. The Stratford production requires him to walk down a flight of stairs which leads under the stage. He goes like a man who can barely see, staring ahead sightlessly. At the second step down, he stops and sits, struggling for strength enough to go on. A moment later, he is up — and suddenly he is holding his head high, too! He disappears from the audience's view with his eyes blazing in a final heroic and heartbreaking gesture of dignity; a man defeated, yet not conquered; a human being who has lost his humanity and found it again. This is a great moment in an extraordinary performance.'

Carnovsky continued to seek and experiment. He played Polonius in *Hamlet* and also played in *The Three Sisters* in Stratford in 1969. That same year he toured as Galileo Galilei in *Lamp at Midnight*. From 1969 until 1972 he was associated with the Long Wharf Theater in New Haven, Connecticut, where he played in *A Swan Song*.

Morris Carnovsky never cared for film-making. There was, he felt, never enough time to develop a character and he found it very unrewarding work. However, he did make a few films. He first appearance was as Anatole France in *The Life of Emile Zola* (1937). He also appeared in *Edge of Darkness* (1943), *Address Unknown* (1944), *Rhapsody in Blue* (1945), *Our Vines Have Tender Grapes* (1945), *Dead Reckoning* (1947), *Saigon* (1948), *Cyrano de Bergerac* (1950) and *A View from the Bridge* (1962).

When he was asked, 'What is an actor?' he had a simple reply: 'Shakespeare tells us in many ways — with many words. He said it for me most aptly in *A Midsummer Night's Dream*: ''The lunatic, the lover, and the poet are of imagination all compact''.'

CAROL CHANNING

*M*any great stage stars have one role with which they are instantly identified; seldom do they have two. Carol Channing is not only Dolly Levi — she is also Lorelei Lee. Only the long Broadway runs of both those characters interrupted her constant wandering the world singing, dancing, joking and acting and entertaining as if it were as natural as breathing. She does not even bother to have a fixed abode. She would never see it, anyway. 'Home' is the Mayflower Hotel in New York.

Carol Elaine Channing was born in Seattle, Washington, on 31 January 1921. Her father, George Channing, was a Christian Science writer, newspaper editor and lecturer and as such was no stranger to touring, nor to playing to packed houses. Carol attended Bennington College in Vermont before making her stage début in the opera *No For an Answer* on 5 January 1941 at the Mecca Temple in New York. After that she understudied Eve Arden as Maggie Watson in *Let's Face It* at the Imperial Theater. She got the job, she says, because she fitted perfectly into Miss Arden's costumes. One night in July 1942 she did play with the star, Danny Kaye.

In December 1942 she played Steve in *Proof Through the Night* and then began to work in nightclubs and cabaret. At the National Theater on 16 December 1948 she opened in the revue *Lend an Ear* and stopped the show, for which performance she received the New York Drama Critics Award. However, it was the following year at the Ziegfeld that she became a star, playing Lorelei Lee, the scatty but cunning blonde in the musical version of *Gentlemen Prefer Blondes*. John Chapman called her 'the funniest female to hit the boards since Fannie Brice and Beatrice Lillie'. Brooks Atkinson, in the *New York Times*, went into raptures: 'Let's call her portrait of the aureate Lee the most fabulous comic creation of this dreary period in history. You will recall Lorelei Lee as the flapper gold digger who made her way through masculine society with a good deal of success in the twenties. In Miss Channing's somewhat sturdier image, Lorelei's rapacious innocence is uproariously amusing . . . she goes through the play like a dazed automaton, husky enough to kick in the teeth of any gentleman on the stage but mincing coyly on high heeled shoes and looking out on a confused world through big, wide, starry eyes. There has never been anything like this before in human society. Miss Channing can also act a part with skill and relish. She has something original and grotesque to contribute to every number. She can also speak the cock-eyed dialogue with droll inflections. Her Lorelei is a mixture of cynicism and stupidity that will keep New York in good spirits all winter . . . Every part [of the show] is alive and abundantly entertaining. And above it all towers the blonde thatch of Miss Channing, who is batting her big eyes, murdering the English language and carrying the whole golden world along with her by sheer audacity. *Gentlemen Prefer Blondes* was always funny. It is even funnier now that the lustrous Miss Channing has taken such a stranglehold on the part.' After eight years' work, Carol Channing became a star overnight, and she deserved much of the credit for the fact that the show ran for 740 Broadway performances. She then toured America with it for two years.

In 1953 Miss Channing toured as Eliza Doolittle in *Pygmalion*, and returned to Broadway that same year to take over the part of Ruth in *Wonderful Town* at the Winter Garden from Rosalind Russell. The numbers had been written for Miss Russell and the critics were disappointed that Miss Channing's bizarre exuberance was toned down. She did, however, subsequently tour with the show. In November 1955 she played Flora Weems in *The Vamp*, not one of her greatest successes, and that year made her first television appearance, in an NBC production of *Svengali and the Blonde*. She became over the years a frequent television performer in all kinds of shows, from variety to quiz games. In 1956 she made her first film, *The First Traveling Saleslady* (RKO), and on 5 September married Charles Lowe, a television producer and writer who became her manager. They subsequently had one son, Chan. (Carol Channing had been married twice before, to Theodore Nadish for two years and to Al Carson for seven.)

Carol Channing opened her own nightclub act at the Tropicana Hotel in Las Vegas in 1957 and toured with it for two years — including in it, of course, her great numbers, 'Diamonds are a girl's best friend' and 'A little girl from Little Rock'. In San Francisco in 1959 she opened a one-woman show called *Show Biz*; the inevitable tour followed, and she then brought it into the Eugene O'Neill Theater in January 1961 retitled *Show Girl*.

Carol Channing was very much touched when the dying Gracie Allen asked her to tour in her place with George Burns. The partnership lasted for a season in 1962 and included a command performance for the Kennedys at the White House. The following year she toured in *The Millionairess* and then became Dolly Levi in *Hello Dolly!* at the St James on 16 January 1964. Howard Taubman wrote of it in the *New York Times*: 'Here in a shrewdly mischievous performance by Carol Channing is the endlessly resourceful widow, Mrs Dolly Gallagher Levi ... Miss Channing's Dolly is all benevolent guile ... Resplendent in a

scarlet gown embroidered with jewels and a feathered headdress and looking like a gorgeous, animated kewpie doll she sings the rousing title song with earthy zest ...' That title song became one of the biggest show stoppers in the history of musical theatre. The show got ten Tonys altogether, and one of them of course went to Miss Channing. She also received the New York Drama Critics Award. Pausing only to entertain at Lyndon Johnson's Inaugural Ball and to make a film called *Thoroughly Modern Millie*, she played Dolly until June 1967 — 1272 performances in all. Carol Channing played to capacity audiences not only for every New York performance but also for every single performance on the road during 141 weeks.

London audiences got their first chance to see the wonder of Carol Channing in April 1970, when she opened at Drury Lane in the revue *Her Ten Stout-hearted Men*, in which she sang, danced and did a devastating impersonation of Marlene Dietrich. Hugh Leonard, writing in *Plays and Players*, was impressed: 'Miss Channing resembles a doll designed for delinquent children. Her hair is a platinum bird's nest, her mouth could probably accommodate a banana sideways ... When we applaud or laugh, she seems to have not the tiniest idea why, but is pleased that somehow she has done the right thing. She laughs with us and then waits for someone to explain the joke. Not that we are fooled for an instant: when heckled by someone who wants her to sing "Hello Dolly!" she gurgles, "I've found a new friend," in tones of girlish pleasure, and it is as chilling as the kiss of death. For the record we are delighted, charmed and tickled pink by Miss Channing's prodigious talents, but never warmed. And to be fair warmth is not on her bill of fare, but its absence robs the evening of perfection.' She was rewarded with the London Critics Award, and then she returned to Broadway, to the Broadhurst, in January 1971 playing four different heroines in *Four in a Garden* but was soon back on tour with her own show. She made her first visit to Australia in 1972. In 1974 she opened again on Broadway at the Palace as Lorelei Lee in a new show called *Lorelei or Gentlemen Still Prefer Blondes*. Then, of course, she took it on the road.

It was 1979 before Carol Channing finally brought her *Hello Dolly!* to London, opening at Drury Lane on 25 September. Robert Zarkon was bewitched: 'It would be foolish to be clever about the impact of a Carol Channing performance but on the first night of this production I had drunk no champagne yet I had bubbles up my nose ... It is amazing how one character actress and ten waiters singing a chorus three times over can bring the house down but it happened each of the almost

2000 times Miss Channing has already performed this theatrical feat.' Carol Channing stayed for a while in London, continuing to bring the house down as Dolly, appearing on television, acting with the Muppets, but a few months later Dolly was back where she belonged — on the road in the United States. In 1984–85 she was also touring in a Jerry Herman musical entitled *Jerry's Girls*. *See photograph opposite page 70.*

JOHN CLEMENTS

John Clements was the most consistently successful actor–manager of the mid-twentieth century. His major talent lay in defining his audience and giving them exactly what they wanted. His shows, as well as his performances, were always solid, respectable and beautifully mounted. There was an attention to detail even though there was often a certain lack of inspiration. With his second wife, the actress Kay Hammond (his first marriage had been to Inga Maria Lillemor Ahlgren), he became a popular and respected entertainer on stage and on the radio. They were always reticent about their personal lives, a trait which also appealed to their audience.

John Clements was born in London on 25 April 1910. He was educated at St Paul's School in London and then went to St John's College, Cambridge. His first appearance on the stage was at the Lyric, Hammersmith, on 1 April 1930, when he played Lucas Carey in *Out of the Blue*. He followed that with Jeremy in *She Stoops to Conquer*. At the Royalty in December 1930 he played Hounslow in *The Beaux' Stratagem*. John Clements appeared in revue at the Little Theatre in December 1930 and then, at the same theatre, in February 1931 played Vettore Capello in *The Venetian*. At the Gate in May 1931 he was Jokaan in *Salomé*. He then left London and toured with Ben Greet's Players, playing juvenile leads in Shakespearian productions. Back at the Palladium for Christmas 1932 he played Jukes in *Peter Pan*. At the Cambridge in March 1933 he was Stephano in *The Lady of Belmont* and in April the same year at the Arts, Laertes in *Hamlet*. At the Savoy that September he was Tony Cleeves in *If Only Father Knew*...and at the Westminster in April 1934 played Ragnar Brovik in *The Master Builder*. At the Embassy in September 1934 he played Lucien in *Napoleon* and at the Gate in November was Fyodor in *Nichevo*.

It was in December 1935 that John Clements founded his first theatre. It was in Palmers Green and he called it the Intimate Theatre. He managed to direct forty-two plays there and to play leading parts in thirty-six of them.

At the Strand in 1937 he played Heathcliff in *Wuthering Heights*, and at his own theatre wrote, directed and played in *Young Society*. He continued at the Intimate playing such parts as Hamlet, Marshall in *Only Yesterday* and Julian Entwhistle in *Alien Corn*. At the outbreak of war in 1939, England was in a state of confusion and all the theatres were closed. John Clements was the first to reopen his, in September with Rattigan's *French Without Tears*.

During the war he directed many plays for ENSA and organized a special revue to entertain the troops. He also played Tony Kenyon in *Skylark* at the Duchess in 1942 and Joe Dinmore in *They Came to a City* at the Globe in 1943.

In 1944 at the Apollo he directed a revival of Noel Coward's *Private Lives* and also played the part of Elyot Chase. Amanda in that production was played by Kay Hammond. John Clements and Kay Hammond were married and continued in a stage partnership that lasted for many years.

John Clements took over the St James's Theatre in 1946 for a season. Audrey Williamson reported that he 'opened a season as actor–manager ... with Margaret Lace's *The Kingmaker* [he played the Earl of Warwick and Kay Hammond played Lady Elizabeth Gray] in many ways the best written and most accurately documented historical biography since Gordon Daviot's *Richard of Bordeaux*. Dryden's *Marriage à la Mode* was chosen by John Clements to follow *The Kingmaker* — a play a little outside the Restoration rut; less ebullient and bawdy and surprisingly combining gallantry with fairy-tale romance ... The mixture of styles is lighthearted and charming and Clements' production enchanted both visually and in wit. He, Robert Eddison and Kay Hammond played with immense humour and polish.'

Following his season at the St James's he joined the Old Vic Company. He played Dunois in *Saint Joan*; Celia Johnson was the Saint, Alec Guinness the Dauphin and Bernard Miles the Inquisitor.

T. C. Worsley noted that '. . . John Clements [was a] wholly admirable Dunois, described in the stage directions as "carrying his armour easily . . . his face marked by active service and responsibility, with the expression of a good-natured and capable man who has no affectations and no illusions". Humble enough to consider these hints, Mr Clements builds up from them a study beautifully proportioned and uniquely appropriate.' Also for the Old Vic, in January 1948 he played Petruchio in *The Taming of the Shrew* and in March of that year was Coriolanus. Audrey Williamson thought he 'shone briefly as an excellent Coriolanus, lacking only the full flash of Olivier's rocket-like performance'. T. C. Worsley elaborated: 'John Clements who played Coriolanus is an actor I particularly admire. He has many physical advantages, a splendid appearance, graceful and virile movement and a voice clear and musical if a little limited in range. These gifts he uses with the greatest intelligence and dignity and, when it is needed, passion. But for Coriolanus he fell a little short. He could not by sheer personality (it would be the only way) tower over the defects of the production and the part.'

In July 1948 John Clements took over the role of Arnold Holt in *Edward, My Son* from Robert Morley, who had written and created it. He played at the Lyric for nine months before returning to management — this time at the Phoenix in May 1949 playing Francis Archer in Farquhar's *The Beaux' Stratagem*. He also directed the play, and Kay Hammond played Mrs Sullen. They were a very popular couple by this time, with their own weekly radio show. They had a record run of 532 performances at the Phoenix — the longest run for a revival of a classic. At the New Theatre in February 1951 John Clements directed *Man and Superman*. He played John Tanner and Kay Hammond played Ann Whitefield. T. C. Worsley said: 'Mr John Clements makes so excellent a Jack Tanner — so explosive and ebullient, but catching too the fundamental good nature underlying the extravagance — that I began (in the first act) to harbour a mean view of him: I wondered whether he wasn't in danger of becoming one of those actor–managers who deliberately surround themselves with inferiors in order to show off (as they hope) their own talents the brighter. But the second act . . . demonstrates that such suspicions were base and baseless.' In June 1951 they added for one performance each week the 'Don Juan in Hell' scene — he played Don Juan Tenorio and his wife played Dona Ana. He directed *And This Was Odd* at the Criterion in October 1951, and in August he and Kay both played in *The Happy Marriage*, which John Clements presented, dir-

ected and had adapted from *Le Complèxe de Philemon*.

John Clements presented and directed a revival of *Pygmalion* at the St James's in November 1953 — he was Higgins, Kay Hammond was Eliza Doolittle. Next they were both in *The Little Glass Clock* at the Aldwych (December 1955) and then he played Arthur at the Saville in July 1955 in *The Shadow of Doubt*. That year he joined the board of directors of the Saville Theatre and personally managed it. He presented *The Wild Duck; The Rivals* (in which he played Sir Anthony Absolute and Kay Hammond played Lydia Languish); *The Seagull; The Doctor's Dilemma; The Way of the World* (he played Mirabell, she played Mrs Millamant). At the Piccadilly he presented *The Rape of the Belt* and played Heracles while his wife was Hippolyte.

From November 1958 until April 1959, when they brought it into the Duke of York's, they both toured in *Gilt and Gingerbread*. At the Piccadilly in October 1959 they were together in *The Marriage-go-Round. Plays and Players* reported: 'The matchless style and polish of the playing of John Clements and Kay Hammond is lavished on the married couple concerned and one can only regret that their artistry, which derives from so much more than mere personality, should be wasted on such trivialities.'

At the Duke of York's in June 1960 John Clements directed *Will You Walk a Little Faster?*, and at the Phoenix in March 1961 played Mr Zuss in *J. B.* He was Sir Lewis Eliot in *The Affair* at the Strand in September 1961 before joining the Old Vic Company once more, this time appearing in New York at the City Center in February 1961 as Macbeth, and then playing the Earl of Warwick in *Saint Joan*. It was his first and only excursion across the Atlantic. Kay Hammond, plagued by ill health, had been forced to retire from the stage.

Back in London he played Colin Elliot in *The Tulip Tree* (Haymarket, November 1962); Paul Jago MA in *The Masters* (Savoy, May 1963) and Edward Moulton-Barrett in the musical *Robert and Elizabeth* (Lyric, October 1964).

In December 1965 John Clements was appointed to succeed Sir Laurence Olivier as director of the Chichester Festival Theatre. He presented plays there each summer until 1973. Felix Barker in *Theatre 73* looked back over Clements' directorship: 'If John Clements did little to nurture playwrights, his other achievements were outstanding. . .Olivier's lustre had been necessary to get Chichester away to a flying start; it was Clements' task to consolidate, improve and keep the spirit of excitement alive . . . where his predecessor would try to be too clever, and therefore have one box-office failure out of three, Clements was more consistently successful in his eight years as director ... occasionally it is a positive virtue to put on something good simply because it is good, rather than because it is audacious and original. Clements never scrambled after effect.'

John Clements also directed many plays there and played in some. In his first season he was Macbeth. Peter Roberts reported: 'John Clements first played Macbeth in an Old Vic production which toured America in 1962. Although this was not given an initial London press preview, accounts from the States suggested that by the end of the tour the actor had a firm grip on a play that in theatre is traditionally supposed to be blessed with an almighty jinx. It's not surprising therefore that when Clements decided to give English theatre-goers a glimpse of himself in a role with which they are unlikely to associate him he should stick to his original director, Michael Benthall, and his original costume designer, Michael Annals. Neither is it surprising that he should hang on to much of the original business, including a final gruesome glimpse of Macbeth's hands stained with the blood of his own death wound. As it turns out the honourable achievement of Clements' performance at Chichester seems to be firmly in the actor's wary realization of his own limitations. It is a reading that has the advantage of clear and incisive delivery of the verse, coupled with certain limited objectives in characterization that are carried off with attack and precision. For me, this is not a performance that scales the grim and giddy heights of the play's wild poetry; rather it is one that proceeds firmly and safely along lower footholds.'

That could really be a review of John Clements' entire career. In 1968 he was knighted. After his successful time at Chichester he continued to act and direct, sometimes in the same productions, notably *The Case in Question* at the Haymarket in 1975. After the death of his beloved wife Kay Hammond in May 1980, Sir John's career moved towards a close.

ALEC CLUNES

'*D*eeply engaged with the theatre, he has yet been ready at times to stand a little apart from the rest of the profession, regarding it with an observant, amused, appreciative eye, immensely aware of all that passes, but not seeking to join the fray until his chosen hour. When he does join, he is apt to do something that the entire stage recognizes, and that lingers with us: he will add the revelation of a gesture, the benison of a look, the high flash of a speech, to our hoarded memories of the craft,' wrote J. C. Trewin in 1958 about Alec Clunes.

Born in Brixton, London, on 17 May 1912, he was christened Alec Sheriff de Moro Clunes. His father was a baritone who toured in musical comedy and then became a stage manager. Alec spent a good deal of time as a child in the wings. He went to Cliftonville School in Margate, where he was noted for his monologue recitations. He had a spell in advertising and journalism when he left school, and worked in amateur theatricals producing and playing for societies at Croydon and at the Tavistock Little Theatre in Bloomsbury. He also founded and edited *The Amateur Theatre and Playwright's Journal*.

After four years as an amateur, Alec Clunes decided to devote himself full-time to the stage. He joined the Croydon Repertory Theatre in June 1934 playing Orlando in *As You Like It*. The *Croydon Advertiser* reported it 'a sound performance, marred by monotonous cadences in delivery'. For a season he trouped the countryside with Ben Greet's Players and then went to the Old Vic in the Waterloo Road, where Lilian Baylis told him: 'You have a good voice, you can carry a spear.' And so he did, in *Antony and Cleopatra*.

In May 1935 he joined a provincial tour of *Grief Goes Over*, in which he played the dope-addict son of Sybil Thorndike, but he left the production before it opened in the West End and went back to the Old Vic where he played the third witch in *Macbeth*, Aslak in *Peer Gynt*, Octavius in *Julius Caesar*, Ferapont in *The Three Sisters*, Clarence in *Richard III*, Dr Antommarchi in *St Helena* and Autolycus in *The Winter's Tale*, where Audrey Williamson said he won his first real triumph. 'He played for youth and a picturesque gypsy flamboyance. He was a vagabond of colour and roaring impertinence and his *joie de vivre* lifted the play.' He was next Edmund in *King Lear*, and James Agate spoke of 'the phosphorescence of evil richly about him'. The next season at the Old Vic he played Berowne in *Love's Labour's Lost* and Harcourt in *The Country Wife*.

At the Phoenix in November 1936 Alec Clunes played Jim Lee in *Hell-for-Leather*, which was set in a pit stop during a Grand Prix race. It had a short run. Then at the Strand in January 1937 he played Roger in *George and Margaret*. The *Times* said his performance was 'well-timed enough to have the air of leisure and could move toward seriousness without losing touch with the nonsensical mood of the play'. At the Ambassadors' the next month he gave a 'gallant figure of the profligate youth devoted to his father' as Harry Dornton in *The Road to Ruin*. At the New Theatre in March 1937 he was Lucentio in *The Taming of the Shrew*, and at the St James's in June of that year, Douglas Hall in *Yes, My Darling Daughter*. He returned to the Old Vic in November to play both Clarence and Tyrrell in *Richard III*. Audrey Williamson found his Tyrrell 'remarkably subtle and intelligent'. In November 1937, for the Stage Society, he played Klas Tott in *Queen Christina* at the Westminster, and at the Whitehall in December he played a novice detective in *I Killed the Count*, which ran through the summer. Alec Clunes went to the Malvern Festival in August, where he played Peter Horlett in *Music at Night*, Tom Buchlyvie in *The Last Trump* and Dunois in *Saint Joan*, with Elisabeth Bergner in the title role. The *Times* said, 'With Dunois on the banks of the Loire, Miss Bergner seemed like a Barrie character trying unsuccessfully to come to terms with a Shavian soldier. At this point the play proceeded rather through the fine acting of Mr Clunes than through her.'

From April until September 1939 Alec Clunes was at the Stratford-on-Avon Memorial Theatre, playing six roles: Petruchio in *The Taming of the Shrew*, Richmond in *Richard III*, Benedick in *Much Ado About Nothing*, the title role in *Coriolanus* and Iago in *Othello*, of which A. V. Cookman said, 'his malignity seemed to spring from a perverted sense of sport'. Of his Aguecheek in *Twelfth Night* Lionel Hale said he presented 'a wild picture of the youngest, ugliest, and most unpopular member of a Victorian bicycling club'.

At the Little Theatre in the Adelphi he played Mr Horner in *The Country Wife* in April 1940, and in May at the New was Godfrey Kneller in *In Good King Charles's Golden Days*. In 1941, because of the war, the Old Vic established its headquarters in Burnley, Lancashire, under the direction of Tyrone Guthrie and Esmé Church — from there they also set out on tours. Alec Clunes played *Young Marlow* in the play of that name, Malvolio in *Twelfth Night* and Taffy in *Trilby*.

Alec Clunes founded the Arts Theatre Group of Actors in May 1942 at the Arts Theatre Club, an intimate theatre seating 324, in Great Newport Street near Leicester Square in London. There he directed the first English production of Clifford Odets' *Awake and Sing*. From 1942 until he gave up the lease in 1950 he produced 160 plays, directing thirty of them but appearing in only eighteen. Ivor Brown called it 'our pocket National Theatre'. When asked about his policy at the theatre Clunes said, 'I haven't a policy. I expect to put on the plays I like and hope the public will like them too.' In June 1942 he played Feste in *Twelfth Night*; the following year he was Vassily in *The Swan Song* and the Stranger in *Magic*. In February 1943 he played Ferrovius in *Androcles and the Lion*, and in March the part of Don Juan in *Don Juan in Hell*. In July he was Sir Harry Wildair in *The Constant Couple*. James Agate said, 'He does not pretend that the hero is one of Congreve's wits, but gives him all of his author's good humour and sincerity which the other neither dreamed of nor aimed at. After fifteen bumpers of burgundy his Sir Harry is still a gentleman.'

He played the Knight of Ripafratta in *Mine Hostess* in August 1944 at his own theatre, but it was at the Arts Theatre, Cambridge, in June 1945 that he appeared as Hamlet. James Agate reported: 'The point about [Clunes'] Hamlet is its extraordinarily human quality. He is a man of finer mould than most, yet willing to sneer. I have not heard the "What a piece of work is man" and "Nay, do not think I flatter" speeches so well delivered these forty years. Never in my life have I heard the prose in this great poem better given. Nor known better deployment of the gentle humour that is as much a part of Hamlet as his sardonicism and melancholy.'

Back at his own theatre in September 1945 he was Charles Surface in *The School for Scandal*, and then played his Hamlet there in October. In July 1946 he played Don Juan, and then toured through Europe for five months for the British Council.

In June 1947 he gave his first performance in five years outside his own company. It was at the Lyric, Hammersmith, where he played Henry Higgins in *Pygmalion*. J. C. Trewin reported: 'Clunes carried off Higgins in a fighting mood. He had seldom put more vigour into a part than into this lusty, gutsy performance. Here was Higgins of Wimpole Street to whom the Tower of Babel would have been merely a happy adventure in phonetics. Here were both the zealot's infuriating single-mindedness and the charm that atoned for all.' Harold Hobson said: 'Mr Alec Clunes attacks Higgins with the zest of a man eating a hearty breakfast after a ten-mile walk.'

Back at the Arts in March 1948, he played Thomas Mendip in the first production of *The

Carol Channing as Dolly Levi in a revival of the award-winning
musical *Hello Dolly!* (New York, May 1978)

Katharine Cornell as Masha in *The Three Sisters* at the
Ethel Barrymore Theatre (New York, 1943)

Lady's Not For Burning. He had kept Christopher Fry on the payroll while he was writing the play. Harold Hobson said of his performance, '... he plays Mr Fry's "poetry" with intelligent zest. Not a tongue twister nor a brain teaser trips his nimble tongue.' And T. C. Worsley: 'To the soldier of fortune Mr Alec Clunes gives every resource of his highly developed art: he speaks the poetry admirably: he moves most expressively: he gives to the character warmth, virility, light, colour, movement: he gives it everything except life and he would give it that if it were there to give.' At the Garrick in May of 1948 he was Robert Browning in *The Barretts of Wimpole Street*. Harold Hobson thought that he smiled too much in the role.

He played Harry Magog in *Gog and Magog* (Arts, December 1948), and Yegor Dimitrich Gloumov in *The Diary of a Scoundrel* (Arts, October 1949). In 1949 he married Stella Richmond, but the marriage was dissolved in 1954.

In June 1950, to celebrate the hundredth production at the Arts Theatre, he directed and played the title role in *Macbeth*. The critics generally agreed that it was not a good choice. But then *Macbeth* seldom is. Audrey Williamson said: 'It was this "haunting" that Clunes himself as Macbeth, like so many before him, lacked; his dagger was prosaic, but within all intellectual — as opposed to the supernatural.'

When the Old Vic reopened on 14 November 1950, Alec Clunes played a highly romantic Orsino in *Twelfth Night*, and followed that in December with Humphrey Waspe in *Bartholomew Fair*. Audrey Williamson found the performance '... a wonderful piece of down-in-the-mouth truculence by an unrecognizable Alec Clunes', and Kenneth Tynan elaborated: 'Waspe has a ferocious maternal regard for his young master, which he expresses by reviling him. Clunes behaves as if there were a hornet's nest in his stomach; he is openly furious, for very little reason, for the greater part of the evening.' He next played Ford in *The Merry Wives of Windsor* and then the title role in *Henry V*, which Kenneth Tynan called the best all-round Shakespeare production the Vic had presented since the war. Of Clunes' performance he said: 'Realizing intelligently that the fire and bite of battle are beyond him, he chooses to emphasize instead the godliness of the repentant prince: he sanctifies his charm by putting it "in God's hand" and often sounds curiously like St Joan ... My only quibble with this triumphantly "gentle gamester" is a look that settles on the actor's face in moments of intense brooding — a bulge-eyed glare which means, to me at least: "I think I've swallowed the spoon".' And T. C. Worsley

thought that 'Alec Clunes makes a most agreeable Harry, of an easy princeliness and an inoffensive gallantry. The schoolboy pattern of a hero certainly, but a perfectly acceptable one. He only fails to produce the fire to match the splendid old patriotic speeches, speaking them not ringingly, but in the quietly encouraging tone of a school captain bucking up the old colours. Otherwise he holds himself gracefully and speaks beautifully, which is all that is needed.'

In 1952 Alec Clunes took over the Winter Garden Theatre and played Moses in *The Firstborn* and Wildair in *The Constant Couple*. For his last season at the Arts he again appeared as Don Juan in *Don Juan in Hell*, directed *Maria Marten* and *The Bespoke Overcoat* and played Bluntschli in, as well as directing, *Arms and the Man*. At the Westminster in July 1953 he played Major C. O. P. Carrington VC in *Carrington VC* and at the Duke of York's in May 1954 played Allan Peters in *The Facts of Life*.

In November 1955, at the Moscow Art Theatre, he played Claudius to Paul Scofield's Hamlet and then opened in the same production at the Phoenix in London in December. Kenneth Tynan was most impressed: 'Alec Clunes is not only the best Claudius I have seen, but in most respects the only one ... returning to the basic principle of acting, he plays Claudius from Claudius' own point of view: as a man who committed a *crime passionnel* after an internal battle which has left scars on his conscience ... we watch the slow crumbling of a man of action who has created through crime a new universe which now falls, stone by stone, about his ears.'

In 1956 Alec Clunes married Daphne Acott, and subsequently they had a son and a daughter. That year he played Professor Peterson at the Fortune Theatre in *Who Cares?* He joined the Shakespeare Memorial Theatre Company for their 1957 season, playing the Bastard in *King John*, Brutus in *Julius Caesar* and Caliban in *The Tempest*. At Drury Lane in March 1959 he took over the role of Henry Higgins in *My Fair Lady* and played it for over a year. In January 1962 he took over the part of Sir Lewis Eliot from John Clements in *The Affair* at the Strand. In 1967 he played the Bishop's ascetic chaplain in an all-star revival of Shaw's *Getting Married*. Hugh Leonard found that he was 'wrong as the Bishop's chaplain but he used every line to such marvellous effect that one could only delight in his presence: his enraged gesture (not in the text) in rending the marriage agreement was sheer inspiration'.

Alec Clunes' last performance was as the Bishop of Chichester in Hochhuth's *Soldiers* in 1968. He died on 13 March 1970.

GEORGE M. COHAN

'As a dancer, I could never do over three steps. As a composer I could never find use for over four or five notes in my musical numbers. As a violinist, I could never learn to play above the first position. I'm a one-key piano player, and as a playwright, most of my plays have been presented in two acts for the simple reason that I could seldom think of an idea for a third act.' Yet ten years after his first Broadway show this man built his own theatre there.

George M. Cohan was born on 3 July 1878 in Providence, Rhode Island. (In later years, with artistic licence, he insisted it was on 4 July, Independence Day.) His family were all vaudeville performers and the theatre was his whole life. He travelled the country, one of the Four Cohans, singing, dancing and acting, and after the performances would spend the night writing. He wrote very quickly, an act in a night. (Later, when he was famous and rich and couldn't get peace and quiet, he would hire a drawing-room on a train in which to work for the night. The destination didn't matter as long as the journey was long enough to give him the time he needed.) He made his Broadway début as Algy Wheelock in *The Governor's Son* at the Savoy on 25 February 1901. It was his own play. Broadway was not impressed. In 1903 he tried at the 14th Street Theater, playing Augie Wright in his own *Running for Office*. Broadway was still unimpressed. He tried a third time, at the Liberty Theater on 7 November 1904, playing Johnny in *Little Johnny Jones*. Again he was ignored.

He took *Little Johnny Jones* out on tour with his family in the cast. He rewrote it, cut it, polished it and brought it back to Broadway containing the songs 'I'm a Yankee Doodle Dandy' and 'Give My Regards to Broadway'. His story of an American jockey unjustly accused of dishonesty in England was a huge success, and for the next fifteen years George M. Cohan had a profound effect on popular theatre. Broadway became his favourite subject. In 1906 he wrote *Forty-Five Minutes From Broadway* for Fay Templeton. That included 'Mary is a Grand Old Name' and 'So Long Mary'. It was also that year that his marriage to the singer Ethel Levy was dissolved; he soon married Agnes Nolan.

Although he could not write music and would whistle his tunes for someone else to transcribe, he was phenomenally successful. His next show, *George Washington Jr*, in which he played George Belgrave (Herald Square Theater, February 1906),

contained 'You're a Grand Old Flag'. In 1907 he played Augie Wright in *The Honeymooners* (which was really *Running for Office* reworked) and also wrote *Talk of the Town*. At the Knickerbocker Theater in April 1908 he opened as Percy Springer in *The Yankee Prince* and that year also wrote *Fifty Miles from Boston*, which contained the catchy 'Harrigan'.

In March 1911 he appeared in his own production, aptly named *Get Rich Quick*, at his very own theatre. Brooks Atkinson tried to explain exactly what he was so famous for on stage: 'He rolled his eyes and dropped his eyelids with a confidential grimace that seemed to be directed at individual members of the audience; he sang through his nose, carried a jaunty cane, wore a hat on the side of his head and danced exuberantly.' He was also patriotic to the point of jingoism. Moreover, George M. Cohan knew his audience. He even had a particularized image whom he named 'Joe Blatz'. He said: 'What the fifteen-year-old, clean-faced, fresh-minded full-of-life American boy or girl likes, the Average American Audience will like' — and he gave it to them. He played Robert Spencer in *The Little Millionaire* (September 1911), Kid Burns in *Forty-Five Minutes from Broadway* (March 1912), Jackson Jones in *Broadway Jones* (September 1912). At Hartford, Connecticut, he was William Hallowell Magee in his own straight play, *Seven Keys to Baldpate*, and at the Astor Theater, New York, in December 1914 played the Patriarch in *The Miracle Man* and both George Babbit and Leo Getrichstein in *Hello Broadway*.

George M. Cohan was a temperamental man — an egoist who was often difficult to work with, and sometimes to live with — but he was also a very generous man with his money. He spread his charity far and wide, both to individuals and to institutions. In 1917, with an all-star revue called *Over There*, he toured the country raising money for the Red Cross. He played an American soldier, and appeared in it also in New York at the Century Theater in May 1918. Back at his own theatre in December, he played Charles Martin in *A Prince There Was*.

In 1919, much to widespread chagrin, he took the side of the theatre managers and owners against the Actors' Equity strike. He became the actors' target because they felt that one of their own had deserted them. Even when the strike was settled he refused ever to sign an Equity contract. He played Richard Clarke in *The Meanest Man in the World* (Hudson, October 1920), the Vagabond in *The*

Tavern (Hudson, May 1921), and John Farrell in *The Song and Dance Man* (Hudson, December 1923), on which John Corbin reported for the *New York Times*: 'Devotees of the well-made play and sticklers for lifelikeness in the Drama will not find much to delight them in *The Song and Dance Man*. Far from being the ''Dramatic Comedy'' which the programme calls it, it is merely a theatric anecdote and rather straggling at that. But all those greater hearts who love the theatre for the sheer glamour and fascination of it will take the offering to their bosoms.'

During the next ten years George M. Cohan produced a great number of shows, revues and revivals. He played Joseph in *American Born* (1925), John Malone in *The Merrry Malones* (1927), Draper in *Gambling* (1930), Joe Townsend in *Friendship* (1931), Mr Daniels in *Confidential Service* (1932), and Parker in *Pigeons and People* (1933).

It was in October 1933 that he surprised — nay, amazed — everyone. He stopped playing George M. Cohan and played Nat Miller, the puzzled father of two teenage boys in Eugene O'Neill's *Ah, Wilderness!* for the Theater Guild. Brooks Atkinson wrote in the *New York Times*: 'As a Connecticut father of the year 1906, Mr Cohan gives the ripest, finest performance in his career, suggesting, as in the case of Mr O'Neill, that his past achievements are no touchstone of the qualities he has never exploited. On the whole, Mr O'Neill's excursion into nostalgic comedy has resulted in one of his best works ... As Nat Miller, the father, Mr Cohan gives a splendid performance. Although that adjective is exact, it seems hardly enthusiastic enough for the ripeness and kindliness and wisdom of his playing. He is quizzical in the style to which we are all accustomed from him, but the jaunty mannerisms and the mugging have disappeared. For the fact is that *Ah, Wilderness!* has dipped deeper into Mr Cohan's gifts and personal character than any of the antics he has written for himself. Ironic as it

may sound, it has taken Eugene O'Neill to show us how fine an actor George M. Cohan is ...' He toured with the part through 1934 and early 1935.

In May of that year he revived *Seven Keys to Baldpate* for the Players, and at the Alvin in March 1936 played Calvin Miller in *Dear Old Darling*. He played Ed Fulton in *Fulton of Oak Falls* at the Morosco in February 1937, and in November at the Alvin played President Roosevelt in the Kaufman and Hart comedy, *I'd Rather Be Right*. Brooks Atkinson reported: '... Mr Cohan is an amiable gentleman whose services to the theater and whose personality have long held him dear in the affections of Gotham playgoers. Put him in as head man in a political garden party and the President of the United States is bound to emerge as a buoyant, tactful man-about-town with a soft spot in his heart for young lovers and a feeling of general confusion about the government. As a matter of fact, Mr Cohan has never been in better form. The audience was his, and lovingly his, all last evening.'

Cohan then tried to revive his old success, *The Tavern*, but it only ran for seven performances. The taste of Joe Blatz had changed. George M. Cohan retired. Still, in 1939 President Roosevelt presented him with the Congressional Medal in recognition of the value of his two songs — 'Over There' and 'It's a Grand Old Flag', and when he died on 2 November 1942 his funeral at St Patrick's Cathedral was a fitting tribute. In 1959 a statue of George M. Cohan was put up at Broadway and 46th Street. No other man of the theatre has had that honour. Brooks Atkinson found it difficult to sum up his career, but tried: 'Since he wrote comedies, musical shows and songs and since he staged them and acted in many of them, it is impossible to classify him neatly. He was a virtuoso theater man. His combination of facility and energy suited the contemporary taste. His shameless flag-waving, his sentimentality, his electricity, his rhythm, his noisiness, his brash personality were the essence of show business.'

CONSTANCE COLLIER

'She is one of the few people I know who is concentrated heart and soul on her job and who has never for an instant, since those days when she used to scramble about among the grease-paint on her mother's dressing table, wished for any laurels other than those legitimately earned in her profession, and never for a moment doubted that for her, as for all of us who belong, the theatre is the most adventurous, exciting and glamorous life in the world ... Constance Collier, as a person, possesses all the range and variety appropriate to an actress of her reputation. I have seen her exceedingly tiresome and radiantly charming, tremendously funny and very tragic, but always, no matter through what crises she may be passing, there emanates from her a vitality and zest for life which makes her the most stimulating and entrancing of companions.' Noel Coward describing Constance Collier in 1929.

Madame Leopoldina Collier, who brought one of the first ballet companies to England and ran a dancing school there, was her grandmother. Her father, C. A. Hardie, was well educated in England and France and came from a prosperous family who virtually shunned him when he decided to become an actor — though talented, he was far from successful. Mother Lizzie Collier was a vagabond actress, a good clog dancer and an excellent second pantomime boy. Constance, named after the character in Shakespeare's *King John*, was born in lodgings in Windsor on 22 January 1878. Her mother rejoined her company only three weeks after the birth, leaving the infant wrapped in a blanket on her dressing table while she was on stage. As Constance grew she was left with the landlady in whichever theatrical digs they found themselves. Mother had begun on the music-hall circuit at the age of six, with her older brother. They were billed 'The Child Wonders'. Constance made her first appearance on stage at the age of three as a fairy in a revival of *A Midsummer Night's Dream* in which her parents were touring, but the first part she actually remembered playing was in another tour with her parents when, at the age of six, she was one of the children in *The Silver King*. Unfortunately she over-acted so much that the audience was reduced to laughter instead of tears at a crucial moment and she was taken off. However, she was an attractive child and after some coaching from the stage manager was given the role of Cissie, the most important child's part in the play.

She was expected to attend school while touring with her parents, but as each week found them in a different town it was virtually impossible. She was sent to a boarding school, where she found the headmistress cruel, the other children incomprehensible and the food sparse. It was the most awful experience of her life, she later recalled. After only one term her mother removed her and her formal education stopped. She did, however, become besotted by Shakespeare and spent her time during her travels studying him. She had learned the part of Lady Macbeth by the time she was 10.

When her mother was out of work life was very difficult, and money very short. Her father, though loving, was pretty useless through a combination of alcoholism and illness. They tried opening a dancing studio in south-east London — Constance played the piano — but it lasted only a month. Unsuccessfully they haunted the casting agents' offices.

In 1893 Constance Collier made her first London appearance, at the Criterion in the chorus of *La Fille de Madame Angot*, and for the six weeks the job lasted they ate properly. Then, lying about her age, she was taken on by George Edwardes at the Gaiety Theatre. There she was given singing and dancing lessons and performed tableaux as a Gaiety girl. In October 1894 she appeared as Ethel Hawthorne in *A Gaiety Girl* at Daly's, and at the Gaiety itself in January 1895 as Lady Jocelyn in *The Shop Girl*. Life changed drastically. Like all the Gaiety girls, she was fêted, showered with gifts and even became engaged to a millionaire thirty-five years older than she was. He was, according to her, 'a little, kind, fat man', but she couldn't even bear to kiss him; she broke off the engagement and lost the allowance he had been paying her. Still, she had tasted the good life and continued to indulge in the lifestyle until she was overwhelmed with debts. George Edwardes bailed her out on condition that she stop partying.

With a revival of *A Gaiety Girl* at Daly's, Constance Collier became a principal with a solo. She had a contract to be photographed three times a week for the postcards that were so popular at the time; dressmakers in Paris and London dressed her for nothing, jewellers lent her their wares and her picture advertised virtually everything. Life was once again sweet, and she was young, beautiful and very naive. She fell in love with a middle-aged actor to whom she became 'engaged' — until she discovered he was already married.

Deciding that there was no future in being a Gaiety girl she tried to become a serious actress.

She did a long provincial tour in a second company production of *An Ideal Husband* — and found it stultifying. Then she got a part in *Tommy Atkins*, which they rehearsed for four weeks and which closed in two. *Her Advocate* did not even last the week.

Constance Collier then became an artist's model to earn her living before getting a small part at the Lyric in January 1896 in *The Sign of the Cross* with Wilson Barrett's company. She played Ancaria, but had the lead for two weeks when Maud Jeffries was ill. She was next in *The Daughters of Babylon* in 1897, and in June 1897 played the title role in *The Maid of Athens* at the Opéra-Comique.

Through a chance meeting with the playwright H. V. Esmond, she got the part of the Gipsy Girl in *One Summer's Day*, starring Charles Hawtrey at the Comedy in 1898. Next she was at the Avenue playing Lady Alexandra Park in *The Cuckoo*, and here she took her first curtain call, at the request of the audience.

At the Comedy in 1899 she was Rachel in *The Ghetto*, and at the Haymarket in 1900 she was Lady Sneerwell in *The School for Scandal* and made a colossal success as Lady Castlemaine in *Sweet Nell of Old Drury*.

Back at the Comedy in 1901 she played Firefly, a nightclub vamp in a bright red wig, in *When We Were Twenty-One*. That same year she was engaged by Beerbohm Tree to play at His Majesty's Theatre. Her first role was that of Pallas Athene in *Ulysses*. 'It was a part,' she said, 'that ran the entire gamut. The part of a glorified fairy queen protecting the hero on every occasion, with the most exquisite lines to speak, the most gorgeous dress with a great golden helmet and a huge spear, very becoming to my particular type of looks . . . the part wound up with a delicious scene of comedy where Pallas Athene disguises herself as a young goatherd and is dressed in a leopard skin.' The critic J. T. Grien didn't quite agree. 'Constance Collier is in appearance more a Queen of Sheba than the goddess of wisdom and tact . . . Miss Collier is all robustness but she spoke with conviction and as her voice is powerful her speech overwhelmed the surrounding clamour and went home to the top-most parts of the house.' *Ulysses* was a resounding success and Miss Collier got a long-term contract with Tree. They rehearsed morning, noon and night and averaged four productions a year. During the run of *Ulysses* she had to honour a previous contract at Drury Lane to play Iras in *Ben Hur*. She managed to be in both plays every night. During her time at His Majesty's she played Roma in *The Eternal City*, of which performance J. T. Grien said: 'Miss Collier gave an estimable

performance of Roma but by no means one approaching greatness. She has plenty of force, both vocal and melodramatic, but her power is limited. She may disturb but she does not move us. She imposes but she rarely impresses.' Constance Collier herself felt that she was 'too inexperienced to hold a play of that sort together and my acting on the whole was pretty bad . . . I gave a performance the public liked, but the critics dragged me from the throne where they had placed me.' (During the run she was threatened and nearly killed by a lunatic religious-fanatic extra.) Also with Tree she played: Mistress Ford in *The Merry Wives of Windsor*, Millicent in *The Man Who Was*, Viola in *Twelfth Night*, Julie de Noirville in *A Man's Shadow*, Portia in *Julius Caesar* and Trilby in the play of that name. She toured with the company playing Viola, Trilby and Portia. In Comyns Carr's version of Dickens' *Oliver Twist* she played Nancy. The play ran for over a year. On the spur of the moment during the run she married Julian l'Estrange, an actor. 'He was a gay, beautiful and irresponsible person and no one who met him could help being affected by his charm and kindliness,' she said, but their separate careers kept them apart so much that it seemed more like 'an intermittent love affair'.

In 1906 she created the part of Poppeia in *Nero* and then played Cleopatra to Tree's Antony. They were commanded by the German Emperor to appear with the play for ten days at the State Theatre in Berlin. At the Shakespeare Festival that year she played Juliet to Henry Ainley's Romeo. At Drury Lane in 1907 she played an Indian girl, Adulola, in *The Last of His Race* and Lady Marion Beaumont in *The Sins of Society*. Of the latter, Max Beerbohm said she 'excellently irradiates despair, determination, remorse, and various other emotions that are in the part. Theatrically as well as morally it is a fine part and it could not be played better.' She then returned to His Majesty's Theatre in January 1908 to play Helena Landless in *The Mystery of Edwin Drood*; and at the Kingsway in May she played Charlotte in *The Latch*.

In October 1908 she made her first trip to America, where at the Garrick Theater in New York she played Ann Marie in *Samson*. Her husband was touring the States. She felt that 'my part in *Samson* wasn't very suitable to me. A depressing and rather colourless heroine who got herself into innumerable muddles and had to be extricated by the rest of the cast — a most irritating lady.' She was back in England by the spring for the Shakespeare Festival, where she played Portia in *The Merchant of Venice*. Then, at His Majesty's in June, she was Mistress Ford in *The*

Merry Wives of Windsor and Portia in *Julius Caesar*. In August at the Coliseum she played Mrs Brand in *The Robber*. That September she travelled back to New York to play the Duchess of Croucy at the Criterion in *Israel*, and then back again to London to play Flora Brasier in *Parasites* at the Globe, opening in May 1910. She then toured America in *Israel*, and opened at the Empire in New York in January 1911 playing Imogen Parrott in *Trelawney of the 'Wells'*. In March 1911, at the Criterion, she was Thais, in which she toured after a quick trip back to His Majesty's to play in *Vision of Delight*. She spent most of 1912 playing Nancy in *Oliver Twist* on both sides of the Atlantic.

The next two years were spent exclusively in America, playing Sara Fennell in *Frisco Sal*, Portia in *Julius Caesar*, Emilia in *Othello*, Roma and Trilby. She returned to England in 1914 and toured the variety theatres playing Alice Hawke in *Getting Out Of It*. The war years were spent mainly giving performances in all-star revivals to raise money for various charities. She produced *Peter Ibbetson* and played Mary, Duchess of Towers, in it. It remained, she said, 'the play I have loved best and taken the greatest joy in acting in my whole career.' She braved the Atlantic during the war to return to America where, at the Amsterdam Theater in May 1916, she played Mistress Ford in *The Merry Wives of Windsor*. She went to Hollywood, where she made a few films, including *Macbeth* with Tree. She toured the United States and in 1918 opened at the Comedy, New York, playing Mrs Cheveley in *An Ideal Husband*. Her husband Julian was at last with her in that production, but he died the same year in the influenza epidemic.

She returned to England and staged *Peter Ibbetson* at the Savoy with Basil Rathbone. She appeared in the film of the *Bohemian Girl* but then her health failed her; she became progressively weaker, not being able even to stand unassisted. She went half blind and was sent to Switzerland, where no treatment seemed to halt her decline until a doctor from Strasbourg treated her with insulin and she made a full recovery. She was the first person in Europe to be given insulin.

At the Globe in September 1923 she played the Duchesse de Surennes in W. Somerset Maugham's comedy of manners, *Our Betters*. James Agate found her '. . . richly comic. She trailed behind her clouds of the port-packing business, yet wore her clothes and her manners with an air. She was, you felt, vulgar only of soul.' The production ran through to January 1925. During the run she wrote, with Ivor Novello, a play called *The Rat*, which they then produced. It ran in London for a year. In February 1925 at the Haymarket she played the Queen to John Barrymore's Hamlet, and at Wyndham's the next year she was the Duchess of Florence in *The Firebrand*. With Ivor Novello again, she wrote *Downhill*. James Agate said that they were 'far too clever not to know that it is the purest trash put together for the purpose of exploiting Mr Novello's personal attractions'. It made them both a great deal of money.

Back in New York, she played Herodias in *John*, which was not a success, and then at the Henry Miller in February 1928 played her first comedy part in America, reviving *Our Betters*. For the next ten years she flitted back and forth across the Atlantic. Noel Coward, describing her in her New York hotel, said she was to be found 'presiding from her bed, attired in a pink dressing gown, with a Pekinese in one hand and a cigarette in the other'. During those years she played Mrs Baxter in *The Mollusc*, the Countess Flor di Folio in *Serena Blandish*, Julia Hurst in *Happy Families*, Anastasia in *The Matriarch*, Judith Bliss in *Hay Fever* (in which, James Agate said, she was 'magnificent, now like the wife of Herod, now like Bernhardt in the role of a Byzantine Empress stung by a horse-fly and neighing with fury, now like someone in *Hypatia* wearing a Graeco-Roman bun'), Carlotta Vance in *Dinner at Eight*, Mrs Duro Pampinelli in *The Torch Bearers*, Madame Bernardi in *Aries is Rising*. In 1941 she toured in *Curtain Going Up* and then in *Our Betters*.

Constance Collier finally settled in Hollywood, where Leslie Halliwell says she spent her later years playing great ladies with caustic tongues and eccentric habits. She died on 25 April 1955 at the age of 77.

FAY
COMPTON

*F*ay Compton was known as the actress who was never out of work. Her versatility was noteworthy, as was her businesslike approach to the stage — not surprisingly, coming as she did from a family that had been involved in the theatre for generations.

Virginia Lilian Emmeline Mackenzie was born in London on 18 September 1894, one of five children of the actor Edward Compton, who founded the Compton Old English Company, and the actress Virginia Bateman, daughter of the American impresario H. L. Bateman. She was educated at Leatherhead Court in Surrey and also studied in Paris. She made her first stage appearance as a child at the Royal Albert Hall on 10 January 1906, in a Christmas play called *Sir Philomir or Love's Victory.*

She was 16 when she joined The Follies (a group of entertainers) at the Apollo Theatre on 20 August 1911. Her elder brother, Compton Mackenzie, who was later to achieve fame as a novelist, was writing material for them. It was traditional in the family that the acting members took the name Compton, and the Fay came from a younger sister's inability to pronounce Virginia. The leader of The Follies was H. G. Pelissier; Fay married him when she was 17, though he was twenty years older than she. He died in 1913 at the age of 39, and she was left with a son. At Pelissier's death the group disintegrated and Fay went into straight farces, playing Denise in *Who's the Lady* (Garrick, November 1913), Miranda Peploe in *The Pearl Girl* (Shaftesbury, March 1914), and Cissie in *The Cinema Star* (Shaftesbury, June 1914). She married the comedian Lauri de Frece and went with him to America, where she first appeared at the Shubert Theater, New York, on 24 December 1914 as Victoria in the light musical *Tonight's the Night.* They toured throughout the United States; when they returned to England the war was on.

Having decided to leave revue, Fay Compton took up straight theatre, working with the top directors of the time — men such as Charles Hawtrey, H. B. Irving and George Alexander. And she attempted a variety of roles. She played Ruth Wilson in *The Only Girl* (Apollo, September 1915), Lady Di in *Follow the Crowd* (Empire, February 1914), Virginia Xelva in *The Boomerang* (Queen's, May 1916), Annabel in *Innocent and Annabel* (Coliseum, June 1916), Lucy White in *The Professor's Love Story* (Savoy, September 1916), Annette in *The Bells* (Savoy, April 1917), Sheila West in *Sheila* (St James's, August 1917),

and Helen Bransby in *The Invisible Foe* (Savoy, August 1917).

In 1917 at Christmas at the New Theatre she was Peter Pan. Fay Compton then played Blanche Wheeler in *Fair and Warmer* (Prince of Wales, May 1918), Sylvia in *The Hanbury Pearls* (Victoria Palace, December 1918), and at last got the chance to play a great emotional part in W. Somerset Maugham's *Caesar's Wife* (Royalty, March 1919). Also at the Royalty she played Silvia in *Summertime* (October 1919) and went on to the Haymarket in February 1920 as the Wife in *Tea For Three.*

It was in April 1920 at the Haymarket that she opened as Mary Rose in J. M. Barrie's play about the young mother who disappears and returns years later, exactly the same, to a world that has changed. W. A. Darlington spoke of her as being 'radiant at the beginning of the play and almost unbearably pathetic at the close'. And Ernest Short said, 'Barrie's creation has never been displayed with a deeper beauty and a fuller pathos'. In *Mary Rose* the part of her husband and then her son was taken by Leon Quartermaine, whom she married after she was widowed for the second time. They were also together at the Haymarket in March 1921 in Maugham's *The Circle* (she played Elizabeth), and in August 1921 when she played Phoebe and he played the dashing Captain Browne in *Quality Street.*

At the Comedy in September 1922 Fay Compton played Mary and Lady Carlton in *Secrets.* W. Macqueen Pope said: 'Fay Compton gave an exquisite performance. She was on stage almost all the time, portraying a woman at varying stages in her life, starting as an old lady, going back to a young wife and then a middle-aged mother, and ending up as an old lady again. As she changed her costumes, make up and wigs, so she changed her character. She hit every note dead in the middle, everything was in perfect time.'

For a charity performance at His Majesty's in February 1923 she played Loyse in *The Ballad Monger,* and at the Haymarket in August 1923 was Princess Flavia in a revival of *The Prisoner of Zenda.* She also played Lady Babbie in a revival of *The Little Minister* (Queen's, November 1923) and Diana Tunstall in *The Claimant* (Queen's, September 1924). Of the latter part, James Agate reported: 'This ninny of the fragile intellect was entrusted to Miss Fay Compton, who seems to me to be playing all those parts which she shouldn't and none of those she should. There is, I suppose, nobody on the English stage possessed of greater power of suggesting purity and innocence: Miss Compton throws this away and dabbles in black-eyed jades like Yasmin. No actress that I know can so mingle dewy pathos and the salt of sanity; yet she must forgo these in favour of gumptionless Dianas.' At the same theatre in December she played Madeleine in *Orange Blossom*.

Except for a brief appearance as Juliet in the Balcony scene at His Majesty's in 1920, Fay Compton did not play Shakespeare until February 1925, when she opened at the Haymarket as Ophelia to John Barrymore's Hamlet. She played the part again with Tearle in 1931 and with Gielgud in 1939. James Agate said she was the best Ophelia he had ever seen; J. C. Trewin explained: 'This was no chit around Elsinore, but the true "rose of May", a girl profoundly hurt; someone who might indeed have mourned as she did for the Hamlet she had lost... she was herself a noble mind o'erthrown. I have not forgotten Fay Compton's Ophelia and those wide, reproachful eyes.'

Still at the Haymarket, Fay Compton played Ariadne Winter in *Ariadne or Business First* (April 1925), and with Leon Quartermaine as her leading man played the Lady in Ashley Duke's comedy *The Man with a Load of Mischief* (June 1925). They continued a successful stage partnership for the next few years, reviving *Mary Rose* (January 1926) and playing in *This Woman Business* (April 1926) and *The White Witch* (September 1926). In the latter Fay Compton played Jenny Bell, and James Agate was sorry that she had. 'Miss Fay Compton was never happy with Jenny who was quite null. And nullity having always refused to be acted, there is no reflection here on Miss Compton's art which simply was not and could not be brought into action.'

In December 1926 she opened at the Duke of York's as Julie in *Liliom*, the play on which *Carousel* was based. It lost a lot of money and was a disaster for all concerned. At the Strand in April 1927 she opened as Constance Middleton in Maugham's *The Constant Wife*. The play had been a great success in New York and it came as a surprise to find that London audiences did not like it. The very next month Miss Compton was playing Lisa Mordaunt in *The Bridge* at the Arts Theatre. For a charity at Drury Lane that same month she was Gianella in *The Wandering Jew*. At the St Martin's in 1928 Fay Compton opened as the Femme de Chambre in *Other Men's Wives* and for a charity in May at the Palace played Suzanne de Tournai in *The Scarlet Pimpernel*.

Although she had made some silent films in England, Fay Compton went to Hollywood for the first time only in 1928 where she co-starred with

Adolph Menjou. She opened in New York at the Empire in October 1928 as Olympia, Princess Orsalini in *Olympia*, but was not a great success. She returned to England where she revived *Secrets* (Comedy, September 1929), toured as Julia March in *Virtue for Sale* (January 1930), played Madeleine Corey in *A Dishonoured Lady* (Playhouse, May 1930) and Dick Whittington in the pantomime at the Palace, Manchester, at Christmas 1930. Pausing to give her Ophelia once again (April 1931), she opened at the Lyric playing Fanny Gray in Dodie Smith's first play, *Autumn Crocus*, and was a great success as the English schoolmistress who falls in love with an innkeeper while on her Tyrolean holiday. She played Dick Whittington again for Christmas that year in Glasgow and then toured in *Autumn Crocus*. She was now acknowledged as one of the country's foremost actresses, a position she maintained for the next twenty years.

In October 1932 she played Camilla Graham in *Once a Husband* at the Haymarket, and at Christmas played her Dick Whittington at the London Hippodrome, after which she toured the variety circuit in *This, That and the Other*. At the Globe in June 1933 she played in *Proscenium* opposite Ivor Novello. It was one of Ivor's last straight plays — he was soon into musicals. Audrey Williamson said that Fay Compton 'brought in drama as an ageing actress who suddenly realized her own incapability of playing Juliet to her young husband's Romeo'. She next played Christina in *Indoor Fireworks* (Aldwych, March 1934), Mary Ventyre in *Murder in Mayfair* (Globe, September 1934), and the Duchess of Shires in *Hervey House* (His Majesty's, May 1935). At the Open Air Theatre in Regent's Park for the summer she played Titania in *A Midsummer Night's Dream* and Rosaline in *Love's Labour's Lost*.

At the Globe Theatre she played Dorothy Hilton in *Call It a Day*. The production opened in October 1935 and ran through January 1937, and then she took it on the road. Back at Regent's Park for the summer Fay Compton, absolutely tireless, played Titania in *A Midsummer Night's Dream*, Calpurnia in *Julius Caesar*, the Lady in *Comus* and Pauline in *A Winter's Tale*. For the rest of 1937 and much of 1938 she toured Australia and New Zealand in *Victoria Regina*, *Tonight at 8.30* and *George and Margaret*. She was back for Christmas 1938, playing Robin Hood in *Babes in the Wood* at Drury Lane. In February 1939 she made her first appearance on the London music hall stage at the Coliseum in *Songs*, and the following month was off on a tour playing Mrs Philips in *Drawing Room*.

Fay Compton again played Ophelia at the

Lyceum (June 1939); this time Hamlet was John Gielgud. They also played at Elsinore. In August 1939 she toured as Sanchia Carson in *Robert's Wife*, and the following April joined the Old Vic to play Regan in John Gielgud's *King Lear*. Audrey Williamson said Fay Compton's Regan 'had an icy venom backed by daemonic cruelty: a performance of astonishing power which left all traces of Mary Rose behind in time and transformed even the liquid silver of the voice into a cold, rock-hard crystal'. Then, for something completely different, she toured in 1940 as the Virgin Mary in *Family Portrait* and later as Doris Gow in *Fumed Oak*. For Christmas she played the Prince in *Cinderella* at the Palace, Manchester. In July 1941 Fay opened at the Piccadilly as Ruth, the second wife, in Noel Coward's *Blithe Spirit*, and stayed there for fifteen months. At the same theatre in October 1942 she played Regina Giddons in Lillian Hellman's *The Little Foxes*. She was the Prince again at Christmas. That year she also found time to dissolve her marriage to Leon Quartermaine.

Fay Compton spent 1943 touring as Madame Sans-Genes in *The Duchess of Dantzig*. She opened at the Phoenix in June 1944 as Hannah Kernahan in *The Last of Summer*, and then scored a two-year run at the Vaudeville as Martha Dacre, the housewife whose work is never done in *No Medals*. In September 1946 she set out on a British Council tour of Belgium, Holland, France and Switzerland playing in *Othello*, *Candida* and *Hamlet*. That year she also divorced her fourth and last husband, the actor Ralph Michael.

Fay Compton played her Candida, and Emilia in *Othello*, at the Piccadilly Theatre from March 1947. She then did some film work before opening at the Strand in February 1948 once more playing Mary in *Family Portrait*. For that performance she received the Ellen Terry Award. Next she played Gina Ekdal in *The Wild Duck* (St Martin's, November 1948), Sister Bonaventure in *Bonaventure* (Vaudeville, December 1949), Yvonne in *Intimate Relations* (Arts, March 1951 and Strand, July 1951), Lora Sutherland in *Red Letter Day* (Garrick, February 1952), Esther Ledous in *The Holy Terror* (Arts, November 1952), and in June 1953 she played Martha in *Out of the Whirlwind*, written by Christopher Hassall for performance in Westminster Abbey during the Coronation season.

Then she went back to the Old Vic for a season, where she played Gertrude in Burton's *Hamlet*, the Countess of Roussillon in *All's Well That Ends Well*, Juno in *The Tempest*, Volumnia in *Coriolanus* and Constance of Bretagne in *King John*. Of her Constance, Audrey Williamson said it 'was all that her long experience, silver voice and

emotional range had led us to anticipate — grief and distraction truly blent, with both the flash of imperiousness and the tenderness of affection'. J. C. Trewin remarked that 'crying Constance' was 'a woman who can be a burden but was seldom so when Fay Compton found in her a dark splendour of grief'.

In September 1954 she opened at the "Q" Theatre as Gertrude Blunt in *Witch Errant*. The following September she toured as Ruth Prendergast in *Tabitha*, and in March 1956 toured as Lydia Sheridan in *Starlight*. She returned to the Old Vic in May 1957 to play Queen Margaret to Robert Helpmann's Richard III. Then in January 1958 she toured as Mrs St Maugham in *The Chalk Garden*.

On Broadway for the first time in more than twenty years, she opened at the 54th Street Theater in February 1959 playing Kate Murphy in *God and Kate Murphy*, but it was an unsuccessful venture.

Fay Compton went back to the Old Vic in October 1959 to play Lady Bracknell in *The Importance of Being Earnest*, which should, as J. C. Trewin pointed out, have been ideal casting. However, at 65 her memory began to fail her. Trewin explained: 'Alas, though the aspect and the potential authority were there, Fay Compton had to stand outside Lady Bracknell — simply because she paraphrased speeches in which she should have been comma perfect: you cannot paraphrase scenes that at least seventy-five per cent of an audience is ready to prompt.' Still, of her next Old Vic performance, as the Comtesse de la Brière in *What Every Woman Knows* in April 1960, Peter Roberts said in *Plays and Players*: 'Fay Compton's Comtesse de la Brière was beautifully done. What a wonderful technique Miss Compton has. Drama students who want to learn to laugh naturally on a stage and at the same time to adopt a French accent that is not an embarrassment should hie them to the Waterloo Road.' She was also an excellent Mrs Malaprop at Croydon in November 1961.

Fay Compton joined Laurence Olivier for his first two seasons at the Chichester Festival Theatre. In 1962 she played Grausis in *The Broken Heart* and Marya in *Uncle Vanya*. She played Mrs Malaprop again, this time at the Lyric, Hammersmith, before returning to Chichester in 1963 to play Marya again as well as Mrs B. in *The Workhouse Donkey*. In September 1963 she toured as Mrs Caution in *The Gentleman Dancing Masters*. She joined Michael Redgrave for the opening season of the Yvonne Arnaud Theatre in Guildford in May 1965, playing Anna in *A Month in the Country* and the Chorus in *Samson Agonistes*; she repeated her performance in *A Month in the Country* at the Cambridge Theatre in September.

Fay Compton appeared frequently on television, but she will probably be best remembered as Aunt Ann, the very oldest member of the family in *The Forsyte Saga*. In 1975 she was awarded the CBE. She died on 12 December 1978.
See photograph opposite page 23.

GLADYS COOPER

Gladys Constance Cooper, actress, theatre manager and Dame of the British Empire, was born in London's Lewisham on 18 December 1888, the eldest of the three children (all daughters) of Charles Frederick Cooper, journalist and editor, and his second wife Mabel, daughter of Captain Barnett of the Scots Greys. She was educated first at home by a French governess, then briefly at school in Fulham; at the age of seven she began regular photographic modelling for the studio of Downey's in Ebury Street.

In the autumn of 1905 she was taken by a school friend to an open audition at the Vaudeville Theatre, and somewhat to her own surprise was offered the title role in a tour of Seymour Hicks' *Bluebell in Fairyland*, which opened at Colchester on her seventeenth birthday. Within another year she had joined George Edwardes' company at the Gaiety, signing a contract for £3 (rising to £5) a week to play as cast, primarily small singing and dancing roles in such musicals as *The Girls of Gottenberg* (1907), *Havana* (1908) and *Our Miss Gibbs* (1909).

Gladys was not, however, the kind of Gaiety girl taken to Romano's by wealthy young men about town; her ambition was to be a serious actress, though all thoughts of a career were interrupted when one night she was seen on stage by Herbert John Buckmaster, a 26-year-old Boer War soldier then working for Ladbroke's. Within days he had arranged an introduction to her, and they were married on 12 December 1908, much to the disapproval of her parents who felt that at 19 she was still too young to leave home.

For a year or so after the marriage she continued to work at the Gaiety but then came the birth (in July 1910) of Joan, the first of her two children by Buckmaster, and when she returned to the stage after that it was at last to the straight theatre; she began to get small roles in comedy at the Royalty Theatre and then joined Sir George Alexander for a revival of *The Importance of Being Earnest* at the St James's. Her first real break came in 1912 with a small but showy last-act role in *Milestones* by Arnold Bennett and Edward Knoblock, which ran for eighteen months. During this time Gladys also took on many other roles at other theatres, provided that they finished early enough in the evening to allow her to get back to the Royalty for her entrance in *Milestones*. When that run ended she went into *Diplomacy* at Wyndham's which lasted another year, throughout which she played for the first time with the man who was to become the most constant and beloved of her stage partners, Sir Gerald du Maurier. By now she was earning £40 a week, and the strain was beginning to tell on her marriage to a man still only earning about half that from Ladbroke's; then, however, came the First War. Buck joined the cavalry and went to France with the Royal Horse Guards, while Gladys spent the Christmas of 1914 also at the Front, though with a concert party organised by Seymour Hicks. By now she was carrying her second child John (born June 1915), and the next year was the only one of her adult life that she was to spend without giving a performance on either stage or screen.

It was in the following year, 1916, that she first began to act at the theatre she was later to manage, the Playhouse on the corner of the Embankment and Northumberland Avenue by Charing Cross, a building that was to become her professional home for the next fifteen years. By 1917 she had joined Frank Curzon in its management, thereby becoming the only woman other than Lilian Baylis at the Old Vic to run a London theatre before the Second World War. The plays that she presented, acted in and sometimes unofficially directed there were to include four Somerset Maugham premieres (*Home and Beauty*, *The Letter*, *The Sacred Flame* and *The Painted Veil*) as well as revivals of *My Lady's Dress*, *The Second Mrs Tanqueray* and *Magda*.

Herbert Buckmaster returned from the war in 1918 to find that the chorus girl he had married a decade earlier had now become a professional actress and theatre manager, neither of them attributes he was looking for in a wife. Accordingly and amicably they were divorced in 1921; he was to marry twice more and make an eventual home at Buck's Club, which he had founded in Clifford

Street and where fifty years after their divorce she would still frequently be found at parties given by him to celebrate yet another first night. They were always to be the best of friends.

Gladys spent the 1920s bringing up her two children and running the Playhouse. In 1928 came a second marriage (to Sir Neville Pearson); by him she had her third and last child Sally, but it was to be a short-lived marriage and by the early 1930s there was little to keep her in England. Changing theatrical tastes brought an end to her years of success at the Playhouse; Maugham had ceased to write plays, and despite her discovery of such interesting new works as *Flies in the Sun* and *The Rats of Norway* (which gave Laurence Olivier one of his early stage successes) and a West End success in *The Shining Hour*, Gladys began to feel that she had lost touch with London theatregoers. The bright young things for whom she had worked so hard and successfully in the twenties were no longer thronging the stalls, and she herself had by now fallen in love with the actor Philip Merivale, who was to become her third and last husband and whose already successful career on Broadway encouraged Gladys to try her luck there too.

Hers was always a cut-and-run philosophy, and by the mid-1930s the London where she had once been a definitive Peter Pan, where she had run her own theatre and brought up her elder children, was a place of the past. America was where she would now live, and despite a catastrophic Broadway start in which she played (unsuccessfully) both Desdemona and Lady Macbeth opposite Merivale (whom she married in Chicago in April 1937) it was indeed America that was to become Gladys's home for the second half of her long life.

She returned to London in 1938 for another brief and unsuccessful Shakespeare season (this in the Open Air Theatre, Regent's Park) and a West End run in *Dodsworth*, by now always appearing in partnership with Merivale. They returned to New York for Dodie Smith's *Spring Meeting* on Broadway and then, in the autumn of 1939, came

an offer from Alfred Hitchcock. He was making his first Hollywood film, *Rebecca*, and wanted Gladys for the small role of Maxim de Winter's sister; she went out to California for three weeks and stayed thirty years.

Gladys fell immediately and totally in love with the sun, the sea and the surroundings of California; though she was never there to get the leading roles that an actress of her stage distinction might have expected, she went under contract to MGM and played in a total of thirty films between 1940 and 1967, of which the most distinguished were *Now Voyager* (for which she got the Oscar nomination in 1943), *Separate Tables* (1958) and *My Fair Lady* (1964). Though Philip Merivale died in California in 1946, Gladys was to live on there alone, making a home for herself and those of her many relatives and friends seeking, however temporarily, a place in the Californian sun.

But during the 1950s and 1960s she also began with increasing frequency to return to the London stage, first in Noel Coward's *Relative Values* (1951) and then in such later successes as *The Chalk Garden* (1956) and the revival of Maugham's *The Sacred Flame* (1967). She bought a house on the regatta stretch of the Thames at Henley and, as the old English colony in California began to disappear, spent more and more of her time back home again amid children, grandchildren and great-grandchildren. In 1967 she became Dame Gladys, a year later she celebrated her eightieth birthday and in November 1971, having just played in another revival of *The Chalk Garden*, she died only a month away from the start of her eighty-fourth year.

She left one son (John Buckmaster, himself for some time an actor), two daughters both of whom married actors (Joan married Robert Morley in 1940; Sally married Robert Hardy in 1960), five grandchildren, two great-grandchildren, and the unforgettable memories of one of the most remarkable and resilient actresses of her generation.
See photograph opposite page 294.

KATHARINE CORNELL

Katharine Cornell was born in Berlin, Germany, on 16 February 1893, but was soon in Buffalo, New York, where her father, a doctor, became manager of the Majestic Theater. She attended Oaksmere School in Mamaroneck, New York, and graduated in 1913. Shortly after that she joined an amateur group called the Washington Square Players, and made her stage début as the Samurai mother in *Bushido* at the Comedy Theater in November 1916. She remained with the company for a year before joining the Jessie Bonstelle Stock Company, with which she toured in such plays as *The Gypsy Trial, Daybreak, Broken Threads, Fanny's First Play, Captain Kidd Jr, Lilàc Time* and *Cheating Cheaters* in ingénue roles before getting the lead in *The Man Who Came Back* for a 1919 tour.

Miss Cornell's first and only London appearance was as Jo in *Little Women* in a series of matinées at the New Theatre, opening in November 1919. Back in Michigan with the Jessie Bonstelle troupe she played Diane in *Seventh Heaven*, and then toured in *The Man Outside*. At the Klaw Theater, New York, she opened in March 1921 as Eileen Baxter Jones in *Nice People*. It was in October 1921 that she had a notable success as the daughter Sydney Fairfield in *A Bill of Divorcement* at the George M. Cohan Theater. That autumn she married the director, Guthrie McClintic, and worked almost exclusively with him thereafter. At the National in January 1923 she played Mary Fitton in *Will Shakespeare*, and then at the Ritz in March of that year Laura Pennington in *The Enchanted Cottage*. In September she was Henriette in *Casanova* at the Empire, and the following January, Shirley Pride in *The Way Things Happen* at the Lyceum. In March 1924 she played Lalage Sturdee in *The Outsider* at the 49th Street Theater, and in October was Suzanne Chaumont in *Tiger Cats*.

It was at the 49th Street Theater in December 1924 that she opened in a role that was to be one of her most enduring — the title role in *Candida*. At the Broadhurst in September 1925 she played Iris Fenwick in *The Green Hat*. The *New York Times* reported that her 'performance was a vibrant one, teeming with emotion that was always just suppressed and expressed in voice of strange, haunting timbre'. She followed that with Leslie Crosbie in *The Letter* (Morosco, September 1927); Ellen Olenska in *The Age of Innocence* (Empire, November 1928); and Madeleine Cary in *Dishonoured Lady* (Empire, February 1930).

During her subsequent tour of *Dishonoured Lady* she read *The Barretts of Wimpole Street* and suggested to her husband that they should produce it. At the time she had no intention of playing in it herself, but he convinced her that she should. Under her own management she opened at the Empire in February 1931 as Elizabeth Moulton-Barrett; Brian Aherne played Robert Browning. Brooks Atkinson in the *New York Times* was ecstatic: 'After a long succession of meretricious plays it introduces us to Katharine Cornell as an actress of the first order. Here the disciplined fury that she has been squandering on catch-penny plays becomes the vibrant beauty of finely wrought character . . . By the crescendo of her playing, by the wild sensitivity that lurks behind her ardent gestures and her piercing stares across the footlights she charges the drama with a meaning beyond the facts it records. Her acting is quite as remarkable for the carefulness of its design as for the fire of her presence.' The entire production was an enormous success and it ran on Broadway for a year — then they toured. Miss Cornell was a great believer in touring the remoter parts of America with her productions, as the great stars had a century before. She opened at the Belasco in New York in December 1932 in the title role of *Lucrece* and then played Elsa Brandt at the same theatre in *Alien Corn* in February 1933.

Katharine Cornell then took her company on a long tour of the United States, during which they visited seventy-seven cities, playing *The Barretts of Wimpole Street, Candida* and *Romeo and Juliet*. But this tour was no fit-up. Basil Rathbone played Romeo, Edith Evans was the Nurse, Brian Aherne was Mercutio and Orson Welles was Tybalt. They brought *Romeo and Juliet* to the Martin Beck Theater in New York for the first time on 20 December 1934. John Mason Brown reported: 'It was a nerve-racking night, fated either to bring her disillusioning failure as a player or to crown her with a new significance in our theater. To say she emerged triumphantly both as an actress and a manageress is but to state an agreeable truth. To add that beyond any shadow of doubt she is today the ''First Lady'' of our stage is but to state another and no less agreeable truth.' Brooks Atkinson spoke of a 'high plane of modern magnificence' and proceeded to trip over himself with superlatives: 'Miss Cornell's [Juliet] is a complete re-creation — with the suppleness of an actress and the imperious quality of an artist who plays from within . . . she is a great actress and that is why her Juliet is a deeply moving idealization of fate.'

They went out on tour again, and when they returned to New York in December 1935 Maurice Evans was playing Romeo and Ralph Richardson was Mercutio. All the critics went to have another look and John Mason Brown said in the *New York Post*: '. . . seldom has a production of such drama as *Romeo and Juliet* mellowed and matured so magnificently . . . When first seen here Miss Cornell's Juliet was possessed of the incandescent stuff from which treasured memories are made. It was exceptional for its lusciousness, its glowing embodiment of everything that is tremulous in young love, its eagerness, its grace, and its lyric intensity . . . She has rounded out the portrait by filling in a hundred and one details that were only indicated in a casual way before. She has, for example, heightened the ecstasy of the love she feels, at the same time that she has added a shimmering sense of humour to her playing of the balcony scene . . . Her Juliet is deeper, surer and more commanding than it ever was . . . She is incontestably the foremost American Juliet of her generation, and I for one am inclined to doubt if her equal has ever been seen anywhere in our time.' And if possible, he liked her *Saint Joan* (March 1936) even better. 'Miss Cornell's Joan is neither bumptious nor sanctimonious. She is the mixture of modesty and assurance Mr Shaw describes. Her modesty is her own; her assurance heaven-sent . . . [*Saint Joan*] comes as a triumph for her not only as a manager but also as an actress. It is one of the finest things she has done.'

Miss Cornell's position in the American theatre was now virtually unassailable. She was the First Lady of the stage and the critics were always respectful.

After touring she opened at the Empire in December 1936 as Oparre in *The Wingless Victory*, then played Candida once more, but closed pre-Broadway with *Herod and Marianne*. At the Ethel Barrymore Theater in April 1939 she opened as Linda Easterbrook in *No Time for Comedy*, which was a success and which she then toured. Next, in 1941 she was Jennifer Dubedat in *The Doctor's Dilemma* and in 1942 played the title role in *Rose Burke* at the Curran in San Francisco. At the Shubert in New York in April the same year she mounted an all-star revival of *Candida* for the benefit of the Army Emergency and Navy Relief Society. Brooks Atkinson said: 'Many of us have seen Miss Cornell's Candida before. It is one of her best parts. If she had never played anything else it would be enough to distinguish her as a great actress for it radiates from her as if it were her own nature — luminous,

tender and entrancingly wise.' She next played Masha in *The Three Sisters* at the Ethel Barrymore Theater before touring with it, and in November 1943 played Stella Boswell in *Lovers and Friends*. The next two years were spent being Elizabeth Barrett Browning yet again — both overseas for the troops and then back in New York at the Ethel Barrymore. In February 1946 she opened at the Cort as Antigone, but the critics did not much care for Anouilh's version of the tragedy, so Miss Cornell did *Candida* again. When she did Shakespeare's *Antony and Cleopatra* at the Martin Beck in 1947 the critics found it all rather refined. Brooks Atkinson said: 'There is more good taste than Shakespeare in this stage version . . . Miss Cornell's wickedness is not very sinful.' Nevertheless, she toured it. In 1949 she played Ana de Mendoza, Princess of Eboly, in *That Lady* and in 1950 toured as Smilja Darde in *Captain Carvallo*.

At the National Theater in 1951 Katharine Cornell played Ethel Barrymore's part in *The Constant Wife*. Kenneth Tynan was over from England to see it. He was not impressed, but it was probably because he had spent his youth being told how great Katharine Cornell was and this was his first glimpse of a legend — always a rather daunting experience. He reported: 'One of the Broadway season's least inspiring achievements has been a lame and static revival of Maugham's *The Constant Wife*, which represents Miss Cornell's coming-of-age as an actress–manager. Miss Cornell, once the first and now almost the last lady of American theatre, makes her every entrance with the martyred look of a woman who has just swept out the attics, put two dozen children to bed, finished the washing-up and painted the scenery as well. Her stock-in-trade mingles quizzical charm with gutsy bossiness, her forehead sags wearily over her eyes and at high moments her simulation of courage and wisdom in extremity gives her a strong resemblance to an industrious nurse in the Orkneys. Her method with Mr Maugham's flimsy witticisms is to bellow them with an expression of incipient nausea; to paraphrase Wilde, she bears distinct traces of what must once have been a quite intolerable condescension.' Miss Cornell toured most successfully with the play for a year. At the Broadhurst in 1953 she appeared as Mary Prescott in *The Prescott Proposals*, and at the ANTA Playhouse in 1955 played the Countess Rosmarin Ostenburg in *The Dark is Light Enough*. In 1958 she played New York and Tel Aviv as Anath Bithiah in *The Firstborn* and in March 1960 played Mrs Patrick Campbell in *Dear Liar* at the Billy Rose Theater and on tour.

Her husband Guthrie McClintic died in

October 1961, and Miss Cornell retired from the stage. Over the years, such was her distinction that she collected honorary academic degrees the way some actresses collect stage awards: nine in all, including Princeton and Smith. She was without doubt a serious actress — her whole life was devoted to the stage — but she was also a no-nonsense actress of the old school. As to the art of acting, she said: 'Every character is both near and far from an actor's personality. The player must understand the person, have a cerebral as well as an emotional sympathy with the role, to act it. Then he has to present it through his own qualities of mind and physique . . . If the actor does live the role at all, it is only in the sense of concentrating on it and it alone, from the moment he reads a script until the last night of the play's run . . . ' Katharine Cornell died in Vineyard Haven, Massachusetts, on 8 June 1974.

See photograph opposite page 71.

TOM COURTENAY

*T*om Courtenay was born in Hull on 25 February 1937, and had he followed in the family footsteps he would be there still, chipping paint off fishing trawlers. He worked with determination at Kingston High School and at 17 came south to University College, London, where he read English literature. He could not really see any point to all the Beowulf and Anglo-Saxon, but although it was the first time in his life he was really unhappy, later he was able to laugh, 'I'm a BA (London, failed).'

It was at college that he began acting for various groups, and then auditioned for the Royal Academy of Dramatic Art. 'So there I was,' he said, '20, with a RADA scholarship, a good loud voice, reasonable health and that was about it. In the theatre it was the time of the angry young men, but my generation was still being trained for drawing-room comedies. Yet I suppose I was lucky in some ways. John Fernald, who ran the school, always seemed to like my work and made me a sort of star pupil. Still I hated the idea of learning technique for its own sake. You have to start with the character and then work outwards. It just isn't possible to do it the other way round, whatever the experts think.'

His first appearance on the professional stage was at the Lyceum Theatre, Edinburgh, in August 1960, where with the Old Vic Company he was Konstantin Treplyef in *The Seagull*. They brought the production to the Old Vic Theatre in London in September that year. Generally the critics praised it, except for Caryl Brahms in *Plays and Players* who thought he was miscast: 'I have reason to know that Mr Tom Courtenay, the Konstantin of this production, is an actor whose instinct guides him towards imagined truth, but Mr Courtenay has a contemporary mind and a contemporary appearance; also a most contem-porary way of speaking. And while I am prepared to accept Mr Courtenay's instinctive truth about his Konstantin, I cannot quite reconcile my Konstantin with his voice and his appearance. There is nothing wrong about Mr Courtenay except his whole personality. In looks the very young actor is loose-slung in the modern manner. He could be a Hamlet, ought to be a Hamlet — but it must be a Hamlet in modern dress (which caper I abominate); the passionately divided princeling of a small provincial court. He is lean, light, with a face that would do for the skull of Yorick. He can be quiet — dangerously quiet. He has the instinctive timing of a very good actor indeed. But above all he is of this year and day and hour and metropolis; and he is purposeful. But Chekhov's Konstantin is of a very quiet lake-side of 1896. His tragedy is that like the seagull, he is not purposeful. Or if he is obsessed, his obsession does not drive him on. Between the two Konstantins lies the gulf of Mr Courtenay's personality. And yet, and in many ways, he is the truest Konstantin that I have ever seen.' Courtenay remained with the Old Vic Company, and in February 1961 played Poins in *Henry IV Part I*, following that in April with Feste in *Twelfth Night*.

In June 1961 Tom Courtenay moved to the West End, to the Cambridge Theatre, where he took over from Albert Finney in *Billy Liar* and soon made the part his own. That same year he made his first film, *The Loneliness of the Long-Distance Runner*. 'After the success of that and *Billy Liar* people wanted me to go on playing that sort of part forever, but I couldn't see how I could advance at all, so I turned down a whole lot of parts in which other actors then made their names,' he said. Instead he joined the National Theatre Company in January 1964 to play Andrei in *Andorra* by Max Frisch, the first foreign play to be presented by the National. Martin Esslin found that: 'Tom Courtenay plays the hero, the boy who is made into a Jew by being treated like a Jew, with subtlety and delicate understanding.' He played the part of Billy Liar in the film, and in 1966 joined the Chichester Festival Theatre playing Trofimov in *The Cherry Orchard* in July and Malcolm in *Macbeth* in August. He continued filming, making such movies as *Doctor Zhivago* and *King Rat*, but he found that though films were more rewarding financially he preferred to work in the theatre and joined Manchester's 69 Company, where he spent two years. There he had a chance to try things, take chances, advance. 'Plays used to come in between films for me,' he has said. 'Now it's the other way round. Manchester has given me confidence in myself.'

He returned to London, to the Garrick Theatre, in May 1969 with a Manchester production of *She Stoops to Conquer*. Michael Billington reported: '...London audiences can now see for themselves how Tom Courtenay has for some time been quietly nurturing his talent in the north and astutely widening his range...One feared that his early success in playing working-class characters would lead to restrictive type-casting and prevent him ever getting a crack at the wide range of classical roles open to him. Thanks to Manchester's Century Theatre and the 69 Company this has not proved so: Courtenay has followed his Romeo and Hamlet with a young Marlow that conclusively gives the lie to the still-current notion that the new generation of actors cannot play stylish period comedy. Without any strain or affectation, Courtenay convinces us that his is a man of noble breeding.'

He returned to Manchester and played the title role in *Peer Gynt*, and Lord Fancourt Babberley in *Charley's Aunt*, which transferred to the Apollo in December 1971. Then, also in the West End, at the Comedy he played Leonard in Alan Ayckbourn's *Time and Time Again*. John Russell Taylor said that he played the part 'with a resourceful variety of slow burns, absent-minded tics, and is sometimes very funny indeed'. Cheryl Kennedy was his co-star, and they were soon married. In May 1973 Tom Courtenay returned to Manchester to play Captain Bluntschli in *Arms and the Man* and was back in the West End (Globe, August 1974) by way of Greenwich (May 1974) playing in another Alan

Ayckbourn — *The Norman Conquests*, a trilogy. *Plays and Players* reported: 'All six characters are acted with skill and intelligence, ensemble playing which in itself is heartening. Tom Courtenay plays the ingratiating Norman with undeniable charm and vanity.' He played in the trilogy for more than a year. 'I couldn't do any one of these plays every night,' he said, 'not for this length of time, but doing all three is fun — and I enjoy getting the chance to be a clown. There is room to change bits, pieces of business, which we do constantly. And they keep getting better. At least my performance does; I'm never at my best on the first night.'

Tom Courtenay's next role could not have been more different. John Lahr describes *The Fool* by Edward Bond, which opened at the Royal Court in November 1975 and in which Courtenay played John Clare: 'Luring his audience into the robust and violent rural world of John Clare, the farm labourer turned poet, at the beginning of England's industrialization in 1815, Bond creates a pageant of exploitation which demonstrates how imagination as well as manpower were victimized by the ruthless pursuit of profit.' He found the play serious, fascinating and 'scrupulously well acted'. In September 1976 Courtenay went back to Manchester to appear in the opening productions of the new Royal Exchange Theatre. In a massive undertaking Courtenay played first Faulkland in *The Rivals* and the following evening the title part in *The Prince of Homburg*. David Mayer reported: 'Tom Courtenay's Faulkland (an inspired piece of casting) is a vastly comic exploration of obsessive grievance-hoarding and masochistic probing for a bitter truth. Courtenay, at moments fretful and exceptitious, gratefully accepts unexpected favourable opinions or kind remarks, then suddenly pauses in mid-thanks...he has become Fate's passive victim.' *The Prince of Homburg* — a massive and difficult play — Mayer found less satisfactory but nevertheless thought that Courtenay acted with 'depth and intelligence'.

Tom Courtenay also made the film of Solzhenitsyn's *A Day in the Life of Ivan Denisovitch*. 'I'm more proud of it,' he said, 'than anything I've ever done. I may not be a lot richer as a result, but I'm pretty sure I'm a better actor.' Most recently he has been seen in the stage and screen versions of Ronald Harwood's *The Dresser* and in a 1984 Manchester revival of Tom Stoppard's *Jumpers*.

CICELY COURTNEIDGE
AND
JACK HULBERT

Although she was the one who received the honours (a CBE and a DBE) Cicely Courtneidge and Jack Hulbert, from their first onstage meeting in her father's production of *The Pearl Girl* until his death in 1978, were mutually interdependent, on stage and off. He was placid, educated, sophisticated but shy, and she was the intuitive, quick-tempered extrovert. They were dearly loved by millions as Cis and Jack.

Esmeralda Cicely Courtneidge was born into a theatrical family on 1 April 1893. Her father was touring (in a show called *Esmeralda*) so she was born in Sydney, Australia, but was brought back to England within the year. Robert Courtneidge, a noted impresario, was also a firm disciplinarian and her training began early. She was a sickly child, and her father decided that the way to health was through hard physical exercise, so every morning began with enforced calisthenics. After school there were dancing, elocution and singing lessons. She was then sent to Switzerland for two years.

At 15 Cicely returned home ready to start her stage career. All those years of lessons had surely readied her; besides she was not totally inexperienced, having made her début at the age of eight playing one of the fairies in her father's production of *A Midsummer Night's Dream* at the Princess Theatre, Manchester. She had also appeared in her father's musical adaptation of Fielding's *Tom Jones* at the Apollo Theatre in London in 1907. But she had to throw herself into an extremely disciplined regime, studying voice, dance and piano before her father gave her a part in his very successful production of *The Arcadians*. She played Chrysea at the Shaftesbury Theatre in July 1909 and stopped the show with her song, 'I Like London. I Like Town'. In 1910 she took the lead when Phyllis Dare had a holiday. In her autobiography Cicely explains that she wasn't greeted with rapture. 'Some of the critics were kind enough to talk about my freshness and vitality. But others had a different story to tell: "This raw, inexperienced child...This unpolished schoolgirl...she had been given the part because of her father's position."' She did, however, continue to work in her father's productions, playing Miyo Ko San in *The Mousmé* (September 1911), Princess Clementine in *Princess Caprice* (May 1912) and Lady Betty Biddulph in *The Pearl Girl* (September 1913). In that show she met Jack Hulbert.

Jack Hulbert was born on 24 April 1892, the son of a doctor. He was educated at Westminster and Cambridge where he read history and psychology and got his BA. But from his first experience as a member of a pantomime audience at the age of five his abiding passion was the theatre.

While at university he appeared in revues and concerts, wrote sketches and played *Jack Straw* (New Theatre, Cambridge, December 1911), Gerald Thornton in *Aching to Act* (February 1913), and Algy Vere in *Cheer Oh!* Cambridge (June 1913). This Cambridge Footlights production then played for one night in London, and Robert Courtneidge, immediately sensing Hulbert's potential, signed him for *The Pearl Girl* to play Robert Jaffrey. At first Cicely was not impressed by him, but she succumbed because he 'had shown such marked enthusiasm in rehearsals of the love scenes'.

On 4 June 1914 they opened at the Shaftesbury in *The Cinema Star*. He played Billy and she played Phyllis. Jack was also partly responsible for the book, an adaptation of a German play with music. It was a disastrous flop in London. Robert Courtneidge lost a lot of money, which was not recouped despite the fact that the company embarked on a highly successful tour of the provinces. In May 1915 at the Shaftesbury they revived *The Arcadians* and at the Pavilion, Glasgow, in July they opened in *A Lucky Escape*. Cicely played Mabel and Jack played Leslie Carter. They then toured again in *The Pearl Girl*, and in September 1915 opened at the Prince of Wales, Birmingham, playing Arthur Hobbs and Cynthia Petrie in *The Light Blues*, which then toured. It was during the tour that her father finally consented to their marriage, which took place at St Paul's Church in St John's Wood. That night they were back on stage in Hull. *The Light Blues* opened at the Shaftesbury in September 1916 and closed within three weeks.

Robert Courtneidge was now so deeply in debt that he had to close the Shaftesbury. Jack Hulbert immediately went into an André Charlot revue called *See-Saw* at the Comedy, and Cicely made a brief appearance in Edinburgh in December 1916 playing Margaret Potts in *Oh Caesar!* It was her last appearance for nearly two years. Jack appeared in May 1917 in another Charlot revue, *Bubbly*, before joining the army.

Desperate for work, Cicely Courtneidge, who up to this time had seen her future as a glamorous

The popular musical comedy team Cicely Courtneidge and Jack Hulbert
in *Full Swing* at the Palace Theatre
(London, May 1942)

Appearing at the Phoenix Theatre in the first production of one
of Coward's greatest successes, the comedy *Private Lives*, are
(from left) Laurence Olivier, (Adrianne Allen,) Noel Coward and
Gertrude Lawrence (London, September 1930)

musical-comedy star, borrowed £100, organized a music hall bill and got a booking at a minor hall in Colchester. She performed a song and dance with a parasol, a sad scene in an army hospital and then finally a male impersonation 'The Knut in the RAF'. The audience response told her that her future was as a comedienne. She began a successful tour of the music halls, specializing in male impersonation. For Christmas 1918 she appeared as Cinderella at the Theatre Royal, Manchester, with Little Tich, and then went back to touring. Her brother-in-law Claude Hulbert toured with her.

When the war was over Jack Hulbert appeared at the opening of the Palais in Paris in April 1919 in the revue *Hullo, Paris,* and returning to England in August was at the Prince of Wales in *Bran-Pie.* As Lord Richard Sandridge he appeared in *Lord Richard in the Pantry* at the Criterion in July 1920, and in December of that year he played Captain Constantine Posch in *A Little Dutch Girl* at the Lyric. During this time Cicely was very successfully touring the variety circuit, and hating the fact that their work kept them apart. Finally, in September 1921 they were booked to appear together in London at the Royalty Theatre in a new revue, *Ring Up.* The critics didn't care for it and it closed, but Jack rewrote it and reproduced it at the Vaudeville, where it ran for three months. Then Cicely went back on the road and Jack continued at the Vaudeville in revue.

It was in 1923 that their stage partnership really took off; it was to continue with phenomenal success for half a century. They appeared together in *Little Revue Starts at Nine O'Clock* (Little Theatre, October 1923) and *By The Way* (Apollo, January 1925), which they took to New York's Gaiety Theater in December 1925. Back in England after a successful New York season where the audiences had loved Cicely dressed as a man, the Hulberts revived the revue at the Gaiety in London, and then in December opened *Lido Lady.* After a tour they opened *Clowns in Clover* at the Adelphi in December 1927 and remained there for two years. Jack had written and produced these revues as well as starring with Cicely in them. They had all been enormously successful and they should have been a very rich couple; however, their business manager was less than astute and they were severely in debt. After touring *The House That Jack Built* and appearing in it at the Adelphi in November 1929, Cicely went back to the music halls while Jack played Bobby Hilary in *Follow a Star* at the Winter Garden in September 1930. They were together at the Piccadilly in January 1931 in *Folly to be Wise.*

The Hulberts spent the next seven years, he exclusively and she mainly, making films — they

were in debt, and that's where the money was to be had. During this time Cicely appeared at the Victoria Palace in February 1934 in *Military Scene,* and reappeared on the regular stage in October 1937 as Sally and Mabel in *Hide and Seek.* Their debts had been discharged. Then, in November 1938, Jack wrote and directed *Under Your Hat,* in which he also starred as Jack Millet, with Cicely as Kay Porter. Jack found it difficult but satisfying doing everything. 'I would have three worries,' he said. 'The first was the show — and you couldn't have a bigger headache than a musical. The next was her [Cicely] — getting her right. And number three is getting Hulbert right — he's playing in it too! I had to sit back in the stalls watching this particular person — in my imagination — acting in the play — but the great advantage was, there wasn't a soul in the world who could interfere. I was in complete command.' *Under Your Hat* was interrupted briefly by the beginning of the war but otherwise it ran until 1940. Jack joined the police force; he spent his days with the force and was on stage every night. (And he kept it up for seventeen years, rising through the ranks until he was eventually in charge of the women's forces at Scotland Yard.)

In 1941, dodging the bombs, they toured in the *Hulbert Follies,* and in April 1942 were back at the Palace in London in *Full Swing.* They followed that the next year with *Something in the Air.* Cicely founded an Ack-Ack Comforts Fund and toured the Mediterranean with ENSA.

After the war Jack produced Cicely in her first solo-starring vehicle, a topical satire on the black market called *Under the Counter.* She played Jo Fox, and opened at the Phoenix in November 1945 with Wilfrid Hyde-White. The British loved it and filled the theatre for nearly two years. Meanwhile, Jack appeared at the Saville in 1946 playing in *Here Come the Boys.*

They took *Under the Counter* to the Shubert Theater in New York in October 1947, hoping to repeat their success, but the Americans were baffled, calling it old-fashioned, dull, silly and anaemic. Nevertheless, Cicely toured Australia with it for a year while Jack went back to England.

Back in London, at the Hippodrome in June 1949 Cicely played Lady Frances Maxwell in *Her Excellency,* which Jack produced. He also produced the last musical composed and written by Ivor Novello, *Gay's the Word,* in which Cicely starred as Gay Daventry, at the Saville in 1951. In that same year she received the CBE, and Jack appeared as James Winter in *The White Sheep of the Family* at the Piccadilly. In 1952 Cicely Courtneidge went back to revue with *Over the Moon* at the Piccadilly, directed by her husband.

They appeared together in Scotland in *The Joy of Living* (1955) and *Star Maker* (1956). At the Cambridge Theatre in July 1956 Jack took over the part of Jimmy Broadbent in *The Reluctant Debutante*, and toured with it in 1957. Meanwhile Cicely was playing Isabel Kilpatrick in *Bachelor Born* (Lyceum, Edinburgh, November 1956, retitled *The Bride and the Bachelor*, at the Duchess, London, December 1956.) Jack played Reginald Fitzgibbon in *The Big Tickle* (Duke of York's, May 1958) and Lucas Edgerton in *Reclining Figure* (New Shakespeare, Liverpool, July 1958). After a tour Cicely opened at the Apollo in April 1959 as Jane Hayling in *Fool's Paradise*.

At last, in November 1960, they were together again in a farce by Ronald Millar called *The Bride Comes Back* at the Vaudeville. It was their first partnership in a non-musical play, and *Plays and Players* reported: 'Jack Hulbert, calm and suave, "throws away" some good comedy lines most effectively and uses to the full his fine ability to hold one's attention while doing very little. Cicely Courtneidge keeps up a tremendous pace and is brilliantly funny, especially in the use of a number of devices which would probably be beyond most actresses half her age. I shall not soon forget the brilliant technique with which she "stumbles" down the staircase on high stiletto heels on the morning after the night before.'

For Christmas 1961 they were in *Mother Goose* at Wimbledon, and then in September 1963 he directed both of them in a tour of *There's a Yank Close Behind Me*, which was retitled *Let's Be Frank* when it opened at the Vaudeville in November. In March 1964 Cicely played the Fairy Queen in *Fielding's Music Hall* at the Prince Charles Theatre, and that November was Madame Arcati at the Savoy in *High Spirits*, the musical version of Noel Coward's *Blithe Spirit*. She toured in 1965 in William Douglas-Home's comedy *The Reluctant Peer*, and at the Haymarket in December 1967 played Marie Tempest's part in a

revival of *Dear Octopus*. Jack had spent 1966 touring as the general in *The Amorous Prawn* but was at the Haymarket to play her husband of fifty years, Charles Randolph. John Russell Taylor said of their contribution to *Dear Octopus*: '. . . Jack Hulbert and Cicely Courtneidge play with the sort of splendid confidence that only a lifetime of being applauded at every entrance can give. Next to me were sitting a couple of not possibly more than 20, who had clearly never seen these grand old monuments of the British theatre before. By the first interval they were incoherent with delight: "The mother," said the young man, "you know. Cicely what's-her-name — she's got such fantastic, such extraordinary . . . vitality!" It is the *mot*, as you might say, *juste* — especially on the lips of someone totally unaware that it was as *juste* twenty years before he was born.'

Cicely and Jack were both at the Duke of York's in November 1968 playing in *Dear Charles*; in 1970 they toured South Africa and the United Kingdom in *Oh Clarence*. At the Vaudeville in March 1971 Cicely was Olive Smythe in *Move Over Mrs Markham*, which ran for eighteen months, while Jack toured first in *Not in Front of the Parents* (1971) and then in *Not Now Darling*. He was at Sadler's Wells in March 1972 playing the Dean of Paddington in *Lord Arthur Savile's Crime*. It was in 1972 that Cicely became a Dame. Then they were back together again on the road, in *The Hollow* (June 1973), *Breath of Spring* (July 1974), *Don't Utter a Note* (September 1974) and finally, in 1976, the autobiographical *Once More with Music*.

Jack Hulbert died in March 1978 and Cicely never recovered from it. Her daughter said, 'They were so close and had been inseparable for so many years that after he had gone she just went steadily down.' On what would have been Jack's eighty-eighth birthday Cicely Courtneidge fell into a coma and never regained consciousness. She died on 26 April 1980.

See photograph opposite page 86.

NOEL COWARD

When Noel Coward, playboy of the West End world, jack of all its entertainment trades and master of most, died in 1973 he was as old as the century and its most constant if often controversial show business reflection. He left behind him over fifty

plays, twenty-five films, hundreds of songs, a ballet, two autobiographies, a novel, several volumes of short stories and countless poems, sketches, recordings and paintings, as well as a volume of post-war diaries and the memories of three generations of playgoers on both sides of the

Atlantic for whom he had been the most ineffably elegant and ubiquitous of entertainers.

He was born in Teddington, Middlesex, on 16 December 1899, just before the last Christmas of the nineteenth century (hence the name Noel); the second son of an unsuccessful piano tuner—salesman and a doting, ambitious mother, he grew up in suburban middle-class South London in conditions which were, he later noted, 'inclined to degenerate into genteel poverty unless carefully watched'. When Noel was 10, his mother answered a call for child actors in the *Daily Mirror* and within three months Noel was on stage at the Crystal Palace in a play by Lila Field called *The Goldfish*. A few months later he was Slightly in *Peter Pan* (Kenneth Tynan was to comment years later that he'd been Wholly in it ever afterwards) and he then settled, like his beloved friend and partner Gertrude Lawrence, into the life of a fairly successful touring child actor; in his own view he was 'when washed and smarmed down a bit passably attractive, but one of the worst boy actors ever inflicted on the paying public'.

He and Gertie first worked together in *Hannele* at Liverpool and Manchester in the spring of 1913; they then went their separate ways for a while and Noel did return engagements in *Peter Pan* and *Where The Rainbow Ends* for the Christmases of the First World War: by 1917 he was already making his first film, *Hearts of the World*, for D. W. Griffith. It starred Lillian and Dorothy Gish but left little impression on Noel beyond 'making up my face bright yellow for the cameras and pushing a wheelbarrow down a street in Worcestershire for which I was paid, I think, a pound a day'.

There followed a brief and undistinguished period of national service in the Artists' Rifles, and as the First World War came to its end Noel was back in the theatre making West End appearances as a juvenile lead in minor comedies and musicals such as *The Saving Grace* and *Scandal*. One of his early heroes, the actor—manager Sir Charles Hawtrey, had already turned him into a light comedian of precision, but Coward's interests and ambitions lay much wider than that. By 1920 he was already writing songs, sketches and some early plays, one of which, *I'll Leave It to You*, made it to the West End from Manchester in that year, though its stay at the New Theatre was not long. Nevertheless it allowed press reports of the 'boy genius' variety since there were precious few other actor—dramatists with their own plays in the West End before twenty-first birthdays. The *Daily Dispatch* wrote in June 1920: 'There is something freakish and Puck-like about the narrow slant of his grey-green eyes, the tilt of his eyebrows, the sleek backward rush of his hair. He is lithe as a fawn: and if you told him, with perfect truth, that he was one of the three best dancers in London his grieved surprise at hearing of the other two would only be equalled by his incredulity.'

Already fascinated by the speed and pace of the American theatre, Coward made one early and unsuccessful sales trip to Broadway soon after the closing of *I'll Leave It to You* with a batch of other playscripts in his suitcase; undeterred by failure he made a number of lasting New York friends including the young Lynn Fontanne and Alfred Lunt, then also struggling for Broadway acclaim. When they had all achieved it, Noel vowed that he would write them a three-handed comedy; just over a decade later that became *Design For Living*.

In the meantime Noel returned to the West End, appeared in another early light comedy of his own (*The Young Idea*, shamelessly pirated from Bernard Shaw's *You Never Can Tell* but with Shaw's avuncular blessing: 'Get away from me and my work, young man, and you will do very well') and by 1923 was also writing songs and sketches for an early Charlot revue, *London Calling*. Coward also appeared here as an actor—singer—dancer, renewing his partnership with Gertrude Lawrence to choreography by the young Fred Astaire, and during its run he also wrote another comedy, *Fallen Angels* (produced 1925), and the drama that was to make his name once and for all. *The Vortex*, which had a quite literally overnight success at the Everyman Theatre in Hampstead in November 1924, was a play about drug addiction (and indirectly also about homosexuality) written and produced at a time when even alcoholism was seldom mentioned on the London stage. The roughly equal amounts of interest, indignation, admiration and money generated by the play which Noel had written, directed and starred in took him at the age of 24 from being a mildly entertaining actor, playwright and composer to being the hottest theatrical property in town — a change that happened so fast and so unexpectedly that it took even him several months and one nervous breakdown to come to terms with it.

Within a year *The Vortex* (described by at least one critic as 'this dustbin of a play', a term used exactly forty years later to describe the only other play to have taken London by similar storm in this century, Osborne's *Look Back in Anger*) had been joined in the West End by two Coward comedies (*Fallen Angels* and *Hay Fever*) and another revue (*On with the Dance*), a quadruple feat achieved before Noel in this century only by Somerset Maugham and after him only by Alan Ayckbourn, neither of whom was also an actor and composer.

Then however the British seemed keen to destroy the reputation that had been so suddenly and multifariously made: in 1927 two Coward plays were in rapid succession booed off the London stage (*Sirocco* and *Home Chat*) and he was actually spat at in the street outside a stage door by irate theatregoers. Only momentarily deterred, Coward started in 1928 on a period of theatrical activity remarkable even by his standards for its variety and success. Within a period of thirty months he wrote and staged three of his greatest successes — the operetta *Bitter Sweet*, the comedy *Private Lives*, and the epic *Cavalcade* — so that by 1931 the boy wonder of the 1920s had settled into an altogether more stable pattern of theatrical triumph, one which was to be characterized in this decade by the continuing partnership with Gertrude Lawrence. Having promised her *Bitter Sweet* and then realized that her voice was not equal to its Vienna-woods score, he instead wrote her the comedy of appalling manners that was *Private Lives*, redolent of Riviera balconies, filled with the potency of cheap music and shot through with the sadness of a couple who could live neither apart nor together, a couple who were in many incidental ways Noel and Gertie themselves.

Six years later Noel and Gertie played together in alternating triple bills of the nine short plays (among them *Red Peppers*, *Shadow Play* and the *Still Life* that became on screen *Brief Encounter*) which made up *Tonight at 8.30* in the West End and on Broadway. Between those two towering landmarks of their relationship, Noel also found time in the mid-1930s to write *Design for Living* for Lynn and Alfred Lunt, *Words and Music* for the producer Charles B. Cochran, and two operettas — *Conversation Piece* for Yvonne Printemps and *Operette* for Fritzi Massary. 'Throughout the thirties,' wrote Noel later, 'I was a highly publicized and irritatingly successful figure, much in demand; the critical laurels that had been so confidently predicted for me in the twenties never graced my brow, and I was forced to content myself with the bitter palliative of box-office success. Which I enjoyed very much indeed.'

But if theatrically the 1930s were Noel's best years, politically he cared for them less and less: having always been bleakly uninterested in politics of any kind (despite the defiant anti-war nature of *Cavalcade* and his unproduced *Post Mortem*) he suddenly found himself on the brink of his own forties increasingly horrified by Chamberlain at Munich and a world that seemed to be rapidly falling apart at the seams. When war came in 1939 Noel was, typically, in rehearsal with not just one but two new plays: the suburban domestic cavalcade he called *This Happy Breed* and the part-

autobiographical comedy *Present Laughter* about an actor whose career is receding even faster than his hair.

He abandoned both plays in mid-rehearsal and went to serve his country first in pre-Occupation Paris as a propaganda officer and then on countless wartime concert tours of the Middle East, Africa and Australia after Churchill had told him that he would be most useful when singing to the troops, leaving Noel to reflect uneasily that if the morale of the British army was at such a low ebb that soldiers could be cheered into battle by his singing of 'Mad Dogs and Englishmen', then the country was in even more trouble than he had realized.

Ironically, however, his most useful contributions to the war effort were achieved on brief home leaves with such songs as 'London Pride', classic films like *In Which We Serve* and *Brief Encounter*, and his own last great comedy, *Blithe Spirit* which (written on a week's holiday in Wales) ran in London virtually throughout the war, gently teaching even troops on leave how laughable death might be.

But then, with the ending of the war, came a considerable slump in Coward's fortunes: his own uncertainty about how to adjust to a world that was suddenly very different showed in the vast range of work he took on in the late 1940s — old-fashioned revues like *Sigh No More*, message plays like *Peace in Our Time*, operettas like *Pacific 1860* and Broadway-type musicals like *Ace of Clubs*, with none of which he or his audience seemed very happy. Early in the 1950s, however, a couple of sturdy light comedies (*Relative Values* and *Quadrille*) restored him to box-office though not critical favour, and then came the last great phase of his career, one which began almost casually when he started singing his own songs in a tent at a theatrical garden party to raise money for charity from passers-by.

From there it was but a short step to cabaret at the Café de Paris and then a rather greater step to a sell-out season at Las Vegas in 1955. Suddenly, in solo cabaret in America, he was restored to the kind of immense personal triumph he had last enjoyed back in the early 1930s, though in England he was vilified for a decision to live abroad in an effort to save a little money for his old age from the hands of the taxman.

America therefore now became the focus for much of his work: he played his own modern-art satire *Nude with Violin* on Broadway and did some early television work including productions of *Blithe Spirit* and *This Happy Breed* as well as a classic ninety-minute live concert with Mary Martin. He also began playing small but highly paid roles in a sequence of a dozen films of the

1950s and 1960s.

Back home in London he wrote a ballet for Helpmann's Festival company, adapted an Oscar Wilde comedy (*After the Ball*) and a Feydeau farce (*Look After Lulu*) and wrote one late, Chekhovian and vastly underrated play about an old actors' retirement home called *Waiting in the Wings*. When that still failed to find critical favour he returned to Broadway for three last musicals (*Sail Away*, *The Girl Who Came to Supper* and an adaptation of his *Blithe Spirit* by Martin and Gray called *High Spirits*) and then at last returned to popularity in his own country with a revival of *Hay Fever* which he himself directed for the National Theatre in 1964: it was that company's first-ever revival of a play by a living British author.

Then came more films, one farewell stage appearance in London in a sequence of three plays all set in the same Swiss hotel (*Suite in Three Keys*) and at the very close of 1969, with his seventieth birthday celebrations, the news that he had at last been awarded by a Labour government the knighthood he had so long deserved. Sir Noel Coward died three tranquil years later at his Jamaican home: he was 73, and recognized at last as the master entertainer of the British theatre in this century.

See photograph opposite page 87.

JANE COWL

'She is everything a famous theatrical star is expected to be: beautiful, effective, gracious, large-hearted, shrewd in everything but business, foolishly generous, infinitely kind to lesser people of the theatre, extremely annoying on many small points and, over and above everything else, a fine actress.' That was the impression Jane Cowl made on Noel Coward. This grand actress of the American stage often struck terror into the hearts of playwrights, directors and fellow actors. Alexander Woollcott reported that a young actor, whom she hoped to persuade to join a touring company she was organizing, was once called into her presence. She explained to him that there would be no stars: 'One night I may star,' she told him, 'but the next I'll be carrying a tray.' He was impressed until, upon relating the conversation to his wife, she told him that the only tray Jane Cowl would be carrying would have the head of John the Baptist on it.

Jane Cowl was born in Boston, Massachusetts, on 14 December 1884. She was educated privately in Brooklyn and then at Columbia University. She began playing small roles in David Belasco's company in 1903 and made her début as a featured player at the Hudson Theater, New York, playing Fanny Perry in *Is Matrimony a Failure?* in August 1909. The following September, at the Maxine Elliott Theater, she was Beatrice in *The Upstart* and the next month Catherine Darwin in *The Gamblers*. She appeared again on Broadway in September 1912 as Mary Turner in *Within the Law*. She married Adolph Klauber, the drama critic of the *New York Times*, and he gave up writing to become a theatrical producer. In August 1915 she played at the Republic as Ellen Neal in *Common Clay*.

Jane Cowl opened in Morristown, New Jersey, in January 1917 as Jeannine in *Lilac Time*, which she co-authored with Jane Murfin. She continued in this role, both in New York and on tour, until 1918. In October 1918 she opened at the Selwyn Theater playing Lady Betty Desmond in *Information Please* (another of her own plays) and the next month was Peggy Lawrence in *The Crowded Hour*. At the Broadhurst in December 1919 she played both Kathleen Dungannon and Moonyeen Clare in *Smilin' Through*, another play which she co-authored and in which she played in 1922. In October 1922 she played the title role in *Malvaloca* at the 48th Street Theater.

It was at the Henry Miller Theater in January 1923 that she had a great success playing Juliet in *Romeo and Juliet*. John Corbin reported in the *New York Times*: 'Of Juliet it is difficult to write with moderation. One reasons that it cannot be as good as it seems, but casts about rather helplessly to find flaws that are intrinsic. Miss Cowl's speech, though quite free from old mannerisms, is ''modern'' and at times colloquial — but so is the speech of Shakespeare, even in moments of torrential lyric beauty and of tragic suffering . . . The one thing essential to the part was always there and was denoted by means so simple and true that they defied analysis. There was youth to begin with, touched with the beauty and mystery of great love. The balcony scene was as familiar as a caress, utterly ingenuous and impassioned, yet it positively sang with lyric exaltation. The potion scene ran the full gamut of womanly trepidation, grisly fear and heroic resolution. Never, in modern memory, has it been rendered with such virtuosity and at the same time with such simple conviction. The ultimate scene in the tomb was perhaps the finest of all in its conception, as it was the most moving. For here Miss Cowl rose to that rare height where gesture is impotent and speech more effective when subdued. It was a moment of absolute tragedy.' She performed it 157 times successively. She continued for a while playing the classic roles: Mélisande in *Pelléas and Mélisande* (Times Square, December 1923), and Cleopatra in *Antony and Cleopatra* (Lyceum, February 1924). In June 1924 she went to Boston to the Selwyn Theater where she played Anna in *The Depths* and then brought it to New York to the Broadhurst in January 1925.

In December of 1925 she and Noel Coward came up against each other at the Empire when she played Larita in his play *Easy Virtue*. Although he had trouble with the censors in England, difficulties were overcome and Jane Cowl made her first and only trip to the West End playing Larita in London at the Duke of York's Theatre in June 1926 for five months.

Back in New York, at the Playhouse in January 1927 she played Amytis, the wife of a Roman senator, in Sherwood's *The Road to Rome*. She played in this through 1928. At the Majestic she again played two parts in one of her own plays — Judy and Columbine in *The Jealous Moon* — and then toured in it. At the Forrest Theater back in New York on April 1929 she played Francesca in *Paola and Francesca*.

Jane Cowl had an enormous capacity for work and never seemed to stop. She played Jenny Valentine in *Jenny* (Booth, October 1929), Viola in *Twelfth Night* (Maxine Elliott, October 1930), Celia Bottle in *Art and Mrs Bottle* (Maxine Elliott, November 1930), Marguerite Gauthier in *Camille* (Curran, San Francisco, September 1931), Sheila Pennington in *A Thousand Summers* (Selwyn, New York, May 1932). In September 1932 she toured as the Lady in *A Man with a Load of Mischief* and then went on with *Camille* (Tremont, Boston, August 1933), Janet Dodge in *Sweet Bells Jangled* (Forrest, Philadelphia, March 1934), Mariella Linden in *The Shining Hour*

(Curran, July 1934). In December she was in New York playing for the Theater Guild (at the Golden Theater) Lady Violet Wyngate in *Rain From Heaven*. Brooks Atkinson reported: 'Out of the muddled tension of the contemporary world S. N. Behrman has spun a silken drawing-room comedy...Lady Violet Wyngate is a wealthy widow who has an instinct for championing lost causes...Jane Cowl gives an infinitely accomplished performance in which charm is seasoned with intelligence and compassion.'

For the summer of 1935 she was in Dennis, Massachusetts, playing Cavallini in *Romance* and returned to New York in November to the Music Box to play Lucy Chase Wayne in *First Lady*, by Katharine Dayton and George S. Kaufman. Lucy Chase Wayne was the wife of the United States Secretary of State and, many critics thought, modelled on Alice Roosevelt Longworth. Brooks Atkinson reported: '...the character of Mrs Wayne is no factitious puppet for wisecracks. Although she is a witty creature, she is also an able woman with a sense of pride in position and loyalty to her husband. At least Miss Cowl plays the part in that spirit of personal magnificence — cascading lines, underscoring the caprices of genuine emotion. What Miss Cowl has brought to the comedy by way of personal beauty, impeccability of manners, humorous vitality and simple command of the art of acting is of inestimable value to the pleasure of the evening.' It ran for 238 performances.

In 1938 she toured the summer theatres in *The Road to Rome* and *Rain from Heaven* and at the Guild Theater in New York in December 1938 opened as Mrs Levi in Thornton Wilder's *The Merchant of Yonkers*. She toured in 1940 as Lady Cecily in *Captain Brassbound's Conversion* and at the Morosco, December 1940, played Katherine Markham in *Old Acquaintance* and subsequently toured with it. At the Playhouse, November 1941, she was Elizabeth Cherry in *Ring Around Elizabeth* and then at the Forrest, August 1942, Candida.

During the Second World War she could be found at the Stage Door Canteen waiting on tables and also touring army bases. Jane Cowl died on 22 June 1950.

LOTTA CRABTREE

'*L*otta, laughing-eyed soubrette, intro-duced a whole new school of technique to the American actress. There was for her none of the grand manner, none of the posing, the declaiming, the abiding tradition that characterized her sister-comediennes. Lotta defied tradition, because her style of acting was in itself to become traditional. She was, above all, natural. No matter how often she did a role, no matter how carefully a piece of pantomime or business was rehearsed, she had the divine gift of making an audience think it fresh and but that moment inspired. Every night at one of Lotta's performances was like a first night. Lotta had only to let mirth shine in her eyes, to laugh her rich, unaffected laughter and her audiences spon-taneously laughed with her.' This is the way DeWitt Bodeen described the phenomenal Lotta Crabtree in *Ladies of the Footlights*.

During her working life she amassed more than four million dollars, built a memorial fountain to herself in San Francisco and entertained not only in one-mule mining towns but also performed for the Prince of Wales. She was one of the first actresses to inaugurate the 'combination system', that is to travel her own cast rather than relying on the local stock company to furnish supporting players.

Constance Rourke in her study of contempo-rary acting said that Lotta Crabtree was 'one of those personalities which belong to the theater but not to drama, which will overpass any proper vehicle with lawless force. She broke the traditions of the stage; she broke tradition as to the place of women in life as well as in theater.' And a fellow actor, Francis Wilson, said: 'It is my belief that Lotta touched comic heights attained by few other comediennes. Others satisfied and delighted; Lotta did this also, but swept you up into a whirl of enthusiasm.'

Charlotte Crabtree was born in New York City on 7 November 1847. At that time her mother was an upholsterer and her father a charming ne'er-do-well who owned a bookshop but seldom ran it properly. In 1851 he went West to seek his fortune in the California gold rush and two years later Mary Ann Crabtree took her daughter Charlotte to California in search of him. They rented a small house on Telegraph Hill in the midst of a colony of actors, and realizing how popular child performers were, her mother instantly enrolled Lotta in dancing classes. Mr Crabtree was located in Grass Valley and they went to join him there. His gold-seeking had been totally

unsuccessful and they opened a boarding house for miners. Lotta made her début when her dancing teacher took her to Rough and Ready, a town three miles away, where atop an anvil at the blacksmith's shop she danced to the rhythm of clapping hands. In the autumn of 1854 the family moved to a new mining town, Rabbit Creek, and opened another boarding house. Lotta's first indoor performance took place when, aged seven, she performed at the local 'theatre', a room attached to the tavern. Mart Taylor who ran the tavern organized a tour for Lotta. She danced jigs, sang sentimental ballads and generally charmed the miners. Mother went along, new baby in tow, and helped her daughter perform in mining towns where the venues ranged from bar-rooms to schools and even to grocery shops. To show their appreciation the audience threw money or gold nuggets. A correspondent, reporting back East to the *Brooklyn Eagle* said that Lotta was 'proclaimed the pet of the miners. Next day she was carried on the shoulders of the men to visit the then celebrated claims . . . when she left us some of the boys followed the party a long way before saying goodbye.'

In 1857 there was a new Taylor touring com-pany. Mary Ann was Arabella and Lotta, La Petite. She did comic patter, a walk-around, the shuffle and of course the sentimental ballads. She played the Gaieties Theater on the Long Wharf in San Francisco following a performance of *Brigham Young*, a play about polygamy — but it was a rough theatre and she fled in fright. On her autumn tour in 1858 she began playing legitimate parts — Gertrude in *Loan of a Lover*. That year she also spent six months at Miss Hurley's Spring Valley School, the longest uninterrupted period of school she was to have. In 1859 and 1860 she played for Tom Maguire in San Francisco at both the Opera House Theater and Eureka Theater. Almost overnight her billing changed from 'La Petite Lotta, the celebrated Danseuse and Vocalist' to 'Miss Lotta, the San Francisco Favorite'. She also appeared at Melodeons, the forerunner of vaudeville.

Having conquered what there was of the West Coast, in 1864 Mary Ann and Lotta headed East. At first she was not a success in New York. The *New York Clipper* said: 'Her style is certainly not intended for a first-class audience, concert halls being her proper stamping ground.' B. H. Whitman took over her management and sent her to Chicago to play five parts in an extravaganza called *The Seven Sisters*. Here she was an instant success. Whitman next sent her to work with Colonel Woods' stock company. She played *Nan the Good for Nothing*, Topsy in *Mr and Mrs White*, and in *Our Gals*. In 1865 they left Woods and took to the road, playing Ohio, Pennsylvania and upstate New York. In Buffalo alone she appeared in eleven plays.

In January 1866 Lotta opened at Willard Howard's Atheneum in Boston. Her plays included *Uncle Tom's Cabin*, *Jenny Leatherlungs* and *Trapping a Tartar*. There was no question now — she was a star. She toured again and then opened at the St Charles Theater in New Orleans playing *Andy Blake*, *Nan the Good for Nothing* and *Ireland as it Was*.

It was 1867 before Lotta got a play all to herself. John Brougham wrote *Little Nell and the Marchioness* for her. The play had its New York première at Wallack's Theater, in September the same year. This time she conquered New York. The *New York Herald* reported: 'The fidelity and effective force with which she sustained each of these opposite characters stamp Lotta as an actress of no ordinary calibre, and she can no longer be regarded as merely one of the prettiest animated toys which has ever enlivened a summer season.' Frank Leslie's *Illustrated Magazine* wrote that she was 'like California wine, bright, sparkling, piquant'. Her theatrical fortunes, in both senses, never turned again, and playwrights rushed to write for her — Edmund Falconer adapted Ouida's *Under Two Flags* and called it *Firefly* — and she played every major city and most of the ones in between. Her social success followed her theatrical: the Grand Duke Alexis of Russia presented her with a diamond bracelet. Her great successes were *Heartsease*, *Zip* and *Musette*. In 1877 she even played Desdemona in the third act of *Othello* at a benefit for Edwin Adams at the Academy of Music in New York.

Though the family had visited Europe a number of times, Lotta had never worked there. In December 1883 she opened at the Opéra-Comique in London, following a blazing trail of publicity. The British were mystified. Reviewing *Musette*, T. P. O'Connor wrote in the *Daily Telegraph* an account of the entire evening: the audience 'could not make head or tail of this "Dramatic Story" [about a gypsy girl being pursued by a Baron] and their vain efforts to follow the thread of the plot and unravel its perplexing mysteries seemed utterly to demoralize them . . . I was a little late coming in but already the whole gigantic horrible disaster had

come. For almost from the first moment after the curtain had risen, a tremendous — almost like an organized — riot had started. Every word of the play was interrupted, every actor hissed and the noise grew in violence as the time went on, until at last it was a hurricane of catcalls, of loud guffaws, of insulting sneers.' The *Times* said simply: 'It would be a kindness to the public and to Miss Lotta herself to relieve her of the trammels of *Musette* and to allow her to caper about the stage in her own way.'

She took the advice, but instead of merely capering, she got Dickens' son to write her an adaptation of *The Old Curiosity Shop*. The British, public and critics alike, forgave her *Musette* and declared her 'brilliantly successful and fascinatingly clever'. They loved her Little Nell. She followed this in May with *Mam'zelle Nitouche*, a comic vaudeville she had picked up in Paris. In this she sang *opéra bouffe*, played the snare drums, marched around in cavalry boots and even sang a Japanese song.

In June she returned to New York, satisfied with her London première. She bought the Park Theater in Boston for a huge sum of money and opened her 1885 season at the New York Grand Opera House. A reviewer said: 'Miss Lotta's methods are peculiar to herself. They may be described briefly as anatomical . . . No one can wink like Lotta. No woman can perform so wide a variety of contortions with her features . . . no one can wriggle more effectively. No one can kick higher or oftener.' In 1887 David Belasco and Clay Green wrote *Pawn Ticket 210* for her and she introduced it at McVicker's Theater in Chicago.

Lotta's last season of touring began in September 1890. She went back to California and toured the entire West. In May she fell on stage and injured her back, and she was never quite the same again. She was 45 and the richest woman in American theatre — in fact one of the richest women in America. There was no need for her to make endless farewell performances. She retired, and she and her mother travelled.

Lotta took up painting and then, after her mother's death, she bought the Brewster Hotel in Boston and moved into it. She owned racehorses, theatres, office buildings, various hotels and a gold mine — as well as jewellery. She spent her time spending money on charity, painting and racing horses. Lotta died at the Hotel Brewster on 25 September 1924 aged 75 — and left over four million dollars in perpetual trust to charities.

MICHAEL CRAWFORD

They do not come much more dedicated than Michael Crawford. Although he dotes on his two children, he is divorced from their mother and his life is devoted to the perfection of his art, which is often athletic, sometimes winsome and always exuberant.

Michael Crawford was born on 19 January 1942 in Salisbury, Wiltshire, and went to St Michael's College, Bexley, and Oakfield School in Dulwich. He was a boy soprano and performer and made his début in the original productions of Britten's *Noye's Fludde* and *Let's Make an Opera*.

His grown-up début was in the West End at the Prince of Wales in April 1965 as Arnold Champion in *Travelling Light*. At the Duke of York's the following April he was what was called 'successfully Byronic' in a curious play called *The Anniversary* which, gothicked up a bit, became a Bette Davis film. He made his New York début at the Ethel Barrymore Theater in February 1967 playing in the double bill, *White Lies* and *Black Comedy*.

At the Strand in June 1971, Michael Crawford created the part of Brian Runnicles in *No Sex Please — We're British*. Peter Roberts reported that it is 'Michael Crawford's evening and it would be a shame if students of the technique of great acting on their way to the culturally more respect-

able Peter Brook *Dream* [Peter Brook's production of *A Midsummer Night's Dream*] next door at the Aldwych failed to catch it whilst it's still at its energetic peak.'

Michael then had a very successful television series in which he played the accident-prone, idiotic but lovable Frank in 'Some Mothers Do 'Ave 'Em'. He tumbled off roofs, roller skated under lorries, fell through floors and his mournful whine became the most imitated voice in the country. When he returned to the West End in May 1974 to Drury Lane playing Billy Fisher in *Billy*, the musical version of *Billy Liar*, he was a star.

He played George in *Same Time Next Year* opening at the Prince of Wales in September 1976. In this he was only required to swing from a beam occasionally and age about twenty-five years while remaining charming and touching. He accomplished it all very well.

Though more touching and real, his next venture, *Flowers For Algernon*, was undervalued and closed quickly. But then in 1981 he became *Barnum* at the Palladium — walking a tightrope while singing, leaping on a trampoline, sliding on a wire from the royal box, dancing, charming, juggling, smiling and generally enchanting the full houses. It was a performance he was still giving at the Victoria Palace in London in 1985.

HUME CRONYN

See Jessica Tandy and Hume Cronyn

CONSTANCE CUMMINGS

'It's like surf-riding: exciting, dashing, dangerous. And you get carried along in spite of anything you're thinking and doing and planning. Something takes over. It's an unpredictable journey, a kind of creativity each time.' That's what Constance Cummings thinks about acting.

She was born on 15 May 1910 in Seattle,

Washington, where her father was a lawyer. She went to St Nicholas School in Seattle and then Coronado High School in California. She had ambitions to be a dancer but made her stage début in 1926 with the Savoy Stock Company playing a prostitute in *Seventh Heaven* in San Diego. She also appeared with them the next year in the chorus of *Silence* and in 1928 toured in the chorus of *Oh, Kay!* On 8 November 1928 Constance Cummings made her New York début in the chorus of *Treasure Girl* at the Alvin Theater and in April 1929 appeared at the Music Box in a revue called *The Little Show*. At the Ritz in March 1930 she was Carrie in *This Man's Town* and then toured in *June Moon*.

In 1931 Constance Cummings went to Hollywood to appear in *Movie Crazy* for Paramount and there she met Benn Levy, the British playwright who was working at RKO. After half a dozen unmemorable films, Constance Cummings made her London stage début at the Comedy Theatre on 22 July 1934 playing Alice Overton in *Sour Grapes*. (The year before she had married Levy, who directed it.) *Sour Grapes* transferred to the Apollo in August 1934. Constance Cummings returned to New York in December, beginning the see-saw between the stages on either side of the Atlantic that characterized her career. Playing Linda Brown, she opened at the Plymouth Theater in *Accent on Youth*. At the Savoy in London she was Regina Conti in *Young Madame Conti* in November 1936, and played the same part at the Music Box in New York in March 1937. At the Broadhurst Theater in New York in November 1937, she played Emma Bovary, directed by her husband in his own adaptation of Flaubert's novel, *Madame Bovary*. The production scandalized the Theater Guild. Benn Levy said: 'People see Madame Bovary as a long-suffering heroine, more sinned against than sinning, which she ain't. Everyone in the book is awful except for poor silly Charles.'

At the Mansfield in January 1938, Constance Cummings played Nellie Blunt in *If I Were You*. Back in London in September she was Katherine in *Goodbye Mr Chips* at the Shaftesbury. In July she was Katharina with the Oxford University Dramatic Society in *The Taming of the Shrew*. She played Dorothy Shaw in *What a Husband Should Do* (Theatre Royal, Brighton, February 1939) and Kate Settle in *The Jealous God* (Lyric, March 1939).

In 1939 the Old Vic Company asked her to appear at the Buxton Festival in August and at Streatham Hill in October playing Juliet in *Romeo and Juliet* (to Robert Donat's Romeo), Miss Richland in *The Good-Natured Man* and Joan in Shaw's *Saint Joan*. Looking back on the experience, she now says that she was 'young and green in judgement — I didn't know how to read the verses. That was a sloppy thing. I should have had more sense.' Audrey Williamson thought Miss Cummings' performances were far from perfect, but of her Juliet said that she caught a 'dancing buoyancy best of all in the scene in which

Juliet waits for the Nurse, where she had a flashing yet child-like impatience. She played always with feeling and ingenuous charm and though fair as a northern lily did not lack the warm blood of the south. Her speech was clear and tuneful and on the whole remarkably free from an American accent.' And of her Joan, Miss Williamson thought that, 'Apart from this lack of ruthlessness with regard to her appearance, Constance Cummings' Joan had fire and inspiration and did not lack solidity of character.'

In March 1942 her husband again directed her, this time in *Skylark*, an American comedy in which she played Lydia Kenyon at the Duchess Theatre. At the Globe in December that year she played Gabby Maple in *The Petrified Forest*, a production which suffered by comparison with the recently released film. She also toured during the war for the Forces playing Helen Hayle in *On Approval*. She returned to New York to play Racine Gardner in *One-Man Show* at the Ethel Barrymore in February 1945. Back in England she toured as Jane Pugh in her husband's new comedy *Clutterbuck*. He found time to write and direct this even though he had recently been elected a Member of Parliament. *Clutterbuck* opened at Wyndham's in August 1946, where it ran for 366 performances. During the next ten years, while raising her family, Constance Cummings stayed on the European side of the Atlantic, playing Luise Klapps in *Happy with Either* (St James's, April 1948), Madeleine in *Don't Listen Ladies* (St James's, September 1948), Laura Whittingham in *Before the Party* (St Martin's, October 1949), Martha Cotton in *Return to Tyassi* (Duke of York's, November 1950), Georgia Elvin in *Winter Journey* (St James's, October 1952), Ann Downs in *The Shrike* (Prince's, February 1953), and Andrea in *Trial and Error* (Vaudeville, September 1953).

In 1957 Frank Hauser invited her to the Oxford Playhouse and her career changed direction. Despite her early brush with the classics, the parts she had been playing were relatively undemanding. In March 1957 Constance Cummings played the title role in *Lysistrata* at Oxford. It was the first English performance of the Greek play in the full version. Only twelve lines had been cut by the Lord Chamberlain. Frank Dibb reported that 'in the title role Constance Cummings had a gracious, radiant quality and at her most militant was never less than infinitely womanly'.

At the Piccadilly in London in December 1957 she was in her husband's *The Rape of the Belt* in which Peter Roberts said her Queen of the Amazons was 'sprightly and sparkling'. She subsequently appeared in it at the Martin Beck

Theater in New York, in November 1960. At the Phoenix in London in March 1961 she played Sarah in *J.B.* and went back to Oxford in February 1962, planning to be in an Aldous Huxley adaptation but there were difficulties, so Frank Hauser decided to put on Sartre's *Huis Clos* and cast Constance Cummings as the tough lesbian, Inez. She was horrified: 'But then,' she said, 'when it came to rehearsal I found I enjoyed it enormously. Not only could I get next to that woman, but I found little seeds of her dreadfulness in myself, things I could build on. It was a marvellous liberation. I'd never opened myself before and taken such a plunge.' And she doubled Inez with the Countess of Amersham in *A Social Success*. Then in April she played Katy Maartens in Huxley's *The Genius and the Goddess*, which transferred to the Comedy in June. John Percival said: 'Constance Cummings, adorably calm and self-possessed, is the still centre at the heart of this teacup storm. She looks ravishing, she throws away her jokes with just the right off-handed intensity, she seems in fact just the actress to play the role which the author intended but failed to write, that of a "richly pagan temperament whose first duty is self-fulfilment". As it is, she plays very well the role of a woman whose first duty is looking after others, a delightfully civilized woman whom it would be a pleasure to meet.' Constance Cummings then crossed the Atlantic to Connecticut where at the Westport Country Playhouse in November 1963 she played Catherine in *The Strangers*. At the Piccadilly in London in May 1964 she took over the awesome role of Martha in *Who's Afraid of Virginia Woolf?* and then at the Malvern Festival in July 1966 played Liza Foote in her husband's political play *Public and Confidential*, bringing it into London to the Duke of York's in August. At the Vaudeville in November 1966 she was Julia Stanford QC in *Justice is a Woman*, and in April 1967 played Jane Banbury in *Fallen Angels*.

It was at the Roundhouse in April 1969 that she took on the role of Gertrude in Tony Richardson's controversial *Hamlet*, which starred Nicol Williamson as the Dane. John Simon saw the production when it opened at the Lunt-Fontanne in New York in May 1969 and he hated every moment of it: 'Constance Cummings' Gertrude,' he said, 'is both wooden and inconspicuous — a bashful marionette.' She

remembers the experience as being not very pleasant.

In 1971 Constance Cummings joined the National Theatre Company, then playing at the New Theatre, and was Volumnia to Anthony Hopkins' Coriolanus and Leda in *Amphitryon 38*. In December 1973 her husband died.

Constance Cummings was awarded the CBE in 1974 for her work on the Arts Council. Then in her mid-sixties, she was approaching her most creative period in the theatre. In 1975 for the National Theatre she played Mary Tyrone in *Long Day's Journey into Night*. Nicholas de Jongh said: 'Cummings is a subtle, quiet sort of player who burns on a slow fuse. I cannot imagine anything more apt and dreadful than her Mary Tyrone, drifting from anxiety into happy morphine-induced oblivion.' In October 1976 she was experimenting at the Gardner Centre, Brighton, with a reportedly incomprehensible play by Albee called *All Over*. Eric Shorter said that her 'final grief is as powerful and impressive as her performance as the mother in *Long Day's Journey*'. In March 1979 Constance Cummings was back on Broadway in an Arthur Kopit play. Dale Harris reported: 'In *Wings*, a long one-acter, she is required by the playwright to hold the stage virtually uninterruptedly for ninety minutes and in that time to show us an entire cycle of human experience — from normality to disintegration and finally to health restored — all of which she achieves brilliantly.' And for her pains, Miss Cummings was awarded a Tony. She came with *Wings* to the National Theatre in August 1979 and Michael Billington found her performance 'very fine indeed. Miss Cummings graduates beautifully from a silver-haired stricken helplessness in which the words she wants to utter emerge jangled and twisted like something from a Carroll nonsense poem into a radiant self-reliance and a delighted re-living of the solitary mysteries of primitive flight.'

After a not very successful revival of *Hay Fever*, Constance Cummings was at the Greenwich Theatre in 1980 playing an 85-year-old woman in A. R. Gurney's play, *The Golden Age*, which was based loosely on Henry James's *The Aspern Papers*.

As Dale Harris commented in the *Guardian* when writing about her: '. . . although she devoted most of her career to West End trifles somehow [Constance Cummings] became a great actress.'

CYRIL CUSACK

'*D*irectors, you know, are always trying to make you believe that actors are small, but we're not; even when we're in bad roles we're huge. That's the trouble with the theatre now: it's far too full of directors telling you to talk louder or softer or move left or right. Any half-good actor knows in his bowels what to do on stage once he gets there. Directors just cloud the brain.'

Cyril James Cusack was born in Durban, Natal, Africa, on 26 November 1910. His mother was a chorus girl (distantly related to Dan Leno) and his father an officer in the Natal Mounted Police. When he was six he was taken to Ireland. 'Mother had enough of the Dark Continent and left my father there,' he says, 'and back in Dublin she married Brefni O'Rorke who was already in the theatre and that was how I started, though I think I was intended to be a lawyer. But we used to tour Ireland fifty weeks of the year so there wasn't much chance of any schooling.'

Despite the touring, Cyril Cusack did attend Dominican College, in County Kildare, and University College, Dublin. He made his first stage appearance at the age of seven playing Willie Carlyle in *East Lynne* on a tour of County Tipperary. He then toured all over Ireland with his stepfather in such plays as *Arrah-Na-Pogue*, *The Sign of the Cross* and *Shot at Dawn*. In 1920 he played the cat in *Dick Whittington* and in 1922 played the donkey in *Ali Baba* and a Babe in *Babes in the Wood*. He also toured the English theatre circuits with his parents in 1924 playing the Boy in *Irish and Proud of It*. In 1928 he joined the Norwich Repertory Company and played the Indian Student in *Tilly of Bloomsbury*, Carruthers in *Mr Wu*, and also appeared in *Milestones*, *The Promised Land* and *Ambrose Applejohn's Adventure*. He toured England in 1928 in *The Terror*.

In 1932 Cyril Cusack returned to Ireland and joined the Abbey Theatre, with which he remained associated until 1945. There he appeared in more than sixty-five productions. Among others, roles he played were the Boy in *The Vigil* (October 1932), Hughie Boyle in *Wrack* (November 1932), Michael in *Drama at Inish* (February 1933), and Irish Countryman in *Parnell of Avondale* (October 1934), Malcolm in *Macbeth* (October 1934), Cassian in *Gallant Cassian* (November 1934), the Son in *Six Characters in Search of an Author* (December 1934), Marchbanks in *Candida* (September 1935), Japhet in *Noah* (November 1935), Andy in *Boyd's Shop* (February 1936), Jo Mahony in *Katie Roche* (March 1936) and Hind in *The Passing Day* (April 1936).

Cyril Cusack made his first appearance on the London stage at the Westminster Theatre on 4 May 1936, playing Richard in *Ah, Wilderness!* Back at the Abbey the parts were getting bigger. He played Joseph Barrett in *The Silver Jubilee* (September 1936), Mr Bunton in *The Jailbird* (October 1936), O'Flingsley in *Shadow and Substance* (January 1937), Quin in *Quin's Secret* (March 1937), Loftus de Lury in *Killycreggs in Twilight* (April 1937), Dan Cusack in *The Patriot* (August 1937), Mangan in *The Man in the Cloak* (September 1937), Kelly in *The Invincibles* (October 1937), Cartney in *Cartney and Kevney* (November 1937), Neddy in *She Had To Do Something* (December 1937), Adam in *Neal Maquade* (January 1938), Ned Hegarty in *Moses Rock* (February 1938), and Hyacinth in *Bird's Nest* (September 1938). During the 1938 Abbey Theatre Festival he played the Fool in *On Baile's Strand*, the Covey in *The Plough and the Stars*, Christopher Mahon in *The Playboy of the Western World* and O'Flingsley in *Shadow and Substance*.

In January 1939 Cyril Cusack opened at the Mercury Theatre in London in *The Playboy of the Western World*. Audrey Williamson called his performance the finest of the younger generation of Irish actors. In June that same year he repeated his performance as the Covey in *The Plough and the Stars* at the "Q" Theatre. At the Gate Theatre in London in May 1940 he played Michel in *Les Parents terribles*.

At the St Martin's in London in February 1941 he played Streeter in *Thunder Rock* and Audrey Williamson thought that he added considerable strength to the production with an intelligent and likable characterization. At the Gate Theatre in Dublin in January 1942 he directed and performed in his own play *Tareis an Aifrinn (After Mass)*.

Having established a distinguished reputation at the Abbey and on his occasional tours of England he was invited by the Tennent management to play opposite Vivien Leigh in *The Doctor's Dilemma* at the Haymarket in 1942. He said, 'The tour was fine, dodging bombs up and down the country, but then we opened in London and on St Patrick's Day I found myself far from home and in a moment of darkness I took a drink or two and the next thing I knew they were replacing me with John Gielgud.' He was not, however, replaced before Audrey

Williamson had a chance to comment on his performance. She said he '... suggested with fine intelligence the feckless unscrupulousness beneath the charm and flame of genius... His Dubedat was perfectly balanced, with the tuberculosis subtly, never flamboyantly, suggested and a death which suddenly lit the stage with a serene yet powerful radiance.'

Cyril Cusack went briefly back to the Abbey but he decided that as a company it was moving too slowly and in 1945 chose independence. His first appearance with his own company was as Tom in *The Last of Summer* at the Gaiety in July 1945. He also played Romeo in *Romeo and Juliet* (co-producing). In 1947 he presented a Shaw season at the Gaiety playing Dubedat in *The Doctor's Dilemma*, Bluntschli in *Arms and the Man*, and Dick Dudgeon in *The Devil's Disciple*. At the People's Palace in London during May 1950 he played Nosey in *Pommy*.

Back in Ireland with his own company he played Christopher Mahon in *The Playboy of the Western World* and Bluntschli in *Arms and the Man* (July 1953), and then toured Ireland with *The Playboy of the Western World*. He then, in June 1954, at the request of the government, presented and repeated his role in that play at the first International Théâtre des Nations season in Paris at the Sarah Bernhardt Theatre.

In February 1955 he presented the first performance of Sean O'Casey's *The Bishop's Bonfire* and played Codger in it. Still at the Gaiety, he played Do-the-Right in *The Golden Cuckoo* (June 1956) and in a double bill played Androcles in *Androcles and the Lion* and the Man in *The Rising of the Moon* (July 1956).

Cyril Cusack made his first appearance on the New York stage on 2 May 1957 at the Bijou Theater playing Phil Hogan in *A Moon for the Misbegotten* and then returned to Ireland where he played Hamlet (October 1957). In 1958 he presented *Casement* in which he played Roger Casement. At the Olympia, Dublin, in March 1959 he played President O'Beirne in *Goodwill Ambassador*. He took this production to the States, hoping for a Broadway run, but it opened at the Shubert, New Haven, Connecticut, on 16 March 1960, and closed in Boston at the Wilbur on 26 March.

In Dublin and Belfast he repeated his performance of Bluntschli in *Arms and the Man* and also played Krapp in *Krapp's Last Tape*. He took these productions to the International Théâtre des Nations at the Sarah Bernhardt Théâtre in Paris in the summer of 1960 and won the International Critics Award. He then toured theatre festivals in Rotterdam, Amsterdam, the Hague, Utrecht and Antwerp. Back in Dublin at the Gaiety in September 1960 he presented *The Voices of Doolin* and played Doolin. He toured this production throughout Ireland. At the Dublin Festival of 1961 he presented his own play, *The Temptation of Mr O*, in which he played the title role.

Cyril Cusack joined the Royal Shakespeare Company in January 1963 to play in *The Physicists* (John Russell Taylor said that he managed 'to suggest that Moebius is a man of principle without making him a prig or a drip') and as Cassius in *Julius Caesar*. In January 1964 he was at the Old Vic with the National Theatre Company (hopelessly miscast, according to Martin Esslin) as Can in *Andorra*. In January 1967 he was back with the Abbey, playing Conn in *The Shaughraun* at the Aldwych World Theatre Season; and at the Dublin Festival in October 1968 he played Gaev in *The Cherry Orchard*. At the Gaiety in Dublin in November 1968 he was Fox Melarkey in *Crystal and Fox* and joined the Abbey Theatre Company for a tour in 1969–70 playing *Hadrian VII*. In November 1970 he played Menenius in *Coriolanus* at the John F. Kennedy Theater in Hawaii. He was Antonio in the National Theatre Company's production of *The Tempest* at the Old Vic in March 1974, and that May played the Masked Man in *Spring Awakening* for them. He went back to the Abbey for the 1974–75 season playing the title role in *The Vicar of Wakefield*. In September 1977 he was with the National Theatre Company in their own building playing Fluther Good, the Carpenter in *The Plough and the Stars*, and he was there again in 1984 as the Inquisitor in *Saint Joan*.

Cyril Cusack's first film was probably Ireland's first film, too. It was produced in Tipperary in 1916. He played Young O'Brien in *Knocknagow or The Homes of Tipperary*. Over the years he made a number of films both in Britain (*Esther Waters, The Small Back Room, The Spanish Gardener, The Spy Who Came in from the Cold*) and in Hollywood (*Soldiers Three, The Secret of Convict Lake, The Blue Veil, The Man Who Never Was*), but as he said, 'Like most actors I did the films to finance the plays, but I was nervous of becoming the Hollywood Irishman.'

He writes and has published poetry in both Gaelic and English and now, looking back over his career, says: 'I've been going a long time, you know, and O'Casey and Shaw have done me very well, and I hope I haven't done them too badly either; but I begin to wish I'd acted less and written more and maybe now I'll just stay in Dublin and get on with the poems and all.'

JIM DALE

Jim Dale has been discovered more times than has America. He was born on 15 August 1935 in Rothwell, Northamptonshire. His father was a steelworker. When he was nine he went to see Lupino Lane starring at the Victoria Palace in *Me and My Girl* and decided he wanted to be on the stage. 'Then you must learn how to move and move fast,' his father said, 'because people are going to be flinging things at you. If they like you they'll fling pennies at you; if they don't it'll be tomatoes. Either way you're going to be dodging things.' Jim spent six years training in ballet and tap dancing and in 1951 made his début as a stand-up comic at the Savoy, Kettering. There he was discovered by a top agent, and though he admits his act was not very good he made a living going round the country in variety for three years. After a spell in the RAF he was discovered by television and starred in the weekly pop-show, '6.5 Special'. He became a teenage idol, wriggling his hips and driving a large pink car. After that he was discovered by the movies and appeared in umpteen 'Carry On' films.

Dale was then discovered by the legitimate theatre. In November 1964 he played William Dawton in *The Wayward Way* at the Lyric, Hammersmith, after which Frank Dunlop, Laurence Olivier's second-in-command at the National Theatre, asked him to play Autolycus in *The Winter's Tale*. It opened in Edinburgh at the Festival and transferred to the Cambridge in London in September 1966. At the Vaudeville in February 1967 he played the Burglar in a play of the same name and at the Edinburgh Festival that August he was Bottom in *A Midsummer Night's Dream*. That production transferred to the Saville the following month. Peter Ansorge reported: 'Jim Dale's ton-up Bottom rushes on to the stage like an ex-pirate station disc jockey late for his stint on Radio One . . . [he] seems very friendly and must be one of the few Bottoms with whom one feels it would be nice to have a drink after the show.'

Jim Dale joined the National Theatre Company at the Old Vic in 1969 and played the Master-of-Ceremonies and the Orderly in *The National Health* (October 1969), Nicholas in *The Travails of Sancho Panza* (December 1969), Costard in *Love's Labour's Lost* (January 1970) and Launcelot Gobbo in *The Merchant of Venice* (April 1970). But it was at the Young Vic under the direction of Frank Dunlop that Jim Dale came into his own. He played a Cockney Scarpino in a free adaptation of Molière's play (for which he wrote the music) in September 1970. Peter Ansorge said in *Plays and Players*: 'As an actor rooted in music hall, [Jim Dale's] performance in Frank Dunlop's opening production of *The Cheats of Scarpino* evoked a genuine response from the young audience . . . Dale, sporting a twenties gangster suit, began at a leisurely pace strumming a melancholy tune, the lyrics of which had been filched from an Italian menu. He proceeded craftily towards the audience tossing the occasional chocolate drop into the delighted palms of a seated child and then began a series of adventures which included a terror-struck flight through the auditorium, a perilous rope-dangling act, suspended from a high balcony, and the miming of an entire army marching threateningly towards its shaking victim who had been persuaded (by Dale naturally) to seek refuge in an empty sack.'

Then he was a whirlwind Petruchio in *The Taming of the Shrew* in November. Robert Cushman found him ' . . . no roaring boy; forswearing his own brand of comic rhetoric he emerges as an unexpectedly quiet performer but possessed of a level of intensity that makes his victory as secure as would any amount of whip-cracking'.

Back with the Old Vic in 1971 Jim Dale played the Architect in *The Architect and the Emperor of Assyria*, Mr Lofty in *The Good-Natured Man*, and Kalle in *The Captain of Köpenick*. Then he set off as Petruchio for a tour of Europe in 1972. He was at the Queen's in July 1973 playing Denry Machin in *The Card*. In March 1974 he set off with the Young Vic Company to New York, where he was to play both Petruchio and Scarpino at the Brooklyn Academy; *Scarpino* transferred to the Circle in the Square and finally, becoming the hottest ticket in town, settled into the Ambassador. New York had discovered Jim Dale. Then for a while the theatre forgot about him, and he thanked his stars for Hollywood and the Walt Disney organisation, which starred him in three films, enabling him to support his wife and four children. It was in late 1979 that Broadway rediscovered Jim Dale when he played the title role in *Barnum*. John Barber reported: 'The whole evening was brought to the boil by the curly-headed charm and the bobby-dazzling professionalism of the man who quietly told me he knew his trade. He did much more than walk a tightrope, ride a unicycle, lead a brass band, do a conjuring turn and dance like an eel crossed with a dervish . . . In Dale we glimpse the miracle of exuberant vitality, articulated through a heart-warming physical prowess. There is no humbug whatever about his talent. The New York critics are at his feet. ''Is there anything Jim Dale can't do? This man can create magic . . . An evening of pure exhilarating fun . . . Abundantly high-spirited . . . bursting with colour . . . Jim Dale pulls out all the stops . . .'' He is a one-man, three-ring, four-star circus!' For his performance Jim Dale was awarded a Tony. Of his Barnum Jim

Dale said: 'Knowing that I can hit a certain standard time and again has really given me tremendous confidence. It's not ego — don't get me wrong. It's the confidence that comes from knowing you're good at your job because you've been so bloody long learning it, and now all those years of graft and all the mistakes are finally paying off!'

ZENA AND PHYLLIS DARE

These two great beauties of the Edwardian era, Zena and Phyllis Dare, made their stage début as children simultaneously, but Zena remained on the stage nearly a quarter of a century longer. Zena was born on 4 February 1887 in London, where three years later, on 15 August 1890, Phyllis put in an appearance. Their father was a clerk in the divorce court. Phyllis was educated at home while Zena attended Maida Vale High School and had a short stint in Brussels.

At Christmas 1899 they made their stage début at the Coronet Theatre in the pantomime *Babes in the Wood*. Zena was understudying the part of the Boy Babe and Phyllis was one of the children. Phyllis next appeared as Christina in *Little Christina* at the Prince of Wales and that Christmas was at the Theatre Royal, Manchester, playing *Little Red Riding Hood*. In April 1901 at the St James's she was Marjorie in *The Wilderness*. Seymour Hicks cast her as Mob, a child in the garret scene in *Bluebell in Fairyland* at the Vaudeville in 1901. He said she 'played very sweetly. But she had a rather childish affectation of speech'. During this period, while spasmodically continuing her education, Zena appeared in pantomime in Scotland, toured for Seymour Hicks playing Daisy Maitland in *An English Daisy* (1902) and played *Cinderella* at the Shakespeare, Liverpool, in 1903. She came back to London in 1904 to play for Frank Curzon at the Strand and then at the Prince of Wales. Curzon released her in September 1904 to create the part of Angela for Seymour Hicks' *The Catch of the Season*. It was her first grown-up part. Hicks had created the part for his wife, Ellaline Terriss, but pregnancy intervened, so he gave it to Zena. He said: 'She was remarkably intelligent, worked hard and had a beautiful face, and on my recommendation she was

given the task of playing this exceptionally big part opposite me in our new production . . . She had stuck to her work at rehearsals like a Briton, and her performance was a charming one, which not only helped us out of our extremely difficult position but spelt her name in golden letters of success which she has made brighter each year by the whole-heartedness and sincerity of all she undertakes.' *The Catch of the Season* ran for 621 performances but in 1905 Phyllis replaced her sister in the role because Zena was contracted to play *The Sleeping Beauty* at Bristol. The next year Zena was hired by George Edwardes, the 'father of musical comedy', to play Lady Madcap in the play of that name, Lady Elizabeth Congress in *The Little Cherub*, and the Girl in *The Girl on Stage*, all at the Prince of Wales.

After playing *Cinderella* in pantomime at Christmas 1905 Phyllis was despatched to Belgium to catch up a little on her education. She came back to the Vaudeville in May 1906 to play in *The Belle of Mayfair*. There was, of course, a pantomime at Christmas and then she toured in *The Dairymaids* until Christmas 1907, when she was Cinderella at the Theatre Royal, Birmingham.

Meanwhile, Zena had rejoined Seymour Hicks. She played Betty Silverthorne in *The Beauty of Bath* at the newly opened Aldwych in 1906 and toured that autumn in her original part in *The Catch of the Season*. At Christmas she was Peter Pan in Manchester, then back at the Aldwych in September 1907 she played Victoria Siddons in *The Gay Gordons*. Zena and Hicks went on a matinée tour giving one-act plays and then, fittingly at Christmas, took the Scottish play *The Gay Gordons* to Glasgow. During 1909 she toured in that and in *Sweet and Twenty*. In March 1909 Zena and Hicks were at the Coliseum in *Papa's*

Wife and at the Hippodrome in November that year Zena played Princess Amaranth in *Mitislaw or The Love Match*. Zena Dare toured during 1910 as the Duc de Richelieu in *The Dashing Little Duke* and at the Hippodrome in August 1910 she opened in *The Model and the Man*. By this time she was a very big star — postcards of her face graced the walls of many houses and the lockers of small boys (including that of the neophyte critic James Agate). However, in January 1911 she married the Hon. Maurice Brett, second son of the second Viscount Esher, and retired from the stage to have a family.

Phyllis had come to London in 1908, to the Queen's with *The Dairymaids*, and at Christmas was at the Adelphi as Cinderella. At the Shaftesbury in April 1909 Phyllis began her first long run. The show was Robert Courtneidge's *The Arcadians*. She played Eileen Cavanagh for over a year. Then for George Edwardes she played Gonda van der Loo in *The Girl in the Train* (Vaudeville, June 1910) and Peggy Barrison in *Peggy* (Gaiety, March 1911). At the Chatelet Théâtre in Paris in June 1922 Phyllis appeared as Prudence in *The Quaker Girl*. Back at the Gaiety in February 1911 she played Delia Dale in *The Sunshine Girl* by Paul Rubens, a prolific composer, a Wykehamist and an Oxford graduate. Phyllis toured *The Sunshine Girl* in 1912 and 1913 before taking over the part of Nancy Joyce in *The Dancing Mistress* at the Adelphi in May 1913. Also at the Adelphi she played Dora Manners in *The Girl from Utah*. She sang in concert at the Victoria Palace in September 1914. In a revival of *Miss Hook of Holland* at the Prince of Wales in October 1914, Phyllis played Sally Hook and the following year she played the title part in *Tina* at the Adelphi. Both these musicals had been written by Paul Rubens, to whom Phyllis was now engaged. But in 1916 Rubens learned that he was seriously ill and in November they announced jointly that the engagement was off. He died a few months later, barely 40.

Phyllis made a brief appearance at the Empire in March 1917 in a revue called *Hanky-Panky*, but was unable to resume her career properly until 1919, when she appeared in May at the Winter Garden playing Lucienne Touquet in *Kissing Time*. The *Times* critic said that her acting and dancing had improved to the point where they were as good as her singing. For Christmas in 1920 she was the Princess in *Aladdin* at the London Hippodrome. She was next in the disaster *Ring Up* at the Royalty in September 1921 but fared better with two Lonsdale musicals — *The Lady of the Rose* (Daly's, February 1922) in which she played Marianne, and *The Street Singer* (Lyric, June

1924) in which she played Yvette. At the Gaiety in December 1926 Phyllis was overshadowed by Cicely Courtneidge and Jack Hulbert when she played Fay Blake in *Lido Lady*; the part of Mary Bannister in Edgar Wallace's *The Yellow Mask* (Carlton, February 1928) did not serve her any better.

It was in March 1929 that Phyllis decided to try the straight theatre and appeared at the Fortune as the Hon. Mrs Willie Tatham in Lonsdale's *Aren't We All?*, but although well received she was soon back in musicals. During 1930 she toured as Stella Trent in *Cheated*. At the Adelphi in November 1932 she appeared in *Words and Music*. She toured again in 1934 as Frieda in *Music in the Air*.

Zena Dare returned to the stage in January 1926 but, at the age of 39, not to musical comedy. She toured as Mrs Cheyney in *The Last of Mrs Cheyney*. Then at the Playhouse in January 1928 she played opposite Noel Coward in S. N. Behrman's *The Second Man*. That year she formed her own company and toured South Africa in *The High Road*, *The Trial of Mary Dugan*, *The Squeaker* and *Other Men's Wives*.

When Zena returned from South Africa she took over from Marie Tempest at the Haymarket, in December 1929 playing Janet Fraser in *The First Mrs Fraser* and then touring with the play. She also toured in *Other Men's Wives* and as Clemency Warlock in *Cynara*. For two Christmases (1931 and 1932) she played Mrs Darling in *Peter Pan* at the Palladium, and in between toured as Leslie in *Counsel's Opinion*. Zena had her greatest success since her preretirement musical days with Ivor Novello. She played his mother in *Proscenium* at the Globe in June 1933, about which Audrey Williamson said she 'incisively sharpened the wit'. The following year she played the murderer's mother, Mrs Sherry, in *Murder in Mayfair*. That year her husband died. In 1936 she was back with Novello in September, this time at Drury Lane. Zena played Phyllida Frame, the manageress of a beauty parlour in his musical *Careless Rapture*. The *Times* pointed out that these roles with Novello 'were exactly suited to her years and to her bent for mild caricature which allowed her to mix frivolity with the romantic sentiment of Novello's work and so made the latter more palatable to his increasingly large public'. Zena left Novello in May 1938 to play Tiny Fox-Coller at the Ambassadors' in M. J. Farrell and John Perry's Irish comedy *Spring Meeting*. She toured the part in 1939.

During the thirties Phyllis had been Lady Beaumont in *The Fugitives* (Apollo, May 1936) and Lady Charity Carstairs in *And the Music Stopped* (New, May 1937), and toured in August

The legendary Marlene Dietrich

Judi Dench in the Royal Shakespeare Company's production of
Mother Courage at the Barbican Theatre
(London, November 1984)

1937 as Dorothy Hilton in Dodie Smith's *Call It a Day*.

In 1940 Zena and Phyllis Dare were together on stage for the first time in over forty years when Zena played Frynne Rodney and Phyllis played Lola Leadenhall in a tour of a revival of Novello's *Full House*. They parted again, however; Zena, according to Ernest Short, 'gave a finely comic performance' as Lady Caroline in a revival of *Dear Brutus* at the Globe in January 1941. The following Christmas she was Mrs Darling again and she toured in 1943 as Fanny Farrelly in *The Watch on the Rhine*. At the Scala in December 1943 Zena was the Red Queen in *Alice Through the Looking Glass* and at the Phoenix in December 1944 played Elsie in Lonsdale's *Another Love Story*. She rejoined Ivor Novello when she took over the role of Lady Charlotte Fayre from Margaret Rutherford in *Perchance to Dream* at the Hippodrome in November 1945.

Phyllis, meanwhile, had played Juliet Maddock in *Other People's Houses* (Ambassadors', October 1941, and Phoenix, March 1942), and toured as Mrs Brown in Rose Franklin's *Claudia*. At the Arts Theatre in Cambridge in April 1945 and on a subsequent ENSA tour she played Mrs Wood in *June Mad*, and then in 1946 toured as Enid Fletcher in *Day After Tomorrow*, bringing it into the Fortune in August. She was back in Edwardian fashions in *Lady Frederick*, playing the Marchioness of Mereston at the Savoy in November 1946. At the Comedy in August 1948 Phyllis played Dorothy Sparkes in *Sit Down a Minute*.

In September 1949 Ivor Novello had a new musical, the Ruritanian *King's Rhapsody*, and parts for both Phyllis and Zena. Zena played his mother and Phyllis his mistress. They opened at the Palace Theatre, where it was an enormous success and continued to run for seven months after Novello's death in 1951. After *King's Rhapsody*, at the age of 61 Phyllis retired to Brighton. She had never married.

Zena stayed on at the Palace and in August 1954 played Julia Ward McKinlock in *Sabrina Fair*. At the Savoy in November 1956 she was Edith Billingsley in *Double Image*, and at the Globe in November 1957 succeeded Joyce Carey as Isobel Sorodin, the bogus painter's widow in Noel Coward's *Nude with Violin*.

Zena Dare's last appearance was as Rex Harrison's mother, Mrs Higgins, in *My Fair Lady* at Drury Lane. She opened in April 1958 and played in London for more than five years before touring for a year. In 1965 Zena Dare retired from the stage. She died on 11 March 1975; her younger sister Phyllis died only a month later, on 27 April.

JUDI DENCH

'Judi Dench has begun her career in a burst of fame and she has the ability and purpose of mind to succeed. If she does reach the heights it will be for one reason above all others; she knows her present limitations and sees clearly that one crowded hour of glorious acting does not make a reputation or an actress.' Thus *Plays and Players*, in a mini-profile, spoke of Judi Dench in 1958. Now, twenty-eight years later, Judi has fulfilled her early promise and she is that rare figure, loved by audiences, critics, directors and fellow actors. She has no need to be a *star* — just a very good actress; and she is the despair of her agent, as she explains: 'There is a joke between us that if anyone offers me a role and asks where is Judi, he tells them: "Probably at the John O'Groats rep doing something worthy."'

Judi Dench was born on 9 December 1934 in York where her father was a doctor. At the age of 12 she went to The Mount, a Quaker school in York. After that she went to art college to study set design but decided she would never be good enough at it. Encouraged by her brother, the actor Jeffrey Dench, she studied at the Central School. Her first professional part was as the Virgin Mary in *A Mystery Cycle* at York and then, right off the deep end, she played Ophelia to John Neville's Hamlet for the Old Vic in September 1957. Peter Roberts found it, 'altogether a most stimulating evening' and thought that Judi Dench's Ophelia was 'as appealing as a tea cosy — which she sometimes makes me think of' — and he meant that as a compliment. That year Judi Dench began a love affair with the critics who almost to a man smothered her not only with affection and praise but also with a kind of protection. She remained a member of the Old Vic Company, during which time she played Juliet in *Measure for Measure*, First Fairy in *A Midsummer Night's Dream*, Maria in *Twelfth Night*, Katharine in *Henry V* (in which she made her New York début), Phoebe in *As You Like It*, Cynthia in *The Double Dealer*, Cecily Cardew in *The Importance of Being Earnest*, Ann Page in *The Merry Wives of Windsor*, Juliet in *Romeo and Juliet*, Kate Hardcastle in *She Stoops to Conquer*, and Hermia in *A Midsummer Night's Dream*. By this time she was 26, and as well as having played so many major roles she had toured the United States, Canada and Yugoslavia.

Judi Dench then joined the Royal Shakespeare Company. She played Anya in *The Cherry Orchard* at the Aldwych in December 1961, and for the Stratford 1962 season was Isabella in *Measure for Measure*, Titania in *A Midsummer Night's Dream* and Dorcas in *Penny for a Song*.

At the Nottingham Playhouse in January 1963 she played Lady Macbeth, and also playing Viola in *Twelfth Night*, she toured West Africa for the British Council. There she was amazed and delighted that audiences cried for operatic-style encores: 'Do it again, the bit where you wash your hands without a basin. Again! Again!'

At the Lyric, London, in May 1963 she played Josefa Lautenay in *A Shot in the Dark* and then joined the Oxford Playhouse Company in April 1964 to play Irina in *The Three Sisters*, Anna in *The Twelfth Hour*, Dol Common in *The Alchemist*, Juliet in *Romeo and Juliet* and Jacqueline in *The Firescreen*. Back at the Nottingham Playhouse in 1965 she once more played Isabella in *Measure for Measure*, Amanda in *Private Lives*, Barbara in *The Astrakhan Coat*, and Joan in Shaw's *Saint Joan*. At the Oxford Playhouse in November 1966 Judi Dench was Lika in *The Promise* and in December Sila in *The Rules of the Game*. *The Promise* transferred to London to the Fortune in January 1967.

In 1968 she was offered the role of Sally Bowles in the musical *Cabaret*. At first she thought they were joking. She had never done a musical and she has an unusual croaky voice which sounds as if she has a permanent cold. So frightened was she of singing in public that she auditioned from the wings, leaving the pianist alone on stage. *Cabaret* opened at the Palace in February 1968. Frank Marcus said: 'She sings well; the title song in particular is projected with great feeling. She isn't really the right build for the flapper period . . . and she lacks the frenetic gaiety. Towards the end, she communicates disillusion and pain most movingly . . . On the whole, Judi Dench has too much warmth and intelligence for the Sally of *Cabaret*.' But it was just that warmth that audiences have always loved.

After a long run, Judi went back the next year to the RSC, where she played Bianca in *Women*

Beware Women, Hermione and Perdita in *The Winter's Tale* and Viola in *Twelfth Night*. With the Company she toured Australia in January 1970. It was in that year that Judi married the actor Michael Williams, another associate member of the RSC. They had known each other for nine years when he suddenly proposed on a sunny day in Adelaide. Judi said, 'Ask me again on a rainy day in London.' So he did. That year also, Judi received an OBE in the Birthday Honours.

For the Aldwych 1970–71 season Judi Dench again played Viola, Hermione and Perdita and added Grace Harkaway in *London Assurance* and Barbara Undershaft in *Major Barbara*. Then at Stratford in 1971 she played Portia in *The Merchant of Venice*, Viola, and the title role in *The Duchess of Malfi*. At Christmas in *Toad of Toad Hall* at Stratford she was the First Fieldmouse, a Brave Stoat and Mother Rabbit. In January 1972 she toured Japan and in April was in *London Assurance* again at the New Theatre in London. That year her daughter, Tara, known as Finty, was born. She went back to York to the Theatre Royal in April 1973 to appear in *Content to Whisper* and back in London at the Apollo in October was Vilma in *The Wolf*. The production transferred to the Queen's and then to the New London.

At Her Majesty's in July 1974, Judi was again in a musical. She played Miss Trent in *The Good Companions*, a pleasant piece but not raved about. *Plays and Players* said: 'In theory and in fact we could have done with a lot more of Miss Dench . . . with what is assigned her she works miracles.' At the Albery in June 1975 she played Sophie Fullgarney in *The Gay Lord Quex* and then returned to the RSC in October. Judi Dench says she is a company person and explains: 'That's why I love the RSC. The important thing is getting to be a part of a family, being with the others. I hate to be alone for long. A sense of trust sets in and you can afford to make a laughing stock of yourself. It's a family feeling where you can let your defences down.' She played the Nurse in *Too True to be Good* at the Aldwych and transferred with it to the Globe in December. For the 1976 Stratford season Judi Dench played Beatrice in *Much Ado About Nothing* and Lady Macbeth. With the RSC she also played Imogen in *Cymbeline* and Juno in *Juno and the Paycock* — for that performance the Variety Club gave her the best actress award. 'I'm going to miss that [part] more than anything I've ever done,' she said. 'Sometimes when a play ends you think, how nice, I will not have to struggle with that again, but it was different with Juno. I felt particularly involved with it, I think partly because I wasn't keen in the beginning. I went in with a lot of trepidation and timidity about doing the Irish but there was fantastic feeling in that cast.'

Judi Dench does not like making films, feeling inadequate in them. Nevertheless she has made five, and *Four in the Morning* won the Critics Award at Cannes. Television is another matter, and she appears frequently in roles ranging from the classic (Madame Ranevsky in *The Cherry Orchard*) to the novelettish (*Love in a Cold Climate*), to the experimental ('Talking to a Stranger', for which she was named Television Actress of the Year), to the documentary ('On Giant's Shoulders'), to situation comedy ('A Fine Romance') and David Hare's Vietnam play *Saigon*. Speaking of her craft she said: 'I like to push myself beyond the limit every now and again.' She

enjoyed a rare commercial success in the West End with Hugh Whitemore's play about the Kroger spy case, *Pack of Lies* (1983 at the Lyric), of which the long run more or less made up for her disappointment at having to leave *Cats* with a broken ankle shortly before the London premiere. Late in 1984 she began an acclaimed *Mother Courage* at the Barbican for the RSC, having had considerable success at London's other subsidised culture palace, the National, playing a youthful Lady Bracknell in *The Importance of Being Earnest*, and the principal character awakening from a twenty-year period of unconsciousness in Pinter's *A Kind of Alaska*.

See photograph opposite page 103.

MARLENE DIETRICH

Stars don't come much more legendary than Marlene Dietrich. Though it's been more than a decade now since her last stage appearances, though her only film appearance in the 1970s was a brief scene in the generally catastrophic *Just A Gigolo*, though her publicity is ever more infrequent (consisting nowadays of gossip-column references to quarrels with American television sponsors or such memorable *faux pas* as her reply when asked why, in the closing months of the life of her old friend Noel Coward, she had not lunched with him: "Because," she said, "I thought he might not last through the meal"), Dietrich remains a constant source of fascination. Marlene watchers keep a close eye on that curtained flat in the Avenue Montaigne, and on her daughter Maria who one day promises us the definitive biography; the rest of us just wait and remember.

> Though we all might enjoy
> Seeing Helen of Troy
> As a gay cabaret entertainer,
> I doubt that she could
> Be one quarter as good
> As our legendary, lovely Marlene.

Thus wrote Coward, introducing Dietrich to a Café de Paris audience in London during the summer of 1954. Dietrich was then already 52 (suggested birth dates had ranged from 1894 to 1912 until an East German clerk located and somewhat tactlessly published an entry in his Register detailing the birth of one Maria Magdalene Dietrich on 27

December 1901 in the Berlin suburb of Schoneberg) and at the time of her Café season she was already well into a cabaret career which was to take her far away from the pre-war Hollywood in which she had made her first starring reputation.

The Dietrich of the post-war years has been first and foremost a stage figure, arguably the greatest feat of theatrical engineering since the invention of the trap door; and despite the continued existence on celluloid (and late-night television) of *The Blue Angel* and *Blonde Venus* and almost all her pre-war film work, it is in solo cabaret that most of us still think of her first.

The 'Marlene' of the 1930s, a German-American creation of the director Josef von Sternberg and some excellent lighting cameramen, was translated by and during the war into 'Dietrich', an infinitely tougher and lonelier figure who, travelling the world first on troop and then on concert tours, had learnt the greatest of all theatrical lessons: waste nothing. Money, time and herself were all exquisitely preserved against need, and although cold to frosty before the footlights Dietrich passed again and yet again that final test of stardom — the ability not just to do something, but to stand there.

Anyone who could collect, as I saw her do at a matinée one wet London Saturday afternoon in 1972, a standing ovation and enough flowers to run her own branch of Interflora must have had something denied to other mortal entertainers. The question is what, and it is not a question immediately resolved by her first appearance in front of a briskly functional orchestra.

There she would stand, an old and defiant German lady swathed in acres of white fur, coolly receiving her applause . . . sifting and apparently checking it for volume and duration, taking it as a sovereign right with no element of mock surprise or humility in her manner. It was patently not wonderful for her to see us, or to be in our wonderful country again, and mercifully she did not even bother to go through the motions of telling us that it was. Hers must be one of the most icily unsentimental star turns ever offered to a paying audience, and it remains absolutely unforgettable.

If you believe that the theatre is, or ever could be, solely about writers or directors or designers, then Dietrich is not for you; her stage presence was a constant reminder of what could be done by the chemistry of the human spirit alone. Dietrich is a musical Mother Courage, owing nothing to anyone except possibly the operator of a single, dazzling spotlight with which she carried on a perpetual and exclusive stage love affair.

She belongs (with Lenya and Coward and Garland and Piaf, and maybe now Midler and Streisand and Minnelli as well) to that exclusive group of singers who demand to be treated and judged theatrically rather than musically. Like Lenya, Dietrich looks as though she were trained in a school of asexual Teutonic drum majors; like Coward she puts a premium on crisp diction; like Garland she can suddenly find a catch in her voice which is nothing less than heart-breaking; like Piaf she knows precisely how slowly a stage can be traversed; like all of them, she is a loner.

There is a theory that Dietrich has grandchildren and neighbours and a passion for vacuuming the houses of her closer friends; I prefer to think of her as being from some other planet, about as closely related to the human race as Titania or Peter Pan.

Anyone who has listened to her LPs, made across twenty years from the early 1950s, will know that her cabaret repertoire remained largely unchanging ('La Vie en Rose', 'Lili Marlene', 'Laziest Gal in Town', 'Lola', 'Falling in Love Again', with a late-sixties addition of 'Where Have All the Flowers Gone?') but to judge Dietrich by her repertoire is like judging Olivier by his ability to wear false noses. Presence is what she is all about, and it is a formidable one. Having her sing to you was not unlike having the Statue of Liberty sing to you; frozen gestures, an eggshell complexion and the kind of lighting (in latter years the masterwork of Joe Davis) that the Louvre gives the Venus de Milo.

Survival, too, is what Dietrich is all about, and the notion is etched across her features in letters of pure alabaster; for better and for worse she has endured. At her considerable best, in songs of war and despair, there was a terrible strength to her voice — a blinding emotional force suddenly unleashed, used and returned equally abruptly to whatever depth of her soul it first came from. I know of no other voice (save perhaps Churchill's) so instantly recognizable, so immediately evocative of time past or so quintessentially theatrical.

Her film presence is the work of many talented technicians — men like Sternberg and Lee Garmes who recognized in the girl from The Blue Angel a talent they could arrange, light and immortalize in countless soft-focus romances of the 1930s. Her stage presence, however, is entirely of her own making, and I still like to think we have not seen the last of it.

To see her in performance was to see one of the major technical show-business feats of our century, and like all great conjuring tricks Dietrich is largely inexplicable. She is not by any of the usual standards a great singer, nor is she a great actress, nor even a great beauty; what she trades in is star quality. 'That Kraut,' said Hemingway with his customarily elegant turn of phrase, 'is the best that ever came out of the ring.'

Dietrich herself has never been the most loquacious of interviewees ('I was born in Germany,' she once confided to me by way of an autobiography, 'and after I was in a film called The Blue Angel Mr Sternberg took me to America') but her career details, first stage then film then cabaret, are well enough known, as is her courageous stand against the country of her birth and her family when in the early thirties it became Hitler's Germany rather than hers. What is less well understood, perhaps, is the reason for her sustained success; once, backstage on the last of her English tours, I asked her why she thought there were still a hundred or so fans outside the stage door. 'Who knows? They certainly don't come to see me just because I take the trouble to look as good as I can. In Russia once they said it was because I represented something — courage, stamina, faith, motherhood, who knows? Laurence Olivier once asked me, "How can you go out there every night all alone — no Shakespeare, no other actors, nothing?" But it's because I go out there alone that I can be myself, and when they applaud they're applauding maybe what I've done, maybe what I've tried to stand for in my life or maybe what they hope I'm going to deliver. Some nights of course they just sit there in stunned silence, amazed that I'm alive and moving at all.'

To evoke nostalgia and then transcend it has perhaps been Dietrich's greatest achievement, that and a healthy sense of what in the theatre constitutes value for money: 'In real life most film people are a disappointment. I on the other hand am better in real life than in the movies.'

'Look me over closely, tell me what you see': what you see now is a formidable German lady in a remarkable state of repair. But even Dietrich, as she is reluctantly beginning to concede, cannot last forever; as for me, I shall tell my children and then my grandchildren that I saw Dietrich work. They may not care, but I do.

See photograph opposite page 102.

ALFRED DRAKE

*A*lfred Drake was born Alfred Capurro in New York City on 7 October 1914. He went to high school in Brooklyn where he began singing solos in the choir at the Church of Our Lady of Good Counsel. After graduation he attended Brooklyn College and received his Bachelor of Arts degree in 1935. He began to study singing in 1932 and was a member of his college glee club. While still at college he began singing in the chorus of Lodewick Vroom productions of Gilbert and Sullivan at the Adelphi Theater, and then he sang the role of Pan in Bach's *Phoebus and Pan* and that of Rocco in *Fidelio* for the Steel Pier Opera Company in Atlantic City. He understudied the role of Leopold in *White Horse Inn* and played Marshall Blackstone and the High Priest in *Babes in Arms* at the Shubert from April 1937, touring with this production until February 1938. He opened at the Windsor in May 1938 as Albert Porter in *The Two Bouquets* and the following February began in a string of revues: *One for the Money* (in which he did a devastating impersonation of Orson Welles), *The Straw Hat Revue* and *Two for the Show*.

For the next few summers he was in stock playing in *After the Ball, Mr and Mrs North, The Gorilla, Dear Brutus, The Yellow Jacket, Her Master's Voice* and *Little Women.* In the winter he could be found working on Broadway playing Norman Reese in *Out of the Frying Pan* (Windsor, February 1941); Orlando in *As You Like It* (Mansfield, October 1941) and Robert in *Yesterday's Magic* (Guild, April 1942).

In 1940 Alfred Drake married Alma Rowena Tollefsen; the marriage was dissolved in 1944, after which he married Esther Harvey Brown and had two daughters.

In March 1943 Alfred Drake opened at New York's St James Theater playing Curly in *Oklahoma!* (Elliot Norton wrote of the first night: 'The opening of *Oklahoma!* was downright daring in its day. The curtain went up on a mid-western farmyard with old Aunt Eller churning butter. No girls, no legs, no dancing! In a moment a voice was heard offstage. Then on walked Alfred Drake, dressed as the cowboy Curly, singing the first and one of the best of all the Rodgers and Hammerstein hits, "Oh, What a Beautiful Morning" . . . In that scene and song, American musical comedy took a new turn away from stilted nonsense towards something like truth and beauty. And Alfred Drake, because he got all that into his manner, his bearing and his exuberant natural singing voice, became in effect the herald of a new era . . .' With that performance Alfred Drake became a star, but he was of the new generation of actors who couldn't bear playing the same part night after night, no matter how commercially successful. After a year he left the show, explaining to the *New York Herald Tribune*, 'I think after an actor has been in a part for a certain length of time, he's exhausted every possibility for improvement. For the first few months, you keep thinking of changes and additions that will make your performance more attractive or more understandable or provide better insight into the character you're portraying. But after that I believe it gets to be completely mechanical. For the good of the show an actor should step out and let a newcomer in.' For his performance Alfred Drake won the New York Drama Critics Award.

He next opened at the International in December 1944 playing Barnaby Goodchild in *Sing Out, Sweet Land* and spent the next year in Hollywood making *Tars and Spars* for Columbia. At the Broadway Theater in December 1946 he opened as Macheath in *Beggar's Holiday*, Duke Ellington's version of *The Beggar's Opera*. Ellington said of the story, which concerned a white hero falling in love with the daughter of a Negro police chief, it was 'really far-out, but no one seemed to notice'.

Playing in *The Promised Valley* and *Pursuit of Happiness* Alfred Drake toured the summer theatres, and back on Broadway in December 1947 he played Larry Foreman in a revival of *The Cradle Will Rock*. At the Plymouth in March

1948 he played Alexander Sorin in *Joy to the World*. In December of that year at the New Century came his next big hit — *Kiss Me, Kate*. Brooks Atkinson wrote: 'We have all been long acquainted with Mr Drake as headman in musical shows. In the part of the egotistical actor who plays Petruchio on stage, Mr Drake's pleasant style of acting and his unaffected singing are the heart of the show. By hard work and through personal sincerity, Mr Drake has become about the most valuable man in his field.' For this performance he won the Donaldson Award. (He repeated his performance for the Hallmark Hall of Fame on NBC television in 1958).

Alfred Drake took his first steps in writing and directing with *The Liar* at the Broadhurst in May 1950, and then staged a production of *Courtin' Time* at the National in June 1951. His next try at directing, *Salt of the Earth*, closed before it got to Broadway and he went back to summer stock playing Laudisi in *Right You Are If You Think You Are* at the Westport Country Playhouse in Connecticut, and John Tanner in *Man and Superman* at the Playhouse-in-the-Park in Philadelphia. At the Lyceum he opened in October 1952 as David Petri in his own adaptation of *The Gambler*. And in March 1953 he played the King in *The King and I* while Yul Brynner had his vacation.

It was in December 1953 at the Ziegfeld Theater that he opened as Hajj in *Kismet*. Praise was universal. Brooks Atkinson said: ' . . . Alfred Drake gives a superb performance. He sings like a thoroughbred with one of the best male voices in the theater. But Mr Drake is also an immensely resourceful actor who can carry off the set pieces with gusto and provide wit and humor on the side.' Elliot Norton said: 'He romps through it, like a breeze through a desert. Where the plot is heavy, he is light of heart and light of foot. Where the music is heavily and sickly sweet, he is airy and antic . . . he stays with the pattern of the play's innocent nonsense while making it plain enough that he knows it is nonsense. Yet isn't it fun, he seems to say!' And Abe Laufe sums it all up: 'Drake's experience as an actor enabled him to make Hajj a romantic, sly, but likeable rogue and to make an incredible tale seem plausible. He dominated the show as he swaggered through the humorous, dramatic and melodramatic scenes.' For this performance Alfred Drake won the New York Drama Critics Award, the Donaldson Award and the Tony.

He brought the role to London to the Stoll Theatre on 20 April 1955 and managed to dazzle the London critics as well — although everyone seemed surprised that he did not appear as tall off stage as he did on. Ronald Barker reported for *Plays and Players*: 'Alfred Drake is one of the biggest stars to come to London from Broadway. He sings superbly, acts as well as he sings and is able to project his personality to the limits of the gallery.'

In the summer of 1957 he joined the American Shakespeare Festival in Stratford, Connecticut, and appeared as Iago in *Othello* and Benedick in *Much Ado About Nothing* (which he subsequently toured with Katharine Hepburn). Of his Iago, Walter Kerr said: 'Mr Drake's scoundrel was a scoundrel who took deep satisfaction in never being obvious, in never having to do more than let the bad habits of the world work for him. He was playing a game with vices that already existed; he needed only to stir the broth lightly, speak politely the expected words and hell's brew would begin to simmer under its own power. Even in defeat — as he stood hands limp at his sides, head cocked as though still trying to puzzle things out — he was not so much a bad man caught as a keen unscrupulous mind baffled that a cog should have slipped. If Mr Drake could not wholly explain Iago [who has?] he drew plainly and precisely the particular shape of his mind, the intellectual canker that nagged him into motion and then, to his astonishment, destroyed him.'

After playing in *He Who Gets Slapped* at Westport, Connecticut, for the summer of 1958, he spent the next few years involved totally in directing.

Back in musicals, he opened at the Broadway Theater in November 1961, as Edmund Kean in *Kean*, and in 1962 revived *Kismet* at the Curran in San Francisco and the Civic Auditorium in Los Angeles. In February 1963 he played the title role in *Lorenzo* at the Plymouth Theater, which was not a success, and then closed pre-Broadway with *The Prisoner of Zenda*. In 1963 he appeared as Claudius at the Lunt-Fontanne Theater to Richard Burton's Hamlet. John Simon was not impressed: 'Alfred Drake does Claudius in three different styles, all of them wrong. There is drawing-room comedy, musical comedy and melodrama, and sometimes he switches in mid-sentence.' Not really fair, perhaps, because the most interesting thing about the entire production was watching the crowds gather to watch Miss Taylor come to see Mr Burton.

In June of 1965 he revived *Kismet* once more and then toured with it, obviously realizing that whether it gave him pleasure to repeat a part or not, it was exactly what the audiences wanted. In November 1966 he played Soren Brandes in *Those That Play the Clowns* at ANTA and in Florida at the Parker Playhouse in February 1967 he played

Kip Roberts in *The Name of the Game*. He was back at ANTA in September 1967 playing Aristobulo in *Song of the Grasshopper*. At the Goodspeed Opera House in Connecticut in the summer of 1968 he was Mr Hyde in *After You Mr Hyde* and played the lead in *On Time*; the latter he partly wrote, and subsequently toured. He played Honore Lachalles in *Gigi* at the Uris in

November 1973 and at the Shea Center in New Jersey in March 1975 played Paul Sillary in *Gambler's Paradise*. He was Mr Antrobus in *The Skin of Our Teeth* at the Mark Hellinger in September 1975. He is Artistic Director of the National Lyric Arts Theater Foundation and has been President of the Players' Club since 31 March 1970.

RUTH DRAPER

Ruth Draper was an original. Never before and never since has there been anyone like her. She was a solo artist who personally peopled the stage with a variety of characters. Although a no-nonsense spinster who packed a suitcase, as only a maiden aunt can, with little parcels for shoes, another for nightclothes, a place for everything and everything in its place, her histrionic ability moved audiences to tears and standing ovations. Never a temperamental performer, she could arrive at the theatre ten minutes before curtain time, eat a ham sandwich and, brushing the crumbs from her hands, walk onto the stage as a roaring Polish prima donna. John Gielgud describes a performance he witnessed: 'The curtained stage was empty save for a few pieces of essential furniture: a sofa, a couple of chairs and a table. Ruth Draper walked on, a tall, dark-eyed woman in a simple brown dress, beautifully cut, and looked out over the auditorium with grave composure. Her authority and concentration were absolute. How swiftly she transformed that stage into her own extraordinary world, transporting us to other places, other countries — a boudoir, a garden, a church, a customs shed; London, New York, Rome, the coast of Maine — creating in each of those imagined settings a single dominant character and then seeming to surround herself, as and when she needed them, with an attendant crowd of minor figures — children, animals, servants, husbands, lovers. Her wit and imagination could not fail to fascinate and never palled, however often I returned to see her famous monologues.'

Ruth Draper was born in New York in 1884. Her grandfather had been the editor of the New York *Sun* and her father was a doctor. She made her first appearance on the stage at the Maxine Elliott Theater in New York in May 1916 as a Maid in *A Lady's Name*, which starred Marie Tempest. It was Ruth Draper's first and last

appearance in a play. She began to write monologues which at first she only performed privately, but in 1920 she gave her first London performance, at the Aeolian Hall in January, and was enthusiastically received. Her reception in England was, for most of her career, warmer than in her native America and she appeared often in London. In June 1926 she was summoned by Royal Command to perform at Windsor Castle for King George V and Queen Mary. Ruth Draper was the first person to have her name in lights at the Theatre Royal, Haymarket, when she appeared there in 1928 because there was a tradition that only the name of the play could be so displayed. Ruth Draper was the play. Her posters were designed by John Singer Sargent. She toured Australia, New Zealand, Ceylon, India and the Malay States in 1938 and 1939 and in 1940 she toured South America. Noel Coward used her as an example of fine acting when he said: 'Ruth Draper is enthralling and she doesn't go leaping around the stage.' Harold Hobson reviewed her performance at the Criterion in November 1947: 'Miss Draper told a simple enough tale of a shrunk and wrinkled mother who saw a vision of her soldier son covered with wounds that would never heal but bidding her not to grieve. She told it with such heart-rending pauses, with so exquisitely musical a voice, with so fine a distinction between the turbulent and wild sorrow that is a present experience, and the past sorrow that has become permanently built into life's fabric, serene and lovely, that I was entranced, enchanted, most deeply moved...' When she returned to the Criterion in 1952, the young critic Kenneth Tynan was there. He said: 'I want to declare Miss Ruth Draper open to the new generation of playgoers, and to trample on their suspicions, which I once shared, that she might turn out to be a museum piece, ripe for the dust sheets and oblivion. She is, on the contrary, about as old-fashioned and

mummified as spring, and as I watched her perform her thronging monologues the other night I could only conclude this was the best and most modern group acting I had ever seen. It seems, in passing, absurd to use a singular verb in connection with so plural a player. Let me put it that Ruth Draper are now at the height of their career . . . Watching her is like being present at a successful audition for the role of a theatrical immortal.'

Ruth Draper opened on Broadway on Christmas Day in 1956 and was finally awarded the triumphant reviews in her native town that she had been accorded world-wide for many years. She played for a week to full houses and then died peacefully in her sleep on 30 December.

GEORGIE DREW

See The Barrymores

JOHN DREW

See The Barrymores

MRS JOHN DREW

See The Barrymores

JOHN DREW II

See The Barrymores

GERALD DU MAURIER

on't force it, don't be self-conscious. Do what you generally do any day of your life when you come into a room. Bite your nails, yawn, lie down on a sofa and read a book — do anything or nothing, but don't look dramatically at the audience and speak with one eye on the right-hand box.' That was the advice given to actors by Gerald du Maurier, who is acknowledged as having started the naturalistic school of acting. He must have known what he was talking about because in the early part of the century he was associated, as actor or producer or both, with more theatrical hits than anyone else on the British stage.

Gerald du Maurier was born in Hampstead, London, on 26 March 1873, the fifth and youngest child of George du Maurier, the noted *Punch* artist and later the author of *Trilby*, the first popular best-seller, and his wife Emma Wightwick. As the youngest and pet of the family, Gerald could do no wrong and developed into quite a show-off. He first attended Heath Mount, a boys' preparatory school, which was near his home, and when his parents moved to a smaller house in Bayswater he became a weekly boarder. At 14 he went to Harrow where he enjoyed football, swimming, mimicking the masters and Henry Irving, but very little else. There he became very keen on amateur theatricals. His parents hoped that he would find a place in the City, but after a short period in a shipping office he declared that the world of finance was not for him, devoted his time to amateur theatricals and began to make a name for himself in them. He was praised for his performance as William III in *Lady Clancarty* at a charity function. He made his professional stage début on 6 January 1894 in John Hare's company at the Garrick Theatre playing Fritz, a waiter in *An Old Jew*. Although the part was small, because of his famous name he was noticed. A critic reported: 'Mr du Maurier in a very few words showed that he had probably found his vocation and that this was only the earliest of better things to come.' So at 21 he was on his way in his chosen profession, and he found the whole thing startlingly easy — he had no trouble securing work. He stayed six months with Hare, playing small parts, and then toured with Forbes-Robertson in *The Profligate* in which he had to serve and clear a whole dinner during the first act; that he did find difficult, but the part of Algy in *Diplomacy* was a piece of cake. All he had to be was a gentleman.

In September of 1895 Beerbohm Tree produced *Trilby* for the first time. They opened in Manchester and Gerald played the small part of Dodor, the French Dragoon, a character based on his uncle. It was, of course, good publicity for the company to have Gerald playing even a small part in his father's work. It opened at the Haymarket in October and ran for 260 performances. During this time Gerald very much enjoyed being the 'man-about-town' and giving champagne suppers.

In November 1896 Gerald went to America with Tree to tour Washington, New York and Baltimore playing in *The Dancing Girl*, *Hamlet*, *The Seats of the Mighty*, *The Red Lamp*, *Trilby* and *Henry IV*. He was fêted everywhere as George's son, and became engaged to an actress called Marguerite Sylva, which infuriated his family. However, both the tour and the engagement failed.

He returned to Her Majesty's on 28 April 1897 playing Lieutenant Ferney in *The Seats of the Mighty*; Chamillac in *The Silver Key*; Count Bohrenheim in *The Red Lamp*; and Ricordot in *A Man's Shadow*. During this period he fell in love with a visiting American actress, the 19-year-old Ethel Barrymore. The affection seemed to be mutual, but she returned to the United States to continue her career.

Gerald left Her Majesty's and joined Hawtrey at the Avenue to play light comedy in *An Interrupted Honeymoon* and in November joined Mrs Patrick Campbell at the Royalty, where he stayed for two years. He played Percy Burlingham in *The Canary*, Strephonal in *The Fantasticks* ('No one was light enough, quick enough, extravagant enough,' wrote one critic, 'with one exception, Mr Gerald du Maurier. He alone seemed to catch the spirit of the piece . . . he acted with infinite humour and grace.'), Ashurst in *Mr and Mrs Daventry*, Sir Sandford Cleeve in *The Notorious Mrs Ebbsmith* and Captain Hugh Ardale in *The Second Mrs Tanqueray*.

At the Prince of Wales in February 1902 he played the part of the Hon. Archibald Vyse in *The Country Mouse*. The part was not a difficult one, and he spent most of his time at the Green Room Club where, his mother said, he drank too much and stayed up too late.

In November 1902 at the Duke of York's he opened as the Hon. Ernest Woolley in *The Admirable Crichton*. Squire Bancroft had said of the play, 'It deals with the juxtaposition of the drawing-room and the servants' hall — always to me a very painful subject.' Gerald played opposite a young actress called Muriel Beaumont. They were married on 11 April 1903, and subsequently had three daughters — Angela, Daphne and Jean.

Gerald du Maurier was never short of work. After *Crichton* closed he went directly to Wyndham's where, in September 1903, he played Lord Rolfe in *Little Mary*, and at the same theatre in May 1904 he was Albert Jerrold in *Cynthia*. At the Duke of York's in September he played Peter in *Merely Mary Ann*.

It was at Christmas in 1904 that he became the first Captain Hook and Mr Darling in Barrie's *Peter Pan*. His daughter Daphne explains his Hook who was, she says, 'a tragic and rather ghastly creation who knew no peace and whose soul was in torment, a dark shadow; a sinister dream; a bogey of fear who lives perpetually in the grey recesses of every small boy's mind.' Gerald found it exhausting playing two performances a day — each lasting four hours. He said, 'There's only one thing I'd rather not be doing and that's sweeping the floors of a mortuary at a shilling a week.'

He kept busy for the next couple of years playing *Pantaloon* (Duke of York's, April 1905), Arthur Frederick Adolphus Taunton in *On the Love Path* (Haymarket, September 1905), in *Peter Pan* (Christmas at the Duke of York's), and the Hon. Jimmy Keppel in *All-of-a-Sudden-Peggy* (Duke of York's, February 1906).

It was at the Comedy in May 1906 that Gerald du Maurier opened in the play that would make him the biggest star of his generation. He played A. J. Raffles, the gentleman crook, in *Raffles*. It was a new genre for the British and they loved it — they also loved his style, his class. *Raffles* ran for a year. (There was, of course, the break at Christmas to play in *Peter Pan*, and the theatres always shut for holidays in August.) He played much the same character in his next big success, *Brewster's Millions*, which opened at the Hicks Theatre in May 1907. He returned to the Duke of York's in March 1908 to his old part in *The Admirable Crichton* and at the same theatre in September 1908 played John Shand in *What Every Woman Knows*. In August he was the Duc de Charmerace in *Arsène Lupin* and of this performance Max Beerbohm said, 'We may congratulate Mr Gerald du Maurier on a part in which there is excellent scope for his peculiar dexterity and grace of style and for his inventive humour.' At the Comedy in March 1910 he played Lee Randall in *Alias Jimmy Valentine* and then at the Duke of York's he was Mr Hyphen-Brown in *A Slice of Life*.

All these parts were basically variations on Raffles, and the critics began to say that was just du Maurier being du Maurier, but the public adored his performance. John Gielgud describes him: 'Gerald du Maurier used to wear old suits on the stage that were beautifully cut, but had obviously hung in his wardrobe for years. How fascinating he was, to men as well as women, although he was not at all conventionally handsome. He could slouch and lounge and flick his leading lady behind one ear as he played a love scene, never seeming to raise his voice or force an emotion, yet he could be infinitely touching, too, without being in the least sentimental.'

In 1910 he went into management with Frank Curzon at Wyndham's Theatre, and opened there in September as John Frampton in *Nobody's Daughter*. He remained at Wyndham's for the next fifteen years, which were the most successful in his career — he was in top form both financially and professionally. He played Charles Lebrun in *Mrs Jarvis* (February 1911), Peter Waverton in *Passers-By* (March 1911), the Governor of Tilbury Fort in *The Critic* (gala performance at His Majesty's, 27 June 1911), Thomas Peeling in *The Perplexed Husband* (September 1911), Sam Weller

in *Bardell v. Pickwick* (Coliseum, 7 January 1912 in aid of the Daily Telegraph Dickens Fund), Geoffrey Lascelles in *The Dust of Egypt* (February 1912), and Noel in *Doormats* (October 1912). In March 1913 he staged a revival of *Diplomacy* at Wyndham's playing Henry Beauclerc. It also starred Gladys Cooper and Owen Nares. In February 1914 they were commanded to appear in this at Windsor Castle. At Wyndham's in April 1914 he opened as Wilfred Callender in *The Clever Ones*, and at His Majesty's in May that year appeared as Henry Corkett in the all-star revival of *The Silver King* given in aid of the King George Pension Fund. That year Gerald du Maurier assumed the responsibility of being President of the Actors' Orphanage. He next played Geoffrey in *Outcast* (September 1914), Charles Sullivan in *A Quiet Rubber* (Drury Lane, December 1914), *Raffles* (December 1914), Harold Tempest in *Gamblers All* (June 1915), Lord Sands in the all-star revival of *Henry VIII* (His Majesty's, 5 July 1915 in aid of the King George Pension Fund), Sir Hubert Ware in *The Ware Case* (September 1915), Our Policeman and a Prince in *A Kiss for Cinderella* (March 1916), and Mr Bantry in *Shakespeare's Legacy* (Drury Lane, April 1916). He then played at the Palace in *The Popular Novelist* (16 May 1916) and for special performances at the Coliseum and the London Opera House in June played his old part in *The Admirable Crichton*. Back at Wyndham's in September he played James Lane Fountain in *The Old Country*, and in December Cuthbert Tunks in *London Pride*.

He was occupied with a good many war charity performances in 1917 as well as reviving *A Pair of Spectacles* at Wyndham's and playing Dick. In October 1917 he played Mr Dearth in *Dear Brutus*. John Gielgud said his drunken painter was 'a masterpiece of understatement, acted with a mixture of infinite charm and regretful pathos'. In June 1918 he played Another in *A Well Remembered Voice*. Then, at the age of 45, he joined the army as a cadet in the Irish Guards. He was hopelessly unsuited to the army; luckily the war ended a few months later.

He returned to Wyndham's in September 1919 playing John Ingleby Cordways in *The Choice*. The following September he was Captain André Le Briquet in *The Prude's Fall* and in March 1921 played Captain Hugh Drummond in *Bulldog Drummond* which made an enormous amount of money, ran for well over a year and was another peak of his career. In May 1922 he revived *Dear Brutus* and the following December revived *Bulldog Drummond*. In February 1923 he opened as Tony and the Earl of Chievely in *The Dancers*, which he wrote with Viola Tree. It was the last of the great Wyndham's successes. He had been knighted in 1922 and was beginning to worry about being 50. (In that way he was more like Peter Pan than Captain Hook.) He played Felix Menzies in *Not in Our Stars*, in February 1924. The critic Ernest Short said: "As the man with second sight [he] was memorable. The tortured expression on the grey features and the haunted look in the eyes will not be forgotten.' Yet the public did not care for it. In April he was playing Prince Michael in *To Have the Honour*. He then revived *The Ware Case*, first for a charity performance for the King George Pension Fund and then for a run at Wyndham's in winter 1924. In March 1925 he played Wilberforce East in *A Man with a Heart*, by Alfred Sutro. It was a failure. Gerald was now disheartened and rather bored with the theatre but he had to keep working. He had made a lot of money and the Inland Revenue now wanted their share — he had, of course, spent it.

Gerald du Maurier left Wyndham's and joined Gladys Cooper and Gilbert Miller at the St James's Theatre for the Lonsdale play, *The Last of Mrs Cheyney*; du Maurier played Arthur Dilling. It was a great success and ran for over a year. As a play, it was eminently enjoyable and equally forgettable.

He stayed on at the St James's with Gilbert Miller and played the part of John Marley, an eminent surgeon who tries to cover up a murder he believes his wife has committed and finds himself accused, in *Interference*. James Agate reported: 'One might say that Sir Gerald du Maurier's performance gives infinite pleasure. But that would be to speak loosely. His acting last night gave one pleasure of a finite, definite, almost concrete sort. You could pin down and nail to the counter each and every one of its many admirable qualities — vigour, ease, precision, attack, balance. He did what only an actor of extreme accomplishment could have done; he remained ten minutes alone on the stage without speaking. There are other roles

besides the philosopher's in which one can be bounded in a nutshell and count oneself a king of infinite space.'

This was the last of Sir Gerald's plays to run a year. He next played Owen Heriot in *SOS*, Dr Henry Fausting in Arnold Bennett's *The Return Journey*, Sandor Turai in a Hungarian translation called *The Play's the Thing* and Paolo Gheradi in *Fame* — all at the St James's in the space of a year. He terminated his association with Gilbert Miller and went to the Playhouse where he revived *Dear Brutus* for a couple of months before returning to *Peter Pan* for Christmas. But the magic had gone. He then made a film of Galsworthy's *Escape*, but he found filming sheer torture.

He joined Gladys Cooper at the Playhouse in June 1930 playing Jim Warlock in *Cynara* by H. C. Harwood and Gore Browne. He played a married barrister who has an affair with a shop girl who subsequently kills herself. It was not a very sympathetic part, but with Gladys as the wife and Celia Johnson as the girl it enjoyed a respectable run of seven months. He then played a small part in a revival of *The Pelican* and then produced *The Church Mouse* and played Baron Thomas Ullrick, but both had very short runs. In August 1931 he was reduced to touring the provinces for the first time in thirty years — he took a revival of *The Ware Case*.

As well as the Orphanage, he now had Denville Hall and the King George Pension Fund to look after, and he proved better at raising money for his charities than for himself. During the tour he raised over £1000 for them. At Wyndham's in February 1932 he played Larry Deans in Edgar Wallace's *The Green Pack*. Wallace died soon after the opening which plunged the proceedings into gloom. Sir Gerald's last play was *Behold, We Love* by John van Druten, in which he opened with Gertrude Lawrence in August 1932 at the St James's. He died on 11 April 1934.
See photograph opposite page 119.

ELEONORA DUSE

Withdrawn, reticent and deeply melancholic, Eleonora Duse drew extremes of rapture and discontent both from her friends and from her audience. She was the kind of actress who had disciples. It was said she could blush at will. She refused to wear stage make-up, her costumes were simple and her style (for the period) naturalistic. Yet Arthur Symons said that Duse reached 'a supremacy in art so divine in her pure humanity, so mystic in the spiritual sense of the word, and so pathetic in her humility, that it has rarely if ever been equalled and which could never or rarely be surpassed'.

She was born in Italy in the village of Vigevano (and not in a third-class railway car, as is sometimes reported) on 3 October 1859. It is true that her mother arrived in the village only the day before. Her parents were part of the famous Duse acting troupe — the last of the *commedia dell' arte*, and constant travellers. And they were very poor. There was no education for Eleonora, who began acting as a small child. By the time she was 12 she was taking over her mother's roles as her mother was too ill to perform. Eleonora played Juliet at 14. That same year her mother died and her father left the company. For several years Eleonora moved about from one acting company to another, barely supporting herself. Then, under the patronage of Giacinta Pezzana, a leading actress who recognized talent when she saw it, she joined a resident company in Naples. There, however, she met a rich playboy who left her pregnant. Her mentor took Eleonora with her to a better company in Turin, and there she was given small parts until her confinement. Her son died within a week of his birth.

Pezzana left Turin and Duse took over her roles. She married a fellow actor, Teobaldo Checchi, and they had a daughter called Enrichetta.

Sarah Bernhardt, fourteen years older than Duse and already an international star, came to Turin; Duse was very impressed. She decided to do Dumas' plays, as had Bernhardt. She made a great success with *La Princesse de Bagdad*, following that with *La Femme de Claude* and *La Dame aux camélias*. She toured Italy in triumph — police had to be called to prevent riots. She came back to Turin with *Frou-Frou*, another great success.

In 1885 she toured South America, which was an artistic success but a financial disaster. Her husband, however, decided to stay in Argentina, and she began a long affair with the composer Arrigo Boito. He coached her in French and gave her a taste for reading philosophy. He translated *Antony and Cleopatra* for her and she performed it in Milan on 24 November 1888. After the disastrous South American tour she refused to go abroad until 1891, when she toured Austria and Russia playing in *La Dame aux camélias*, *Fedora*, *La Locandiera*, *A Doll's House*, *Odette*, *La Femme de Claude*, *Antony and Cleopatra*, *Magda*, *Françillon* and *Divorçons*.

She made her American début in New York at the Fifth Avenue Theater on 23 January 1893, playing Marguerite Gautier in what the Americans insisted upon calling *Camille*. The *New York Herald* reported that she was 'indubitably one of the subtlest and most interesting actresses of the modern school . . . a phenomenal histrionic psychologist rather than a great actress in the hitherto accepted sense of the word. She depicts with an unerring touch the subtlest and most delicate emotions. Her method is simplicity itself. Never for a moment does she raise her voice, which is colorless and not capable of great variety of expression, above the tone which is ordinarily heard within the walls of a drawing room . . . [she] speaks and gesticulates in the most natural way imaginable . . . not an original style but one that has been refined and gilded to a wondrous nicety . . . she is not capable of sustained dramatic effect. That last touch which distinguishes great talent from positive genius was decidedly wanting.' The response to her on the whole was definitely mixed, and she was also absolutely hopeless at publicizing herself. She refused to give interviews, attend dinners, indeed even show herself, off the stage. And often she cancelled performances when she felt distressed or uncomfortable. She was prone to headaches, a bad chest and a rotten temperament. On the whole, she did not care for America.

Eleonora Duse made her first appearance on the London stage at the Lyric Theatre on 24 May 1893. She performed her usual repertoire but here she found the critics more intelligent and the audiences more appreciative. She toured Europe and was commanded to appear before Queen Victoria in 1894. She played the title role in *La Locandiera*, by Goldoni, as presumably the only thing suitable in her repertoire of fallen women. A. B. Walkley reported in the *Times*: 'No doubt it is as a great tragic actress that Signora Duse will pass into history. Hers is the tragic mask, with its knitted brow and its mouth drawn down at the corner . . . Yet those of us who have seen her as the Miandolina of Goldoni will always put that memory of her before everything else; we shall say that, tragic actress though she may be by temperament and choice, it is in her one brief moment of comedy that she casts over us her most potent spell. For my own part, I count it a unique thing. Night after night, year after year I have gone to theatre after theatre, and, though I have not found all barren, yet on the whole I should be inclined to sigh over a misspent life if it were not for the thought of Duse in *La Locandiera*. For the sake of that one supreme pleasure I might be tempted to go through it all again.'

She returned to America in 1896 for another tour, this time an undisputed star, and was received as one by critics and audiences. The New York *Dramatic Mirror* said: 'In *Magda*, she excites one intellectually and emotionally. This is the hardest and the highest thing for an actor to accomplish — to make one think and feel intensely at the same moment, to keep the brain and the heart of the spectator straining to fever pitch . . . She makes one tingle with excitement . . . she touches the summits of realism.' It was also in 1896 that she began a passionate romance with the Italian poet Gabriele D'Annunzio. They fought their way across Europe for ten years, sometimes being faithful, sometimes not, involving everyone they met in their passion. He went so far as to make notes on their most intimate moments and incorporate them in a novel about her. But the worst thing he did to her was write plays for her — florid, overbearing, overwritten, overplotted, over-the-top melodramas which she loved.

Of her Hedda Gabler Max Beerbohm said: ' . . . in this as in every other part that she plays [she] behaved like a guardian angel half-asleep at her post over humanity. Her air of listlessness in this instance happened to be apt; but otherwise showed not a shadow of comprehension on her part.' But then Max was not a disciple. 'Am I over-whelmed by the personality of Duse? Of course I ought to be — there can be no question of that. But the wretched fact remains that I am not. True I see power and nobility in her face: and the little shrill soft voice, which is in such strange contrast with it, has a certain charm for me. I admire, too, her movements, full of grace and strength. But my prevailing emotion is hostile to her. I cannot surrender myself and see in her the "incarnate womanhood" and the "very spirit of the world's tears" and all those other things which other critics see in her. My prevailing impression is that

of a great egoistic force; of a woman overriding with an air of sombre unconcern, plays, mimes, critics, and public . . . ' Her romance with D'Annunzio ended — or rather, he left her. She came to England in 1906. John Gielgud saw her playing in *Ghosts* at the New Oxford Theatre. He said she 'looked infinitely sad and distinguished with her white hair, and wearing a plain black dress with a shawl draped over her shoulders . . . her acting seemed very, very simple. She had marvellous hands and all her movements were weary and poetic'.

Eleonora Duse retired from the stage for fifteen years. She had grown disillusioned with it, and indeed with life, and lived as a recluse — though a demanding recluse — in Asola, Italy. From her friends she asked for attention, care and concern and she gave little of herself. Lack of money forced her to resume her career in 1921. She returned to the Teatro Balbo in Turin in May, appearing in *The Lady from the Sea*. She toured again. St John Ervine said, 'She has the power which no other actress known to me possesses, of transmitting physical qualities to her very clothes; when she drops her shawl from her shoulders at the end of the second act after a period of trouble, it seems to be as weary as she is, to have gathered weariness into its folds, so that it drops almost to the ground in sheer fatigue.' And Alexander Woollcott in New York: ' . . . it was a performance by a non-descript company with forlorn scenery — a performance in Italian of a Norwegian romance that was no great shakes when it was new in its own land . . . [yet Duse's] performance of Ellida Wangel was among the few truly and exhilaratingly beautiful things which we have seen in our time . . . [this critic] left the Metropolitan with the feeling that he had never seen any human being of such luminous and transcendent beauty . . . when she moves across the stage it is as though the loveliest sculpture you had ever seen were come magically to life before your eyes . . . '

Eleonora Duse went on a massive coast-to-coast tour of America, and in Pittsburgh caught pneumonia. She died there on 21 April 1924. And then ensued the farce. Mussolini, whom she detested, declared her a national hero and arranged, after a funeral mass in New York, for the body to be shipped back to Italy for a state funeral in Rome amid a national day of mourning. Mussolini got a lot of publicity from Eleonora Duse, who loathed both.

JEANNE EAGELS

Jeanne Eagels' story is the kind upon which Hollywood melodrama existed. She was born in Kansas City, Missouri, on 26 June 1890 and it was there that she was bitten by the theatre bug when she played Puck in *A Midsummer Night's Dream* at the age of seven. As soon as she could, she travelled to New York to become a star but found herself working instead in a casting office as a clerk. She was extremely beautiful but turned down offers from Florenz Ziegfeld to join the Follies because she was determined to be a serious actress. It took her years of small parts to achieve her aim. She first appeared at the New York Theater on 6 March 1911 as Miss Renault in *Jumping Jupiter* and in September 1912 she played Olga Cook at the Lyceum, New York, in *The Mind-the-Paint-Girl*. Jeanne spent the next two years on the road in *The Crinoline Girl* and *Outcast*. Then in March 1916 she played Kate Merryweather in *The Great Pursuit*. She toured with George Arliss as Lady Clarissa in *Disraeli*. In February 1917 she was Lucy White in *The Professor's Love Story* at the Knickerbocker Theater and in September of that year Mrs Reynolds in *Hamilton*.

It was in September 1918 at the Belasco Theater when she played Ruth Atkins in *Daddies* that the critics first called her promising. The parts began to get better. In October 1919 she was Mary Darling Furlong in *A Young Man's Fancy* at the Playhouse, New York, and in February 1920 at the same theatre she played Jacqueline Laurentine in *The Wonderful Thing*. In January 1921 at the Century Theater, Jeanne Eagels was Eugenie de Corlaix in *In the Night Watch*.

Finally, in November 1922 at the Maxine Elliott Theater her promise was fulfilled when she opened as Sadie Thompson in *Rain*. John Corbin in the *New York Times* reported: 'Miss Eagels ...rises to the requirements of this difficult role with fine loyalty to the reality of the character and with an emotional power as fiery and unbridled in effect as it is artistically restrained...The house...fairly rose to Miss Eagels and acclaimed her.' Stark Young in *New Republic* said: 'Miss

Eagels has pathos and a wit of her own, and an oddly likeable and wistful effect of naturalness. And she has from the moment she comes on the stage the gift of being entertaining, which is at the bottom of all good acting everywhere. You like to have her on the stage no matter what she does.' *Rain* ran for two years in New York and then Jeanne Eagels toured with it. In 1925 she made a disastrous marriage with Edward Harris Coy which was dissolved in 1928.

Jeanne Eagels kept *Rain* going for five years before she found another part that suited her: the role of Simone in *Her Cardboard Lover*, which she opened at the Empire in March 1927. By this time she had begun drinking to excess; still her artistry was evident. The *Boston Transcript* reported: 'It was a visibly nervous Miss Eagels, all fidget and misgiving, who entered shakily upon the scene. There was the squeak of new, self-conscious shoes about her.'

Miss Eagels also toured *Her Cardboard Lover* but began to miss performances and was suspended from stage work for eighteen months by Actors' Equity. She went to Hollywood to work in movies but her problems continued, and by the time her suspension was lifted she had taken an overdose of sleeping pills — she died in New York on 3 October 1929.

Her director in *Rain*, John D. Williams, wrote her obituary in the *New York Times* in which he said: '...In my score of years in the theater Miss Eagels was one of the two or three highest types of interpretative acting intelligences I have met...[she is] another tragic example of one who, with all she had yet to give to the theater, not of mere representation but of high interpretation, actually extinguished a great gift through an idealistic but unmeasured struggle for the summit of her art. That was the apex, that was the strain and stress, that was the zone of her heart and mind. That, too, was the scene of her triumphs and troubles. Anything or anybody impeding her way, even one of her own failures, was an obstacle to be fought as if by a crusader.'

MAXINE ELLIOTT

Jessie C. Dermot was born in Rockland, Maine, on 5 February 1868 and educated by the Sisters of Notre Dame in Massachusetts. At the age of 16 she married George MacDermott but the marriage did not last. She needed to support herself and being extraordinarily beautiful she went to New York, where at that time beautiful women had no difficulty finding a place on the stage. Now called Maxine Elliott, which had a nicer ring to it than her original name, she made her début at Palmer's Theater on 10 November 1890 playing Felicia Umfraville in *The Middleman*. At that theatre she also played in *John Needham's Double*, *Old Soldiers*, *A Fool's Paradise*, *Judah* and *The Professor's Love Story*. In 1893 she appeared at the American Theater in *The Prodigal Daughter*, *The Voyage of Suzette* and *Sister Mary*. The following year she joined Rose Coughlan's company, where she played in *To Nemesis*, *London Assurance*, *Diplomacy*, *A Woman of No Importance* and *Forget-Me-Not*. She was taken on by the impresario Augustine Daly in 1895 and was seen at his New York Theater in *The Heart of Ruby*, *The Orient Express*, *The Two Gentlemen of Verona*, *Nancy & Co*, *The Honeymoon*, *A Midsummer Night's Dream*, *The Transit of Leo* and *The Two Escutcheons*. Maxine Elliott made her London stage début at Daly's Theatre on 2 July 1895 as Sylvia in *The Two Gentlemen of Verona*, and that same month played Hermia in *A Midsummer Night's Dream*.

By this time Maxine Elliott was acknowledged as the most sensationally beautiful woman on Broadway. She left Daly's company in 1896 (the year she was divorced from George) and went to the Fifth Avenue Theater where in April she opened as Eleanor Cuthbert in *A House of Cards*. She then went on a tour of Australia with the actor Nat Goodwin, whom she married in 1898. Brooks Atkinson said that Mr Goodwin was such a connoisseur of beautiful women that he married several of them. The Goodwins lived at 326 West End Avenue, which was so far from the theatre district that Maxine Elliott drove herself up and down Fifth Avenue to work, stopping the traffic as everyone craned to get a look at her. She worked exclusively with her husband for a number of years, playing mainly small parts to his leading ones. She was Margaret Ruthven in *A Gilded Fool*, and Kate Vernon in *In Mizzoura*. Of her performance as Alice Adams in *Nathan Hale*, the critic Lewis C. Strong said: '. . . Maxine Elliott first

made it plain that she could act as well as pose with pictorial effectiveness. Nor did she act with violent theatricalism, impressively performing a cut and dried histrionic "stunt", but she acted as the great ones act, from within outward, with sincerity, with truth, with the positive possession of artistic feeling and personal conviction.'

In 1899 she and Nat took their company to London, where she played Mrs Weston in *The Cowboy and the Lady* at the Duke of York's in June. Of this performance Max Beerbohm said: 'Miss Maxine Elliott showed such intelligence and skill as would have won her a leading-ladyship even had she been but ordinarily beautiful.' And of their second offering he said: 'Mr Nat Goodwin and Miss Maxine Elliott are such admirable comedians, so quick, sure and sympathetic that no one need grudge a second visit, still less a first.'

Back in New York at the Knickerbocker Theater in February 1900 she played Phyllis Ericson in *When We Were Twenty-one*. In May 1901 she played Portia in *The Merchant of Venice*. Henry Austin Clapp reported: 'The actress's radiant beauty is effective at almost every point, her mirth is charming and contagious, her love-making is full of tenderness. But she misses many fine points in the text.' So she abandoned Shakespeare and returned to London in September to play *When We Were Twenty-one* at the Comedy. She toured the United States in 1902 as Sally Sartoris in *The Altar of Friendship*.

In 1903 Maxine Elliott was publicized for the first time as 'star' of the show when she opened as Georgiana Carley in *Her Own Way* under the management of Charles B. Dillingham. Brooks Atkinson explains that 'Clyde Fitch had a special talent for writing female characters that female stars could act agreeably'. Fitch wrote *Her Own Way* for Maxine Elliott and indeed she looked a great actress, although one critic insisted upon harking back to her beauty and called her 'the Venus de Milo with arms'. By this time she was tired of being called a great beauty and pleased to be called an actress. She told *Theater Magazine* (significantly the interview was being conducted as she drove the interviewer down Fifth Avenue): 'Beauty is only a fifth wheel. It is of no help to a woman at the beginning of her career. On the contrary, it is a positive hindrance to be a so-called stage beauty. It challenges attention and one's poor beginnings as an artist stand out more glaringly because of the prominence one would so gladly escape during those first two or three years.' She played *Her Own Way* for a couple of years at the Garrick in New York and then in 1905 played at the Lyric in London. She was again at the Lyric in 1907 when she was Mary Hamilton in *Under the Greenwood Tree*.

In Philadelphia in September 1908 she opened as Bettina in *Myself, Bettina* and played the same role in New York in October. In November she was in Boston playing *The Chaperon* and on 30 December 1908 she appeared in that play at the opening of the Maxine Elliott Theater on 39th Street in New York. Few living actresses have had a theatre named after them and this one, a gem of comfort and elegant décor, was the most costly theatre of its time. It was reputedly financed by J. P. Morgan. That same year Maxine Elliott was divorced from Nat Goodwin. She never remarried.

Returning to England in April 1909 she appeared at the Lyric as the Duchesse de Langeais in *The Conquest* and that same year toured the

United States in *The Chaperon* and as Yuki in *Sayonara*. She was in Boston in December 1909 playing Deborah in *Deborah of Tod's* and at Daly's in New York in January 1910 playing Eve Addison in *The Inferior Sex*. She toured that play in 1911. At His Majesty's in London in September 1913 she played Zuleika in *Joseph and His Brethren*.

In 1916 she made a few films, notably *The Eternal Magdalen* and *Fighting Odds*, which captured her beauty for posterity. She was back on stage, to the Broadhurst in New York, in December 1917 playing Lady Algernon Chetland in *Lord and Lady Algy* and she toured it in 1919.

Maxine Elliott opened in February 1920 for the last time in the theatre named for her, playing Cordelia in *Trimmed in Scarlet*. Then at the age of 52 (though she only admitted to 49), she retired from the stage. She died twenty years later in Cannes on 5 March 1940.

EDITH EVANS

'You must control the audience,' Edith Evans said. 'Never give them too much opportunity for applause and laughter and tears. Don't indulge yourself by showing off; the moment that you begin to find that you can do something well, you must control it and do it more selectively. In a farce you must play as if you had a practical joke inside you but you're not going to let anybody know you think it's funny.'

Edith Mary Evans was born in London on 8 February 1888. Her father was a civil servant and there was a brother, but he died in childhood. She went to St Michael's School in Chester Square. She was happy and naturally imitative, but as a child had no contact with the stage, nor did she have any ambitions towards the theatre. At 15 she was apprenticed to a milliner and very much enjoyed her work, delighting in the fabrics and colours with which she worked. In the evenings, rather for the fun of it, she went to a dramatic class run by Miss Massey in Victoria Street. Miss Massey founded the Streatham Shakespeare Players, an amateur group; in October 1910 Edith Evans played Viola in *Twelfth Night* for her, and in April 1912 she was Beatrice in *Much Ado About Nothing*. That performance was seen by the producer William Poel, and he hired her to play Gautami in Kalidasa's *Sakuntala* which he directed at the

Cambridge University Examination Hall that August. In December he engaged her to replace Hermione Gingold as Cressida in *Troilus and Cressida* for the Elizabethan Stage Society at King's Hall, Covent Garden. After that, Miss Evans said, she found it very difficult to go back to her hats — and against all advice she turned professional. In May 1913 she again played Cressida for Poel, this time at the Shakepeare Memorial Theatre at Stratford. In June she played the Maid in George Moore's *Elizabeth Cooper* at the Haymarket Theatre. Moore had wanted her to play the leading part, so impressed was he by her acting, but he was dissuaded because she was an unknown. Despite the dire warnings, Edith Evans had no trouble finding employment. She was Knowledge in *Everyman* for William Poel at Crosby Hall in Chelsea in July 1913, and the next year in January was the Queen in Poel's production of *Hamlet* at the Little Theatre. In February, also at the Little Theatre, she played Isota in *The Ladies' Comedy*.

In 1914 Edith Evans was taken on by the management of Vedrenne and Eadie to play a variety of small parts and to understudy at the Royalty Theatre in Dean Street, Soho. The engagement was to give her a whole range of characters of all shapes and sizes. She played Mrs Taylor in *Acid Drops*, Moeder Kaatje and Miss Sylvia in *My*

Edith Evans and Cedric Hardwicke in George Bernard Shaw's
comedy *The Apple Cart* at the Queen's Theatre
(London, August 1929)

Gerald du Maurier was the barrister Jim Warlock and Celia Johnson
played the shop girl in the drama *Cynara* at the Playhouse Theatre
(London, August 1930)

Lady's Dress and Mrs Read in *Milestones*.

Edith Evans appeared in her first film in 1915. It was made at Walton-on-Thames Studios and was called *A Welsh Singer*. In February 1916 she was Lady Frances Ponsonby in *The Conference* for the Pioneer Players at the Royal Court Theatre, then back at the Royalty played Miss Myrtle in a revival of *The Man Who Stayed at Home*. That year she also filmed *East is East*.

In November 1917 Edith Evans worked with Ellen Terry at the London Coliseum playing Mistress Ford in scenes from *The Merry Wives of Windsor*, and the following February was with her playing Nerissa in the Trial Scene from *The Merchant of Venice*. Then she played the Nurse in *The Dead City* at the Royal Court Theatre for the Stage Society. She toured the variety theatres with Ellen Terry in May 1918 and in July was the Witch of the Alps and Destiny in Lord Byron's *Manfred* at Drury Lane for the Stage Society.

Edith Evans was never out of work. During the next few years she played Ann Rutherford in *Rutherford and Son*, Nina in *The Player Queen* (May 1919, Covent Garden), Sir Randell in *The Return from Parnassus* (June 1919, Apothecaries Hall), Nerissa in *The Merchant of Venice* (October 1919, Royal Court), the Wife and Salvation Officer in *From Morn to Midnight* (March 1920, Lyric, Hammersmith), Captain Dumain in *All's Well That Ends Well* (May 1920, Ethical Church, Bayswater), Moeder Kaatje and Lady Appleby in *My Lady's Dress* (June 1920, Royalty), Mrs Hunter in *Wedding Bells* (August 1920, Playhouse), Aquilina in *Venice Preserv'd* (November 1920, Lyric, Hammersmith), Madame Girard in *Daniel* (January 1921, St James's), Mrs Van Zile in *Polly with a Past* (March 1921, St James's), Ann Ratcliffe in *The Witch of Edmonton* (April 1921, Lyric, Hammersmith), Mrs Chester in *Mother Eve* (April 1921, Ambassadors'), Mrs Barraclough in *Out to Win* (June 1921, Shaftesbury), Lady Utterword in the first production of *Heartbreak House* (October 1921, Royal Court), Mrs Faraker in *The Wheel* (February 1922, Apollo), and Cleopatra in *All for Love* (March 1922, Phoenix Society).

By this time she was the darling of the critics, but the public still did not seem aware of her presence. This was partly because as a character actress she remade herself for each appearance. There was no 'Edith Evans', only the characters she played. In September 1922 she played the maid who changes places with her impoverished mistress in Roland Pertwee's *I Serve* at the Kingsway Theatre. James Agate, writing in the *Saturday Review*, said: 'Her Kate is the most finished piece of acting on the London stage today, perfect both

spiritually and in externals, whether as the ultra-ladylike maid or the slightly vulgar chatelaine. It is the portrait of a great artist who possesses the gift of observation, a fine sense of comedy and the pathos of Mrs Kendal.' The play was, however, soon off, and in November Edith Evans was playing Cynthia Dell in *The Laughing Lady* at the Globe. In December she was again at the Globe playing Ruby in *The Rumour* for the Stage Society. For one performance only at the Prince of Wales Theatre in February 1923 Edith Evans played in *Taffy*. In October 1923 she was at the Birmingham Repertory Theatre playing various parts in Shaw's *Back to Methuselah*. She played Mistress Page in *The Merry Wives of Windsor* at the Lyric, Hammersmith, in December 1923.

It was in February 1924 that Edith Evans had a real triumph as Mrs Millamant in *The Way of the World*. W. A. Darlington reported: '. . . she gave the passionate few one of the most memorable evenings of their lives as Millamant in Congreve's *The Way of the World* . . . she became, not a heartless coquette, but a woman of lively but carefully concealed intelligence playing a game for her own amusement and that of anybody quick enough to appreciate it. You could tell by the lilt of her voice how much she delighted in her own affectations . . .' James Agate said she was 'impertinent without being pert, graceless without being ill-graced'.

In March at the Strand Theatre she was Daisy in Elmer Rice's *The Adding Machine* and in June at the Savoy was Suzanne in *Tiger Cats*. Ernest Short said that her 'voice, features and movements all suggested the predatory wild beast'. Edith Evans played Mrs George Collins in *Getting Married* by Bernard Shaw at the Everyman Theatre, Hampstead, in July and in September was at special matinée revivals of Parts One and Five of his *Back to Methuselah* at the Royal Court Theatre. In December she was Helena in *A Midsummer Night's Dream* at Drury Lane, and for the first time the critics were not totally enthusiastic — but quick to point out that it was not her fault. Herbert Farjeon thought that she had tried to read too much into the part and had discovered too late that nothing was there. Agate, however, still thought it 'a richly comic performance'. In March 1925 Edith Evans was at the Everyman Theatre in Hampstead playing Ann in *The Painted Swan* and in May at the Scala was Evadne in *The Maid's Tragedy*.

Edith Evans was finally taken into the Old Vic Company for their 1926 season. She had approached Lilian Baylis before about joining them, as she was anxious to learn to play Shakespeare, but she had been rejected as too ugly. After her performance as Millamant, however, Miss Baylis reconsidered. During her first season there Edith Evans played Portia in *The Merchant of Venice*, Queen Margaret in *Richard III* (of which performance Farjeon said: 'As she advances on Richard, you could swear that she holds a thunderbolt in her upraised cursing arm'), Katharina in *The Taming of the Shrew*, which pleased both the critics and the public, Mariana in *Measure for Measure*, Cleopatra in *Antony and Cleopatra* (in which part she for once did not please Agate, who said: 'She has not enough passion and vulgarity for Cleopatra, or you may say that she has too much fastidiousness'), the Angel in *The Child in Flanders* by Cecily Hamilton, Mistress Page in *The Merry Wives of Windsor*, Kate Hardcastle in Goldsmith's *She Stoops to Conquer*, Portia in *Julius Caesar*, Rosalind in *As You Like It*, Dame Margery Eyre in *The Shoemaker's Holiday*, the Nurse in *Romeo and Juliet*, and Beatrice in *Much Ado About Nothing*. Of that first Old Vic season, Edith Evans said: 'From the moment I entered until we finished the season I never missed a performance, lost seventeen pounds in weight and on the only free day we were given from rehearsal, ran off and got married; so it was altogether a momentous season for me.' The wedding that took place on 9 September 1925 was not as spontaneous as it sounds. Edith Evans had known George (Guy) Booth since she was a milliner's apprentice. They had been sweethearts for years and then became lovers. He survived the First World War, and when he came back was amazed to find what a dedicated actress she had become — but he doted on her. He went abroad, working in the oilfields in South America, and on his return they married, though he was soon abroad again. They kept the marriage very quiet — most of her fellow actors did not even know that Edith was Mrs Booth.

In June 1926, her stint at the Old Vic óver, Edith Evans was Maude Fulton in Maugham's *Caroline* at the Playhouse and in September Rebecca West in *Rosmersholm* at the Kingsway Theatre. She played Katharina in a scene from *The Taming of the Shrew* at a Drury Lane matinée in aid of the Shakespeare Memorial Theatre at Stratford.

In January 1927 Edith Evans played Mrs Sullen in *The Beaux' Stratagem* at the Lyric, Hammersmith, and that September was tempted into her own management with Leon M. Lion. They presented *The Lady in Law* at Wyndham's Theatre with Edith playing Maître Bolbec, but the play was simply not good enough and was soon taken off. In November she played Mrs Millamant once more, and it was again a great success. By March 1928

she had given up management and was at the Royal Court Theatre playing the Serpent, the She-Ancient and the Ghost of the Serpent in Shaw's *Back to Methuselah*. In July she was at the Arts playing Miriam Rooth in *The Tragic Muse* and in September was Josephine in *Napoleon's Josephine* at the Fortune. The following January she was Florence Nightingale in *The Lady with a Lamp*, which opened at the Arts Theatre and then transferred to the Garrick. In August she was Orinthia in the first English production of Shaw's *The Apple Cart* at the Malvern Festival, and also at the festival played Lady Utterword in *Heartbreak House* once more. She was in *The Apple Cart* when it was produced at the Queen's Theatre in September. Her next two roles were at the Arts Theatre: she played Constance Harker in *Wills and Ways* (December 1929) and Diana in *The Humours of the Court* (January 1930). Guy had come home in 1927 and together they bought a farm in Kent which he looked after. Edith continued to live in London at the Albany in Piccadilly, joining him only occasionally. In June 1930 she revived the part of Mrs Sullen in *The Beaux' Stratagem* at the Royalty and gave a special performance of *Plus ça change* in aid of the Oxford Preservation Trust.

In September 1930 she was once more lured back into management, presenting *Delilah*, in which she played the title role at the Prince of Wales. It lasted three nights and one matinée. In March 1931 she was playing Mrs Carruthers in *O.H.M.S.* at the Arts and then at the New Theatre, and in May at the Royalty she revived *Tiger Cats*. In September she played Laetitia in Congreve's *The Old Bachelor* at the Lyric, Hammersmith, and in November appeared for the first time on the New York stage at the Maxine Elliott Theater playing Florence Nightingale in *The Lady with a Lamp*. America was polite but not overwhelmed. In February 1932, for the second time, she played the Nurse in *Romeo and Juliet* — this time at the New Theatre, Oxford, in John Gielgud's production. In March she returned to the Old Vic and played Emilia in *Othello* and Viola in *Twelfth Night*. The following month she revived Lady Utterword in *Heartbreak House* at the Queen's Theatre.

In January 1933 Edith Evans had her first real commercial success playing Irela in *Evensong*. The character was based on Melba. She took the play to New York's Selwyn Theater in January 1933 but did not repeat the success it had had in London.

She returned from Amercia, and still clutching an American accent took over the role of May in Kaufman and Hart's *Once in a Lifetime* at the Queen's Theatre. The next month she played

Gwenny in Emlyn Williams' adaptation of *The Late Christopher Bean*. This time she had a Welsh accent.

In May 1934 Edith Evans played the Duchess of Marlborough in *Viceroy Sarah* at the Arts Theatre, and in December she was back in New York, at the Martin Beck Theater playing once more the Nurse in *Romeo and Juliet*. This time she was with Katharine Cornell's company. John Mason Brown wrote: 'Miss Evans' Nurse is in itself a lesson in acting. It dodges all the tiresome low-comedy tricks lesser players bring to the part. It has the completeness of a full-length portrait and is spoken with great skill. It is the highly distinguished performance of a highly distinguished performer.' And Brooks Atkinson wrote in the *New York Times*: '[Edith Evans] played a guileful, temperamental, bawdy Nurse that was as fresh as if the part had never been acted before.' While she was in New York her husband died of a brain tumour; she immediately sailed for home, but missed the funeral.

It was in April 1935 that Edith Evans played Agatha Payne in *The Old Ladies* at the New Theatre. Charles Morgan reported: 'Miss Evans' performance . . . is creative and cumulative — a slow nightmare of macabre genius. The body, the eyes, the hands are terrible enough, but the mouth wears the very shape and colour of the mind's disease. The whole figure, in its stained and mountainous velvets, is like some insane doll that increases continuously in physical stature and spiritual decay.' It was a performance that truly curdled the blood, and *The Old Ladies* achieved a moderate run. In October she was once more the Nurse in John Gielgud and Laurence Olivier's *Romeo and Juliet*, at the New Theatre. Still at the New Theatre, in May 1936 Edith Evans played Irina Arcadina in *The Seagull*. Audrey Williamson said that her performance 'brought the character to flamboyant life; the complete actress in temperament and tantrum, in selfishness and parsimony, she still managed to suggest that intoxicating warmth and ardour of passion that chained Trigorin and Konstantin to her, even though they realized the desperation behind her sense of waning power.'

From October to December Edith Evans was once more with the Old Vic Company in a variety of roles. She played Lady Fidget in Wycherley's *The Country Wife* and Mother Sawyer in *The Witch of Edmonton* as well as Rosalind in *As You Like It*, which she revived in February 1937 at the New Theatre. Of her Rosalind, Audrey Williamson said she 'has set a standard for our time. For me . . . it remains the loveliest performance by a woman in approaching twenty years of playgoing

. . . as Rosalind she had a radiance that seemed to proceed from beauty, youth and all the bewitching graces of femininity: she was young love incarnate.' And moreover Edith Evans was in love — with her leading man, Michael Redgrave. In March at the New she played Katharina in *The Taming of the Shrew* and then at the Globe Theatre began an eighteen-month run of *Robert's Wife*, in which she co-starred with Owen Nares. In August 1939 at the Globe she played Lady Bracknell for the first time in *The Importance of Being Earnest*. It was a part she would revive and record on film — and it grew to haunt her. No one could resist trying to imitate her sliding, lilting voice when she expressed shock and amazement at the circumstances of being found in a handbag. She, the most versatile of actresses, did not care for being identified with one performance, no matter how lovingly.

In March 1940 Edith Evans played Muriel Meilhac in *Cousin Muriel* at the Globe. In August of that year she embarked on a provincial tour with *The Millionairess*. It was planned to bring it into the Globe in September, but this was abandoned because of the bombing in London.

Edith Evans appeared in revue for the first time in October 1940 when she created the role of the Hop-picker at Wyndham's in Herbert Farjeon's *Diversion*. And she continued in *Diversion No. 2* in January. In December she was back in the straight theatre playing Katharine Markham in John Van Druten's *Old Acquaintance* at the Apollo. She revived Lady Bracknell at the Phoenix in October 1942 and then in December appeared in revue for the forces in Gibraltar. In March 1943 she returned to Shaw's *Heartbreak House*, playing Hesione Hushabye at the Cambridge Theatre, and then toured the play for ENSA both in Britain and abroad. She returned in 1944 to join Murray Macdonald at the Garrison Theatre in Salisbury, where she entertained the troops with a number of plays. The following year she took a production of *The Late Christopher Bean* to the forces in India, and returning to the Criterion Theatre in September she played Mrs Malaprop in *The Rivals*. At the New Theatre in June 1946 Edith Evans played Katerina Ivanovna in Rodney Ackland's adaptation of *Crime and Punishment*. Then in December, well into her fifties, Edith Evans made a mistake by playing Cleopatra to Godfrey Tearle's Antony in Shakespeare's play. The part had not suited her even when she was younger, and Kenneth Tynan reported uncharitably: 'Edith Evans gave us a Cleopatra who was really Lady Bracknell cruelly starved of cucumber sandwiches.' In 1948 she made two films — *The Queen of Spades* and *The Last Days of Dolwyn*. In October of that year she rejoined the Old Vic Company and played Lady Wishfort in *The Way of the World*. T. C. Worsley said: 'Hers is a dazzling performance which alone makes it worth while to sit through the attendant horrors at the New Theatre.' And of her next offering, as Madame Ranevsky in *The Cherry Orchard*, he said: 'More than any other Madame Ranevsky I have seen does she bring with her the whole past of this feckless, emotionally self-indulgent and warm creature.'

At Wyndham's Theatre in March 1949 she played Lady Pitts in James Bridie's controversial *Daphne Laureola*. T. C. Worsley said that here she was seen 'displaying a mastery of her medium, an assurance and a variety that are unmatched on the stage today'. And Harold Hobson was ecstatic: 'Bridie is sustained by Dame [she had been elevated in 1946 for services to ENSA] Edith's shattering performance, upon which, for brilliance, I believe the very constellations will look down with jealousy. Every smile is like the rising of the sun, and every syllable she speaks, a song.' In 1950, when she took *Daphne* to the Music Box in New York, Edith Evans got her usual reception — liked her, hated the play — so she was back in England in time to speak the Prologue before *Twelfth Night* at the reopening of the bombed out Old Vic Theatre.

In April 1951 she played Helen Lancaster in *Waters of the Moon* with Sybil Thorndike at the the Theatre Royal, Haymarket, where they stayed for more than two years, during which time she committed her Lady Bracknell to celluloid. In April 1954 she was directed by Peter Brook in *The Dark is Light Enough* at the Aldwych Theatre. Her next part was to be in André Roussin's farce *Nina*, but before the play opened in Liverpool she had a nervous breakdown. By the autumn she had recovered enough to do television work and on the opening night of commercial television she appeared in scenes from *The Importance of Being Earnest*. On 12 November she played Mrs Smith on television in Wynyard Browne's *A Question of Fact*, and the following January repeated *The Old Ladies* for television.

Edith Evans returned to the stage in March 1956 playing Mrs St Maugham in *The Chalk Garden* at the Alexandra Theatre in Birmingham, and opened in London at the Haymarket in April.

With the Old Vic in 1958 she played Katharine

of Aragon in *Henry VIII*. Kenneth Tynan said: 'Her death scene lifted her to those serene, unassertive heights where at her best she has no rivals. The quiet large face, with its prehensile upper lip, shifted and quaked according to the dictates of the character, an unabashed queen in great extremity.' In July she toured Paris, Antwerp and Brussels with the production. In 1959 Edith Evans joined the Royal Shakespeare Company at Stratford-on-Avon to play the Countess of Rousillon in *All's Well That Ends Well* and Volumnia in *Coriolanus*. Mr Tynan did not like this performance so well: 'Edith Evans looks overpowering, but her fussy, warbling vibrato swamps all too often the meaning of the lines . . .' That year she played in two films, as Ma Tanner in *Look Back in Anger* and the Mother Superior in *The Nun's Story*. In 1960 she gave a poetry recital in Canada and did television work on both sides of the Atlantic. The following year, with the RSC, she played Margaret in *Richard III* and made her last appearance in the Nurse in *Romeo and Juliet*. Television, films and recitals took her into 1963, when in November she played Violet in *Gentle Jack* by Robert Bolt at the Queen's Theatre. In October 1964 she was directed by Noel Coward as Judith Bliss in a revival of his play *Hay Fever* at the National Theatre, and the following May she played Mrs Forest in *The Chinese Prime Minister*. It was her last stage appearance in a play. She did television work and films, most notably *The Whisperers* for which she was nominated for an Oscar and received best actress awards from the New York Film Critics, the British Academy and the Berlin Film Festival. Roger Clifford devised a stage entertainment for her called *Edith Evans . . . and Friends* which she played at various venues in 1973 and 1974. Her last stage appearance was in this at the Phoenix Theatre in October 1974. Dame Edith Evans died in Kent after a heart attack on 14 October 1976.

John Gielgud wrote of her: 'Edith Evans was the finest actress of our time. She was not always easy. There was something rather aloof about her . . . at different times she tried to take up dancing, farming, attempted to drive a car or skate, to do the everyday things that an ordinary woman does. But she was always driven back to the theatre.'

See photograph opposite page 118.

MAURICE EVANS

Maurice Evans was born in Dorchester, Dorset, on 3 June 1901. He attended the Grocers' Company School in London and was a singer as a boy. His father was an analytical chemist and a keen amateur playwright, and it was in his father's adaptations of Thomas Hardy's novels that Maurice Evans began to act. He was a music publisher at the time. His first appearance on the professional stage was as Orestes in *The Oresteia of Aeschylus* at the Festival Theatre in Cambridge on 26 November 1926 and he remained at Cambridge playing in a variety of parts. Maurice Evans was first seen on the London stage on 25 August 1927 when at Wyndham's he played PC Andrews in *The One-Eyed Herring*. In February 1928 he played Stephani in *Listeners* and in April Sir Blayden Coote in *The Stranger in the House*. Other small parts followed in quick succession: Jean in *The Man They Buried* (Ambassadors', June 1928), Hector Frome and Edward Clements in *Justice* (Wyndham's, July 1928), Borring and Graviter in *Loyalties* (Wyndham's, August 1928). In September 1928 Maurice Evans was at the Little Theatre playing Wyn Hayward in *Diversion*. Sir George Arthur remembered that it was in this play Maurice Evans 'showed us unmistakably the stuff of which he is made ... those of us who saw him here for the first time were a little startled by his technique and there were some of us to give rein to happy memories in recognizing a voice of the same or nearly the same timbre as that with which Forbes-Robertson used to hold us spellbound.'

He next played Second Lieutenant Raleigh in *Journey's End* (Apollo, December 1928 and Savoy, January 1929). In this anti-war play set in the trenches of the First World War he had his first big success, as he managed to portray the suffering of both mind and body in his characterization. At Streatham Hill in April 1930 he played the Young Frenchman in *The Man I Killed*, and at the Savoy in September was the Sailor in *The Queen Bee*. He then succeeded Colin Clive as Professor Agi in *The Swan* at the St James's in October and in December played Owen Llewellyn in *To See Ourselves*. For the next four years he was never out of work and established a reputation as a 'West End actor'. He played Marius in *Sea Fever* (New, June 1931), Eric Masters in *Those Naughty Nineties* (Criterion, August 1931), Ralph in *After All* (tour, 1931), Nigel Chelmsford in *Avalanche* (Arts, January 1932), Jean Jacques in *The Heart Line* (Lyric, April 1932), Peter in *Will You Love*

Me? (Globe, September 1932), the Rev. Peter Penlee in *Playground* (Royalty, November 1932), Guy Daunt in *Cecilia* (Arts, March 1933), Dick in *The Soldier and the Gentlewoman* (Vaudeville, April 1933), Arnold Waite in *Other People's Lives* (Wyndham's, July 1933), Aristide in *Ball at the Savoy* (Drury Lane, September 1933), and Edward Voysey in *The Voysey Inheritance* (Sadler's Wells and Shaftesbury, May 1934).

Maurice Evans joined the Old Vic Sadler's Wells company for their 1934–35 season. Audrey Williamson, writing in 1948, said: 'It is doubtful if any Old Vic leading actor has surpassed Maurice Evans' range of characters and achievement in his single nine-month season at this theatre. While many actors before and since have taken both tragedy and comedy in their stride, his was the rarer type of versatility which encompassed both with a natural ease that made it difficult to affix a label to him at all.' He was Octavius Caesar in *Antony and Cleopatra*. Of his Richard II, Audrey Williamson said: 'Evans, in fact, turned over and exposed every facet of the part with the loving care of a connoisseur examining a prized jewel.' Next came Benedick in *Much Ado About Nothing* and then the Dauphin in *Saint Joan*. Miss Williamson reported that he played the character 'as a shrivelled monkey of a man with a lisp, brilliantly underlining the shrewd wit while preserving the ineffectual pathos'. She was equally impressed by his Iago in *Othello*: 'Maurice Evans, brilliant and sinuous as quicksilver, caught the essence of Iago and gave a performance which, although light-weight, drove the play before it with a Machiavellian force.' He was an hilarious Petruchio in *The Taming of the Shrew* and followed that with the title role in *Hippolytus*, Adolphus Cusins in *Major Barbara* and the small part of Silence in *Henry IV Part 2*, while he prepared his full-length Hamlet (known to the players as '*Hamlet* in its eternity'). Miss Williamson again: 'Evans' Hamlet was quick with life, and practically everything was in it except the fatal irresolution. It lacked natural melancholy and natural antipathy to violence, and the intellect was a shade too calculating to suggest a mind torn by doubt and girded to action only by extreme emotional stress. This Hamlet would, one suspected, have dispatched the King within a few scenes and with no shriving time allowed. Given this defect, a matter of personality rather than interpretation, it was a performance of mobility, suffering and whiplash intelligence, every word lucid in meaning and with reserves of genuine pathos and tenderness.'

Guthrie McClintic was in the audience looking for a Romeo for his wife Katharine Cornell's Juliet, and Maurice was his man. Maurice went to the United States and replaced Basil Rathbone in the part, touring in *Romeo and Juliet* in October 1935 and making his first appearance on the New York stage at the Martin Beck Theater on 23 December 1935 in the same part. Broadway critics were very impressed. John Mason Brown said this was 'the first Italianate Romeo of our time; a lyric creation filled with the true ardor and the beauty of the text'. In March 1936, at the same theatre and still with Miss Cornell, he played the Dauphin in Shaw's *Saint Joan*. This, John Mason Brown said, 'showed Mr Evans was more than an unusually talented romantic. It made clear that a gift for the slyest of sly comedy was also at his command.' At the Lyceum in New York in October 1936 he played Napoleon Bonaparte in exile in *St Helena*. In this, Mr Brown said he 'gave a performance so remarkable in its illusion and its force that those of us who had already tossed our hats into the air because of him could scarcely wait for them to fall to earth again so that we could toss them even higher'.

Maurice Evans astounded Broadway in February 1937 when he played Richard II at the St James Theater. Brooks Atkinson of the *New York Times* said: 'Evans' strutting Richard, who succumbed to his enemies with tattered dignity and pathos, was fresh and disarming and transformed Shakespeare out of respectability into a dramatic humanist.' And John Mason Brown was beside himself: 'It is one of the finest Shakespearian performances the modern theater has seen. It is rich in sensitivity. It is possessed of those final qualities of illumination, divination and revelation which stamp the work only of such actors as can be truly said to function as interpretive artists ... in Maurice Evans the English-speaking theater possesses by all odds its finest and most accomplished actor at the present time.'

Richard II ran for an astonishing 171 consecutive performances; the Drama League named Maurice Evans best actor of the year. The English critic James Agate, who was visiting New York, went to see what all the fuss was about; he was not so impressed, feeling that Evans' features were too boyish for tragedy. 'A great actor,' he wrote in his diary, 'must include the forbidding in his facial range: when last I saw Maurice he could do no better in this line than stave off with impudence.' He did, however, keep his opinions to himself, as he felt he would have been lynched on Broadway if he dared to suggest that Mr Evans was anything

less than perfection. After the Broadway run, Maurice Evans toured the production.

In November 1937 he pointed out his versatility by playing Falstaff in *Henry IV Part 1* at the Forrest Theater in Philadelphia. Brooks Atkinson reported: 'By adding a robust Falstaff to his gallery of Shakespearian portraits, Maurice Evans adds a little more stature and range to his eminence as an actor ... He is fabulously made up and he rolls humorously through the play. As usual he knows how to space the phrases of Elizabethan dialogue so that they speak lucidly to modern minds.'

Under his own management, financed mainly by Michael Todd, Maurice Evans opened at the St James Theater in October 1938 as Hamlet. This was the first time the uncut text had been played in America. It ran from 6.30 p.m. to 11.15 p.m. with only a half-hour break. And Broadway was again at his feet. Brooks Atkinson said: '... he acts a Hamlet of modern sensibilities who does not love words for their own sake but for their active meaning. This is a Hamlet of quick intellect who knows what is happening all through the play. He dominates by alertness. He is frank; and above everything else, he is lucid ... It is refreshing and exciting to see it played for sheer drama.' And John Mason Brown was once more throwing his hat in the air: 'His Dane was an extrovert, a man of action, a bounding Legionnaire. He broke away from the tradition of those pale-faced neurotics, those sad Jung men who, brilliant or befuddled, had inclined increasingly to mope about the palace, lamenting their lack of will and burrowing into their subconscious. Mr Evans' Hamlet was politically minded.'

The production achieved a run of 131 performances, the longest for a *Hamlet* up to that time. Maurice Evans followed it at the same theatre with his Falstaff in January 1939 and then played Hamlet again in December 1939, this time at the 44th Street Theater. He revived *Richard II* at the St James in April 1940 and then, for the Theater Guild, played Malvolio in *Twelfth Night* with Helen Hayes. They toured this into 1941. In August 1941 Maurice Evans declared his allegiance and became a United States citizen.

In November 1941, at the National Theater, and under his own management, he was Macbeth with Judith Anderson as his Lady. This too ran for 131 performances. Mr Evans had done what three years before everyone would have said was impossible — he made Shakespeare not only popular on Broadway but a hit everywhere. They toured *Macbeth* into 1942, when Maurice Evans joined the army. From December 1942 until June 1945 he was in charge of the Army Entertainment Section, Central Pacific section. And what did

Mr Evans himself give the troops? *Hamlet*, of course. 'We are giving you,' he told them, 'a *Hamlet* without the intellectual trimmings.' His cut version became known as the *G. I. Hamlet* or the Jeep Version. Instead of being unsure, this was the 'certain' Prince of Denmark. And the soldiers loved it. After the war, Evans performed this version at Columbus Circle Theater and John Mason Brown reported: 'If anything [this cut version] is more virile. He is all male, a man who, in Mr Evans' fashion, is fresh from the army.' This too ran for the magical 131 performances and then Maurice Evans toured it round the United States until April 1947.

In October 1947 he abandoned Shakespeare for a while, but sticking close to the British classics played John Tanner in his own production of Shaw's *Man and Superman*. This ran for 293 performances at the Alvin Theater in New York. Brooks Atkinson called its opening 'the first crackle of brilliance... As the voluble Tanner, who considerably outsmarts himself, Mr Evans is at his best in a holiday mood. The speeches are long and the phrasing complex, but Mr Evans keeps them refreshingly intelligible and he does not forget that *Man and Superman* is very funny stuff. To people familiar with Mr Evans' career, there are shadows of Shakespeare chasing across the performance, particularly in the scenes between Tanner and his chauffeur. Perhaps it is only the architecture of Mr Evans' performance which makes them seem like a Shakespearian monarch bantering words with a jester. Or perhaps this is the way Shaw conceived them. Whatever the reason, they are thoroughly enjoyable.'

In March 1948 he supervised the production of *The Linden Tree* and then took *Man and Superman* on the road until reviving it at the City Center in May 1949. At the Coronet in October 1949 Maurice Evans appeared as Andrew Crocker Harris in *The Browning Version* and as Arthur Gosport in *Harlequinade*. He played Dick Dudgeon in Shaw's *The Devil's Disciple* at the City Center in January 1950 and then at the Royale the next month before touring the summer theatres with it. He was artistic supervisor of the City Center from 1949 until 1951, and for his unpaid services he received a special Tony Award in 1950. At the City Center in January 1951 he revived *Richard II* and then in December played Hjalmar Ekdal in *The Wild Duck*.

Departing from his tradition of appearing in the classics he opened at the Plymouth in October 1952 playing Tony Wendice in the modern thriller *Dial M for Murder*, with which he stayed until May 1954. During the run he was involved with the production of *Teahouse of the August Moon* and *No Time for Sergeants*.

He was at the Plymouth again in October 1956 and back with Shaw when he played King Magnus in *The Apple Cart*, touring with it in 1957. At the Billy Rose in October 1959 he co-presented and played Captain Shotover in *Heartbreak House*. At the 46th Street Theater in October 1960 he was the Rev. Brock in *Tenderloin* and at the Playhouse in February 1962 HJ in *The Aspern Papers*.

He returned to Shakespeare, indeed to the Shakespeare Festival in Stratford, Connecticut, in a Shakespearian recital which he gave with Helen Hayes. They toured it until March 1963.

In 1965 Maurice Evans toured in *The Grass Is Greener* and then, after virtual retirement from the stage, at the Kennedy Center for the Performing Arts in 1973, he gave a solo Shakespeare recital entitled *Shakespeare and the Performing Arts*.

Maurice Evans made a few films, the most notable being *Androcles and the Lion* (1952) and *Gilbert and Sullivan* (1953). His television work was more spectacular. For the Hallmark Hall of Fame he recreated his most important roles, and he received an Emmy for his performance as Macbeth in 1961.

The man who convinced Americans that Shakespeare could be fun retired in the 1970s — back to England.

ALBERT FINNEY

'*I* grew up secure, and it was dull. Part of the reason I became an actor is that I like my life insecure.' But Albert Finney's 'insecurity' is self-manufactured. He became a star in 1960 when he played Billy Liar on stage and was voted most promising newcomer by the Variety Club for his performance in the film *Saturday Night and Sunday Morning*. It was he who made regional accents not only acceptable but very nearly compulsory.

Albert Finney was born on 9 May 1936 in Salford, Lancashire, where his father was a bookie — or as they were called in those days, a gambling commission agent. At the Salford Grammar School Finney failed his GCE exams in five subjects, but was extremely good at animal impressions and also in the title role of *The Emperor Jones*. At RADA he resisted all attempts to make him talk 'posh'. 'I was very unhappy in the first two or three terms,' he says. 'They tried to teach me standard English which, coming from Salford, sounded just like another regional accent. It wasn't until I realized that there was music in my voice and that the voice belonged to only me that I began to settle there. I simply refused to let RADA wipe my personality clean.'

After drama school he joined the Birmingham Repertory Company, where in April 1956 he made his professional début playing Decius Brutus in *Julius Caesar* and followed that with the title roles in *Hamlet*, *Henry V* and *Macbeth*. 'I have views about how Shakespearian parts should be spoken and acted, and I believe that Elizabethan performers spoke with what we would regard as heavy regional accents. They certainly didn't talk posh.' At Birmingham he also played Francis Archer in *The Beaux' Stratagem*, Face in *The Alchemist* and Malcolm in *The Lizard on the Rock*. Finney made his London début with the Birmingham company at the Old Vic on 30 July 1956 playing Belzanor in *Caesar and Cleopatra*. In 1957 he married Jane Wenham, an actress with the company, and they had one son, Simon.

Finney was much too young and inexperienced for his major roles at Birmingham. Charles Laughton went to see his Macbeth and proclaimed it 'bloody terrible' but still brought Finney to London to play Soya Marshall in *The Party* which Laughton directed and in which he also starred together with his wife Elsa Lanchester. It opened at the New Theatre in May 1958. Kenneth Tynan cared neither for the play nor for its star performers, but thought that Finney 'has brought

to London from Birmingham those qualities of technical assurance and latent power that are the fruits of hard training and the buds of great acting'. (It was Tynan who on seeing Finney play Troilus in a student production of *The Face of Love* at RADA called him a 'smouldering young Spencer Tracy'.) Peter Jackson, writing in *Plays and Players* about *The Party*, said: 'Albert Finney, fresh from repertory in Birmingham, has little to say but gives depth and feeling to Henrietta's complex boyfriend, a mixed-up mechanic with no head for figures. His short scene with Laughton over the gin glasses is the most electric moment of the evening.'

Laughton persuaded Finney to come with him to Stratford in April 1959 to the Shakespeare Memorial Theatre for their hundredth season. The parts for Finney were not very attractive. He played Cassio to Paul Robeson's Othello. Caryl Brahms thought the whole thing a 'vulgar, dark, inaudible, over-set, over-dressed, over-produced piece . . . Mr Finney made little impact in the general murk — his tunic was more stylish than his art.' He was Lysander ('plebeian' — Caryl Brahms) in Peter Hall's production of *A Midsummer Night's Dream* in June, and in July played the First Roman Citizen and also understudied Laurence Olivier in *Coriolanus*. He in fact played for an injured Olivier for one performance. 'I started to get cocky,' he recalls, 'and imitate Olivier and make the company laugh.' In August he was Edgar in *King Lear*.

It was in January 1960 that he returned to London, opening at the Royal Court in Lindsay Anderson's production of *The Lily-White Boys*, a play with songs and music. Peter Roberts was not impressed: 'Albert Finney, as the leading delinquent, gives a rather thin performance and is quite out of his depth when this character is elevated to the Establishment, the final courtroom speech being poorly handled.' But everyone was impressed when he opened at the Cambridge Theatre in September 1960 as Billy Liar, the boy who could not tell the difference between daydreams and reality. 'Albert Finney,' Bill Lester wrote in *Plays and Players*, 'accomplishes these changes of mood and tempo with a rare consummate skill.' And Tynan reported: 'Mr Finney is a true fascinator, as Richard Burton was at his age.' Finney left the highly successful *Billy Liar* after eight months to play the title part in John Osborne's *Luther* at the Sarah Bernhardt Theatre for the Théâtre des Nations in Paris in July 1961. There he was named best actor of the season. He repeated the role at the Holland Festival before opening in London at the Royal Court in July 1961. At last Caryl Brahms liked him — and seemed to forget her earlier criticisms. 'Finney,' she wrote, 'at all times a compulsive actor, is more than compelling as Luther. He *is* Luther. His quiet, strong and admirable performance threw me in a frame of mind to swear that had he been born into a springtime world he would have turned his back on it as did the early Luther. This was the most convincing performance that I can remember ever to have seen.' Tynan, of course, had always appreciated him: ' . . . no finer Luther could be imagined than the clod, the lump, the infinitely vulnerable Everyman presented by Albert Finney, who looks, in his moments of pallor and lip-gnawing doubt, like a reincarnation of the young Irving, fattened up for some cannibal feast.' *Luther* went to the Edinburgh Festival in August and then returned to London to the Phoenix in September.

Back at the Royal Court in February 1962 Finney played Feste in *Twelfth Night*, and was then taken with an urge to direct. After playing the title role in Tony Richardson's film of *Tom Jones* (for which he received an Oscar nomination) Finney went to the Citizens' Theatre, Glasgow, where he was told he could direct *The Birthday Party* and *The School for Scandal* if he would first play the title part in Pirandello's *Henry IV*. Finney agreed, and Tynan reported: 'He is greatly miscast; too young, too moon-shaped of mien and frankly inept at conveying the razor-edged intellect that underlies Henry's lunacy; but the thrust of his temperament carried him over these hurdles to hard-won triumph. His very presence, relaxed and watchful, the long arms dangling, the heavy head balefully swaying in search of opposition, imparts a sense of danger that is authentically feudal; as he lopes crabwise around the stage, we are unnerved by the knowledge that at any moment he may do something violent and unpredictable . . . only a handful of living actors can make a whole audience gasp and recoil with a single syllable, and one of these is Mr Finney.'

Albert Finney made his New York stage début at the St James Theater on 25 September 1963, once again playing Luther. Broadway critic John Simon called it a 'boldly sculptured, stinging performance' and Finney received a Tony for it. Then he spent a year going around the world, whether to express his independence or to run away from his celebrity, he was not sure. But he came back to London and joined the National Theatre Company at the Old Vic to play Don Pedro in *Much Ado About Nothing* in February 1965. Also with the company, at the Chichester

Festival that summer he played John Armstrong in Arden's *Armstrong's Last Good Night* (which John Russell Taylor found a 'powerfully animal performance') and Jean to Maggie Smith's *Miss Julie* in a double bill with *Black Comedy* (in which he played Harold Gorringe). Of his performance in *Miss Julie* John Russell Taylor said: 'Though well enough cast as Jean [he] seems unengaged and does not quite project the sort of flashy animal magnetism the character should have.' Back at the Old Vic he was again Armstrong in October 1965 and in February 1966 played Victor Chandebise and Poche at that theatre in *A Flea in Her Ear*. Hugh Leonard said: 'Mr Finney plays his dual role with a brilliant subtlety, so that one thinks of him throughout as two characters rather than as one clever actor.' For this performance he received the *Evening Standard* Best Actor Award.

Together with Michael Medwin, Albert Finney formed Memorial Enterprises Ltd, an independent production company for television films and plays, and he directed and starred in their first film, *Charlie Bubbles*. In July 1967 they presented *A Day in the Death of Joe Egg* at the Comedy Theatre in London and in February 1968 took it to Broadway to the Brooks Atkinson Theater, where Finney played Bri, the role Joe Melia had in London. John Simon said: 'Albert Finney is — he can't help it — a star, which is too much for the will-o'-the-wisp Bri; yet how charmingly he plays down his bravura, how intelligently he conveys the ambiguities of wit, the ambivalence of feeling that did not grow up. And his impersonation of an Oxbridge vicar, the last word in muscular Christianity ludicrously trying to be with it — indeed, just the way his pipe smokes him rather than vice versa — is a piece of unalloyed histrionic brilliance.' And Clive Barnes, writing in the *New York Times*, agreed: 'Mr Finney — mildly but gamely miscast — is superb, running the gamut of manic immaturity with a raw-nerved semi-hysteria.'

Back in England, at the Royal Court in January 1972 Finney played Mr Elliot in *Alpha Beta*, the story of a doomed marriage. Rachel Roberts played his hapless wife. Michael Billington reported: 'Finney got the externals absolutely right as the boozy, randy, adolescent Peter Pan of a husband. Everything was authentic: the cutting, grating Liverpool accent that sounded as if it had been transmitted through a clogged sewer-pipe, the exuberant drunkenness which meant that when aiming a puff at a cigarette he actually missed, the tell-tale narcissism that entailed a slight duck when he passed a mirror . . . At the same time, through conscious application to outer detail he gave one a complete chart of the man's inner life.' *Alpha*

Beta transferred to the Apollo in March 1972.

For three years, from 1972, he was an associate artistic director of the Royal Court Theatre where he directed a number of plays, including *The Freedom of the City* and *Loot*, and played in *Krapp's Last Tape* (January 1973) and *Cromwell* (August 1973).

At the Globe Theatre in February 1974 he opened as Phil in *Chez Nous*. Ronald Bryden said: 'Albert Finney's Phil is moving in his flushed ecstasy over his son, but the character's too flimsily introduced to carry the weight of the revelation forced on it.'

Albert Finney rejoined the National Theatre in December 1975. First at the Old Vic and then in the opening production of the Lyttelton in March 1976 he played Hamlet. Michael Coveney summed up the critical response: 'Finney . . . gives us a blazing open-minded fanatic who would drop acid and walk on burning coals if there was a half-chance that, at the end, some important truth would be uncovered . . . From the very beginning, there is no repose in this performance, no relaxation . . . Finney has never had to banish sentimentality from his acting — it just doesn't figure in his technique . . . Finney is a gloriously physical performer. He is engaging, sexy, mischievous, witty and merciless.' And more than one critic thought he should have been named actor of the year for that performance as well as his *Tamburlaine the Great* at the Olivier Theatre in October 1976.

In 1977 he separated from his second wife, the French actress Anouk Aimée, and then concentrated for a while on filming. In June 1978 he opened as Macbeth at the Olivier Theatre with Dorothy Tutin as his Lady. Dave Robins, writing in *Plays and Players*, was unimpressed by Peter Hall's production, calling it a 'series of lifeless tableaux performed with the artificiality of a second-rate opera'. He did not go quite as far as Laughton had done all those years before and call Finney's Scot 'bloody awful' — but he did not like the performance. 'As Macbeth he rants and raves about the stage, part Richard III, part Quasimodo, part late seventies Henry Irving. By the end of the evening it was not clear whether he had played Macbeth as pompous and self-important or whether this was simply an aspect of his own personality coming through.'

There are, Albert Finney tells interviewers, still a lot of parts he is keen to play on stage. One of them is Lear and he says: 'En route to that I'd like to do Shylock and Richard III. And I'd quite like to do Falstaff and Sir Toby Belch. I don't want to do them all next week and all at once. There is plenty of time.'

In 1984, after a long absence from films, Albert Finney formed with Richard Johnson and Diana Rigg a theatre company: he directed and starred in its first two productions, *The Biko Inquest* (at Riverside) and a revival of John Arden's *Serjeant Musgrave's Dance* (at the Old Vic). *See photograph opposite page 135.*

MINNIE MADDERN FISKE

Minnie Maddern was born on 19 December 1865 in New Orleans, Louisiana, where her father, Thomas Davey, was a theatrical agent. She made her début as the Duke of York in *Richard III* at Little Rock, Arkansas, when she was three, using her mother's maiden name, Maddern; two years later she made her first New York appearance playing Sybil in *A Sheep in Wolf's Clothing* at the French Theater on 30 May 1870. She was soon well known as Little Minnie Maddern and went on as a child actress to play Little Fritz in *Fritz, Our German Cousin* (Wallack's Theater, July 1870), in *Hunted Down* (Kelly and Leon's, January 1871), the Duke of York in *Richard III* (Niblo's Garden, April 1871), Dollie in *Chicago Before the Fire*, (Théâtre-Comique, June 1872), Prince Arthur in *King John*

(Booth's, May 1874), and Richelieu in *The Two Orphans*. During this time she had a smattering of education at convents in Cincinnati and St Louis. By the time she was 13 she was playing the Widow Melnotte in *The Lady of Lyons*, and at 15 she was a fully fledged star. Minnie Maddern played Ralph Rackstraw in *HMS Pinafore* in 1879.

In May 1882 she was at the Park Theater in New York playing Chip in *Fogg's Ferry*. That same year she married Le Grand White but the marriage was short-lived; they divorced in 1888. She went on to play Mercy Baxter in *Caprice* (New Park, August 1884), Alice Glendenning in *In Spite of It All* (Lyceum, New York, September 1885 and on a subsequent United States tour) and Mrs Coney in *Featherbrain* (Madison Square Theater, May 1889).

On 19 March 1890 she married Harrison Grey Fiske, the extremely rich editor and owner of the New York *Dramatic Mirror* and retired from the stage to become a lady of leisure. However, in January 1894 she played the part of Nora for a charity production of Ibsen's *A Doll's House* and the response to her performance was so great that she returned to the stage, as the heroine in her husband's play *Hester Crewe*. She had grown up now and was not afraid of plays that said something, a rarity at the time on Broadway; in February 1894 she played Nora once more in *A Doll's House* at the Empire Theater, shocking a number of people but delighting others. She was subsequently Gilberte in *Frou-Frou* (Garden Theater, March 1894), toured in *The Queen of Liars* in 1895, which she brought to New York's Garden Theater in March 1896 under the title *Marie Deloche*, and played the heroine of *Césarine* (Garden, March 1896). She wrote and appeared in *A Light from St Agnes*, and at Miner's Theater on Fifth Avenue in March 1897 she played Tess in Lorrimer Stoddard's version of *Tess of the d'Urbervilles*. The New York *Dramatic Mirror* wrote: 'The Fifth Avenue Theater was the scene last Tuesday evening of a dual achievement. One of the most vitally human and emotion-compelling novels of the century was successfully set forth in the form of a play; and an American actress who in lesser cities, in other dramas, had been greeted as the greatest player of her sex at last enjoyed metropolitan acceptance ... It would be a work of long detail to describe the excellencies of Mrs Fiske's acting in this role. As Tess she shows the perfections of stage art. It is her greatest character. She convinces from first to last. She is Tess in her refined reticence when thrown into contact with the coarser feminine natures about her, from whose primitive amusements she holds aloof ... The murder enacted by Mrs Fiske is one of the most marvelously natural and thrillingly effective things ever seen on the stage. There is only one other actress living who could conceive and execute the scene with a power so reserved and yet adequately suggestive and wholly untheatrical, and the tongue of that actress is Italian ... [but] even Duse will not fill the physical eye.' Of course it must be noted that the editor of that journal was still Mr Fiske; nevertheless, Mrs Fiske's Tess was also a great popular success. In May 1897 she played Cyprienne in *Divorçons* and in 1898 was Saucers in *A Bit of Old Chelsea* and Madeleine in *Love Finds the Way*. The following year she was Magda Giulia in *Little Italy* and then performed one of her most famous roles, that of Becky Sharp in a dramatization by Langdon Mitchell of William Makepeace Thackeray's novel *Vanity Fair*. Lewis

C. Strang wrote of her performance: 'There is really very little use in bothering oneself about Mr Thackeray in connection with Mr Mitchell's play ... As a matter of fact *Becky Sharp* had very little Thackeray in it ... [in fact] it was truly one of the most colourless dramas, from first to last, that ever was put upon the stage. Yet, in the face of this trustworthy fact, I am going to declare that I have passed few evenings in the theater more delightful than the several for which *Becky Sharp* was responsible. Mrs Fiske explained the paradox — Mrs Fiske, whose captivating impersonation of Becky Sharp inspired rhapsodies. One is tempted to spread on paper a synonym book of adjectives — brilliant, sparkling, scintillating, that sort of thing — but these, after all, are merely superficialities; they convey an idea of the manner, but they give no notion of the spirit of Mrs Fiske's characterization. They tell nothing of the marvellous way in which her conception of Becky got across the footlights, nor of the wonderfully sympathetic understanding of the character that was vouchsafed those who sat in orchestra chairs. Never knew I insincerity to be shown with such convincing sincerity.'

All these triumphs had taken place in New York at the Fifth Avenue Theater, and during these years Mrs Fiske had been engaged in a running battle with the syndicate which had a monopoly on New York theatres, dictating to producers and actors. By 1899 Klaw and Erlanger, who ran the syndicate, had had enough of her and evicted her from their theatre in the middle of the successful run of *Becky Sharp*. Her husband then bought the Manhattan Theater, which he renovated at great cost, turning it into one of the most attractive theatres in New York. There Minnie Maddern Fiske played in *Miranda on the Balcony* and *The Unwelcome Mrs Hatch* (1901), and in 1902 she played Mary in *Mary of Magdala*. The following year she played in *Hedda Gabler, A Bit of Old Chelsea, Divorçons* and *Césarine*. In 1904, also at the Manhattan Theater, she had the title role in *Leah Kleschna* and in April 1906 was the heroine in *Dolce*. In October 1906 she opened in Milwaukee playing Cynthia Karslake in Langdon Mitchell's new play, *The New York Idea*, which was a breakthrough in comedy at the time, being satirical of social customs without snobbishness. She opened in the same part at the Lyric Theater in New York in November. By this time Mrs Fiske, as well as being exceedingly active in the theatre, was involved in passionate crusades against the killing of wild animals for fur and of birds for feathers. It was the one activity, apart from the theatre, to which her life was devoted. At the Lyric in December 1907 she played Rebecca West in

Ibsen's *Rosmersholm*. It ran for 199 consecutive performances at a time when Ibsen was considered immoral and shocking to the still Victorian Broadway audiences. Mrs Fiske argued that Ibsen was the genius of the age and continued to play him successfully, both critically and commercially.

At Hackett's Theater in November 1908 she played the parish scrubwoman, Nell Sanders, in *Salvation Nell,* and at the Lyceum in March 1910 was Lona Hessel in *The Pillars of Society.* In April 1910 she played the title role in *Hannele* and in November of that year opened at Chicago as Mrs Bumpstead-Leigh in the play of that name. She revived *Becky Sharp* at the Lyceum in New York in March 1911 and followed that with a New York production of *Mrs Bumpstead-Leigh.* She toured for the next two years playing in *The New Marriage* and *Julia France.* Back in New York in February 1912, she was Lady Patricia Cosway in *Lady Patricia* and at the Hudson Theater in November played Mary Page in *The High Road.* She then took to the road again. Mrs Fiske was not a believer in the repertory system of casting, calling it an 'outworn, impossible, harmful scheme'. She believed that actors should be cast for their parts, and in her touring companies she did just that, filling houses throughout the country. It was as well she did, because in 1915 her husband declared bankruptcy and she had to pay the bills. She attracted large audiences and generally good reviews, though she was sometimes criticized for her lack of gesture and at times was accused of unintelligibility. Franklin Pierce Adams wrote in the *New York Tribune:*

> Somewords she runstogether,
>> Some others are distinctly stated.
> Somecometoofast and s o m e t o o s l o w
>> And some are syncopated,
> And yet no voice — I am sincere —
>> Exists that I prefer to hear.

Her husband was now not only bankrupt but increasingly unfaithful, and Minnie Maddern Fiske, except for her devotion to animals, lived for the theatre alone. At the Gaiety, New York, in January 1916 she played Juliet Miller in *Erstwhile Susan*, and at the Criterion in November 1917 she was George Sand in *Madame Sand.* That year she also toured America with an all-star cast in *Out There,* raising $683 632 for the Red Cross. At the Cohan Theater in April 1918 she was Madame Eulin in *Service,* and the next year at the Henry Miller Theater played Nellie Daventry in *Mis' Nelly o' New Orleans.* In January 1921 she

played Marion Blake in *Wake Up, Jonathan* and at the National Theater in April 1923 was Patricia Baird in *The Dice of the Gods.* It was at the Belasco in September 1923, when she played Mary Westlake in *Mary, Mary, Quite Contrary,* that the fledgling actress Helen Hayes came under her spell. As Miss Hayes reported in her autobiography: 'I had never seen such spontaneity of acting. She was a superb comedienne. Mrs Fiske had a butterfly touch and she fluttered through the play, barely lighting on the furniture: an ephemeral thing, catching the light, always trembling on the brink of audacity. She was yellow-bright, sunlight. I was dazzled by her. It was immediately apparent that I was witness to one of those performances of which every actor dreams, and which he may achieve only once in a lifetime . . . The perfect one, where you are lost in your art and can do no wrong . . . I attended the Henry Miller Theater [every Thursday] for the rest of the season . . . She gave exactly the same performance every single time. There wasn't a smile or a shrug that was a fraction of a second early or late. A crumb was brushed off her jabot at precisely the same moment as she was fashioning a particular syllable. All that incredible spontaneity was calculated to a sigh.'

Also at the Henry Miller, she played Helen Tilden in *Helena's Boys* in April 1924, and at the Mansfield in January 1927 she returned to Ibsen as Mrs Alving in *Ghosts.* At the Knickerbocker in March 1928 she played Mistress Page in *The Merry Wives* of *Windsor* and then toured as Beatrice in *Much Ado About Nothing.*

Minnie Maddern Fiske revived *Mrs Bumpstead-Leigh* at the Klaw in April 1929 and then took to the road again. Her last performance was in Chicago; she died three months later on 15 February 1932.

Brooks Atkinson summed up the career of Minnie Maddern Fiske: 'Her last years were undistinguished and a little desperate. She appeared in a succession of potboilers. But her total career was one of the most honorable on Broadway. At a time when nearly everyone else was content with humbug, she acted on the stage in a sharp, naturalistic style, and she was the champion of intelligence in the theater. Since she did what she wanted to do, it would be patronizing to feel sorry for her, particularly at the end. But as she hurried around the country, rehearsing her company almost every day and playing almost every night, she surrounded herself with loneliness. A brilliant public figure had a joyless private life and few of the comforts of companionship and devotion.'

LYNN FONTANNE

See The Lunts

JOHNSTON FORBES-ROBERTSON

'Never at any time have I gone on the stage without longing for the moment when the curtain would come down on the last act. Rarely, very rarely have I enjoyed myself in acting. This cannot be the proper mental attitude for an actor, and I am persuaded ... that I am not temperamentally suited to my calling. For years I have fought hard against this ''ego'' but seldom would I reach that impersonal exaltation, so to speak, which it seems to me an actor should be able to attain.' For someone who felt like that about it, Johnston Forbes-Robertson had a spectacular career. He was hailed as the finest romantic actor of his day, and the greatest Hamlet ever.

He was born in London on 16 January 1853, the son of John Forbes-Robertson, a Scottish art critic and journalist. He planned to be a painter but acting came naturally to him (he was followed into the profession by three brothers, his daughter, Jean, and a nephew) and his first part was that of Macbeth at a Christmas party in 1866. Fully intending to be an artist, he was admitted to study at the Royal Academy in 1870 but being the eldest of a large family, whose ancestry Bryan Forbes reports can be traced back to King Duncan of *Macbeth* fame, he felt he should earn a living, and reluctantly became an actor, studying elocution under Samuel Phelps. He was, according to Hesketh Pearson, eminently suited to the stage, 'blessed with every possible quality for success as an actor: classical features, an engaging manner, a natural elegance of speech and movement and a rich, melodious voice.' He made his professional début on 5 March 1874 at the Princess Theatre when he succeeded the late Charles Harcourt as Chastelard in *Mary, Queen of Scots*. His next appearance was with Ellen Terry on the occasion of her triumphant comeback at Astley's Theatre, where in April 1874 he played James Annersley in *The Wandering Heir*. He then toured with her. In September he was at Manchester playing Prince Hal in *Henry IV Part 2*. In December he rejoined Phelps at the Gaiety, where he played Fenton in *The Merry Wives of Windsor*, Lord Glossmore in *Money*, Beauseant in *The Lady of Lyons*, Hastings in *She Stoops to Conquer* and Lysander in *A Midsummer Night's Dream*.

It seems that Forbes-Robertson had made the right choice of career — he was never out of work. He played Chevalier de Vaudray in *The Two Orphans* (Olympic, April 1875), Borders in *The Spendthrift* (Olympic, May 1875), and then a number of roles at the Haymarket including Mark Smeaton in *Anne Boleyn* (February 1876). Back at the Gaiety in 1876 he was Orsino in *Twelfth Night* and Baron Steinfort in *The Stranger*, and at the Lyceum in June he played the Abbé de Larse in *Corinne*. His first great success came at the Haymarket in September 1876 when he played Geoffrey Wynyard in W. S. Gilbert's *Dan 'l Druce, Blacksmith*. He returned to the Olympic in 1877 and played Jeremy Diddler in *Raising the Wind*, Arthur Wardlaw in *The Scuttled Ship*, George Talboys in *Lady Audley's Secret*, Sandro in *The Violin Maker of Cremona*, Clement Austin in *Henry Dunbar*, Edgar Greville in *The Turn of the Tide*, Gerard Seton in *The Ne'er Do Well*, Richard Goodwin in *The Miser's Treasure*, Hercule in *Belphegor*, Squire Lockwood in *Love of Life* — among other parts.

He was then engaged by the Bancrofts at the Prince of Wales; there he was at first Count Orloff in *Diplomacy*, later taking over the role of Julian Beauclerc.

In 1879 he went to the Lyceum to play Pierre Latouche in *Zillah* and Orsini in *Lucrezia Borgia*, and to originate the role of Sir Horace Welby in *Forget-Me-Not*. Then in August he went back to the Bancrofts to play Dick Fanshawe in *Duty* and Sergeant Jones in *Ours*. When the Bancrofts moved to the Haymarket he was with them and opened there in January 1880 as Lord Glossmore in *Money*, going on to play Krux in *School*. At the Prince of Wales he played Koenraad Deel in *Anne-Mie*.

In 1880 he was at the Court Theatre supporting Madame Modjeska as Maurice de Saxe in *Adrienne Lecouvreur*, Armand Duval in *Heartsease*, Romeo in *Romeo and Juliet* and Don Carlos in *Juana*. He moved from the Court to the Princess with Modjeska and played the Comte de

Valreas in *Frou-Frou*. He was back at the Court in April 1882 playing Claude Glynne in *The Parvenu*.

Henry Irving asked Forbes-Robertson to join him at the Lyceum in 1882, and there he played Claudio in *Much Ado About Nothing*. In November 1883 he rejoined the Bancrofts, and remained with them until they left the Haymarket in 1885. There he played the Earl of Caryll in *Lords and Commons*, Sir George Ormond in *Peril*, Captain Absolute in *The Rivals*, Julian in *Diplomacy*, Sir Charles Pomander in *Masks and Faces* and Petruchio in *Katherine and Petruchio*. Then he toured the provinces with Mary Anderson, and went with her to America where he made his New York début on 12 October 1885 at the Star Theater as Orlando in *As You Like It*.

Back in London in 1887 he played Captain Absolute in *The Rivals* at the Opéra-Comique and then in September rejoined Mary Anderson, this time at the Lyceum, playing Leontes in *The Winter's Tale*. He designed the costumes for that production. At the Prince of Wales in January 1888 he was Nigel Chester in *Tares*, and at the Royalty in June played Arthur Dimmesdale in *The Scarlet Letter*. He then went to the Shaftesbury where he played Orlando and Claude Melnotte before joining John Hare for six years at the Garrick. Notable among his roles were Dunstan Renshaw in *The Profligate*, Baron Scarpia in *La Tosca*, Robert in *Dream Faces*, Dennis Heron in *Lady Bountiful*, Hugh Rokeby in *Robin Goodfellow*, Julian in *Diplomacy*, George D'Alroy in *Caste*, Walter Forbes in *Mrs Lessingham* and Alfred Evelyn in *Money*. While at the Garrick he took time off to visit America again, where at Proctor's Theater, New York, he played Hugon in *Thermidor* in October 1891, also finding time back in London to appear at the Lyceum in January 1892 as Buckingham in *Henry VIII*.

In January 1895 Johnston Forbes-Robertson rejoined Irving at the Lyceum to play Lancelot in *King Arthur* and made one more excursion to the Garrick in March to play Lucas Cleeve in *The Notorious Mrs Ebbsmith*.

Each autumn Irving toured America, and in September 1895 he left the Lyceum to the management of a reluctant Forbes-Robertson, who only became a manager because it seemed cowardly not to — his heart was still in painting. With Mrs Patrick Campbell as his leading lady he produced during his first season: *Romeo and Juliet*, *Michael and His Lost Angel*, *For the Crown*, *Magda* and *The School for Scandal*. He moved on to the Fifth Avenue Theater in February 1897 where he played Lord Nelson in *Nelson's Enchantress*. In the summer of 1897 he toured as *Othello*. Then in

September 1897 at the Lyceum he played his Hamlet for the first time — he was 44 years old. To say it was well received would be a massive understatement. Ernest Short wrote: 'The dignity, grace of movement. and integrity of the man, together with the significance and charm of his elocution made his far and away the best Hamlet of his generation. Here was beauty in full measure, coupled with an understanding of the text which alone made this Prince of Denmark perfect of its kind.' When Irving saw Forbes-Robertson's Hamlet he refused ever to play it again himself, and told Forbes-Robertson that now he would have to go and show it to the world. He did. In February 1898 he took his company to Berlin where he performed his Hamlet and Macbeth and also played Aubrey in *The Second Mrs Tanqueray*.

Sharing management with Mrs Patrick Campbell, Forbes-Robertson opened at the Prince of Wales in June 1898 as Golaud in *Pelléas and Mélisande*, and in September played Macbeth. The following September he played Ito Arumo in *The Moonlight Blossom*, and in October the part of Jacques Bernez in *The Sacrament of Judas*. He then toured, also playing Mr Lepic in *Carrots* and Dick Dudgeon in Shaw's *The Devil's Disciple*.

In 1900, much to Mrs Patrick Campbell's annoyance, he married his favourite leading lady, the American Gertrude Elliott, sister of Maxine, and twenty-one years younger than he was. He took over the Comedy Theatre in April 1901 and played Count David Tezma in *Count Tezma;* at the Lyric in January 1902 he played Mark Embury in *Mice and Men*. This was one of his greatest commercial successes and ran for nearly a year. He revived *Othello* for December, and then in February 1903 had another success with Kipling's *The Light That Failed* in which he played Dick Heldar. He then toured America with *Love and the Man*. Back in London in June 1904, he played Jim Poulett in *The Edge of the Storm*. Neither critics nor audiences were impressed. Max Beerbohm reported: ' . . . Poulet should appear to be, as the author drew him, just a plain, decent Briton. Mr Forbes-Robertson cannot help appearing to be something more than that — a disability which is, in other impersonations, the secret of his hold on us.' In September 1905 Forbes-Robertson opened the Scala Theatre with *The Conqueror*, playing Morven, Lord of Abivard. Max Beerbohm hated that play: 'Morven is an impossible hero for poetic drama. That a man should be fascinated by a little girl of ten years old and should intend to marry her later on, and finally should return for this express purpose after the lapse of eight years, is not at all an impossible idea. But it is an idea which makes the soldier a slightly ridiculous or perhaps a slightly unpleasant figure. Not even Mr Forbes-Robertson could be expected to make Morven wholly dignified or delightful. He, moreover, was handicapped by the fact that Morven was a soldier — a trampling and bloodthirsty soldier. Mr Forbes-Robertson's method does not blend well with even the most modified forms of militarism. He is at his best in the last act, when Morven shows a more civilian side to his nature and renounces his chosen bride because she does not love him. I have seen Mr Forbes-Robertson renouncing his heart's desire in more last acts than I should care to count. But I never saw him do it more beautifully than last Saturday evening.'

He next revived *For the Crown,* and then produced *Mrs Grundy* in which he played Edward Sotheby. After touring the provinces he went back to America, where his Hamlet was received rapturously. Walter Tallmadge Arndt, writing in *Current Literature* in 1905, said: 'The Hamlet of Forbes-Robertson is not new to America, yet one cannot repeat too often the assertion that without a doubt his is the greatest interpretation of the Prince of Denmark on the modern stage. Nor will we attempt to limit the interpretation of the term ''modern'' to the past year — or the past decade. Let it suffice to remark that we must not forget that we are apt to have a reverential awe for the interpretations of past generations that is due almost entirely to the accumulating force of tradition. It is simply part of our natures to feel certain that the Hamlet of Betterton or of Garrick was great, even had we not contemporary critics to tell us so. It is in no iconoclastic spirit, therefore, but merely with a true appreciation of the hallowing effects of time, that we rank Forbes-Robertson's impersonation with the great Hamlets of dramatic history.

'What must at once and most forcibly strike everyone who sees the play is that Mr Robertson's Hamlet is a *real* man. Naturalness is the keynote of the character as he plays it. A man of emotional moods, of irrational moments he is — but never is there anything of the madman about him. Never for an instant does he rant, not even in his ''Get thee to a nunnery'' scene, where if anywhere there might seem to be justification. Throughout the play, from beginning to end there is a consistency, and to us, a most pleasing repression. For this very repression he has been called to account by some of the elder critics who recall Booth in his prime. They declare that because of this, Mr Robertson's Hamlet is lacking in depths of emotional power, in breadth of conception. We must confess to a belief that what it possibly lacks here is more than made up in the pulsing naturalism, the poetic coloring,

the subtle, intangible lights and shades, that in a too forceful impersonation must necessarily be minimized if they are not entirely overlooked.

'Compare it, for instance, with Irving's portrayal of the Prince, which we have had ample opportunity to admire here in America. Both are remarkable for their artistic qualities, but Irving's is artistic artificiality, while Mr Robertson's is artistic naturalness. Irving is always Irving acting Hamlet; Forbes-Robertson lives his Hamlet . . .'

During that tour Forbes-Robertson also produced Shaw's *Caesar and Cleopatra.* Shaw had written the play specifically for Forbes-Robertson after he had seen his Hamlet in 1897. It had been conceived as a vehicle for both him and Mrs Patrick Campbell but Mrs Pat did not care for it, so it waited until 1906 when it was first seen and well received in America.

In August 1906 Forbes-Robertson returned to England, to Manchester, where he played Shylock in *The Merchant of Venice;* in Leeds in September 1907 he played Caesar once more in *Caesar and Cleopatra.* He brought the production to London, to the Savoy in November 1907, and most of the critics and audiences felt the same way as Mrs Patrick Campbell about the play. But Hesketh Pearson was an exception that history would vindicate. He later wrote: 'I saw *Caesar and Cleopatra* three times during that month's run at the Savoy and I cannot remember enjoying any piece of acting so much as Robertson's Caesar. There has been nothing to compare with it on the stage of my time: a great classical actor interpreting to perfection a self-inspired classical part. There may have been passages in his Hamlet that were not rendered as effectively as similar passages in the performances of other actors, though no one can have been so completely satisfying in the part; but there was not a movement or an inflection in his Caesar that could have been bettered; and if the play had to wait for another artist to perform the leading character so superbly as Forbes-Robertson, it would never again be seen on the stage. I ought to add that the acting of Cleopatra by his wife, Gertrude Elliott, was worthy of his Caesar.'

In March 1908 Forbes-Robertson played Captain Yule at the Lyceum, Edinburgh, in *The High Bid.* That September he opened a season at the St James's Theatre in a part that was to be his most commercially successful — and also to become something of a millstone around his neck. It was Jerome K. Jerome's *The Passing of the Third Floor Back.* Hesketh Pearson explains: 'It was the sort of thing that unites the clergy of all denominations. Praises of it were chanted in churches and chapels throughout Great Britain and America and the dramatic critics joined their voices to the chorus of alleluias. The plot is simple. A Christ-like personage takes a room in a third-rate Bloomsbury boarding house, comes into contact with its vicious but entertaining inmates, irons out their characters in the course of the play, and leaves them virtuous but tedious. It was exactly what one would expect from a professional humorist ...' Max Beerbohm called it 'vilely stupid', nevertheless the play transferred to Terry's Theater. In February 1909 Forbes-Robertson was playing at His Majesty's in *The High Bid* once more and also in *A Soul's Flight*. *The Passing of the Third Floor Back* opened at the Maxine Elliott Theater in New York in October 1909. Forbes-Robertson came back to London for the gala performance at His Majesty's in June 1911 and then returned to America in October to tour *The Passing of the Third Floor Back*.

In 1912 Forbes-Robertson, still the reluctant actor, decided to retire, and in the autumn he began a farewell tour of the provinces in England playing in his major successes. His farewell season in London was at Drury Lane, beginning at the end of March 1913 and lasting until 6 June. During the final week a knighthood was bestowed upon him, and his last performance was as Hamlet. Max

Beerbohm noted: 'One of the reasons for the great popularity of Mr Forbes-Robertson's Hamlet was that he so notably brightened the play up.'

Now Sir Johnston Forbes-Robertson, he toured the United States from 1913 to 1916, playing Hamlet for the last time on 26 April 1916 at Harvard University. He revived *The Passing of the Third Floor Back* for the War Charities in 1917 and in June 1918 appeared at Wyndham's as Mr Don in *A Well-Remembered Voice*.

In 1921 he lectured on Shakespeare at the Wigmore Hall, and for the King George Pension Fund for actors he played the Hon. Sir Richard Petworth in *The Ware Case* at the Adelphi in June 1924. His absolutely final performance was at the Forbes-Robertson Clan Matinée at the St James's on 17 May 1927 when he played the Priest in *Twelfth Night*, at the age of 74.

Johnston Forbes-Robertson lived on for another ten years; he died on 6 November 1937. Despite his long and distinguished career as an actor, he was probably most proud of the fact that his portrait of the actor Samuel Phelps as Cardinal Wolsey hangs in the Garrick Club in London. *See photograph opposite.*

DAVID GARRICK

Small men are often exceedingly ambitious; standing at barely five feet four inches, David Garrick was no exception. The son of a British army officer, Captain Peter Garrick, David was born on 19 February 1717 in Hereford. He attended Lichfield Grammar School and while there his interest in theatre was awakened by a group of strolling players. He first appeared on stage in an amateur production of *The Recruiting Officer* in which he played Sergeant Kite.

Garrick's family could not afford to send him to university, but he studied under Samuel Johnson at his academy near Lichfield. Soon both Garrick and Johnson were heading for London. Garrick studied for the bar at Lincoln's Inn in 1737. He received an inheritance from an uncle who had earlier instructed him in the wine trade, and opened a wine business of his own in London, just off the Strand and near Covent Garden. It was the right area for him, as he could hang around the coffee-houses and pretend to be part of the theatrical milieu. He was soon acting in amateur theatricals, writing theatrical criticism in *Gentleman's*

Magazine and dabbling in playwriting. In 1741 he decided to give up the wine business and throw himself wholeheartedly into the theatre. He made his first professional appearance (under the name of Lyddal) at Ipswich, where he played Aboan in *Oroonoko*. Coming back to London he was frankly amazed that neither Covent Garden nor Drury Lane took up his offer to join them. However, he made his London début — at a small, unlicensed theatre in Goodman's Fields in October 1741. There he played Richard III, and the critics found a new naturalness in his performance. Alexander Pope, not noted for being kind, said: 'That young man never had his equal and never will have a rival.' He was still not playing under his own name; the playbills simply called him a gentleman. He went on to play Clodio in *Love Makes the Man*, Charmont in *The Orphan*, Jack Smutter in *Pamela*, the title role in *The Lying Valet*, and Bayes in *The Rehearsal*. He first appeared under his own name in *The Fair Penitent*, playing Lothario. London was fascinated by this newcomer and flocked to Goodman's Fields. He was soon snapped up

Johnston Forbes-Robertson as Othello (London, 1906)

Albert Finney directed and starred in his theatre company's
production of *The Biko Inquest* at the Riverside Studios
(London, January 1984)

by Drury Lane, and played three parts with them to finish off the season. By this time he was living with Peg Woffington and the two of them went off to Dublin for the summer, where she was the star and he the supporting player.

David Garrick made his official début at Drury Lane on 5 October 1742. That first season with them he played nineteen parts, including Charmont in *The Orphan*, Bayes in *The Rehearsal*, Clodio in *Love Makes the Man*, Captain Plume in *The Recruiting Officer*, Fondewife in *The Old Bachelor*, Lear, Hamlet, Archer in *The Beaux' Stratagem* and Millammur in *Wedding Day*. He also played Drugger in *The Alchemist* with great success. A portrait of him in this part was painted by Zoffany; Fanny Burney, writing of the handsome Garrick in the role, said: 'Never could I have imagined such a metamorphosis as I saw, the extreme meanness, the vulgarity, the low wit, the vacancy of countenance, the appearance of unlicked nature in all his motions.' The season was a great success and Drury Lane was constantly full, though the management was very bad and the company full of disquiet. In January 1744 Garrick played Macbeth — almost as written by Shakespeare — and he followed that with Zaphna in Voltaire's *Mahomet* and Sir John Brute in *The Provok'd Wife*. His Othello (February 1745) was not a success. He was simply physically not right for the part, even though (or maybe because) he blacked up and wore a huge turban, and he soon dropped it from his repertoire. He then played a season at Covent Garden, notably opposite Mrs Cibber in *Fair Portrait*.

In 1747 David Garrick became the artistic and administrative director of Drury Lane. He gathered a notable company around him and tried to encourage more ensemble playing rather than star outbursts. In his first production as director he spoke the prologue Samuel Johnson had written for *The Merchant of Venice* and Macklin played the lead. He did Dryden and D'Avenant's version of *The Tempest* and the following season Springer Barry's *Hamlet* and *Othello, Much Ado About Nothing, Romeo and Juliet* and Johnson's *Irene*.

On 22 June 1749 Garrick married Eva Maria Veigel, a mysterious young beauty who danced under the name of Mlle Violette. She immediately gave up her career and they settled down to respectability.

The rivalry between Drury Lane and Covent Garden was in those days intense. Covent Garden, devoted to mindless spectacle and hence able to offer a great deal of money, lured away the best of Garrick's company. The rivalry culminated in a *tour de force* run of *Romeo and Juliet* at both theatres — a kind of contest of which the public

soon tired. Garrick managed to keep his production on for eleven nights to Covent Garden's ten and declared himself the winner. He also took on the rivals at their own game and at Christmas staged a spectacular pantomime, *Queen Mab*, which ran for a month — in days when productions changed nightly. He also had a great success with the comedy *Gil Blas*, David Mallet's masque *Alfred* (which introduced the song 'Rule Britannia') and Congreve's tragedy, *The Mourning Bride*. Garrick excelled in comedy roles and often presented a double bill of tragedy and farce in the same night.

He had one disaster in 1755 when he presented *The Chinese Festival*, a French ballet, and although he kept trying to tell the public that the director was Swiss-French they would have none of it, and feeling strongly about France at the time mobs wrecked the theatre. He managed to continue successfully, however, with his own adaptations of Shakespeare's *The Winter's Tale, The Taming of The Shrew* and *The Tempest*. And he did *Antony and Cleopatra* almost as it was written.

Garrick continued to make innovations in the theatre, and in the process of running Drury Lane amassed a fortune. But what he cared about most was his own standing as an actor (one of his finest performances was as Posthumus in his own adaptation of *Cymbeline*, which he introduced during the 1761 season), so although he encouraged good acting in his company he did not go out of his way to encourage potential rivals to his stardom. Any actor who showed signs of eclipsing him was left to wander the provinces seeking work.

Garrick was beginning to feel that through familiarity he was losing the appreciation of his audiences, so in 1763 he decided to take an extended holiday. He and his wife travelled widely through Europe, visiting grandly and studying theatrical techniques. After two years he was summoned back to the stage by Royal Command — just what he had been waiting for — and appeared in November 1765, as Benedick in *Much Ado About Nothing*, to overflowing houses. Having learned his lesson he now acted less often; his every appearance became an event. He wrote more, most notably, with George Colman, a comedy called *The Clandestine Marriage*, and he continued to introduce changes in staging.

During Shakespeare's jubilee year in 1769 he was given the Freedom of the city of Stratford and, deeply touched, organized a pageant there. The next season he had to organize a Shakespeare Commemoration at Drury Lane to recoup his losses on that project. He also produced with great success his own *King Arthur* and *The Institution of the Garter or Arthur's Round Table*.

David Garrick had his last season at Drury

Lane during the winter of 1775–76. He played all his old roles and people came from all over the country and from abroad to see him. The house was always full and the audience always enthusiastic. His last appearance was on 10 June 1776, and all the proceeds from the evening went to his fund for destitute actors.

David Garrick had made acting respectable. After a London reign of thirty years as the greatest actor in England, he retired to his mansion in Hampton Court, which was filled with exquisite paintings and furniture, having become not only exceedingly rich but a gentleman as well. Unlike some actors he never made returns to the stage, except for one Royal Command performance at Windsor. After a year of being plagued by a variety of illnesses he died, quite suddenly, on 20 January 1779.

JOHN GIELGUD

John Gielgud, one of four children, was born at 7 Gledhow Gardens in South Kensington on 14 April 1904. His mother was the daughter of actress Kate Terry-Lewis and the niece of Ellen Terry. His father, Frank Gielgud, was a stockbroker and the grandson of the famous Polish actress Aniela Aszpergerowa. As a child John was taken not only to concerts and museums but also to the theatre, where he saw the great actor—managers George Alexander, Beerbohm Tree and du Maurier. He was stage-struck as a boy, and when he was 12 spent as much time and all the pocket money he could raise watching *Chu-Chin-Chow*. At Westminster School he spent his free afternoons at the ballet.

At 17 John Gielgud auditioned for Sir Frank Benson's wife Constance and was given a scholarship to her stage school. Between terms at Lady Benson's school he walked on at the Old Vic, unpaid, in four plays — *Hamlet*, *Peer Gynt*, *Wat Tyler* and *King Lear*. He had his first speaking part on 7 November 1921 when as the Herald in *Henry V* he said: 'Here is the number of the slaughter'd French.'

In 1922 his cousin Phyllis Neilson-Terry gave him a job touring in *The Wheel*, in which he understudied four parts and was an assistant stage manager. He played occasionally but realizing he was not sufficiently trained, auditioned for and was awarded a scholarship to RADA. When he finished at RADA he opened in December 1923 as Charles Wykeham in *Charley's Aunt* at the Comedy. In January 1924 he joined J. B. Fagan's repertory company at the Oxford Playhouse. In May that year at the Regent he played his first Romeo to Gwen Ffrangcon-Davies' Juliet in Barry Jackson's production, and also played a dope-fiend sculptor in a silent film called *Who Is the Man?* He returned to the Oxford Playhouse that autumn and was released in the spring to take over from Noel Coward

in the role of Nicky Lancaster in *The Vortex* at the Little Theatre. Then *The Cherry Orchard* was transferred from Oxford to the Lyric, Hammersmith, and Gielgud played Peter Trofimov. The play transferred once more, to the Royalty Theatre in Dean Street, and ran on through the summer. Never out of work, Gielgud next played Konstantin Treplev in *The Seagull* (Little, October 1925), Sir John Harrington in *Gloriana* (Little, December 1925), Robert in *L'École des cocottes* (Princess, December 1925), and Ferdinand in *The Tempest* (Savoy, January, 1926). In February and March 1926, at a converted cinema in Barnes, he played Baron Nikolai in *The Three Sisters* and George Stibelev in *Katerina* directed by Theodore Komisarjevsky, who had a great influence on his acting style.

At the New Theatre in October 1926, Gielgud once again took over from Noel Coward, this time playing Lewis Dodd in *The Constant Nymph*. Pausing to play Dion Anthony in *The Great God Brown* for the Stage Society at the Strand in June 1927, he spent the rest of that year touring Great Britain in the Coward play.

John Gielgud made his New York début at the Majestic Theater on 18 January 1928, playing Grand Duke Alexander in Alfred Neumann's *The Patriot*. It lasted only twelve performances.

Back in London, at Wyndham's in March 1928, the centenary of Ibsen's birth, he was asked to play Oswald to Mrs Patrick Campbell's lead in *Ghosts*. They played matinées only and usually to a very sparse audience. His next outing was not much more successful. He played Dr Gerald Marlow in a farce called *Holding Out the Apple* at the Globe. It ran only six weeks but for those weeks he saw his name in lights in the West End for the first time. In August at the Shaftesbury he played Captain Allenby in *The Skull*, which he described as a ghastly thriller. In October he was

Felipe Rivas in *The Lady from Albuquerque* and Alberto in *Fortunato* at the Court, moving in November to the Strand where he played a pianist called John Marston in *Out of the Sea*. It had not been a good year for plays. The next, 1929, also started badly when he played Fedor in *Red Rust* at the Little Theatre, but it improved in April when he took over from Leslie Banks playing Henry Tremayne in *The Lady with a Lamp* at the Garrick and worked with Edith Evans and Gwen Ffrangcon-Davies. At the Arts in June he played Bronstein in *Red Sunday*.

Taking an enormous cut in salary, at the invitation of Harcourt Williams, Gielgud then joined the Old Vic Company in September 1929. That season he played Romeo, Antonio in *The Merchant of Venice*, Cleante in *The Imaginary Invalid*, Richard II, Oberon, Mark Antony in *Julius Caesar*, Orlando, the Emperor in *Androcles and the Lion*, Macbeth and Hamlet. *Hamlet* transferred to the Queen's Theatre in April 1930. Eventually, over fifteen years, Gielgud was to play Hamlet more than 500 times in six different productions; this, the first, Gielgud feels was probably his best.

At the Lyric, Hammersmith, in July 1930 John Gielgud played John Worthing in *The Importance of Being Earnest* for the first time and then in September rejoined the Old Vic Company. That season he played Hotspur in *Henry IV Part 1*, Prospero, Lord Trinket in *The Jealous Wife*, Antony in *Antony and Cleopatra*, and at the reopening of Sadler's Wells Theatre in January 1931 he played Malvolio in *Twelfth Night*, following that with Sergius Saranoff in *Arms and the Man*, Benedick, and *King Lear*.

In May 1931 John Gielgud went back to the West End to His Majesty's where he played Inigo Jollifant in *The Good Companions*. At the Arts in November he played Joseph Schindler in *Musical Chairs*, transferring with it to the Criterion in April 1932.

It was in 1933 that John Gielgud became the kind of star who is hailed in the streets when he directed and played the title role in *Richard of Bordeaux*. Ernest Short wrote: 'John Gielgud, as Richard, put up the performance of his career. Here was all the Terry charm, coupled with the capacity to display a character which was gracious, generous and wayward in the early scenes, hysterical and short-tempered in the King's encounters with his barons and dignified and pathetic when facing death.' After a tentative start of two Sunday-night performances at the Arts Theatre, *Richard of Bordeaux* opened in February 1933 at the New Theatre and ran for a year. Gielgud directed *Spring 1600* at the Shaftesbury in

January 1934 and *Queen of Scots* at the New in June 1934. At Wyndham's in July he played Roger Maitland in *The Maitlands*, which was less than successful. However, in November he directed and played the title role in *Hamlet* and notched up a record 155 performances. Sybil Thorndike said: 'Those who saw the Hamlet of John Gielgud have a memory of something hauntingly beautiful for which to be grateful all their lives.' At the New in April 1935 he directed *The Old Ladies*, and in July at the same theatre under a mass of grey hair played Noah. Still at the New, in October he directed Laurence Olivier as Romeo while himself playing Mercutio. In November they swapped roles. Altogether *Romeo and Juliet* played 186 performances — the longest run ever achieved for that play and still a theatrical legend. In May 1936 Gielgud played Boris Trigorin in *The Seagull*; by this time he had become as noted for his playing of Chekhov as he was for his playing of Shakespeare.

In 1936 he crossed the Atlantic once more and opened at the Empire in October, this time triumphantly as Hamlet. John Mason Brown reported: 'Not since John Barrymore made Elsinore his own has a Hamlet of the interest of John Gielgud's been seen — and heard — in New York. If to some of us the Mr Barrymore who was remains even now the Hamlet we shall continue to see in our mind's eye as the perfect embodiment of the Prince, it will be Mr Gielgud's voice in the future we shall hear lending its colour to many of the nobler speeches. Such a voice, such diction, and such a gift for maintaining the melody of Shakespeare's verse even while keeping it edged from speech to speech with dramatic significance is a new experience to those of us who since the twilight days of Forbes-Robertson have seen a small army of actors try their wings, and sometimes our patience, as Hamlet.' And Brooks Atkinson wrote: 'He is young, slender and handsome, with a sensitive, mobile face and blond hair, and he plays his part with extraordinary grace and winged intelligence. For this is no roaring, robust Hamlet, lost in melancholy, but an appealing young man brimming over with grief. His suffering is that of a cultivated youth whose affections are warm and whose honor is bright. Far from being a traditional Hamlet, beating the bass notes of some mighty lines, Mr Gielgud speaks the lines with the quick spontaneity of a modern man. His emotions are keen. He looks on tragedy with the clarity of the mind's eye.' But — win some, lose some — Mr Atkinson continues: 'What Mr Gielgud's Hamlet lacks is a solid body of overpowering emotion, the command, power and storm of Elizabethan tragedy. For it is the paradox of Hamlet that vigorous actors, who know a good deal less about the character than Mr Gielgud does, can make the horror more harrowing and the tragedy more deeply felt.'

Back in London, at the Queen's in May 1937, Gielgud directed *He Was Born Gay* and played the 'lost' Dauphin in this Emlyn Williams play about Marie Antoinette's son. Although it ran for only twelve performances, Gielgud took over the management of the Queen's in September and between then and May 1938 played Richard II, Joseph Surface in *The School for Scandal*, Vershinin in *The Three Sisters* and Shylock in *The Merchant of Venice*. He directed *Spring Meeting* at the Ambassadors' in May 1938, and in September at the Queen's played Nicholas Randolph in Dodie Smith's play about the family, *Dear Octopus*. At the Globe in January 1939 he was once more John Worthing in *The Importance of Being Earnest* and at the same theatre in April he directed *Scandal in Assyria*. He presented *Rhonnda Roundabout* there in May.

In June 1939 Gielgud once again played Hamlet. This time it was at the Lyceum, which was scheduled for demolition but was in the end turned into a dance hall. His was the last theatrical performance in the famous building. Gielgud then went to Elsinore to play the Dane at Kronborg Castle.

The Importance of Being Earnest raised its head once more in August 1939. He toured with it and returned to the Globe in December. In March the following year Gielgud directed *The Beggar's Opera* at the Haymarket, and when Michael Redgrave became ill played Captain Macheath himself.

John Gielgud returned to the Old Vic on 15 April 1940. It was an auspicious occasion. The theatre had been closed because of the declaration of war and this was its reopening. It was also Harley Granville-Barker's first personal supervision of a Shakespeare production. Gielgud played a Renaissance King Lear in glowing satin. His daughters were played by Cathleen Nesbitt, Fay Compton and Jessica Tandy. Ernest Short thought that Gielgud was 'just less than great as the old King. The terror and the pity of Lear, if not the power were there.' But Audrey Williamson thought he 'suggested a genius of spirit that lifted the passion to the highest plane of tragic imagination'. In May 1940 Gielgud played Prospero in an Old Vic production that coincided with the fall of France and the disaster of Dunkirk. Audrey Williamson reported: 'A younger Prospero than most, beardless and spectacled, he gave the character a certain wry humour and scholastic irony ... Gielgud's vocal and temperamental range covered all the moods with ease, and at the end seemed to gather together all the conflicting chords of the play in a serene harmony.' It was the last production before the Old Vic was severely damaged in the bombings.

At the Globe in 1940, in aid of the Actors' Orphanage, John Gielgud played in Coward's *Fumed Oak* and *Hands Across the Sea*. He then toured the army and RAF garrison theatres with the Coward plays for ENSA; during the war, he also toured extensively overseas, entertaining troops in Malta and Gibraltar as well as Burma. He also managed to remain active in the West End to entertain those at home. He directed and played Will Dearth in *Dear Brutus* at the Globe in January 1941, directed *Ducks and Drakes* at the Apollo in November 1941 and at the Piccadilly in July 1942 directed and played the title role in *Macbeth*. At the Haymarket in January 1943 he played Louis in *The Doctor's Dilemma*. *Love for Love*, in which he played Valentine as well as directing, ran at the Phoenix for a year in 1943. He managed to direct five plays in 1944; from October 1944 to May 1945 he ran a repertory season at the Haymarket in which he played Arnold Champion-Cheney in *The Circle*, Valentine in *Love for Love*, Hamlet, Oberon, and Ferdinand in *The Duchess of Malfi*. He then directed *Lady Windermere's Fan* there. Of his 1944 Hamlet James Agate wrote: 'Mr Gielgud is now completely and authoritatively master of this tremendous part. He is, we feel, this generation's rightful tenant of this "monstrous Gothic-castle of a poem". He has acquired an almost Irvingesque quality of pathos, and in the passages after the play scene an incisiveness, a raillery, a mordancy worthy of the Old Man. He imposes on us this play's questing feverishness. The middle act gives us ninety minutes of high excitement and assured virtuosity ... In short, I hold that this is and is likely to remain the best Hamlet of our time.'

After the war Gielgud toured as Raskolnikov in *Crime and Punishment*, a part for which he felt too old but nevertheless brought into the New Theatre in June 1946. In January 1947 he set out on a tour of Canada and the United States, taking *Love for Love* and *The Importance of Being Earnest*. Congreve was not a success, but Wilde was. While abroad he also played Raskolnikov, and Jason in *Medea*.

Returning to England, he directed Tennessee Williams' *The Glass Menagerie* at the Haymarket in July 1948 and *Medea* at the Globe in September. In November he played Eustace Jackson in *The Return of the Prodigal*. Harold Hobson said, on the occasion of Gielgud's return to the West End after an absence of two years: 'Mr Gielgud not only acts well himself, but he is the cause of good acting in other men.'

After directing *The Heiress* at short notice at the Haymarket in February 1949, Gielgud directed Christopher Fry's *The Lady's Not for Burning* at the Globe with the assistance of Esmé Percy. It opened in May and John Gielgud played Thomas Mendip, to everyone's praise. Harold Hobson wrote: 'John Gielgud's Thomas Mendip, a character in search of the gallows, dirty-gartered, half-shaved, with stubbly hair and not yet cleansed from the mud of Flanders, has many a resounding gale of rhetoric with which to make the echoes ring and sing and thunder. Too often the threat of the nightingale is allied to the brain of the Hottentot, but in Mr Gielgud we do not know which to admire the more — his alert, understanding mind, or his superb physical endowments. Both are needed in this play, both are used and at the end, when he walks out into the night, a free man with the unburned lady, and prays God to have mercy on their souls, one almost believes these two characters, which have sometimes been only a witty mist of words, have souls indeed.' T. C. Worsley said: 'Mr Gielgud speaks the difficult verse most intelligently as well as most beautifully, he strikes the romantic attitude when he can and the part brings in the comedy timing he has now perfected.'

The Lady's Not for Burning ran for 294 performances in the West End. During the run Gielgud directed *Much Ado About Nothing* (Stratford, June 1949), *Treasure Island* (Apollo, September 1949), *Shall We Join the Ladies?* and *The Boy with a Cart* (both Lyric, Hammersmith, January 1950). He then went to the Memorial Theatre, Stratford-on-Avon, where during the 1950 season he played Angelo in *Measure for Measure*, Benedick in *Much Ado About Nothing* (Peggy Ashcroft was Beatrice), Cassius in *Julius Caesar* and King Lear. With his performance of Angelo, T. C. Worsley thought that at last John Gielgud had got away from the echoes of his Hamlet, which had pervaded his later Shakespearian work. He went on to say: 'In this characterization of a thin, spinsterish walking Legality there are no traces of the romantic gestures, no echoes of youthful tones.'

John Gielgud took *The Lady's Not for Burning* to New York to the Royale Theater, where it opened in November 1950 to rapturous acclaim. Brooks Atkinson wrote in the *New York Times*: 'Mr Gielgud has long given evidence of his mastery of style in acting; and the performance he has directed is a perfect piece of work ... Mr Gielgud's misanthrope is sharply drawn, spoken with easy virtuosity, droll in tone and inflection. This is acting as expert as the memorable Wilde comedy he brought us several years ago ... Mr

Fry ought to be very grateful to Mr Gielgud. For it seems likely that no one else could make a dry comic antic out of so much undisciplined abundance.'

Returning to London in June 1951, John Gielgud appeared at the Phoenix as Leontes in *The Winter's Tale*, and at the Criterion in December he directed *Indian Summer*. Still at the Phoenix, in January 1952 he played Benedick in his own production of *Much Ado About Nothing*. (This time Diana Wynyard played Beatrice.) He then directed *Macbeth* for Stratford.

With Peter Brook, Gielgud ran a season at the Lyric, Hammersmith, opening in December 1952 with his own production of *Richard II* in which he cast Paul Scofield as the King, feeling himself too old to re-create the part. In February 1953 Gielgud played Mirabell in *The Way of the World*. His Millamant was Pamela Brown. The final play of the season was *Venice Preserv'd*, which opened in May. It had not been performed since the eighteenth century, and since it had two major men's parts, Gielgud decided it would be good for himself and Scofield. Kenneth Tynan had reservations: 'The play's major flaw is that Otway [the playwright] allows Jaffier far too much self-pity, a mood of which John Gielgud as an actor is far too fond. The temptation sometimes proves too much for him: inhaling passionately through his nose, he administers to every line a tremendous parsonical quiver. But pictorially, if not emotionally, this is a very satisfying performance.' It was the only production of the three to lose money.

It was also in 1953 that John Gielgud was knighted; in that year he took his company to Rhodesia (now Zimbabwe) in July to the Rhodes Festival in Bulawayo, where once more he played Richard II. After a much-needed holiday at the game reserves he returned to London, where at the Haymarket in November he played Julian Anson, a dreary, ineffectual civil servant, in *A Day by the Sea*, also directing the production. (It was in this play that Sir John made his first television appearance, in March 1959.) He directed *Charley's Aunt* at the New in February 1954, and at the Lyric, Hammersmith, in May of the same year directed his own adaptation of *The Cherry Orchard*. In April 1955 he directed a confused Vivien Leigh and an obstinate Laurence Olivier in *Twelfth Night* at Stratford and undertook a tour of the provinces and the Continent with the Shakespeare Memorial Theatre Company playing Benedick and King Lear. In July he brought both plays to London, to the Palace. He directed *The Chalk Garden* at the Haymarket in April 1956 and in November directed *Nude with Violin* at the Globe, playing Sebastian. Tynan was unenthusiastic: 'When Sir John Gielgud appears in modern dress on the London stage for only the second time since 1940, selecting as his vehicle Noel Coward's *Nude with Violin*, one's expectations are naturally low. Sir John never acts seriously in modern dress; it is the lounging attire in which he relaxes between classical bookings; and his present performance as a simpering valet is an act of boyish mischief, carried out with extreme elegance and the general aspect of a tight, smart walking umbrella.'

Sir John first directed opera in June 1957. It was *The Trojans* at Covent Garden. He went back to Stratford in August to play Prospero in *The Tempest* and appeared in London in the same production in December at Drury Lane. In May 1958 he was at the Old Vic playing Cardinal Wolsey in *Henry VIII*. At the Globe in February 1959 he played James Callifer in *The Potting Shed* and it was at the same theatre that he directed *Variations on a Theme* in May. The company then toured Paris, Antwerp and Brussels.

Sir John directed *Five Finger Exercise* at the Comedy in July 1958. That September he set out on a tour of his one-man show — a Shakespearian anthology called *Ages of Man*. He travelled through Canada and the United States, ending up at the 46th Street Theater in New York in December. Back in London, in June 1959 he directed *The Complaisant Lover* at the Globe and in July opened at the Queen's in his *Ages of Man*. Kenneth Tynan reported: 'I have always felt that Sir John Gielgud is the finest actor on earth from the nek up, and having heard his Shakespeare recital, *Ages of Man*, I am in no mood to revise that opinion ... The impact of his performance is not, however, exclusively aural; as I've said, Sir John's physical inexpressiveness does not extend above the collar stud. Poker-backed he may be; poker-faced he certainly isn't. Whenever pride, scorn, compassion, and the more cerebral kinds of agony are called for, his features respond promptly and memorably.' (Sir John had been dogged throughout his career with criticism of his movement. It went right back to the days at Lady Benson's school, when she said he walked like 'a cat with rickets'.)

In the autumn of 1959 he took his *Much Ado About Nothing* to America, where he played Benedick to Margaret Leighton's Beatrice in Boston at the Cambridge Drama Festival and in New York at the Lunt-Fontanne Theater. He remained in New York to direct *Five Finger Exercise* at the Music Box in December and when he returned to London he once more performed *Ages of Man*, this time at the Haymarket in April 1960. In September he played Prince Ferdinand Cavanate in *The Last Joke* at the Phoenix. Much of 1961

was spent directing — Benjamin Britten's opera *A Midsummer Night's Dream* (Covent Garden, February), *Big Fish, Little Fish* (ANTA, New York, March) and *Dazzling Prospect* (Globe, June). For the RSC in October he played in Zeffirelli's *Othello*, which Tynan hated: 'In [Gielgud's] hand Othello dwindles into a coffee-stained Leontes; instead of a wounded bull, dangerous despite its injuries, we have an heraldic eagle with its wings harmlessly clipped ... his voice has no body, no nakedness, no explosive power.' At the Aldwych in December, Sir John rounded off the year by playing Gaev in his own adaptation of *The Cherry Orchard*.

Pausing to direct *The School for Scandal* at the Haymarket in April 1962, he took *Ages of Man* to Haifa, Jerusalem and Tel Aviv. He returned to the Haymarket in October and took over the role of Joseph Surface before taking that production of *The School for Scandal* to the Majestic in New York in January 1963. He stayed in New York to perform *Ages of Man* at the Lyceum.

Back in London, at the Haymarket in August 1963 Sir John played Julius Caesar and co-directed *The Ides of March*, then he set off on a tour of Australia and New Zealand with his Shakespeare recital.

At the Lunt-Fontanne in New York he played the Ghost (on tape) and directed Burton's *Hamlet*, and at the Philharmonic Hall there he appeared in a recital, *Homage to Shakespeare*, in March 1964. He then toured Scandinavia, Finland, Poland and the USSR in *Ages of Man*.

In New York at the Billy Rose Theater in December 1964 he played Julian in Edward Albee's *Tiny Alice*. Martin Gottfried wrote: 'John Gielgud's Julian is masterful, building a fearfully human being through candor and sheer goodness into a dreadfully innocent victim.'

Back in England, at the Yvonne Arnaud Theatre in Guildford he directed *Ivanov* in August 1965 and played the title part. It moved into the Phoenix in London in September and crossed the Atlantic in May 1966 to the Shubert in New York. In winter 1966 Sir John toured South America and the American universities for the British Council in a recital of Shakespeare. At the Old Vic in November 1967 he was Orgon for the National Theatre Company's production of *Tartuffe* and that same month he directed Robert Morley in Peter Ustinov's *Halfway Up the Tree* at the Queen's.

In March 1968 Sir John played Oedipus at the Old Vic and that August at the Coliseum directed another opera — *Don Giovanni*. It was at the Apollo in October 1968 that he had an enormous success playing the Headmaster in Alan Bennett's *Forty Years On*, and at the Lyric in February 1970 he was Gideon in *The Battle of Shrivings* — more a debate than a play. He received the *Evening Standard* Award for Best Actor when he played Harry in *Home*. He performed it at the Royal Court in June and at the Morosco in New York in November 1970.

Sir John spent summer 1971 at the Chichester Festival Theatre playing Julius Caesar in *Caesar and Cleopatra*, and was back at the Royal Court in March 1972 as Sir Geoffrey Kendle in *Veterans*. In September he directed Coward's *Private Lives* at the Queen's and then, with the National Theatre Company still at the Old Vic, he played Prospero once more in March 1974. He played Shakespeare himself at the Royal Court that August in *Bingo*.

At the Royal in York in November 1974 Sir John played Milton in *Paradise Lost* and repeated it for the Apollo Society at the Old Vic in December. In 1975 he directed the American tour of *Private Lives* and *The Constant Wife* before playing the down-at-heel poet, Spooner, to Ralph Richardson's wealthy man of letters, Hirst, in *No Man's Land*. They opened at the Old Vic in April 1975, moved to Wyndham's in July and then went to the Lyttelton with it in April 1976. He directed *The Gay Lord Quex* at the Albery in between. In February 1978 Julian Mitchell's *Half Life* trans-

ferred from the National's Cottesloe Theatre; in it Sir John played an Oxford don, Sir Noel Cunliffe. Milton Shulman reported: 'It is a long time since so much polished wit and stimulating reflections have been heard on the English stage. It is a role impeccably tailored for Gielgud's grandest manner.'

As well as his knighthood, Sir John Gielgud has also been appointed Chevalier of France's Légion d'honneur and has numerous honorary doctorates. Although primarily a stage actor, he has made some notable appearances in films, among them *Murder on the Orient Express* and *Arthur* and has done some admirable work on television, especially *Brideshead Revisited*.

A writer as well as an actor, Sir John has written *Early Stages* (1939), *Stage Directions* (1963), *Distinguished Company* (1972); it is in *An Actor and His Time* (1979) that he sums up and explains his massive achievements in the theatre: 'I am quite useless at almost everything except where the theatre is concerned and so I have always been completely occupied working there ... Acting has rid me of my frustrations and satisfied many of my ambitions. It is more than an occupation or a profession; for me it has been a life.'
See photograph opposite page 151.

WILLIAM GILLETTE

'*I*'m a pretty fair stage carpenter, and not altogether bad as an actor after I have written myself a good part that suits me.' William Gillette was born in Hartford, Connecticut, on 24 July 1855. His was by no means an acting family. His father Francis had been a senator from that state, and William was well educated at Hartford, Yale, Harvard, Boston University and the Massachusetts Fine Arts Institute. He had a first-class mind, but never stayed at university long enough to get a degree. He made his first appearance on stage in *Across the Continent* at New Orleans in 1875 when he was still at Yale. His parents discouraged his acting ambitions but a neighbour in Connecticut, Mark Twain, encouraged him and indeed helped him find a job in Boston.

William Gillette, tall and lean with chiselled features, made his first professional appearance on 15 September 1875 at the Globe Theater in Boston playing Guzman in *Faint Heart Ne'er Won Fair*

Lady. He then went to the Boston Museum where he was in *A Gilded Cage*, and played Malcolm in *Macbeth*, Benvolio in *Romeo and Juliet*, Montano in *Othello*, Rosencrantz in *Hamlet*, and Wilford in *The Hunchback*, among other parts. People began to notice him when he played Prince Florian in *Broken Hearts*. After Boston, William Gillette joined Ben McCauley's Company at Cincinnati and Louisville.

In *The Professor*, a play he had written himself, William Gillette made his New York début at the Madison Square Theater on 1 June 1881. He toured as Douglas Winthrop in *Young Mrs Winthrop* throughout 1883 and 1884, returning to New York in September to the Comedy Theater to play the Rev. Job McCosh in *Digby's Secretary*, his own adaptation of van Moser's *Der Bibliothekar*. His next play was a melodrama about the Civil War called *Held by the Enemy*, and he appeared in it at the Criterion in Brooklyn in February 1886, playing Thomas Henry Bean. He also appeared in it at the Madison Square Theater in August. At the Standard in New York in November 1894 he played Augustus Billings in his own farcical version of a French comedy, *Too Much Johnson*. His next play, *Secret Service*, also about the Civil War, was to become one of his most famous. He first appeared in it as Lewis Dumont at the Garrick, New York, on 5 October 1896 and he made his London début at the Adelphi in the role on 15 May 1897. Lewis Strang wrote: 'The success of this play was largely due to Mr Gillette's acting and to his gift for forming and maintaining an atmosphere of actuality. It was no small feat to establish sufficient interest in a spy to make him the hero of the play. Particularly difficult was it to arouse this sympathy, not by an appeal to patriotic sentiment, but by the dramatic strength of the character. Yet this was what Mr Gillette did, as was shown by the full acceptance of the drama south of the Mason and Dixon line and in England. Simplicity and sincerity, intensity and force are the qualities that have made Mr Gillette a thoroughly convincing actor.'

William Gillette next wrote a starring vehicle for himself based on the works of Arthur Conan Doyle about the detective, Sherlock Holmes. Conan Doyle gave him permission to do what he would with the character, and what Gillette did was to create a very successful play, which first appeared at the Garrick Theater, New York, on 6 November 1899, became famous all over the western world, and which he was still reviving in 1935. Brooks Atkinson described it thus: 'A detective play of terse dialogue, great sleight-of-hand, at least one novel device (the red tip of a lighted cigar in a pitchblack room), and terrific excitement.' When Gillette appeared in the play at the Lyceum in London in 1901, J. T. Grein hated the play but he had to concede: 'Mr William Gillette is a splendid actor. We have seen him in *Secret Service* and in *Too Much Johnson* and everyone has given him the praise due to a talent of rare versatility. As Sherlock Holmes he is less happy, simply because the character allows of no grip. The attempt to enact a part which is all incident and contains not an atom of concrete inwardness, is like trying to play ball with bubbles. The thing is beyond the power of man. Still, Mr Gillette, with his remarkably pointed delivery, his striking countenance and presence, his innate sense of humour, now and again infuses a little vitality into the paste-board figure of the famous detective. Sometimes he flagged and spoke his lines in undertones and monotony which provoked gallery protest. But on the whole he carried the part through with the assurance and the volubility of a dexterous conjurer bent on bewildering the

audience at all cost. The performance will confirm Mr Gillette's reputation as an actor of great resources, but I fear that at best his fame as an artist will remain unimpaired by his thankless experiment.' That thankless experiment, called *Sherlock Holmes*, made Gillette a very rich man as well as a very famous one.

Back in New York, in November 1903 he played Crichton in J. M. Barrie's play *The Admirable Crichton*. For a benefit performance at the Metropolitan Opera House in March 1905 he played in *The Painful Predicament of Sherlock Holmes* — a one-act play he had written. Then in September of that year he went back to London where he opened at the Duke of York's playing Doctor Carrington in his new play *Clarice*. He stayed for a while, playing also in *Sherlock Holmes*. He then toured the United States with *Clarice*, bringing it into New York to the Garrick in October 1906. His next play was adapted from the French; he opened at the Criterion in New York in October 1908 playing Maurice Brachard in *Samson*.

The next two years he spent fighting off tuberculosis, and reappeared on the stage in October 1910 in Boston where he played Sherlock Holmes once more, as well as reviving his other famous roles. William Gillette never attempted the great roles — he was a believer in playing to type. He wrote: 'Actors of recent times who have been universally acknowledged to be great have invariably been so because of their successful use of their own strong and compelling personalities in the roles which they made famous. And when they undertook parts, as they occasionally did, unsuited to their personalities, they were great no longer and frequently quite the reverse.' Lewis Strang summed up Gillette's style: 'In spite of his success and facility in both farcical and melodramatic characters, Mr Gillette is by no means a versatile actor. He is essentially the same in every part in which he appears, always cool, collected and unabashed. In farce, by contrast, this sang-froid yields a wealth of fun; in melodrama it serves to increase immeasurably the power of a dramatic situation. Indeed Mr Gillette's methods of expressing emotion are so much his own, so individual, that they may almost be called mannerisms. His points he makes quietly, a twitching of the fingers, perhaps, or a compression of the lips, or a hardening of the muscles of the face. He rarely gesticulates, and his bodily movements often seem purposely slow and deliberate. His composure is absolute and his mental grasp of a situation is complete. In a sense he is wonderfully restful; but he never fails to make himself understood and he is never ambiguous . . .'

At the Empire in New York in October 1914, William Gillette played Beauclerc in *Diplomacy* but the following year was reviving *Sherlock Holmes* and *Secret Service*. At the Booth Theater in February 1917 he played Henry Wilton in *A Successful Calamity* and at the Empire in December 1918 played Mr Dearth in J. M. Barrie's *Dear Brutus*, acting with the very young Helen Hayes. According to Brooks Atkinson it was a memorable appearance: 'No one who saw the production will ever forget the dramatic contrast between the tall, thin, sedate man and the excellent sprite.' After playing Dr Paul Clement in *The Dream Maker* in 1921, William Gillette retired from the stage to his estate in Connecticut where he had built himself an eccentric castle as well as a three-mile private railway. The estate at Hadlyme is now a state park.

In 1929 he returned to the stage, to the New Amsterdam in November, in a revival of *Sherlock Holmes*. John Mason Brown was there and reported: '... the Master Detective he plays, without ever raising his voice or making a single violent movement, is as vivid and commanding an example of the powers of understatement as our theatre knows. One feels from the moment he first courts danger ... that this lean man with his dry casual voice, his fine clean-cut head and his authoritative calm, is somehow beyond the reach of evil ... relief from the uncertainty of most melodramatic plots also grants you more leisure in which to revel in Mr Gillette's playing. It lets you watch him as he takes his time over single sentences, note the masterly way in which he handles his pauses, and observe him as he doubles up on all the negatives of his acting until they are skilfully changed into positives of a compelling kind.' He played a farewell tour in the role in 1931 and 1932, and broadcast it on radio in 1935. William Gillette died on 29 April 1937, at the age of 81.

HERMIONE GINGOLD

The awesome eccentricity of Hermione Gingold has been captured for future generations in the film *Gigi*, but it is on stage that she gives full expression to that peculiar and hilarious strangeness that is pure Gingold.

She was born on 9 December 1897 in London, and her parents named her Hermione Ferdinanda Gingold. ('Would I have chosen such a name?' she said later.) Her father, James, was a wealthy stockbroker. Unfortunately, when she was still a child he lost all his money on the market.

Miss Gingold first appeared on stage in a kindergarten production of *Henry VIII* in which she played Cardinal Wolsey. She made her professional début when she was barely 11, on 19 December 1908, playing the Herald in *Pinkie and the Fairies* at His Majesty's. She attended Rosina Filippi's stage school and made many appearances on stage as a child. When she was 16 she appeared in *The Marriage Market* at Daly's and then for the Old Vic the following year was Jessica in *The Merchant of Venice*. She married the publisher Michael Joseph, with whom she had two sons, but the marriage ended in divorce. She was also divorced from her second husband, the songwriter Eric Maschwitz.

At the Ambassadors' in May 1921 she played Liza in *If* and at the Criterion in August 1922 the Old Woman in *The Dippers*. She was at the Gate Theatre from 1931 to 1933, continuing her career as a serious actress. There she played in *Little Lord Fauntleroy*, and was the second daughter in *From Morn to Midnight*, Lavinia in *One More River*, Lily Malone in *Hotel Universe* and Vidette in *I Hate Men*.

At the 'Q' in November 1934 she played Camille in *Mountebanks* and back at the Gate in December 1935 appeared in *This World of Ours*. At the Saville in April 1936 she was in *Spread It Abroad* and at the Arts in September 1936 played May in *Laura Garrett*. In April 1937 she was at the Mercury playing the Leading Lady in *In Theatre Street*.

It was in March 1939 that Hermione Gingold really found her theatrical niche — in *The Gate Revue*, which transferred to the Ambassadors'. Still at the Ambassadors' in May 1940 she appeared in *Swinging the Gate*. At the Comedy in 1941 she was in *Rise Above It* and at the Phoenix in June 1942 in *Sky High*. In June 1943 she began a revue at the Ambassadors', called *Sweet and Low* which in its various incarnations (*Sweeter and Lower*, *Sweetest and Lowest*) kept that theatre full for the best part of six years. T. C. Worsley said: 'She is, indeed, the archetypal Theatre Gossip ... To watch Miss Gingold's tongue roll round a familiar name and then quietly drop it off with all the mud sticking on is to watch art raising a foible to the stature of a Humour.' She moved to the Comedy in November 1948 in another revue, *Slings and Arrows*, and Harold Hobson noted: 'Miss Gingold blossoms into gargoyles as if she were Notre Dame itself.'

Abandoning revue briefly in November 1949 she played Mrs Rocket in Noel Coward's *Fumed Oak* and Jane Banbury in his *Fallen Angels*, both at the Ambassadors'.

Hermione Gingold was depressed by post-war London and she sailed for America, making her début there at the Brattle Theater in Cambridge, Massachusetts, in March 1951 playing in the revue *It's About Time*. She made her New York début in December 1953 at the Imperial in the revue *John Murray Anderson's Almanac* and in summer 1956 toured America in *Sticks and Stones*. At the Huntington Hartford in Los Angeles in November 1956 she starred in *The Sleeping Prince* and then toured summer theatres in 1957 and 1958 in *Fallen Angels*.

Hermione Gingold returned to Broadway in March 1959 when she played Mrs Bennet in Abe Burrows' musical adaptation of Jane Austen's *Pride and Prejudice* at the Alvin. It was called *First Impressions* and Kenneth Tynan was there to see it. He reported: 'As played by Hermione Gingold, Mrs Bennet is no longer the vague, fussy provincial matchmaker of Jane Austen's imagination but a burbling dragoness fully capable (as she never is in the novel) of withering her husband with a single fire-darting glare. Needless to say, much of what Miss Gingold does is strangely hilarious. No actress commands a more purposeful leer; and in nobody's mouth do vowels more acidly curdle. But she upsets the equilibrium of the Bennet family and hence of the play.'

In April 1960 she was at the Plymouth in a revue, *From A to Z*, and then toured in July as Julia Maltby in *Abracadabra*. At the Martin Beck in September 1962 she took over the part of Clara

Weiss from Molly Picon in *Milk and Honey* and at the Phoenix in January 1963 succeeded Jo van Fleet as Madame Rosepettle in Arthur Kopit's *Oh Dad, Poor Dad, Mama's Hung You in the Closet and I'm Feelin' So Sad*. She then toured it before returning to New York, to the Morosco, in August.

At the Chandler Pavilion in Los Angeles in August 1967 she played Celeste in *Dumas and Son* and in 1969 played in *Charley's Aunt* in New Jersey.

Back in London in 1969 she played Agnes Derringdo, a retired Mata Hari called back to service in *Highly Confidential* at the Cambridge. Helen Dawson reported: 'It was a surprise and a pleasure, to find her famous powers of entertainment intact; to relish for the first time her gurgling voice, the throaty delight in double meanings and the blandly comic acceptance of the features which nature bestowed upon her; reassuring to find all this so apparently indestructible. It's not often that myth is so well preserved.' Miss Dawson, however, felt 'It would be dishonest to recommend the play, but for those who have not yet seen Hermione Gingold, I would recommend the first act and then a quiet dinner.'

Hermione Gingold returned to New York to play Madame Armfeldt in Sondheim's award-winning *A Little Night Music* at the Shubert in February 1973, and repeated the part in London at the Adelphi in April 1975. Michael Coveney found: 'Madame Armfeldt presides sphinx-like over the proceedings, an unmovable object played with irresistible force by Miss Gingold.'

Having been, as she puts it, 'very chintzy' with her money Miss Gingold has always had the luxury of working only when she chooses to, yet still views the prospect of retirement with horror. She dotes on her dog, collects china and dabbles in interior decorating.

LILLIAN GISH

*F*rom tours of Victorian melodrama at an early age, through the birth of cinema, to Broadway at its peak and on to episodes of 'The Love Boat' on television, Miss Lillian Gish has kept pace with a century of entertainment and the changing expectations of the audience.

She was born in Springfield, Ohio, on 14 October and although the year is in dispute we can

settle for 1893. But it was in New York that her father, a candy salesman, deserted his family, leaving her mother to raise Lillian and her younger sister Dorothy. Becoming an actress was a matter of necessity (what else could a child do to help support the family?); becoming a star was a matter of hard work and talent. Lillian Gish made her stage début in Rising Sun, Ohio, in *In Convict's*

Stripes in 1902. Touring the country in melodramas left little time for schooling. As a child she danced in a Sarah Bernhardt production in New York. 'All I can remember,' she said many years later, 'is this apparition with flame-red hair and a swooping voice speaking French.'

In January 1913, at the Republic Theater, she played Marganie in *A Good Little Devil*. The leading part was played by Mary Pickford. The Gishes soon followed Miss Pickford to California, where they became part of Hollywood history and legend, appearing in such D. W. Griffith classics as *Hearts of the World, Broken Blossoms, Birth of a Nation* and *Orphans of the Storm*.

In 1930 Louis B. Mayer told her that the public was rather bored with her and that there was no future for her in the new sound movies, so she returned to New York and opened at the Cort Theater in April 1930 as Helena in *Uncle Vanya*. Her first stage appearance in seventeen years was greeted rapturously by the audience, and Brooks Atkinson reported in the *New York Times* that she was 'fragile and pliant as the young wife of a pretentious scholar'. In 1932 she went west again, this time to Colorado, where in July she opened as Marguerite Gautier in *Camille*. The production came to New York, to the Morosco Theater in November that year, and John Mason Brown found it fascinating. 'Wrong as her performance may have been according to tradition it was the only living thing in a dead script. Her frail innocence was a new explanation of Marguerite's professional success, and a fairly convincing one at that. Though Miss Gish failed to rise to her acting opportunities by not seeming to act at all, her negative Marguerite was not without its gleaming moments. At such times it illumined Dumas's empty script like a candle, a very bright candle, flaming in a hollow pumpkin. Even the sins of her Camille had a radiance about them which made them shine like good deeds in a naughty world.'

At the Longacre in April 1933 she was playing Effie Holden (a character closely based on the famous Lizzie Borden) in *9 Pine Street. Newsweek* reported: 'Something that George Jean Nathan [the critic who was for years begging Lillian Gish to marry him] has been asserting for years, but had not been proved, was demonstrated last week ... Lillian Gish is an actress ... In her previous appearances on the legitimate stage there was no denying the fascination of her personality, but that personality was always the same and she seemed to drift through a play ... what matters now is that Lillian Gish gives what can only be described as a brilliant performance.'

She followed that with *The Joyous Season* at the Belasco in January 1934 in which she played

Christine Farley and then played the Young Whore in *Within the Gates* at the National in October that year. According to John Mason Brown she brought 'a new strength — a new and much deeper voice — to a part that abounds in difficulties'.

Lillian Gish made her British début at the King's Theatre, Glasgow, in March 1936 playing Charlotte Lovell in *The Old Maid*.

Back in New York in October 1936 at the Empire she was Ophelia in the famous John Gielgud *Hamlet*. John Mason Brown said: 'Although completely negative until the mad scene, Lillian Gish's Ophelia then turns into the most effective, if untraditional Ophelia we have yet witnessed.' The following September she played Martha Minch in Maxwell Anderson's *The Star Wagon* and John Mason Brown wrote that in it she gave 'The best, most fully rounded performance of her stage career as the inventor's wife who must change from the scold she now is, to the laughing girl she once was and become the tender and reconciled wife of the final scene. Never has her aggressive innocence been displayed to better advantage.'

As Grace Fenning in *Dear Octopus* she opened at the Broadhurst Theater in January 1939 and then in 1940 appeared in Chicago as Vinnie in *Life with Father*, before touring it. She was Jane Gwilt in *Mr Sycamore* at the Guild Theater in November 1942. It was not until 1947 that she again appeared on stage, this time touring the summer theatres as Marquise Eloise in *The Marquise* and Leonore in *The Legend of Leonore*. In December 1947 at the National Theater in New York she played Katerina Ivanova in a dramatization of Dostoevsky's *Crime and Punishment*, and then spent much of 1950 touring in the title role of *Miss Mabel*; in October she returned to New York, to the Martin Beck Theater, to play Ethel in *The Curious Savage*, and in 1951 took *Miss Mabel* on the road again.

In 1953 Lillian Gish starred as Mrs Carrie Watts in Horton Foote's *The Trip Bountiful* at the Henry Miller Theater. Harold Clurman, writing in the *Nation*, said: 'Lillian Gish seems to me better in *The Trip Bountiful* than in any other play in which I have seen her.' Miss Gish toured with her sister Dorothy in *The Chalk Garden* in 1956 and then went to Germany, where she dedicated the Congress Hall, Berlin, playing in a programme of one-act plays.

At the Phoenix Theater in New York in October 1958 she was Agatha in *The Family Reunion* and Catherine Lynch at the Belasco, December 1960, in *All the Way Home*. For the 1962–63 season in Chicago she played Mrs Moore in *A Passage To India*, and back in New York at the

54th Street Theater in March 1963 she was in a revival of *Too True to be Good* playing Mrs Mopply.

For the summer of 1965 at the Shakespeare Festival Theater in Stratford, Connecticut, Lillian Gish played a fluttery Nurse in *Romeo and Juliet* and then in November at the Ziegfeld played the Dowager Empress in *Anya* — a musical version of *Anastasia*. At the Longacre in January 1968 she played Margaret Garrison in *I Never Sang for My Father*. She then devised a one-woman show called *Lillian Gish and the Movies — The Art of Film 1900-28* and met packed houses and standing ovations when she trekked around the world with it — now aged about 77 — visiting Russia, France and Great Britian.

In 1973 she returned to New York and Chekhov, opening in June at the Circle in the Square playing Marina in Mike Nichols' production of *Uncle Vanya*. At the St James in November 1975 she appeared in the revue, *A Musical Jubilee*.

Despite her distinguished theatrical career (not to mention the legendary cinematic one) Lillian Gish admits to a few mistakes: 'I turned down Blanche Du Bois when Tennessee Williams brought me a first draft of *A Streetcar Named Desire*, I guess because I couldn't really understand her, and then one day a writer told me he had the idea for a comedy about murder and

insanity. I told him that sounded like a terrible idea and he told me it was called *Arsenic and Old Lace* — and I didn't get to do that one either.' But she has no regrets about remaining single: 'Somehow marriage seemed like a full-time job, and I deeply loved and admired my mother who'd had a disaster with hers, so I thought, well, if she can't make a go of it, what on earth makes me think I ever could? I had to look after her and then Dorothy when they got ill towards the end of their lives, and that was maybe twenty years altogether, and though I've had a lot of very good friends I've always liked them too much to want to ruin their lives by marrying them.'

Brooks Atkinson sums up Lillian Gish's talent: 'Miss Gish has never failed the author or the audience. She believes that it is the duty of the actor to help make the play intelligible and interesting. She has no patience with the introspective school of acting. To her, what motivates the actor is a matter of no importance; what moves her audience is.' And in an interview in 1977 Miss Gish summed up her life: 'I've never known what to do except work; if you start acting when you're five there isn't a lot of point in trying to find something else to do when you're 84. I expect I'll still have a couple of days' shooting to do when they bury me.'

JOYCE GRENFELL

Joyce Grenfell was born in Montpelier Square in London on 10 February 1910. Her father, Paul Phipps, was a noted architect, and her mother, Nora Langhorne, was an American and sister to Nancy Astor. As a child Joyce frequently crossed the Atlantic, and although she seemed to epitomize English gentility she absorbed a good deal of both cultures. She was greatly influenced by the famous monologue creator and performer Ruth Draper, who was a distant cousin of her father. On visits to London, Miss Draper would entertain Joyce and her younger brother Tommy in the nursery. After a variety of schools, including one in Paris which 'finished' her, in 1927 Joyce Grenfell went to RADA, where she remained only one term and played a dairymaid in a French play.

On 12 December 1929 she married Reginald Pasco Grenfell, a chartered accountant and eventual company director whom she had known for years. (Although childless, the marriage was a

long and happy one.) As a young married woman she got together with a group in Tunbridge Wells to organize a charity entertainment. The group called themselves The Bright Spots and performed other people's material. She wrote occasional verses for *Punch* and became radio critic for the *Observer*. All this time she had been entertaining her friends and relatives with her humorous monologues. She was asked by Herbert Farjeon to join his revue, and made her professional début on 21 April 1939 performing her own material in *The Little Revue*, which starred Hermione Baddeley and Cyril Ritchard at the Little Theatre. She describes the experience: 'I began, as all real Women's Institute lecturers begin: "Madam President — fellow Institute members — good evening." I spoke in the dainty way of the original speaker and I suppose the audience recognized the authenticity of what I said and how I said it. We were off. I said a line. They laughed. I said another.

They laughed. It was a sort of game, with me holding back the next line till the very last moment and then letting them have it. I felt as if I were playing superlative tennis with a challenging opponent — long, even rallies and then a sharp change of pace — and my point.' Joyce Grenfell the entertainer was launched. She performed in three editions of *The Little Revue*. That year she also made her first record, a BBC broadcast, and performed privately at the home of Lady Halifax to entertain the King and Queen after dinner.

At Wyndham's in October 1940 Joyce Grenfell appeared in *Diversion*, sharing the bill with Edith Evans, Peter Ustinov and a very young Dirk Bogarde, among others. *Diversion No. 2* was at the Ambassadors' the following January. She began composing songs with Richard Addinsell and worked at the Red Cross Hospital set up at the Astors' estate in Cliveden. In August 1942 she spent three weeks at the Ambassadors' trying to prop up her old friend Herbert Farjeon's sinking revue, *Light and Shade*, but was unsuccessful. During 1944–45 she travelled with ENSA touring hospitals in Algeria, Malta, Sicily, Italy, Iran, India and Egypt. Back in London in August 1945 she was at the Piccadilly in Noel Coward's revue, *Sigh No More*. The critic James Agate was not very impressed with the evening, but found things to like, including 'The shattering "Backfischerei" of Miss Joyce Grenfell — Lewis Carroll is the father of that grin with which the maddening child greets misfortune, a grin which grows and Grows and GROWS.'

In 1946 Joyce Grenfell was awarded the OBE for services to the armed forces. She then wrote two new monologues for herself for a new revue, *Tuppence Coloured*. It included the 'Odyssey', about an American tourist's view of post-war England, and the 'Artist's Room', in which she played four different members of the audience going backstage after a piano recital. She also performed a new song she had written, 'The Countess of Coteley', and clowned in an Echo song and dance she had composed. *Tuppence Coloured* opened at the Lyric, Hammersmith, in September 1947. Harold Hobson wrote: 'With Nicholas Phipps and Arthur Macrae to write the most literate lyrics of any revue in London, Richard Addinsell to compose much of the music, Victor Stiebel designing dresses and Joyce Grenfell, Elisabeth Welch and Max Adrian in the cast, there is on the stage at Hammersmith enough talent to keep three-quarters of London's theatres full for three-quarters of the year ... Miss Grenfell's Countess [is] especially to be commended.' The show transferred to the Globe, where it ran for more than a year. Her next revue was in May 1951 at the St Martin's and was called *Penny Plain*. At this time she was also appearing regularly in films such as *Genevieve*, *The Belles of St Trinian's* and *The Million-Pound Note*.

In June 1954 Joyce Grenfell opened at the Fortune in the first entertainment built entirely around her talents. She wrote and starred in it, calling it *Joyce Grenfell Requests the Pleasure*. She made her New York début in this at the Bijou Theater in October 1955. This was her last performance sharing the stage with other people. Apart from a pianist (William Blezard), after 1955 Joyce Grenfell was strictly a solo performer. She toured extensively in the United States, Canada, Australia, New Zealand and Great Britain. She also continued recording and appeared very successfully on television. Her very last performance of songs and monologues was given on 21 June 1963 at Windsor Castle at the command of the Queen. Joyce Grenfell then retired to write two very successful volumes of autobiography. She died in 1979.

ALEC GUINNESS

*A*lec Guinness, the first of the modern classical actors periodically to desert the legitimate stage for the film world (at a curtain call on stage he once said how nice it was to be back in the profession having been working in the industry), is a very quiet star indeed. He is rather tired of being called faceless and chameleon; his acting has been praised, and duly awarded, on stage, film and television.

Alec Guinness was born in London on 2 April 1914, son of a Scottish banker whom he never saw. His stepfather, a Scottish army officer, left for New Zealand when Alec was three. Alec went to boarding school in Southborne when he was eight and got his first chance to perform at Roborough, his secondary school in Eastbourne, where he played a messenger in *Macbeth*.

Finishing school at 18, he went to work for an

advertising agency, a job which he not only disliked but at which he was particularly inept. He was not paid much so he walked everywhere and as often as possible to the theatre. His early perambulations are a key to his performances. 'I don't really get into a part until I can imagine how a man walks. The walking stems from the days when I never had any money and I was forced to walk everywhere. I was always in between jobs and there was nothing much to do except follow people. So I would imitate their walk.'

He finally summoned up his courage and telephoned John Gielgud, a complete stranger, to ask him how to become an actor. Gielgud recommended that he take voice lessons from Martita Hunt, which Guinness did, and although at first she proclaimed him no-talent, he persisted and was eventually awarded a scholarship to the Fay Compton Studio of Dramatic Art. He happily gave up his job, but after seven months at the drama school he could no longer afford to continue — not if he wanted to eat — so he sought employment on the stage.

Alec Guinness made his professional stage début walking on as a junior counsel in *Libel* at the Playhouse on 2 April 1934. That September at the Cambridge Theatre he played three minor parts. Then Gielgud, who had been keeping an eye on him, gave him the parts of Osric and the Third Player in his production of *Hamlet* at the New Theatre in November 1934. In July 1935, still with Gielgud, he played the Wolf in *Noah*. Playing Tiger in the production was a young actress named Merula Salaman, whom he married in 1938. Guinness doubled Sampson and the Apothecary in Gielgud's famous production of *Romeo and Juliet* which starred Olivier and Peggy Ashcroft in October 1935, and in May 1936 he was the Workman and later played Yakov in Chekhov's *The Seagull*.

In September 1936 Alec Guinness joined the Old Vic, for whom he played Boyet in *Love's Labour's Lost*, Le Beau and William in *As You Like It*, Old Thorney in *The Witch of Edmonton*, Reynaldo and Osric in *Hamlet*, Aguecheek in *Twelfth Night* and Exeter in *Henry V*. He played Osric, Reynaldo and the Player Queen in June 1937 at Elsinore with the Old Vic and then joined John Gielgud's company at the Queen's Theatre, where he was Aumerle and the Groom in *Richard II*, Snake in *The School for Scandal*, Feoditch in *The Three Sisters* and Lorenzo in *The Merchant of Venice*. In June 1938 in Richmond he played Louis Dubedat in *The Doctor's Dilemma*. By now, aged 24, Guinness had inherited the title 'most promising'.

In September 1938 he rejoined the Old Vic and played Arthur Gower in *Trelawney of the 'Wells'*, a complete *Hamlet* in modern dress, and Bob Acres in *The Rivals*. Then he toured Europe and Egypt with the company, playing in *Hamlet*, *The Rivals* and *Libel*. Back at the Old Vic in June 1939 he played Michael Ransom in *The Ascent of F6* and the following month was in Perth for the Scottish Theatre Festival playing Romeo. He adapted Dickens' *Great Expectations* for the stage and played Herbert Pockett at the Rudolf Steiner Hall in December 1939. In March 1940 he was Richard Meilhac in *Cousin Muriel* at the Globe, and then went back to the Old Vic in May to play Ferdinand in *The Tempest* before touring as Charleston in *Thunder Rock*.

By this time Alec Guinness had a son and the world had a war. He enlisted in the Royal Navy in 1941 as an ordinary seaman and was commissioned a lieutenant in April 1942; he served in the Mediterranean on an escort ship. When the ship was laid up for repairs in New York, Guinness got leave to make his Broadway début at the Henry Miller Theater playing Flight-Lieutenant Graham in Terence Rattigan's *Flare Path*. It closed in ten days. Also during the war he appeared as Lord Nelson in a Pageant in London in the spring of 1945. He was discharged from the navy and made his reappearance on the London stage playing (at the Lyric, Hammersmith, in June 1946) Mitya in his own adaptation of Dostoevsky's *The Brothers Karamazov*, directed by Peter Brook. They went on to do the first English-language production of Sartre's *Huis-Clos* at the Arts in July 1946; it was called *Vicious Circle* and Guinness played Garçin. In September that same year he rejoined the Old Vic. There he played the Fool in *King Lear*, and Harold Hobson said he was 'so pale and anxious of face despite his smile, infinitely dejected at a jest misfired'. Hobson was also impressed by his Eric Birling in the next production, *An Inspector Calls*. 'As the young wastrel of the family, yet with a spark of sympathy left in him, Mr Alec Guinness shows himself a notable newcomer to the Old Vic Company. There is a paleness, a weariness of face about him that recalls Fred Astaire. I have no doubt he dances less skilfully than Astaire, but he acts extraordinarily well.' After playing Comte de Guiche in *Cyrano de Bergerac* and Abel Drugger in *The Alchemist*, he scored a real triumph as what W. A. Darlington called an 'unforgettably subtle and impressive King Richard II'. Hobson raved: 'The feeling and thinking are touched to fine issues. I have never heard the great speeches more beautifully delivered. In the scenes in Wales in particular, that music which at first only Mr Guinness hears surges through the theatre. He has a whole orchestra in his voice: the wailing violin, the thundering trumpet, the lamenting cello.' And he continued to rave when Guinness went on to play the Dauphin to Celia Johnson's St Joan. 'Mr Alec Guinness's Dauphin is a triumph. It suggests a sharp-nosed, half-witted schoolgirl in its red stockings and its yellow smock, and it replies to all the bullying it encounters with a flouncing and sulky resentment that is endearing as well as comic.'

Still with the Old Vic in 1948, Alec Guinness played Khlestakov in *The Government Inspector*, of which performance Harold Hobson said: 'He is as delicate as a butterfly and as silly as a moth; and when, his brief flirtation with fortune over, his tongue resumes its common accent with his threadbare coat, you can see a light die within him. Curiously, with this pale and fragile actor, whose gaiety seems always haunted by sadness, there is no pathos here; but the declension is a cruel thing.' Guinness then played Menenius Agrippa in *Coriolanus* before producing *Twelfth Night* for the Old Vic Company at the New Theatre in September 1948.

At the Savoy in 1949 Alec Guinness played Dr James Y. Simpson, the discoverer of the anaesthetic properties of chloroform, in *The Human Touch*. Harold Hobson reported: 'Alec Guinness's outbursts of indignant pity at the wickedness of unnecessary suffering rang through the theatre like the tolling of a great bell.'

In Edinburgh for the Festival in August 1949, Alec Guinness played the Uninvited Guest in T. S. Eliot's *The Cocktail Party* and went with it to New York to the Henry Miller Theater in January 1950. Although no one on Broadway understood it, the play was a great success, and Brooks Atkinson, writing in the *New York Times*, enthused: 'As the psychiatrist, Alec Guinness is superb — casual and amusing in the early scenes but rising to considerable spiritual eminence in the last act.' He was voted best actor in the New York Drama Critics Poll.

Back in London, at the New Theatre in May 1951 he directed and played the lead in *Hamlet* and in April the following year at the Aldwych he was the Scientist in *Under the Sycamore Tree*. He went to Toronto for the Stratford Shakespearian Festival in July 1953, where he played Richard III and the King in *All's Well That Ends Well*.

Alec Guinness played a Roman Catholic cardinal under pressure in a police state in *The Prisoner* at the Globe in April 1954. It was about this time that he himself became a Roman Catholic, having been an atheist. 'I read a lot,' he said, 'I thought a lot. It seemed a simple step. There was no drama.'

At the Winter Garden in May 1956 he played Boniface in Feydeau's *Hotel Paradiso*. Caryl Brahms wrote a dissertation on his performance in *Plays and Players*: 'What other actor can so touchingly acquaint us with the strength that is part of weakness — or equally the weakness that lies at the heart of strength? . . . Then there is that unobtrusive but undeniable range he can command . . . Guinness has only to enter, eternally hopeful upon the scene and we, the playgoers, are instantly implicated . . . There are, of course, two kinds of comics — the improviser or natural clown who plays his business off the cuff, and the careful, calculating performer who times his effects precisely and sets his performance at the beginning of the run and does not vary his playing by the flicker of an eyelash. Guinness is an actor who plays according to plan. And a perfection of planning goes into each gesture, every look . . . Without recourse to the hysteria of farce, he contrives to be hysterically funny. He does not, then, subscribe to the convention by which no player enters but at a run, no word is uttered but in a squeak or in a big bass boom. Guinness, quite simply, is — and we are in the aisles.'

In 1959 Alec Guinness was knighted in the Queen's Birthday Honours. It was not until 1960 that he returned to the stage, and then it was in the title role of Rattigan's play about T. E. Lawrence, *Ross*, at the Haymarket in May 1960. Caryl Brahms was still in raptures: 'A most impressive performance by Guinness holds the play, which is fragmentary, together. Gentle as a tear and swift and light and kind and authoritative . . . There was nothing of the Ealing Comedian, no clever business — only the timing of a histrionic angel, the sweetness from which Guinness is never wholly divorced.' For this performance he was given the *Evening Standard* Best Actor Award. He next appeared on stage at the Edinburgh Festival playing Berenger the First in Ionesco's *Exit the King*, which he brought to the Royal Court Theatre in Sloane Square in September 1963. The following year, in January, he played Dylan Thomas in *Dylan* at the Plymouth Theater, New York. It ran for eight months and Guinness received not only the Tony Award but also the Newspaper Guild of New York Page One and the Aegis Theater Club Awards for best actor.

Back in London at the Phoenix in January 1966 he played von Berg, a Christian with a conscience in wartime occupied France, in Arthur Miller's flawed *Incident at Vichy*. He was deemed, as ever, interesting to watch. But his next outing, this time as Macbeth at the Royal Court in October 1966, was not a success. He had an almost unintelligible Simone Signoret as his Lady, and Hugh Leonard summed it up: 'It says much for Sir Alec's gift for anonymity that although he is standing and speaking in full view of the audience, with only Banquo and the witches present, it is two or three minutes before we notice him. If ever the Invisible Man is dramatized, Sir Alec will be ideal casting; but Macbeth is not his part.'

At Wyndham's the following October Sir Alec got into drag to play Mrs Arminster in Simon Gray's black comedy, *Wise Child*. He revived *The Cocktail Party*, playing at Chichester (May 1968), Wyndham's (November 1968) and the Haymarket (February 1969). Then he had a real disaster at the Yvonne Arnaud Theatre in Guildford in July 1970 playing John in Bridget Brophy's anti-nuclear play *Time Out of Mind*, but returned to form at the Haymarket in August 1971 playing the blind father in John Mortimer's *A Voyage Round My Father*. Michael Billington wrote: '... he brilliantly suggests the character's blindness: the hand plays lightly over the surface of tables and chairs as if he were intuitively searching them out, the head constantly turns to acknowledge a new speaker or seek out a moving figure and the eyes have none of that hard, unfocused quality that is the cliché way of presenting stage blindness. Guinness may not naturally possess the character's intransigent selfhood, but his artistry is nonetheless impeccable.'

According to Helen Dawson he gave a 'delicious and subtle performance' as Dr Wickstead in Alan Bennett's *Habeas Corpus* at the Lyric in May 1973, and he was marvellous but barely stretched for his performance as Dudley in an adaptation of Ivy Compton-Burnett's novel *A Family and a Fortune* at the Apollo in April 1975.

In October 1976 he co-devised and played Jonathan Swift in an entertainment based on the life and writings of the satirist at the Queen's, and then returned to Alan Bennett for his next venture — playing an expatriate in *The Old Country*.

In 1981 Sir Alec scored an enormous success on BBC television playing George Smiley the spymaster in John Le Carré's *Tinker, Tailor, Soldier, Spy* and followed that with the sequel, *Smiley's People*. He had been shy of television but these two series were made on film, and Guinness had successfully begun filming in 1946 when he starred in *Great Expectations*. His successes in that field include *Oliver Twist*, *Kind Hearts and Coronets*, *The Lavender Hill Mob*, *The Ladykillers*, *The Bridge on the River Kwai* (for which he won an Oscar), *Lawrence of Arabia*, and most recently, *Star Wars*, in which he played the wise old Kenobe, and David Lean's *A Passage to India*.

Alec Guinness comments about his career: 'I've been lucky all my life. Once I got started I've only had a few weeks out of work, not of my own choice. I'm much more relaxed as an actor now, not to say any better. I'm probably more real, or perhaps just lazy.'

In 1984 Sir Alec returned to the stage to play Shylock in *The Merchant of Venice* at the Chichester Festival.
See photograph opposite.

LUCIEN GUITRY

'*I* have always acted,' said Lucien Guitry, 'everywhere, in every place, at every minute — always, always!' And as to his stage performances he explained: 'I have an audience of three. One is deaf as a post, the other is blind as a mole, and the third is the most intelligent man in the world, cultured, sensitive and appreciative beyond all expectation ... only he doesn't understand French. My job as an actor is to convince all three of them.'

Lucien Guitry, the youngest of four children, was born on 13 December 1860 in Paris, where his Normandy-born father ran a thriving cutlery business. He had typhoid at the age of nine and it caused a severe loss of memory — so severe that Lucien had to re-learn everything. The process somehow caused his mind to become abnormally retentive, so that for years he could carry entire scripts of plays in his mind.

Both his parents were stage-struck, constantly reciting plays around the house, and Lucien took to skipping school and spending his time studying plays. At 15 he was taken on at the Conservatoire to study acting, but he was as bored there as he had been at school. In spite of some success at the Conservatoire, Lucien broke his contract and instead signed a three-year contract with the Théâtre de Gymnase, where he played many parts including Armand in *La Dame aux camélias*. He attracted the attention of the tempestuous Sarah Bernhardt, who took him on her annual tour to London in 1882. There he played in *La Dame aux camélias*, *Hernani* and *Adrienne Lecouvreur*. It was said that while the Divine Sarah often chose

Alec Guinness as Abel Drugger in Ben Jonson's comedy
The Alchemist (London, May 1947)

John Gielgud in one of his greatest roles, Hamlet (London)

her leading men for their talent in the bedroom as well as their talent on the stage, Guitry was chosen solely because he was a tremendous actor. In fact he had brought Renée de Pont-Just with him from Paris, abducting her against the wishes of her father (a noted writer, journalist and duellist), and Sarah was a witness at their wedding in London, at St Martin in the Fields, on 10 June.

Guitry signed a contract to play nine consecutive winter seasons in Russia — at the Mikhailovsky Theatre in St Petersburg. The theatre mounted a new production each week and between 1882 and 1891 he played over fifty roles there, ranging from Shakespeare to adaptations of the novels of Zola. The family spent their summers in Paris and winters in Russia; when the marriage broke down and Lucien's wife had custody of the children, Lucien kidnapped his third son, Sacha, and took him off to Russia with him for the season.

Lucien Guitry returned to Paris in 1891 and worked at the Odéon and Théâtre de la Renaissance with Réjane and Bernhardt; he became the most respected, admired and popular actor in France. James Harding describes him: 'He was tall, handsome like a Roman emperor and deep-voiced. His speech was low and even and he gained his effects by subtly grouping and building up phrases more or less in the same tone, a complex artifice which gave the most complete illusion of truth . . . his ''silences'' were as telling as the words he pronounced . . . He never tore a passion to tatters and always aimed to be master of himself and of his audience . . . he introduced a new style of naturalistic acting which sounded the death knell of the declamatory boulevard manner which had flourished when he entered the theatre.'

For a few months in 1901 he joined the Comédie-Française as a producer, but left to take over the management of the Théâtre de la Renaissance, a position he held until 1910 and during which time he continued to embellish his own reputation as well as to introduce outstanding actors and contemporary playwrights such as France, Brieux, Borget and Capus. He earned vast amounts of money and spent it all on pictures, antiques or the woman currently in residence, who was usually his present leading lady.

In 1902 his international reputation was enhanced when he appeared at the Garrick Theatre in London with Jeanne Granier in *La Veine* and at the Adelphi in June and July of 1909 playing in *L'Assommoir*, *Le Voleur*, *L'Emigré*, *Crainquebille* and *Samson*.

In February 1910 Lucien Guitry was asked to create the part of Chantecler in Rostand's play of the same name at the Théâtre de la Porte Saint-Martin. Max Beerbohm hurried across the Chan-

nel to have a look at it, and reported: ' . . . Guitry is magnificent. He is, indeed, too magnificent. Not for a moment do we wonder at the awe he inspires in the hens: we share it. Whenever he turns his full-face to us — that face wrought in iron, or hewn out of rock, that face fashioned for heroic villainy or villainous heroism (we know not which), with its glittering eyes and minatory nose, and all-compressing, all-compelling lips, that face more than ever grim now in the shadow of the great beak above it — we quail as in the presence of some great Viking revisiting the earth and behaving in his old fashion. Yes, it is as such that Guitry behaves throughout the play. He has humour but always it is grim, never comedic; and never is there a touch of the grotesque. And thus while he personally succeeds by sheer force and splendour, the play itself loses much of its quality.'

At the Vaudeville in Paris in March 1911 he played Georges Portal in *Le Tribun* and in June of that year went on a tour of South America. It was so successful that with the proceeds he bought a prime piece of land in Paris. A subsequent South American tour paid for the building of a house to his requirements around a magnificent staircase, and a third tour saw it exquisitely furnished.

Also in 1911, in Paris he played in *L'Assaut* at the Gymnase, and the Hajj in *Kismet* at the Théâtre Sarah Bernhardt, a production he mounted at his own (vast) expense. He built a lake on stage and even went to the East to make sure he had the *mise-en-scène* right. Even with a full house every night there was no hope of getting his money back. At the same theatre in 1913 he was Colonel Eulin in *Servir*.

At the Gymnase in March 1914 he played the title role in *Pétard* and at the Gaîté, in 1918 after the war, he played in *Miette*. He went back to the Porte Saint-Martin in 1917 where he appeared in the title role of his own comedy, *Grandpère*. He followed that the next year with his own *L'Archeveque et ses fils* and then performed in a revival of *Samson*.

After a thirteen-year estrangement he asked his son Sacha to write a play for him. It was *Pasteur*, based on the life and discoveries of the great scientist. In it Lucien gave one of his finest performances. In 1920 Lucien, Sacha and Sacha's wife, Yvonne Printemps, went to London to the Aldwych for a season and the audiences were so massive that they had to extend their stay. Of *Pasteur* Arnold Bennett said: 'It seems a lot to say, but at every moment he was perfect.' And C. B. Cochran, the showman, enthused: 'As Lucien Guitry began the long, agonizing vigil, upon the result of which all Pasteur had fought for depended, the audience was held with that tense-ness which one experiences only once in a lifetime. And then the curtain fell, with the audience gasping, and then breaking into frenzied applause.'

Back in Paris Sacha had taken a lease on the tiny Théâtre Edouard VII. There Lucien played in Sacha's play *Le Comèdien*, which was almost the story of his own life. For the last seven years of his life he acted almost solely in Sacha's plays. They included *Le Mari, La Femme et l'amant* and *Mon Père avait raison*. He did, however, revive some of his early successes, and at the Théâtre Edouard VII put on a Molière season to mark the playwright's tricentenary in 1922. He played in *Le Misanthrope, Tartuffe* and *L'Ecole des femmes*. In these productions Lucien broke with tradition and played them for a realistic blend of tragedy and comedy. James Harding said: 'They were done at the peak of Lucien's career and represent, together with the acting style he bequeathed, his lasting revolutionary contribution to the theatre.'

Lucien was struck not only with coronary trouble but also with terminal grief after the accidental death of his son Jean; he died, no longer with a will to live, of a heart attack on June 1925 after telling his son Sacha simply to write a play about Mozart. At his funeral Antoine, a fellow actor, said: 'In the name of French actors, I salute the greatest of all actors.'

SACHA GUITRY

' *M* y surname was made, so I made myself a first name.'
Alexandre Georges Pierre Guitry was born on 21 February 1885 in St Petersburg, Russia, where his father, Lucien, was playing a winter season at the Mikhailovsky Theatre. His Russian nurse called him Sacha and so did everyone else for the rest of his life. As a baby his summers were spent in Paris and his winters in Russia. When he was four his parents divorced, and his father abducted him from Paris, where his mother had custody, to spend his last Russian season with him in St Petersburg. Sacha's mother went on the stage herself playing small parts and understudying, and Sacha's childhood revolved around the theatre. Holidays were spent with Sarah Bernhardt. He adored the theatre and the famous friends of his father, who was an enormous star.

Although Sacha had appeared on the stage with his father in St Petersburg when he was five, Lucien Guitry was not pleased when, as a young man, Sacha wanted to follow him into the theatre. Lucien did not want Sacha tarnishing the name of Guitry. Finally his father relented and Sacha was given a small part in his current play, a costume drama, on condition that he take the name of Lorcey. One evening he arrived late at the theatre, and when he finally made his entrance he had forgotten his wig. In a fury over such unprofessional behaviour his father fined him one hundred francs. Sacha protested, they quarrelled and he left the theatre. They neither saw nor spoke to each other for thirteen years.

In 1905 Sacha played a summer season near Dieppe at St Valéry-en-Caux, without distinction. But during that season he wrote *Nono*, a play about a young man trying to rid himself of an older mistress; it was performed first at the Théâtre des Mathurins on 6 December 1905, and both it and Sacha, who played in it, were immediate successes. His second play, *Chez les Zoaques*, was an even greater success and when the leading man left the cast Sacha took his place. James Harding reports that 'despite having no rehearsal he played with an ease and charm that captivated the audience ... He could not only write plays but could act them with an air of improvization as attractive as the spontaneity of the dialogue.'

Sacha then had a run of ill-received plays until 1911 when he starred in his own *Le Veilleur de nuit*. He followed that with *Un Beau mariage*, of which the critic Paul Leautaud wrote: 'I find that he really has more talent than his father, who is always the same in his roles.' Sacha continued to star in his successes: *La Prise de Berg-op-Zoom, La Pèlerine écossaise* and *Les Deux converts*, which opened at the Comédie-Française in March 1914.

Sacha made his first film in 1914 in response to the German invasion. In it he showed the greatest Frenchmen in the arts, including Renoir, Monet, Rodin, Antoine, Bernhardt and Henri Robert, a famous lawyer.

In 1916 he wrote one of his biggest successes, *Faisons un rêve*, a play for three characters — a husband played by Raimu, a lover played by Sacha, and a wife played by Sacha's wife Charlotte.

Sacha then presented the first of his biographical plays, *Jean de la Fontaine*. In his historical and biographical epics Sacha took many liberties with fact, but most agreed that he captured the spirit. In *Jean de la Fontaine* the mistress was played by Yvonne Printemps, who soon took the part into reality. Charlotte, though still deeply in love with Sacha, simply faded from the scene when she saw the affair in progress.

In 1918 he starred in and wrote *La Revue de Paris* and *Deburau*, the story of the great French mime. It was in the latter that his father finally saw him; they were reconciled, and he then wrote *Pasteur* for his father. Yvonne and Sacha were married that year and for the next five years the triumvirate ruled the stages of Paris, appearing all together first in Sacha's *Mon Père avait raison*, which broke all box office records in that city. He took a lease on the intimate Théâtre Edouard VII, in which over the next decade he produced more than a dozen of his own plays.

Sacha first appeared in London at the Aldwych on 11 May 1920, playing Robert Chapelle in *Nono*. The triumvirate appeared in a number of Sacha's plays and were so successful in London, both socially and on stage, that the season had to be extended. The *Sunday Times* critic wrote: 'Polish of acting is a special prerogative of the French. It is second nature to them, and with these players the smoothness, the shine, the grace, the flexibility of their performances eclipse all the nature and many vulgarities of the story.' And the *Times* found 'delight in the smooth voluble patter of Sacha Guitry'. The Guitrys made almost annual appearances in London after that, appearing at the Prince's, the New Oxford and the Gaiety.

For the Divine Sarah, Sacha wrote two plays — *Comment on écrit histoire* and *Un Sujet de roman*.

In 1925 he fulfilled his father's dying wish and wrote *Mozart*, in which he himself played the part of Grimm. In 1927 he wrote *Marietta*, a play about a young girl who captivates Napoleon. Yvonne was of course the girl, and he himself played two roles — those of Napoleon and a journalist. He did this mainly because Napoleon was not in the last act and he could not bear to be off the stage.

The Guitrys toured America and Canada in 1929, and in 1931 Sacha was declared a Chevalier of the Légion d'honneur. On 25 April 1932 he celebrated thirty years on the stage with a banquet, naming the dishes after some of his triumphs. That year also his marriage to Yvonne Printemps broke down and Sacha took a six-month break from the stage. He returned in April 1933 with *Chateaux en Espagne* and his new love Jacqueline Delubac, who co-starred. On his fiftieth birthday he married the 25-year-old Jacqueline.

Sacha Guitry made his first sound film in 1931, a version of his play *Le Blanc et le noir*. In it were Raimu and Fernandel. He threw himself into cinema — directing, writing and acting, and made dozens of films while at the same time writing, directing and starring in plays. In 1936 alone he made five films and wrote five plays as well. *Le Mot de Cambronne*, first produced in 1936 at the Théâtre de la Madeleine, was his hundredth play and dedicated to Edmond Rostand, who many years before had given him the idea for it.

In 1938 he wrote a one-act play *Dieu sauve le roi* to entertain King George VI and the Queen at the Palais de l'Elysée during a state visit, and on the French President's return visit to London the following year Sacha appeared with Seymour Hicks at the India Office in a sketch he had written called *You're Telling Me*. The two of them then topped the variety bill at the Coliseum three times a day for a fortnight with the sketch.

His next play, *Un Monde fou*, was his last with Jacqueline Delubac, who could no longer bear living with a jealous workaholic. Once more Sacha tried a new marriage, this time with Généviève de Sereville. They were wed in July 1939.

Sacha Guitry continued to work both on stage and in the cinema during the Occupation. This caused many Frenchmen to accuse him of collaboration with the enemy. It had also, however, given him the opportunity to help many of his countrymen. In April 1944 his bored fourth wife, who was thirty years his junior, left him.

At the Liberation Guitry was arrested and spent sixty days in prison before he was totally cleared of all accusations of collaboration. The way his countrymen had vilified him left a great burden of sorrow. In 1947 he married the 28-year-old Lana Marconi. 'The others,' he told her, 'were only my wives, but you, *chérie*, you will be my widow.' Sacha made his return to the theatre, from which he had been banned, in 1948 with *Le Diable boiteux*. For Queen Elizabeth II's Coronation in 1953 Sacha Guitry appeared at the Winter Garden in London in his *Ecoutez bien, messieurs*, but it was evident that the spark had gone. His last appearance on stage in Paris was that same year in *Palsambleu* in which he had cunningly written himself into a wheelchair. He played a deaf centenarian. He then retired from the stage, and as a symbol of his determination not to return he grew a beard. He did, however, continue to make films until 1957, when he was completely stricken with a disease of the nerves that required endless injections of morphine to ease the pain. It was a long and painful time and he died on 24 July 1957; his last audience consisted of twelve thousand people filing past his coffin. In his seventy-two years he had written and starred in more than 120 plays.

UTA HAGEN

*U*ta Thyra Hagen was born on 12 June 1919 in Göttingen, Germany, where her father was a teacher and her mother an opera singer. The family moved to the United States and Uta graduated from high school in Madison, Wisconsin. She then attended the University of Wisconsin where she made her stage début at the Bascom Hall in July 1935 playing Sorrel in *Hay Fever*. She studied at RADA in London for a year and on her return to the United States played Ophelia in *Hamlet*, directed by Eva Le Gallienne at the Cape Playhouse in Dennis, Massachusetts, in August 1937. Uta Hagen made her New York début with the Lunts in March 1938 playing Nina in *The Seagull* at the Shubert; John Mason Brown said: 'Uta Hagen's Nina is a lovely and sensitive characterization.'

In July 1938 she played Louka in *Arms and the Man* and the Ingenue in *Mr Pim Passes By* at the Ridgefield Summer Theater in Connecticut; in August at the Westport Country Playhouse she was Suzanna in *Suzanna and the Elders*. In the autumn she joined the National Company tour of *The Seagull*. On 8 December 1938 she married the actor José Ferrer. (The marriage lasted for ten years and produced one daughter.)

Uta Hagen played Edith in *The Happiest Days* at the Vanderbilt in New York in April 1939. In August she went to New Jersey to the Paper Mill Playhouse where she was a Chinese Girl in *Flight into China* and a Nurse in *Men in White*. In summer 1940 she was at the Mt Kisco Playhouse playing the Secretary in *Topaze* and at the Ann Arbor Drama Festival in Michigan in May 1941 played Ella in *Charley's Aunt*, with which she then toured. In summer 1941 she was at the Suffern County Playhouse in New York playing Ellen Turner in *The Male Animal* and the Woman in *The Guardsman*.

She played the Wife in *The Admiral Had a Wife* which closed before it reached Broadway in December 1941. In summer 1942 she toured as Desdemona in the Theater Guild's production of *Othello*, and in September 1942 she opened at the Plymouth on Broadway playing the title role in *Vicki*.

She was at the Shubert in October 1943 playing Desdemona while Paul Robeson played the Moor and her husband José Ferrer played Iago. Lewis Nichols reported in the *New York Times* that Uta Hagen was 'a very pretty, soft-spoken heroine and victim whose death scene is the most moving of the play'. They toured the production the following

September and returned with it to New York in May 1945 to the City Center.

In March 1947 Uta Hagen opened as Olga Vorontsov in *The Whole World Over* at the Biltmore and that July at the Yardley Theater in Pennsylvania played Mrs Manningham in *Angel Street*. She spent the summer touring in *Dark Eyes*. She then appeared in two German-language productions at the Barbizon-Plaza Theater in New York. She played Gretchen in *Faust* (October 1947) and Hilda in *The Master Builder* (January 1948).

At the New York City Center she played Mrs Manningham in *Angel Street* at the end of January 1948 and that June succeeded Jessica Tandy as Blanche Du Bois at the Ethel Barrymore Theater in *A Streetcar Named Desire*. Harold Hobson reported that 'Uta Hagen's long speech in which she reveals the horrible tale of her marriage to a degenerate, held them [the audience] completely'. She toured in the role until June 1949 when she returned to the Ethel Barrymore Theater with it, where she played until February 1950. She toured again before playing it yet again in New York at the City Center in May.

Uta Hagen opened at the Lyceum in November 1950 as Georgie in *The Country Girl*. For that performance she received the Donaldson Award, the Tony and the New York Drama Critics Award.

On 5 January 1951 Uta Hagen married Herbert Berghof, the actor–director and teacher with whom she had been working since 1947 at his acting studio in New York.

At the Cort in October 1951 she played St Joan and followed that in May 1952 at the City Center as Tatiana in *Tovarich*. She toured *Tovarich* for the summer, also appearing in *The Play's the Thing*. Back in New York in October she played Hannah King in *In Any Language* at the Cort and then toured for the summer of 1953 as Jennet Jourdemayne in *The Lady's Not for Burning* and Georgie in *The Country Girl*.

Uta Hagen played Grace Wilson in *The Magic and the Loss* at the Booth Theater in April 1954 and spent the summer touring in the title role in *Cyprienne*. She played Lavinia in *Michael and Lavinia* at the Theater by the Sea in September 1954 and the following February was in the Bahamas, again playing Jennet Jourdemayne in *The Lady's Not for Burning*. She went back to Michigan to the Ann Arbor Drama Festival in May 1955 where she played all the female roles in *The Affairs of Anatol*; she repeated the performance at the Edgewater Beach Hotel in Chicago that July. Back in New York in October 1955 she played Agata in *Island of Goats* at the Fulton and in April 1956 at the Phoenix she played Natalia Petrovna in *A Month in the Country*. Still at the Phoenix in December she played Shen Te in *The Good Woman of Setzuan*.

In August 1959 Uta Hagen was playing Argia in *The Queen and the Rebels* at the Bucks County Playhouse in New Hope, Pennsylvania. At the Grace Church Theater in New York City she played Angelique in the American première of *Port Royal* in May 1960. In Canada at the Vancouver International Festival in August 1961 she played Leah in *Sodom and Gomorrah*, and then at the Billy Rose Theater in New York in October 1962 she opened as Martha in Albee's *Who's Afraid of Virginia Woolf?* Harold Taubman reported in the *New York Times:* 'As the vulgar, scornful, desperate Martha, Miss Hagen makes a tormented harridan horrifyingly believable,' and Kenneth Tynan said that the part 'could not be better acted than by Uta Hagen, lecherously booming'. For this performance she received another Tony as well as the New York

Drama Critics Award and the Outer Circle Award. Uta Hagen made her London début in this part at the Piccadilly Theatre on 6 February 1964. Hugh Leonard said: 'Martha is a superb creation, honey-tongued, bawdy, obtuse, perceptive, tender, lustful, and — at any given moment — lethal. Miss Hagen and Mr Hill wage total war on each other with the most exquisitely refined playing one could ever hope to see.' And Charles Marowitz: 'Of the performances of Uta Hagen and Arthur Hill, one must not dwell too much on the indescribable. No one on the West End stage is playing with this degree of involvement and contact. Only a conscious artist like Hagen, one of New York's leading teachers as well as actresses, would be able to produce the wealth of unconscious artistry now on view at the Piccadilly Theatre.' Miss Hagen won the London Critics Award for Best Female Performance. Her next appearance was at the Lyceum in March 1968 when she played Madame Ranevskaya in *The Cherry Orchard*.

Uta Hagen lives in Greenwich Village, New York, where she teaches acting and writes about both acting and cooking.

KAY HAMMOND

*D*orothy Katherine Standing was born in London on 18 February 1909, the daughter of actor Sir Guy Standing KBE and his actress wife, Dorothy. As a child she learned both French and English and was informally coached in elocution by Mrs Patrick Campbell, a close family friend. She was educated at Banstead in Surrey, and then studied at RADA. She made her stage début on 25 June 1927 as Kay Hammond at the Regent Theatre, playing Amelia in *Tilly of Bloomsbury*. The next month, at the same venue she played Ellen in *Plus Fours*. Many small parts followed: in August 1927 she was at the Globe Theatre understudying in *Potiphar's Wife*, and she then played Valerie Hildegarde in *77 Park Lane* (St Martin's, October 1928), Beatrice in *Nine Till Six* (Arts and Apollo, January 1930), 'Foxey' Dennison in *The Last Chapter* (New, May 1930) and Babs in *Dance with No Music* (Arts, July 1930). In the Cochran revue *Ever Green* at the Adelphi in December 1930 a critic called her 'teenaged Miss Hammond — a pretty girl with a funny voice', although she was nearly 22. She continued to play many small parts until

November 1936, when she opened at the Criterion as Diana Lake in Rattigan's *French Without Tears*, her first leading role. She scored a triumph, and it ran for two years. Still at the Criterion, in March 1939 she played Adeline Rawlinson in *Sugar Plum*.

From July 1941 until February 1944, at the Piccadilly, St James's and Duchess theatres successively, Kay Hammond played Elvira in Noel Coward's *Blithe Spirit*. (She filmed it in 1945.) She continued in a Coward play, the revival of *Private Lives*, in which she played Gertrude Lawrence's part of Amanda and John Clements played Coward's original role. The revival began at the Apollo Theatre in London in November 1944 and continued through a tour in 1946. By this time Miss Hammond and Mr Clements were married and at the beginning of a stage partnership that was to last for many years.

Under her husband's management at the St James's, in May 1946 Kay Hammond played Lady Elizabeth Gray in *The Kingmaker*. Audrey Williamson said: 'Kay Hammond cleverly suggested this head "clear as crystal" and rock-like will, under the fragile exterior of an elegant feminine beauty.'

Also at the St James's, in July 1946 she played Melantha in Dryden's *Marriage à la Mode*. Kay Hammond was then stricken with the ill health that was to plague her all her life, and was forced to retire from the stage for nearly two years. She made her return in May 1949 appearing with her husband as Mrs Sullen in *The Beaux' Stratagem* at the Phoenix. Audrey Williamson reported: 'Kay Hammond as the ill-wedded Mrs Sullen was in particular exquisite — a pouting period beauty with a sidelong glance and a perfection of wit in the pointing of her lines. In spite of her famous ''plummy'' yet attractive drawl, she has a style and intelligence in dialogue surpassed only by Edith Evans among modern actresses of Restoration Comedy.' Harold Hobson thought 'Kay Hammond's Mrs Sullen, pouting, flirtatious, but with a substratum of common sense, a Millamant with her feet on the ground, delicious to gaze on and very, very funny'. And the *Observer* critic said: 'It was delightful to have Miss Kay Hammond back in full health. As Mrs Sullen she looked exquisite in Miss Haffenden's well-chosen costumes, and she can point any scene of comedy with a pretty pout or the turn of a most expressive eye. In giving firmness and clarity to the stylish dialogue of the period she frequently fails, but she amply radiates the kind of mischief which the part demands.' *The Beaux' Stratagem* ran for more than fifteen months — longer than a classic revival had ever done before in the English-speaking theatre.

At the New in February 1951 the couple went on to do Shaw's *Man and Superman*, Kay Hammond playing Ann Whitefield. From June of that year they frequently played the full text and then she played Dona Ana de Ulloa in the 'Don Juan in Hell' scene. The critic T. C. Worsley was annoyed by her performance. 'Miss Hammond is simply impossible in Shaw. Her particular trick of speech, by which in modern comedy she gets all her characteristic effects, is a slow over-articulated drawl, insinuating an innuendo. For most of Shaw an opposite technique is required. Miss Hammond doesn't just lack speed, which it might be possible to get away with; she completely holds things up.'

At the Duke of York's in August 1952, Kay Hammond played Helen Mansell-Smith in John Clements' version of a French comedy by Jean Bernard Luc, *The Happy Marriage*. Patrick Gibbs thought it a repetitive piece but found the acting charming. 'The wife,' he wrote, 'with her combination of vagueness with quick wit would be tiresome in real life. On the stage she is a gift for

Kay Hammond, who makes her bewitchingly attractive.'

The Clements were back at the St James's in November 1953 with Kay Hammond playing Eliza Doolittle in a revival of Shaw's *Pygmalion*. She had taken voice lessons in an attempt to modify her distinguishing drawl. The *Times* reported: 'It may be that before the curtain rose we were chiefly curious to know how Miss Hammond would adapt her mannered diction to the various demands made upon it by the phonetic education of Eliza Doolittle. The very first scene more or less put an end to this curiosity. Shaw's rendering of Cockney dialect may be wonderfully exact but most actresses make it sound excruciatingly unreal. Miss Hammond gave the impression that we were listening to something real, something euphonious, and something slightly comic. She was equally good in her elaborate handling of the new small talk at Mrs Higgins' ''At Home'', and even better when the work of art has been perfected and is on the point of coming painfully to life. In short, Miss Hammond shows that she can when she wishes completely shed a mannerism which has come to be regarded as part of her stage personality.'

Of her role as Gabrielle in *The Little Glass Clock* at the Aldwych in December 1954 Ronald Barker said she 'is brilliant for she gets many laughs when the audience are quite unable to hear what she is saying'.

At the Saville in February 1956 her husband revived *The Rivals* and Kay Hammond played Lydia Languish. Frank Granville-Barker said her performance 'is always charming but unhappily not so invariably audible'. And W. A. Darlington said: 'Kay Hammond is a lovely but subdued Lydia who hardly goes in search of all the comedy the part contains.' She had to bow out of the cast for a few weeks during the run as she was suffering from bronchitis. The next production at the theatre was *The Way of the World*, in which she played Mrs Millamant that December. This was not a success. Frank Granville-Barker said: 'Here is no imperious beauty commanding universal masculine respect but an eighteenth-century dumb blonde.' And W. A. Darlington wrote: '... Millamant is the play's great creation and unless she is brilliantly played all the rest is a jumble of incomprehensible plot, from which Congreve's wit and invention can struggle free only at moments. Last night at the Saville, in John Clements' production, this fearful responsibility fell on Kay Hammond; and the load was too much for her.' In December 1957 the Clements were at the Piccadilly and Kay Hammond played Hippolyte in Benn Levy's *The Rape of the Belt*. Of her performance as the Queen of the Amazons Peter Roberts said: 'Kay Hammond is her glowing, languorous self.' At the Duke of York's in April 1959 she played Louise Yeyder in *Gilt and Gingerbread*, a modern comedy by Lionel Hale. *Plays and Players* called it 'a large and delightful part. In recent years her very considerable talents have been seriously threatened by excessive mannerisms, but here [she]

restrains herself to a remarkable degree.'

Kay Hammond last appeared on the stage at the Piccadilly, where the Clements opened in October 1959 in *The Marriage-Go-Round*. Ill health then forced her into retirement. Her husband, who was knighted in 1968, looked after her until her death on 5 May 1980.

CEDRIC HARDWICKE

The fifth-favourite actor of George Bernard Shaw (the playwright himself told him that the first four were the Marx Brothers), Cedric Hardwicke was born in a Queen Anne house in Lye, Stourbridge, Worcestershire, on 19 February 1893. The first book he ever read was the complete works of Shakespeare, and he had soon learned pages by heart, much to the annoyance of the family, to whom he constantly recited. In spite of being sent to board at Bridgnorth School at the age of 14, his theatrical ambitions continued to grow. His father wanted him to be a doctor, and to please him Cedric sat the entrance exams for Cambridge Medical School; much to Cedric's delight he failed to gain a place. So at 17 he went to London to Herbert Beerbohm Tree's Academy of Dramatic Art (later RADA). While a student there he made his first professional stage appearance, walking on as a gentleman of the court in *The Monk and the Woman* at the Lyceum in 1912; eventually he took up the part of Brother John and was able to speak. He played in *The Devil Himself*, a dreadful one-acter by Major Yeldam at the Lewisham Hippodrome, and then went back to His Majesty's, Tree's theatre, as an understudy and walk-on in *Drake*, but left after six weeks when he was offered the dual roles of lift boy and butler in Arthur Bourchier's production of *Find the Woman* at the Garrick. This ran for over a hundred nights, and he was next seen at the Garrick in Stanley Houghton's *Trust the People*. Then, completely out of theatre work, he made his first film (in which he played six parts), *Riches and Rogues*.

Hardwicke joined Frank Benson's company in 1913 touring the provinces, South Africa and Rhodesia. It was as Sir Harry Bumper in *The School for Scandal*, when he had merely two words to say on stage, that he got his first newspaper review. The performance of the Benson company, the local critic in Ipswich wrote, was marred 'only

by Mr Cedric Hardwicke, who overdid his part the least little bit'. While he was in South Africa the First World War broke out. On his return home he toured with Miss Darragh in *The Unwritten Law* and then appeared at the Old Vic in 1914 as Malcolm in *Macbeth*, Tranio in *The Taming of the Shrew* and a gravedigger in *Hamlet*, among other roles. He left the company when its director Lilian Baylis suggested he work for nothing on Shakespeare's birthday matinée, and joined the army. He served in France until 1921, and was officially the last British officer to leave the war zone — three years after the war ended.

Cedric Hardwicke returned home in 1921 to find that the theatre had changed in his absence, and he could see no place for himself within it. Then he chanced upon Barry Jackson's Birmingham Repertory Theatre. He was taken on in January 1922, and made his company début as an Arctic explorer in a one-act curtain-raiser to *Candide*. He was deemed hopeless as a juvenile and developed into their leading character man, playing Faulkland in *The Rivals*, Hobart in *Advertising April*, Simon in *The Shoemaker's Holiday*, General Grant in *Abraham Lincoln*, Captain Shotover in *Heartbreak House* (with which GBS was very impressed), Tachimo in *Cymbeline*, Sir Toby in *Twelfth Night*, Professor Goodwillie in *The Professor's Love Story*, Darnley in *Mary Stuart*, M. Pierrot in *L'Enfant prodigue*, Haslam, the Archbishop and the He-Ancient in *Back to Methuselah* (which was actually directed by GBS) and Churdles Ash in Eden Phillpotts' *The Farmer's Wife*.

In February 1924 Barry Jackson moved his company to London to the Court Theatre in Sloane Square where he presented *Back to Methuselah*, with Cedric Hardwicke in his original parts; it was a great success. They followed that with *The Farmer's Wife* in March, Hardwicke once more playing the bent old Devonshire labourer, Churdles

Ash. At first the public did not care for this broad, almost farcical comedy but although they played to near-empty houses for weeks, Jackson had faith in the play and eventually the tide turned and they played 1329 performances to standing room only. Everyone believed that Hardwicke, then only 31, was indeed a septuagenarian, so skilful was his make-up and performance. It was during this run that he met the actress Helena Pickard, whom he married.

Cedric Hardwicke next played Caesar in Shaw's *Caesar and Cleopatra* with Gwen Ffrangcon-Davies at the Kingsway in April 1925. It was not a success, but Shaw still regarded him not only as a great actor but now also as a friend. In June of that year he was playing Wooton, the butler with only twenty lines in *The New Morality,* and in August the First Gravedigger in Barry Jackson's modern dress production of *Hamlet.* At the Scala for the Renaissance Society in October he played Flamineo in *The White Devil* and closed the year playing Iago in *Othello* at the Prince's for the Fellowship of Players. He then toured the music halls in an Eden Phillpotts one-acter called *Point of View,* and when he brought it into the Coliseum for a season saw his name in lights for the first time.

At the Haymarket in November 1926 he played Richard Varwell in another Devon comedy, *Yellow Sands.* The following November for an Adelphi matinée he played Sir Peter Teazle in *The School for Scandal;* he returned to the Court in March 1928 to play once again his old parts in *Back to Methuselah.*

Cedric Hardwicke opened a long run at Drury Lane in May 1928 when he played Captain Andy in the musical *Show Boat.* During that run, for the King George Pension Fund he played Mr Hempseed in *The Scarlet Pimpernel* in May, and in July directed *My Lady's Mill* at the Lyric. At the Malvern Festival in August 1929 he premièred *The Apple Cart* playing King Magnus, a part longer than Hamlet that Shaw had written for him. It transferred to the Queen's in London where to everyone's surprise it ran very successfully for nine months. He then played, again, the First Gravedigger in an all-star revival of *Hamlet* at the Haymarket in April 1930. In August he went back to the Malvern Festival and played the Bishop in *Getting Married,* Captain Shotover in *Heartbreak House,* Lickcheese in *Widowers' Houses,* and Edward Moulton-Barrett in *The Barretts of Wimpole Street.* That last play came to the Queen's in London in September and ran through to the end of 1931. For the Stage Society at a special performance at the Prince of Wales he played Lickcheese again in *Widowers' Houses* and then stayed at the Queen's in 1932 where he

revived *The Farmer's Wife* and *Heartbreak House,* and also played Karl Kling in *Caravan.*

At the Malvern Festival in August 1931 he played the Prologue and Abel Drugger in *The Alchemist* and the Burglar in Shaw's *Too True To Be Good.* On the second night of that play his son Edward was born. *Too True To Be Good* opened at the New in September; it was not a success, though James Agate reported: 'Mr Cedric Hardwicke possesses not only a sense but a tact of the stage which is second to none. Guided surely by this, he did not attempt to turn a trumpet solo into a duet, but played oboe to Mr Richardson, delivering the final speech with all that beauty of tone and phrasing which comes from acquired talent and natural artistry. Both players showed us how the English language should be spoken.'

Cedric Hardwicke was now living a very social life in a large house near the Thames at Runnymede. He began to work under the management of Gilbert Miller and played Sidney Ardsley at the Globe in November 1932 in *For Services Rendered* by W. Somerset Maugham. That year for the King George Pension Fund he played James Hanley in *Bulldog Drummond.* At the Queen's in February 1933 he was Lord Bretton in *Head-On Crash* and at the St James's in May 1933 played Dr Haggett in *The Late Christopher Bean,* which ran for over a year. He was knighted in the 1934 New Year Honours. At the Lyric in April 1935 he began another long run as Prince Mikail in *Tovarich.*

Having by this time achieved everything he had set out to do in London, under Gilbert Miller's auspices he sailed for New York where he opened at the Little Theater in December 1936 in *Promise* which unfortunately failed. He next played Dr Clitterhouse at the Hudson in March 1937, and that ran for six months. He returned to England that summer to play Edward Fritton in *Return to Sanity* at the Malvern Festival and then went back to New York to the Golden in January 1938, where he had a massive hit playing Canon Skerritt in *Shadow and Substance.* Brooks Atkinson reported in the *New York Times:* 'Sir Cedric's portrait of Canon Skerritt is an actor's masterpiece. The whole man is present in the severity of his acting — snobbery, learning, insouciance, sardonic contempt, formal religious devotion and personal tenderness.' John Mason Brown wrote: 'Sir Cedric Hardwicke gives as the austere canon the finest performance for which he has so far been responsible in America. His characterization is a masterpiece of acting which burns its way into the memory ... It is proudly arrogant and authoritative throughout but it smoulders with a pent-up passion.' He subsequently toured the

United States in the part through 1939.

Cedric Hardwicke then went to Hollywood, where he made a number of films, and he stayed there until 1944 at the request of the British Government, which said that English actors could be of more use there during the war for propaganda purposes than they could be at home. In September 1941 he played General Burgoyne in *The Devil's Disciple* at Santa Barbara, and in April 1944 staged *Sheppey* at the Playhouse in New York. Later in 1944 Cedric Hardwicke returned to England and toured as Jonathan Dale in *The House on the Bridge*. He made his reappearance on the London stage at the Westminster in March 1945 playing Richard Varwell in a revival of *Yellow Sands*, and then toured this play for ENSA on the Continent.

Returning to New York in 1945 he directed Gertrude Lawrence in a revival of *Pygmalion*, which opened at the Ethel Barrymore in December; and at the Cort Theater in February 1946 he played Creon to Katharine Cornell's *Antigone*. The production was not very well received, but Lewis Nichols did write in the *New York Times:* 'One scene, that with Cedric Hardwicke as Creon, finds the play and the two characters fully alive, but after that they drift again to the shadows ... Mr Hardwicke's performance is excellent and it does not detract from that to say Creon is the one honest role ... Mr Hardwicke looks the tired but strong man; his voice and expressions are as logical as the even array of his thoughts.' In April of that year at the same theatre he was playing Mr Burgess in *Candida*. He directed *An Inspector Calls* at the Booth in October 1947 before returning to England, where he directed *Ambassador Extraordinary* at the Aldwych in June 1948. Sir Cedric then joined the Old Vic Company at the New Theatre from September to November 1948, playing a variety of parts.

In *Twelfth Night*, Harold Hobson said, 'Sir Cedric Hardwicke gives us a Sir Toby Belch purged of grossness. Here is no bloated sot, but a man who, though he brawls in wine cellars now, has once sung in ladies' chambers ... it has not always been a matter of drunken afternoons; there have been bright mornings ... This is a distinguished performance, beautifully still.' And Audrey Williamson wrote: 'Pinkly amiable, distinctively profiled, his only gesture of flamboyance a daisy stuck, probably in a moment of defiance, in his hat, he suggested a sun of the aristocracy declining in a West full of pioneer promise, with gold still happily for the digging while the world produced Aguecheeks for the expert gentleman miner.' No one, however, was very pleased with his Dr Faustus. Miss Williamson said: 'Sir Cedric

Hardwicke as Dr Faustus did not so much toss the Helen speech away ... as kill it with indifference ... It was an intelligent and civilized performance where the lines were concerned, but it had no blood in it, no surge of passion either of lust or of agony.' And Harold Hobson reported that he 'attacks Faustus's big speech with the élan of an elderly grocer who doesn't quite know what all those ration books are for'. Audrey Williamson thought his next performance for the Old Vic in *The Cherry Orchard* was 'highly distinguished', and while not totally convinced, T. C. Worsley thought that his was a 'most authoritative performance, which persuades you, even a little against your will, that his polished version of Gaev is the right one'.

Sir Cedric returned to the United States and toured the summer theatres in 1949 playing Sir Robert Morton in *The Winslow Boy*. At the National in New York in December 1949 he played Caesar and Lilli Palmer played Cleopatra in Shaw's play, which Hardwicke also directed. In Los Angeles in June 1950 he played William Collins in *Getting Married* and toured in 1950 as Professor Winke in *Captain Carvallo*. In New York in November 1951, together with Charles Boyer, Charles Laughton and Agnes Moorehead (calling themselves The First Drama Quartet) Cedric Hardwicke opened in *Don Juan in Hell*. Brooks Atkinson was delighted: 'Attired in evening clothes and standing before microphones they pretend that they are going to read their parts from a manuscript of the drama. But they are actors. The reading they gave last evening at Carnegie Hall is a thrilling performance ... Cedric Hardwicke is in fine fettle as The Statue or Shaw's professional Englishman. He plays it with grace, subtlety and wit.' The group found this a delightful and easy evening to tour and they did, quite a lot.

At the Royale, New York, in April 1953 he played Charles Pine in *Horses in Midstream*, also directing the production. He appeared at the Longacre in March 1954 as Montagu Winthrop in *The Burning Glass*. He went on to direct *A Day By the Sea* (ANTA, September 1955), *Androcles and the Lion* (Chicago, October 1956), and *Miss Isobel* (Royale, New York, December 1957). He spent the summer of 1958 touring in *An Inspector Calls* and had a final great success in 1959 when he played Koicho Asano in *A Majority of One*, which ran at the Shubert on Broadway for 556 performances and then toured the United States.

'I can't act. I have never acted. And I shall never act,' Cedric Hardwicke told James Agate one Friday night in 1945. 'What I can do is to suspend my audience's power of judgement till I've finished. There are good actors and there are great actors. The great actor takes care that the audience shall have eyes and ears for no one else.'

Sir Cedric Hardwicke died in University Hospital, New York, on 6 August 1964. *See photograph opposite page 118.*

JULIE HARRIS

Julie Ann Harris was born in Grosse Pointe, Michigan, on 2 December 1925, where her father was an investment banker. She attended Yale Drama School for a year and then became one of the original students at the Actors' Studio, where she spent four years, while playing at night. She made her New York début playing Atlanta in *It's a Gift* at the Playhouse in March 1945. The following March she walked on at the Century in the Old Vic productions of *Henry IV Part 2* and *Oedipus.* In October 1946 at the Booth she played Nelly in a revival of *The Playboy of the Western World.* That August she had married for the first time.

She played the White Rabbit in *Alice in Wonderland,* in April 1947 at the International, and then Arianne in a pre-Broadway tryout of *We Love a Lassie* which closed out of town. She played one of the Weird Sisters in Michael Redgrave's production of *Macbeth,* which opened at the National in March 1948, and in September that year was Ida Mae in the Actors' Studio production of *Sundown Beach* at the Belasco. But she became impatient with the Studio. 'I quite like working fast,' she said, 'and I always learnt all the lines before the first rehearsal, which was strictly against Studio rules.'

At the Fulton in November 1948 Julie Harris was Nancy Gear in *The Young and the Fair*; at the Mansfield in April 1949 she was Angel Tuttle in *Magnolia Alley* and back at the Fulton again in October she played Delisa in *Montsarrat.*

It was at the Empire in January 1950 that the 25-year-old Julie Harris opened as the 12-year-old Frankie Addams in Carson McCullers' *Member of the Wedding* to rave reviews. Brooks Atkinson, writing in the *New York Times,* said: 'In the long, immensely complicated part of the adolescent girl, Julie Harris, a very gifted young actress, gives an extraordinary performance — vibrant, full of anguish and elation by turns, rumpled, unstable, egotistic, and unconsciously cruel.' *Member of the Wedding* ran for over a year and Julie Harris received the Donaldson Award for her performance. She then went to Hollywood and recreated the role for Columbia Pictures.

Julie Harris's next opening on Broadway was in November 1951 when at the Empire she played Sally Bowles in *I Am a Camera.* Brooks Atkinson raved again: 'With the assistance of a remarkable actress, John van Druten has put together an impromptu acting piece ... The actress is Julie Harris, who was playing a restless tomboy in the same theatre two years ago. Now she is playing a glib, brassy, temperamental woman of the world — all cleverness, all sophistication. She plays with a virtuosity and an honesty that are altogether stunning and that renew an old impression that Miss Harris has the quicksilver and the genius we all long to discover on the stage.' And Kenneth Tynan said that she 'plays Isherwood's Sally Bowles as a sort of Daisy Ashford gone to seed, with frank piercing eyes and the softness of marshmallow. Miss Harris's Sally is a frail, alcoholic adolescent with grubby fingers. She bursts with unrealized affectations, and is for ever latching herself on to a bullrush length cigarette-holder, like a peignoir suspended from a clothes hook. She brings with her an aura of cigarettes stubbed out in pots of cold cream; of moths and flames; and of a most touching wit. I expect Miss Harris to mature astonishingly and to become, very shortly, one of the nobler ladies of the modern stage.' She received another Donaldson and added the New York Drama Critics Award this time; but, she said, 'I never really got it right; in those days we weren't allowed to talk about things like abortion and the script really didn't have a lot in common with what eventually became *Cabaret.* Sally should really have been played all along by Vanessa Redgrave: she was a rebel, all I managed was a runaway schoolgirl.' Nevertheless she toured with the production and filmed it.

In 1954 Julie Harris divorced and remarried. That year, also, she opened at the Longacre playing Colombe in *Mlle Colombe.* At that same theatre in November 1955 she opened as St Joan in Anouilh's *The Lark* and then toured with it through December 1956. As Mrs Margery Pinchewife, she opened at the Adelphi in November 1957, and at the Helen Hayes Theater in October 1959 she played Ruth Arnold in *The*

Warm Peninsula.

Julie Harris spent summer 1960 at Stratford, Ontario, playing Juliet in *Romeo and Juliet* and Blanche in *King John*. She played Brigid Mary Mangan in *Little Moon of Alban* at the Longacre in December 1960 and in 1961 she took the part of Josefa Lantenay in *A Shot in the Dark*.

At ANTA in December 1963 she played June Havoc in *Marathon '33* and in June 1964 at the Delacorte played Ophelia in *Hamlet*. Next she was Annie in *Ready When You Are* at the Brooks Atkinson in December 1964 and then in November 1965 was Georgina in the musical, *Skyscraper*. She played Blanche Du Bois in *A Streetcar Named Desire* for summer stock at the Tappan Zee Playhouse in Nyack, New York, and came back to Broadway to the Morosco in December 1968 to play Ann Stanley in *Forty Carats*. The critic Martin Gottfried loathed this comedy about May—December marriages, saying it 'stands for all that is ugly and fraudulent and even sick in this country ... Julie Harris tried very hard, in a Method way, to understand the motivations of the mother, which would have been a neat trick considering the play's refusal to make her simply in love. Miss Harris also tried very hard, in a Method way, to play comedy, and like all Method actors, failed because of sheer overseriousness.' However, Miss Harris did get a Tony for her performance.

At the Repertory Theater in New Orleans she played in *The Woman* in 1970 and then back at the Morosco in March 1971 played Anna Reardon in *And Miss Reardon Drinks A Little*, then touring for a year in the part. At the Ethel Barrymore in April 1972 she played Claire in *Voices;* in December she got her second Tony for her performance as Mrs Lincoln in *The Last of Mrs Lincoln* at ANTA. At the Vivian Beaumont the following December she was Mrs Rogers in *The Au Pair Man* and back at the Morosco in December 1974 played Lydia Cruttwell in *In Praise of Love.*

Julie Harris introduced her one-woman show playing Emily Dickinson in *The Belle of Amherst* at the Longacre Theater in April 1976. She subsequently toured in it and for the first time appeared in London, at the Phoenix in September 1977. She had by then married for the third time.

As well as the screen versions of plays already mentioned, Julie Harris starred in *East of Eden*, *Reflections in a Golden Eye* and *Requiem for a Heavyweight*, among other films. She has also received two Emmys, one for her performance in *Little Moon of Alban* and another for *Victoria Regina*, both shown on NBC's Hallmark Hall of Fame.

ROSEMARY HARRIS

Rosemary Harris was born in Ashby, Suffolk, on 19 September 1930. Her father was in the Royal Air Force, and Rosemary was educated in England and in India. She made her first appearance on stage at Westwind School in Penzance in 1946 when she played Mrs Otherly in *Abraham Lincoln*. In 1949 she made her professional début when she joined the Phoenix Players of the Bognor Regis Repertory Company at the Roof Garden Theatre. She stayed with them until 1950, playing more than thirty-two roles in weekly rep. In January 1950 she joined the Falcon Players in Bedford and in a year with them played more than forty parts. Rosemary Harris then went into rep in Margate and Eastbourne with Winwood Productions and in her final bout of weekly rep with the Penzance Repertory Company played seventeen parts between June and August 1951.

Moving to London, Rosemary Harris studied at RADA and understudied Gillian Lutyens as Sally and Yvette Wyatt as Peggy in *The Gay Dog* at the Piccadilly Theatre. Rosemary Harris made her New York début at the Martin Beck Theater on 13 November 1952 when she played Mabel in *The Climate of Eden* (which won her a Theater World award) and her London début at the Aldwych on 14 May 1953 as the Girl in *The Seven-Year Itch*. In 1954 she toured Brighton, Edinburgh, Dublin and Paris as Lucasta Angel in *The Confidential Clerk*. She joined the Bristol Old Vic for the 1954—55 season, and played Beatrice in *Much Ado About Nothing*, Elizabeth Proctor in *The Crucible*, Françoise Piquetot in *Image in the Sun*, Portia in *The Merchant of Venice*, Isobel in *The Enchanted*, Mrs Golightly in *The Golden Cuckoo* and Hermione in *The Winter's Tale*. Of her performance in *The Crucible* Kenneth Tynan noted: 'Rosemary Harris catches exactly the wan aridity of Proctor's wife.' In September 1955 she joined the Old Vic Company in London and played

Calpurnia in *Julius Caesar.* Audrey Williamson said: 'Rosemary Harris was a young but beautiful and sympathetic Calpurnia, fulfilling Granville-Barker's description of "a nervous, fear-haunted creature" without loss of quiet dignity.' She also played Dorcas in *The Winter's Tale* and Desdemona in the Richard Burton—John Neville *Othello*. Kenneth Tynan said: 'Rosemary Harris's Desdemona [was] a moth of peace who might profitably have beaten her wings more vigorously.' But Audrey Williamson thought her Desdemona was 'both beautiful to look at and deeply felt, a matter of real tears and genuine devotion shocked but not losing dignity when savaged and with a rather winning cajolery and gay lightness in the earlier scenes with Othello'. She then appeared as Cressida in a modern-dress version of *Troilus and Cressida.* Audrey Williamson said: 'Rosemary Harris unexpectedly flamed as Cressida, a Cressida red-haired and sensuous, feeling her passions genuinely enough and only at the end realizing the true lightness of her nature.' The Old Vic took *Troilus and Cressida* to the Winter Garden Theater in New York in December 1956. Writing in the *New York Times* Brooks Atkinson said: 'As Cressida Rosemary Harris is admirable. Her slow, sensual, treacherous strumpet is everything that Shakespeare had in mind.'

Rosemary Harris stayed on in New York, where in February 1958 at ANTA she played Jere Halliday in *The Disenchanted*. She joined the Group 20 Players in Wellesley, Massachusetts, for their 1958–59 season and played Eliza Doolittle in *Pygmalion*, Beatrice in *Much Ado About Nothing*, Ann Whitefield in *Man and Superman* and the title role in *Peter Pan*. At the Helen Hayes Theater in New York she played Lennie in *The Tumbler* in February 1960 and then joined the Association of Producing Artists Repertory Company, which was directed by her husband (she married Ellis Rabb on 4 December 1959). Between 1960 and 1962 she toured the United States playing Lady Teazle in *The School for Scandal*, Bianca in *The Taming of the Shrew*, Cecily in *The Importance of Being Earnest*, Gabrielle in *Anatole*, Phoebe in *As You Like It*, Ann Whitefield in *Man and Superman*, Nina and Madame Arkadina in *The Seagull*, Viola in *Twelfth Night*, Titania in *A Midsummer Night's Dream*, and Virginia in *The Tavern*.

In England, at the Chichester Festival in July 1962 Rosemary Harris played Constantia in *The Chances* and Penthea in John Ford's *The Broken Heart*. Kenneth Tynan said she was 'a calm, unpainted Penthea looking at once ravaged and ravishing'. She rejoined the APA at the University of Michigan at Ann Arbor, and from August 1962

to March 1963 played Regina in *Ghosts*, Lady Teazle in *The School for Scandal*, Virginia in *The Tavern*, the Girl in *We Comrades Three*, the Duchess of Gloucester in *Richard III* and Portia in *The Merchant of Venice*.

She returned to Chichester in July 1963 where, directed by Laurence Olivier, she succeeded Joan Greenwood in a revival of their production of *Uncle Vanya*. Peter Roberts reported: 'Rosemary Harris ... plays this artificial part a good deal less artificially and though her performance is not quite as well integrated as the rest (Olivier, Redgrave, Plowright, Thorndike, Casson and Compton), she does not destroy but contributes to the elaborate counterpoint of thought and feeling from which Chekhov's dialogue flowers.'

At the Old Vic in October 1963 Rosemary Harris played Ophelia in the National Theatre Company's inaugural production of *Hamlet* in which Peter O'Toole played the Dane. Again Peter Roberts reported: 'The production's freshest aspect is its treatment of Ophelia. This is a character who has suffered from a hangover of the Victorian conception of her ... The Ophelia of Rosemary Harris is a different creature altogether and the part is recreated in the feminine image of our time where girls, unlike their Victorian forbears, are credited with a measure of intelligence, initiative and experience. Harris's Ophelia has long discarded her schoolgirl plaits and pigtails. She is a poised and gracious courtier whose passionate embrace of Hamlet in the nunnery scene suggests a very positive creature who has thought of Hamlet in terms more basic than the exchange of girlish trinkets. This makes better sense of the mad scene which Miss Harris brings off superlatively well, the strange repetitions of consonants hinting that her loose behaviour may partly be explained by the fact that the girl in desperation has taken to drink.' She then, for the National Theatre Company, repeated her Chekhov Ilyena and played the First Woman in *Play* in April 1964.

Rosemary Harris went back to Michigan and rejoined the APA in September 1964 when she played the title part in *Judith*, Natasha in *War and Peace* and Violet in *Man and Superman*. In December the company went to New York to the Phoenix Theater and John Simon reported on her performance in Giraudoux' *Judith*: 'Rosemary Harris failed to give us a Judith who goes from charming socialite through frightened virgin and profoundly aroused woman, all the way to a fanatic who allows God's angel — if it is God's angel — to persuade her to bask in a macabre sanctity she herself had most disclaimed. What we got was a rather good impersonation of Audrey Hepburn — in other words, the imitation of an imitation.'

Back at Ann Arbor in October 1965 she played Megara in *Herakles* and at the Lyceum in New York in November 1965 was Alice in Kaufman's *You Can't Take It With You.*

Rosemary Harris received the Tony for her next performance, as Eleanor in *The Lion in Winter.* It opened at the Ambassador Theater in New York in March 1966. Martin Gottfried called her magnificent and said she made the Queen 'a fascinating, bitchy, desperate, abandoned woman'. John Simon, however, said she 'once again demonstrates the difference between a highly competent, technically proficient actress and a truly fine or even great one: her Eleanor is always calculated for maximum effect, with nothing smacking of mere humanity allowed to peep through.' In June 1966 she went back to the role of Alice in *You Can't Take It with You* at the Lyceum; and for the APA in their 1966–67 season at the Lyceum she played Gina in *The Wild Duck,* Signora Ponza in *Right You Are,* Natasha in *War and Peace,* and Lady Teazle in *The School for Scandal.*

Back in London, at the Lyric in February 1969 she played Karen Nash, Muriel Tate and Norma Hubley in Neil Simon's *Plaza Suite* for which she received the *Evening Standard* Best Actress Award. Her marriage to Ellis Rabb was dissolved and she married John Ehle.

At the Ahmanson Theater in Los Angeles in March 1970 she played Irene in *Idiot's Delight*

and in New York at the Billy Rose in November 1971 was Anna in *Old Times.* At Stratford, Connecticut, in 1972 she took the title role in Shaw's *Major Barbara* and at the Vivian Beaumont Theater in New York she played Portia in *The Merchant of Venice* in March 1973 and Blanche Du Bois in *A Streetcar Named Desire* in April.

In December 1975 she played Julie Cavendish in *The Royal Family* at the Brooklyn Academy of Music. This send-up of the Barrymores soon transferred to the Helen Hayes Theater. John Barber wrote: 'Her performance has made her the talk of New York; quick-witted, gleamingly mischievous, sparkling with intelligence. Her porcelain good looks suggest a Kaendler figure but the wicked speed of diction betrays the imp within . . . Miss Harris is a wonder. Her hands always a trace too carefully placed, her voice just a decibel too histrionically hoarse, she cannot even embrace her man without making it compulsively dignified and wistful and girlish withal. But the fashion-plate posturing, hiding her insecurity, is only just visible. Judging precisely how to underdo overdoing it, she gives the play a new dimension. A spoof on a Broadway family becomes a wry analysis of the cost to human integrity of a life of pretence.'

In the early 1980s Miss Harris was back in London for acclaimed revivals of *Heartbreak House* and *All My Sons.*

REX
HARRISON

'I was a seedy child, good for nothing but a bit of cricket. My family couldn't afford drama schools. So I learned in seaside reps how to stop people coughing on damp Wednesday afternoons. Styles change but truth in acting doesn't. I've always tried to be the sort of actor who works from the inside outward to develop a character. It takes time and concentration, but the aim is to make the performance look easy so that the audience may even think "I could do that". It is possible by concentrating on the outside of a character — the walk, the voice, the accent, the make-up, the wardrobe — to give a dazzling performance, but it will rarely move an audience unless the inward portrayal is true. I'm very serious in this respect and whatever the final verdict on me as an actor may be, I'm hopeful that the seriousness of my intention will be accepted.'

Thus wrote Rex Harrison after fifty years on the stage. He is one of a handful of actors who can play high comedy 'seriously'.

Harrison was born on 5 March 1908 in Huyton, Lancashire. His father was a stockbroker and an enthusiastic amateur sportsman. He was educated at Liverpool College, where he developed a great love for both cricket and the stage. At 16, with a little behind-the-scenes help from his father, he was taken on by the Liverpool Playhouse. He first appeared there in September 1924 when he had one line in *Thirty Minutes in a Street* — and he fluffed the line. He stayed there for two and a half years playing very small parts and generally helping out. The director of the company, William Armstrong, strongly suggested that he should give up the idea of acting for a living, but Rex, in 1927, went to London to do the rounds of the agents and picked up work touring in road productions of *Charley's Aunt*, *Potiphar's Wife*, *Alibi*, *The Chinese Bungalow*, and *A Cup of Kindness*. He made his first London appearance at the Everyman Theatre in November 1930 playing the Hon. Fred Thrippleton in *Getting George Married*. At the Prince of Wales in February 1931 he played Rankin in a thriller, *The Ninth Man*, and James Agate commented: 'The actor, whose name escapes me, did something more by bringing a new method, a new style of entertaining.' He then played in repertory at Cardiff and took to the road again as Ralph in *After All*. He enjoyed touring and in 1932 was in *Other Men's Wives* and *For the Love of Mike*. And the following year he was touring in *Road House* and *Mother of Pearl*. In May 1934 he was at the Whitehall in London playing Peter Featherstone in *No Way Back*. That year Rex also played his first and last Shakespeare — four small parts in *Richard III* at the Prince of Wales Theatre. In November he was John Murdoch in *Our Mutual Father* and at Fulham that same month Anthony Fair in *Anthony and Anna*. In February 1935, briefly at the St Martin's, he played Paul Galloway in *Man of Yesterday*. He then went to Nottingham, where he was playing in *The Wicked Flee* when Tyrone Guthrie cast him to play in Robert Morley's *Short Story*, with a distinguished cast headed by Marie Tempest and starring the master of comedy and style A. E. Matthews. Rex could not take his eyes off Matthews all through rehearsal, and indeed even after they opened (Rex playing Mark Kurt) at the Queen's in November 1935. He learned much. He was next at the Aldwych playing Rodney Walters in *Charity Begins...* in January 1936.

Rex Harrison made his New York début at the Booth Theater on 2 March 1936 playing Tubbs Barrow in *Sweet Aloes*, a play by Joyce Cary which starred Evelyn Laye, but it came off in three weeks and Rex was soon back home. He fared better with his next venture, a comedy about polar explorers called *Heroes Don't Care*, which ran for seven months at the St Martin's. He was then given a contract with Alexander Korda; and he began his film career with *Men Are Not Gods*, and then made *Storm in a Teacup* with Vivien Leigh.

His first great West End success came in November 1936 when he opened in Terence Rattigan's *French Without Tears* as the Hon. Alan Howard. He played at the Criterion for over a year, though filming all day and playing in the theatre at night wore him out.

At the Haymarket in January 1939 he played Leo in Coward's *Design for Living*. A very successful run was interrupted by the declaration of war and the closure of the theatres, so they took the play on the road. During the tour he met Lilli Palmer, who was touring in *You, of All People* with Leslie Banks. Wanting to do something for the war effort Rex Harrison joined the Home Guard. His attempts at something more meaningful were dismissed — officials kept saying he was better off entertaining. At the Haymarket in March 1941 he played Gaylord Easterbrook in *No Time for Comedy*, which ran for a year, all through the Blitz. In 1942 he finally convinced the powers that be to let him into the RAF, where he spent two years in photographic reconnaissance. In 1944, released from the RAF and in need of some fast money, Harrison made a series of films, including *Blithe Spirit*, *I Live in Grosvenor Square* and *The Rake's Progress*. He then did a European tour of *French Without Tears* for ENSA.

In 1945, under contract, Rex Harrison went to Hollywood to make *Anna and the King of Siam*. He made several more films but found Hollywood not to his liking. He battled with the columnists who 'made' stars, and found himself involved in a scandal over the suicide of actress Carole Landis. He was happy to escape to Broadway, where in December 1948 he opened at the Shubert Theater as Henry VIII in Maxwell Anderson's *Anne of a Thousand Days*. John Mason Brown reported: 'His king has all the faults with which history cursed Henry and he cursed history. As a monarch able to mistake his earthly lust for his divine right, he is cruel, remorseless, and headstrong. He is selfish, too, and gruff and commanding. He is to the palace born. The hot blood in his veins is royal. Haughty though he is, his eyes are lighted by wit. Formidable when he is crossed, he is charming when having his way. Mr Harrison manages to suggest weight without being fat himself, or resorting to undue padding. He also succeeds in suggesting the physical changes which overtake Henry in the ten years' span of Mr Anderson's drama. He does this in such subtle ways as stance or gesture. But, most of all, he manages to capture the fatal vitality of the sovereign in his playing. Mr Harrison's mind is as much a part of his performance as his appearance. If the verse he reads were Shakespeare's he could not take greater pains to preserve the music of what he has to say.' For this performance Rex Harrison received a Tony.

Returning to London in May 1950, Rex Harrison played the Uninvited Guest in *The Cocktail Party*, a part Alec Guinness had originated at the Edinburgh Festival and was to play on Broadway. T. C. Worsley reported: 'That Mr Rex Harrison is miscast goes without saying. All the same he nearly wins through in the second act ... Mr

Harrison is soft, tentative, engaging ... charms his way along. But in the consulting room scene in the second act he does impose a kind of ascendancy. It would surely help if he could only assert some authority earlier on ... In his first serious exchanges with the husband he should come down on top of the words, not slide smilingly up to them. Not only does the sense demand a harder and more authoritative note, but it is also demanded by the very fact of our finding Mr Rex Harrison here at all. An actor like Mr Harrison, who had traded on his personality in parts cut to measure, must assert his difference early when he is to be taken quite differently.' And Audrey Williamson said: 'Harrison was polished, grave and immaculate but lacked I think the sense of unexplained spiritual power.'

Rex Harrison returned to New York and had a great success there with *Bell, Book and Candle* at the Ethel Barrymore Theater in November 1950. At the New Century in February 1952 he played here ward in *Venus Observed* and at the Shubert in January 1953 he was the Man in Peter Ustinov's *The Love of Four Colonels*. This was the first time he also directed. That year he made a film called *The Constant Husband* and fell madly in love with Kay Kendall. But he had committed himself to directing *Bell, Book and Candle* for the London stage and starring in it himself with his then wife, Lilli Palmer. They opened at the Phoenix in October 1954; though relations were extremely strained, professionally it did not show, as *Plays and Players* reported: '... it is an amusing evening in the theatre thanks to the Harrisons. They play with a delicate, featherweight touch which is a joy to watch. They transform this ordinary dialogue into something which passes for wit.' He directed *Nina* at the Haymarket in July 1955 and then went back to New York.

March 15, 1956 was an historic occasion at the Mark Hellinger Theater on Broadway. It was the opening night of *My Fair Lady*, with Rex Harrison playing Henry Higgins. Brooks Atkinson said simply, after noting that it was the greatest musical ever written: 'The part of Henry Higgins was played by Rex Harrison with virtuosity and subtleties of inflection that brought wit and humour into a romantic story.' Rex Harrison played on Broadway for two years, during which time he learned that Kay Kendall was dying of leukaemia. He never told her, and they were married on 23 June 1957.

Rex Harrison left the Broadway production of *My Fair Lady* to open in it at Drury Lane in April 1958. That December he directed Kay in *The Bright One* at the Winter Garden. He helped her through her last film, *Once More with Feeling*,

before she died.

In December 1959 Rex Harrison opened at ANTA in New York as the General in Jean Anouilh's *The Fighting Cock*. It ran for only 87 performances and those were played to half-empty houses. He had better luck back in London, where he opened at the Royal Court in October 1960 in Chekhov's *Platonov* in which he played the title part, a schoolteacher of considerable intellect who decided to concentrate on his physical attractiveness. Kenneth Tynan said: 'Edgy and tentative in the first expository act, he now (in the second) expands and relaxes. This bearded satyr, febrile and wild-eyed, rides a perfect switchback from euphoria to misery. He makes the farce funny, by impeccable timing; and touching an instant later, by his ability to convert querulous complaints into emotional assets ... he even looks Slavic.' *Platonov* brought him not only the *Evening Standard* Best Actor Award (which he shared with Alec Guinness for his performance in *Ross*) but also Rachel Roberts, whom he married in 1962 in Genoa.

At the Edinburgh Festival, and at the Royal Court in September 1961 he played Sir Augustus Thwaites in *August for the People*. Peter Roberts reported: 'Rex Harrison, as Sir Augustus Thwaites, the aristocratic owner of one of the stately homes of England thrown open at half-a-crown a time to the coach party masses, had a part that exactly suited him. Mr Harrison is expert at giving breathlessly polished performances of characters without feeling and it is precisely Sir Augustus Thwaites' dilemma that he is not able to enter into the drama of life so studiously built up around him. Rex Harrison has exactly the right measure of hauteur and nobody will deny the fine technical accomplishment of his performance.' It was scheduled to run for a month at the Court but it closed after only eleven performances when Rex was released from his contract to hurry off to the doomed filming of *Cleopatra*. However, despite all the troubles of that production, he did get an Academy Award nomination for his portrayal of Caesar. For his next film, *My Fair Lady*, he gained the award itself. Rex Harrison then spent a year making *Dr Doolittle*, which lessened his love of animals, and filmed *A Flea in Her Ear* with his wife, Rachel Roberts.

He returned to the stage in 1969, to the Lyric in London where he played Lionel Fairleigh in *The Lionel Touch*. (He met Elizabeth, ex-Mrs Richard Harris, during this period. They married in 1971 and divorced before the decade was out.) The play, about an ageing roué, hopeless around the house and at supporting his family but desperately charming, was not worthy of the performance he gave.

In 1973 he toured North America playing the title role in Pirandello's *Henry IV*. He brought the part to London to Her Majesty's in February 1974. In New York John Simon wrote: 'Rex Harrison now is all wrong. Looking and acting like a cross between Paul Scofield's Lear and the Man of La Mancha in the Nicaraguan production, he plays everything on much the same level, except for going very slow at times, and at others speeding up to the point of incomprehensibility. Though he does convey the humorous aspects of the part, the grandeur and the pathos are quite beyond him.' In London Alan Seymour reported: 'Rex Harrison's famous voice, yelping in that pleasing, familiar manner, murmuring so lightly, even whispering and holding a large house in that imposing auditorium with his whisper — disappoints only in not quite letting go with the ultimate fury of which this demoniacal character is surely possessed . . . a little more risk-taking would have made Mr Harrison's Henry not only a fine, intelligent and impressive performance as it is, but an electrifying and unforgettable one.'

Harrison returned to New York to the Morosco in December 1974 to play Sebastian in *In Praise of Love*, and in 1976 came back to England to play M. Perichon in *M. Perichon's Travels* at Chichester. Then he was on the road again — nearly full circle — except that this time he was back as his triumphant Henry Higgins in *My Fair Lady*, and in a later tour of *The Kingfisher*.

In 1983 Harrison had considerable London and Broadway success as Shotover in a revival of *Heartbreak House*, and a year later he returned to the Theatre Royal, Haymarket, with Claudette Colbert in Lonsdale's *Aren't We All?* He remains the master Shavian and light comedian of his generation: timing has always been his strongest suit, apart from the suit itself. Nobody has done more to keep the art of stage tailoring alive: 'If you weren't the best light comedian in the country,' Coward once told Harrison, 'you'd only be fit for selling secondhand cars in Great Portland Street.' In 1985 he was back on Broadway in *Aren't We All?*

Charles Hawtrey

'He was born,' said Seymour Hicks, 'with a silver spoon in his mouth and the gods had engraved on it as a gift to him the most priceless of all gifts — humour.'

Charles Hawtrey, the man whom Noel Coward once said taught him everything he knew about the stage, was born on 21 September 1858, the eighth child of a housemaster at Eton. After being educated at Eton, at a school his father opened near Slough, and at Rugby, he went to Pembroke College, Oxford, but left after a couple of terms and made his professional stage début at the Prince of Wales Theatre in Tottenham Street on 23 October 1881 as Edward Langton in *The Colonel*. He described it as a 'straight-away part requiring very little else beyond being able to dress in evening clothes, with quite fifty lines to speak'. He was, however, given lessons for an hour or so each day by the stage manager. 'He taught me a great many elementary rules which were most helpful — such as the actions of my hands and arms, walking on the stage, holding myself as easily as I could, and above all things, he would never let me put my hands in my pockets.' In spring 1882 he played Jack Merryweather in *The Marble Arch*, supporting Beerbohm Tree. He then played in a

tour of *The Colonel*, and at the Gaiety in April 1883 was Charles Livingstone in *That Rascal Pat* and Mr Bultitude's Body in *Vice-Versa*. At the Imperial in May 1883 he was in a revival of *The Colonel*, and then toured playing Herbert in *Equals*, Maurice Lawley in *Stage Land* and Douglas Cattermole in *The Private Secretary*, his own adaptation of van Moser's *Der Bibliothekar*. At the Court Theatre in March 1884 he played Geoffrey Wynyard in *Dan'l Druce*, the part created by Forbes-Robertson. A newspaper critic wrote of his performance: 'Mr Hawtrey as Geoffrey, looked to me more like a bicyclist [which at that time was a terrible term of reproach] or a member of the Clapham Rovers Football Team.'

Hawtrey condensed his play, *The Private Secretary*, into three acts and considerably rewrote it. Then, raising £1200 from friends, he produced it at the Prince of Wales Theatre opening in March 1884. Beerbohm Tree played the lead. After a shaky start it eventually caught on, though the critic from the *Globe* wrote: 'The talents of capable actors are frittered away on worthless parts and not all their efforts could save this play from a dismal fate.' Hawtrey transferred the play to the Globe under his own management and took the part of

Douglas Cattermole himself. By July it had recouped its money, and despite pirated versions of the play which ran in the provinces and in America, Hawtrey made a lot of money.

In 1885, now manager of Her Majesty's Theatre, he revived *Secret Service* and produced *Excelsior*, taking over from the impoverished Milan Scala Company. In April 1886 Charles Hawtrey opened as Osmond Hewitt at the Globe in *The Pickpocket*. The critics didn't care for this play either, and this time they were right — it only had a six-month run. That June he married Madeline Sherriffe. (Their son Anthony, born in 1909, also became an actor.) In September he took over the management of Prince's (retaining that of the Globe) and produced *Harvest*, in which he played Basil Brooke. Returning to the Globe in January 1887 he played Reginald Sparker in *Lodgers*. He next played Felix Featherstone in *The Snowball* in March 1887 and then his first leading part, that of Arthur Hummingtop in *The Arabian Nights* in November 1887. This was a farce by Sydney Grundy, and also was adapted from a play by van Moser. He took over the Comedy Theatre, to which he transferred this piece, and on the eve of the transfer was served notice of bankruptcy, for the first but certainly not the last time. On this occasion he won the money he needed playing baccarat, and discharged his debts before any proceedings could be taken. He remained in charge of the Comedy until 1893, and there he produced *Uncles and Aunts*, which had a successful nine-month run, *Tenterhooks* in May 1889, in which he played Jasper Quayle, *Pink Dominoes* in November 1889, in which he played Charles Gregthorne, and *Nerves* in June 1890, in which he played Captain Armytage. He later said: 'Although I had no wish or ambition to become a manager [I] had management as it were thrust upon me. The result of this was that in plays that I afterwards produced, I was able to choose the characters and parts that I felt I could play and not the ones that other managers had given me, when they rarely and grudgingly gave me an engagement.'

He continued at the Comedy, playing Captain L'Estrange in *May and December* (November 1890), Charles Shackleton in *Jane* (December 1890), Reginald in *Godpapa* (October 1891), John Maxwell in *The Grey Mare* (January 1892), Mr Graham in *Time is Money* (April 1892), the Poet in *The Poet and the Puppets* (May 1892), Charles Prothero in *Today* (December 1892), and Harry Briscoe in *The Sportsman* (January 1893).

He was again bankrupted by his next production, which was at the Trafalgar Square Theatre in November 1893. He played Tom Stanhope in *Tom, Dick and Harry*, which lost a good deal of

money. For the next couple of years, as a bankrupt, he was out of management, though for other people he played Major Kildare in *Mrs Dexter* (Strand, February 1894), Viscount Oldacre in *The Candidate* (Criterion, July 1894), Chauncey Pottleton in *Hot Water* (Prince's, August 1894), Horace Dudley in *A Gay Widow* (Court, October 1894), William Brown in *Dr Bill* (Court, December 1894), and Lord Goring in *An Ideal Husband* (Haymarket, January 1895).

In September 1895 he went back into management, reviving *The Private Secretary* at the Avenue Theatre. In November that same year he appeared as Matthew Ponderbury in *Mrs Ponderbury's Past*. He took over the Comedy Theatre once again in October 1896, when he appeared as Martin Heathcote in his own play, *Mr Martin*. He then played the Hon. Stacey Gillam in *A White Elephant* (November 1896), Herbert Jocelyn in *Saucy Sally* (March 1897), Major Dick Rudyard in *One Summer's Day* (September 1897), and Lord Algernon Chetland in *Lord and Lady Algy* (April 1898). In September 1898 he transferred *Lord and Lady Algy* to the Avenue. There he also played Hugh Farrant in *The Cuckoo* (March 1899) and Horace Parker in *A Message from Mars* (November 1899). This transferred to the Prince of Wales in April 1901. He then went to America and made his New York début at the Garrick Theater in October 1901 playing in *A Message from Mars*.

Charles Hawtrey returned to London to the Prince of Wales in April 1902 playing Brooke Trench in *The President*, and in May he was William Waring in *There and Back*. He went back to America for two seasons in 1903, and was the first Englishman to play in vaudeville, touring throughout the United States.

Returning to the Avenue in June 1905 Charles Hawtrey was once more in *A Message from Mars*, and at the Criterion that August he played Charlie Graham in *Time is Money*. He opened as Frederick Ware in *Lucky Miss Dean* at the Coronet in September 1905 and then toured with it. He brought it back to London to the Haymarket in November. The following month he was playing Arthur Kingsbury in *The Indecision of Mr Kingsbury*, with which the critic Max Beerbohm was not very happy: 'That he consented to play the part assigned to him is evidence of infinite submissiveness. He knew that he was in the prime of life, and that he could not, by taking thought, change himself into a stripling. He must have known also, that only by a man of extreme youth could the part of Mr Kingsbury be played appropriately. The whole play depends on the fact that Mr Kingsbury is extremely young.'

By March 1906 Charles Hawtrey was in a revival of *The Man from Blankley's*, which finished the season successfully. In January 1907 he was Captain Dorvaston in *Lady Huntworth's Experiment*, and at the Vaudeville in April 1907 he was John March in *Mr George*; he revived *Mrs Ponderbury's Past* in June and *The Cuckoo* in November. In January 1908 he was Charles Ingleton in *Dear Old Charlie*, and opened in March 1908 playing the title role in Somerset Maugham's *Jack Straw*. Max Beerbohm reported: 'Mr Hawtrey, as the hero, has a part that skilfully gives him all his usual chances, with a few new ones thrown in. The effect of him in an auburn and bifurcated beard is in itself so startling as to ensure the success of the first act. And at the end of the second act, before making a silent exit, he has occasion to turn and wink at the other persons of the play. Some twelve years ago the United States of America were profoundly stirred by "the Cissie Fitzgerald wink". I shall not be surprised if the Hawtrey wink created an equally deep impression here. In its slowness, its solemnity, its richness, it is as memorable as it is indescribable and can be likened only to an eclipse of the sun.' The play could have run and run but had to close because Hawtrey had appendicitis. The following March he returned to the Vaudeville in Maugham's adaptation of a French play, *The Noble Spaniard*. This costume drama was not so successful and in May he was playing Sir Charles Morgan in *What the Public Wants*.

At Wyndham's in October 1909 he played Recklaw Poole in *The Little Damozel* with May Blaney in the title role, and in April 1910 he was Bernard Darrell in *The Naked Truth*. He returned to the Prince of Wales in October 1910 playing George Bullin in *Inconstant George* and in April 1911 was Edouard Maubrun in *Better Not Enquire*. He played the part of Mr Flat in *Money* at the Command Performance at Drury Lane in May 1911. That June, at a Gala Performance at His Majesty's, he played Sneer in *The Critic*. At the Prince of Wales in September he played John Harcourt in his own adaptation of *The Great Name* and in October appeared there as Jacques Calvel in *The Uninvited Guest*. In December he was Horace Parker in *A Message from Mars* yet again, and at the Savoy for Christmas produced *Where the Rainbow Ends*, a play for and starring children that was to become a Christmas classic. Forty children played gnomes, dwarfs, fairies, hyenas and other assorted beasts, and nine others had the principals' roles — one of those was Noel Coward.

In February 1912 he revived *Dear Old Charlie*, and took it to New York to the Maxine Elliott

Theater in April. At the Apollo Theatre in January 1913 he played Dr Lucius O'Grady in *General John Regan* and in June was Vincent Cray in *The Perfect Cure*.

There was an all-star revival of *London Assurance* at the St James's Theatre on 27 June 1913 in aid of the King George Pension Fund and Charles Hawtrey played Cool, the valet. At the Apollo in September he was Dionysius Woodbury in *Never Say Die*, and in March 1914 Richard Gilder in *Things We'd Like to Know*. At the all-star revival of *The Silver King* in May 1914 he was the Tipsy Passenger, and at the Coliseum in July 1914 played the Hon. Wylie Walton in *The Compleat Angler*. Back at the Apollo, in September he played William Hallowell Magee in *Seven Keys to Baldpate*, in December was Horace Parker in a revival of *A Message from Mars*, and in January 1915 played Lord Charles Temperleigh in *A Busy Day*.

At an all-star revival in aid of the Actors' Benevolent Fund at Covent Garden in February 1915 he played Moses in *The School for Scandal*; at the Apollo in May he played Lord Marston in *Striking*. That spring Charles Hawtrey set out on a tour of the variety theatres in *The Compleat Angler*, returning to the Coliseum in July 1915 as Sam in *The Haunted Husband*. Still at the Coliseum, in November 1915 he played Jack Annerley in *Q*. In January 1916, with Gladys Cooper at the Playhouse, he produced *Please Help Emily* and played Richard Trotter in it. In September he was back at the Coliseum in variety playing Jimmy in *Waiting at the Church*. He was Anthony Silvertree in *Anthony in Wonderland* at the Prince of Wales in February 1917 and went back to the Coliseum in July to play Peter in *His Wedding Night*.

At the Garrick in October 1917 he was Blinn Corbett in *The Saving Grace*, and took the part of Lord Strathpeffer in the all-star revival of *The Man from Blankley's* at His Majesty's in December 1917. Back with Gladys Cooper at the Playhouse in April 1918 he played Hilary Farrington in *The Naughty Wife*, and followed that in August 1919 playing William in Somerset Maugham's *Home and Beauty*. In August 1920 he was at the St James's playing James Smith in *His Lady Friends*.

His health now began to deteriorate quickly and he was often forced off the stage. However, at the Playhouse in April 1921 he played Garry Ainsworth in *Up in Mabel's Room*, and in July 1921 he doubled the characters of the pirate and his respectable descendant in *Ambrose Applejohn's Adventure*. He played 570 consecutive performances of this at the Criterion and at the same time produced seven plays for other managements. Charles Hawtrey was knighted in 1922, and died on 30 July 1923.

Sir John Gielgud has written that he 'saw him in a number of plays and he never seemed to do anything at all. He was fat with a lazy manner, not good-looking at all, but with impeccable timing —

and a deadpan perfection in comic situations.' Somerset Maugham put the same sentiment another way: 'With his magnetic personality, his incomparable humour and unfailing charm he was a great comedian. He became an adept in stage pre-varication in a style quite his own, never flurried, always natural, quiet and persuasive.'

HELEN HAYES

'Without the compensation of glamour, I am hard put to explain the durability of my career and the loyalty of the audience. Perhaps it is just identification. I was once the typical daughter, then 'the easily recognizable wife and then the quintessential mother. I seem always to have reminded people of someone in their family.'

For many years Helen Hayes shared with Katharine Cornell the title of First Lady of the American Theater. She was born in Washington, DC, on 10 October 1900. Her father was a travelling salesman, and her mother travelled as much as possible with rather strange stock companies in an attempt to bring some glamour into her life and to avoid domesticity. As a very small child Helen was looked after by her paternal grandmother and attended Holy Cross Academy, where she was first seen on stage as Pease-Blossom in *A Midsummer Night's Dream*. She made her professional début aged five as Prince Charles in the Columbia Players' production of *The Royal Family* at the National Theater in Washington. She went on to play in *Little Lord Fauntleroy, The Prince Chap* and *The Prince and the Pauper*. She generally did two plays a summer, and attended the academy when there was time.

Then her mother decided that Helen was ready for greater things and took her to New York, where she reminded Lew Fields, who had once seen Helen perform, how much he had liked the child. With his help, Helen made her New York début playing Little Mimi in *Old Dutch* at the Herald Square Theater on 22 November 1909. She went on to play Psyche Finnegan in *The Summer Widowers* at the Broadway in 1910 and Fannie Hickes in *The Never Homes* in 1911. She also made her first film, *Jean and the Calico Cat*.

Twelve is an awkward age, and the Broadway parts dried up. Helen was 16 before she returned to New York regularly. Then, at the Hudson in September 1916 she played Pollyanna Whittier in

Pollyanna with great success and toured it through 1918. It was then that she began to notice her lack of training. 'On tour in *Pollyanna* I started out like a house afire. Across the country my reviews became less and less enthusiastic. I simply could not repeat a good performance at will.'

She returned to New York to the Globe, where in September 1918 she opened as Margaret Scho-field in *Penrod*. That December she was at the Empire playing opposite William Gillette with great success in *Dear Brutus*. Her career at this point was being run not only by her mother but also by the impresario George C. Tyler. He moulded her, decided what was good for her, and even commissioned plays for her. He intended to make her a star, and used all the methods Holly-wood later adopted in the building of names. In June 1919, back in Washington, she was Dorothy Fessenden in *On the Hiring Line* and then at the Hudson that September played Cora Wheeler, the archetypal teenager in *Clarence*, with Alfred Lunt. She realized that if she were to go on she would have to learn stage technique, and took coaching from Frances Robinson Duff and her mother Madame Duff. They were always at her side for the first rehearsals of plays, and they stayed there for years, much to the annoyance of the directors. After Miss Duff's death, Constance Collier took her place. Helen also studied boxing until she could move like a featherweight champion, as well as fencing and interpretive dance.

Helen Hayes' name was first up in lights at the Park Theater when she took the title role in *Bab* in October 1920. Tyler had commissioned the play especially for her from some Mary Roberts Rein-hardt short stories. *The Wren*, which opened at the Gaiety in October 1921, was also written espec-ially for her, but it was not a success because the character was too close to her real personality for her to come to terms with it. By November at the same theatre she was playing Mary Anne in *Golden Days*. In 1922 she played Elsie Beebe in

George S. Kaufman and Marc Connelly's *To the Ladies*, which Alexander Woollcott called 'a wise and merry and artful comedy'. It ran for two years, and then Helen Hayes toured it for nearly two more. The year 1924 brought her four parts: Mary Sundale in *We Moderns*, Constance Neville in *She Stoops to Conquer*, Catherine Westcourt in *Dancing Mothers*, and Dinah Partlett in *Quarantine*.

She was determined to play something 'heavier' and in spite of her mother's protests played Cleopatra in Shaw's *Caesar and Cleopatra* in April 1925, at the opening of the Theater Guild's new theatre on 52nd Street. Brooks Atkinson reported that she, at the beginning of her career, and Lionel Atwell, at the end of his, were part of one of the most mediocre productions ever given by the Theater Guild.

Helen Hayes had by now met Charles MacArthur, a writer, charmer, wit, heavy drinker and married man. His friends were against the match, her friends were against the match and the Catholic Church of which she was an ardent member forbade the match. Yet she was determined to go ahead with it. At the Ritz in November 1925 she was Georgia Bissell in *Young Blood*, and in April 1926 took on the part of Maggie Wylie for the first time in *What Every Woman Knows*. Brooks Atkinson wrote in the *New York Times*: 'Notwithstanding [some] deeply moving scenes Miss Hayes is not yet quite up to the interpretation of so full-bodied a part. And although her abilities have broadened and taken firm root since her first diaphanous and fragile embodiments of Barriesque creation [*Dear Brutus*], this Maggie is a woman of tougher substance than Miss Hayes communicates . . . Miss Hayes relies too much upon her charm in the portrayal of so real and complex a personage.' She was, however, to have further attempts at the role, and Atkinson's final comment on the performance some years later was: 'Miss Hayes does not have a personality that dazzles the public; she does not behave like a star . . . but put her on the stage and raise the curtain, and something happens to the audience. She was perfectly cast when she played in Barrie's *What Every Woman Knows* — a mousy, unassertive woman who has a powerful influence on other people.'

While she was playing Norma Besant in *Coquette* at the Maxine Elliott Theater in 1927, MacArthur's play *The Front Page* opened. It was a hit, he proposed, and they were married on 17 August 1928. After the tour of *Coquette* she opened at the Broadhurst in September 1930 as Nellie Fitzpatrick in *Mr Gilhooley*. She followed that the same year with Peggy Chalfont in *Petticoat Influence* at the Empire in December 1930. That year her daughter

Mary was born. She caused great public interest as the 'Act of God' child — which the courts allowed when Helen had to leave a play, breaking her contract, because of her pregnancy.

Helen Hayes next played Lu in *The Good Family* at the Henry Miller Theater in November 1931. She then took a break from the theatre for a while, concentrating on the domestic side of her life (with Charlie for a husband this was always rather chaotic but, as she said, never boring) and on filming. In 1933 she made the transition from popular star to serious actress when she played the title role in Maxwell Anderson's *Mary of Scotland*. Brooks Atkinson wrote: 'As Mary, Miss Hayes is at her best. Slight as she is in stature (and Mary was six feet tall) Miss Hayes raises herself to queendom by the transcendence of her spirit. The girlish charm of her arrival in Scotland, the grimness with which she tries to control her destiny, the womanly horror in the murder scene, the bravery with which she meets Elizabeth summon emotions that none of her previous roles have required. She is the mistress of them . . . she speaks verse with the warmth and clarity of an artist.'

After Mary, Helen Hayes took on another Queen, and was once again triumphant — in fact *Victoria Regina* was her masterpiece. She based her conception of the character on her grandmother, herself a Victorian, and it worked. John Mason Brown reported: 'Miss Hayes succeeds with Victoria as she succeeded with Mary, in being a queen without ever forgetting she is a woman. She does not resort to any of the "Lady-Come-To-See" tricks by means of which most stage queens betray that at heart they are commoners' children whose notions of royalty are as naive as Daisy Ashford's. Miss Hayes has the good sense and the artistic perception to realize what makes a queen a queen is not the costume she wears when she rides through the streets in a gold coach to open Parliament, but the blood coursing through her veins and the spirit born of it.' And Brooks Atkinson sums up: 'The girlish innocence, the eager propriety of her wooing of Albert, the unaffected joy of her devotion to him, her pettish anger when her authority was challenged, the moving humility of her surrender from Queen to wife, her courage and her simplicity were parts of a memorable stage composition.' For her performance Helen Hayes won the Drama League of New York Medal. She had already won an Oscar in 1931 in Hollywood for her performance in *The Son of Madelon Claudet*. Her husband had written it; it was her first major film. *Victoria Regina* opened at the Broadhurst in December 1935, and taking in the tour, Helen Hayes played the part into 1938.

During that time she also managed three matinée performances of Portia in *The Merchant of Venice*. She revived *What Every Woman Knows* briefly at the Suffern County Playhouse in September 1938, and then went back to Broadway to the Martin Beck Theater and *Victoria Regina*. Still at the Martin Beck in October 1939 she played Miss Scott in *Ladies and Gentlemen*. At the St James in November 1940 she played Viola in *Twelfth Night*, in which part Brooks Atkinson felt that 'she lacked style. She missed Viola's high breeding, her lighthearted unsophisticated Viola was more pathetic than romantic.' *Candle in the Wind*, in which she played Madeline Guest at the Shubert in October 1941, was not a success, but a play based on the life of Harriet Beecher Stowe, called simply *Harriet*, in which she opened at the Henry Miller Theater in March 1943, was an enormous triumph. She had wanted to do something meaningful during the war, as well as the work she did entertaining the troops and raising money, and this was it. It ran on through 1945.

Helen Hayes received a Tony for her performance as Addie in *Happy Birthday*, which opened at the Broadhurst in October 1946. She made her London début playing Amanda in Tennessee Williams' *The Glass Menagerie* at the Haymarket in July 1948. The English critics were puzzled and none too pleased with the play, though T. C. Worsley conceded: 'Miss Hayes flutters and flutes triumphantly through this part, with the absolute assurance of the master artist who convinces us that it could only have been like this.' It is a pity that she could never work up the courage to play either of her queens in London.

With her daughter, Mary, Helen Hayes went to the Falmouth Playhouse in summer 1949 to play in *Good Housekeeping*. It was during that summer that Mary was stricken with polio and died. Helen Hayes was distraught but her friends finally persuaded her to take the part of Lucy Andree Ransdell in Josh Logan's *The Wisteria Tree*, which opened at the Martin Beck in March 1950. Brooks Atkinson explains that acting was a kind of therapy for her: 'Broadway audiences supported her in it, not only because of her gallant acting, but because they understood her problem. The relationship between actress and public became increasingly personal.' She produced Barrie's *Mary Rose* at ANTA in 1951, and the next year appeared there herself as Mrs Howard V. Larue II in *Mrs Nothing*. She appeared in a season of revivals of her starring parts at the Falmouth Playhouse the summer of 1954 and continued revivals in New York through 1955.

Helen Hayes appeared first in Paris as Mrs

Antrobus in *The Skin of Our Teeth* at the Sarah Bernhardt in June 1955, and came with the production back to New York to ANTA in August. Charles MacArthur, her husband of thirty years, died on 21 April 1956. For consolation, Helen Hayes returned first of all to her Church and then to the stage. She played Amanda once more in *The Glass Menagerie* at the New York City Center in November 1956, and the following November at the Morosco was the Duchess of Pont-au-Bronc in *Time Remembered* with Richard Burton and Susan Strasberg; it ran for 248 performances.

At the Helen Hayes Theater in October 1958 she played Nora Melody in O'Neill's A *Touch of the Poet*, and in the summer of 1959 in her local theatre at Nyack, New York, she played Lulu Spencer in *An Adventure*. She went to Palm Beach in January 1960 to play in *The Cherry Orchard* and then back to Nyack for the summer where she played Mrs St Maugham in *The Chalk Garden*.

Sponsored by the United States State Department, the following winter Miss Hayes toured twenty-eight different countries through South America and Europe, playing in *The Glass Menagerie* and *The Skin of Our Teeth*.

For the American Shakespeare Festival at Stratford, Connecticut, in 1962 she and Maurice Evans got together a Shakespearian entertainment called *Shakespeare Revisited*, which they then toured. Back in New York in 1964 she appeared in *The White House* at the Henry Miller Theater, in which she played Abigail Adams, Dolly Madison, Mrs Lincoln, Mrs Cleveland and Mrs Wilson — all Presidents' wives.

The Helen Hayes Repertory Company, which sponsored university tours of Shakespeare recitals, was formed in 1964. While on a State Department tour of the Far East in the winter of 1965 she played in *The Glass Menagerie* for Japanese television. She toured the United States in April 1966 with her repertory company, and at the Lyceum in New York in November 1966 played Mrs Candour in *The School for Scandal* and Signora Frola in Pirandello's *Right You Are*. Of the latter, Martin Gottfried reported: 'The lone misperformance of the evening was that of Helen Hayes as the mysterious Signora Frola. Working in a thin, colorless voice and apparently acting off the top of her head, Miss Hayes seemed entirely unaware of the rigors of style or the demands of group acting. Off somewhere on her own, she missed the not-terribly-difficult details of her interesting character.' In December 1966 she was in *We Comrades Three* and the following December played Mrs Fishe in *The Show-Off*. John Simon did not care for it: 'As the crusty, sensible mother,

Helen Hayes does everything under the sun — or more precisely under the spotlight — to make an audience drool, shriek with helpless laughter and eat her up alive. She's as American as cutie-pie, as adorable as a big fat baby that has just peed in your lap, and if canny, senescent whimsy could be bottled, there is enough here to make an entire convention of geriatricians pie-eyed drunk.' Nevertheless Miss Hayes repeated the performance in September 1968 and then toured with it. In October 1969 she played the part of Mrs Grant (a role based on her mother) in her late husband's *The Front Page* at the Ethel Barrymore Theater, and in February 1970 she was at ANTA in Jimmy Stewart's revival of *Harvey*, playing Veta Louise Simmons. John Simon did not care for that either: 'With knowing technique and adorable fussiness galore, she succeeds in depriving the protagonist of his antagonist, and converting Veta Louise, whom

you should love to hate, into someone you hate to love.' At Catholic University in her native Washington, DC, she played Mary Tyrone in O'Neill's *Long Day's Journey into Night* in a farewell stage performance.

At one time known as the Triple Threat because of her work on stage, screen and radio, Helen Hayes has achieved awards in all three (she received her second Oscar for *Airport*). She has worked tirelessly for innumerable charities and holds honorary degrees from at least ten universities.

'I had never yearned to be an actress,' she wrote in her autobiography, 'because I always was one. I never dreamed of a career — because I always had one. For sixty years I've heard, "Two minutes, Miss Hayes," and I've sprinted onto the stage. It's become a reflex. Pavlov's Actress, that's me.'

EILEEN HERLIE

T he critics have, throughout her career, either loved her or hated her — but they have never been indifferent to her.

Eileen Herlie was born O'Herlihy to a Scots mother and an Irish father in Glasgow on 8 March 1920. She was educated at Shawland's Academy, also in Glasgow, and when she was 15 paid her first visit to the theatre, where she saw Matheson Lang in *Wandering Jew* and determined to become an actress. Parental opposition, however, was strong. She became a secretary in Scotland, and in the meantime made her first appearance on the stage at the Lyric, Glasgow, with the Scottish National Players in *Sweet Aloes* in 1938. She then toured with the Rutherglen Repertory Company and on 12 August 1942 married Philip Barrett, an impresario who had bought the stage rights to Daphne du Maurier's *Rebecca*. Eileen toured with it in 1942, playing the second Mrs de Winter, and when the Ambassadors' Theatre in London suddenly became vacant on Boxing Day she made her London stage début in that part. She repeated the role in April 1943 at the Scala, and in May played Peg in *Peg o' My Heart* there. In 1944 she toured as Regina in *The Little Foxes*, and then joined the Old Vic Company at the Playhouse, Liverpool, where during 1945 and 1946 she appeared in a number of roles: Mrs Fanny Wilton in *John Gabriel Borkman*, Varvara in *Lisa*, Paula in *The Second Mrs Tanqueray*, Lady Sneerwell in *The*

School for Scandal, Anna Christopherson in *Anna Christie*, the Queen in *Hamlet*, Dol Common in *The Alchemist*, and Stella de Gex in *His Excellency the Governor*.

At the Lyric, Hammersmith, in November 1945 she played Andromache in a modern-dress production of *The Trojan Women*. Audrey Williamson reported that she was 'statuesque and beautiful in grief, yet just failing to tear the heart when the child was torn from her arms to be killed'. She continued at the Lyric, where she played Mary in *The Time of Life* (February 1946) and Alcestis in *The Thracian Horses* (May 1946). It was in September 1946, when at the same theatre she played the Queen in Cocteau's *The Eagle Has Two Heads*, that after seven years in the theatre she became a star overnight. The lugubrious Hannen Swaffer wrote: 'Not even the oldest living playgoer can recall an achievement such as that of which Eileen Herlie can now rightly boast. In a suburban theatre holding only 800 people she rose to fame in a night. Scarcely had the excited and prolonged cheers fallen on her performance ... when Noel Coward was in her dressing-room almost too moved to pay tribute to her. That meant that before more than a day had passed the entire acting profession would be at her feet.' The reviews were raves, and in February 1947 the play transferred to the Haymarket. A few critics were not totally enthralled. Audrey Williamson said that

Eileen Herlie 'achieved a technical *tour de force* and (rare on our stage today) really looked and behaved like a queen. Personally I found her lacking in depth and flexibility of emotion, yet pictorially she was regal and vivid, with a mask of tragic beauty.' And Harold Hobson, newly installed at the *Sunday Times*, was amazed at the rapture with which Miss Herlie's performance was greeted. 'For twenty-one consecutive minutes,' he reported, 'the flow of words from her lips is punctuated only by her own pauses and by peals of off-stage thunder. It is a tremendous feat. I think of the music-hall artist handcuffed in a tank of water; I think of the triple-century test match innings; I think of this speech; and henceforth my symbols of endurance more than human are: Houdini, Hutton and Herlie. To deliver a speech like this, with constant variation of pace and strength, without flagging or fizziness, is a great strain on the throat, voice muscles, larynx: and it places Miss Herlie among, if not the great actresses, at least the notable athletes . . . But though she discharges her task with energy, intelligence and spirit, she did not once move me, except perhaps in her scream at the assassin's entrance.'

At the Edinburgh Festival in August and the Globe Theatre in London in September 1948 Eileen Herlie played *Medea*. Harold Hobson reported: 'Miss Herlie is challenged on the one hand to present the pathos of a discarded woman, and on the other to show the fury of a baulked tiger. To my mind, she gets nearer the second effect than the first. For a great part of her performance her mouth is like a gaping wound: one almost expects cascades of blood to come pouring out of it; and she has a gesture of scrabbling the flesh off her naked arms that is perfectly horrible. All this is good. But with the other part of the character she fails through monotony of voice . . . she can bellow and she can whisper, as you can turn the radio up or down. But though she can alter the volume of her voice, her range seems limited. She never takes the ear by surprise.' The *Times* critic reported: 'This exacting part of Medea — who is nearly always on the stage and for ever sounding the top note of jealous fury — offers Miss Eileen Herlie the finest opportunity that has yet come her way. In this translation the opportunity is cruelly whittled down. She altogether fails to make Medea great, but then the grain of the text is against her, nearly always encouraging the diminution of true values. The vengeance which should fill the heavens only makes the earth creepy. She is a pathological ''case'' infinitely horrible and pathetic but never terrible, much too near to the madness which is a corruption of reason for us to see ourselves in the presence of a transcendent

hatred which quickens and clarifies reason. Miss Herlie is fettered to the leaden-footed dialogue, yet there are passages in which she might break through at any rate for while. She remains fettered and we are left wondering if she has yet learned to use her emotional energy, her tragic personality, to awe-inspiring effect.' Sidney W. Carroll, the former dramatic critic on the *Sunday Times*, wrote to that paper deploring the critics' views on *Medea*. He said that 'Eileen Herlie's Medea is one of the greatest tragic performances seen in an English theatre (in over forty years). She redeems completely a vulgar and abbreviated version of the tragedy by a dramatic exhibition of Asiatic revenge and hatred that terrifies while it enthrals, a classic purity of diction, a maturity of technique, a passion and a pathos no other actress could surpass.'

Eileen Herlie opened at the Haymarket in August 1950 as Paula in *The Second Mrs Tanqueray*. T. C. Worsley reported: 'She makes her Paula intense and low-toned, a beautiful and sad misfit with echoes of tragedy about her. It is a very consistent, thoughtful performance but . . . Miss Herlie seems to have discarded the author's hints. There is no volatility, nothing of the mercurial about her playing. The extremities of undisciplined emotionalism — that's what one wants from Paula Tanqueray, together with charm and sexual appeal. And without them neither play nor part quite makes sense.'

In February 1953 she joined John Gielgud back at the scene of her first triumph, the Lyric, Hammersmith. There she played Mrs Marwood in *The Way of the World* and in May took the part of Belvidera in *Venice Preserv'd*; of the latter Kenneth Tynan wrote: 'The spectacle of Miss Herlie reeling and writhing in coils is both pleasing and appropriate but something in her voice, a touch of fulsomeness, suggests an energetic saleswoman rather than a tragic heroine.'

At the King's, Glasgow, in November 1953 she played Irene Carey in *A Sense of Guilt* and returned to the Haymarket in London in November 1954 to play Mrs Molloy in *The Matchmaker*. Ronald Barker said: 'Eileen Herlie is delicious as Mrs Molloy the Milliner. Her beauty and gaiety make us realize more than ever that she must keep us entranced with more comedy performances.' Eileen Herlie made her Broadway début in this role at the Royale in December 1955; the play ran for 488 performances. Staying in New York, she opened at the Phoenix in December 1957 playing Emilia Marty in *The Makropoulos Secret*. At the Shakespeare Festival in Stratford, Ontario, in June 1958 she was Paulina in *The Winter's Tale* and Beatrice in *Much Ado About Nothing*.

In November 1959 Eileen Herlie played Ruth

Gray in *Epitaph for George Dillon* at the John Golden Theater in New York, and repeated the performance at the Henry Miller Theater when the play was revived in January 1959. At the Shubert in October 1959 she appeared as Lily in *Take Me Along*. At the Winter Garden in March 1962 she played Elizabeth Hawkes-Bullock in the musical *All American*, and in February 1963 was Stella in *Photo Finish*. It was in April 1964 that she played Gertrude in John Gielgud's production of *Hamlet*. She was Lady Fitzbuttress in November 1967 at the Brooks Atkinson in Peter Ustinov's *Halfway Up the Tree*, and at the Ivanhoe in Chicago in 1971 played Martha in *Who's Afraid of Virginia Woolf?* and Clare in *Outcry*. At the Ethel Barrymore in New York in March 1973 she

opened as Countess Matilda Spina in Pirandello's *Emperor Henry IV* with Rex Harrison. John Simon noted: 'As the fatal Countess Matilda Spina, who is supposed to be "imperious and too beautiful", Eileen Herlie is shrill and painfully homely.'

At the Helen Hayes Theater in October 1973, Eileen Herlie played Queen Mary in the play about the abdication of Edward VIII, *Crown Matrimonial*, and then toured the United States with it. Back at the Ivanhoe in Chicago in October 1975 she was Essie Sebastian in *The Great Sebastians*.

Eileen Herlie made her first film in 1947, playing a small part in *Hungry Hill* for Korda. She was notable as the Queen in Laurence Olivier's *Hamlet*, and also appeared in *Freud*.

WENDY HILLER

'*I*t's no good trying to plan a career or consulting oracles or picking through entrails,' Wendy Hiller said. 'All you can do is press on and take the work as it comes.'

Wendy Margaret Hiller was born in Bramhall, Cheshire, on 15 August 1912. Her father Frank had started there as a spinner in the cotton trade, but by the time of her birth had become a mill director. She went to Winceby House School in Bexhill, and straight from school became an assistant stage manager with the Manchester Repertory Theatre, where she made her stage début in September 1930 playing the maid in *The Ware Case*. She continued to understudy and to play small parts through 1932 when she toured with the company in *Evensong*. She was sacked from the company because they told her she was not a good enough actress, and while she sat at home and waited, wondering what she was going to do next, they called her back. They had received Ronald Gow's adaptation of the novel *Love on the Dole*, about the depressed areas in the 1930s, and needed a girl who could do a convincing Lancashire accent — that was Wendy. She opened as Sally Hardcastle in May 1934, toured through that year and came to London to the Garrick in June 1935, where she became an instantaneous success. She made her New York stage début at the Shubert Theater in February 1936 in the same part, and was again triumphant. George Bernard Shaw was so impressed with her performance that he asked her to play St Joan and Eliza Doolittle, which she did at the Malvern Festival in 1936, and then made

the film version of *Pygmalion*. On 25 February 1937 she married the playwright Ronald Gow, who wrote *Love on the Dole*.

Wendy Hiller returned to the stage in 1943 when she toured factory centres playing Viola in *Twelfth Night*. At the Apollo in January 1944 she opened in a revival of *The Cradle Song* playing Sister Joanna. James Agate reported: 'It is exquisitely acted by a cast keeping perfect balance between frustration and breathless devotion ... Miss Wendy Hiller knows all about the starved Sister Joanna, but I wish her peasant inflections ... didn't sound quite so like the modern crooner.' At the New in July 1945 she was Princess Charlotte in *The First Gentleman*, and Audrey Williamson said she 'gave the young Princess a mixture of strong will and clear-cut charm'.

In 1946 Wendy Hiller joined the Bristol Old Vic Company for the season, playing Tess in her husband's adaptation of the Hardy novel *Tess of the d'Urbervilles*, Portia in *The Merchant of Venice* and Pegeen Mike in *The Playboy of the Western World*. *Tess* transferred to the New Theatre in London in November 1946, and on to the Piccadilly in May 1947. Of this performance, Harold Hobson wrote: 'With rosy cheeks that any intelligent apple would envy, Miss Hiller is physically well suited to Hardy's opulently earthy heroine: temperamentally too: she causes Tess's love for Angel to seem a blessing and benediction, and confounds morality by making murder only a very little thing.'

It was in an adaptation of Henry James's

Washington Square called *The Heiress* that Wendy Hiller next appeared in New York; she played Catherine Sloper. She opened in September 1947 at the Biltmore, and Brooks Atkinson reported: 'She is an admirable actress, highly esteemed in America as well as England and well-remembered for her acting in *Love on the Dole* and *Pygmalion*. But in an effort to contribute some dramatic contrast to the plain part of Catherine Sloper she has made her a rather painfully abnormal person in the early half of the drama and her composure toward the end of it is not exhilarating. Nothing Miss Hiller has been able to do alters a general impression that poor Catherine is better off inside the discreet, impeccable pages of Henry James.'

Back in London, in May 1949, at the Piccadilly she played Ann Veronica Stanley in her husband's adaptation of the H. G. Wells novel *Ann Veronica*, and Harold Hobson reported: 'Wendy Hiller reveals Ann's essential tenderness; you can see the femininity beneath the feminism.' At the Haymarket in January 1950 she returned to the part of Catherine in *The Heiress* when Peggy Ashcroft left the English production of the play. In April 1951 at the same theatre she began a two-year run as Evelyn Daly in N. C. Hunter's *Waters of the Moon*, with Edith Evans and Sybil Thorndike. T. C. Worsley called it 'essentially a cosy middle-brow, middle-class piece, inhabited by characters by no means unfamiliar in brave old theatre-land ... there is the maid-of-all-work daughter of the house, whom Miss Wendy Hiller plays with real pathos as Wendy Hiller ...' In January 1955 she played Margaret Tollemache in *Night of the Ball* at the New; Ronald Barker called it a 'trite, novelettish story'.

Wendy Hiller joined the Old Vic Company for their 1955–56 season, where she played a variety of roles. Of her Portia in *Julius Caesar* Audrey Williamson said: 'Wendy Hiller put passion and loyal affection into Portia, though her voice seemed harsh and her diction disjointed for Shakespeare.' But she was happier with her performance in *The Winter's Tale*: 'The beauty of the scenery and costumes was matched by the beauty of Wendy Hiller as Hermione, a charming figure sewing among her women and showing us for once a woman racked by human anguish at the trial — her innate queenliness sustained by the barest margin of nervous physical control and grief cracking the poetry in a way that distressed the purist but gave the human tragedy more scope.' Audrey Williamson said of *Othello* (which had John Neville and Richard Burton alternating Othello and Iago): 'Wendy Hiller's Emilia was outstanding, clearly defining the woman's fascinated passion for her husband, as if her experience of

Iago had not necessarily dulled her realization that his character had its enigmatic and mischievous flaws.' That season Wendy Hiller also played Mistress Page in *The Merry Wives of Windsor*, and Helen in a modern-dress production of *Troilus and Cressida*.

She returned to New York in May 1957, where she played Josie Hogan in *A Moon for the Misbegotten* at the Bijou, and back in London at the Haymarket in June 1958 she followed Celia Johnson as Isobel Cherry in *Flowering Cherry*. Wendy Hiller went to Dublin, to the Gaiety, in June 1959 to play Marie Marescaud in *All in the Family* and returned to New York to the Lyceum that October with *Flowering Cherry*. At the Piccadilly in London in November 1960 she played Carrie Berniers in *Toys in the Attic*, and at the Theatre Royal in Windsor in October 1961 she was Mary Kingsley in *Mr Rhodes*.

In February 1962 Wendy Hiller opened once more in New York, this time at the Playhouse as Miss Tina in *The Aspern Papers*, and back in London at the Lyric in December 1963 she starred in another Henry James adaptation, this time *The Wings of the Dove* in which she played Susan Shepherd. At the Birmingham Repertory in February 1965 she played Elisabeth in *A Measure of Cruelty*, and at the Edinburgh Festival in September 1966 was Martha in *A Present for the Past*. At the Duke of York's in London in February 1967 she opened as Nurse Wayland in a revival of Somerset Maugham's *The Sacred Flame*. The production was generally considered rather dated, and of her own performance Michael Billington reported: 'Wendy Hiller makes the rigorous Nurse Wayland understandable if not exactly sympathetic: one feels her soul is as starched as her uniform.'

She returned to the Edinburgh Festival in August 1968 playing Irene in *When We Dead Awaken*, and was at the Lyric in London in 1970 playing Enid in *The Battle of Shrivings*. At the Arts, Cambridge, in February 1972 she played Mrs Alving in *Ghosts*, and returned to London in October that year, opening at the Haymarket as Queen Mary in *Crown Matrimonial*, the story of the abdication of Edward VIII. W. Stephen Gilbert reported for *Plays and Players*: 'Wendy Hiller, whom I've found resistible in the past, won me with her firm characterization and her skill with a deadly line — "I've been so lucky with my daughters-in-law ... so far." When she entered in her toque as an older Mary, we all gasped. She *was* the woman who waved to me outside Sandringham when I was five.'

In 1975 Wendy Hiller was created a Dame. That year she starred in the excellent Peter Hall production of Ibsen's *John Gabriel Borkman* at the Old Vic for the National Theatre Company in January, and in October at the Albery she played a bizarre poetess, Edith Grove, in *Lies*. According to Geoff Brown: 'Edith is a commanding figure, whether she be placing garden weeds under chair cushions or reminiscing about the life and strange tasks of her late ecclesiastical husband. But the pleasures gradually fade away, particularly as Wendy Hiller phrases her sentences and pronounces her words with wearisome eccentricity.'

In March 1976 Wendy Hiller returned to the National Theatre Company, this time at the Lyttelton Theatre on the South Bank, and once more played Gunhild Borkman in the production of *John Gabriel Borkman* which co-starred Ralph Richardson and Peggy Ashcroft.

Wendy Hiller has had a long and distinguished film career stretching back to 1937. Especially notable is her work in the Shaw films of *Pygmalion* and *Major Barbara*, and she received an Academy Award for her appearance in *Separate Tables* in 1959. She played the mother in *Sons and Lovers* and Lady Margaret in *A Man for All Seasons*. Of her film work Wendy Hiller said: 'After I'm dead I'll be a cult and they'll have entire seasons of me. Thank heaven I won't have to sit through them.'

In 1984 she returned to the stage in a revival of *The Aspern Papers* at the Theatre Royal, Haymarket.

STANLEY HOLLOWAY

*A*lthough his monologues would brand him a North Country lad, Stanley Holloway was in fact born in the East End of London on 1 October 1890. His father was a law clerk. Stanley had a natural singing voice and his talent was encouraged by his uncle, who taught him songs and verses. He soon discovered that performing was the one sure way to become the centre of attention, and as Master Stanley Holloway, Boy Soprano, he specialized in 'O Dry Those Tears', 'The Lost Chord' and 'Rest in the Lord'. When his voice broke he worked first as a clerk in a boot polish factory and then at a Billingsgate fish market. By 1910 he had developed a pleasant baritone and he took to the seaside with a concert party called Pepper's White Coons, with whom he specialized in strong ballads. Concert parties, he said, were 'hard work but a great training ground because, although I was a baritone, if ever they needed a policeman or a bus conductor for a sketch I'd be in. You had to do a bit of everything.'

In 1913 Stanley Holloway went to Milan to study opera, but then the First World War came along. He served in the Connaught Rangers, a Yorkshire regiment, which is how he learned the North Country accent. After the war he returned to concert parties and was noticed by Leslie Henson, and so he moved from concert parties to music hall. Stanley Holloway made his first London appearance at the Winter Garden Theatre on 20 May 1919 when he played Captain Wentworth in *Kissing Time*. In September 1920 he was René in *A Night Out* at the same theatre.

At the Royalty in June 1921 he opened as an original member of *The Co-optimists* — really an extended concert party dressed up in Pierrot costumes with skull caps and ruffles. *The Co-optimists* lasted at that theatre for six years. In 1921 Stanley Holloway also made his first film, when he played the juvenile lead in the silent *The Rotters*. Over the years he was to make more than fifty films, including *The Lavender Hill Mob*, *My Fair Lady*, *This Happy Breed* and *Passport to Pimlico*. Yet he always preferred the theatre to film. 'It's the immediate impact on an audience that's so rewarding. You deliver a line and — wham, back comes a laugh or applause, or a chuckle.'

In November 1927 Stanley Holloway returned to musicals at the London Hippodrome, where he played Bill Smith in *Hit the Deck*. At His Majesty's in September 1928 he was Lieutenant Richard Manners in *Song of the Sea*, and at the Vaudeville in April 1929 he was in *Cooee*. In 1929 *The Co-optimists* were revived.

Stanley Holloway was in the *Savoy Follies* in July 1932 and at the Lyceum in October 1932 in *Here We Are Again*. At Drury Lane in April 1934 he was Eustace Titherley in the decidedly un-Chekhovian *The Three Sisters*, and made his first pantomime appearance at the Prince of Wales in Birmingham in December 1934. He played Abanazar in *Aladdin*, and went on to play the same part in following years at Leeds, Golders Green, Edinburgh and Manchester.

Continuing in stage revues, Stanley Holloway played in *All Wave* (Duke of York's, November

1936), *London Rhapsody* (London Palladium, April 1938), *All The Best* (tour, June 1938), *Up and Doing* (Saville, April 1940, May 1941), and *Fine and Dandy* (Saville, April 1942). Stanley Holloway could deliver over forty monologues, some of which he wrote himself, such as the 'Sam' monologues of which there were more than ten; the first, however, 'Sam, Pick Oop Tha Musket', remained the most popular. Another classic series, about the Ramsbottoms and poor Albert who gets eaten by a lion, was written by Marriott Edgar, Edgar Wallace's brother.

At the New Theatre in May 1951 Stanley Holloway played his first straight role — the First Gravedigger in the Festival of Britain *Hamlet*, a role he had already filmed with Olivier. He appeared with the Old Vic Company at the Edinburgh Festival in 1954 as Bottom in *A Midsummer Night's Dream*. About being offered the part he said: 'I was surprised and yet again I wasn't. I had been used to doing this, that and the other. They said they only wanted me for Bottom because I had a fairly strong voice and they were touring big places where they needed somebody who could be heard.' The Old Vic Company toured Canada and the United States with this production, and in it Stanley Holloway made his New York début at the Metropolitan Opera House in September 1954. It was because of this performance that he was the first to be offered a part in the as yet unwritten *My Fair Lady*. He opened as Alfred P. Doolittle at the Mark Hellinger Theater in New York in March 1956. Everything about the show was praised, and as Kenneth Tynan said: 'Stanley Holloway is the

fruitiest of Doolittles.' And Brooks Atkinson wrote in the *New York Times*: 'As Alfred P. Doolittle, the plausible rogue, Stanley Holloway gives a breezy performance that is thoroughly enjoyable.' At the age of 66 Stanley was having his greatest success. He left the American cast to return to England to re-create the part at Drury Lane in April 1958. Now with a new popularity in his professional life, Stanley Holloway mounted a one-man entertainment at the Ethel Barrymore Theater in New York in October 1960 called *Laughs and Other Events*. That same year he was awarded the OBE. At the Forrest in Philadelphia in April 1964 he played Lester Linstom, Irving, the Policeman, and Lester Lenz in *Cool Off*. In 1970 at the Canadian Shaw Festival he played Burgess in *Candida*. It was not until 1972 that Stanley Holloway had his next straight role. He opened at the Cambridge Theatre in February in David Ambrose's political three-hander, *Siege*. Stanley played the head steward in a men's club frequented by the Prime Minister, played by Michael Bryant, and the ex-Prime Minister, played by Alastair Sim. Robert Waterhouse reported in *Plays and Players*: 'Stanley Holloway devotees, flocking to see him for the first time up West since *My Fair Lady*, will be disappointed by the very few minutes he is on stage.' He went back to the Canadian Shaw Festival in 1973 to play William in *You Never Can Tell*. In 1977, aged 87, Stanley Holloway toured Australia with Douglas Fairbanks Jnr in *The Pleasure of His Company*. He died following a stroke on 30 January 1981.

MICHAEL HORDERN

*A*lthough he was 26 before he set toot on the professional stage, Michael Hordern became one of Britain's most brilliant classical character actors.

Michael Murray Hordern was born in Berkhamsted on 3 October 1911. He went to Brighton College, and though his two elder brothers had studied at Oxford, his family could not afford to send him there. He joined a firm called the Educational Supply Association, and for five years he was an exercise book salesman, earning not a bad living. He appeared as an amateur at the St Pancras People's Theatre and then, quite by chance, was offered a job in the West End, understudying Bernard Lee and assistant stage managing. He took

the job — and quite a cut in salary.

He made his first appearance on the professional stage at the People's Palace in March 1937, when he played Lodovico in *Othello*. He then toured in Scandinavia and the Baltic capitals as Sergius in *Arms and the Man*, and Henry in *Outward Bound*. He went into rep at the Little Theatre in Bristol from 1937 to 1939. At the Whitehall in April 1940 he played PC James Hawkins in *Without the Prince*, and then played the Stranger in the same play. From 1940 to the end of the war he served in the navy, part of the time being spent on the aircraft carrier *Illustrious*.

After the war Michael Hordern returned to the stage playing Torvald Helmer in *A Doll's House* at the Intimate Theatre, Palmer's Green, in January 1946. He went on to the Aldwych in July of that year as Richard Fenton in *Dear Murderer*. At Covent Garden at Christmas he was Bottom in *The Fairy Queen*. In June 1947 at the Saville he played Captain Hoyle in *Noose*.

He made his first appearance at Stratford-on-Avon at the Memorial Theatre in December 1948 when he played Mr Toad in *Toad of Toad Hall* for Christmas. He repeated the performance the following Christmas. 'It was magic,' he said later, 'absolutely marvellous; it was one of the happiest memories of my career. The chorus of the weasels and stoats gave me as a first-night present this toad, this brass stud box — an opening toad. And I said I will keep it on my dressing room table in whatever theatre I'm playing, wherever I'm playing to remind me that whatever I'm playing, I am not as tired as I was when I played Mr Toad. That still goes; King Lear, Prospero, you name it, nothing was as tiring as Mr Toad.'

At the Embassy in April 1949 he was Pascal in *A Woman in Love* and toured that autumn as the Rev. John Courtenay in *Stratton*.

Michael Hordern went to the Arts Theatre in 1950, where in April he played Nikolai Ivanov in *Ivanov*, and in June was Macduff in *Macbeth*. Audrey Williamson said that he was haunting as Macduff, and of his Ivanov, T. C. Worsley reported: 'Perhaps an actor with star quality might have imposed on us more successfully than Mr Michael Hordern, and won our sympathy for Ivanov by his own personality. But such a performance would have raised the level of expectation all round. As it is, Mr Hordern is rich in intelligence, sensitivity and grasp, and with very few exceptions, the company give his impressive playing the right kind of support.' He played Christopher in *Party Manners* at the Prince's in October 1950 and in September 1951 was back at the Arts playing Paul Southman in *Saint's Day*.

Michael Hordern joined the Shakespeare Memorial Theatre Company for the 1952 season and played Menenius in *Coriolanus*, Caliban in *The Tempest* and Jaques in *As You Like It*. Of this last performance Kenneth Tynan said he 'played him with a marvellous sense of injury, yet beneath the shaggy melancholy you felt a fine tempered mind, drawn still towards wit and beauty . . .' That season he also played Sir Politick Would-Be in *Volpone*. At the Edinburgh Festival in 1953 he played Polonius in *Hamlet* and joined the Old Vic Company for their 1953–54 season. He played Polonius once more to Burton's Hamlet, and Audrey Williamson said: 'Michael Hordern's Polonius, not excessively old, fussed very humanly although a little distractedly for the pompous

politician.' Of his performance in *All's Well That Ends Well* that season, she said: 'Michael Hordern's shifty adventurer Parolles [was] seedy under the plumage, with wit enough to play on Bertram's gullibility for his own ends, yet caught in the end by his own cleverness, cowardice and unscrupulous betrayal of his friends. This was a rogue, clever but not wise, abject in terror yet not without pathos in realization of defeat.' But it was his playing of King John that distinguished him, according to Miss Williamson: 'The electric current in this production came from Michael Hordern's John and it was not less dynamic because the lightning sometimes flickered and wavered with the character. This was a superb study of a half-king capable of bold diplomacy and a royal challenge, but without the character to sustain them — a neurotic of violent impulses, and violent fears, brilliant in the scene of repudiating and striking Hubert . . . and feverishly anguished in death, where one felt sickness of mind as well as body. The performance put the actor unmistakably in the front classical rank and tragic class; a position to which he has been moving, after a not very successful career, ever since the two performances which first put him in the critical eye, the senile artist in John Whiting's controversial *Saint's Day* and Ivanov in Chekhov's rarely played tragedy, both at the Arts Theatre.' She was equally enthusiastic about his Prospero: '. . . there is bitterness in Prospero and anger and disillusion too: he has faced the worst in man and his forgiveness at the end comes not without effort. Hordern, a natural character actor, compassed this spiritual conflict finely and created a figure of genuine dignity, master of the island, who could rule with iron as well as affection. The lined face was compelling, not old but worn by experience; and the verse was resonantly and beautifully spoken with an intelligence and instinct for its structure and rhythm that overcame to a very large degree the slight edge of granite.'

Michael Hordern returned to the West End in July 1955, when he played Georges de Fourville in *Nina*, and was at the Saville in October playing Sir Ralph Bloomfield Bonington in Shaw's *The Doctor's Dilemma*. At the Lyric, Hammersmith, in April 1958 he was in the John Mortimer double-bill, playing Tony Peters in *What Shall We Tell Caroline?* and Morgenhall in *The Dock Brief*. These plays transferred to the Garrick in May 1958.

He rejoined the Old Vic Company in October 1958 to play Pastor Manders in *Ghosts*, Mr Posket in *The Magistrate*, and Cassius in *Julius Caesar*. His 'refined Cassius has a sinister bedside manner', Peter Jackson reported. That season he played the title role in *Macbeth*, and Peter Roberts said: 'Michael Hordern, that lean and hungry-looking Cassius of our first dozen best actors, would not have been everybody's first choice as Thane of Glamis, Cawdor or King. His voice lacks texture, the richness and resonance necessary to project Macbeth on the grand scale he obviously intended. But it is a voice capable of some remarkably effective trills. He will squeeze you out a phrase in that quick nervous staccato of his and — lo! — for a second you glimpse the inner man he is playing.'

Michael Hordern made his New York début at the Cort Theater in October 1959 playing Alexander Chabert in *Moonbirds*, but the play only survived three performances. He came back to London and narrated Stravinsky's *Oedipus Rex* at Sadler's Wells in April 1960. After making some films he joined the Royal Shakespeare Company at the Aldwych and was the Father in *Playing with Fire* and Harry in *The Collection* in a double-bill in June 1962. In October he played Ulysses in *Troilus and Cressida*, and in January 1963 he was Herbert George Butler in *The Physicists*, a part which John Russell Taylor said he played 'with cool comic flair'.

At the Theatre Royal, Stratford East, in May 1965 he once more played Paul Southman in Whiting's curious mixture of naturalism and surrealism, *Saint's Day*. This was only the second production of the play, and Hordern had been in the first, fourteen years before at the Arts. At the Duke of York's in March 1967 he was Philip in *Relatively Speaking*, the first of Alan Ayckbourn's enormous West End successes. He played George Riley at the St Martin's in March 1968 in Tom Stoppard's *Enter a Free Man*, Stoppard's first play, but the second to be produced. Back with the Royal Shakespeare Company at the Aldwych in January 1969 he played Tobias in Edward Albee's sinister *A Delicate Balance*.

At the Nottingham Playhouse in October 1969 he played the title role in Jonathan Miller's production of *King Lear*. It visited the Old Vic in February 1970, and Martin Esslin reported: 'Michael Hordern's King is a magnificent creation: there is a nervous fussiness in the opening scenes which explains the antagonism this old man arouses in his daughters, but this expands and unfolds its tragic madnesses: Hordern's timing of the silences from which snatches of demented wisdom emerge is masterly and illuminates the subterranean mental processes of his derangement.'

In May 1970 at the Criterion, Michael Hordern played an agnostic, randy, septuagenarian vicar with a wife in a wheelchair — the title role in *Flint*, by David Mercer. Writing in *Plays and Players* Robert Waterhouse said: 'Michael

Hordern's inspired reading of the character, gaunt, self-effacing, nervously uninhibited, allows for introspection and self-doubt ... a lovable character, in fact, particularly in the hands of Michael Hordern.'

In January 1972 he was awarded the CBE in the New Year Honours List and joined the National Theatre Company at the Old Vic to play George Moore in Tom Stoppard's *Jumpers*. 'With *Jumpers*,' he said, 'I'm more or less around from the beginning. At least when I did *Lear* there was a period of forty-five minutes when I wasn't on stage and could go off to my dressing room, take off my wig and put my feet up before going back for the storm scene. Shakespeare was pretty decent that way. But in *Jumpers* my first speech is thirteen minutes long, and it's all about the existence of God! When I first got the script I could not understand a single bloody word Stoppard had written. I mean I just didn't know how the hell I was going to learn it all.' But he did — and brilliantly. Well, mostly. Michael Billington said: 'Once or twice one of Stoppard's brightly coloured balls falls to the ground, partly because Michael Hordern's moral philosopher sometimes substitutes academic mannerism for apprehension of the argument. But this is not to deny that Hordern's simian habit of scratching his left earlobe with his right hand or leaning on his desk as if doing intellectual press-ups is very funny to watch or that he is brilliant at displaying cuckolded curiosity.' In March that year, still with the company, he was John of Gaunt to Ronald Pickup's Richard II. 'John of Gaunt,' Frank Cox wrote, 'is in the safe hands of Michael Hordern, a good gruff account of this time-honoured gentleman.' In May he was Gaev in *The Cherry Orchard*.

In October 1975 Michael Hordern was at the Royal Court playing a decadent, hypocritical judge in Howard Barker's *Stripwell*. Jonathan Hammond found the play very uneven and unsure of itself and its message. 'Stripwell's ambiguities are therefore viewed half affectionately and half contemptuously,' he wrote in *Plays and Players*, 'and this comes over well in Michael Hordern's portrayal of bumbling, sometimes endearing ineffectiveness, as skilful and accomplished a performance as one would expect from this actor.'

Michael Hordern has appeared in nearly seventy films, notably *Joseph Andrews*, *England Made Me*, *The Spy Who Came in from the Cold* and *Barry Lyndon*. He has also worked extensively on television and is not opposed to commercials, having been an amusing Mr Blackwell in the Crosse & Blackwell soup advertisements. But acting is just the way Michael Hordern earns his living and supports his family. 'I don't like

London,' he said, 'and do not want to see my name in lights in Shaftesbury Avenue. The thought of a long commercial run in the West End fills me with no pleasure.' He finds the subsidized companies too big and bureaucratic; and what he really likes doing is fishing. 'Once the curtain is down,' he said, 'I leave the theatre and theatre people and get as far away from them and all the shop talk as I can —

preferably to my cottage in Berkshire. I love the country, and the reality of my life is to be found not so much behind the footlights, but at the side of a river with a fishing rod.'

In 1983 he played in a National Theatre production of *The Rivals*, and was awarded a knighthood in the New Year Honours of 1984. *See photograph opposite page 263.*

ALAN HOWARD

A committed company actor, an ensemble player, Alan Howard has become a star almost in spite of himself. He was born in London on 5 August 1937 — and into a starry family. His father is the comedian Arthur Howard, his mother actress Jean Compton Mackenzie; his uncle was Leslie Howard; Fay Compton was his great-aunt and it was his great-uncle Compton Mackenzie who raised him in Scotland during the war. 'You can't call mine an easy family background for an actor,' he says, 'although there were two different traditions there: the Comptons who had been actors for more than a hundred years and were both more professional and more unscrupulous, and then the Howards who were newer at the business and yet more indulgent. The Comptons said if I was going to be an actor I had better be bloody good at it, where the Howards just tried to put me off the whole thing.'

Alan Howard began as he meant to go on — with a company. In 1958 he joined the Belgrade in Coventry, where he made his stage début in April as the footman in *Half in Earnest*. He remained with the company until 1960, and during that time among other roles he played Frankie Bryant in Arnold Wesker's *Roots* and Dave Simmonds in *I'm Talking About Jerusalem*. The first transferred to the Royal Court in June 1959 and the second to the Duke of York's in July that year. For a season, at the Royal Court in June and July 1960, he played in the Wesker trilogy: Monty Blatt in *Chicken Soup with Barley*, Frankie Bryant in *Roots* and the first removal man in *I'm Talking About Jerusalem*.

At the Pembroke in Croydon in January 1961 he played Kenny Baird in *A Loss of Roses*, and returned to the Royal Court in February to play de Piraquo in *The Changeling*. At the Chichester Festival in summer 1962 he was the Duke of Ferrara in *The Chances* and Nearchus in *The Broken Heart*. He went to the Mermaid in April 1961, where he played Loveless in *Virtue in*

Danger, and transferred with it to the Strand in June 1963. At the Arts in August 1963 he played Fotheringham in *Afternoon Men*.

It was in 1964 that Alan Howard played his first Shakespeare — Bassanio in *The Merchant of Venice* and Lysander in *A Midsummer Night's Dream* on a tour of South America and Europe organized by Tennent Productions. He returned to London in May 1965, where at the Phoenix he played Simon in *A Heritage and Its History*, the first Ivy Compton-Burnett novel to be dramatized. He then went to the Playhouse in Nottingham to be Angelo in *Measure for Measure* and Bolingbroke in *Richard II*.

In 1966 Alan Howard joined the Royal Shakespeare Company, where he found a happy home. 'Life with the RSC,' he says, 'is a very attractive kind of existence in a way, and it means there's always a base from which to work.' For the RSC he has played Orsino in *Twelfth Night*, Burgundy in *Henry V*, Lussurioso in *The Revenger's Tragedy*, Jaques in *As You Like It*, Young Fashion in *The Relapse* and Edgar in *King Lear*. Peter Roberts was not quite happy with the last: 'Alan Howard's lean and for the most part nude appearance as Edgar cum Poor Tom doesn't quite come off yet.' Professionally growing up in the subsidized theatre, the roles for Mr Howard became bigger. In 1968 he was a magnificently tattooed Achilles in *Troilus and Cressida* and Benedick in *Much Ado About Nothing*. The following year he was Lussurioso in *The Revenger's Tragedy* and Bartholomew Cokes in *Bartholomew Fair*. In 1970 he played Mephistopheles in *Doctor Faustus*, Hamlet, Theseus and Oberon in *A Midsummer Night's Dream* and Ceres in *The Tempest*.

Alan Howard made his New York début with the RSC at the Billy Rose Theater in January 1971 in *A Midsummer Night's Dream*.

During the 1971–72 season he revived some earlier roles and added Nikolai in *Enemies*, Dorimant in *The Man of Mode* and the Envoy in

The Balcony. At the Traverse in Edinburgh in July 1972 he played Cyril Jackson in *The Black and White Minstrels*. From August 1972 to August 1973 he toured the world in the RSC production of *A Midsummer Night's Dream*.

He returned to Hampstead in November 1973 to play Erich von Stroheim in *The Ride Across Lake Constance*, and transferred with it to the Mayfair in December. Also at Hampstead, in January 1974 he repeated his performance as Cyril Jackson in *The Black and White Minstrels*.

Back at the Aldwych with the RSC in May 1974 Alan Howard played Carlos II in *The Bewitched*. *Plays and Players* reported: '... the virtuoso performance of the evening is Alan Howard's in the enormous and almost literally back-breaking part of Carlos II. Peter Barnes [the author] uses the fact that epileptics have moments of almost superhuman lucidity in the post-epileptic state to give his grotesque anti-hero speeches of sudden eloquence and poetic insight. This demands an actor of immense range who can make the transition from blathering idiocy to subtlest lyricism without breaking the unity of the character; behind the disease, the image of the man he could have been had he developed healthily must always somehow remain visible as a potentiality, just as the straight limbs must somehow be potentially there inside the diseased twisted legs and arms. Alan Howard manages all those enormous tasks with elegance and ease.'

The next two years were spent playing Prince Hal in the two parts of *Henry IV*, as well as Jack

Rover in *Wild Oats*. That part was made famous by his great-grandfather Edward Compton, who played it at Stratford in 1882 and in London at the Strand in 1883. Alan Howard commented: 'One forgets how much easier it is for most of us today; an actor in the time of Jack Rover and *Wild Oats* would have sixteen or seventeen leading roles permanently memorized; and be able to perform any one of them at about one day's notice anywhere in the country.'

It was a much awarded time for Alan Howard — from the *Plays and Players* London Critics Award to the West End Managers Award. David Mayer said of his performance in *Wild Oats*: 'Rover, whose speech is wholly a mangled patchwork of lines from his stroller's repertoire, Shakespeare, Otway, Buckingham, Fielding, Rowe and lesser dramatists, might be obscure to modern audiences familiar only with hardcore Shakespeare, but Alan Howard gets round this difficulty by reminding us of his years of barnstorming with the RSC, broadly sending up his own Hamlet and Henry and Edgar, even to the point of self-parodying stance and inflection with unabashed pleasure. He conveys, as well, Rover's astonishment that these lines out of context are primed with more good sense and profound emotion than ever he expressed before groundlings in fit-up theatres.' He went on to play Coriolanus and Henry VI for the RSC before returning to the twentieth century theatre in C. P. Taylor's *Good*, as the semi-detached professor drifting through an increasingly Nazi Germany.

BOBBY HOWES

*T*he *Times'* obituary said that Bobby Howes 'will be remembered chiefly as a comedian whose personality, humble but hopeful as it was once described, had, provided with a suitable foil and support, been the centrepiece of successful British musical comedies of the 1930s.'

He was born in Battersea in London on 4 August 1895 and it was there, at the Battersea Palace in 1909, that he made his stage début with 'Sally Fern and her Boy Scouts'. He trained in acrobatics and dancing and took voice lessons, and in 1912 was one of the Gotham Quartette appearing at the Tivoli Music Hall. He spent the next few years touring with concert parties and appearing in variety theatres.

After the First World War he was hired by Jack

Hylton for the Metropolitan Musical Hall where he appeared in December 1919 in *Seasoned to Taste*. He then toured in *All in One* and *Pot Luck*. Bobby Howes made his first West End appearance under the auspices of Jack Hulbert at the Little Theatre. He opened on 2 October 1923 in *The Little Revue Starts at 9* and the following March was in *The Second Little Revue*.

In April 1924 he was at the Prince's Restaurant in *The Five O'Clock Follies* and at the Garrick Theatre in December played Gilbert Stirling in *Six Cylinder Love*. He was in *The Midnight Follies* at the Hotel Metropole in June 1925 and at the Vaudeville in September appeared in *The Punch Bowl*. At the Gaiety Theatre in December he played Octave in *The Blue Kitten* and then went back to music hall, playing the Coliseum, the

Alhambra and touring in *We* and subsequently in *Tricks*. He was back in London at the Vaudeville in November 1926 appearing in *Vaudeville Vanities*.

In May 1927 Bobby Howes opened in a true musical comedy — heavy on plot and sentiment. He played Freddy Royce in *The Blue Train*, and the *Times* reported that he was 'a born entertainer, expressive of foot and face'. In November he was at the Theatre Royal, Birmingham, playing Sam Slider in *The Yellow Mask*. It came to the Carlton Theatre in London in February 1928.

Teamed with Binnie Hale, he opened at the Adelphi in February 1929 playing Jim, a neglected orphan in the Vivian Ellis and Richard Myers musical, *Mr Cinders*. The *Times* called him 'Chaplinesque'. He opened at the London Hippodrome (where he was to become a firm favourite) in June 1930 as Jimmy Canfield in *Sons o' Guns*. In January 1931 he was Chips Wilcox in *The Song of the Drum* at Drury Lane. At the Saville in October 1931 he opened as Bob Seymour in *For the Love of Mike*, and in June 1932 at the same theatre was Bobbie in *Tell Her the Truth*. In March 1933 he was Bobby Bramstone in *He Wanted Adventure*.

Back at the London Hippodrome in September 1934 with Binnie Hale he was in *Yes, Madam?* Also starring with them was Vera Pearce, a large lady who chased him around the stage a lot. He continued at the Hippodrome playing Tommy Deacon in *Please Teacher* (October 1935), Jimmy Rackstraw in *Big Business* (February 1937) and in October 1937 Tommy and Mike in *Hide and Seek* with Cicely Courtneidge. This was nominally a musical comedy but in fact a revue. At the Adelphi in October 1938 he was Bobby Lockwood in *Bobby Get Your Gun*, and at the Queen's two months later appeared in the optimistically titled *All Clear*. He was again with the aggressive Vera Pearce in *Shephard's Pie* at the Prince's in May 1941. In September of the same year he succeeded Stanley Lupino as Tony Meyrick in *Lady Behave* at His Majesty's, and then toured the part before returning to London with it in March 1942.

He went back to the Hippodrome in November 1942 as Jerry Walker in Cole Porter's *Let's Face It*. Ernest Short reported: 'The highlight of the piece was Bobby Howes portraying in dumb-show the whole career of a soldier, from medical examination on enlistment day to the big moment of decoration for duty well and fully done. Here was miming worthy of miming's long tradition in musical shows.'

At the Prince's in December 1943 he played Joe Pendleton in *Halfway to Heaven* and then **toured in July 1944 as Sapiens in *By Jupiter*.** At the Winter Garden in December 1944 he went into pantomime playing Buttons in Cinderella, and spent the following year in variety at the Victoria Palace. He teamed up with Jack Hulbert at the Saville in April 1946 in *Here Come the Boys*.

Bobby Howes had his first straight role at the St James's in October 1947 where, under the direction of Basil Dean, he played Harry Smith in *The Man in the Street*. He returned to revue in March 1948 when he took over from the stricken Sonnie Hale and opened at the Duke of York's in *Four, Five, Six!* Harold Hobson said: 'Bobby Howes has never been better; there is a shy subdued glory about his performance; his Hyde Park orator, a mouse with his breast torn by a lion's rage, is masterly. This is first-class revue.'

At Christmas in Wolverhampton he was Buttons in *Cinderella*. In August 1949 he was Billy Warren in *Roundabout*, and returned to the part of Buttons at Christmas that year in Brighton. Christmas 1950 found him in London — at Wimbledon playing the Queen of Hearts in a pantomime of that name, and he spent 1951 touring as Philip Hudson Jnr in *Double Alibi*. In February 1953 he played Ben Rumson, the founder of a Californian boom town, in the musical *Paint Your Wagon* at Her Majesty's. His daughter Sally Ann Howes scored a great success in the show. At the 'Q' in January 1956 he played Milo Cantrell in *Start from Scratch* and toured in 1958 as Archie Rice's father, Bill, in Osborne's *The Entertainer*. At the Theatre Royal, Brighton, in April 1959 he played Roger Spelding in *Visit to a Small Planet*.

Now at normal retirement age, Bobby Howes made his New York début at the City Center as Finian, the Irishman who stole the leprechaun's pot of gold, in a revival of the musical *Finian's Rainbow*.

He returned to the London stage in December 1960 where he played Dr Nairn at the Phoenix in *The Geese Are Getting Fat*, which starred Michael Wilding. Peter Carthew wrote in *Plays and Players*: 'It is a feeble, insulting, patronizing piece of nothingness, a meaningless charade ... Luckily most of the cast are able to rise above their material ... But Bobby Howes, whose last-minute appearance in a tiny part received a justly generous welcome, is unnecessary and he knows it.'

Bobby Howes returned to the musical as Finian for a tour in March 1961, and then toured the following February as Stan Dunnock in *A Gazelle in Park Lane*. He ended his career in December 1964, just short of his seventieth birthday, in Melbourne, Australia, once more playing in *Finian's Rainbow*. He died in London on 27 April 1972.

JACK HULBERT

See Cicely Courtneidge and Jack Hulbert

HENRY IRVING

'There is no nobler episode in the story of the English theatre,' wrote Ernest Short, 'than Henry Irving's thirty years of management at the Lyceum. His personal dignity, fine taste and generous expenditure were coupled with a sense of spiritual intimacy and powers of creative characterization such as the London stage had not seen for half a century.'

He had a tendency to drag one leg, his voice often became distorted when striving for dramatic effect, but he had a magnetic personality, a distinguished appearance and, as Bram Stoker wrote, 'the finest man's hands I have ever seen ... Size, and shape, proportion and articulation were all alike beautiful and distinguished and distinctive ... With them he could speak. It was not possible to doubt the meaning which he intended to convey ... The weakness of Charles I, ... the vulture grip of Shylock; the fossilized age of Gregory Brewster; the asceticism of Becket.'

He was born Henry Brodribb on 6 February 1838 in Keinton Mandeville, Somerset. His father was something of a failure, and the family's hopes were pinned on Henry, who was brought to London aged 11 to study at Dr Pinches City Commercial School in Lombard Street. He began acting quietly in school productions; when he was 12 he saw Samuel Phelps at Sadler's Wells playing Hamlet — and decided that his future lay on the stage. First of all, however, in 1851 he became a junior clerk in a solicitor's office and then worked in the same capacity for Thacher, Spink and Co., East India Merchants. He had a pronounced stammer which he knew would hamper his stage acceptance, so he joined elocution and dramatic classes taught in the city by Harry Thomas. He also swam in the Thames before work each morning to strengthen his lungs. With the elocution school, he appeared as Captain Absolute in a semi-public performance of *The Rivals* and the *Theatrical Journal* gave him his first review, saying that he acted with 'intelligent tact and with great credit to Mr Thomas'.

His mother, like most religious people of the time, considered the theatre not a nice place to work and disapproved strongly of her son's ambitions. But he was not deterred. The Royal Soho Theatre put on plays for amateurs, and on 11 August 1856 Henry Irving (he had thought Brodribb an unsuitable name for a glittering stage star) made his first appearance there playing Romeo. Through this he made the acquaintance of William Hoskins, an actor in Phelps' company who, agreeably impressed by Henry's ability and ambition, coached him. When Hoskins left Phelps to go to Australia he offered the boy a place in his company, but Irving declined. It was also said that he declined an offer to join Phelps at Sadler's Wells and accepted instead an introduction to the manager of the Lyceum Theatre, Sunderland, where he was taken on. He made his professional stage début there in September 1856 playing the very reduced part of the Duke of Orleans in Lytton's *Richelieu*. In February 1857 he went to the Theatre Royal, Edinburgh, where he remained for two and a half years playing over 400 parts — and there was a new role to learn every two days. While in Edinburgh he also appeared at the Queen's Theatre and the Opera House. The company gave him a farewell benefit on 13 September 1859 and he very successfully played Claude Melnotte in *The Lady of Lyons.*

Henry Irving's London début was at the Princess Theatre. He was incensed when he found that he was only given six lines in *Ivy Hall* and soon left. He hired Crosby Hall and gave some readings, and from there was hired to go to the Queen's Theatre in Dublin, where in March 1860 he opened as Cassio in *Othello.* What happened in Dublin would have put most aspiring actors off the stage for life. Irving had been hired to replace a very popular actor who had been sacked. The gallery, and indeed hired claques, caused an uproar at each performance. Irving was booed, hissed and assaulted, but he carried on.

He went back to Scotland, this time to the Theatre Royal, Glasgow, for a few months, where he played various small parts and a notable Macduff. In 1860 he was at the Theatre Royal, Manchester, where he received good reviews as Mr

Dombey in *Dombey and Son*. Edwin Booth was in Manchester at the time and Irving welcomed the chance to study the great actor at close range. There, too, he fell in love with an actress, Nellie Moore, but he was too poor and unsuccessful even to contemplate continuing the liaison. Irving played his first Hamlet in 1864 in Manchester, and the *Guardian* said he 'possessed neither the robust physique nor the vocal power' for the part. At the Theatre Royal in Oxford he played Hamlet, Macduff and Claude Melnotte again.

In 1865 Irving went back to the Prince of Wales Operetta House in Edinburgh and then on to Bury where he played Hamlet, Oxford where he played Iago and Macduff, and Birmingham where he played Bob Brierley in *The Ticket of Leave Man*. In Liverpool he was Philip Austin in *A Dark Cloud* and then played the title role in *Robert Macaire*, which brought him good reviews. 'He was merrily miserable, jocosely wretched and laughed with a grim determination — an echo suggesting a gallows-shriek.' He then played in Newcastle-on-Tyne.

In 1866, after ten years of poverty-stricken traipsing through the provinces, Irving's luck finally changed. Dion Boucicault gave him the part of Rawdon Scudamore in *The Two Lives of Mary Leigh*, for a pre-London tryout in Manchester. It was not an enormous success there but Boucicault had faith in it and sold it to Mrs Cawley at the St James's Theatre in London on the condition that she take Irving with it. She was impressed by him and agreed as long as he was willing to stage manage as well. He was not in fact exactly willing, but he did it. Before putting on Boucicault's play that season she staged the comedy *The Belle's Stratagem*. Irving had only a small part in that and he didn't very much like it, but he threw himself into it for his London début and happily 'stopped the show'. When Boucicault's play, now called *Hunted Down*, opened Irving was at last a name to be reckoned with. He followed his appearance in that with performances as Joseph Surface and Robert Macaire. He then went to Paris to the Théâtre des Italiens, where he played in *Our American Cousin*, and then toured the provinces again — Bath, Bristol, Manchester, Liverpool and Dublin — but this time the money was much better.

Back in London, in December 1867 at the Queen's Theatre he played with Ellen Terry in Garrick's adaptation of *The Taming of the Shrew*, *Katharine and Petruchio* — it was not a success. Irving found that he was a better draw as a villain, and next played Bob Gassett in *Dearer than Life*, Bill Sikes in *Oliver Twist* and Robert Redburn in *The Lancashire Lass*. He also played Charles Surface in *The School for Scandal* and Faulkland in *The Rivals*. He was reunited with Nellie Moore, who played Nancy in *Oliver Twist* and the title part in *The Lancashire Lass*; but during the latter's run she contracted scarlet fever and died.

Henry Irving went on another provincial tour and returned to two small London theatres, the Standard and the Surrey, before opening at the Haymarket in July 1869 as Captain Fitzherbert in *All for Money*. Three days later, mainly on the rebound from Nellie and also because her father was so opposed to the match, he married Florence O'Callaghan, daughter of India's Surgeon-General. It was a mistake.

In autumn 1869 he played the villain in Boucicault's *Formosa* at Drury Lane and the critics hated it. But he was more successful at the Vaudeville the following year, when he played Digby Grant in *Two Roses*. The *Globe* critic praised 'his delineation of the hollow-hearted meanness, the contemptible presumption and the disgusting hypocrisy'. It had a long run.

An American named Bateman had taken a lease on the Lyceum Theatre, mainly to star his daughter Isabel, and he convinced Irving to play in *Fanchette* and *Pickwick* with her. Then Irving persuaded him to put on *The Bells*. It was an uphill struggle, but on 25 November 1871 Irving opened at the Lyceum as Mathias in *The Bells*. The cheering echoed on for weeks. Donald Brook summed up the critical response: 'Irving's deeply studied insight into this conscience-stricken character, tortured by the obsession and by the strain of trying to preserve a calm demeanour, enabled him to hold his audience spellbound. It was an incredible display of histrionic skill, and even the sourest critics had to admit that another great actor had "arrived" on the English stage.' After the performance Irving had a triumphant supper party in which he bathed in his new-found celebrity. His wife, a month short of giving birth to their second child, was sulking. In the cab on the way home she said to him, 'Are you going to go on making a fool of yourself like this all your life?' At that Irving got out of the cab, and he never spoke to her again. It was, however, five years before they separated officially.

He next played Jeremy Diddler in the farce *Raising the Wind* and took both plays on a provincial tour. For the 1872 season Irving gave 200 performances of *Charles I* — not a brilliant play, but the audiences were coming to see Irving rather than the play. In September 1873 he took the title role in *Richelieu* and the *Standard* reported: 'We have dwelt more emphatically on those passages denoting the actor's capacity for expressing vigorous passion as it undoubtedly forms his strongest side, but that there is no deficiency of pathos in his nature was abundantly proved in the various passages of tender expansion.'

In October 1874 he played Hamlet, with Isabel Bateman as Ophelia. The first-night curtain fell to triumphant applause. The critic Edward R. Russell wrote: 'He has noticed that Hamlet not merely is simple-minded, frankly susceptible, and naturally self-contemplative, but has a trick — not at all uncommon in persons whose most real life is an inner one — of fostering and aggravating his own excitements. This discovery of Irving is a stroke of genius and will identify his Hamlet as long as the memory of it endures. The idea will be handed down and the mechanical execution of it will probably be imitated but the vivid flashing, half-foolish, half-inspired hysterical power of Irving in the passages where it is developed is a triumph of idiosyncrasy, which, even with the help of the traditions he is founding, is not very likely to be achieved by any other actor.' And so psychological acting was founded. *Hamlet* ran over 200 performances at the Lyceum — unheard of at that time for Shakespeare. In September 1875 he attempted Macbeth without much success, but it did run for a few months. In February his Othello was, as is so often the case, outshone by the actor who played Iago, but in April 1876 he was successful as Philip of Spain in Tennyson's *Queen Mary.* He toured the provinces with all these, and met with full and enthusiastic houses everywhere.

In January 1877 he restored *Richard III* to its original text, and after a much applauded performance was bequeathed Edmund Kean's sword. He then played the dual roles of Lesurques and Dubose in the melodrama *The Lyons Mail* and went on another tour. By this time he was successful and popular enough to be the subject of much sniping, and was particularly hurt by a pamphlet called 'The Fashionable Tragedian' by William Archer and Robert William Lowe.

In March 1878 he created what was to become one of his most popular roles, Louis XI. He had, however, run into personal difficulties: Isabel Bateman had fallen in love with him, and he found the situation intolerable. So, with great understanding on the part of Miss Bateman, the lease on the Lyceum was relinquished to him and the Batemans disappeared from his life. While on a most successful provincial tour he had the Lyceum refurbished, and he reopened on 30 December 1878 as Hamlet with Ellen Terry as Ophelia. Joseph Knight wrote: 'The representation of

Hamlet supplied on Monday night is the best the stage during the last quarter of a century has seen, and it is the best also that is likely, under existing conditions, to be seen for some time to come. Scenic accessories are explanatory without being cumbersome, the costumes are picturesque and striking and show no needless affectation of archaeological accuracy; and the interpretation has an ensemble rarely found in any performances, and never, during recent years, in a representation of tragedy.' At the Lyceum Irving also continued to produce popular melodrama, farce and comedy. In November 1879 he was an 'old, haggard, halting and sordid' Shylock while Ellen Terry was Portia in *The Merchant of Venice,* which ran seven months. He then produced *The Corsican Brothers* and on 3 January 1881 premièred Tennyson's tragedy *The Cup* playing Synorix while Terry played Camma. He played Iago to Edwin Booth's Othello, and gave an unconvincing performance as Romeo in *Romeo and Juliet.* In October 1882 he was Benedick and Terry was Beatrice in *Much Ado About Nothing.* The critic Dutton Cook reported that he was 'a valorous cavalier who rejoices in brave apparel and owns a strong feeling for humour; over his witty encounters with Beatrice there presides a spirit of pleasantness; his rudest sallies are so mirthfully spoken as to be deprived of all real offensiveness; he banters like a gentleman and not like a churl; he is a privileged railer at women, a recognized jester at marriage, but a popular person nevertheless.' The play ran for eight months.

With the Lyceum Company, Irving then set out on his first American tour. In America the company played *The Bells, Charles I, Louis XI, The Merchant of Venice, The Lyons Mail, The Belle's Stratagem, Hamlet* and *Much Ado About Nothing,* and were much acclaimed. His New York début was at the Star Theater on 29 October 1883, when he played Mathias in *The Bells.*

On their return to England the company reopened with *Much Ado About Nothing* and then played *Twelfth Night,* but Irving's Victorian-villain interpretation of Malvolio was not a success. Their second American tour included Canadian cities.

Back at the Lyceum in May 1885 Irving played Dr Primrose in *Olivia,* an adaptation of *The Vicar of Wakefield,* and in December opened *Faust* which, running for 375 performances, broke all records at the Lyceum. His standing both in society and in intellectual circles was noted when he was invited to address Oxford University on 26 June 1886.

In October 1887 Henry Irving embarked on his

third American tour, this time visiting New York, Philadelphia, Chicago and Boston. He always took his entire company on these tours, sparing no expense and usually finding a place for wives and children.

In his thirteenth season at the Lyceum he once again attempted Macbeth — it was still not his role. He performed *The Bells* at Sandringham for Queen Victoria by royal command in April 1889.

Still at the Lyceum, in January 1892 he mounted an extremely expensive production of *Henry VIII* in which he played Cardinal Wolsey. Although it ran for six months it was impossible even to begin to get his money back. He played King Lear in November of that year, and the following February made a great success of Tennyson's *Becket*. 'Becket is a noble and a human part,' Henry Irving said. 'I do not see how anyone could act it and feel it thoroughly without being a better man for it. It is full of some of the noblest thoughts and elements of introspection that may come to us in this life of ours.' He gave a command performance of the part at Windsor in March and then embarked on another American tour. On 8 November 1893 they presented *Becket* at the opening of the Abbey Theater in New York. The New York *Tribune* reported: 'It was very brilliantly played; and every appreciative spectator of it must have been pleasurably excited, exalted and deeply impressed. The manifestations of public delight were numerous and emphatic. There were four calls after each act.' He went on to comment on Irving's performance, saying that his 'impersonation of Becket [was] remarkable for many attributes of complex character and felicitous impersonation — the piercing sidelong glance and peculiar motion of the head not being omitted — was especially remarkable for the fervent heat and steadfast glow of torrid intellectual power; for fitful tumults of noble passion; for moments of great tenderness; for the consistent preservation of imperial authority; for the sustainment of a perfect illusion; and at the last for a wonderful realization of sublime and saint-like ecstasy.'

Back in England, in September 1894 the company premièred Conan Doyle's *Story of Waterloo* at the Prince's Theatre in Bristol. Irving played Corporal Gregory Brewster. The following January, Ellen Terry played Guinevere and Forbes-Robertson played Lancelot while Irving took the title part in a production of *King Arthur* designed by Sir Edward Burne-Jones. In the Birthday Honours of 1895 Henry Irving was knighted for services to art, becoming the first British actor to be so honoured.

Before embarking on another American tour, during which he refused to advertise his

knighthood, he played *Don Quixote*. In New York he opened in October with *Macbeth*. The *New York Times*, after a long review of the glittering audience, reported: 'As a whole, Mr Irving's performance of Macbeth will be regarded as an interesting interpretation, for the complete, beautiful, rich and careful manner in which the tragedy is presented, rather than for anything new that it suggests in the leading characters. Extravagance of action, incoherency of speech, all those things that are called "mannerisms" will be regarded as unimportant in reaching a conclusion as to the merit of the presentation . . . Though Mr Irving's face showed hardly any evidence of "make-up", and was bare except for a moustache cut short over the mouth and falling straight downward at the corners, he looked strangely unlike his pictures, and not less strangely unlike the ideal Macbeth. He seemed stalwart, a man habituated to war and arms, as different as it is possible to conceive from the Irving of other roles. But the voice, the intonations, the booming nasals, the pauses that disjoint sentences — these were all familiar, too familiar, wearisomely familiar.'

He returned to London in summer 1896 and in a not very successful revival of *Cymbeline* played Iachimo. In December he injured his knee and was off the stage for two months, which cost him a good deal at the box office. He did, however, mount a very profitable provincial tour in 1897.

He had one of his most expensive failures at the Lyceum in 1898 when he played the title role of *Peter the Great* in a play by his son, Laurence. He was beset by throat trouble and it was not a very good play — it was off in a month. In February his scenery store was burned and more than £30,000 worth of property destroyed. It was not only too costly but also impossible to reproduce quickly, so his repertoire at the Lyceum was severely limited. In May he had another failure with *The Medicine Man*. However, there was some good news. In June he received an honorary doctorate of letters from Cambridge University, and that autumn managed to recoup some money with another provincial tour. The bad luck returned when he was struck with pneumonia and pleurisy and was off the stage for months. The Lyceum was costing a great deal of money, and in hopes of sorting out the finances in April 1899 he gave up sole ownership of it and turned it into a company; he played *Robespierre* there, a play specially written for him at his own request by Sardou.

The theatre was changing around him. There were the new dramatists, Ibsen and Shaw. Irving neither understood them nor had any desire to play their works. He went on a sixth American tour.

In 1901 he played *Coriolanus*, a notoriously

unpopular Shakespeare, and he lost money. He recouped some, however, in a massive twenty-nine-week American tour.

By 1902 Ellen Terry had left his company, but she returned occasionally, especially to help him raise money. In July 1902 she once more played Portia to Irving's Shylock in *The Merchant of Venice*, the last production at the Lyceum. The local authority had decreed that a good deal of structural work must be carried out if the building was to continue as a theatre. Neither Irving nor the company could afford to do it, and the Lyceum became a music hall. That autumn Irving went on another provincial tour and gave a command performance of *Waterloo* at Sandringham for the King.

In April 1903, Irving opened as Dante. He was always convinced there was a play there somewhere, and persuaded Sardou to write it. However, it was a failure, playing only eighty-one performances; never stingy with production costs, Irving lost a lot of money. He took it on a provincial tour, and then in October on to America, where they did not like it either. Henry Irving's last American performance was on 25 March 1904 at the Harlem Opera House, when he played Louis XI.

In September in Cardiff Irving began a long provincial tour, which he planned to be his last. It was triumphant and he was fêted wherever he went. However, the tour had to be curtailed when he collapsed in Wolverhampton and was off the stage for two months.

He returned to London and from 29 April to 10 June he played a repertory season at Drury Lane. A critic on the first night reported: 'From the moment when Sir Henry Irving came on the stage his triumph was assured. Such a shout of approval as rang through the house has seldom been heard in a theatre ... The same frenzied welcome attended the Archbishop throughout and there was not a scene in which Becket appeared that did not bring down shouts of acclamation.'

On 15 June, for the benefit of an actor friend, he played *Waterloo* at His Majesty's Theatre. Unknown to anyone at the time, that was his last London appearance. He resumed his tour of the provinces and at Bradford on Friday, 13 October 1905, coming off the stage after a performance of *Becket*, he collapsed and died, aged 67. His ashes were buried in Westminster Abbey on Friday, 20 October.

Ellen Terry said that Henry Irving was 'quiet, patient, tolerant, impersonal, gentle, close, crafty, incapable of caring for anything outside his work'.

But the critic A. B. Walkley was more poetic in his description of the man: 'To touch the imagination in the playhouse world of Romance and withal, to bring the great outer Philistine world to its knees — to set our ears ringing with the "chink-chink" of the Polish Jew's sleigh bells, and to get elected to the Athenaeum Club *honoris causa* — is an achievement verging on the paradoxical; it is running with the hare and hunting with the hounds. Alone among actors, Mr Irving has taken this double first; a success on the stage and off it.'

GLENDA JACKSON

'*I*f she'd gone into politics,' said Glenda Jackson's husband of eighteen years, 'she'd now be Prime Minister. If she'd taken to crime she'd be Jack the Ripper.' And as she herself explains her concentration: 'I work to live and I have a strong puritan ethic. I was taught to earn my pleasures and to earn through work. To work at my best I have to be interested, and what interests me more than anything are the difficulties the work presents. Even if I am working in rubbish, the strictures I place on myself make the acting difficult.'

Glenda May Jackson was born on 9 May 1936 at her grandmother's house in Birkenhead, Cheshire, where the whole family was living. She was the eldest of four girls. Her father was a bricklayer and her mother took on cleaning jobs to help support the family.

Glenda, named after the actress Glenda Farrell, went to Hoylake Church School and from there got a place at West Kirby County Grammar School. As a child she was a keen ballet dancer but grew too tall to continue and, though judged to have a very able intelligence, left school with only three 'O' levels. An avid reader, however, she aspired to be a librarian but found herself working behind the medicine counter at Boots the chemist in Chester. She hated the job and spent her evenings in amateur theatricals, eventually taking elocution and fencing lessons at night in Liverpool. She was then accepted to study at RADA and as a student made her stage début at Worthing in *Separate Tables* in February 1957.

Her career had a very slow start. 'I spent the first ten years mainly out of work,' she says. She played Ruby in *All Kinds of Men* at the Arts in London in September 1957 and at the Lyric, Hammersmith, in March 1962 was Alexandra in *The Idiot* with the Ikon Company. It was noted as a brave try. At the Mermaid in June 1963 she played Siddie to John Neville's Alfie and transferred with the production to the Duchess in July. The following year she joined the Royal Shakespeare Company and appeared in the experimental Theatre of Cruelty season at LAMDA in January 1965. At Stratford that year she played the Princess of France in *Love's Labour's Lost*. Peter Roberts reported: '. . . of the quartet of lovers the deepest impression is made by Glenda Jackson's Princess of France. There is a certain hard, almost metallic, edge to her delivery of the verse which at first seems uncalled for but which it is soon evident is an essential quality of her stage personality and which distinguishes her work from twenty other young actresses who might tackle the role with equal competence.' In July at the Aldwych she was Eva in Michel Saint-Denis's production of Brecht's *Puntila*. John Holmstron said she gave 'an amusingly stylized performance as Puntila's spoilt tomboy daughter, petulantly flushed and flouncing'. In August she was back at Stratford in David Warner's *Hamlet*. 'As for Glenda Jackson as Ophelia,' Hugh Leonard wrote, 'one can only yammer in admiration. This was a regular man-eater: a highly sexed young woman, cracking under the strain of a disintegrating love affair. Unlikely? . . . perhaps, but it works. Never has a character been portrayed so completely despite such a minimum of material as in this instance. While watching Miss Jackson, one could hear the click of numerous minds snapping shut all over the auditorium. I say, the hell with them: this is acting!' In October, still with the RSC, Glenda was a reader in *The Investigation*, and then in November played Charlotte Corday in *Marat/Sade*. She made her New York début in this part at the Martin Beck Theater in December and received the Variety Drama Critics Award as the most promising actress. Back at the Aldwych in October 1966 she took part in Peter Brook's *Us* which was voted the best production of the year by the London critics in *Plays and Players*.

At the Royal Court in April 1967 Glenda Jackson played Masha in *The Three Sisters*, and it was she who became central of the three. David Benedictus wrote: 'Glenda Jackson's controlled intensity will always fit her for roles of incipient

hysteria, which roles she plays compellingly.' In November that year she was at the Fortune in David Pinner's *Fanghorn*, a play Michael Billington described as 'an arbitrary mixture of Iris Murdoch and J. M. Barrie: a piece of black whimsy.' He went on to say that 'Glenda Jackson's Tamara, clad in a black leather dress slit up the front, had the authority and intelligence one invariably associates with this actress'.

Her next stage appearance was as Katherine Winter at the Duchess in April 1973 in John Mortimer's flawed *Collaborators*, and at Greenwich in February 1974 she played Solange in Genet's *The Maids* with Susannah York and Vivien Merchant. Charles Marowitz said: 'Jackson only gets limited mileage out of what has now become the J-Effect, viz., great bursts of emotional effusion unexpectedly cut short by flat, catatonic delivery . . . '

At the Aldwych in July 1975 she played *Hedda Gabler* and then toured the provinces, the United States and Australia in the part. Glenda Jackson then played Vittoria Corombona in *The White Devil* at the Old Vic in July 1976. David Zane Mairowitz, writing in *Plays and Players*, criticized her performance for being 'full of her famous cynicism and world-weariness which infects the stage from her very first entrance. Once again Jackson gives the impression she knows the entire plot from the outset, so that we never get Vittoria's freshness or vitality.'

Back with the RSC Glenda Jackson played the Egyptian Queen in Peter Brook's production of *Antony and Cleopatra*, and she was judged to be vocally a match for her Antony, Alan Howard. She scored a great success as Stevie Smith in the dramatic version of the poet's life both on stage and on film.

Glenda Jackson's first film was Peter Brook's *Marat/Sade;* she then went on to work in dramatic roles in such films as Ken Russell's *The Music Lovers* and *Women in Love* (for which she won an Oscar) and in light comedy such as *A Touch of Class* which also gained her an Oscar. In television she was especially notable in the series 'Elizabeth R' in which she played the first Queen Elizabeth.

Glenda Jackson's marriage to Roy Hodges has ended but they had one son, to whom she is devoted and who is also the cause of her modern angst. 'I am a working mother and I'm of the generation that will always be burdened with a sense of guilt at not having been at home all the time, not being a minute-by-minute mother. I've had to learn to live with that guilt and hope that it doesn't become too punitive.' However, when it comes to her acting, Miss Jackson knows exactly what she is doing: 'The performance you give in your head when you first read a script will be a million times better than the one you ultimately give on a stage or on film. But that is what you are always striving for — the performance in your head.'

In 1983 she returned to the stage in Bothe Strauss's controversial *Great and Small*, and the following year played the leading role in a rare London revival (at the Duke of York's) of O'Neill's five-hour marathon *Strange Interlude* which she took to Broadway in 1985, after an Old Vic *Phaedra*.

See photograph opposite page 198.

DEREK JACOBI

Although he may still lack the commercial box-office drawing power of some of his contemporaries, there are those who would argue that Derek Jacobi is an almost perfect example of the mid-century classical company actor: there is, indeed, no other who has managed to play (as he did in one single 1982–84 Royal Shakespeare Company season) four leading roles of the size of Peer Gynt, Benedick, Prospero and Cyrano de Bergerac.

Born in London on 22 October 1938, Jacobi was educated at Leyton County High School and then at St John's College, Cambridge, by which time he had already started to play leading roles with the National Youth Theatre of Michael Croft, a more prolific and successful training-ground than any drama school of the time. At Cambridge he went on to act with the Marlowe Society and the Cambridge Amateur Dramatic Club, then going straight into the Birmingham Repertory Company where he made his professional debut in September 1960 in *One Way Pendulum*. He then auditioned unsuccessfully for Stratford, but in 1963 was invited by Olivier to go to Chichester for the start of an eight-year alliance with the National Theatre Company there and at the Old Vic.

For the National, Jacobi started as Brother Martin in the Joan Plowright *Saint Joan*, and then played Laertes to the Hamlet of Peter O'Toole, which in 1963 officially opened the company's stay at the Vic. There, too, he played Cassio to Olivier's Othello, Simon Bliss in Noel Coward's own production of *Hay Fever*, and Felipillo in Shaffer's *Royal Hunt of the Sun* (all 1964). In the following year he played Brindsley Miller in Shaffer's *Black Comedy*, and Don John in Zeffirelli's *Much Ado About Nothing*.

In his remaining years with the National, Jacobi continued to rise through the ranks as the most consistently successful and distinguished of all the younger home-grown stars established there during the Olivier regime. His parts included Tusenbach in *The Three Sisters*, Touchstone in *As You Like It*, the King of Navarre in *Love's Labour's Lost*, Edward in *Macrune's Guevara*, Adam in *Back to Methuselah*, Myshkin in *The Idiot*, Lodovico in *The White Devil*, and Sir Charles Mountford in *A Woman Killed with Kindness*.

In 1972, with the Olivier regime at the National already drawing to a close, Jacobi returned to the Birmingham Rep to do the double that Sir Laurence himself had once made famous — the title role in *Oedipus Rex* followed by Mr Puff in *The Critic*. Then, ever the company man, he joined Prospect for a lengthy English, European and Middle Eastern tour in which he played the title role in *Ivanov*, Buckingham in *Richard III*, Aguecheek in *Twelfth Night* and Pericles, returning to London in the latter role at Her Majesty's in 1974.

That summer he also went back to Chichester for Rakitin in *A Month in the Country*, before joining the RSC for the first time to tour in two poetry recitals, *The Hollow Crown* and *Pleasure and Repentance*. At the Arnaud Theatre, Guildford, in 1975 he played Will Mossop in *Hobson's Choice* before rejoining the touring Prospect Company where he stayed for the remainder of the 1970s. But Prospect were not always on the road: in these years they established London seasons at both the Albery and the Old Vic, and as the company's leading man Jacobi was able to do a vast range of classical and modern work.

For Prospect in these years he played Rakitin again in *A Month in the Country*, Cecil Vyse in *A Room with a View*, Hamlet, Caesar in *Antony and Cleopatra*, Ivanov again, Thomas Mendip in *The Lady's Not For Burning*; he also played in such anthologies as *The Grand Tour* and *The Lunatic, the Lover and the Poet*, and toured most if not all these productions through Scandinavia, Australia, Japan, as well as China, where Prospect were the first modern Western theatrical visitors.

Jacobi then scored an immense television success as the stammering title character in Robert Graves' 'I Claudius', and has made appearances in such movies as *The Day of the Jackal*, *The Odessa File* and *The Human Factor*.

It was, however, when he rejoined the RSC in 1983 that he came fully into his own with that great quartet of leading roles played at both Stratford and the Barbican: he and Sinead Cusack then took the RSC on to New York in a 1984 double of *Much Ado* and *Cyrano* which established him for the first time as a Broadway star.

JOSEPH JEFFERSON

'... Joseph Jefferson was destined to be a star and destined to be a comedian. He has accomplished within the range of comedy more than most of his contemporaries have accomplished with all the advantages of tragedy,' wrote a critic in 1869. 'He shines alone in his sphere. Belonging to a gentle family of actors, he has added the American quality, and is an American gentleman and an American actor, to whom universal homage has been paid, and of whom we of America may be justly proud ... He is the most able exponent, if not the leader, of that natural school which reproduces without caricature, acts without exaggeration — is, and not merely seems to be. He blends French wit with English humor, so that it is impossible to mark where the one begins and the other ends. His lithe figure and nervous organization, peculiarly American, give him a telling mobility of limb as well as of feature, to which a characteristic quickness of apprehension is a corresponding mental trait. His expression follows the thought with the trueness and rapidity of perception. His appreciation is apt, his taste is excellent, and he is wary in availing himself of every means that may be legitimately used for stage effect; yet he realizes fully the principle of that superlative art which conceals art. One of the most remarkable properties of Mr Jefferson's acting is that he accomplishes everything in the most quiet and unpretentious way, which inspires so genuine a sympathy for the character itself that no one pauses to inquire by what means the effect is produced.'

Joseph Jefferson was born in Philadelphia, Pennsylvania, on 20 February 1829. His father was a scenic artist and actor, his mother an actress, and his grandfather had also been an actor. He had an older stepbrother. The entire family's life revolved around the theatre. Although they were travelling artists they were in no way bohemian, and Joseph had a strictly moral upbringing in which prayer played a great part.

He could never remember his earliest moments on stage because whenever a play called for a baby he was taken on 'in arms' — a property child. His first recorded stage appearance was at the Washington Theater in Washington, DC, where for a benefit performance one night Thomas D. Rice, famous as a 'black face' performer, brought Joseph on stage, a miniature version of himself. The four-year-old Jefferson sang alternate stanzas of 'Jump Jim Crow' to the delight of the audience, who threw not only small coins but also silver dollars.

In 1837 the family found themselves at the Franklin Street Theater where on 30 September, aged six, Jefferson made his New York début as a pirate. The family were on their way to the new city of Chicago where there was to be a new theatre, along with everything else, and the promise of good steady work. In Chicago the company played at the New Theater but were soon on their way over prairies in open wagons to Galena and then on to Dubuque over the frozen Mississippi. After a few months' stop in Springfield, where they built a new theatre, they were on the road again. They arrived in Mobile in October 1842 during the yellow fever outbreak, and Jefferson's father died there the following month. Jefferson did, however, have the good fortune to see the great actors of his time, Macready and Booth. Life continued to be hard for the Jefferson family, who travelled from place to place entertaining wherever they were able to do so.

In 1846 Jefferson went to Philadelphia to join his stepbrother Charles at the Arch Street Theater. There he played a number of parts, including the Chorus in *Antigone*. But Joseph Jefferson was soon on the road again. 'There is nothing a young actor enjoys more than itinerant theatricals,' he wrote. 'It is so grand to break loose from a big tyrant manager in the city and become a small tyrant manager in the country. I was one of those juvenile theatrical anarchists who, after having stirred up a rebellion in the greenroom, would shout to my comrades, ''Let's all be equal, and I'll be King''.'

But back he went to Philadelphia where the manager of the Amphitheater told him, 'You do not look like a comedian. You have a serious, melancholy expression, you look more like an undertaker.' Nevertheless he hired him. Jefferson's task was not an easy one. As he explained: 'The low comedian of a melodramatic theater is generally used as a stop-gap and his artistic efforts are confined to going on in ''front scenes'' and amusing the audience, if he can, by speaking some long dry speeches, supposed to be full of humor, while the carpenters are hammering away behind and noisily arranging an elaborate set. Under these conditions it is very difficult to gain the confidence of an audience, or to distract their attention away from the painful fact that there is a hitch in the scenery.'

Joseph Jefferson moved on to New York, where he had two seasons in metropolitan stock. There he played Marrall in *A New Way To Pay Old Debts* while Booth played Sir Giles Overreach. There, too, he married Margaret Clements Lockyer on 19 May 1850.

He entered into management with John Ellsler in Savannah, Georgia, and from there travelled through the South. Then he was back in Philadelphia playing 'first comedy' at the Chestnut Street Theater, where he was Dr Pangloss in *The Heir-in-Law*. In 1853 he was the stage manager at the Baltimore Museum for Henry C. Jarrett, and among other roles played Moses in *The School for Scandal*. The following year he was manager for John T. Ford in Richmond, Virginia. In June 1856 he sailed for Europe, where he visited England and then went on to France to see where his maternal grandparents had come from.

In September 1857 Joseph Jefferson was in New York at Laura Keene's Theater where he was engaged as the leading comedy actor. Of his performance in *The Heir-in-Law* a critic said a 'nervous, fidgety young man by the name of Jefferson appeared as Dr Pangloss, into which character he infused a number of curious interpolations, occasionally using the text prepared by the author.' He also dramatized George Lepard's revolutionary story *Blanche of Brandywine*, which proved a great success.

It was during the 1858—59 season in New York that the turning point in Jefferson's career came when he played Asa Trenchard in *Our American Cousin*. He left the company and took the play on a starring tour. He returned to New York to the Winter Garden's first season under the direction of Dion Boucicault. There he played Caleb Plummer in *Dot*, an adaptation of Dickens' *Cricket on the Hearth*. He was also Salem Scudder in *The Octoroon*.

Jefferson then decided to play Rip Van Winkle, but found the extant adaptations of the story lacking. He assembled a costume for the part before writing a line, and then with a script completed opened at Carusi's Hall in Washington. He felt the character was right but the play was still wrong.

In February 1861 his wife died. He left his three younger children in school in New York and took his eldest son with him to California where, in San Francisco, his *Rip Van Winkle* failed to draw audiences. They sailed for Australia in September 1861; in Sydney, Jefferson rented a theatre and performed *Rip Van Winkle, Our American Cousin* and *The Octoroon* to great acclaim. They then went to Melbourne, where they played 164 consecutive nights at the Princess Theatre, later touring the mining and country towns. After a long holiday he returned to the stage in Melbourne and then went to Tasmania, where for the first time he played Bob Brierley in *The Ticket of Leave Man*. They went to play in New Zealand and then returned to Australia, spending in all four years there.

In April 1865 they sailed from Melbourne to England via South America, landing in Southampton in June 1865. There Dion Boucicault reworked *Rip Van Winkle* for him, and Jefferson opened at the Adelphi in September 1865 and played 170 nights. He went on to play it in Manchester and Liverpool before sailing back to New York.

Joseph Jefferson married for the second time on 20 December 1867 while on a tour of the midwest. He then toured constantly throughout the United States and returned to Europe in 1875. He met with enormous acclaim throughout Britain, with the exception of Dublin.

When Joseph Jefferson played *Rip Van Winkle* in New York at the Fifth Avenue Theater in 1878 the New York *Daily Tribune* reported: 'To say that Mr Jefferson reappeared last night as Rip Van Winkle is to imply that a beautiful work of dramatic art was set before the public in a profoundly earnest spirit, and that it was greeted with deep delight and unaffected cordiality by a large and enthusiastic assemblage ... to observe Mr Jefferson's audience became nearly as great a pleasure as to observe the artist himself. Beauty in art and sincerity in its ministration naturally awaken the sympathetic response of kindliness and sweetness, combined with the poetic instinct ... There will be, as there have been, many Rip Van Winkles: there is but one Jefferson. For him it was reserved to depart altogether from the character as it exists in the pages of Irving; to idealize the entire subject; to elevate a prosaic type of good-natured indolence into an ideal emblem of poetical freedom; to construct and translate in the world of fact the Arcadian vagabond of the world of dreams. In the presence, accordingly, of his wonderful embodiment of this droll, gentle, drifting human creature — to whom trees and brooks and flowers are familiar companions, to whom spirits appear, and for whom the mysterious voices of the lovely midnight forest have a meaning and a charm — the observer feels that poetry is no longer restricted to canvas, and marble, and rapt reverie over the printed page, but walks forth crystalized in a human form, spangled with the freshness of the diamond dews of morning, mysterious with hints of woodland secrets, lovely with the simplicity and joy of rustic freedom, and fragrant with the incense of pines.'

Rip Van Winkle was Jefferson's masterpiece. He also altered and condensed Sheridan's *The Rivals*, playing Bob Acres most successfully. 'I have often been taxed with idleness for not studying new parts and adding them to my repertoire,' he wrote. 'The list of plays that I have acted of late years is certainly a very short one, and the critic who becomes weary of witnessing them over and over again naturally protests against their constant repetition ... Believe me, it requires more skill to act one part fifty different ways than to act fifty parts all the same way.'

Jefferson continued his very successful starring tours. He always played to full houses and the receipts allowed him to buy a plantation in Louisiana. He was something of an intellectual concerning his art. As Otis Skinner reported, he was 'a man who made the acting of comedy a science'. Of his profession Jefferson wrote '... the work of an actor is fleeting; it not only dies with him, but, through his different moods, may vary from night to night. If the performance be indifferent it is no consolation for the audience to hear that the players acted well last night, or to be told that he will act better tomorrow night ... The great value of art when applied to the stage is that it enables the performer to reproduce the gift [of talent] and so move his audience night after night, even though he has acted the same character a thousand times. In fact, we cannot act a character too often, if we do not lose interest in it. But when its constant repetition palls on the actor it will as surely weary his audience. When you lose interest — stop acting.'

Joseph Jefferson himself never lost interest and he never stopped acting. He died in Palm Beach, Florida, on 23 April 1905.

CELIA JOHNSON

C elia Johnson, whose wide-eyed beauty and British understated demeanour has been captured forever in the film of Noel Coward's *Brief Encounter*, had a long and distinguished stage career.

She was born in Richmond, Surrey, on 18 December 1908. Her father was a member of the Royal College of Surgeons. Celia Johnson was educated well, at St Paul's Girls School and also on the Continent. She then studied at RADA and made her first stage appearance in August 1928 at the Theatre Royal in Huddersfield, where she played Sarah in *Major Barbara*. Her London début came in January 1929 at the Lyric, Hammersmith, where she succeeded Angela Baddeley as Currita in *A Hundred Years Old*. In August 1929 she toured as Thérèse Meunier in *Typhoon* and was back in London at the Kingsway in March 1930 playing Suzette in *The Artist and the Shadow*. The following month she played Loveday Trevel-

yan in *Debonair*, and because it was rather short the balcony scene from *Romeo and Juliet* was introduced as a curtain raiser. At the Playhouse in June she played Doris Lea in *Cynara* with Gerald du Maurier and Gladys Cooper, and at the Arts in September was Elle in *L'Occasion*, which was played in French.

At the Vaudeville in March 1931 Celia Johnson played Elizabeth in *The Circle* and at the Savoy in June was Grezia in *Death Takes a Holiday*. She followed Madeleine Carroll at the Criterion in July 1931 as Phyl in *After All*.

Celia Johnson made her New York début at the Broadhurst Theater on 5 November 1931, playing Ophelia to Raymond Massey's Hamlet. John Mason Brown reported that her performance had 'a touching pathos when its mad scenes are reached'.

She returned to London and in February 1932 was at the Globe playing Judy in *Punchinello*. At the Apollo in March she was Elsa in *The Man I Killed* and at the St James's in June played Leone Merrick in *The Vinegar Tree*. In August she was at the Haymarket playing the Hon. Cynthia Lynne in *Tomorrow Will Be Friday*.

Celia Johnson started 1933 at the Embassy, where she played Betty Findon in *Ten Minute Alibi* and then succeeded Edna Best as Stella Hallam in *Another Language* at the Lyric. In February she was back at the Arts playing Celia Desmond in *These Two*, and that same month at the Haymarket was again playing Betty Findon in *Ten Minute Alibi*. At the Embassy in May 1933 she was Sheila Grey in *Sometimes Even Now* and at the St Martin's in September was Janet Carr in *The Key*. In October, she began to enjoy her first long run when she played Ann Hargraves in *The Wind and the Rain*, which lasted two years.

In 1935 Celia Johnson married Peter Fleming, the writer and explorer who also ran a large country estate near Henley-on-Thames. At the St James's Theatre in February 1936 she was cast as Elizabeth Bennet in *Pride and Prejudice* and in August 1937 was Judith in *Old Music*. In May 1939 she played Jacqueline Hochepot in *Sixth Floor* and at the Queen's in April 1940 was Mrs de Winter in Daphne du Maurier's *Rebecca*. She succeeded Vivien Leigh at the Haymarket in September 1942, playing Jennifer in *The Doctor's Dilemma*. She then took five years off to start a family.

Celia Johnson returned to the stage with the Old Vic Company at the New Theatre in December 1947 when she played the title role in Shaw's *Saint Joan*. It was an admired but not totally successful performance. T. C. Worsley said: 'Miss Celia Johnson is a sincere and gifted player ... To Saint Joan, for all her sincerity, she is at no point suited, not in voice, presence or weight. This is no fault of hers, but her acting fails to redeem it.' And Harold Hobson: 'This Joan's fighting is as temporal as it is temporary. It has known no spiritual ambushes, no mental snare. It fights against principalities and against powers but not against spiritual wickedness, for spiritual wickedness is something it cannot even realize. The faith of this Joan, who is wide-eyed in wonder, in appearance slender and gentle and yielding as the willow, soft-voiced as a summer breeze, angelic as a choir of surpliced children, has never had to know increase ... Miss Johnson's is a performance of clear spiritual perception ... Its clarity is greater than its power, its beauty more notable than its authority. Its radiance illuminates Joan's face, but whether it would have driven the English out of France is another matter.' And Audrey Williamson summed up all the criticism and the

praise: 'It was the charm and beauty of Celia Johnson's performance that, fragile of form, wondering and rapt of face, with enormous eyes like pools reflecting some radiance in the skies, it left us in no doubt that here was sainthood in some form ... Its very spiritual frailty, though touching deeply, lacked the piercing lance of suffering that can only come from the *strength* of Joan's passion.'

In 1950 Celia Johnson toured in Italy with the Old Vic Company playing Viola in *Twelfth Night*. Back in London in May 1951 she was Olga in *The Three Sisters* and at the Westminster in June 1954 played Laura Hammond in *It's Never Too Late*.

At the Cambridge in May 1955 Celia Johnson played Sheila Broadbent in William Douglas-Home's comedy *The Reluctant Debutante*. Frank Granville-Barker reported: 'The comedy could have been placed in no more capable hands than those of Celia Johnson and Wilfrid Hyde-White, whose timing and throwaway of lines are impeccable. The former's portrayal of harassed social ambition is thoroughly captivating.'

In November 1957 at the Haymarket with Ralph Richardson she played Isobel Cherry in Robert Bolt's *Flowering Cherry*, and at the St Martin's in December 1958, according to Bill Lester, she behaved 'impeccably in a not very exacting part' — that of Hilary in Hugh and Margaret Williams' *The Grass Is Greener*. In the 1958 Birthday Honours Celia Johnson was made a CBE. She then, in 1960, directed *Special Providence* at the St Martin's.

In November 1960 at Wyndham's she played Pamela Puffy-Picq in François Billetdoux's *Chin-Chin* with Anthony Quayle. Peter Roberts said: 'Miss Johnson continues to get the utmost comedy out of the precise and orderly Englishwoman she is playing and at the same time makes the onlooker feel pity for the character's desperate unhappiness.' And Kenneth Tynan agreed that her performance had 'just the right nervy niceness for Pamela and the right rebuking stare, spectrally disquieted and British to the core'. At the Haymarket in November 1962 she was Clare Elliot in *The Tulip Tree*, and at the Phoenix in October 1963 played Helen Hampster in Giles Cooper's cross between a comedy and a farce, *Out of the Crocodile*.

Celia Johnson joined the National Theatre Company at the Old Vic in June 1964 to play Mrs Solness in *The Master Builder* with Maggie Smith and Michael Redgrave. Martin Esslin reported: 'Celia Johnson gives Mrs Solness a sickly pallor, a suffering air that is both heartrending and bound to drive any man condemned to live with it to distraction. And in her final confession about her dolls she suggests frightening depths of madness. And this fabulous performance is entirely in the style of the period.'

In March 1965 she took over the part of Judith Bliss in Noel Coward's *Hay Fever*, and at the Chichester Festival in July 1966 played Madame Ranyevskaya in *The Cherry Orchard*. Peter Roberts, writing in *Plays and Players*, had his doubts about this performance: 'This Madame Ranyevskaya is small-scale, edgy, giggly and rather a dolt. This is a perfectly valid and courageous reading in so far as it's bound to disappoint those who regularly turn up at *The Cherry Orchard* to break their hearts over a romantic woman, not shrug their shoulders at a pathetically foolish one. One reservation though. Miss Johnson is a mannered actress who has thrived on her mannerisms in parts ranging widely from Ibsen's Mrs Solness to the Coward housewife in *Brief Encounter*. But a new mannerism — a sort of pop-eyed stare — is developing and it does not work as well as the others. At one moment this Madame Ranyevskaya looks perfectly normal. At another she takes on the appearance of a raving lunatic. It is extremely disconcerting.'

At the Duke of York's in March 1967 Celia Johnson played Sheila in Alan Ayckbourn's *Rela-*

tively Speaking, and in January 1969 went to Toronto to the O'Keefe Center, where she played Judith Bliss in *Hay Fever*. She then brought the production back to London to the Duke of York's in February 1968.

In Nottingham at the Playhouse in November 1970 she played Gertrude in Alan Bates' *Hamlet* and came with the production to London to the Cambridge Theatre in January 1971.

At the Savoy in October the same year Celia Johnson took over the part of Lady Boothroyd in *Lloyd George Knew My Father*, and in 1974, at the Oxford Festival in September and at Wyndham's in October, she played Sybil Hathaway in William Douglas-Home's *The Dame of Sark*. It was in another Douglas-Home play, *The Kingfisher*, that she starred in 1977 with Ralph Richardson. Celia Johnson was created a Dame in 1981. She made her final appearance, starring once more opposite Sir Ralph Richardson, in Angela Huth's play, *The Understanding*; they played a few previews at the Strand Theatre but then, on Sunday, 25 April 1982, during a bridge game at her home in Nettlebed, she suffered a stroke and died.

See photograph opposite page 119.

JAMES EARL JONES

James Earl Jones was born on 17 January 1931 in Tate County, Mississippi. His father Robert was an actor and his mother a tailor, but Jones was brought up mainly on his family's farm in Mississippi. He graduated from Norman Dickson High School in Michigan, and then attended the University of Michigan. His first acting experience was at the university. He served with the United States Army as a first lieutenant and then went into summer stock in Michigan at the Manistee Summer Theater, appearing there regularly from 1955 to 1959 in *Stalag 17*, *The Caine Mutiny*, *Velvet Gloves*, *The Tender Trap*, *Arsenic and Old Lace*, *Desperate Hours*; and there, for the first time, he played the title role in *Othello*. He had always realized his start would be slow. 'It never bothered me that actors had a hard time, and black actors in particular. My father was an actor and I saw how difficult it was for him. I knew I had to accept a low standard of living for some years.'

He went to New York first in 1957, where he studied acting with Lee Strasberg and Tad Danielewsky. He had the job of understudy to Lloyd

Richards as Perry Hall in *The Egghead*, which opened at the Ethel Barrymore Theater in October 1957. He played Sergeant Blunt in *Wedding in Japan* at the Graystone Hotel in 1957, and in January 1958 opened at the Cort Theater playing Edward in *Sunrise at Campobello*. He played Jessie Prince in *The Pretender* the following year.

In February 1960 he played Harrison Thurston in *The Cool World* at the Eugene O'Neill Theater, and that summer in Central Park for the New York Shakespeare Festival played Williams in *Henry V* and Abhorson in *Measure for Measure*.

His performance as Deodatus Village in Genet's *The Blacks* at St Mark's Playhouse in May 1961 had Howard Taubman singling him out in the *New York Times* as someone to watch. Rejoining the New York Shakespeare Festival in the summer of 1961, James Earl Jones played Oberon in *A Midsummer Night's Dream* and Lord Marshall in *Richard II* in Central Park.

He played Roger Clark in *Clandestine on the Morning Line* at the Actors' Playhouse in October 1961, Ace in *The Apple* at the Living Theater in

December of that year and in January 1962 was Ephraim in *Moon on a Rainbow Shawl* at the East 11th Street Theater. For these performances he received the Village Voice Off-Broadway Award (Obie), and also the Theater World Award for his performance in *Moon on a Rainbow Shawl*.

At the Music Box in April 1962 James Earl Jones played Cinna in *Infidel Caesar* and that summer was back with the Shakespeare Festival playing Caliban in *The Tempest* and the Prince of Morocco in *The Merchant of Venice*. At the Corning Summer Theater in New York that year he played Henry in *Toys in the Attic*.

At the Writers' Stage in October 1962 James Earl Jones played Mario Saccone in *P.S. 193* and then succeeded Ramon Bieri as Macduff in a New York Shakespeare Festival production of *Macbeth* at the Hecksecher Theater in November. In January he was back at the Writers' Stage, playing George Gulp in *The Love Nest*. He went to the Pocket Theater that May, where he succeeded Melvin Stewart as Mr Ash in *The Last Minstrel*. At the Delacorte in August he was Camillo in the New York Shakespeare Festival production of *The Winter's Tale*.

For the Equity Library at the Masters' Institute in October 1963 he played the title role in *Mr Johnson*. He was Rudge in *Next Time I'll Sing to You* at the Phoenix in November 1963, and the following March, Zachariah Pieterson in *Blood Knot* at the Cricket. In July 1964 he played the title role in *Othello* at the Delacorte Theater, and took this production to Martinique, where in April 1965 he also played Ekart in *Baal*. He returned to the Delacorte, where in June 1965 he played Junius Brutus in *Coriolanus* and in August played Ajax in *Troilus and Cressida*.

He was Philipeau in the opening production at the Vivian Beaumont Theater in October 1965 — *Danton's Death*. Generally disappointed with the production, the critic Martin Gottfried hoped, in print, that Jones was simply the victim of 'mixed-up direction'. For summer 1966 he played Macbeth for the New York Shakespeare Festival, and at the Longacre in September was in the revue *A Hand Is on the Gates*.

James Earl Jones made his first European tour during summer 1967, playing the title role in *The Emperor Jones*.

At the Arena Stage in Washington, DC, in December 1967 he opened as Jack Jefferson in *The Great White Hope*. This play was based loosely on the career of Jack Johnson, who in 1908 became the first black heavyweight boxing champion of the world. Martin Gottfried reported: 'In this performance Jones passed over the line from being a very good actor to being a great one

... Shaving his mannerisms as he did his head, and in phenomenal physical shape, he worked with every acting tool under inspired control — vocal technique, physical sense, intellectual understanding. Bravura actors are almost extinct in America and now there is Jones.'

For the summer he went to the Purdue University Theater where in Lafayette, Indiana, he played Lonnie in *Of Mice and Men* and then in October arrived with *The Great White Hope* at the Alvin Theater in New York. John Simon wrote: 'Physically, he is just the shiny-pated, swift-footed, barrel-chested, debonair giant Johnson must have been; quick-witted, too, and jovial, charmingly embodying that real or imagined animality that white men fear for real or imaginary reasons. His emotional range is no less colossal; from bubbling badinage through ironic jabs to overwhelming grief at the death of his girl — human, animal, titanic — Jones encompasses everything with the precision and ease of a master.' He remained at the Alvin in that role for more than a year, and won the Tony for his performance.

At the Circle in the Square in June 1970 Jones played Boesman in the South African Athol Fugard's *Boesman and Lena*, and in November was back on Broadway at the Longacre playing Tshembe Matoseh in *Les Blancs*. In 1978 James Earl Jones found himself at the centre of a vocal controversy when he played in a one-man show, *Paul Robeson*. Robeson's son objected strongly to the play. It lasted only 45 days at the Lunt-Fontanne Theater, then transferring to the Booth, it folded. He brought it to Her Majesty's in London for a short engagement, and Harold Atkins reported in the *Daily Telegraph*: 'Those who knew Robeson will never forget his great humanity and dignity and Mr Jones captured these to a great extent. At beginning and end, though, the taped voice of Robeson himself conveys deeper inner notes than Mr Jones attains, though it is a good performance of integrity and simplicity ... Mr Jones succeeds in suggesting that Robeson was of influence in whipping forward greater awareness of the negro point of view in the United States.'

James Earl Jones made his first film appearance in *Dr Strangelove* in 1963 and was nominated for an Academy Award for his performance in *The Great White Hope* in 1970. His many television appearances include an unsuccessful attempt as Paris, the chief of detectives, in a series and an acclaimed performance as the author Alex Haley in 'Roots — the Second Generation'. He was also, of course, the voice of the immortal Darth Vader in *Star Wars*.
See photograph opposite page 199.

EDMUND KEAN

'Never has an actor appeared who owed less to the acting of others; he disdained imitation; he was himself alone,' wrote Kean's friend John W. Francis in his book *Old New York, or, Reminiscences of the Past Sixty Years*.

Consciously or unconsciously, Edmund Kean broke with the classical tradition established by Garrick and introduced the Romantic Age to the theatre. He, too, was a small man but on the stage he towered. His childhood is cloaked in mystery and legend, and he himself was given to saying he was the bastard son of the Duke of Norfolk, but that seems unlikely. He was born in London, probably in 1789, the son of Ann Carey, an unsuccessful actress who was herself the daughter of a failed actor. She abandoned him soon after his birth and went off with a group of strolling players. An actress named Miss Tidswell looked after him in a manner of speaking, and took him with her to Drury Lane when she was acting there. It is said that he was Cupid in one of Noverre's ballets at the Opera House when he was three, and at seven was an imp dancing around the witches' cauldron in Kemble's *Macbeth*.

Somehow he survived, though it is also rumoured that he ran away to sea when it was suggested that he might go to school. He found that he could earn money by giving imitations in taverns of the leading actors of the time. At one point he joined a travelling circus.

In 1804 he joined Samuel Jerrold's company at Sheerness, where he began playing principal Shakespearian parts. The following year he was in Belfast playing small roles — but Mrs Siddons noted his potential. Near to starvation, he joined Mrs Baker's company in Tunbridge Wells, where he was well paid but not allowed to play the leading roles; to him this was more important, so he went back to Sheerness — but left there in 1808 pursued by local tradesmen, to whom he was in debt. He joined another travelling troupe where he met and married Mary Chambers, an actress who was minimally talented and nine years older than himself. The wedding took place at Stroud on 17 July 1808. After the marriage they were dismissed from the company because the manager did not like having married people on the stage. He said they had no appeal for the audience. They walked from Birmingham to Swansea to join Andre Cherry's company, where they stayed for two years. Kean played many principal roles, including Hamlet and Richard III. Ever belligerent, particularly after a

session with the bottle, Kean quarrelled with Cherry and was sacked. He and his wife walked back to London with their two baby sons, and when they arrived found that Edmund was still unemployable there. He set off on a tour of Weymouth, Exeter and Plymouth theatres, but was dismissed for drunkenness. He got another job which took him to Taunton and Dorchester, where in November 1813 he was playing Alexander the Great to near-empty houses. However, the manager of Drury Lane was in front and he engaged him for three seasons at his London theatre. At last Kean would have his chance — though it came too late for his elder son, Howard, who died of malnutrition in Dorchester.

On 26 January 1814, in the middle of a violent snowstorm, to a half-empty theatre and with an uninterested company, Edmund Kean walked on to the stage of the Drury Lane Theatre to give his revolutionary interpretation of Shylock in *The Merchant of Venice*. William Hazlitt, writing in the *Morning Chronicle*, said: 'His style of acting is, if we may use the expression, more significant, more pregnant with meaning, more varied and alive in every part, than any we have almost ever witnessed. The character never stands still; there is no vacant pause in the action; the eye is never silent.'

On 12 February Kean scored an enormous success with Richard III. Lord Byron said: 'Life, nature, truth, without exaggeration or diminution. Richard is a man and Kean is Richard.' There was now no looking back — in March he was Hamlet, in May Othello and then Iago. On 25 May he gave a benefit performance of a terrible melodrama, *Riches*, and made £1150; the audiences swooned at everything he did. Not only had he made himself a very rich man (his son Charles took to playing with gold guineas), but he had saved the fortune of the theatre by filling it every night. Aware of the fickleness of audiences, Kean decided to make money while he could and that summer toured Cheltenham, Bristol, Gloucester, Birmingham and Dublin.

On 3 October 1814 he was back at Drury Lane with *Richard III*. The rival house Covent Garden challenged his supremacy with a new star, Elizabeth O'Neill, in an attempt to draw the audiences to their doors. Kean countered with a production of *Macbeth* which was a great success. In January he played in *Romeo and Juliet* with Mrs Bartley. He was totally unsuited to the role, but at that moment he could do nothing wrong.

However, he was not a happy man. His wife had become addicted to social climbing; Kean disliked the drawing-room — where he felt he was put on display — and preferred the tavern. He took literally to drink, gambling and loose women, to everyone's despair, though the money and the applause were both still profuse. In the 1814 season he played Richard III, Penruddock in *Wheel of Fortune*, Zanga in *The Revenge* and Abel Drugger in *The Alchemist*. He went to Ireland in the summer of 1815, where he scored a triumph. His wife moved to a grand house in Clarges Street, Piccadilly, determined on respectability. She filled the house with servants — and Kean contributed a pet lion, to her evident despair. Still terrified that his success would not last, Kean would go off to the provinces to make a quick fee when he was committed to playing at Drury Lane. However, so great was his attraction for the audience that the management put up with it. On 12 January 1816 he played Sir Giles Overreach in Massinger's *A New Way to Pay Old Debts*. The final scene was described by the *Morning Chronicle* as 'a climax of terrible destruction and awful desolation of a mind buoyed up by false hopes, the failure of which overwhelms it in blank desperation and universal wretchedness'. In March he introduced Massinger's *The Duke of Milan*. By this time he was earning a colossal sum, in excess of £10,000 a season, but his drinking and carousing were catching up with him and he began missing performances. To placate the audiences the managements made up stories of ill-health.

The young actor Junius Brutus Booth was beginning to make a name for himself as a Kean lookalike. He modelled himself on the great star and audiences began to say there was no difference. Kean invited the young man to play Iago to his Othello on 20 February 1817. The aspect of challenge in the performance was a great crowd puller; Kean acted Booth off the stage and back to the provinces. Kean had great success that season with *Timon of Athens*, *Oroonoko* and the *The Iron Chest*, though he did not fare as well with *Manuel*, *The Jew of Malta*, or Byron's *Bride of Abydos*.

Drury Lane was once again facing ruin. Kean was the only draw they had; the supporting actors were bad and the management was terrible. Kean made a bid for the management himself but was outbid by Robert Elliston, who took it over. Kean's only new success of the 1819 season was *King Lear*. In August of that year he gave a short season of his old favourites before departing on a tour of America where, his reputation preceding him, they were clamouring for his appearance.

In New York tickets were in such demand that they had to be auctioned, all profits being given to charity. He made his New York début on 29 November 1820 playing Richard III at the Anthony Street Theater. The New York *Evening Post* reported: 'We were assured that certain imitations of him were exact likenesses; and that certain actors were good copies; that his excellencies consisted in sudden starts, frequent and unexpected pauses, in short a complete knowledge of what is called stage struck, which we hold in contempt. But he had not finished his soliloquy before our prejudices gave way and we saw the most complete actor, in our judgement, that ever appeared on our boards. The imitations we had seen were, indeed, likenesses, but it was the resemblance of copper to gold; and the copies no more like Kean "than I to Hercules".' He was feted all over New York, Boston, Baltimore and Philadelphia, and earned enormous sums. In May, however, he returned against advice to Boston — the wrong season for theatregoers — and after two nights of playing to nearly empty houses declined to go on for the third. It caused a scandal, greatly played up by the newspapers.

There was much rejoicing at his homecoming when he played in *Richard III, The Merchant of Venice* and *Othello* at Drury Lane. However, the season itself was not an unqualified success. His popularity was waning. He started a liaison with Charlotte Cox, the wife of a City alderman who also happened to sit on the Drury Lane Committee. Alderman Cox took Kean to court over Charlotte and there was the most enormous scandal. General uproar, hissing and booing greeted his stage appearances. He told his audiences that he refused to justify his private conduct, but they would not be appeased and the newspapers continued to fuel the flames with stories of his dissolute habits. Demonstrations broke out everywhere against him when he attempted a provincial tour. His wife, distressed and furious that she was now a social outcast too, took refuge in their home on the Isle of Bute and felt he was getting what he deserved.

In September 1825 Kean went once more to America, thinking that they would have forgotten his ungraceful exit. There, too, he was greeted with abuse. He swallowed his pride, however, and begged to be given a chance. New York forgave him, but in Boston, where he had committed his offence, they threw cabbages and wrecked the theatre; Kean had to flee town in a disguise. He was given a warm welcome in Canada, and then had a successful autumn in New York. He returned to Drury Lane on 8 January 1827, where all was forgiven and he had a warm and friendly audience for his Shylock. But his abused body was now reacting, he no longer had sufficient energy for his old roles and his performances became unpredictable. On 21 May he attempted to introduce a new one, *Ben Nazir*, but he could not learn the lines and the performance was a fiasco.

After a quarrel, Edmund Kean left Drury Lane and went over to the opposition at Covent Garden. By this time his son Charles had left school and was determined to act, though Edmund did everything he could to discourage it, including getting him a job with the East India Company. Drury Lane now hired Charles, hoping to attract audiences with the promise of the great Kean's son. But the boy was young and inexperienced, and the ploy did not work. Kean went on to play Shylock successfully at Covent Garden but he was sustained by constant doses of brandy. In summer 1828 he had a short and disastrous season at the Odéon in Paris. He came back and, deciding to stop fighting Charles, played Brutus in *Julius Caesar* with him in October in Glasgow. By this time Edmund Kean was living with an extravagant Irishwoman called, appropriately enough as a consort for the great Shakespearian, Ophelia. She did nothing to help the now very sick actor. On 5 December he managed to acquit himself admirably in the title role of *Virginius*, but he collapsed after the performance. By May he had recovered sufficiently to give a season in Dublin and Cork.

On his return to London, Fanny Kemble was being hailed as the new star of Covent Garden, so he went back to Drury Lane. On 8 March 1830 he attempted to play Henry V but once more it was a fiasco. 'Want of a memory,' he said, 'is not want of

heart.' The Richard III that followed, however, was deemed to be one of the best of his entire career.

In summer 1830 he staged a very successful farewell season at the Haymarket; on 19 July at the King's Theatre in a final farewell, he performed scenes from all his important successes. In that one performance he raised more than £1000 and encouraged by this he tramped through the provinces enjoying similar success wherever he took his 'farewells'. Then, to the surprise of all who had said farewell to him, he returned to London to Drury Lane to play Richard III in January.

He acquired a house in Richmond, and next door a theatre that he thought would be a great source of income. However, remembering his days of starvation as a young actor, he paid his own actors very well indeed and through a combination of generosity and plain extravagance was soon having to appear at other theatres to cover his costs at Richmond. His financial difficulties did no more to help his health than did the brandy. And Drury Lane had a new star anyway — Macready.

In an attempt to raise some money, on 25 March 1833 at Covent Garden he played Othello and his son Charles, now beginning to make a name for himself, played Iago. Edmund Kean collapsed during the third act and had to be carried from the stage. He seemed to recover slightly, but died on 15 May. The Dean of Westminster refused to allow his burial in Westminster Abbey, and he was finally laid to rest in the old parish churchyard in Richmond.

THE KEMBLES

Roger **Kemble**, founder of one of England's greatest acting dynasties, was born in Hereford in 1721. He worked as a barber until he was 30, when he succumbed to the acting bug and joined John Ward's travelling company. In 1753 he married **Sally**, Ward's actress daughter, and inherited the company and the circuit when his father-in-law retired. It was a good circuit, covering the English West Midlands — north to Lancashire and south to Warwickshire and Gloucestershire. His wife continued to act while raising twelve children.

Their eldest child, **Sarah**, was born on 5 July 1755 in Brecon, Wales. She was baptized into her mother's Protestant faith, as were subsequent daughters. The sons were baptized Roman Catholics, following their father's religion. The Kembles'

eldest son, **John Philip**, was born on 1 February 1757 in Prescott, Lancashire; the next child, **Stephen**, was born in 1758 in Herefordshire.

The Kemble children's earliest appearances on stage remain unrecorded, but they led a nomadic life acting with the family all over the circuit. There is evidence that they were all on stage together in Worcester in 1767 when the 12-year-old Sarah played Princess Elizabeth in *Charles I* while John Philip played James, Duke of York. With an eye to society and respectability, the Kemble parents insisted that their children should be well educated. John Philip went first to a preparatory school in Worcester, then on to the Catholic College at Sedgeley Park near Wolverhampton before being sent to the Benedictine School in Douai, France, where he was to train for

Glenda Jackson (with Edward Petherbridge) in a revival of
Eugene O'Neill's drama *Strange Interlude* at the Duke of York's Theatre
(London, April 1984)

James Earl Jones plays the title role in *Othello*
(New York, October 1982)

the priesthood. Sarah was sent to Thornloe House, a school for genteel young ladies, where she excelled herself in all her studies. She rejoined her parents' touring company and, to their horror, fell in love with William Siddons, a member of the company who was deemed suitable only for supporting roles and who was, moreover, eleven years her senior. That she should fall in love with an actor was bad enough — but to fall in love with an unsuccessful one! Finally, her parents saw that they had no hope of dissuading her, and on 26 November 1773 her father gave her in marriage to William Siddons at the Holy Trinity Church in Coventry. They all immediately began touring again; Sarah's most important roles during this time were Charlotte in *The West Indian* and Leonora in *The Padlock*.

In 1774, asserting their independence, the Siddons left the Kemble troupe and joined up with Chamberlain and Crump. It was while playing in Otway's *Venice Preserv'd* that Sarah was befriended by the Hon. Henrietta Boyle, a fortuitous meeting because Miss Boyle thereafter furnished Sarah with the expensive wardrobe so useful to a young actress which Sarah could not possibly have afforded herself.

The Siddons' first child, Henry, was born in Wolverhampton in October 1774. Sarah was soon back on the road and on the stage. She was seen in Cheltenham playing Colista in Rowe's *The Fair Penitent* by one of Garrick's scouts for Drury Lane, who was most impressed. The following year the Siddons joined Joseph Younger's company. Garrick sent Henry Bate to see Sarah, again when she was performing in Cheltenham. Bate wrote back that he judged she would be 'a valuable acquisition to Drury Lane. Her figure must be remarkably fine when she is happily delivered of a big baby ... Her face ... is one of the most strikingly beautiful for stage effect that ever I beheld: but I shall surprise you more, when I assure you that these are nothing to her action and general stage deportment which are remarkably pleasing and characteristic; in short I know no woman who marks the different passages and transitions with so much variety and at the same time propriety of expression ...'

Drury Lane's rival, Covent Garden, was also after Sarah Siddons at this time and her husband William acted as her manager. After her second child was born, on 5 November 1775, she came to London, and on Friday, 29 December, billed as 'a Young Lady' and playing Portia in *The Merchant of Venice*, Sarah Siddons made her London début at Drury Lane. She had not been welcomed by the female stars of the company, who viewed her with jealousy, she was exhausted after the recent birth

and move south, she was highly nervous of the prestigious house and moreover she was used to small provincial theatres. She was not very good. In January she played a boy disguised as a woman in Ben Jonson's *Epicoene* and on 1 February was the heroine in *The Blackamoor Washed White*. The *Morning Chronicle* reported: 'All played well except Mrs Siddons who, having no comedy in her nature, rendered that ridiculous which the author evidently intended to be pleasant.' On 15 February she was the ingénue in Hannah Crowley's first play, *The Runaway*, and also played in the farce, *Love's Vagaries*. In May she played Mrs Strickland in *The Suspicious Wife* with Garrick, and her performance drew mild approval from the critics. Sarah Siddons then played Lady Anne in Garrick's farewell performance of *Richard III*. Garrick retired and Drury Lane no longer required the services of Sarah Siddons. She had not made a great success of her London début, and had to swallow her pride and return to the provinces to earn a living for the family. She spent six years away from London, during which time three more children were born: Maria in 1779, Frances Emilia (who died in infancy) in 1781 and Eliza Ann in 1782.

Sarah toured — mainly Liverpool, Birmingham, Manchester and York — playing the lead in Murphy's *The Grecian Daughter*, Rowe's *The Fair Penitent* and Home's *Douglas*. She also played Hamlet, and no one seemed surprised.

In September 1778 she joined the Bath-Bristol Company, the most respected outside London. There she added to her repértoire Lady Townley in *The Provoked Husband*, the Countess in *The Countess of Salisbury* and Elvira in Hannah More's tragedy, *Percy*. Of the last, the *Bath Chronicle* wrote that she was 'in the judgement of the town the most capital actress that had performed here these many years'. That year Drury Lane began asking her to come back to them in London; but Sarah remained in Bath for four seasons, until 1782.

Meanwhile, her brother John Philip left Douai feeling that he definitely had no vocation for the priesthood. Against the wishes of his father, who was still looking for respectability for his children, he declared himself an actor and on 8 January 1776 was with Chamberlain and Crump's theatrical company playing the title role in Nathaniel Lee's tragedy *Theodosius* in Wolverhampton. He embarked upon the life of a strolling player. He next joined Tate Wilkins' company and played most successfully (among other parts) Captain Plum in Farquhar's *The Recruiting Officer*, Macbeth, Orestes in *The Distrest Mother*, and in *Zenobia*. When, in January 1781, he played his Hamlet at the Theatre Royal in York he had an established reputation in the northern counties, as well as in Edinburgh and Dublin.

On 10 October 1782 Sarah Siddons, then aged 28, appeared once more at Drury Lane. This time she was playing the lead in *Isabella, or The Fatal Marriage*. To report that she had an enormous success would be serious understatement. The *Morning Post* said: 'A late hour prevents us from dwelling on the merits of this accomplished woman who beyond all comparison is the first tragic actress now on the English stage.' (Between November and the following June, Sarah Siddons repeated the role sixteen times to full and enthusiastic audiences.) On 30 October she played Euphrasia in *The Grecian Daughter*, and on 8 November the title role in *Jane Shore*, a part she was to revive fourteen times that season. Boaden reported the reaction to the latter: 'We then [the audience] indeed, knew all the luxury of grief; but the nerves of many a gentle being gave way before the intensity of such appeals, and fainting fits long and frequently alarmed the decorum of the house filled almost to suffocation ...' One of her performances that season, in *The Fatal Interview*, was not successful, so she went on to play Colista in *The Fair Penitent* on 29 November and on 14 December played Belvidera in *Venice Preserv'd* for her own benefit, taking home £800. In acknowledgement of her great success she was given Garrick's dressing room. On 18 March 1783 she introduced Zara in *Zaire* into her repertoire. In all, from October to June of that 1782–83 season Sarah Siddons gave more than eighty major performances. Not only did she become a star, filling the house to overflowing at each performance, but she also did an enormous amount to raise the reputation of the theatrical community. She attracted royalty back into the audience, and moreover was commanded to play both at Windsor and what was then still Buckingham House. And where royalty went, there went the rest of society.

Still mindful of her family, she brought her younger sister **Frances Kemble** into the Drury Lane company, where she stayed for three seasons. She was attractive but not as talented as her sister. (She married a dramatic critic and eventually began a school for young ladies in Bath for which she charged exorbitant fees, rather trading on Sarah's name.) Although she was socially much in demand, Sarah Siddons remained shy and almost reclusive, a trait which was often misinterpreted as arrogance. She was sought after as a subject for portrait painters and eventually sat for many of them, including Reynolds and Gainsborough.

Sarah Siddons spent summer 1783 in Dublin, where she opened at the Smock Alley Theatre in June in *Isabella*. Her brother John Philip had been heading the resident company there, playing as many as thirty-eight leading roles in a season, including Hamlet, Othello, Iago, King Charles, Richard III, Shylock, Byron, Mark Antony, Romeo, Macbeth and Henry V. Elizabeth Inchbald, with whom he was noticeably in love, was also in the company. Mrs Siddons did not like Ireland. She was used to a certain respect from Drury Lane audiences, and she did not care for the familiarity with which the Irish treated her. However, the amount of money she was earning made up for her discomfort.

John Philip preceded her back to London, where he, too, was now engaged at Drury Lane, and on 30 September 1783 made his début there as Hamlet. Boaden described his London début: 'On Mr Kemble's first appearance before the spectators, the general exclamation was "How very like his sister!" and there was a very striking resemblance. His person seemed to be finely formed, and his manners princely ... there struck me to be in him a peculiar and personal fitness for tragedy. The first great point of remark was that his Hamlet was decidedly original ... He had seen no great actor whom he could have copied. His style was formed by his own taste or judgement, or rather grew out of the peculiar properties of his person and his intellectual habits. He was of a solemn and deliberate temperament — his walk was always slow, and his expression of countenance contemplative — his utterance rather tardy for the most part, but always finely articulate, and in common parlance seemed to proceed rather from organization than voice.' Six days before that, brother Stephen made his London début at the rival Covent Garden playing Othello. *London Magazine* reported that Stephen 'seemed to labour earnestly but in vain'. He eventually became the manager of the Theatre Royal in Edinburgh, and is remembered mainly for his playing of Falstaff — he was fat enough not to need the stuffing. Hazlitt recorded, rather cruelly: 'We see no more reason why Mr Stephen Kemble should play Falstaff than why Louis XVIII is qualified to fill a throne because he is fat and belongs to a particular family.' Another sibling, **Elizabeth Kemble**, also joined Drury Lane in 1783. (In 1785 she married a dentist and went to America, where she achieved some success as a tragic actress.) Nepotism was commented on at the time but tolerated because of the enormous talent of Sarah and John. It was sister Julia Ann, large, clumsy and cross-eyed, who caused the trouble. Her appearance barred her from satisfying her ambition to be an actress so instead she settled for celebrity. She lectured on chastity in the dubious Temple of Hymen, published a notorious novel and tried to kill herself in

Westminster Abbey. Sarah eventually promised to give her £20 a year to stay at least 150 miles out of London.

Sarah Siddons began her 1783–84 Drury Lane season with a command performance of *Isabella*. On 30 November John Philip and Sarah made their first appearance together at Drury Lane in the domestic tragedy *The Gamester*, in which they were jointly praised. When Sarah played Constance, however, she outshone her brother's King John. Sarah introduced six new characters into her repertoire that season, including Isabella in *Measure for Measure*, the title role in *The Countess of Salisbury* and Sigismunda in *Tancred and Sigismunda*. That, together with her domestic responsibilities, left her very tired by the end of the season and rather unwell, yet her summer tour encompassed Edinburgh, Dublin, Belfast, Cork and Limerick. She was confined to bed for two weeks in Ireland with a fever and to her distress was accused, falsely, of refusing to appear for the benefit nights of two other actors. So great was her celebrity that this caused a furore in the press.

When she returned to Drury Lane on 5 October to play in *The Gamester* with her brother and William Brereton (the source of some of the accusations) the audience was so hostile and noisy that she had to make a speech from the stage, in which she said, 'The stories which have circulated against me are calumnies ...' The howling subsided; however, she never overcame her reputation for stinginess. Having known poverty too well, she was in truth very close with money even though she now earned a great deal, but she did not deserve to be called 'Lady Sarah Save-all'. In the 1784–85 season she made seventy-one appearances and introduced eight new characters, including Margaret of Anjou in *The Earl of Warwick*, and Matilda in *The Carmelite*. Her real triumph came on 2 February 1785, when she played Lady Macbeth. It was to become her greatest role.

On 8 December 1787, John Philip married Mrs Brereton, and the following month became the manager of Drury Lane; he succeeded Sheridan, who had become immersed in politics, though he remained owner of the theatre. That month, too, he had a great success playing King Lear, with Sarah as his Cordelia. He continued the season with a successful Iago, Prospero and Petruchio, but was not so successful as Macbeth or Romeo, though he triumphed as Coriolanus and Wolsey.

While continuing as manager of Drury Lane, in 1789 John Philip Kemble took over in partnership the Liverpool Theatre; on 1 October at the Lane he played Shakespeare's Henry V, which had not been seen on the London stage for twenty years. James Boaden reported: 'As a coup de théâtre, his starting up from prayer at the sound of the trumpet, in the passage where he states his attempted atonement to Richard the Second, formed one of the most spirited excitements that the stage has ever displayed.' An educated man and a scholar, more proud of his library than anything else, John Philip indulged in revising Shakespeare. *Henry V* was judged to be one of his better attempts — *The Tempest*, which followed, was not so successful.

Sarah went on strike during the 1789–90 season declaring that Sheridan, who still owned the Lane, was not paying her according to contract. The Drury Lane Theatre was by this time in a terrible state and had to be demolished. The new Theatre Royal, Drury Lane, opened on 12 March 1794, with a series of musical extravaganzas. The first dramatic presentation was on 21 April, when Sarah played Lady Macbeth and brother **Charles**, who had also left Douai determined to be an actor, played Malcolm. John Philip was Macbeth. In December he played Bertram in his own adaptation of *All's Well That Ends Well*. He was then the Duke in *Measure for Measure*, which part Boaden said Kemble played with 'a dignity, a venerable propriety and picturesque effect never surpassed'. Seeing Sarah's Isabella once more that season, Boaden said it remained 'a model of cloistered purity and energy and grace'. That was also the year when Sarah's last child, Cecilia, was born.

In 1803 John Philip and Sarah moved from Drury Lane to Covent Garden. He went as the leading tragedian, stage manager and owner of one-sixth of the total assets. She went as the great Sarah Siddons. In September John Philip opened once more as Hamlet and the *Gazetteer and New Daily Advertiser* reported: 'His recitation is evidently his great talent and here, in our mind, he has no equal. His tones are beautifully modulated, his emphasis critical and instructive, and he so accurately possesses and conveys the meaning of the Poet that it is a feast to hear him.' Sarah was struck with very bad rheumatism, and moreover Master Betty fever raged in London, so brother and sister retired from the stage until it had abated. But in the 1805–06 season Sarah appeared thirty-nine times at Covent Garden. On 3 November 1806 they had a most successful revival of *Coriolanus* with Sarah playing Volumnia.

In March 1808, while Sarah was playing a season in Edinburgh, William Siddons died in Bath and she entered a period of mourning although they had in effect been separated for years. It was not a good year. That September, after a lavish production of *Pizarro*, Covent Garden was destroyed by fire. While it was being rebuilt the company played a full season at the King's Theatre and at the Haymarket, Sarah playing over forty times. Covent Garden was rebuilt within a year, but at great expense. The following year Sarah began to think about retirement, although in the 1811–12 season she played a tremendous fifty-seven performances. But it was time to retire. Crabbe Robinson, reporting on her performance in June 1812 of *Comus*, wrote: '. . . for the first time in my life I saw Mrs Siddons without any pleasure. She was dressed most unbecomingly with a low gypsy hat and feathers hanging down one side. She looked old and I had almost said ugly — her fine features were lost in the distance. And her disadvantages of years and bulk were made as prominent as possible.' In February 1812 John had played Brutus in *Julius Caesar*. He, too, was thinking about retirement, stricken with both asthma and gout. His round of farewell performances went on for five years; on 22 June 1812 Sarah played Lady Macbeth and announced her retirement from the London stage. Petitions were organized calling for her return, and even Lord Byron tried to get her to perform for a season. She did make occasional reappearances until 1819, and thereafter continued to give private readings in her house.

John Philip Kemble died in Lausanne, Switzerland, on 26 February 1823, leaving Charles, to whom he had passed on his shares, to struggle on with Covent Garden. **Charles Kemble** had been born in 1775 and was married to Maria Theresa de Camp, who at the age of five had been a London star at the head of a troupe of child dancers. Their daughter Frances Anne, to become known as **Fanny Kemble**, was born in London, near Oxford Street, on 27 November 1809. She grew up to be intellectual and withdrawn, and longed to be a novelist. However, in an attempt to attract audiences the family decided that Fanny should go on the stage. On 5 October 1824, she made her London début at Covent Garden playing Juliet. She was so nervous that she had literally to be pushed onto the stage. A London critic reported: 'We dreamt for a while of being able to analyse her acting and to fix in our memory the finest moments of its power and grace, but her attitudes glided into each other so harmoniously that we at last gave over our enumerating how often she seemed a study to the painter's eye and a vision to the poet's heart.' In her first season Fanny scored a palpable hit with Covent Garden audiences, and rescued her father from financial ruin. Untrained as she was, it was very difficult for her to step into the great Sarah Siddons' shoes, but that first season Fanny played in her aunt's famous roles — Belvidera in *Venice Preserv'd*, Euphrasia in *The Grecian Daughter* and even as Isabella. Society fell over itself to welcome her; praise was intemperate.

Only a few kept their heads. When Charles Greville saw her in *The Gamester* he reported: 'She had a very great success — house crowded and plenty of emotion — but she does not touch me though she did more than in other parts; however she is very good and will be much better.' She began her first provincial tour in Bath and went on to Dublin in July, drawing large audiences everywhere.

Fanny Kemble opened her second Covent Garden season playing Bianca in *Fazio*. Crabbe Robinson reported: 'Fanny Kemble is certainly a superior actress — and I should think the best we have and this in spite of her small figure and insignificant face . . . In the alternation of love and jealousy [is] ample room for the display of passion and on several occasions she reminded me successfully of her illustrious aunt, Mrs Siddons.' She went on that season to play Julia in Sheridan Knowles' new play *The Hunchback* and Lady Teazle in *The School for Scandal*, though she found playing comedy very difficult. She also played Constance in *King John*. She continued to play each winter at Covent Garden with her father, and each summer they set off on extremely profitable provincial tours.

On 8 June 1831, just a month short of her seventy-sixth birthday, Sarah Siddons died. The following night Fanny Kemble played Lady Macbeth. In April 1832 her own five-act play, *Francis I*, was produced at Covent Garden. From the proceeds of the published version she launched her brother on a military career. She gave her last performance at Covent Garden on 22 June that year and on 1 August sailed with her father from Liverpool to America. Charles Kemble made his American début at the Park Theater, New York, on 17 September 1832 playing Hamlet, and Fanny made hers the following night playing Bianca in *Fazio*. The *New York Mirror* reported: 'Miss Fanny Kemble did not disappoint expectations. Of higher praise she cannot be ambitious for never was expectation raised to such a pitch . . . Her action is most easy and elegant, with more of the French than the English manner in it; and perfectly original in our eyes, accustomed as they are to something more staid and homely.' She also played Juliet to her father's Romeo.

They sailed by river boat from New York to Philadelphia, where they found gratifyingly full houses, and then returned to New York, adding *Much Ado About Nothing* to the repertoire. Baltimore followed and then Washington, DC, where they were fêted by President Andrew Jackson. In July they played in Boston, and then in Albany before returning to New York they played in *The Stranger*. All this time Fanny kept a journal, which was not always very complimentary to her American hosts and caused an uproar when it was published.

On 7 June 1834 Fanny Kemble married Pierce Butler, the son of a leading Philadelphia family, and Charles was left to return to England alone. Her first child, Sarah, was born in May 1835, but Fanny found herself discontented with America, her husband and domesticity. Finally in 1845 she returned first to her father in England, and then went to Italy where she spent a year with her sister Adelaide and Adelaide's husband.

Fanny Kemble returned to the stage in Manchester in 1846 where she played in *The Honeymoon* and was Julia in *The Hunchback*. She toured the provinces, including Liverpool and Dublin. In an amateur production of *Hernani* and *The Hunchback* at the St James's Theatre in London, Fanny played the leads. She acted at the Princess Theatre and then toured again — Bristol, Bath, Exeter, Plymouth, Glasgow, Perth and Dundee. By this time her father was devoting himself to solo play readings.

In 1848 Fanny Kemble joined Macready at the Princess Theatre in London where they played in, among other things, *Macbeth* and *Othello*. It was not an easy partnership as they had two completely different styles — hers intellectual and his physical. In March that year she gave the first of her Shakespeare readings at the Highgate Institute.

Fanny's husband filed for divorce on the grounds of desertion and she returned to America determined to prove that he had driven her out. She performed her Shakespeare reading in New York to raise money for the lengthy legal battles and was so successful at raising money that she had enough to buy a house in Lenox, Massachusetts. She was not so successful in her legal battles and her husband retained custody of the children.

In 1850 Fanny returned to England, and continued to perform her readings very successfully. Crabbe Robinson said of her Hamlet: 'She has a fine, clear voice and reads with admirable distinctness, so that at the bottom of a long room I scarcely lost a word . . . I thought her occasionally too violent and exaggerated but generally the expression was such as I could [have] sympathy with. She gave great effect to the light and comic tone of Polonius but on the contrary was somewhat bombastic as Laertes.' Fanny Kemble travelled all over Britain with her readings. Her father was by now very deaf and in need of support, and in November 1854 Charles died.

In 1856 Fanny returned to America, where her eldest daughter was old enough to be out of her father's control. They shared their summers in Lenox and in the autumn Fanny set out on her tours. In the early 1870s Fanny retired to write her reminiscences (which were first published in the *Atlantic Monthly* under the title 'Old Woman's Gossip') and become a doting grandmother — both her daughters had married. She returned to England in 1877, and the following year published *Records of a Girlhood*, which was an immediate success. She struck up an intimate friendship with Henry James and followed her first literary success with *Records of a Later Life* and two volumes of *Further Records*. Fanny then wrote a satirical farce, *The Adventures of John Timothy Homespun in Switzerland* and at the age of 80 finally wrote her first novel, *Far Away and Long Ago*.

Fanny Kemble died on 13 January 1893 and was buried near her father in Kensal Green Cemetery. The Kembles had finally passed from the theatrical scene.

MADGE KENDAL

*A*lthough in later years she resembled no one so much as the widowed Queen Victoria both in dress and in manner, Madge Kendal was the greatest comedienne of her generation. 'I defy any other actress, living or dead, to get a laugh out of some of the poor lines with which Mrs Kendal simply rocked the house,' said Mary Jerrold, an actress in the Kendal Company for more than three years. 'And what control she had! One moment she would have her audience roaring with laughter and in a flash she could have them quiet as mice.'

Margaret Shafto Robertson was born on 15 March 1849 in Grimsby, Lincolnshire, the twenty-second — and last — child of the actress and comedienne Margherita Elisabetta Marinus and her husband William Robertson, who was an actor and theatrical manager. Her eldest brother, T. W. Robertson, became a revolutionary playwright and two other siblings, E. Shafto Robertson and Fanny Robertson, went on the stage but without achieving the success of their youngest sister.

When her father's company required a child on tour Madge was available, and she made her stage début on 20 February 1854 playing Marie in *The Orphan of the Frozen Sea* at the Marylebone Theatre. At the same theatre she was the child in a number of other plays.

In 1869 she went to the Theatre Royal in Bristol, where five years earlier she had played Eva in *Uncle Tom's Cabin*. There she played in *Puss in Boots* (1860), *Cinderella* (1862) and *Little Goody Two Shoes* (1863) while being educated, mostly in music. In March 1863 she formally joined Mr Chute's companies in Bristol and Bath, which were well-esteemed theatrical training schools. There she played everything — burlesque, farce, comedy, melodrama, tragedy and pantomime. On 4 March 1863 at the opening of the Theatre Royal, Bath, she played both Alice in the farce *Marriage at Any Price* and a singing fairy in *A Midsummer Night's Dream*. She remained in Chute's company until 1865, then went to Bradford, where she played leading parts.

On 29 July 1865, still Madge Robertson, she made her grown-up London début at the Haymarket playing Ophelia to Walter Montgomery's Hamlet. She followed this with Blanche of Spain in *King John* and then in August was Desdemona to the American black actor (known as the African Roscius) Ira Aldridge's Othello. Madge continued the season at the Haymarket playing Cupid in *Ixion* and Jessica in *The Merchant of Venice*. She went to the Theatre Royal, Nottingham, with Montgomery and subsequently to Hull in 1866, where she played Anne Carew in Tom Taylor's *A Sheep in Wolf's Clothing*, Julie to Samuel Phelps' Richelieu in the play of that name, and Lady Macbeth to his Macbeth. She also appeared there as a gossamer-winged butterfly in a musical extravaganza. Madge followed Hull with starring engagements at Liverpool and Nottingham, playing Juliet in *Romeo and Juliet*, Peg Woffington in *Masks and Faces* and Pauline Deschappelles in *The Lady of Lyons*. At Drury Lane on Easter Monday 1867 Madge played the heroine Edith Fairlam in Andrew Halliday's *The Great City*, a production that delighted audiences with the introduction of a real horse and hansom cab on the stage.

In autumn 1867 she went to the Haymarket, where she joined E. A. Sothern and the other comedians in Mr Buckstone's company. There she played Georgina in *Our American Cousin*, Alice in *Brother Sam*, Ada Ingor in *David Garrick*, Blanche Dumont in *A Hero of Romance*, Marguerite in *A Wife Well Won* and Hippolyta in *She Would and She Would Not*. In that production W. H. Kendal, another member of the company,

played Don Octavio. The company went on a provincial tour, and Madge had a great success at Hull in *Passion Flowers*.

Returning to London in December 1868, at the opening production of the Gaiety Theatre on 21 December Madge Robertson played the principal female part, Florence, in *On the Cards*, an adaptation of the French *L'Escamoteur*. In 1869, also at the Gaiety, she played Lady Clara Vere de Vere in her brother T. W. Robertson's five-act play *Dreams*. She returned to the Haymarket Company for a tour, and played in *As You Like It, Twelfth Night, She Stoops to Conquer, The School for Scandal, The Rivals, The Heir-in-Law* and *The Country Girl*. At St Saviour's Church in Manchester on 7 August 1869 she married W. H. Kendal — the only other young member of the company. On the eve of their wedding Madge's father made them promise always to act together, and so they did. On their wedding night they were on stage as Rosalind and Orlando in *As You Like It*.

They stayed with the Haymarket Company until 1874. Madge said of the older actors in the company: 'The fine veterans were only too glad to give me all the assistance in their power. When I played in any of the classical parts I always had one of them to tell me that this was the way in which some of my great predecessors in the part had performed it, and so I had the advantage of knowing all the traditions of the stage.' She played Charlotte in the *The Hypocrite*, of which performance her biographer T. Edgar Pemberton said: 'I can conscientiously say that I have never seen anything so perfect on the stage. The sweet, vivacious, graceful and altogether winsome Charlotte of that evening will ever linger in the memories of those who were fortunate enough to witness the impersonation.' In October 1869 Madge Kendal created the part of Lilian Vavasour in Taylor and Dubourg's *New Men and Old Acres*. A critic at the time reported: '. . . the acting of Miss Robertson [as she was still known] who sustained the part of Lilian, might alone have sufficed to secure success for a work of far inferior merits. A young lady who talks slang, corrupted by the society of a sporting cousin, would be a dangerous part in ordinary hands, but Miss Robertson's performance in no part degenerated into anything like vulgarity. There was a neatness and finish not only in her delivery of the words, but in all her movements, including that indefinable filling up of time known to the actors as ''business'' which belongs to the very best school of comedy acting. Nor is she much less at home in the more pathetic portions of her part.'

When she played Florence Marigold opposite

her husband in *Uncle's Will* they were both praised for their handling of the witty repartee. In November 1870 she was Princess Zeolida and he was Prince Philamor in W. S. Gilbert's *The Palace of Truth*. In December 1871 they were together in Gilbert's *Pygmalion and Galatea*, in which she triumphed. They played Queen Selene and Sir Ethois in another of Gilbert's plays, *The Wicked World*, in 1873 and both triumphed in two comedies, *His Own Enemy* and *Twenty Minutes Conversation Under an Umbrella*. In 1874 Madge played Mrs Van Brugh in Gilbert's four-act prose play, *Charity*, and a contemporary critic reported the audience reaction as 'a triumph more spontaneous and overwhelming than had often been accorded an artist. The audience literally rose to greet her.' Also during that time at the Haymarket, Madge Kendal played Ellen Petworth in *Barwise's Book*, Lydia Languish in *The Rivals*, Lady Teazle in *The School for Scandal*, Rosalind in *As You Like It*, Kate Hardcastle in *She Stoops to Conquer*, Miranda in *The Busy Body*, Ada in *Faded Flowers*, Ethel in *A Little Change*, Mrs Whymper in *His Own Enemy*, Mrs Sebright in *The Overland Route*, Lady Gay Spanker in *London Assurance*, Jessie Meadows in *Single Life*, Elinor Vane in *A Madcap Prince*, and Mrs Honeyton in *A Happy Pair*.

The Haymarket Company broke up in autumn 1874 and the Kendals went out on their own on tour beginning at the Prince of Wales Theatre in Birmingham on 16 November, where for six consecutive nights they appeared in *Romeo and Juliet*, *The Lady of Lyons*, *The Hunchback*, *As You Like It*, *East Lynne*, *Uncle's Will* and *Weeds*. At the Opéra-Comique in 1875 they played Kate Hardcastle and Young Marlowe in *She Stoops to Conquer*, and went on to the Gaiety where a critic wrote of their performance of *As You Like It*: 'One side of the character of Rosalind is shown by Mrs Kendal with admirable clearness and point. So suited to her style are the bantering speeches Shakespeare has put into the mouth of Rosalind, they might almost have been written for her ... What was wanting was the underlying tenderness that more emotional artists are able to present.'

The Kendals joined John Hare at the Court Theatre in Sloane Square in 1875, where in March Madge opened in the name part of a new comedy by Charles Coghlan called *Lady Flora*. She went on to play Mrs Fitzroy in *A Nine Days' Wonder*, and in December Lady Hilda in W. S. Gilbert's fairy comedy, *Broken Hearts*. She played Susan Hartley (a part she would repeat many times) in Palgrave Simpson's adaptation of a Sardou comedy called *A Scrap of Paper*.

In September 1876 Madge Kendal and her husband moved on to the Prince of Wales Theatre in the Tottenham Court Road under the management of the Bancrofts. There Madge played Lady Ormond in *Peril*, a comedy based on Sardou but thoroughly anglicized. She went on to play Clara Douglas in *Money*, Lady Gay Spanker in *London Assurance* and Dora in *Diplomacy*. This last, based on Sardou's *Dora*, the Kendals played for twelve months, including a tour. Joseph Knight reported: 'Mr Kendal revealed as Captain Beaucere, the hero, an amount of force that he had not previously displayed and carried off the honours of the evening.' Although Madge maintained throughout her life that her husband was the better actor, pointing out that he could blanch at will, it was usually Madge who carried away the honours.

They returned to the Court Theatre where they revived *A Scrap of Paper* in January 1879. In February she played the Countess d'Autreval in her brother's adaptation from the French, *The Ladies' Battle*, and in April played Kate Greville in *The Queen's Shilling*, an adaptation of *Un Fils de famille*.

In 1879 W. H. Kendal went into partnership with John Hare at the St James's Theatre, the most luxurious in London at the time. They opened in October with *The Queen's Shilling*. On 18 December they introduced a play-poem, *The Falcon*, by Alfred Tennyson, in which Madge played Lady Giocanna and her husband was Count Alberaghi. She then played Mrs Sternhold while he took the part of John Mildmay in Tom Taylor's *Still Waters Run Deep*. They revived *The Ladies' Battle* with a farce called *A Regular Fix* in which it was said that W. K. distinguished himself as Sir Hugh de Brass. They played in *William and Susan*, a modernized version of *Black-Eyed Susan*. An adaptation of *Le Roman d'un jeune homme pauvre*, *Good Fortune*, in which Madge played Isobel Ransome, was not a success so they hurried on with Pinero's *The Money Spinner*, in which Madge played Millicent Boycott, an unsuccessful card sharp. This play had only two acts so they finished the evening with *A Sheep in Wolf's Clothing* in which Madge played Anne Carew. The next presentation was *The Lady of Lyons* followed by a controversial adaptation of the French *Corolie*. Madge then played Mrs Pinchbeck in *Home* and Mrs Frank Preston in yet another French adaptation, *The Cape Mail*. In 1881 Pinero's *The Squire*, in which Madge played Kate Verity, was the management's greatest achievement to date, though it was curiously like Hardy's *Far From the Madding Crowd*. They followed it with *Impulse*, another French adaptation in which the Kendals took the relatively minor roles of Captain Crichton and Mrs Beresford. Madge played Nora Desmond in *Young Folks' Ways* and then had a triumph as Clair de Beaupre in Pinero's *The Iron Master*, a version of *Le Maître de forges*. Her husband, always to be found somewhere in the plays, was Philippe Derblay this time. In January 1885 they mounted a sumptuous revival of *As You Like It*. Madge Kendal played Lilian Selkirk in *The Castaways* and then Agnes Roydant in Pinero's *Mayfair*, which was adapted from Sardou's *La Maison neuve*. This play was judged to be 'too spicy for English palates', so they pressed on with a revival of *Impulse*. Next, another French play, *Antoinette Rigaud*, was at the St James's, in which Madge played the name part, prompting a critic to write: 'Indiscreet gentlemen are always coming to ladies' bedrooms at the St James's Theatre. Mrs Kendal is continually attacked in this unseemly fashion. Yesterday in *Mayfair*, today in *Antoinette Rigaud.*'

In May 1886 the company presented Grundy and Edwards' adaptation in five acts of the French *Martyre*, which they called *The Wife's Sacrifice*. A critic reported: 'Mrs Kendal's interpretation of the Countess was remarkably fine. In speaking of Mrs Kendal's performance I use the word interpretation because she is one of the few actresses who aim at giving a complete, consistent rendering of character. She is for the time being the woman she represents. She loses herself entirely in her part, and in this respect she might with advantage be imitated by her younger sisters in the theatrical profession. Her interpretation of the life of this unhappy woman was rich with thought, illuminated by intelligence and rendered unusually interesting by its completeness. It was not merely striking here and there, but it was all acting should accomplish, a perfectly consistent rendering of character.' She next played Mrs Spencer Jermyn in Pinero's *The Hobby Horse*.

In February 1887 the Kendals gave a command performance of the two-act comedy by W. S. Gilbert, *Sweethearts*, for Queen Victoria at Osborne House, and Madge was rewarded with a brooch shaped like the royal crown made of diamonds, sapphires and rubies. In March 1887 they staged a revival of Tom Taylor's historical drama *Lady Clancarty*, in which Madge played the title role. She then played Lady Amyot in a revival of George W. Lovell's *The Wife's Secret*, but the play was deemed rather old-fashioned. After a season of revivals of their greatest successes the partnership between Hare and Kendal was dissolved, and the Kendals left the St James's Theatre on a provincial tour, returning to London to the

Court Theatre in March 1889 where Madge played Lady Vivash in *The Weaker Sex* and in May was Kate Desmond in *A White Lie*. That autumn they set out on their first American tour, making their début at the Fifth Avenue Theater in New York with *A Scrap of Paper*, on 7 October 1889. The New York *Dramatic Mirror* reported: 'Everybody attended the American début of Mr and Mrs Kendal ... that is to say everybody that could get seats or standing room ... If Mr Kendal's welcome was decidedly cordial, Mrs Kendal's was distinctly enthusiastic. So long-continued was the applause with which she was greeted that it became almost disconcerting to the fair, fine-looking actress, who stood, smiling and bowing before the first American audience she had ever faced. The reports of Mrs Kendal's skill as a comedienne were not exaggerated. Her art is as fine as old point lace, and yet it is laid upon a temperament so genuinely sympathetic and so pliant and transitional that there is no sign of effort, no direct exhibition of method in anything she does. Originality marks much of her work. It does not strike one unpleasantly, as departures from convention frequently do, because it is dominated by taste, feeling, a keen appreciation of the relations of cause and effect and that feminine, subtle instinct, which means scope of action within the limits of the boundary lines of artistic propriety. We have never before seen such a brilliant and clever Susan as Mrs Kendal presents. Refined and natural, in every aspect it perfectly realizes the creation of the dramatist ...' The Kendals also presented New York with *The Iron Master*, of which J. Ranken Towse wrote: 'Mrs Kendal comprehended the part of the heroine perfectly and played it with a most sympathetic sincerity. In the trying scene in which her worthless lover's perfidy is explained to her with every refinement of feminine malice, she portrayed the struggle between wounded love and natural pride with rare perception, truthfulness, and histrionic skill. There was poignant anguish in every motion of her swaying figure and in the lines of her tortured face and her resolute rally from a threatened faint was an eloquent illustration of high moral courage vanquishing physical weakness ...'

They returned to London briefly and then set off on a second and more extensive American tour, increasing their repertoire which now included *The Squire*, in which Madge played the heroine. Of this Towse said: 'Her impersonation was exceptional on account of its physical beauty, its refinement of manner — a manifestation not too common among aristocratic stage heroines — its elaborate artistic finish, and its exquisite feeling ... her acting was not supremely eloquent but it was very human, touching and skilful... She also played Lady Marsden in *All for Her*, Helen Rutherford in *The Senator's Wife*, Violet Huntley in *Marriage* and Katherine Vail in *Prince Karatoff*.

In October 1891 the Kendals set off on what they billed their third and last American tour. It lasted until May 1892 and in all they visited thirty-five cities. They reappeared on the London stage at the Avenue Theatre in January 1893, where they gave the audiences *A White Lie*, *The Iron Master* and *Prince Karatoff* — now called *A Silver Shell* — as well as *A Scrap of Paper*.

During a short provincial tour in 1893, Madge Kendal played *The Second Mrs Tanqueray* for the first time, in Leicester. William Archer reported: 'What of Mrs Kendal's reading of the part of Paula? It is the work of an accomplished comedienne who has at her command all the resources of her art. Comparisons are odious, and I do not propose to compare Mrs Kendal with Mrs Patrick Campbell except on one point. She certainly puts a greater depth of feeling into the later acts, and on the whole (I should say) she does rightly.' They then took Paula off to America, where the voice of 'public morality' screamed in offended virtue. One critic reported: '. . . Mrs Kendal has won and holds her position as the most popular actress on the English-speaking stage because she has always been not only a good actress, but a good woman . . . Why should she pain her admirers, and risk her popularity after all these good years, by devoting her talents to the exemplification of how an abandoned woman would behave under certain distasteful circumstances?' And the New York *Dramatic Mirror* said: 'Mrs Kendal's acting as Paula does not demand careful analysis. It is a crude, noisy, and vulgar performance. The actress seems to have done her utmost to emphasize the adventuress' most disagreeable characteristics. She makes the woman unspeakably coarse in bearing, voice and gesture. In no sense is it an artistic personation, or one that does credit to Mrs Kendal's reputation as a painstaking actress. Of subtlety and finesse it has none, either in intention or in execution . . .' In spite of all this, she played to packed houses. During the Kendals' fifth tour of America, which lasted from September 1894 until May 1895 and during which they visited over forty cities, they played in *The Second Mrs Tanqueray*, *Lady Clancarty*, *Still Waters Run Deep*, *A Scrap of Paper*, *All for Her* and *The Iron Master*.

Madge Kendal appeared back in London at the Garrick Theatre in June 1896 playing Mrs Armitage in *The Greatest of These*. George Bernard Shaw reported: 'Mrs Kendal, forgetting that London playgoers have been starved for years

in the matter of acting, inconsiderately gave them more in the first ten minutes than they have had in the last five years, with the result that the poor wretches became hysterical and vented their applause in sobs and shrieks.'

The Kendals toured the provinces for two years, Madge playing Sara Leaster in *A Flash in the Pan*, Dorothy Blossom in *The Elder Miss Blossom* and Mrs Grantham in *Not Wisely But Too Well*. They brought *The Elder Miss Blossom* to London to the St James's Theatre for a brief season in September 1898. A critic reported: 'Unluckily for all who love genuine art *Miss Blossom* has to retire. She has been the noblest thing of the dramatic year, the one emphatic proof that Mrs Kendal is the greatest actress we possess.' Soon, the Kendals were back on tour: Madge played Margaret Hulestone in *The Poverty of Riches*, Mildred Archerson in *The Likeness of the Night*, and the Duchess of Cluny in *The Secret Orchard*; she reappeared at the St James's in London in September 1901 again playing in *Miss Blossom* and *The Likeness of the Night*, before setting off on tour once more. This time she played Mrs Trecarrel in *St Martin's Summer* and Mrs Hamilton in *Conscience* (subsequently retitled *Mrs Hamilton's Silence*).

At His Majesty's Theatre in June 1902 she played Mistress Ford in *The Merry Wives of Windsor* with Beerbohm Tree and Ellen Terry. On the Kendals' 1903 tour of the provinces, Madge played Anne McLeod in *One People* and came to London in that role to the Coronet in May. After a tour playing Marjorie Lyall in *Dick Hope* she performed it at the Coronet in December 1903. The Kendals met with full houses and enthusiastic audiences all over the country. 'I am always called a lucky woman,' Madge wrote; 'but I don't think it's all luck. I am vain enough to think that some of it is hard work — very hard work — constant and everlasting work. You must never cease to study. As you get older, you must fill up the wrinkles with intelligence.'

In 1904 she toured as Lady Audrey Whitby in *The Housekeeper* and the following year was Nora in *The Bird at the Neck*. She played in *The Housekeeper* and *Dick Hope* at the St James's in autumn 1905. In 1906 she was on the road as Mrs Hyacinth in *A Tight Corner* and in 1907 as Judith Carlusen in *The Melcombe Marriage*. In April of that year she played *A Tight Corner* in London at the Coronet and then set out as Mrs Stannas and Lady Marrable in *The Other Side*. In 1908 she was Constance Livingstone in *The Whirlpool* and Madame Armières in *The House of Clay*, which she played in London at the Coronet in October of that year.

Then, with no fuss, the Kendals retired from the stage. 'Like the Arab,' she said, 'we folded our tents and stole away.' They had had four children, with whom they were not on the best of terms; Madge attributed her husband's death on 6 November 1917 to a broken heart caused by the divorce of his youngest daughter, an actress.

Madge Kendal was awarded the DBE in 1926, and the following year received the Grand Cross of the Order. She died in Hertfordshire on 14 September 1935, aged 87.

Bert
Lahr

'*B*ert Lahr should be preserved like a fine old wine, or in one, it doesn't matter which,' wrote Walter Kerr in *Life* magazine. 'As the years go along his tang gets headier, his lifted pinky daintier, his moose call to the great beyond gets mellower and mellower and, furthermore, he is beginning to carbonate.'

The great comic was born Irving Lahreim in New York City on 13 August 1895. His father Jacob was an upholsterer but there was no money to spare and Bert resented it. As a child he enjoyed reading and penmanship as well as the theatre, but hated school. His first appearance on stage, however, was in school at the age of 14 when in a 'kid act' he mimicked the grown-ups and their strange accents. His performance moved one of his teachers to exclaim: 'If you don't go on the stage, you'll probably go to jail.' When told to repeat the eighth grade he left school and got a job as a tailor's delivery boy. Within six months he had been fired from fourteen jobs. With a group of school friends he auditioned unsuccessfully at Loew's 145th Street Theatre. 'My idols,' he said later, 'were the Dutch comedians Solly Ward and Sam Bernard, because I was born in a German neighborhood and knew the accents.'

In 1910 he joined the professional group, The Seven Frolics, and changed his name to Bert Lahr. The next five years were spent in and out of work in a thriving industry. He toured during this time with *College Days* and *Garden Belles*. In September 1917 he entered burlesque and regular employment on the Columbia touring circuit, or the Wheel as it was known, in the second comedy slot in *The Best Show in Town*. He was constantly improving his technique and listening for the audience to tell him what was funny. In New York, 'Clipper' reported that he performed 'in a most pleasing and different way than is usually seen ... He is a newcomer to burlesque and a welcome one.' There were packed houses for the forty-week tour and Lahr was signed to a three-year contract, two shows a day, seven days a week. He nearly

regularized his relationship with fellow burlesque performer, Mercedes La Fay (real name Delpino), when they declared themselves married.

Lahr served a nine-month tour of duty with the Naval Reserve in 1919 and then performed in the burlesque *Folly Town* on Broadway for two months. He was again second comedian but was soon promoted to first comedian, and starred in *Roseland Girls* for the 1920–21 season. He also took on the role of general manager during the tour. It was during this run that he performed his famous 'Lord Onion' sketch and embarked upon a programme of self-improvement.

His greatest burlesque success came with *Keep Smiling* in the 1921–22 season. *Variety* reported: 'Mr Lahr has a real sense of travesty — something which can hardly be said of more than one burlesque comic. He knows how to handle the ins and outs of dialogue and situation perfectly. He's clean, inclined to be a bit boisterous at times, and works like a Trojan always, but he never gives the appearance of straining for effect in the slightest degree. With all the facility of expression of the experienced burlesquer at his command, Lahr combines this practised touch with the life and spirit that springs from the ground up.'

In 1922 he went onto the vaudeville circuit, and for four years he and Mercedes performed the same act — with different titles. They did not present the sophistication that vaudeville audiences were used to. In Los Angeles the local critic reported: 'Comedy of a slightly lower type is offered by Lahr and Mercedes ... The act is designed to appeal to the masses, but the middle classes can find plenty of things to be amused at ...' In Cincinnati a critic reported: 'Lahr as a comedy cop proves himself one of the most amusing comedians in vaudeville.' Lahr and Mercedes, together twenty-four hours a day, on stage and off, had an often stormy relationship, but by 1925 they were playing that Mecca of vaudeville, the Palace in New York, and packing the house.

The following year they toured in *Orpheum Time* coast-to-coast. Lahr saw his name in lights on Broadway for the first time in 1927 in *Harry Delmar's Revels*. Unfortunately the revue lasted only sixteen weeks. The exposure did, however, net him a five-year musical comedy contract, and the following year he was playing a noisy, punch-drunk prize fighter in De Sylva, Brown and Henderson's *Hold Everything*. The *New York Times* reported: 'As a pug who concludes his bouts more frequently on the nose than on the feet, Lahr supplies most of the uproarious comedy in this carnival ... he dances, grimaces, rolls his eyes and sings with that sort of broad abandon that is instantaneously appreciated in the abdomen.' The show ran at the Broadhurst Theater for nearly two years. After her mother's death, Mercedes had gradually begun to deteriorate mentally and, now pregnant, was becoming even more disturbed. They finally married in August 1929; their son Herbert was born the same year, and Lahr toured in *Hold Everything*. In 1930 Lahr was back on Broadway in *Flying High*, in which he played a pilot in a cross-country airmail race. He filmed it for MGM in 1931.

Flo Ziegfeld's last extravaganza was the ill-conceived *Hot-Cha!* in which Lahr starred in 1932 — it ran only fifteen weeks. By this time Bert Lahr had made a name for himself on radio. In *George White's Music Hall Varieties*, in 1933, Lahr attempted satire for the first time, and by 1934 in *Life Begins at 8.40* he was playing more sophisticated material. Brooks Atkinson was not convinced it was a wholly good idea. 'He is a low comedian,' Atkinson wrote in the *New York Times*. 'Most of the material in *Life Begins at 8.40* is too subtle in manner to release his native exuberance. Having no more than one stop to his instrument of comedy, he does remarkably well with what he has.' John Mason Brown, however, thought it was fine: 'Mr Lahr proves conclusively he is not the single-tracked zany he once seemed fated to be ... [he] succeeds in adding much to the pleasures of a pleasant evening by being, as we like to have him be, a Lahr unto himself.'

George White's Scandals of 1936 ran only 110 performances. He next appeared with Bea Lillie in *The Show Is On*, conceived, staged and designed by Vincente Minnelli in 1936. Brooks Atkinson noted in a wholly ecstatic review: 'As for Mr Lahr, they have given him the uproarious things that he can do with cartoon gusto — singing a burlesque banality in a woodsman's shirt, ruining the mannerisms of swing-music in a lethal travesty, wooing passionately in a full dress suit. None of Mr Lahr's stretch-mouthed talents have been wasted ...'

In 1938 Bert Lahr went to Hollywood, and made five movies that first year. It was in 1939, however, that he played the Cowardly Lion in *The Wizard of Oz*, a part for which he will always be remembered. Surprisingly after this great success, MGM dropped his contract and he returned to New York to star in *Du Barry Was a Lady* with Betty Grable and Ethel Merman.

Lahr made a string of forgettable B movies and joined in the money-raising effort for the war, but in 1944 he returned East to star in *Seven Lively Arts*, which was produced by Billy Rose to reopen his newly acquired Ziegfeld Theater. The score was by Cole Porter, sketches by Kaufman and Hart, and as well as Lahr it starred Bea Lillie, Alicia Markova and Benny Goodman. Rose called it 'the last word in escapism, a super Christmas tree, a grab-bag of fun, anything you want to call it', and spent $1,350,000 on the production. However, the audiences called it outdated and it closed after 183 performances. Lahr spent the next year touring with the Invisible Rabbit in *Harvey*.

On Christmas Eve 1946 Lahr was back on Broadway in a show called *Burlesque*. His son, John, the critic, writing in the 1970s said that this was the first time Lahr had starred in a show that reflected only his taste. He took Sid Caesar's vehicle, *Make Mine Manhattan*, on the road in 1948 and then made a film for Warner Brothers. In 1951 Bert Lahr starred in Broadway's last big-time revue. Conceived and directed by Abe Burrows, it was called *Two on the Aisle* and lasted for 267 performances.

After making a few films, Lahr returned to the stage in 1956 playing Estragon in Beckett's *Waiting for Godot*. With Tom Ewell he opened at the Coconut Grove Playhouse in Miami. They were supposed to play Washington, Boston and Philadelphia before the Music Box in New York, but the producer lost faith in the play and it was dropped. However, a new production with Lahr and E. G. Marshall arrived at the John Golden Theater in New York in April 1956, and Brooks Atkinson reported: 'Bert Lahr has never given a performance as glorious as his tatterdemalion hobo who seems to stand for all the stumbling, bewildered people on earth who go on living without knowing why ... Mr Lahr is an actor in the pantomime tradition who has a thousand ways to move and a hundred ways to grimace in order to make the story interesting and theatrical and touching too ...' This enigma by Beckett was Lahr's favourite part. The production established Beckett in America as an important dramatist even though the play ran for only ten weeks. Richard Watts wrote in the *New York Post*: 'Mr Lahr, in addition to being enormously funny and touching in the role, somehow managed to seem a kind of liaison between the narrative and the audience, a sort of spiritual interpreter whose warmth and humanity extended across the footlights and caught up every spectator in a shared experience.' And the review of which Lahr remained most proud came from Kenneth Tynan, who said: 'Bert Lahr, no less, the cowardly lion of *The Wizard of Oz*, played the dumber of Samuel Beckett's two timeless hoboes, and by his playing bridged, for the first time that I can remember, the irrational abyss that yawns between the world of red noses and the world of blue stockings.'

For television that year, Lahr starred in *Androcles and the Lion* and *The School for Wives*, and he returned to Broadway in 1957 playing Boniface in Feydeau's *Hotel Paradiso*, with Angela Lansbury making her first stage appearance. Harold Clurman reported on the old French farce for the *Nation:* 'The New York production is louder, faster, closer to burlesque. The changes ... help our audience which can more readily accept departures from realism when they are unmistakable.' In all, the reviews were good, yet the show soon closed, and Lahr did Gore Vidal's *A Visit to a Small Planet* in summer stock.

In 1959 revue was tried once more on Broadway. An impressive cast was assembled: as well as Lahr, Nancy Walker, Dick Van Dyke and Shelley Berman starred in *The Girls Against the Boys*, but it only lasted two weeks. Lahr went off

on tour with Ustinov's *Romanoff and Juliet.* The following summer he did a repertory tour with the American Shakespeare Festival playing Bottom in *A Midsummer Night's Dream* and Autolycus in *The Winter's Tale.* He received a Best Shakespearian Actor of the Year Award for his portrayal of Bottom.

In 1962 in *The Beauty Part* by S. J. Perelman, Lahr played five parts, ranging from a lady editor to a theatrical agent, but the show died on Broadway. Before the Perelman he had starred in *Foxy*, a musical adaptation of Ben Jonson's *Volpone*, which began in the Yukon; in February 1964 *Foxy* opened at the Ziegfeld Theater on Broadway. Richard Gilman found the musical 'atrocious', the adaptation 'subcretinous', and the songs 'unbelievably dreary', but added: 'When all that is mercifully dispensed with and Lahr stands forth in the circle of his own being, we can begin to live again and better.' *Foxy* closed after eighty-five performances. but Bert Lahr received the Tony for the Best Musical Star Actor. That year he also played in *The Fantasticks* for television's Hallmark Hall of Fame.

In 1966 he played Pristhetairos in Aristophanes' *The Birds* at the Ypsilanti Greek Theater Festival in Michigan. It was a strange exercise which the *Times* of London said offered 'the spectacle of Lahr in spirited but unequal combat with literature'.

Bert Lahr was making a film, *The Night They Raided Minsky's*, when he collapsed with suspected pneumonia; it was in fact cancer. He died two weeks later, on 4 December 1967.

LILLIE LANGTRY

*E*milie Charlotte Le Breton was born on 13 October 1853 on the Isle of Jersey, where her father was a conservative Anglican clergyman. There were already five boys in the family when little Emilie arrived and a sixth followed her birth; always a tomboy, she managed to hold her own with them while growing up. She was educated at home by a series of tutors, and by the age of 15 was astonishingly beautiful and also very well aware of it.

At 16 she made her first trip to London, where she found herself out of her depth in society and horrified by her own lack of sophistication. She returned to Jersey and began studying in earnest — particularly Shakespeare and Ben Jonson.

In 1874 a large yacht came into the harbour at Jersey. The owner was Edward Langtry, a friend of

one of her brothers and five years older than she was. She fell in love with the yacht and married Mr Langtry, on 9 March 1874. A year later they moved to London. There the cult of the Professional Beauties was at its height. These were lovely married ladies who dressed well. They were encouraged by the new photographers, who dispensed their pictures eagerly. After a dull year Lillie was 'discovered', and had soon become the latest Professional Beauty, so the invitations flooded in and she accepted them all. Millais painted her with her native flower and she became known as the Jersey Lily. In that first year of her celebrity eleven oil portraits of her were painted and she developed a long and lasting friendship with Oscar Wilde; as her fame grew, so the marriage disintegrated. Lillie became an immediate fashion setter (and remained so for fifty years). She soon became the mistress of the Prince of Wales and during her time with him she acquired a spectacular jewellery collection. She also became pregnant. Because of her condition she retired to Jersey, having been *de facto* separated from her husband for some time. Her daughter Jeanne was born in March or April 1881 and kept a secret.

Now Lillie needed to earn money for herself and the child, whom she left in Jersey with a governess. She decided to become an actress. Through Oscar Wilde she met Henrietta Hodson Labouchire, an actress who taught diction, movement and technique. Lillie studied hard and made her début on 19 November 1881 at the Twickenham Town Hall in a charity performance where she did a one-act play, *A Fair Encounter.* Encouraged by the reaction of her artist friends she determined that she would succeed as a professional actress. Henrietta, as well as being her teacher, acted as her manager.

On 15 December 1881 Lillie played Kate Hardcastle in *She Stoops to Conquer* at the Theatre Royal, Haymarket. Again it was a charity performance. The *Times* reported: 'Mrs Langtry was not only lovely which we expected, but surprised us by displaying a potential as an actress.' The *Pall Mall Gazette* said: 'The standing of Ellen Terry has not been threatened nor will it be, but Mrs Langtry will become an expert in the art of playing comedy.'

Lillie got a small part in Tom Robertson's *Ours*, which opened at the Haymarket on 19 January 1882, and she became a professional. She then repeated the role of Kate Hardcastle. On a provincial tour she played *She Stoops to Conquer*, *Ours*, *As You Like It* and *An Unequal Match.* She opened in Manchester, where she took twenty-three curtain calls, and the whole tour was completely sold out. Then, breaking with tradition, and completely damning herself in the eyes of Society, she became the first woman to endorse a commercial product. It was Pears Soap.

After a trial season of *As You Like It*, *An Unequal Match* and *The Honeymoon* at the Imperial Theatre in London and an extravagant farewell party organized by the Prince of Wales, on 14 October 1883 Lillie Langtry, armed with an advantageous contract from an American producer, sailed for the United States. She was greeted in New York by theatrical managers, thirty newspaper reporters, a brass band and Oscar Wilde. Commenting on this arrival and New York's first glimpse of the lady, the *New York Times* wrote: 'One may see a hundred as pretty on Fifth Avenue at any time, but if they could carry themselves with the ease, grace and self-possession of Mrs Langtry,

they would be envied. She was asked all sorts of questions, sensible, idiotic, impertinent and irrelevant, and good naturedly answered them all. She does not disappoint those who have been singing her praises.' So great was the public demand to see her that the tickets for the first night were auctioned, and the box office takings broke all records. She made her début on 30 October at Wallack's Theater playing Hester Grazebrook in *An Unequal Match.* William Winter wrote in the *New York Tribune:* 'The crudities of her performance were obvious last night, although I may not be regarded as a gentleman for telling the truth. However, her freshness, charm and promise are equally great and it is to be hoped that she will make progress in her elected profession. If she does, she will be hailed as an actress with the enthusiasm that now trumpets her appearance as a great beauty.'

That first season in New York Lillie met and captivated the 22-year-old millionaire Frederick Gebhard Jun. The critics did not like her performance in *As You Like It*, but the scandal that erupted over her relationship with Gebhard assured increased box office takings. Lillie also became her own manager that season, having had a row with Henrietta.

In January 1883 Lillie Langtry set out on a United States tour in a private railroad car (obtained by Diamond Jim Brady), with Gebhard in tow. She opened at the Globe Theater in Boston where the critics damned her performance, calling her amateur and shallow. However, the two-week engagement there was completely sold out, due partly to the furore caused by the publicity over her travelling arrangements. The tour took her through Philadelphia, Chicago, St Louis, New Orleans, Memphis and Milwaukee; she was earning an unprecedented $6000 a week.

In April at the Fifth Avenue Theater in New York she opened in W. S. Gilbert's *Pygmalion and Galatea*, and alternating it with *She Stoops to Conquer* she played six weeks there before touring until June. She then returned to England, where Langtry still refused to give her a divorce.

On 1 July 1883 she went to Paris to study drama with Joseph Regnier — from eight in the morning till late into the night for three months. Sarah Bernhardt and Benoit Coquelin were so impressed with her endeavour and perseverance that they worked with her for a few weeks. In October she went back to America, where she opened in New York with *The Highest Bidder* and played there until January 1884. Then she began a tour which lasted until late June. In August she returned to England. There, after a holiday, she opened a season at the Prince of Wales

Theatre in Coventry Street in January 1885, playing in repertory *Princess George*, *The School for Scandal* and Sardou's *Peril*, translated by Clemence Scott. The *Daily Telegraph* reported: 'She proves herself an actress of genuine merit, even though her range may be limited.' She next set off on a completely sold out provincial tour which included York, Liverpool and Edinburgh.

Then, in February 1886, she went with Fred Gebhard on a continental holiday, though she required a bodyguard to protect her from her fans. For three months the couple were received everywhere by royalty. In the autumn they returned to America, where Fred gave her a town house in New York; she played her London repertoire from September to March 1887, and then toured coast-to-coast in her private railroad car.

In order to obtain a divorce in America she became a United States citizen in July 1887. In the autumn she returned to New York to play in *As in a Looking Glass* with Maurice Barrymore and then they took it on tour. Her earnings were consistently high, she invested her money wisely, and 1887 she was one of the world's most independently wealthy women.

Lillie now decided the moment for attempting the classics had come. She hired Charles T. Coghlan to direct and play Macbeth to her Lady Macbeth. She also poured a small fortune into the production. William Winter reported on the results: 'She was admirable and rose to greatness; she was grand and exquisite.' *Macbeth* ran four months on Broadway and then toured. She premièred *Esther Sandraz* by Sidney Grundy in Chicago. That year when she returned to London she found that Oscar Wilde had written a play specially for her. It was *Lady Windermere's Fan*, but she declined to play it, declaring herself far too young for the part. She rented the St James's Theatre, and after recovering from measles followed by influenza (when she was said to be at death's door), she opened as Rosalind in *As You Like It* in mid-November 1889. The *Times* was impressed: 'Mrs Langtry is a bewitching Rosalind. The improvement in her acting is astounding, and must be seen to be appreciated.' The theatre was sold out for a full four months.

In April 1890 Lillie Langtry opened at the Prince's Theatre with Charles Coghlan in *Antony and Cleopatra*. It was a lavish production, and it was said that she fully deserved her fourteen curtain calls. The *Daily Telegraph* called her 'the finest Cleopatra of our time'. The production closed just a few days before Christmas, having become one of her greatest successes.

At the Criterion Theatre in May 1892 Lillie played a bad woman with a heart of gold in *The Fringe of Society*, which sold out for eight weeks. That September she rented the Haymarket and produced the comedy melodrama, *The Queen of Manoa*.

After taking a year's holiday, Lillie returned to the Comedy Theatre in March 1894 in *The Social Butterfly*, and in the late summer went to the United States for a sixteen-week tour, followed by five weeks in New York in *Esther Sandraz* and *Peril*. She then opened in New York at Palmer's Theater, in Clyde Fitch's *Gossip* in March 1895. The critics found her overdressed, one reporting: 'Mrs Langtry's brilliant company of diamonds, sapphires and the largest ruby in captivity is ably supported by Mrs Langtry and several other living actors.' The New York *Dramatic Mirror* said: 'Mrs Langtry was seen at her best in the light comedy scenes. She frequently delivered her lines with sparkling humor. She was not seen to advantage, however, in scenes requiring any great degree of dramatic force or depth of emotion. Still, it is only fair to say that if she did not thrill the audience in the strong dramatic climax of the second act, and in other stirring episodes of the play, she at least acquitted herself with artistic credit, and, in some instances, was even moderately effective.'

In autumn 1895 she brought *Gossip* to London's Comedy Theatre. The critics hated it but she played to full houses through May 1896, and then toured the provinces equally successfully for two months. Her divorce and the existence of her child finally became public knowledge and Lillie disappeared from the stage for a while. On the day that she became the first woman whose horse won the Cesarewitch and the first woman to enter the Jockey Club, her husband died in an insane asylum. There was nothing she could have done about him — she had been supporting him for years — but it did not help her image.

In 1898, with a private fortune estimated at more than two million dollars and aged 45, Lillie Langtry formally retired from the stage. The following year she married Hugo de Bathe, the heir to a baronetcy, who was not well off and was nineteen years her junior. She kept the marriage a secret, but when she returned to the stage, to the Haymarket in autumn 1899, somehow the secret of the marriage was revealed and the entire run of Sidney Grundy's *The Degenerates* was sold out before the opening night. Hugo went off to the war in South Africa, and in January 1900 Lillie went to the United States to play *The Degenerates* for eighteen weeks in New York at the Garden Theater. The *New York Herald* reported: 'Every seat in the house was occupied, from orchestra rail to back bench of the gallery ... Mrs Langtry's entry on the scene was marked by long continued applause. It was quickly seen that she had not lost a detail of her beauty or personal charm during her long absence. She was in every way the Mrs Langtry of old, as handsome as ever, as distinguished in bearing — the same wonderfully engaging eyes and smile — as when she had said "au revoir" to New York a few seasons ago. As an actress she has improved since she was last here. She acts with the technique of theatric art more completely at her command, acts with an assurance that added experience has brought, a confidence, an ease of effort and a consequent increase of effect that stamps her in all ways as one who has steadily advanced ...'

She then went on tour. In Philadelphia both she and the play were condemned. The play was banned in Pittsburgh and Detroit, but sold out in Boston, Buffalo, Louisville, St Louis, Memphis, Nashville and Chicago. She returned to England to tour the provinces and proudly opened St Helier's new theatre.

Lillie Langtry next leased the huge Imperial Theatre in London and at great expense installed electricity and completely redecorated it. She had no hope of getting her money back. The theatre was successfully reopened in October 1902 with *Crossways*, for which she was billed as co-author with J. Hartley Manners. She then went on a provincial tour. On 9 December she gave a Command Performance at the Imperial, the proceeds of which went to Queen Alexandra's Charity. The next day she sailed once more for the United States and played to packed houses and respectable reviews in New York. She toured coast to coast in her new private railroad car and dined at the White House with President Theodore Roosevelt. During the tour, under pressure from the author she planned a single performance in Providence, Rhode Island, of a newly commissioned play, *Mrs Deering's Divorce*, by Percy Fandall. She had no confidence in the play and was only doing it, and half-heartedly at that, to fulfil a contractual obligation. She thought in Rhode Island no one would notice. She was amazed and delighted by the response from both critics and audiences, and quickly added it to her repertoire.

In 1903 she returned to the United States, to New York, and then undertook another marathon coast-to-coast tour with *Mrs Deering's Divorce*. The *New York Times* reported: 'Mrs Langtry has made a career of shocking the American theatre-going public, and this time she goes too far beyond the bounds of good taste by unnecessarily removing her clothes on stage. She cannot be faulted for wanting to demonstrate that her figure

would be the envy of a woman of thirty, but one expects a greater sense of propriety when an actress of Mrs Langtry's stature steps on stage.' Although she was completely covered by a full-length slip, Lillie knew she would cause a sensation when she removed her gown and then put on a dressing wrap in full view of the audience. She was as usual right, and it was house-full signs every night and a furore in the press coast-to-coast. She extended the tour to Canada.

At the age of 51, and now a grandmother, Lillie embarked on a South African tour which included *As You Like It*. The tour lasted a year from spring 1905 to 1906. That summer she returned home and had an excellent racing season. She then commissioned a twenty-minute skit and embarked on the vaudeville circuit, where there was a lot of money to be made. She entered vaudeville with a melodrama, *Between the Daytime and the Night*, in which she played the unfaithful wife who is shot by her husband, and has a great dying speech. Her first vaudeville appearance was at the Fifth Avenue Hotel on 1 October 1906. The nine months in vaudeville, although highly profitable, exhausted her and she returned to England where she spent the summer racing; the autumn and winter found her in Monaco, losing heavily at the Casino. Her luck returned in February, however: when playing roulette she became the woman who broke the bank at Monte Carlo.

In April 1908 at the Haymarket, Lillie opened in a new Sidney Grundy play, *A Fearful Joy*, but times had changed and it ran only three months. She then wrote a novel called *All at Sea* under the name, Lillie de Bathe.

Lillie spent 1909 and early 1910 playing British vaudeville in a condensation of *The Degenerates* called *The Right Sort*. In May 1910 King Edward VII died and she went into seclusion for the summer, sailing to the United States in the autumn to pick up the vaudeville circuit there. She continued thus for three years in vaudeville in Britain and America, spending her summers racing.

In April 1913 she made a film, *His Neighbor's Wife*, for Adolph Zukor's Famous Players Company in New York. Lillie spent the first year of the First World War at Drury Lane, playing in Sidney Grundy's *Mrs Thompson*. The following year she performed the play in New York. She gave over her entire salary for the endeavour to the Red Cross. Despite the danger, Lillie criss-crossed the Atlantic continually during the war and organized many benefits. In 1917 she wrote an autobiography for Hearst's newspapers and a lot of money, but managed to reveal absolutely nothing. She played the Coliseum in London while the

Zeppelins were bombing but then at the end of the war retired to Monaco with a lady companion, installing her husband, who agreed to act as escort when needed, in Nice. She became the best amateur gardener on the Riviera — with a gold cup to prove it. There was another attempt at autobiography in 1925 called *The Days I Knew* — still she told nothing.

Lillie Langtry died on 12 February 1929, and was buried in the churchyard of St Saviour's in Jersey.

See photograph opposite.

ANGELA LANSBURY

*H*aving appeared in more than twenty-five films, playing parts ranging from the surly cockney housemaid in *Gaslight* through Laurence Harvey's mother in *The Manchurian Candidate* to Miss Marple, and having been nominated numerous times for an Oscar, Angela Lansbury could be considered a formidable film actress. It must be remembered, however, that the winner of four Tonys is also a formidable stage star.

Angela Lansbury was born in London on 16 October 1925. Her father was a lumber merchant (he died when she was nine) and her mother was the actress Moyna MacGill. Miss Lansbury went to South Hampstead High School for Girls from 1934 to 1939 and then began her drama training at the Webber Douglas School. With her two younger brothers she was evacuated to America when the war began and she continued her studies at Feagin School of Drama in New York. After a brief time as a singer and impersonator in a Montreal club she went to Hollywood with her mother, where they were both put under contract to MGM. Angela played Elizabeth Taylor's older sister in *National Velvet* and soon had two Oscar nominations under her belt — for *Gaslight* and *The Picture of Dorian Gray.*

Angela Lansbury made her stage début in New York at the Henry Miller Theater on 11 April 1957, playing Marcelle in the farce, *Hotel Paradiso.* At the Lyceum in October 1960 she was widely praised for her performance as Helen in *A Taste of Honey.* She made her musical début at the Majestic in March 1964 playing Cora Hoover Hooper in Stephen Sondheim's *Anyone Can Whistle.* The critic Martin Gottfried described her as 'a mayoress who struts like the young Bette Davis' and bemoaned the fact that the show closed within the week. However, in May 1966 Miss Lansbury had a triumph on Broadway at the Winter Garden as *Mame.* Stanley Kauffmann, writing in the *New York Times*, said: 'In short Miss Lansbury is a singing dancing actress, not a singer or dancer who also acts ... In this marathon role she has wit, poise, warmth and a very taking coolth.' For this performance she received her first Tony. *Mame* played the Curran in San Francisco and toured the country.

At the Mark Hellinger Theater in February 1969 Angela Lansbury opened as Countess Aurelia, the Madwoman of Chaillot, in *Dear World* — and captured another Tony. She was not so successful as Prettybelle Sweet in *Prettybelle,* which played the Shubert in Boston in February 1971 and went no further.

Angela Lansbury made her London début in January 1972 at the Aldwych Theatre with the Royal Shakespeare Company in Peter Hall's production of Edward Albee's *All Over,* in which she played the Mistress. Martin Esslin reported: '... both Peggy Ashcroft and Angela Lansbury have succeeded in filling the vague outlines of the writing — of its archetypal universality — with as much naturalistic flesh and blood as could be desired ... Angela Lansbury gives the Mistress the features of those terrifying women who, however old they may become, retain some of the horrid doll-like qualities of the sweet little things they once were — a little girl in her middle 60s.' She returned to America in July of that year to play *Mame* once again — this time at the Westbury Music Fair.

In March 1973 at the Shubert in New York she appeared in *Sondheim: A Musical Tribute* and then returned to London in May to play Rose (which part Ethel Merman had created on Broadway) in *Gypsy* at the Piccadilly Theatre. Robert Cushman said: 'Miss Lansbury's Madame Rose is a slow, steady build towards magnificence.' She subsequently played the part in Los Angeles and on tour in the United States, before coming into the Winter Garden on Broadway with it in September 1974 and getting another Tony Award. She played *Gypsy* during summer 1975 at the Westbury Music Fair in Long Island.

Back in London, for the National Theatre

Lillie Langtry as Cleopatra in Shakespeare's *Antony and Cleopatra* at the Prince's Theatre
(London, 1890)

In *Payment Deferred*, Charles Laughton played the murderer
William Marble (New York, 1931)

Company, first at the Old Vic in December 1975, and then at the opening of the Lyttelton Theatre in March 1976, she was Gertrude to Albert Finney's

Hamlet. Angela Lansbury won her fourth Tony Award in 1979 for her performance as Mrs Lovett in Stephen Sondheim's *Sweeney Todd.*

CHARLES LAUGHTON

Charles Laughton was born on 1 July 1899 in Scarborough, England, where his parents ran the Victoria Hotel. He first went to school at a convent run by French nuns and became fluent in their language. From 1912 to 1918 he attended the Jesuit Stonyhurst College where he excelled in debating and in Latin recitation, but where he was not very happy. There he made his first stage appearance playing the innkeeper in *The Private Secretary*, and drew his first review — 'We hope to see more of C. Laughton' — in the school magazine.

During the First World War he served as a private in the Royal Huntingdonshire Regiment and saw action at Vimy Ridge in France, where he was gassed. After the war he was sent to London to learn the hotel business at Claridge's and spent every spare moment at the theatre. He returned to Scarborough and worked at the Pavilion Hotel, which his parents then owned, and performed in amateur theatricals with the Scarborough Players, appearing in *Trelawney of the 'Wells', The Dear Departed, Hobson's Choice* and *Becky Sharp.* He trained for the stage at RADA under the tutelage of Theodore Komisarjevsky and Alice Gachet, and made his London début at the St James's Theatre on 26 March 1926 with other students from RADA, playing scenes from Molière, Shaw, Shakespeare and Chekhov. About his performance as Dr Sutcliffe in Tom Robertson's *School*, the *Times* critic wrote: 'Although the part is not a very promising one, Charles played it with assurance.' Laughton received the Bancroft Gold Medal for this role.

Charles Laughton made his professional début on 26 April 1926 as Osip in Gogol's *The Government Inspector*, produced by Komisarjevsky at the Barnes Theatre. It transferred that May to the Gaiety Theatre. He was next seen in July at the Everyman, playing Rummel in *Pillars of Society*. Back at Barnes he was Ephikhodof in *The Cherry Orchard* in September and Vassily Solyony in *The Three Sisters* in October. Seldom out of work, he was Ficsur in *Liliom* (Duke of York's, December 1926), General Markeloff in *The Greater Love* (Prince's, February 1927),

Cantavalle in *Naked* (Royalty, March 1927), Sir James Hartley in *Angela* (Prince's, March 1927), and Creon in *Medea* (Prince's, April 1927). He was at the Criterion in June 1927 playing Frank K. Pratt in *The Happy Husband*, most successfully. Then, at the Court in October he was Count Pahlen in *Paul I*. It was also at the Court in November that he had another success playing the title role in *Mr Prohack*. In this play he met Elsa Lanchester, who was playing a secretary; they married in 1929.

He was at the Little in February 1928 playing Mr Crispin in Hugh Walpole's *A Man With Red Hair*. The *Times* critic reported: 'Mr Laughton has made so subtle, so revoltingly brilliant a study of sadistic obsession that the man, and through him the play, is well nigh intolerable. Mr Laughton by face, by voice, above all, by imaginative bodily movement, compels suspension of disbelief,' Although an artistic success, the play was too horrifying to succeed commercially, and in April Charles Laughton was at the Arts playing Ben Jonson in George Moore's *The Making of an Immortal*. However, Michael Morton's play, *Alibi*, based on an Agatha Christie story, in which Laughton played Hercule Poirot, opened at the Prince of Wales in May 1928 and ran for several months. Laughton then made three short two-reel films for Ivor Montagu — their only distinction being the fact that they were written by H. G. Wells. At the Haymarket in December 1928 he was Mr Pickwick in the Dickens story.

He opened at the Strand in July 1929 playing Jacques Blaise in *Beauty*, and at the Apollo in October was sadly miscast in *The Silver Tassie*. He was Brigadier-General Archibald Root at the Vaudeville in January 1930 in *French Leave*. Charles Laughton's next great success was at Wyndham's in April 1930 when he played Tony Perelli in Edgar Wallace's *On the Spot*. The character was based on the real life Al Capone. The *Times* reported: 'It is Mr Laughton who gives the evening a distinction beyond the ingenuity of its contrivances. The insolence, the vanity, the weary skill of a masterly criminal are all in his study of Perelli.' The play ran for just under a year in

London and the Laughtons toured with it.

He was next in London at the St James's Theatre in May 1931 playing the unhappy murderer, William Marble, in Jeffrey Dell's version of C. S. Forester's *Payment Deferred*. It was a great success and he took it to New York, where he opened at the Lyceum on 24 September 1931, making his American début. Brooks Atkinson reported: 'Mr Laughton makes him [William Marble] a study in broad Hogarthian strokes. It is gross, repulsive, and treacherous; it is also whinnying and pathetic. It is fatuous, cheap and coldly cruel. Without Mr Laughton to play in a flamboyant style of cartoon drawing, *Payment Deferred* might be a soggy play. But with him it is darkly engrossing ...' However, even with Mr Laughton it closed on Broadway in three weeks. They got another three weeks out of it in Chicago and then he returned to Broadway, to the Booth Theater in February 1932, and played Hercule Poirot in *The Fatal Alibi*; it ran for forty performances.

Charles Laughton then returned briefly to London before being summoned to Hollywood where he made *The Old Dark House, The Devil and the Deep* with Tallulah Bankhead, *The Sign of the Cross* and *Payment Deferred*. Back in England, he made one of his most successful movies for Korda, *The Private Life of Henry VIII*, which won him an Oscar. He returned to Hollywood for *White Woman* before joining the Old Vic—Sadler's Wells Company in October 1933 for a season, during which he played Lopakin in *The Cherry Orchard*, King Henry in *Henry VIII*, Prospero in *The Tempest*, the Rev. Canon Chasuble in *The Importance of Being Earnest*, Tattle in *Love for Love* and Angelo to Flora Robson's Isabella in *Measure for Measure*. Of the last the *Times* reported: 'We are given the man of affairs, smiling, precise, and self-confident as well as the sensualist, and Mr Laughton sees to it that what is horrible in the overwhelming of a formidable talent by the senses is given its full value. But throughout the evening this performance is rich and satisfying, full of subtle penetration and expressive gesture.' That season he also played Macbeth.

Returning to Hollywood, he made *The Barretts of Wimpole Street, Les Misérables, Ruggles of Red Gap*, and *Mutiny on the Bounty*. His success in films allowed him to indulge his passion for collecting works of art — and his knowledge of painting stood him in good stead when he made *Rembrandt* for Korda.

On 9 May 1936, Charles Laughton became the first English actor to appear on the stage of the Comédie-Française when he played Sganarelle in the second act of Molière's *Le Médecin malgré lui*, in the original French. At the London Palladium in December 1936 he was Captain Hook in *Peter Pan* while his wife flew around in the name part.

With Erich Pommer in 1937 he founded the Mayflower Picture Corporation but it was not successful and he returned to Hollywood where he made *The Hunchback of Notre Dame*. He became involved in War Bond tours and hospital visits during the war, while continuing to make films. He was away from the stage until July 1947, when he appeared at the Coronet Theater in Los Angeles in Brecht's *Galileo*, playing the title part. He had worked closely with Brecht on the adaptation. He brought it to Broadway to the Maxine Elliott Theatre in December 1947 and Brooks Atkinson reported: 'He is casual and contemptuous: he is ponderous and condescending, and there is a great deal of old-fashioned fiddle-faddle in his buffeting of the books and his giving of orders to underlings ... both as a play and a performance, *Galileo* is fingertips playmaking. And the production is stuffed to the ears with hokum. Nothing the play says justifies Mr Brecht's humble and fearful prayer for science in the brief epilogue.'

Laughton went back to California and began teaching drama there, his students including Jane Wyatt and Shelley Winters. He became a United States citizen on 29 April 1950 in Los Angeles. Laughton then took to performing one-night stands all over the country, giving readings from the Bible and from standard works. He appeared in Hollywood in June 1950 in *The Cherry Orchard* and then at the New Century in New York in November 1951 he was the Devil in *Don Juan in Hell*, which he played with Charles Boyer, Sir Cedric Hardwicke and Agnes Moorehead, and also directed. Brooks Atkinson wrote in the *New York Times:* 'Since The First Drama Quartet is composed of extraordinary actors their reading, as they call it, of Shaw's *Don Juan in Hell* is a mighty and moving occasion ... This is not only a performance but an intellectual crusade ... As the Devil, moon-faced Mr Laughton acts with diabolical gusto and gives dramatic weight to the whole performance. The long, closely reasoned speeches he gives with great spontaneity, putting the emphasis where it belongs, using the words carefully, pointing the meaning with gestures and movements. Call it a masterful performance and you cannot be wrong.' They toured the country with it.

In 1953 Laughton adapted Stephen Vincent Benet's poem and directed a production of *John Brown's Body* — with Raymond Massey, Tyrone Power and Judith Anderson in the cast. They played sixty-eight cities in ten weeks, including New York. In January 1954 Laughton edited and directed a production of *The Caine Mutiny Court Martial* which starred Henry Fonda and ran at the Plymouth Theater for a year. At the Martin Beck Theater in October 1956 he played Andrew Undershaft in a production he directed of *Major Barbara*.

He returned to London in May 1958 where at the New Theatre he directed Jane Arden's *The Party* and played Richard Brough. Kenneth Tynan reported: 'An expert at cringing and cajoling, he can make miracles of wit out of lines which in other mouths would seem mere explosions of petulance. But he is not a realist, and Miss Arden's play is nothing if not realistic. Mr Laughton's role is that of a downtrodden Kilburn solicitor with a history of alcoholism, vaguely stemming from incestuous feelings towards his daughter, who despises him ... Mr Laughton offers neither danger nor defeat, just an extravagant booby harmlessly letting off steam.'

At Stratford-on-Avon during the 1959 season at the Shakespeare Memorial Theatre he was a not very successful King Lear, and of his performance as Bottom in Peter Hall's production of *A Midsummer Night's Dream*, Tynan said he was '... a ginger-wigged, ginger-bearded Bottom ... Fidgeting with a lightness that reminds one (even as one forgets what the other actors are talking about) how expertly bulky men dance, he blinks at the pit his moist reproachful eyes, softly cajoles and suddenly roars, and behaves throughout in a manner that has nothing to do with acting, although it perfectly hits off the demeanour of a rapscallion uncle dressed up to entertain the children at a Christmas party.'

Charles Laughton received an Academy Award nomination for his performance in the film *Witness for the Prosecution* and his adaptation of *Galileo* was produced at the Mermaid Theatre in London in June 1960.

His health deteriorated suddenly and rapidly, and Charles Laughton died of bone cancer after a short illness on 15 December 1962.
See photograph opposite page 215.

GERTRUDE LAWRENCE

'S ometimes, in *Private Lives*, I would look across the stage at her and she would simply take my breath away: nobody I have ever known, however brilliant or however talented, has contributed quite what she contributed to my work. Her quality was to me unique and her magic imperishable.' Thus Noel Coward, paying tribute to the actress for whom he wrote many of his best plays and songs, after her sudden and unexpected death from cancer in 1952 at the age of only 54. Gertrude Lawrence may not always have been the best, but she was certainly the brightest. Others of her generation were better singers, better actresses, better dancers; Gertrude Lawrence was a better star. For her the Gershwins wrote *Oh, Kay*; for her Noel Coward wrote *Private Lives* and *Tonight at 8.30* and 'Parisian Pierrot'; for her Richard Rodgers and Oscar Hammerstein wrote *The King and I*. It was Gertrude Lawrence who first sang Coward's 'Someday I'll Find You', she who made hits out of the Gershwins' 'Someone To Watch Over Me' and 'Do, Do, Do', she who first sang Kurt Weill's 'Jenny' in *Lady in the Dark* and the Cole Porter score for *Nymph Errant*. For a brief but memorable time she was First Lady of the revue and musical comedy stage on Broadway and in the West End.

She was a bright, particular star who rose above the considerable limitations and variations of her talent to personify the brittle glamour of a post-First World War generation which was hiding its disenchantment and disillusion under a tight and often cynical smile. When she died, all the theatre lights were dimmed not only along Broadway, where until only a few weeks earlier she had been playing Mrs Anna in *The King and I*, but also in the West End, which apart from one brief post-war appearance in a play by Daphne du Maurier she had forsaken in 1936 after the run of *Tonight at 8.30*. It was a unique tribute to an actress who had started out in 1911 at Olympia as one of 150 child choristers in *The Miracle* and who was inclined to view her entire career from then onward as something of a miracle in itself.

She was born Gertrude Alexandra Dagmar Klasen on — suitably enough — Independence Day, 4 July 1898, though she later took to putting 1901 on all documents, a practice not unknown among actresses of her generation. Her father was a Dane whose family had moved from Schleswig-Holstein to London when he was two: later, as Arthur Lawrence, he achieved some success on music-hall bills as a *basso profundo*, some said none too profound. He took to drink, however, and Gertie's mother left him soon after the birth of their only child.

Gertrude Lawrence was therefore brought up by her mother against a South London background of genteel poverty much like Coward's, though he was always quick to insist that her later tales of dancing barefoot to barrel-organs outside Dickensian pubs were pure fantasy. By 1908 her mother had found Gertie a job as a child dancer in *Babes in the Wood* at Brixton: a year later Gertie was at the Italia Conti stage school, and by the time she first met Coward on a train going to Liverpool for a 1913 *Hannele* she was already in his recollection 'a vivacious little girl with ringlets, wearing a black satin coat and a black velvet military cap with a peak. Her face was far from pretty, but tremendously alive: she was very mondaine, carried a handbag with a powder puff, and frequently dabbed at her generously turned-up nose. She confided to me that her name was Gertrude Lawrence but that I was to call her Gert because everybody did ... she then gave me an orange, told me a few mildly dirty stories, and I loved her from then onwards.'

She was then 14; he had just turned 13. Privately, it was the start of a beautiful if sometimes stormy friendship. Professionally, it was the most important meeting of both their lives.

After *Hannele*, Gertie went out on tour in a number of tacky revues and worked her way slowly toward the Vaudeville Theatre in London, where with Beatrice Lillie she began to make her name towards the end of the First World War in a succession of André Charlot's intimate revues. At first she was always Bea's understudy, but funny ladies who could also sing and act a bit were at that time somewhat thin on the ground and it did not take Charlot long to realize that in Lawrence and Lillie he had a new and unique pair: 'Lillie and Lawrence, Lawrence and Lillie' ran a popular verse of the time, 'if you haven't seen them, you're perfectly silly'.

Gertie stayed with Charlot for the next ten years, appearing in revue after revue (including *London Calling*, which was to reunite her with Coward and in which she sang his 'Parisian Pierrot') and travelling with the Charlot company, which also included Jack Buchanan, to Broadway where in the early 1920s the Lillie–Lawrence–Buchanan trio became the first English stars to take modern Broadway by storm. Their style of intimate revue was at that time virtually unknown in America, and it was with considerable success that they played successive winter seasons on Broadway and then toured, even reaching Hollywood in 1926. There, however, Gertie decided that her time with Charlot had reached the end of its useful-

ness to them both: her eyes were now set on musical comedy rather than revue, and later that year she played Kay in *Oh, Kay* for P. G. Wodehouse and Guy Bolton in both London and New York.

Other musicals followed, notably the Gershwins' *Treasure Girl*, and then in 1930 came the London and Broadway seasons in Coward's *Private Lives* that were to establish her as a light comedienne of classic talent and Lawrence and Coward as a team rivalled only by Fred Astaire and Ginger Rogers — who were, after all, mere celluloid creations.

After *Private Lives* she did a succession of undistinguished straight plays and got herself deeper and deeper into debt: after an early and unsuccessful marriage to one of her stage managers (which produced her only child, Pamela) Gertie remained for some time resolutely unmarried, a bachelor girl watched over by a succession of glamorous lovers ranging from Philip Astley to Douglas Fairbanks Jun; but none of them ever taught her the elements of economy, with the result that she was to reach the bankruptcy courts on more than one occasion.

Coward, however, was by now engaged on an ambitious new project designed as a money-maker for them both; in the light of her mercurial character, and frequent changes of stage mood, this was to be not just one but a sequence of nine new plays under the overall title *Tonight at 8.30*: they played the three-month seasons that were always Coward's upper limit (for reasons of boredom) in the West End and on Broadway in 1936 — and that, amazingly, was the end of one of the most remarkable stage partnerships of the century. Coward return to London; Gertie decided that her future lay in America, where soon afterwards she married her second and last husband, the Cape Cod theatre owner and manager Richard Aldrich. 'Dear Mrs A', cabled Coward on their wedding day in 1940, 'Hooray Hooray, at last you are deflowered. On this as every other day I love you: Noel Coward.'

So by now Noel and Gertie were separated by her marriage, by the Atlantic, and by the war: her own Broadway career flourished (*Susan and God* 1937, *Skylark* 1939, *Lady in the Dark* 1941, *Pygmalion* 1945) and though she did return to London briefly at the war's end to star in a Daphne du Maurier play, *September Tide*, the West End to which she returned was no longer a place she remembered or cared for. Her London theatre world had ended as surely as Coward's with the outbreak of war, and Gertie hastened back to the theatre on Cape Cod which had become her last home.

In 1949, while making a Hollywood film of

Tennessee Williams' *The Glass Menagerie*, she happened upon a book called *Anna and the King of Siam* which had already once been filmed by Irene Dunne and Rex Harrison. Gertie, however, decided that here would be the perfect musical, and persuaded Rodgers and Hammerstein to make it into one for her. Gertie's hope had been that Noel might consent to play the King, but his usual loathing of long runs forbade that and the role went instead to a young and unknown Yul Brynner. The success of *The King and I* on Broadway in 1951 was the greatest that Gertie had known since her days with Noel back in the 1930s; sadly, it was also to be her last. During the run, increasing ill-health led to a rapid decline in her performance and Rodgers and Hammerstein asked

Noel if, for the good of their show as well as of Gertie herself, he could persuade her to leave the cast. Gertie refused on the grounds that she had never given up before and was not about to start now; besides, she had one great dream left. She wanted to play *The King and I* at Drury Lane for the Coronation summer of 1953, and she feared that if she left the show on Broadway she might forfeit that chance. The one thing, friends thought, that might change her mind would be if Noel was to write for her a new and less demanding comedy. There was one on his typewriter when, on a Folkestone racecourse on 6 September 1952, he happened to see an evening paper headline announcing her sudden death.

See photograph opposite page 87.

WILFRID LAWSON

'*T*hroughout the vicissitudes of his career he retained the respect and affection of directors and fellow actors, and he had not ceased to be in demand,' wrote the *Times* in his obituary.

A hard-drinking, eccentric and unforgettable character actor, Wilfrid Lawson was born on 14 January 1900 at Bradford, Yorkshire. He was educated at Hanson School and technical college and became a professional actor at the age of 16. His first stage appearance was at the Pier Theatre in Brighton in 1916, when he played Gecko in *Trilby*. During the First World War he was a pilot in the RAF, and after the war for nearly ten years he remained in the provinces playing over 400 parts for various repertory companies. Wilfrid Lawson made his London début at the Elephant and Castle Theatre on 6 February 1928 playing Mark Ingestre in *Sweeney Todd*. He was then at the Court Theatre from December 1929 to March 1930 playing Major Pekoff in *Arms and the Man*, Alfred Doolittle in *Pygmalion*, Roebuck Ramsden in *Man and Superman*, Sir Patrick Cullen in *The Doctor's Dilemma*, Colonel Craven in *The Philanderer*, First Gravedigger in *Hamlet*, and John Tarleton in *Misalliance*. Also at the Court, in March 1931 he played Mr Gilbey in *Fanny's First Play* and Sir George Crofts in *Mrs Warren's Profession*. At the Lyric, Hammersmith, in December 1931 he was the comic policeman in *Aladdin*.

In April 1932, Wilfrid Lawson joined Barry Jackson's Company and at the Queen's Theatre he played Membel in *Heartbreak House*. In June he

was Arthur Kober in *Evensong*. He had his first real, powerful success at the Shaftesbury in May 1933 when he played John Brown of Harper's Ferry in *Gallows Glorious*. At the Lyric that August he was Unteroffizier Keller in *The Ace* and at the Coliseum in February 1934 he played Prince Sansthanaka in *The Golden Toy*. He went to the Old Vic in September 1934 and played Mark Antony in *Antony and Cleopatra*. At the Playhouse in November 1934 he was George Morel in *Hurricane*.

Working once more with Barry Jackson he played Edward Moulton-Barrett in a revival of *The Barretts of Wimpole Street* at the Piccadilly in January 1935. At the Playhouse that May he was John Builder in *A Family Man* and at the Malvern Festival from July through August he played Volpone, Mr Gilbey in *Fanny's First Play* and Mr Tarleton in *Misalliance*.

Wilfrid Lawson made his New York début at the Henry Miller Theater on 20 December 1935 playing Thomas Foxley, KC, in *Libel*, and at the Guild in November 1936 he played Richard Wagner in *Prelude to Exile*. Brooks Atkinson reported for the *New York Times*: 'As Richard Wagner the megalomaniac, voluptuary rascal and magnificent mendicant, Wilfrid Lawson gives an accomplished performance that one should respect more than one can. He is enormously versatile and agile without really conveying an impression of a volcanic composer.' At the Fulton in February 1937 he was Benedict Arnold in *A Point of Honour*.

Returning to London in June 1937 he played

King James in *The King's Pirate* at the St Martin's and at the Royalty that September he was Walter Ormund in J. B. Priestley's 'time play', *I Have Been Here Before*. Audrey Williamson said that the part was 'finely played by Wilfrid Lawson, an actor big enough to grasp the spiritual nettles, as well as the emotional opportunities involved', and the author said that Lawson gave 'a performance to make your hair stand on end'. He played the same part at the Guild Theater in New York in October 1938 but the play failed there.

At the Garrick in January 1939 he played Bill Cooper in *Hundreds and Thousands*, and at the Westminster in May he was Stephen Moore in *Bridge Head*. At the outbreak of the Second World War, Wilfrid Lawson rejoined the RAF and served with it for two and half years. He was offered a leading part in the Hollywood film of *How Green was My Valley* in 1940 but was refused an exit visa.

It was July 1942 when Lawson returned to the stage, as Captain McGrath in *Lifeline* at the Duchess. At the Cambridge Theatre in January 1943 he played Gideon Bloodgood in *The Streets of London*, and at the Opera House in Manchester that March he was André Legrand in *Devil's Own*. At the Mercury in February 1947 he was Dan Hillboy in *The Beautiful People*. He set out on a tour of the United States in April 1947 playing Edward Moulton-Barrett in *The Barretts of Wimpole Street*. He returned to London and in February 1953 was at the Arts Theatre playing the Captain in Strindberg's *The Father*. At the Savoy that September he played Korrianke in *The Devil's General*. The General was Trevor Howard. Richard Buckle said: 'Wilfrid Lawson presents a fine, grotesque portrait of the General's gruff, deformed, devoted servant.'

At the Globe in April 1954 he was the Cell Warder while Alec Guinness had the name part in *The Prisoner*. Ronald Barker reported: 'Wilfrid Lawson as the Warder is a ripe type and the most successful character, because he is human and we can believe in him.' In July 1954 at the Phoenix he was the 81-year-old Lon Dennison who has become a nuisance to his children in *The Wooden Dish*, directed by Joseph Losey. The play was set in Texas and Ronald Barker said that Lawson's performance 'consists of a bag of tricks, odd angular movements and a sing-song voice which would be more in keeping in an opera than a straight play. Lawson makes no attempt at an American accent and is as liable to jump over a chair as carry a stick.' At the same theatre in October 1954 he played Sidney Reditch, the

amateur investigator of black magic, in the highly successful *Bell, Book and Candle* with Rex Harrison and Lilli Palmer. Ronald Barker was still not impressed by his performance. 'Only Wilfrid Lawson,' he wrote, 'was on a distinctly different plane. This was not a light comedy performance but a heavy character from a different world.' Of his performance as Geraldine Page's father in *The Rainmaker* at the St Martin's in May 1956, Frank Granville-Barker said that he 'movingly shows the mellow kindliness of Lizzie's father'. At the Arts in September 1957 he was Thomas Johnson in *All Kinds of Men*. The critic Peter Roberts hated the play and the production, but thought that 'Wilfrid Lawson, as the ne'er do well friend who makes up for a sinful life by dying that a murderer might live, gave a performance of a fine, colourful, fruity order.'

At the Royal Court the following September he was Sailor Sawney in Arden's *Live Like Pigs*. In this, Peter Roberts said he 'gives the same compelling and highly individual performance he has treated us to for years'. Also at the Royal Court, in September 1959 he played Sailor Mahan in Sean O'Casey's *Cock-A-Doodle-Dandy*, directed by George Devine. Frank Granville-Barker said: 'Wilfrid Lawson throws in a hilarious scene as an old man trying desperately to prove he has not yet lost his virility.'

At the Arts in May 1962 Wilfrid Lawson played Luka in Gorki's *The Lower Depths* for Peter Hall's RSC. Clive Barnes reported that his performance was 'too mannered for my taste, the peculiarly pathetic note of poetry he manages to add almost as a counterpoint to every phrase becomes tedious with repetition'. His last stage appearance was at the Old Vic in September 1962 when he played the Button Moulder in *Peer Gynt*. Charles Marowitz thought it 'the cleverest production of *Peer Gynt* we shall probably ever see...with Wilfrid Lawson's Button Moulder once again we find this actor bringing on his own special rhythm which, in every production I have ever seen, is at least five times slower than anyone else's. Lawson's dominant quality is of a man making desperate internal efforts to control himself. This produces a peculiarly outstanding performance which asks to be judged in isolation.'

Wilfrid Lawson made many films. Most important was his Alfred Doolittle in Gabriel Pascal's film of Shaw's *Pygmalion*, in 1938. He was also the gamekeeper in Tony Richardson's *Tom Jones* and he played King Priam in *The Viking Queen* just before his death on 12 October 1966.

EVELYN LAYE

Evelyn Laye was born on 10 July 1900 in London. She attended school in Brighton and Folkestone, and was barely 15 when she made her stage début at the Theatre Royal, Brighton, playing a mute Chinese servant in *Mr Wu*. Her father was Gilbert Laye: his concert party, The Fascinators, was disbanded because of the war and Evelyn was the only one in work for a time.

It was at the East Ham Palace on 24 April 1916 that she made her London début in a revue called *Honi Soit*, and then toured with the show, but she was something less than a triumph. 'On tour,' she later recounted, 'we played the ports and garrison towns. I threw my fluffy cotton snowballs into the audience singing, ''I Want You to Snowball Me'', and they did. They snowballed me with anything that came to hand — orange peel, toffee papers, the occasional apple core.'

In December 1916 Evelyn Laye opened at the Lyceum in Edinburgh playing Pyrrha in *Oh Caesar!* and then toured in that show. The following Christmas she was at the Theatre Royal in Portsmouth playing *Goody Two Shoes*.

On 14 February 1918 she became a Gaiety girl when she succeeded Moya Manning as Leonie Bramble in *The Beauty Spot* at the Gaiety Theatre. She remained at the Gaiety for nearly three years, playing Madeline Manners in *Going Up* (May 1918), the flapper Dollis Pym in *The Kiss Call* (October 1919), and Bessie Brent in *The Shop Girl* (March 1920). At the Queen's Theatre in March 1921 she was Mollie Moffat in *Nighty Night* and the following month was Mary Howells in *Mary*. She appeared in *The League of Notions* at Oxford in August 1921, and in October was at the London Pavilion in *Fun of the Fayre*. In August 1922 she was the Prologue and Helen in *Phi-Phi* and then was engaged for Daly's Theatre, where she played Sonia in a revival of *The Merry Widow* in May 1923; in December of that year she took the title part in *Madame Pompadour*. She was Alice in *The Dollar Princess* at the King's Theatre, Glasgow, in December 1924 and brought the part to Daly's in February. That June at Daly's she was Cleopatra in the piece of that name, and in November 1925 she was at the Adelphi playing Betty in *Betty in Mayfair*. She opened at the same theatre in September 1926 playing Molly Shine in *Merely Molly*. That year she married another musical comedy star, Sonnie Hale.

At the Palace in March 1927, Evelyn Laye succeeded Winnie Melville as Princess Elaine in *Princess Charming*, and at Daly's in December 1927 she was Lili in *Lilac Time*. At the Piccadilly in April 1928 she was in *Blue Eyes*, and then returned to Daly's and *Lilac Time* in December. She played Marianne in *The New Moon* at Drury Lane in April 1929. She was by this time the biggest musical comedy star in England, and she crossed the Atlantic where she made her New York début at the Ziegfeld Theater on 5 November 1929 in Noel Coward's operetta, *Bitter Sweet*. Under the headline, 'Evelyn Laye is Radiant', Brooks Atkinson reported in the *New York Times*: 'What makes Evelyn Laye so rare a presence in the leading part is not merely her fragile beauty but the daintiness with which she acts and sings in the precise spirit of the play. As an actress she catches the ardor of the romantic love scenes of the first act, she trips through the dramatic episodes with a skill equal to Mr Coward's composition. She has, moreover, a voice sweet in quality and full in tone.'

Back in London in November 1930 she took over the London lead in *Bitter Sweet* from Peggy Wood, who created the role in England. She played once more at the Lyceum in April 1931.

In July 1931 she toured in *Madame Pompadour* and in October toured in *Bitter Sweet*. At the Adelphi in London in January 1932 she opened in the title role in *Helen!*, and at the London Hippodrome in June 1933 she was Peggy in *Give Me a Ring*. The following year she married the actor Frank Lawton; the marriage lasted for thirty-five years, until his death in 1969.

Evelyn Laye played in *Bitter Sweet* again in October 1935 on the West Coast of America at the Shrine Auditorium in Los Angeles. Then back on Broadway, at the Booth Theater in March 1936 she played Belinda Warren in *Sweet Aloes*. She returned to England in May 1937 when she opened at the Lyceum in London playing Princess Anna in *Paganini*.

Now the toast of two continents, she returned to New York to the Majestic Theater in December 1937 to play Natalie Rivers in *Between the Devil*. When she went back to England she made her first appearance on the variety stage in London at the Palladium in June 1938. In Birmingham, at the Theatre Royal in December 1938 she played Prince Florizel in the pantomime *The Sleeping Beauty*. At the Savoy in February 1940 she appeared in *Lights Up*. Ernest Short reported that she was specially good as Cora Pearl singing 'Only a Glass of Champagne'. And he went on to write about her various performances in this variety evening: 'Miss Laye displayed an unexpected sense of characterization in a number of roles; for example, as the uniformed assistant of Carlo the Illusionist whose best tricks she botched with obstinate persistence. The turn was in quaint contrast to her earlier appearance in Ronald Jeans' "Four Stages of Marriage" in which the sentiment ranged from the ecstasy of the honeymoon era to the exasperated boredom of marital maturity. As her pretty self, Evelyn sang a Noel Gay number, "You've Done Something to My Heart".' At the Coliseum in September 1942 she played Violet Gray in *The Belle of New York* and at the Piccadilly in August 1943 she was Marie Sauvinet in *Sunny River*. For Christmas 1943 she was the Prince in *Cinderella* at His Majesty's and then toured around the country, entertaining in theatres in the middle of the Blitz. At the Prince's in March 1945 Evelyn Laye played Katherine in *Three Waltzes* and then toured in the role. From April 1946 she toured as Laura Kent in *Elusive Lady* and in 1948 toured as Lady Teazle in *The School for Scandal*. For Christmas that year she was at the Palladium being Prince Charming once more in *Cinderella*.

At the Lyric Theatre in May 1949 she opened as Marina Verani in *Two Dozen Red Roses*. Harold Hobson found it an 'ingeniously worked out comedy...Clever but [with] no wit in the dialogue.' She toured from September 1950 as Stella in *September Tide* and at Wimbledon that year was in another Christmas pantomime, playing Joscelyn in *Queen of Hearts*. It was also at Wimbledon, in July 1953, that she appeared in *The Domino Revue*; at the Scala that Christmas she was Mrs Darling in *Peter Pan*.

Evelyn Laye's appearance at the Hippodrome in April 1954 as Marcelle Thibault in *Wedding in Paris* was considered her proper return to the West End, and drew from the audience a four-minute standing ovation. Frank Granville-Barker reported: 'How delightful it is to have Evelyn Laye back with us! Once more she is in her rightful place as leading lady of British musicals, sweeping gaily across the Hippodrome stage with her usual vivacity, poise and assurance.' She was next at the Cambridge in July 1957 playing Lady Marlowe in *Silver Wedding*, and from February 1959 she toured in the title role of *The Marquise*.

In December 1959 Evelyn Laye opened as Lady Fitzadam in The *Amorous Prawn*. Peter Roberts reported for *Plays and Players*: 'As a General's wife who turns her husband's official army residence into a private guest house during his absence, she has plenty of scope for graciousness, charm and comedy.' It ran in the West End for two years.

At the Prince of Wales in January 1964 Evelyn Laye succeeded Joan Bennett as Edith Lambert in *Never Too Late*. She opened at the Ashcroft, Croydon, in April 1965 as Lady Catherine in Somerset Maugham's *The Circle*, and transferred with it to the Savoy in June. Hugh Leonard said: 'Miss Laye, whom I have never seen before, must be a dream to play with. Her timing is faultless, she never hogs the stage...and she is that rare thing: a comedienne who doesn't try to be funny.'

Evelyn Laye opened at the Alhambra in Glasgow in April 1966 playing Annie Besant in the musical, *Strike a Light*; it came into the West End to the Piccadilly in July, but was not successful. At the Phoenix in October 1967 she played Muriel Willoughby in Hugh and Margaret Williams' *Let's All Go Down the Strand*. Michael Billington reported that she had 'nothing very much to do but stand around and be scored off by other characters'. She took over briefly the part of Lady Hadwell in *Charlie Girl* while Anna Neagle had a holiday from the Adelphi in March 1969, and in November of that year she tried again with a new British musical — *Phil the Fluter* — at the Palace, in which she played Mrs Fitzmaurice. John Russell Taylor reported: 'Evelyn Laye is given a real part, and plays it with every sign of relish: as a rich society woman with a shady past and a rip-roaring taste for handsome young men, she is like enough to the Evelyn Laye we have always known to carry along old admirers, but amusing enough in her own right to please people who have never even heard of her.' The show unfortunately closed in February. She resurrected *The Amorous Prawn* in September 1970 and toured with it. At the Strand Theatre in June 1971 Evelyn Laye opened in *No Sex Please — We're British* playing Eleanor Hunter. Peter Roberts said that she discharged her duties 'as a sort of gracious clothes horse for so many Norman Hartnell creations I lost count'. It was her last West End appearance.

In August 1976 she toured as Leonora Fiske in *Ladies in Retirement* — but somehow never considered retirement for herself. In 1978 she set off on a sixteen-week, sixteen-stop tour of the provinces with *Pygmalion*, and in 1980, although a fortune teller had said that she would die at the age of 77, set off to Nottingham to play in *A Little Night Music*. For her eightieth birthday, which she celebrated at the Strand Theatre, her friends endowed the London Academy of Music and Dramatic Art with an Evelyn Laye Award — an annual prize for the best performance in a musical. In February 1982 she was at Cheltenham's Everyman Theatre recalling a lifetime on the stage. Evelyn Laye had been awarded the CBE in 1973 and into her eighties showed no sign of final retirement. 'I have never been able to give up the theatre,' she said. 'It has always been my first love. I like the smell of it, the smell of the stage door, my dressing room, applying my make-up and of course, my audiences.'

EVA LE GALLIENNE

*E*va Le Gallienne, the high priestess of classical drama in America, believed the classics should be available in the theatre to the public much as books were in a library. She was born in London on 11 January 1899. Her father was the British poet Richard Le Gallienne, and her mother the Danish writer and journalist Julie Norregaard Le Gallienne. She was educated in France at the College Sevinge and then, at the age of 14, attended RADA in London. She made her stage début in London as a Page in *Monna Vanna* at the Queen's Theatre on 21 July 1914; thereafter, apart from her Yorkshire terriers, the theatre was her life. In London, she played Elizabeth in *Laughter of Fools* at the Prince of Wales in May 1915 and subsequently Victorine in *Peter Ibbetson* at His Majesty's in July 1915.

She moved to New York, where she made her début as Rose in *Mrs Botany's Daughters* at the Comedy in October 1915 and then played Jennie in *Bunny* at the Hudson (January 1916), Mary Powers in *The Melody of Youth* at the Fulton (February 1916) and Patricia Molloy in *Mr Lazarus* at the Shubert (September 1916). She toured the West Coast in this production in 1917 and then appeared in *The Cinderella Man*, *Rio Grande* and *Pierre of the Plains* at the Alcazar in San Francisco that same year.

Eva Le Gallienne returned in October 1917 to New York, where she played Dot Carrington in *Saturday to Monday* at the Bijou. She then played Ottoline Mallinson in *Lord and Lady Algy* at the Broadhurst in December, before joining Ethel Barrymore's company at the Empire in February 1918 to play the Duchess of Burchester in *The Off Chance*, following in May with Delia in *Belinda* at the same theatre. A tour of *The Off Chance* took her through the summer of 1919. She returned to the Henry Miller Theater in New York in September to play Eithne in *Lusmore*. In December 1919 Eva Le Gallienne opened at the George M. Cohan Theater as the Parisienne in *Elsie Janis and Her Gang*. She played Elsie Dover in *Not So Long Ago* at the Booth in May 1920, before touring with the production through the spring of 1921.

It was in April 1921 when she appeared at the Garrick as Julie in *Liliom* that she captivated New York audiences. She then played Simonetta Vespucci in *Sandro Botticelli* at the Provincetown Playhouse in March 1923. That May she returned to New York to the 48th Street Theater, to play Julia in *The Rivals*. She was again captivating as the Princess Alexandra in Molnar's *The Swan* at the Cort in October 1923. She stayed on at the Cort, and there in February 1924 played Hannele in *The Assumption of Hannele*. At the Gaiety in March of that year she played Diane de Charance in *La Vierge Folle*. *The Swan* moved to the Empire Theater in August 1924 and then she toured it until October 1925, returning to Broadway to the Comedy that month to play Marie in *The Call of Life*.

Eva Le Gallienne opened her own production of *The Master Builder* in November 1925 at the Maxine Elliott Theater for special matinées on Tuesdays and Fridays. The *New York Times* reported: 'Miss Le Gallienne revealed every facet on the character of Hilda Wangel. Her entrance, knapsack in place, dressed in muddy tramping togs, was bold to the extreme. Sparing of gesture and mere artistry, she created a vibrant illusion of strength, directness, and eerie perception. For the part of Hilda is not confined within the limitations of this workaday world, obedient to the rules governing phlegmatic characterization. When everyone in the last scene mourns Solness as dead, she is still transfixed, gazing with ecstasy into the heights where for a moment he stood on the tower of his new house, high above the plain. For her, he has fulfilled his existence; the incident of death does not matter. Miss Le Gallienne's performance expressed that preternatural transcendence beyond the physical directions of the play.' Next Miss Le Gallienne turned again to Ibsen and played Ella Rentheim in her own production of *John Gabriel Borkman* at the Booth in January 1925 before touring with it.

In 1926 Eva Le Gallienne founded, organized and directed the Civic Repertory Company in West 14th Street, off-Broadway. She opened the theatre on 25 October 1926 playing Imperia in her own production of *Saturday Night*. She then played Hilda Wangel again in *The Master Builder*, Masha in *The Three Sisters*, Ella Rentheim in *John Gabriel Borkman*, Mirandolina in *The Mistress of the Inn*, and Viola in *Twelfth Night*.

She opened 1927 playing Sister Joanna in *The Cradle Song*. Brooks Atkinson reported that she and her actors 'suffuse *Cradle Song* with beauty ... If Miss Le Gallienne's company at the 14th Street Theater had produced nothing else well this year, the finely modulated performance of *Cradle Song* would still make the season distinguished.' She continued at the 14th Street Theater as Aunt Isabel in *Inheritors* (March 1927), Jo in *The Good Hope* (October 1927), Sara Peri in *The First Stone* (January 1928), Princess Orloff in *Improvisations in June* (March 1928), Hedda in *Hedda Gabler* (March 1928), Dorimene in *The Would-Be Gentleman* (October 1928), and Varya in *The Cherry Orchard* (October 1928). In November 1928 with J. Blake Scott she directed *Peter Pan* and played the title role — the first to do so in America since Maude Adams. The *New York Times* said: 'She was a gallant, buoyant, clean-cut figure and gave Peter plenty of élan and boyish grace. She even expressed something of the aloofness of Peter... Mrs Eva Le Gallienne's own dances... were airily and expertly executed.'

In January 1929 she directed the double-bill, *The Lady From Albuquerque* and *On the High Road*. The following month she directed *Katerina*. She then directed *A Sunny Morning* as well as playing Dona Laura in the production which opened in April. In September she directed and played Masha in *The Seagull*, and then in October directed *Mademoiselle Bourrat*. Eva Le Gallienne played Anna Karenina in *The Living Corpse* in December 1929, and the following month directed another double-bill and played in both — Juanita in *The Women Have Their Way* and Lady Torminster in *The Open Door*. Eva Le Gallienne directed and played Juliet in *Romeo and Juliet* in April 1930 and that October she directed *The Green Cockatoo* and *Siegfried*, appearing as Genevieve in the latter. She directed and played Elsa in *Alison's House* in December.

Eva Le Gallienne opened the year 1931 as Marguerite in *Camille*. George Nathan thought her performance underdone, and rather cruelly said it was the first Camille he had ever seen die of catarrh. In October she played Julie in *Liliom* once more, this time directing as well, and the following month she was Cassandra Austen in *Dear Jane*. With Florida Friebus she adapted *Alice in Wonderland* for the stage and opened in December as the White Queen. Brooks Atkinson found her totally delightful and said: 'To a long history of

interesting projects, Miss Le Gallienne has now added the most original of all.' But now her theatre on 14th Street had to close. It had always run at a loss of about $100,000 a year; the deficit was taken up by private subsidy. The Depression changed that. Her patrons could no longer afford the luxury of subsidizing the arts. She took *Alice in Wonderland*, *A Doll's House*, *The Master Builder*, *Romeo and Juliet* and *Hedda Gabler* on a tour in the hopes of raising enough money to continue the Civic Repertory Company, but failed.

In November 1934 she produced *L'Aiglon* at the Broadhurst Theater. She also directed it and played the Duke of Reichstadt. John Mason Brown reported: 'Miss Le Gallienne has the physique to be visually convincing as "The Eaglet". She wears her white uniform and her purple greatcoat well. She bows in a courtly manner, affects a mannish stride, gestures gracefully and endows Rostand's weakling with much charm. If her performance begins tamely and continues unevenly, it does have its satisfactory stretches. And in the last scene of all, it does find her at her topnotch best, playing so simply, so earnestly and with such beauty that she manages to make the proud hokum of the little Duke's death immensely touching ... Miss Le Gallienne sets off a number of firecrackers before the evening is over but she illumines the part with no skyrockets.' In December she revived *Cradle Song* and *Hedda Gabler* at the Broadhurst. Of the latter John Mason Brown said: 'Her Hedda is not a subtle woman: she is merely a despicable one ... She denies Hedda the icy coquetry which is implied in the text.'

Eva Le Gallienne toured in 1935 in *Rosmersholm*, *Camille*, *The Women Have Their Way* and *A Sunny Morning* and brought the repertory into the Shubert Theater in New York in December. In June 1936 she was in Westport, Connecticut, at the Country Playhouse as Angelica in *Love for Love*, and that November at the Guild in New York City played Mathilda Wesendonck in *Prelude to Exile*. At the Westchester County Playhouse in Mt Kisco, New York, in June 1937 she played Mirandolina in *The Mistress of the Inn*. It was at the Cape Playhouse in Dennis, Massachusetts, in August 1937 that she first played Hamlet. She returned to New York, to the Cort Theater in October 1938 where she played Marie Antoinette in *Madame Capet*. In *Frank Fay's Music Hall* at the 44th Street Theater in March 1939 Eva Le Gallienne played Juliet in the balcony scene from *Romeo and Juliet*, and then took Amanda in *Private Lives* on a summer tour. Through 1940 and 1941 she toured the United States in *Hedda Gabler* and *The Master Builder*.

In October 1941 she produced and directed

Ah, Wilderness! for the Guild and then, temporarily succeeding Mary Boland who was ill, she played Mrs Malaprop in *The Rivals* in St Louis, Missouri. She directed the New York production of *The Rivals* which opened at the Shubert in January 1942. At the Broadhurst the following May she played Lettie in *Uncle Harry*.

At the National Theater on 25 January 1943, Eva Le Gallienne opened as Lyubov Andreyevna in *The Cherry Orchard*, which she also directed. At the Biltmore in October she was Thérèse Raquin in *Thérèse*.

Together with Cheryl Crawford and Margaret Webster, Eva Le Gallienne established a repertory company at the International Theater in Columbus Circle which they called the American Repertory Company. It opened on 6 November 1946 with Miss Le Gallienne playing Queen Katherine in *Henry VIII*, a play adapted by Margaret Webster. Brooks Atkinson was impressed. 'As Katherine of Aragon, Miss Le Gallienne is capping her career with one or two vividly acted scenes,' he wrote in the *New York Times*. 'Katherine, pleading her case fearlessly before her wayward husband and a disingenuous cardinal, gathers stature and nobility from Miss Le Gallienne's acting and the scene of her death acquires poignancy from her neat artistic integrity.' She followed *Henry VIII* with the Comtesse de la Brière in *What Every Woman Knows* and Ella Rentheim in *John Gabriel Borkman* — both opening in November. In April 1947 she was once more the White Queen in *Alice in Wonderland*. But the company failed, and closed with debts of over $100,000. Many organizations and individuals tried to rescue her by paying off the debts.

In February 1948, Eva Le Gallienne was back on Broadway at the Cort Theater playing Mrs Alving in *Ghosts* and in *Hedda Gabler*. She toured as Miss Moffat in *The Corn is Green*, the production opening in New York at the City Center in January 1950. At the Woodstock Playhouse that summer she was Signora Amaranta in *Fortunato*.

Eva Le Gallienne opened at the Royale in New York City in January 1954 as Lady Starcross in *The Starcross Story*, and in February 1955 was at the Holiday playing Marcia Elder in *The Southwest Corner*. She presented a reading, *An Afternoon with Oscar Wilde*, at the Théâtre de Lys in Greenwich Village in January 1957. Eva Le Gallienne then played Queen Elizabeth in *Mary Stuart*, directed by Tyrone Guthrie, at the Phoenix in October 1957. Irene Worth had the title role. Brooks Atkinson reported: 'Miss Le Gallienne and Miss Worth in perfect contrast of style and personality give headlong performances that are vivid in the theatre and are bound to be memorable

afterwards. This is the finest performance Miss Le Gallienne has brought us for a long time. Her Elizabeth is an ascetic-looking woman with a wealth of passion when she is aroused by treachery or a threat to her security. Her guile with her advisers is amusing, her cautiousness and uncertainties are disarming and her assertions of authority are brutal when she is desperate. Thin, pale, fastidious, with a small voice that can express great emotion, Miss Le Gallienne gives a big performance in a small compass.' The production toured the United States and Canada. She closed out of town playing Lavinia Prendergast in *Listen to the Mocking Bird*.

Eva Le Gallienne then toured with the National Repertory Theater playing Elizabeth in *Mary Stuart* and in *Elizabeth the Queen*. From October 1963 to April 1964 she toured as Madame Arkadina in *The Seagull* and Madam Desmermortes in *Ring Round the Moon*; she played *The Seagull* in New York at the Belasco in April 1964. For the National Repertory Company tour of 1964–65 she directed *Liliom* and *Hedda Gabler*, and at the White Barn Theater in Westport, Connecticut, in August 1965 co-presented *The Bernard Shaw Story*. In 1965–66 she toured with the National Repertory as the Countess Aurelia in *The Madwoman of Chaillot* and Hecuba in *The Trojan Women*, returning to Connecticut that summer to co-produce *Come Slowly, Eden, Seven Ages of Bernard Shaw, Israeli Mime Theatre* and *The Effect of Gamma Rays on Man-in-the-Moon Marigolds*.

In 1968 with the APA Repertory Company at the Lyceum, Miss Le Gallienne played Queen Margaret in *Exit the King* and directed her own translation of *The Cherry Orchard*. She joined the American Shakespeare Festival Theater in Stratford, Connecticut, in 1970 to play the Countess in *All's Well That Ends Well*, and went to Seattle, Washington, in February 1975 to direct *A Doll's House*. Back at the White Barn in Connecticut that August she was Mrs Orpha-Woodfin in *The Dream Watcher*, and at the Brooklyn Academy of Music in December played Fanny Cavendish in *The Royal Family*, which transferred to the Helen Hayes Theater.

Miss Le Gallienne has garnered more than a handful of honorary degrees during her lifetime, as well as a special Tony Award in 1964. She has written two volumes of autobiography and a children's book, and has translated numerous plays as well as writing a study of Eleonora Duse. But she is first and foremost a person of the theatre, while remaining a very private individual. As she told the *Christian Science Monitor*: 'I really don't know why I came into the theater, because I am not a theatrical person at all. The outside trappings of the theater do not interest me. I do not care for publicity. I appreciate it when people are kind enough to send me telegrams, or come back to say they have enjoyed the performance. I would really, though, much rather slip into the theater each evening and do my work quietly, because it is the work that I like doing.'

VIVIEN LEIGH

Vivien Mary Hartley was born on 5 November 1913 in Darjeeling, where her father Ernest was a junior partner in a firm of exchange brokers. Her French-Irish mother was extremely cultured, and from an early age instilled good taste into Vivien, her only surviving child.

When Vivien was seven she was sent to school in England as a boarder at the Convent of the Sacred Heart in Roehampton. Even as a child she was extraordinarily beautiful and self-possessed, and at school was both envied and resented. She was no scholar, but showed great interest in music and dance and made her stage début at school playing Mustardseed in *A Midsummer Night's Dream*.

At the age of 13 she began a five-year tour of schools on the continent, in France, Germany and Italy, becoming fluent in all three languages. She also studied acting at the Comédie-Française under Mlle Antoine. She returned to England and enrolled at RADA, but in 1932 married a young barrister, Herbert Leigh Holman. Still longing to be an actress, she had one line in the film *Things Are Looking Up*, in which she played a schoolgirl, and was next seen in *The Village Squire*, *Gentleman's Agreement*, and *Look Up and Laugh*; she was never less than stunning.

Vivien Leigh made her professional stage début at the Q Theatre on 25 February 1935 playing Guista in *The Green Sash*. The following May she was at the Ambassadors' Theatre playing Henriette in *The Mask of Virtue*. The curtain rose and there she was, sitting mid-stage facing the audience, who gasped at her beauty and then broke into applause before a word had been spoken. She was immediately signed by Alexander Korda to a five-year film contract. But he did not cast her immediately, and at Oxford for the OUDS she played the Queen in *Richard II* in February 1936, and at His Majesty's in April 1936 she was Jenny Mere in *The Happy Hypocrite* with Ivor Novello. That June she played Anne Boleyn in *Henry VIII* at the Open Air Theatre, and then made *Fire Over England* for Korda; her co-star was Laurence Olivier. They fell passionately in love and the rest

is recorded history. Meanwhile, on stage at Wyndham's in February she was playing Pamela in *Because We Must*. In March she was Jessica Morton in *Bats in the Belfry*, and in June Olivier took her to Elsinore to play Ophelia to his Hamlet. At Christmas she was at the Old Vic in Tyrone Guthrie's magical production of *A Midsummer Night's Dream*, which according to Audrey Williamson was to haunt the Old Vic consciousness for many years to come. Vivien Leigh played Titania; the music was by Mendelssohn, the choreography by Ninette de Valois, the design by Oliver Messel. Robert Helpmann was Oberon and Ralph Richardson was Bottom. In September 1938 she was at the Gate playing the title role in *Serena Blandish*.

Miss Leigh followed Olivier to Hollywood, where he was making *Wuthering Heights*, and landed for herself the plum role of Scarlett O'Hara in *Gone with the Wind*. The part brought her not only international stardom and an Oscar, but immortality as well.

Both Leigh and Olivier had by this time managed to extricate themselves from previous marriages, and in California in August 1940 they became not only man and wife but a formidable acting duo, though the stage partnership was to come later — first they starred together in the film *Lady Hamilton*. Vivien Leigh made her Broadway début at the 51st Street Theater playing Juliet to her husband's Romeo in Shakespeare's play. It was not a success, and as they had put their own money into the production it was all lost. They returned to England, Olivier to the war and Vivien to set up house for them; she was an expert if increasingly eccentric hostess.

She opened at the Haymarket Theatre in March 1942 as Jennifer Dubedat in a revival of Shaw's *The Doctor's Dilemma* and remained there for a year.

She then toured the Middle East with Beatrice Lillie in a concert party for the troops. She opened at the Phoenix in May 1945 as Sabina in her husband's production of Thornton Wilder's *The Skin of Our Teeth*. James Agate reported on her success: 'On the visual side, owing to Mr Olivier's ingenious inventive producing backed by some brilliantly co-ordinated teamwork, the play must be reckoned a complete success. Through it all, lovely to look at, flitted and fluttered Miss Leigh's hired girl, Sabina, an enchanting piece of nonsense-cum-allure, half dab-chick and half dragon fly. The best performance of this kind since Yvonne Printemps.' *The Skin of Our Teeth* played also at the Piccadilly in 1946. In 1947 Olivier was knighted and he and his wife set off with the Old Vic on a ten-month tour of Australia and New Zealand, playing in *Richard III*, *The School for Scandal* and *The Skin of Our Teeth*. The Old Vic Company returned to the New Theatre in January 1949, where Vivien played Lady Anne in *Richard III* and Lady Teazle in *The School for Scandal* while Olivier played Richard III and Sir Peter. Of the latter production Audrey Williamson said that Vivien was 'as lovely and finely drawn as a picture by Gainsborough. Completely and effortlessly "in period", she achieved wit and grace with porcelain delicacy and a charmingly teasing hint of the minx, in the pointing of a line, that did not preclude a stab of genuine contrition and feeling … she had the right idea of both the style and character of the part …' T. C. Worsley, however, was not completely captivated by her performance: 'Miss Vivien Leigh has been endowed by nature with the most fetching appearance, but she does not succeed in suggesting with it a Lady Teazle. One traces in her voice and her gesture neither the country squire's daughter nor the fashionable wife: what one gets from her is just what one doesn't want for this century — an artshop daintiness.' That Old Vic season she also played Antigone, and Ivor Brown said: 'This is a new Miss Leigh altogether, with a new and strong vocal range, a fanatical force of character and the calm intensity of an unshakable devotee.' Harold Hobson reported: 'In repose, Vivien Leigh's Antigone has a beautiful, statuesque classic calm.'

In 1949 Olivier directed her as Blanche Du Bois in Tennessee Williams' *A Streetcar Named Desire*, which opened at the Aldwych in October, and remained there playing to capacity houses for eight months. Audrey Williamson said she was 'an actress perfect for the part of Blanche in her suggestion of moth-like vulnerability, of a waxen flower of beauty that can only radiate in the softest of lights. The lightness of the woman was brilliantly conveyed with the right needle-point of wit; but there was also present a thin veil of nervous hysteria, the iridescent flushes of a tottering reason, an undercurrent of sheer terror that were not only dramatic but moving. The emotional intensity suggested a new power in the actress, and the ending had quietness and deep pitiability.' She

committed the role to celluloid in Hollywood opposite Marlon Brando, and received her second Oscar.

In 1951 at the St James's Theatre she appeared opposite her husband, in his productions of Shakespeare's *Antony and Cleopatra* and Shaw's *Caesar and Cleopatra*, playing the Egyptian Queen in both. It was generally reckoned that she was much better at Shaw than at Shakespeare. According to T. C. Worsley: ' … she is not and never will be, a classical tragic actress. She simply lacks stature all round … She lacks, as an actress, extravagance of temperament.' (Extravagance of temperament was not something she lacked off the stage — the Oliviers had a stormy personal life; and she was racked with health problems, both mental and physical.) They took both productions to New York to the Ziegfeld Theater in December 1951.

Returning to London in November 1953 Vivien Leigh played Miss Mary Morgan in *The Sleeping Prince*. Kenneth Tynan accused Olivier of lowering himself by pushing his wife into the spotlight. He declared that Vivien was not an equal to Olivier, no matter how hard she tried.

They joined the Shakespeare Memorial Theatre Company at Stratford-on-Avon in 1955 and Vivien played Viola in *Twelfth Night*, Lady Macbeth, and Lavinia in *Titus Andronicus*, directed by Peter Brook. Of her Lady Macbeth, Tynan wrote: 'Vivien Leigh's Lady Macbeth is more niminy-piminy than thundery-blundery, more viper than anaconda, but still quite competent in its small way.'

At the Lyric in London in April 1956 she played Lady Alexandra Shotter in Noel Coward's *South Sea Bubble* — it was not a success for either of them. She spent May and June of 1957 touring Paris, Vienna, Belgrade and Zagreb with the Shakespeare Memorial Theatre Company for the British Council playing Lavinia in *Titus Andronicus*, and played the same part at the Stoll Theatre in London in July. It was the last time she and Olivier were on stage together.

At the Apollo in April 1958 Vivien Leigh played Paola in Giraudoux's *Duel of Angels* with Claire Bloom as the other angel, and then in July 1959 at the Royal Court was Lulu d'Arville in Noel Coward's adaptation of Feydeau's farce, *Look After Lulu*. Bill Lester, writing in *Plays and Players*, said: 'Miss Leigh would delight even as a stooge to a red-nosed comedian, but it does seem a pity that there isn't something more for her talents.' However, the production transferred to the New Theatre in September.

She opened in New York at the Helen Hayes Theater in April 1960, again playing Paola in *Duel of Angels*. This time Mary Ure was her opposite number. *Newsweek* magazine reported that Miss Leigh, 'the vixen who stalks away from the field of honor [is] evil triumphant. Older, surer, and as handsome as she ever was as Scarlett O'Hara, Miss Leigh plays her role with the look of Lilith and the deadly dedication of a Lady Macbeth.' She toured with the play. She also toured during 1961 and 1962 with the Old Vic Company in Australia, New Zealand and South America, playing Viola in *Twelfth Night*, Paola in *Duel of Angels* and Marguerite in *The Lady of the Camellias*.

Vivien Leigh made her musical début at the Broadway Theater in March 1963 playing Tatiana in *Tovarich*, the musical version of an old Claudette Colbert–Charles Boyer film of the thirties. Jean-Pierre Aumont was her leading man. *Time* magazine reported: 'Miss Leigh divertingly peps up the proceedings. She shimmies a madcap

Charleston that ought to be recorded on a film strip of memorable moments from forgettable musicals. She torch-sings an affecting lament for lost first love in a bistro baritone that huskily recalls early Marlene Dietrich . . . she plays the regal scamp all evening, ornamenting with a playfully aristocratic touch the shoddy show goods with which Broadway's indomitable pitchmen hope to mulct the theater-going audience.' For this performance she received a Tony Award in 1963.

Her health continued to fail; she played Contessa Sanziani in *La Contessa* on a tour in England in April 1965, and was planning to return to the West End in Edward Albee's *A Delicate Balance* when she died in London of tuberculosis on 8 July 1967. The London theatre world paid her the tribute of turning off their lights that night. *See photograph opposite page 262.*

MARGARET LEIGHTON

Margaret Leighton was born on 26 February 1922 in Barnt Green in Worcestershire, where her father worked in the cotton trade. Until she was 15 she attended the Church of England College in Edgbaston, Birmingham, but from her earliest teens knew she wanted to be on the stage. 'In ignorance, I just liked the idea of it,' she said, 'and I felt sure I could make a living at it.' In 1938 she auditioned for Sir Barry Jackson at the Birmingham Repertory Theatre, and he took her on as an assistant deputy stage manager. She made her first appearance there as Dorothy in *Laugh With Me* on 4 September 1938. In January 1941 she joined Basil C. Langton's Travelling Repertory Company, and before she returned to the Birmingham Rep in December 1942 played many parts — in *The Cricket on the Hearth*, *The Doctor's Dilemma*, *Ah, Wilderness!*, *I Have Been Here Before*, *The Importance of Being Earnest*, *The Devil's Disciple*, *The Late Christopher Bean*, and *Arms and the Man*, to name but a few. She remained at Birmingham until 1944 when she decided to audition for the Old Vic Company. Olivier and Richardson came to Birmingham to see her play and asked her to join them at the New Theatre. Margaret Leighton made her London début on 31 August 1944, playing the Troll King's Daughter in *Peer Gynt*. In September she played Raina in *Arms and the Man*, and Audrey Williamson reported: 'Margaret Leighton, tall, slender and fair

as an arum lily was an enchanting Raina, with a shy humour lurking behind the romantic dignity.' Also that September she played Queen Elizabeth in *Richard III*, and in January 1945 she was Elena in *Uncle Vanya*. The following September and October she played Lady Percy in *Henry IV* and Mrs Dangle in *The Critic*.

Margaret Leighton went with the Old Vic Company to America and made her New York début on 6 May 1946 playing Lady Percy in *Henry IV*. She stayed on there in repertory. When she returned to England with the company W. A. Darlington reported: 'Whatever it may have done for their reputations, this American tour certainly developed the skill of some of the younger members of the company, more particularly of Margaret Leighton. Before she sailed she was just a pretty and promising actress, and I admit without shame that I had, up to then, found her a little dull. She was anything but dull when she came back. She had crossed more than the ocean — she had put behind her that invisible line which divides promise in an artist from achievement. She had always been good to look at, but good looks matter surprisingly little on the stage unless they are illuminated from within; as she now was. In the third season of the Old Vic at the New Theatre she had become a personage, clearly bound for the heights.' During that third season, from September 1946 to April 1947, Margaret Leighton played many varied roles. According to Harold Hobson she was a 'swooning

Regan' in the production of *King Lear* in which Laurence Olivier played the King and Alec Guinness was the Fool. Audrey Williamson elaborated: 'The languorous pure Saxon beauty of this Regan, a model for Rossetti, made the cruelty and sensuality the more horrifying: it was like honey turned rancid.' She was Roxanne in *Cyrano de Bergerac* and was, according to Williamson, 'all moonlight and silver; beautiful as Cyrano's dream but with a certain rippling amusement that softened the character's tendency to romantic vapidity'. She was Sheila Birling in Priestley's *An Inspector Calls*, Dame Pliant in *The Alchemist*, and the Queen in *Richard II*.

At the Criterion Theatre in June 1947 she played three parts — Harriet Marshall, Wilhelmina Cameron and Hope Cameron — in one play, *The Sleeping Clergyman*, with Robert Donat. Harold Hobson said that it was 'a play that has some of the best acting in London...Miss Leighton, as a betrayed young woman, a murderess, and an international pacifist, whose intensity of conviction, beside the thundering force of Mr Donat, seems pale only because it has passed from red heat to white, gives three impressive performances. In particular, her young murderess has a subdued, breathless excitement that is strangely disturbing; it twines itself round the heart and almost strangles it. Never, whilst I've been about, has Miss Leighton played as well as this before.'

Margaret Leighton made her first film in 1947 playing Flora MacDonald to David Niven's *Bonnie Prince Charlie*. The film did not do very well, but it was regarded as a personal success for Miss Leighton. That year also she married the publisher Max Reinhardt.

In December 1949 Margaret Leighton was at the Duchess Theatre playing Tracy Lord (the part made famous in the United States by Katharine Hepburn) in *The Philadelphia Story*. She moved on to the New in May 1950 playing Celia Coplestone in T. S. Eliot's *The Cocktail Party*. T. C. Worsley reported: 'Miss Margaret Leighton gains in the first act by putting more feeling into the scene where she is discarded. But she tries to put too much, or the wrong kind, into her conversion scene. Spiritual states are doubtless very difficult to represent, but her staring eyes and strained intensities did not convince me.' On the other hand, Audrey Williamson thought that her 'honey-toned Saxon beauty framed in gold like a waxen Sienese Madonna gave an additional poignancy to the girl's fate'.

The following May she was at the Aldwych playing Masha in *The Three Sisters* with Renee Asherson and Celia Johnson. T. C. Worsley said she 'was quite excellent in her last scene and indeed made the best impression of the three sisters throughout'.

In 1952 she joined the Shakespeare Memorial Theatre Company at Stratford-on-Avon for the season. There she played Lady Macbeth to Ralph Richardson's Macbeth, directed by John Gielgud. Kenneth Tynan said: 'Margaret Leighton seized her big solo opportunity, waking up to give us a gaunt, pasty, compulsive reading of the [sleepwalking] scene which atoned for many of her earlier inadequacies ... [however] to cast a woman as attractive as Miss Leighton in the part is like casting a gazelle as Medusa.' Next she was Ariel in *A Midsummer Night's Dream* and, finally that season, Rosalind in *As You Like It*. Tynan said she 'was giving a highly ornamental exhibition of technique as Rosalind. Fulsomely she showed us all her tricks, but the impression left was somehow chilly, in the manner of some of Lynn Fontanne's lesser achievements. This Rosalind was a gay and giggly creature — loads of fun, game for any jape, rather like a popular head girl — but a tiring companion, I felt, after a long day.' Margaret Leighton's Orlando in *As You Like It*, Laurence Harvey, did not find Tynan's observation true. They began a lengthy and passionate affair in Stratford that summer.

Returning to London, at the Haymarket in May 1953 Margaret Leighton played Orinthia in a revival of Shaw's *The Apple Cart* and at the Edinburgh Festival that autumn she played Lucasta Angel in T. S. Eliot's *The Confidential Clerk*. This transferred to the Lyric in London in September 1953. According to Caryl Brahms: 'She played her confession scene so movingly as to suggest that she does not realize what a good actress she is, for if she did she would rely more often on her inspired art and less frequently on her brilliant artifice.'

The following September Margaret Leighton was at the St James's in Rattigan's double-bill, *Separate Tables*. She played Mrs Shankland in *The Window Table*. Ronald Barker said: 'Margaret Leighton, looking beautiful, reveals an unsuspected depth in her acting. Never before has she been so moving, so sincere. Gone are the petty affectations which have spoilt her work in the past.' And of her performance as Miss Railton-Bell in the second offering, *Table Number Seven*, Barker said: 'As the drab girl Margaret Leighton reveals a sense of character based on observation which we seldom see in the theatre today. But above all, she shows an imaginative quality which is painful to watch.' She repeated the parts at the Music Box in New York, opening there in October 1956, and was awarded the Tony for her performances. Max Reinhardt divorced her on grounds of misconduct with Laurence Harvey, whom she married in Gibraltar (where he was filming) in 1957.

Margaret Leighton was at the Globe Theatre in London in May 1958 playing Rose in *Variations on a Theme*, Rattigan's misguided journey around *La Dame aux camélias*. She returned to New York in September 1959 to play Beatrice in Sir John Gielgud's production of *Much Ado About Nothing* at the Lunt-Fontanne Theater. Sir John wrote: 'I thought my production had become rather old-fashioned. They reproduced the scenery poorly and it was not well lit. It looked like a Soho trattoria and lacked the lovely classical Italian quality that it had in England.' However, he added that Margaret Leighton was 'absolutely enchanting'.

She returned to London to the Cambridge in February 1960 playing Elaine Lee in *The Wrong Side of the Park* by John Mortimer, and in March was at the Queen's Theatre playing Ellida in Ibsen's *The Lady from the Sea*. Caryl Brahms reported: 'Miss Leighton, in one sea-green tea-gown after another, played the Lady with the thing-about-the-lake with the right kind of willowy strength and managed to look attractive with her mouth open, like the fish gasping for air which was the image she was feeling for but . . . she never made me feel she was a woman torn.'

Margaret Leighton then returned to New York, where in December 1961 at the Royale she opened as Hannah Jelkes in Tennessee Williams' *The Night of the Iguana*. Brooks Atkinson said the play was 'acted with an eerie sense of fore-boding by Margaret Leighton, Bette Davis and Alan Webb'. For this performance Miss Leighton received a Tony Award, a Variety Award and a Newspaper Guild Page One Award. At the Plymouth in New York she opened in October 1962 as Pamela Pew-Pickett in *Tchin-Tchin*. Back at the Royale in January 1964 she played She in *The Chinese Prime Minister*. At the Philharmonia Hall in March 1964 she appeared in *Homage to Shakespeare*, a programme in celebration of the Shakespeare Quatercentenary. That year she married Michael Wilding, the film actor turned agent, and former husband of Elizabeth Taylor. After a brief, fruitless trip to Hollywood she returned to New York where she appeared in a Tennessee Williams double-bill at the Longacre in February 1966, playing Trinket in *The Mutilated* and the title part in *Gnädiges Fräulein*.

Margaret Leighton returned to London, where she opened in March 1967 as Stephanie in *Cactus Flower* at the Lyric. It was the part in which Lauren Bacall triumphed on Broadway. Hugh Leonard reported: 'She sails through *Cactus Flower* like a Rolls purring through a slum. It is debatable whether she saves the play or shows up

its tawdriness by, through some strange alchemy, transforming her character from a puppet into a human being . . . The vehicle may be shabby but Miss Leighton is a magnificent passenger.' Back in New York in November 1967 she opened at the Ethel Barrymore playing Birdie in *The Little Foxes* with George C. Scott and Anne Bancroft. John Simon reported: 'Margaret Leighton's pathetic Birdie is rather too young, too shrill, too deliberate to be truly pathetic and her accent is just a little bit South of Viven Leigh's Scarlett O'Hara and just as convincing. But at least she tries.'

John Clements invited Margaret Leighton to the Chichester Festival in July 1969 to play Cleopatra to his Antony, and for this performance she received the Variety Club Award for Best Performance by an Actress. Helen Dawson, however, writing in *Plays and Players*, thought they were both just too old for *Antony and Cleopatra*. Also, she wrote, 'Margaret Leighton is finely elegant, angularly egocentric, an aristocrat among ladies. But not a majesty; not a politician. As an actress she has perfected the art of steering round the hard edges of mid-twentieth century woman: this is where her roots are, and this is where she is special. The aura of pre-Christian Egypt (and on some occasions 20th Century Fox Egypt) hangs uneasily about her. And where is the gypsy-witch who so fascinated Shakespeare? She may be lurking there, and if she had been unearthed the combination with Margaret Leighton's already proven qualities might have been astonishing. But this Cleopatra at Chichester is too self-critical to dare such abandon.'

At the Apollo in London in February 1970 she played Lettice Mason in *Girlfriend*, a play about homosexuality which closed very quickly. About this time Margaret Leighton began to display distressing and painful symptoms which were later diagnosed as multiple sclerosis. She did not, however, let them interfere with her return to Chichester in summer 1971, where in May she played Mrs Malaprop in *The Rivals* and in July, Elena in *Reunion in Vienna*. The latter transferred to the Piccadilly in London in February 1972. Ivan Hewlett reported: 'Margaret Leighton's Elena has progressed from being the dominant performance at Chichester to being a sheer delight, the only figure embodying the intended romantic mystery.'

In 1974 Margaret Leighton was delighted to receive a CBE. Her last stage appearance was at the Apollo in April 1975, when she played Matty Seaton in Julian Mitchell's adaptation of Ivy Compton-Burnett's *A Family and a Fortune*, with Alec Guinness. This part she acted in a wheelchair, and despite great pain she played for a year. When the production closed she deteriorated very quickly, and died on 13 January 1976.

LOTTE LENYA

The name Lotte Lenya is inextricably tied to that of her husband, Kurt Weill, and his collaborator Bertolt Brecht.

Lotte Lenya was born Karoline Blamauer in Hitzing, Vienna, on 18 October, in either 1898 or 1900. Her father was a city coachman and her mother a laundress. After the First World War she was drawn to the theatrical capital of the German-speaking world, Berlin, where in 1920 she joined a small company devoted to the production of Shakespearian plays. The playwright Georg Kaiser and his wife took her under their wing and it was they who in 1924 introduced her to Kurt Weill. She and Weill married in 1926.

The first collaboration between Bertolt Brecht and Kurt Weill was the short opera *Songspiel* (later to be known as *Little Mahagonny*) which opened at the Baden-Baden Chamber Music Festival in 1927. Lenya (the stage name derives from her nickname, Lenja) played Jenny. The controversial success of *Songspiel* led to further collaboration on *The Threepenny Opera* (*Die Dreigroschenoper*), which opened at the Theater-am-Schiffbauerdamm in Berlin in August 1928. Lenya alternated Lucy and Jenny. It became an enormous European hit and Lenya became a star. At the Stadttheater in Berlin in 1929 she played Jocasta in *Oedipus* and the following year at the Volksbuehne was in *Danton's Death* and *The Awakening of Spring*.

At the Theater-am-Kurfurstendamm, also in 1930, she played Pionière in *Ingolstadt*, and in 1931 played Jenny in Brecht and Weill's *Aufstieg und Fall de Stadt Mahagonny* (*Rise and Fall of Mahagonny*, an expanded *Songspiel*) there; the following year at the Volksbuehne she was in *Song of Hoboken*.

The Nazis came to power. Kurt Weill was Jewish, so he and Lenya left Germany for Paris where, at the Théâtre des Champs-Elysées, she sang Anna I in *The Seven Deadly Sins*. Although Weill once said, 'My melodies always come to my inner ear in Lenya's voice,' this was the only piece he and Brecht wrote especially for her. Lenya gave concerts in Paris and London and then, in 1936, went to America with her husband. On 7 January 1937 she made her New York début as Miriam in Max Reinhardt's production of *The Eternal Road*. She appeared as Cissie in *Candle in the Wind* at the Shubert Theater in October 1941 and as the Duchess in *The Firebrand of Florence* at the Alvin in March 1945. Then it was not until after Kurt Weill's sudden heart attack and death in 1950 that she devoted herself to the stage once more. At the

time she said she 'wanted to crawl into a hole and never come out', but the following year she married the former editor of *Harper's Bazaar*, George Davis, who actively encouraged her to resume her career. She became a missionary of her late husband's work. In early 1951 Lenya gave a concert performance at the Town Hall, NYC, of *The Threepenny Opera* and in October at the Martin Beck Theater played Socrates' wife, Xantippe, in *Barefoot in Athens* by Maxwell Anderson, a close friend and colleague of Weill. At the Théâtre de Lys in Greenwich Village Lenya re-emerged at the forefront of theatrical life when once more she played Jenny in *The Threepenny Opera*. This was Marc Blitzstein's English adaptation of the work. The *New York Times* reported: 'Miss Lenya . . . delivers her role with the necessary strength and authority.' The show had to close because the theatre was previously booked but a year later it reopened and lasted for nearly seven years, though Lenya left the production occasionally to do other things, including a definitive recording of the works of Weill. In 1957 her second husband died.

At the New York City Center in 1958 Lenya was once more Anna I in *The Seven Deadly Sins* in an acclaimed staging of the work by the New York City Ballet. In 1962, back at the Théâtre de Lys, Lenya opened in George Tabori's adaptation of Brecht's work, the revue *Brecht on Brecht*, in which she joined Viveca Lindfors, Anne Jackson, Dane Clark, George Voskovec and Michael Wager. Howard Taubman reported: 'The flashes of Brecht's theater glow brilliantly. Miss Lenya's singing of the song of Mother Courage, with the pride of a marcher in the ranks, has a grim vitality.' They toured the United States, subsequently bringing *Brecht on Brecht* to London to the Royal Court in September 1962. That November Lenya married the painter Russell Detwiler.

At Carnegie Hall on 8 January 1965 Lenya sang in *A Kurt Weill Evening*. 'In a Kurt Weill work I am as nervous as a cat,' she said. 'A burden falls on my shoulders. I feel a crushing responsibility.' Her next Broadway venture was not Weill: Lenya played Fräulein Schneider in the musical *Cabaret* at the Broadhurst, opening in November 1966. Walter Kerr reported in the *New York Times* that the music offered Miss Lenya ' . . . several enchantingly throaty plaints, notably a winning acceptance of the way things are, called "So What?" ' Miss Lenya has never been better, or if she has been, I don't believe it.' She won a Tony

Award for this performance. Lenya's third husband died in 1969 and she continued to spread the gospel of Weill and Bertolt Brecht. In 1973 she was a notable Mother Courage in Los Angeles.

Lotte Lenya had begun her film career in Germany in 1930 with *The Threepenny Opera*, and in later years was nominated for an Academy Award for her performance in *The Roman Spring of Mrs Stone* (1961).

Apart from her definitive recordings of Weill, Lotte Lenya will possibly be best remembered by future generations for her performance as Rosa Kleb, the deadly Spectre agent trapped forever in celluloid in *From Russia with Love*.

Alone at the end of her life she kept a close watch over productions of Weill's work. Her renditions of his songs had made her a legend ('I prefer to be a legend than an old scrap heap,' she said) — and it was her performance that gave his music life. When asked what she considered the most important quality in an actress she replied: 'To come out on stage and know instantly whether you have your audience in your hands. That happens to me all the time.' Lotte Lenya died on 27 November 1981.

BEATRICE LILLIE

Beatrice Gladys Lillie was born on 29 May 1898 in Toronto, Canada, the second daughter of ambitious and musical Lucie Shaw and her husband John Lillie, who at the time of the birth was working as a guard at the city prison. Beatrice came to London after she left school, and her mother hoped to turn herself and her two daughters into a successful trio. This was not to be.

Beatrice managed to make her London début at the Pavilion in April 1914 in *The Daring of Diane*. It was that October that she first appeared in a revue by André Charlot, *Not Likely*, at the Alhambra Theatre. Her first personal success came in her second Charlot revue — *5064 Gerrard* in March 1915, also at the Alhambra. Dressed in farmer's overalls and carrying a milk pail she sang 'Take Me Back to Michigan'. She quickly became, according to the critics, 'one of the most dapper and accomplished of contemporary male impersonators'.

As a boy in *Now's The Time* (Alhambra, October 1915) she sang a duet with Lee White called 'Up the River', and then, in white tie and tails, was Lord Lionel Lyonesse singing 'Where the Black Eyed Susans Grow'. By the time she had been through *Samples* (March 1916), *Some* (June 1916), *Cheep* (April 1917) and *Tabs* (May 1918), all at the Vaudeville, she had given up her earlier ambition of singing sad songs and decided to settle for being a comedienne. She had become a great favourite with audiences and with gossip columnists. Noel Coward reported that the revue of *Cheep* was 'the first time that Beatrice Lillie appeared in her true colours as a comic genius of the first order'.

In December 1918 Beatrice Lillie opened at the Prince's Theatre, Manchester, as Jackie Sampson in *Oh, Joy!* — her first book musical as opposed to a revue. It was the English version of the American *Oh, Boy!* She came to London to the Kingsway Theatre with the production in January 1919. In August of the same year Beatrice Lillie was back in revue at the Prince of Wales in *Bran-Pie*.

At the beginning of 1920 Beatrice Lillie married the extravagant Robert Peel. In December their son, also Robert, was born. Beatrice was soon back on stage, at the Playhouse in April 1921 where she played Geraldine Ainsworth in a farce called *Up in Mabel's Room*. With her mother to look after her son, Beatrice went back to revue at the Vaudeville where she was in *Now and Then* (October 1921) and *Pot Luck* (December 1921). At the Prince of Wales in September 1922 she was in *A to Z* and at the Little Theatre the next month was in *The Nine O'Clock Revue*, for which her sister had written the music and which ran for a year.

Beatrice Lillie made her New York début at the Times Square Theater on 9 January 1924 where, with Gertrude Lawrence and Jack Buchanan, she opened in *André Charlot's Revue of 1924*. The *New York Times* reported: 'There is no one in New York quite comparable to Beatrice Lillie. In appearance she is an exaggerated Lynn Fontanne, and it is in burlesque that she shines. The opening of the second act found her as a fifty-year-old soubrette, still bent upon singing the giddy ballads of her youth. And in "March With Me", a bit of patriotism near the finish, she rose to superb heights.' The show was originally booked for six weeks — it ran for nine months, then toured the country for six months. It was while they were in Chicago that she learned of her father-in-law's death; her husband inherited a baronetcy, and the comic Bea Lillie became Lady Peel.

In March 1925 she returned to England, where at the Prince of Wales Theatre there was such demand for tickets to the *Charlot Revue* that they took the unprecedented step of having two first nights on the same evening, playing at eight and midnight. She returned to New York to the Selwyn Theater for the *Charlot Revue of 1926* and then toured with it, ending up at Hollywood's El Capitain Theater. She stayed there to make her first film, *Exit Smiling*. It was also in 1926 that Beatrice Lillie made her first appearance in cabaret at Charlot's Rendezvous Club.

At the Fulton Theater in New York in December 1926 she opened as Lily Valli in *Oh, Please*, a farce revue in two acts. Brooks Atkinson wrote in the *New York Times*: ' . . . Miss Lillie, an incomparable comedienne in the highly intelligent vein of Charlie Chaplin, has no patience with the stuffy sentimentalities and mawkish romance of the musical stage . . . [she] is a comedienne with a divine spark, a mimic of the highest skill, and everything she does is shot through with a piercing sense of humor . . . she ridicules every traditional staple of musical comedy, everyone of the cast, everyone in the audience, and nearly everything she does herself. The friendliest of first night audiences was completely captivated whenever she was on the stage — responsive to every meaningful flick of her eye-lashes, every fleeting expression on her face.'

But Walter Winchell reported: 'No star, perhaps, ever received such wretched and abominable support as that which Lady Peel drew last night. When an ensemble maiden wasn't catching her ice skates in the star's frock, or a youth didn't forget his lines, or a curtain refused to lift, or Conductor Previn didn't muff a music cue, a stage mechanic or two interfered with Miss Lillie's solos . . . This affectionate spectator wept for her.' Miss Lillie toured with this show.

At the Globe in January 1928 she was Tilly in *She's My Baby*. The *New York Times* critic reported: 'whenever Beatrice Lillie was on stage . . . the audience succumbed to her extraordinary comic genius. The "musical comedy farce" in which she appeared was wretched enough, the good Lord knows; even Miss Lillie could not be wholly indifferent to it . . . It is no secret that Miss Lillie is no ordinary musical stage comedian trading in cracks and buffoonery. She is not only subtle and mischievous, but so brilliantly intelligent, so restrained with every stroke, that she can twist "Don't we have fun!" into the funniest line ever

spoken. Whether she is ringing every banal change on the sentimental ballad-bawler's artistry or looking behind her chair to see who poked her from the rear, Miss Lillie keeps her clowning in terms of the intellect. Through all her low travesties she holds the image of one idea before her audience; and she does not spare her own skill in her burlesque of every musical comedy convention. It is, as the initiated say dryly, "so much clean fun". Miss Lillie is good — hell, she's perfect . . .'

Beatrice Lillie returned in 1928 to London, where she appeared at the Palladium. Back in New York in November of the same year she was at the Selwyn in Noel Coward's *This Year of Grace*. She played the Palace in February 1930 and then toured the United States in vaudeville, on the Orpheum circuit. In one of her skits, *After Dinner Music*, written for her by Noel Coward, she played an ageing *prima donna*.

In London in September 1930 in *Charlot's Masquerade* at the newly opened Cambridge Theatre she did an Irish jig in wedgies, a clog dance in galoshes and a skit about Hollywood, of which she was none too fond. In June 1931 she was back in New York at the Music Box, where in *The Third Little Show* she sang Coward's 'Mad Dogs and Englishmen'. She was at the Palace again in January 1932. In April 1932 for the Theater Guild at their own theatre Beatrice Lillie played Sweetie the Nurse in George Bernard Shaw's *Too True To Be Good* with Claude Rains and Leo G. Carroll. The *Herald Tribune* reported: 'The Guild subscribers and the Shavians speak of it with proper respect but unregenerate outsiders call it Beatrice Lillie's show.' By December she was back in revue at the St James Theater with Bobby Clark in *Walk a Little Faster*, which lasted 119 performances.

Beatrice Lillie was back in London at the Savoy in November 1933 in revue. In 1934 her private life was marred by the tragedy of her husband's death from peritonitis following an appendicitis operation. In January 1935 Bea Lillie was again in variety at the Palladium. She returned in September to New York, where at the Winter Garden she was in *At Home Abroad* with Eleanor Powell, Ethel Waters and Reginald Gardiner. Cole Porter wrote 'Mrs Lowsborough-Goodby' for her. In December 1936 she was in *The Show Is On* with Bert Lahr at the same theatre. It ran for nearly a year, during which time Bea Lillie performed in cabaret after the show each night at the newly opened Rainbow Room in the Rockefeller Center. She then had another stab at Hollywood, where she made *Dr Rhythm* with Bing Crosby.

After returning to London, in May 1938 she was at the Adelphi with Flanagan and Allen in

Charles Cochran's *Happy Returns*. In this show she did a burlesque of Evelyn Laye playing Helen of Troy. She also managed to find time during the run to play in cabaret twice nightly at the Café de Paris. She returned to Broadway in January 1939 to the Music Box in Coward's *Set to Music*.

Beatrice Lillie began touring to entertain the troops in October 1939, when she went to Scapa Flow. She was in revue at the Queen's in December 1939, in *All Clear*. At the Globe in July 1940 at a benefit for the Actors' Orphanage she appeared in Coward's *Tonight at 8.30*, and then toured the bases throughout Britain with it. With ENSA in 1940 she was in *Plays and Music*, and continued to entertain the troops throughout 1941. It was in Manchester in April 1942, on the opening night of Cochran's revue, *Big Top*, that she learned her son, who had joined the Navy, was missing in action, presumed dead. She managed to come with the production to London to His Majesty's Theatre in May 1942, and at the end of that year she once again took up travelling to entertain the troops, visiting the Mediterranean, Africa and the Middle East until 1944, when illness forced her to cease. She received the African Star for her efforts.

In February 1944, still not fully recovered, she played Frieda Appleby in Robert Morley's *Staff Dance* at the New Theatre in Oxford, but the production never made it to London. She went to New York in December, where at the Ziegfeld Theater she appeared in *Seven Lively Arts*, for which she received the Donaldson Award. In London at the Garrick in April 1946 she was in *Better Late*. At the Century Theater in New York in April 1948 she was in *Inside USA* with Jack Haley. Brooks Atkinson described the revue: 'It was as contemporary as a newspaper; it was a sharp comment on America.' It was in this revue that Bea originated her famous pearl twirling bit. She toured with this revue until 1950.

Beatrice Lillie then devised *An Evening with Beatrice Lillie*. She began touring the summer theatres with it in 1952, and opened at the Booth Theater in New York in October 1952. Brooks Atkinson wrote in the *New York Times*: 'Beatrice Lillie is the funniest woman in the world and her program of songs and sketches is admirable and hilarious . . . You leave Miss Lillie's show full of laughter, and full of admiration also. For she is a brilliant artist and craftsman as well as an uproarious buffoon . . . her style is always demure on the surface; the manner is dry, the gestures sharp and spare, the pace is like quicksilver and the whole thing adds up to the most brilliant comic spirit of our times.' It ran nearly a year at the Booth and then she toured it through the United States and

Canada until 1954, when she went to entertain the troops in Tokyo and Hong Kong.

In October 1954 Beatrice Lillie opened her *Evening with . . .* at the Court Theatre in Liverpool and then brought it into London, to the Globe, in November. Ronald Barker wrote in *Plays and Players*: 'Other generations may have had their Mistinguette and their Marie Lloyd. We have our Beatrice Lillie and seldom have we seen such a display of perfect talent . . . As to the accusation that she still perpetuates the period of the twenties, she is a sufficiently great artist (I use these words after careful consideration) to revitalize her material at every performance. There is nothing démodé about her. She is as fresh and smart as the Dior H line and much more attractive.' Beatrice Lillie toured through Britain with the show until September 1955. The following January she took it to Miami and Palm Beach in Florida, and then toured the summer theatres in the United States with a solo entertainment, *Beasop's Fables*. At the Winter Garden Theater in New York in March 1957 she appeared in the Golden Jubilee edition of the *Ziegfeld Follies* with Billy de Wolfe. The following year at the Broadhurst she took over the title part of *Auntie Mame* from Ros Russell. Brooks Atkinson went along to have a look at her Mame and wrote: 'Her impact goes deeper than clowning. It discovers a tender relationship between the comic beldame and her little nephew. By the time you read this, Miss Lillie will have made *Mame* her own.' Beatrice Lillie opened in the part at the Adelphi Theatre in London in September 1958, where she ran for more than a year. Caryl Brahms wrote: 'Miss Lillie has a way with words. Almost she pipes and they dance for her. She treats words with respect and a profound understanding, for a word is to Miss Lillie what a prop is to a clown — the thing is to win a laugh with . . . And underlying the speaking of the line and the staccato personality of the speaker is the wit and steely strength and the infectious friendliness of the unique Bea Lillie with the face of an urchin and the smile of a cherub; outrageous and real in a breath. And like a conjurer her tricks are at her fingertips — dexterous, clean, clear.'

At the Alvin Theater in New York in April 1964 Bea Lillie played Madame Arcati in *High Spirits*, a musical version of Coward's *Blithe Spirit*. Miss Lillie's performances on film have not been among her best mainly because, as with all great performers, she needs an audience. It is an essential part of her act. Notably, though, she appeared in *Around the World in Eighty Days* and *Thoroughly Modern Millie*.

She retired to her Queen Anne house at Henley, where she has been nursed through years of illness by her manager John Philip. The two great New York critics of the mid-1900s summed up her genius. First Brooks Atkinson: '... Beatrice Lillie [was] a comic genius. A slight, elegant lady with sharp features, a modish personality and a small tight, abashed grin, Miss Lillie had an incomparable gift for raillery. She overwhelmed the audience, not by broad strokes, but by gleams and grimaces. Her mind was hard, and it was always far ahead of the audience's. It hated sentimentality, pretentiousness and buncombe. Standing a little to one side of the main action, she undermined everything by the bright irradiations of her intelligence. She could turn a

sentimental ballad about the fairies at the bottom of her garden into a devastating comment on the whole range of culture.'

And her talent was summarized by John Mason Brown: '...her comedy always appears effortless. It never seems to have exhausted itself. Something is always left in reserve. This is but a part of the ever quickening intelligence Miss Lillie brings to the words she speaks and her all-expressive pantomime. She knows how to poke fun at the gravity which befits Lady Peel in such a ludicrous manner that delighted audiences must sometimes wonder if her proper title is not Lady Banana Peel.'

ROGER LIVESEY

Roger Livesey was born in Barry, South Wales, on 25 June 1906, the third son of Sam Livesey, a distinguished touring actor. As a child he attended Westminster City School and became a pupil of Italia Conti. Roger made his stage début at the age of 11 playing the Office Boy in *Loyalties* at the St James's Theatre on 21 November 1917. His father was also in the cast, and Roger decided to follow his older brothers into a stage career. He subsequently appeared as Jimmy in *A Pair of Sixes* (Queen's, September 1920), Spot in *The Windmill Man* (Victoria Palace, December 1921), Benjy Sturgis in *If Four Walls Told* (Royalty, April 1922), Ike Levi in *Love in Pawn* (Kingsway, March 1923), Jim Street in *The Man in the Next Room* (Ambassadors', July 1924), Henry in *Fata Morgana* (Ambassadors', September 1924), Alfred in *The Cuckoo in the Nest* (Aldwych, July 1925), and Snout in *A Midsummer Night's Dream* (Winter Garden, December 1926). Roger Livesey then toured the West Indies with Florence Glossop-Harris and spent two seasons acting in South Africa.

When he returned to England it was to the Ambassadors', where in September 1929 he opened in *The Misdoings of Charley Peace*. At the same theatre in October 1930 he was Tuck in *A Grain of Mustard*. He was Detective Curwen in *Sensation* at the Lyceum in October 1931, and at the Arts the next month he was Geoffrey Preston in Ronald MacKenzie's *Musical Chairs* with John Gielgud. In January 1932 he was at the Queen's playing Richard Coaker in *The Farmer's Wife* and in April was Martin Rothaker in *Caravan*. For the

Arts Theatre Club at the New in June 1932 he played Bolingbroke to John Gielgud's Richard in *Richard of Bordeaux*, and in September at the Criterion went back into *Musical Chairs*.

Harcourt Williams invited Roger Livesey to join the Old Vic–Sadler's Wells Company at the Waterloo Road; he stayed with them for two years working under the direction of Tyrone Guthrie. He played the Duke to Flora Robson's Isabella, and Caliban in *The Tempest* when Charles Laughton was Prospero. Then, with his father Sam playing his stage father, Sir Sampson, and his brother Barry playing Valentine, Roger Livesey played Ben in Congreve's *Love for Love*.

He returned to the West End in May 1934 playing Alfred in *Martine* and Fontaney in *The Poet's Secret*. In June at the Globe he was Harold Parker in *Meeting at Night*. In August he was Jim Milburn in *Sour Grapes* at the Apollo and he scored a great success at the Little Theatre in November 1934 playing Hsieh-Ping-Kuei in the Chinese play *Lady Precious Stream*. Audrey Williamson reported that he exercised 'all the family charm and gusto on an invisible horse as the romantic gardener'. At the Royalty in February 1936 he was Frank Burdon in *Storm in a Teacup*. Roger Livesey had already begun his film career, and was notable as the beggar in Korda's *Rembrandt* whom Charles Laughton, playing the title role, used as his model for King Saul.

His father died shortly before Roger made his New York stage début at the Henry Miller Theater on 1 December 1936 playing Mr Horner in *The Country Wife*; Ruth Gordon had the title role. The following month he married the actress Ursula

Jeans, whom he had met during his time under Guthrie at the Old Vic. He stayed in New York to play Frank Burdon once more in *Storm in a Teacup*, which had been retitled *Storm over Patsy* for its production at the Guild Theater, and he returned to London where he took over the part of Macduff from Ellis Irving in Olivier's *Macbeth*, playing it, according to Audrey Williamson, 'with a husky and rugged sympathy'. The huskiness was due to throat cancer, which would plague him throughout his career. At the Ambassadors' in May 1938, he played Sir Richard Furze in *Spring Meeting*, and then returned to the Old Vic in February 1930. There he played Dr Stockman in Ibsen's *Enemy of the People*. According to Audrey Williamson 'Livesey was perfectly cast, and his joviality and absent-minded bustle made the doctor a living character from the first moments of the play'. His throat trouble recurred and Wilfrid Walter took over the role. Still for the Old Vic he played Petruchio and his wife played Kate in the *commedia dell'arte* production of *The Taming of the Shrew*, which was to be the last at Waterloo Road before the war. Miss Williamson saw this performance also and reported: 'Roger Livesey, battling with gusto against a rather unserviceable voice, gave indication of being an interesting and surprisingly subtle Petruchio in any other production and in the meantime a highly acrobatic and uproarious one in this.' At the Piccadilly in July 1940 Roger Livesey played Anthony Anderson in *The Devil's Disciple* with Robert Donat, and at the Globe in January 1941 he was Matey in John Gielgud's production of *Dear Brutus* with Zena Dare. He made a number of notable films during the war, particularly Powell and Pressberger's *The Life and Death of Colonel Blimp*, in which he played the title role, *I Know Where I'm Going* with Wendy Hiller, and *A Matter of Life and Death*, which was the Royal Film Performance choice for 1946. He toured in 1943 in Lillian Hellman's *The Watch on the Rhine*, and brought it into the Aldwych in August 1943. At the Theatre Royal, Glasgow, in February 1944 he was Philip in *The Fifth Column*, and at Wyndham's that September played Lieutenant-General Hume Banbury in Peter Ustinov's *The Banbury Nose*. With his wife he toured for ENSA in *Dear Brutus*, *The Watch on the Rhine* and *Springtime for Henry*. After the war, at the New in June 1947, Roger Livesey and Ursula Jeans were the leading couple in J. B. Priestley's *Ever Since Paradise*.

Roger Livesey played Hoederer in Jean-Paul Sartre's *Crime Passionel* at the Lyric, Hammersmith, in June 1948. T. C. Worsley reported: 'Mr Livesey's acting seems to me a most exceptional piece of work. From the moment when

he walks in we seem to see the whole man; it is all there in his grunt and chuckle, the set of his shoulders, the cigarette he rolls, his intonations, his accent, his bear-like shamble.' And Harold Hobson said: 'Roger Livesey plays Hoederer with friendliness and charm. He makes him the embodiment of a reasonableness rough but sweet.' In February 1950 he was George Bernard in *Man of the World*, an experimental play produced by the Company of Four and directed by Kenneth Tynan.

The Old Vic reopened in November 1950, and Roger Livesey played Sir Toby Belch in Hugh Hunt's production of *Twelfth Night*, while Ursula Jeans played Olivia. T. C. Worsley praised his performance: 'Mr Roger Livesey is a rich, bursting Sir Toby, who never misses an opportunity for a bit of business but never gives us too much, never a belch or a stagger in excess, and he remains — that priceless attribute in an actor — always in perfect command.' That same season he was Adam Overdo in *Bartholomew Fair*, of which performance T. C. Worsley wrote: 'From the moment when he charms us into his confidence, we simply wait for his return in one disguise or another. It is his large commanding air that enables his character to bulge out in a dozen expressive excrescences.' And Kenneth Tynan said that his 'immense sloth is here perfectly matched to his part, that of a perambulant JP, who, heavily disguised, investigates the "enormities" of the fair. The disguise, of course, renders him about as effectively incognito as a walrus in a ballet-skirt ... The whole performance is portentously Victorian, as if Pinero had written a part for a porpoise.' He was the Chorus in *Henry V* in which part, according to Tynan, he 'moaned quite genially, trotting on and off stage like a St Bernard'. According to Audrey Williamson he 'provided persuasive mental colour ... He had not the voice for the great swell of poetry in the part — for the lofty surge and furrow's sea, for the invisible and creeping wind and the little body with a mighty hurt — but his muse, if not of fire, was one of quiet illumination; the voice perhaps rather husky.'

He was Brassbound and his wife was Lady Cicely in *Captain Brassbound's Conversion*, and in *The Merry Wives of Windsor* Ursula Jeans played Mistress Ford and he was, according to Beverley Baxter, 'a great Falstaff. An obese glutton with the soul of a troubadour.'

At the Arts Theatre in October 1951, he was Hank Moreland in *Third Person*, transferring with the production to the Criterion in January 1952. That April at the Duke of York's he was Professor Mortimer in *The Mortimer Touch*, and at the St Martin's the following April played Charles Delaney in *The Teddy Bear*. In 1953 he went to

Hollywood, where he was in an Errol Flynn movie; he then intended to open on Broadway with Ursula Jeans in *Escapade*, but illness forced him from the production. Back in London at the Saville in August 1954 he was Marcus McLeod in *Keep in a Cool Place*, by William Templeton. Frank Granville-Barker had reservations about both the play and the performance. 'Such a weak play as this depends on a star name to attract the public and the choice of Roger Livesey may be in some respects a wise one. Pleasant as it is to see him back in the West End, however, Livesey is not the right person to play the part of a testy arrogant Scot. Whatever he tries to do to make the character convincing, all his efforts are no match against his irrepressible personal charm, which tends to make nonsense of the situation.'

Roger Livesey was Stephen Leigh in *Uncertain Joy* at the Court in March 1955, and at the Lyric, Hammersmith, in February 1956, he played John Tarleton in Shaw's *Misalliance*. Frank Granville-Barker thought it not a clever piece of casting: 'Roger Livesey was a particular disappointment, for his doddering bonhomie as John Tarleton reduced the part to tedious nonsense. Unless the audience is made aware of Tarleton's intellectual drive, the savour of *Misalliance* is lost.' Roger Livesey and Ursula Jeans toured Australia and New Zealand between 1956 and 1958, playing in *The Reluctant Debutante* and *The Great Sebastians*. Then Mr Livesey played Laurence Olivier's screen father in the film of *The Entertainer*.

At the Westminster Theatre in London in April 1960 he played Marcus Heatherington in *A Lodging for the Bride*, which did not last very long. However, in October 1961 at the Oxford Playhouse he took the role of Captain Shotover in Shaw's *Heartbreak House*, which came to London in November to Wyndham's. Peter Roberts wrote: 'Roger Livesey is an impressive Shotover, but the huskiness of his voice tends to blur the edge of his lines and can make for monotony.' At St Martin's in October 1962 he was Inspector Gates in *Kill Two Birds*, an inept thriller which also starred Tony Britton. He was Bernard Dulac in *Head of the Family* at the Hampstead Theatre Club in January 1963, and in April 1964 was at the Oxford Playhouse as Chebutykin in Chekhov's *The Three Sisters*. The following April he toured as Colonel Pocock in *The Elephant's Foot*, and in December came to the Strand Theatre in London playing the Earl of Caversham in *An Ideal Husband*; he played this part for over a year. At the Round House in March 1969 he was the First Player and also the Gravedigger to Nicol Williamson's Hamlet, directed by Tony Richardson. He played the same parts at the Lunt–Fontanne Theater in New York in May 1969. He toured South Africa in July 1970 in *Oh Clarence!*

Roger Livesey did some very good work on television, notably in *The Winslow Boy*, *The Master Builder* and *The Physicists*; he will probably be best remembered for his role as the Duke of St Bungay in the BBC serialization of Trollope's *The Pallisers*. His wife died in 1973, and Roger Livesey himself died on 4 February 1976.

ROBERT LORAINE

*H*arry Loraine's father was a very rich ship-builder who refused to let his son use the family name of Bilcliffe in his chosen profession — acting. So Harry used his mother's name and he and his wife, Nellie, who was twenty years his junior, became a quite famous theatrical team travelling the country. Their most popular production was *Mystery of a Hansom Cab*. Their son Robert was born in New Brighton, near Liskard, Cheshire, on 14 January 1876. As a child, Robert was very precocious. He read voraciously and attended rehearsals. He was not allowed to act with his parents but he did occasionally hold the prompt book, and he quickly memorized his parents' repertoire. His career began in Liverpool in sailors' dives — bars where plays were performed nightly. He joined a touring rep company, and after two years was taken on by Ben Greet's Pastoral Players, with whom he stayed another two years, touring all over England and gradually working up to starring roles.

He finally made it back to London, where he discovered his father beset by money problems and his mother desperately ill. Robert, having been a star on tour, made his London début at the Strand Theatre on 22 May 1894 as Alfred Dunscombe in *The Ne'er Do Well*. He appeared at the Standard Theatre, Bishopsgate, in September as Arthur Tredgold in *The Lights of Home*, and at the Criterion in July 1895 appeared as De Mauprat in the first act of *Richelieu* for his father's benefit night.

He then went back to touring, as Georges Bernay in *The City of Pleasure*, returning to London in January 1896 as Toni in *The Prisoner of Zenda*. His mother died two nights after the opening. Also at the St James's in December he played Jaques de Boys in *As You Like It* and in July 1897 he was Captain Hentzau in *The Prisoner of Zenda*. It was while he was in this production that he met the beautiful actress Julie Opp, who was playing a Court Lady; they were married two days before she left for New York as the second lead in Pinero's *Princess and the Butterfly*. She spent eighteen months in New York and Loraine left her the night she returned after an argument over the house he had bought and furnished for them to share. The marriage was never consummated.

While Julie was in New York, Loraine had become a star. He had an enormous success with *The White Heather*, in which he played Dick Beech, at Drury Lane in 1897. He followed that with his performance as Kit French in *Admiral Guineau* at the Avenue in 1897 and then returned to the St James's in 1898 as Claudio in *Much Ado About Nothing*. However, it was again at Drury Lane, in 1898, that he had his next great success, playing the Indian Prince Kassim Wadia in *The Great Ruby*. He was Dudley Keppel in *One of the Best* at the Princess in 1899 and then d'Artagnan in *The Three Musketeers* at the Garrick in 1899. That same year at the Garrick he was in *Change Alley*, and at the Metropole in September he played Hervey Blake in *The Rebels*. Then he went off to serve in the Boer War in search of adventure. Although he served with distinction there was never quite enough action to satisfy his romantic nature.

After the war he made his American stage début in New York under Frohman's management at the Knickerbocker Theater on 4 March 1901 playing the lead, Ralph Percy, in *To Have and to Hold*, an indifferent version of Mary Johnson's novel *By Order of the Company*. Loraine was a great success and became known as 'New York's most beautiful man'. At Daly's Theater in January 1902 he was Noel, Viscount Doughton, in the musical comedy *Frocks and Frills*. He was successful, he was famous and he was earning a great deal of money — but being known as 'Beautiful Bob' and walking through non-roles was not to his liking.

At the age of 26 he returned to England, where he was the visiting star with his old company, Ben Greet's Pastoral Players, in *Henry V*. They opened in Stratford and then toured around the country before a short run in London at the Metropole, Camberwell. It was during this period that he began riding from town to town on a white horse.

Back in London in April 1902, Robert Loraine played Enrico Carbayal in *The President* at the Prince of Wales and in July was William in *There and Back*. At Wyndham's in June 1903 he was in *The Queen of the Roses*, and at the Avenue that same month he was Tom Faggus in *Lorna Doone*.

He returned to America in 1903. He played David Garrick in *Pretty Peggy* opposite Grace George's Peg Woffington on a tour, and then wrote a vaudeville sketch for himself which he took round the circuit — it was called *A Little Tragedy in Tientsin* and in it he played Ah Chang, an ancient Chinese who kills his unfaithful wife. The novelty of it was that he never spoke. In 1904, at Rochester, New York, he played in *The Liars*, *Americans Abroad*, *The Mysterious Mr Bugle* and *Diplomacy*, and at the Lyric in New York in September 1904 he was Lieutenant Von Lauffen in *Taps*. He opened at the Garrick in Philadelphia in December 1904 as King Edward IV in *The Lady Shore*, and at the Criterion in New York in March 1905 he was Danvers Macgregor in *Nancy Stair*. He was in *The Lady Shore* once again at the Hudson Theater in New York in March 1905, and the following month was at the Manhattan Theater as the Invermorach in *The Proud Laird*. As well as being 'Beautiful Bob', Robert Loraine was now known as a fine actor, but he was unhappy with the parts he was playing. He wanted to do something new in the theatre, something important. He wanted to do Shaw's *Man and Superman*, but all the managers said it was uncommercial; he tried without success to raise the money. Then Charles Frohman rescued him and took over the project, leaving Loraine in complete charge of the production but footing the bill himself. Loraine, talking about his desire to perform Shaw, said: 'I tried to infuse into the acting all the mental agility and spiritual sincerity of the author. My efforts were not only for the sake of the money I would make, they sprang from the desire to spread the tidings of a new and exhilarating view of life. I was also determined to vindicate my argument that the public would always support the best.'

Robert Loraine opened as John Tanner at the Hudson Theater in New York in September 1905 and broke all house records. The play closed in May 1906 and reopened on tour in September, playing one-night stands all over the country and breaking attendance records wherever it went. The company travelled across the country in two white railway coaches with *Man and Superman* painted in yellow along the sides. This was not unusual — most travelling companies had their own coaches with their name emblazoned thereon; what was unusual was that they also travelled with horseboxes, and at every town Robert Loraine would make his entrance on a white charger.

In May 1907 Robert Loraine appeared in London at the Court Theatre playing John Tanner in *Man and Superman*. One critic reported: 'He *was* John Tanner. In every movement, turn, gesture, and thought he was the living man. He did not deliver long speeches of dialectical fireworks as though he had committed them to memory. He said them on the spur of the moment. They were all impromptu! It was the performance of a superman; a man almost too much alive, who might easily become too manly, too much of a good thing.' The critic Ernest Short, writing some years later, recalled: 'Good as Loraine was in the part, he did not eclipse the memory of Granville-Barker, the first London John Tanner. Loraine played the victorious Tanner of the early acts perfectly, but when it was Ann's turn to be the conqueror the tragedy suggested by Granville-Barker proved beyond Loraine.' Shaw himself said, 'Oh, if I only could have Loraine for the first half and Granville-Barker for the second, what a Tanner that would be!' In June he added *Don Juan in Hell*, and William Archer said it was 'a really immense achievement', while the *Daily Telegraph* said, 'Anything better than Mr Loraine's performance we have never seen.' Max Beerbohm explained: 'His excellence is not merely in that variety of pace and intonation necessary in long speeches and so seldom achieved by actors trained up on a stage where only snippets of speech are fashionable. He seems to be really thinking, really evolving the ideas he has to express, and really rejoicing too in his mastery of debate.' Sticking with Shaw, Loraine spent five months as Bluntschli at the Savoy in *Arms and the Man*, and then at the Haymarket in May 1908 was St John Hotchkiss in *Getting Married*.

At the Aldwych in September 1908 Loraine played Joseph Brooks in *Paid in Full*. The following month he was at Wyndham's playing Stephens in *Bellamy the Magnificent*, and the next month was Harry Telfer in *Dolly Reforming Herself* at the Haymarket. Of the latter Max Beerbohm wrote: 'Miss Ethel Irving as Dolly, and Mr Loraine as the husband, are exactly suited to each other's methods; and the great scene, though it will be played by many comedians in the future, will never, I imagine, be played better.' Still at the Haymarket in February 1909, he had a great success as Young Marlowe in *She Stoops to Conquer* and at His Majesty's in April he was praised as Charles Surface in *The School for Scandal*. At the Lyric Theatre in May the same

year he was Prince Hal in *Henry IV* and at the Comedy in September played Thomas Freeman in Maugham's *Smith*. He was Bob Acres in *The Rivals* at the Lyric in April 1910, and at Stratford that same month played Benedick in *Much Ado About Nothing*. He returned to London that September to play Jan Redlander in *The Man From the Sea*.

Robert Loraine opened at the Duke of York's in February 1911 as the Rev. Canon Theodore Spratte in *Loaves and Fishes*, and the following month was at the Comedy as Henry Longton in *Playing With Fire*.

Back in England, he appeared in November 1913 at the Comedy Theatre as Dick Blair in *A Place in the Sun*. At the same theatre, in February 1914 he was Mr Parbury in *The Tyranny of Tears*.

At the outbreak of the First World War he joined the Royal Flying Corps. He was nearly killed by a bullet which pierced his lung, his kneecap was also shot away, and his hair turned white. He was awarded the Military Cross and in the Birthday Honours of 1917 the DSO.

Before the war he had acquired the English-language rights to *Cyrano de Bergerac*, and he made his return to the stage in it at Edinburgh in March 1919. The company then played Newcastle and Glasgow before coming to London, to the Garrick Theatre, in March 1919. The critic A. B. Walkley reported: 'It sent a playhouseful of English people into ecstasies of enjoyment, almost to intoxication ... *Cyrano* is audaciously, triumphantly, flamboyantly romantic in its magnificent swagger, in its sacrifice of everything in life to the rounded phrase and the beau geste, in its sheer unbridled joy of living. Romantic to the very tip of Cyrano's nose. And Mr Loraine has produced it romantically with beautiful romantic scenery and dresses, with an almost continual accompaniment of romantic music and, happiest stroke of all, with fearlessly romantic acting. His death is a thing of pure romantic beauty ... When the play was over last night, the house gave Mr Loraine a demonstration of delight — delight with his performance, delight at seeing the actor once more at his work — which fairly unnerved him, as well it might. He could only stammer out his thanks. Some of the stage crowd gathered behind him had already resumed their airmen's uniform. And that gave the last touch of romance to this romantic evening.' Sidney Carroll said: 'Although the pantomimic size of the nose deprives the actor of almost all facial expression, we never for a moment lose our insight into the man's soul. Such is the magic of fine words, finely spoken, of great thoughts eloquently expressed, that the nose disappears. And this bizarre mixture of all that is grotesque and all that is lovely thrills us with the desire to enjoy our manhood, makes our pulses throb with a zest for life, it points the road to unselfishness, it teaches us to despise the mean.' Although the production was an enormous success it was also very expensive, and C. B. Cochran, the producer, found he was not making any money from it and wanted to close it. Loraine took over the production himself through the transfers to the Garrick in late March and then on to the Drury Lane Theatre and finally into the Duke of York's. At the Duke of York's in December 1919 he revived *Arms and the Man*, then took a holiday in Switzerland.

J. M. Barrie was keen to get him into his next play, *Mary Rose*, and flying himself back for a discussion with Barrie, Loraine became lost over the Alps. He was an excellent flyer, but a very poor navigator. He was missing for more than two days and presumed dead. In fact he was greeted by the news of his death when he finally made it back to London, having abandoned the fuel-less plane in Holland and completing his journey home by boat and train. *Mary Rose* opened at the Haymarket Theatre in April 1920 with Fay Compton in the title part and Loraine playing Harry and Simon Blake. It was Fay Compton's triumph, but W. A. Darlington reported: 'Robert Loraine's performance was an admirable one also, but unhappily my most vivid picture of him is at the moment of his first entrance as Mary Rose's youthful lover. Loraine was at the time 44 years of age and stockily built, and when he first came on the effect of an exuberantly boyish make-up was that he looked older than Time. As soon as he began to act the scene this impression was dispelled, but it has lodged in my memory all the same. Loraine was a forceful actor, not easy to forget, and in this instance he gave me a very nasty shock.'

After *Mary Rose* Loraine set off on a trip round the world. On a ship coming from Bombay to London he met Winifred Lydia Strangman, whom he married. All the money that Loraine had made over the years — and he had made a lot — had gone in productions, or on horses or aeroplanes. Now that he was married he had to earn some. He opened at the Ambassadors' in November 1921 playing the title role in *Deburau*, but it was off in three weeks. He then managed to make some money from a forgettable film. At the Duke of York's in January 1922 he was in a detective play, being Robert Andrew in *The Nightcap*. It was not very good. In June he was Angelo Pageant in *Pomp and Circumstance*; by November he was at the St James's playing Dale Conway in *The Happy Ending*, which became known as the Unhappy Ending. By this time he

had not only a wife but a daughter as well (two more daughters would eventually complete the family), and they were living in two rooms. However, fire destroyed all his *Cyrano* sets, which were in store, and the insurance money provided Loraine with some capital. He bought a house in Roehampton.

In August 1923 he played Rudolf Rassendyl and King Rudolf in a revival of *The Prisoner of Zenda*, and then the following February he was at the Lyric, Hammersmith, playing Mirabell to Edith Evans' Millamant in *The Way of the World*, with great success. At the Savoy in June 1924 he played (again with Edith Evans) André Chaumont in Leon M. Lion's *Tiger Cats*. It was an enormous success and Loraine purchased the American rights. He opened in New York in it at the Belasco Theater in October 1924 with Katharine Cornell — and it was off in six weeks. After many more idle and unsuccessful months, his fortunes turned. He opened at the Everyman Theatre in Hampstead in August 1927 in Strindberg's *The Father*. The little theatre was soon overflowing and they transferred to the Savoy, playing Barrie's *Barbara's Wedding* as a curtain raiser. James Agate reported: 'By resisting every temptation to overplay — and the piece offers many — he brought out all that it holds of terror, pity and wonderment.' Ernest Short said: 'Such power had not been present in a theatre for a generation.' They transferred to the Apollo, which Loraine had rented at a most advantageous price, for an indefinite period. In November he revived *Cyrano de Bergerac* at that theatre; his wife played Roxanne. However, all his scenery and costumes having been destroyed by fire, he tried to reconstruct it too cheaply, and on the first night the scenery fell about the stage. It came off in three weeks. He had more success with Strindberg's *The Dance of Death*, which he opened in January. Then Edgar Wallace, whose name was magic in the West End, wrote *The Man Who Changed His Name* for him to play with Dorothy Dickson. It opened in March 1928 — but for once Wallace was wrong. The play was not a success; it was too short and badly written. To save face Wallace kept the play running with his own money and Loraine left it to make a film and to look for a new play.

He opened in June 1929 as Tice Collins in *This Thing Called Love*. It was a trivial comedy in which Loraine had to use every trick he had learned in forty years on the stage to wring laughs from the audience. He then revived *The Father* and *Barbara's Wedding* in August. One of the Sunday critics reported: 'I have seen Loraine in *The Father* three times. The effect produced by the play and the actor gains by repetition. I sat with my eyes glued on the stage and he never left it. I consider his performance to be the greatest of this generation. Anyone with a love for acting must see Loraine. Not should — MUST!' In November he went to the Criterion as the dissolute artist Max Lightly in Benn Levy's *Art and Mrs Bottle*, playing opposite Irene Vanbrugh, and at Christmas he played matinées of *Treasure Island* at the Strand.

The theatre business, however, was bad. He ran

up a massive overdraft trying to hang on to his tenancy of the Apollo, but finally had to relinquish it. His final years brought him little success and some actual failures. He died on 23 December 1935. Ernest Short wrote later: 'In the generation after Henry Irving and the famous actor—managers, Robert Loraine was one of the few actors in Britain to whom the word genius could justly be applied.'

THE LUNTS

'The Lunts can march through a play like welcome invaders, entering a conquered kingdom. Their energies are boundless, their zest overpowering. They can sweep magnificently through the right kinds of scripts. Without meaning to, or having anyone object, they can turn them into so many red carpets for their royal progresses. Quite rightly their high spirits, their technical virtuosity, their skill in displaying each other to advantage, their contagious pleasure in what they are doing and their unstinting dedication to their job, are qualities which have won for them the affectionate admiration of a huge army of devoted playgoers.' Thus wrote John Mason Brown in 1938. To put it more succinctly here is Sir Ralph Richardson: 'We often hear about the superiority of English stars. We have some very good performers, but America has something better — the Lunts.'

Lynn Fontanne was born in Woodford, Essex, on 6 December 1887, one of four daughters of Jules Pierre Antoine Fontanne and his wife Frances. Her father, English-born of French ancestry, was a printer and inventor, and very successful at both. As a schoolgirl Lynn became obsessed with the idea of becoming an actress and luckily a friend of her mother happened to be a friend of Ellen Terry, who was taking a few pupils in between engagements. Lynn, through a recommendation from Miss Terry, got a part in the chorus in the pantomime *Cinderella* at the Drury Lane Theatre during the Christmas 1905 season. 'All through the rehearsals they kept threatening to fire me,' she reported, 'because I couldn't tell my right from my left in the dance numbers.'

When the pantomime season was over Lynn Fontanne spent the next couple of years doing walk-on parts, until in 1909 she got the part of Rose in a tour of Somerset Maugham's *Lady Frederick*. At the Garrick Theatre in the West End she appeared in *Where Children Rule* in December 1909, and the following June she had her first West End speaking role as Lady Mulberry in *Billy's Bargain*.

Lynn Fontanne made her Broadway début on 7 November 1910 at Nazimova's 39th Street Theater playing Harriet Budgeon in *Mr Preedy and the Countess*, a routine comedy which did not thrill New Yorkers. It closed within three weeks, and she returned to England. At the Criterion in February 1911 she played Gwendolen in *The Young Lady of Seventeen*, and at the Vaudeville that September she was Mrs Gerrard in *A Story in a Tea Shop*. Remaining with the Weedon Grossmith management she spent 1912 and 1913 touring the provinces as Gertrude Rhead in *Milestones*. The provincial critics praised her glowingly. She came back to London to the Royalty Theatre in April 1914, where she played two parts (Mrs Collison and Liza) in *My Lady's Dress*. Also in the cast were Gladys Cooper and Edith Evans. One critic reported: 'Miss Cooper gives a pathetic study of a hump-backed girl with a selfish sister whom Miss Lynn Fontanne enacts to the life.' That October she played in *Milestones* at the Royalty. Four parts came her way in 1915: the Nurse in *Searchlight* at the Savoy (February), the title part in *Terrorist* at the Playhouse (May), Ada Pilbeam in *How to Get On* at the Victoria Palace (July), and a role in *The Starlight Express* at the Kingsway (December).

In 1916 Lynn Fontanne sailed once more for New York, this time to join Laurette Taylor's company. She began with them in Rochester playing Winifred in *The Wooing of Eve*, in March. They then tried out *The Harp of Life*, in which Miss Fontanne played Olive Hood, and brought it to Broadway to the Globe Theater in November.

THE • LUNTS

All the reviews were very complimentary. The *Morning Telegraph* enthused: 'One of the delights of the performance is the exquisite acting of a newcomer, Lynn Fontanne, who established a reputation for uncommon ability overnight. Miss Fontanne comes from England and it is earnestly hoped that she never returns.' In March 1917, she was Princess Lizzie in *Out There* at the same theatre. 'The acting,' reported the *Dramatic Mirror*, 'is of a high order throughout, with Lynn Fontanne again illustrating her remarkable aptitude for characterization in the role of the unpleasant sister . . .' In November she once more played in *The Wooing of Eve*, this time at the Liberty Theater, and in December at the Criterion she was Miss Perkins in *Happiness*. Charles Darnton, writing in the New York *Evening World* said: 'Lynn Fontanne does a capital bit of work as a hare-brained social waster.'

At the Lyric in 1918 the company did *Scenes from Shakespeare*, and while Laurette Taylor played Katharina from *The Taming of the Shrew* and Portia from *The Merchant of Venice*, Lynn Fontanne supported her as Bianca and Nerissa. Lynn Fontanne then left Laurette Taylor's company and replaced Laura Hope Crewe as Mrs Rockingham in *A Pair of Petticoats* at the Bijou Theater in May 1918. That September she played Mrs Glendenning at the Knickerbocker in *Someone in the House*. She went to Chicago in June 1919 where she appeared in *A Young Man's Fancy*. She was then cast as Anna Christophersen in a Eugene O'Neill play entitled *Chris*. They opened in Philadelphia, where the *Philadelphia Record* reported: 'Lynn Fontanne, charming in her young womanhood and in complete sympathy with the role of the daughter, won deserved admiration.' The play was not, however, ready for New York. There was a lot of script revision to be done so they closed in Philadelphia. She rejoined the Taylor company and returned to London, where they opened at the Garrick Theatre in May 1920 with *One Night in Rome*. Miss Fontanne played Zephyr. The play did not please the audiences and they responded on the first night by heckling and throwing stink bombs. It did, however, last for 104 performances.

Miss Fontanne returned to the United States for her first enormous success, the role of Dulcinea in *Dulcy* by Marc Connelly and George S. Kaufman. She opened in Chicago as the young wife who is constantly opening her mouth only to put her foot in it, and arrived in New York at the Frazer Theater to delight the critics in August 1921. Heywood Broun writing in the *New York Tribune* said: 'This is an exceedingly merry performance. The humor of a young woman

supposed to be a deadly bore might actually become so in less skilful hands, but Miss Fontanne preserves the spirit of mockery and the authors have been wise enough to let the bromides swirl into drifts.'

By this time Lynn Fontanne had met a young actor, Alfred Lunt, who courted her for about two years. 'I think his mother was being a little troublesome about losing him,' Lynn commented later. On a Friday morning, 26 May 1922, they took the subway to the City Hall in New York, stopped a couple of passers-by to act as witnesses, and were married. They went back to their respective theatres that evening. It was the beginning of a long and very happy marriage — the stage partnership had not yet begun.

Alfred Davis Lunt was born in Milwaukee, Wisconsin, on 19 August 1892. He was stage-struck at an early age. He studied oratory at Carroll College in Waukesha, Wisconsin, and while there appeared in at least twelve productions in two years. He then went to Boston intending to study at Emerson College, but on his first day there went to the Castle Square Theater, asked for a job and got one. He opened two days later playing the Sheriff in James Montgomery's *The Aviator*. There he stayed for three years, playing first bits and then larger small parts. He then joined Margaret Anglin's company and toured with her for eighteen months in such plays as *Green Stockings*, *Beverly's Balances* and *As You Like It*. He supported her at the open-air theatre at the University of California at Berkeley in *Iphigenia in Tauris* and *Medea*. Alfred Lunt then toured the vaudeville circuit with Lillie Langtry in *Ashes* before returning in 1916 to Margaret Anglin's company.

Alfred Lunt made his Broadway début playing Claude Estabrook in *Romance and Arabella* at the Harris Theater. He was noticed by the critics, but only just. He then went on tour again, this time playing George Tewkesbury Reynolds in *The Country Cousin*. Booth Tarkington saw him in this role and wrote *Clarence* for him. Lunt opened in the part at the Hudson Theater in September 1919, and the critics raved. In *New York Call* Louis Gardy wrote: 'Alfred Lunt, one of our most artistic comedians, carries off the acting honors in the role of Clarence. He is, without question, the most capable of all the players who have portrayed a Tarkington character on the stage.' He played Clarence for two years and then went into another Tarkington comedy, playing Ames in *The Intimate Strangers* opposite Billie Burke. Louis V. DeFoe reported in the *New York World* that Lunt's was 'a deft bit of comedy acting with its suggestion of good manners, half credulity and embarrassed mys-

tification.' At the Ritz Theater in September 1922 he played Count Alexander de Lussac, the title part in *Banco*. Then in May 1923, he and his wife played together for the first time. It was at the 48th Street Theater. He was Charles II and she was Lady Castlemaine in *Sweet Nell of Old Drury*. That August at the Ritz, Lynn played Ann Jordan in *In Love with Love* and Alfred opened in November at the same theatre as David Peel in the ill-fated *Robert E. Lee*. It closed after only fifteen performances. In January 1924 he had his first 'serious' success as Tom Prior in Sutton Vane's *Outward Bound*, at the Ritz. John Corbin reported in the *New York Times*: 'Mr Lunt finds large scope for his powers as a comedian and finally does a bit of emotional acting of the very first order.'

The Lunts then joined the Theater Guild and opened in October 1924 in *The Guardsman* by Ferenc Molnar, directed by Philip Moeller. In the *New York Times* Stark Young wrote: 'Lynn Fontanne portrayed the actress often delightfully, with now and again a kind of prima donna charm and no little technical fluency; she could heighten to advantage her whole performance and give it more brilliance and point. Alfred Lunt's acting was less convincing. His natural turn for cues and transitions often helped him out, but he fell a long way short of both Lynn Fontanne and Dudley Briggs, who played the bachelor friend in a manner that was exactly right in every sense.' E. W. Osborn, writing in the *Evening World*, disagreed. He said the Lunts were 'a comedy pair who need fear no compare. Their swift transition from the spats and dissension of an afternoon in their dear little home to the flirtatious byplay of the evening at the opera is wonderfully smooth and complete, and they rise most happily to the moment of confounding revelations in the third act.' And it was Alexander Woollcott writing in the *New York Sun* who was the most prescient: 'They have youth, great gifts and the unmistakable attitude of ascent and those who saw them last night bowing hand in hand for the first time may well have been witnessing a moment in theatrical history.'

The Lunts opened the Theater Guild's 1925–26 season in September playing Raina and Captain Bluntschli in Philip Moeller's production of Shaw's *Arms and the Man*. They then played in *Goat Song* and *At Mrs Beam's*. The 1926–27 season opened with Alfred miscast as Maximilian in Werfel's *Juarez and Maximilian*, but in November Lynn had a great success as Eliza Doolittle in Shaw's *Pygmalion*. Reginald Mason was her Higgins. Charles Brackett reported in the *New Yorker*: 'Lynn Fontanne's vibrant young Eliza Doolittle makes one's memory of Mrs Patrick Campbell in the part seem like a faded cigarette

card.' While she carried on with Eliza, her husband, with another Theater Guild company, opened at the John Golden Theater in *Ned McCobb's Daughter*. The *New York Herald Tribune* reported: 'Strangely metamorphosed since the close of *Juarez and Maximilian*, Alfred Lunt represented a wholesale bootlegger with unction, gusto, and immense vitality'. Together they played in Jacques Copeau's adaptation and production of *The Brothers Karamazov*.

In April 1927 they opened together in S. N. Behrman's *The Second Man*, and in November were in Shaw's *The Doctor's Dilemma*, in New York. This they had opened in Chicago during a tour which also included *The Guardsman* and *Arms and the Man*. Of *The Doctor's Dilemma* Alexander Woollcott wrote: 'It may be doubted if ever anywhere the crucial roles of the dying blackguard of an artist and his exalted, exalting wife have been so illuminatingly acted as they were last night by Alfred Lunt and Lynn Fontanne. It may be doubted if ever anywhere in our time they will be so well acted again . . . I should like to linger long over the most phosphorescent quality of Mr Lunt's performance, the gleam of his diablerie. I should like to write much of the dauntless humility of this all-conquering Jennifer.'

In January 1928, Alfred Lunt played the title role in Eugene O'Neill's *Marco Millions*, and that same month Lynn opened as Nina Leeds in O'Neill's *Strange Interlude*. Brooks Atkinson said that she played with 'power, concentrated aggression and magnetism . . .'. In December they got together again in the comedy *Caprice*. Brooks Atkinson said they were 'a matchless pair of volatile comedians . . . When they run their lines together they accent the meaning even while they confuse the words.' They took this play to London and Alfred made his début there at the St James's Theatre on 4 June 1929. Returning to New York, they opened at the Guild Theater in December 1929, in *Meteor*, a comedy which S. N. Behrman had written for them. The play-was flawed but the Lunts were transcendent.

The following year they had a deserved success in Maxwell Anderson's *Elizabeth the Queen* — Lynn played the title role and Alfred was the Earl of Essex. They were rewarded with seventeen curtain calls on the first night. The next autumn they were in Robert E. Sherwood's comedy about an Austrian archduke and his one-time mistress, *Reunion in Vienna*. John Mason Brown reported in the *New York Post*: 'When the Lunts are in topnotch form — as they generally are in comedy — there are no two players in our theatre who can equal them or excel them. Their acting not only has a zest about it which is irresistible, but it has a precision equal to its energy.' *Reunion in Vienna* had a long Broadway run and then a long tour.

Before their rise to stardom, when he and they were struggling young actors together, Noel Coward promised the Lunts, even before their marriage, that when they were all famous he would write a vehicle for them to play together. *Design for Living* opened for a limited (135 performances) season at the Ethel Barrymore Theater in January 1933. John Mason Brown enthused: 'It is the most brilliant comedy acting New York has seen in years. It is perfect in its smallest details, filled with unction which each of these players brings to the theatre.' And Brooks Atkinson said: 'They are an incomparable trio of high comedians and they give *Design for Living* the sententious acting that transmutes artificial comedy into delight.'

The Lunts returned to England to the Lyric Theatre in January 1934, with *Reunion in Vienna.* W. A. Darlington wrote in the *Telegraph*: '... the acting of Mr Lunt and Miss Fontanne in their play is high comedy acting of exquisite quality.'

The Lunts returned to New York, where in January 1935 they were Stefan and Linda in Noel Coward's *Point Valaine* at the Ethel Barrymore Theater. It was the closest they came to failure, and the show closed after fifty-five performances.

They quickly went into rehearsal of Shakespeare's *The Taming of the Shrew* and opened the production, whose cast included Sidney Greenstreet, at the Nixon Theater in Pittsburgh in April 1935. They came to the Guild Theater on Broadway at the end of September and the critics enthused. John Mason Brown reported: 'The Lunts have treated Shakespeare as if he were our contemporary or we his ... They have subjected an old farce to the most respectful kind of disrespect. They have freed it of its dust, taken advantage of its every unimagined playing possibility, and staged and acted it with such skill and unction that it still succeeds in romping its way through scene after scene as one of the major laugh-getters of our time ... Miss Fontanne's Katharine has energy and fire, and more than serves its laughing purpose. Mr Lunt's Petruchio takes its place among his most distinguished performances. It misses no chances. It finds him reading Shakespeare with surprising ease. It is richly humorous, has tremendous drive, benefits by an unfailing invention, and it is a memorable achievement in acting.' *The Taming of the Shrew* ran for 129 performances on Broadway.

They returned to Robert E. Sherwood for their next venture, *Idiot's Delight*, and again opened in Pittsburgh — this time in the middle of a flood. Most of the audience arrived in rowing boats. They brought the play to the Shubert in New York in

March 1936, preceded by nationwide publicity. John Mason Brown wrote: '... as actors who know their business and are masters of it, those two are a peerless team. As the song-and-dance man and the mysterious Russian lady ... who is more Russian than the Romanovs they supply enough art and entertainment in their own rights to make anyone happy.' The play won the Pulitzer Prize that year. They closed it for a brief vacation on their farm in Wisconsin but by the end of July were back on Broadway, where they played another 179 performances before touring with it.

They returned to Broadway, to the Shubert Theater (again for the Theater Guild) in November 1937, in Jean Giraudoux's *Amphitryon 38*. The translation was by S. N. Behrman and the music by Samuel L. M. Barlow. Richard Watts reported for the *Herald Tribune*: 'It is worth repeating that both Miss Fontanne and Mr Lunt are delightful. Miss Fontanne looks very handsome in her Grecian robes and her playing never ceases to be gay and charming. Mr Lunt, whether in the whiskers of Jupiter or the disguise of the absent Amphitryon, is invariably engaging, and in the moments when he is baffled by Alkemena's loyalty to her husband or annoyed by suggestions that the world he made is not perfect he is a complete joy.'

In March 1938, still at the Shubert, the Lunts opened in Stark Young's translation of Chekhov's *The Seagull*. For once the critics were not wholly charmed. John Mason Brown wrote: 'His Trigorin fits easily into the ensemble. He is quiet, unassuming and co-operative. His second-act scene, in which he discourses on the trials of literary fame, is charmingly played. His whole performance is acted not only from within the character he is creating but well within the demands of the ensemble ... Miss Fontanne is not so successful in meeting either need. Her red-wigged Irina does not seem to have been approached from within ... There is no subtlety ... Miss Fontanne forces us to wonder how, if her Irina cannot give a better performance in masking her faults in her daily life, she could ever be the great actress she is supposed to be on the stage ...' They returned to London to the Lyric Theatre in May 1938 to play in *Amphitryon 38*. Audrey Williamson wrote: 'Lynn Fontanne, subtle in humour, magical in seductiveness, gave the part a shimmer of poetry, and the perfection of teamwork attained by herself and Alfred Lunt made their scenes together seem as complete and finely chiselled as sculpture. Lunt himself made the most of Jupiter's childish and human vanities, but he did not miss the majesty of the end when, transformed into the splendour of godhood, he took the stage like a Grecian statue.'

They then spent until February 1940 touring

the United States in *Amphitryon 38*, *The Seagull* and *Idiot's Delight*. They returned to Broadway to play in *The Taming of the Shrew* once more, this time at the Alvin for the benefit of the Finnish Relief Fund, and opened in April at the same theatre in Robert E. Sherwood's regretful call to arms, *There Shall Be No Night*. John Anderson wrote in the New York *Journal American*: 'Miss Fontanne is superb as the American-born wife of the Finnish scientist, and plays with a tragic perception as affecting and as sharply inflected as her sense of comedy. Mr Lunt gives the part of Dr Valkonen the sort of illuminated scientific touch that reveals the personal tragedy of a mind overwhelmed by brute matter, and he has also directed the performance.' Their son was played by Montgomery Clift.

Alfred Lunt then directed Helen Hayes in Maxwell Anderson's *Candle in the Wind*. It was the first time he had not appeared in his own production for Broadway. Louis Kronenberger was not impressed: 'Alfred Lunt's direction,' he wrote, 'seems somewhat over-reverent, making a slow play even slower.'

Together again, the Lunts opened at the Martin Beck Theater in November 1942, in S. N. Behrman's *The Pirate*, and once more stunned the critics. Writing in the *New York Times* Lewis Nichols said, '. . . they can do anything. Miss Fontanne is roguish, coquettish, practical by turns . . . Mr Lunt can be bumptious or pleading, and, in addition to all that, he can break an egg to make an omelette and then find it turn into a rabbit.'

Lynn Fontanne had a great desire to be back in her native England while it was under bombardment and Alfred of course wanted to be with her, so they took Sherwood's *There Shall Be No Night* to the Aldwych in December 1943. Since Russia was now an ally of England, she could not be depicted as an aggressor so the play was rewritten and the situation transposed from the Russian invasion of Finland to the German invasion of Greece. James Agate wrote: 'This actress is a brilliant comedienne, a mistress of the art of insinuation, extremely skilled in the hoodwinkery of gestures of which Duse was the greatest exponent. Hoodwinkery? Well, let me say the art of restraint suggesting the pent-up torrent, of avoidance hinting at virtuosity resisted . . . On the other hand Mr Lunt works by accomplishment rather than by implications. His fun is brilliant, his pathos is open and declared and at times unbearable. To sum I will say the play is lovely theatre.' They played at the Aldwych during the Blitz and one night a bomb fell next to the theatre, blowing one member of the cast right out of it — but the cast dusted themselves off and went on with the performance.

Remaining in England, in December 1944 they opened as Sir John Fletcher and Olivia Brown in Terence Rattigan's *Love-in-Idleness*. James Agate reported: 'Mr Lunt and Miss Fontanne were superb in the first act and good in the second; if their performances crumbled away at the end it was merely because the comedy had lost its sincerity.' During 1945 they toured the continent in *Love-in-Idleness* playing for the troops, and then returning to the United States toured there from December 1945, finally bringing the play (now retitled *O Mistress Mine*) into the Empire in New York in January 1946. Lewis Nichols wrote in the *New York Times*: 'The Lunts have never been better, gayer, more amusing. One swallow may not make a summer, but two Lunts can throw a great deal of weight on the credit side of what has not always been a good season. The welcome mat has been set out to good purpose this time.'

In 1949 the Lunts celebrated their twenty-fifth anniversary as a theatrical acting team. Brooks Atkinson wrote a tribute in the *New York Times*: 'For so triumphant a couple they are singularly humble. That is one of the astonishing things about them. Over a quarter of a century their record is so brilliant that they can hardly be unaware of their quality. Their names are a guarantee of packed houses across the country. They have never let the public down — nor, for that matter have they ever let down authors, other actors or producers . . . Their talents are thoroughly individual, but they perfectly blend. Miss Fontanne's voice is low and sultry, Mr Lunt's high and querulous. They both know the theatrical value of walking, but Miss Fontanne's walk is mischievously undulating and Mr Lunt's is towering and bent forward. Around and around the play goes this witty, sophisticated comic dance, which, as a matter of fact, the Lunts might have learned from their chicken yard in Genesee Depot. The brilliant gaiety of their acting is not a gift that has come freely. Having worked at acting for a number of years in a wide variety of parts, they have earned it the hard way . . .' They celebrated their silver jubilee by playing Emily Chanler and Thomas Chanler in S. N. Behrman's *I Know My Love* at the Shubert Theater, opening in November of that year. Ward Morehouse wrote in the *New York Sun*: 'Alfred Lunt, the world's best actor, is again playing love scenes with Mrs Lunt, the brilliant other half of the theatre's first stage team, and Broadway seems a wonderful place once more . . . Alfred Lunt is again mumbling and sputtering, jerking his head and rolling his eyes as he explosively stalks Miss Fontanne, his prey for all of a quarter of a century, about the drawing-room.

She is again gay and winning, taunting and knowing — arch, airy and elusive.' Of Lunt's direction of the production Howard Barnes wrote in the New York *Herald Tribune*: 'Lunt has directed the work to perfection even when Behrman has been more intent on graceful prose than dynamic action.' They toured *I Know My Love* through 1950.

In 1951 Alfred Lunt staged Mozart's *Cosi Fan Tutte* at the Metropolitan Opera House. Olin Downes reported for the *New York Times*: 'His production appears to us in every way to serve a double and profoundly artistic purpose. It is comprehending of Mozart, and it is in the truest sense a modern realization of a classic masterpiece.'

The Lunts opened at the Phoenix Theatre in London in September 1952, in Noel Coward's *Quadrille*. Kenneth Tynan wrote: 'The excuse for this monstrously over-loaded tea-trolley of a play is, of course, the presence in it of Alfred Lunt and Lynne Fontanne who play together, as the millionaire and the marchioness, like sandpaper on diamond. Mr Lunt comes off best, since he is not required to sound witty; shambling and guileless, he has the strength and stature of a displaced Zeus... Miss Fontanne, at his side, performs with the crackle and sheen of a new five-pound note; given one sprig of verbal wit to adorn it, this would be a gorgeous banquet.'

Returning to New York, Alfred directed Audrey Hepburn and Mel Ferrer in Giraudoux's *Ondine* at the 46th Street Theater, and then in November 1954 he and Lynn appeared at the Coronet Theater in *Quadrille*. The critics on that side of the Atlantic were no more taken with Coward's play than were the English critics, but as Richard Watts Jun. wrote in the *New York Post*: 'It is an ancient statement about Alfred Lunt and Lynn Fontanne that they would be delightful to watch if they were reading the telephone directory, and there may have been cases when I have suspected that they and their audiences would have been better off if that had been what they were doing... This is light, deft acting at its peak, even if the play is far from completely worthy of such artful playing.' It ran for 150 performances.

At ANTA in January 1956, they opened as Rudi and Essie Sebastian in *The Great Sebastians*, a vaudeville mind-reading act who find themselves involved in a Communist intrigue while playing in Prague. Brooks Atkinson wrote: 'As usual, the Lunts are giving a bright performance in a dullish play... Everything they do is meticulous, pertinent, fluent and funny... Golly, what they could do if they selected a script as subtle and skilful as they are!' They followed their Broadway season

with another coast-to-coast tour, and then appeared on television in the play, their first venture into the medium. The Lunts returned to England in December 1957 and toured as Claire Zachanassian and Anton Schill in Dürrenmatt's *Time and Again*, which was retitled *The Visit* when they brought it to New York in May 1958, and opened the new Lunt-Fontanne Theater. They toured it coast-to-coast the following year, and then returned to England, where in June 1960 they opened the new Royalty Theatre with the production. Kenneth Tynan reported: 'Miss Fontanne plays the super-capitalist with blood curdling aplomb, and Mr Lunt, her sacrifice, makes memorable use of his defeated shoulder, his beseeching hands and the operatic blast of his voice.'

After *The Visit* the acting partnership retired. Brooks Atkinson wrote: 'For years they had been squandering talent on trivial comedies cut to their measure. But their acting in *The Visit*, which marked the conclusion of their long stage career, reminded theatre-goers that they were great actors in any genre — perfectionists in details, magnetic in style.' Retirement took them to their beloved Genesee Depot, a home that had become a minor shrine to American theatricals. As Carol Channing said: 'Genesee Depot is to performers what the Vatican is to Catholics. I'm complete there. The Lunts are where we all spring from.' They had spent their acting lives on stage, making only two films, *The Guardsman* in 1932 (which they said paid for the swimming pool), and the wartime *Hollywood Canteen*. After retirement they ventured out occasionally. Alfred directed *First Love* at the Morosco Theater in December 1961. On television in 1963 Alfred played the narrator in *The Old Lady Shows Her Medals* and Lynn was Mrs Oliver Wendell Holmes in *The Magnificent Yankee*. (This brought her a second Emmy — the first was for *The Great Sebastians*.) In September 1966, Alfred Lunt directed *La Traviata* for the Metropolitan Opera House's opening week at the Lincoln Center. Their last appearance together was on the Dick Cavett Television Show in 1970 when they joined their friend Noel Coward.

Alfred Lunt died, aged 84, on 3 August 1977 after undergoing surgery for cancer. After his death Lynn said: 'We had a very happy time, and I don't think if we had to do it all again we'd do much differently. The best thing in a way about our marriage was retirement; after all those years of work we had a long marvellously peaceful time in the garden. Alfred did so love that garden.' Lynn Fontanne died on 31 July 1983.
See photograph opposite.

Alfred Lunt and Lynn Fontanne in Robert E. Sherwood's *Idiot's Delight*
(New York, May 1939)

Alec McCowen in his one-man show, *Kipling*, at the Mermaid Theatre
(London, May 1984)

ALEC MCCOWEN

Alexander Duncan McCowen was born in Tunbridge Wells, England, on 26 May 1925. His father was a pram salesman and a devoted Christian evangelist; his mother, Mary Walkden, had been a dancer before her marriage. Alec went to Skinner's School in Tunbridge Wells and then on to RADA; he has always been a dedicated loner.

He made his first stage appearance at the Repertory Theatre in Macclesfield in August 1942 playing Micky in *Paddy the Next Best Thing*, and remained in repertory there until 1945, when he toured India and Burma for ENSA playing in *Love in a Mist*. He then went to York Repertory Company where, barely 20, he played a centenarian Spaniard while the company's 'old man', who was in fact 75, played his son. Alec McCowen remained in rep until 1949, and had one season at St John's in Newfoundland.

He made his London début at the Arts Theatre in April 1950 playing Maxim in *Ivanov*, and at the same theatre that September was Georges Almaire in *The Mask and the Face*. In November he played Kitts in *Preserving Mr Panmure*. He went to the Lyric, Hammersmith, in January 1951 and was in *The Silver Box*; that April he was at the Westminster playing Brian in *The Martin's Nest*.

Alec McCowen made his first appearance on the New York stage on 20 December 1951 at the Ziegfeld as the Messenger in *Antony and Cleopatra*, and returned to the Arts where in May he played Hugh Voysey in *The Voysey Inheritance*. In November he was the Announcer in *The Holy Terrors*.

He had his first long run at the St James's Theatre, where he played Daventry in *Escapade*. It opened in January 1953 and ran for more than a year. During that time, for special performances for the Repertory Players he was Larry Thompson in *Serious Charge* at the Adelphi and Julian Heath in *Shadow of the Vine* at Wyndham's.

At the New Bromley Theatre in June 1954 he was Toulouse-Lautrec in *Moulin Rouge*. He went to the Haymarket in November 1954 to play Barnaby Tucker in *The Matchmaker*. The production was directed by Tyrone Guthrie, and had opened at the Edinburgh Festival. Ronald Barker reported: 'Arthur Hill and Alec McCowen, as the merchant's clerk and apprentice, both give performances which will help to place them in the race for stardom.'

Alec McCowen had a notable success at the Garrick Theatre in September 1955 when he played Vicomte Octave de Clerambard in *The Count of Clerambard*. At the Hippodrome in June 1956 he played Dr Bird in *The Caine Mutiny Court Martial* which starred Lloyd Nolan.

No Laughing Matter, translated by Lucienne Hill from the French of Armand Salacrou, was a major Parisian hit which ran for three years in Paris. Playing Lancelot Berenson, Alec McCowen opened in it at the Arts in January 1957. It did not fare as well in London, but Frank Granville-Barker reported: 'Alec McCowen's cringing bewilderment as Lancelot is quite masterly, and he shows once again — as he did in *Clerambard* last year — that he can play in a French style as easily as an English one.' In August 1958 he opened at the Edinburgh Festival playing Michael Claverton-Ferry in T. S. Eliot's *The Elder Statesman*, and transferred with the production to the Cambridge Theatre in September. Caryl Brahms enthused: 'Mr Alec McCowen made me forget that the wastrel son was speaking lines. His first burst of passionate rebellion is a small tour de force that only a fine actor could accomplish — and many of us have known for some time now that in Mr McCowen we have a fine actor.'

He joined the Old Vic Company for the 1959–60 season, during which he played Mr Brisk in *The Double Dealer*, Touchstone in *As You Like It*, Algernon Moncrieff in *The Importance of Being Earnest*, Ford in *The Merry Wives of Windsor*, and the Dauphin in *Saint Joan*, and he took over the title role in *Richard II*. He remained with the company the following year and played Oberon in *A Midsummer Night's Dream*, Malvolio in *Twelfth Night*, and what Kenneth Tynan called an 'electrically played' Mercutio in *Romeo and Juliet*.

As a complete change of pace, in February he went to the Garrick in the revue *Not to Worry*, and in May was at the Piccadilly playing Sebastian in *Castle in Sweden*, Françoise Sagan's first stage play. Mark Taylor wrote in *Plays and Players* that McCowen gave 'a performance of such throw-away assured professionalism as to hold the play together'.

In September 1962 he joined the Royal Shakespeare Company at Stratford, where he played Antipholus of Syracuse in *The Comedy of Errors*. Peter Roberts said he had 'comic resources of his own which he was able to spin out when Shakespeare's don't go quite far enough'. That October he played the Fool to Paul Scofield's King Lear. Both productions came to the Aldwych in

December. In September 1963 Alec McCowen played Father Riccardo Fontano at the Aldwych in what was probably the most controversial play of the decade, *The Representative*. *The Comedy of Errors* and *King Lear* toured the USSR, Europe and the United States from February through June 1964. When they played New York, the critic John Simon called McCowen's Fool 'saucily sophisticated'.

Returning to England in July 1965 Alec McCowen opened at the Yvonne Arnaud Theatre in Guildford playing Ronald Gamble in the farce *Thark*, and transferred with the production the following month to the Garrick. At the Strand in November he was the Author in Anouilh's *The Cavern*.

In September 1966 he played Arthur Henderson in John Bowen's *After the Rain*. He played the same role at the Duchess in London in January 1967 and at the Golden, New York, in September the same year. John Russell Taylor did not much care for the play but thought it one of McCowen's best performances.

The role of Fr William Rolfe in *Hadrian the Seventh* began in Birmingham in May 1967. It continued at the Mermaid in London in April 1968 and went on to New York to the Helen Hayes Theater in January 1969. For this performance Alec McCowen won the *Evening Standard* Award for Best Actor of 1968. John Russell Taylor wrote: 'As we all know, Mr McCowen has a superb face for playing clerics and fanatics and since Hadrian is both he has found an ideal role. The more so in that Hadrian is, deliberately, a very funny man, his impossible character being constantly alleviated by his wit and even in success, has blazing good humor. This, too, Mr McCowen can manage wonderfully well; his comic timing is immaculate, and the lightning shifts of mood are beautifully done. Indeed, I cannot recall an occasion on which this splendid underestimated actor has been better used, and even were the play far less interesting, his performance alone would make it essential viewing for anyone anxious to see the best that contemporary British theatre has to offer.'

Back in Birmingham in January 1970 he did his obligatory Hamlet, and in August was at the Royal Court playing Philip in Christopher Hampton's *The Philanthropist*. John Holstrom said he played the academic philologist 'irresistibly behind an elaborate semaphore of tiny wincing smiles'. The production transferred to the Mayfair in September 1970 and went on to the Ethel Barrymore on Broadway in March 1971. Alec McCowen won the Variety Club Award the same year.

In August 1970 he took over the title role in *Butley* from Alan Bates at the Criterion. He had

his first job directing at the Hampstead Theatre Club in December 1972.

In February 1973, Alec McCowen opened for the National Theatre at the Old Vic where, opposite Diana Rigg, he played Alceste in *The Misanthrope*. The Molière play was translated and freely adapted by Tony Harrison and directed by John Dexter. W. Stephen Gilbert reported: '. . . McCowen gives by his scrupulous standards, an extravagant performance. And it works beautifully. This Alceste is believably both a captive of Celimene's set and prickly idealist. McCowen never sends up the part, yet he knows just when to make us laugh at Alceste and when to annex our laughter. It's a fine fusion of art and craft and you'd be daft to miss it.' For this performance McCowen again got the *Evening Standard* Award. In July 1973, still at the Old Vic, he played the psychiatrist Martin Dysart in Peter Shaffer's *Equus*. Helen Dawson said: 'Alec McCowen handles the moods and manoeuvres of the interrogation with that mixture of steely impatience and faltering humanity which is becoming his trademark.' During this performance, McCowen himself went into psychoanalysis.

At the Albery Theatre in May 1974 he was with Diana Rigg again. This time she was Eliza and he was Professor Higgins in Shaw's *Pygmalion*; it was a critical and commercial success. He was Alceste again at the St James in New York in March 1975 and at the Old Vic in July. At the Criterion in June 1976 he was Ben Musgrave in Felicity Browne's *The Family Dance*. In February 1977 he was back as the psychiatrist in *Equus*, playing at the Helen Hayes Theater in New York. At the Edinburgh Festival that year he was Antony in the Prospect Theatre Company's *Antony and Cleopatra*, which transferred to the Old Vic in November.

It was in 1978 that he devised a solo performance for himself of St Mark's Gospel. This he performed at the Riverside Studios, at the Mermaid and at the Comedy as well as in New York. He returned to Wyndham's Theatre in October 1979 where he played Frank in *Tishoo!*, and to the National Theatre in May 1980 where he appeared with Geraldine McEwan in the Rattigan double-bill, *The Browning Version* and *Harlequinade*.

In July 1981 he was back with St Mark's Gospel at the Globe Theatre. Anthony Thorncroft described the performance in the *Financial Times*: 'On a stage decked only with a table and three chairs he recites the King James version of St Mark. Recites, however, is hardly the word. The effect must be similar to the impact of Homer declaiming the *Odyssey* and Chaucer his *Canterbury Tales*. Alec McCowen does not dramatize the work with a range of voices and affected gestures but interprets it as an unfolding story, a saga. The result is that this, the shortest and the oldest of the Gospels, comes across with a meaning quite beyond the words read on the printed page or an interpretation from the pulpit ... McCowen manages to avoid "acting". Instead, he gives a reading with an uncanny ear for the right emphasis, for the flow of the events. It is a marvel not because it shows off the dramatic skills of a professional actor but because it opens up thought on the Gospel in a way quite outside the capabilities of a thousand scholars...' He was at the Mermaid in London in February 1982 playing Adolf Hitler, aged 92, in Christopher Hampton's *The Portage to San Cristobal of A.H.* The play was not a success but Michael Billington wrote in the *Guardian*: 'Alec

McCowen's delivery of the final speech is one of the greatest pieces of acting I have ever seen.'

Alec McCowen made his first film in 1952, when he appeared in *The Cruel Sea*, and has since been seen in many others including Hitchcock's *Frenzy*. He has never married, and lives in a large flat in Chelsea with a grand piano. 'I suppose the reason that I am as I am today is that I am in love with freedom,' he says. 'I was a maverick at school — I didn't care for the team things. I like to think of life as an adventure. If you ask me what I love, I would immediately think of my car ... It's just that I can take off and go somewhere when I get in it.' In 1984 McCowen returned to the stage with a highly acclaimed solo show about Rudyard Kipling. *See photograph opposite page 247.*

GERALDINE McEWAN

Geraldine McKeown was born on 9 May 1932 in Old Windsor, Berkshire, where her father was a printer. She gained a scholarship to Windsor County School. 'The plays we did at school always loomed large in my life,' she said. 'I was the one who recited poems on Speech Day.'

She always longed to be an actress but had no idea of how to go about it. Luckily her mother's best friend worked at the snack bar of the Theatre Royal at Windsor and she got a few walk-on parts there while she was still at school. Geraldine also began taking private elocution lessons, though she and her family could ill afford it. She made her stage début at Windsor in October 1946 as an attendant of Hippolyta in *A Midsummer Night's Dream*. When she left school she went to work in an office but spent most of her time and a good deal of postage writing for acting jobs, unsuccessfully. But at last she was taken on as assistant stage manager at Windsor. It was there that she met Hugh Crutwell, a director who would go on to become principal of the Royal Academy of Dramatic Art and also her husband. His first impression of her was that he did not think her up to the job, but she remained as stage manager and the parts she was allowed to play got bigger until in 1951 she played a young Irish girl, Christina Deed, in a new comedy, *Who Goes There?*, which was taken to the West End with her still in it. The producer thought McKeown too difficult a name, so it was as Geraldine McEwan that she opened at the

Vaudeville in April 1951 — and was proclaimed a star. 'Bring on the new girl!' the first night audience shouted.

She was now cast as a comedienne. At the Vaudeville in May 1952 she played Janet Andrews in *Sweet Madness* and at the Q Theatre in September was Janet Blake in *For Love or Money*. She opened at the Comedy Theatre in December 1952 as Anne Purves in *For Better, For Worse* ... and stayed there for eighteen months. She spent all that time on voice and movement lessons, not wishing to be taken as a light comedienne. She auditioned for Stratford, but they were not yet ready for each other. On 17 May 1953 she and Hugh Crutwell married.

Her next play was at the Saville in May 1955, when she played Julie Gillis in *The Tender Trap*. Frank Granville-Barker reported that she 'oozes husky-throated charm as the girl who bags her quarry'. During summer 1955 she was at Brighton and Streatham playing the title role in *Patience*, and in November of that year was co-starring with Dirk Bogarde in a play directed by Peter Hall at the Apollo. It was called *Summertime* and Frank Granville-Barker was still impressed by her, though a bit worried. 'Geraldine McEwan has charm and polish but there is a monotonous quality in her voice ...' However, Peter Hall was summoned to the Shakespeare Memorial Theatre in Stratford and he brought Geraldine McEwan with him. In July 1956 there she played the Princess of France in *Love's Labour's Lost*, and Lisa Gordon-Smith wrote in *Plays and Players*: 'Geraldine McEwan compensates for her unShakespearian vocal delivery (which she is obviously trying to overcome and nearly succeeds in doing) by a delightful appearance and a very good representation of that witty but never un-royal Princess.'

She was back in London at the Royal Court in February 1957 playing the 12-year-old Frankie Adams in Carson McCullers' *A Member of the Wedding*. *Plays and Players* said she 'itches and gawks and does what a courageous and resourceful adult actress can to create the puzzlement of this odd and restless final stage of childhood'. At the Palace Theatre that December she took over the role of Jean Rice in *The Entertainer* from Joan Plowright.

In 1958 she returned to Stratford and Peter Hall for the season. She played Olivia in *Twelfth Night*, and according to Peter Jackson: 'To force Olivia to play for laughs while surrounded on all sides by comedians with far better lines does not give the actress a fighting chance, but Geraldine McEwan, with her piping voice and plaintive little gestures, draws such sympathy from the audience that the approach is justified.' In *Much Ado About Nothing* Frank Granville-Barker was disappointed by her Hero: '[She was] negative and passive in her virtue and the charm of her husky voice smacks more of the English 1920s than the Italian 1850s.' However, Kenneth Tynan thought that her Marina in *Pericles* directed by Tony Richardson was 'sweetly candid'. She travelled with the company to Moscow and Leningrad in December 1958.

She was Marie Renaud in Alan Melville's *Change of Tune* at the Strand in May 1959 — but not for long. With the RSC at the Aldwych in December 1960 she was once more Olivia in *Twelfth Night*, and she returned to Stratford for the 1961 season, where she played with Christopher Plummer in *Much Ado About Nothing*. Peter Roberts reported: 'Geraldine McEwan has graduated from Hero in the last Stratford production to Beatrice in the present one and she fully deserves the promotion. She could probably have continued in the commercial theatre trading on the idiosyncratic voice and personality that won her fame in trivialities like *Who Goes There?* Instead she has taken on what seemed an impossible challenge in the classical field and is now a fully accomplished Shakespeare player giving us a Beatrice at whose birth a star certainly danced.' However, Kenneth Tynan was not impressed by her Ophelia in Ian Bannen's *Hamlet*. 'Geraldine McEwan is at once a passionless Ophelia and a glum reminder of our theatre's perennial deficiency in girls with a natural talent for emotional acting.'

In March 1962 she opened at the Arts Theatre as Jenny Acton in Giles Cooper's black comedy *Everything in the Garden*, and transferred with the production in May to the Duke of York's. She then took over the part of Lady Teazle in *The School for Scandal* at the Haymarket in October, and made her Broadway début in this production at the Majestic in January 1963. That September she returned to England and opened at Wimbledon in the double-bill *The Private Ear and the Public Eye*, returning to the United States with the production, which played the Morosco on Broadway in October 1963 before touring the country.

She next toured in England during February 1965, playing Fay in Joe Orton's *Loot*. In July 1965 she was at Chichester with the National Theatre Company playing opposite Albert Finney in Arden's *Armstrong's Last Goodnight*. She went with the company to Moscow and Berlin in September playing Angelica in *Love for Love*, and then played both roles at the Old Vic in October. In 1966 with the National Theatre Company she played Raymonde Chandebise in *A Flea in Her Ear*, which transferred to the Queen's, and Alice in Strindberg's *The Dance of Death*. Of the latter, Martin Esslin wrote: 'The casting of Geraldine McEwan, a brilliant comedienne, as Alice was another masterstroke. She has the sense of the grotesque, the timing and the comic invention needed for the part, and at the same time she succeeds triumphantly in evoking sympathy for the sufferings of this insufferable woman.' The company went to the United States and also toured Canada. In New York Martin Gottfried reported on her Raymonde: 'Geraldine McEwan was splendid as the wife although, strangely, she played the role in high English (in the Joan Greenwood–Glynis Johns–Fenella Fielding style) while everyone else was doing French.'

Staying with the National Theatre Company, in 1968 she played Queen Anne in Brecht's *Edward II* and Victoria in *Home and Beauty*. In 1969 she was Millamant in *The Way of the World*, Ada in *Rites* and Vittoria Corombona in *The White Devil*. At the New Theatre, still with the National Theatre Company, she opened in July 1971 playing Alkemena in *Amphitryon 38*, directed by Laurence Olivier and co-starring Christopher Plummer. Stanley Price, writing in *Plays and Players*, did not care for the production but noted: 'On the credit side, and one is immensely grateful for it, there is the playing of Geraldine McEwan as Alkemena. Miss McEwan's voice and comic stylization, so invariably and ideally suited to the Elvira of *Blithe Spirit*, are both used here to fine effect to make of the vamp-like wife a funny, sensual and appealing character; a girl willing and able to argue the hind legs off a God.'

With Keith Michell at the Comedy Theatre in May 1973 she gave dramatized readings of the letters of Robert Browning and Elizabeth Barrett in a programme entitled *Dear Love*, and at Greenwich in December was seen as Zoe in *Not Drowning But Waving*. She was at the Globe Theatre in February 1974 with Albert Finney and Denholm Elliott in Peter Nichols' *Chez Nous*; Ronald Bryden wrote: 'Geraldine McEwan's Diana is a marvellously skilled comic creation from moment to moment, but nothing in the writing of the part can connect her catty fastidiousness with the past attributed to her.' She was Susan, the comically adulterous wife, in a revival of *The Little Hut* at the Duke of York's in October 1974, and at the Criterion in June 1975 was with Roderick Cook and Jamie Ross in the revue compilation, *Oh Coward!*

Geraldine McEwan went to Chichester for their season in 1978 to play the title part in *Look After Lulu*, and transferred with the production to the Haymarket in October. Ned Chaillet reported for the *Times*: 'Miss McEwan is Lulu, the erotic enthusiast whose capers lead into unexpected marriage, and she proves herself a mistress of double meaning and sexual innuendo, lowering her voice to the limits of suggestiveness and moving with a lively, stylized kick to her heels.' In May 1980 she returned to the National Theatre for the Rattigan double-bill, *The Browning Version* and *Harlequinade*.

Although she has never made a film ('More than anything else I'd love to do a film,' she told a reporter, 'but somehow I don't get asked.') she has done notable television work, especially the series of Muriel Spark's *The Prime of Miss Jean Brodie*. Geraldine McEwan has also devised a one-woman show based on the writings of Jane Austen.

In the 1983–84 season at the National Theatre Geraldine McEwan played Mrs Malaprop in a production of *The Rivals* to considerable critical delight.

See photograph opposite page 263.

IAN McKELLEN

*I*an McKellen was born in Burnley, Lancashire, on 25 May 1939. He spent his childhood in a family that was neither rich nor poor. His father was the borough engineer and surveyor of Bolton, and his mother the daughter of a Congregationalist minister and a keen amateur performer. Luckily one of his father's friends owned the Bolton theatre and there the young McKellen could watch from backstage for free. He still admires the old music-hall tradition that he first saw up north. He went first to Wigan Grammar School and then on to Bolton School where, as he puts it, they 'encouraged drama with the same enthusiasm as they trained us for sport or self-sufficiency'.

As a teenager Ian McKellen declared his intention of being an actor, but by the time he went up to Cambridge, to St Catharine's College, he planned to be a teacher. There, however, he found the most extraordinary generation of students, who included Trevor Nunn, Derek Jacobi, Corin Redgrave and the playwright-to-be Simon Gray. They were all encouraged in their theatrical aims by George Rylands, a don and the adviser to the Marlowe Society, who instilled in that generation the most scrupulous attention to the classic texts. McKellen became president of the Society and in his first year at Cambridge he played a Justice Shallow that was talked about for years after. His determination to be an actor returned suddenly. 'It was outside the stage door of the Arts Theatre, Cambridge, in 1959,' he said, 'when Richard Cottrell, whom I worked with later, congratulated me on a notice I'd had from Alan Dent in the *News Chronicle* for my Justice Shallow in *Henry IV Part 2*. Richard said that would be very useful in getting my first job. Until then I hadn't thought I was good enough to be an actor. But at that exact moment I suddenly realized it was where I was heading.' After Cambridge, in 1961 McKellen joined the Belgrade, Coventry, and went on to repertory seasons at Ipswich from 1962 to 1963, where among other roles he played the title parts in *Henry V* and *Luther*. He then went on to the Nottingham Theatre, where in December 1963 he played Aufidius in John Neville's *Coriolanus* and in April, Arthur Seaton in *Saturday Night and Sunday Morning*. In June in Nottingham he was Sir Thomas More in *A Man for All Seasons*.

Ian McKellen made his London début at the Duke of York's in September 1964, playing

Godfrey in James Saunders' *A Scent of Flowers*. Then for the National Theatre Company he played Claudio in *Much Ado About Nothing*, the Protestant Evangelist in *Armstrong's Last Good Night*, and Captain de Foenix in *Trelawney of the 'Wells'* at the Chichester Festival in July 1965. In November that year he went to the Hampstead Theatre Club, where he played Alvin in *A Lily in Little India*. He transferred with the play to the St Martin's in the West End in January 1966. Michael Billington reported: 'Mr McKellen endows the voluble Alvin with a tousled charm and plays him with obvious insight.' In May 1966 he was at the Royal Court playing Andrew Cobham in Arnold Wesker's *Their Very Own and Golden City*. Martin Esslin said: 'Ian McKellen runs the gamut from fiery youth to doddering dotage with a wealth of fine characterization.'

At the Mermaid in September 1966 he was in a double-bill playing the title part in *O'Flaherty VC* and Bonaparte in *The Man of Destiny*. At the Oxford Playhouse in November he opened with Judi Dench and Ian McShane in Aleksei Arbuzov's *The Promise*. This play, translated by Ariadne Nicolaeff, about three young people in Leningrad — the scientist, the fanatic and the poet — transferred to the Fortune Theatre in London in January 1967; Ian McKellen also made his Broadway début in the part of Leonidik at the Henry Miller Theater in November 1967. The same group also made the film version.

At the Lyric in the West End in February 1968 he was in Peter Shaffer's double-bill, *The White Liars* and *Black Comedy*, playing Tom and Harold Gorringe.

He joined the Prospect Players and toured in November 1968 as Richard II. At the Liverpool Playhouse in May 1969 he was Pentheus in *The Bacchae*. It was at Liverpool that he directed his first production, *The Prime of Miss Jean Brodie*. For the Edinburgh Festival in August 1969 he was back with Prospect playing the title roles in Shakespeare's *Richard II* and Marlowe's *Edward II*. He toured in both these parts all over the country, and stopped off in London with them at the Mermaid in September 1969 and at the Piccadilly in January 1970. Michael Billington reported on his performances: 'McKellen shrewdly exploits the differences between the two monarchs. Broadly speaking, his Edward is a man who discovers that inside him is a king; his Richard is a king who pays too little heed to the internal man. The tragedy is that for both of them the self-knowledge acquired comes too late. What strikes you about the performances, though, is the combination of sheer animal magnetism and interpretive intelligence. McKellen also shows that rage and almost

indescribable relish for acting, as if the stage were both a natural stomping ground and a spiritual gymnasium for the exploration of personality, that makes for heady theatrical excitement.'

At the Royal Court's Theatre Upstairs in July 1970 he was Darkly in *Billy's Last Stand*, and then in October he began a tour for the Cambridge Theatre Company playing Captain Plum in *The Recruiting Officer* and Corporal Hill in *Chips with Everything*.

Back with the Prospect Company, Ian McKellen toured from March through July 1971 as Hamlet and came into the Cambridge Theatre in the West End with the production in August. There had been a surfeit of Hamlets that season, and perhaps Peter Ansorge was suffering from it when he reported for *Plays and Players*: 'Though McKellen begins his foggy night in Elsinore somewhat clumsily — in woollen socks and a pullover — his main motivation seems to be in cornering Claudius as quickly and as neatly as possible. This unfortunately sugars over most of the interesting psychological issues in the play . . . Also McKellen gives a sudden shuddering emphasis to lines which seem to bear little or no relationship to his or any other interpretation of the play.'

He played Svetlovidov in *Swan Song*, the inaugural production of the Crucible Theatre, Sheffield, in November 1971, and then in Watford at the Palace in March 1972 he directed *The Erpingham Camp*.

Ian McKellen then became a founding member of the Actors' Company — a classical touring actors' co-operative where all the members shared big and small parts. They began at the Edinburgh Festival in 1972, McKellen playing Giovanni in *'Tis Pity She's a Whore*, the Page-boy in *Ruling the Roost* and Prince Yoremitsu in *The Three Arrows*. He directed *A Private Matter* at the Vaudeville in February 1973 and then with the Actors' Company at the Edinburgh Festival before their 1973 tour he played Michael in *The Wood-Demon*, a footman in *The Way of the World* and Edgar in *King Lear*. But although very much approving of the idea of the Actors' Company in theory, Ian McKellen became bored with playing small parts. He joined the Royal Shakespeare Company, and made his début with them as Dr Faustus at the Edinburgh Festival in 1974, coming to the Aldwych with it in September. In November, also at the Aldwych, he played the title role in Frank Wedekind's *The Marquis of Keith*. Martin Esslin reported: 'Ian McKellen underlines the Marquis's limp, but at the same time shows his animal vitality by the intensity of the contortions of his body, when, for example, to emphasize a point in an argument he leans across a table so that only his toes and his elbows hold him suspended, like a gymnast on the barre. His voice is the rich instrument of the born mob-orator with the histrionic inflections of a barnstorming actor; and he conveys all the wit and sheer intelligence, the exuberant, innocent overconfidence which makes the amoralist more honest than the respectable squares who surround him. A memorable performance.' Also with the RSC that season he played Philip the Bastard in *King John*.

At the Savoy in April 1975 he directed *The Clandestine Marriage*, and in June at the Young Vic played Colin in *Ashes*. He returned to the RSC to play Aubrey Bagot in Shaw's *Too True to Be Good*, which was at the Aldwych in October 1975 and transferred to the Globe in December. Alan Brien, who did not care for the production, wrote: 'Ian McKellen, as the burglar-preacher, can only unify the role by continually titillating us with odd looks, gestures, little dances, bodily quirks and vocal variations which distract us.' For the RSC's 1976 Stratford season he was Leontes in *The Winter's Tale*, Macbeth, and Romeo in *Romeo and Juliet* — a part he admits he came to too late. For the Edinburgh Festival that autumn he devised a solo show, *Words, Words, Words*, and returned to Stratford the next season to repeat *Macbeth* and play Face in *The Alchemist*.

At the Festival Hall in July 1977 he was Alex in Tom Stoppard's *Every Good Boy Deserves Favour*, and returned to the Edinburgh Festival with a solo show, *Acting Shakespeare*. For the 1977–78 Aldwych season with the RSC he was in *Romeo and Juliet*, *Pillars of the Community*, *The Alchemist* and *Days of the Commune*. He also created a sensation that season at the RSC's small London establishment, the Warehouse, when he played his Macbeth.

During 1978 he was on the road directing a small-scale RSC tour, and also playing Sir Toby in *Twelfth Night*, and Andrei in *The Three Sisters*.

At the Royal Court in May 1979 he opened as Max in *Bent*. Ned Chaillet reported: 'McKellen's performance . . . is further demonstration of his mastery of the stage. In this play alone, his range is immense. He swoops through Coward-like control of comedy to all the pain of a destroyed human being. It should now be clear that McKellen is a great actor.' That year he won his third award from the Society of West End Theatre Managers — best actor three years in a row.

He then went to America, where Peter Hall directed him as Salieri in Shaffer's *Amadeus*. The production opened on Broadway and *Time* magazine reported: 'It is a portrait in depth of a shallow man, a forgotten eighteenth-century court composer so bedeviled by jealousy, the shock of his own mediocrity and the daunting genius of his principal rival that he encouraged Mozart's ruination and hastened his death. Full of wit and passion and measured extravagance, the performance has become perhaps the most warmly admired of the Broadway season.' Ian McKellen won a Tony Award for that performance. He had already received a CBE at home, for his theatrical work in general.

'Acting,' he says, 'is rather like being a cartoonist. But you mustn't exaggerate, you mustn't coarsen or change what you've found. It's not being a good mimic, though you can pick up something about a character and plug that. Acting is all to do with being conscious of what you are doing as well as being unconscious. It's being possessed but not possessive. Subjective and objective. It's really only an extension of what we all do every day. We think we know what impressions we give other people. We are all wonderful actors.'

In 1984, after a solo Shakespeare recital in America, McKellen joined the National Theatre as one of its directors and to play in *Venice Preserv'd*, *Coriolanus* and Chekhov's *Wild Honey*.
See photograph opposite page 278.

SIOBHAN McKENNA

Siobhan McKenna was born on 24 May 1922 in Belfast, Ireland. Her father was a professor of mathematical physics and her mother designed hats. She was convent-educated, making her first stage appearance as Charity in a school religious play. She earned a first-class honours degree at the National University in Galway. She appeared with the Gaelic Repertory Theatre in Galway from 1940 to 1942, playing in Gaelic-language productions and translating them herself. She played the title role in *Mary Rose*, Bessie Burgess in *The Plough and the Stars*, Mrs Grigson in *Shadow of a Gunman*, the Wife in *Tons of Money*, Miriamne in *Winterset*, Lady Macbeth, and Bella in *Gaslight*. She spent a year at the National University at Dublin, and then joined the Abbey Players where she played Nicole in *Le Bourgeois Gentilhomme* and appeared in *The End House*, *The Railway House*, *Marks and Mabel*, *The Countess Kathleen*, *The Far Off Hills* and *The Dear Father*.

On 7 July 1946 she married the actor Denis O'Dea, and that same year left the Abbey Players. She felt that she did not have the temperament to remain part of a permanent company. 'It wasn't that I didn't believe in team acting. Each time you do a play you become like a family working together. But you don't have to belong to an institution to do it.'

Siobhan McKenna made her London début playing Nora Fintry in *The White Steed* at the Embassy Theatre on 3 March 1947. At the Q in 1949 she was Helen Pettigrew in *Berkeley Square*, and the same year she played Maura Joyce in *Fading Mansion* at the Duchess. She returned to Ireland, where she played the title role in a Gaelic-language production of Shaw's *Saint Joan* both in Galway and at the Gaiety in Dublin.

In London in June 1951 she was Regina in *Ghosts* at the Embassy, and went to the Edinburgh Festival playing Pegeen Mike in *The Playboy of the Western World* and appearing in *The White-Headed Boy*. In November the same year Siobhan McKenna played the title role in *Héloïse* at the Duke of York's in London. Kenneth Tynan reported: 'Siobhan McKenna, flinty of mien, offers a pinched Héloïse which, in its pallor and intensity, recalls the spooky lady in Charles Addams' drawings.'

She went to Stratford for the 1952 season, where she played Virgilia in *Coriolanus*, Celia in *As You Like It*, Lady Macduff in *Macbeth* and Virginia in *Volpone*. In April 1953 she was in

Scotland at the Royal Theatre, Glasgow, playing April in *Purple Dust*, and then returned to Ireland to Dublin's Gaiety Theatre, where she played Beauty in *The Love of Four Colonels* and the title role in *Anna Christie*. In 1954 she played St Joan once again, this time at the Gate Theatre in Dublin, and went back to the Gaiety as Luka in *Arms and the Man* and Pegeen Mike in *The Playboy of the Western World*. She finally brought her St Joan to London, to the Arts Theatre in September 1954. Kenneth Tynan reported: '... this actress lets us see life stripping Joan down to her spiritual buff. The beaming clown of the opening scenes has undergone, by the end, an annealing: all that is mortal about her is peeled away, and sheer soul bursts through. "God is alone" had tears flowing everywhere in the house, and during the epilogue one scarcely dared look at the stage...the richest portrait of saintliness since Falconette shaved her head for Dreyer's film *La Passion de Jeanne d'Arc*.' For her performance she received the London *Evening Standard* Award as Best Actress of the year.

Siobhan McKenna made her American début as Miss Madrigal in Enid Bagnold's *The Chalk Garden* at the Ethel Barrymore Theater on 26 October 1955. The following August she played St Joan at the Sanders Theater in Cambridge, Massachusetts, and took it to the Phoenix in New York in September. She then went to Canada to the Stratford, Ontario, Shakespeare Festival, where in June 1957 she played Viola in *Twelfth Night*. Back in New York in November she was at the Cort playing Margaret Hyland in *The Rope Dancers*. At the Théâtre de Lys in January 1958 she played the title role in *Hamlet*.

'Hamlet fascinated Sarah Bernhardt and fascinates me,' she said. 'He has one of the most extraordinary minds in drama in his thoughts and philosophy of life. With me it was simply an experiment. I was asked to play any role I wanted and chose Hamlet.'

At the Drama Festival in Cambridge, Massachusetts, in July 1959 she played Viola in *Twelfth Night* and Lady Macbeth. The following January she took on the part of Isobel in *Motel* in a production intended for Broadway, but it closed on the road.

Siobhan McKenna returned to Europe, where once more she played Pegeen Mike in *The Playboy of the Western World* first at the Dublin Theatre Festival and then at the Piccadilly Theatre in London in October 1960. Kenneth Tynan said: 'As

Pegeen Mike, Siobhan McKenna gets her arms akimbo and her voice bountifully throbbing. All she lacks is tenderness; instead of a nice girl pretending to be a termagant, she gives us a real termagant.' That year she also filmed the Synge play.

Her next stage venture was at the Comedy Theatre in 1962, when she played Anna in *To Play with a Tiger* by Doris Lessing. Her role was that of an Australian writer living in Earls Court; Bill Lester, writing in *Plays and Players*, said 'she was masterly, portraying the whole of the world's unhappiness in a single glance'.

At the Dublin International Theatre Festival in 1963 she played the title role in Bertolt Brecht's *St Joan of the Stockyards* at the Gaiety Theatre, and the following year presented an evening of solo readings at the Shelbourne Theatre. She repeated her performance in *St Joan of the Stockyards* in London at the Queen's Theatre in June 1964; Martin Esslin, the Brecht authority, reported: '... no ox in the stockyards of Chicago could have been as brutally butchered as this play is in this performance ... Siobhan McKenna simply does her St Joan from Shaw, wide-eyed innocence and all ...'

For the Dublin International Theatre Festival in September 1964 she played the title role in *Laurette* at the Olympia Theatre, and at the Strand Theatre in London in November 1965 she was Marie-Jeanne in Anouilh's *The Cavern*. Mary Holland did not care for the production — among its faults, she wrote, '... there is Siobhan McKenna as Marie-Jeanne, the cook. She should be dour, dignified, grimly controlling her emotions with a sour peasant realism. Miss McKenna plays her like a relic of the Celtic twilight, an ageing Pegeen Mike who has been trailing her flannel petticoat, her long red hair and lines of Synge around an Irish mist for far too long. She keens the lines like sentimental verse, absorbing murder, abortion, poverty, into ever elocuted cadences, and never apparently notices anybody or anything else on the stage.'

She returned to Ireland to the Gaiety Theatre, where in August 1966 she played Juno in *Juno and the Paycock*. In September 1967 for the Dublin International Theatre Festival she was Cass in *The Loves of Cass Maguire*, and the following year played Madame Ranevsky in *The Cherry Orchard*. Back in London at the St Martin's in July 1969 she played Pearl in *On a Foggy Day* by John Kerr. She co-starred in this production with Margaret Lockwood, and although Rosemary Say did not like the play, she said: 'Siobhan McKenna's frigid tight-lipped widow stays genteel even when swilling down whisky or demonstrating her sexual

inhibitions with outstretched limbs and a look of fixed terror.' Siobhan McKenna's next play was, she said, the only one she had ever done that she herself did not like. It opened at the Strand in February 1970 and was called *Best of Friends*. At the Playhouse in Oxford in April the same year she performed a one-woman show, *Here Are the Ladies*, and brought it to London to the Criterion in July.

She was at the Mermaid in July 1973 playing Juno Boyle in *Juno and the Paycock*, taking over the production before the opening when the director Sean Kenny died. Alan Seymour reported: 'As Juno the Irish Mother Courage, Siobhan McKenna is notably unhistrionic, playing with directness and simplicity and a kind of understated strength which makes her utterly believable, though a shade lacking in that ironic humour which is surely present in the writing.'

Returning to Ireland for the Dublin International Theatre Festival in September 1974 she played at the Olympia in *The Morgan Yard* and the following year at the Gate Theatre once more performed her solo show. Still at the Gate Theatre, in June 1975 she played Julia Sterroll in Coward's *Fallen Angels*, and in June 1976 was Josie in *A Moon for the Misbegotten*. That same year she played Dublin and New York as Bessie Burgess in *The Plough and the Stars*, then came to London for the Greenwich Festival in February 1977, as Jocasta in *Sons of Oedipus*. During 1977 she played Canada, Dublin and London as Sarah Bernhardt in *Memoir*, a play by the Canadian writer John Morell. The critics were sharply divided about its merits. Michael Billington wrote: '... it is a poor evening that reduces a famous theatrical sorceress to an implausible player of biographical charades'; but Irving Wardle said: 'It is a quiet and fastidious portrait ... shaped with a skill that disarms prejudice against two-character plays ... Mr Morell creates a delicate comedy drawn less from the events of the past than from the immediate bond between the tempestuous mistress and the humourlessly thin-blooded servant.' And of Miss McKenna he added: '... most of her performance is low-pitched and ruefully comic, retreating into near-crestfallen apology whenever she blows up. She delivers only three extracts from Bernhardt's star repertory, all done with a gentle regret that reveals the character as a whale of a star. It is a beautiful performance ...'

That year her husband died after sixteen years of crippling arthritis, and Siobhan McKenna flew to America to 'get away for a good while and close the door', but she did not have a successful time there. One night in March 1979 she opened as

Margaret in Christopher Isherwood's *Meeting by the River* — and closed the same night. The following year, however, she had a great success at the Abbey Theatre in Dublin when once more she played Juno in *Juno and the Paycock*. Since then she has largely been working in television.

MICHÈAL MACLIAMMÒIR

Michèal MacLiammòir was born in Cork, Ireland, on 25 October 1899. Soon after his birth his father, a miller, moved the family to London, taking the English translation of the name, Willmore. It was as Alfred Willmore that Michèal made his stage début at the Little Theatre in London on 28 January 1911 playing King Goldfish in *The Goldfish* with Lila Field's children's group. His father took him to Sir Herbert Tree for an audition at His Majesty's Theatre, and he first appeared there in September 1911 as Young Macduff and the Bloody Child in *Macbeth*. For Christmas at the Duke of York's that year he was Michael Darling in *Peter Pan*, and returned to His Majesty's in June 1912 to play the title role in *Oliver Twist*. He went back to *Peter Pan* at Christmas, this time playing John. In September 1913 he was Benjamin in *Joseph and His Brethren* at His Majesty's and that Christmas was once more playing John in *Peter Pan* at the Duke of York's.

His voice broke, and Michèal abandoned the stage for a while. He spent two years in Spain — and then studied painting at the Slade School during 1915 and 1916. He described his style as a cross between Beardsley and Blake. At the Haymarket in February 1917, he played Cornwallis in *Felix Gets a Month*, and then he returned to Ireland, where he painted and designed for the Irish Theatre and the Dublin Drama League. He was greatly influenced by the writings of Yeats, and had dreams of building an artistic Utopia in Ireland. A. J. Leventhal, later a professor of modern literature at Trinity College, Dublin, knew him in those days and described him thus: 'He is remarkable for three things — his painting, his dreams and his hair. He paints in intense water-colour concentric circles that fly off into ornamental flames with bull's eyes to focus attention. His dreams bring him to the Egypt of the Ptolemies, where he is on the point of being sacrificed to some mammal god when he recognizes his sister in the veiled swaying figure of the priestess. The sister dreams the same dream and, we are assured, there is a cousin addicted to the same habit of living his pre-natal lives, who appears to have been the offerer of the sacrifice ... MacLiammòir's hair is a shock in the double sense that it rises in a round mass of curls from his head and startles the pilosial convention of male prudes. He is nineteen, speaks Spanish in his sleep, knows by heart Wilde's plays, hates bridge, sings the Volga boatsong, is anti-English in the Gaelic press and tells fortunes.'

From 1921 he travelled extensively in Europe, painting and staging exhibitions of his work. During this time he acquired, as he put it, 'almost as many languages as a head waiter'. He also came under the influence of Diaghilev's Ballets Russes.

He returned to Ireland and the stage in 1927, when he joined his brother-in-law Anew McMaster's Shakespeare Company playing such parts as Bassanio, Laertes and Cassio. In this company he met Hilton Edwards, newly come from the Old Vic, and a personal and private partnership began which was to last until his death. They opened the Galway Gaelic Theatre in 1928 and produced twenty plays there. It was the only Gaelic-speaking theatre in the world, and their first production was MacLiammòir's own *Diarmuid Agus Grainne*. That autumn together they founded the Dublin Gate Theatre Company, opening on 14 October 1928 with Ibsen's *Peer Gynt*. Ireland and this theatre were to be MacLiammòir's major involvement. At the Gate he and Hilton produced more than 350 plays in over thirty years. Nine of the plays were written by MacLiammòir himself. Among the roles he played were Romeo, Othello, Mark Antony, Faust, Brand, Liliom, Raskolnikov, Peter in *Berkeley Square*, Robert Emmett in *The Old Lady Says No!* and Hamlet. The *Irish Times* remembered his career: 'No layman could possibly understand the knowledge, research, skill and sheer back-breaking work that went into every Gate production ... the same applied to all MacLiammòir's performances — and I could list twenty or thirty great MacLiammòir performances from memory alone. I never saw Barrymore's Hamlet, but of all that I have seen none approached MacLiammòir's. The same goes for his Romeo and his Antony, though his Iago and his Richard II didn't reach me — but

I'd have given a lot to see him play Richard III in recent years. Spot-lit impressions come back from dozens of good, bad and mediocre plays: *Night Must Fall*, the poet in *The Old Lady* ..., a changeling Celtic god in his own *Where Stars Walk* and dozens more.'

The Dublin Gate Theatre Company came to London, to the Westminster Theatre in June 1935 where MacLiammòir played in *Hamlet* and *The Old Lady Says No!* They toured Egypt and the Balkan states in 1938. In February 1947 they came to the Vaudeville Theatre in London, where MacLiammòir played Lee in his own play, *Ill Met By Moonlight*. At the Embassy during November and December of that year he played Larry Doyle in *John Bull's Other Island* and the Speaker in *The Old Lady Says No!*, as well as Martin in his own *Where Stars Walk*.

Michèal MacLiammòir made his American début at the Mansfield Theater in New York on 10 February 1948 playing Larry Doyle, and subsequently the Speaker and Martin. Back home at the Gate in December 1950 he played Mr Wogan in his own play, *Home for Christmas*. In September 1954 he was at the Lyric, Hammersmith, playing Judge Brack to Peggy Ashcroft's Hedda Gabler, and at the Gaiety in Dublin in August 1956 he designed, wrote and appeared in the revue *Gateway to Gaiety*.

At the Edinburgh Festival in August 1957 he was Dom Cristovao de Moura in *The Hidden King*, and at the Lyric, Hammersmith, in May 1958 played Michael Marne in *The Key of the Door*. He designed the sets and costumes for *The Heart's a Wonder* at the Westminster in September 1958, and in November that year back in Dublin at the Olympia he played Gypo Nolan in his own adaptation from Liam O'Flaherty's novel, *The Informer*.

He returned to New York in September 1959, where at the Lunt-Fontanne Theatre he played Don Pedro in *Much Ado About Nothing*. In 1960 Michèal MacLiammòir began a new career which was to be extremely successful. He devised a one-man show for himself, based on the work and life of Oscar Wilde, called *The Importance of Being Oscar*. He performed it first at the Dublin International Theatre Festival that September, and the following month brought it to the Apollo Theatre in London. Kate O'Brien reported: 'Michèal MacLiammòir, Ireland's greatest actor, ranks in versatility and culture with the world's greatest. But his deep love of Ireland and of her language and literature has kept him too much homebound, many of us thought — spending his complex gifts within a space and scene too small for them. Now,

however, he has had a truly superb idea, and has worked it out superbly. Here is Wilde, one of the most gifted, most memorable and most endearing of all Irishmen, brought back to the London he enlivened and the London stage he so exquisitely enriched — and brought there by another Irishman, like him greatly gifted, like him brilliant, memorable and endearing. And the work is carried through with a grace and skill which are enough as almost to make Oscar himself, in his very appreciations, a little envious perhaps?' And the *Irish Times* said of his impersonation of Lady Bracknell during the evening: 'Only Michèal, dressed in a dinner jacket, could have created such a dazzling illusion of full-flowing gown, pince-nez and shawl.' He was kept busy with *The Importance of Being Oscar* for two years touring through Europe, the United States, South America and South Africa.

At the Dublin International Theatre Festival in September 1962 he played Iago in *Othello*, a role he had undertaken in the Orson Welles 1949 film of the play. He returned to London in April 1963 to the Aldwych, where once more he performed *The Importance of Being Oscar* and the next month introduced another one-man show, *I Must Be Talking to My Friends*. At the Dublin International Theatre Festival in October 1963 he played Conrad Apfelbaum in *The Roses Are Real*, and came to London to the Vaudeville Theatre with the play in January 1964. He then toured Australia and New Zealand with *The Importance of Being Oscar*. He toured both his solo shows in 1965 and 1966, touching down in London a couple of times with them.

Again at the Dublin International Theatre Festival in October 1969 he played Jonathan Swift in *Swift* and translated *The Liar* from the Irish. After designing *The Seagull* for the Abbey Theatre in October 1970 he appeared in London in yet another one-man show, *Talking About Yeats*.

As well as all his entertainments and plays, Michèal MacLiammòir wrote volumes of autobiography, poems and books on the theatre in Ireland. In 1972, for services to Irish theatre, he was given the Irish Actors' Equity Award. He was made a Freeman of the City of Dublin and a Chevalier de la Légion d'honneur in 1973. He died in Ireland on 6 March 1978. His friend and partner of nearly fifty years said: 'Ireland has lost a great Irishman, who loved his country in peace all his life and served her in peace all his life, not without honour and distinction beyond her shores. This he was always careful and anxious to do, and this wish formed the basis of his work, in which he always tried to show Ireland as he wanted her to be.'

WILLIAM CHARLES MACREADY

William Charles Macready never wanted to be an actor. All the time he was acting — and indeed at the head of his profession — he still did not want to be an actor. But if that is what he had to do, he was determined to be good at it.

He was born in London on 3 March 1793, the fifth of eight children of William Macready, a small-part actor at Covent Garden, and his wife Christina Ann Birch, an actress. By the time William Charles was five years old his father had decided that he was never going to be a star in London, and became manager of a stock company in the Midlands. In 1809 his father was gaoled for debt, and William Charles left Rugby School to take over the management of the company. Thanks to his determination the company was soon solvent again — so his father returned to management.

William Charles, having studied fencing and movement, made his stage début in Birmingham playing Romeo in his father's company. He was successful, and continued in it up and down the country. In 1812 he played in Newcastle with Sarah Siddons in one of her farewell tours in *The Gamester* and *Douglas*. It was then that she gave him the famous advice — 'Study, study, study and don't marry until you are thirty.' He took it.

In 1816 he got a five-year contract with Covent Garden, and made his London début at that theatre on 16 September playing Orestes in Ambrose Philips' version of Racine's *Andromaque, The Distrest Mother*. He next played a Negro in *The Slave*. He alternated with Charles Young the parts of Othello and Iago. He spent the summer season with his father's circuit and returned to Covent Garden, where he was still disillusioned with roles he was playing. However, because of Charles Kemble's illness he was able to play Romeo to Miss O'Neill's Juliet, and in March he created the part of Rob Roy in Pocock's adaptation of the Scott novel. William Charles wanted to leave the stage and go to Oxford to study for the Church; but when he did manage to borrow the money necessary for this he gave it to his brother to buy an army promotion. That determined it — he would have to remain an actor to pay back the debt.

During the 1819-20 season at Covent Garden he had some notable successes. Of his Richard III Leigh Hunt wrote: 'We certainly never saw the gayer part of Richard to such advantage. His very step, in the more sanguine scenes, had a princely gaiety of self-possession, and seemed to walk off to the music of his approaching triumph.' He per-

formed an admirable Coriolanus, and in May took the title role of *Virginius* by Irish schoolmaster and actor Sheridan Knowles. The *Morning Herald* spoke of his 'great and still-growing genius' and went on: 'Austere, tender, familiar, elevated, mingling at once terror and pathos, he ran over the scale of dramatic expression with the highest degree of power.'

Macready became spoken of as Kean's rival, though they had totally different personalities as well as talents. As Hazlitt, who preferred Kean, wrote: 'He has talent and a magnificent voice, but he is, I fear, too improving an actor to be a man of genius. That little ill-looking vagabond Kean never improved in anything. On some plays he could not, and in others he would not.' Macready had devoted himself to restoring Shakespeare to the original. He also devoted himself to the perfection of roles — constantly rehearsing himself and others.

In 1822 Charles Kemble took over the management of Covent Garden. Macready was praised for his performances there of Wolsey, King John, Macbeth and Shylock. For the 1823-24 theatre season he went to Drury Lane, where he had a great success as Hamlet, Macbeth, Leontes and in a Roman tragedy by Sheridan Knowles. On 24 June 1824 he married the actress Catherine Atkins.

In January 1825 he had a triumph as Romont in Massinger's *Fatal Dowry*, but soon afterwards was stricken with a serious illness which left him debilitated. However, though now aware of his physical limitations, he came back with a great success playing William Tell in a drama constructed partly by himself and partly by Knowles. He embarked in September 1826 on an eight-month tour of America, and was warmly received. Francis Courtney Wemyss wrote of his first engagement in Philadelphia: 'Mr Macready was the first star of the season. He opened on the 10th of January, 1827 as Macbeth and at once received that approbation which his high character as an actor deserved. He played Hamlet, Virginius, William Tell, Pierre, Coriolanus, Damon and Petruchio...'

In November he was back at the Lane as Macbeth, and in the spring of 1828 was overwhelmed by his reception in Paris, where for a short season he played Macbeth, Othello and Virginius. Of the latter the newspaper *La Réunion* wrote: 'Who would believe that a man to whom nature has refused everything — voice, carriage, and face — would rival Talma, for whom she has left nothing undone?' He then spent two years in the provinces touring and helping to run the Bristol company after the death of his father. He returned to the Lane in 1830 with *Virginius*, and the following year had his only major success in comedy as the timid husband Oakely in George Coleman's *The Jealous Wife*. In 1832 he played Iago and Othello with Kean — and Kean won.

Alfred Bunn, a vulgar showman whom Macready disliked, took over the management of both the Lane and Covent Garden, so Macready went into management in Bath and Bristol where he remained until 1835. The venture had, however, cost him money. He returned to Drury Lane for the 1835-36 season. It was still under Bunn's management and after sulking for a while over the parts he was given by Bunn and the salary he was being paid, Macready finally exploded and attacked him physically. Bunn sued and Macready had to pay damages.

Fed up with managers, Macready took over Covent Garden himself in July 1837. He strove to improve the quality of Shakespearian texts — ridding them of the tamperings of people who thought they knew better. He was highly successful with *Macbeth*, *Lear* and *Coriolanus*, but his greatest success that season was the non-Shakespearian *Richelieu*. He took over the Drury Lane Theatre in 1841 and opened with a production of *The Merchant of Venice*, playing Shylock. The following season he had success with *As You Like It* and *King John*. But the man who had never wanted to be an actor was now looking forward to retirement. Only one thing stood in his way. He wanted to have enough money to enjoy it — and he was not going to make any money in management.

In September 1843 he sailed for a twelve-month tour of America. The *Spirit of the Times* carried this report: 'Of the few Shakespearian tragedies now belonging to the acting drama, *Macbeth* may be cited as the most attractive. The performance of this character by Mr Macready on Wednesday last, was greeted by a full, and we were happy to add, fashionable audience . . . we claim Mr Macready's performance as the best stage delineation we have witnessed, as avoiding many popular errors of the actor and the critic . . . ' His tour was not only a critical but also a financial success. He spent the next years touring the English provinces — and increasing his savings.

His farewell tour of America in 1848-49 resulted in riots in New York, where the American actor Edwin Forrest had been claiming that his lack of success in England was due to Macready's intervention. Feeling ran high at that time in the theatrical world, and onstage Macready was pelted by fruit in varying states of decay. Outside the theatre where he was attempting to play Macbeth

(Forrest was at another theatre in the same city also playing the role in an attempt to upstage Macready) a riot broke out. Police responded by firing into the crowd, causing thirty-one injuries and seventeen deaths. Macready was smuggled out of the theatre and hurried on to Boston where, deeply disturbed by the whole incident, he nevertheless managed to give a reading as a thank you to his friends.

He spent the next two years touring the English provinces, and made his farewell appearance at Drury Lane on 26 February 1851 playing Macbeth. After a public dinner given in his honour he retired at last to Dorset. His wife died the following year; in April 1860 he remarried and went to live in Cheltenham until his death on 27 April 1873.

While Macready was still enjoying his long retirement the historian Dr John W. Francis summed up his work thus: 'Mr Macready is less of a comedian than tragedian, but in this latter, the materials are ample to demonstrate that, in the maturity of his faculties, his efficiency justly placed him at the head of the English stage. He cannot be entirely classed with the exclusive followers of nature, though he borrowed largely from her resources; and it would be unjust to his original powers to attribute his excellencies to his adoption of the cold and formal school of actors. Hazlitt, a discriminating dramatic critic, pronounced him by far the best tragic actor that had come out, with the exception of Kean. But Mr Macready has other and higher claims to our regard and esteem. He studied and enacted Shakespeare less for objects of pecuniary result than to bring out for increased admiration the matchless beauties and the deep philosophy of the great author in the purity of his own incomparable diction; and he made corresponding efforts to eradicate the corruptions which annotators and playwrights have introduced. He loathed the claptraps of sentiment with which the stage was so often burthened . . . Assuredly he deserves all praises for his unceasing toil and his noble ambition. Mr Macready has been ever scrupulously careful about assuming a part in plays which tended to the exaltation of the baser passions, and the increase of licentiousness. The regularity of his own life added to the self-gratification he enjoyed from so scrupulous a line of conduct in his professional duty. Believing that a great ethical principle for the improvement of morals and the diffusion of knowledge resided in the stage, he, above all things, wished Shakespeare to be exhibited as he is, unencumbered with the trapping of other minds, and I have little doubt that in his happy retirement he finds solace in the conduct he adopted.'

FREDRIC MARCH

Fredric March became a film star before he became a stage star — he won an Academy Award in 1932 for his performance in *Dr Jekyll and Mr Hyde*, was nominated for one in 1937 for his performance in *A Star is Born*, won again in 1947 for *The Best Years of Our Lives* and was nominated for the fourth time in 1947 for *Death of a Salesman*. However compelling an actor he was on screen, his stardom in the theatre was equally brilliant.

Frederich McIntyre Bickel was born in Racine, Wisconsin, on 31 August 1897. His father was a merchant banker, and after completing his education at Racine High School and the University of Wisconsin, Fred Bickel tried banking for a time, but after serving with the army in the First World War he gave up banking and studied acting with Eva Alberti. His first stage appearance was in Baltimore at Ford's Theater on 7 December 1920, when he played the Prompter in David Belasco's production of *Deburau*, adapted from the French of Sacha Guitry by Harley Granville-Barker. The play came into the Belasco Theater in New York on 20 December and although the *New York Times* raved about the production young Fred Bickel was not pointed out as a great star of the future. He did, however, understudy Lionel Atwill, who was playing the title part, and got to play it himself for a week. He toured through 1921 in *Shavings* and returned to New York to the Booth Theater in February 1922 playing Tom Fowler in *The Law Breaker*. In August 1923 he was Henry Williams in *Zero* at the 48th Street Theater.

By May 1924 Fred Bickel was no more, and Fredric March played Donald Clemens in *The Melody Man* at the Ritz. He toured during the rest of 1924 and part of 1925 as Emmett Carr in *Tarnish*. He was at the Selwyn in New York later in 1925 playing Bruno Monte in *Puppets* and at the Belmont in September playing Richard ·Knight in *Harvest*. At the National in March 1926 he was Dick Chester in *The Half-Caste* and at the Charles Hopkins Theater in December played Jimmie Chard in *The Devil in the Cheese*.

On 30 May 1927 he married the actress Florence Eldridge. They subsequently had two children, and often worked together. They began their married life with a Theater Guild tour of the United States in *Arms and the Man*, *The Silver Cord*, *Mr Pim Passes By* and *The Guardsman*. In 1928 at the Curran Theater in San Francisco and the Belasco Theater in Los Angeles, Fredric March played Anthony Cavendish in *The Royal Family*.

The Marches stayed in California and Fredric made his movie début for Paramount playing in *The Dummy*. He made more than forty films during the next ten years, many of them with his wife. The parts ranged from light comedy through heavy drama and even into costume period pieces. There seemed to be no way Hollywood could pin down his screen persona — he remained first and foremost an actor.

They returned to New York in January 1938, where they were at the Broadhurst Theater in *Yr Obedient Husband*. The following January Fredric March played Martin Gunther in *The American Way* at the Center Theater. At the Guild Theater in November 1941 he was Elliott Martin in *Hope for a Harvest*. At the Plymouth Theater in November 1942 Fredric March and Florence Eldridge played Mr and Mrs Antrobus in *The Skin of Our Teeth*, while Tallulah Bankhead was Sabina. In *A Bell for Adano* (an adaptation of John Hersey's novel) at the Cort in November 1944 he played Major Victor Joppolo and the *Saturday Review of Literature* reported: 'As Joppolo, Fredric March gives the best performance of his career. If visually he is handsomer than the Joppolo we saw in Mr Hersey's pages, if vocally the Bronx is scarcely more to him than a point of reference, the fact remains that spiritually he is to the full the novel's Major . . . He plays glibly and gaily his hilarious comedy scenes with the young Lieutenant who is Yale enough to make even the Navy blue. His goodness comes to him without effort and without sententiousness. His Joppolo remains as poseless as he must be. The projection of virtue behind the footlights is an accomplishment as single as the task is challenging . . .'

At the Mansfield Theater in December 1946 he played Clinton Jones in *Years Ago*, and at the Broadhurst in March 1950 he was General Leonidas Erosa in *Now I Lay Me Down to Sleep*. He played Dr Stockmann in December 1950 at the same theatre in Arthur Miller's adaptation of Ibsen's *An Enemy of the People*, which was meant to be an attack on McCarthyism. At the Coronet Theater in March 1951 he was Nicholas Denery in *The Autumn Garden*.

More films intervened, including Miller's *Death of a Salesman* and the magnificent *Inherit the Wind*, but he was back on Broadway at the Helen Hayes Theater in November 1956 playing James Tyrone in O'Neill's *Long Day's Journey Into Night* with his wife, Jason Robards and Bradford Dillman. Brooks Atkinson reported in the

New York Times: 'The performance is stunning. As the aging actor who stands at the head of the family, Fredric March gives a masterly performance that will stand as a milestone in the acting of an O'Neill play. Petty, mean, bullying, impulsive and sharp-tongued, he also has magnificence — a man of strong passions, deep loyalties and basic humility. This is a character portrait of grandeur.' For this performance Fredric March received the New York Drama Critics Award for the Best Actor in a Straight Play and also won the Tony. They took the production to Paris during the Broadway summer break in July 1957 and played at the Sarah Bernhardt Theatre during the Theatre of Nations season.

Fredric March next appeared on Broadway in November 1961 playing the Angel of the Lord in Paddy Chayefsky's *Gideon*. The production was directed by Tyrone Guthrie and Douglas Campbell played the title role. *Time* magazine reported: 'To watch March and Campbell shade in the lights and shadows of this relationship is to see something like acting genius at work. March hisses and rumbles like an active volcano, and his "I am the Lord" is an eruption of molten lava. At times, March seems to take an actorish delight in playing the Lord, but he is awesome when, with magnetic all-seeing eyes, he probes for Gideon's soul in a speck of human dust . . .' This was March's last Broadway appearance. During the spring of 1965 he toured for the State Department with his wife, and they subsequently visited Greece, Egypt, Italy and the Near East giving readings and scenes from plays. He died on 14 April 1975 at the age of 77.

JULIA MARLOWE
AND
E. H. SOTHERN

Sarah Frances Frost was born on 17 August 1866 in Caldbeck, a tiny village near Keswick in Cumberland, England. When she was a child the family moved to Cincinnati, Ohio. Sarah, now known as Fanny Brough (her mother's maiden name), was a serious girl, a voracious reader who worked long and hard as a chambermaid in her mother's boarding house until one day in October 1876 she saw an advertisement in the local newspaper for children to sing and act in a juvenile performance of *HMS Pinafore*. The tour was organized by Colonel Robert E. J. Miles and the children were coached and looked after by his sister-in-law, the actress Ada Dow. Fanny was hired to be in the sailors' chorus, and she made her first stage appearance at Vincennes, Indiana, in 1876; she was soon given the part of Sir Joseph Porter.

The children's troupe, numbering fifty, was a great success throughout the middle west. With the company she also appeared as Suzanne in *The Chimes of Normandy* and the Page in *The Little Duke*. The company disbanded in November 1877 and returned to Cincinnati, where Fanny found that her mother had divorced and remarried. Fanny did not take kindly to her stepfather, who decreed that all the children should learn a trade. Fanny spent one day in a biscuit factory and three months learning to use a telegraph machine. She then became an apprentice dress designer, which job brought with it free entrance to theatrical performances — and occasionally she was hired for a walk-on part.

Eventually her talent was recognized by Ada Dow, who took Fanny under her wing. She would tutor and manage the girl at her own expense, looking forward to the day when she would get her money back. They went to New York, where for three years Fanny studied assiduously — texts, voice, movement, and technique. She was tireless in her very solitary studies.

When she thought the time was ready for her serious début, she felt dissatisfied with her name. From her study of *The Hunchback*, one of her favourite plays, she took the name of Julia and Marlowe came from the poet Christopher Marlowe, whom she admired and thought of as undervalued. She would revive his name. A company was formed for a two-week tour of New England, and Julia Marlowe made her début on 25 April 1887 in New London, Connecticut, playing Parthenia in the German play *Ingomar*. The *New London Day* reported: 'Of Miss Marlowe a certain future may be predicted from her Parthenia last night. It is an exacting part but the young artist need not fear comparison with her seniors in the same walk. Added to her remarkable histrionic abilities are charms of person which seem indispensable when happily combined'; and the *New London Telegraph* was equally impressed: 'Miss

Julia Marlowe is an actress to the manner born, and judging from her performance last night, her career will not close till she has climbed to the diamond ridge of artistic fame. Miss Marlowe's Parthenia was a marvelously correct interpretation, and her classic beauty helped to make the character one of the most attractive and engaging we have ever seen upon any stage.' During this brief tour she also played Pauline in *The Lady of Lyons* with equal success throughout New England. But although the critics enthused, the box office takings were not inspiring.

Julia's mother and stepfather, having made a success of an hotel in Cincinnati, agreed to finance a New York début, and she appeared in that city for the first time at a specially organized matinée at the Bijou Theater on 20 October 1887. There were many such matinées at this time organized for aspiring actresses, most of whom had more money than talent, and the critics were resentful at having to attend. They approached Julia Marlowe's début cynically, but they stayed to cheer. The *New York Times* critic, Mr Dithmar, wrote: 'Julia Marlowe — remember her name, for you will hear of her again … Her work was marred by none of the failings of the novice. Her touch was always sure, and she impresses the critical observer with a sense of her ability to calculate beforehand the actual effect of every look and gesture. This is a faculty that three-fifths of the actors on the stage do not possess … Her voice is strong and pleasing and if she has a singing voice it ought to be a pure contralto … And best of all she speaks the English language very well … Of her permanent success there can be no doubt.' Managers fought for her, but she determined that her next venture would be Shakespeare, and accordingly opened at the Star Theater in December 1887 playing Juliet in *Romeo and Juliet*. The critics on the whole praised her performance but were puzzled by some of her innovations. In December she appeared for the first time as Viola in *Twelfth Night*.

After her week at the Star Theater she embarked on a six-week tour of the country, adding to her repertoire Julia in *The Hunchback* and Rosalind in *As You Like It*. Again she was critically acclaimed but did not make any money. She and Miss Dow returned to New York, where the managements sought her to star in modern, commercial plays. But she would have none of it, and was soon off on tour again.

The Fifth Avenue Theater in New York was rented for a period of eight weeks. Julia Marlowe opened with her Rosalind in *As You Like It* and followed that with *The Hunchback* and *Pygmalion and Galatea*; again she met with critical success and little money. She toured again, and in Septem-

ber 1890 opened in Memphis, Tennessee, a new theatre named in her honour, with her interpretation of Beatrice in *Much Ado About Nothing*, a part she had been studying and working on for two years. In Philadelphia in 1890 her career nearly came to an end when she was stricken with typhoid fever, but happily she recovered and remained unscarred although doctors had very nearly lanced her hideously swollen face.

By this time Julia Marlowe had had four full seasons on stage, meeting with critical acclaim but still not making much money. This nearly changed when she was engaged to play opposite Edwin Booth at the Chicago World's Fair — but Booth died.

In 1892 Julia Marlowe revived Sheridan Knowles' *The Love Chase*. Robert Taber played Wildrake, and Mrs John Drew was the Widow Green while Julia played Constance. That season she also played Charles Hard in *Rogues and Vagabonds*, and the following year introduced Imogen in *Cymbeline*, Letitia Hardy in *The Belles' Stratagem*, Thomas Chatterton in *Chatterton* and Colombe in *Colombe's Birthday* into her repertoire. In May 1894 she married Robert Taber, and the following season Mr Taber took over the stage direction while the posters read Julia Marlowe Taber and Robert Taber. The public did not like it, considering that Mr Taber had achieved through marriage what he could never have achieved through talent. Managers were loath to book them as a double act, although they had been acting together for seasons. During the 1894–95 season Julia introduced her Lady Teazle in *The School for Scandal* and Prince Hal in *Henry IV Part 1*. At Palmer's Theater during March 1896 Julia Marlowe appeared as Juliet, Kate Hardcastle, Rosalind, Prince Hal, and Julia in *The Hunchback*. Then she toured for four weeks in an all-star revival of *The Rivals*, playing Lydia Languish. This production came into the American Theater for a limited run in May 1896. Back on tour again, she introduced *Romula* in Milwaukee in September 1896, and in January 1897 at Buffalo played Mary in *For Bonnie Prince Charlie*. This came into New York to Palmer's in February 1897. In March she was at the Broadway playing in *Chatterton* and at the Knickerbocker Theater the following January she was the Countess in *Countess Valeska*.

The manager Charles Frohman saw her for the first time in *Valeska* and said: 'This is the greatest emotional actress in America but it will be a heartbreaking task to find plays equal to her strength.' At last Julia Marlowe had a real popular success. She then proceeded to revive her Shakespeare productions before spending the summer in Switzerland.

Vivien Leigh as Lady Teazle (with Cyril Maude playing Sir Peter Teazle)
in the Quarrel scene from *The School for Scandal* at the Haymarket Theatre
(London, April 1942)

Geraldine McEwan and Michael Hordern in Sheridan's *The Rivals*
at the National Theatre (London, April 1983)

For the 1898–99 season Julia Marlowe played the title role in a French comedy, *Colinette*, and both in New York and on tour had a great success, so she had another summer in Europe. In October 1899 she opened at the Criterion in New York playing the title role in *Barbara Frietchie* — it too was a great success.

In January 1901 Julia Marlowe opened as Mary Tudor in a comedy — a strenuous comedy at that — *When Knighthood Was in Flower*. This was such an enormous success that at last Miss Marlowe was financially independent. At the Criterion in New York in December 1902 she played Charlotte Oliver in *The Cavalier*. Though some critics bemoaned the fact that she was not in something more substantial, they granted that she was very good and the audiences came in droves.

In 1903 she was not very successful as Lady Branchester in H. V. Esmond's *Fools of Nature*, so she revived *When Knighthood Was in Flower* and again played to standing room only. She then revived *Ingomar*, and met with equal success. James Huneker wrote in the *New York Sun*: 'She is a creature apart on the English-speaking stage. There is not a woman player in America or in England that is — attractively considered — fit to unlace her shoe. One must go to Paris, Berlin, Vienna or Rome to find her peer.'

Edward Hugh Sothern was born on 6 December 1859 in New Orleans, Louisiana. His father Edward Askew Sothern was an actor who, although acclaimed in many roles in his native England and his adopted America, became known for his impersonation of Lord Dundreary in *Our American Cousin*. E. H. was educated in England, but made his first stage appearance in New York when he was 20, at the Park Theater playing the cabman in *Brother Sam* in which his father had the lead. He then spent some time in repertory at the Boston Museum, and returned to England where he made his London stage début on 8 October 1881 playing Mr Sharpe in *False Colours* at the Royalty Theatre. On the same evening he also played Marshley Bittern in *Out of the Hunt*. Remaining in England, he took over the part of Arthur Spoonbill in *Fourteen Days* at the Criterion in June 1882 from his brother, Lytton. Under the management of Charles Wyndham he played in other theatres around the provinces.

E. H. Sothern returned to the United States in 1883, and toured with John McCullough in *Called Back*, *Lost* and *Three Wives to One Husband*. He then toured with Helen Barry in *The Fatal Letter* and next appeared in New York in April 1884 playing Eliphaz Tresham at the Union Square Theater in *The Fatal Letter*. In May that year at the Star Theater he was Melchizidec Flighty in *Whose Are They?*, which he wrote for himself. In October he was at Wallack's playing in *Nita's First*.

With Helen Dauvray at the Union Square Theater in February 1885 he was Alfred Vane in *Favette* and at the Star Theater in April was Knolly in *Mona*. He played John in *In Chancery* in June at Madison Square and in September was Jules in *A Moral Climate*.

E.H. Sothern spent the next twelve years as a leading man in the Lyceum Company, for which he played a number of roles, the most noteworthy being that of Rudolf Rassendyl in *The Prisoner of Zenda*, which he introduced in September 1895. The *New York Dramatic Mirror* reported: 'Mr Sothern does the best work of his career in the dual role of the King and the Englishman. He has laid aside many of the mannerisms that used to mar his acting. In this play he is easy and natural in the comedy scenes, and strong and convincing in the serious scenes. In the prison where, as the imprisoned King, he lies dying on the floor of his cell, he displayed remarkable emotional strength. He has to wear a hideous red wig throughout the play and it should go to his credit that he was willing to make the sacrifice of his vanity to the artistic demands of the playwright.' *The Prisoner of Zenda* established E. H. Sothern as a star.

When he left the Lyceum Theater, E. H. Sothern continued in the romantic tradition playing d'Artagnan in *The King's Musketeers* at the Knickerbocker in February 1899, transferring the production to Daly's in September. In October at Daly's he was in *The Song of the Sword*. At the Knickerbocker in March 1900 he was Heinrich in *The Sunken Bell* and back at Daly's in April played Sir Geoffrey Bloomfield in *Drifting Apart*.

Although he made his reputation as a romantic actor, E. H. Sothern was a devout student of Shakespeare. He wanted to mount a spectacular and precise *Hamlet*; his ambition was finally achieved on 17 September 1900 at the Garden in New York. However, during the first week he was stabbed in the foot by Laertes' sword during a fight scene and blood poisoning set in; the production and the tour had to be cancelled. When he recovered and the tour was resumed, his entire production was destroyed when the Grand Opera House in Cincinnati burned down. However, he was soon back in the romances that his audiences dearly loved. At the Garden Theater in September 1901 he played the title role in *Richard Lovelace* and the following month introduced the part of François Villon in *If I Were King*. He opened at the Hollis Street Theater in Boston in April 1903 in the title role in *Markheim*, and at the Herald Square Theater in New York in October was

Robert, the King of Sicily, in *The Proud Prince*, before resuming touring.

In 1904 a partnership was arranged between Julia Marlowe and E. H. Sothern, and they appeared together for the first time at the Illinois Theater in Chicago on 19 September 1904 as Romeo and Juliet. It was said that their performance inspired thirty-one curtain calls. Barrett Eastman reported: 'It must be admitted that neither Miss Marlowe nor Mr Sothern appeared to the best advantage on that occasion but each of them has a record of so much worthy and distinguished endeavor and accomplishment that both were entitled to a suspension of judgement at least. It was plain to anybody with any discrimination that they were not doing themselves justice and that it was very unfair to pass judgement upon them at that time. All this was demonstrated the very next night when a truly marvelous improvement was shown and night by night the improvement continued.' The next week she played Beatrice and he played Benedick in *Much Ado About Nothing* and in October they opened in *Hamlet*. The couple moved by way of Pittsburgh to the Knickerbocker Theater in New York, where they remained through October and November. They went on to Boston and then travelled across country, playing the larger cities all the way to California. Their first season in partnership was an artistic and financial success.

For the 1905–06 season they added *The Taming of the Shrew* and *The Merchant of Venice* to their repertoire, and in November he played Malvolio while she was Viola in *Twelfth Night*. The season carried on with the inevitable tour, after a time at the Knickerbocker Theater. They ended the season with a benefit performance in Chicago for the victims of the San Francisco earthquake. That season also saw the end of their relationship with their manager Charles Frohman, who worked with the Klaw and Erlanger syndicate: in a dispute over money Marlowe and Sothern left the syndicate and carried on under the aegis of the Shuberts. They would from then on receive not a salary but a percentage of the profits.

The 1906–07 season opened at the Lyric Theater in Philadelphia with Julia Marlowe playing the title part and Sothern playing the Duc d'Alençon in Percy MacKaye's *Jeanne d'Arc*. They also introduced Sudermann's *John the Baptist*, in which Sothern played John and the critics wondered if Julia Marlowe really ought to be playing Salome and doing the dance of the seven veils. Audiences, however, were intrigued, and Miss Marlowe was always tasteful. Next he was Heinrich and she was Rautendelein in *The Sunken Bell*, and the critic of the *Washington Times* was

lavish in his praise of Mr Sothern: 'It may be that he had done something better than his impersonation of Heinrich, the master bell founder, but a memory extending over the majority of his characters from his Lord Chumley and Jack Hammerton down to his Duc d'Alençon in *Jeanne d'Arc* fails to recall it. He plays the idealist thoughtfully and intelligently, of course, but he does more; he plays it as only an idealist could. He plays it with a fire and enthusiasm that approach closely to genius.' After a season in New York at the Lyric Theater and a short post-New York tour, on 29 March 1907 the company sailed for England on the steamship *America*.

This was to be Sothern's first appearance on an English stage in twenty-four years, and Julia Marlowe's début. They were understandably nervous of opening with Shakespeare in his own country, so first performed *The Sunken Bell* at the Waldorf Theatre in April 1907. The critics and the audiences agreed they did not care for the play. One critic wrote: 'International courtesy would lead one to attribute the undoubted dullness of last night's performance to the players if they were English. But the players were American, and the well-mannered critic is in a quandary. But shall this balk him? Not in the least. The way out is easily found to a critic of any spirit as thus: Miss Marlowe and Mr Sothern have, indeed, come to England with so great a reputation that it is preferable to reserve criticism until they have been seen in a more understandable play.' The critics did not much like *Jeanne d'Arc* either, but praised the players. The English censor prevented them from performing *John the Baptist*, so they proceeded with *Twelfth Night*, despite their worries about performing Shakespeare, and won plaudits, as they did for *Romeo and Juliet* and *Hamlet*. Although the critics came around to praising the couple in the end, the audiences were not interested in seeing the Americans. For the final weeks of the engagement they put on *When Knighthood Was in Flower* and recouped some of their losses. They were fêted on the last night of their English sojourn by Beerbohm Tree at a farewell supper on the roof of his theatre. When they returned to New York they played at popular prices at the Academy of Music, bringing in an audience who hitherto could not have afforded to see their Shakespeare. They did the same in Philadelphia and then took a long European holiday.

In 1907 they temporarily disbanded the artistic partnership. Sothern formed his own independent company and at the Garrick Theater in Chicago in September 1907 opened as Raskolnikov in Laurence Irving's adaptation of *Crime and Punishment* called *The Fool Hath Said in His*

Heart. He then revived *Hamlet* and *If I Were King* before appearing in his father's old part of Lord Dundreary in *Our American Cousin*. He came to the Lyric Theater in New York in these productions in January 1908. In April he was Don Quixote in Paul Kester's play of the same name, which was written specially for him. At Daly's in March 1909 he played the title role in *Richelieu*.

During this time Miss Marlowe, too, had formed her own company. She played in a new comedy by J. B. Fagan called *Gloria*, which most people thought not worthy of her talents, but she also staged revivals of *Romeo and Juliet* and *As You Like it*. Julia Marlowe opened the 1908–09 season playing Yvette in Mary Johnston's verse play *The Goddess of Reason* at the Majestic in Boston. She appeared in the same part at Daly's in New York in February.

On 8 November 1909, together again, Julia Marlowe and E. H. Sothern played *Antony and Cleopatra* at the opening of New York's prestigious New Theater. It was a highly social opening — newspaper reports concerned themselves more with what the audience was wearing than with what was going on on stage. The theatre itself proved to be a disaster, and the play — to put it kindly — was not suited to the talents of the stars. Miss Marlowe and Mr Sothern left the New to its own devices, formed another company and returned to touring the country.

At New Haven, Connecticut, in November 1910 they appeared for the first time in *Macbeth*. The production and its stars were universally praised. *Macbeth* arrived at the Broadway Theater in New York in December 1910; again the critical praise was unanimous, and it was a triumph at the box office. They then toured their Shakespearian repertoire across the country in a kind of triumphant procession. They spent the summer of 1911 in Europe and in August were quietly married in London. Sothern had been extricated from a previous marriage by divorce the year before, and Julia Marlowe's first marriage had been

similarly ended. They continued to tour their Shakespeare repertory, introducing special performances for schoolchildren in the various centres they visited.

In April 1914 Sothern appeared at the Garrick Theater in Chicago as *Charlemagne* and at the Booth Theater in New York in October 1915 he played Jeffery Panton in *The Two Virtues*. In November he was Dundreary in *Lord Dundreary*. Julia Marlowe announced her retirement from the stage that year.

In 1916 Sothern was Garrick in *David Garrick* and at the Shubert in April that year revived *If I Were King*. His wife was soon back on the stage with him touring in Shakespeare revivals. In 1921 they were at the Century Theater in New York for a four-week season. The *New York Times* reported on their four-hour *The Merchant of Venice*: 'Mr Sothern's Shylock is a cruel Shylock, untouched by any consideration save his revenge. He is powerful of will and unbroken even at the end. He leaves the scene of the trial with his shoulders back and a sneer for the mocking of Gratiano... [Julia Marlowe's] charming voice and faultless diction are the great things in listening to this Shakespearian revival.' In 1924 ill-health finally forced Julia Marlowe really to retire. They presented all their scenery, costumes and props for ten productions to the Memorial Theatre at Stratford-on-Avon, so they could not go on touring even if they changed their minds. Sothern continued on the stage, playing Edmund de Verron in *Accused* at the Belasco Theater in September 1925. At the Lyceum in December 1926 he was Tiburtius in *What Never Dies*. In 1928 he took to the lecture circuit and remained a great expert, lecturing on drama until his death on 28 October 1933. Julia Marlowe received honorary doctorates from George Washington University (1923) and Columbia University (1943) and remained in retirement until her death on 12 November 1950, aged 84.

MARY MARTIN

Mary Virginia Martin was born in Weatherford, Texas, on 1 December 1913. Her father Preston Martin was a lawyer and her mother Juanita a violin teacher. Mary was a tomboy and a performer from the time she could walk. She began to learn the violin (although she was never very successful with it) when she was five, soon moved on to elocution and had her first singing lessons at the age of 12, during which the teacher had to beg her to stop singing all the time. Her family had a pass to the local cinema, and Mary Martin maintains that it is there she learned her stagecraft, from watching virtually every movie ever made. She danced like Ruby Keeler, sang like Bing Crosby and learned all of Busby Berkeley's routines.

Mary started a dancing school in the town. In her first season she managed to teach her pupils everything she knew about dancing — which was not quite enough, so her parents financed a trip to California where she studied at the Fanchon and Marco School of the Theater. When she returned, thoroughly hooked on show business, she found that her parents had built her a new school. The following summer she returned to study at Fanchon and Marco and got a job with their touring troupe, the Fanchonettes, singing in the wings while they danced. She then returned to Texas, where by this time she had over 300 pupils and three schools, but she found that teaching dancing was not very fulfilling. She had married very young; her husband was now a young lawyer working in her father's office, her mother was very happy looking after her son, so Mary Martin went off to Hollywood. She managed to get work singing on radio programmes and in night clubs, her first job being at the Trocadero.

Mary Martin auditioned for every studio in Hollywood, and while she was trying to carve out a career for herself her father managed to get her a divorce by proxy in Texas. A Broadway producer heard her singing at the Trocadero one night and signed her to a contract, so she went East — but the show she was destined for was postponed and she made her Broadway début at the Imperial Theater on 9 November 1938 playing Dolly Winslow in *Leave It to Me*, in which she sang Cole Porter's *My Heart Belongs to Daddy* and got a standing ovation. Walter Winchell shouted her name from the rooftops and she was on the cover of *Life* magazine. Paramount Pictures offered a contract, which she accepted. She stayed in Hollywood until 1943 making films with Bing Crosby, Dick Powell, Jack Benny, Robert Preston and Fred MacMurray. In Hollywood she met Richard Halliday, a screenwriter who would become her manager and the moving force in her career and in her life. Once more she eloped, this time to Las Vegas where on 5 May 1940 they married.

Late in 1942 Mary Martin was offered two stage parts — one was *Dancing in the Streets*, which was being produced by the man responsible for her first Broadway success, and the other was the Rodgers and Hammerstein show provisionally called *Away We Go*. She chose the first, which opened in Boston at the Shubert in March 1943 and closed there. *Away We Go* subsequently acquired the title *Oklahoma!*

By October 1943, however, Mary Martin was back on Broadway in *One Touch of Venus* in a part originally written for Marlene Dietrich by S. J. Perelman, Ogden Nash and Kurt Weill. While listing the assets of this new show Lewis Nichols reported in the *New York Times*: '. . . there is Mary Martin too, the Mary Martin whose heart once belonged to daddy and who shows in *One Touch of Venus* that Hollywood has done her no harm whatsoever. In this new musical she is a statue that comes to life and falls in love with a barber; she is also a lady of high charm, an engaging quality and the ability to toss a song over the footlights, which is the only place to send a song. Her heart this morning will probably be Broadway's generally.' The show ran for 567 performances, and Abe Laufe in a study of Broadway musicals said: 'Miss Martin made the show a personal triumph, not only carrying the burden of the plot but also by being a visual delight. Even the male critics commented on her extensive wardrobe, specially designed by Mainbocher.' She toured in the part until June 1945, and by December she was on the road again, this time playing Tchao-Ou-Niang in *Lute Song*, a musical based on a Chinese legend. Her stage husband was Yul Brynner. They opened in New York at the Plymouth Theater in February 1946 but only played 142 performances. Mary Martin returned to Hollywood, where she made another film, the story of Cole Porter called *Night and Day*.

On 19 December 1946 Mary Martin made her London stage début at the Drury Lane Theatre playing Elena Salvador in Noel Coward's *Pacific 1860*. Although it ran for nine months, neither the part nor the music really suited her. She returned to the United States and toured all over during 1947 and 1948 playing Annie Oakley in *Annie Get Your Gun*, the Irving Berlin cowboy hit in which Ethel Merman had scored on Broadway. Then in April 1949 she opened in her own Rodgers and Hammerstein show on Broadway at the Majestic, playing Nellie Forbush in *South Pacific*. Brooks Atkinson wrote in the *New York Times*: 'Since we have all been more or less in love with Miss Martin for several years, it is no surprise to find her full of quicksilver, pertness and delight as the Navy nurse. She sings some good knock-about melodies with skill and good nature, making something particularly enjoyable out of the stomping jubilation of "I'm Gonna Wash That Man Right Out of My Hair" and blowing out the walls of the theatre with the rapture of "I'm in Love with a Wonderful Guy".' With her co-star, Ezio Pinza, she stayed on Broadway until June 1951 and then journeyed to London once more to the Drury Lane Theatre, where she opened in November. Kenneth Tynan castigated his colleagues for complaining that *South Pacific* was not the same as *Oklahoma!* and continued: 'Skipping and roaming round the stage on diminutive flat feet, [Mary Martin] has poured her voice directly into that funnel to the heart which is sealed off from all but the rarest performers, and which was last broached, I believe, by Yvonne Printemps. After one burst of morning joy she explains that "it's an America-type song, but we sort of put in our own words", and this artful spontaneity is in everything she does. Later, with a straw hat pulled over her eyes and a beam comically broad, she stands astride, turns up her toes and sings: "I'm in Love with a Wonderful Guy". Aldous Huxley once wrote of the Caroline poets that "They spoke in their natural voices, and it was poetry." Miss Martin's style is similar; the technique is informal and the effect, unless we are to imprison the poor word, poetic.'

After a tour, Mary Martin opened at the Alvin Theater in New York in November 1953 playing opposite Charles Boyer in her first straight play, *Kind Sir*. It was not a very successful venture; the critics, feeling kindly, simply reviewed the clothes, which were again by Mainbocher. It did, however, become a very successful film called *Indiscreet* with Ingrid Bergman and Cary Grant. At the Curran Theater in San Francisco in July 1954 Mary Martin played *Peter Pan* for the first time. She did it again in Los Angeles in August and came to New York to the Winter Garden in October. Brooks Atkinson reported: '...Miss Martin, looking trim and happy, is the liveliest Peter Pan in the record book. She has more appetite for flying and swinging than any of her more demure predecessors, and she performs as actor, dancer, and

singer with skill and enjoyment. Peter Pan may have been a proper Victorian originally. He is a healthy fun-loving American now...Peter Pan with a Texas accent is fun.'

In 1955 she was Sabina in a State Department production of Thornton Wilder's *The Skin of Our Teeth*, which also starred Helen Hayes, George Abbott and Don Murray. Her son Larry Hagman (later of 'Dallas' fame) was also in the production as was her daughter Mary Heller. They opened at the Sarah Bernhardt Theatre in Paris in June and toured the United States with it during July and August playing at the ANTA Playhouse in New York in September. In 1955 Mary Martin also played Peter Pan on television. She played it again the following year and, happily for future generations, that performance was recorded.

At the Curran Theater in San Francisco in June 1957 she revived *South Pacific*, and in August, *Annie Get Your Gun*. The next year she toured the United States in a one-woman show, *Music with Mary Martin*.

In November 1959 at the Lunt-Fontanne Theater Mary Martin opened in what was to become the last and biggest of all the Rodgers and Hammerstein hits, *The Sound of Music*. She of course played the novice, Maria. Although the critics all deplored the writers' return to operetta styles of pre-*Oklahoma!* days, they did admit that Mary Martin was still a massive star. Kenneth Tynan said she 'can still brandish a note as blithely and suddenly as the best of them, though the sunlight of her voice is somewhat dimmer than it used to be...[Her] buoyancy is corklike and enchanting, despite a tendency to address the members of the audience as if they, like the Trapps, were her stepchildren.' Brooks Atkinson in the *New York Times* had no reservations whatsoever about Mary Martin's performance: 'Although Miss Martin now playing an Austrian maiden has longer hair than she had in *South Pacific*, she still has the same common touch that wins friends and influences people, the same sharp features, goodwill and glowing personality and the same plain voice that makes music sound intimate and familiar.' For this performance she received both the Tony and the New York Drama Critics Award. She played the part for more than two years.

Her next Broadway venture was not so successful. It was a musical version of the life of the actress Laurette Taylor, called *Jennie*. It opened at the Majestic in October 1963 but did not stay very long. It was three years before she returned to Broadway. In the intervening years she played Dolly Gallagher Levi in *Hello Dolly!* around the United States, in Tokyo and in Vietnam, finally ending up at Drury Lane in London. For her return to Broadway she had Robert Preston for her co-star. In fact there were only the two of them in the musical version of *The Fourposter* called *I Do! I Do!* It opened at the 46th Street Theater in November 1966 and was a feat of technical endurance if nothing else, though Walter Kerr, as well as praising the stars' agility and audience-holding powers, referred to that 'mellow sound that comes from her throat like red wine at room temperature'. She toured in this role for a year.

Mary Martin's television appearances have always been notable. As well as the magical *Peter Pan* there was *Annie Get Your Gun* and

Together with Music in which she co-starred with Noel Coward.

After the tour of *I Do! I Do!* Mary Martin returned with her husband to Brazil, where they had a home, a farm, a chicken ranch, and a shop. There they completed a book on needlepoint — a recreation about which Miss Martin is most knowledgeable. Richard Halliday died there suddenly in 1973; Mary moved to California, where she wrote her autobiography, and looked around for songs to sing, shows to do and friends to amuse. Occasional concert appearances have been her only professional engagements since then.

RAYMOND MASSEY

R aymond Massey became so identified with the role of Abraham Lincoln for a period during his long career that a wit remarked he would not be happy until he was shot.

He was born in Toronto, Canada, on 30 August 1896. His father was the head of a huge family business which manufactured farm machinery world-wide. Although his mother died when he was seven, it was she who instilled in him a love of the theatre. Raymond Massey went to Appleby School in Toronto and then to the University of Toronto, spending all his spare time at the theatre. During the First World War he served in France, where he was shell-shocked, and returned home to become a gunnery instructor at Yale's Reserve Officers' Training Corps. In 1919 he went to Siberia with the army to fight with the White Russians against the Bolsheviks, then attended Balliol College, Oxford. When he was 23, having left Oxford without taking a degree, he married an art student, Margery Freemantle, and returned to Canada where he went into the family business. In his spare time he acted at the University of Toronto, and eventually sailed for England determined to be an actor.

His first professional stage appearance was with the Everyman Theatre Company in July 1922, where at the Winter Garden Theatre in New Brighton he played Jack in *In the Zone*. They returned to the Everyman in London and Raymond Massey stayed with them, acting small parts and understudying in several plays.

He next played the part of Roberts, an aged, philosophical head waiter of a country inn in *The Heart of Doris*, which starred Aubrey Smith. After two weeks in Brighton and Cardiff they

changed the name to *Glamour* and opened at the Apollo Theatre in London in October 1922. The name change did not help and they lasted a mere ten performances. He returned to the Everyman, where in a children's musical, *Brer Rabbit*, he sang and danced in blackface. His next part was as James Bebb in a boarding house comedy, *At Mrs Beam's*, which opened at the Everyman in February 1923 and transferred to the Royalty in April where it played 300 performances. During the run he was able to act and stage-manage Sunday night performances for stage societies, which were flourishing at the time, and this gave him valuable experience.

For Christmas 1923 he was Jones in *The Rose and the Ring*, a musical adaptation of the work of William Makepeace Thackeray that was produced by Lewis Casson. In February 1924 he played Stanley Pitt at the Criterion in *The Audacious Mr Squire*, but was soon back with Lewis Casson for the first production of Shaw's *Saint Joan* which starred Sybil Thorndike and opened at the New in March 1924. Massey played Captain La Hire and Canon d'Estivet.

For the Repertory Players in March 1925 he directed *Tunnel Trench* at the Prince's and also played Lieutenant Gaythorne. In May that year he was back with Lewis Casson and Sybil Thorndike at Wyndham's, where he played Jonty Drennan in *The Round Table*. At the Court Theatre in July 1925 he played Captain Rickman in *Prisoners of War*; the production transferred to the Playhouse in August.

Raymond Massey, in partnership with Allan Wade and George Carr, took a long lease on the Everyman Theatre in Hampstead and entered into management. There he directed a number of plays as well as playing Robert Mayo in *Beyond the Horizon*, Rufe Pryor in *Hell-Bent for Heaven*, Edmund Crowe in *The Rat Trap*, Mr Man in *Brer Rabbit*, and Tommy Luttrell in *The White Chateau*. The tenancy at the Everyman, though an artistic success, was financially not viable, and Raymond Massey returned to the West End in April 1927 where at the Ambassadors' he played Khan Aghaba, an Arab chieftain who does not want his country's oil exploited, in H. M. Harwood's *The Transit of Venus*. The critics praised his performance but the play failed. At the Apollo Theatre for the Venturers Society he played the Rev. MacMillan in *An American Tragedy* in June, and in September he was at the Globe playing Reuben Manassa in another play by Harwood, *The Golden Calf*. This was his first leading role in the West End. Again he had a personal success but the play failed. His next venture was at the Playhouse in January 1928, when he played Austin Lowe in S. N. Behrman's *The Second Man* with Noel Coward, Zena Dare and Ursula Jeans. At the St Martin's in May 1928 he was Alister Ballantyne in *Four People*, and the next month was at the New playing Joe Cobb in *Spread Eagle*, which had only a three-week run. It was at the Garrick in September 1928 that he took on the role of Lewis Dodd in *The Constant Nymph* for an eight-week limited season. The part had previously been played by Noel Coward and John Gielgud. Ivor Brown reported: 'Dodd III, Mr Raymond Massey, brings an amiable waywardness. It is the rough wind which shakes the darling bud which is Tessa, it is not an east wind but a wild, rough, westerly caress. He has tenderness as well as abruptness, with the result that his being so loved is more credible and his conduct at the party less unnatural.'

At the Globe Theatre in May 1929 he was Randolph Calthorpe in Dorothy Brandon's *The Black Ace*, which was an unmitigated disaster. By mutual agreement he and Margery divorced and on 30 October 1929 he married the actress Adrianne Allen.

At the Ambassadors' in January 1930 he played Raymond Dabney in *The Man in Possession* with *In the Zone*, in which he played Smitty, as a curtain-raiser. He was next in a musical disaster at the New Theatre in October 1930. It was Benn Levy's adaptation of Marcel Pagnol's French hit *Topaze*, and co-starred Alice Delysia. The *Times* wrote of his performance: 'Mr Massey gives two extremes — an absolute innocence in the poor schoolmaster, an absolute coarseness and greed in the blackmailer that he becomes ... Brilliant though Mr Massey's separated performances are, they have not the connecting link

that might have made them a representation of one continuously recognizable human being.'

At this point he thought he would probably never work again and was extremely grateful when, through the auspices of Gerald du Maurier, he got the role of Sherlock Holmes in a film, *The Speckled Band*. He would eventually go on to make more than seventy films.

He need not have worried about his value to the stage. In 1931 in less than six months he directed four major plays, and played the leading part in one of them. That was *Late Night Final* at the Phoenix in June 1931. In this play by Louis Weitzenkorn about newspaper life, which had been a hit as *Five Star Final* on Broadway, he played Randall. There was a cast of thirty and it was an instant success. Eventually Godfrey Tearle took over his part and Massey went to make his Broadway début at the Broadhurst Theater on 5 November 1931 as Hamlet, in a production designed, produced and directed by Norman Bel Geddes which was controversial to say the least. John Mason Brown wrote: 'Mr Massey has fine, simple moments. He frequently strikes attitudes that are visually right, for he postures well even though he moves badly. He fences with fire, upbraids his mother with spirit and wanders effectively in and out of the spotlights' rays. Beside many old-timers he may seem naturalness itself. But he is still very far from being the Hamlet of the lines he is speaking ... Mr Massey's acting is so uneven that he is only every other inch a Hamlet ... He pouts rather than ponders; is surly instead of ironic; and is not so much melancholy as morbid ...' The *New Yorker* wrote: 'My only criticism of Mr Raymond Massey in the new Geddes production of the great tragedy would be that he is not enough of a ham ... Mr Massey is quite natural, his voice is the voice of an ordinary man (an ordinary man who doesn't like actors) and he gives the impression of being just what Hamlet probably was: a very young man with something on his mind ...'

At this point Adrianne Allen signed a two-year Hollywood contract, and Massey went with her to California. Universal Studios signed him as a director and a writer but he was soon acting in his first Hollywood film, *The Old Dark House*, with Charles Laughton and Boris Karloff. His contract, however, was a disaster — he had nothing to do except script a few animal sounds for a movie, so he gave it up and returned to London where he and his wife co-starred in a Frederick Lonsdale comedy, *Never Come Back*, at the Phoenix in October 1932, but it lasted only six weeks. At the Globe in January 1933 he co-starred with Yvonne Arnaud in *Doctor's Orders*. Although it was directed by

Gerald du Maurier it was not successful. He went to the Playhouse in April 1933 where he directed *The Rats of Norway* playing Hugh Sebastian. He co-starred with Gladys Cooper; Laurence Olivier was also in this successful production. In August he was at the Lyric playing Kurt von Hagen in a German *Journey's End* type of play called *The Ace*, which the public did not like. Nor did they care for Robert Sherwood's *Acropolis*, in which he played Creon. This ran for only eleven performances in November.

His next venture was, however, an unqualified success. He played David Linden in Keith Winter's *The Shining Hour*, also co-producing with Gladys Cooper. His wife Adrianne was in the cast as well. They rehearsed in London and opened at the Royal Alexandra Theater in Toronto in February 1934. That same month they took it to the Booth Theater on Broadway, and in September came to London with it to the St James's. After closing the play Massey spent a year on Korda's film of H. G. Wells's *The Shape of Things to Come*.

Raymond Massey opened at the National Theater in New York in January 1936 playing the title role in *Ethan Frome*. Brooks Atkinson reported for the *New York Times*: 'As Ethan Frome, the young farmer trapped between love and duty, Raymond Massey gives the best performance he has disclosed in this country — graceless, desperate yet kind withal.'

In 1937 he spent nine months in Hollywood making such films as *The Prisoner of Zenda* and *The Hurricane*, and then returned to England for Korda's *Drums*.

Back in London's West End in March 1938 he directed and played the part Alfred Lunt had created on Broadway in Robert Sherwood's *Idiot's Delight*. He stayed at the Apollo for six months in this anti-Nazi play and then returned to New York, where he opened at the Plymouth Theater in October playing Abraham Lincoln in Sherwood's *Abe Lincoln in Illinois*. Brooks Atkinson wrote: 'Mr Massey has an exhaustingly long part to play. He is the center of every scene; he has a great many lines and several long speeches to deliver. An actor might be forgiven for not mastering all the details. But Mr Massey, too, has drawn inspiration from the theme he is conveying, and he plays it with an artless honesty that is completely overwhelming at the end. Fortunately he looks the part. But he goes deeper than surface resemblance. He has the artistic stature to measure the great things that lie beneath. From the careless, good-natured boy to the towering man of melancholy who goes on leaden feet to face his destiny is a long road for any actor to travel in one night. But Mr Massey tells the whole story in terms of humanity with the

diffident eloquence of a man who knows what it means.' This play ran two years on Broadway and then Massey made the film. During this time he and Adrianne Allen were divorced; he married Dorothy Ludington Whitney, and Adrianne married Mr Whitney — it was all very amicable.

At the Shubert Theater in New York in March 1941 he played Sir Colenso Ridgeon in Shaw's *The Doctor's Dilemma* with Katharine Cornell playing Jennifer. The next month he was James Havor Morell in *Candida*. That year he also began a contract with Warner Brothers, and in the next fifteen years made eighteen pictures with them. In 1942, anxious to do something about the war, he joined the Canadian army, where he spent a year on the adjutant-general's staff shuffling papers.

He was back at the Plymouth Theater in November 1943 with Katharine Cornell. He played Rodney Boswell in *Lovers and Friends*. It was not a very good play, but with that couple it worked. In March 1944 he became a United States citizen, and in 1945 toured European bases playing the Stage Manager in *Our Town* for the USO.

In December 1945 he was Henry Higgins while Gertrude Lawrence was Eliza in *Pygmalion* at the Ethel Barrymore Theater. It ran for 179 performances, breaking the house records for a non-musical. At the Hudson in September 1947 he was Prof. Lemuel Stevenson in *How I Wonder*, and spent 1949 playing the lawyer in *The Winslow Boy* in summer theatres. He directed and played Strindberg's *The Father* at the Cort Theater in November 1949, and toured the summer theatres in 1950 in *Our Town*.

With Judith Anderson and Tyrone Power at the Civic Auditorium in Pasadena, California, in November 1952 he gave a reading of the epic poem *John Brown's Body*. They subsequently performed it at the New Century Theater in New York, and on a nine-month tour of the United States. At the opening of the American Shakespeare Festival Theater in Stratford, Connecticut, in July 1955 he played Brutus in *Julius Caesar* and Prospero in *The Tempest*.

Raymond Massey once more played Abraham Lincoln. This time it was in *The Rivalry*, which consisted of excerpts from six debates between Stephen Douglas and Lincoln, but the play never got any further than Seattle, Washington, in September 1957. It suffered, according to Massey, from too much authenticity.

At the ANTA in New York in December 1958 he was, according to Kenneth Tynan, 'as imposing as a riven oak' playing Mr Zuss in Archibald MacLeish's *JB*. It was Massey's last Broadway appearance, and he stayed with the role for 196 performances before Basil Rathbone took over. He then tried *The Rivalry* once more on a tour of the United States.

In 1960 he became familiar to a world-wide audience as Dr Gillespie in the television series 'Dr Kildare', which ran for five years.

After thirty-two years away, Raymond Massey returned to make his final appearance on the London stage at the Duke of York's in May 1970, playing Tom Garrison in *I Never Sang for My Father*. John Russell Taylor reported on what he called a play for American tourists: 'Raymond Massey, the star of the piece, gives a good big star performance, roaring away like an old but still unpredictable lion.'

By this time severely crippled by arthritis, Raymond Massey made his last stage appearance in a wheelchair at the Ahmanson Theater in Los Angeles in December 1975, co-starring with Richard Chamberlain, Dorothy Maguire and Eleanor Parker in Tennessee Williams' *The Night of the Iguana*. He then retired and wrote two books of memoirs before his death in 1983.

JESSIE MATTHEWS

Jessie Matthews was the seventh of the sixteen children of George and Jane Matthews. She was born on 11 March 1907 in Soho, London, where her father ran a market stall. The family was extremely poor and lived in cramped conditions, but having seen Pearl White in the film *Perils of Pauline* Jessie became enamoured of the screen and of the stage. She was a natural dancer and by the time she was eight she was organizing school ballet concerts. And she was constantly urged on in her performances by her older sister Rosie, who taught her poems to recite and worked on her elocution.

Her formal dance training began at the age of ten when she was enrolled with Madame Elise Clerc, and she made her stage début on 29 December 1919 at the Metropolitan Theatre, Edgware Road, in Seymour Hicks' production of *Bluebell in Fairyland*. The following Christmas she did a butterfly dance and a sailor's hornpipe in George Shurley's pantomime, *Dick Whittington*, at the Kennington Theatre. When Madame Clerc went to the United States Jessie moved on to Terry Freedman, who ran a company called Terry's Juveniles. For Christmas 1921 she was at the Alexandra Theatre in Stoke Newington in *Babes in the Wood*. The local paper reported: 'The palm for dancing goes to Miss Jessica Matthews, a sprightly elf, who gives an extremely clever and graceful display.' The following Christmas she was at the Lewisham Hippodrome in *Red Riding Hood* and the same paper said she 'dances with exceptional grace as Snowdrop'. Jessie took over the title part during the run.

Having now left school, Jessie Matthews joined C. B. Cochran and opened at the Palace Theatre in May 1923 in his *Music Box Revue*. In this production she had a song by Irving Berlin. However, the show closed in August after only 119 performances—the seventh Cochran flop in a row. Jessie made her first film during this period, a silent one called *The Beloved Vagabond*, in which she played Pan. In September she was hired by André Charlot for *London Calling*, a revue which starred Noel Coward and Gertrude Lawrence. Jessie was only a stand-by chorus girl at the Duke of York's, but Mr Charlot decided to take her to America with the company, and after a disastrous Atlantic City tryout *Charlot's Revue of 1924* opened at the Times Square Theater in New York in January 1924; it starred Jack Buchanan, Bea Lillie and Gertrude Lawrence. When the production, which was a great success, moved to the Selwyn Theater in April, Jessie became understudy to Miss Lawrence and was often allowed by her to perform the 'Parisian Pierrot' number. After the show closed on Broadway they went on tour; on Friday, 13 February 1925, Gertrude Lawrence was taken into hospital in Toronto suffering from pleurisy, and at the Princess Theater Jessie Matthews took over the lead. After the tour she was back at the Prince of Wales Theatre in London, and back in the chorus of the Charlot revue.

In October 1925, however, she opened at the same theatre in the *Charlot Revue of 1925* playing the second lead after Dorothy Dickson. One critic reported: 'Jessie Matthews sang, danced and acted as if her whole heart was in her task. It looks as if Charlot has found another Hermione Baddeley.' For a six-month tour of the provinces Jessie had the lead. On 16 February 1926 Jessie married Henry Lytton Jr, her co-star on the tour.

The 1926 Charlot revue was specially written for Jessie Matthews. It opened at the Prince of Wales in October. The *Daily Chronicle* said: 'Miss Matthews achieved a triumph that would have turned the head of many an actress who has been twenty years on the stage.' And James Agate was delirious. 'It was obvious as soon as this little actress came on that she possessed freshness and natural high spirits in keeping with her tip-tilted nose, wide smile and china-blue saucer eyes . . . She sang a clever little song with a complete semblance of spontaneity and danced as one delighted to be dancing. But even so, I was not prepared for her admirable French maid, who she presented with all the verve and distinction and sense of fun of Spinelli at her best. It must be remembered, too, that in giving us a French soubrette Spinelli is pretending to be what she is, whereas Miss Matthews succeeds in being to the life what she very obviously isn't. This little sketch revealed talent of a singularly high order.' But Charlot sent her to America to join *Earl Carroll's Vanities* at the Earl Carroll Theater, and that helped neither her career nor her marriage. The American show was devoted mainly to semi-clad models and show-girls, and Jessie Matthews had a disaster there in January 1927, both in New York and on tour.

When she returned to London she signed a four-year contract with C. B. Cochran. Her first show, written by Rodgers and Hart and called *One Dam Thing After Another*, opened at the London Pavilion in May 1927. Her leading man was Sonnie Hale and the show was an enormous hit. One of her songs, 'My Heart Stood Still', became her trademark. The production closed after a standing-room-only season in December.

The next Cochran revue, *This Year of Grace*, was written and directed by Noel Coward. It opened at the London Pavilion in March 1928, and again Sonnie Hale was her leading man. They sang the haunting 'A Room with a View', and it was obvious that although both were married to other people, they were not entirely acting the love scenes. The show was again an enormous hit, and a personal one, too, for Jessie Matthews. The *Sunday Express* ranked her with Evelyn Laye (Sonnie Hale's wife) and Cicely Courtneidge, calling them the three brightest female stars in the West End. St John Ervine, writing in the *Observer* about Jessie, said: 'She grows in grace and is charming and dainty in all she does.'

The third Cochran revue in which she starred opened in March 1929. It was Cole Porter's *Wake Up and Dream*, and contained the classic 'Let's Do It'. It was another enormous success. Her private life, however, was in turmoil and it was now that the notorious West End feud between herself and Evelyn Laye began. Cochran sent Jessie Matthews to the Selwyn Theater in New York in December 1929 with *Wake Up and Dream*, but with Jack Buchanan as her leading man.

The fourth Jessie Matthews–Cochran revue,

Ever Green, was written by Rodgers and Hart. It opened at the Adelphi Theatre in December 1930 and gave her the gorgeous number 'Dancing on the Ceiling'. Having both obtained divorces, on 24 January 1931 Sonnie Hale and Jessie Matthews married at the Hampstead Registry Office.

After *Ever Green* closed in July, Jessie made the film *Out of the Blue* but was back on the stage, this time at the Gaiety, in December 1931 with Sonnie Hale and Stanley Lupino in *Hold My Hand*. It was her first opportunity as a comedienne.

British–Gaumont then signed her to a film contract for two years, during which time she made such films as *There Goes the Bride*, *The Midshipmaid*, *The Good Companions* and *Friday the Thirteenth*. She was soon a very big film star. In May 1933 she opened at the Strand Theatre with her husband in *Sally Who?* The production closed in a month but she was still the only international British film star. She made *Waltzes from Vienna*, directed by Hitchcock, and the film *Evergreen* which brought her some fabulous offers from Hollywood, but she chose to stay in England and nurture a now failing marriage.

She made her return to the stage after six years in *I Can Take It*, an enormous show with her husband co-starring and managing. It opened at the Sheffield Empire in January 1939 for the start of a tour and was due to open at the huge London Coliseum in September. But the Second World War began, and the prospect of a huge show costing a fortune — his own — to mount in such precarious times frightened Hale and he cancelled the opening. Instead he backed them in a smaller play in which the financial risks were less, and they toured the revue *Come Out to Play*, opening in London at the Phoenix in March 1940. The revue lasted only nine weeks in the West End and then toured for a further six before closing.

For Christmas 1940 Jessie Matthews was back in pantomime after eighteen years. She played the title role in Emile Littler's production of *Aladdin* at the Prince of Wales Theatre in Birmingham. It was so successful that they played for three months. The next December was not so successful. She crossed the Atlantic for a musical, *The Lady Comes Across*; it was constantly postponed, rewritten many times and finally opened at the Shubert Theater in New Haven, Connecticut. It closed the next week at the Shubert Theater in Boston.

Back in London, in August 1942 she played Sally in *Wild Rose*, a revival of Dorothy Dickson's great hit *Sally*. It opened at the Prince's Theatre and stayed there for six months. The *Daily Telegraph* reported: 'Her spirits were as high and her dancing as light as ever, and her devoted public welcomed her back with acclamation. It was obvious that even if *Wild Rose* had been a less excellent show than it is, she would have still carried it to success.' Unfortunately that year her husband ran away with their adopted daughter's nanny, and Jessie went into a decline, becoming a virtual recluse. She was coaxed out of it to do troop concerts, and she even directed a twenty-minute propaganda film.

Jessie Matthews' days of stardom were over, but she did not see it. She began a tour of a specially written revue, *Maid to Measure*, at the Royal Lyceum in Edinburgh in December 1947. It was a nostalgic show and a great success on the road. It came to London to the suburban King's Theatre in Hammersmith in April 1948. She received an eight-minute ovation on her first entrance. Harold Hobson reported: 'She came forward and stood with her head dropped downwards on her breast in response to the enormous applause, with a moving blend of humility and authority, as a queen might look who was being contrite. Was Miss Matthews really moved by her reception? I doubt it. There was the same terrific enthusiasm at the finish, and it renewed itself after she had made her speech, in which she struck, I thought, an unfortunate note when she introduced the presenter of the show, Leigh Stafford, as "Someone who still has faith in me". Why this suggestion that all the world had deserted her? As the cheering went on, she stood in the centre of the stage once more, with her lips quivering. But she was sufficiently in control of the situation to nod almost imperceptibly to the conductor to prevent him from striking up a tune to bring the applause to an end. She has the same big and melting eyes, the same piquant nose, the same too ambitious voice, the same roguish childish charm, the same svelte and agile legs. We must, we simply must, have her back in the West End. The gaiety of nations is a mockery without her.' West End managers believed Mr Hobson and the show moved to the Cambridge Theatre in May, but nostalgia was not all that commercial and it closed after only thirty-six performances.

Jessie Matthews next played Harriet Stirling in a straight comedy, *Sweethearts and Wives*, which opened at the Theatre Royal in Brighton and came to Wyndham's in February 1949. The *Evening Standard* said: 'If business men still get tired then there may be a public for this nonsense.' There was not and it closed in under a month.

At the suburban Q Theatre she guest-starred for a week as Madeleine in *Don't Listen Ladies*, and then in May had two weeks at the King's, Hammersmith, in two Rattigan plays, *The Browning Version* and *Harlequinade*. In August she replaced an ill Zoe Gail at the Cambridge in the

successful *Sauce Tartare* and continued the run for five months, during which time she developed an enormous row with her co-star Renee Houston, which did not help her growing reputation for being difficult and unreliable. This was to be her last West End appearance for sixteen years.

After touring, first in England and then in Australia and New Zealand, she returned to England, and to the provinces, touring first as Olivia Brown in *Love in Idleness*. In 1954 she toured as Amanda in Coward's *Private Lives* and the following year as Denise Darvel in *Dear Charles*. In December 1955 she toured South Africa in *Larger than Life*, going on to Australia, where she opened at the Theatre Royal, Sydney, in December 1956 as Jessica in *Janus*. She also played in Adelaide and Melbourne.

At the Royal Court Theatre in Liverpool, England, in July 1957, she played Gloria Faraday in *Nest of Robins*. It was a publicist's dream. The play was written by and co-starred her ex-husband, Sonnie Hale. They were both now prepared to cash in on their notoriety. However, she suffered from growing paranoia throughout the tour and by the end of August the show closed on the road.

Jessie Matthews spent some years away from England, returning in 1960, to find that she was always welcome in the West End for charity shows. She stopped the show in that year's *Night of 100 Stars* Palladium concert. She got some radio work and went on a six-week Arts Council tour of Wales in *Five Finger Exercise*. For Christmas 1960 she was at the Bristol Old Vic playing Fairy Snowflake in *Dick Whittington* and then had three weeks in Northampton playing in Maugham's *The Sacred Flame*.

In May 1961, she embarked on a provincial tour of *Port in a Storm*, playing Alicia Storm in a terrible farce which co-starred the 80-year-old Ralph Lynn. She then revived *Larger than Life* for a provincial tour. A critic in Sunderland reported that he 'found little to commend in the spectacle of Miss Matthews, attired in a negligee, playing the coquette. It was embarrassing to say the least. And for those older patrons in the near-empty theatre last night, the nostalgia of the moment must have been overshadowed with a tinge of regret at the decline of this latter day idol.'

Salvation came at last in the shape of a radio soap opera, 'Mrs Dale's Diary', in which for six years she played the doctor's wife.

In August 1966 she tried the West End again, playing Violet Deakin in *A Share in the Sun* at the Cambridge. It ran a bare two and a half weeks. In July 1969 she was back in the provinces, playing the Theatre Royal, Norwich, in *Cockles and Champagne*. That Christmas she was in pantomime at the Congress, Eastbourne, playing the Duchess of Monte Polo in *Puss in Boots*. She received the OBE in the 1970 Birthday Honours, which helped to bring the audiences for her summer season in Bournemouth, in which she played Judith Bliss in *Hay Fever* and Mrs Bramson in *Night Must Fall*. At Cardiff the following January she was June Buckridge, the lesbian who is sacked from a long-running radio soap opera, in Frank Marcus's *The Killing of Sister George*. It might have been a bit close to home, but the *Western Mail* reported: 'A gruelling, real portrayal. Miss Matthews is funny as the butch aging actress whose radio role has almost taken her over; pathetic as she sees her radio identity killed off to promote broadcast ratings; and bitterly sad when her lesbian companion moves on to more successful pickings.' At the Theatre Royal in York in October 1972 she was Lady Catherine Champion-Cheney in *The Circle*, and she made a brief return to London to the Royalty Theatre in July 1973 for matinées of *The Water Babies*, in which she

played Mrs Doasyouwouldbedoneby. Ian Christie reported in the *Daily Express*: 'It is hardly the most notable role of her career, but as a good and rather senior fairy she sings pleasantly and contributes to the overall gaiety.' *The Water Babies* played only four weeks of its scheduled six-week run.

Still with a strong and pleasant voice, she appeared at the Shaftesbury Theatre in London in October 1976 singing all her old favourites in *The Jessie Matthews Show*, and then toured the provinces with it. She toured in 1978 playing the Duchess of Berwick in *Lady Windermere's Fan*, and took her concert to the United States, to the Mayfair Music Hall in Santa Monica. Luckily, Jessie Matthews at her best — before the traumatic marriages, the nervous breakdowns, the mental disturbances — has been captured on celluloid, and future generations can still thrill to her 'Dancing on the Ceiling' in *Evergreen*. She died on 20 August 1981, of cancer.

ETHEL MERMAN

*E*thel Merman, the lady with the legendary lungs of brass who never took a single singing lesson and was said to hold a note longer than the Chase Manhattan Bank, was born in Astoria, Long Island, New York, on 16 January 1909. Her mother was of Scots descent and her father, Edward Zimmermann, of German origin. He was professionally an accountant but also an amateur pianist and organist.

Ethel Merman could sing as soon as she could open her mouth, and as a child sang at every possible venue from the Lutheran Church to the Masonic Lodge — stopping off at every women's club along the way. She was also a keen cinema-goer as a child, and worried that she would be an unacceptable star because she was not beautiful. She attended public schools in Long Island and did a commercial course throughout high school where she learned to type and take shorthand, two skills she spent her life being proud of. After graduation she went to work in an office but was soon singing in clubs after work. Always a practical lady, she vowed never to give up the typing and shorthand until she was sure she could make a living singing — and not in the back of the chorus.

Her big break came with a two-week engagement at the Club Little Russia in New York, where

the theatrical agent Lou Irwin saw and heard her and signed her to a nine-year contract. The first thing he got her was a Warner Brothers contract, but the movies did not know what to do with the little girl with the big voice; she made only a short film for them, and ended up on the cutting-room floor. They released her from her contract and she got a job with Jimmy Durante singing in cabaret at the new Broadway club, Les Ambassadeurs, in 1929. She had to give the job up when she entered hospital for a tonsilectomy. She left hospital, voice intact, for a seven-week season at the Roman Pools Casino in Miami Beach. Next she teamed up with pianist and arranger Al Siegel, and they opened at the Ritz Theater in Elizabeth, New Jersey. *Variety* reported: '. . . A new singing team has come into existence with interesting arrangements by Siegel. And the girl can sing.' Together they did vaudeville dates and she performed Sunday Night impromptus at the Pavilion Royal, where Guy Lombardo was playing.

It was there that she was seen by the producers of a new Gershwin show, *Girl Crazy*, planned for Broadway to star Ginger Rogers. Merman was hired — and she opened at the Alvin Theater in October 1930 playing Kate Fothergill. Among her numbers was 'I Got Rhythm' and she explained: 'I held a note for sixteen bars while the orchestra played the melodic line — a big tooty thing — against the note I was holding. By the time I'd held that note for four bars the audience was applauding. They applauded through the whole chorus and I did several encores.' Miss Merman had stopped the show. The *New York Times* reported: '. . . a peculiar song style was brought from the nightclubs to the stage to the vast delight last evening of the people who go places and watch things.' And *Time* magazine wrote: '*Girl Crazy*'s chief claim to fame lies in the fact that it was the cradle for the birth of another blues singer, Ethel Merman. Her trim little body was dragged up by the hair from a nightclub to the boards of the Alvin . . . Her baby stare belies knowing anatomical curves . . . She approaches sex in a song with the cold fury of a philosopher. She aims at a point slightly above the entrails, but she knocks you out just the same.' The show ran forty weeks on Broadway and Ethel took to singing at the Central Park Casino after the curtain fell. After the show closed she worked at the New York Paramount, and then opened in *George White's Scandals* at the Apollo in September 1931. Her classic number from this show was 'Life is Just a Bowl of Cherries'. Also on stage with her were Rudy Vallee, Ray Bolger and Ethel Barrymore, and the show ran seven months. After a time as a vaudeville headliner, Ethel Merman returned to Broadway, to the Apollo, in November 1932 playing Wanda Brill in *Take a Chance*. She stopped the show on this occasion with 'Eadie Was a Lady'. After the show closed on Broadway she went with it to Chicago.

At the Alvin in November 1934 she opened as Reno Sweeney in Cole Porter's *Anything Goes*. The *New York Times* reported: 'If Ethel Merman did not write "I Get a Kick Out of You" and also the title song of the show she has made them hers now by the swinging gusto of her platform style.' She went to Hollywood for her first film there, *We're Not Dressing*, but again most of her scenes ended up on the cutting-room floor. The same thing happened to her in *Alexander's Ragtime Band*, which starred Alice Faye.

With Jimmy Durante and Bob Hope at the Alvin in October 1936 she played Nails Duquesne in *Red, Hot and Blue!* They played forty weeks and then moved on to Chicago. She had her first solid comic scenes on stage directed by Josh Logan in *Stars in Your Eyes*, which opened at the Majestic in February 1939. At the 46th Street Theater in December 1939 she was May Daly in *Du Barry was a Lady* with Bert Lahr and Betty Grable; the music was again by Cole Porter, and the play ran 408 performances.

In October 1940, Ethel Merman had her name

above the title for the first time. It was at the 46th Street Theater, and she played Hattie Maloney in *Panama Hattie*. She had the great Porter number 'Let's Be Buddies' which left not a dry eye in the house. Abe Laufe, recalling her performance, wrote: 'Merman's perfect enunciation immeasurably helped the Porter lyrics. Merman was not and is not, as some critics have suggested, merely a shouter. Volume is not her only attribute; her ability to be heard in the last row of the balcony is due to her extraordinary ability to project her voice and enunciate.' Perhaps it was the euphoria of at last being above the title, perhaps not — on 16 November 1940 in Maryland, Ethel Merman married actor's agent Bill Smith. The marriage lasted three days only, but it was a year before they tidied things up with a Mexican divorce. That was the year she married the newspaper man, Robert Levitt.

She was back on Broadway in January 1943, again at the Alvin and again in a Cole Porter show, this time playing Blossom Hart in *Something for the Boys*. Lewis Nichols wrote in the *New York Times*: 'Ethel Merman gives a performance that suggests all Merman performances before last night were simply practice . . . Ethel Merman in good voice is a raucous overtone to the trumpets of a band; it is a soft trill for a torch song, it is tinny for parody and fast for one of Mr Porter's complicated lyrics. Accompanying the Voice are all the necessary gestures, the roll of the eyes or the wave of the hand to suggest friendly ribaldries or separations forever more. In "Hey, Good Lookin'" she is loud, in "He's a Right Guy" she's soft; it is one of Mr Porter's lines that sums it up pretty well; she is "the missing link between Lily Pons and Mae West."'

After *Something for the Boys* she decided to go into a new show called *Sadie Thompson*. Ethel Merman actually rehearsed for a week but could not understand a word of it, especially the lyrics, so she left. She was replaced by June Havoc, but the show closed in under forty performances.

Ethel Merman then played her strongest role to date. She was Annie Oakley in Irving Berlin's *Annie Get Your Gun*, which opened on Broadway at the Imperial in May 1946 and ran there for three years — 1147 performances in all. The *New York Times* reviewed the opening: 'By now, Miss Merman is regarded as heaven's gift to the musical show, and there is nothing about the new one to detract from that reputation.' Brooks Atkinson wrote: 'Her brass band voice, her infectious sense of rhythm and her razzle-dazzle performance gave the songs remarkable beat and relish.'

After a short break she was back on the Imperial stage in October 1950 playing Sally

Adams in Berlin's *Call Me Madam*. Brooks Atkinson said: 'She is still lighting up like an inspired pin ball machine, and still blowing the music lustily throughout the theatre...We were all eating out of Ethel's hand last evening for she was acting in the grand manner without being snobbish or pretentious.'

In March 1953, with a new husband, she moved to Denver, Colorado, proclaiming that she was through with Broadway and would be happy to concentrate on a couple of television spectaculars a year — and perhaps a film. She made *Call Me Madam* in 1953 and *No Business Like Show Business* in 1954, both for Fox, but by December 1956 she was back on Broadway at the Imperial, playing Liz Livingstone in *Happy Hunting*. It was in May 1958, however, that the next really big success came her way when she opened at the Broadway Theater playing Rose in *Gypsy*. Brooks Atkinson wrote in the *New York Times*: '...*Gypsy* is Miss Merman's show. Mr Styne has given her some good greased horn music which she delivers with earthy magnificence in her familiar manner...She concludes the proceedings with a song and dance of defiance. Mr Styne's music is dramatic; Miss Merman's performance expressed her whole character — cocky and aggressive but also sociable and good hearted. Not for the first time in her fabulous career, her personal magnetism electrifies the whole theatre. For she is a performer of incomparable power.' Kenneth Tynan reported: '[Ethel Merman is] the most relaxed brass section on earth, singing her heart out and missing none of her own inimitable tricks, among them her habit of sliding down to important words from a grace note above, which supplies the flick that precedes the vocal whipcrack. But Miss Merman not only sings; she acts. I would not say that she acts very subtly; Rose, after all, with her dreams of glory, her kleptomania, her savage parsimony and her passion for exotic animals and Chinese breakfasts, is scarcely a subtle character. Someone in the show describes her as ''a pioneer woman without a frontier'' and that is what Miss Merman magnificently plays.'

Ethel Merman became ill shortly after *Gypsy* opened, and the box office receipts dropped for the several weeks during which she was off. They picked up on her return, however, and the play lasted for 720 performances. For this role she received the New York Drama Critics Award for the Best Female Lead in a Musical. She toured the United States from March through December of 1961 with the show.

Ethel Merman was in cabaret at the Flamingo in Las Vegas in October 1962 and finally made her London début in March 1964, not in a musical play but in cabaret at the Talk of the Town. In Los Angeles at the Valley Music Theater in July 1965 she revived *Call Me Madam*, and at the New York State in May 1966 revived *Annie Get Your Gun*, which she brought to the Broadway Theater in September and then subsequently toured. She was in *Call Me Madam* once again at the Coconut Grove Playhouse in Miami in 1968, and in March 1970 took over as Dolly Gallagher Levi at the St James Theater in *Hello Dolly!* From then on her appearances were in concert and cabaret and on television. She received a special Tony Award in 1974.

The *Saturday Review of Literature* summed up Ethel Merman's talents thus: '...Miss Merman is Broadway. She is Broadway with its flash in the flesh; Broadway making noon of darkness and ready to turn each night into New Year's Eve ... Hearing is believing in Miss Merman's case. Her voice is one of the less larklike sounds known to contemporary ears. It is also one of the most jubilant. She may create fission in the middle ear, but she never lets a number, a note, or an audience down. Miss Merman sings volumes; rowdy, racy, joyful volumes. Though very much of an individualist, her vocal powers are choral. So athletic is her throat that it is hard to understand how anyone who had not heard Miss Merman could have invented the calliope.. No metronome can equal her precise timing. This does not mean that she is mechanical. She lets each song fly, no matter how often she may have repeated it, with as much joy as if she had just discovered it. She is all over the place. She works like a stable, not a.horse. Her work is so palpably her pleasure that we enjoy it in her fashion, forgetting the labor involved. To tell the truth, we relish it the more because of the reckless expenditure of energy it represents. Her personality is pure benzedrine ... As a comedienne, Miss Merman is as American as the Fourth of July ...'

Ethel Merman, the 'golden foghorn' who more than any other defined and characterized the Broadway musical at its Showbiz best, died after a heart attack early in 1984.

BERNARD
MILES

*L*ord Miles of Blackfriars, the only actor apart from Olivier to be given a peerage, was born in Uxbridge on 27 September 1907. His father was a market gardener. Bernard went to the Uxbridge Country School and then on to Pembroke College, Oxford, but left without taking a degree, although later, after his theatrical success, the College made him an honorary fellow.

He taught for a year in a school in Filey and made his first stage appearance at the New Theatre in London on 1 September 1930 playing the Second Messenger in *Richard III*. During most of 1931 he remained backstage as property master and scene painter at the People's Theatre, but he did secure a small part in *Saint Joan* which he played at His Majesty's and also on tour. At the Westminster in December 1934 he played the Workman in *The Fisher of Shadows*. For the next five years he worked backstage in repertory companies. It was at Sheffield, where he was stage-managing, that he met the actress Josephine Hinchliffe and they married. He was at Windsor being a stage carpenter when one of the actors was held up in the fog and Bernard Miles went on for him. It was then that he decided he preferred to be on the stage rather than behind the scenes. 'There was nothing like the applause, nothing. The theatre is the home of the ego. In-built in all of us is the conviction that we are God's gift to creation and the audience confirms this. You stand in the middle of the stage with all the lights on you and people roar with laughter every four minutes, and there's no feeling like it.'

He made his first film, *Channel Crossing*, in 1937 — he went on to appear in more than forty films during the next fourteen years. He was back in London at the New Theatre in September 1938 playing Moore in *Can We Tell?*, and then appeared at the Players Theatre the following year in *Late Joys*. He was in *The Little Revue* at the Little Theatre in April 1939, and at the Globe in July 1940 played Briggs in *Thunder Rock* He was in revue at Wyndham's during the winter of 1940–41 and then toured with the Old Vic as Iago in *Othello*. He repeated the role at the New Theatre in July 1942. The Czech actor Frederic Valk played the title role, and Audrey Williamson reported: 'Bernard Miles' Iago was pedestrian of speech and an unmistakable whiff of Cockney gave an unexpected aroma to his performance.' Bernard Miles had developed the ability to master any regional accent.

In September 1942, for the first time, Bernard Miles went into the production side of theatre with John Mills. He produced *Men in Shadow* at the Vaudeville Theatre, and in December took over the leading part of Lew Messenger. At the Scala in March 1946 he was George Watkins in *A Century for George*, and Abel Honeyman in his own play *Let Tyrants Tremble*.

He joined the Old Vic for their 1947–48 season at the New Theatre, playing Christopher Sly in *The Taming of the Shrew*, and the Bishop of Carlisle in *Richard II*. In Celia Johnson's *Saint Joan* he was Robert de Baudricourt and the Inquisitor. Of the latter performance Harold Hobson said: 'Another excellent performance is Mr Bernard Miles' Inquisitor whose long speech is delivered with a calm and insinuating elegance.' But it worried T. C. Worsley: 'He held our attention marvellously with his long and difficult speech. But should he have that touch of the sinister? Should he not be grand instead of shabby?' That season he also played Antonovitch in Gogol's *The Government Inspector* with Alec Guinness. Harold Hobson thought that his 'blustering Mayor is amusing for the first half hour; after that, still red-cheeked and clumsily assertive, he becomes a village bore'. On tour with the Old Vic he played Face in *The Alchemist*.

In July 1950 he went on the Palladium music-hall stage with his rustic monologues, and that same year began the establishment of an Elizabethan-style playhouse, the Mermaid, in the grounds of his house in St John's Wood. In September 1951 he produced Purcell's *Dido and Aeneas*, which starred his friend Kirsten Flagstad, and *The Tempest* in which he played Caliban. The following year he presented *A Trick to Catch the Old One* and *Macbeth*, spoken entirely in seventeenth-century English, with himself in the title role. Kenneth Tynan reported: 'Mr Miles himself embraces the dialect like an old friend (which in his case it is) and goes dourly to work. His Macbeth is a rowdy, shamefaced upstart, a Mummerset Mephistopheles who rarely rises above the spiritual level of the thugs he employs. Gaudy and ostentatious, he struts like a prize rooster, vivid in scarlet and gold.'

The Lord Mayor of London asked the Mileses to transfer their little theatre to the Royal Exchange to celebrate the Coronation, and in May 1953 they began a three-month season there presenting *As You Like It*, *Eastward Ho!*, *Macbeth* and *Dido and Aeneas*.

Bernard Miles then decided that he liked the

idea of having a theatre in the City of London, found a bombed-out warehouse on the Thames at Puddle Dock, and with Josephine began the construction of his new Mermaid Theatre. 'I think I'm a bit of a missionary,' he said. 'Acting and not doing anything else bores me. I want to start things and organize them, and this theatre is something I really believe in.' The theatre opened in May 1959 with his adaptation of Henry Fielding's *Rape Upon Rape* into the musical play *Lock Up Your Daughters*, which had great success. For Christmas he presented his own adaptation of *Treasure Island*, in which he played Long John Silver. When asked who was the greatest Long John Silver of all he said, 'I think I am. I walk on one leg, I move like a cat, I have perfected a set of physical accomplishments in the role that have never been equalled.' Bernard Miles remained the controlling hand in the Mermaid Theatre. As he told *Time* magazine: 'I could have become established as one of Britain's outstanding character actors, instead of which my dedication has been to the Mermaid.' And though the Mermaid gave him a creative outlet for performing, adapting and producing — as well as running the restaurant — his living has largely been made from television commercials, his rustic impersonations having many selling qualities. In 1960 he produced a modern dress version of *Henry V* and directed Bertolt Brecht's *Life of Galileo*, playing the title role himself. That Christmas he made his Candadian début at the O'Keefe Center in Toronto playing his Long John Silver. Back at the Mermaid for 1961, he played the title part in *John Gabriel Borkman*, directed *The Andersonville Trial*, *The Long Sunset* and *The Bed Bug*. In May

1962 he revived *Lock Up Your Daughters*, playing Squeezum himself, and transferred with the production to Her Majesty's in August 1962. He directed *The Witch of Edmonton* in November 1962 and in March 1963 played Ezra Fitton in *All in Good Time*, which transferred to the Phoenix in April. The next few years were mainly spent directing, but he also played Schweyk in *Schweyk in the Second World War* (August 1963), *Oedipus* (May 1965), the Archbishop in *Left-Handed Liberty* (June 1965), Organ in *The Imaginary Invalid* (April 1966), and Charlie Pappalardo in *Climb the Greased Pole* (November 1967). In January 1966 he devised a one-man show called *On The Wagon*, and every Christmas there was his *Treasure Island* with his resident parrot, who spent the rest of the year in his office. In 1969 he became Sir Bernard Miles and the following year played Falstaff in both parts of *Henry IV*. He continued to play in his one-man show, do his Long John Silver at Christmas and play small parts at the Mermaid as well as branching out into larger ones on occasion. In October 1978 the Mermaid closed for a rebuilding programme. 'It was a slum,' Sir Bernard said. By the time the rebuilding was completed at an estimated cost of over two million pounds, Sir Bernard had taken his seat in the House of Lords. 'My acting days are over,' he said, although he was reluctant to relinquish control of 'his' theatre. 'Acting is a very time-consuming, a very enjoyable, but over-indulgent occupation.'

In 1981 he became Lord Miles, and began to move towards a kind of retirement interrupted by a 1982 *Cherry Orchard*.

HELENA MODJESKA

Helena Modjeska was one of ten children of the beautiful Josephine Mary Misel. She was in the second batch, by the second husband Michael Ophid, a gentleman and a teacher. She went to a convent school in Cracow, Poland, where she had been born on 12 October 1840, and studied under the actor and music teacher Herr Axtman. In 1856, pregnant by her childhood sweetheart, an impoverished painter, she married the rich German Gustav Sinnemayer, who was twenty years older than she. As she could not bear to have a German name, he changed his last name to please her, to Modrzejewski. Her son Rudolph was born 'prematurely', causing a scandal

in Cracow, but Gustav was still delighted with his beautiful and talented young bride and moved the family to Bochnia, where he put considerable money and effort into making her a star — albeit in a small town. He imported name stars to play with her in Shakespeare and French and Polish operettas, and they toured local towns. But Helena soon tired of being provincial — and also of her husband. She returned to Cracow and another liaison with her childhood love, which again resulted in pregnancy. She continued to act and tour, even with her baby and young son. The baby, a daughter named Marylka, died in infancy. Soon afterwards, after begging to be reconciled with her,

Ian McKellen in the National Theatre's production of *Coriolanus*
(London, 1985)

Robert Morley as the Bishop in *A Time to Laugh* at the Piccadilly Theatre
(London, April 1962)

Gustav died mysteriously. Helena returned to Cracow, where she starred. One of her fellow performers described her effect in Cracow: 'Her audiences were stirred to the depth by her. In all my stage experience, I have never seen another actress who can compare with her. A genius was hidden in this woman. She was great in comedy and as great in straight drama. Her Viola — ah, sheer poetry! Lady Macbeth — exciting! But her powerful role was Mary Stuart. People trembled in the audience and behind the scenes. Her voice was of tremendous range — from a whisper that dripped with emotion to a magnificent and awful power.' She also produced Polish plays and was known as an ardent patriot in the face of Russian domination. Her Paris début at the Comédie-Française at the age of 26 as Racine's Iphigénie was organized by her admirer Count Bozenta, who became her manager and an excellent press agent, arranging sell-out tours of the European capitals. She married him, full name Karol Bozenta Chapowski, on 12 September 1868, and her childhood lover killed himself.

For a while she acted at the Imperial Theatre of Warsaw, but was so depressed by the political situation that she went to America with her husband and son. She refused offers to act there and instead went to California, where she bought an orange farm and studied English. She finally made her American début on 13 August 1877 at the Baldwin Theater in San Francisco, playing the title role in *Adrienne Lecouvreur* in English. George H. Jessop was there and reported to friends: 'As the first lines fell from her lips, tinged as they were by a strangely marked foreign accent, the knowing ones shook their heads. But not for long. We soon saw that no ordinary artist was before us. We recognized and bowed to the charm that has swayed so many thousands since. The diminutive audience felt the spell, and a warm round of applause as the curtain fell attested the interest that the fair foreigner had awakened. To be brief, each succeeding act was a culminating triumph, and I could not have believed that so small an audience could have manifested so great a volume of enthusiasm.'

Although she had many offers she returned to her orange farm, where she milked cows, cooked and wrote pastoral poems for a time. However, she soon signed a two-year touring contract with Henry Sargent. She made her New York début at the Fifth Avenue Theater as Adrienne Lecouvreur in December 1877. She then played Marguerite Gautier in *Camille*. The *New York Sun* critic reported: 'Modjeska's representation of the part is unlike any other that we have had here ... it is far more poetic in its passion, more effeminate in its

pathos, and far more beautiful in its many exquisite shades of tenderness and grief. The Camille of last evening represented a woman whose exquisite sensibilities had not been destroyed, whose impulsive nature knew no other discipline than that of affection, whose fate was worse than her life. The excellences of the portrayal consisted in its perfect symmetry and consistency, and in the marvellously delicate manner in which the intervening emotions between the extremes of great love and awful despair were manifested ... Nothing could be finer than her sportive mood in the gayer scenes. Her assumption of a reckless gaiety to hide her sorrow, her wanton manner suddenly interrupted by a recollection, her superb grace of action and her charming naïveté made up a picture of the woman of pleasure and beauty such as we have seldom seen.'

She also played Peg Woffington and the leads in *Frou-Frou* and *East Lynne*. Charles Wingate reported on the season: 'Although the personality of Madame Modjeska is charming, with her graceful figure, her beautiful face and her sweetly modulated voice, yet this is not the attribute to which her success is due. The auditor has been drawn by that magnetism which comes from warm enthusiastic absorption in the character of the moment and from the consequent natural expression of all the passions of a woman's heart. Coldly studying the role of the night, one feels that each movement and inflection has been planned with the mind of a careful student; but even as he watches, his enforced coldness must disappear, and the subsequent warmth of sympathy conceals the conscientious actress and reveals only the fictional woman, with all sorrow and joys, loves and hates.'

She toured major American cities with Edwin Booth in 1879–80, playing in *Romeo and Juliet*, *Hamlet, Macbeth, The Merchant of Venice* and the non-Shakespearian *Richelieu*. She played Camille at the prestigious Boston Museum, and there is a story that she and Bernhardt had a contest over who played scenes from Camille better. The contest was conducted in the nude — before a totally female audience of course — and Modjeska won.

She conquered London in 1880, and in the autumn of 1883 mounted a tour with her own company which included Maurice Barrymore as her leading man. His wife, Georgie Drew Barrymore, was also in the company and the children toured with them. Modjeska became very attached to Little Ethel and was a great influence on her.

Helena Modjeska became an American citizen, though remaining a Polish patriot. Her son Rudolph became an engineer and built the San Francisco–Oakland Bridge. In later years she toured with Otis Skinner as her leading man, and was the acknowledged female player of Shakespearian women in the world. At the World's Fair in Chicago in 1893 she made a violently anti-Russian speech, thereby closing the doors to a serious return to Poland. She did go back, however, in 1902, when she toured minor theatres raising money for local projects. Her health by this time

was bad — she had both kidney and heart ailments and tended toward depression.

On 2 May 1905 a testimonial to honour her was given at the Metropolitan Opera House. She died in California of Bright's disease on 8 April 1909; her body was sent back to Poland, where it is buried in the old Cracow cemetery.

ROBERT MORLEY

Robert Morley was born in Semley, Wiltshire, on 26 May 1908. He was the second child and only son of Major Robert Morley, retired from the Fourth Royal Irish Dragoon Guards, a noted gambler at the tables, on the horses and with life generally, and of Gertrude Emily Fass, known as Daisy and very much a woman of her time, solitary, shy and subject to attacks of the vapours, who wanted nothing so much as that her son should be 'something in the Empire'. Robert disliked his schooldays. He moved about a good deal as the family fortunes rose and fell, and attended Wellington College but did not stay the course. After a stab at education on the Continent he went to RADA; he made his first appearance on the professional stage while a student there, in a Christmas production of *Treasure Island* at the Strand Theatre with Arthur Bouchier. Young Morley played an elderly pirate. He left RADA before the final student production and began his ten years 'on the road'.

His first tour, which lasted nearly a year, was with Russell Thorndike in a play Thorndike had adapted from his own novel, *Dr Syn*. Robert played the Squire of Dymchurch. He was next the assistant stage manager of a long tour of *And So to Bed*. At the Playhouse in Oxford, under the direction of J. B. Fagan, he was a butler in *The Importance of Being Earnest*, and appeared in J. M. Barrie's one-act play, *Half an Hour*. While there he also got his first review. It was of his performance in Shaw's *Arms and the Man*, and the local critic wrote that 'Robert Morley acted well as the Russian peasant Servant'. In 1933 he was at the Festival Theatre in Cambridge for a season directed by Norman Marshall, among other roles playing Herod in *Salome*. At the Royalty Theatre in London in November 1933 he was Oakes in *Up In the Air* and was then back on the road touring with Sir Frank Benson in H. V. Neilson's Shakespeare Company. During 1934 he toured as the Rev. Vernon Isopod in *Late*

Night Final, and during 1935 was Gloucester in *Richard of Bordeaux*, still on the road. That year he wrote his first play, *Short Story*, which was produced at the Queen's Theatre in London with an all-star cast including Marie Tempest, A. E. Matthews, Sybil Thorndike and Rex Harrison.

For the summer of 1936 he and his actor friend Peter Bull established a summer theatre in the Women's Institute building at Perranporth in Cornwall. There Robert played a variety of roles, in *Rope*, *Springtime for Henry*, *To See Ourselves* and *The Murder in the Red Barn*, as well as helping in the box office and shifting scenery.

Robert's great chance came in September 1936 when he opened at the Gate Theatre playing Oscar Wilde in a play of that name by Sewell and Leslie Stokes. It was to be a six-week run at this club theatre — at that time the subject of homosexuality could not be passed for a major theatre by the censor. The *Saturday Review* reported: 'I cannot speak too highly of Mr Robert Morley's unforgettable performance as Wilde. His was no easy task but he carried it out with a delicacy and yet a forcefulness which I could not over-praise if I tried. I have added Mr Morley to my collection of actors who really know how to act.' The house was packed for the entire run.

In May 1937 he played Alexandre Dumas in *The Great Romancer* at the New Theatre for a special Sunday night performance. So great was the critical response that the show opened for a run at the Strand Theatre in June. The *Evening News* raved: 'With what an assured sweep of swagger he endows the hero! How cleverly he manages his voice so as to give a continuous air of impromptu wit to his conversation! How delicately he introduces the little touches of sentiment ...' Robert Morley was declared a star overnight, but the production lasted only twelve days, so he went back to Perranporth with Peter Bull. That summer they staged the première of Morley's new play

Goodness, How Sad, and Robert played the part of Chasuble in *The Importance of Being Earnest*. Then in September he returned to London to the Old Vic, where, directed by Tyrone Guthrie, he played Henry Higgins in *Pygmalion*.

Robert Morley made his first film in 1938. It was in Hollywood and with Norma Shearer. He played Louis XVI in *Marie Antoinette*, and was nominated for an Academy Award for his performance.

On 10 October 1938 he made his New York début at the Fulton Theater as Oscar Wilde. Brooks Atkinson wrote in the *New York Times*: 'Speaking some of the most perfect apophthegms an actor ever got hold of, Mr Morley knows how to phrase them with grace and humor and how to distinguish a cultivated wit from a common wisecracker. As far as the part goes, one feels instinctively that this is the truth of Oscar Wilde, who was no cheap phenomenon but a "lord of language" as he once immodestly phrased it. Mr Morley is an actor of very superior stature whose coming into our theater is an event.' He played more than eight months on Broadway, and then returned for the 1939 summer season at Perranporth. This closed early when war was declared. Robert had hoped for an American tour of *Oscar Wilde* but the war cancelled that, and he signed with Gabriel Pascal to play in the film of *Major Barbara*. It was eleven months in production during which time, on 22 February 1940 at Caxton Hall in London, he married Joan Buckmaster, daughter of Captain Herbert Buckmaster of Buck's Club, and the actress Gladys Cooper.

Robert's next venture into the theatre after *Major Barbara* was as Decius Hess in *Play with Fire*. It closed on tour. He was luckier with his next play — the Kaufman and Hart *The Man Who Came to Dinner*, which opened at the Savoy in December 1941 with Robert playing Sheridan Whiteside. His first son, appropriately named Sheridan, was born on the first night — and the reviews were good too. The play ran for two years in the West End and then toured. During the run Robert made some films which included *The Foreman Went to France* and *The Young Mr Pitt*.

In February 1944 he toured as Charles in his own play *Staff Dance* with Bea Lillie, but the production never made it to London. He opened at the New Theatre in July 1945 playing the Prince Regent in *The First Gentleman*. After a transfer to the Savoy it ran for more than a year in London.

Robert Morley opened at the His Majesty's Theatre in May 1947 playing Arnold Holt in the play he had written with Noel Langley, *Edward, My Son*. It transferred to the Lyric Theatre in Sep-

tember and went on running there with John Clements in the Arnold Holt part while Morley opened on Broadway with it at the Martin Beck Theater in September 1948. He took it on to Australia and New Zealand in 1949 and finally, after three years in the part, returned to England in 1950. In August he opened once more at the Lyric, this time playing Philip in *The Little Hut*, directed by Peter Brook. *The Little Hut* ran for more than two years. At the same theatre in April 1954 he played Hippo in *Hippo Dancing*, which he had adapted from the French of André Roussin. The *Daily Telegraph* reported: 'A curious play and not really a very good one ... All the same I think it will draw the public. The tremendous gusto of Mr Morley's performance, if it does not carry him off by spontaneous combustion early in the run, will be an irresistible attraction.' It ran more than a year. At the Globe Theatre in March 1956 he played a dual role, that of Oswald Petersham and his son Jonah, in *A Likely Tale* which Kenneth Tynan referred to simply as 'irrelevant theatre', and was soon into rehearsal for his first musical play. It was *Fanny*, in which he played Panisse, and it opened at Drury Lane in November 1956. Robert Morley, tone-deaf, never really came to terms with the orchestra. At this time, with his agent Robin Fox, Robert entered into management. Their first production starred Yvonne Arnaud in a play Robert had written with Dundas Hamilton, *Six Months' Grace*, but their second was the more successful. Robert directed Ian Carmichael in *Tunnel of Love*, which ran at Her Majesty's for a year.

In November 1958 he opened at the Piccadilly Theatre as Sebastian Le Boeuf in another adaptation from the French, *Hook, Line and Sinker*, but this one ran only four months. He then directed *Once More with Feeling* at the New Theatre, and in March 1960 played the Japanese Mr Asano in *A Majority of One*. 'Morley with eyebrows thinned, face yellowed and the famous expressions disciplined,' wrote one critic, 'manages to convince us that, while still manifestly Robert Morley, he is also a Japanese textile tycoon.'

He played the title part in Ronald Gow's *Mr Rhodes* at the Theatre Royal in Windsor in October 1961, and back at the Piccadilly in April 1962 he was the Bishop in *A Time to Laugh*, one of his few real disasters. It closed in three weeks. He spent the 1966–67 season touring Australia in his one-man show, *The Sound of Morley*, and returned to London to the Queen's in November 1967 playing Sir Mallalieu Fitzbuttress in Peter Ustinov's *Halfway Up the Tree*. Irving Wardle said: 'The main justification for this play is that it tempted Robert Morley back on the London stage.'

It ran for more than a year in the West End. Next he was Frank Foster in Alan Ayckbourn's *How the Other Half Loves* at the Lyric. It ran for two years in London, and he then played it in Canada and in Australia in 1973. At the Savoy in August 1976 he played Barnstable in *Ghost on Tiptoe*, which he wrote with Rosemary Anne Sisson. Jeremy Kingston reported in *Punch*: 'Robert Morley is hard to resist: a powerful personality, always fun to watch and nearly always worth watching. He stomps about the stage, heaving himself from chair to sofa, crushing the spirit out of defenceless cushions . . . but the plays he now stars in tend to be less sturdy than he, and this is a pity. He has always disparaged his abilities, holding them, like Coward, to be little more than "a talent to amuse". But he does also have the talent to move, which his plays permit him to exercise just once or twice but never more often.' *Ghost on Tiptoe* ran for a year. His next play was a solidly constructed farce — Ben Travers' *Banana Ridge*, which Robert played at the Savoy in 1976. In 1978

he returned to the one-man show format with *Robert Morley Talks to Everybody*, in which he told stories of his life, acted out scenes from plays and recited poetry; but he found it very hard work, physically and emotionally, and missed the camaraderie of the theatre. With John Wells he wrote *Picture of Innocence*, in which he played a high court judge who also happens to be a transvestite. He toured this and played it in Canada but decided, probably wisely, that the West End was not ready for the sight of him in blue eyeshadow, wig and twinset.

Robert Morley has made more than sixty-five films, and has starred in television productions in England, the United States and Australia. He has also become a most welcome guest on that television phenomenon, the 'chat show', and during the 1970s and 1980s as the commercial spokesman for British Airways in America. He received the CBE in the 1957 New Year Honours. *See photograph opposite page 279.*

ZERO MOSTEL

Samuel Joel Mostel was born on 28 February 1915 in Brooklyn, New York, where his father was a rabbi. He went to Seward Park High School in New York and, determined to be a painter, studied at City College of New York and earned a Bachelor of Arts, after which he went on to graduate art study.

He tried a number of occupations to subsidize his painting, including working on the docks, in factories, and actually teaching art, for the WPA. His lectures became famous. Al Hirschfeld, the caricaturist, said, ' . . . he used to imitate wallpaper, a percolator, all sorts of abstract things. You could see the steam coming from the top of his head.'

He made his first stage appearance at clubs in Greenwich Village, where he was one of the first stand-up comics to delve into political satire. Press agent Ivan Black gave him the name Zero, but the actor himself said it was a comment on his academic prowess. As a comic in the clubs he had instant success, his salary rising from $40 to $4000 a week in the short span of a year.

Zero Mostel made his Broadway début in April 1942 in a vaudeville production called *Keep 'em Laughing* at the 44th Street Theater. The following year he was serving in the army as a private in the infantry.

He made his film début in 1943, though he was miscast by MGM as Paliostro and Rami in *Du Barry Was a Lady*.

Zero Mostel was back on Broadway in *Concert Varieties* at the Ziegfeld in June 1945, and at the Broadway Theater in December 1946 he played Hamilton Peachum in *Beggar's Holiday*. He went to Hollywood, where he appeared in a string of movies in the early fifties before becoming a victim of the McCarthy witch hunts. The blacklist closed the doors of filming to him for a time and he returned to Broadway, where he played Glubb in *Flight into Egypt* at the Music Box in March 1952. In July of that year he was at the Brattle Theater in Cambridge, Massachusetts, playing in his own adaptation of *The Imaginary Invalid*. At the Downtown National Theater in New York he was Maxie Fields in *A Stone for Danny Fisher* in October 1954, and he played Dan Cupid in *Lunatics and Lovers* on tour during 1955. Back on Broadway in December 1956 he was Shu Fu in *The Good Woman of Setzuan* at the Phoenix, and was Doc Penny in *Good as Gold* at the Belasco in March 1957.

In June 1958 Zero Mostel opened at the Rooftop Theater in New York as Leopold Bloom in *Ulysses in Nighttown*. This production, conceived and directed by Burgess Meredith, was Padraic Colum's version of the 'Nighttown' section of James Joyce's *Ulysses*. Brooks Atkinson reported for the *New York Times*: 'Zero Mostel is the perfect Leopold Bloom. Around him the dreams and hallucinations, the feeling of guilt, the delusions of grandeur spiral off into a mad rigadoon. But Mr Mostel's Bloom provides a solid center of gravity — derby hat, cutaway coat, mustache, resonant voice, bulging eyes, clumsy hands, the Philistine among revelers ... it is Mr Mostel who pulls the whole production together with his solid characterization of the amiable, commonplace Bloom.' He received the Village Voice Off-Broadway Award (Obie) for this performance. The production came to London, to the Arts Theatre, in May 1959 and Caryl Brahms reported for *Plays and Players*: 'In Mr Zero Mostel who plays Leopold Bloom, we find an inspired clown, granted that his face, a putty moon, does his tumbling for him. His broad loose hands, his ambling and his giggle, his large eyes swimming with self-reproach, or shining with absurd defiance, his squalors and his grandeurs are peculiar to himself. He is a stomach of a man.' The production went on to Amsterdam, The Hague and Paris, where Mostel was named the best actor at the International Festival.

At the Longacre in January 1961 he was John in Ionesco's *Rhinoceros*. Brooks Atkinson was not entirely taken with the play but said: '... it did provide a great clown and actor Zero Mostel with a chance to change from man to rhinoceros before the eyes of the audience, and Mr Mostel accomplished that impossible transubstantiation magnificently for 240 performances.' During the run of *Rhinoceros* it was reported he said to a friend: 'Tonight I gotta concentrate. This afternoon, I got it all wrong and turned into a cow by mistake.' He toured the United States with this production, and won a Tony Award as best actor in 1961.

In May 1962 he opened at the Alvin Theater on Broadway playing Pseudolus and Prologus in the musical *A Funny Thing Happened on the Way to the Forum*. He got his second Tony for this performance and continued in it for nearly two years before making the film version.

As Tevye the Milkman he opened at the Imperial Theater in September 1964 in *Fiddler on the Roof*. Howard Taubman reported: 'Mr Mostel looks as Tevye should ... does not keep his acting and singing or his walking and dancing in separate compartments. His Tevye is a unified, lyrical conception ... And in Mr Mostel's Tevye [Broadway] has one of the most glowing creations in the history of the musical theater.' And Martin Gottfried wrote: 'Mr Mostel's praises have been sung to the skies, but it is time to sing them to the heavens. To see him dance is to see an angel in underwear, to listen in on his conversations with God is to be privy to the secret of life ... There is no one else on earth who can shake a belly slowly ... God must surely be Mostel's friend, he talks with Him so easily. God is not so easy to talk to on a Broadway stage ...' *Fiddler on the Roof* went on to become Broadway's longest-running musical, although Mostel stayed with it only a year. He did, however, receive the New York Drama Critics Award for his performance, as well as his third Tony.

At the Kalita Humphreys Theater in Dallas, Texas, in March 1968 he took the title role in *The Latent Heterosexual*. In October 1971, at the Long Island Music Fair, he once more played in *Fiddler on the Roof*, and in November 1973 there he played in *A Funny Thing Happened on the Way to the Forum*. At the Winter Garden in March 1974 he revived *Ulysses in Nighttown* and spent 1976 touring in *Fiddler on the Roof*.

Zero Mostel was in Philadelphia, preparing for out of town tryouts of Arnold Wesker's version of *The Merchant of Venice*, in which Mostel played Shylock, when he was stricken with a respiratory illness and taken to hospital. He died on 8 September 1977 from cardiac arrest. As Clive Barnes wrote of Mostel's last revival of *Fiddler on the Roof*: 'Mr Mostel has no real right to be charming. But he could charm the birds off the trees in a deserted aviary. He is the kind of monster you would unavailingly search Loch Ness for, and, in passing, make into a legend.'

OWEN NARES

Owen Nares was undoubtedly a star — a matinée idol — and he was indeed beautiful. He was also a very serious actor, though he would probably have been an even better one if he had stretched himself beyond pleasant roles.

His maternal grandfather was the great scenic artist William Roxby Beverley, and his uncle was an actor, as was his elder half-brother. His father, William Owen Nares, was a great sportsman who founded the Berkshire County Cricket Club, a country gentleman who earned his living by running a school for army candidates.

Owen Nares was born on 11 August 1888 in Maiden Erleigh, Berkshire, but soon the family moved to Reading and then to Sonning. There, Owen, taking after his father, became a great sportsman — he played cricket, rowed, and even golfed at a tender age. He made his first stage appearance, aged six, at the Sonning Village Hall where he played a Page in a play in aid of the local cricket club. The family went to the local theatre in Reading every week and saw many of the great stars of the time on tour. He remembered that he saw his first London play at the Haymarket when he was seven. It was Barrie's *The Little Minister* and made a lasting impression on him.

When Owen Nares was 14, at Speech Day at Reading School he played the First Lord in *As You Like It*, and the following year the school hired the County Theatre in Reading for a special matinée of *Ion*, the Greek tragedy by Reading's old boy, Sir Thomas Noon Talfourd. Owen played the lead, a part originated by Macready. His mother was highly impressed with his performance and determined that he should be a professional actor. She wrote to Sir Herbert Beerbohm Tree at His Majesty's, where he saw Owen during the interval of a matinée of *Richard II*. 'He ought to be on the stage,' the great Tree pronounced, 'he's got a Greek head.'

Nares left school soon afterwards, and his half-brother Evelyn, who was touring with Seymour Hicks, arranged an introduction to Rosina Filippi, the acting teacher with whom Nares studied for six months in London. He was still with her when he got his first professional part, on 28 January 1908, walking on at the Haymarket in *Her Father*, which starred Marie Lohr. He then wrote to the stage manager of the prestigious St James's Theatre and got a job as 'walking understudy' to Reginald Owen in Pinero's *The Thunderbolt*. No appearance was necessary unless the actor fell ill, so during this time Owen Nares played with Miss Filippi's company in open-air shows at Ranelagh.

In autumn 1908 Owen Nares went off on a tour in *The Thief*, playing Harry Leyton with the St James's Company. Also in the company was the actress Marie Polini, and before the Christmas break they became secretly engaged. After the spring tour he returned to the St James's, where he had small parts — in May 1909 it was in *Old Heidelberg* and in September *Mid-Channel*.

It was then discovered that Owen Nares had incipient tuberculosis, and he spent nearly a year in a sanatorium in the Chilterns. All his life he was plagued by ill health, but somehow managed to remain an active sportsman as well as a constantly employable actor both on stage and in films, though he was uninsurable.

In autumn 1910 he set off on a tour of *Old Heidelberg* playing Karl Heinrich, Sir George Alexander's London role. In January 1911 he was at the Little Theatre playing Bobby Lechmere in Henry James's ghost play, *The Saloon*. Before the spring tour of *Old Heidelberg* he married Marie Polini, though soon afterwards she went on tour with Marie Tempest. He was Kenyon Shawardine in *The Crucible*, a comedy by Hemmerde and Neilson, at the Comedy Theatre in June 1911 with Henry Ainley, but it was not a success and he was back at the St James's in September playing Tony Sitgrave in *The Ogre* by Henry Arthur Jones. It starred George Alexander, and there Owen Nares met Gladys Cooper, who also had a small role. The production, however, was not a success, and the following month they presented a revival of *Lady Windermere's Fan*, in which Nares played Cecil Graham.

He was briefly in the *The Great Gay Road* by Tom Gallon at the Court Theatre and then, in January 1912 at the Little Theatre, he had his first real success, playing the Hon. Archibald Graham in Cosmo Hamilton's *The Blindness of Virtue*. The author reported: 'Owen Nares, unknown to London, was watched with immense interest and instant liking and when, at the end of the third act, he rose to a great height of genuine and poignant emotion, he brought down the house.' Nares, however, had to leave this success still running because of a prior contract at the Royalty to play Lord Monkhurst in *Milestones*. He was only in the last act but it was a showy part, and opposite him played Gladys Cooper. *Milestones* ran for nearly a year but as he was not needed until the last act he worked in curtain raisers and sketches at other theatres, including the Prince's, the Haymarket and the Court.

In March 1913, Gerald du Maurier revived *Diplomacy* at Wyndham's and Owen Nares played Julian Beauclerc, the part originated by Forbes-Robertson. The production ran for fourteen months and included a Royal Command performance at Windsor Castle.

He was in an 'all-star' revival in aid of the King George Pension Fund on 22 May 1914 at His Majesty's playing Frank Selwyn in *The Silver King*. He opened at the Haymarket in June 1914 playing Captain Furness in *Driven*, but business was not good once war had broken out.

He was briefly at the Vaudeville in October playing John Woodhouse in *The Cost*, and the following month went to His Majesty's where he played his first and last Shakespearian role — Prince Hal in *Henry IV Part 1*. One paper reported: 'As Prince Hal, Mr Owen Nares experienced great difficulty with his armour; but that was nothing to the difficulty he experienced with his part!' To his great relief the production lasted only a month, and he was soon playing the title role at the same theatre in *David Copperfield*. That February at Covent Garden he was Sir Toby in *The School for Scandal* for a charity matinée. After *David Copperfield* he was in two failures at the St James's Theatre: *The Panorama of Youth* in May 1915 and *The Day Before the Day* the following month.

He was deemed unfit for active service during the war, but even though he was onstage nearly every night he worked during the day at King George's Hospital as assistant transport officer. He next spent a season in the music halls in a sketch with Mademoiselle Dorziat. During that time, for charity matinées he played Thomas Cromwell in *Henry VIII* and Peter in *Peter Ibbetson*, which remained his favourite part.

At the Duke of York's in October 1915 he played the Bishop and Thomas Armstrong in the American success, *Romance*. It starred and was produced by Doris Keane. She, however, was not well on the opening night and the notices were lukewarm; audiences were not encouraged by a Zeppelin attack on the second night. After playing to sparse audiences for a fortnight they were given notice by the management to quit the theatre. However, almost immediately business improved so in November they moved to the Lyric, where the show ran to full houses for two years. Nares left after twenty-one months and opened at the Globe Theatre in October 1917 playing Edward Hamilton in *The Willow Tree*. That was not a success, and in December he was at the Palace in his first musical play, *Pamela*, in which he was

Guy Tremayne. Then at the Victoria Palace in September 1918 he played Philip in a sketch by A. A. Milne, *The Boy Comes Home*. Back at the Palace in September 1918 he was in another musical revue, *Hullo! America*, which starred Elsie Janis. When he left the show he was succeeded by Maurice Chevalier.

On 8 March 1919 he entered into management in conjunction with Sir Alfred Butt at the Queen's Theatre. During his time there he played the Count Paul de Virieu in *The House of Peril*, Anthony Quintard in *The Cinderella Man*, and Arthur John Carrington in *Mr Todd's Experiment*. Those three plays took him through two years, and when he retired from management he went to the Playhouse, in August 1920, where with Gladys Cooper and Edith Evans he starred in the American comedy, *Wedding Bells*. At the Comedy in December 1921 he played Peter Bevans in *The Charm School*, and the following May at the Aldwych was Kit Harwood in *Love Among the Paint Pots* and Larry Darrant in *The First and the Last*. He then toured the provinces in *The Charm School*. He returned to London in July 1921 where at the Aldwych he played Jim Chevrell in *James the Less*; at the Duke of York's in March 1922 he was Oliver Bashforth in *The Enchanted Cottage*.

In August 1922 he joined Bertie Meyer and produced a touring schedule for *If Winter Comes* in which he played Mark Sabre. They took over the management of the St James's in London and brought the show into town in January 1923. The following month he played Hugh Paton in *Half an Hour* for a charity matinée at His Majesty's.

At the Queen's in November 1923 he was the Rev. Gavin Dishart in *The Little Minister* — a part he had longed to play since he was seven, when he first saw the play.

With Gladys Cooper in March 1924 he revived *Diplomacy*, once again playing Julian Beauclerc. They opened at the Adelphi, and including the later tour played 350 performances. While it was running he played Marston Gurney in *The Ware Case* for a charity matinée at the Aldwych. At the St James's Theatre in 1925 he played Maurice Sorbier in *Grounds for Divorce*, and followed that with Anthony Walford in *The River* before going on a tour of South Africa with *Diplomacy*, *Grounds for Divorce*, *Romance* and *The Last of Mrs Cheyney*. He was back in London at the Playhouse in October 1926 in a revival of *Romance*. At the St Martin's in March 1927 he played Jeremy Dairiven in *No Gentleman*, and at the Queen's the following month he took over from Nicholas Hannen playing John Freeman in *The Fanatics*. While that run continued he played Pietro Morelli in *The Wandering Jew* for a charity matinée at Drury Lane.

During 1928 he played Cary Liston in *Two White Arms* and Georges Duhamel in *The Man They Buried* in London at the Ambassadors' and on tour. Returning to London in January 1929 he played Tony Ambersham in *Living Together* at Wyndham's and in April at the Duke of York's was Kenneth Vail in *These Few Ashes*. At the Palace in June he played Jim Brooks in *Hold Everything* and in September he was Garry Anson in *The Calendar*.

Owen Nares was at the New Theatre in 1930 playing Victor Gresham in *The Last Chapter* in May, and Desire Tronchais in his own production of *Desire* in July. The following month he took over from Raymond Massey at the Ambassadors' playing Raymond Dabney in *The Man in Possession*. He spent early 1931 touring the provinces in *Cynara*, in which he played Jim Warlock, and in June came into the Embassy as Peter in *Delicate Question*. At the Strand in August he was Logan in *Counsel's Opinion*.

At the Apollo in April 1932 he played André Poole in *Pleasure Cruise*, and at the Haymarket in October 1932 was Gerald Graham in *Once a Husband*. He was still at the Haymarket in January 1933, playing John Rockingham in *Double Harness*. He went to the Lyric in April, where he played Jimmie Lee in *When Ladies Meet*, and then on to Wyndham's in November where he was Toby Strang in *Man Proposes*. In March 1934 he played Robert Van Brett in *Double Door* at the Globe, and in May was at the Comedy playing Henry in *All's Over Then*. That was not a success, and the same month he took over from Godfrey Tearle at the Criterion playing Sir John Corbett in *Sixteen* before going to the Vaudeville in October to play Roger Storer in *Lovers' Leap*.

He opened 1935 at the Globe playing Randolph Warrender in *Youth at the Helm*, and in October, still at the Globe, was Roger Hilton, the respectable accountant in Dodie Smith's *Call It a Day*. His son played his stage son in this production, which ran for fifteen months. At the same theatre, in July 1937 he played John Fothergill in *They Came by Night*; and in November, also at the Globe — which by this time must have seemed very like home — he began an eighteen-month run as Robert Carson in *Robert's Wife* by St John Ervine. Audrey Williamson reported: 'Edith Evans and

Owen Nares played admirably in the leads; her overruling enthusiasm and courage were finely matched with his quiet and pleasant integrity.' In 1942 at the Globe, Owen Nares played the Leslie Howard part in Sherwood's *The Petrified Forest*, while the other two principal parts were played by Constance Cummings and Hartley Power. Unfortunately the production, though very good, suffered by comparison with the already released Humphrey Bogart film.

Owen Nares began in films in 1913 and played many roles, both in silent and in talking roles, but he never took the cinema seriously — it seemed to him just 'too easy'. He died on 31 July 1943 aged only 54. The critic W. A. Darlington summed up his career thus: 'With Owen Nares I had a valued personal friendship, which went, I suppose, as deep as any friendship can between an actor and a practising critic. It was an episodic relationship developed chiefly on the pleasantly neutral ground of cricket-field and golf-course. Mixed with my strong liking for him was a growing respect ... Owen's face was his fortune up to a certain point and his misfortune beyond it, that his absurd good looks made a matinée idol of him when he was in himself a serious actor; and ... the delicacy of those good looks, while it attracted women, was apt to create in some men — especially the hearty athletic kind of men — a violent antipathy and contempt ... When I came to know him well I was ashamed to remember that I had myself had a prejudice against him on the same account; for the delicacy of his appearance was the outward sign of an extremely delicate constitution ... What made the situation more ironic was that he was a very fine natural game-player ... I have laid stress on my admiration for Owen Nares's character and my affection for his memory in order to emphasize the point he illustrates, that a theatre in which an actor of his type could rank as a leader was a theatre lacking in quality, in variety, and in resource. Seriously though he took his profession, and earnestly though he worked to deserve his success, he was not (and I am sure he did not consider himself) an artist of any high degree of talent. He was a man essentially of his hour, a mark to aim at for all the intelligent young men with easy manners and well-cut coats who were now streaming onto the stage. What Owen Nares had done, they aspired to do — that and no more.'

ANNA NEAGLE

'The public adore her — especially the women — because she has all the appeal of a terribly nice person. She is the sort of good neighbour everyone would like to have. No star has ever been less theatrical than Anna Neagle. She gives the impression of being a genuine person, who looks most elegant through choosing simplicity as her guiding motif. Backstage with her colleagues she is just as congenial. She never demands star treatment and because of that always gets it.' Thus does the director Freddie Carpenter sum up Anna Neagle.

She was born Marjorie Robertson in 1904 in Forest Gate, London, the youngest child and only daughter of a sea captain, Herbert William Robertson, and his wife Florence Neagle. As a child she had dancing lessons with Judith Espinosa, not in preparation for a career on the stage — her father remained set against that for some time — but merely as little girls take dancing lessons. She made her stage début in a 1917 Christmas Show at the Ambassadors', where she danced with other pupils in J. B. Fagan's *The Wonder Tales*. After leaving school she decided that the quickest way to a job was as a dancer. Her first job was at the Duke of York's in June 1925 when she was hired by André Charlot for the chorus of *Bubbly*. She spent the next five years in the chorus — she was in Charlot's revue at the Prince of Wales Theatre in September 1925, and in March 1926 was at Drury Lane in the chorus of *Rose Marie*. In October 1926, she opened in the chorus of the *Charlot Revue of 1926* at the Prince of Wales and was back at Drury Lane in April 1927 in the chorus of *The Desert Song*. She was in the chorus of Noel Coward's *This Year of Grace* at the London Pavilion in March 1928. During this time she also danced in cabaret after the shows at the Trocadero. 'When I was in the chorus,' she said, 'I had no idea what it meant to an actor given the responsibility of playing a leading role. Nor did I realize the price idolized players had to pay for their stardom. Even so, it was exciting to be in shows with such famous people as Bea Lillie, Gertie Lawrence, Jack Buchanan, Jessie Matthews and Edith Day, and a great advantage to be chosen to work with them in their numbers.'

In March 1929 she was a dancer in *Wake Up and Dream* at the London Pavilion, and went to New York with the show where she made her American début at the Selwyn Theater on 30 December 1929. While in New York she developed a great desire not to go back into the chorus and took singing and tap lessons. She returned to England to be offered the second understudy to Jessie Matthews and a job in the chorus of *Ever Green* by Cochran, but turned it down. She began auditioning for work, but was always paralysed with fear. She finally got a small part in a film, *The Chinese Bungalow*, and the producer persuaded her to change her name — Marjorie Robertson became Anna Neagle.

Jack Buchanan, who had starred in her New York show, was producing *Stand Up and Sing* and needed an ingénue. He decided that if they tailored the part carefully she could do it, and she opened in it playing Mary Clyde-Burkin at Southampton in December 1930, coming to London to the Hippodrome in March 1931. Herbert Wilcox, the film producer, who was looking for someone to star opposite Buchanan in *Goodnight, Vienna* saw her in it and decided she would do nicely. From then he organized her career as well as could any Svengali. He also fell in love with her and asked her to marry him, the only snag being that he was already a husband and the father of small children.

After making a great success with her early Wilcox movies, Anna Neagle next appeared on stage in May 1934 at the Regent's Park Open Air Theatre playing Rosalind in *As You Like It* and Olivia in *Twelfth Night* (opposite Jack Hawkins). For Christmas 1937 she was Peter Pan at the London Palladium. That same year she had an enormous success in the film of *Victoria the Great*. She went to Hollywood in 1939, where she made more films. After the outbreak of war she and Herbert Wilcox returned to England, and in 1943 — he had finally managed a divorce — they married. She went on an ENSA tour in England and on the Continent in 1944 with Rex Harrison and Roland Culver in *French Without Tears*.

In 1944 she toured before a planned London opening as Emma Woodhouse in Gordon Glenn's adaptation of Jane Austen's novel, *Emma*. It was a very successful tour, and they opened at the St James's Theatre in London in February 1945. Unfortunately the German doodle-bugs arrived at the same time, and the show closed. It remains, however, Anna Neagle's favourite part.

Anna Neagle went back to films and made an enormous success with such titles as *Piccadilly Incident*, *The Courtneys of Curzon Street*, *Spring in Park Lane* and *Odette*. She was the International Top Box-Office Actress, according to the British Exhibitors Box-Office Poll, from 1949 through 1952. In 1952 she returned to the stage and toured in *The Glorious Days*, an entertainment specially written to cash in on her film successes. She played Carol Beaumont, Nell Gwynn, Victoria and Lilia Grey in this production, which opened at the Palace in London in February 1953. On stage Anna Neagle was never the darling of the critics, but perhaps Kenneth Tynan went fractionally too far when he wrote: '*The Glorious Days* can best be described — to adapt a phrase of George Kaufman's — as Anna Neagle rolled into one. Here she is, anthologized at last, available once nightly in the large economy size; dipping into the fabled store of her talents, she brings up a horn of plenty from which she pours, with cautious rapture, three dwarf acorns. First, she acts, in a fashion so devoid of personality as to be practically incognito; second she sings, shaking her voice at the audience like a tiny fist; and third, she dances, in that non-committal, twirling style, once known as "skirt-dancing" which was originally invented (or so Shaw tells us) to explain the presence on stage of genteel young women who could neither sing nor act.' The show ran for 256 performances.

She appeared in her first straight play at the Strand in 1960, playing Stella Felby in Ronald Millar's *The More the Merrier*. In July 1961 she was at the Lyceum, Edinburgh, playing Ruth Peterson in *Nothing Is for Free*, a title which proved too sadly true for Anna Neagle and her husband Herbert Wilcox. The film company went bankrupt, which meant selling all their possessions and property and moving to a small flat in Brighton. They thought of opening a string of dance schools à la Arthur Murray, with Anna's name, but that too failed. However, they managed to keep the rent paid and the cats fed. Anna Neagle toured as Jane Canning in a thriller called *Person Unknown* in 1963, and then in December 1965 all was well when she opened as Lady Hadwell at the Adelphi in *Charlie Girl* with Joe Brown, Hy Hazell, Derek Nimmo and David Toguri. The critics absolutely slaughtered it but John Russell Taylor noted that, though the plot was out of the

Ark, the evening was tailored to suit the talents of those involved and what was so very wrong with that? Anna Neagle herself said, 'I think it was the sort of family show audiences had been waiting for . . . There were good tunes.' They must have been because *Charlie Girl* played 2000 performances at the Adelphi. During the run, in the Birthday Honours of 1969 she became a Dame. She took *Charlie Girl* to Melbourne in 1971 and to Auckland in 1972, playing in it for a total of six years and four months.

When she returned to England, feeling unwell, she discovered she had cancer, but the operation was completely successful and she was soon back on the stage, this time opening in May 1973 as Sue Smith in a revival of *No, No, Nanette*. *Plays and Players* called it a 'creaking disaster', and Michael Coveney reported: 'Miss Neagle walks pleasantly but unimpressively down the stairs and sings the song ['I Want To Be Happy'] again. She then dances to the tune, which, with the lumbering intrusion of a vulgar simultaneous tap routine in the chorus, winds the scene up into an orgy of magnificently anti-climactic proportions. Would Miss Neagle's energy hold out for the whole scene? It did and her achievement in this respect is wondrous to behold.' This 'creaking disaster' ran eight months in London.

At the Duke of York's in 1975 she took over from Celia Johnson as Dame Sibyl Hathaway in William Douglas-Home's *The Dame of Sark* and then toured in March 1976 as Janet Fraser in *The First Mrs Fraser*. For the Silver Jubilee in 1977 she appeared at the Theatre Royal in Windsor in *Most Gracious Lady*, and at the Shaftesbury in London in October of that year was the Comtesse de la Brière in *Maggie*. Then in 1978 she began a massive tour playing Henry Higgins' mother in *My Fair Lady*. By this time Herbert Wilcox, the guiding force in her career, had died, but Anna Neagle showed absolutely no sign of retiring from the stage.

JOHN NEVILLE

John Neville was born on 2 May 1925 in Church Road, Willesden, a northern suburb of London. His father was a mechanic for the local council and he had one younger sister. He was an extremely average schoolboy who enjoyed games and was not over-enthusiastic about studying. He produced his first play — *Pyramus and Thisbe* — at school, and played Starveling when he was 11. By the age of 14 he was an ardent Shakespearian.

He was given a scholarship to RADA , but in 1943 was drafted into the Navy and it was October 1947 before he was able to enter RADA. He was still there when he made his stage début at the New Theatre, walking on in Alec Guinness's *Richard II*. After leaving drama school he was Bassanio in *The Taming of the Shrew* mornings and afternoons at Camberwell Palace and Toynbee Hall for children. Then he went to Regent's Park Open Air Theatre for the 1948 season, where he played Chatillon the Ambassador in *King John*, the First Lord in *As You Like It* and Lysander in *A Midsummer Night's Dream*.

He then went to Lowestoft for a season in weekly rep and then on to the Birmingham Repertory Company where he played small parts from January 1949 through March 1950. There he met the actress Caroline Hooper; they were married in December 1949. They left Birmingham for London, but it was only a roundabout way of getting to the Bristol Old Vic where John Neville, now a father, spent three consecutive seasons from September 1950 through June 1953. The first season he was Richard in *The Lady's Not for Burning* and then Fenton in *The Merry Wives of Windsor*, a part that did not call for much apart from standing around and looking handsome, which he managed very nicely. *The Blind Goddess* gave him a crack at a character part, which he enjoyed. In 1951 he was Charles Surface in *The School for Scandal*, and in September of that year was in Anouilh's *The Traveller Without Luggage*. In February 1952 the Bristol Old Vic journeyed to the London Old Vic for a few weeks. John Neville was playing Valentine in *The Two Gentlemen of Verona*. The *Times* reported: 'Mr John Neville, looking rather like the young Mr Gielgud, brings to his wooing the hint of ease and aristocracy which is called for by comedy of this kind.' After London he went to Denmark to film some Hans Christian Andersen stories for television before returning to Bristol, where he was now given leading roles. He doubled the twins in *Ring Round the Moon* and played the Duke in *Measure for Measure*. His last Bristol part was Henry V; the critics were divided over it. For many years he would be haunted by his comparison with Gielgud, and this time was no exception. *Punch* reported: 'On all sides Mr Neville has been accused of imitating Sir John. The grounds seem to me to be slight. A more valid criticism is that in voice and manner he is still too limited for the full sweep of the part.'

John Neville joined the Old Vic Company at the beginning of their five-year plan to produce the entire first folio. For the 1953–54 season he was Fortinbras to Richard Burton's Hamlet, Lewis the Dauphin in *King John*, Orsino in *Twelfth Night*, Cominius (in a grizzled beard) in *Coriolanus*, Ferdinand in *The Tempest* and Bertram in *All's Well That Ends Well*. According to Derek Granger, in the last he had 'exactly the measure of cold superiority the part demands'.

For his second Old Vic season (1954–55) he played Macduff to Paul Rogers' Macbeth, and Berowne in *Love's Labour's Lost*, which according to Alan Dent was 'swift and humorous and lyric'. In January 1955 he opened as Richard II. J. C. Trewin reported: 'Neville's voice ruled the night. In early arrogance it glittered imperiously, like the crown he wore. In defeat it had a shining sorrow that waned to the afterglow at Pomfret.' He received one of the longest ovations in the modern history of the theatre, and took twenty-three curtain calls. Overnight he became a gallery hero, pursued by squealing girls and fawning reporters. That season he also played Orlando in *As You Like It*, with Virginia McKenna as Rosalind. He was Hotspur in *Henry IV Part 1* and Pistol in *Henry IV Part 2*. George Scott wrote: 'It is no disparagement to say that his Hotspur might have been anticipated. He has the stature, the presence and the vigour ... But his Pistol was an all-dominating, full-blooded triumph ... The bawdy lusty gestures of his hands, the eupeptic villainy of his expressions, do not weary; they are measured out nicely within the narrow limits of his part.'

The third season he was Mark Antony in *Julius Caesar*. The *Times* critic wrote: 'Once Caesar is dead and his own life is at stake, we can almost see the instinct of self-preservation growing in him with ugly consequences. His delivery of the oration over Caesar's body is magnificent in its variety and the real man stands plainly revealed in his harsh contempt for Lepidus and his instinctive respect for Octavius in the list-pricking scene.'

That same season he was also a controversial Bohemian spiv as Autolycus in *The Winter's Tale*. Richard Burton returned to the Old Vic Company to play *Henry V*, and Neville was the Chorus. The fans were sharply divided in their loyalty and gallery war broke out. Philip Hope Wallace reported: 'John Neville as Chorus, could not move a muscle without eliciting a loud bravo: Richard Burton dared not twitch his crown without waking a counter-cheer from the O.P. [Opposite prompt] side of the balcony.' This intense public reaction was pandered to when it was decided to alternate the two stars in the principal roles in *Othello*. Of Neville's playing of the title role, Kenneth Tynan said: 'In the grace notes Mr Neville was exemplary, the moments of sacrificial tenderness; he conveyed, even at the raging climax, a sense of pain at the treachery of Iago, whom once he had loved. The part's quiet dawn and its quiescent sunset were both there. What escaped the actor was the intervening tempest.' Of his Iago, Tynan said he was 'a capering spiv'. The critics were as sharply divided over the playing of the two actors as were their fans. Who was the better? Why was it a contest at all? But it was, and Milton Shulman sourly reflected: 'Shakespeare, I'm afraid, floored them both.' Also during that season Neville was Troilus in a modern dress *Troilus and Cressida*, and Romeo to Claire Bloom's Juliet.

John Neville then went with the Old Vic Company, first on a tour of Canada and then on to two and a half months at the Winter Garden Theater in New York followed by a tour around the United States. He made his New York début in October 1956 playing Romeo, and followed that with Richard II, Macduff, and Thersites in *Troilus and Cressida*. Brooks Atkinson wrote in the *New York Times* of his leading role: 'John Neville's Richard is a brilliant portrait that grows in stature as the King loses authority. There is nothing in Richard's unheroic character that Neville has not found some way to express in the unhurried flow of his performance.'

He returned to the Old Vic in London for the 1957–58 season, which he opened in September as Hamlet. Harold Hobson said it was 'the most satisfying, beautiful, most touching Hamlet I remember'. Kenneth Tynan wrote: 'John Neville resists agony with lips prefectorially stiff, and simply won't let go of his voice. Always there is effort, audible vocal effort, with the actor pushing for climaxes he might be able to reach if only he would stop pushing. He is first rate, however, in the hysteria that follows the interview with the ghost, which I have never seen better done.' He was Angelo in *Measure for Measure*, a production which was not a success and survived for only

fifteen performances. That year he had his first directing assignment, *The Summer of the Seventeenth Doll* at Bristol, and he played Henry V on television. At the Old Vic he was also Sir Andrew Aguecheek in *Twelfth Night*, and Harold Hobson said: 'Mr Neville makes of him a gentle, generous figure, whose grief it is that his taste and sensibility outdistance his intellect by a million miles.' He then toured Europe and the United States in *Hamlet* and *Twelfth Night* until February 1959.

John Neville had completed an enormous Shakespearian record — twenty-two parts in nineteen plays. It was time for something else, a modern play. He opened at the New Theatre in July 1959 as the eccentric, temperamental conductor Victor Fabian in the American light comedy, *Once More with Feeling*, playing opposite Dorothy Tutin and directed by Robert Morley. It lasted only fifty-two performances. In October he took over from Keith Michell at the Lyric as Nestor in the musical *Irma La Douce*, and loved every minute of his six months in it. During that time he also played Alfred Douglas in Robert Morley's film, *Oscar Wilde*. At the Arts Theatre in September 1960 he played Jacko in *The Naked Island*; at the Queen's in March 1961 he was with Vanessa Redgrave and Margaret Leighton in Ibsen's *The Lady from the Sea*; and at the Palace in Watford in May 1961 he played the Evangelist in *The Substitute*. The following September he joined the Nottingham Playhouse Company, where he was appointed associate director in December.

He was the theatre director there from 1963 to 1967. He played a variety of roles at Nottingham, including Macbeth, Sir Thomas More in *A Man for All Seasons* and Petruchio in *The Taming of the Shrew*. At the Haymarket in April 1962 he played Joseph Surface in *The School for Scandal* with Ralph Richardson and Margaret Rutherford. Caryl Brahms said he was an 'elegantly villainous Joseph'. In July 1962 he was at the opening of the Chichester Festival Theatre playing Don Frederick in Beaumont and Fletcher's *The Chances*, and Orgilus in John Ford's Jacobean bloodbath *The Broken Heart* with Fay Compton and Laurence Olivier. He returned to Nottingham in October 1962, where he directed *Twelfth Night* and played d'Artagnan in a musical he had adapted from *The Three Musketeers*. That year he also directed *A Subject of Scandal and Concern*.

In February 1963 for the British Council he toured with the Nottingham Playhouse Company in West Africa playing Macbeth. He opened at the Mermaid Theatre in London in June 1963 playing the title role in Bill Naughton's *Alfie*. He was the disarmingly charming, cocky, lady-killing spiv, and Martin Esslin said he 'carries his mammoth part with infinite wit and variety'. He transferred with the show to the Duchess, but in December returned to Nottingham where the new Playhouse had been constructed. There he starred in the opening production, *Coriolanus*. He stayed there directing and playing a number of roles, ranging from Richard II through Faust to Willy Loman, until 1967, when he had a blazing row with the board of directors whom he called 'a mediocre and lacklustre bunch of city men'.

At the Palace in December 1968 he played Henry Gow and Alec Harvey in a musical, *Mr and Mrs*, and at the Fortune in May 1969 he directed *Honour and Offer*. John Neville returned to the Mermaid in March 1970 to play King Magnus in *The Apple Cart*. Hugh Leonard said: 'The weight of the evening falls, of course, upon John Neville. At first sight Magnus seems to be no more than Mr Neville wearing a crown. Then we notice the melancholy. As a King Magnus is temperate, urbane, astute; as a man he is a disaster area . . . the loneliness of the man haunts one. What he gives us is subtle, eloquent, comic and — predominantly — very sad.' For Prospect Productions at the Edinburgh Festival in August 1970 he played Garrick in *Boswell's Life of Johnson* and Benedick in *Much Ado About Nothing*, and then toured the United States as Humbert Humbert in *Lolita*.

John Neville returned to the Chichester Festival in July 1972, where he played Sir Colenso Ridgeon in *The Doctor's Dilemma* and Macheath in *The Beggar's Opera*. Of the latter performance Helen Dawson wrote: 'As Macheath, John Neville occasionally looks a bit like Richard II fallen among thieves, and initially a shaky nasal Cockney twang sounded as though it was going to bung up his delivery. But, with a little less stiffness along the vertebrae, he'll make an attractively relaxed roué of a hero. Already his "If the heart of a Man", without playing for sentimentality, brings a catch to the throat and a tear to the eye.'

John Neville was then invited to go to Canada for a month to direct a production of *The Rivals* at the National Arts Centre in Ottawa, and he accepted happily. From there Winnipeg invited him to play Judge Brack in *Hedda Gabler* and then Ottawa invited him back for Prospero in *The Tempest*. He found he was getting better offers there than he could expect back home, and when the city of Edmonton, Alberta, asked him to take over a roughly converted Salvation Army citadel with no wing space, no flies and only 300 seats he accepted the challenge. There within two years he had built up a young Canadian company that could play the classics as well as modern plays and musicals. He also managed to build a new arts complex with two theatres, a cinema and classrooms.

In 1975 he returned to New York, where he took over the role of Sherlock Holmes at the Broadhurst Theater, but was soon back at the Citadel in Edmonton where he remained until 1977, occasionally bringing in stars like Peggy Ashcroft, who appeared there with him in *Dear Liar*. He made a fleeting appearance with Dame Peggy at London's National Theatre in September 1977 playing in Beckett's *Happy Days* before taking the production off to Canada.

In 1978 he moved on to Halifax, Nova Scotia, to a 500-seat ex-vaudeville theatre. 'People in Edmonton think I'm crazy to leave, having just got the new building open, but I want to move on precisely for that reason,' he said. 'There's not so much of a challenge there now, whereas Halifax needs the doctor. I'll be inheriting a deficit of a hundred and fifty thousand dollars and I want to see if I can write it off in the first year there. Then maybe we can think about a new theatre: I've already opened two and I'd quite like to go for the hat trick.'

In 1986 John Neville took over as director of the Shakespeare Festival in Stratford, Ontario.

IVOR
NOVELLO

David Ivor Davies was born in Cardiff on 15 January 1893, the son of David Davies, a tax collector and Clara Novello Davies, a music teacher and head of the Royal Welsh Ladies Choir which established an international reputation. Ivor had music lessons from his mother from a very early age, and by the time he was eight was obsessed by theatre — playing constantly with a toy theatre his mother had bought him. When he was ten, calling himself Ivor Cardiff to avoid being accused of cashing in on his famous mother's reputation, he took first prize in the National Eisteddfod at Aberystwyth singing a Bach aria. He won a scholarship to Magdalen College School in 1903, where he sang in the famous choir — solo soprano — until his voice broke. 'I am told,' he later said, 'that my singing then was exceptional, that it was quite the thing in Oxford musical circles in 1905 and 1906 to go and hear the solo boy at Magdalen.'

Ivor Novello wrote songs and playlets and studied harmony and theory. From the age of 12 he had been the piano accompanist to the Royal Welsh Ladies Choir during holiday tours. He had his first song, a waltz called 'Spring of the Year', published when he was 16. The following year he went with his mother to live in London where he spent his days composing and his evenings playing at concerts. He wanted desperately to go on the stage but his mother insisted his life was in music. In 1911, having composed the music for a travelling pageant, he went to Canada and the United States. Back in London, in 1914 he made a brief appearance in the revue *As I Used to Be* at the Little Theatre, where he played the harpsichord and had two lines; but as the show closed within two weeks he never considered it his stage début. That same year he wrote 'Keep the Home Fires Burning', which made him not only famous but also very rich. He gave more than seventy concerts in the war areas of France before being commissioned in the Royal Naval Air Service as a flight sub-lieutenant. He served in the office of the Air Ministry and at night wrote *Theodore and Co.* for Leslie Henson, which opened at the Gaiety in September 1916 and ran there for eighteen months.

He was by this time an enormous celebrity because of his songs, and his good looks were a help too. He was seduced into film-making — his first, *The Call of the Blood*, was filmed in Sicily and Rome; he became a film star overnight, and quickly made two more films. He continued composing for the stage, though his ambitions to be on it were discouraged by his friends. He would not be deterred, and made his stage début at the Ambassadors' on 3 November 1921 playing Armand Duval in *Deburau*. At the Kingsway in March 1922 he was the Chinese hero Wu Hoo Git in *The Yellow Jacket*, and then in June was the Spanish boy Javier in *Spanish Lovers*. He went to the United States, where he made the film *The White Rose*, with D. W. Griffith. The publicity people were calling him the next Valentino. Then, back in London at the Playhouse in August 1923, he played a French theatrical manager aged 45 in *Enter Kiki*, which starred Gladys Cooper in the title role.

On film he played the title role in *Bonnie Prince Charlie*. Though he was now an enormous film star in England he was still composing seriously, and he longed still to conquer the stage. He had written a film script which he could not get produced, and with the help of Constance Collier he turned it into a stage play. As actor–manager he opened *The Rat* in Brighton in January 1924 and on the opening night took thirty-nine curtain calls. There followed an enormously successful tour and subsequently it opened at the Prince of Wales in London in June. The *Tatler* critic reported: 'His performance must surely amaze even his staunchest admirers. Both in his lighter, more devil-may-care moods and in his scenes of passion and despair he is wonderfully effective and affecting. Indeed, the play is not only a success for him as part-author, but especially as chief actor.' *The Rat* transferred in September to the Garrick, where it ran until February when Novello put on a revival of *Old Heidelberg*, which was not a success.

In April 1925 he took over the part of Laurence Trenwith in a revival of Pinero's *Iris* at the Adelphi, and the box-office takings trebled. At the same theatre in May he played Peo in a charity matinée of *My Lady's Dress*. After making the film of *The Rat* he opened at the Palace in Manchester in December 1925 as Roddy Berwick in *Down Hill*, another play he had written with Constance Collier. In February 1926 he was at Wyndham's as Benvenuto Cellini in *The Firebrand*, which ran for only ten weeks and that to very bad business, but from June at the Queen's he had a good six months with *Down Hill*.

Ivor Novello went to the Duke of York's in December 1926 with Fay Compton and Charles Laughton in *Liliom*. He played the title part but it lasted for only three weeks, and at the Prince of

Wales in February he revived *The Rat*. In November 1927 at Daly's he played Sirio Marson in Noel Coward's famous theatrical disaster, *Sirocco*. 'A rather curious fact about my stage career,' Novello noted, 'is that although I make no claims that my plays are in any way better than anyone else's, they are apparently right for me. Whenever I have been in a play written by anyone else it has failed.'

He abandoned the stage and signed with Michael Balcon to become the top star for Gainsborough Pictures. However, in September 1928 he was at the Palladium appearing in *The Gate Crasher* and the following month was at the Globe playing Max Clement in his own play, *The Truth Game*. It was a light comedy which kept him for six months in London. After a provincial tour he brought it back to Daly's. He next wrote *Symphony in Two Flats* in which he played David Kennard, a tragic young composer who loses his sight. Opposite him was Benita Hume. They opened at the New Theatre in October 1929 and had another success. During the run he continued to make films during the day and remained Britain's number one box-office star. It was during this period that he made his first talking film.

Ivor Novello made his New York début at the Shubert Theater in September 1930 playing in *Symphony in Two Flats*. As he noted, 'We opened in a heat wave and closed in a heat wave. Unfortunately it was the same heat wave.' *Symphony* ran a bare seven weeks. But at the Ethel Barrymore Theater in December he opened *The Truth Game* which ran for six months.

He signed a Hollywood contract with MGM, but they had enough stars and really wanted him as a writer. There, strangely enough, he wrote *Tarzan, the Ape Man*, and for himself, two more plays with which he returned to London in 1932. He opened at the Prince of Wales in March 1932 playing Prince Felix in *I Lived with You*. James Agate reported: 'This piece was obviously written by Mr Novello for the good actor Mr Novello, and it should succeed since I can imagine nothing more likely to be popular than a theme of Dostoevsky treated in the manner of Ian Hay.'

Novello then took over the part of Lord Bay Clender in his other play, *Party*, which was running at the Strand, while Sebastian Shaw had a holiday for the month of August. In September he set out on a provincial tour of *I Lived with You*, during which he wrote *Fresh Fields*, which opened in January 1933 and ran for fifteen months. He did not have such success himself as an actor playing Seraphine in *Flies in the Sun* at the Playhouse, which opened the same month and ran only a few weeks. In June at the Globe he played Lieutenant-Colonel Sir Geoffrey Bethel and Gray Raynor in his own *Proscenium*, a sentimental story of theatre folk which kept him at the Globe for seven months. At the same theatre in September 1934 he was the French pianist Jacques Clavel in his own *Murder in Mayfair*, which ran for six months. Sidney W. Carroll wrote: ' . . . to say that this man is not a first rate actor is just nonsense. See him in his present thriller, *Murder in Mayfair*. Note the consistency of the portraiture, his nervous sincerity and concentration, how he acts with every one of his fingers, how every mood of the temperamental foreign pianist works itself out to perfection, and how subordinate he can be when the situation calls for deference to the other players.'

For a while Novello tried to combine working in films during the day and acting at night, but he found he was exhausting himself and determined to star in no more films after *I Lived with You*. He kept to that, apart from *Autumn Crocus*, which he made in 1935.

Ivor Novello devised, wrote and composed *Glamorous Night*. It was a musical play which called for an orchestra of at least forty and a cast of 120, as well as magnificent scenic effects including a luxury liner sinking on stage. It opened at Drury Lane in May 1935, and he played Anthony Allen. The *Daily Mail* reported: 'It has taken Mr Ivor Novello, writing and composing his first full-scale musical play and acting the leading male role himself, to provide Drury Lane Theatre Royal with the biggest hit it has had for many years.' Although the play was full of his lilting music, Novello himself did not sing. He gave that up when his voice broke and explained: 'My singing voice finished at the age of sixteen and a half. Now it's like the croak of a tired bullfrog and I would not dream of asking an audience to pay to hear me.' *Glamorous Night* ran to capacity at the Lane until the end of November 1935, when it had to quit the theatre to make room for the scheduled pantomime. Novello was not pleased. At the same theatre in November for a charity matinée he played Romeo in the Balcony scene from *Romeo and Juliet*.

He was next at His Majesty's in April 1936, playing the Regency rake Lord George Hell in Clemence Dane's *The Happy Hypocrite* with Vivien Leigh and Isobel Jeans. James Agate reported: 'Mr Novello plays Lord George with great sincerity. His make-up for the first act is very effective and exactly gives the note of Caligula with a touch of Sir John Falstaff. He acts all the latter part of the play with a disarming simplicity; to have such a profile and pretend not to know it would write him down as an artist of enormous sensibility. It is a beautiful performance throughout.' However, following true to form, Novello in a non-

Novello play did not work and it had a short run. He next played Michael in his second musical play, *Careless Rapture*, which ran for ten months from September 1936 at Drury Lane. The following September he played two parts, the Duke of Cheviot and Otto Fresch, in his third musical, *Crest of the Wave*. On the first night he received over 5000 telegrams, and the show ran at the Lane for a year to standing room only. At the Winter Garden in December 1937 for a charity matinée he played Charles Surface in *The School for Scandal*.

In September 1938, as a complete change, he opened at Drury Lane, starring in Shakespeare's *Henry V*. The critics were impressed. James Agate wrote: 'Novello has fire where fire should be; the prayer before the battle and the reading of the list of the dead are admirably done. And the soliloquy beginning with "Upon the King" has an admirable cogency.' Novello had planned an entire Shakespeare season, but the war intervened and the Lane closed. However, slowly the theatres reopened and in March 1939 Novello was back at the Lane in his fourth musical, *The Dancing Years*, in which he played a Viennese composer. It ran at the Lane until October, when he went on tour in a small comedy he had written called *Second Helping*. This came into the Lyric in April 1940 retitled *Ladies into Action* and co-starred Lilli Palmer. The *Daily Mail* critic wrote: 'After his recent concern with very-large-scale musical productions at Drury Lane, together with a shot at *Henry V* at the same theatre, this little bedroom comedy must have seemed small beer to Mr Novello; it is a pleasant tipple nonetheless. It develops at times into something more exciting than beer, but never, however, becomes champagne.' James Agate reported: 'Mr Novello is excellent. The piece itself? It is one of those comedies in which everybody does a great deal of getting into bed and nobody seems to get out of it.' In June he revived *I Lived with You* for a tour and in September set out on a tour of *The Dancing Years* which lasted until February 1942, when he returned to the Adelphi in London with it, staying there a further two years.

In August 1944 he toured Belgium and Normandy as Bruce Lovell in *Love from a Stranger* and was back in *The Dancing Years* in October

for another tour of the provinces.

He opened at the Hippodrome in April 1945 playing three parts, Sir Graham Rodney, Valentine Fayre and Bay in his latest musical *Perchance to Dream*. He had been told that the musical had changed and that he was hopelessly old-fashioned – but he thought not. Harold Hobson reported: 'Whatever one may have thought of this, in one's superior way, as a contribution to Higher Thought, it cannot be denied that it was a superb piece of stage craft, bright and shining in presentation as one of the new pennies promised for these holidays.' And James Agate wrote: '... the curtain, when it went up, took with it the entire audience, which remained in its seventh heaven until after three hours and a half the curtain descended and automatically brought the audience down with it. Mr Novello's nonsense had obviously suited their nonsense. The actor himself? I don't feel that he is at home in the age or perhaps the country of Pierce Egan. I feel that his genius requires a steeper setting, a balmier baskier air, that his spiritual home is the Tyrol. I wonder whether in his next production Mr Novello will wear a feather? I rather think he should.' The public were well pleased. Everyone was singing 'We'll Gather Lilacs' and the show ran at the Adelphi until 1947.

Ivor Novello's last appearance was in the Ruritanian *King's Rhapsody*, which opened at the Palace Theatre in September 1949. Ivor Brown reported: 'Mr Novello continues to conquer. *King's Rhapsody* is everything the Novellites can desire. Mr Novello, author, composer and actor, can with his tranquillity stand up to all the bounding Oklahomans and Brigadooners in the world. He is far the biggest box-office attraction of our native stage, and he has earned his victories by honest service of the public appetite. Sweet tooth is sweetly served, and what is more — abundantly. He hands out no trivial fables, but lashings of plot, with plentiful changes of scene ... Ivor Novello himself (as the deposed king) sadly rules and gladly deserts Murania, looking half Hamlet, half Antony and wholly the darling of his public.' On 5 March 1951, having written *Gay's the Word* for Cicely Courtneidge, Ivor Novello came offstage to the usual tumultuous applause — and died of a heart attack three hours later.
See photograph opposite.

Gladys Cooper and Ivor Novello in *Flies in the Sun* at the
Playhouse Theatre (London, February 1933)

Joan Plowright (left) and Maggie Smith in William Congreve's
comedy *The Way of the World* at the Theatre Royal
(London, October 1984)

LAURENCE OLIVIER

*L*aurence Olivier was born in Dorking on 22 May 1907, the third and youngest child in the family, which soon moved to London. His father was a Church of England clergyman. When he was nine, Laurence Olivier was sent to board at All Saints, a Church of England choir school near Oxford Circus. He did not care for sports, but distinguished himself as an actor even at that tender age. In his second year there he played Brutus in *Julius Caesar* for the school Christmas production and Sybil Thorndike, who saw the performance, noted: 'The small boy who played Brutus is already an actor.' The next Christmas he was Maria in *Twelfth Night*.

When he was 13 his mother died suddenly and he was desolate. His father had always discouraged his acting, and after seeing him play the following Christmas, forbade him to act again.

In 1921, when he was 14, Olivier was moved to St Edward's School in Oxford, noted as a training-ground for clergymen. However, the headmaster there persuaded his father to relax his ban on acting. He noted that the boy needed to act for his spirit — it was the one thing he was good at, and it might just lead him to the pulpit. During the 1922 Easter holidays at Stratford-on-Avon, Olivier was in *The Taming of the Shrew*. It was then that he determined to be an actor, though still despairing that his father would ever allow it. For the 1923 Christmas production he was Puck in *A Midsummer Night's Dream*. He began going over the top and indulging in onstage pranks. The local paper wrote: 'The boy who played Puck, although he has a potent stage presence, emoted with frantic and altogether unnecessary effect, as though playing a joke on his fellow cast members, indeed on the audience.' However, his future stepmother saw the performance, and succeeded in convincing his father that the boy should indeed be an actor.

He received a scholarship to the Central School of Speech Training and Dramatic Art run by Elsie Fogerty in London, and began there in July 1924. By November he had a walk-on part in the West End, playing the Suliot Officer in *Byron* at the Century Theatre. He was in a one-act play in Brighton and then joined up for a winter season in a travelling rep run by Lena Ashwell; he was sacked from it for fooling around on the stage. His father, worried by the company his son was keeping and by his growing reputation for mischief, spoke to Sybil Thorndike about him. Her husband, Lewis Casson, after admonishing the young Olivier, engaged him for a season as an assistant stage manager and understudy in *Henry VIII* and *The Cenci*. He also played small parts in the productions at the Empire.

In April 1926 he took the small part of the Minstrel in *The Marvellous History of Saint Bernard* with the Birmingham Repertory Company at the Kingsway Theatre. The production closed because of the general strike, and Olivier went with the company to Clacton-on-Sea for a summer season. It was there that he met Ralph Richardson who would become his life-long friend. He toured with the company as Richard Croaker in *The Farmer's Wife* in July 1926. From January to April 1928 the company played at the Royal Court in London and Olivier had a number of interesting parts. He was Malcolm in *Macbeth*, Marcellus in *Back to Methuselah* and the Young Man in Elmer Rice's *The Adding Machine*. Of the last of these St John Ervine wrote: 'Mr Laurence Olivier as the young man ... gave a very good performance indeed — the best, I think, in the play. He had little to do but he acted.' Olivier then got the title role in Alfred Lord Tennyson's verse play, *Harold*. St John Ervine reported: 'Mr Laurence Olivier, the Harold, varies in his performance, but he is excellent on the whole and has the makings of a very considerable actor in him. His faults are those of inexperience rather than of ineffectiveness. The good performance he gave in *Macbeth*, added to the good performance he gives in *Harold*, makes me believe that when romantic and poetic drama return to their proper place in the theatre, Mr Olivier will be ready to occupy the position of a distinguished romantic actor.' Olivier was not pleased then to be given the small part of a Lord in *The Taming of the Shrew*. He left the company in mid-June 1928, when at the Royalty he replaced Patrick Susands as Gerald Arnwood in *Bird in Hand*. Opposite him played Jill Esmond. In December 1928 for the Stage Society he played Captain Denis Stanhope in R. C. Sherriff's *Journey's End*. There were only two special performances, on 9 and 10 December. Eventually, however, the play was put on in the West End where it ran for two years — without Olivier who had opted for the title role in *Beau Geste* opposite Madeleine Carroll. It opened at His Majesty's in January 1929 but it was a colossal failure and closed in four weeks. In March at the New Theatre he was the Oriental Prince Po in *The Circle of Chalk*; that too folded in a month. The domestic comedy *Paris Bound*, in which he played Richard Parish, opened at the Lyric in April and closed soon afterwards. He then played John Hardy in a suspense drama, *The Stranger Within*, which opened at the Garrick in June 1929 and closed a few days later.

Besides having a terrible time with his choice of plays, Olivier was missing Jill Esmond, who was working in New York, so he opted to go there, and made his American début at the Eltinge Theater on 11 September 1929 playing Hugh Bromilow in *Murder on the Second Floor*. The show flopped; however, he had a firm reconciliation with Jill Esmond. He returned to London in December of that Depression year, and played Jerry Warrender at the Fortune Theatre in *The Last Enemy* and in March at the Arts was Ralph in *After All*. There was not much stage work around, but he kept himself occupied with film work. At All Saints' Church in London on 25 July 1930 he and Jill Esmond married.

In September 1930 he played Victor Prynne at the Phoenix in Noel Coward's *Private Lives* and the show had the expected success. Coward took it and him (along with Jill Esmond to replace the pregnant Adrianne Allen) to Broadway, where they opened at the Times Square Theater in January 1931. Brooks Atkinson reported for the *New York Times*: 'For the most part it is a duologue between Mr Coward and Miss Lawrence. Jill Esmond as the deserted bride and Laurence Olivier as the deserted bridegroom are permitted to chatter foolishly once or twice in the first act, and to help keep the ball rolling at the end.' It was not a great part, but Olivier badly needed to be in a success at that point and he was eternally grateful to Coward, who taught him a good deal about the stage.

The Oliviers went to Hollywood in the spring of 1931, where they took up contracts with RKO. There Olivier made *Friends and Lovers* and *The Yellow Ticket*, but he realized that it was Jill they were truly interested in.

In April 1933 he finally had a stage success in the melodrama about a boys' boarding school, *The Rats of Norway*, directed by and starring Raymond Massey. Olivier opened at the Playhouse in it playing the schoolteacher Steven Beringer. His next stage venture, playing Julian Dulcimer in *The Green Bay Tree* at New York's Cort Theater in October 1933, was a great success, and he remained in it for six months. Back in London in April 1934 he was directed by Noel Coward and played Richard Kurt in *Biography*, which unfortunately ran only a few weeks, so in June he played Bothwell in *Queen of Scots* at the New Theatre.

At the Lyric Theatre in October of that year he played Anthony Cavendish, a thinly disguised John Barrymore, in *Theatre Royal*. Agate called it 'a

hair-raising performance . . . the portrait is lifesize and life-like.' It was also a very athletic performance, and one night, leaping over some banisters, Olivier fractured his ankle and had to leave the show.

At the Shaftesbury Theatre in March 1935 Laurence Olivier produced and played the part of Peter Hammond in *The Ringmaster*, which closed after only ten performances. He was accused of inaudibility by the critics. His next venture was at the Whitehall in May, when he played Richard Harben in *Golden Arrow*. That was a box-office disaster and one critic reported: 'Throughout the evening Mr Olivier had not one single word to say that was worth speaking or hearing.' He spent the summer filming for Korda.

In October 1935 he opened at the New Theatre playing Romeo in John Gielgud's production of *Romeo and Juliet*. James Agate wrote: 'Mr Olivier's Romeo suffered enormously from the fact that the spoken poetry of the part eluded him. In his delivery he brought off a twofold inexpertness which approached virtuosity — that of gabbling all his words in a line and uttering each line as a staccato whole cut off from its fellows. Apart from the speaking, there was poetry to spare. This Romeo looked every inch a lover, and a lover fey and foredoomed. The actor's facial expression was varied and mobile, his bearing noble, his play of arm imaginative, and his smaller gestures were infinitely touching . . . Taking the performance by and large, I have no hesitation in saying that this is the most moving Romeo I have ever seen.' The management hit on a box-office ploy and the following month Gielgud took over as Romeo while Olivier played Mercutio. Thereafter they alternated and the production played to full houses for 187 performances. At this point Olivier met Vivien Leigh, a young, keen actress who already adored him, and his personal life fell into turmoil. Korda cast him opposite Vivien Leigh in the historical film, *Fire Over England*, and their passionate affair developed at about the same time that his wife had his son, Tarquin.

From January through November 1937 he was with the Old Vic Company. There he played Hamlet, which was a great box-office if not critical success. He was Toby Belch in *Twelfth Night*, Macbeth, and the King in *Henry V*, which was a critical success. In June he went to Kronborg Castle in Denmark to play Hamlet, and took Vivien with him as Ophelia. At the New Theatre in December 1937 with the Old Vic Company, Olivier played Macbeth, and was next Iago to Ralph Richardson's Othello, directed by Tyrone Guthrie. He played Vivaldi in *The King of Nowhere* and Caius Marcius in *Coriolanus* directed by Lewis Casson. Olivier returned to Hollywood where, as Heathcliff in *Wuthering Heights*, directed by William Wyler, he at last became a film star.

In April 1939 (while Vivien was still in Hollywood becoming a star herself with *Gone with the Wind*) at the Ethel Barrymore Theater, Olivier was a Broadway success when he played Gaylord Easterbrook in *No Time for Comedy* with Katharine Cornell. Brooks Atkinson wrote: 'Laurence Olivier, a most remarkable young actor, knows how to play a part from the inside. He had a hundred ways to express as an actor what the author has put into the lines.'

Back in Hollywood Olivier made *Rebecca* and *Pride and Prejudice*, and then in San Francisco in April 1940 he and Vivien opened in their own production of *Romeo and Juliet*. They also played in Chicago and opened in New York at the 51st Street Theater in May 1940. Although Vivien had just won an Oscar, the reviews for *Romeo and Juliet* were extremely negative and they lost a fortune.

They returned to Hollywood, where they married on 31 August 1940, having finally been released by their respective spouses. Then for Korda, under instruction from Churchill, they starred together in *Lady Hamilton*, a propaganda film which England hoped would encourage America to enter the war. In the end England did not need the film (although it was a huge success) — there was Pearl Harbour. They returned to England in January 1941 and Olivier made another propaganda film, *49th Parallel*, before joining the Royal Navy Fleet Air Arm. He was released in spring 1943 to direct and star in the film of *Henry V*.

In 1944 he was appointed a co-director of the Old Vic Company and in August was at the New Theatre playing the Button Moulder while Ralph Richardson played the title role in *Peer Gynt*. For the rest of the season he was Sergius in Shaw's *Arms and the Man*, the Duke of Gloucester in *Richard III* and Astrov in *Uncle Vanya*. For the 1945–46 season he played Hotspur in *Henry IV Part 1*, while in *Part 2* he was Justice Shallow. He then made an enormous impression when he played the title role in *Oedipus Rex*. John Mason Brown reported: '... Mr Olivier's Oedipus is one of those performances in which blood and electricity are somehow mixed. It pulls lightning down from the sky. It is awesome, dwarfing, and appalling as one of nature's angriest displays. Though thrilling, it never loses its majesty ... When the fearful realization at last inundates him ... Mr Olivier released two cries which no one who has heard them can hope to forget. They are the dreadful, hoarse groans of a wounded animal. They

well up out of a baby that has been clubbed by fate. They are sounds which speak, as no words could, for a soul torn by horror, for a mind numbed by what it has been forced to comprehend ... The subsequent moments when Oedipus appears, self-blinded with the blood trickling down his face, are almost more terrible than audiences can bear.' But Olivier decided to demonstrate his versatility and also send them home laughing, and the same night played Mr Puff in Sheridan's *The Critic*. He appeared with the company at the Comédie-Française in July 1945, and in May 1946 took the repertoire to New York where the Old Vic Company played at the Century Theater. In September 1946, back at the New Theatre in London, he directed and played the title role in *King Lear* and then devoted himself to the film of *Hamlet*, which won him an Oscar. He became the youngest actor to be so decorated when he was knighted in 1947.

In February 1948 he set out with the Old Vic Company on a tour of Australia and New Zealand, and stepped on a few toes when he selected plays that would be starring vehicles for himself and Vivien. The plays were *Richard III*, *The Skin of Our Teeth* and *The School for Scandal*. While on the tour he was notified that his contract as director of the Old Vic would not be renewed. However, it was to the New Theatre that he returned in January 1949. The first night back he was Sir Peter Teazle in *The School For Scandal*. Harold Hobson reported: '... it was a great occasion and Britain's capital gathered all her beauty and her chivalry to welcome the country's most popular actor ... This Sir Peter is crusted as old port; when he thinks he has said a good thing, he smiles to himself enchantingly; he is delightful in the lulls of domestic storms; and in his crabbedly reluctant manifestations of affection touching and endearing.' He followed that with his Richard III of which Hobson wrote: '... in the company of Barry Sullivan, Kean, Irving and Kemble, Olivier need not be ashamed ... From the moment when, before the first word of the play was spoken, Olivier's malign hunchback hobbled across the stage ... this performance amused, delighted and astounded.' (Olivier was to commit it to film in 1956.) He directed Vivien in *Antigone* and also played the Chorus, as well as directing *The Proposal*. He then directed his wife in Tennessee Williams' *A Streetcar Named Desire*, and Edith Evans and Peter Finch in *Daphne Laureola*.

In January 1950 he launched Laurence Olivier Productions at the St James's Theatre with Christopher Fry's *Venus Observed*, in which he played the Duke of Altair. The critic T. C. Worsley was disappointed after Olivier's massive Shakespearian performances. He wrote: 'Sir Laurence Olivier as the duke has a part that calls for nothing but an easy command and a negligent air. Sir Laurence supplies both.' In May he played Antony and Caesar while his wife played Cleopatra in Shaw's *Caesar and Cleopatra* and Shakespeare's *Antony and Cleopatra*. T. C. Worsley said of the double: 'It enables Sir Laurence Olivier to bring off a very neat left and right. His Caesar is a most convincing creation: the offspring clearly of a great late nineteenth century ruling family, accustomed to producing political bishops and idealizing politicians, conscious of their own greatness, just but firm, eminently reasonable on the outside but tough as leather on the inside ... [his Antony] seems to me exactly right to the last hair ... It is a superb performance.' Kenneth Tynan, however, was not so well pleased: 'Sir Laurence, with that curious chivalry which some time or other blights the progress of every great actor, gives me the impression that he subdues his blow-lamp ebullience to match her [Vivien Leigh]. Blunting his iron precision, levelling away his towering authority he meets her halfway.' However, they ran with the productions for six months in London and for four months at the Ziegfeld Theater in New York, where Brooks Atkinson called his Caesar a masterpiece. At the New Century Theater in New York in February 1952 he directed *Venus Observed*. He then made the film of *The Beggar's Opera* while Vivien was making *Elephant Walk*. Her health, mental and physical, had been very delicate and during this film she finally cracked and was replaced by Elizabeth Taylor.

For the Coronation year Olivier and Vivien Leigh teamed up again for Rattigan's *The Sleeping Prince* at the Phoenix Theatre in London, where she played the chorus girl and he the Grand Duke for an eight-month run. They then went to Stratford for the 1955 season, during which he played Macbeth. Tynan wrote: 'The marvel of Sir Laurence Olivier's reading is that it ... turns the play inside out, and makes it (for the first time I can remember) a thing of mounting, not waning excitement. Last Tuesday Sir Laurence shook hands with greatness, and within a week or so the performance will have ripened into a masterpiece: not of the superficial, booming, have-a-bash kind, but the real thing, a structure of perfect forethought and proportion lit by flashes of intuitive lightning.' He was also Malvolio in *Twelfth Night*, and of his performance in the title role of *Titus Andronicus* Tynan wrote: 'Sir Laurence Olivier's Titus, even with one hand gone, is a five-finger exercise transformed into an unforgettable concerto of grief. This is a performance which ushers us into the presence of one who is, pound for pound, the

greatest actor alive.' Bernard Levin said that it was 'not so much on the heroic scale as on a new scale entirely, the greatness of which has smashed all our measuring rods and pressure gauges to smithereens'. Olivier then filmed the Rattigan play, retitled *The Prince and the Showgirl*, and directed Marilyn Monroe as his co-star.

At the Royal Court Theatre in April 1957 he played the third-rate music-hall star Archie Rice in Osborne's *The Entertainer*. They had to close after five weeks so that Olivier could tour as Titus Andronicus throughout Europe. They reopened at the Stoll Theatre in July 1957 and then moved to the Palace in September. *The Entertainer* went to Broadway to the Royale Theater in February 1959, and Olivier subsequently starred in the film. It was during this time that he met Joan Plowright, who was his daughter in the play. His marriage to Vivien now existed in name only and he and Joan Plowright began a liaison. Of his performance in New York in *The Entertainer*, Brooks Atkinson wrote: 'In case anyone doubts that Laurence Olivier is a versatile actor, consider the subject closed. He is versatile. In John Osborne's *The Entertainer* which opened at the Royale last evening, England's most illustrious classical actor plays the part of a seedy vaudeville actor at a seaside resort in the north of England at the time of the Suez crisis. Archie Rice, as he is called, is a glib, cheap, unscrupulous actor and promoter who is going down for the last time, dragging everyone else down with him. Mr Olivier misses neither the personality nor the significance of the character. In the vaudeville scenes, he tap-dances, he sings in the nasal tones that are usual in the lower ranks of the profession; he tells blue jokes in a cheap accent and throws the usual insults at the orchestra leader. His shoulders swivel with a kind of spurious bravado. Wearing his hat at a flashy angle, swinging his stick smartly, Mr Olivier is the very model of the worn-out, untalented music-hall performer who is on the downgrade. Even a quick glimpse of Britannia (a lusciously fabricated nude) does not upset the cool vulgarity of his characterization.'

Laurence Olivier then spent some time filming — *The Devil's Disciple* and *Spartacus* — but in July 1959 was back on stage at the Memorial Theatre in Stratford-on-Avon playing the title role in *Coriolanus*. Tynan reported: 'This Coriolanus is all-round Olivier. We have the wagging head, the soaring index finger, and the sly, roaming eyes of one of the world's cleverest comic actors, plus the desperate, exhausted moans of one of the world's masters of pathos. But we also confront the nonpareil of heroic tragedians as athletically lissom as when he played Oedipus a dozen years ago. No actor uses rubato, stealing a beat from one line to give to the next, like Olivier. The voice is soft steel that can chill and cut, or melt and scorch . . .' And of the end Tynan wrote: 'He is poised now, on a promontory some twelve feet above the stage, from which he topples forward, to be caught by the ankles so that he dangles, inverted like the slaughtered Mussolini. A more shocking, less sentimental death I have not seen in the theatre; it is at once proud and ignominious, as befits the titanic fool who dies it. The image and the echo of this astonishing performance have taken root in my mind in the weeks that have passed since I witnessed it. The dark imprint of Olivier's stage presence is something one forgets only with an effort, but the voice is a lifelong possession of those who have heard it at its best. It sounds, distinct and barbaric, across the valley of many centuries, like a horn calling to the hunt, or the neigh of a battle-maddened charger.'

He next had a very different role playing Berenger in Ionesco's *Rhinoceros*. This production opened at the Royal Court in April 1960 and transferred to the Strand for a successful run in July. At the St James Theater in New York in October the same year he opened in the title role of Anouilh's *Becket*. Howard Taubman reported for the *New York Times*: 'A role like Becket has obvious attractions for an actor like Laurence Olivier who has never stood still. He plays the part with admirable scope. The courtier is limned with elegance and spirit; the man of God has dedicated simplicity and sad consoling wisdom. Mr Olivier's performance almost created the illusion that M. Anouilh has penetrated the character of Becket.' In March 1961 he was touring with the production playing the part of Henry II when, in Connecticut, he married Joan Plowright. He went back to New York to the Hudson Theater in May, again to play the King.

Laurence Olivier returned to England in July 1962 and opened the Chichester Festival Theatre. There he directed *The Chances* and *The Broken Heart* in which he played the Prologue and Bassanes. He also played Astrov in his own production of *Uncle Vanya*. In London at the Saville Theatre in December 1962 he played Fred Midway in *Semi-Detached*. Returning to Chichester for the 1963 Festival he revived *Uncle Vanya*.

The National Theatre Company came into being in 1963 with Laurence Olivier at its head. He directed the inaugural production at the Old Vic in October. It was *Hamlet*, and starred Peter O'Toole. That same season at the Old Vic Olivier once more played Astrov and then was Captain Brazen in *The Recruiting Officer*. In 1964 he took on the massive role of Othello, for which he lowered his voice to a register never before heard from him, and was also Halvard Solness, *The Master Builder*. He directed *The Crucible* in 1965 and began to devote himself more to administration for the National Theatre Company. In September 1965 they visited Moscow and Berlin, where Olivier played Othello, and Tattle in *Love for Love*. At the Old Vic he was once more Tattle the following month. In 1966 he directed *Juno and the Paycock* for the company. He played Edgar in *The Dance of Death* and directed *The Three Sisters* in 1967.

By 1967 Olivier and Joan Plowright had three small children. Olivier had cancer, but still he toured Canada with the company playing in *Love for Love* and *The Dance of Death*, and was Plucheux in the farce, *A Flea in Her Ear*. For the next two years he performed cameo parts in films and for the stage directed *The Advertisement, Love's Labour's Lost* and *The Three Sisters*. He took over the part of A. B. Raham in *Home and Beauty*. In 1970 he was an extraordinary Shylock in Jonathan Miller's production of *The Merchant of Venice*. That year he was given a life peerage. In 1971 he directed *Amphitryon 38* and played the massive role of James Tyrone in O'Neill's *Long Day's Journey Into Night*. In 1973 he was Antonio in *Saturday, Sunday, Monday* and John Tagg in *The Party*. That same year he reluctantly handed over the directorship of the National Theatre to Peter Hall.

Olivier's health deteriorated severely. He contracted dermatomyositis and he looked much older than his years. However, acting was his life and he overcame the ill-health to direct television productions, to film and once more to play King Lear, for television.

Olivier has never been short of awards. As well as his Oscars he has three Emmys, innumerable foreign orders from such countries as Sweden, France and Yugoslavia, his peerage, honorary doctorates from the universities of Oxford, Edinburgh, Manchester and London. 'I'm sure,' he once told an interviewer, 'if I didn't act for a year, I would be utterly miserable. I'm sure I would.'
See photograph opposite page 87.

JAMES O'NEILL

'*H*is face is beautiful — beautiful in its cameo-like profile, and beautiful in its mobile expressiveness. His eyes are large, dark, and lustrous, dreamy in repose, flashing in action. His mouth is sensitive, yet firm, the shade of sadness blending with its smile giving a strange interest to the whole countenance. His movements are grace itself; his attitudes are superbly picturesque. His voice is rich, mellow, and musical; and it is susceptible to a wide range of expression. His speech is tinged with a bit of the brogue that adds to, rather than detracts from, his many singular graces.' Thus Harrison Grey Fiske, the editor of the *New York Dramatic Mirror*, described James O'Neill in 1896; but O'Neill is probably best remembered as the prototype for James Tyrone in his son Eugene's play, *Long Day's Journey Into Night*.

James O'Neill was born on 14 October 1847 in Thomastown, County Kilkenny, Ireland, but within a few years his parents took him — together with his nine brothers and sister — to New York after the great Irish potato famine, and the family settled in Buffalo.

At the age of ten James had to go to work to help support the family and found a job as clerk in a store. Later he went into a machine shop, which paid better, and then into business with his brother in Cincinnati. In his spare time he played billiards in a hall across from the National Theater. One night the stage manager crossed the road looking for supernumeraries. O'Neill described his début as one of the lords in *The Colleen Bawn* at the National Theater in Cincinnati: 'That night we went to the theater early and the wardrobe man dressed me in a marvelous velvet suit with lace ruffles at my wrists. I looked into the mirror. "I don't look so bad," I said. "Indeed you don't," said the wardrobe man, "and you're going to have a line." "What's a line?" "I mean you have to speak — to say something." A little later I led in the beaux, and when the beautiful leading lady said, "I must have a husband," I stepped forward, and with a deep bow said, "Madame, take me!" How the blushes mounted my boyish cheek.' He was soon in the stock company. When he played James, King of Scotland, in *Queen Elizabeth*, a local newspaper wrote that 'Mr O'Neill must be reminded that King James was not an Irishman', so O'Neill set about losing his brogue. He joined Edwin Forrest's Company and went barnstorming around the country. The company, as was usual in those days, became stranded and O'Neill made his

way back to Cincinnati where he joined Colonel Bob Miles' Company as a walking gentleman. Next came Ford's Theater Company in Baltimore, where he played leading juvenile roles for two years. In 1872 he joined the company at McVicker's Theater in Chicago, where he acted with Charlotte Cushman and Adelaide Neilson. He and Edwin Booth alternated Iago and Othello. In 1873 he was with Hooley's Stock Company in Chicago playing Hamlet and Richelieu. Then after a spell in stock in San Francisco he joined up with A. M. Palmer's Stock Company at the Union Square Theater in New York City. He had two seasons there, during which time he played the Prince in *The Danisheffs*, Jean Renaud in *A Celebrated Case* and Pierre in *The Two Orphans*. In 1875 he was again with Hooley's company in San Francisco at Maguire's Opera House.

After a two-year courtship he married the well-bred, convent-educated Ella Quinlan in New York. Together they went back to San Francisco, where this time he was in E. J. Baldwin's Company. Ella, though loving him dearly, never cared for the theatrical set and began her life of isolation. In California he was induced into playing the Christus in Salmi Morse's adaptation of the Oberammergau pageant, *The Passion Play*. According to reporters it was all done in the best possible taste, and people were even seen kneeling in the theatre, but the police declared it sacrilegious and closed the show, fining O'Neill $50. O'Neill, himself a devout Catholic, was horrified at the reaction.

In 1882 at the Booth Theater in New York, James O'Neill played Edmond Dantes in *The Count of Monte Cristo*. He immediately recognized what a success it was and bought all the rights — including the production. Harrison Grey Fiske wrote of his performance: 'In the role of Dantes he demonstrates his mastery of the technique of stage art, and exhibits the versatility of his talents. Whether as the rollicking, nimble sailor of the prologue, or the emaciated convict making his bold stroke for liberty, or the gentle-voiced sad-eyed priest, or the opulent Count of Monte Cristo, he is equally effective. Each phase of this complex character is perfectly shown; and the rapid alternation of the primal passions — love, hate, revenge — is powerfully exhibited.'

O'Neill spent the following years travelling the country, seldom playing anything but *The Count of Monte Cristo*. It made him a very rich man, but he invested his money unwisely. He was at that time making up to $40,000 a year. His son remembered as a boy watching James O'Neill on the stage. He said that people never tired of seeing Monte Cristo rip the sack in which he had been thrown into the canvas ocean. 'I can still see my father dripping with salt and sawdust, climbing on a stool behind the swinging profile of dashing waves,' Eugene said much later. 'It was then that the calcium lights in the gallery played on his long beard and tattered clothes, as with arms outstretched he declared the world was his. That was the signal for the house to burst into deafening applause that overwhelmed the noise of the storm manufactured backstage.'

O'Neill played the Count for more than twenty-four years. It never failed him. William Winter wrote of one of his many reappearances in New York: 'The most important dramatic event that occurred in New York last night was the re-entrance of that public favorite, Mr James O'Neill, which was made at the Academy of Music, before a numerous and brilliant audience — that great theater indeed, being crowded in every part — in the character of the Count of Monte Cristo, with which for many seasons, his name has been closely

and honorably associated. Mr O'Neill was warmly welcomed, cordially applauded and many times called before the curtain, and this tribute of respect he merited by giving a fine performance.'

Occasionally O'Neill ventured into something else — most notably *The Three Musketeers* — but not for long. On 6 December 1918 he was struck by a car while getting off a streetcar at Broadway and 27th Street and he never fully recovered. Soon afterwards he had a stroke which left him bedridden. He returned to his home in New London, Connecticut, but was taken to the Lawrence Memorial Hospital where he died on 10 August 1920, an unhappy, bitter man. He felt he had squandered his talents by taking the easy, profitable option of giving the public what they wanted — *The Count of Monte Cristo*. The *New York Times* wrote in his obituary: 'O'Neill was one of the last of the old school of actors well grounded in their profession, always effective and a lover of all that is true and good in dramatic art, always holding up with authority the best traditions of the American stage.'

PETER O'TOOLE

Peter O'Toole was born on 2 August 1932 in Connemara, Ireland. A year later his father, who was a gambler, moved the family to England, to Leeds. O'Toole left school at 14 and tried a variety of jobs, including newspaper copy boy, jazz band drummer, vacuum-cleaner salesman and seaman. When his national service was over he spent the last of his money on a ticket to see Michael Redgrave as King Lear at Stratford. So impressed was he that he hitch-hiked to London where, at the Royal Academy of Dramatic Art, he demanded an audition. So impressed were they that they gave him a scholarship. His first professional job had been at the Civic Theatre, Leeds, but after his RADA training he joined the Old Vic Company in September 1955 for the seven-line part of the Cabman in *The Matchmaker*. He remained with the company for four years, playing a great variety of parts. In the first year, as well as the Cabman he was Covino in *Volpone*. The following year he was the Duke of Cornwall in *King Lear*, Herbert in *The Empty Chair*, Bullock in *The Recruiting Officer*, Peter Shirley in *Major Barbara*, Maupa in *The Queen and the Rebels*, Cardinal Malko Barberini in *The Lamp at Mid-*

night, Lodovico in *Othello* and Baron Parsnip in *The Sleeping Beauty*. He made his first London appearance that year in July with the Bristol Old Vic Company at the London Old Vic, where he played Peter Shirley in *Major Barbara*. In 1957 in Bristol he was Mr Jaggers in *Great Expectations*, Alfred Doolittle in *Pygmalion*, Lysander in *A Midsummer Night's Dream*, Jimmy Porter in *Look Back in Anger*, the Angel in *Sodom and Gomorrah*, the General in *Romanoff and Juliet*, Mrs Millie Baba in *Ali Baba and the Forty Thieves*, and Uncle Gustave in *Oh, My Papa*. The last play, a Swiss musical comedy set in the nineteenth century, also played in London at the Garrick during July 1957. By 1958 Peter O'Toole had the big roles at Bristol. That year he was John Tanner in *Man and Superman*, Paddy in *The Pier*, Jupiter in *Amphitryon 38*, and Hamlet. He spent September 1958 touring as Roger Muir in *The Holiday* and opened at the Royal Court in London in January 1959 playing Private Bamforth in *The Long and the Short and the Tall*. Of this performance Kenneth Tynan wrote: '... in the case of Mr O'Toole, as the cynical Cockney who befriends the Japanese captive, I sensed a technical authority that may, given discipline and purpose, presage greatness. To convey violence beneath banter, and a soured embarrassed goodness beneath both is not the simplest task for a young player, yet Mr O'Toole achieved it without sweating a drop.' The play transferred to the New Theatre in April 1959 but ran only three months.

Peter O'Toole joined the Shakespeare Memorial Theatre Company for their 1960 season at Stratford. There he played Petruchio to Peggy Ashcroft's Kate in *The Taming of the Shrew*, Thersites in *Troilus and Cressida* and Shylock in *The Merchant of Venice*. Of the last Peter Roberts wrote: 'Peter O'Toole's Jew was decidedly tragic . . . [he] delivered the well-worn lines with remarkable freshness, often choosing mezza voce where so many of his predecessors have pulled the stops right out.' Hugh Herbert wrote many years later in the *Times* about that performance: 'The performance that very nearly turned him into a major Shakespearian actor twenty years ago drew its power largely from the fact that his starting point was not the then-traditional griping old money lender, but a dashing, young mercantile adventurer, with some pretension to a kind of nouveau riche nobility. So when he broke, he broke utterly, and the contrast, the sense of pain and disaster was all the greater.'

At the Phoenix in February 1963 he played the title role in Brecht's *Baal*. Martin Esslin wrote: 'Peter O'Toole, whom I regard as probably the greatest potential force among all actors of the English-speaking world, magnificent as he is, is totally miscast in the part of Baal. If Baal appears handsome as a young god . . . the central mystery of the character is lost. Even if O'Toole's Baal were not a poet but a barrow-boy, not a genius but a moron, women would still pursue him to the ends of the earth, so his genius, his almost supernatural life force ceases to matter.'

In October 1963 Peter O'Toole played the title role in an almost uncut version of *Hamlet* which, directed by Laurence Olivier, was the inaugural production of the National Theatre Company at the Old Vic. Of his Hamlet Peter Roberts wrote in *Plays and Players*: 'The performance is conceived in an arch, beginning on a low level of melancholy developing through a middle period of self-torture and torment giving way to a final acquiescence to fate and so to death. This is not the poetic aesthete nor the babbling neurotic. It is simply a man of sufficient nobility and complexity to give the performance tragic stature.'

At the Piccadilly in June 1965 he was Peter in David Mercer's *Ride a Cock Horse*. Charles Marowitz wrote of this: 'Peter O'Toole, once again the self-destructive hero, is now well-versed in moral and physical deterioration. He plays the comedy like a music hall veteran and sometimes suggests that the serious stuff is there only on sufferance. He rages beautifully but the characterization has no overall shape and so a bevy of fine moments don't add up to anything whole.'

O'Toole went back to Ireland in August 1966, where at the Gaiety Theatre in Dublin he played Captain Jack Boyle in *Juno and the Paycock*. At the same theatre in October 1969 he was John Tanner in *Man and Superman* and at the Abbey Theatre in Dublin that December he played Vladimir in *Waiting for Godot*. He rejoined the Bristol Old Vic Company in October 1973 and played the title role in *Uncle Vanya*, D'Arcy Tuck in *Plunder* and King Magnus in *The Apple Cart*. He gave a solo reading of *Justice* there in January 1974. For the Dublin Festival in October 1976 Peter O'Toole played three parts in *Dead-Eyed Dicks*. After seventeen years away which included filming — *Lawrence of Arabia*, *Lord Jim*, *The Lion in Winter* and *Man of La Mancha*, among others — a couple of Oscar nominations, a divorce from his actress wife Sian Phillips after twenty years of marriage and two daughters, and a major operation, in September 1980 Peter O'Toole made his return to the London stage. He opened at the Old Vic in the title role of *Macbeth* — and he and the production received some of the worst notices since Pearl Harbour. However, he did draw the biggest advance booking of any modern Old Vic production, and when they went on the road with it they broke house records all over the country. He resigned from the board of the Old Vic after his fellow directors disowned the production. And who could blame him. In the end, however, *Macbeth* netted £20,000. 'I just wanted a crack at *Macbeth*,' he said when it was all over, 'on the principle of getting the worst over first. In the history of the British theatre there have only been three actors who have pulled it off: Macready, Garrick, Wolfit. And now me. It took time, but eventually it came together. I enjoyed every second of it. My favourite moment on the first night was when I'd killed Duncan. As I came down the stairs dripping with blood, an ambulance howled all the way up Waterloo Road. I got the giggles. The audience got the giggles. It was bloody marvellous.'

More successfully, O'Toole made West End appearances in two Shaw revivals, *Man and Superman* (1983) and *Pygmalion* (1984).

GERALDINE PAGE

Geraldine Page was born in Kirksville, Missouri, on 22 November 1924. Her father, Leon Elwin Page, was on the faculty of the College of Osteopathy there. The family moved to Chicago when Geraldine was five. She went to High School in Chicago and after that, wanting to be an artist, got a scholarship to the Chicago Academy of Fine Arts. She first appeared on the stage at the Englewood Methodist Church in Chicago in 1940 playing in *Excuse My Dust*. Soon afterwards she decided she wanted to be an actress. As she explained: 'It was after seeing Laurette Taylor doing nothing and making it everything that I decided to be an actress. Father wanted me to be a writer instead.' She studied for the stage in Chicago at the Goodman Theater School, and went to New York in 1945 where she first appeared at the Blackfriars Guild on 25 October playing the Sophomore in *Seven Mirrors*. She then spent four summers (1945–48) at the Lake Zurich Summer Playhouse in rep and three winters (1947–49) at the Woodstock Winter Playhouse. In the summers of 1950 and 1951 she was at the Shadylane Summer Theater.

Back in New York, at the Circle in the Square Theater in 1951 she played the Pagan Crone in *Yerma* and at the same theatre in April 1952 she was Alma in a revival of Tennessee Williams' *Summer and Smoke*. With that production she became a star. Brooks Atkinson wrote in the *New York Times*: 'Geraldine Page's portrait of the lonely, panicky spinster of Glorious Hill, Mississippi, is truthful, perceptive and poignant.' By this time Geraldine Page was studying with the actress Uta Hagen. She remained a constant believer in study and psychiatry to get to the depths of a character, and became a leading exponent of the Method school of acting, studying with Elia Kazan. At the Vanderbilt Theater in January 1953 she was Lily Barton in *Midsummer*, and her name was above the title. At the Royale Theater in February 1954 she was Marcelline in *The Immoralist*, and had a great success at the Cort that October playing Lizzie Curry in *The Rainmaker*. Brooks Atkinson reported: 'As a comedienne, Miss Page has some unexpected qualities. She is fresher than the play and equally funny.' She toured with *The Rainmaker* from March through May 1955. Then at the John Golden in February 1956 she played Amy McGregor in *The Innkeepers* before making her London début at the St Martin's in May, once more playing Lizzie in *The Rainmaker*. Returning

to the United States, she played in repertory at the Studebaker Theater in Chicago from October through December. That year also she married the violinist Alexander Schneider.

Geraldine Page returned to New York in July 1957, where she took over the parts of Mrs Shankland and Miss Railton-Bell from Margaret Leighton in Rattigan's double bill, *Separate Tables*, first at the Music Box and then on tour.

In March 1959 Geraldine Page opened on Broadway at the Martin Beck Theater in Tennessee Williams' *Sweet Bird of Youth*, playing Alexandra del Lago. Brooks Atkinson reported: 'Geraldine Page gives a fabulous performance as the decaying movie queen. Loose-jointed, gangling, raucous of voice, crumpled, shrewd, abandoned yet sensitive about some things that live in the heart, Miss Page is at the peak of form in this raffish characterization.' And Kenneth Tynan said her performance was 'a display of knock-down flamboyance and drag-out authority that triumphantly quells all doubts about this actress's ability to transcend her mannerisms.' For this portrayal Geraldine Page received the New York Drama Critics Award for Best Actress. She then toured with the production.

In January 1962, having by this time married the actor Rip Torn, she was in Philadelphia at the Locust Theater playing Sister Bonaventure in *The Umbrella*. She returned to Broadway to the Hudson Theater in March 1963 playing Nina Leeds in a revival of O'Neill's *Strange Interlude*. Howard Taubman wrote that the part '. . . offers wonderful opportunities to an actress. Geraldine Page has seized them in her own way . . . With the slightly quavering girlish voice of her first entrance, Miss Page suggests the young woman whose preoccupation is largely with herself. If O'Neill's insistence on her irresistibility is not credible, Miss Page subdues this disbelief. As Nina ages, Miss Page discovers subtleties of gesture that convey both the brittleness of her emotions and the emptiness of her heart.'

At the Morosco in June 1964 Geraldine Page played Olga in *The Three Sisters*. The critic Martin Gottfried cared neither for the production nor for her performance. 'Geraldine Page as Olga', he wrote, 'merely trundles out every one of her Tennessee Williams heroine mannerisms, but without their former conviction.' Miss Page succeeded Kim Stanley in the part of Masha in the same production in August that year.

At the Henry Miller Theater in November

1964 she played Julie Cunningham in *PS I Love You*, and was at the Eugene O'Neill Theater in February 1966 playing Oriane Brice in *The Great Outdoors*.

Geraldine Page scored a great success at the Ethel Barrymore in February 1967 playing Baroness Lemberg in *White Lies* and Clea in *Black Comedy*, the Shaffer double bill. At the Music Box in October 1969 she played Angela Palmer in *Angela* and then in 1971 toured in *Marriage and Money*. She went to Philadelphia in July of that year, where at the Playhouse in the Park she was in *The Marriage Proposal* and *The Boor*. At the Playhouse in January 1973 she played Mary Todd Lincoln in *Look Away*, and returned to the Circle in the Square (the scene of her first triumph) on 29 April 1974 for a benefit gala. For the summer of 1974 she was playing Regina Giddons in *The Little Foxes*, both at the Academy Festival in Lake Forest, Illinois, and at the Walnut, Philadelphia. Then at the Music Box in October she was in *Absurd Person Singular*, remaining in the production for more than a year.

Geraldine Page has also had great success in films, her most notable being Williams' *Summer and Smoke* and *Sweet Bird of Youth*, Lillian Hellman's *Toys in the Attic* and Woody Allen's *Interiors*. She also received two Emmy Awards for television appearances, in *A Christmas Memory* and *The Thanksgiving Visitor*.

LILLI PALMER

*L*illi Palmer — actress, painter, writer — was born in Germany on 24 May 1914. Her father, Alfred Peiser, was a surgeon and her mother, Rose Lissmann, was an actress before her marriage. A born performer, at the age of ten Lilli was acting under the pine trees at the Open Air School in Berlin her own version of Fritz Lang's *The Nibelungs* for the entertainment of her classmates. When she was older and wanted to go to acting school her father, who had always hoped she might be persuaded to become a doctor, insisted that she finish high school, so she went to classes in the mornings and in the afternoons attended the Ilka Grüning School of Acting. After two years of this gruelling schedule she managed both to complete her academic career and to finish her professional training. She made her stage début at the Rose Theatre in Berlin in June 1932 playing Rolly in *Die Eiserne Jungfrau*. For her graduation exercise at the Ilka Grüning School she performed the Bells monologue from *Saint Joan* and a comic scene from Sardou's *Cyprienne*. She got a job with the Darmstadt State Theatre, where she was cast mostly in musical comedies, including *White Horse Inn*, *Gypsy Princess* and *Happy Journey*. With the rise of the Nazis, Lilli Palmer, a Jew, found her contract cancelled. She went to Paris, knowing there was no future for her on the stage in Germany, and worked in nightclubs and cabaret, including the Moulin Rouge, but barely made a living.

In 1935 Lilli Palmer went to England, armed with an introduction to Alexander Korda, the film-maker, and began her career in films. She made her first appearance on the London stage at the Garrick Theatre in March 1938 when she played Katia in *Road to Gandahar*. In October that year she was at the Apollo playing Eve in *The Tree of Eden*, and at the Strand in February 1939 she was another Eve in *Little Ladyship*. At the Apollo in December 1939 she played Elsie Sorel-Easton in *You, of All People* and at the Lyric in April 1940 she was Felicity Van der Loo in *Ladies into Action*. At the Haymarket in March 1941 she played Amanda Smith in *No Time for Comedy*, which starred Rex Harrison; that ran for more than a year, and in January 1943 she and Harrison were married. They had a son the following year and in November 1945 set off for Hollywood where they both had film contracts to take up.

Four years later, her husband became involved in the scandal following Carole Landis' suicide and they went to New York, where Lilli Palmer made her Broadway début in Jean Pierre Aumont's *My Name Is Aquilon*, at the Lyceum Theater on 9 February 1949. She played Christine Benoit-Benoit, and the *New York Times* reported: 'Miss Palmer is the finest thing that has happened to the Gotham stage for quite a long time.' Despite that, the show lasted only a month. She opened at the National Theater in December 1949 starring opposite Cedric Hardwicke in Shaw's *Caesar and Cleopatra*. On the opening night Hardwicke had a bad cold which lessened his impact but Brooks Atkinson reported: 'Lilli Palmer is not only in good health but in radiant spirit and her Cleopatra is nothing short of ideal. Miss Palmer has personal beauty that is notable on its own account. But her limpid, girlish, roguish Cleopatra is also a superb exposition of character that would delight the old man of English letters if he could see it . . .'

At the Ethel Barrymore Theater in November 1950 she co-starred with her husband in *Bell, Book and Candle*, playing the urban witch Gillian Holroyd. The critics praised their playing together and the show ran a year. At the New Century in February 1952 she was Perpetua in *Venus Observed* and at the Shubert in January 1953 played Beauty in *The Love of Four Colonels*, both with Rex Harrison, and they were welcomed as an excellent husband and wife team.

By the time the duo arrived back on the London stage, at the Phoenix in October 1954 once more playing in *Bell, Book and Candle*, the marriage was breaking up. But the tension was not noticeable from the stalls, and Ronald Barker reported: '. . . it is a very amusing evening in the theatre thanks to the Harrisons. They play with a delicate, feather-weight touch which is a joy to watch.'

After the divorce, Lilli Palmer concentrated on films in Europe and America. Married to Argentinian actor and writer Carlos Thompson, she made her home in Zurich and did not return to the stage until 1966, when she played in Noel Coward's *Suite in Three Keys* at the Queen's — opening in April. John Russell Taylor reported that in all three plays Lilli Palmer was 'called upon to do little more than embody ageless Continental seductiveness which of course she could hardly help doing anyway, but does it admirably.'

After this brief excursion she returned to films. In 1975 she wrote a best-selling autobiography, and followed that with best-selling novels. Her paintings, too, have been highly praised.

JOAN PLOWRIGHT

Joan Plowright was born on 28 October 1929 in Brigg, Lincolnshire, where her father was editor of the *Scunthorpe and Frodingham Star*. She won prizes for essays in Scunthorpe Grammar School and her father hoped she would be a journalist, but she was encouraged in her acting ambitions by her mother Daisy, who was herself involved in amateur theatricals. When she was 15 she went to London to answer an ad in *The Stage*, and was politely sent home. She then took a summer drama course at Hull University, and when she was 17 spent a year at the Laban Art of Movement Studio in Manchester. From there she got a scholarship to the Old Vic School. She went with her father's admonition — 'I'll give you six months' — and her mother's rather left-handed encouragement — 'You're no oil painting, my girl, but you have good, useful eyes and, thank God, you have my legs and not your father's.' Joan Plowright made her first appearance on stage in repertory at the Grand Theatre, Croydon, where in July 1951 she played Hope in *If Four Walls Told*. She became a member of the Bristol Old Vic Company and toured with them to South Africa. It was after that tour that she married the actor Roger Gage, whom she had met at the Old Vic School. 'We got engaged on the boat,' she explained. 'I think it was all that hot sun. We were married for seven years and did remain friends after the divorce.' She joined the West of England Repertory Company, a travelling group involved mostly in one-night stands, and made her London début at the Westminster in July 1954 playing Donna Clara in *The Duenna*. At the Duke of York's in June 1955 she was in Orson Welles' production of *Moby Dick*, and Roger Gellant remembered a 'small, frightened, half-demented creature with eyes like boot-buttons' — that was Joan playing the cabin boy. She then went to the Nottingham Playhouse, where she spent a season playing leading parts before she was recruited to the English Stage Company under the directorship of George Devine at the Royal Court in London. She joined them in April 1956 to play Mary Warren in *The Crucible*. She went on to a variety of roles, including Baptista in *Don Juan*, the Receptionist in *The Death of Satan*, Miss Tray in *Cards of Identity* and Mrs Shin in *The Good Woman of Setzuan*. In December 1956 she played Margery Pinchwife, the title role in a revival of Wycherley's *The Country Wife*, with Laurence Harvey as the rake. Frank Granville-Barker reported: 'Joan Plowright jumps to the forefront of our young actresses with her lively performance in the title role: she is all cunning and mischief, a richly endearing flirt.' The production transferred to the Adelphi in February 1957.

Back at the Royal Court in May 1957 she played the Old Woman in *The Chairs* and Elizabeth Compton in *The Making of Moo*.

Kenneth Tynan wrote that 'Joan Plowright, all boggling fervour and timorous glee, makes a wonderful North-country mouse of the Old Woman'. At the Palace in September 1957 she took over the role Dorothy Tutin had played at the Court in *The Entertainer*, John Osborne's play which starred Laurence Olivier. She played Jean Rice, Olivier's daughter in the play — and their romance began.

Joan Plowright made her New York début at the Phoenix Theater in an Ionesco double bill in which she played the Old Woman in *The Chairs* and the Pupil in *The Lesson*. Of the first, Brooks Atkinson wrote in the *New York Times*: 'It is extremely well played by Miss Plowright as the old crone with sore feet, a loose plate, cracked voice and benevolent spirit.' And of the second play he wrote: '... no one needs a syllabus to appreciate the cherubic acting of Miss Plowright, now in the part of a schoolgirl ... [her] bright eyes, shining face and varieties of animation are very funny indeed.' The following month, at the Royale, she returned to the part of Jean Rice.

Joan Plowright was back in London, at the Royal Court in June 1958, where once more she played the Ionesco double bill, and then in August took the title role in Shaw's *Major Barbara*. Peter Roberts, writing in *Plays and Players*, said: 'In the hands of Miss Joan Plowright she was a twinkling bright as well as fair lady — an Edwardian angry young woman, in fact, with an astonishing amount to say to startle Atomic Age audiences.'

In November that year she took a break from the Royal Court and joined Robert Morley at the Piccadilly Theatre to play Arlette in *Hook, Line and Sinker*. The production was not a great critical success but Peter Roberts said: 'Glamorized to a degree, Miss Plowright does her excellent best to suppress that individual quality that made her Margery Pinchwife such a delight in favour of a more impersonal brittle style totally unsuited to her undoubted gift for good old English humour.'

In May 1959 she was at the Belgrade, Coventry, playing Beatie Bryant in Arnold Wesker's *Roots*. The production came to the Royal Court Theatre in June and the next month transferred once more to the Duke of York's. Kenneth Tynan had a few reservations: 'Joan Plowright's Beatie seemed to me a touch too pawky, suggestive less of rural Norfolk than of urban Lancs ... All the same she grips one's attention throughout and rises glowing to the challenge of the final scene.'

At the Royal Court in April 1960 she and Olivier were together once more on stage in Ionesco's *Rhinoceros*. Frank Granville-Barker said: 'Joan Plowright, in a less complicated role [than Olivier's] is also excellent. Her portrayal of the warm-hearted but empty-headed office girl was maddeningly true.'

Joan Plowright went back to New York, where in October 1960 she opened at the Lyceum Theater playing Josephine in *A Taste of Honey*. This performance won her the New York Drama Critics Award for 1961. Olivier was also playing on Broadway, and in March the same year he and Joan Plowright married in Connecticut. 'By the time I married Larry,' Joan said, 'my name was over the title of the play. I'd won my awards, I could choose my scripts, the climb was over. Only then was I ready for babies.' They subsequently had three.

When the Oliviers returned to England it was to open the Chichester Festival Theatre in July 1962. In the opening production, *The Chances*, Joan Plowright played Constantia. Clive Barnes wrote: 'As a poppet of a doxie, her whole manner affectionately rumpled and voice thick with nubility, Plowright romped through the play as if Buckingham had written it specially for her. Perhaps he did.' That opening season Plowright also played in *Uncle Vanya*. Peter Roberts reported: 'In the part of the plain and unloved Sonya, Joan Plowright finds an ideal outlet for the unique blending of eagerness, warmth and sincerity which is characteristic of her work as an actress. Her performance still retains a certain English regional quality which, whilst it colours and gives strength to her acting, is also, in a minor way, a limitation.' And Kenneth Tynan said: 'Joan Plowright drains every tear-duct in the house with her final, defiant avowal of faith in the future.'

At the Edinburgh Festival in September 1963 she played the title role in Shaw's *Saint Joan*, and the following month joined the first National Theatre Company at the Old Vic playing that part and reviving her Sonya in *Uncle Vanya*. Of the former Charles Marowitz wrote: 'Her Joan is hell-bent for heaven and one almost resents her pushy martyrdom. What in fact happens, is that Plowright is doing what she does best; glowing and throbbing with wilfulness and resolve, inspiring and being inspired by a sense of high purpose and a better-world-to-come. Even as one admires the heat of her acting, one realizes it is diminishing the impact of the play and reducing its complexity.' The following year she was a much-admired Maggie Hobson in *Hobson's Choice*, and Hilda Wangel in *The Master Builder*. Children intervened; in 1967, when she went back to the National Theatre Company, she took over the part of Beatrice in *Much Ado About Nothing* and played Maria in *The Three Sisters*. Martin Esslin said of the latter: 'Joan Plowright is, as always, warm, intelligent, witty and capable of generating powerful emotional climaxes. Hers is a wonderful performance.' That year she also played Dorine in *Tartuffe*, and *Plays and Players* enthused: 'Joan Plowright as Dorine is perfect: what wit! what irony! what sweetness!'

In 1968 she played Teresa in *The Advertisement* and John Bowen analysed the performance. 'Joan Plowright's Teresa, unconcentrated, self-pitying, abandoned by her husband and unable to think or talk of any subject but their life together, is clearly a tiresome woman, but she does not tire us. The actress shows us the pain beneath the tiresomeness and the depth of boredom and loneliness which she is boringly trying to cover over with talk ... What is more easy to notice is the perfection of Joan Plowright's comedy timing.' That year, in contrast, she also played in *Love's Labour's Lost*, and Helen Dawson reported: 'As Rosaline, Joan Plowright is bustling and bubbling, her wit darting irrepressibly.'

In 1969 with the National Theatre Company she was the Voice of Lilith in *Back to Methuselah Part II* and the following year was Portia in Jonathan Miller's production of *The Merchant of Venice*. Peter Ansorge said her Portia 'was an original creation: a new rich, snobby spinster who, apart from a determination to buy a husband ... was utterly indifferent to the events taking place around her ... Her appearance at the trial scene made no sense at all and her conventional delivery of "The quality of mercy" in saintlike whispers undercut much of the originality that had fired Plowright's performance in the earlier scenes.' The following year she played Mistress Anne Frankford in *A Woman Killed with Kindness* and Silla in *The Rules of the Game*.

At the Chichester Festival Theatre in 1972 she played Jennifer Dubedat in *The Doctor's Dilemma* and Katharina in *The Taming of the Shrew*, which Ivan Howlett said was a 'subdued but infinitely subtle performance'. At Greenwich in May 1973 she was Rebecca West in *Rosmersholm*, and then returned to the Old Vic to play Rosa in Eduardo da Filippo's *Saturday, Sunday,*

Monday, directed by Franco Zeffirelli. The following year she played Stella Kirby in *Eden End*. The very successful *Saturday, Sunday, Monday* transferred to the Queen's in October 1974.

The following October she joined the Lyric Theatre Company, where she alternated the part of Irena Arkadina in *The Seagull* with that of Alma in *The Bed Before Yesterday*. Of the Chekhov Helen Dawson wrote: 'Miss Plowright's Arkadina is the summation of "actressy" actresses — highly wrought and self-absorbed, a self-conscious star who is unsure of her own scale outside the theatre. Her hands, lost without props and stage directions, pick tensely at her shawl ... it is a sustained comic performance.' And of the Ben Travers farce, Sandy Wilson wrote: 'To be honest I had not fully realized that she is one of the greatest comediennes of our generation until I saw her play Alma Millett, but I will go further than that and say that this performance is the funniest to be seen in London since Bea Lillie went into retirement.'

In November 1977, also at the Lyric, she had great success in another da Filippo play, *Filumena*. John Barber reported: 'It allows Miss Plowright to spend three acts looking noble, hard-done-by and as queenly as the statue on the prow of a ship.' It ran for two years before going to Broadway, where it opened at the St James in February 1980. Since then she has played in *The Cherry Orchard* at the Haymarket and *Cavell* and *Way of the World* at Chichester.

Joan Plowright, who received a CBE in the 1970 New Year Honours, remains firmly a theatre star and sees no prospect of retirement. In fact, now that her children are grown she considers she is entering a third phase of her life and indeed of her career. 'I just can't see myself retiring,' she said. 'What's more, there may be another generation of us, as the children are already horribly keen to act. I've told them only to go into the theatre if it's as necessary as breathing; otherwise they'll have to watch out, particularly with a name like theirs.'

See photograph opposite page 295.

CHRISTOPHER
PLUMMER

Arthur Christopher Orme Plummer was born on 13 December 1929 in Toronto. His father John was Secretary to the Dean of Science at McGill University. His mother Isabella for a time headed the Canadian Handicrafts Guild. Plummer went to Montreal High School and then on to Jennings Private School in Montreal. His first theatrical assignment was as lighting designer for a high school production of *A Midsummer Night's Dream*.

In 1950 he joined the Canadian Repertory Theatre in Ottawa, where he played Lieutenant Victor O'Leary in *John Loves Mary* and Faulkland in *The Rivals*. He stayed with the company for two years, playing over 100 parts. For the winter of 1952 he joined the Bermuda Repertory Theatre and played Old Mahon in *The Playboy of the Western World*, Gerard in *Nina*, Anthony Cavendish in *The Royal Family*, Ben in *The Little Foxes*, Duke Mantee in *The Petrified Forest*, the Father in *George and Margaret*, Hector Benbow in *Thark* and Bernard Kersal in *The Constant Wife*. In October 1952 he joined the national touring company of *The Constant Wife* and understudied John Emery in the role of Bernard Kersal.

Christopher Plummer made his New York début at the Royale Theater on 13 January 1954 playing George Phillips in *The Starcross Story*. At the Booth Theater in September that year he played Manchester Monaghan in *Home Is the Hero*. In February 1955 he was at ANTA playing Count Peter Zichy in *The Dark Is Light Enough*, for which he received the Theater World Award. He went to Europe in June 1955, where at the International Festival at the Sarah Bernhardt Theatre in Paris he played Jason in *Medea*. The following month, at the Shakespeare Festival in Stratford, Connecticut, he played Mark Antony in *Julius Caesar* and Ferdinand in *The Tempest*. Back on Broadway in November he was at the Longacre playing the Earl of Warwick in Anouilh's *The Lark*.

Christopher Plummer returned to Canada in June 1956, where at the Shakespeare Festival in Stratford, Ontario, he played the title role in *Henry V*. He went to the Edinburgh Festival with the production in August the same year. Back in New York in December he played Lewis Rohnen in *Night of the Auk* at the Playhouse. That year he also married the actress and singer Tammy Grimes.

Back at Stratford, Ontario, in summer 1957

Plummer played the title part in *Hamlet* and Sir Andrew Aguecheek in *Twelfth Night*. He then made his first films, in the role of the Playwright in *Stage Struck* for Buena Vista and appearing in *Wind Across the Everglades* for Warner Brothers. He spent summer 1958 at Stratford, Ontario, playing Benedick in *Much Ado About Nothing*, Leontes in *The Winter's Tale* and Bardolph in *Henry IV Part 1*.

In December 1958 he opened at ANTA playing Nickles in Archibald MacLeish's *JB*. Admiring the performance, Kenneth Tynan wrote that Christopher Plummer was 'the flexible, saturnine young Canadian whose range, widening every season, has already put him within striking distance of most of the light-heavyweight roles in the American and European repertoire'. Back at Stratford, Ontario, in June 1960 he played the Bastard in *King John* and Mercutio in *Romeo and Juliet*.

Christopher Plummer joined the Royal Shakespeare Company in Stratford-on-Avon in April 1961, where once more he played Benedick in *Much Ado About Nothing*. Peter Roberts reported: 'Mr Plummer has a fine voice and a fine presence, and he is not afraid to use his hands, pointing a line with a delicacy and variety of gesture that one does not see often outside the Comédie-Française.' He then, bravely, took on the title role in *Richard III*, so closely identified with Laurence Olivier. Peter Roberts was again complimentary: 'Christopher Plummer, for all that he reminds one at times of Olivier, brings a personal twist to many familiar lines and scenes and is particularly good in the exchange with Buckingham.' At the Aldwych Theatre in London in July 1961 he played King Henry in Anouilh's *Becket*. Kenneth Tynan said: 'This is an actor of real stage-seizing power, unafraid of the big gesture, and endowed with a stabbing voice of kaleidophonic virtuosity.' The production transferred to the Globe in December and Plummer received the *Evening Standard* Award for Best Actor. In July that same year he was back at Stratford, Ontario, playing the titles roles in *Macbeth* and *Cyrano de Bergerac*.

In November 1963 he was again on Broadway at the Lunt-Fontanne Theater playing the title role in Brecht's *Arturo Ui*. The production closed within the week, though the critic Martin Gottfried reported: 'Christopher Plummer gave the performance of a lifetime. The excitement was palpable.' He played Francisco Pizarro in *The Royal Hunt of the Sun* at ANTA in October

1965, and in July 1967 returned to Stratford, Ontario, where he played Mark Antony in *Antony and Cleopatra*.

Christopher Plummer received Canada's highest civilian honour on 25 September 1970 when he was made a Companion of the Order of Canada.

In June 1971 Laurence Olivier invited him to join the National Theatre Company at the New Theatre in London. He first played Jupiter and Amphitryon in *Amphitryon 38* with Geraldine McEwan. Stanley Price, writing in *Plays and Players*, was not impressed: 'No doubt a star vehicle was intended for Christopher Plummer as guest artiste, but despite a hard-sell programme note about him signed by Olivier himself, Mr Plummer fails to rise to the occasion. He makes little distinction in his playing of Jupiter or Amphitryon or of Jupiter in the guise of Amphitryon. He has some comic moments as the straight Amphitryon when he appears to be groping towards a characterization of an amiable, golf-playing young militarist summoned too soon from the nuptial couch, but he never maintains these moments.' His next assignment for the National was playing Danton in *Danton's Death*, directed by Jonathan Miller. Hilary Spurling wrote: 'Christopher Plummer ... plays Danton with a weary bland perplexity which puts one in mind less of a revolutionary hero than of one of Sheridan's heavy fathers.' Back in New York, at the Palace Theater in May 1973 he played the title role in a musical *Cyrano*, for which he got the Tony Award for best actor in a musical — even though the said musical lasted a mere two weeks on Broadway. By this time he had married his third

wife, Elaine Taylor, whom he had met when filming *Lock Up Your Daughters*. At the Eugene O'Neill Theater in November 1973 he played Anton Chekhov in Neil Simon's play, *The Good Doctor*.

With fellow Canadian Zoe Caldwell he devised and appeared in *Love and Master Will*, which they presented at the Opera House of the Kennedy Center in Washington, DC, in September 1975. In November 1978 he was Edgar in *Drinks Before Dinner*, and in 1982 was at the Winter Garden Theater on Broadway playing Iago to James Earl Jones' Othello, and filling the house every night in that usually Shakespeare-allergic city. John Barber, the English critic, reported: 'Christopher Plummer's Iago is a far more remarkable creation [than Jones' Othello]. I thought the actor began by working too hard to arrest attention — spitting, clapping, slapping a table-top, on occasion mincing with an Olivier-like effeminacy. Then I realized that this restlessness expressed the impatience of the hatred in his heart. This is a real character, a hypocritical soldier who stands too punctiliously to attention, is always too obsequiously respectful of his betters. His glassy eyes, deep-set and malign, and his disdainful efficiency suggest the dangerous contempt of a mean, bored man who cannot endure being a supernumerary, and who lies and stabs in the dark to avenge and amuse himself.' For this performance Christopher Plummer was nominated for a Tony.

He has worked often in films — most notably in *The Sound of Music*, *Inside Daisy Clover* and *The Royal Hunt of the Sun* — and first performed on television in 1951, returning frequently to play in both classical and modern scripts.

ERIC PORTMAN

*E*ric Portman was born on 13 July 1903 in Halifax, Yorkshire. His father was a wool merchant. He went to Rushworth School in Halifax, where he was an enthusiastic performer in plays and became a member of the Halifax Opera Society. When he left school he went to work in a Leeds department store but soon bored of the work, and when the famous Shakespearian actor Henry Baynton was visiting the Grand Theatre, Leeds, Eric Portman went backstage after the performance and got himself a job with the company. He made his stage début at the Victoria Theatre in Sunderland in 1924.

Eric Portman made his London début that same year at the Savoy Theatre playing Antipholus of Syracuse in *The Comedy of Errors*. He next played Mowbray in *Richard II*, and at the Strand Theatre in 1925 he was Worthing in *White Cargo*. He spent 1936 touring in a repertory of modern plays and in February 1927 he was at the Rudolf Steiner Hall playing Orestes in *Electra*. The following month he was at the Old Vic playing Horatio in *Hamlet*, and joined the Old Vic Company at the Lyric, Hammersmith, where between September 1927 and January 1928 he played a variety of parts, including Lucentio in *The Taming of the*

Shrew, and Claudio in *Much Ado About Nothing*. Between February and May 1928, with the Old Vic Company, Eric Portman played Romeo, Charles Surface, Edmund in *King Lear,* Arcite in *The Two Noble Kinsmen,* Laertes in *Hamlet* and Strength in *Everyman*. At the Arts Theatre in October 1928 he was Erhard Borkman in *John Gabriel Borkman* and Kaleve in *Caravan*.

At the Queen's Theatre in January 1929 Eric Portman played Berthold in *The Mock Emperor*, and at Wyndham's in March he was Stephen Undershaft in *Major Barbara*. He returned to the Arts in July as Robert in *The Hell Within*, and at the Q the following month played Edward Adishan in *Portrait of a Lady*. He was at the Vaudeville in November playing Tony in *The Roof*, and at the Court in February 1930 once more played Laertes in *Hamlet*. In March he was Le Vicomte in *The Lion Tamer* at the Gate and Joseph Percival in *Misalliance* at the Court. The next month, back at the Lyric, Hammersmith, he played Crowley Tukes in *Out of the Blue* and Young Marlow in *She Stoops to Conquer*. At the Royalty in June he was Aimwell in *The Beaux' Stratagem* and at the Embassy in October played Lelio in *The Liar*.

Eric Portman returned to the Gate in February 1931 to play Eben in *Desire Under the Elms*, and in September at the Lyric, Hammersmith, was Bellmour in *The Old Bachelor*. At the Duchess in November he was Ragnar Brovik in *The Master Builder*, and back at the Gate in February 1932 played Paul in *Which …?* He went to the Embassy in October 1932 where he played George d'Alroy in *Caste*, Captain Absolute in *The Rivals* and Georg von Hartwig in *Midsummer Fires*.

At the Prince's in May 1933 he was Count Orloff in *Diplomacy*, and in September of that year was at Wyndham's playing Ernest Turner in *Sheppey*. At the Apollo in November he was Thomas Lawrence in *Mrs Siddons*, and the following month was at the Playhouse playing Hubert Capes in *The World of Light*. In 1934 he played Robert de Vere in *Richard of Bordeaux* at the New Theatre and at the Embassy that September was Murat in *Napoleon*.

For the Repertory Players in November 1934 he played Carlo Monreale at the Piccadilly in *Our Mutual Father* while the same month he was at the Shaftesbury playing Dante Alighieri in *For Ever*. In March 1935 he opened at the Westminster playing Adrian Adair in *Chase the Ace*, and the production transferred to Daly's in May. In July at the Criterion he played Edward Tranley in *This Desirable Residence*. He opened in January 1936 at the Arts playing Lord Byron in *Bitter Harvest*, transferring in May to St Martin's. At the New in June 1937 he played Victor Brun in *The Great*

Romancer, and at the Open Air Theatre in Regent's Park that July was Brutus in *Julius Caesar*.

Eric Portman made his New York début at the Broadhurst Theater in November 1937 playing Rudolph Boulanger in *Madame Bovary*, and returned to London to the Gate in April 1938 as Crown Prince Rudolph in *The Masque of Kings*. At the Comedy in August 1938 he was Richard Dahl in *Give Me Yesterday*. He returned to New York in October 1938, where at the Guild Theater he played Oliver Farrant in *I Have Been Here Before*. Back in London, at Wyndham's in May 1939 he played Blaise Lebel in *The Intruder* by François Mauriac, in which Audrey Williamson said he was 'livid of face and twisted of mind, [and] gave a performance of sinister power'. At the Embassy in November 1939 he played Mark Antony in a modern-dress production of *Julius Caesar*, which transferred to His Majesty's in December. At the Torch Theatre in February 1940 he played Stanley Smith in *Jeannie* and in April transferred with the production to Wyndham's.

In 1940 Eric Portman entered films seriously and became a household name with his performance in *49th Parallel*. He had made his film début in Hollywood's version of *The Prince and the Pauper* after he was spotted by a Hollywood scout when he played Lord Byron in *Bitter Harvest*. For three years he was voted in a *Motion Picture Herald* poll among the first ten money-making stars in British productions. Among the films he appeared in were *One of Our Aircraft Is Missing, We Dive at Dawn, A Canterbury Tale* and *Wanted for Murder*.

Eric Portman toured England in February 1943 as Henry Quincey in *Uncle Harry*, and at the Duke of York's in May 1944 played Stephen Marlowe in *Zero Hour*, but it was not until September 1948 that he returned to the stage full-time. He opened that month at the Phoenix playing Andrew Crocker Harris in *The Browning Version* and Arthur Gosport in *Harlequinade* — Rattigan's double bill with the overall title *Playbill*. Harold Hobson reported: 'Mr Portman's playing is as quiet as Mr Rattigan's writing. There is a moment in the play when Mr Portman hesitates, polishing his glasses. The action is barely perceptible, but Mr Portman makes it show how all the pride of a man's life can be killed at one blow.' And of *The Browning Version* T. C. Worsley wrote: 'Mr Eric Portman gives one of the brilliant performances of the year. He keeps and holds very exactly the details of the personality, the tics of speech and the uncontrollable jerks of mannerism which a lifetime has stamped on the mask; then when he reaches to the moment for the real man to break through he triumphantly avoids the mawkish.' For this performance he received the Ellen Terry Award as best actor of the year.

At the Prince's Theatre in May 1950 Eric Portman played the title role in *His Excellency*, and T. C. Worsley reported: 'The evening is a triumph for Mr Portman ... [he] provides something here that is unusual on the English stage, a star performance that is nevertheless not a mere personality performance. This is the art of acting from the inside of a character at its highest and Mr Portman keeps it up all the way through the play. Not one gesture or inflection is commonplace or conventional. Every detailed touch contributes; every movement is genuinely in that part.' He was Marshall in Peter Ustinov's *The Moment of Truth* at the Adelphi in November 1951, and Worsley said: 'This old man is nothing but an old bore, and though Mr Eric Portman does everything that can technically be done to make us feel about him, we pass through the last part of the play almost wholly untouched.'

At the Opera House in Manchester in September 1952 Eric Portman played Sir Robert Briston in *The Guilty Party* and returned to London to Wyndham's in April 1953 as Father James Brown in Graham Greene's *The Living Room*. Kenneth Tynan reported: 'Though I must applaud Eric Portman's unselfishness in accepting the role of the priest, I must deplore the waste involved. His legs are cut off at the knees and his temperament is cut off at the mains. Mr Portman is an active actor miscast in a passive part. His game struggle to repress his natural exuberance produces an effect which I can only describe as vocal costiveness.'

For the Repertory Players in February 1954 he played Mark Heath in *Shadow of the Vine* at Wyndham's and was back in another Rattigan double bill in September at the St James's when he played Mr Martin in *Table by the Window* and Major Pollock in *Table Number Seven*, the overall evening termed *Separate Tables* and the parts specifically written for him by Rattigan. Tynan reported: 'It is Eric Portman who commands the stage, volcanic as the journalist, but even better as the major, speaking in nervous spasms and walking stiff-legged with his shoulders protectively hunched. He has the mask of a true mime, the *comédien* as opposed to the *acteur*.' And writing in *Plays and Players*, Ronald Barker said of *Table by the Window*: 'Eric Portman as the broken-down politician with heavy drooping shoulders, podgy figure, hesitant walk and rough, unkempt appearance is perfectly in key. The performance is so right that one is apt to take this great talent for

granted.' Of the second play he wrote: 'Rattigan sketches in the details of this boasting, lying, pitiful man as only a master can. To match it Portman gives one of his finest performances, mingling extreme sensitivity with broad strength. This is as good a performance as England can show.' Eric Portman went with the production to the Music Box in New York in October 1956 and toured America with it until January 1958.

He remained in America, where in May of that year he played Mr Rochester in *Jane Eyre* at the Belasco and in October at the Helen Hayes was Cornelius Melody in *A Touch of the Poet*. Of the latter Brooks Atkinson wrote: 'The acting of Miss Hayes, Miss Stanley and Mr Portman brought a random script vigorously alive.' At the Lyceum in New York the following October he was Cherry in *Flowering Cherry*, and at the Ambassador in January 1962 he played Mr Fielding in *A Passage to India*.

Eric Portman returned to England in April 1964 when he opened at the Comedy Theatre in the title part of Robin Maugham's based-on-fact play, *The Claimant*. Hugh Leonard called it 'an anti-play — acted by and large by anti-actors', and said of Mr Portman: 'He went on to give a performance so fidgety that one expected him momentarily to say, "Sorry, wrong theatre," and flee the stage.'

In July 1965 he was Edward Kimberley in *The Creeper* at St Martin's, and Martin Esslin reported: 'Edward Kimberley ... a millionaire, 57 years of age, lives in retirement in a vast mansion, Highgate, with an old family retainer and a succession of young men "companions" whom he keeps up all night by playing the piano to and gin rummy with them ... Eric Portman is the ideal cast for Edward Kimberley, the part is simply made for him.'

In July 1969 ill-health forced Eric Portman to retire from both the stage and the screen. He took an advertisement in the *Times* which read: 'Eric Portman would like to thank all those who have sent such understanding messages with regard to his enforced retirement from the stage and TV. Luckily he is still allowed to do radio work (if it should come his way). He remembers with gratitude the parts he has played in England and America and the immense fun he has always enjoyed with his friends both in and out of the dressing room.' He went to work on a radio programme based on his own misfortune of having a weak heart. Unfortunately it was never completed, and Eric Portman died in his converted labourer's cottage at St Veep in Cornwall on 7 December 1969, aged only 66 years.

ROBERT
PRESTON

Robert Preston Meservey was born in Newton Highlands, Massachusetts, on 8 June 1918. When he was two the family moved to Los Angeles, where his father worked in the garment industry and his mother, after the birth of his younger brother, in a record shop. She also happened to be a regular member of the Theater Guild and rather encouraged her son when he decided to be an actor. It was at Lincoln High School in Los Angeles that he first thought of it. As he explained: 'When I acted, I was immediately good at it. I didn't go through any of the tortures of doing something I didn't like.'

He made his first appearance on stage in *Kearney from Killarney* and then spent some time parking cars at the racetrack before being taken on by Patia Power's Company in *Julius Caesar*. He joined the Pasadena Playhouse in 1936 and worked in Shakespearian repertory and other plays — forty-two in all during his two years with them. By 1938 he had a movie contract with Paramount. With the Pasadena Players was an actress named Catherine Feltus; she and Preston married on 8 November 1940. Preston continued in films until 1951 playing second leads and heavies, with a break during the war when he served in England as an intelligence officer. He was completely fed up with the roles he was getting when he heard that José Ferrer was looking for someone to replace him playing Oscar Jaffe in *Twentieth Century* on Broadway at the Fulton Theater. Preston leapt at the chance, though the play only had another two weeks to run. He decided to stay in New York and at the City Center in April 1952 he played Joe Ferguson in *The Male Animal*, which remains one of his favourite roles. The production transferred to the Music Box in May that year. The following April he played Peter Hogarth in *Men of Distinction* at the 48th Street Theater, and at the same theatre in 1954 he was Clem Scott in *His and Hers*. At the Booth in April 1954 he was George Wilson in *The Magic and the Loss*, and at the Longacre that October played Joe McCall in *The Tender Trap*. He was Gil in *Janus* at the Plymouth in November 1955. In January 1957 at the Playhouse he was Jean Monnerie in *The Hidden River*. Though none of the plays was memorable, he did at least break the Hollywood mould in which he had been set, and proved to people that he could play a variety of roles.

It was in December 1957 that Robert Preston began a three-year tenancy of the Majestic Theater when he opened as Harold Hill in *The Music Man*. Brooks Atkinson wrote in the *New York Times* of his performance: 'As the infectious bunko man, Mr Preston could hardly be improved upon. His expansive energy and his concentration on the crisis of the moment are tonic.' And the *New York Post* reported: 'It has been recognized for quite a while in this vicinity that Mr Preston is a very fine actor, a notable comedian and a talented player of serious roles. But we never had seen him in a musical comedy or in a part that so dominated an evening, and his portrayal of a good-natured con man, an itinerant vendor of trombones and other band instruments, with both larceny and sentiment in his heart, combines racy, humorous and charming characterization with a pleasant ability to put over a song or a dance. He really comes into his heritage.' For this performance Preston won both the Tony Award and the New York Drama Critics Award.

Robert Preston was not so successful with his next venture, *We Take the Town*, a musical about the Mexican Revolution in which he played Pancho Villa. It opened at the Shubert in New Haven, Connecticut, on 19 February 1962, and closed at the Shubert in Philadelphia on 17 March. At the 54th Street Theater in March 1963 he played the Burglar in a revival of *Too True to Be Good*, and at the Lyceum in December that year was Nat Bentley in *Nobody Loves an Albatross*.

His next big success was at the Lunt-Fontanne Theater in October 1964, when he played Benjamin Franklin in *Ben Franklin in Paris*. Gilbert Millstein reported in the *Saturday Evening Post*: 'There is a reasonable chance that just as Lincoln and Raymond Massey once began to seem almost interchangeable, so will Franklin be identified with Preston — all big square teeth and craggy avid face; splayed nose sniffing at everything in a spirit of olfactory and scientific inquiry; and roving pale-gray eyes constantly on the lookout for complaisant women.' But Preston had had enough of being typecast in his Hollywood days, and in his next Broadway play, at the Ambassador in March 1966, he played King Henry II in *The Lion in Winter*.

At the 46th Street Theater in November 1966 he opened with Mary Martin in a musical version of *The Fourposter* called *I Do! I Do!* The two of them occupied the stage alone for the duration, and their singing, acting and dancing overwhelmed the critics — though none of them was mad about the material. Walter Kerr said of Preston's Michael: 'He is at his untouchable best when the show asks him to be pompous and blissfully obtuse ... My own preference is for the sight of Mr Preston's putting Harry Richman to shame in a blazing green dressing-gown slithering one patent-leather shoe along the floor as he whirls time with a walking stick and a high silk hat.' Preston received his second Tony and New York Drama Critics awards for this performance, and he spent 1968 touring in the part.

Preston's Broadway success led to better film parts, and he was very successful with *The Dark at the Top of the Stairs* and *All the Way Home*, not to mention the Hollywood version of *The Music Man*.

Preston and his wife live in Rye, New York, but when playing on Broadway he can be found every night after the show in Sardi's bar.

'Acting is all I've ever done,' he says. 'I've nothing else to make comparisons with when anyone asks me whether I've ever wanted anything else out of life. It's given me enough satisfaction so that I haven't wanted or had to look for anything else. For a man without hobbies, I stand in a wonderful spot, where what I do is my best hobby and everything else is a poor second.'

ANTHONY QUAYLE

An only child, born into a family of wholesale manufacturing druggists on 7 September 1913 in Ainsdale, Lancashire, Anthony Quayle was cosseted for a time in middle-class comfortable surroundings. 'But oh, God, it was humdrum,' he says. 'It was something about those flat Lancashire fields and the cotton mills and the coal mines. The theatre was a wonderful escape into other worlds. It was as if I were shut in this box, and there were these incredible doors through which you could escape with people who lived, loved and cried.' He went to Rugby School from 1927 to 1930, but by this time his father had disappeared and Quayle had to think about earning a living. He found it hard to decide between journalism and the theatre but opted for the latter because, as he put it, 'the girls were prettier and because I thought I'd have a better chance of making some money quickly to help my mother'. He went to RADA for a year and then got a job on the halls as straight man to a comedian called Naylor Grimson, billed as 'The Meanest Man on Earth'. That lasted for a year and then Anthony Quayle made his legitimate stage début at the Q Theatre on 28 December 1931 playing Richard Coeur de Lion and Will Scarlet in *Robin Hood*. At the Festival Theatre in Cambridge he played Hector in *Troilus and Cressida*, and then in June 1932 was Aumerle to John Gielgud's Richard of Bordeaux at the New Theatre. He played Ferdinand in *Love's Labour's Lost* at the Westminster in July 1932; that September he joined the Old Vic Company, where he spent the season playing small parts. In 1933 he played a Shakespearian season at the Chiswick Empire and then in March 1934 was Bennie Edelman in *Mag-*

nolia Street at the Adelphi. In July that year he was Matt Burke in *Anna Christie* at the Imperial Institute, and at the New in November played Guildenstern in *Hamlet*.

Anthony Quayle was at the Ambassadors' in October 1935 playing Captain Coutine in *The Soldier's Fortune*, and returned to the Old Vic in February 1936 where he played St Denis in *St Helena*. That same month he was at the St James's playing Mr Wickham in *Pride and Prejudice*.

He made his New York début at the Henry Miller Theater in December 1936 playing Mr Harcourt in *The Country Wife*. He travelled to Elsinore with the Old Vic Company in June 1937 playing Laertes in *Hamlet*, and at the Westminster the following month was Horatio in the same play. At the Queen's in September 1937 he was the Duke of Surrey in *Richard II*, and in November at the St James's Theatre played Beppo in *The Silent King*.

Anthony Quayle went back to the Old Vic in December 1937, playing Demetrius in *A Midsummer Night's Dream* and Cassio in *Othello*. Audrey Williamson said he was 'a competent Cassio who grew mournful in his cups and yielded like wax to Iago's prompting'. In March 1938 at the Gate he played the Earl of Essex in *Elizabeth, La Femme sans homme*, and transferred with the production to the Haymarket the following month. He returned to the Old Vic in September, where he played Ferdinand in *Trelawney of the 'Wells'*. He also played Laertes in the modern-dress production of *Hamlet* in which Alec Guinness was the Prince. Audrey Williamson wrote: 'Anthony Quayle brought a stricken stillness to Laertes' grief and played the duel scene with a fine appreciation of the boy's uneasy sense of guilt.' Of his next role for the Vic, that of John Tanner in *Man and Superman*, she said: 'There was plenty of character and elocutionary fire about this performance.' That season he also played Captain Absolute in *The Rivals*, and then from January to April he toured the Continent and Egypt with the company. During the tour he also played the King in *Henry V*.

In 1939 Anthony Quayle joined the Royal Artillery. As he tells it: 'I had an unconventional war, fascinating and with periods of extreme discomfort. For a while I was staff officer to the C.-in-C., Gibraltar, at the time of the North African landings, which meant that I came into contact with Churchill and Eisenhower and de Gaulle, all of whom used us as a staging post in the days when they couldn't fly over Europe. I was there when Sikorsky's plane crashed — I put him in the coffin with my own hands. Then I was sent into occupied Albania by the SOE: all in all it was an intriguing time to be alive and I'd not have missed a day of it.' He had joined as a gunner, and in 1945 was demobilized as a major. It was also during the war that Quayle had his first attempt at directing: in Gibraltar there was a little theatre, and his commanding officer asked him to devise some shows for the troops.

After the war Anthony Quayle made his reappearance on the London stage in September 1945 at the Criterion, where once again he played Jack Absolute in *The Rivals*. He then directed Rodney Ackland's version of *Crime and Punishment* at the New Theatre in June 1946; Frank Granville-Barker termed it a magnificent production. At the Piccadilly Theatre in December 1946 he was Enobarbus in *Antony and Cleopatra*, and Audrey Williamson reported: 'His red-bearded, rough-hewn soldier was in exactly the right key and showed the player for the first time to be a character actor of coming note.' At the same theatre in March 1947 he was, according to Frank Granville-Barker, a 'glowingly evil' Iago to Jack Hawkins' Othello, and Harold Hobson praised the 'instant excellence of Mr Anthony Quayle's Iago. Mr Quayle's mouth-wiping, nose-scratching Iago was not born in Venice; the polish of the cities is not on him; he wears a rough jerkin, and his manner is not smooth either; he is a stubborn, scheming country lad who has come into Venice from the fields lying beyond the canals and the piazzas. This is a very notable performance.' At the Lyric, Hammersmith, in December he directed a scintillating production of *The Relapse*, which transferred to the Phoenix in January 1948. That year he joined the Shakespeare Memorial Theatre at Stratford-on-Avon as both a director and an

actor, and that first season played Iago, Claudius and Petruchio. In October he was appointed director of of the theatre and kept the post for eight years, though he occasionally took time out to direct productions in the West End. For the 1949–50 season he played Macbeth, and Benedick in *Much Ado About Nothing*. Of the latter Harold Hobson wrote: 'Mr Quayle's Benedick is less like a bright courtier of the Italian Renaissance than one of Dr Arnold's muscular young Christians. His heart is true as steel, but his tongue is not a rapier.' He also played Henry VIII, and Hobson reported: 'Anthony Quayle's Harry is half Renaissance tyrant, half petulant schoolboy, a satisfying performance.' T. C. Worsley said he was a 'ponderous but cunning King'. In October 1949 he took the company on a tour of Australia and New Zealand which lasted through February 1950. For the 1951 Stratford season Quayle directed a Cycle of Histories and played Falstaff. John Barber said: 'With a large body, deep voice and winning smile, he is obviously cast for Falstaff ... not even a Hallowe'en turnip make-up could disguise the electric quality without which Falstaff must seem a heartless poltroon.' The company then returned to Australia and New Zealand for another tour. In 1952 Quayle was created a CBE.

For the 1954 Stratford season Anthony Quayle directed and played the title role in *Othello*. Frank Granville-Barker praised his direction but was less happy with his performance. 'At no time,' he wrote, 'does this Othello convince of his native nobility, nor has he the voice to bring the music from the poetry.' That season he was also Bottom in *A Midsummer Night's Dream*, and Frank Granville-Barker said it was 'an excellent comic performance that never lapsed into caricature'. Of his Pandarus in *Troilus and Cressida* that same season Ronald Barker wrote: 'Quayle gives one of his best character studies, the laugh, high-pitched voice and decaying teeth well suggesting the flabby old man.'

He played Falstaff again during the 1955 season, this time in *The Merry Wives of Windsor*, and Ronald Barker had some reservations: 'Anthony Quayle has made a good shot at Falstaff. Perhaps at the moment he is a little young for the part, but in ten years' time he will be the best Falstaff of his generation. Here is the note of dignity and authority without which no Falstaff can succeed.' That season he was also Aaron to Olivier's Titus Andronicus. Frank Granville-Barker said: 'Anthony Quayle's Aaron is excellent in its spine-chilling contrast [to Titus]. There is no nobility here, but a revelling in evil for its own sake that makes Iago almost a suburban gentleman in comparison.' That season *Plays and Players* were able to report that he was the only administrator running a theatre in this country and making a profit.

At the Winter Garden Theater in New York in January 1956 Anthony Quayle played the title part in *Tamburlaine the Great*, directed by Tyrone Guthrie. *Plays and Players* reported: 'Anthony Quayle has played magnificently the most difficult and the longest part of the English theatre, with artistry and heroic ease, using his voice deftly.' And Brooks Atkinson wrote in the *New York Times*: 'The part is bellowing and flamboyant. Made up like an Asiatic tyrant, Mr Quayle plays with enormous agility and physical prowess, and he spends most of the evening shouting at the top of his voice. But out of the tumult a tangible character appears. An able actor, Mr Quayle has a big part under control.'

Back at Stratford in July 1956, Anthony Quayle directed *Measure for Measure* and then resigned from the directorship of the theatre. He had in his eight years there elevated a rather shaky summer festival to the level of world eminence. 'I realized,' he said, 'that the next few years would have to be full of finance sub-committees, and I really couldn't bear that so I trundled off.' And became once more a freelance actor.

He was at the Comedy Theatre in October 1956 playing Eddie in *A View from the Bridge*. Richard Buckle reported: 'Anthony Quayle's jerky, grunting, violent, unbalanced portrait of Eddie is remarkable; he becomes like a beast at bay.' In May 1957 he once more played Aaron in *Titus Andronicus*, this time at the Paris Festival, and toured with the production through Venice, Belgrade, Zagreb, Vienna and Warsaw, and then settled with it into the Stoll in London in July 1957.

He returned to New York, to the Coronet Theater, in April 1958, where he directed *The Firstborn* and also played Moses. He took the production to the Habimah Theatre in Tel Aviv in July. In September 1958 at the Edinburgh Festival he played James Tyrone in O'Neill's *Long Day's Journey into Night* and came to London with the production to the Globe Theatre. Peter Roberts reported: 'Behind Anthony Quayle's magnificent-looking James Tyrone there is a strange lack of power, so that this man never seems to be quite the giant O'Neill intended.'

He was at the Royal Court in July 1959 playing Marcel Blanchard in Noel Coward's adaptation of the Feydeau farce, *Look After Lulu*, and transferred with the production to the New Theatre in September. In November 1960 he was with Celia Johnson at Wyndham's in *Chin-Chin* playing Cesar Grimaldi. Peter Roberts said:

'Anthony Quayle, in my opinion, gives the performance of his career as Cesar. Beginning as a prosperous business man, the character dwindles into a street tramp, the victim of his unquenchable love for his faithless wife.' However, Tynan wasn't satified. He called it 'a doughty, craftsman's performance that lacks nothing except the authentic flavour of Italy. From Italian lips the words flow; from Mr Quayle's they have to be pushed.'

At the Garrick in September 1963 he co-directed and played Nachtigall in *Power of Persuasion*, and at Her Majesty's in May 1964 was Sir Charles Dilke in *The Right Honourable Gentleman*, of which Hugh Leonard wrote: '... the character of Dilke, as written, is virtually unplayable. He is either a martyr or an accomplished hypocrite and Mr Quayle is obliged to plump for one or the other of these alternatives. He chooses to portray Dilke as a grievously wronged man, but the author's ambiguous intentions turn the character into a pompous nonentity.'

In January 1966 Quayle played Leduc in Miller's *Incident at Vichy* at the Phoenix, and at the same theatre that October directed *Lady Windermere's Fan*. He returned in April 1967 to New York, where he played the title part in Brecht's *Galileo* at the Vivian Beaumont. The critic John Simon thought he was '... dependable, assured, meticulous in elocution and ultimately unexciting. Quayle has a provocative all-purpose slouch and a serviceable pucker of the eyes and areas adjoining, but he never ventures far beyond this utility base, and his performances, instead of gallant conquests of uncharted seas, are mere periploi.' Walter Kerr, writing in the *New York Times*, said: 'With an alert mind, attentive eyes, and a kindly care for the sound of words, Mr Quayle establishes the classroom tone that is going to mark the whole occasion, but establishes it with geniality as well as with precision.' Quayle remained in New York, where in November at the Atkinson Theater he played General Fitzbuttress in Peter Ustinov's *Halfway Up the Tree*.

At the St Martin's Theatre in London in February 1970 he was Andrew Wyke in *Sleuth*. Michael Billington reported: 'Anthony Quayle is almost unimprovable as the thriller writer, steeped in his fantasy-world of scholarly sleuths, egghead puzzles and eccentric games.' And when the production moved to the Music Box in New York in November, John Simon said that Quayle gave an 'unabashedly, gloriously theatrical performance'.

Though he had directed some productions for the National Theatre and the West End stage, Anthony Quayle did not appear on the London stage again until October 1976 when he played Rodion Nikolayevich at the Aldwych for the Royal

Shakespeare Company's production of *Old World*. In May 1978 he took over the part of Hilary in Alan Bennett's *The Old Country* at the Queen's, and in September was at the Old Vic playing Sir Anthony Absolute in his own production of *The Rivals*. Michael Billington reported: 'Quayle's own performance as Sir Anthony Absolute is also a delight. On the one hand he is a choleric club man with Healeyesque eyebrows and plum-coloured countenance, forever looking as if he is about to break up the furniture. On the other hand he conveys the cheeriness that is the obverse of his anger.'

At the same theatre in October, he was directed by Toby Robertson in the title role of *King Lear*. B. A. Young said: 'No one with any respect for the theatre would want to miss Mr Quayle's Lear and it is a compliment both to him and to the rest of the production to say that he does not command the evening but inhabits it.' Michael Billington called it a 'sterling performance', and Irving Wardle wrote in the *Times*: 'It is a reading of compelling interest by a master Shakespearian who has come to terms with his own limits. Prime among these is the fact that despite his bull-like physique, Mr Quayle is vocally lightweight and temperamentally bounded by a robust common-sense that blocks the expression of extreme emotions ... Direct pathos is alien to this actor, but the sight of the bullying old man descending to earth and asking quiet, conversational questions

about the nature of the world he has always taken for granted is moving in the extreme.'

Anthony Quayle made many films, notably *Ice Cold in Alex*, *The Guns of Navarone*, *Lawrence of Arabia* and *Anne of a Thousand Days*, and has also had great success on television. His talents, however, are not limited to acting: he is the author of two novels, is an intrepid sailor, and spent two years as guest professor at the University of Tennessee, organizing a new theatre and lecturing on drama.

'I don't regret anything in my life,' Quayle says, 'and I wouldn't change a moment of it. I have always cared, but have never consciously chased success. People who do pursue it as a goal eventually find themselves atrophied. As for eternity and leaving something behind, I don't give a damn what I leave. Who cares about some silly old image on the screen? What good is image once you're dead? It is today and it is quality that counts. All I would want is a year or eighteen months free to scratch a message on rocks for my children and grandchildren ... hopefully a good piece of writing in which I tell them how it was.'

In 1984, Quayle fulfilled a long-standing wish to form his own theatrical touring company: his first production for Compass was *The Clandestine Marriage* which opened at the Albery in June. In 1985 he received a knighthood and opened at the Old Vic in *After the Ball*.

See photograph opposite page 326.

DENIS QUILLEY

Denis Quilley was born in Islington, London, on 26 December 1927. He went to the Bancroft School in Woodford Green, Essex, and when he was barely 17 got a job with Barry Jackson's Birmingham Repertory Company as an assistant stage manager, but during 1945 moved on to playing medium-sized roles. There were then two years of national service, during which time he had his nose broken in a boxing match. In 1947, along with 250 other young men, he went to audition for a part in *The Lady's Not for Burning*. He was hired as Richard Burton's understudy. Claire Bloom had the female lead and her understudy was Stella Chapman. In January 1950 at the Globe Theatre, London, Quilley and Miss Chapman took over the parts; they were also married that year.

At the Phoenix Theatre in April 1950 Quilley

played Leading Seaman Kendall in *Red Dragon*, and then joined the Old Vic Company for a tour of Italy playing Fabian in *Twelfth Night*. Back in London with the Young Vic Company in December at the Old Vic he was Richard Shelton in *Black Arrow*, and the following month played Gratiano in *The Merchant of Venice*. At the Duke of York's he took over the part of Mathias in *Point of Departure*.

Denis Quilley spent 1952 with the Nottingham Repertory Company. He has said how much he enjoys repertory 'because although you are always tired and overworked, you never get bored'. In April 1953 he was at the Royal Court in the revue *Airs on a Shoestring*, which ran for more than 700 performances. Then, at the Duke of York's in July 1955, he had his first leading role in the West End playing Geoffrey Morris in *Wild Thyme*. His wife

Stella was also in the production. Frank Granville-Barker reported: 'The outstanding performance is given by Denis Quilley, a newcomer to London's musical stage. Unlike the average undisciplined musical-comedy juvenile, he is an actor turned singer. He knows how to give a wholly sympathetic study of character, he sings with strong, clear, pleasing tone and he possesses good looks and agility. It seems unfair, in fact, that one person should have so much.' At the Piccadilly in December 1955 he played Laurie in *A Girl Called Jo*, and in November 1956 he was Tom Wilson in *Grab Me a Gondola* at the Lyric, Hammersmith. He transferred with the production to the Lyric in the West End, where it ran for two years.

Denis Quilley then went to the Bristol Old Vic in September 1958 where he played Captain Brassbound in *Captain Brassbound's Conversion* and Orlando in *As You Like It*. At the Saville in April 1959 he played the title role in a musical version of *Candide* and at the Piccadilly in May 1960 he was Mike Polaski in *Bachelor Flat*. Peter Roberts described the latter as a trifling American comedy, but added: 'Denis Quilley makes the most of the amorous student.'

At the Everyman in Cheltenham in September 1960 he played Mark Raven in *Wildest Dreams*, and then in November took over the part of Nestor-le-Fripe in *Irma La Douce* at the Lyric. He made his New York début at the Plymouth Theater in June 1961 in this role and then toured the United States with it. Back in London in June 1963 he was Benedick in *Much Ado About Nothing* at the Open Air Theatre in Regent's Park.

Denis Quilley was at Drury Lane in November 1963 playing Antipholus of Ephesus in *The Boys from Syracuse*, and the following November at the Savoy was in the musical version of Noel Coward's *Blithe Spirit*, called *High Spirits*, playing Charles Condomine.

In April 1966 he went on a long tour of Australia playing Robert Browning in *Robert and Elizabeth*. Back in England in January 1969 he went to the Playhouse, Nottingham, as Archie Rice in *The Entertainer* and then took over the title role in *Macbeth*. He played Krogstad in *A Doll's House* at the Gardner Centre at the University of Sussex in January 1970, and at Greenwich in February was Alec Hurley in *Sing a Rude Song*. He transferred with the production to the Garrick in May.

Denis Quilley was summoned to the National Theatre Company by Olivier in March 1971 to play Aufidius in *Coriolanus*, then Scofield in *Tyger* and Jamie in *Long Day's Journey into Night*. The following year with the company he was Henry Bolingbroke in *Richard II*, and Frank Cox

reported: 'Denis Quilley brings to Henry Bolingbroke a splendid practicality; this is a man of iron, uncomplicated and nobody's fool, physically assured, the type for whom things seem to fall naturally into place — even things like the crown of England.' During 1972 he was also Crabtree in *The School for Scandal*, Banquo in *Macbeth*, and according to Alan Brien was 'a bouncy, open-faced star bull-shitter' Hildy Johnson in *The Front Page*. In 1973 he took over the title role in *Macbeth* and also played Luigi Ianiello in *Saturday, Sunday, Monday*, Andrew Ford in *The Party* and Lopakhin in *The Cherry Orchard*. Of the last Charles Marowitz wrote: 'Denis Quilley's gregarious Lopakhin manages to suggest not only that the character has peasant roots but that he has also developed bourgeois traits with which to disguise them. It is a lucid, telling, physically stated performance.' In 1974 he played Caliban to John Gielgud's Prospero in *The Tempest*, directed by Peter Hall. Michael Coveney said: 'It is a pity that Denis Quilley's full-blooded redskin wasn't allowed to develop the political consciousness he was so excitingly gaining during the middle acts.'

In August 1975 at the Yvonne Arnaud Theatre in Guildford he played John Tanner in *Man and Superman*, and was back at the Old Vic with the National Theatre Company in December playing Claudius in the Finney–Hall *Hamlet* which opened the Lyttelton Theatre in March 1976. With the Young Vic he played Hector in *Troilus and Cressida* in June 1976. Then at the Olivier Theatre in October he bashed his brains out against the prison bars as Bajazeth in the epic *Tamburlaine the Great*.

He joined the Royal Shakespeare Company at the Aldwych in February 1977 playing the outrageously camp Captain Terri Dennis in *Privates on Parade*. Charles Marowitz reported: 'As the fruity compere who directs the stray band of military mummers, Denis Quilley is invited, in almost every scene, to go whistling over the top; an invitation he discreetly declines, producing instead a delicately controlled performance which perfectly balances comment and caricature.' In this production he impersonated Vera Lynn, Marlene Dietrich and Carmen Miranda and won himself the SWET award for best comedy performance. He transferred with the production to the Piccadilly Theatre in February 1978. Before that at the Albery in June 1977 he played Morell in *Candida*, with Deborah Kerr.

At the Garrick in October 1978 Denis Quilley played Sidney Bruhl in the thriller *Deathtrap*. David Robins wrote in *Plays and Players*: 'Denis Quilley ... is excellent as Bruhl. Urbane, witty, utterly unscrupulous ... Yet one cannot help feeling that an actor of Mr Quilley's ability can have essentially one-note parts like this for breakfast.' His next role was indeed a challenge. At Drury Lane in July 1980 he played the title role in Sondheim's *Sweeney Todd*. 'This,' Quilley said, 'is the toughest thing I've done but I've worked hard on it. I studied the music, I worked with a coach and then with the music director so by the time we started rehearsals I had that part of it under my belt.' Unfortunately, despite a splendid performance by Quilley the show closed after only

five months, although it was named the best musical of the year by the drama critics.

In 1985 he opened at Chichester as Antony to the Cleopatra of Diana Rigg.

Denis Quilley has worked on television and in films, most notably in *Murder on the Orient Express* and *Privates on Parade*. He lives in Hampstead with his wife and three children, and most enjoys musical evenings when he plays the piano, the flute and the cello.

RACHEL

*E*lizabeth Felix was born on 28 February 1821 in Mumpf, Switzerland, the daughter of a Jewish peddler who came from Metz in Lorraine and made his way with his family to Paris by way of Lyons. As a child Elizabeth sang in the streets with her elder sister while her parents sold their wares, and when they settled for a while in Lyons the children took to singing in cafés, a practice they continued when they reached Paris. In 1832 she was apprenticed to Etienne Choron, director of the Institut Royal de la Musique Réligieuse, but Choron soon decided that her voice was not good enough so she studied classical French drama with Pagnon Saint-Aulaire, a former Comédie-Française actor. In April 1835 he hired the Salle Molière so that his pupils could perform on stage there. By 1836 Elizabeth was at the Conservatoire of the Comédie-Française, but only for a brief time because she soon got a job at the Gymnase, one of the smaller theatres of Paris. She made her début there on 24 July 1837 in a play based on Sir Walter Scott's novel *The Heart of Midlothian* called *La Vendenne*. It was at this début that Elizabeth Felix adopted the stage name of Rachel, which she got from a popular opera of the time, Halévy's *La Juive*. Her début was well reviewed by the influential critic Jules Janin in the *Journal des Débats*.

Rachel then joined the Comédie-Française company and made her début with them on 12 June 1838 as Camille in Corneille's *Horace*. During July and August she also played in Corneille's *Cinna*, Racine's *Andromaque*, Voltaire's *Tancrède* and Racine's *Iphigénie*. But it was summer in Paris, she was unknown, the classical plays were not very popular and all this added up to near-empty houses, until Jules Janin returned from his holiday and wrote: 'Be advised that at the moment I am speaking to you there exists at the

Théâtre-Français itself, I repeat, at the Théâtre-Français, an unheralded victory, one of those happy triumphs of which a nation like ours is rightly proud ... Now at last we have the most stunning and marvellous young girl whom the present generation has seen on the stage. That child (learn her name!) is Mademoiselle Rachel ... A strange thing: a young, ignorant, artless girl, falling among the ancient tragedies. She resuscitates them, blowing vigorously on these venerable embers.' The audiences hurried to see her and to acclaim her. By November she was the sensation of Paris and making an enormous salary playing in Racine's *Bajazet*. She began her social climb and chose her lovers, of whom there were many, with an eye to advancement. Prince Napoleon was numbered among her conquests. One of her favourite roles was that of Camille in *Horace*, and a contemporary actor described her performance thus: 'Instead of the classic elevation of voice and those loud outbursts of grief which carry away the audience and force applause, Mlle Rachel, either through fatigue, calculation or disdain of received traditions, uttered those words [at the play's climax] hoarsely, and with concentrated feelings, so that the public which expected something different, did not applaud.' They were, however, overwhelmed by her new method with the old tragedies. She acted rather than declaimed them.

In May 1842 Rachel chose London for her first appearance abroad, where the *Times* critic called her Andromaque 'electrifying' and the *Athenaeum* critic reported: 'Few who saw her went away without those deeper chords being touched which belong to terror rather than grief.' All of London society and royalty were at her feet. She performed at Marlborough House for Queen Victoria on 3 June. During her London stay she also performed *Mary Stuart* and *Bajazet*, in French, of course.

Rachel always performed in French. She was invited to perform at Windsor Castle and Queen Victoria gave her a bracelet. She was to end up with a magnificent collection of jewellery presented by admirers, most of them royal. In October 1841 she returned to the Comédie-Française in *Horace*. The audience resented her having gone abroad — the adoration of Paris should surely be sufficient — but she soon won them back. Throughout her career Rachel was to prove a mixed blessing to the Comédie. She could certainly fill the houses, but when in Paris she only performed two days a week while everyone noted that on tour she performed nightly. She was also constantly on leave making her way around the capitals of Europe. Her detractors called her contract a paid vacation. She also went on provincial tours, and in 1842 went on her first Belgian tour.

Back in Paris in January 1843 she added *Phèdre* to her repertoire, and it was her greatest success. The critic G. H. Lewes wrote: 'Whoever saw Rachel play Phèdre may be pardoned if he doubts whether he will ever see such acting again.'

Rachel's silver service and letterhead incorporated her motto *Tout ou rien* and that was the way she lived her life, on stage and off. In the 1840s she had two sons, by different fathers. In 1846 she toured the Netherlands. When she returned to the Comédie-Française after the February 1848 revolution it had been renamed the Théâtre de la République. Rachel once more played in *Horace*, and at the end gave a rendering of *Marseillaise* during which she waved the tricolour and finally clutched it to her breast. The audience was much impressed by her patriotism. Backstage she was rowing with the Comédie director and tried to resign but was contractually bound. In 1850 she tried playing the romantics — Dumas and Hugo — but was unsuccessful.

During the summer and autumn of 1850 Rachel toured the southern German capitals and the major cities of the Austrian Empire, ending up in Vienna where she said her success 'surpasses all the others I have ever had'. In 1851 she toured Italy, and returned to England during the Crystal Palace Exposition. Charlotte Brontë said: 'Rachel's acting thrilled me with horror. That tremendous force with which she expresses the very worst passions in their strongest essence forms an exhibition as exciting as the bull fights of Spain and the gladiatorial combats of old Rome and (it seems to me) not one whit more moral.'

Rachel travelled with her actor–manager brother Raphael, and in 1852 they were touring Germany where they performed before the King and Queen as well as the Tsar and Empress of Russia. Of her performance in *Athalie* Gautier wrote: 'Mlle Rachel possesses that one superior endowment which makes a great tragedienne: authority. When one sees her, one understands her power; in her bearing, her gesture, her glance one recognizes a queen.'

Rachel went to Russia in 1853 where she was given diamonds and rubies as well as a great deal of money. In St Petersburg she said: 'I was treated like a monarch. Not like a pasteboard monarch in a tragedy with a crown of gilt cardboard, but like a real sovereign, the true minted article.' She performed daily even when the Crimean War started in February 1854 and France and Russia had severed diplomatic relations. When Rachel returned from Russia, her younger sister Rebecca died. Rachel, herself never well — and not helped by constantly burning the candle at both ends — was under a severe emotional strain. She was once more fighting with the management of the Comédie. They wanted her to play *Medea* and she refused, mainly because they asked her. She was seen in a bad and violent play, *Rosemonde*, and in *Le Czarene* by Scribe. That summer Ristori arrived in Paris for the first time from her native Italy. The critics praised her — some even over-praised her to tease Rachel — and audiences flocked to her. She was acclaimed as the greatest actress of them all. Rachel would have none of it. That summer she played in *Horace*, *Andromaque*, *Polyeucte*, *Phèdre* and *Mary Stuart*, and her public came back to her.

In July Rachel went to London for what was to be her last appearance there (she played in England five times), and on 11 August 1855 with her father, brother, three sisters and theatrical company she sailed for America. Rather than be managed by Americans and have to split the money from what she hoped would be a highly lucrative tour, her brother Raphael organized it. And he made many mistakes. The advance publicity, though massive, was not correctly geared to the Americans, whom they did not understand. And the ticket prices for her performances were the highest ever charged in the United States, which the public resented.

Rachel, feeling not at all well, made her American début at the Metropolitan Theater in New York on 3 September 1855 playing Camille in *Horace*. All the expatriate French turned out to see her and wave the flag, and all New York society came to see Rachel. She next played *Phèdre* and followed that with *Adrienne Lecouvreur*, Hugo's *Angelo*, *Bajazet* and *Jeanne d'Arc*. The audience, however, did not care what the play was — they just came to see Rachel. During her time in New York, despite the critics calling her 'the greatest actress that ever lived', the box-office takings

declined — the houses were far from full. It was a commercial success, however, if not the bonanza Rachel had hoped for; it was also a massive critical success. The *New York Sun* reported: 'The appearance of Rachel as she entered as Camille that night at once riveted the gaze. No words can convey the impression. As she began to speak, the impression became more confirmed; as she advanced it ripened into conviction. There was but one feeling — she surpassed expectation.'

She went next to Boston, where she was well received, but she had caught a cold which was the beginning of the end. After Boston she returned for another spell in New York and then went on to Philadelphia, where on 19 November she collapsed and had to cancel the rest of her tour. She travelled to South Carolina in search of some sunshine where she might rest and recover. There, at the request of friends, on 17 December in Charleston she played *Adrienne Lecouvreur*. It was to be her last performance and a fellow actor called it 'the most painful spectacle I shall ever experience ... I saw her barely able to remain on her feet, barely able to speak, coughing at each word, holding her breath to stifle this cough, gripping my arm in order not to fall, and despite her suffering, I saw her find the energy to carry on to the end of her part with an indomitable courage.'

Rachel went further south, to Havana, Cuba, intending to play there when she had recovered, but by New Year's Eve she knew it was a forlorn hope and sent the company home. Shortly she followed them to Paris, and then sought relief in Egypt. She returned to Paris where she formally and finally resigned from the Comédie on 10 June 1857. That winter she was not well enough to make the journey to Egypt so went instead to Cannes in the south of France, where she died on 3 January 1858. A military guard of honour attended her funeral, Alexandre Dumas was one of the pall bearers, and the Grand Rabbi of Paris officiated.

After her death Edmond Got wrote of her: 'Mlle Rachel was an incomparable theatrical structure, rather than a perfect artist in the widest sense of the word; for she was hardly ever anyone but Camille in all her roles, especially after the provinces and the foreign countries had unbalanced in her the lesson of the masters, and driven her to the limits of her strength. But what a voice! What pronunciation! What range! And even what beauty, no matter what is said.' Prince Napoleon, a former lover, said simply: 'A woman who deceives you with such grace is irreplaceable. Where will we ever find another artist who can be Phèdre incarnate and a burlesque queen an hour later.'

MICHAEL REDGRAVE

Summing up the methods of the greatest English actors of a generation, the critic Kenneth Tynan wrote: 'There is, you see, a gulf fixed between good and great performances; but a bridge spans it, over which you may stroll if your visa is in order. Mr Redgrave, ignoring this, always chooses the hard way. He dives into the torrent and tries to swim across, usually sinking within sight of the shore. Olivier pole-vaults over in a single animal leap; Gielgud, seizing a parasol, crosses by tight-rope; Redgrave alone must battle it out with the current. The ensuing spectacle is never dull, but it can be very painful to watch.'

Michael Redgrave was born in Bristol on 20 March 1908. His mother, Margaret Scudamore, was an actress, and his father, Roy Redgrave, was an actor who had a long and good career in Australia. His mother did not want her son on the stage and encouraged him in an academic career, which began at Clifton College and continued at Magdalene College, Cambridge. After Cambridge,

believing his mother when she said he was too tall to be an actor, he became a schoolmaster at Cranleigh School. There he directed the boys in *Hamlet*, *King Lear* and *The Tempest*, but managed to play all the leading roles himself. One day he saw the Michel Saint-Denis company and knew he had to be either a director or an actor, so at the age of 25 he presented himself for an audition to Lilian Baylis at the Old Vic. She agreed to take him on, but he had already fixed up an audition with the Liverpool Playhouse, and there the director offered him more money so it was there that he made his professional début, on 30 August 1934 playing Roy Darwin in *Counsellor-at-Law*. He spent two years at Liverpool, and there met the actress Rachel Kempson, whom he married on 18 July 1935.

Tyrone Guthrie saw Redgrave at Liverpool and offered him a job at the Old Vic in London in a company that included Olivier and Guinness. Michael Redgrave made his London début on 14

September 1936 playing Ferdinand in *Love's Labour's Lost*. That season he also played Mr Horner in *The Country Wife*, Warbeck in *The Witch of Edmonton*, and Laertes to Olivier's Hamlet. Of the last Audrey Williamson said: 'Michael Redgrave was a fine Laertes, magnificent of speech and presence and moving without loss of vitality.' His hit of the season, however, was as Orlando in *As You Like It*. Edith Evans was Rosalind, and the two were very much in love at the time. Later, talking about the brief affair, Redgrave explained: 'Edith always had a habit of falling in love with her leading men; with us it just went rather further ...' Of his performance as Orlando Audrey Williamson wrote: 'He made the youth a handsome, well-spoken stripling, with a strong measure of charm and enough virility to force one to believe him when he said he felt the spirit of his father grow strong within him.'

In February 1937 the production of *As You Like It* transferred to the New Theatre. At the Embassy the following month he was Anderson in *The Bat*, and returned to the Old Vic in April where he took over from Marius Goring as the Chorus in *Henry V*.

At the St Martin's in May 1937 Michael Redgrave played Christopher Drew in *A Ship Comes Home*, and at the Embassy the following month he was Larry Starr in *Three Set Out*. In September John Gielgud invited Redgrave to join his company for a season at the Queen's Theatre, and there he played Bolingbroke in *Richard II*, Charles Surface in *The School for Scandal* and Baron Tusenbach in *The Three Sisters*.

At the Phoenix in October 1938 he was Alexei Turbin in *The White Guard*, an adaptation from the Russian, and Audrey Williamson reported: 'Michael Redgrave's part of the elder brother and military commander, Alexei, was short ... but he gave it an authority that was of enormous service in the early scenes.' For Christmas of that year he was Sir Andrew Aguecheek in *Twelfth Night*. At the Westminster in March 1939 he played Harry, Lord Monchensey, in T. S. Eliot's *The Family Reunion*, and Miss Williamson wrote later that it was 'perhaps his best leading performance before the war, suggesting a new flexibility of emotion, and neurotic imagination, if not perhaps quite the full stormy pathos of Harry's tormented spirit'. He spent the rest of 1939 touring as Henry in *Springtime for Henry*, and was back in London at the Haymarket in March 1940 playing Captain Macheath in *The Beggar's Opera*. Audrey Williamson said that 'with an untrained but pleasant baritone, [he] was an attractive Macheath'. At the Neighbourhood Theatre in June he was Charleston in *Thunder Rock*, and transferred to

the Globe in July.

He entered the Royal Navy in July 1941 as an ordinary seaman, but was discharged on medical grounds in November 1942. Having spent most of 1942 in the Reserve, he still managed to direct *Lifeline* at the Duchess in July, and in October directed *The Duke in Darkness* at the St James's, in which he also played Gribaud. This was based on an episode in the French Civil War of 1580 and had an all-male cast. Audrey Williamson wrote: 'Redgrave gave the finest performance of his career as the crazed servant Gribaud.' In March 1943, also at the St James's, he played Rakitin in *A Month in the Country*. T. C. Worsley reported: 'His performance is exemplary. His Rakitin stands, so to speak, at just that distance from himself that the ironist commonly keeps ... and when he moves into passion it is with an admirably restrained intensity that leaves us feeling as we should about all these people.' In June at the same theatre he directed matinées of *Parisienne* and played Lafont.

Michael Redgrave directed *Blow Your Own Trumpet* at the Playhouse in August 1943 and in September at the Phoenix directed *The Wingless Victory*. He co-directed and played the title role in *Uncle Harry* at the Garrick in March 1944. James Agate wrote: 'Mr Michael Redgrave plays the shabby poisoner so well that here and now I take the responsibility of advising him to give up the intellectual drama and devote himself to the profession.' In June 1945 he directed and played Colonel Stjerbinsky in *Jacobowsky and the Colonel* at the Piccadilly. Agate was not as well pleased with this performance. 'I have no doubt,' he wrote, 'that Mr Redgrave tried to be funny the other evening; indeed one could see him trying. But seriousness deeper than anything even Matthew Arnold conceived, and not funning, is the good actor's forte; he dissects absurdity where he should warm to it.'

At the Aldwych in December 1947 Michael Redgrave played Macbeth. Harold Hobson reported: 'Now Mr Redgrave has a fine presence and a keen intelligence, but from time to time he reminds me of Iceland, the place where the depressions come from. Macbeth, of course, is constantly on the rack; but Mr Redgrave too often seems merely in the dumps ... His performance, like the production, at last becomes energetic, concentrated and vehement. But his start is slow, he looks as wild as the Great Glen of Mull; and in the strain after speed and barbarian vigour, the poetry alas is lost.' T. C. Worsley called it a straight telling of the plain story and had other views: 'Mr Redgrave within the limits that he sets himself — and they are proper limits — gives a performance that commands our acceptance, fine and finished, with the gradations exactly marked and movingly rendered.' Michael Redgrave made his New York début in this role at the National Theater on 31 March 1948.

Back in London in November 1948 he was at the Embassy playing the famous Robert Loraine part, the Captain in *The Father*. Audrey Williamson said: 'Michael Redgrave gave a good emotional performance with a sense of breaking nerve, but somehow failed to convey the full macabre intensity, the feeling of one possessed, in the final scene.' He played the same part at the Duchess Theatre in January 1949. At the Embassy in April that year he was Etienne in *A Woman in Love*, as well as directing the production. He also did the adaptation, which was from Georges de Ponto-Riche's *Amoureuse*. Harold Hobson said: '. . . as a doctor whose bedside manner is more than professional, he strides and storms as though farce were his spiritual home, bringing to it at the same time an intellectual tang that makes his performance very rewarding.'

Michael Redgrave joined the Old Vic Company at the New Theatre for their 1949–50 season, and played Berowne in *Love's Labour's Lost*, Marlow in *She Stoops to Conquer*, Rakitin in *A Month in the Country* and Hamlet. Of his Hamlet, T. C. Worsley wrote: 'He moves with a new grace and certainty. His voice, musical and flexible, has discovered in itself a new richness. He employs broadly three registers: a grief that has a sweet unforced tenderness in the earliest scenes; a hard piercing cry that strikes straight from the top of passion and hits it squarely, from the moment when his father's spirit breaks down this frozen grief; and a completely relaxed, almost smiling easiness which is first used as he sits among the Players and which pervades that last act from the graveyard scene onwards up to the very end . . . Of the many virtues in this rendering the prime one to my mind is Mr Redgrave's absolute mastery of the vocal line. He is beautifully sensitive to the words as poetry and gives us, from the very start, the assurance that he will value at its full worth every nuance of every phrase, every supporting syllable of the whole poetic structure. And he keeps his word. It is an exemplary performance as a piece of verse speaking, without tricks, mannerisms or affectations, but immensely various, always absolutely true, always perfectly in tune. The sense, we feel, has been mastered as a whole and, delivered as near perfectly as may be, with the progression exactly and carefully marked, it makes us, too, understand it all over again. It is a performance not to be missed and one that is even more impressive on the second seeing than the first.' Redgrave also played Hamlet at the Zurich

Festival, the Holland Festival and at Elsinore.

In 1951 he joined the Shakespeare Memorial Theatre Company at Stratford-on-Avon. There he played Richard II, and T. C. Worsley reported: 'Mr Redgrave, in fact, is set to play his character, in a sense, against the production. The lyricism of his part, which distils the very essence of a sweet adolescent self-pity, is over-shadowed. Mr Redgrave gives an extremely sensitive and lyric performance and if it doesn't, as it should, absolutely engulf us, isn't this because the production is deliberately designed to see that it does not?' However, on seeing it again Worsley changed his mind. 'Mr Redgrave's Richard does now just what it didn't quite do before,' he wrote. 'It catches us up completely in pity for the King.' That season Redgrave also played Hotspur and Chorus in the Cycle of Histories and directed *Henry IV Part 2*. And as if that were not enough, he played Prospero in *The Tempest*. Worsley thought that this was one of his best performances and went on: '. . . from the first Mr Redgrave distils an extraordinary human warmth and a dominating largeness of heart . . . Nothing is more difficult for some reason than the portrayal of goodness in any medium, fiction, drama or acting. Mr Redgrave brings off the difficult feat so successfully that his forgiving of those who have wronged him seems in action neither forced nor condescending nor priggish.'

He returned to London in April 1952, where at the St James's Theatre he played Frank Elgin in Clifford Odets' *Winter Journey*, and Kenneth Tynan said that '. . . it is the best serious performance he has given us for years'. That year he received the CBE.

Michael Redgrave rejoined the Shakespeare Memorial Theatre Company for their 1953 season, and played Shylock in *The Merchant of Venice*. Kenneth Tynan reported: 'His conception of Shylock is highly intelligent — a major prophet with a German accent, a touch of asthma, and lightning playing round his head. But who cares for conceptions? It is the execution that counts. And here Mr Redgrave's smash-and-grab methods tell against him. His performance is a prolonged wrestling match with Shylock, each speech being floored with a tremendous vein-bursting thump; the process also involves his making a noise like a death-rattle whenever he inhales, and spitting visibly whenever he strikes a "p" or "b". Some things he did superbly . . . There were also hints that Mr Redgrave did not deny Shylock a sense of humour . . . But he simply could not fuse the villainy of the part with its sardonic comedy.' He also played *Antony and Cleopatra* that season with Peggy Ashcroft, of which Tynan wrote: 'Michael

Redgrave does not so much fill the part as overflow it ... he sometimes goes too far ... If he can let up a little on the lust and rid himself of a few more mannerisms ... he will be giving a first-rate performance.' Redgrave must have been on the point of feeling that there was no pleasing the foremost drama critic that season, until he played King Lear and Tynan wrote: 'Michael Redgrave has played King Lear and won. For once the complex armoury of this actor's mind has found a foe worthy of its steel ... The technical apparatus with which he besieges his parts has sometimes looked a little over-elaborate, recalling the old metaphor about the sledgehammer and the nut. But Lear is a labyrinthine citadel, all but impregnable, and it needed a Redgrave to assault it.' Redgrave played his Antony again when the production transferred to the Prince's in London in November 1953 and he also played it in January 1954 on a tour of Holland, Belgium and Paris.

At the Apollo in June 1955 Michael Redgrave played Hector in *Tiger at the Gates*. This time Tynan reported: 'It is Michael Redgrave, as Hector, who bears the evening's brunt. He is clearly much happier in the emotional bits than in the flicks of wit which spark and speckle them, but even so, this is a monumental piece of acting, immensely moving, intelligent in action and in repose never less than a demi-god.' He played the same part at the Plymouth Theater in New York in October 1955 and received the New York Drama Critics Award. He remained in New York, and in April directed *A Month in the Country* there at the Phoenix. In November he directed and played the Prince Regent in *The Sleeping Prince* at the Coronet. He returned to London in January 1958 where at the Saville he played Philip Lester in *A Touch of the Sun*, in which his daughter Vanessa made her London début. Redgrave received the *Evening Standard* Award for Best Actor for this performance. That June he joined up with the Shakespeare Memorial Theatre Company once more to play Benedick and, aged 50, to have another go at Hamlet. Tynan wrote: 'The case of Michael Redgrave is perennially absorbing, even to those who deny that he is a great actor. On he plunges, struggling and climbing and stumbling, bursting with will and intelligence and seeking always to widen the range of his remarkable physical and vocal equipment. Never, to my knowledge, has he run away from an acting problem: he'll wrestle with them all. A serious actor in short. Yet something is missing. We admire, but are not involved ... Even so, he is always fascinating to watch. His present Hamlet is a packed, compendious affair, much richer in detail than the one he gave us eight years ago at the Vic

... Mr Redgrave's Hamlet, like his Lear, is most convincing when closest to madness.' He also played the Danish Prince in Leningrad and Moscow with the company during 1958 and 1959.

In June 1959 he received a knighthood, and he was back in London in August at the Queen's Theatre playing HJ in his own adaptation of *The Aspern Papers*. Peter Roberts, writing in *Plays and Players*, said: 'The signal achievement of Sir Michael's adaptation is that he has managed to make the most of the purely theatrical effectiveness implicit in the novel, without, in the process, sacrificing the complex and subtle qualities of James's art ... Acting and production are remarkable both for their quality and for their integration. Sir Michael, as HJ, is throughout the evening chiefly concerned with suggesting that gentleman's ill-concealed eagerness to be in possession of the old lady's papers, and the tension he conveys is well-nigh unbearable.' He was with his daughter Vanessa at the Queen's in August 1960, playing Jack Dean in *The Tiger and the Horse*, and Peter Roberts reported: 'Michael Redgrave gives a performance bristling with technical accomplishment which, however, rarely comes to life.'

Michael Redgrave went to New York to the Ethel Barrymore Theater in November 1961, playing Victor Rhodes in *The Complaisant Lover*, and returned to England to the Chichester Festival opening to play the title role in the all-star production of *Uncle Vanya*. It was highly praised, and Peter Roberts wrote: 'Olivier as Astrov and Redgrave as Vanya between them offer acting on the highest level the contemporary English theatre has to offer. The precision, calculation and control of Olivier fused with the performance of Redgrave, which was compounded from an inner nervous tension and an intellectually evolved portraiture, combining to give one of those thrilling experiences in the theatre which are as rare as they are welcome.'

He was next at Wyndham's in November 1962 playing Lancelot Dodd in *Out of Bounds*, a part that according to the critic Clive Barnes was markedly beneath his talents. In July 1963 at Chichester they revived *Uncle Vanya* and once more he played the title role. He again received the *Evening Standard* Award for Best Actor.

In October 1963 Michael Redgrave played Claudius in the National Theatre Company's inaugural production of *Hamlet* at the Old Vic. He was upset when he heard that Olivier, the head of the company, referred to his Claudius as 'rather dim'. Peter Roberts, on the other hand, reported: 'Michael Redgrave's pleasure-loving Claudius is a rounded performance of great interest, and it is good to see a company being able to put an actor of his calibre in such a small but key role.' He repeated his *Uncle Vanya* in November 1963 for the National, and in January 1964 played Henry Hobson in *Hobson's Choice*. He said himself that *Hobson's Choice* was well outside his range. 'I couldn't do the Lancashire accent and that shook my nerve terribly — all the other performances suffered.' In June 1964, still with the National Theatre Company, he played Halvard Solness in *The Master Builder*, which he said 'went wrong'. At this time he had incipient Parkinson's disease, though he did not know it. Of his performance Martin Esslin wrote: 'Sir Michael Redgrave, with all his skill and penetrating intelligence, or perhaps because of them ... simply cannot suggest the element of demonic charm, of genius that Solness must have if he is not to emerge simply as a cad and petty egoist — and a very stupid fellow as well.'

Michael Redgrave left the National Theatre Company and went to Guildford, where he directed the opening festival for the Yvonne Arnaud Theatre. He played Samson in *Samson and Agonistes*, and once more Rakitin in *A Month in the Country*, but this time he played opposite Ingrid Bergman and Martin Esslin reported: '... it seems that in order not to show up the weakness of his partner too much, he has chosen not to act Rakitin at all, or only on the same coarse farce level. This nineteenth-century blend of Cyrano and Hamlet thus turns into a mere fumbling fool. It is enough to break one's heart to see so fine an actor committing such a subtle act of self-immolation.' Nevertheless, the production came into the Cambridge in London in September 1965, though Redgrave was far from well. He turned to directing opera at the Glyndebourne Festival: in 1966 it was *Werther* and in 1967 *La Bohème*.

At the Mermaid Theatre in July 1971 he played Mr Jaraby in William Trevor's *The Old*

Boys, and had a very nasty experience. As he said, 'My memory went, and on the first night they made me wear a deaf aid to hear some lines from the prompter and it literally fell to pieces and there were little bits of machinery all over the floor, so then I knew I really couldn't go on, at least not learning new plays.' Nevertheless, in April 1972 at the Haymarket he very successfully took over the part of the Father in *Voyage Round My Father*, and spent 1972 and 1973 touring Canada and Australia with the part.

Michael Redgrave's first film appearance was in 1938, and although he was never as prolific as other theatrical knights some films are notable — *The Lady Vanishes*, *The Browning Version*, *The Importance of Being Earnest*, *The Dam Busters* and *Oh! What a Lovely War*.

Looking not back on his career but ahead he said: 'I think I'll have left a good few memories behind me and one or two films I needn't be altogether ashamed of, and whatever happens to me from now on doesn't really matter terribly. The curious thing about death, you know, is that you worry about other people's much more than your own. When my time comes I'll be glad to take off quite quickly while things are still fairly good.' Sir Michael died, after a long illness, on 21 March 1985.

He left behind a notable progeny, his daughters Vanessa and Lynn Redgrave and his son Corin Redgrave. 'I always knew,' he said, 'that Vanessa was going to be an actress: there are some days when her politics drive me mad and other days when I see her touch greatness as an actress, and am immensely proud ... Corin has given up his career for his politics and I'm sorry about that because he could be a fine actor, but mercifully Lynn escaped the politics altogether and just concentrates on her work and the children.' *See photograph opposite page 343.*

VANESSA REDGRAVE

On the night of 30 January 1937, Michael Redgrave was on the Old Vic stage playing Laertes to Laurence Olivier's Hamlet. When the curtain fell, Olivier walked to the footlights and said, 'Ladies and gentlemen, tonight a great actress has been born. Laertes has a daughter.' Michael's wife, Rachel Kempson, was also an actress and a member of the Old Vic

Company, so it was not surprising that after a childhood of theatrical conversation and games, and being educated at the Queensgate School in London, Vanessa studied at the Central School of Speech and Drama. She made her stage début at the Frinton Summer Theatre in July 1957 playing Clarissa in *The Reluctant Debutante*. At the Arts Theatre in Cambridge in September of that year she played Mrs Spottsworth in *Come On Jeeves*, and made her London début on 31 January 1958 as Caroline Lester in *A Touch of the Sun*. Her father played her stage father in the production, and Peter Roberts said Vanessa was a 'fine specimen of gawky English schoolgirlhood' in this play by N. C. Hunter. She was with Joan Plowright at the Royal Court in August, playing Sarah Undershaft in *Major Barbara*, and at Christmas that year was at Leatherhead playing the Principal Boy in *Mother Goose*. She was taken into the Shakespeare Memorial Theatre Company at Stratford-on-Avon for the 1959 season; though she played Helena in *A Midsummer Night's Dream* with Albert Finney and was Valeria in Olivier's *Coriolanus*, it was an unremarkable Shakespearian début.

Vanessa Redgrave returned in March 1960 to the West End, to the Comedy Theatre, where she played Rose Sinclair in *Look on Tempests*, which starred Gladys Cooper and Ian Hunter. Caryl Brahms said: 'The part of the young wife gives a very young actress, Miss Vanessa Redgrave, a chance. How good she is, and how true her portrayal of the troubled, loyal young woman, longing only to comfort and to be comforted.' In August of that year she was at the Queen's Theatre playing Stella Dean in Robert Bolt's *The Tiger and the Horse*, in which her father starred. Peter Roberts wrote: 'Vanessa Redgrave plays the seduced girl and gives a truly remarkable performance. There is no question of the daughter of a famous father getting a part for which she is no match. On the contrary, on the strength of this performance alone, Miss Redgrave has a great career before her.' At the same theatre in March 1961 she opened in Ibsen's *The Lady from the Sea*, and completely enthralled Kenneth Tynan who wrote: 'To witness the scene in which Miss Redgrave embraces her tutor's offer of financial help, rejects it upon learning that it involves marriage, and eventually, tentatively, reaccepts it, as her need to escape stagnation overrides her distaste for an unpropitious match, is to relive the painful, illusion-shedding transition that marks the end of youth. If there is better acting than this in London, I should like to hear of it.'

Vanessa Redgrave went back to Stratford in July 1961 when she joined the Royal Shakespeare Company and played a remarkable Rosalind in *As You Like It*. Peter Roberts wrote in *Plays and Players*: 'That special inner radiance that has swiftly brought her to the front of her profession is here very much in evidence. She is excited. She is in love. She glows warmly and sincerely. She struts boyishly yet has immense grace. In the end she wins your heart.' Caryl Brahms was not so enthusiastic about her next role for the RSC, that

of Katharina in *The Taming of the Shrew*. 'Courageous it was for an actress so young to have a bash at the Shrew,' she wrote, 'and a bash is exactly what she gave us.' Vanessa Redgrave remained with the RSC in 1962, also playing Imogen in *Cymbeline*, of which Mark Taylor wrote: 'Vanessa Redgrave must be weary of the word "radiant". I offer a few dictionary alternatives — "glowing", "shining", "beaming with happy emotion". But "radiant" is still the word that springs to mind when her Imogen, all pale-gold hair, simple garment and love, strides the stage. How strong and positive is the purity of this Imogen; how clearly and unaffectedly Miss Redgrave speaks her poetry, the slight huskiness of voice caressing the ear. We can never doubt that, come what may, this Imogen's innocence will remain unsullied.' On 28 April 1962 Vanessa Redgrave married the director Tony Richardson, and pregnancy kept her off the stage for a while.

In March 1964 she was at the Queen's Theatre in London playing Nina in *The Seagull*. Also in the cast were her mother, Rachel Kempson, Peggy Ashcroft and Peter Finch. Martin Esslin said that her performance was '. . . wholly admirable. This is a part that all too often tempts an actress into sentimentality and mawkishness . . . Vanessa Redgrave avoided the temptation with the finest tact: in the first three acts she has the angular coltishness of a girl from the provinces which emphasizes the vulnerability and innocence of the character better than any sweet-girlish attitudinizing could, and in the last act she presents a woman destroyed by love and on the verge of madness and degradation, a spectacle which is poignant and heartrending precisely because it lacks any element of the death of Little Nell or *East Lynne*.' At Wyndham's in May 1966 Vanessa Redgrave played the fascist Scottish schoolmarm, Jean Brodie, in *The Prime of Miss Jean Brodie*. It was a remarkable performance which won her the *Evening Standard* Award as Best Actress of the Year for the second time. (The first was in 1961 for *The Lady from the Sea*.) Mary Holland wrote of her performance: 'With flat brown bun, flowing clothes, angular gestures of uncommon grace and refined Scots voice, she takes Miss Spark's creation of fire, air and unselfconscious oddity and makes her physically alive on stage . . . She makes the spiky dialogue and mannerisms, the visions and the quirky expression of them her own, fills in the dottiness and aggravation as well as the irresistible romance of the character.' Vanessa found it an extremely difficult part. The character was so alien to her own self that she 'split right open — my greatest fear was that I would actually go mad on stage.' Successful though her performance was, it was her experience with Jean Brodie that sent her fleeing from the stage. In 1967 she went to Hollywood, where she played the errant Queen in *Camelot*.

In 1967 Vanessa Redgrave received the CBE, and when she returned to the stage in January 1969 it was to the University Theatre in Manchester, where she played Gwendolen Harleth in *Daniel Deronda*. At the Young Vic in November 1971 she was Susan Thistlewood in Robert Shaw's *Cato Street*, and though her marriage to director Tony Richardson was over she was directed by him in a rather bizarre version of Brecht's *The Threepenny Opera* set in the gangster 1920s. It opened at the Prince of Wales Theatre in February 1972. Hugh Leonard said: 'Vanessa Redgrave as Polly was excellent although at times one was reminded of a battleship in a mill-pond. In short, the part was lightweight: she could have done it standing on her head, and so she did — apart from her attempt at turning a cartwheel.'

At the Shaw in May 1972 she was Viola in *Twelfth Night*, directed by Michael Blakemore. Hugh Leonard reported: 'Miss Redgrave was such a believable "boy" as almost to swamp the lovelorn Viola underneath. She has a phenomenal gift of allowing us instant access to her thought . . . Viola is not an exceptionally difficult role, but Miss Redgrave made of it a great one — never more so than in Shakespeare's beautiful elongation of the reunion between Viola and Sebastian.'

At the Bankside Globe Theatre in August 1973

she was Cleopatra to Julian Glover's Antony in Shakespeare's play, updated by director Tony Richardson to the 1920s. Although she was 36, Nicholas de Jongh wrote of her: 'Vanessa Redgrave cannot be blamed for her youth but that must rob her Cleopatra of the grand desperation at which her appropriately lurid costumes hint. At the end she abandons her wilful girlishness, uneasily between love and caprice to achieve an enraptured dignity in death and desolation.' That November she was at the Phoenix playing Gilda in Michael Blakemore's production of Noel Coward's *Design for Living*, and Sandy Wilson wrote in *Plays and Players* that it was '. . . her most beautiful performance in every sense of the word. Whether bundled in a sleazy kimono or draped in yards of gold jersey, she *is* Gilda, the divine intellectual slut, slenderly androgynous, an ideal creature of her period, as she glides, pounces, perches bewitchingly at a cocktail bar or, in one glorious moment, jumps up and down in girlish temper on the line, "We can pretend that we're happy".'

For many years Vanessa Redgrave's militant, left-wing, flag-waving politics have taken precedence over her acting career, but the moments when she does step on a stage or before a camera are breathtaking in their depth. In the summer of 1984 she was at the Theatre Royal, Haymarket, with Christopher Reeve and Wendy Hiller in a revival of her father's adaptation of *The Aspern Papers*.

RALPH
RICHARDSON

Ralph Richardson was born on 19 December 1902 in Cheltenham, where his father was involved in the family leather-manufacturing business. During his childhood Ralph was taken by his mother to live in Brighton. After seeing a performance by Frank Benson as Hamlet he determined to be an actor. In December 1920 he went to Frank Growcott, who ran the St Nicholas Players in an old bacon factory behind the station at Brighton, and promised him one pound a week for ten weeks to take him on. If he worked out, Ralph said, then Growcott would pay him one pound a week. With the St Nicholas Players Richardson was involved backstage, mostly with sound effects. He did manage to play the steward in *Twelfth Night* and a local critic noted his appearance. He said his make-up was excellent and

he 'gave a thoughtful impression of the conceited steward'.

He joined Charles Doran's Shakespearian Company and made his professional début at the Marina Theatre in Lowestoft in August 1921 playing Lorenzo in *The Merchant of Venice*. He also played Banquo and Macduff in *Macbeth*, and a local critic said he was 'well-graced' and played 'with great distinction'. He toured the provinces with Doran's company, and at the Gaiety Theatre, Dublin, in February 1923 was Mark Antony in *Julius Caesar*. A local critic was very impressed by his performance: 'One of the finest performances of the night was the Mark Antony of Mr Ralph Richardson. Of course, the great test piece, if it may be so called, is the Oration over the body of the dead Caesar, and this was delivered by the artist

At the Ambassadors' Theatre, Anthony Quayle played Captain Coutine
(with Lesley Waring as Sylvia) in *The Soldier's Fortune*
(London, 1935)

Ralph Richardson as Falstaff in *Henry IV* at the New Theatre
(London, 1945)

with quite remarkable elocutionary effect. It had indeed this rare quality, that the actor seemed not to be giving utterance to a set speech, but rather to the spontaneous expression of his feelings, delivered in the most affecting tones of voice, and with gestures most natural.'

In 1923 a beautiful young actress, Muriel Hewitt, joined the Doran company and the mutual attraction was immediate. Richardson left the company in July 1924 to tour in Nigel Playfair's production of *The Way of the World*, and Kit Hewitt went with him. They were married on 18 September 1924. That December they joined the prestigious Barry Jackson Birmingham Repertory Company and set out together on a year's tour of Eden Philpotts' *The Farmer's Wife*. They did manage a fortnight in London in the middle of the tour. Back at home base, the young Kit's talents were much easier to spot than Richardson's and he found himself a junior member of the company. One of his contemporaries, and at first a rival, was Laurence Olivier. In July 1926, for the Greek Play Society, Richardson was at the Scala Theatre playing the Stranger in *Oedipus at Colonus*. His first real West End role was at the Haymarket, when he opened in November 1926 playing Arthur Varwell in Eden Phillpotts' *Yellow Sands*. His wife was in the cast with him, and the play ran for 610 performances.

He was back in London again at the Court in March 1928 playing Zazim and Pygmalion in *Back to Methuselah*. One critic reported: 'Ralph Richardson, the young actor who stands on the pedestal and makes that long biological speech about creating life synthetically, is sure to be heard of in the future.' The following month he was in a modern-dress version of *The Taming of the Shrew*, playing Tranio. Horace Hornsell wrote: 'It was a stroke of something like genius on this actor's part to bring the refinements of modern Cockney to the speaking of Shakespeare's archaisms, and the idiosyncrasy that so refreshed the character was so cleverly sustained that one felt that Shakespeare would have enjoyed it too. Thus, one of the first entries on the credit side of this production is the fact that it converted what are usually tedious and indistinguishable supers into individuals, and that it gave Mr Richardson the opportunity which he took magnificently, to turn Tranio into a star.' That month he also played Gurth in *Harold*.

At the Arts Theatre in June 1928 he was Hezekiah Brent in *Prejudice*, and back at the Court in August played Ben Hawley in *Aren't Women Wonderful?* In November the same year at the Garrick he played James Jago in *The Runaways*, and spent the following year touring

South Africa. He returned to the Dominion in February 1930 where he played Gilbert Nash in *Silver Wings* and at the Savoy in May was Roderigo in *Othello*.

Ralph Richardson joined the Old Vic Company and opened in September 1930 playing the Prince of Wales in *Henry IV Part 1*. The *Daily Telegraph* reported: 'The Prince Hal of Mr Ralph Richardson was vivacious, but a figure of modern comedy rather than of Shakespeare.' That season he also played Sir Harry Beagle in *The Jealous Wife*, Bolingbroke in *Richard II* and Caliban in *The Tempest*. Ivor Brown said he was an 'excellent Caliban, conceived like an old man of the China Seas'. Of his performance in *Antony and Cleopatra* that season the *Morning Post* reported: 'Mr Ralph Richardson's Enobarbus places him among the first Shakespearian actors on the English stage.' At the reopening of the Sadler's Wells Theatre in January 1931, Ralph Richardson played Sir Toby Belch in *Twelfth Night*. James Agate was not totally happy with the performance. 'Mr Richardson,' he wrote, 'avoided making Sir Toby a mere tosspot, but avoidance is not the whole of this part.' That season he also played Bluntschli in *Arms and the Man*, Don Pedro in *Much Ado About Nothing* and the Earl of Kent in *King Lear*.

At the Malvern Festival in August 1931 Ralph Richardson was Nicholas in *A Woman Killed with Kindness*, Courtall in *She Would If She Could* and Viscount Pascal in *The Switchback*. He returned to the Old Vic for the 1931–32 season, where he played a vast range of parts including Philip Faulconbridge in *King John*, Petruchio, Bottom, Henry V, Ralph in *The Knight of the Burning Pestle*, Brutus, General Grant in *Abraham Lincoln*, Iago, and the Ghost and the First Gravedigger in *Hamlet*. James Agate reported: 'Mr Ralph Richardson is making progress in the right way, that is by going back a little and coming on a great deal more. His recent Petruchio was not good, but his present performance of Bottom is very fine indeed. In the fairy scenes he abandoned clowning in favour of a dim consciousness of a rarer world and of being at court there. This was new to me, and if Mr Richardson had not the ripeness of some of the old actors, his acting here was an agreeable change from the familiar refusal to alternate fruitiness with anything else. Most of the old players seem to have thought Bottom, with the ass's head on, was the same Bottom, only funnier. Shakespeare says he was "translated", and Mr Richardson translated him.'

For the Malvern Festival in 1932 he played Merrygreek in *Ralph Roister Doister*, Face in *The Alchemist*, *Oroonoko*, and Sergeant Fielding in

Too True To Be Good, which he brought to the New Theatre in September. At the Globe in November he was Collie Stratton in *For Services Rendered* and in February 1933 he was at the Queen's playing Dirk Barclay in *Head-on Crash*. At the Apollo in May he played Arthur Bell Nicholls in *Wild Decembers* and in September had the title role in Somerset Maugham's *Sheppey*. The *Times* critic wrote: 'Mr Richardson with an artist's patience builds up little by little a character in whom the miracle of conversion is acceptable, a saint with his feet on earth.' The production ran less than 100 performances. At the Palladium for Christmas he was Mr Darling and Captain Hook in *Peter Pan*.

In February 1934 he opened at the Globe playing John MacGregor in James Bridie's *Marriage Is No Joke*. The production closed six nights later. At the Duchess in September he was Charles Appleby in Priestley's *Eden End*, a great critical success which ran only 162 performances. The following March he had the title role in Priestley's new play, *Cornelius*, which ran less than two months.

He toured America in October 1935 playing Mercutio in *Romeo and Juliet*, and made his New York début at the Martin Beck Theater on 23 December 1935 playing both Chorus and Mercutio in that play, which starred Katharine Cornell. Back in London, in February 1936 he was at the Shaftesbury playing Emile Delbar in *Promise*. He teamed up with Laurence Olivier for a production of Priestley's *Bees on the Boat Deck* at the Lyric in May 1936, in which he played Sam Gridley; it closed in four weeks.

Finally, he had a great West End success when he played the title role in *The Amazing Dr Clitterhouse*. It opened at the Haymarket in August 1936 and ran more than a year. In November 1937 he was at the St James's playing Peter Agardi in *The Silent Knight*.

Ralph Richardson was back at the Old Vic in December 1937 playing Bottom again in *A Midsummer Night's Dream*, and in February 1938 he took on the title role in *Othello*. Harold Hobson reported: 'Ralph Richardson killed himself from the start with a disastrous make-up; no man looking like a golliwog can persuade us that he is talking like a god.'

In February 1939 he was at the New Theatre playing Robert Johnson in Priestley's *Johnson over Jordan*, which ran for two and a half months. It was his last stage appearance for more than five years; on 21 September 1939 he reported to the Royal Navy Air Station at Lee-on-Solent as a sub-lieutenant. He served until 1944 (retiring with the rank of lieutenant-commander), when he and

Olivier were given the task of re-forming the Old Vic. That first season as co-director he played Peer in *Peer Gynt*, Bluntschli in *Arms and the Man*, Richmond in *Richard III* and Vanya in *Uncle Vanya*. Although James Agate thought his Peer Gynt was 'excellent', of the Uncle Vanya he said: 'I just cannot believe in Mr Richardson wallowing in misery; his voice is the wrong colour.'

Ralph Richardson had married the actress Meriel Forbes on 26 January 1944 at the Chelsea Register Office. He had first met her when they played together in *The Amazing Dr Clitterhouse*. His first wife Kit had died in October 1942, aged only 35, after a long and tragic illness.

In 1945 the Old Vic Company toured Germany and played in Paris at the Comédie-Française. They returned to the New Theatre in September 1945, and Richardson played Falstaff in both parts of *Henry IV*. Of the first part Agate wrote: 'He had everything the part wants — the exuberance, the mischief, the gusto ...' And of the second part: 'Wisely, Mr Richardson is content in this second part not to do but to be ... Here is something better than virtuosity in character-acting — the spirit of the part shining through the actor.' And Audrey Williamson praised him as 'the greatest of modern Falstaffs'. That season he also played Tiresias in *Oedipus Rex*, and the non-speaking Lord Burleigh in *The Critic*. The company took these productions to New York to the Century Theater in May 1946.

Back in England the following season at the New Theatre, Richardson played Inspector Goole in Priestley's *An Inspector Calls*. Harold Hobson reported: 'Mr Ralph Richardson plays Inspector Goole with quiet calm and a half-quizzical smile. His occasional bursts of indignation when some member of the family is particularly recalcitrant or unsympathetic are very impressive; and if at times he has faintly the air of the Recording Angel getting his notes together, the audience at the end will find him justified.' That season he also played Cyrano de Bergerac, Face in *The Alchemist* and John of Gaunt in *Richard II*. That year, 1947, he was knighted.

The directorship of the Old Vic moved on to other hands and in 1948 Ralph Richardson was at Wyndham's in his own production of *Royal Circle*, in which he played Marcus. Of this, his return to the commercial stage, Hobson wrote: 'Richardson dominates the entire production as the amorous king with a fishing rod who is forced to abandon his vacation by diplomatic complications, and turns from angling to ogling. He dominates the production, that is if domination is a quality pertaining to a performance that is as light as a soufflé, as airy as a bubble and as gay as a mayfly.'

At the Haymarket in February 1949 he was Dr Sloper in *The Heiress*, while Peggy Ashcroft took the title role. T. C. Worsley: 'Sir Ralph Richardson brings all the tricks at his command to the part and, the doctor falling mortally sick at the last scene, he has a chance ("good theatre") of impersonating a dying man.' Hobson said he played the Doctor '. . . finely. He has a stiff sarcastic deliberation that is most effective.'

T. C. Worsley reported that Sir Ralph was 'wasting his talent' when he played David Preston in R. C. Sherriff's *Home at Seven* at Wyndham's in March 1950. At the Aldwych in May 1951 he was Vershinin in *The Three Sisters*, and Worsley said that '. . . he has developed almost to a point of schizophrenia his tricks of voice, which, by now, bear simply no relation to the words he is saying. Whenever he is not speaking, when interjecting a smile or a grunt, or just acting, he is masterly as he used to be.'

In 1952 Sir Ralph joined the Shakespeare Memorial Theatre Company at Stratford-on-Avon, and that season played Prospero in *The Tempest* and the name part in *Volpone*. Of the latter Kenneth Tynan wrote: 'I thought Richardson's Volpone a little too fantastical and quite deficient in stature and authority . . . You might say, quite fairly, that this was a semi-precious performance: lots of glitter, but not much real worth.' He also played Macbeth that season, and directed by John Gielgud had a disaster.

At the Globe in March 1953 he played John Greenwood in R. C. Sherriff's *The White Carnation*, and Tynan wrote: 'As monarch of the chaos, Sir Ralph is perfectly at home. Being a ghost, he can wander about without the disturbing necessity of making human contact with any of the other members of the cast. Freed of this worry he guides the play through its shallows with the touch of a master helmsman. It is a magnificent performance, and I mean no irony when I nominate Sir Ralph the best supernatural actor of his generation.' At the Haymarket in November that year he played Dr Farley in *A Day by the Sea*.

In 1955 he toured Australia with his wife, playing in *Separate Tables* and *The Sleeping Prince*. He was back at the Old Vic in September 1956 playing the title part in *Timon of Athens* and Tynan reported: 'Sir Ralph Richardson brings his familiar attributes: a vagrant eye, gestures so eccentric that their true significance could only be revealed by extensive trepanning, and a mode of speech that democratically regards all syllables as equal . . . Yet there was in his performance, for all its vagueness, a certain energy, and it was a relief to hear Timon's later tirades spoken with irony instead of fury.'

In New York in January 1957 he opened at the Coronet Theater playing General St Pé in Anouilh's *The Waltz of the Toreadors*. Brooks Atkinson wrote in the *New York Times*: 'For a classical actor, Ralph Richardson knows better than most how to act with the gusto of a low comedian . . . Mr Richardson's changes of pace are fabulous. In the midst of a military roar and posture he suddenly drops his voice to a conversational level, and the laughter out front is probably all out of proportion to what is said. He gives a heroic performance that is just short of heroic conclusions. The disparity is as witty — wittier perhaps than the dialogue.' Writing in the *Christian Science Monitor* John Beaufort said: 'The profound humanity and gallantry which invariably characterize Sir Ralph's stage portraiture bestow upon General St Pé an unstrained quality of mercy which expresses his faltering and largely unrealized virtues without condoning his vices.'

Back in London, at the Haymarket in November 1957 Richardson opened as Cherry in Robert Bolt's *Flowering Cherry*. Tynan said: 'He rides, not rough-shod but with spring-heeled lightness, over everyone else on the stage. Mr Bolt's hero is an apparently normal suburbanite who lives in a world of fantasy: Sir Ralph gives us all of the fantasy and none of the normality.' Nevertheless he played Cherry for more than 400 performances at the Haymarket and then toured with the production. Caryl Brahms praised his performance and said that '. . . as the unheroic Cherry, Sir Ralph Richardson is resolutely, immoderately natural — one can feel that naturalistic technique flexing in every muscle — a queasy giant of ordinariness caught in his own canary cage.'

At the Globe in June 1959 he was Victor Rhodes in Graham Greene's *The Complaisant Lover*, and at the Phoenix in September 1960 was with John Gielgud in Enid Bagnold's *The Last Joke*. In April 1962 he went to the Haymarket, where he was directed this time by John Gielgud, and played Sir Peter Teazle in *The School for Scandal*. Caryl Brahms found his performance 'unexpectedly real', and went on to say: 'Sir Ralph's justly rueful, rotund, ripe and heartfelt Sir Peter was indeed neighbour and friend to every one of us in that theatre.' The production toured the United States from November until January 1963, when it played in New York at the Majestic Theater.

In June 1963 Richardson played the Father in Pirandello's *Six Characters in Search of an Author*, which opened the new Mayfair Theatre in London and was, according to Martin Esslin, a masterpiece. 'Ralph Richardson plays the character of the Father, a theatrical conception asking to be embodied on the stage: there is hardly another part in the entire repertoire more suitable for Richardson, whose exquisite mannerisms nowadays tend to militate against one's acceptance of everyday character . . . here where he incarnates not a real person but a figment of theatrical imagination these very mannerisms are triumphantly right and give his performance a definitiveness of perfection.'

The following February he opened at the Royal Theatre, Brighton, playing Shylock in *The Merchant of Venice* and Bottom in *A Midsummer Night's Dream*, and then went with both productions on a British Council tour of South America and Europe which lasted from March through May 1964. Back at the Haymarket in September he played the Sculptor looking for the face of God in Graham Greene's *Carving a Statue*. In January 1966 he was at the same theatre playing the Waiter in Shaw's *You Never Can Tell*. Martin Esslin reported: 'Sir Ralph Richardson [is] incomparable as the old waiter, warm-hearted, superior, wise and contemplating the proceedings with an inimitable tremor of his grizzled head.' This was followed in September by an all-star revival of Sheridan's *The Rivals* in which Sir Ralph played Sir Anthony Absolute. According to David Benedictus: '. . . he is choleric and gouty certainly, the script demands that he shall be, but his most engaging quality, his love for his son in spite of himself, shines through every line.' The following September, still at the Haymarket, he played Shylock in *The Merchant of Venice*, and Michael Billington said his performance was the 'sole justification of the production'. He went on: 'It is Richardson's technique, riveting and idiosyncratic, that gives the performance its grandeur.' Sir Ralph surprised everyone by playing Dr Rance in Joe Orton's anarchic farce, *What the Butler Saw*, at the Queen's in March 1969. That year also he received an honorary doctorate from Oxford.

He was at the Royal Court in June 1970, once more playing with John Gielgud and this time directed by Lindsay Anderson in David Storey's *Home*. John Russell Taylor said: 'Richardson's bluff commonsensical quality with its suggested reserves of deep if slightly embarrassed feeling matches perfectly Gielgud's slight otherworldliness.' The production transferred to the Apollo in July, and in November they went to New York to the Morosco. Clive Barnes wrote: 'The acting and staging is as near perfection as can be hoped for. The two men bleakly examining the little nothingness of their lives are John Gielgud and Ralph Richardson giving two of the greatest performances of two careers that have been among the glories of the English-speaking theater.' Walter Kerr called *Home* 'an evening of endings' and enthused about

Sir Ralph ' . . . testing the ground before him with a cane to make certain it is there, putting each foot down as though it might not quite match the other, managing to suggest in the vacant oval of his eyes and mouth that eyes and mouth have lost all definition . . .'

Back at the Royal Court in August 1971 Ralph Richardson played Wyatt Gilman in John Osborne's *West of Suez*. Mary Holland reported for *Plays and Players*: 'This is a compelling piece of stagecraft, but whether it is acting or art is another matter. It seemed to me Sir Ralph at his most raffish, giving his vintage performance of an old poseur who demands everyone's undivided attention.' The production transferred to the Cambridge in October 1971.

The following July he was at the Savoy in William Douglas-Home's *Lloyd George Knew My Father*. Martin Esslin said: 'Sir Ralph Richardson [as General Sir William Boothroyd] gives a magisterial performance which makes him, beyond a shadow of a doubt, unchallenged world champion portrayer of gaga doddering dears. Who *could* rival the mastery of his incomprehension when he is — or pretends to be — deaf; who in the whole wide world could compete with him in the perfection of senile symptoms brilliantly observed and masterfully executed? The result is a character study of truly devastating cruelty.' Sir Ralph toured in this play — in 1973 he was in Australia and in 1974 in North America.

Sir Ralph joined the National Theatre Company at the Old Vic in January 1975 when he played the title role in Ibsen's *John Gabriel Borkman*. Helen Dawson said: 'He combines frailty and strength in an extraordinary physical tension; at times leashed by an almost manic power.' In April 1975 he was back with John Gielgud making up what Michael Coveney called 'the funniest double-act in town' in Harold Pinter's *No Man's Land*. The production transferred to Wyndham's in July 1975.

Sir Ralph Richardson began his film career in 1933 in a horror movie called *The Ghoul*. There were propaganda films during the war, and made notable appearances in *Richard III*, *Our Man in Havana* and *Oh! What a Lovely War*.

Sir Harold Hobson has said of him: 'Sir Ralph is an actor who, whatever his failure in heroic parts, however short of tragic grandeur his Othello or his Macbeth have fallen, has nevertheless, in unromantic tweeds and provincial hats, received a revelation. There are more graceful players than he upon the stage; there is none who has been so touched by Grace.' He died on 10 October 1983. *See photograph opposite page 327.*

DIANA
RIGG

Diana Rigg shot to international stardom through the television series 'The Avengers' in the 1960s, when she played the seductive karate-trained superspy Emma Peel, but her first and natural medium is the theatre.

She was born on 20 July 1938 in Doncaster, Yorkshire, but at the age of two months returned with her mother to Jodhpur, India, where her father was manager of the State Railway. She stayed in India until she was eight, then returned to England. At school she developed a love of poetry and of speaking verse, and encouraged by her elocution teacher determined to be an actress. She enrolled at RADA, and made her professional début in a RADA production of *The Caucasian Chalk Circle* in which she played Natella Abashwili at the Theatre Royal, York, during the York Festival in summer 1957.

She filled in time as a model until she got a job as assistant stage manager at the Chesterfield Repertory Company. There she worked on lighting, prompting and as a stage hand, and occasionally walked on. In summer 1958 she was in rep at Scarborough. In 1959 she joined the Shakespeare Memorial Theatre Company (that became the Royal Shakespeare Company in 1961) at Stratford-on-Avon, where she had the female equivalent of spear-carrying parts and understudied. She played the role of Diana in *All's Well That Ends Well* for six nights when the principal actress, Priscilla Morgan, was unwell, and the *Stratford Herald* reported that 'she gave a light and amusing performance'. She also played Andromache in *Troilus and Cressida*.

Diana Rigg made her London début with the RSC at the Aldwych in January 1961 when she played Second Ondine and Violanta in Giraudoux's *Ondine*. That season she also played Phillipe Trincante in *The Devils*, Gwendolene in *Becket* and Bianca in *The Taming of the Shrew*. In 1962 at the Aldwych she played Madame de Touruel in *The Art of Seduction*.

Back in Stratford in April 1962 Diana Rigg was Helena in *A Midsummer Night's Dream*, and *Plays and Players* reported: 'Diana Rigg's drooping, swooping Helena has the most outrageously comic invention and she makes the most of it. This girl is rapidly proving herself one of our best Shakespearian actresses.' She also played Lady Macduff in *Macbeth* and Adriana in *The Comedy of Errors*. *Plays and Players* said of the latter: 'Diana Rigg, whose work with the company has become consistently more interesting this season,

contributes a delightful study in wayward femininity as Adriana.' Of her Cordelia in *King Lear*, R. B. Marriot wrote: 'Diana Rigg is the best Cordelia I have ever seen; entirely believable, a princess of mind and spirit, as well as utter truthfulness and compassion.'

At the Aldwych in January 1963 she was Monica Stettler in *The Physicists*, and toured the provinces that spring with the company, returning with *The Comedy of Errors* to Stratford for the summer and to the Aldwych in December. Still at the Aldwych, in February 1964 she once more played Cordelia and then set out on a British Council tour which covered Europe and the USSR.

Diana Rigg made her New York début at the State Theater in May 1964 with the company in *King Lear* and *The Comedy of Errors*. She ended her first stint with the RSC that summer with a command performance of *The Comedy of Errors* at Windsor Castle. The following year she was acclaimed for her part in the television series 'The Avengers' and was nominated for an Emmy. In 1966 she returned briefly to the RSC to play Viola in *Twelfth Night*, opening in June in Stratford. Harold Hobson called her Viola a 'creation of great delicacy and sweetness' and went on to say: 'Of the whole company she alone speaks the verse as it should be spoken with a proper appreciation of its music and its pathos.'

Diana Rigg spent the next few years filming, notably the RSC's version of *A Midsummer Night's Dream*, *On Her Majesty's Secret Service*, and Stuart Burge's *Julius Caesar*, in which she played Brutus' wife, Portia. She returned to the theatre in May 1970 when at Wyndham's she played Héloïse in *Abelard and Héloïse*. Harold Hobson wrote: '. . . Héloïse, in Diana Rigg's radiant and moving performance, is strong enough in earthy affection simply to put guilt aside to be so quietly enraptured that the thought of damnation is a stranger to her.' In 1971 she played the role in Los Angeles, and in March opened in New York with it at the Brooks Atkinson Theater. One New York critic wrote: 'Diana Rigg, as Héloïse, the sensitive, brilliant woman, renders the finest single performance I have seen this season.' The play lasted only fifty-two performances on Broadway, but she did receive a Tony nomination that year.

In 1972 Diana Rigg joined the National Theatre Company and opened with them as Dottie in Tom Stoppard's *Jumpers*. Harold Hobson reported: '. . . if the radiant splendour of her appearance is not enough, Miss Rigg is witty and poised and returns Mr Stoppard's intellectual service from the racket of a champion.' That season she also played Lady Macbeth, directed by Michael Blakemore. Jack Pitman said it was '... an eloquent and persuasive characterization; one of authority and discipline'. The second year with the National she added the role of Celimene in *The Misanthrope*. Robert Brustein wrote in the *Observer*: 'Oddly enough the most complicated character in this production is usually the most superficial — Celimene, the coquette, and Diana Rigg's performance in this role confirms her growing authority as an actress.'

At the Albery in May 1974 she played Eliza Doolittle in *Pygmalion*. Robert Cushman said her Eliza was 'a rare comic creation, compact of dignity, fire and mischief'.

Diana Rigg returned to the National Theatre for an American tour in 1975. They played in Washington, DC, at the Kennedy Center and then, in March, were at the St James Theater in New York. John O'Connor wrote in the *New York Times*: 'Perfectionists will not cavil at Diana Rigg as Celimene. Speaking of Miss Rigg, I am in danger of babbling in a public place. Draped with outrageous seductiveness in Tanya Moiseiwitsch's bitchily classic gowns, her oval ode of a face framed in a hymeneal wig of antique golden curls, clipping off rhymes like Delilah clipping off sideburns, Rigg exactly captures Celimene's passion which counterpoints Alceste's.' She received another Tony nomination for this part. She returned to London with the production and in September 1975 opened at the Old Vic playing the Governor's Wife in

Phaedra Britannica, an Anglo-Indian version of Racine's *Phèdre*. She was named in *Plays and Players* by the London critics as the best actress of the year for this role.

On 30 May 1977 Diana Rigg had her first child, a daughter. She returned to the National Theatre in January 1978 when she played Ilona in *The Guardsman* at the Lyttelton Theatre. B. A. Young reported in the *Financial Times* that she gave 'a thoroughly human performance as Ilona, true and sensitive, and never tainted by excessive theatricality'.

In November 1978 she opened at the Phoenix Theatre as Ruth Carson in Tom Stoppard's *Night and Day*. Jack Kroll reported in *Newsweek*: 'Diana Rigg is awesome in the power of her presence. Beauty, wit, bitchery and vulnerability seem to whirl about her like a pride of playfully savage ocelots.' And Harold Hobson said: 'Miss Rigg looks very delectable and acts her most complicated part with great distinction.' Once more the London critics voted her best actress of the year in *Plays and Players*. She was asked to take the play to Broadway, but plagued by back trouble she left the part to Maggie Smith and settled down to edit a book made up of unpleasant reviews received by actors and actresses, called *No Turn Unstoned*. With characteristic good humour she included one of her own: of her celebrated nude scene in *Abelard and Héloïse* John Simon wrote in *New York Magazine*: 'Diana Rigg is built like a brick mausoleum with insufficient flying buttresses.'

In 1985 she was back on the British stage in *Little Eyolf* at Hammersmith and as Cleopatra at Chichester.

ADELAIDE RISTORI

A delaide Ristori was born on 29 January 1822 at Cividale to the north-west of Venice. Her father Antonio Ristori and her mother Maddalena were members of Caviechi's wandering troupe of actors. At only three months Adelaide was a stage prop in the farce *The New Year's Gift* and by the time she was four years old she was a regular member of the company. When she was 10 she played small speaking parts and at the age of 15 was playing Francesca da Rimini. Her father got her a position as an ingénue with one of the top Italian companies, the Royal Sardinian, which was based in Turin for a part of the year and toured Italy for

the rest. By the time she was 18 she was at the top of the company.

Italy was at the time in political turmoil. New plays were not being written and the old ones were heavily censored. By 1855 Ristori had had enough of performing in the political climate and thought about retiring from the stage, but instead settled on a tour of France and a visit to Paris, the artistic centre of the world. In May the Royal Sardinian Company set out on a conquest of Paris which they duly accomplished. At the Salle Ventadour on 22 May Ristori opened with *Francesca da Rimini*, and the influential critic Jules Janin praised her highly and favourably in comparison with Rachel. The audiences poured in. Edmond Got said she was '. . . a talented artist, who seems to compose her roles with intelligence and a sure hand, but angular and almost always overemphatic'. In Italy Ristori's reputation was based on Goldoni comedies, and she duly performed two for the Parisians. She also played in Alfieri's *Mirra*, which was very like *Phèdre* and thereby invited further comparisons with Rachel. She also played *Maria Stuarda*, an adaptation of Schiller's *Mary Stuart*, one of Rachel's most popular roles. Ristori was idolized by the critics and playwrights and the Emperor Napoleon sent her a valuable bracelet. She obtained from the Salle Ventadour the promise of three annual spring seasons.

Ristori's reputation firmly established by her reception in Paris, the company then toured France, Belgium and Germany and word of her genius preceded them. Everywhere she was acclaimed. The company made a triumphant home-coming tour of Italy.

When Ristori returned to Paris in 1856 the reception was distinctly cooler. The Parisians had made a star of a foreigner, and rather regretted it — particularly as their own Rachel had retired. Nevertheless her reputation was established, and she followed it to London, Warsaw, Madrid, the Hague, Amsterdam, Budapest, St Petersburg, Moscow, Egypt, Turkey and Greece. Everywhere she aroused enthusiasm, except in Paris where she was now bitterly resented. Her principal plays during this time were Giacometti's *Elizabeth Queen of England* and *Queen Marie Antoinette* (which he wrote specially for her), Legouve's *Medée*, *Macbeth* and *Mirra*. Everywhere she went she was applauded and fêted; she was not only a great actress but had also married a marchese, and her husband travelled with her.

Adelaide Ristori made her American début at the 14th Street Theater in New York on 20 September 1866 playing in Legouve's *Medée*, and took twenty curtain calls. She then toured twenty-one cities playing Medée, Mary Stuart, Queen Elizabeth, Phèdre, Judith, Pia de Tolomei, Francesca da Rimini, Adrienne Lecouvreur, Tisbe, Camma, Myrrha, Deborah, Norma and Lady Macbeth. Her net profit was $270,000. She returned to Europe in June but was back in America in September, where she remained for nine months giving 181 performances and playing also in Cuba. For that tour she added the parts of Marie Antoinette and Isabella Suarez.

In 1869 Ristori undertook a tour of South America, and in 1871 toured the Balkans with a caravan of horse-drawn carriages. From April 1874 through January 1876 she accomplished a round-the-world tour which she reckoned covered 35,283

miles on water and 8365 miles on land. She was seen in South America, in the United States from coast to coast (where she performed the sleep-walking scene from *Macbeth* in English), in Hawaii, New Zealand and Australia. In 1879 she visited Scandinavia for the first time and so great was her success that she returned there the following year.

In 1881 Ristori's husband died. The unsuitable marriage had lasted thirty-four years; they had a son and daughter. Ristori decided to retire from the stage.

Ristori made her last United States tour in 1884 when she performed Lady Macbeth, Mary Stuart, Elizabeth, and Marie Antoinette in English. The New York *Daily Tribune* said: 'Her use of English is surprisingly efficient.' During that tour she played in *Macbeth* opposite Edwin Booth. Ristori then returned to Italy and definitely retired from the stage. On her eightieth birthday in 1902 she was much honoured. Special newspaper editions were published, medals were struck, all the Italian dramatic companies devoted the evening performance to her honour. The King of Italy called on her at home and every school in Rome delivered a lecture in her honour. That evening in the presence of the King and Queen of Italy she was the guest of honour at the Teatro Valle and received more than 3000 telegrams.

Adelaide Ristori died on 9 October 1906. William Winter, the New York drama critic, described her technique: 'The conquering characteristic of Ristori's acting was its humanity. She was faithful to actual life; and that fidelity appeared in her presentment of classic ideals as well as in her portraiture of the heroines of history. She was not a spiritual actress; her art methods were, distinctively, rugged rather than delicate; and her mind seemed deficient in the attribute of poetry. But all her dramatic persons were women of flesh and blood, and she was always definite in depicting them. She ranked in the school of natural, as contrasted with the school of ideal, tragedians. Those thinkers upon acting who attach more value to imagination in conceiving of ideals, and to intellectual character in expressing them, than to frenzies of the person and the eccentricities of ebullient emotions, were able, while rejoicing in her magnetism, to enjoy it with something of the coolness of patience. She was, unquestionably, a great actress; she possessed many attributes, physical and mental, which made her one of the foremost women of her time; but she lacked the ineffable quality which has always been found to animate and hallow the highest forms of human genius.'

CYRIL RITCHARD

Cyril Trimnel-Ritchard was born in Sydney, Australia, on 1 December 1897 and attended St Aloysius' College there before becoming a medical student at Sydney University. He later abandoned medicine, and made his stage début at the age of 20 at His Majesty's Theatre in Sydney as a member of the chorus in *A Waltz Dream*. He worked in Australia until 1924 for the Williamsons and then went to America, where he made his New York début in February 1925 at the Fulton Theater in the revue *Puzzles of 1925*. In June that year he made his London début at the Duke of York's in a revival of the revue, *Bubbly*. In November he was taken by André Charlot to the Prince of Wales where he appeared in *Charlot's Revue*. At the Vaudeville in February 1926 he was in *RSVP*, and then went to the Hotel Metropole in cabaret, *The Midnight Follies*. At the Carlton in April 1927 he was Tony Lester in *Lady Luck*, and at the Winter Garden the following April played the Hon. Peter Malden in *So This Is Love*. He was at the Gaiety in March 1929 playing Jack Stanton in *Love Lies*, and in April 1930 played the London Hippodrome with *The Co-Optimists*. Back at the Gaiety in June 1931 he was Harry Drake in *The Love Race* and in May the following year played the Hon. Aubrey Forsyth in *The Millionaire Kid*.

Cyril Ritchard went back to Australia in February 1932 and stayed there until 1936, appearing in a number of roles. He married Madge Elliott on 16 September 1935. Back in England in August 1936 Ritchard was at the Saville Theatre playing in the revue, *Spread It Abroad*. He went to the Comedy in December in *To and Fro*, and in April 1937 at the Q played Hugo Arnold in *The Constant Sinner*. At the Arts that June he was Charlie Paget in *In the Best Families* and at the Ambassadors' in September played Nicky in *People in Love*. That December he was at the Garrick playing Sir John Shaley in *Bedtime Story* and the following month went to the Little Theatre in the revue, *Nine Sharp*, which kept him occupied for over a year. He followed in April 1939 at the same theatre in *The Little Revue*, and for Christmas 1939 he went to the Palace Theatre in Manchester, where he appeared for the first time in pantomime. He was back at the Saville Theatre in April 1940 in *Up and Doing* and in July 1941 produced his first revue at the Ambassadors'. He was at His Majesty's in May 1942 in *Big Top*, and then at the Phoenix in October played Algernon Moncrieff in

Wilde's *The Importance of Being Earnest*.

At His Majesty's in March 1943 he played Prince Danilo in *The Merry Widow*. This production toured the army bases in England as well as Egypt, the central Mediterranean, France, Belgium and Holland until 1945, touching home base briefly at the Coliseum in September and December 1944.

At the Palace Theatre in London in March 1945 Cyril Ritchard played Gabriel von Eisenstein in an English version of *Die Fledermaus*. In August he was at the Piccadilly Theatre in *Sigh No More*. Cyril Ritchard returned to Australia in 1946, where in May he opened at the Theatre Royal in Sydney in Noel Coward's *Tonight at 8.30*. The following May he went to New York where at the Royale he played Tattle in *Love for Love*, returning to London in December 1947. He opened at the Lyric, Hammersmith, that month playing Sir Novelty Fashion in *The Relapse*. The production transferred to the Phoenix in January 1948. Audrey Williamson called his performance 'brilliantly funny', and Harold Hobson said it was 'a gorgeous creation of wit, wigs, taste and paste'. Back in New York at the Cort in December he played Georgie Pillson in *Make Way for Lucia*, and he returned to London to the Piccadilly in May 1949 where he played Hubert Manning in *Ann Veronica*. At the Saville in February 1950 he was the Hon. Vere Queckett in *The Schoolmistress*.

Cyril Ritchard went back to the United States, and in May 1950 at the Brattle Theater in Harvard Square, Cambridge, he played Sparkish in *The Country Wife*. In November he opened in New York at the Morosco, repeating his role in *The Relapse*. The following April he played in *Castle in the Air* in Nassau before returning to his home city to appear in Coward's *Private Lives*. He then directed two New York productions before returning to London to the New Theatre, where in April 1952 he played Adrian Blenderbland in *The Millionairess*, which starred Katharine Hepburn. Kenneth Tynan said he 'lent a flustered dignity, like that of a goosed hen, to the nonentity Blenderbland'. The production opened at the Shubert Theater in New York in October. Ritchard stayed on in that city to direct *Misalliance* at the New York City Center, and returned to London to the Hippodrome in May 1953 to appear in the revue, *High Spirits*. He returned to New York in December, to direct some revue sketches at the Imperial and then a new production of *The Barber* of Seville at the Metropolitan Opera House.

In October 1954 came the part for which he will always be remembered — the dual role of Mr Darling and Captain Hook in the musical version of *Peter Pan*, which starred Mary Martin in the title role. It opened at the Winter Garden, and Brooks Atkinson wrote in the *New York Times*: 'As the bloodthirsty Captain Hook, Cyril Ritchard gives a superb performance in the grand manner, with just a touch of burlesque.' The performance won him two Donaldson Awards and a Tony. He directed *The Reluctant Debutante* in October 1956 at the Henry Miller Theater in New York, and at the Metropolitan Opera House in December directed *La Perichole* in which he played the part of Don Andres. At the Booth Theater in February he directed Gore Vidal's *A Visit to a Small Planet* and played Kreton. At the Longacre in October 1958 he played Biddeford Poole in *The Pleasure of His Company*, and ran for a year. He directed *Look After Lulu* at the Henry Miller Theater and went back to the Metropolitan in 1959, where he directed *The Gypsy Baron* and *The Marriage of Figaro*.

In May 1960 he set out on a tour of the United States in *The Pleasure of His Company*, subsequently touring Australia with it until December. Back in New York in April 1961 he not only directed *The Happiest Girl in the World* at the Martin Beck Theater but also played six roles in it. He directed *Everybody Loves Opal* at the Longacre in October and at the Music Box in January 1962 played the title-role in *Romulus*. He was at the 54th Street Theater in March 1963 playing Colonel Tallboys in a revival of Shaw's *Too*

True to Be Good. He directed *The Mackerel Plaza* for the Westport Country Playhouse in Connecticut in summer 1963 and in September at the Ethel Barrymore Theater played Felix Rankin in his own production of *The Irregular Verb to Love*. He directed *Roar Like a Dove* at the Booth Theater before opening in May 1965 at the Shubert in Anthony Newley's *The Roar of the Greasepaint — The Smell of the Crowd* in which he played Sir. He then directed a tour of *Where's Charley*, and in 1967 at Stratford, Connecticut, directed *A Midsummer Night's Dream* in which he played Bottom and Oberon. He went to Florida in 1968 where he played in *Lock Up Your Daughters* at the Coconut Grove, and returned to New York in March 1969 where he narrated *Peter and the Wolf* at the City Center. In December 1970 he directed *La Perichole* at the Metropolitan Opera, once more playing Don Andres, and then spent summer 1971 touring in *The Pleasure of His Company*.

Cyril Ritchard returned to Broadway in April 1972 to the Majestic Theater where he played Osgood Fielding Jr in *Sugar*, a musical version of the film *Some Like It Hot*. Although the critic John Simon said the production 'made me feel that Ivor Novello was alive and well and more winsome than ever', it ran a year very successfully. Ritchard directed *The Jockey Club Stakes* at the Cort Theater in January 1973, and then in November 1975 he made his last stage appearance at the St James Theater. He had made it full circle and was back in a revue — *A Musical Jubilee*.

Cyril Ritchard died on 18 December 1977, having just turned 80.

BRIAN RIX

Brian Rix was born on 27 January 1924 in Cottingham near Hull in the East Riding of Yorkshire, the youngest of four children. His father was a shipowner and his mother was deeply involved in amateur theatre. She sang the lead in Gilbert and Sullivan shows and had her own amateur concert party, called Mrs Fanny Rix and her Bright Young Things. By the end of his school days Brian thought only of the theatre. His older sister had gone to drama school in Stratford-on-Avon and introduced Donald Wolfit into the household — and the young Brian was enamoured. Although he had acted under his mother's direc-

tion in Hornsea, Brian Rix made his professional début in Wolfit's company on 24 August 1932 when he played a Courtier in *King Lear* at the Prince of Wales Theatre in Cardiff. He remained with Wolfit's company on tour, playing small parts in *A Midsummer Night's Dream*, *Twelfth Night* and *Hamlet* through April 1943, and during that time made his London début with the company when he played Sebastian in *Twelfth Night* as they touched down at the St James's Theatre in January. Rix's RAF call-up was deferred and he joined the White Rose Players, a repertory company in Harrogate, staying with them from

May 1943 through July 1944. There he acted in his first farce, *Nothing But the Truth*, and the *Yorkshire Evening Post* reported: 'Brian Rix, in the lead, enhances the favourable impression he has already made since joining the company recently.' One of his greatest successes with the company was in Emlyn Williams' *Night Must Fall*. The *Harrogate Herald* reported: 'We do not often get the chance of complimenting Brian Rix on his handling of a major part, but this week praise must not be stinted for his Danny.'

He was called up in July 1944 and remained in the RAF for nearly four years. On his release, with money borrowed from his father and his uncle he set up his own company, the Ilkley Repertory Company, which he opened with *Nothing But the Truth*. That company failed and he moved on to Bridlington, with the company re-titled the Viking Theatre Company, in November 1948. In January 1949 he opened a second company at the Hippodrome, Margate. That year the actress Elspeth Gray joined; they were married on 14 August 1949. They toured for six months with an army farce by Colin Morris, *Reluctant Heroes*, which opened at the Whitehall Theatre in London in September 1950. The reviews were mixed but the *Evening Standard* reported that the 'biggest triumph was 26-year-old actor–manager Brian Rix's performance as a "dumb" Lancashire recruit'. And Ivor Brown said: 'He [the author–actor Colin Morris] and his team have knocked up some good old music-hall gags and goings-on; in the performance of this they confront us with an abounding will to please.' *Reluctant Heroes* remained at the Whitehall for nearly four years, during which time a film was made of it. Rix also produced *Long March* and directed *Tell the Marines*.

In August 1954 Brian Rix opened at the Whitehall playing Fred Phipps in *Dry Rot*. Frank Granville-Barker, writing in *Plays and Players*, called it an incomprehensible farce of the shamelessly knockabout variety in which Rix helped 'to keep the pot boiling with a broadly comic performance'. This also ran for nearly four years. Rix's next production at the Whitehall was *Simple Spymen*, which opened in March 1958 and in which he adopted nine disguises. This ran until August 1961, when Rix presented *One for the Pot* in which he played the part of Hickory Wood. Of this production Lisa Gordon Wood wrote in *Plays and Players*: 'Brian Rix has done it again, only more so. This is farce with all the required ingredients and a few not often to be seen, including Mr Rix as four quite different people, and often, so does the quickness of the exit deceive the eye — several at once, seemingly. It would be

interesting to discover how far (and how fast) he runs at each performance; his achievement in this direction would appear to make the Olympic champions look small.' That year he broke the record of over ten years' continuous presentation of farce by one management in one theatre — and went on to lengthen it. *One for the Pot* ran at the Whitehall until July 1964, when Rix presented *Chase Me Comrade*, playing the part of Gerry Buss. Three years later Rix moved from the Whitehall to the Garrick Theatre, where he attempted to introduce a repertory programme of farce, and from March to September he presented and played in *Stand by Your Bedouin*, *Uproar in the House* and *Let Sleeping Wives Lie*. The repertory idea did not catch on, and from September *Let Sleeping Wives Lie* ran alone for eighteen months. Still at the Garrick, in October 1969 Brian Rix played Hubert Porter in his own production of *She's Done It Again*. He spent the spring of 1971 touring in four farces by Vernon Sylvaine and then, back at the Garrick in September, he played Barry Ovis in *Don't Just Lie There, Say Something*.

Brian Rix appeared in his first pantomime in December 1973, when he played Billy in *Robinson Crusoe* at the New Theatre in Cardiff. At the Cambridge Theatre in September 1974 he presented *A Bit Between the Teeth*, playing Fogg. Then he returned to the Whitehall in 1976 where he played Colin Hudson in *Fringe Benefits*. In 1976 Brian Rix retired from the stage, after a thirty-year reign as the king of farce. He told reporters: 'It's a great relief to make the break. I'm not a naturally funny man and I found it a strain to go on stage and be funny night after night. I just got so tired of the eternal cry of "Drop 'em!" I never minded losing my dignity as an actor in farce but I began to hate the loss of dignity on public occasions. Everywhere I went, people still expected me to act the fool and drop my trousers and it became boring and unacceptable. I couldn't envisage going on to my dotage like that and eventually came to the conclusion that it was a rather silly way for an elderly man to carry on — diving under beds and into cupboards and pinching girls' bottoms.' Brian Rix went into a theatrical management partnership, but by 1981 he had given up the theatre business; he took on full-time the job of general secretary for the National Society for the Mentally Handicapped. The previous year he had been awarded the CBE for his services to charity. It is unlikely that his record as farce actor–manager will ever be broken, but as he declared when retiring, 'I'm capable of, well, not necessarily better, but different things.'

JASON ROBARDS

ason Robards was born in Chicago, Illinois, on 26 July 1922. His father, also called Jason, was an actor of repute who moved the family to Beverly Hills. In Hollywood he made a certain success in silent films, but with the coming of talkies his career went into a decline, and the family moved into progressively smaller houses. Finally his wife could bear it no longer and left. Robards Jr went to Hollywood High School and when he was 17 enlisted in the navy. He was on duty as Radioman Third Class on the USS *Honolulu* when the Japanese attacked Pearl Harbour. During the war he was three times aboard warships which were damaged by the enemy, and he accumulated thirteen battle stars and the Navy Cross for Valour. After the war he studied for the stage with Uta Hagen at the American Academy of Dramatic Art, and made his first stage appearance at the Delyork Theater in Delaware in July 1947 in *Out of the Frying Pan*. Jason Robards made his New York début at the Children's World Theater in October 1947 playing the rear end of a cow in *Jack and the Beanstalk*. That year he also walked on in *The Mikado* at the Century Theater, and married Eleanor Pitman.

At the 48th Street Theater he understudied and was assistant stage manager in *Stalag 17*, and then toured for a year with the play in the role of Witherspoon. He was back assistant-stage-managing at the Playhouse in April 1952 for *The Chase*. He played Ed Moody in *American Gothic* in 1953 at the Circle in the Square, and at that same theatre in May 1956 had a great success as Hickey in the four-and-three-quarter-hour production of O'Neill's *The Iceman Cometh*. Brooks Atkinson reported: 'Jason Robards Jr plays Hickey, the catalyst in the narrative, like an evangelist. His unction, condescension and piety introduce an element of moral affectation that clarifies the perspective of the drama as a whole. His heartiness, his aura of good fellowship give the character of Hickey a feeling of evil mischief it did not have before.' This was the beginning of his notable association with O'Neill's work. At the Helen Hayes Theater in November 1956 Robards played Jamie in *Long Day's Journey into Night* and won the New York Drama Critics Award as the most promising actor. The part made his name as an actor but was very destructive to him as a person. 'One of the most damaging things for me, I realize now,' he says, 'was playing a drunk in the play *Long Day's Journey into Night*. In the play, the drunk's father is a failed artist and his mother a

drug addict. It was only after years of analysis I realized I was acting out events in my own life on stage.'

In June 1958, Jason Robards joined the Stratford Festival Company in Stratford, Ontario, to play Hotspur in *Henry IV Part 1* and Polixenes in *The Winter's Tale*. Back in New York in December 1958 he played Manley Halliday in *The Disenchanted*, and this performance gained him another Drama Critics Award as well as the Tony. In August 1959 in Cambridge, Massachusetts, he played the title role in *Macbeth*, and returned to the New York stage to the Hudson Theater in February 1960 playing Julian Berniers in Hellman's *Toys in the Attic*, for which he once more won the New York Drama Critics Award. At ANTA in March 1961 he played William Baker in *Big Fish, Little Fish*. That year he married Humphrey Bogart's widow, the actress Lauren Bacall.

At the Eugene O'Neill Theater in April 1962 he was Murray Burns in *A Thousand Clowns*, and back at ANTA in Washington Square he played Quentin in Miller's *After the Fall* in January 1964. Martin Gottfried said: 'Jason Robards Jr, as Quentin, handles the enormous central role magnificently [with] a staccato delivery that can only be the voice of a man speaking to himself.' Kenneth Tynan, however, thought he 'played on a plaintive cawing note', though Brooks Atkinson said he 'acted with great authority'. At the same theatre in March he was Seymour Rosenthal in *But for Whom Charlie*. At the Royale in December 1964 he played Eric Smith in *Hughie* and toured California with the production in 1965. He was back in New York at the Broadway in November of that year playing the Vicar of St Peter's in *The Devils*, and at the Ambassador in October 1968 was Captain Starkey in *We Bombed in New Haven*. He played Frank Elgin in *The Country Girl* at the Billy Rose in March 1972.

On 8 December 1972 Jason Robards was driving to his home in Malibu when a car crash left his face a mangled wreck. It took three operations and $50,000 to rebuild it. A year later, in December 1973, he opened at the Morosco playing James Tyrone Jr in *The Moon for the Misbegotten*. In November 1974 he was in the same play at the Ahmanson Theater in Los Angeles and in June 1975, still in Los Angeles, he played Eric Smith once more in *Hughie* at the Zellerbach Auditorium. At the Brooklyn Academy of Music in February 1976 he was James Tyrone in his own production of *Long Day's Journey into Night*. By this time he was married to his fourth wife, Lois O'Connor, who had been the assistant to the film director Sam Peckinpah, and they live in a large house in Connecticut with their two children.

Jason Robards has had notable successes in films, particularly in *Julia*, in which his portrayal of the writer Dashiell Hammett won him an Academy Award. He won another Oscar for his performance as the *Washington Post* editor Ben Bradlee in *All the President's Men*.

PAUL ROBESON

Born 9 April 1898, the son of a slave who managed to escape and subsequently worked his way through university, Paul Robeson first achieved fame at high school and subsequently at Rutgers and Columbia universities as one of America's greatest young footballers and a member of the 1918 All-American team. He studied for the Bar and was admitted, but in 1921 took to the stage where a weekly salary proved tempting. He made his début in 1921 at the Lafayette Theater in New York in *Simon the Cyrenian*, and a year later made his English stage début in *Voodoo* opposite Mrs Patrick Campbell.

He then played a season at the Provincetown Playhouse where, in May 1924, he first made his name as Jim Harris in Eugene O'Neill's *All God's Chillun*. Press reports that he would be cast opposite a white woman who would kneel at his feet caused a predictable furore, but O'Neill was so delighted with his performance that in the following year he wrote *The Emperor Jones* for Robeson. In this, he opened at the Comedy Theatre in London in 1925 before taking it to Broadway in the following year, and it was there in 1928 that he also took over the role of Crown in the first production of *Porgy and Bess*. Later that same year he was back at Drury Lane as Joe in *Show Boat*, the part which is perhaps most immediately identified with him on stage and screen because of his legendary singing of 'Old Man River'.

Robeson subsequently toured Europe and America with song recitals before playing his first Othello (with Peggy Ashcroft as Desdemona) at the Savoy in May 1930. He went on to the London production of O'Neill's *The Hairy Ape* and a revival of *All God's Chillun* with Flora Robson in 1933, before turning his back on the commercial theatre and working instead for the Unity in plays with strong socialist propaganda.

In the 1940s he returned to his native America and played Othello for the first time there, in Boston in 1943. That production went on to Broadway and broke all records for a Shakespearian play; Robeson was the first black actor to have attempted the role since Ira Aldridge in the 1860s.

But his career was then severely interrupted by the State Department's refusal to give him a passport for overseas travel during the McCarthy years, and Robeson did not return to England or *Othello* until 1959 when he played the part for the last time at the Shakespeare Memorial Theatre in Stratford in a production which also featured Sam Wanamaker, Albert Finney, Vanessa Redgrave and Diana Rigg. He then retired to his home in America, continued to sing and to campaign actively for black rights, and died after a mild stroke on 23 January 1976. We shall, I suspect, never see a greater Othello.

FLORA ROBSON

Flora Robson was born on 28 March 1902 in South Shields, County Durham, where her father was a marine engineer. He recognized that she had a beautiful, musical voice and took pride in teaching her to recite. They moved to North London when she was a small child and there she did well reciting in local competitions. When she was six her father took her to see Henry Ainley in *Faust* at His Majesty's Theatre and she determined to be an actress. After she finished Palmer's Green High School she enrolled at RADA and came away in 1921 with the bronze medal.

Flora was never a beauty — in fact she was plain — and the way ahead was not easy for her. She did, however, get a one-line part playing the Ghost of Queen Margaret in *Will Shakespeare* and made her professional début in that part at the Shaftesbury Theatre on 17 November 1921. The following year she joined up with Ben Greet's Pastoral Players, and performed in repertory in the open air in twenty plays. In 1923 she was invited to join J. B. Fagan's company at the Oxford Playhouse and there she performed in repertory for two seasons. One of her fellow actors was Tyrone Guthrie, who was to have a great influence on her career. After a brief appearance as Annie in *Fata Morgana* at the Ambassadors' Theatre in London in September 1924, she could find no more stage work and returned home to her parents, who were then living in Welwyn Garden City, where she found a job as a personnel–public relations worker at the Shredded Wheat factory. She remained there four years, and also directed the company's amateur theatre group. She was then recommended by Guthrie to the Cambridge Festival Theatre under the direction of Anmer Hall, and in October 1929 she returned to the stage. She spent eighteen months there and considered her greatest achievement to be her role in *Six Characters in Search of an Author*. Flora Robson returned to London, to the Little Theatre, in January 1931 where she played Tatiana in *Betrayal*, and the following month she was at the Gate playing the young wife, Abbie Putnam, in *Desire Under the Elms* with Eric Portman. In May she was Herodias in *Salome*, and at the Westminster that October she made a great success playing the drunken harlot, Mary Paterson, in James Bridie's *The Anatomist*. The critic St John Ervine wrote: 'Here is an actress. If you are not moved by this girl's performance, then you are immovable and have no right to be on this earth. Hell is your place.' In April 1932 she was at the St James's Theatre playing Bianca in *Othello*, and the following month she was at the Lyric playing Olwen Peel in J. B. Priestley's first play, *Dangerous Corner*. For the Sunday Players at St Martin's in June 1932 she played Mercia in *The Storm Fighter* and then in November was at the Globe playing Eva in Somerset Maugham's *For Services Rendered* with Ralph Richardson. Although it was judged a great success, she missed Guthrie's direction. During 1933 she was seldom out of work, playing Lady Audley in *Lady Audley's Secret* in January at the Arts, Penelope Otto in *Head-on Crash* at the Queen's in February, Ella Downey in *All God's Chillun* at the Embassy in March, and Narouli Karth in *Vessels Departing* in July.

Flora Robson was invited to join the Old Vic–Sadler's Wells company headed by Charles Laughton for their 1933–34 season, and she accepted happily, mainly because Guthrie would be directing all the productions. During the season she played Varya in *The Cherry Orchard*, Queen Katharine in *Henry VIII*, Isabella in *Measure for Measure*, Gwendolen Fairfax in *The Importance of Being Earnest*, Mrs Foresight in *Love for Love*, Ceres in *The Tempest*, and Lady Macbeth. She returned to the West End to the Haymarket in May 1934 where she played Elizabeth Enticknap in *Touch Wood*.

Alexander Korda gave her a four-year film contract, which ended all her money worries; as he did not have a part for her at the time he got James Bridie to write *Mary Reed* for her, and it was produced at His Majesty's in November 1934. Flora Robson played the title role, an eighteenth-century woman pirate, and Audrey Williamson said she 'gave a fine performance in the picaresque leading role'. At the Embassy Theatre in June 1935 she opened as Liesa Bergmann in *Close Quarters*, and transferred with the production to the Haymarket the following month. In December 1935 at the Playhouse she had the title role in *Mary Tudor*, and at the Westminster Theatre in April 1937 she played Anna Christopherson in *Anna Christie*. At the Shaftesbury in June 1937 she played Mrs de Meyer in *Satyr* and at St Martin's in October was Lady Catherine Brooke in *Autumn* — a performance she regarded as her greatest stage success. She was still at St Martin's in August 1938, when she played Anya in *Last Train South*.

Flora Robson had a great success in Korda's film *Fire Over England*, in which she played

Queen Elizabeth, and in 1939 she went to Hollywood to film. She made her New York début at the Henry Miller Theater in March 1940 playing Ellen Creed in *Ladies in Retirement*. At the St James in October 1941 she was the Duchess of Marlborough in *Anne of England* and then toured the summer theatres in 1942 playing Elizabeth in *Elizabeth the Queen*. At the Playhouse in New York in October 1942 she was Rhoda Meldrum in *The Damask Cheek* and the following June appeared at the Belasco Theater in Los Angeles in Grand Guignol plays.

Flora Robson returned to England in April 1944 for the reopening of the Lyric, Hammersmith, where she played Thérèse Raquin in *Guilty*, an adaptation of the Zola novel. Audrey Williamson reported: 'This was emotional acting of rare power in which face, voice and gesture mirrored the sickening agony and fear of a character not strong enough to face the consequences of murder. Obliged to play against her physical type, she nevertheless painted a nervously vital portrait of the sensuous and passion-fevered Thérèse.'

Flora Robson always enjoyed touring, bringing life to what she called drab provincial centres. In February 1945 she began a provincial tour playing the title role in a play called *Ethel Fry*, and in October toured as Agnes Isit in *A Man About the House*, which opened at the Piccadilly Theatre in London in February 1946. At the Westminster that August she played Margaret Hayden in *A Message for Margaret*, and then in March 1948 she returned to New York to the National Theater to play Lady Macbeth. At the Theatre Royal, Windsor, in July the same year she played Lady Cicely Waynflete in *Captain Brassbound's Conversion*, and opened with the production in London at the Lyric, Hammersmith, in October.

At the Westminster Theatre in May 1949 Flora Robson had a great success as the disturbed mother who turns to shoplifting in *Black Chiffon*. T. C. Worsley said: 'Miss Robson is magnificent in this part. Is there any other actress playing today who can suggest so much feeling with so little fuss? ... So real is her behaviour, so totally convincing the illusion she creates, that we hardly notice during the play the improbabilities or the skirtings which the play tails off into.' And Harold Hobson wrote: 'Flora Robson is true and unexaggerated, as she always is in the presentation of emotional distress.' She appeared again in the play in New York in September 1950 at the 48th Street Theater.

Returning to England in April 1951 she played Lady Brook at the Q Theatre in a revival of *Autumn*, and in June went to the Phoenix playing Paulina in *The Winter's Tale*. In 1952 Flora Robson received the CBE, and the same year played Miss Giddens in *The Innocents* at Her Majesty's Theatre. In November 1953 she played Sister Agatha at the Duchess in *The Return*, and then spent the following year touring as Rachel Lloyd in *No Escape*. In February 1955 she opened at the Duchess Theatre playing Sarah Ashby in *A Kind of Folly*. Flora Robson's acting abilities were never in doubt, but once again her judgement in choosing plays was. This was an obscure, heavy-handed and intellectual (if that is not a contradiction in terms) farce, and Ronald Barker reported: 'Flora Robson, a superb emotional actress, has not the ease required for light comedy or farce. She makes us feel so deeply that we are afraid to laugh.' At the Duke of York's in May 1956 she played Janet in *The House by the Lake*. Writing in *Plays and Players*, John Foss called it 'a dismal little thriller [with] neither dialogue nor theatre and Flora Robson's ability is wasted on the few unconvincing pieces of business she has been given ... Unfair to Flora Robson.' However, the production ran for more than 700 performances.

At the Old Vic in November 1958 she played Mrs Alving in *Ghosts*, and transferred with the production to the Prince's in April 1959. Flora Robson went to the Queen's Theatre in August the same year where she played Miss Tina in *The Aspern Papers*. Peter Roberts reported: '... Flora Robson, as Miss Tina, gives a performance that must surely rank as the greatest in her career. Watch her, for instance, in the second act when she appears in an unfamiliar best dress with an unfamiliar coiffure. She is in a state of agitated expectancy yet has spoken no line that hints of a new dress, coiffure, or, indeed, of agitation. But she conveys all these things, and much more, in a few seconds.' For this performance she received the *Evening Standard* Award as Best Actress in 1960. In June that year she was created a dame, and spent from August through December touring in South Africa in *The Aspern Papers*. In May 1961 she was back in London at St Martin's playing Grace Rovarte in Lesley Storm's play, *Time and Yellow Roses*. Peter Carthew called it a heavy and lifeless melodrama, but went on to praise Dame Flora: 'Dame Flora's radiance seemed to be a little dimmed on the night I saw her, but she had brought her harp to the party all right and the pull of her acting was, as always, wonderful to feel.'

At the Connaught Theatre in Worthing in November 1961 she played Miss Moffat in *The Corn Is Green*, and then took the production on a tour of South Africa in early 1962 before returning with it to the Flora Robson Playhouse in Newcastle-on-Tyne in October. She spent early 1963 touring once more, this time playing Liesa Bergmann again in *Close Quarter*, and in December returned to London where at the Duchess Theatre she played Gunhild Borkman in *John Gabriel Borkman* while Donald Wolfit had the title role. In 1964, back at the theatre named after her in Newcastle, she played Lady Bracknell, and then at the Edinburgh Festival in 1966 she was Hecuba in *The Trojan Women*. She was on tour again in April 1967 playing Winifred Brazier in *Brother and Sister*, and returned to London to the Haymarket and great applause in February 1968 when she played Miss Prism in an all-star revival of *The Importance of Being Earnest*. Helen Dawson wrote: 'Flora Robson almost makes it Miss Prism's play — stumbling with embarrassed gestures, grabbing back words she accidentally let out, greeting her Reverend's every phrase as though it were a revelation. Her joy in the last act at retrieving her handbag is a high-point of stage ecstasy.'

At the same theatre in October, the same company performed Anouilh's *Ring Round the Moon*, and Helen Dawson was disappointed: 'Flora Robson seemed a little unsure of how frivolous she was allowed to be as the Mother with an eye to the main chance.'

In November 1969 she opened at the Westminster Theatre playing Agatha Payne in *The Old Ladies*, and Hugh Leonard reported: 'Flora Robson played the villainous Mrs Payne with a gleeful sense of black humour. Self-preservation was the keynote, whether Dame Flora was popping a slice of cake into her reticule or negotiating the stairs with the concentration of a bomb-disposal expert.' The production transferred to the Duchess in December. The following August at the Edinburgh Festival she appeared in the title role in *Elizabeth Tudor*. Flora Robson was last seen on the stage nearly four years later when she narrated *Peter and the Wolf* at the Brighton Festival. She had retired to Brighton — not, however, into seclusion, because there she spent her time keeping her eye on the local theatres and hospitals, and engaging in charitable work and her hobby of making tapestry. Dame Flora died in July 1984.

See photograph opposite page 342.

MARGARET RUTHERFORD

A unique face, a unique figure, a unique comic ability graced Margaret Rutherford — but she resented all of them. In her soul she was Juliet. 'There have been many parts I yearned to play,' she said. 'How I would love to have been a great traditional actress like Bernhardt, Duse or Ellen Terry.' But she was destined to enter the consciousness, and indeed the hearts, of theatregoers as the epitome of eccentric, middle-aged ladies; as the *Times* put it: 'They were unconscious of their eccentricity; that they combined it with shrewdness and an air of authority and that they liked the world and felt at home there were among the reasons why a large public found them irresistible.'

Margaret Rutherford was born in South London, in Balham, on 11 May 1892. Her mother died when she was only three and after that she was raised by a devoted aunt, who happened to be enamoured of the theatre. Very early on Margaret shared her love of the stage and determined to be on it, but it was a very long and a very uphill struggle. At school she developed a great love for music, poetry and the spoken word. She was involved in local amateur theatricals, poetry recitals and took private drama tuition. Her aunt died when Margaret was 33 and left her a small amount of money. Not much, but enough for Margaret to gain the security to try her hand at her heart's desire — the stage. She got herself an introduction to Lilian Baylis at the Old Vic and was taken on as a student — albeit a rather ageing one — in September 1925. That month she played an Attendant on Portia in *The Merchant of Venice*. In October she was a Bridesmaid in *The Taming of the Shrew* and in November a Citizen in *Measure for Measure* and a Slave in *Antony and Cleopatra*. Then in December she got her first speaking part, that of the Fairy with the Long Nose in *Harlequin Jack Horner and the Enchanted Pie*. That month, too, she spoke the off-stage voice for Edith Evans' Angel Gabriel in *The Child in Flanders* by Cicely Hamilton. In January 1926 she was a Merrymaker in *The Merry Wives of Windsor* and the following month she had one line as a Citizen in *Julius Caesar*. In March she was once more a Citizen, but without a line, in *The Shoemaker's Holiday*. She played Lady Capulet in April in *Romeo and Juliet* and appeared in the *The Old Vic Follies* in Shakespeare's Birthday Programme. She ended her time with the Old Vic as a Guest in *Much Ado About Nothing*. Then it was back to Wimbledon, the bicycle and teaching, for a while.

In November 1928 Margaret Rutherford was taken on by Nigel Playfair at the Lyric, Hammersmith, as an understudy and played for a short while as Dona Filumena in *A Hundred Years Old* when Mabel Terry-Lewis was indisposed. From April until December 1929 she worked with the English Repertory Players at the Grand Theatre, Fulham, where she had a number of roles ranging from that of Madame Vinard in *Trilby* to La Vengeance in *A Tale of Two Cities*. She played a spy in *The Three Musketeers* and the Chinese Chi Li in *The Green Beetle*, altogether managing twenty-seven roles that season. In October 1930 she went to the Little Theatre in Epsom, where she played Mrs Coade in J. M. Barrie's *Dear Brutus*. The following month she was summoned to the Playhouse at Oxford where she played Mrs Frush in *Thark*, Mrs Janet Rodney in *March Hares* and Mrs Wislack in *On Approval*. There she also met her future husband, Stringer Davis, who was at Oxford acting and directing. She returned to Epsom for Christmas, where she played Mrs Pudie in Ian Hay's *The Sport of Kings*.

At the beginning of 1931 Margaret Rutherford went back to Oxford where she played Mrs Sturgis in *If Four Walls Told*, Dona Barbarita in *The Romantic Young Lady*, Madame Denaux in *French Leave*, Mrs Fred Livingston in *The First Year*, Mrs Delisse in *The Unfair Sex* and Lady Bracknell in *The Importance of Being Earnest*. In April she returned to London, where she had a season of repertory at the Greyhound Theatre in Croydon. In the six months she was there she played eighteen parts in plays ranging from Ibsen and Maugham to Pinero and Coward. She returned once again to Oxford in October, where she played Florence Rooke in *Interference* and Mrs Morland in *Mary Rose*. The following month she was Miss Bourne in *The Ghost Train*, Mrs Leverett in *Rookery Nook* and Mrs Ebley in *The Last of Mrs Cheyney*. She ended her spell with the Oxford repertory in December playing Agatha Whatcombe in *Ambrose Applejohn's Adventure*.

In 1932, seeming not to be advancing very quickly in her career, Margaret Rutherford joined the Greater London Players, who toured the suburbs in repertory for one-night stands. With them she played, among other roles, Mrs Tabret in *The Sacred Flame*, Miss Mayne in *Autumn Crocus*, and Miss Willesden in *London Wall*. At last, in 1933 came the breakthrough. She went to the Lyric, Hammersmith, in April to play Mrs Read in James Dale's *Wild Justice*. She was the

murderer's charwoman; the play transferred to the Vaudeville Theatre in May, and at the age of 41 Margaret Rutherford made her West End début. But the work did not come pouring in. In February 1934 she was at the Cambridge Theatre, but understudying Jean Cadell and Muriel Aked in *Birthday*. In April she was engaged for a single performance for the Scandinavian Society at the Westminster Theatre to play Aline Solness in Ibsen's *The Master Builder*, which starred Donald Wolfit and was directed by him. The production then transferred to the Embassy Theatre for a run. People in the profession at last began to notice her, and when Athene Seyler dropped out of a production of *Hervey House* which was due to open at His Majesty's Theatre in May 1935 the director Tyrone Guthrie contacted Margaret, who opened in the production. In November, Guthrie engaged her to play Miss Flower in Robert Morley's first play, *Short Story*, which after a tour opened at the Queen's Theatre. James Agate reported: 'As a ruthless village spinster [Margaret Rutherford] entrances and convulses the house every moment she is on the stage.'

At the Lyric Theatre she opened in September 1936 playing Mrs Palmai in *Farewell Performance*, which starred Mary Ellis and unfortunately lasted only nine nights. That year, however, she began her film career, which was to be long and successful, if limited. She was back on stage in February 1939 playing Aunt Bella in *Tavern in the Town* at the Embassy Theatre in Swiss Cottage, and in July at the same theatre played Emily Deveral in *Up the Garden Path*. She returned to the West End to the Phoenix Theatre in January 1938 playing the Mother in *The Melody that Got Lost*, and finally had her first great stage success in May at the Ambassadors' Theatre, where she played Bijou Furze in *Spring Meeting*, written by M. J. Farrell and John Perry and directed by John Gielgud. Ivor Brown wrote: '. . . she presents a fussy, irritable, absurd old maid with a great contempt for marriage and a wide, if secret knowledge of the turf, where she punts secretly . . . If sometimes one feels that the kind of fevered gamester's eagerness and the slash of spinsterish temper which Miss Rutherford so forcibly puts into the play are too large and too vivid for the compass of comedy, it is also true that her performance is in many ways vastly amusing, as one soon discovers when she is packed off to bed during far too much of the second act.' Audiences found her performance extremely funny — but Margaret Rutherford saw only the tragic side of the part she was playing and resented the laughter. Gielgud had a difficult time getting her to accept

Flora Robson (with Basil Sydney) in *A Man About the House*
at the Piccadilly Theatre
(London, February 1946)

Michael Redgrave as Charles Surface in *The School for Scandal*
at the Queen's Theatre
(London, 1937)

the notion that the laughter was wholly sympathetic.

In 1939 she was again directed by Gielgud, this time in Wilde's *The Importance of Being Earnest* in which she played Miss Prism. The production played for eight charity matinées at the Globe Theatre in January and then began its run at the same theatre in August. The *Times* reported: 'Miss Rutherford's bridling over the restored handbag, as if it were a favourite cat long lost and now astonishingly mewing in her lap, [is] as restrained and effective a piece of drollery as one could wish for.'

Margaret Rutherford had a complete change of pace when, directed by George Devine, she very successfully played the brooding, vengeful Mrs Danvers in Daphne du Maurier's *Rebecca* at the Queen's Theatre in April 1940. In July 1941 she was the inimitable Madame Arcati in Noel Coward's *Blithe Spirit* at the Piccadilly Theatre. At first she did not want the role, not wishing to offend mediums, whom she considered good and sincere people, but in the end she received their plaudits as well as those of the general public. Although the production continued to run, she left it after a year. She concentrated for a while on filming, making such notable movies as *The Demi-Paradise*, *Yellow Canary* and *English Without Tears*. In September 1944 she went on an ENSA tour of the Continent, playing Louise Garrard in *Love from a Stranger*, and in December, alternating with Sybil Thorndike, played the Queen of Hearts and the White Queen in *Alice in Wonderland*. During the production she got to fly from a wire and she considered it 'one of the major thrills of my life'.

In April 1945 at the London Hippodrome she played Lady Charlotte Fayre in Ivor Novello's *Perchance to Dream*. John Trewin wrote: 'Her part hardly exists; but ingeniously she makes a personage of a phantom and at the end — in Mr Novello's odd little ghost scene behind the gauzes — a phantom of a personage.' Early in the run, on 26 March 1945, she married her old friend Stringer Davis.

On 11 April 1946 she once more played Miss Prism in *The Importance of Being Earnest*, this time for a single matinée in aid of the King George Pension Fund at the Haymarket. The production was destined to tour abroad, but Edith Evans, who played Lady Bracknell, did not want to go so — reluctantly, as she felt she could not live up to Miss Evans' performance — Margaret Rutherford took over the role for the tour, which visited Canada and the United States before opening on Broadway at the Royale Theater on 3 March 1947. Brooks

Atkinson reported: 'As the overbearing Lady Bracknell, Miss Margaret Rutherford is tremendously skilful — the speaking, the walking and the wearing of costumes all gathered up into one impression of insufferability.'

Back in London at the Apollo Theatre in March 1948 she had a great success as Miss Evelyn Whitchurch in *The Happiest Days of Your Life*. That year she also made the evergreen film, *Passport to Pimlico*. In January 1950 she played Madame Desmortes in Anouilh's *Ring Round the Moon*, adapted by Christopher Fry for the Globe Theatre. T. C. Worsley said it was a 'wonderfully rich and highly enjoyable virtuoso performance — but too deliberate and heavy for such light tongued comedy'. However, Audrey Williamson reported: 'Margaret Rutherford gave racy gusto to an elderly and sardonic aristocrat in a wheelchair.'

Margaret Rutherford had one of her rare failures in July 1952 when she played the title role in Frank Baker's *Miss Hargreaves* at the Royal Court Theatre, but in February 1953 she was back at the top playing Lady Wishfort in Congreve's *The Way of the World* at the Lyric, Hammersmith, directed once more by John Gielgud. Eric Keown wrote: 'Top marks go to Miss Margaret Rutherford, most happily cast as Lady Wishfort, whom she plays with enormous gusto in the grand manner, waving her jaw menacingly at her enemies and behaving like a splendidly padded windmill, very funny and curiously touching.' And Harold Hobson: 'In her raddled, vain, manhunting, farcical and absurd rhetoric can be heard the echo of the authentic music of her vanished and betrayed romantic youth; there is something disturbingly sad, as well as uproariously funny, in this beauty become scarecrow. This is a Lady Wishfort who, slightly eccentric, might easily be encountered in St James's Park; yet if one met her, by moonlight, gliding round the corner of a broken staircase in a ruined castle, one would be startled, but not surprised. Here is a performance that satisfies the eye by its picturesqueness, the ear by the impeccable musical control that underlies its apparent blustering, and that moves the imagination.'

The following February she played the White Queen in *Alice* once more, at the Prince's Theatre, and on 18 March for the theatrical charities played Mrs Ackroyd-Smith in a sketch entitled *Homecoming* by Arthur Macrae at the London Palladium's Midnight Cavalcade. In December she was in Anouilh's *Time Remembered* at the Lyric, Hammersmith, and transferred with the production to the New Theatre in April 1955. Ronald Barker, writing in *Plays and Players*, said: 'Margaret Rutherford, as the eccentric aristocratic Duchess, never for a moment conveys the elegance and charm which make the madness so effective. Instead we have a sensible country woman, quite out of her depths in this odd charade and turning the high comedy into farce.' Her next role was, however, entirely tailored to her talents: she played the eccentric Mirabell Petersham in Gerald Savory's *A Likely Tale* at the Globe Theatre with Robert Morley in March 1956. At the charity matinée *Night of 100 Stars* at the Palladium on 28 June that year, she appeared in Morley's sketch, *Progress in Work*.

At the Saville Theatre in December 1956 she was once more Lady Wishfort in a revival of *The Way of the World*, and as Kenneth Tynan had reported earlier: 'Margaret Rutherford is filled with a monstrous vitality: the soul of Cleopatra has somehow got trapped in the corporate shape of an entire lacrosse team. The unique thing about Miss Rutherford is that she can act with her chin alone: among its many moods I especially cherish the chin commanding, the chin in doubt, and the chin at bay. My dearest impression of this Hammersmith night is a vision of Miss Rutherford, clad in something loose, darting about her boudoir like a gigantic bumblebee at large in a hothouse.' And Frank Granville-Barker wrote: 'Richest of all the impersonations is Margaret Rutherford's Lady Wishfort, a gaudy galleon of lecherous womanhood ploughing her way through a sea of amorous troubles. Her exchanges of boudoir Billingsgate with her maid Foible, her almost obscene gambolling when she hears that a man is coming to her with the worst intentions, her sudden collapse into pathos when trapped by Fainall — all are played with vigour, yet never overdone.'

Margaret Rutherford once more played Lady Bracknell, at the Dublin Festival in May 1957, and then spent much of that and the following year touring Australia, as Miss Whitchurch in *The Happiest Days of Your Life* and the Duchess in *Time Remembered*.

She returned to London, and at the Garrick in June 1959 played Minerva Goody in *Farewell, Eugene*. With her in the production was Peggy Mount, and it was a perfect vehicle for both of them. She went to the Helen Hayes Theater in New York in September 1960, where she once more played Minerva.

She did not have a success with her next London appearance, which was at the Globe Theatre in May 1961 when she played Bijou Furze in *Dazzling Prospect*, once more directed by John Gielgud. Bill Lester reported for *Plays and Players*: 'Whether an individual enjoyed it or not depended entirely on whether or not he liked Margaret

Rutherford. If he did, then it was a play which suited her to the full and a cast backed up admirably her every eccentricity. If he did not, then no effort of director or cast could have mitigated the boredom. Evidently a lot of people did not.' She did, however, receive an OBE that year, and in October she was at the Pembroke Theatre in Croydon appearing in a programme of extracts from dramatic works called *Our Little Life*.

Margaret Rutherford was back in Restoration comedy at the Haymarket Theatre in April 1962 playing Mrs Candour in *The School for Scandal*. Caryl Brahms wrote: 'She does not merely get her laughs, she acts for them and can be (even though it is not called for here) heartbreaking as well as so funny it hurts. Her Mrs Candour draws up scandal as the sun draws up water from the earth — strongly, naturally, inevitably. And her glee in sniffing the sweet incense of some wrecked reputation is equalled only by our own as we watch suspicions becoming certainties.'

Margaret Rutherford turned again to filming for a while, and in 1964 was awarded an Oscar for her supporting performance in the Burton–Taylor drama *The VIPs*. She had a serious nervous breakdown, and when she returned to the stage to the Saville in May 1965 she was still living in a nursing home and accompanied every night to the theatre by a doctor. She was playing Mrs Laura Partridge in the American comedy, *The Solid Gold Cadillac*; Hugh Leonard did not care for it at all. 'As a vehicle for Miss Rutherford,' he wrote, 'it fails on nearly all counts.' That December at the Jeanetta Cochrane she played the Prologue in *The Gulls*, and at the Chichester Festival in July the following year she was Mrs Heidelberg in *The Clandestine Marriage*. John Russell Taylor found her performance 'a trifle subdued'. At the Haymarket in October 1966 she was Mrs Malaprop in *The Rivals*. It was a difficult experience for her; her memory was no longer trustworthy, and she admitted that many of the malapropisms were her own. 'As in all comedy,' she said, 'the timing had to be precise. Catch the split second and the laughs come. Miss two beats and they are gone. Sensing the timing in a period piece is always difficult, but combining a crop of malapropisms with this was very wearying.' David Benedictus reported: 'Margaret Rutherford as Mrs Malaprop looking like some masterpiece of the confectioner's art, had a rather unhappy evening but is nonetheless inimitable; at odd moments throughout the play she uttered shrill animal noises.' With *The Rivals* Margaret Rutherford ended her stage career. All her life she had been terrified of forgetting her words; now it had indeed happened. There were still films, however. Not only did she have the

Oscar, she had had a string of successes playing Miss Marples in Agatha Christie stories.

She was awarded the DBE in the New Year Honours of 1967 but her last years were spent in increasing unhappiness as her mind failed completely; even her beloved Stringer Davis could not penetrate the fog which surrounded her. She died on 22 May 1972, aged 80.

PAUL SCOFIELD

*P*aul Scofield was born on 21 January 1922 at Hurstpierpoint near Brighton, where his father was headmaster of the village school. In 1935 while he was at Vardean School, he appeared at the Theatre Royal in Brighton as an extra in a crowd scene in *The Only Way*. After leaving school he became a student at the Croydon Repertory Theatre School, and when war broke out and that was closed down he joined the London Mask Theatre School run by John Fernald. One of its advantages was that the students got walk-on parts at the Westminster Theatre, to which it was attached. In January he walked on in Eugene O'Neill's *Desire Under the Elms*, and in April he spoke his first lines on the London stage when he played the Third Clerk and the First Soldier in Drinkwater's *Abraham Lincoln*. In each part the line was 'Yes, Sir'. In August he was again a mute walk-on in J. B. Priestley's *Cornelius*. Two of the teachers at the school, Eileen Thorndike (Sybil's sister) and Herbert Scott, evacuated some of the students in autumn 1940 to Bideford in north Devon. In the spring they opened the Bideford Repertory Company, and there Scofield played a number of roles. In one night alone he was King Lear, Macbeth and Petruchio in the programme of Shakespearian extracts that opened the theatre. He went on to play Dan in *Night Must Fall*, Tom Pettigrew in *Berkeley Square*, Albert Feather in *Ladies in Retirement*, Prosper in *Granite*, Richard Greatham in *Hay Fever*, George Pepper in *Red Peppers*, Alec Harvey in *Still Life* and Henry Gow in *Fumed Oak*. That summer the company moved to the Houghton Hall in Cambridge where Paul Scofield played the title role in André Obey's *Noah*.

In autumn 1941 he set off on an ENSA tour, playing at first Vincentio and then Tranio in Robert Atkins' production of *The Taming of the Shrew*. In spring 1942 he was engaged by Sybil Thorndike and Lewis Casson to play the Messenger for a tour of *Medea*, but after a few rehearsals went down with mumps. He was better by March and went on a tour of *Jeannie* playing the Hotel Clerk. In June he set off again, this time playing Ainger in

John van Druten's *Young Woodley*. In the autumn he was at the Repertory Theatre in Birmingham, a member of the Travelling Repertory Theatre, and he played Stephen Undershaft in *Major Barbara* and Horatio in *Hamlet*. There he met the actress Joy Parker, who was playing Ophelia. They both set off on a tour of munitions hostels in *Arms and the Man*. He was Sergius Saranoff and she played the Bulgarian Maid. Before their next play, Steinbeck's *The Moon Is Down*, opened at the Whitehall Theatre in London, Paul Scofield and Joy Parker married. In the autumn they were off on another tour of munitions hostels, with Paul Scofield playing Donald in *Three-Cornered Moon*, an American comedy by Gertrude Tonkonogy.

Paul Scofield was in Travelling Repertory Theatre productions at the Theatre Royal, Bristol, in January 1944, playing the Stranger in *The Cricket on the Hearth* and Tybalt in *Romeo and Juliet*. In the spring it was back to the munitions hostels, playing Oliver Farrant in J. B. Priestley's *I Have Been Here Before*.

In autumn 1944 the Scofields joined Sir Barry Jackson's company at the Birmingham Repertory Theatre. There Paul played a number of parts, including Prince Po and the First Coolie in *The Circle of Chalk*, Reginald Bridgnorth in *Getting Married*, the Clown in *The Winter's Tale*, William d'Albini in *The Empress Maud*, Toad in *Toad of Toad Hall*, Valentine in *Doctor's Delight*, a Fisherman in *Land's End*, Young Marlow in *She Stoops to Conquer*, Constantin in *The Seagull*, and Jerry Devine in *Juno and the Paycock*. By the end of the first season he was a glowing star in Birmingham and the local critics praised his every performance. He began, however, as he would always continue in his career, as an actor and not as a personality. His appearance changed with every role — and his private life always remained private.

The second season at Birmingham brought a young director of genius, Peter Brook, to the company; he directed Scofield as John Tanner in *Man and Superman*, the Bastard in *King John*, and Doctor Wangel in *The Lady from the Sea*. That season Scofield also played a number of roles in *1066 and All That*, adapted by Reginald Arkell.

Sir Barry Jackson was made director of the Shakespeare Memorial Theatre in 1946 and Scofield went with him to Stratford, where that first season he played Cloten in *Cymbeline*, Don Adriano de Armado in *Love's Labour's Lost*, the title role in *Henry V*, Oliver in *As You Like It*, Malcolm (the best in living memory, according to most of the critics) in *Macbeth*, and Lucio in *Measure for Measure*. So successful was his first Stratford season that at the end of it he was offered a Hollywood contract, but had no difficulty in turning it down. His home was the stage. At the Arts Theatre Club in November he played Tegeus-Chromis in Christopher Fry's *A Phoenix Too Frequent*. Harold Hobson reported: 'Here is an actor of presence and potentiality. He has a trick of ending a phrase on a rising note, with a sudden, detached and meditative tone.'

Scofield returned in April 1947 to Stratford where Harold Hobson said of his Mercutio in *Romeo and Juliet* (which was directed by Peter Brook): 'Mr Paul Scofield's Mercutio has little gaiety, but at this point his gravity is richly rewarding. It is gravity moonstruck: he is a Mercutio who really has seen the fairies and wishes, perhaps, that he had not.' That season his parts were, as ever, varied. He played Mephistopheles in *The Tragical History of Doctor Faustus*, Lucio in *Measure for Measure*, Don Adriano de Armado once more in *Love's Labour's Lost*, Sir Andrew Aguecheek in *Twelfth Night*, and the title role in *Pericles*. In October the company had a short London season at His Majesty's Theatre, and there Scofield repeated his Mercutio and Sir Andrew. In December he was at the Lyric, Hammersmith, playing Young Fashion in *The Relapse*, and transferred with the production in January 1948 to the Phoenix Theatre.

In April, Paul Scofield was once more at Stratford. That year he played Philip in *King John* and Bassanio in *The Merchant of Venice*. It was also the year that he gave the audiences Hamlet for the first time. The production was directed by Michael Benthall, and dressed up as Victorian. Scofield alternated playing the title role with Robert Helpmann. T. C. Worsley thought that the production seemed to be designed around Helpmann and that Scofield did not fit into it so well. However, he reported: 'This much talked of young actor certainly has gifts, youth, looks and above all, attack. He can take the stage, but does not give the impression of knowing quite what to do with it when he has it, and of having to fill in with tricks that are rather dangerously growing on him.'

A. V. Cookman said that Scofield played Hamlet as 'a spiritual fugitive who seeks not so desperately the fulfilment of his earthly mission as some steadfast refuge for the hard-driven imagination. Only in death the refuge is found. It is the distinction of Mr Scofield's playing that makes us free of this imagination, and its inner distractions have for us such intense dramatic reality that the melodramatic bustle of the court appears unreal, like the shadows outside Plato's cavern.' That season Paul Scofield was also a magnificent Clown in *The Winter's Tale*, Roderigo in *Othello*, and Troilus in *Troilus and Cressida*. Of the last Harold Hobson wrote: 'Nothing could be better, sadder than Paul Scofield's delivery of the "Distracted with the salt of broken tears", in which a lack of vocal melody is more than made up for by a miracle of timing.'

Paul Scofield had his first major starring role in the West End in March 1949 when he opened at the St James's Theatre in Terence Rattigan's uncharacteristically epic play, *Adventure Story*. In it Scofield played Alexander the Great, and Hobson wrote: 'Paul Scofield's Alexander is drawn and haunted, memorably so. All this fine actor's performances have something of the other world about them ... His Alexander might, by sheer tension and desperate resolve, have conquered the world, but he looks like a man who has heard the banshee howl.' And T. C. Worsley said: 'Mr Paul Scofield is a young actor graced with the most enviable array of gifts. An excellent presence, fine looks, a musical voice and that indefinable magnetism which can by itself take an audience. But these endowments are only the foundation. Whether he uses them to become an actor, or whether he will be content to drift into becoming a gallery-idol or a film star is yet to be seen.' A strange review about someone who had played so many major parts — and had already turned down a Hollywood contract. Scofield was, however, only 27 at the time. In October of that year he played Constantin in Chekhov's *The Seagull* at the Lyric, Hammersmith. The production transferred in November to the St James's Theatre and Worsley wrote: 'To play him flat is to create areas of calm just where there ought to be areas of storm. Notice how tame this flatness makes the fiasco of his play; and this is not just a case of a low-toned start which is meant to build up through the play. Mr Scofield mutes his part deliberately from start to finish.' For a special matinée at the London Coliseum on 20 November 1949 Paul Scofield played Romeo in the Balcony scene of *Romeo and Juliet* with Peggy Ashcroft as his Juliet.

In January 1950 he opened at the Globe Theatre playing the dual roles of Hugo and Frederic, twin brothers in Anouilh's *Ring Round the Moon*, directed by Peter Brook. T. C. Worsley, who never seemed to be satisfied with Scofield's performances, wrote rather grudgingly: 'Mr Paul Scofield moves through the double role gracefully and with style, though I think he could afford a little more swagger as the wicked twin.' *Ring Round the Moon* ran at the Globe for two years.

Scofield opened at the Phoenix Theatre in January 1952 playing Don Pedro, the Prince of Aragon, in *Much Ado About Nothing*, and in August was Philip Sturgiss in Charles Morgan's *The River Line* at the Edinburgh Festival. The play came to the Lyric, Hammersmith, and then on to the Strand Theatre, where it settled in for a run. However, Scofield left the cast before Christmas to play the title role in *Richard II* at the Lyric, Hammersmith, directed by John Gielgud. In February 1953 he was still in the Lyric, Hammersmith, company, playing Witwoud in Congreve's *The Way of the World*. Kenneth Tynan said he gave 'a beautifully gaudy performance, pitched somewhere between Hermione Gingold and Stan Laurel'. In May at the Lyric, Hammersmith, he played Pierre in Otway's *Venice Preserv'd* directed by Peter Brook, and Tynan wrote: 'Paul Scofield's Pierre, smouldering under a black wig, is the strongest, surest performance this actor has given since he came to London.' Scofield left the Lyric, Hammersmith, and in December opened at the Piccadilly Theatre playing Paul Gardiner in Wynyard Browne's *A Question of Fact*. Richard Buckle, writing in *Plays and Players*, said: 'Paul Scofield was far less mannered than I have ever seen him: his performance is natural, balanced, varied in colour and telling in effect. The schoolmaster is a kind of genius in a small way, and this Paul Scofield proves beautifully able to suggest. He switches brilliantly from humour to bravado, from ferocity to tenderness. I like his smile and his way of pacing up and down like a tiger.' For the Sybil Thorndike Jubilee matinée at Her Majesty's on 31 May 1954 Paul Scofield played Charles Surface in the Screen scene from *The School for Scandal*. In December that year he was back in an Anouilh play, *Time Remembered*, at the Lyric, Hammersmith. He played Prince Albert Troubiscoi and the production transferred to the New Theatre. The critic Ronald Barker said that he 'saves the production from disaster by his understanding of the mood, with its melancholy and humid nostalgia. His angular movements are dramatically correct and his appreciation of the poetic quality of the dialogue is fully realized.'

In 1955 Paul Scofield played Hamlet once more, in a remarkable production directed by Peter Brook. This was the first English company to play in Moscow since the 1917 revolution, and the pro-

duction became known thereafter as the Moscow *Hamlet*. It opened at the Phoenix Theatre in the West End in December, and Kenneth Tynan reported: '. . . no living actor is better equipped for Hamlet than Paul Scofield . . . He plays Hamlet as a man whose skill in smelling falseness extends to himself, thereby breeding self-disgust . . . Mr Scofield's outline is impeccable. What is surprising is the crude brushwork with which he fills it in. Vocally and physically he is one long tremendous sulk; a roaring boy at large, and not (as when he played the part before) a scholar gipsy. The new Mr Scofield protests much too much . . . too many speeches are mechanically gabbled; and the actor's face is a mask devoid of pathos . . .' However, Caryl Brahms wrote: 'With this interpretation Mr Scofield has left his salad days behind — too far behind, perhaps. Gone is the coltish amble, the strangulated voice, endearingly halfway between a coo and a creak, the over-frequent recourse to an unhouseled soul whose counsels once appeared to be kept in the general direction of the gallery. This Hamlet is precisely and decisively placed, stylishly enacted, beautifully spoken. His movements are purposeful and swift, his frenzies carefully considered. He leaves the playgoer in no doubt that, in his own good time, he would have dealt faithfully, lethally and in cold blood with Claudius. The sanest, least petulant of a long line of sable princes, he still brought what poetry there was to a prosaic production.' That year, too, his first film came out. It was *That Lady*, which starred Olivia de Havilland, and in which he very successfully played Philip of Spain.

In the 1956 New Year Honours list Paul Scofield was awarded the CBE. That April he played the Priest in the adaptation of the Graham Greene novel, *The Power and the Glory*. Kenneth Tynan wrote that Paul Scofield 'brings off a prodigious success as the trudging, wizened hero-victim. Puffing on a cheroot, with lines of resignation etched as if by acid on his cheeks and forehead, Mr Scofield exudes, drunk or sober . . . a Goya-esque melancholy. This is the authentic face of Mexico, fly-blown and God-bitten.' And of this production, directed by Scofield's old friend Peter Brook, Frank Granville-Barker wrote: 'Scofield himself is the very personification of seediness, hopelessness and failure. His shambling gait, his careworn face, the gentle melancholy of his drunkenness — all add up to a portrayal of absolute fidelity to his author's wishes. It is one of those rare performances in which feeling and technique merge into a whole.' (For this performance Scofield won the *Evening Standard* Drama Award.) In June 1956, at the Phoenix Theatre again, he played Harry, Lord Monchesney, in T. S. Eliot's *The*

Family Reunion, and Philip Squire wrote in *Plays and Players*: 'Paul Scofield brings a vibrant intelligence to Harry and speaks the character's mind as freely as the play allows though the blank verse occasionally halts for it.'

At the Piccadilly Theatre in May 1957 Paul Scofield played Fred Dyson in Rodney Ackland's *A Dead Secret*, and Caryl Brahms reported: 'Now that his work shines out as the fine, honest, graceful acting that it is, freed of archness and self-pity, balanced, squarely stanced, wide, generous and informed, only that voice, hanging about it like limp seaweed, holds him back with its lack of warmth, its curious flatness.'

The following year, at the Saville in April, Paul Scofield made his first appearance in a musical play, *Expresso Bongo*. Caryl Brahms thought him 'more of a butterfly than a grubby agent on the golden bandwagon' but the critics writing in *Plays and Players* voted it one of the best performances of the year. In June 1959 Paul Scofield was back in a Graham Greene play when he played Clive Root in *The Complaisant Lover* at the Globe. Richard Buckle reported: 'Paul Scofield edged his way in and out of his caddish part with the crooked and faltering assurance which has for decades proved irresistible to women of all ages.'

A truly great part came the way of Paul Scofield in July 1960, when at the Globe Theatre he played Sir Thomas More in Robert Bolt's *A Man for All Seasons*. Kenneth Tynan could not come to terms with either the subject matter or the play, and wrote of Scofield's performance: 'What remains is More the gentle reasoner, and this Paul Scofield plays to the hilt, at once wily and holy, as unastonished by betrayal as he is by fidelity. He does the job beautifully, but where, in this obsequious piece of acting, is the original Scofield who burst upon us, some twelve years ago, like exquisite thunder? ... It is true he has never given a bad performance, but it was not in negatives like this that we formerly hoped to praise him ...' Caryl Brahms, however, wrote: 'It must be seen because as Thomas More, Paul Scofield gives the finest of a career of fine performances. More is in safe hands, true hands, being in Mr Scofield's hands. For Scofield knows him with his mind and with his heart, which means that he completely convinces us that he is that grey, dry, loyal, wise and witty man; and that if in life More was something less grey, dry, loyal, wise and witty, it is life and not the actor who has failed to show us the whole truth.'

In summer 1961 Paul Scofield went to the Shakespeare Festival at Stratford, Ontario, where he played the title part in *Coriolanus* and Don Armado in *Love's Labour's Lost*. Then in November he made his Broadway début at the

ANTA Theater, where he once again played Thomas More in *A Man for All Seasons*. Howard Taubman wrote in the *New York Times*: 'Because the nature of Sir Thomas More deepens rather than alters and because his emotions are merely suggested in the quiet sparkle of his mind, the role is enormously exacting. Paul Scofield brings dignity and reserve to it. The crinkle of an eye emphasizes the pithiness of a phrase; the droop of a shoulder sums up the weight of an unbending conscience. Mr Scofield is so fine an actor that he can permit himself the repose that lets others shine in crucial scenes ... Yet this Sir Thomas can reveal his agony as he says farewell to his wife and daughter and his pride as a man in his final declaration in court.' The performance won Scofield a Tony; and when he repeated it on film he won an Oscar.

At the Royal Shakespeare Theatre in Stratford-on-Avon in November 1962, Paul Scofield played the title role in Peter Brook's production of *King Lear*. Irving Wardle wrote: '... although he has sublime passages in the latter half of the production ... these are the exceptions: the general level of his performance is bleakly negative: it leaves an impression more of determination to avoid clichés than of any positive expressive intent. And he remains to the end a robust figure, far removed from the image of the wasted monarch, fourscore and upward, whose life is held by the slenderest thread.' Nevertheless, Scofield again collected the *Evening Standard* Drama Award for this performance, and appeared in the same production in London at the Aldwych in December 1962 and in Paris at the Théâtre Sarah Bernhardt in May 1963. The production then toured Berlin, Prague, Budapest, Belgrade, Bucharest, Warsaw, Helsinki, Leningrad and Moscow during early 1964. It ended up at the State Theater, Lincoln Center, in New York in May, and Howard Taubman, writing in the *New York Times* was immensely impressed. 'Mr Scofield's Lear has size but it remains within the proportions of modern man's sensibility. In his first scene he allows himself the signs of old age — a cracked, quavering voice and a trembling arm — as he exhorts his daughters to expatiate on the extent of their love. When Goneril later crosses him, he can overturn the table and set his knight roaring in anger. And in the tempest his powerful voice can contend with the elements without resort to ranting. Although Mr Scofield commands the grand manner, he is at his noblest and most moving as his anguish increases and his mind turns inwards and cracks ... Mr Scofield finds subtleties of movement, expression and speech to convey the deepening of his awareness and humility ... At the end, when he carries in the slain Cordelia, he is like a man who has summoned up unexpected reserves of physical strength and moral courage.'

Paul Scofield remained with the Royal Shakespeare Company for the next few years. At Stratford in July 1965 he played the title role in *Timon of Athens*, directed by John Schlesinger. Peter Roberts reported: 'At first he seems too big for the role: the Scofield manner and Scofield inflexions are so pronounced as to verge on caricature. It is like watching a tenor who has built his voice up for Wagner trying to scale it down again for Mozart. But, of course, there is little in Timon of Athens that is Mozartian and by the time this Timon's frenzied geniality has snapped, the howl of anguish that follows is harrowing indeed. The actor, in fact, is sufficiently in command to rush the incantatory manner of ecclesiastical delivery and pull if off as well.' At the RSC's London home, the Aldwych, in January 1966 Scofield played Ivan Alexandrovich Khlestakov in *The Government Inspector*; and in November he was Charlie Dyer in *Staircase*, of which performance John Russell Taylor wrote: 'Paul Scofield, acting away like mad as Charles, is really much too heavyweight an actor for the role.' For Christmas that year, at the Aldwych he played the Dragon in *The Thwarting of Baron Bolligrew*. Scofield returned to Stratford in August where he played the title role in *Macbeth*, directed by Peter Hall and with Vivien Merchant as his Lady.

Peter Roberts wrote: 'Paul Scofield is particularly fine with the dagger speech, where his fluttering hands reach out for the evasive weapon. His ''She should have died hereafter'' is also very fine . . . Nonetheless it must be said that Scofield displays an exceedingly elaborate armoury on the verse which isolates him from the rest of the cast, who adopt a more naturalistic technique. Certainly the growling whimper, the staccato line, the sudden whispered close-up do produce some startling effects.' Scofield toured Finland and Russia in the Scottish play during November and December and brought it into London to the Aldwych in January 1968.

In July that year Scofield left the RSC and appeared at the Royal Court playing Laurie in John Osborne's *Hotel in Amsterdam*. Benedict Nightingale wrote that it was '. . . a ripe part for Paul Scofield, who exploits the same nagging, nasal, trumpeting whine he used in *Staircase* to much more serious effect.' The production transferred to the New Theatre in September and moved on to the Duke of York's in December. He was back at the Royal Court in February 1970 playing the title role in *Uncle Vanya*, and Stanley Price reported: '. . . I have rarely been moved by Scofield. His in-

terpretations and the style he uses for their effect seem the product of head rather than heart. His technique is prodigious, his integrity unswerving. Once his decision is made his skill imposes a total pattern. Yet frequently the character can seem more like a disguise, and thus the profounder moments are missed . . . His Vanya is a lost soul that has lost itself . . . Scofield's Vanya never achieves . . . vulnerability. One has never believed totally in his passion for Yeliena: there has been too much play acting in it.'

Paul Scofield joined the National Theatre Company at the Old Vic in March 1971 when he played Wilhelm Voigt in *The Captain of Köpenick*, John Mortimer's adaptation of the Carl Zuckmayer play, which was directed by Frank Dunlop. Helen Dawson wrote: 'From his first entrance there is that exciting amalgam of his own confidence in the character, and the fact that the spectator has no idea where this confidence will lead him. During the rest of the performance he never lets you, or himself, down . . . As usual, Scofield's voice lies at the heart of the character . . . And every so often, Scofield looks out into the distance, through heavy, dejected lids and the eyes gleam through the slits, reflecting a sharp, crafty intelligence.' In June he was at the New Theatre playing Leone in Pirandello's *The Rules of the Game*, and Mary Holland reported: 'Grey, glacial, precise, never wasting a movement nor a word, he dominated the play with his cold vision — an ideal of living-empty emotion, in which a man may control his fate only by his indifference to it.'

In April 1973 Paul Scofield went back to the Royal Court, where he played Alan West in Christopher Hampton's *Savages*, spending most of the evening with his hands tied behind his back and some of it with his head in a bag, having been kidnapped; the production transferred to the Comedy Theatre. At Leeds Playhouse in November 1974 Paul Scofield played Prospero in *The Tempest*, and brought the production into London to Wyndham's in February 1975. He played the title part, in April 1976, in *Dimetos* at the Nottingham Playhouse and transferred with the production to the Comedy.

He still lives happily in Sussex with his wife, and holds honorary doctorates from Glasgow and Kent universities. In the late 1970s Scofield joined Peter Hall's National Theatre company to play Volpone, appearing also in *The Madras House* and *Othello* and then scoring a considerable London success as Salieri in the first production of Peter Shaffer's *Amadeus*.

See photograph opposite page 374.

SARAH SIDDONS

See The Kembles

DONALD SINDEN

Donald Sinden was born in Plymouth, Devon, on 9 October 1923. He left school at 15, having not made much academic progress, and became a joinery apprentice, studying draughting at night school. Then his cousin, a keen amateur actor who was scheduled to open in a production for the Brighton Little Theatre Company, was called up into the RAF and asked Donald to take over his part. Incredulous, Donald agreed and made his stage début in *A Modern Aspasia*, which was written by a local author for the company. This was in 1940, and he was seen by Charles Smith who ran Mobile Entertainments Southern Area (MESA). Sinden had been judged unfit for active service because of his asthma and he was offered a job by Smith with MESA, which would fit in with wartime occupation requirements — the job entailed helping in an ambulance or answering phones — so Sinden signed up with Smith. He made his début with the company on 26 January 1941 playing Dudley in *George and Margaret*. For nearly four years he remained with the company travelling through village halls, Nissen huts and camps entertaining the troops with a repertory of plays which included *Fresh Fields*, *Private Lives*, *Good Morning Bill*, *French Without Tears* and *The Man in Possession*. All this time he also worked to complete his apprenticeship, which he did in 1944. Faced with the decision of what to do with his life — acting or joinery — he sought the advice of Charles Smith, who was convinced of his acting potential and summoned the great drama critic James Agate to give Sinden his opinion. Agate noted the meeting in his diary: 'He is the son of a chemist, and according to Charles has some notion of acting. Will I say whether in my opinion he should go on the stage or stick to cabinet-making ... Enough height, an attractive head, something of the look of a young Ainley, a good resonant voice, vowels not common, manner modest yet firm ... I tell him to stick to Shakespeare, beginning at the bottom of the ladder. Which advice may ruin his career ...' So in March 1944 Donald Sinden decided to become an actor. He got a scholarship to the Webber-Douglas School of Dramatic Art, and was then recruited into ENSA for a tour of Europe, India and Burma with *The Normandy Story*. Sinden went on to the Leicester Repertory Company for six months during winter 1945, and in spring 1946 joined Sir Barry Jackson's company at Stratford-on-Avon, having been recommended by both Charles Smith and James Agate. That season he played Dumain in *Love's Labour's Lost*, Arviragus in *Cymbeline* and Pride in *Dr Faustus*. He was re-engaged for the following season; with three months in between he and his friend and fellow actor, John Harrison, put together a dramatic recital called *Curtain Up*, with which they toured village halls. During the 1947 Stratford season he added the parts of Paris in *Romeo and Juliet*, Sebastian in *The Tempest*, Aumerle in *Richard II* and Lorenzo in *The Merchant of Venice*. He also met the new company member, a young actress named Diana Mahony, whom he later married. The Shakespeare Memorial Theatre Company had a London season at His Majesty's which opened in October 1947 and with them Sinden made his London début playing Aumerle in *Richard II*. He also played Romeo that season, as the actor who had the part, Laurence Payne, and whom Sinden was understudying, was taken ill.

Sinden made his television début playing the detective in an adaptation of Caryl Brahms' *A Bullet in the Ballet*, and then took over as a walking understudy to nine parts in *Off the Record* in the West End. Sinden became a member of the Bristol Old Vic Company. With them he appeared at the St James's Theatre as Rosencrantz in *Hamlet*, a performance which according to himself was 'unmemorable'. He was at the New Theatre in September and October 1948 with the Old Vic Company headed by Cedric Hardwicke and Edith Evans, and he played Sebastian in *Twelfth Night* and Envy and the Scholar in *Dr Faustus*.

At the Haymarket in January 1949 Donald Sinden opened as Arthur Townsend in *The Heiress*, which starred Ralph Richardson and Peggy Ashcroft. He had only seven lines, but he said them for every one of the 644 performances that the play ran, although the rest of the cast changed around him.

In 1950 he rejoined the Bristol Old Vic Company where he played in *The Lady's Not for Burning*, *The Good-Natured Man*, *The Merry Wives of Windsor* and *Puss in Boots*. When he returned to London the managements were not exactly waiting with open arms. He got an understudy job with *Waters of the Moon* and a few weeks' work at the Q Theatre. He was then cast as the Brazilian, Manuel del Vega, in *Red Letter Day*, which opened at the Garrick in February 1952. The play lasted for three months; more importantly it brought him an Ealing Studio screen test, a major part in the film *The Cruel Sea*, and eventually a seven-year contract with Rank, which in the end stretched into eight years of steady employment.

He was still under contract to Rank, and filming in the daytime, when he returned to the West End to play Mervyn Browne at the St Martin's in *Odd Man In*, an adaptation from the French by Robin Maugham which had a three-person cast — Sinden, Derek Farr and Muriel Parlow. Derek Conrad reported: 'Donald Sinden, as the stranger who becomes very much a friend in the household, has a fine gift for comedy. He gets laughs from the dialogue, his moves and the situations. His technique is almost imperceptible and achieves maximum results.' *Odd Man In* ran for six months in the West End. In December 1958 he was at the Cambridge playing a young man from Eton, Bob Brewster, in *Who's Your Father*, an upper-class comedy/farce by Denis Cannan which lasted only two and a half weeks. At the Strand in June 1959 he was Frank Marescaud in *All in the Family*, another adaptation from the French in which Sinden played the black sheep of the family. That lasted five weeks. At the Queen's in July 1960 he was Brian Curtis in *Joie de vivre* and at Christmas at the Scala played Captain Hook and Mr Darling in *Peter Pan*.

That year his Rank contract came to an end. He thought for a while of giving it all up, starting an entirely new profession and leaving acting behind, but at the Phoenix in March 1961 he played the title part in MacLeish's *JB*. Peter Carthew reported: 'Donald Sinden was a shade too young and eager for the middle-aged JB. But it was good to see him given at last a part worthy of his talents.' His next appearance was at the St Martin's in August 1961 when he played Edward Bromley in *Guilty Party*. *Plays and Players* termed it a run-of-the-mill whodunit; Sinden termed it a life-saver.

In April 1963 Donald Sinden joined the Royal Shakespeare Company at Stratford-on-Avon, and

during that season played Sebastian in *The Tempest*, Solinus in *The Comedy of Errors*, and Richard Plantagenet in *Henry VI* and *Edward IV* in the cycle to be known as *The Wars of the Roses*. He repeated his performances at the Aldwych that winter and returned to Stratford the following season to play in *The Wars of the Roses* for Shakespeare's quatercentenary celebrations. Frank Cox reported: 'Donald Sinden's York proceeds from an infectious relish of the early soliloquies to a resounding climax with Peggy Ashcroft's Queen Margaret when in the cruel and blazingly rhetorical Wakefield scene between them they triumph over the perils of bombast and overplaying; their full-blooded treatment of the two great speeches of this truly awful scene stands as a symbol of the best qualities of the production as a whole.' At the Aldwych in October 1964 he played Mr Price in *Eh?*, and the critic John Holmstrom called it a crashing piece of miscasting. Then in 1965 Donald Sinden toured South America for the British Council playing George Bernard Shaw in *Dear Liar* and Willie in *Happy Days*.

He returned to the West End to the Globe Theatre in June 1966, playing Robert Danvers in *There's a Girl in My Soup*. For the RSC in August 1967 at the Aldwych he played Lord Foppington in *The Relapse*. Frank Marcus wrote: 'Donald Sinden, in a brilliant performance, begins the day in the cadences of Malcolm Muggeridge, and is gradually turned into a rouged puppet by his dozen or so attendants. At heart he remains a rather foolish, puzzled man, desperately anxious to do the correct fashionable thing.' He then directed *Relatively Speaking* for a tour, and in June 1968 opened at the Strand playing Gilbert Bodley in *Not Now Darling*. Writing in *Plays and Players* Frank Cox said: '. . . I record my admiration for the superprofessionalism of Donald Sinden in the thankless leading role. Mr Sinden, matchless in the real comedy of *The Relapse* and *Girl in My Soup* alike, and riveting as York in *The Wars of the Roses*, here brings style, elegance and masterly timing to a part unworthy of his talent. There is an almost surreal quality in the way that he tosses into the air some of the feeblest of puns and double-meanings and worries them ingeniously into a sort of humour . . . In this form it would have been good to have seen him in a proper comedy, instead of a collection of puerile witticisms.' He returned once more to Stratford and to the RSC in August 1969 when he played Malvolio in *Twelfth Night* and the title role in *Henry VIII*, directed by Trevor Nunn. Robert Cushman reported: 'Donald Sinden comes nearest to success, a King who grows in authority before our eyes and whose battles with his conscience come near to establishing the play with a central conflict. His long, nervous speech of self-justification at his wife's trial was a triumph.' He toured Japan and Australia in 1970 as Malvolio, and at the Aldwych for the 1970–71 season he played that as well as repeating his *Henry VIII*, and added the part of Sir William Harcourt Courtly in *London Assurance*, of which performance Helen Dawson raved: '... Donald Sinden's glorious Sir William Harcourt Courtly, rouged and corseted like a pantomime dame; so ill-at-ease in the country that he hesitates even to remove his hat for fear of what may fall on his wig. It is a hugely funny performance, made all the funnier because behind the foppish trimmings beats a nervous human heart, taking refuge in artifice and London manners because they protect him from the uncertainty of reacting to bumping outside intrusions.' *London Assurance* transferred to the New Theatre in April 1972.

In September that year Donald Sinden was at the Duchess with Joan Greenwood in Terence Rattigan's double bill, *In Praise of Love*, which consisted of a terrible curtain raiser, *Before Dawn*, and a wonderful short play about love and death, called *After Lydia*.

He toured the United States with the RSC in *London Assurance* in the autumn of 1974 and appeared in the production at the Palace in New York during December. He returned to England to the Chichester Festival in May 1975 where he played Dr Stockmann in Ibsen's *An Enemy of the People*. W. Stephen Gilbert said that there was '... a performance from Donald Sinden which, though a perfectly legitimate reading, seems to me to diminish the play. Sinden is a specialist in comic acting and I yield to no one in my admiration of his technique and his ability to create a complete character. Here, though, Sinden plays a figure who graduates through a partly comedic development to a heroic stance. The balance clearly is problematical. What, for instance, do you do with a line like, ''Some people in this town look on me as a bit eccentric''? ... Sinden, not surprisingly, has looked for a roundness of character. He has found a vein of expansiveness, of good-hearted enthusiasm in the role and made it his modus operandi. This means in practice that we go along with Stockmann because he's endearing — we like him ... And so he plays dangerously near a Capra-esque hero, standing up against the corrupt world as much out of naïveté as out of concern for the truth. Consequently, the play loses much of its expressionist power and begins to look disappointingly like a bourgeois comedy.'

Donald Sinden played Arthur Wickstead in *Habeas Corpus* at the Martin Beck Theater in New York in November 1975 and returned for the Stratford season the following year, when he played Benedick in *Much Ado About Nothing*. Since then he has played both *King Lear* and *Othello* for the RSC at Stratford and the Aldwych, and enjoyed a long London run in a revival of Coward's *Present Laughter*. In 1984 he toured Europe for the British Council with a Haymarket production of *School for Scandal*, before appearing in a Ray Cooney farce, *Two Into One*, and then going to Chichester for a 1985 *Scarlet Pimpernel*.

As well as his hit films, which included *The Cruel Sea* and *Doctor in the House*, Sinden had a massive television success with Elaine Stritch, playing her bossy butler in 'Two's Company'. He has also had published two volumes of autobiography.

OTIS SKINNER

Otis Skinner was born in Cambridge, Massachusetts, on 28 June 1858. His father, the Rev. Charles Skinner, was a Universalist preacher, and they moved to Hartford, Connecticut, when Otis was a teenager. He attended Brown Grammar School, and although an omnivorous reader he was a mediocre student and left school early, becoming a clerk in an insurance company. He was soon bored by the dull routine and turned to more physical work in the shipping department of a large company. His brother Charles was working in New York as a reporter, and on a trip to visit him Otis went to the Lyceum Theater where he was so impressed by a production of *The Hunchback of Notre Dame* that he determined to be an actor. Returning to Hartford, he organized rather unsuccessful amateur theatricals, but did manage to become the Hartford correspondent for the *New York Dramatic News*, which gave him free entry to any professional production that came to his city. He wrote endless letters to theatrical managements seeking work in the business and finally, after many months, was taken on by William Davidge, the actor—manager of the grandly titled Philadelphia Museum — a ramshackle outfit that was known locally with derision as 'Davidge's Snake Shop' because of a display of stuffed reptiles in the foyer. Otis Skinner made his professional début there in November 1877 playing Jim, an old Negro, in *Woodleigh*. He went on that first season to play ninety-two character roles, but often the salary was not forthcoming. When Davidge was forced to close the theatre because of mounting debts Skinner got four weeks' work at the Chestnut Street Theater, where he played infinitely better roles with better actors. It was as Malcolm in *Macbeth* that he was noticed by George K. Goodwin, manager of the reputable Walnut Street Theater, and engaged for the 1878–79 season at that theatre. He played there in repertory for two years, and then had a week at Mrs John Drew's Arch Street Theater where he played in six English comedies in as many nights.

Otis Skinner made his New York début with the Kiralfy Brothers at the Niblo Gardens when he played Maclow, the Beggar of the Mountains, in *Enchantment*, a lavish spectacular which included music, melodrama, trapeze artists and ballet. This was in September 1879. In December he played Sir Francis Mowbray in *Hearts of Steel*. In March 1880 he was taken on by Edwin Booth at Booth's Theater, where he played the Wounded Officer in *Macbeth*. The following month he played with Booth in *Richelieu*, *Much Ado About Nothing*, *Richard III*, *Othello*, *The Fool's Revenge*, *Hamlet*, *The Merchant of Venice*, *The Taming of the Shrew* and *Ruy Blas*. His roles were small, but he learned a good deal from working with the master. Skinner was then taken into Lawrence Barrett's company, and spent three years with them touring and occasionally touching down in New York, where among other roles he played Paolo in *Francesca da Rimini* at the Star Theater in August 1883.

In October 1884 he joined John Drew and Ada Rehan and other great stars in Augustin Daly's company at Daly's Theater. He remained with Daly until 1888, playing a variety of parts. It was with this company that he made his London début at Toole's Theatre in July 1884, playing Paul Hollyhock in *Casting the Boomerang*. The company again visited London in 1886, playing at the Strand Theatre. Skinner was Harry Damask in *A Night Off* and also appeared in *Nancy and Co*. The company then went on to play Glasgow, Edinburgh, Dublin, and on the Continent in Germany and France. In his final year with the company they visited London again, this time appearing at the Gaiety Theatre where Skinner played in *The Railroad of Love* and *The Taming of the Shrew*.

Back in New York he played Paul Falshawe in *The Love Story* at Tompkin's Fifth Avenue Theater in August 1889, and then joined the Booth—Modjeska Company at the Broadway Theater from October through December, playing Claudio in *Much Ado About Nothing*, Bassanio, Laertes, Macduff, de Mauprat in *Richelieu* and Seragino del'Aquila in *The Fool's Revenge*. He then toured with the company playing second leads until 1890, when in June he went to the Globe Theatre in London with a disastrous production of *Romeo and Juliet* in which he played the lead; though the critics derided the show they were impressed by Skinner. At the same theatre in August he played Percy Gauntlett in *This Woman and That*.

On December 1890 he appeared at Miner's Fifth Avenue Theater in New York playing Thibault and La Hire in *Joan of Arc*. Then Otis Skinner was taken on by Madame Modjeska as her leading man. With her he played Orlando in *As You Like It*, the title part in *Henry VIII*, Sir Edward Mortimer in *Mary Stuart*, Leonatus in *Cymbeline*, Benedick in *Much Ado About Nothing*, and Major Schubert in *Magda*. He spent three years touring with Modjeska, and during this time she also took on a young actress-apprentice, Maud Durbin. After a time playing Captain Absolute in *The Rivals* with Joseph Jefferson, Otis Skinner started his own touring company and hired Maud Durbin as his leading lady. His first season consisted of a romantic comedy by Clyde Fitch, *His Grace de Grammont*, set in the Restoration period, and an adaptation of Victor Hugo's *Le Roi s'amuse* made by his brother Charles and called *The King's Jester*. They opened in Rochford, Illinois, and then went on to Chicago, where they met with great success; the rest of the tour brought good notices but unsatisfactory houses. Otis was, however, not depressed — he had fallen in love with his leading lady, whom he married at the close of the season on 21 April 1895 in New York. That year he received an honorary MA from Tufts University.

Otis Skinner spent the next six years touring to generally good notices but bad houses. During this time he played in *Hamlet*, *Richard III*, *Romeo and Juliet*, *The Merchant of Venice*, *The Lady of Lyons*, *The Liars*, *In a Balcony*, *Shenandoah*, *Francesca da Rimini* and *Prince Otto*, among other plays. In 1903 he co-starred with the ageing Ada Rehan on a tour that included *The Taming of the Shrew*, *The Merchant of Venice* and *The School for Scandal*. This tour was financially successful, which was just as well, because his daughter Cornelia had been born in Chicago on 30

May 1902 and his wife gave up the stage.

Otis Skinner was seen at the Lyric Theater in New York in October 1904 playing the title role in *The Harvester*, an adaptation of *Le Chemineau*. In February 1906, after more touring, he came under Charles Frohman's management to play the Abbé Daniel in Henri Lavedon's *The Duel* at the Hudson Theater in New York. After a successful run there he took it on an extensive tour. He opened at New Rochelle in September 1907 as Colonel Philippe Brideau in *The Honour of the Family*, which was based on Balzac's *Le Ménage du Garçon*. His playing of this role has been called one of the immortal comedy characterizations of the American stage, and John Mason Brown reported: '... it has lasted a lifetime in the memory of those of us fortunate enough to see it.' They went on the road with it for a few months before opening at the Hudson Theater in New York in February 1908.

In January 1910 he opened at the Garrick Theater in New York playing Lafayette Towers in *Your Humble Servant*, and the following January at the Criterion in the same city he was Denis Roulette in *Sire*. He was offered the part of the beggar Hajj in Edward Knoblock's *Kismet* but at first turned it down. His perceptive wife, however, insisted that he take it, and he opened in the role at the Knickerbocker Theater in New York on Christmas Day, 1911. It became his most famous role. Walter Prichard Easton reported: 'The one part in this naive and romantic fable which links its picturesque episodes together and gives it a personal and dramatic interest is that of Hajj, the beggar, and, of course, Mr Skinner is amply able to fill the bill, the more as that slight note of unreality in his acting which sometimes mars his impersonations of serious romantic roles or roles in modern plays, here admirably blends with the glamor of dreamlike fable. His impersonation is consistently the beggar, though the part is rather sketched broadly than characterized in detail. Never for an instant is he anything else, be his borrowed robes ever so grand. It is lit with a grim, masculine humor, it is touched with tenderness for his daughter and with fierce passions of revenge. But humor, tenderness, passion, are all held in the key of romantic fable and so while he counts the bubbles that arise from the drowning Wazir there is no horror in the episode, and when he goes to sleep again at last in his beggar's robes there is no sorrow — only a half smile for the round-the-circle logic of it, and the pleasant finish to a good tale told. And Mr Skinner's speech is a perpetual de-

light. He was trained in the days when the ability to speak well was supposed to be part of an actor's equipment ...' Skinner played Hajj for a year in New York and then for a further two years on tour.

He was back in New York at the Liberty Theater in October 1914, when he played Montgomery Starr in *The Silent Voice*, and at the Empire in April 1915 was Jean Renaud in *A Celebrated Case*. At the Cohan Theater in December of that year he played Antony Bellchamber in *Cock o' the Walk*. Booth Tarkington wrote the part of the Italian hurdy-gurdy man, Antonio Camaradonio, in *Mister Antonio* especially for Skinner and he had a great success with it in New York at the Lyceum where he opened in September 1916 and subsequently on tour. He returned to the Lyceum in September 1918 where he played Albert Mott in *Humpty-Dumpty*. Otis Skinner then spent 1919 touring in *The Joy of Peter Barban*.

At the Criterion in New York in January 1920 he played the title role in *Pietro*, and in Chicago the following January he was Hanaud in *At the Villa Rosa*. In September 1921 at the Empire in New York he played Juan Gallardo in *Blood and Sand* and introduced New York audiences to his daughter Cornelia, who had a small part. She went on to become successful as both an actress and a writer. Skinner was next seen in New York at the Hudson Theater in November 1923 when he played the title role in *Sancho Panza*, and at the Knickerbocker in May 1926 he played Falstaff in *Henry IV Part 1*. At the Booth Theater in December 1926 he was once more Colonal Bridau in a revival of *The Honour of the Family*, and he was Falstaff once more in March 1928, again at the Knickerbocker, but this time the play was *The Merry Wives of Windsor*. In Chicago in April 1929 he played Papa Juan in *A Hundred Years Old* and took the production to the Lyceum in New York in October. He spent 1931–32 touring with Maude Adams and played Shylock.

Back in New York at the Broadway Theater, for the Players Club in June 1932 he was Thersites in *Troilus and Cressida* and, again for the Players Club, in May 1933 at the Alvin he played Uncle Tom in *Uncle Tom's Cabin*. He went to Westport in July of that year, appearing in *The Nobel Prize*.

Otis Skinner made only two films and both of them were *Kismet* — a silent version in 1916 and a talking one in 1930. He was a successful writer, and his books include *Footlights and Spotlights* and *Mad Folk of the Theatre*. He died in New York on 4 January 1942, aged 83.

MAGGIE SMITH

Maggie Smith was born in Ilford, Essex, in 1934 but grew up in Oxford where she attended the Oxford Girls' High School. There, too, she studied for the stage at the Oxford Playhouse School. It was in 1952 that she made her first appearance on the stage, when with the OUDS she played Viola in *Twelfth Night*. At Oxford she worked with the fringe group which included Patrick Dromgoole and Ned Sherrin. A comedienne by nature, she was working in a small London cabaret theatre called the Watergate when Leonard Sillman signed her to appear in *New Faces of 1956* at the Ethel Barrymore Theater on Broadway. She returned to London to the Lyric, Hammersmith, where she was in a revue written by Bamber Gascoigne called *Share My Lettuce*. Billed as a diversion with music and co-starring Kenneth Williams, it was a sophisticated intimate revue. Peter Roberts reported: 'Maggie Smith here gives promise of being on the brink of a career which will closely follow that of Beatrice Lillie.' Well, enthusiastic but not quite right. The show did, however, transfer to the Comedy Theatre in the West End in September 1957.

In November 1958 Maggie Smith made her straight acting début at the St Martin's playing Vere Dane in *The Stepmother*. Based on a novel, the play was judged not very theatrical and she refers to it as a thudding flop. 'It didn't worry me at the time,' she said. 'When you start it's not so desperate, one's got a confidence of some kind. You think it will be all right if you know your lines.' It was, however, the play and not Miss Smith that the critics attacked. Bill Lester, writing in *Plays and Players*, said her ' . . . portrayal of the tough blonde longing for the bedworthiness of her dead husband is very good indeed. Her down-to-earth attitude successfully demolishes the pompous façade of father and son.' She joined the Old Vic Company for their 1959–60 season where her first role was that of Lady Plyant in Congreve's *The Double Dealer*. She was next directed by Wendy Toye as Celia in *As You Like It*, and Caryl Brahms reported: 'Miss Maggie Smith, comedienne that she is, seizes with both hands every laugh that Celia gives her, and quite a few she and Miss Toye have dreamt up for themselves.' Peter Roberts thought she was too young as Mistress Ford in *The Merry Wives of Windsor*, and of her Queen to John Justin's *Richard II* he said: 'Maggie Smith does what she can in a part for which Shakespeare himself did so little.' She finished off the Old Vic season playing Maggie Wylie in Barrie's *What*

Every Woman Knows, and Peter Roberts said she 'found just the right appealing quality' for the role.

At the Strand Theatre in June 1960 she played Daisy in Ionesco's *Rhinoceros*, and then in October set out on a tour playing Kathy in *Strip the Willow*. She went to the Theatre Royal in Bristol in March 1961 where she played Lucile in Anouilh's *The Rehearsal*, and came with the production to the Globe in London the following month. They moved on to the Queen's in May, then back to the Globe in July and ended their London tour at the Apollo in December. Caryl Brahms wrote: 'Maggie Smith, fresh from shining at the Old Vic, made a fair enough start as a very young girl whom she played with a directness and simplicity.'

At the Globe Theatre in May 1962 she was in a double bill playing Doreen in *The Private Ear* and Belinda in *The Public Eye*, and the performances won her the *Evening Standard* Award as Best Actress of 1962. In September that year she was at the Mermaid in a reading of *Pictures in the Hallway*.

She opened at the Queen's in February 1963 in the title role of Jean Kerr's Broadway smash, *Mary, Mary*, and John Russell Taylor reported: 'I can see that a lot of mannerisms in this part come from Lucille Ball and that the performance is very cunningly contrived line by line and gesture by gesture. And still the result is wholly personal and quite enchanting.' For this performance she received the Variety Club of Great Britain Award as Best Actress. Maggie Smith joined the National Theatre Company at the Old Vic in December 1963, where she played Silvia in *The Recruiting Officer*. Martin Esslin wrote: 'Maggie Smith is a first rate actress, but when transformed into a boy she is anything but strapping, a pigeon-chested little runt of a fellow. As to sensuality: an iceberg must seem hot in comparison.' The following year she was Desdemona in Olivier's *Othello*, and John Holmstrom reported: 'One word of praise to Maggie Smith for a Desdemona of considerable dignity and delicacy. Her face, perhaps, is too ineradicably sly, and the mournful little voice, so perfect in comedy, is sometimes a problem in tragedy. But she was sweetly serious, beside sporting a most wringable neck.' Also in 1964 she was Hilde Wangel in *The Master Builder* and Myra in Noel Coward's *Hay Fever*. Of the latter Hugh Leonard wrote: 'Miss Smith possesses an angularity which is temperamental no less than physical; she seems to belong to the 1920s. Her timing is impeccable. For the most part, she regards her ill-mannered hosts with a deadpan balefulness, but her right hand is the giveaway: it wields her cigarette-holder and handbag like a rapier and a mace respectively, seemingly owing not the slightest allegiance to the parent body. This was a superb performance.'

Still with the National Theatre Company, in 1965 she played Beatrice in Zeffirelli's production of *Much Ado About Nothing*. Peter Roberts thought the whole production was fascinating but rather too tricksy, and added: 'All Maggie Smith can give is a blowsy sharp-tongued gal who wears her blonde curls at a rakish angle.' That year she was with Albert Finney in Strindberg's *Miss Julie*, playing the title part, and Hugh Leonard said: 'Miss Smith wasn't nearly patrician enough. To fall spectacularly, one needs height first and foremost; and it is Julie's pretensions which dictate her suicide ... Miss Smith is always delightful to watch and listen to; but this isn't her part.' This production was part of a double bill which included Peter Shaffer's virtually actor-proof *Black Comedy*. That year she also co-starred with Robert Stephens in John Osborne's adaptation of the Lope de Vega play, *A Bond Honoured*. In 1967 she married Stephens and they had two sons.

At Chichester in 1969 she played Margery Pinchwife in *The Country Wife*, and Hugh Leonard wrote: 'As Margery, Maggie Smith is memorable. Her appetites are as great as those of Lady Fidget and Co., but to them sex is the bread of life, while to Margery it is the cake. Well-scrubbed, shining with an innocence which can never be wholly lost — which make Pinchwife's cuckoldry all the more inevitable — Miss Smith is delightful. The letter writing scene is by no means an actor-proof *tour de force*, but Miss Smith almost makes it seem so.' That same year Maggie Smith won her first Oscar, as best actress for her performance in *The Prime of Miss Jean Brodie*. She began making films in between theatre seasons in 1957, and by the time she got her second Oscar, for *California Suite* in 1979, she had totalled six nominations. Still, she says, 'I think films are totally baffling. It's desperately hard. When you're on stage you have the time to gather yourself together. If you have a performance that evening, you have the day to prepare. In filming, you have to be ready when they're ready. To have a film career you really have to want a film career. It's greedy to want both. I would choose the stage if I had to.'

In 1970, still with the National Theatre Company, she played Mrs Sullen in *The Beaux' Stratagem* in Los Angeles and in London, where she also played Masha in *The Three Sisters* and the title role in *Hedda Gabler*. That year she received the CBE in the New Year Honours List.

At the Queen's Theatre in September 1972, co-starring with her husband, she played Amanda Prynne in Coward's *Private Lives*. Once again she received the Variety Club's award for best actress and transferred with the production to the Globe in July 1973. The critics were, however, beginning to write with increasing regularity about her 'mannerisms'.

She played in *Peter Pan* for Christmas at the Coliseum, and then in March 1974 opened at the Vaudeville Theatre playing Connie Hudson in *Snap*. While far from pleased with the play, Alan Brien wrote: '... it is Maggie Smith, all those knees and elbows and pointed toes like an umbrella in a thunderstorm, or a sleepwalking bat, or a spider escaping from treacle, who keeps us continually watching her in incredulous delight. She seems forever enmeshed and tangled in her clothes and in her ideas, blinded by her hat, struck dumb in mid-sentence, falling over her own ankles, colliding with her own syntax. It is like an extended music-hall act, a unique circus turn, grafted onto the outline of a promising farce which has lost its way.' She then went on a tour of America in *Private Lives*, playing in Los Angeles, and in February 1975 on Broadway at the 46th Street Theater. That year she divorced Robert Stephens and two months later married Beverley Cross. 'I should have done it this way from the start,' she said. She also went to Stratford, Ontario, where for four years she worked in Robin Phillips' theatre company. There she blossomed, and collected more glowing reviews from visiting British drama critics than she had ever enjoyed when resident in London. She played Cleopatra and Millamant and Masha, among other roles. There she also created the part of Virginia Woolf in Edna O'Brien's *Virginia*, which she brought to London on her return in 1981. John Barber wrote of her performance at the Haymarket: 'Smith suggests a mind shimmering with intelligence — a mind so perceptive she is often cattily funny and so sensitive she often finds the world insupportable. The play is a revelation of raw-nerved femininity ... Her performance demonstrates the impressive range of an artist who can express the enchanted glee of a child and in the next instant show a countenance folded in sorrow at the thought of her fears and the years and the coming of madness. Her return is most welcome.' The London *Evening Standard* welcomed her back with another award — as best actress of 1981, though her next stage appearance was not until 1984 when she again played Millamant, this time at the Chichester Festival. *See photograph opposite page 295.*

E. H. SOTHERN

See Julia Marlowe and E. H. Sothern

ROBERT SPEAIGHT

Robert Speaight was born at St Margaret-at-Cliffe near Dover in Kent on 14 January 1904. He was educated at Wick Preparatory School in Hove and then at Haileybury, where he seemed constantly to be winning prizes for elocution. During the summer holidays in 1922 at Angmering-on-Sea he mounted an amateur production of *The Merchant of Venice* in which he played Shylock, and for some inexplicable reason the *Times* reviewed it. 'This Shylock was a vengeful old man rather than a symbolic figure of racial passion. His hate of the debtor outweighed the anguish for the loss of his daughter. These things apart, the performance was remarkably good, and the stage sense was apparently instinctive. It was a good fault, perhaps, that Mr Speaight paid meticulous attention to elocution, but it robbed his acting of a certain amount of freedom. His make-up was excellent and it was a very remarkable performance for a youth.'

Speaight won a scholarship to Lincoln College, Oxford, where he intended to read history but instead was persuaded to study English. At Oxford he joined the OUDS, eventually becoming secretary. He was the First Player in *Hamlet*, directed by J. B. Fagan, in his first season there. In 1925 he was a much praised Peer Gynt, and the following year his Falstaff in *Henry IV Part 2* reduced the critic James Agate to tears of pleasure. He called Speaight the best Falstaff since Louis Calvert.

Robert Speaight made his professional début at the Liverpool Repertory Theatre in September 1926 playing the Stranger in *Portrait of a Gentleman*. He spent a year with the company. He made his London début at the Arts Theatre in October 1927 playing Arrighi in *The Duchess of Elba*, and also began broadcasting for the BBC that year. During November and December 1927 he toured Egypt with Robert Atkins' Company, and at the Holborn Empire in February 1928 he played Lucius Arruntius in *Sejanus: His Fall*. At the Court in April he was Tostig and then had the title role in *Harold*. At the Prince of Wales in July he played Barnabas in *Paul Among the Jews* and then at the Apollo in October he had his first major London role in Komisarjevsky's adaptation of The

Brothers Karamazov which was called *The Brass Paperweight*. Speaight played Smerdyakov, the epileptic murderer — renamed Paul in the adaptation. Charles Morgan wrote that his performance showed 'all the colours, and none of them too high, of vengeance and spite'. It was a great critical success, but it ran for only four weeks.

Speaight had more luck with his next part — that of Lieutenant Hibbert in R. C. Sherriff's *Journey's End*. This was mounted first by the Stage Society for a Sunday night at the Apollo Theatre in December 1928. It was such a success that it transferred, with cast changes (notably Colin Clive replacing Laurence Olivier), to the Savoy in January 1929 and ran there and on tour until June 1930. It was Speaight's first experience of a long run; although the financial security was welcome he found it rather boring and determined during this period to be a writer as well as an actor. He began work on his first novel, eventually to be called *Mutinous Wind*. He also worked on the special Sunday matinées which were so prevalent at the time. At the Royalty Theatre for the Elizabethan Stage Circle in July 1929 he played the Duke of Byron in *The Conspiracy*. At the Arts in January 1930 he was Frederick in *The Humours of the Court*, and at the Haymarket in April 1930 he was the First Player in an all-star production of *Hamlet*. This production was repeated in May for the King George Pension Fund.

At the Arts Theatre in October 1930 he played Borgheim in *Little Eyolf*. That month, also, he was received into the Roman Catholic Church, a step he had been contemplating since his Oxford days. At the Everyman Theatre in January 1931 he played Eric Halle in *Danger! High Tension*, and at the Players the following month was Julian in *Sense and Sensibility*. He went to the Haymarket in March for a limited run of *Hamlet*, in which he played Osric and the Player King. At the Old Vic in April 1931 he played Edmund in Gielgud's *King Lear*. The following month he was at the Gate playing Herod in *Salome*.

In September 1931 Robert Speaight joined the Old Vic–Sadler's Wells Company. Gielgud had left, but Richardson was still there. Speaight opened with the title role in *King John* while Ralph Richardson had what amounted to the lead, the Bastard. Also that season he played Demetrius in *A Midsummer Night's Dream*, Fluellen in *Henry V*, Humphrey in *The Knight of the Burning Pestle*, Roderigo in *Othello* and Malvolio in *Twelfth Night*. His Cassius in *Julius Caesar* was a great success but his Hamlet failed to create a stir of any kind. That year his first novel was published to a certain amount of critical acclaim and he began work on the second, *The Lost Hero*.

At the Q Theatre in October 1932 he played Alfred Field in *Crime on the Hill* and Alan Alston in *The Call*. The following month at the Arts he was Nahor in *The Gates of Ur* and in November at the Little he was Cecil Sykes in Shaw's *Getting Married*. He returned to the Q in January 1933 where he played Somers in *The Scoop*, and at the Westminster in March he was Judas in *Caesar's Friend* and transferred with the production to the Piccadilly in May. The following month he was at the Shaftesbury playing Ivan Ivanoff in *If I Were You*, and at the Lyric in August he was Soldat Muller in *The Ace*. Robert Speaight was at the Duke of York's in November 1933 playing John Lascelles in *The Rose Without a Thorn* and went to the Q in February 1934 where he played the Refugee in *Nurse Cavell*, transferring with the production to the Vaudeville in March. It did not last, however, and that month he was off on a provincial tour of Bridie's *A Sleeping Clergyman*, playing Robert Donat's part of Cameron.

At the Arts Theatre in May 1934 he played Robert Harley in *Viceroy Sarah* and at the Little Theatre the following month was the Austrian Official in *The Little Man*. Also at the Little, in October 1934 he was Titus Oates in *Royal Baggage* and that month at the Savoy played Kira in *Two Kingdoms*. In June 1935 he accepted the role with which he would become identified — and also typecast. At the Chapter House of Canterbury Cathedral he played Becket in T. S. Eliot's *Murder in the Cathedral*. Audrey Williamson reported: 'It was a performance with the noble ring of elocution and of mind: deeply sincere, at all times intellectually lucid, perhaps a little lacking in the flexibility and passion of temperament that could mark Thomas as a man who could feel the torture of insidious temptation.' He played the same part at the Mercury Theatre in London in November 1935 and at the Duchess Theatre, the Old Vic and the Tewkesbury Festival. He toured Great Britain and Ireland with it during 1936 and 1937 and made his New York début in the role at the Ritz Theater on 16 February 1938. There it was a great critical success but the public was not very interested. Meanwhile, at the Canterbury Festival

in June 1936 he had appeared as Thomas Cranmer in *Thomas Cranmer of Canterbury*.

He was again in religious drama in June 1938, when at Canterbury he played Artaban in Christopher Hassall's *Christ's Comet*, a play based on the legend of the fourth Wise Man. At the Westminster Theatre in September 1938 he played Ulysses in a modern-dress production of *Troilus and Cressida*, and then in October set out on what was to be a lucrative tour throughout Britain and on to New York playing Laurence Olivier's London part, Vivaldi, in *A King of Nowhere*. However, the money ran out on the first week of the tour. Orson Welles hired him for the part of the Chorus in his Shakespeare anthology, *Five Kings*, which opened in Boston, Massachusetts, at the Colonial Theater in February 1939, but then somehow went wrong, partly because it ran more than six hours. Robert Speaight found himself giving a course on modern poetry at Notre Dame University. On his way back to England he played in Henri Gheon's *The Comedian*, directed by Walter Kerr at the Catholic University in Washington.

The Ministry of Information sent Speaight back to the United States at the beginning of the war to report on public opinion there. In 1941 he returned to England, where he joined the wartime BBC to write and produce features to boost morale, and was the voice of Christ in the serial plays, 'The Man Born to be King'. He moved on to the BBC European Service, and in 1945 went to France as the correspondent for *Time and Tide*.

He began his numerous British Council tours and recitals, which took him all over Europe and America. He went to the Mercury Theatre for a series of new plays in the Poets Season which ran from September 1945 till August 1946, and appeared as Elijah in *The Old Man of the Mountains*, Antony and the Old Man in *This Way to the Tomb*, Spencer Harding in *The Shadow Factory* and the Hebrew in *The Resurrection*. He repeated his performances in *This Way to the Tomb* at the Garrick Theatre in September 1946. Back at the Mercury in February 1947 he played Jonah Webster in *The Beautiful People* and in January 1948 he was Abraham in *The Dragon and the Dove*. The following month it was back to *Murder in the Cathedral*. At Covent Garden in July 1948 he was Christian in *The Pilgrim's Progress*. That summer at the first Aldeburgh Festival he gave a poetry recital with Celia Johnson. There he met the painter Bridget Bramwell, whom he married.

At Wyndham's in September 1949 he played Benjamin Robert Haydon in *John Keats Lived Here*. Then followed more British Council tours and teaching assignments. At the Assembly Rooms in Chichester in May 1951 he played Myself in *The Four Men*, which he also directed. At Westminster Abbey in June 1953 he was St Peter in *Out of the Whirlwind*, and back at the Chapter House in Canterbury in July was Cardinal Pole in *His Eminence of England*. At Lichfield Cathedral in September he was St Chad in *St Chad of the Seven Wells*; and it came as a great relief after all these saints to play the sinister Tama Domikis Harklip in Charles Morgan's political melodrama, *The Burning Glass*.

In August 1954 he toured and appeared at the Paris Festival playing Sir Claude Mulhammer in *The Confidential Clerk*, and in May 1955 he was back in church at the Peterborough Cathedral playing the Chronicler in *Upon this Rock*. He went to the Edinburgh Festival in 1955, where he played King Agis in *A Life in the Sun*. Putting acting aside for a time he directed *Antony and Cleopatra* in Geneva in 1947 and the next two years served as adjudicator at the Canadian Drama Festivals.

He returned to the Edinburgh Festival in 1956 where he played Don Pedro de Miura in *The Strong Are Lonely*, taking over from Robert Harris and working with Donald Wolfit. His appearance at the Edinburgh Festival the next year was his last on the stages of England for all practical purposes. It was not meant to be. He played Dom Diogo in *The Hidden King* by Jonathan Griffin; it was a poem-pageant which he described as 'exceptional in its alliance of intellectual vigour with tragic passion and romantic trappings'. Micheàl MacLiammòir was in it with him, and said: 'I think we're going to like it better than they are' — referring to the audience. He was right and Speaight found himself very disillusioned, feeling that a theatre that had no place for *The Hidden King* was not a place he wanted to be.

In 1960, for the Australian Elizabethan Theatre Trust he played Becket in *Murder in the Cathedral* in Sydney and in 1962 for them he was Sir Thomas More in *A Man for All Seasons*. At the Olympia Theatre at the Dublin Festival in September 1963 he was the Promoter in *Inquiry at Lisieux* and at the Gaiety in Dublin that same month played the Prime Minister of Cardoman in *The Last PM*. In August 1967 he toured as Edward Moulton-Barrett in *Robert and Elizabeth* and in 1972 for the Missouri Summer Repertory Company in the United States he directed *Murder in the Cathedral*.

As well as writing four novels and a book of memoirs, Robert Speaight became a noted biographer, publishing books on Thomas à Becket, George Eliot, William Poel, Hilaire Belloc, William Rothenstein, Eric Gill, Teilhard de Chardin, Vanier and Georges Bernanos. He also wrote *The Companion Guide to Burgundy*. Robert Speaight was given a CBE in the New Year Honours in 1958, and in 1959 was appointed officer of the Légion d'honneur. He died on 1 November 1976.

KIM STANLEY

P atricia Kimberley Reid was born in Tularosa, New Mexico, on 11 February 1925. Her father was a professor of philosophy at the University of New Mexico and her mother was a painter and interior decorator. She attended the University of New Mexico for a while, and it was there that she made her first stage appearance, in *Thunder Rock* in 1942, though it was from the University of Texas that she received a BA in psychology in 1945. Taking the stage name of Kim Stanley she went to California, where she studied acting at the Pasadena Playhouse for a year. In winter 1946 she appeared in the Louisville, Kentucky, stock company where she played the Manicurist in *Boy Meet Girl* and then in summer of 1947 she was in stock at Pompton Lakes, New Jersey, where she played Corliss Archer in *Kiss and Tell* and Prudence in *The Pursuit of Happiness*. Miss Stanley then moved on to New York, where she worked as a waitress and as a model and joined the Actors' Studio. In December 1948 she made her New York début at the Carnegie Recital Hall playing Iris in *The Dog Beneath the Skin*. In 1949 she appeared at the Provincetown Playhouse in *Him*, at the Cherry Lane in *Yes Is for a Very Young Man*, and at the Equity Library in November in the title role in *Saint Joan*. That same month she took over the role of Elisa in *Montserrat* from Julie Harris at the Fulton Theater on Broadway. At ANTA in January 1951 she played Adela in *The House of Bernarda Alba* and at the Playhouse in April 1952 she was Anna Reeves in *The Chase*. At the Music Box in February 1953 she was Millie Owens in

William Inge's much-praised *Picnic*, and in October 1954 she was at the Playhouse in *The Travelling Lady* playing Georgette Thomas, repeating the performance for television.

At the Music Box in March 1955 Kim Stanley played Cherie in William Inge's *Bus Stop*, and Brooks Atkinson reported in the *New York Times*: 'As the nightclub singer, Kim Stanley is superb. Still the travelling lady, she gives a glowing performance that is full of amusing detail — cheap, ignorant, bewildered, but also radiant with personality.' For this performance Miss Stanley received the Donaldson Award and won the New York Drama Critics Award as Best Actress. In January 1957 she opened at the Belasco playing Virginia in *A Clearing in the Woods*.

Miss Stanley made her London début on 30 January 1958 at the Comedy Theatre playing Maggie in Tennessee Williams' *Cat on a Hot Tin Roof*. Kenneth Tynan did not care for the production at all but was most impressed with Miss Stanley, saying she 'has all the qualities for the part, an anxious lyricism, a limpid voice, tear-puffed eyes and indomitable gallantry; but, as pregnant women are said to be eating for two, she found herself quite early on acting for four. It was like watching a first rate squash player hammering away at a court without walls.'

Richard Buckle reported in *Plays and Players*: 'Her performance in this most difficult part is a triumph of subtlety and vitality. Her first-act duel with Brick is almost a monologue, and it is wonderful to watch her, obsessed by the sole idea of becoming his wife again, going at him with her drill of nervous energy, charged by love and will power, only to retreat and crumble miserably before the laconic implacability of his replies — then reviving, gathering strength and persuasiveness, rallying, as if inspired, to her vocational task

again. During these bouts Miss Stanley's face changes from a mask of feminine charm to the battered hopeless face of an older woman, and, as the noble impulse stirs her, changes back to beauty. The way she switches from catty defensiveness in brushes with her brother-in-law and his wife to a consoling warmth with which to envelop the moaning Big Mama is magical too ...'

In August 1958 Kim Stanley married the actor and director Alfred Ryder and they eventually had a daughter. That year too, her first movie, *The Goddess*, was released, and she was nominated for an Academy Award. In October she opened at the Helen Hayes Theater in New York playing Sara Melody in *A Touch of the Poet*.

At the Morosco in October 1959 she played Lea de Lonval in *Cheri*. That year she was given the ANTA Award for her outstanding contribution to the art of living theatre. At the Music Box in April 1961 she played Elizabeth von Ritter in *A Far Country* and at the Booth Theater in January 1963 she was Sue Barker in *Natural Affection*. That year she also received an Emmy for her performance on television in 'A Cardinal Act of Mercy' — an episode in the 'Ben Casey' series.

At the Morosco Theater in June 1964 she played Masha in the Actors' Studio production of *The Three Sisters*, directed by Lee Strasberg. The critic John Simon, never very keen on the Actors' Studio or its products, wrote: 'As Masha, Kim Stanley is up to her tried and trying tricks: the long pause before speaking, the soft and slightly quavering delivery, the staring off into astral space, the lurking threat of hysterics.' Kim Stanley repeated the role in London when the Actors' Studio made its début at the Aldwych in May 1965 during the World Theatre Season. Since then her work has largely been in American films and television.

MAUREEN STAPLETON

*I*t seems a big leap from being the greatest interpreter of Tennessee Williams' emotional heroines to being the acclaimed star of Neil Simon's comedies, but Maureen Stapleton has been much praised for making that leap.

She was born Lois Maureen Stapleton in Troy, New York, on 21 June 1925. She went to the Catholic Central High School in Troy but every afternoon as soon as school was out she hurried to the cinema, where she stayed watching whatever

happened to be on the screen until it closed. She spent two years studying acting in the evenings at the Herbert Berghof Acting School in New York City, and made her New York début playing Sarah Tansey in *The Playboy of the Western World* at the Booth Theater in October 1946. In November 1947 she was at the Martin Beck Theater playing Iras in *Antony and Cleopatra*, which starred Katharine Cornell and Godfrey Tearle. She played Miss Hatch in *Detective Story* at the Hudson in

March 1949 and that July she married the business manager Max Allentuck. The marriage ended in divorce ten years later.

Maureen Stapleton opened at the Coronet Theater in February 1950 playing Emily Williams in *The Bird Cage*, but her great success was to come the following February, when at the Martin Beck Theater she played Serafina in Tennessee Williams' *The Rose Tattoo*. He had written the part for Anna Magnani, but her English was not up to a Broadway production. It won Miss Stapleton a Peabody Award and a Tony as best actress. The *New York Times* reported: 'Maureen Stapleton's performance is triumphant. The widow is unlearned and superstitious and becomes something of a harridan after her husband dies. Miss Stapleton does not evade the coarseness of the part. But neither does she miss its exaltation. For Mr Williams has sprinkled a little stardust over the widow's shoulders and Miss Stapleton has kept the part sparkling through all the fury and tumult of the emotion . . .' She toured in this part in April 1952.

In January 1953, also at the Martin Beck, she took over the part of Elizabeth Proctor in *The Crucible* from Beatrice Straight, and the following month at the Ethel Barrymore Theater she opened as Bella in *The Emperor's New Clothes*. She went to the City Center in December 1953 where she played Anne to José Ferrer's Richard III. In May she was Masha in *The Seagull* at the Phoenix and at the Playhouse in April 1955 she played Flora in *Twenty-Seven Wagons Full of Cotton*.

Maureen Stapleton returned to the Martin Beck Theater in March 1957 where she played Lady Torrance in *Orpheus Descending*, by Tennessee Williams. Walter Kerr wrote in the New York *Herald Tribune*: '. . . When Maureen Stapleton, as a woman who has been handed over to an ailing husband in a "fire sale", apologizes and hurls out an epithet in the same running breath, when her eyes blaze with the vision of the new confectionery she is going to add to her dry-goods store, when she fumbles in embarrassment over the proposition she is making to the young wanderer who works for her, the shadow of a genuine human being begins to rise on the stage. Miss Stapleton's fiercely intelligent eyes always carry conviction; you're sure she does know and feel everything the author says she knows and feels . . .'

At the Morosco in December 1958 Maureen Stapleton opened as Ida in S. N. Behrman's autobiographical play, *The Cold Wind and the Warm*. Kenneth Tynan said that the 'match-making aunt is played with uproarious, upholstered aplomb by Maureen Stapleton, who can cock an eyebrow and purse a lip with more wit than many actresses can find in the whole of Oscar Wilde . . .' And Walter Kerr wrote: 'It is an expansive and honest pleasure to watch Maureen Stapleton, as matchmaker for a Jewish neighborhood and foster-mother to practically everyone in sight, turn a speculative eye on an attractive and available spinster, invent a handful of splendid lies to account for the failure of a promised suitor to show up, and, in a burst of breathless efficiency, hustle the lass off to the corner drugstore where there are prospects with every milk shake.' At the Hudson Theater in February 1960 she played Carrie in Hellman's *Toys in the Attic*, a role she found very difficult.

In 1963 Maureen Stapleton married the playwright David Rayfiel. At the Brooks Atkinson Theater in May 1965 she played Amanda Wingfield in a revival of Tennessee Williams' *The Glass Menagerie*. At the City Center in October 1966 she once again played Serafina in *The Rose Tattoo* and transferred with the production to the Billy Rose Theater the following month.

In February 1968 she took on three roles at the Plymouth in Neil Simon's *Plaza Suite*, and at the Lyceum in February 1969 she played Beatrice Chambers in *Norman, Is That You?* She was at the Plymouth in December 1970 in another Neil Simon comedy, playing Evy Meara in *The Gingerbread Lady*, a once-popular pop-singing star turned to the bottle. John Simon, the critic, said: 'Matters are not helped by Maureen Stapleton's neither looking, nor moving, nor sounding like a famous pop singer of only a few years ago. The actress delivers her lines with impeccable timing and emphasis, but she sorely lacks any sort of grace, charm, poise or sexiness that would suggest either music or glamor in her past.' Simon's main complaint, however, was about the play, which most critics dismissed as a series of one-line gags. Allene Talmey, writing in *Vogue*, explained: 'His plot is a bore but his lines are a succession of funnies that rise properly from situation and his people. And they succeed for the moment. What he has done brilliantly, however, is to build a character for Stapleton who manages with almost no special makeup to look like Tugboat Annie with a potato nose when she does not look like Rocky Graziano trying to get up in the third round. Stapleton makes it, for she is a collage of theatrical magic, entirely made by Stapleton.'

In March 1972 she was at the Billy Rose Theater playing Georgie Elgin in *The Country Girl*, and at the Ambassador that November played Mildred Wild in *The Secret Affairs of Mildred Wild*. She revived *The Rose Tattoo* once again at the Walnut Theater in Philadelphia in

November 1973, and in April 1974 she appeared in a benefit gala at the Circle in the Square in New York. She went to Los Angeles to the Mark Taper Forum in November that year to play Juno Boyle in *Juno and the Paycock*, and back in New York at the Circle in the Square in December 1975 she was again in Tennessee Williams' *The Glass Menagerie*.

Maureen Stapleton began filming in 1960 with *Lonelyhearts*, and made many notable appearances including roles in *The Fugitive Kind*, *Bye, Bye Birdie* and Woody Allen's *Interiors*. Her television appearances include *All the King's Men*, *Tell Me Where It Hurts* and *Queen of the Stardust Ballroom*; she received an Emmy Award for her role in *Save Me a Place at Forest Lawn* in 1967.

TOMMY STEELE

Thomas Hicks was born on 17 December 1936 in South London just off the Old Kent Road, where his father and mother were working class and almost professional about it. He went to Bacon's School for Boys in Bermondsey, but left in 1951 after a verbal fight with his geography master. His mother was keen for him to work at the Savoy Hotel but he went instead to work as a pantry boy for Cunard on a liner sailing to New York; he worked his way up to assistant gym instructor with Cunard during his four and a half years with them. For two of these years he was based in New York and sailed between there and Bermuda and the West Indies and was much influenced by the native music, which ranged from jazz through calypso to the beginnings of rock and roll. He acquired a guitar and a sort of technique which he used on board for entertainments. On leave in London he worked at various West End coffee bars with the new rock and roll music he had learned in the United States and was offered a recording contract. His 'Rock with the Cavemen' was an instant hit and he did not return to sea. By this time a very successful British pop star, he made his stage début at the Empire Theatre, Sunderland, in November 1956 in variety. He first appeared, apart from coffee house performances, in London at the Dominion Theatre in May 1957. In December 1958 Harold Fielding cast him as Buttons in a lavish production of Rodgers and Hammerstein's *Cinderella*, and such was Tommy's pop stardom that he was allowed to add one of his numbers to the score. In 1960, the same year that he married former dancer Ann Donoughue he made his legitimate début at the Old Vic in November, when he played Tony Lumpkin in *She Stoops to Conquer*. Caryl Brahms reported: 'Mr Steele is one of Nature's comics: a small live-wire born to play Buttons, which he did with considerable aplomb at the Coliseum two winters ago. A perky Cockney sparrow as friendly

as he is high, who having no acting technique, as such, to fall back upon, must needs make mugging do, pulling faces to show us what he thinks and feels — but since these faces bear a strong resemblance to one another they leave us very much where we were. Pace, good-humoured comeback, personality; these are Mr Steele's equipment when he leaves the world behind — his world that is of pop-song and ''guee-tar''. A broth of a boy kicking reality around a bit. There is nothing slow and rural in his Tony Lumpkin. This one never slept it off in the lee of a hayrick or subsided beneath a hedgerow on his wavering way home. His haystack is well within the sound of Bow Bells, his ditch not further from the sound of them than Shoreditch, his country brogue a Brummagem accent.'

It was two years before Tommy Steele was back on stage again, two years of searching for the proper vehicle for this star, and Harold Fielding commissioned one especially for him — the musical version of H. G. Wells' novel *Kipps*, which was called *Half a Sixpence* and opened at the Cambridge Theatre in March 1963. Harold Hobson said his was a 'superbly funny and touching performance'; John Russell Taylor wrote at greater length: 'Whatever the critics have thought about *Half a Sixpence* in general, they have nearly all rushed to repeat, as though it is an article of faith, that Tommy Steele is a Good Thing and the sort of performer who gives one faith in the integrity of British youth, the working classes' continuing capacity for self-improvement, and all that. All this seems to me dangerously complacent, insultingly patronizing to Mr Steele himself, and just untrue. He had talent and personality, and no doubt still has them, but he has allowed himself, it seems, to be so moulded by his advisers that neither is at all appreciable in this particular show. He beams amiably at the audience throughout — in fact to my taste he's too damned winsome by half — and looks like a nice, good-natured young man. But he doesn't begin to act the part, to tell us, even in the fairly elementary terms of the average musical, what sort of man Arthur Kipps is, rather than what sort of man Tommy Steele is. And even the Tommy Steele characterization is lacking in bite: he goes through the evening obediently doing what he is told, like an animated puppet, but never strikes directly across the footlights as a full-sized theatrical personality ... It would be a pleasure to see again the real Tommy Steele we once knew — he might even be rather good in the role — but the Tommy Steele we meet here seems to have been devised by a committee.' The show ran for twenty months in London and then went on to New York, where it opened at the Broadhurst in April 1965. Tommy Steele later consolidated his success with the film version.

Tommy Steele opened at the Queen's in London in December 1968 playing Truffaldino in *The Servant of Two Masters*, and Hugh Leonard reported: 'The main flaw in the current revival of Goldoni's *The Servant of Two Masters* is that the supporting cast ... are acting in a play, while Tommy Steele is giving a one-man variety show. He addresses the audience so often and intimately as to make Frankie Howerd, by contrast, seem uncommunicative; his manner is so boyishly sunny that at any moment one feared he was about to exhort us to cry out: "We do believe in feyness!"; he turns dialogue into patter and stage business into parlour acrobatics ... Fair enough: no one, apart from misanthropes and Malcolm Muggeridge, could possibly dislike Mr Steele: he burns up more energy on our behalf than the Christmas illuminations, even if he is lacking actual expertise; but by treating the play itself as his own irrelevant backdrop he gives us rather a thin evening ... Instead of seeming harassed, Mr Steele enjoys himself enormously, as if it was all of no consequence; he makes the other characters and the play itself seem superfluous ... Perhaps I have been less than kind to Mr Steele who, although wrong for the play, is a charmer.'

Tommy Steele returned to his own milieu in December 1969 when at the Palladium he played Dick Whittington in the pantomime. He then went on to cabaret in Las Vegas. He returned to the Adelphi to a revue, *Meet Me in London*, in April 1971, and then continued in variety at the Palladium in April 1973. At the same theatre in December 1974 he took the title role in *Hans Andersen*, a musical based on the Danny Kaye film. It was a lavish production which ran for almost two years in London and then toured most successfully. In September 1976 he toured with *The Tommy Steele Anniversary Show*. He returned to London in October 1979 with a one-man show at the Prince of Wales Theatre which was scheduled to run for twelve weeks. But it set a record for a one-man musical in the West End — it ran sixty weeks. That year Tommy Steele was awarded the OBE in the New Year Honours.

In 1983 he opened a long London run at the Palladium in the first-ever staging of *Singin' in the Rain*.

ELAINE STRITCH

Elaine Stritch was born on 2 February 1925 in Detroit, Michigan, where her father was a rubber company executive. She was very properly educated at the Sacred Heart Convent in Detroit and then at a finishing school, but she was determined to be a Broadway star and went to New York in 1944, where she studied at the Dramatic Workshop of the New School for Social Research. She made her first stage appearance at the New School in April that year playing a Tiger and a Cow in the children's show, *Bambino*. At the City College Auditorium in June 1945 she appeared as the Parlourmaid in *The Private Life of the Master Race* for the Theatre of All Nations. Then in April 1946 she played Betty Lord in the pre-Broadway tryout of *Woman Bites Dog* at the Walnut Street Theater in Philadelphia. The show never made it to Broadway, so Elaine spent the summer at the Westport Country Playhouse in Connecticut playing Lady Sybil in *What Every Woman Knows*.

She made her Broadway début as Pamela Brewster in *Loco* at the Biltmore on 16 October 1946. The following February she succeeded Jane Middleton playing Miss Crowser in *Made in Heaven* at the Henry Miller Theater. She had another unsuccessful pre-Broadway tryout in April 1947, when she played Robert in *Three Indelicate Ladies* at the Shubert in New Haven, Connecticut.

At the John Drew Theater in Easthampton in summer 1947 she appeared in the revue *The Shape of Things* and then at the Rooftop Theater in October was Regina Giddons in a revival of *The*

Little Foxes. She was back in revue in December at the Coronet in *Angel in the Wings*. At the Westport Country Playhouse in August 1949 she played Dallas Smith in a summer tryout of *Texas Li'l Darlin'* but that never made it to Broadway, so at the Booth in October 1949 she played June Farrell in *Yes, M'Lord*.

In October 1950 at the Imperial Theater Elaine Stritch understudied Ethel Merman as Sally Adams in *Call Me Madam*, and took the show on the road, playing the lead herself from May 1952 until April 1953. Before setting out, however, she managed to play the part of Melba Snyder in a revival of *Pal Joey* at the Broadhurst. The Critics Circle named it the best musical of the year, and Elaine Stritch made "Zip" an even greater showstopper than it had been before. In July 1953 she was back at the Westport Country Playhouse, as Carol Frazer in a tryout of yet another show that did not make it to Broadway, *Once Married, Twice Shy*. She went to Louisville, Kentucky, in July 1954 to the Iroquois Amphitheater to play the title role in *Panama Hattie*. Back on Broadway at the 46th Street Theater in October she was Peggy Porterfield in *On Your Toes*, a musical which Rodgers and Hart had written in 1936.

It was back to the straight theatre in March 1955 when Elaine Stritch played Grace in William Inge's *Bus Stop*. Brooks Atkinson wrote in the *New York Times*: 'Elaine Stritch's loose-jointed, tough-talking restaurant keeper is vastly amusing.' In March 1957 she played Gertrude Muldoon at the Cort in *The Sin of Pat Muldoon* and in October 1958 she was at the Lunt-Fontanne playing Maggie Harris in *Goldilocks*.

Elaine Stritch was in Jutland, New Jersey, in June 1959 at the Hunterdon Hills Playhouse playing Leona Samish in *The Time of the Cuckoo*. She was back on Broadway at the Broadhurst Theater in October 1961 playing Mimi Paragon in Noel Coward's *Sail Away*. Coward very much wanted her in the show in London; when she arrived she said: 'He really had to talk me into coming here. He bought me a red-leather, gold-tooled passport case, then took me to lunch and had three violinists play "A Nightingale Sang in Berkeley Square" in my ear until my mind blew.' But eventually Miss Stritch and London fell mutually in love. When she opened at the Savoy on 21 June 1962 in *Sail Away*, Charles Marowitz, although he called the musical old-fashioned, reported: 'The female musical-lead is the most masculine character the American theatre has ever produced. She is the quintessence of robustness, muscularity and aggressive high spirits ... Elaine Stritch possesses all her qualities, plus a cunning sense of timing and an ability to switch off levity

and turn on seriousness which, in the context of a modulating musical comedy, is a useful trick to know. The girl wins us over by implying that she shares our distaste for the generally vapid things she has to say.'

Although she made forays back to Broadway and points beyond, at this time in her life the Savoy Hotel began to be home to Elaine Stritch. It was only here, as she put it, that she could claim to have more servants than the Queen. In April 1963 she took over the role of Martha in matinée performances of *Who's Afraid of Virginia Woolf?* In 1963 she had another pre-Broadway tryout, this time farther afield; in October at the Curran Theater in San Francisco she opened as Stella in *The Time of the Barracudas*, but this never made it to Broadway either. She spent part of 1965 touring as Martha in *Who's Afraid of Virginia Woolf?* and the rest of it touring as Anna in *The King and I*.

In Providence, Rhode Island, at the Trinity Square Theater in December 1966 she played Babylove Dallas in *The Grass Harp*, and back in New York at the City Center the following May she was Ruth in *Wonderful Town*. The rest of 1967 was spent touring in *Any Wednesday*. Back in New York in May 1968 she played Amanda Prynne in Coward's *Private Lives* at the Theatre de Lys and then toured as Vera Charles in *Mame*, eventually taking over the title role.

At the Alvin Theater in April 1970 she played Joanne in Stephen Sondheim's *Company*. She also played it in Los Angeles in May 1971, and returned to London to Her Majesty's in January 1972. Robert Cushman reported: '. . . And always there is Elaine Stritch, the good-humoured bad-time girl, tossing off her routines with a look-no-hands abandon and mowing down the opposition with every acid line.' This time she really settled into the Savoy Hotel. At the Hampstead Theatre Club in March 1973 she played Leona Dawson in Tennessee Williams' *Small Craft Warnings*, and Peter Buckley reported in *Plays and Players*: 'Elaine Stritch has taken this wonderful creation and shaped something even more extraordinary out of it. Rarely has the London theatre seen a performance of such intensity, such whiplash drive, such virtuosity, such pure theatrical magic. It is a huge part, full of words and thundering emotions, driving and brutal, and Miss Stritch does it and the play a glorious honour.' The production transferred to the Comedy the same month. In the cast of the Williams play with Elaine Stritch was an actor called John Bay, who had been in love with her ever since he first saw her in Sardi's twenty years before. They married during the run. She was 47, he was 46 and she explained: 'From the age of 17 to 47 I lived with my career. I didn't know nothin' about anything else. When I was young I was too selfish, too interested in myself.'

At the Phoenix Theatre in October 1974 Elaine Stritch played Evy Meara in Neil Simon's *The Gingerbread Lady*, and Alan Brien wrote: 'Elaine Stritch as Evy strides across the stage on her compass legs, as if on stilts, savaging the cowed friends who gather to cheer her up following her stay in a home for alcoholics. A burnt-out torch singer, who has broken many a house record for falling off stools, she still retains the nervous, flickering electric presence of the professional entertainer, sketching in with a flick of muscular shoulder, the wave of a tendril hand, the cock of a bouffant head halo-ing an ageing cupid face, a brilliant caricature of the performance she once

gave. She is an ideal mouthpiece for the lines which snap like a whip, or snake tight like a lasso.'

While in England Miss Stritch also had an enormous success with a number of series on television of the situation comedy, 'Two's Company', in which she teamed with Donald Sinden. She played an American writer, and he was her ever-so-English butler, and the series ran for five years. Then she began writing and starring in the series 'Nobody's Perfect' for British television. In 1982, tired of hotel living and desirous of putting down roots, Elaine and her husband returned to the United States, where they bought an old house in upstate New York. Then tragedy struck — John had a malignant brain tumour, and he died in November 1982.

JESSICA TANDY AND HUME CRONYN

Jessica Tandy was born in London on 7 June 1909. She was often ill as a child but she attended Dame Alice Owen's Girls School in London from 1919 to 1924 and then worked for three years at Ben Greet's Academy of Acting also in London. She made her professional début playing Sara Manderson in *The Manderson Girls* at Playroom Six in London on 22 November 1927. It was a tiny backroom theatre in Old Compton Street; Miss Tandy played a 'gay, fascinating woman' and was expected to supply her own costumes. 'I wore odd clothes, capes, broadbrimmed hats. I was very, very poor,' she said. 'It was a real struggle.' Jessica Tandy then joined the Birmingham Repertory Company where she played Gladys in *The Comedy of Good and Evil* and Ginevra in *Alice-Sit-by-the-Fire*. She was Lydia Blake in a touring production of *Yellow Sands*. At the Court Theatre in London in February 1929 she played Lena Jackson in *The Rumour*, and at the Arts in April was the Typist in *The Theatre of Life*. She was Maggie in *Water* at the Little in June and she finished 1929 at the Haymarket Theatre playing Aude in *The Unknown Warrior*.

In March 1930, Jessica Tandy made her Broadway début playing Toni in *The Matriarch* at the Longacre, and she returned to England that summer where she played Olivia in *Twelfth Night* for the Oxford University Dramatic Society. She

was back in New York in October playing Cynthia Perry in *The Last Enemy* at the Shubert Theater.

At the St Martin's in London in February 1931 she was Fay in *The Man Who Pays the Piper* and at the Lyric in April she played Audrey in *Autumn Crocus*. At Wyndham's in November she was Ruth Blair in *Port Said*, and also that month at the Arts she played Anna in *Musical Chairs*. For the Repertory Players in January 1932 she was in *Below the Surface* and the following month at the Phoenix played in *Juarez and Maximilian*. From April to June 1932 she was at the Cambridge Festival playing in *Troilus and Cressida, See Naples and Die, The Witch, Rose Without a Thorn, The Inspector General* and *The Servant of Two Masters.* She returned to London in July where she opened at the St Martin's as Carlotta in *Mutual Benefit*. In October at the Duchess she was Manuela in *Children in Uniform*, at 23 playing the part of a 13-year-old. That year, too, she married the actor Jack Hawkins, and released her first film, *This Is the Night*, for Paramount.

Jessica Tandy began 1933 at the Arts Theatre playing Alicia in *Lady Audley's Secret*. In May she was at the Embassy playing Marikke in *Midsummer Fires* and in July was at Regent's Park playing Titania in *A Midsummer Night's Dream* in the Open Air. In November she took over from Maisie Darrel playing Betty in *Ten*

Minute Alibi at the Embassy. At the Fulham Shilling Theatre in January 1934 she was in *The Romantic Young Lady* and the following month at the Cambridge played Rosamund in *Birthday*. Jessica Tandy spent April and May 1934 in Manchester at the Hippodrome playing Viola in *Twelfth Night* and Anne Page in *The Merry Wives of Windsor*. She returned to London in October when she opened at the Duke of York's as Eva Whiston in *Line Engaged*.

At the New Theatre in November 1934 Jessica Tandy played Ophelia to John Gielgud's *Hamlet*. 'I did play Ophelia rather differently from the way she had been played before,' she said. 'Some of the notices didn't like my performance at all. They'd always been used to Ophelia being played by rather namby-pamby ladies, very sweet and innocent and so forth.' Also at the New and also with John Gielgud, in July 1935 she played Ada in *Noah*. Audrey Williamson reported: 'Jessica Tandy, in a tiny part, brought a moment of fleeting spirituality as a young girl conscious of coming danger.' At the Whitehall Theatre in November 1935 she played Anna Penn in *Anthony and Anna* and in August 1936 was at the Queen's playing Marie Rose in *The Ante-Room*.

She had a great success at the Criterion in November 1936 playing Jaqueline in Terence Rattigan's *French Without Tears*. At the Arts the following month she played Pamela in *Honour Thy Father*. In February 1937 Jessica Tandy joined the Old Vic Company where she played Viola in *Twelfth Night*. Audrey Williamson wrote of her performance: 'Jessica Tandy's Viola, softly spoken, brought to flower much of the rare regretful beauty, the inescapable heartache, of the speeches about unrequited love. Her wit was grave, girlish and pretty rather than dry and sparkling, as the wit of this remarkably resourceful and varied heroine should be.' In April, with the company, she played Katharine in Olivier's *Henry V*. In June she was at the St James's playing Ellen Murray in *Yes, My Darling Daughter*.

Jessica Tandy was in Priestley's *Time and the Conways* at the Ritz in January 1938 and at the Duchess in May played Leda in *Glorious Morning*. She returned to New York in January 1939 where she opened at the Cort Theater playing Nora in *The White Steed*, but was back in London in the Open Air at Regent's Park in July, once more playing Viola in *Twelfth Night*. She then set off on a tour of Canada playing in *Charles, the King*, *Geneva* and *Tobias and the Angel*. In January 1940 she played the Deaconess in *Geneva* in New York at the Henry Miller Theater. In April she was back with the Old Vic Company playing Cordelia in John Gielgud's *King Lear* directed by

Harley Granville-Barker. Audrey Williamson said: 'Jessica Tandy's Cordelia had a delicate and wistful grace: a performance full of sweetness if a little lacking in that strength of will she derives from her father. No Cordelia could have more tenderly complemented Gielgud's playing in the tent scene.' In May she was Miranda to Gielgud's Prospero in *The Tempest*, and Miss Williamson said she 'was a Miranda of ethereal enchantment: a delicate spring flower that seemed to have blossomed miraculously in this arid soil'.

Jessica Tandy was back in New York in September 1940 where at the Biltmore she played Dr Mary Murray in *Jupiter Laughs*. At the St James in October 1941 she was Abigail Hill in *Anne of England* and at the Guild Theater the following April she played Cattrin in *Yesterday's Magic*. She then went off to Hollywood to film, and there she met the actor Hume Cronyn, whom she married on 27 September 1942.

Hume Cronyn was born in London, Ontario, on 18 July 1911. He graduated from Ridley College in 1930 and went on to McGill University, where he studied art. It was at McGill that Cronyn appeared with the Montreal Repertory Theatre and also with the McGill Players, in productions which included *The Adding Machine*, *Dr Faustus*, *From Morn to Midnight*, *The Road to Rome*, *Alice in Wonderland* and *The Red and White Revue*. He made his professional début at the National Theater in Washington, DC, with Cochran's Stock Company playing in *Up Pops the Devil* in spring 1931. He studied at the American Academy of Dramatic Art from 1932 to 1934, spending the summers of 1932 and 1933 in Austria studying with Harold Kreutzberg. In summer 1934 he joined Robert Porterfield's Barter Theater Company as production director. With the company he played Austin Lowe in *The Second Man*, Dr Haggett in *The Late Christopher Bean*, Jim Hipper in *He Knew Dillinger*, and Doke Idum in *Mountain Ivy*.

Hume Cronyn made his Broadway début as a Janitor in *Hipper's Holiday* at the Maxine Elliott Theater on 18 October 1934. This was *He Knew Dillinger* retitled, and in the production Cronyn also understudied Burgess Meredith as Hipper.

From March to September 1935 Hume Cronyn toured with the Jinty Players as Stingo and Sir Charles Marlow in *She Stoops to Conquer*, and as Gideon Bloodgood in *The Streets of New York*. He toured from October to June 1936, playing Erwin Trowbridge in *Three Men On a Horse*. He returned to New York in September 1936, where he took over from Garsin Kanin playing Green in the farce *Boy Meets Girl* at the Cort Theater. He also played the part on tour.

In January 1937 at the Martin Beck Theater he played Elkus in *High Tor* and also again understudied Burgess Meredith, who was playing the lead. In August he took over from Eddie Albert playing Leo Davis in *Room Service* at the Cort, and went with the production on the road. He returned to New York in March 1938 when at the Windsor he played Abe Sherman in *There's Always a Breeze*. The following month at the 44th Street Theater he was Steve in *Escape This Night*. In February 1939 he was at the Ethel Barrymore Theater playing Harry Quill in *Off to Buffalo*. He spent the summers of 1939 and 1940 in stock at the Lakewood Theater in Skowhegan, Maine. In New York in October 1939 he played Andrei Prozoroff in *The Three Sisters* at the Longacre, and in March 1940 he was Peter Mason in *The Weak Link* at the John Golden Theater. In December for the Group Theater at the Belasco he played Lee Tatnall in *Retreat to Pleasure*.

In May 1941 Hume Cronyn produced and appeared in a revue for the Canadian Active Service Canteen, and at the Bucks County Playhouse in New Hope, Pennsylvania, in the summer played Joe Bonaparte in *Golden Boy*. Back in New York City in September he played Harley L. Miller in *Mr Big* at the Lyceum.

Hume Cronyn began 1942 producing *Junior Miss* for the United Services Organisation and then in March, still for the USO, he co-produced and appeared in a revue called *It's All Yours*. He toured military installations in California in May 1944 in an Actors' Laboratory production of *The Male Animal*; and in October that year he toured Canada in a vaudeville sketch in aid of War Bonds. Also in 1944, he was nominated for an Academy Award for his performance in *The Seventh Cross*, a film in which he acted with his wife, Jessica Tandy. They remained filming in Hollywood for several years, and during this time Cronyn directed Jessica Tandy in an Actors' Laboratory production of Tennessee Williams' one-act play, *Portrait of a Madonna*. This led to her being cast as Blanche Du Bois in Williams' *A Streetcar Named Desire*, which opened at the Ethel Barrymore Theater in December 1947. Brooks Atkinson wrote in the *New York Times*: 'Miss Tandy has a remarkably long part to play. She is hardly ever off the stage, and when she is on stage she is almost constantly talking — chattering, dreaming aloud, wondering, building enchantments out of words. Miss Tandy is a trim agile actress with a lovely voice and quick intelligence. Her performance is almost incredibly true. For it does seem almost incredible that she could understand such an elusive part so thoroughly and that she can convey it with so many shades and impulses that are accurate,

revealing and true.'

For this performance Miss Tandy won both the Tony and Twelfth Night Club awards; she spent two years playing Blanche, including the Broadway run and the tour. She then went back to Hollywood. In July 1949, while they were detained in California, Cronyn directed her in *Now I Lay Me Down to Sleep* at Stanford University in Palo Alto.

In August 1950 they appeared together at the Brattle Theater in Cambridge, Massachusetts, in *The Little Blue Light*, and in November that year Miss Tandy opened on Broadway at the Coronet Theater playing the title role in *Hilda Crane*, directed by Hume Cronyn. At the Ethel Barrymore in October 1951 she played Agnes and he played Michael in Jan de Hartog's *The Fourposter* for which they received the Commedia Matinée Club's Award. They opened at the Phoenix Theater in New York in December 1953 with a production (which Cronyn co-produced) of *Madam, Will You Walk?* in which Jessica Tandy played Mary Doyle and Hume Cronyn played Dr Brightlee. From September through December 1954 they toured the country in a concert recital entitled *Face to Face*. They repeated their roles in *The Fourposter* at the New York City Center in January 1955. Then, in April at the Longacre, she played Mary Honey while he played Curtis and Bebbett Honey in *The Honeys*.

In September that year at ANTA he was Julian and she was Frances Farrar in *A Day by the Sea*. They then, in 1957, toured in a summer stock production of *The Man in the Dog Suit*. The following summer they toured with *Triple Bill*, which consisted of three one-act works and a monologue. Jessica Tandy played Lucretia Collins once more in *Portrait of a Madonna*, and Angela Nightingale in *Bedtime Story*. Hume Cronyn played the Doctor in *Portrait of a Madonna*, Jerry in *A Pound on Demand*, John Jo Mulligan in *Bedtime Story*, and Professor Ivan Ivanovitch Nyukhin in the monologue, *Some Comments on the Harmful Effects of Tobacco*.

The Man in the Dog Suit opened at the Coronet in October 1958, and *Triple Bill* at the Playhouse in April 1959. In December that year Jessica Tandy played Louise Harrington in Peter Shaffer's *Five Finger Exercise* at the Music Box, and Kenneth Tynan said she 'hits the right note of frayed edginess'. She toured with the production during 1960 and 1961. The New York Drama League gave her the Delia Austria Medal for this performance. In March 1961 Hume Cronyn played Jimmy Luton in *Big Fish, Little Fish* at ANTA; for this performance he received the Delia Austria Medal also, and was nominated for the Tony. Jessica Tandy went to Stratford, Connecticut, in

June 1961, where at the American Shakespeare Festival she played Lady Macbeth, and Cassandra in *Troilus and Cressida*. She came back to London for the first time in over twenty years (she had become a United States citizen in 1954), taking the part of Edith Maitland in *Big Fish, Little Fish* while Hume Cronyn retained his award-winning role, Jimmy Luton. It opened at the Duke of York's Theatre in September 1962 — and played only nine performances.

They went to the Minnesota Theater Company, at the Tyrone Guthrie Theater in Minneapolis, for its first season in summer 1963. There Cronyn played Harpagon in *The Miser*, and Tchebutkin in *The Three Sisters*, while Tandy played Olga; he was Willie Loman in *Death of a Salesman* while she played Linda in the same production. That season Jessica Tandy also played Gertrude in *Hamlet*.

In April 1964 at the Lunt-Fontanne Theater in New York he played Polonius in Richard Burton's *Hamlet* and was judged to be the best thing in it. For this performance he received the New York Drama Critics Award and a Tony. They were together again at the Martin Beck Theater in October 1964 in *The Physicists*, in which she played Doktor Mathilde von Zahnd and he played Herbert George Beutler. At the Plymouth Theater in November he produced *Slow Dance on a Killing Ground*.

President Johnson invited the couple to the White House in February 1965 to perform together in *Hear America Speaking*. That summer they returned to Minneapolis to the Tyrone Guthrie Theater, where they were Madame Ranevskaya and Yepihodov in *The Cherry Orchard*. Jessica Tandy also played Lady Wishfort in *The Way of the World* and the Mother-in-law in *Caucasian Chalk Circle*, while Hume Cronyn played the Duke of Gloucester in *Richard III* and Harpagon in *The Miser*. In September 1966 they were both at the Martin Beck Theater in New York in Albee's *A Delicate Balance*. Hume Cronyn played Tobias and Jessica Tandy was Agnes, for which performance she received the Leland Powers Honors Award. They toured in the production from January through June 1967. At the Mark Taper Forum in Los Angeles Hume Cronyn once again played Harpagon in *The Miser* in March 1968, and this time Jessica Tandy played Frosine. She was in Niagara-on-the-Lake in Ontario for the Shaw Festival in July 1968, when she played Hesione Hushabye in *Heartbreak House*. In August 1969 Hume Cronyn was at the Stratford Festival Theater in Canada once more, this time playing Fr Rolfe in *Hadrian VII*. He toured the United States in this role until May 1970. Mean-

while Jessica was at the Ivanhoe Theater in Chicago in October 1969 playing Pamela Pew-Pickett in *Tchin-Tchin*, and back in New York in January 1970 at the Vivian Beaumont playing Marguerite Gautier in *Camino Real*. In January 1971 she took over from Dandy Nichols playing Marjorie at the Morosco in *Home*. In March she played the wife in Edward Albee's *All Over* at the Martin Beck Theater, directed by John Gielgud. John Simon reported: 'Jessica Tandy gives a bravura performance as the wife, all the more so since it must be done with delivery rather than dialogue.' Hume Cronyn spent summer 1971 touring as the Grandfather and Willie in *Promenade All!* and in November was at the Ahmanson in Los Angeles playing Commander Queeg in *The Caine Mutiny Court Martial*. They spent summer 1972 touring together in *Conflict of Interest*.

In November 1971 they opened at the Forum in a season of Beckett plays. In *Happy Days* he played Willie and she played Winnie. John Simon wrote: 'Miss Tandy has a theatrical quality, a larger-than-lifesizeness achieved partly by looking too studiously lovely for her age (and in this case for her role) partly by having a diction that smacks of the elocution teacher resolutely addressing some particularly backward pupils and partly by having a certain aristocratic hauteur that is really too good, too special for Winnie.' Cronyn was the Player in *Act Without Words 1* and Krapp in *Krapp's Last Tape*, of which John Simon wrote: 'Hume Cronyn was a fine Krapp, uncoy and unlovable in his old, corporeal presence, in which he gave out with some of the best stage wheezing I ever heard: a wheeze almost good enough for a death rattle.' Jessica Tandy was the Mouth in the twenty-three-minute tour de force, *Not I*, which earned her the Obie and Drama Desk awards. Cronyn also played Krapp at the St Lawrence Theater Center in Toronto, the Arena Stage in Washington, DC, and on tour throughout 1973.

At the Ethel Barrymore Theater in New York in February 1974 they mounted a double bill, *Noel Coward in Two Keys*, which consisted of *Come into the Garden Maud* and *A Song at Twilight*. After Broadway they took the productions on tour. They toured throughout 1975 in dramatic readings entitled *The Many Faces of Love*, and in 1976 returned to the Stratford, Ontario, Festival where Jessica played Lady Wishfort in *The Way of the World* and the title role in *Eve*. They were both in *A Midsummer Night's Dream*; he played Bottom and she played Hippolyta and Titania. That season he was also Shylock in *The Merchant of Venice*.

In October 1977 the couple were back on Broadway at the John Golden Theater in a production of Don Coburn's *The Gin Game*, which Cronyn co-produced and in which he played Weller Martin while his wife played Fonsia Dorsey. It was directed by Mike Nichols, and the play won the Pulitzer Prize. John Barber reported: 'I doubt if I shall see better acting this year here (in New York) or anywhere else, than is offered by Hume Cronyn and his wife Jessica Tandy in *The Gin Game*, a play for two people that is at once a funny, perceptive and frightening picture of old age. Both are performers of infinite distinction . . . In the play they appear far older than they are, as a seedy couple lately assigned to a retired folks' home. They reach towards friendship, much needed by both, when he teaches her how to play gin rummy. For him, the game banishes memories of a career

he has ruined with bad temper and know-it-all bluster. Cronyn suggests with suppressed twitches, alligator grins and his showy shuffling of the deck, the sensitivity and the vulnerability of the old man. While Tandy, with her wrinkled stockings and complacent habit of singing as she sorts her cards, demonstrates an inborn lack of instinct for dealing with a man.' The performance won Miss Tandy another Tony, and the production took them on to London to the Lyric in July 1979 and to Russia that autumn. As Gordon Gow wrote in *Plays and Players*: 'Taste and professionalism and a true dramatic sense are the hallmarks of the Cronyns. Their long careers are linked with some of the finest plays.'

LAURETTE TAYLOR

*L*aurette Cooney, the daughter of Irish immigrants, was born in Mt Morris Park, New York City, on 1 April 1884. She was a rebellious and imaginative child, who when set the task of writing about her life for a school essay invented a new beginning for herself, denying her father and saying she was the illegitimate daughter of a Spanish count. She read her fiction aloud to the class and reduced it, including the teacher, to tears. The teacher contacted Mother and convinced her that Laurette belonged on the stage. She made an inauspicious stage début in vaudeville in Gloucester, Massachusetts. It did, however, lead to a booking at Boston Athenaeum in 1903, and she went on to star in *The Child Wife* and *From Rags to Riches*, in which she made her New York début at the New Star Theater on 2 November 1903. She toured with the part of the soubrette in *The King of the Opium Ring* which brought her to Seattle, where she met the playwright Charles A. Taylor whom she later married. She starred in his productions of *The King of the Opium Ring*, *Escaped from the Harem* and *Yosemite*. According to the writer John Chapman, Taylor 'taught Laurette a certain kind of truth in acting; that you must make what you are doing and saying seem true'.

Charles Taylor died in 1908 and Laurette was left with two small children, a son and a daughter. Acting was all she knew and really all she cared about so she carried on, travelling in stock and then coming to the Lyric Theater in New York in May 1909 as May Keating in *The Great John Ganton*.

At the Maxine Elliott Theater in August she was Eleanor Hillary in *The Ringmaster* and at the Hackett Theater in December she played Ruth Dakon in *Mrs Dakon*. At Hartford, Connecticut, in April 1910 she played Lilian Turner in *The Girl in Waiting*, and in June at Wallack's Theater she had her first real success when she was Rose Lane in *Alias Jimmy Valentine*. According to Brooks Atkinson: '. . . then everyone understood that her spontaneity behind the footlights was indeed acting, and perhaps the most original and virtuoso acting of the time.'

At the Lyceum Theater in February 1911 she was Mici in *The Seven Sisters*; at Daly's in January the following year she was praised highly as Luana in *The Bird of Paradise*. Her greatest success, however, was to come at the end of 1912, when she played Peg in *Peg o' My Heart*, written for her by the English playwright, J. Hartley Manners. She and Manners were married during rehearsals and he went on to write fourteen plays for her — they became for a time an unbeatable theatrical partnership.

Peg o' My Heart opened in Rochester, New York, at the Shubert Theater in November 1912. It came to the Cort Theater (the opening production) in December and ran there for over 600 nights — the longest run of any dramatic play up to that time. Still at the Cort, in March 1914 she played Doleen Sweetmarsh in *Just as Well*, Jenny in *Happiness* and the Dupe in *The Day of the Dupes*.

Laurette Taylor made her English début at the

Devonshire Park Theatre in Eastbourne on 5 October 1914, playing Peg. She made her London début on the tenth of that month at the Comedy Theatre. The Zeppelin raids on the city put an end to her London run the following year, after more than 500 performances. She returned home in November 1915 and at the Globe Theater in New York that month played Sylvia in *The Harp of Life*. In March 1917 she played a Red Cross Nurse in *Out There*, and joined an all-star cast for a tour which raised more than 600,000 dollars for the Red Cross. At the Liberty Theater in November 1917 she was Miss Alverstone in *The Wooing of Eve* and at the Criterion the following month Jenny in *Happiness*, a sentimental comedy about a Brooklyn errand-girl teaching a rich man the secret of happiness. She made a brief excursion away from her husband's plays when in April 1918 she played Portia, Juliet and Katharine in scenes from Shakespeare's plays. In December she was L'Enigme in *One Night in Rome*.

Laurette Taylor returned to London in May 1920, where at the Garrick she played in *One Night in Rome*. She returned to New York in February 1921 and appeared in a revival of *Peg o' My Heart* at the Cort Theater. Alexander Woollcott wrote in the *New York Times* that Laurette Taylor's performance was 'one of the finest characterizations in comedy which has graced the American stage in our time. Peg with her bundles and her dog Michael under her arm, Peg with her tousled red hair, her gusty laugh, her skating walk and her fugitive smile, her wonderful wistful smile — our Peg is back in Forty-eighth Street and that thoroughfare seems a more cheerful place on that account ... To one seeing the play again after seven years it seems as though the role had somehow mellowed and sweetened with the years, and as though a hundred and one new touches of warmth and laughter had been added to it. One fancies Miss Taylor forever and forever recreating it, but perhaps this is just an illusion wrought by her skilful suggestion of always seeming to be playing the part for the first time in her wide-eyed and gratified existence.'

Theatre critics were, however, by now complaining about the lack of substance in Mr Manners' plays. John Corbin wrote in the *New York Times* that she 'had probably the greatest talent, the highest spirit of our times', but that both were 'subdued to the level of J. Hartley Manners' improvizations'. So Mr Manners wrote a serious play, *The National Anthem*, which was a denunciation of the jazz age and in which Laurette played Marian Hale. It opened at the Henry Miller Theater in January 1922 — and it flopped. They were still happily married, but this was the end of

their theatrical partnership. Laurette Taylor moved on to other playwrights. At the Vanderbilt Theater in February 1923 she played Sarah Kantor in *Humoresque*. She was at the 48th Street Theater in May playing Nell Gwynn in a revival of *Sweet Nell of Old Drury*, and at the same theatre in March 1925 she played Young Pierrot in *Pierrot the Prodigal*. At the Knickerbocker Theater in June 1925 she was Rose Trelawney in *Trelawney of the 'Wells'*, and at the Plymouth that November was Lisa Terry in *In a Garden*. She went to Chicago in 1927 where she appeared in *The Comedienne*, and back at the Shubert in New York in March 1928 she was Fifi Sands in *The Furies*. That year her husband died and she was desolate. She sold everything in the house — and all the letters, clippings and pictures that recalled their life together she burned.

Laurette Taylor made a brief reappearance on the stage at the Playhouse in New York in March 1932 when she appeared in a J. M. Barrie double bill of *The Old Lady Shows Her Medals* and *Alice-Sit-by-the-Fire*. Brooks Atkinson reported on the latter: 'As the artful wife in *Alice-Sit-by-the-Fire* which was revived at the Playhouse last evening, she does not tamely remind us of what a superb actress she is. It is as though we had never seen her before. In every scene of this trivial playlet she appears to be creating something fine and rapturous that has never been on the stage before ... it is a piece of magic in her virtuoso hands. Her undulating motion, the receptive tremor of her listening, her liquid speech, her limpid gestures, her awareness of the whole comedy, and, best of all, her tender, beaming smile bathe *Alice-Sit-by-the-Fire* in genius ... she is a lyric comedienne with a touch of pathos. The word "magnificent" is often recklessly used in the rush of play reviewing. Let it be used here scrupulously. Miss Taylor is magnificent.'

In 1938 she returned again to the stage, starting cautiously with a tour of summer theatres in *Tomorrow's Sunday*, *Mary, Mary, Quite Contrary* and *Candida*, and then in December opened at the Playhouse in New York in a revival of Sutton Vanes' *Outward Bound* in which she played Mrs Midgit. Brooks Atkinson said that her 'well-remembered radiance gives a glow and a heart-beat to the old charwoman's humility ...' She then went away from the theatre for another six years, but when she returned it was with a real bang. It was again at the Playhouse and it was in March 1945 that she opened as the Mother in Tennessee Williams' *The Glass Menagerie*. John Mason Brown reported: '... the evening's performance — more accurately, the season's — is Miss Taylor's. She casts upon the play and upon the audience the kind of spell one dreams of falling under in the theater. The mother she acts is a drudge, plump and frowsy. A nag, too. Yet Miss Taylor leads us back into that mother's white-columned past while never sparing us the sordidness of her present. Miss Taylor has only to mention youth to summon it.' And Lewis Nichols wrote in the *New York Times*: ''Memorable'' is an over-worked word but that is the only one to describe Laurette Taylor's performance ... Miss Taylor's picture of a blowsy, impoverished woman who is living on memories of a flower-scented Southern past is completely perfect. It combines qualities of humor and human understanding.' She played the part for over a year. Laurette Taylor died on 17 December 1946 in New York.

GODFREY TEARLE

Godfrey Tearle was born in New York on 12 October 1884 into an acting family. His father was Osmond Tearle, a famous English actor and his American mother was Marianne Conway. He was at first educated privately and then at Carlisle Grammar School. He made his stage début in Burnley in 1893, when he played the Duke of York in *Richard III*, and joined his father's touring company in 1899. He toured with Osmond Tearle playing a variety of roles until Tearle's death in 1901, when Godfrey took over the company. In 1902 he took it to South Africa where they toured for two years, Godfrey himself playing over fifty roles in repertory. They returned to England in 1904, and he spent another two years touring in the provinces playing such parts as Hamlet, Othello, Brutus, Romeo, Sir Peter Teazle and Young Marlow. He was extremely attractive, but with women falling at his feet he married a young actress in his company, Mary Plante, who acted under the name of Mary Malone. They often worked together, but it seems her acting was not of his calibre.

Godfrey Tearle made his London début at the King's Theatre, Hammersmith, in May 1906 playing the Earl of Bothwell in *Mary Queen of Scots*. In September 1907 he was at His Majesty's Theatre playing Sigismund in Oscar Asche's production of *Attila*, and the following month was Silvius in *As You Like It*. In November he played Lodovico in *Othello*. He then set off again on a provincial tour playing the Rev. Edgar Linnell in *The Hypocrites*.

In September 1908 Tearle went to work for Beerbohm Tree at His Majesty's playing Valentine in *Faust*. It was, as was usual with Tree, a hugely lavish production. Although he did not find Tree congenial, Tearle stayed with him at His Majesty's playing Trip in *The School for Scandal*, Kit French in *Admiral Guinea*, Master Page in *The Merry Wives of Windsor*, Octavius in *Julius Caesar*, Marcellus in *Hamlet* and Lorenzo in *The Merchant of Venice*.

In September 1909 he set out on a tour with *The Builder of Bridges*, playing Walter Gresham, and *His House in Order* in which he played Major Maurewarde. In November he was back in London at the St James's, playing Noel Darcus in *Lorrimer Sabiston, Dramatist*. He went to the Globe in February 1910 where he played the Rt Hon. Robert Colby in *The Tenth Man*, and in April was Prince Olaf in *The Prince and the Beggar Maid*. In August he was at the Coronet playing George d'Alroy in *Caste* and Angus MacAllister in *Ours*, and back at the St James's in September was Captain Henry Townshend in *D'Arcy of the Guards*. He went to the Little Theatre in November to be Adam Lancaster in *Just to Get Married*, and toured for Christmas playing the Grand Duke Sergius in *The Balkan Princess*. In May 1911 Godfrey Tearle played William Laud in *Margaret Catchpole*, and at the Comedy that September was Pierre Vareine in *The Marionettes*. The following month he was at the Little playing Arden in *The Sentimentalists* and at the Globe in February 1912 he was John Madison in *The Easiest Way*. He was Orestes in *Iphigenia in Tauris* at the Kingsway in March, and at the Duke of York's in June was Viscount Litterly in *The Amazons*. He returned to the St James's in October 1912 when he played Marcel Beaucourt in *The Turning Point*, and there in January he was Calaf, Prince of Astrakhan, in *Turandot, Princess of China*. At the Aldwych in March he was Lord Arlington in *Her Side of the House* and at the Little the following month played Percy Robinson in *The Cap and Bells*. He returned to Shakespeare at the Court in April 1913 when he played Cassius in *Julius Caesar*, but by June he was back to less spectacular roles at the Comedy playing Louis Percival in *Jim The Penman*.

Godfrey Tearle was in an all-star revival of

London Assurance at the St James's playing Charles Courtly in aid of the King George Pension Fund in June and in September he was at the Duke of York's playing Captain Rattray, RN, in *The Adored One*. In November he was Valentine Brown in *Quality Street* at night while in the afternoons he was Captain Hook in *Peter Pan*. Although he was always in work and a much-admired actor, earning a good deal of money, it was not until February 1914 that he became a fully-fledged star. That month he opened as Frank Taylor in Somerset Maugham's *The Land of Promise*, which was a kind of modern-day *Taming of the Shrew*. At last he could combine his acting talent with his enormous good looks and stage personality in a substantial role; until then it had been classical parts which stretched him, or attractive amorous parts which utilized his charisma.

At the Haymarket in September 1914 he was Gregory Jardine in *The Impossible Woman* and in November Dicky Lascelles in *The Flag Lieutenant*. For the Actors' Benevolent Fund an all-star *The School for Scandal* was staged at Covent Garden on 2 February 1915, in which Godfrey Tearle played Careless.

At the Haymarket in April 1915 he played Bert in *Five Birds in a Cage* and James in *Quinneys*, and at the St James's in May he was the renegade Monk in *The Monk and the King's Daughter*. Another all-star revival for the King George Pension Fund was staged at His Majesty's on 5 July 1915 and in this one he played Sir Henry Guildford in *Henry VIII*. His last performance, before going into the services, was at the Adelphi in November 1915 when he played Carlo in *Tina*.

Godfrey Tearle returned to the stage in April 1919 when he played Philip in *The Boy Comes Home* at the Hippodrome in Newcastle-on-Tyne. He was at the Coliseum in April in the same role. Also at the Coliseum, in September he was Dennis Camberley in *The Camberley Triangle*, and at the Savoy the following month he played Michael Devlin in *Tiger Rose*.

At the end of 1919 Godfrey Tearle went to America, where at the Belasco in Washington he played Silvio Steno in *Carnival*, coming to New York to the 44th Street Theater in that same role. He came back to England, where at the Coliseum in March 1920 he played Brutus and Cassius in scenes from *Julius Caesar*. At the Queen's the same month he was Edward Gibbs in *The Fold*.

It was June 1920 when he opened at Drury Lane playing Boris Androvsky in the spectacular *The Garden of Allah*. As Jill Bennett describes the role: 'The story tells of a monk who falls passionately in love and breaks his vows of poverty, chastity and obedience. He marries the woman he loves, but his conscience and faith will not let him be happy. He gives her up and returns to the monastery. Godfrey was ideal casting for the hero. He had purity and masculinity and physical passion. He had a good deal of poetic suffering to do, and a ten-minute soliloquy. As for the production, it had everything a theatregoer's heart could desire. There was a baby camel, a desert caravan, dancing dervishes in howling winds, and — the pièce de résistance — a real sandstorm.' Needless to say *The Garden of Allah* enjoyed a long run. From this melodrama Godfrey Tearle went to the Court in April 1921, where he played the title role in J. B. Fagan's revival of *Othello*. Then it was on to the Playhouse in September to play Lafe Regan in *The Sign on the Door*. At the Comedy in November he was Waverly Ango in *The Faithful Heart* and at the Savoy in April 1922 he played Wilford Ashfield in *The Card Players*. At the Adelphi in June 1922 he was Captain Nick Ratcliffe in *The Way of an Eagle* and at the Globe in November, Daniel Farr in *The Laughing Lady*. He went to the Empire in December to play the title role in *Harlequin* and for the King George Pension Fund in February 1923 at His Majesty's he was Gringoire in *The Ballad Monger*. At the Queen's in March 1923 he took over from Norman McKinnell as John Brown in *Bluebeard's Eighth Wife* and at the Apollo in May he was John Shand in *What Every Woman Knows*.

In 1924 Tearle took on the management of the Apollo Theatre and opened there in February playing John Star in *The Fairy Tale*. The following month he directed *The Fake* and played the part of Geoffrey Sands. He took the production to America, where he opened at the Hudson Theater in New York in October 1924. When he returned to London in January 1925 it was to the Queen's, where he played Jim Warren in *Silence*. In March he was Hugh Westcourt in *Dancing Mothers*. For the Fellowship of Players in May 1925 at the Prince of Wales's he was Hamlet, and in June at the Queen's was the Man in *Salomy Jane*. He played in *The Fake* once again at the Lyceum the following month. At the Prince's in September he was Weston in *White Cargo* and he had another major Shakespearian role for the Fellowship of Players in December when he played Othello. At St Martin's in January 1926 he was David Campbell in *Scotch Mist* and took over from Wilfred Shine at the Little in May playing Owen Keegan in *Autumn Fire*. For the Venturers' Society in June 1926 he played Rufz Quenbo in *Martinique* at the Shaftesbury, and at the Adelphi in August he took over from Francis Lister playing Bob Holden in *Aloma*. He toured in January 1927 playing Hugh Ferrers in *Dawn* and at the Strand in September was Chico in

Seventh Heaven. It was back to the classics in November when he played Mirabell in *The Way of the World* at Wyndham's. Godfrey Tearle spent 1928 touring as Philip Conway in *The Acquittal*, and returned to London to the Little in January 1929 when he played Maurice in *Jealousy*. He opened at the Q in March playing John Rool in *The Berg* and transferred with the production that same month to His Majesty's. The following month at the Arts Theatre and the Little Theatre he had the title role in *Captain Banner*. He embarked in July 1929 on a tour of *This Thing Called Love* playing Tice Collins, and returned to the Playhouse the following January playing Hardress Mackenzie in *The White Assegai*. Then it was back on tour again as General Herrera in *Bandits*. At the Haymarket in April he was playing Horatio in an all-star *Hamlet* for the King George Pension Fund, and the performance was repeated in May. At the Royalty the following month he was Francis Archer in *The Beaux' Stratagem* and in August toured as Mervyn Allington in *Slings and Arrows*. Back in London at the Cambridge in February 1931 he was Kong in a play of the same name, and at the Haymarket in March had the title role in an all-star *Hamlet*. At the Phoenix in September 1931 he took over from Raymond Massey in *Late Night Final*, and at the Comedy in December played Waverly Ango in a revival of *The Faithful Heart*.

In 1932 Godfrey Tearle became the first president of British Actors' Equity. At His Majesty's in February he played Mark Antony in *Julius Caesar* and in March was Brutus in the same play. In April, on a South African tour, he played in *Cynara, Michael and Mary* and *Seventh Heaven*, returning to London in October when at the Whitehall he was Jack and Lance Donovan in *Road House*. At St Martin's the following September he was Andrew Kerr in *The Key*. At the Alhambra in January 1934 he had the title role in *Henry V* and the following month played Mark Antony in *Julius Caesar*. The critic J. C. Trewin remembered that it was the last of the old Shakespeare seasons there. 'It was received rather roughly then. New ways of acting and directing Shakespeare had begun to be seen. But I remember how excited I was by Godfrey Tearle's ease. He was in supreme command, almost a lazy command. He spoke Shakespeare with understanding and appreciation and almost with relish. Most of the speaking then, except for the Gielgud school, was pretty bad. It was sheer joy to sit back and listen and look.'

At the Criterion in April 1934 he was Sir John Corbett in *Sixteen* and at the Strand in June played David Norton in *Living Dangerously*. At the Apollo in October he was Captain Concannon and

Sir Richard Carstairs, KC, in *Hyde Park Corner*. At Daly's in July 1935 he was Sir Francis Dearden in *The Unguarded House* and at the Apollo the following May played Black Jack and Tracy Eagan in *The Fugitives*. At His Majesty's in December he played King Saul in the play Barrie had written specially for Elisabeth Bergner, *The Boy David*.

Godfrey Tearle went on tour in February 1937 playing Dr Clitterhouse in *The Amazing Dr Clitterhouse*. The following February back in London at the Comedy he was Hugh Willis in *The Island*. He took over the management of the Lyric in September, and played Commander Edward Ferrers in *The Flashing Stream*. Audrey Williamson reported: 'Godfrey Tearle made a completely convincing mathematician till the last scenes when the nervous breakdown failed to move ...' He took the production to the Biltmore in New York in April 1939 and then returned to England where he toured with it. At His Majesty's in December the same year he was Brutus in a modern-dress *Julius Caesar*, and at the Apollo in February 1940 he played Maddoc Thomas in Emlyn Williams' *The Light of Heart*, which Audrey Williamson said was 'noted for a performance of crumbling power by Godfrey Tearle as an ageing actor of heroic gifts, fatally degenerating through drink and loss of memory'. There then followed a period of filming and at the Piccadilly Theatre in December 1946 Godfrey Tearle was, according to Miss Williamson, 'an Antony in heroic ruin, passionate and tragic', in *Antony and Cleopatra*. In November 1947 he played the same part at the Martin Beck Theater in New York with Katharine Cornell as his Cleopatra, and Brooks Atkinson reported: 'As Antony, Godfrey Tearle has style and force, and ably portrays the whole varying sequence of one of the great tragic parts. Tick him off a little for being no great lover in a part steeped in ardor, but credit him beautifully for his intelligence and understanding.'

Godfrey Tearle had married Stella Freeman, and after her death four years later had married once again but this marriage, to Barbara Mary Palmer, had ended in divorce. In August 1948 he went to the Stratford-on-Avon Memorial Theatre to play the title role in *Othello*. Harold Hobson reported: 'The characteristic feature of Godfrey Tearle's Othello lies in this fact: that it gives a more assured impression than any other Othello I have seen of being capable of delivering nobly the part's great speeches, and yet deliberately, apparently of set purpose, as if disdaining their splendour ... throws them one by one away. I should add that, in throwing them away, Mr Tearle does not act like a rich man wantonly wasting his gold and silver: he acts like a rich man who scatters his gold and silver because he knows he possesses abundant wealth of another kind ... His voice is resonant, it is deep and musical; it can encompass great things without effort. At no point in the evening did Mr Tearle make any attempt to use this fine instrument to its full capacity. Vocally, complete simplicity was the keynote of his performance ... here is a dominating character, a man so easily noble of presence that he does not require to tell us he comes from men of royal liege, of such commanding stature of mind that he needs no arresting words to prove it ...' The following April at Stratford he repeated this part and also played Macbeth, directed by Anthony Quayle and with Diana Wynyard as his Lady. T. C. Worsley wrote: 'What is essential for Macbeth is that he should seize our sympathy for himself from the very outset ... Mr Tearle never did this, nor even attempted it. He threw away almost the whole of the first act, line after line, speech after speech ... Too harassed from the start, too haggard with doubt too soon, he played all the time right below his Lady Macbeth making himself a mere junior partner ... The second act was better, much better ... He drove himself through the banquet with a kind of nervous intensity that was highly effective ... It was a brillant flash: but too late and all too brief. The third act was again less successful ... In Mr Tearle

there seemed no strength, no core — for there never had been that from the start; there was only the sort of despairing haphazard striking all round him that any cornered man, even the least physically courageous, might muster at such a moment ... Mr Tearle is one of our leading Shakespearian actors and though he shows here that he can be flatter than one would ever have imagined, he cannot be bad ...' However, Harold Hobson, who saw the production on a different night, reported: 'He is from the first the powerful soldier, wild and shaggy in appearance, and wielding a vast sword that would have been no toothpick to Goliath ... he develops his performance into a husband who flares in passion no less than in ambition ...' At Stratford that year Godfrey Tearle met the neophyte actress Jill Bennett and they fell in love. After filming *Decameron Nights* in Spain in the winter of 1949 he succeeded Sir Ralph Richardson at the Haymarket playing Dr Sloper in Henry James's *The Heiress*.

In the 1951 Birthday Honours Godfrey Tearle accepted a knighthood. He spent time filming, mainly Ealing comedies, and then at the New Theatre played the title role in *The Hanging Judge*. But his health was deteriorating — he had a weak heart, and he died in hospital on 8 June 1953, Jill Bennett by his side.

MARIE TEMPEST

M ary Susan Etherington was born in London on 15 July 1864. She went to school first at Midhurst and then was sent to a strict convent in Belgium. At the age of 16 she was taken by her grandmother, who had brought her up, to Paris for a while to learn the language and study music. When she returned to London it was to study at the Royal Academy of Music; while she was still a student there she first sang in public at St James's Hall, and determined to go on the stage.

In 1883 Mary Etherington became Marie Tempest (she took her stage name from her godmother, Lady Susan Vane-Tempest) and began her career singing in the provinces, where she was praised by local critics. She made her London début on 30 May 1885 at the Comedy Theatre playing Fiammetta in Suppé's comic opera *Boccaccio*. The critics all agreed that she had a charming voice but then divided. One said she showed 'no trace of the amateur' while another declared she had 'every-

thing to learn as an actress'. In November 1885 she was Lady Blanche in *The Fay o' Fire* at the Opéra-Comique, and the following month was back at the Comedy playing the title role in *Erminie*. In June 1886 she opened at Drury Lane as Rosella in *Friboli* and that October was at the Prince of Wales playing Countess Bianca in *La Béarnaise*. She took over the title role in *Dorothy* from Marion Hood at the Prince of Wales Theatre in February 1887 and transferred with it to the Lyric, where she played until 1889. In June that year at the Lyric she had the title role in Cellier's *Doris*, and in November at the same theatre opened as Kitty Carroll in Edward Solomon's *The Red Hussar*, to great acclaim.

Marie Tempest made her New York début at Palmer's Theater on 5 August 1889 in *The Red Hussar*. One local critic reported: 'Pretty? Well, not exactly pretty. Her nose is retroussé and her cheek bones are too high to give regularity to her features, but she has a lovely mouth and a pair of

Paul Scofield as Othello (with Michael Bryant and Felicity Kendal)
at the National Theatre
(London, March 1980)

Ellen Terry played the role of Mistress Page in the Coronation
revival of *The Merry Wives of Windsor* at His Majesty's Theatre
(London, June 1902)

eyes that can smile with the archness of a coquette, and almost at the same time reveal a world of passion.' And another wrote: 'It was a success and from the last notes of the song, Marie Tempest was received into the affections of New York theatregoers . . . After that the opera seemed to be but a secondary consideration and the other players were but foils. Tempest only could fill the stage.' She then toured the United States and Canada with the J. C. Duff Opera Company, playing the roles of Kitty and Dorothy again, Carmen in Bizet's opera, Arline in *The Bohemian Girl*, the title role in *Mignon* and Mabel in *The Pirates of Penzance*. In October 1891 she was back in New York at the Casino playing Adam in *The Tyrolean*. The following January, at the same theatre, she was Nanon in an opera of that name and in February played Christel in *The Tyrolean*. Still at the Casino, in November 1892 she was Francesca in *The Fencing Master*, and in October 1893 she played Celeste in *The Algerian* at the Garden in New York.

She returned to London in 1895, bringing her mother and sister with her, and opened at Daly's in February playing Adele in *An Artist's Model*. It was the beginning of her reign there as the queen of musical comedy; she even used the special royal entrance rather than the stage door. In April 1896 she played O Mimosa San in *The Geisha*, and in June was Maia in *A Greek Slave*. She became the first actress to have her clothes designed by couturiers instead of theatrical costumiers. In 1898 she met Cosmo Gordon-Lennox; she was most impressed with this extremely rich aristocrat and they soon married. He not only indulged her completely — she had a passion for shopping, redecorating her house, and fine clothes — but also introduced her to intellectuals and the world of literature.

In October 1899 Marie Tempest opened at Daly's in the title part of *San Toy*, but it was to be her last opening at Daly's. She had a row with the manager, George Edwardes, over the costume — he wanted her to wear trousers and she adamantly refused. The partnership was over. She left musical comedy behind, and opened as Nell Gwynn in Anthony Hope and Edward Rose's *English Nell* at the Prince of Wales Theatre in August 1900. At the same theatre in February 1901 she had the title role in *Peg Woffington*, and in August was Becky Sharp in an adaptation of *Vanity Fair*. In all of these she had as her director Dion Boucicault, who taught her to be a straight actress, and she spent the rest of her life perfecting the techniques she had learned from him. In April 1902 at the Haymarket she was Polly Eccles in *Caste*, and then in 1902 she was hired by Charles Frohman to play Kitty Silverton in her husband's adaptation from

the French, *The Marriage of Kitty*. This play remained in her repertoire for thirty years. It was also the beginning of her association with the American impresario Frohman, for whom she was to work for eight years. In November 1903 she opened at the Hudson Theater in New York with *The Marriage of Kitty*, and in November 1904 she returned to London where at the Criterion she played Suzanne Trevor in *The Freedom of Suzanne*.

In February 1906 Marie Tempest was at the Duke of York's playing Peggy O'Mara in *All-of-a-Sudden-Peggy*, and that September she made her first appearance in variety with a selection of songs at the Palace in London. In April 1907 she was at the Comedy Theatre in London playing Margaret Verrall in *The Barrier* and in December at the same theatre played Angela Courland in *Angela*.

It was in February 1908, when at the Comedy Theatre she played Lady Barbara in *Lady Barbarity*, that she met the actor William Graham Browne. (Her marriage had already floundered.) She and Browne began a partnership that worked both on and off the stage. On stage he took a secondary role but often directed her, and off stage was her complete guide — and something of a guardian. In April at the Comedy she played Mrs Worthley in *Mrs Dot* by Somerset Maugham, which ran for over a year. In January 1909 she opened at the Comedy in the title role in *Penelope*, and in December took the play to the Lyceum in New York. In April at the Empire in New York she was Polly Eccles in *Caste* and in September at Atlantic City played Irma Lurette in *A Thief in the Night*. She was at the New Theater in New York in January 1911 playing Becky Sharp once more, and she returned to Europe in April where at the Lyceum in Edinburgh she was Miss Lily in *Lily the Bill-Topper*. Marie Tempest was at the Hippodrome Theatre in London in May 1911 playing the Lady in *The Shearing of Samson* and appearing in *Circe and the Pigs*. At the Duke of York's in June she revived *The Marriage of Kitty*. For the Coronation Performance of *The Critic* at His Majesty's Theatre in June 1911 she played the Confidante, and at the Royalty in October took the part of Flora Lloyd in *The Honeymoon*. She was Molly Blair in *At the Barn* at the Prince of Wales in April 1912, and the *Times* reported that it was a performance of '. . . sincerity, intensity, perfect finish in detail, and a curious felicity of style'. In September at the same theatre she played Pauline Cheverelle in *Art and Opportunity* and in November was Kate Morre in *An Imaginary Conversation*. That same month she played Frivol in *The Malingerer*. In January 1913 she opened in the title role of Jerome K. Jerome's *Esther Casaways* but it was a short run, because as one critic explained: 'We want to hear Miss Tempest laugh ... we do not want to see her sad and harassed.' In March she was Lady Wetherall in *The Handful*, but this was not a great success either.

For the King George Pension Fund at the St James's Theatre on 27 June 1913 she played Pert in *London Assurance*. In September she took on the management of the Playhouse in London where she opened with *Mary Goes First*, playing the title role. In February at the Playhouse she was Lady Sophia Flete in *Thank Your Ladyship* and in May was the Countess of Wynmarten in *The Wynmartens*. In June 1914 she was Lady Henrietta in *The Duke of Killiecrankie*. By this time she was enormously in debt. The war in Europe did not help box office receipts, and Marie Tempest and Browne set off on a world tour which opened at the Royal Alexandra Theater in Toronto in October 1914 and during which she acted in New York, Chicago, Australia, New Zealand, South Africa, India, the Straits Settlements, China, Japan, the Philippines and through the United States before returning to England eight years later. While she was in Australia her husband died in Europe, having served with the medical corps in France, and she and Browne were married immediately — it was 1921. The tour was a triumph and the takings in Australia alone allowed her to pay all her English debts.

Marie Tempest returned to London in February 1923 and at the Duke of York's Theatre played Annabelle Leigh in *Good Gracious, Annabelle*, a play which had been a great success on the tour. The English did not care for it and on that night their delight at having her home again was overwhelmed by their dislike of the material. And the audience was vociferous in its dislike. She described her feelings to her biographer Hector Bolitho: 'How long I stood there, leaning against the wings I do not know. Dimly I remember clapping my hands over my ears, trying to shut out that cruel noise. Able to bear it no longer, I rushed to my dressing room and closed the door behind me ... after thirty-seven years as a trouper I had been booed for the first time and in London ... But I am still unrepentant about the play ... the time was unwise, maybe. But the play was fresh and clever and I still believe that we were right and that the audience, fed on the fluffy plays of the war, was wrong. That night killed something in me. I've never felt quite the same about my "dear public" since.' However, to keep her spirits up and 'show the world' she quickly moved to an even bigger house in Regent's Park. She also quickly revived the old standby *The Marriage of Kitty*, and ran for nearly a year with it. At the Comedy Theatre in

January 1924 she played Alice Grey in Barrie's *Alice-Sit-by-the-Fire* and in March was Lady Messilent in *Far Above Rubies*.

Marie Tempest returned briefly to operetta in July 1924 when at the Lyric, Hammersmith, she played Mrs Nolan in *Midsummer Madness*. Then at the Queen's in December she played Madame Fougasse in *Orange Blossom*. In January, for charity, she played Emily Carewe in *The Baker's Dozen* at the Palladium and in April at the Ambassadors' she was Mrs Duro Pampinelli in *The Torch Bearers*. For the King George Pension Fund on 11 May 1925 she played Lady Appleby in *My Lady's Dress* at the Adelphi.

In June 1925 she opened in her first big London success in ten years. It was Noel Coward's *Hay Fever*, and Coward had written the part of Judith Bliss with her in mind. *Punch* reported: '... the most delightful thing of the evening was to see Miss Marie Tempest coming into her own again with a part which gave every scope for her really distinguished sense of comedy and her admirable technique ... [she] moved the house to a storm of spontaneous applause by the exquisite singing of a little chanson d'amour, and it was in perfect voice — not a note strained or even thin ...' *Hay Fever* ran for 337 performances.

In April 1926 Marie Tempest played Angela Fane in *The Cat's Cradle* at the Criterion, and the *Times* reported: 'People agitate for a brighter London, but so long as Miss Tempest is there to brighten it, why worry? Her talent is as fresh and brilliant as ever. Perhaps we ought rather to say, her temperament, for with all her technical accomplishment — and she brought that to the last refinement of virtuosity — it is not so much the artist in the woman that thrills us with delight as the woman herself. She seems to radiate the joy of living, to drive it home to us by her mere presence, by the inspiring notes of her voice, and by the depths of worldly experience and indulgence for our human foibles in her glance. Briefly she is a perpetual refreshment and source of pleasure: something for which the theatre exists and by which it triumphantly justifies its existence.'

In September 1926 she played Alicia Crane in *The Scarlet Lady*, also at the Criterion, and at the same theatre in February 1927 she opened in the title role of *The Marquise*, another play Coward wrote for her. At the Ambassadors' in June 1927 she played Mrs Patrick in *The Spot on the Sun*, and in January 1928 was at the Savoy playing Sophia Elphinstone in *The Masque of Venice*. The following month she was at St Martin's playing Olivia in *Mr Pim Passes By*, and in July was back at the Criterion playing Dultitia Sloane in *Passing Brompton Road*. In February 1929, still at the

Criterion, she was Lady Mary Torrent in *Her Shop*.

She and Henry Ainley had an excellent vehicle in St John Ervine's *The First Mrs Fraser* at the Haymarket in July 1929. Marie Tempest played Janet Fraser. She was still at the Haymarket in April 1931, playing Mrs Wickham in *Five Farthings*, and in June was Helen Forbes in *Marry at Leisure*. In November she moved to the Phoenix, where she played Empress Elizabeth in *Little Catherine*, and in February 1932 she was at the Ambassadors' playing Mary Melbourne in *So Far and No Farther*. In June at the St James's she was Laura Merrick in *The Vinegar Tree* and in August at the Haymarket played Lady Immingham in *Tomorrow Will Be Friday*. Marie Tempest went to the Lyric in April 1933 where she played Bridget Drake in *When Ladies Meet*, and in December she was at the Queen's playing Lady Jane Kingdom in *The Old Folks at Home*. At the Lyric in October 1934 she played Fanny Cavendish in *Theatre Royal* and Audrey Williamson reported: 'Marie Tempest acted a courageous death scene — standing to the last — with an exquisite and unearthly poise.'

On 28 May 1935 Marie Tempest's golden jubilee on the stage was celebrated at a special matinée at Drury Lane. She appeared in an act each from *The Marriage of Kitty* and *Little Catherine*. King George and Queen Mary were there and over £5000 was raised for the Marie Tempest Ward at St George's Hospital, for the benefit of actors.

At the Queen's Theatre in November 1935 she played Georgina Leigh in Robert Morley's first play, *Short Story*, and in February 1937 she was Flora Lowell at the same theatre in *Retreat from Folly*. That year she was made a dame, but it was also the year that her husband Willie Browne died. At the Haymarket in February 1938 she played Mary Berkeley in *Mary Goes to See* and at the Queen's in September 1938 had a great success in what was to be her last appearance. She played Dora Randolph in Dodie Smith's *Dear Octopus*.

Marie Tempest began rehearsals for another play but found that her memory failed her. She simply could not learn the lines.

She went home stoically and six months later, on 14 October 1942, she died, aged 78. Eric Johns summed up her career: 'She had perfected a number of technical tricks that never failed to conjure laughs out of an author's flimsiest lines. People who flocked to see Marie Tempest did not care a jot for the play. All they wanted was to enjoy her sparkling performance. The play was no more than a vehicle and she did not venture to play the great classic parts, as Ellen Terry had done. She was frequently content with a mediocre script offering her an opportunity to perform her celebrated tricks of which the public never seemed to tire. She was a martinet in the theatre. She always had her own way.'

ELLALINE TERRISS

Ellaline Terriss was born on 13 April 1871 at the Ship Hotel at Stanley in the Falkland Islands, where her father, who had once tried acting, was a sheep farmer. The family soon moved back to England, where William Terriss finally, at the age of 26, settled down to become a successful and respected actor.

From her earliest days Ellaline was taught singing and dancing, and entertained her parents' guests at home. Her first true stage performance was as an amateur in *Caste* at the Club in Bedford Park. Then when she was staying up north with friends who managed a theatre she was allowed for a week to dance in the pantomime *Sinbad the Sailor* with Vesta Tilley. She was 15, and knew that she loved the stage. When she returned home she mounted a production of the one-act play, *Cupid's Messenger*, in her sitting room to impress her father. She did. On 14 February 1888 she was suddenly summoned by Beerbohm Tree (who had heard from Terriss of her success) to play the part in *Cupid's Messenger* that she had learned, as the actress whose role it was at the Haymarket was taken ill. Within a few hours of the summons Ellaline was acquitting herself well on the professional stage. She played the part for a week. Her father decided she was ready for full-time employment on stage and arranged an interview with the impresario Charles Wyndham at the Criterion. Ellaline was immediately given a three-year contract. In February 1888 she played Madge in *Why Women Weep*, and the following month she was Lottie in *Two Roses*. Although much of her first year was taken up with understudy rehearsals she also played Ada Ingot in *David Garrick*, Nellie Bassett in *Betsy* and at Terry's Theatre was Lucy in *Dream Faces*. At the Strand Theatre in 1889 she played Grace Wentworth in *The Balloon* and Lucy Maynard in *Aesop's Fables*. At the Criterion she was then Prudence in *Truth*, the Maid in *The School for Scandal*, Jane Gammon in *Wild Oats* and Minnie in *Shylock and Co*. The Criterion was noted for comedy and her father thought it would be a good idea if she widened her range, so in August 1891 Ellaline left Charles Wyndham and went to the old Princess Theatre in Oxford Street to play in melodrama. There she opened as Arrah Meelish in Boucicault's *Arrah-Na-Pogue* and Clement Scott reported: 'The heroine should naturally be the first to pass in review, and I think I may say that all were charmed with the fresh, natural acting of Miss Ella Terriss.' She did a whole season of melodrama, which included Rose Egerton in *After Dark*, Tom Chickweed in *Alone in London*, and Nell in *The Great Metropolis*.

After that it was back to comedy, but this time to the Court Theatre in Sloane Square. Ellaline played Lady Belton in *Marriage*, Mrs Duncan in *Faithful James*, Daphne in *The Guardsman*, Lady Wilhelmine in *The Amazons*, and Louise in *The Other Fellow*. She and Seymour Hicks, whom she had earlier encountered through her father, came face to face when they played together in a curtain raiser. Within eight days he proposed, and in spite of some opposition from her father they married within a few weeks.

On Boxing Day 1893 Ellaline Terriss opened at the Lyceum as Cinderella, and had her first major success. Clement Scott reported: 'Miss Ellaline Terriss makes an absolutely ideal Cinderella. Everything stagy and theatrical vanishes from the mind. The new Cinderella is cut clean out of a lovely picture book.' And another critic wrote: 'But better than all is the poetical Cinderella of Miss Ellaline Terriss, the most bewitching little heroine of pantomime ever seen, a heroine worthy of the Lyceum.' She made her New York début in the role at the Abbey Theater on 30 April 1894 and played for ten weeks. Hicks was an Ugly Sister. They returned to England in October and she played Thora in *His Excellency*, and in *Papa's Wife* at the Lyric before they both joined George Edwardes at the Gaiety. Her first role at this theatre was to be Bessie Brent in *The Shop Girl*, but she became ill and could not open until April 1895; the play ran 546 performances. At the Gaiety she was also May in *My Girl*, which she described as a melodrama with music, and Dora Wemyss in *The Circus Girl*, which gave her her famous song, 'Just a Little Bit of String'.

By this time she and her husband were very successful, living in style and mixing in fashionable society. More difficult times were ahead, however.

She left during the run of *The Circus Girl* in 1897 when she became pregnant. Unhappily, her son lived only two days, and while she was still convalescing her father was stabbed to death by a mad jealous actor near the Adelphi. Her mother died a few months later. Ellaline returned to the Gaiety and to *The Circus Girl*, which ran for 497 performances altogether. Her last role as a Gaiety girl was Winifred Gray in *The Runaway Girl*, which ran for 593 performances.

She then left Edwardes and musical comedy and went to the impresario Charles Frohman at the Criterion, where in 1899 Ellaline played Mrs Richard Mainwaring, Jr, in *My Daughter-in-Law*, which was a moderate success. Her next play, however, an adaptation from the French called *The Masked Ball*, in which she played Suzanne, was a total failure. The Hicks then embarked on a United States tour of *My Daughter-in-Law*. They returned to the Vaudeville, which was run by Frohman, but in reality Seymour Hicks managed it for the next five years. There in September 1900 she played Josephine Furet in *Self and Lady* and in December was Alice in *Alice in Wonderland*. In April 1901 she was Joan Trevelyan in *Sweet and Twenty*, and their greatest success came at Christmas when she played Bluebell in *Bluebell in Fairyland*.

In September 1902 she played Phoebe Throssel in J. M. Barrie's *Quality Street*, and the production ran for 459 performances. In December 1903 she played in a musical with libretto by Hicks called *The Cherry Girl* — Ellaline was the Queen. Soon she discovered she was again pregnant — and this time she was safely delivered of a daughter, Betty. In 1905 she went on a provincial tour of *The Catch of the Season*, playing Angela.

As well as acting and writing Seymour Hicks was very busy building theatres. The first of these was the Aldwych, which they opened in December 1905 with *Bluebell in Fairyland*. In March Miss Terriss was the Hon. Betty Silverthorne in *The Beauty of Bath* which ran very successfully, transferring in December for the opening of the Hicks Theatre (now called the Globe). It was a full-scale musical comedy and ran 287 nights. Back at the Aldwych in September 1907 she was Peggy Quainton in *The Gay Gordons* and spent most of 1908 touring in that and in *Sweet and Twenty*.

The Hicks entered variety for the first time at the Palace Theatre in December 1908 playing in a sketch called *Fly-by-Night*. At the Hicks Theatre in February 1909 she was the Duc de Richelieu in *The Dashing Little Duke* and at Wyndham's in January 1910 played Lucy Sheridan in *Captain Kidd*. She then undertook a music-hall tour that covered the country, playing in sketches such as

Cook's Man, *The Pink of Perfection* and *A Lady at Large*, mainly with her husband. At the Coliseum in April 1921 she was in a spectacular sketch called *Joan of Arc*, and in May she and Seymour Hicks went to South Africa where they toured the music halls.

They returned to London in October, where at the Coliseum she played in *After the Honeymoon* and in November was in the sketch, *The Slum Angel*. They toured the music halls until July 1913, when once more Ellaline played Ada Ingot in *David Garrick* at the Coliseum. In October she joined her husband on tour to play Josie Richards in *Broadway Jones*, and back at the Coliseum in December she was Mrs Chesson in *Always Tell Your Wife*. *Broadway Jones* was at the Prince of Wales in February 1914, and in December of that year at the Lyric she was Elphin Haye in *The Earl and the Girl*. The Hicks had been in financial difficulties for some time — running the theatres, an extravagant life-style and poor box office had contributed to it — but now the war put the finishing touches and disaster struck. All the theatres were sold as well as Ellaline's jewellery.

They spent Christmas 1914 at the Front in France giving a concert for the troops. At the Comedy Theatre in April 1915 Ellaline Terriss played Hélène de Treville in *Wild Thyme*. They spent the rest of the year touring in variety, and in December 1916 once more played in *Bluebell in Fairyland*, this time at the Prince's Theatre. In 1917 at the Palace she was Peggy Goode in *Cash on Delivery* and she spent 1918 touring as the Wife in *Sleeping Partners*. At the Coliseum in January 1919 she played Josephine Pettigrew in *After the Honeymoon* and toured during 1920 in *Sleeping Partners*.

After a serious illness and surgery, she and her husband went on a tour of Australia in 1924 playing in *The Man in Dress Clothes*, and returned to London to Golders Green in May 1925 where once more she played in *Sleeping Partners*. *The Man in Dress Clothes* was revived at the Lyceum in November 1925, and at the Savoy in July it was *Sleeping Partners* once again. Ellaline Terriss then discovered the cinema and made two films — *Blighty* and *Land of Hope and Glory*.

In April 1927 at the Coliseum she played Lady Mary in *Mint Sauce* and in December that year went with her husband to Canada. She was very keen to retire but at the Lyceum in March 1929 she was once more Germaine in *The Man in Dress Clothes*.

Ellaline did take some years off, and made her final appearance on the stage at the Victoria Palace in May 1935 when she played Mrs Thornton in *The Miracle Man*. Unfortunately it was not a success, but during the time at the Victoria Palace her husband received his knighthood and she became Lady Hicks.

In 1939 they set off to the Middle East, where they entertained troops. They made their way back to South Africa and were marooned there until after the war. They returned to England in 1946. Seymour Hicks died on 6 April 1949; Ellaline Terriss lived on until 16 June 1971, when she died aged 100.

ELLEN TERRY

E llen Alice Terry was born in Coventry on 27 February 1849. Her father and mother, Benjamin and Sarah, were provincial actors, well known and as established as strolling players could hope to be in those times. Ellen Alice was their fourth daughter. The children were expected to go on the stage as soon as possible, and her elder sister Kate had made a name for herself very early in Charles Kean's company. Her mother had moved to London to supervise Kate, taking the younger children with her and leaving Ellen in the North with her father. Father and daughter were together for nearly two years, during which time he educated her in the art of the stage and constantly improved her elocution. She had small parts on stage with her parents, but it was when they all settled in London that she made her début there, at the Princess Theatre on 28 April 1856 as Mamillius in Charles Kean's production of *The Winter's Tale*. That October she played Puck in Kean's *A Midsummer Night's Dream*. Her father decided to start a theatrical company at Ryde in the Isle of Wight, and during the first season there Ellen played in *To Parents and Guardians* and *Boots at the Swan*. She returned to Kean's company at the Princess where she played Fairy Goldenstar at Christmas in the pantomime *The White Cat*, and was then promoted to the part of Dragonetta. In April 1858 she was Karl in *Faust and Marguerite*, and in October played Prince

Arthur in *King John*. In November she was Fleance in *Macbeth* and for Christmas played the Genius of the Jewels in *King o' the Castle*. The Kean management of the Princess Theatre ended in 1859, and at the last performance on 13 June Ellen Terry played Tiger Tom in *If the Cap Fits*. She had been well received by the London critics and public but now she was out of a job. She toured during 1859–60 with her sister Kate, playing Hector Melrose in *Home for the Holidays* and five parts in a sketch called *Distant Relations*.

She was back in London in September 1861 playing Puck once more in *A Midsummer Night's Dream*, but this time it was at the Lyceum. She then spent nearly a year in Madame de Rhona's Royalty Theatre Company where she played Clementine in *Atar Gull*, Letty in *The Governor's Wife*, Mabel in *A Lesson for Husbands*, Florence in *A Chinese Romance* and Louisa Drayton in *Grandfather Whitehead*.

In September 1862 she joined her sister at the Theatre Royal, Bristol, where she played, in repertory, pieces of burlesque, farce and melodrama. At the Theatre Royal in Bath, which was under the same management, she played Titania in *A Midsummer Night's Dream* in March 1863. That same month she went to the Haymarket Theatre to play Hero in *Much Ado About Nothing*, Lady Touchwood in *The Belle's Stratagem* and Gertrude Howard in *The Little Treasure*. In June 1863 she was at the Princess once more, but this time playing Desdemona to Walter Montgomery's Othello. She returned to Bristol in September where she played Isabella in *A Game of Romps*, Flora in *The Duke's Motto*, Nerissa in *The Merchant of Venice*, and Hero once again.

At the Haymarket Theatre in London in October she played Julia in *The Rivals*, Sir Tristram in *King Arthur* and Mary Meredith in Tom Taylor's *Our American Cousin*. It was Tom Taylor who introduced the Terry sisters to the painter George Frederick Watts, who fell in love with Ellen and wanted to paint her forever. He was 47 and she not yet 17 when they married in February 1864; she spent ten months posing for her husband, but then they separated. On 20 June 1866 she made an appearance at a benefit for her sister Kate at the Olympic playing Helen in *The Hunchback*. She also appeared with Kate, who was a big star, in Bristol in March 1867 playing Marion Vernon in *Henry Dunbar*, and at the Adelphi in London in May playing Keziah Mapletoft in *A Sheep in Wolf's Clothing* and Margaret Wentworth in *Henry Dunbar*. At the Holborn Theatre in June that year she was Madeline in Tom Taylor's *The Antipodes* but this was a failure. She went on her sister's farewell tour during September and October playing Hero in *Much Ado About Nothing*, Helen in *The Hunchback*, and Ann Carew in *A Sheep in Wolf's Clothing*. At the new Queen's Theatre in Long Acre in October 1867 she was Rose de Beaurepaire in *The Double Marriage* and in November played Mrs Mildmay in *Still Waters Run Deep*.

On 26 December 1867 she acted with Henry Irving for the first time when at the Queen's she played Katharina to his Petruchio in a shortened version of *The Taming of the Shrew*. The *Times* reported that her concluding speech of capitulation was 'a model of quiet elocution, so sensibly, so feelingly, and with so unequivocal an appearance of moral conviction is it delivered'. In February 1869 she played Katherine in *A Household Fairy*, a comedy by Francis Talfourd. But at this time in her life Ellen Terry was not interested in the theatre. She was in love, and interested in only one thing — being with Edwin Godwin, who when she had first met him in Bristol was an architect but by this time — à la William Morris — was an artist concerned with total environment. Ellen was happy to be involved with her home and children and felt no yearning for the stage, but as Godwin's behaviour became more erratic she began to worry about her children's future. When quite by accident she met the playwright and impresario Charles Reade and he invited her back to the stage — for the sum of £40 a week — she took the opportunity. She reappeared at the Queen's Theatre on 28 February 1874 when she took over the part of Philippa Chester from Mrs John Wood in Reade's *The Wandering Heir*. She toured with Reade's company in that part, also playing Susan Merton in *It's Never Too Late to Mend* and Helen Rolleston in *Our Seamen*. She then went to the Crystal Palace with Charles Wyndham, playing Volante in *The Honeymoon* and Kate Hardcastle in *She Stoops to Conquer*.

In April 1875 she joined the Bancrofts at the Prince of Wales where she was a great success as Portia in *The Merchant of Venice*. Godwin was the architectural consultant on the production. Alice Comyns Carr reported on Terry's performance: 'What Ellen established as the characteristic of her performance in an age when pompous, rhetorical, windy and monotonous acting was still the rule, was an utter naturalness of manner which came directly from her own essential nature. As soon as she put her foot on the stage she did not assume artificial limbs and an artificial voice — she intensified by careful study and the thoughtful invention of ''business'' her own natural reaction to whatever part she was playing. Her high spirits led her to find her fullest realization in comedy; her own suffering led her to understand the human aspect of pathos and compassion.' And Joseph Knight wrote: 'More adequate expression has seldom been given to the light-heartedness of maidenhood, the perplexities and hesitations of love ... The famous speech on mercy assumed new beauties from a correct and exquisite delivery ...' Also at the Prince of Wales, she played Clara Douglas in *Money*, Mabel Vane in *Masks and Faces*, and Blanche Haye in *Ours*. At the Princess in August 1875 she was Pauline in *The Lady of Lyons*.

In November 1876 she joined John Hare at the Court where she played Kate Hungerford in *Brothers*, Lilian in *New Men and Old Acres*, Lady Juliet in *The House of Darnley*, Mrs Merryweather in *Victims* and the title role in *Olivia*. She and Godwin had finally parted in November 1875. One of the actors at the Court with Ellen Terry was Charles Wardell (whose stage name was Charles Kelly), and in 1877 she married him, though the marriage broke up in 1881. At the Gaiety Theatre in 1877 Ellen Terry played Lady Teazle in *The School for Scandal*, and in August 1878 she toured with her husband in *New Men and Old Acres*, *All Is Vanity* and *Dora*.

On 30 December 1878 Ellen Terry began what was to become one of the theatre's most famous and successful partnerships when she played Ophelia to Henry Irving's Hamlet at the Lyceum. It was a great success. Joseph Knight wrote that she was '... picturesque, tender and womanly throughout'. That season she was also in *The Lady of Lyons, Eugene Aram*, and played Queen Henrietta Maria in *Charles I*. She spent summer 1879 touring with her husband, and returned to the Lyceum where she played Portia in *The Merchant of Venice*. It ran 250 nights. Henry James, however, was not unduly impressed with her performance and reported: 'Her manner of dealing with the delightful speeches of Portia with all their play of irony, of wit and temper, savours to put it harshly of the schoolgirlish. We have ventured to say that her comprehension of a character is sometimes weak, and may illustrate it by a reference to her whole handling of this same rich opportunity. Miss Terry's mistress of Belmont giggles too much, plays too much with her fingers, is too free and familiar, too osculatory in her relations with Bassanio.' She toured in autumn 1880 playing Beatrice in *Much Ado About Nothing* for the first time. She then returned to the Lyceum, where she played Iolanthe on 20 May.

In 1881 she was Camma in Tennyson's *The Cup*, Letitia Hardy in *The Belle's Stratagem* and Desdemona with Irving and Booth in *Othello*. The following year at the Lyceum, Ellen Terry was Juliet while Irving was Romeo. The production

was beautiful, but they were both far too old. She continued her support of Irving playing Beatrice in *Much Ado About Nothing* and Viola in *Twelfth Night*. Beatrice was one of Terry's best parts and received unanimous praise from the critics. It ran from October 1882 until June 1883.

In autumn 1883 Irving took his Lyceum company to America where on 31 October Ellen Terry made her New York début (she made ten United States tours altogether) at the Star Theater playing Queen Henrietta in *Charles I*. The company also played *The Bells, The Belle's Stratagem, Richard II, The Lyons Mail, Louis XI* and *The Merchant of Venice*. Of Terry's Portia, William Winter wrote: 'When Ellen Terry embodied Portia — in Henry Irving's magnificent revival of *The Merchant of Venice* — the essential womanliness of that character was for the first time in the modern theatre adequately interpreted and conveyed. Upon many playgoing observers indeed the wonderful wealth of beauty that is in the part — its winsome grace, its incessant sparkle, its piquant as well as luscious sweetness, its impetuous ardour, its enchantment of physical equally with emotional condition, its august morality, its perfect candour, and its noble passion — came as a surprise ... The stage Portia of the past has usually been a didactic lady, self-contained, formal, conventional and oratorical. Ellen Terry came, and Portia was figured exactly as she lives in the pages of Shakespeare — an imperial and yet an enchanting woman, dazzling in her beauty, royal in her dignity, as ardent in temperament as she is fine in brain and various and splendid in personal peculiarities and feminine charm ... Ellen Terry's achievement was a complete vindication of the high view that Shakespearian study has always taken of that character ...'

During the tour, which was most profitable, the company also went to Baltimore and Chicago. They returned to the Lyceum for three months before embarking on their second American tour, which ran from September 1884 to early 1885. The 1885 season at the Lyceum opened with *Hamlet* and then in May, Ellen Terry played the title role in *Olivia*. In December she was Margaret in *Faust*. (It was to become one of her favourite parts and had a long run spanning two seasons.) During the winter of 1887–88 the company made a provincial tour of Britain and their third American tour, which included seasons in New York, Philadelphia, Chicago and Boston.

In December 1888, back at the Lyceum, Irving played Macbeth and Ellen Terry was his Lady. *The Stage* reported: 'It is difficult to speak of the Lady Macbeth of Miss Terry. So perfect has she been in everything else at the Lyceum that we are loath to differ from her admirers upon the merits of a performance that has evidently been the outcome of great labour and perseverance. Miss Terry has based her entire reading of the character upon the supposition that Macbeth is loved by his wife, that all her evil promptings are but the outcome of her loving thought for his future; and it must be owned that Miss Terry in following out this theory plays the part in a generally consistent manner. But the question arises, did such a love exist? ... Miss Terry's performance is most interesting, graceful, and at times most poetical, but it does not suggest the author's creation. The sleep-walking scene is full of charm by reason of Miss Terry's personality. She looks like a beautiful picture, the conception of a poetic mind. But her pure white clinging garments and pain-strained face call for admiration rather than pity and awe.'

In September 1890 Ellen Terry played Catherine Duval in *The Dead Heart* and the following September introduced Lucy Ashton in *Ravenswood*. American tours with Irving intervened and throughout the rest of the partnership Terry continued to introduce new roles into her repertoire, which included Queen Katherine in *Henry VIII* (January 1892), Cordelia in *King Lear* (November 1892), Rosamund in *Becket* (February 1893), Guinevere in *King Arthur* (January 1895), Imogen in *Cymbeline* (September 1896), the title role in *Madame sans gêne* (April 1897), Catherine in *Peter the Great* (January 1898), the Hon. Sylvia Wynford in *The Medicine Man* (May 1898), Clarisse in *Robespierre* (April 1899) and Volumnia in *Coriolanus* (April 1901).

Throughout their partnership there was speculation over whether Irving and Terry were lovers. That they were in love was never in doubt, but of whether they were lovers there has been no consensus. Irving lost the Lyceum in 1902 and Terry was with him at the final performance of *The Merchant of Venice* on 19 July. They had one final season together in Bristol that December. Meanwhile Ellen Terry had joined Beerbohm Tree and Mrs Kendal at the His Majesty's in June, where she played Mistress Page in Tree's Coronation revival of *The Merry Wives of Windsor*. On 15 April 1903 she began management of the Imperial Theatre where she produced *The Vikings* and revived *Much Ado About Nothing*.

On 14 July 1903 Ellen Terry acted for the last time with Henry Irving when she played Portia in an all-star revival of *The Merchant of Venice* at Drury Lane in aid of the Actors' Benevolent Fund. When he was taken ill two years later in Wolverhampton she rushed to his side to help, but there was a new woman in his life and she found him cool.

Ellen Terry toured for a while, adding *The Mistress of Robes*, *The Good Hope* and *Eriksson's Wife* to her repertoire. In 1905 Charles Frohman brought her to the Duke of York's Theatre to play Alice Gray in J. M. Barrie's *Alice-Sit-by-the-Fire*. She subsequently toured the provinces and the United States in this play. Max Beerbohm did not think it was the right vehicle for her: ' ... Miss Terry is really too exuberant, too impulsive. The play is not big enough for her ... One longs for Shakespeare, who, alone among dramatists, can stand up to her; and one wishes the theatre itself were bigger — better proportioned to the wildly ample sweep of her method.'

Ellen Terry and George Bernard Shaw had been corresponding lovingly for many years, though they had never met. He wrote the part of Lady Cicely Waynflete in *Captain Brassbound's Conversion* for her, and indeed based the character on the personality she had revealed in her letters. They met only briefly during the rehearsals, and found that they could not sustain face to face the rapport that they had on paper. *Captain Brassbound's Conversion* opened at the Court Theatre in March 1906, and Beerbohm reported: 'Miss Ellen Terry was duly vivacious last Tuesday. But she was, also, very nervous. She was often at a loss when it was most necessary that she should take her cue instantly. And, in the relief of having remembered her cue, she often spoke with disastrous emphasis. I should not like those of the rising generation who saw the performance to imagine that Miss Terry was within measurable distance of her best ...'

On 27 April, in celebration of her stage jubilee, she appeared at His Majesty's Theatre as Mistress Page in *The Merry Wives of Windsor*. On the following afternoon she was at the Adelphi as Francesca in *Measure for Measure*, and in the evening resumed her part in the Shaw play at the Court. The ticket queues for each of her performances stretched for blocks. As tribute to her, on 12 June a special performance was mounted at Drury Lane in which all the notable personages of the stage appeared, including Caruso, Lillie Langtry, the Vanbrughs, Mrs Patrick Campbell and Charles Wyndham. Gertie Miller was there, and Rejane and Beerbohm Tree and even Duse.

With her in the cast of the Shaw play at the Court, which continued through all the celebrations, was a young American actor, James Usselmann, who used the stage name James Carew. According to Shaw, Terry took one look at this 36-year-old man (she was 59) and decided to marry him. Terry was by this time living near

Tenterden in Kent, with her now grown and decidedly jealous daughter Edith in a house nearby. She married James Carew in 1907 during the American tour of *Captain Brassbound's Conversion*; but what with Edith's jealousy and his natural youth, Mr Carew became more trouble than he was worth and was soon amicably despatched. In 1908 Ellen Terry was Elizabeth of York in *Henry of Lancaster*, and at His Majesty's in May she played Mistress Page once more in *The Merry Wives of Windsor*. That year, too, she played Aunt Imogen in Graham Robertson's *Pinkie and the Fairies* for Christmas.

In October 1910 Terry set out on an American tour with a series of lectures on Shakespeare's heroines. She returned to England to the Kingsway in May 1911 as Nell Gwynn in *The First Actress*. Also that month, she gave her lectures at the Haymarket. For a gala performance in June at His Majesty's she was once more Mistress Page and then resumed her lectures, this time at the Savoy. She played Kniertje in *The Good Hope* at the King's Hall, Covent Garden, in November 1912, and then with the Pioneer Players at the Savoy Theatre in January 1914 was the Abbess in *Paphnutius*. She was, however, according to her biographer Roger Manvell, living on past glories. Audiences came to see the memories that she revived or the legend rather than the actual performance.

She spent 1914 touring and lecturing in Australia and America; when she returned home in July 1915 she appeared at the Haymarket in a children's play, *The Princess and the Pea*. She discovered the cinema and began filming, in all making five films.

In 1917 Ellen Terry went on the variety stage with an excerpt from *The Merry Wives of Windsor* and toured the halls. She was at the Coliseum in February 1918 in the trial scene from *The Merchant of Venice*. At the Lyric Theatre in April 1919 she played the Nurse in *Romeo and Juliet* and then for Christmas 1920 at the Everyman Theatre in Hampstead she read the prologue to an old English nativity play. After that her performances were only intermittent and for charity. At the Palace Theatre in March 1922 she was Mrs Long in *Pride and Prejudice* and in June played the Old Woman in *The Shoe*. That year she received an honorary doctorate from St Andrew's University. In 1925 she was created a dame, and that year she made her last appearance on stage when she played Susan Wildersham at the Lyric, Hammersmith, in Walter de la Mare's *Crossings*.

Ellen Terry had a stroke early in July 1928, and died on 28 July at Smallhythe. Her funeral was in the village church, and when the procession moved on to London to Golders Green for cremation people lined the route, throwing bouquets of flowers. Her ashes are kept at St Paul's in Covent Garden, and her cottage in Kent is a theatrical museum.
See photograph opposite page 375.

SYBIL THORNDIKE

A star (as A. P. Herbert once said) not only of the stage but of life, Agnes Sybil Thorndike was born on 24 October 1882 at Gainsborough in Lincolnshire. Like Olivier she was a clergyman's child: the eldest of the four children of the Rev. Arthur Thorndike and his wife Agnes (Bowers). The others were Russell and Eileen and Frank, all of whom went into the theatre for some time as, later, did all four of Sybil's own children and many of her grandchildren. Sybil was the only one to be born in Lincolnshire; before she was two, her father was appointed a minor canon of Rochester Cathedral and the family moved to Kent where they stayed throughout the rest of her childhood. Ruthless in her pursuit of amateur theatricals, Sybil made her parlour début at the age of four, and within three years was regularly performing for family and cathedral friends in Rochester a melodrama called *The Dentist's Cure* and subtitled *Saw Their Silly Heads Off* (after *Sweeney Todd*) which she and Russell had written and produced—the beginnings, perhaps, of a fascination with Grand Guignol which was to lead to her celebrated seasons at the Little Theatre in the 1920s.

Around the time of Sybil's tenth birthday, her father was offered the living of the nearby St Margaret's parish and the family moved from Minor Canon Row (immortalized by Dickens in *Edwin Drood*) to more spacious vicarage quarters. By now there was little doubt that Sybil would be going into public performance of one kind or another, although it might well have been musical rather than dramatic since her mother was an excellent pianist. But Sybil suffered from piano cramp, and although she persevered for a while with the dogged tenacity that was already a hallmark of her personality, it was soon clear that she would need another career.

Mrs Thorndike, remembering Sybil's interest in Kentish village plays, arranged for her to audition for Charles Wyndham; on the morning of the arranged meeting, however, Sybil awoke feeling violently sick, and her father decided it was a warning from God about life on the wicked stage. Instead, Sybil finished her schooling locally (by now her father had taken up the plum living of the diocese at Aylesford, 'the little cathedral of Kent') but then, undeterred by her earlier sickness, went again to London, this time to audition for Ben Greet, who agreed that she should join his company on 24 August 1904 as they set off to tour America; in the preceding weeks she was to walk on with the company during a summer season at Cambridge where she made her professional début in the grounds of Downing College on 14 June as Palmis in *The Palace of Truth*.

The following two years were spent largely with Greet in America, touring the length and breadth of the country in often rough conditions playing a clutch of lesser roles (including 'Lucianus nephew to the King' in the Play scene of *Hamlet* and Ceres in the masque of *The Tempest*) as well as stepping into the breach frequently enough for actresses higher up the company afflicted by the rigours of primitive touring schedules and appalling transport. Thus by 1907 Sybil had played 112 parts in all for Greet on the road, ranging from Viola, Helena, Gertrude and Rosalind, to Ophelia, Nerissa and (Kansas City, 1905) Everyman. It was a baptism of fire, but on those American tours Sybil, still in her twenties, learnt the elements of her trade, of which the most important remained sheer survival.

On her final return to London in 1907 she landed a Sunday-night job with the Play Actors' Society as an American girl in a farce called *The Marquis*; by one of those accidental miracles of which theatrical biographies are largely composed, Bernard Shaw was in front for the play's sole performance, and next morning asked Sybil if she would be willing to understudy Ellen O'Malley in a revival of *Candida* for Miss Horniman. They were to play a split week in Belfast, the first three evenings being taken up with Shaw's *Widower's Houses* in which Sybil noticed, playing Trench, 'a young man called Lewis Casson'.

That one Belfast week in the spring of 1908 was to condition the remaining seventy years of Sybil's public and private life; it established an alliance with Shaw (who in 1923 was to write *Saint*

Joan for her) and with Casson, whom Sybil married the Christmas after that first meeting and with whom she was to celebrate a diamond wedding anniversary in 1968, by which time she was over 80 and he over 90.

At the time of her wedding Sybil was a permanent member of Miss Horniman's pioneering repertory company at the Gaiety, Manchester; the following year she joined the Charles Frohman company at the Duke of York's in London, before returning briefly to America to tour and appear on Broadway as Emily Chapman in W. Somerset Maugham's *Smith*. Then, in June 1912, she returned to the Gaiety, Manchester, to play Beatrice in Stanley Houghton's *Hindle Wakes*, a major play of the 'northern' school of semi-documentary dramas, and until the outbreak of the First World War she was to remain a leading player for Miss Horniman's company in Manchester and on their occasional London visits with productions of which Lewis Casson was, increasingly, the director.

By now the Cassons had three children, born to Sybil during short breaks from repertory work at the Gaiety; when war was declared Lewis at once joined the army and Sybil moved the rest of the family down to London where she had been offered a season at the Old Vic by Lilian Baylis. In the event, she was to stay at the Vic for four years, playing Rosalind, Lady Macbeth, Portia, Beatrice, Imogen, Ophelia, the Fool in *King Lear* (male actors being hard to come by in wartime), Kate Hardcastle and Lydia Languish and Lady Teazle among a vast range of other and sometimes lesser roles: 'Miss Thorndike will be a great actress,' wrote a *Sunday Times* critic, ' so long as she learns to keep her hands beneath her shoulders.' But those wartime seasons at the Vic, some of them played during the earliest air raids, forged and fired and confirmed for London audiences the blazing talent that was soon to hallmark her St Joan.

But first came the Greeks: Sybil played Hecuba in Gilbert Murray's translation of the Euripides *Trojan Women* for a series of special matinées at the Vic in October 1919; by March 1920 she was at the Holborn Empire (though again for matinées only) as Hecuba and Medea, performances to which she would also add Candida for good measure. Then came a two-year run at the Little Theatre in a series of Grand Guignol melodramas which was something of a family concern: Sybil and her brother Russell would co-star with Lewis (who also directed) in plays like *The Hound of Death*, *The Kill* and *Fear*, in which they were gainfully employed scaring the living daylights out of theatregoers, never more so than in *The Old Ladies* where Sybil had her eyes gouged out by the knitting needles of the crazed fellow-inmates of an asylum.

But as the vogue for horror drew to a close, the Cassons themselves set up in management of the New Theatre; they opened with *The Cenci*, and at one of its matinées Sybil was seen by Bernard Shaw who on returning home said to his wife, 'I have found my Joan.'

The play he then wrote for Sybil opened at the New Theatre in March 1924, and marked the early but unchallenged climax of her career; as she herself said, looking back on it fifty years later, 'I felt that I never wanted to do anything else, that I'd reached something I could never reach again, and I was just so grateful that the audience was there night after night to see me do it.'

Saint Joan initially ran 244 performances, and Sybil was to go on reviving it at regular intervals at home and abroad until her final performance of the role in March 1941. Throughout the late 1920s and 1930s she also did a great deal of other classical and modern work, often under her husband's direction, and ranging from *Jane Clegg*, through Emilia to Robeson's 1930 *Othello*, to Miss Moffat in Emlyn Williams' 1938 *The Corn Is Green*.

As the Second World War started, the Cassons toured the Welsh mining villages and towns, bringing *Macbeth* and *Medea* and *Candida* to audiences who had often never seen them before, and in 1944 Sybil joined the legendary Olivier–Richardson Old Vic season at the New, playing Margaret to Olivier's Richard III and Aase to Richardson's Peer Gynt as well as the Nurse in *Uncle Vanya* and, in 1946, Jocasta in *Oedipus Rex*, among many other roles.

Then began a gentle post-war decline; the great years of Shaw and the Greeks and Miss Horniman all belonged to a lost pre-war world; Sybil was already in her early sixties and, though still indefatigable, now had to spend her time in minor West End comedies or guest-starring in films. The 1950s brought her considerable successes (*Waters of the Moon, A Day by the Sea*) in London but it was now only on long and gruelling tours of Australia and South Africa that the Cassons were to be seen in their more classical work.

But in 1963, when Olivier was forming at Chichester the company he would take with him to open the National Theatre at the Old Vic, both Cassons were in his *Uncle Vanya* again, Sybil now playing the old nurse Marina. From that, as if to prove her now septuagenarian versatility and vitality, she went into a short-lived musical of *Vanity Fair* (1962) murmuring, 'Never be sorry to attempt something new — never, never, never.'

But the stage roles now were fewer and further between, and in 1966 the Cassons made their farewell appearance in London with a revival of *Arsenic and Old Lace*. Then came the diamond wedding and the opening of the Thorndike Theatre in Leatherhead, where she was to make her final appearance in October 1969, six months after the death of her beloved Lewis. When, in 1970, she was made a Companion of Honour, the highest award the Crown can give an actress, it seemed only right and proper. Then, on 9 June 1976, after two heart attacks within four days, Sybil Thorndike died at her flat in Swan Court, Chelsea. 'The most loved actress since Ellen Terry,' said John Gielgud at her Westminster Abbey memorial service, and one might add also the best.

HERBERT BEERBOHM TREE

A notable character actor both on and off the stage, Herbert Beerbohm was born in London on 17 December 1853. His father Julius was of Lithuanian descent, and came to England (by way of Paris) where he became a grain merchant and father of nine. Herbert went to school in England and at Schnepfeuthal in the Thuringian Mountains in Germany; when he returned to England he joined his father's business but found no joy in it. He was a natural mimic and spent his spare time in amateur dramatics. While still an amateur he played Chille Talma Dufard in *The First Night* at the Duke's Theatre, Holborn, in June 1876 and also at the Opéra-Comique in April 1877. At the Olympic in February 1878 he was David in *Woodcock's Little Game*. That same month at the Globe Theatre for charity he was Grimaldi in *The Life of an Actress* and this performance led to an offer of a short touring job. He turned professional, took the stage name of Beerbohm Tree and toured as Colonel Challice in *Alone*, Admiral Kingston in *Naval Engagements*, and in *Milky White*. In June 1878 he was at the Old Park Theatre in Camden Town playing Lord Ingleborough in *Engineering*, and was then taken on by Henry Neville at the Olympic Theatre to play character roles. In July he was the French Grandfather (at the age of 25) in *A Congress at Paris*, and Laffleur in *The Two Orphans* in September. In November he was in *A Republican Marriage* and in December played Daniel Gunter in *Jolliboys Woes*. In May 1879 Tree went to the Criterion, where he played Algernon Wrigglesworth in *Campaigning*, and then at the Garrick Theatre in Leman Street in June 1879 had a great success as Bonneteau in *A Cruise to China* and in *M.D.* At the end of 1879 he was touring as the wicked old rake Marquis de Pontsable in Offenbach's comic opera, *Madame Favart*. He returned to London in April 1880, where at the Prince of Wales Theatre in Tottenham Street he played Prince Maleotti in *Forget-Me-Not* with Genevieve Ward. The following month he played Mont Prade in a French production of *L'Aventurière*. For a special matinée at the Imperial Theatre on 3 July 1880 he was Sir Andrew Aguecheek in *Twelfth Night*.

In November 1880 Beerbohm Tree was hired by Charles Wyndham for the Criterion, where he played Scott Ramsey in *Where's the Cat?* In January the following year at the Criterion he was the Marquis de Château-Laroche in *Brave Hearts*, and then had a great success in May as Lambert Steyke in *The Colonel* at the Prince of Wales and then on tour. *The Colonel* lasted him until June 1882, during which time he played a number of special matinées.

In June 1882 at the Theatre Royal, Brighton, he played Solon Trippetow in *The Mulberry Bush*, which was retitled *Little Miss Muffet* when it came to the Criterion in September. At the Adelphi in March 1883 he was James Greene in *Storm Beaten*. That same month at the Olympic he played Lord Boodle in *A Great Catch*. More matinées followed. At the Theatre Royal in Brighton in May he was Digby Grant in *Two Roses*, and that same month he played William Roffy in *Knowledge* back at the Gaiety, where he also played Malvolio in *Twelfth Night*. At the Crystal Palace in July he was John Drummond in *Blow for Blow*.

That year he found time to marry Maud Holt, an aspiring actress who had come to him for advice. At first their married life was rather a struggle, but their financial problems were solved when at the Globe Theatre in September he played Prince Borowski in Sydney Grundy's *The Glass of Fashion*. He then went to the Prince of Wales Theatre and in January 1884 played Chrysal in a revival of *The Palace of Truth*; in March there he was Philip Dunkley in *Breaking a Butterfly*. That same month he played Herbert in his own one-act play, *Six and Eightpence*, and at the end of that

month had an enormous success as the Rev. Robert Spalding in *The Private Secretary*. He topped that success with his next role, in May 1884, as Paolo Macari in *Called Back*, which ran for a year. He banished the boredom of a long run by playing in many special matinées during that time.

At the Court Theatre in August 1885 he took over the role of Mr Poskett from Arthur Cecil in Pinero's *The Magistrate*. In September he went to the Haymarket, where he played Sir Mervyn Ferrand in *Dark Days*. In January the following year, still at the Haymarket, he played Prince Zabouroll in *Nadjesda* and the next month was Herr Slowitz in *A Woman of the World*. That same month he played Cheviot Hill in *Engaged*, and in April was Baron Hargeld in *Jim the Penman* which ran until January 1887, when he opened as Stephen Cudlit in *Hard Hit*.

Beerbohm Tree went into management at the Comedy Theatre in April 1887, where he played Paul Demetrius in *The Red Lamp*. This ran 185 performances at the Comedy, and then he took on the Haymarket, where he rearranged the seating and installed electricity, transferring *The Red Lamp* there on 15 September. It was the beginning of his ten-year reign at the Haymarket as actor—manager. In his first year there he played the poet Gringoire in *The Ballad Monger*, Heinrich Borgfeldt in *Partners* (January 1888), Vincent in *Incognito* (January 1888), Iago in the third act of *Othello* (March 1888), Narcisse Rameau in *The Pompadour* (March 1888) and Mr Wilding in Haddon Chambers' *Captain Swift* (June 1888). In January 1889 he produced his first Shakespeare at the Haymarket, *The Merry Wives of Windsor*, in which he played Falstaff; one critic reported: '. . . no actor has ever leered more naturally, or has expressed the dominant desire in his mind by facial expression more strikingly than does this latest Falstaff.' In April he was Matthew Ruddick in *Wealth*, and in September played both Lucien Laroque and Luversan in *A Man's Shadow*. He played the title role in *King John* at a Crystal Palace matinée in September, and at the Haymarket the following April had another enormous success as the Abbé Dubois in Sydney Grundy's *Village Priest*. In October 1890 at the Crystal Palace he was Sir Peter Teazle in *The School for Scandal*, and at the Haymarket in November played the title role in Henley and Stevenson's *Beau Austin*. He then mounted some revivals and in January 1891 opened as the Duke of Guisebury in Henry Arthur Jones' *The Dancing Girl*, which gave him his longest run yet at the Haymarket. He and his actress wife were by this time enjoying fashionable society.

He toured the provinces in autumn 1892, and

while at the Theatre Royal, Manchester, in September played Hamlet for the first time. He introduced it to London at the Haymarket in January 1893, where it played to great success and controversy. W. S. Gilbert said it was 'funny without being vulgar'. During 1893 at the Haymarket he was Issachar in *Hypatia*, Lord Illingworth in Wilde's *A Woman of No Importance*, Dr Thomas Stockmann in *An Enemy of the People*, and the Devil in *The Tempter*. During the following year he played Philip Woodville in *The Charlatan*, the King in *Once Upon a Time*, his own adaptation from the German, Sir Philip Marchant in *A Bunch of Violets*, Kenyon Wargrave in *A Modern Eve*, and Harold Wynn in *John-a-Dreams*.

Herbert Beerbohm Tree set out on his first American tour in 1895 and made his New York début at the Abbey Theater on 28 January when he played Demetrius in *The Red Lamp*. In April he returned to the Haymarket, where he revived *John-a-Dreams*, and in May played Boris Ipanoff in a revival of *Fedora*. On his autumn tour of the provinces he introduced du Maurier's *Trilby*, in which he played Svengali, for the first time at the Theatre Royal in Manchester on 7 September. The following month he introduced it to London and it was an enormous success — so successful in fact that on the proceeds Tree decided to build himself a new theatre across the road from the Haymarket. In 1896 he played matinées of *Henry IV*, in which he took the part of Hotspur and was scorned by the critics, though the public always liked him. He was a great admirer of Shakespeare and never hesitated to play the major roles, though it was as a character actor that he was at his best. Sir George Arthur explained: 'Tree's flair for make-up was truly remarkable, far exceeding that of any other actor; he could alter the shape of his head as easily as he could rearrange his features, but unfortunately he could not remodel his hands, which were the weak part of his physique. Although the cares of production might cause him to be a little vague about his words on a first night, it was always evident that word-perfect or not, he not only looked but really felt the character he was assuming.'

He went on another American tour in 1896 but the takings were disappointing. He was now in financial trouble, as the new theatre (called Her Majesty's) was costing more than he had bargained for. He opened it on 28 April 1897 with Gilbert Parker's *The Seats of the Mighty*, in which he played Tinoir Doltaire and which he had previously produced in New York. It was a disaster, and he quickly revived his more successful productions including *The Silver Key* in which he played the Duc de Richelieu. In November he was Petruchio

in *The Taming of the Shrew*, and the following January played Mark Antony in *Julius Caesar*, which put him back into profit. In June he played Robin in *Ragged Robin* and in November was d'Artagnan in *The Musketeers*. The following year he played Colonel Stacey Carnac in *Carnac Sahib* and the title role in *King John*.

Tree opened 1900 with a production of *A Midsummer Night's Dream* in which he played Bottom. Tree was never noted for his subtlety, and in the case of stage pictures he left nothing to the imagination — his stage was populated with real animals and real trees. His rehearsals were usually chaos in which he was either vague or feigned vagueness. Depending on whose memoirs you read he was funny, lovable and caring but eccentric, or a boorish, bullying egomaniac; he remained as controversial as his productions. In May 1900 he was Rip in *Rip Van Winkle*, and in October played the name part in *Herod*. The following year the theatre became His Majesty's on the accession of King Edward, and Tree played Malvolio in *Twelfth Night*, Robert Macaire in *Macaire*, and Count d'Orsay in *The Last of the Dandies*. In February 1902 he played Ulysses, and in June for his Coronation production was once more Falstaff in *The Merry Wives of Windsor*, with Ellen Terry and Mrs Kendal. In October he played Baron Bonelly in *The Eternal City*, and the following February was Prince Dmitri Nehludoff in *Resurrection*. In May 1903 he had what he termed his greatest failure when he played Roger Martens in *The Gordian Knot*, and the following month he was Austin Limmason in *The Man Who Was*. In September he played the title role in his elaborate production of Shakespeare's *Richard II*, and he finished the year as Zakkuri in *The Darling of the Gods*.

In 1904 Tree established the Academy of Dramatic Art in Gower Street, which he then handed over to a governing body to run. That same year he mounted a production of *The Tempest* which included the usual elaborate scenery, and real water, and was termed by most critics a demeaning of Shakespeare that put the bard on the same level as a Christmas pantomime. Tree played Caliban and the audiences loved it, though *Blackwood's Magazine* complained: 'The play which now enthrals the uncritical audience is Shakespeare's only in name and title. The whole frame and fabric of the drama are misinformed. Shakespeare, for reasons which doubtless appeared excellent to him, composed *The Tempest* in five acts. This arrangement does not commend itself to Mr Tree, who ruthlessly cuts it down to three.'

In January 1905 his Benedick, in an equally lavish *Much Ado About Nothing*, was a failure but he followed it with two of his biggest successes. In May he played Isidore Izard in Grundy's *Business Is Business*, and in July was Fagin in an adaptation of Dickens' *Oliver Twist*.

The following January he mounted a spectacular version of Stephen Phillips' *Nero* in which he played the title role, but the lead part was Agrippina, played by his wife. His next big role was in May when he had the title role in *Colonel Newcombe*. In December he played Mark Antony in *Antony and Cleopatra* and in March 1907 was Arthur Blair-Woldingham in *The Van Dyck*.

He opened as John Jasper in *The Mystery of Edwin Drood* in January 1908 and in February was Gaston de Nerac in *The Beloved Vagabond*. In April he was Shylock in *The Merchant of Venice*, but although this was one of his better impersonations he suffered by comparison with Henry Irving, whose party-piece it was. In September he was Mephistopheles in *Faust*, and the following April once more played Sir Peter Teazle in *The School for Scandal*. Herbert Beerbohm Tree was knighted in the Birthday Honours of 1909, and that September played the priest in *False Gods*. He finished the year as the composer in *Beethoven*.

He played the title role in *The O'Flynn* in February 1910 and then took on the part of Cardinal Wolsey in *Henry VIII* in September. The following September he was Macbeth, but as Hesketh Pearson wrote: 'He had an odd personality, quite unfitted to heroic parts, a curious throaty delivery which prevented him from speaking blank verse naturally and rather bizarre gestures, more in tune with burlesque than with poetry.' In November he was Count Frithiof in *The War God*, and the following April was a rather curious Othello. He mounted a Shakespeare Festival at His Majesty's during May and June 1912, when he revived *The Merchant of Venice*, *Twelfth Night*, *Henry VIII* and *The Merry Wives of Windsor*; in June he also revived *Oliver Twist*.

He had another failure in March 1913 when he played Derek Arden in *The Happy Island*, and the following month quickly revived *The School for Scandal*. In May he played M. Jourdain in *The Perfect Gentleman*, and in June had another Shakespeare Festival during which he played Mercutio for the first time.

In aid of the King George Pension Fund, in

June 1913 at the St James's, Tree played Sir Harcourt Courtly in an all-star production of *London Assurance*. Back at His Majesty's in September he was Jacob in *Joseph and His Brethren*, and in January 1914 he revived *The Darling of the Gods*.

Although George Bernard Shaw often criticized Tree for vulgarity, it was to him that he brought his *Pygmalion*, and after many stormy rehearsals and rows between the author, Tree and his Eliza, Mrs Patrick Campbell, the play opened on 11 April 1914, to great acclaim and very good box office.

For the King George Pension Fund that year he was Gaffer Pottle in *The Silver King*. In August he played the title role in a revival of *Drake*, when all the profits went to war charities. That November he revived *Henry IV*, and in December played Wilkins Micawber and Dan Peggotty in an adaptation of *David Copperfield*. The 1915 production for the fund was at Covent Garden, and once more Tree played Peter Teazle in *The School for Scandal*. He revived *Oliver Twist* at His Majesty's in April and in May played the Marquis de Sévigné in *The Right to Kill*. In July he was Cardinal Wolsey in an all-star revival of *Henry VIII* for charity, and then, with *Chu-Chin-Chow* running profitably at his theatre, Tree went to Hollywood to do some filming. He made his final tour of the United States in 1916. One of the plays he presented during this tour was *Henry VIII*, and John Ranken Towse wrote in *Nation*: 'The production of *Henry VIII* which Sir Herbert Beerbohm Tree has transferred from His Majesty's Theatre in London, to the New Amsterdam Theater in New York, will give more satisfaction to the lovers of spectacle than to students of the acted drama. To the former it will be an unalloyed delight, to the latter a notably brilliant, imposing, realistic but somewhat disappointing show. It is an artistic and antiquarian rather than a histrionic triumph; is, in short, more of a production than a performance.' And that really summed up the story of his life. In 1917 he returned to England, where he had a cottage in Birchington, on the Kent coast. He fell down the stairs there on 16 June, injuring his knee; the subsequent operation was a success, but when a blood clot struck, the patient died suddenly, on 2 July 1917, aged 64.
See photograph opposite page 390.

DOROTHY TUTIN

Dorothy Tutin was born in London on 8 April 1930, daughter of a naval architect. She went to St Catherine's School in Bramley, Surrey, leaving when she was 15 to study music. She spent a year studying the piano and the flute and singing, but decided that she was not talented enough. Her parents persuaded her to go to RADA.

Her first stage appearance was at the club theatre, The Boltons, where in September 1949 she played Princess Margaret of England in *The Thistle and the Rose*. She joined the Bristol Old Vic Company in January 1950, where among other parts she played Phoebe in *As You Like It*, Anni in *Captain Carvallo* and Belinda in *The Provok'd Wife*. She returned to London for the Old Vic's 1950–51 season. She was meant to be understudying Anouk Aimée as the Princess of France in *Henry V*, which starred Alec Clunes, but Miss Aimée was unavailable and Tutin got the role. Kenneth Tynan reported: 'Maybe the completest performance, apart from Clunes' was Dorothy Tutin's spry little Queen-to-be: a frisk of impertinent babyhood, but a princess withal, with commanding Oriental eyes.' That season she also played Ann Page in *The Merry Wives of Windsor* and Win-the-Fight-Littlewit in *Bartholomew Fair*. Of the latter Audrey Williamson wrote: ' . . . the most vivid and enchanting memory is Dorothy Tutin's piquant, brown-eyed, ecstatic little puritan wife eager for pork and mischief.'

At the Lyric, Hammersmith, in September 1951 Dorothy Tutin played Martina in *Thor With Angels* and then made a great success as Cecily in the film of *The Importance of Being Earnest*. She was invited to play Hero in John Gielgud's producton of *Much Ado About Nothing* at the Phoenix in January 1952; dissatisfied with her playing, she was about to give up the stage when she was cast as Rose Pemberton in Graham Greene's *The Living Room*. She played a Catholic girl driven to suicide through her guilt at having an affair with a married man. Kenneth Tynan reported: 'Her role is half of what must be the most fully documented love affair in dramatic literature; we are privy to all her secrets, sexual and spiritual alike. Miss Tutin's performance is masterly: the very nakedness of acting. In her greatest sorrow she blazes like a diamond in a mine.' *The Living Room* made her name on stage but it also ruined her soprano singing voice. As she explained: 'I rehearsed *The Living Room* at such a pitch for the first week because the director pushed me and pushed me. Then, the second week, he said I should shout and be more angry. I was being British and where was my temperament? So I went on stage and I screamed and choked—and that caused my trouble. I went to a voice specialist who said I had to be silent for nine days. We opened in Edinburgh in ten.' The nodules healed but the singing voice never fully returned.

Dorothy Tutin opened at the New Theatre in March 1954 playing Sally Bowles in *I Am a Camera*, and Caryl Brahms reported: 'Miss Tutin, that player with a gift of tears for those who are attuned to weep with her, now shows that she has also a great appetite for comedy. She somehow contrives to combine the satiric with the entirely credible. Sally Bowles looks like the two-dimensional scribble of a cartoonist at his most inspired; she sounds like Tallulah Bankhead's daughter. The method is the same. And so, or very nearly so, is the voice—that kind of curdled cooing that could only come from a turtle-dove with laryngitis. And I, for one, can't wait for Christopher Fry to write a play for her.' Miss Tutin's next play was indeed a Christopher Fry, a translation of Anouilh's *The Lark* in which she opened at the Lyric, Hammersmith, playing Joan of Arc in March 1955. The production was not a success — it was compared unfavourably with the *Saint Joan* of Siobhan McKenna and Bernard Shaw which was already playing in the West End. Moreover, as Ronald Barker wrote: 'Dorothy Tutin is temperamentally wrong for Joan. The essential quality for any actress who plays the part is a natural simplicity. Dorothy Tutin is urbane and sophisticated. All that human intelligence and talent can do has been done, but nothing can disguise the fact that this girl would have been more at home in a coffee bar than with cows in a field. I have always felt that the stumbling block to this actress playing any period part was her voice, which is unmistakably modern. When she can shed that modernity her range will be greatly increased. Her performance is big and brilliant, but never convinces or moves one and in consequence fails to hold the play together.'

At the Saville in December she was Hedvig in *The Wild Duck*. Caryl Brahms, who did not care for Ibsen's play, bemoaned the fact that she played the part at all but noted that it was inevitable. All serious young actresses played Hedvig. She went on: 'We who have been watching Miss Dorothy Tutin's quiet excellence ripening into rip-roaring stardom, who have treasured her sincerity, the purity of her portrayals, their youthful rounded contours, their freshness with just that spicing of acid that gives a pippin its perfection, have known that sooner or later Ol' Debbil Hedvig would get her. She has. And all that is matter-of-fact in Miss Tutin's utterance is at war with the adolescent rashness of Hedvig as her author has it ... And yet with such a direct simplicity does Miss Tutin attack the part that she touches our tears in spite of our misgivings.'

In September 1956 Dorothy Tutin began a tour of *The Gates of Summer*, in which she played Caroline Traherne, and in April 1957 she was back in London, at the Royal Court, playing Archie Rice's (Laurence Olivier's) daughter, Jean Rice, in John Osborne's *The Entertainer*. The following April she joined the Shakespeare Memorial Theatre Company at Stratford-on-Avon where she played Juliet in *Romeo and Juliet*, and, directed by Peter Hall, Viola in *Twelfth Night*. Peter Jackson wrote: 'Dorothy Tutin's golden Viola is wonderfully boyish, breathless and bewildered and always completely audible. She is alive and to be alive in a cast like this [it included Geraldine McEwan, Richard Johnson and Patrick Wymark] means working double overtime.'

That season she was also Ophelia in Michael Redgrave's *Hamlet*. Peter Roberts said: 'Dorothy Tutin's Ophelia is no cloying, sweet gentle creature. A wild, nervy girl, she is obviously in need of a course of tranquillizers even in the early scenes, which makes her later madness more convincing.' She played the same part when she toured with the company to Leningrad and Moscow in December 1958. In July the following year she was in the West End with John Neville playing Dolly in Robert Morley's production of the Broadway hit *Once More With Feeling*, and she returned to Stratford for their 1960 season when she played Portia to Peter O'Toole's Shylock in *The Merchant of Venice*. Peter Roberts compared her conception of the role to that of Ellen Terry, and went on: 'Whilst I like to think of Portia as a greater and more serious character than Miss Tutin gives her credit for, I was nevertheless delighted with her charming performance.' That season she also played Cressida in *Troilus and Cressida* and repeated her performance in *Twelfth Night*, which she brought to London to the Aldwych in December 1960 and for which she received the *Evening Standard* Award as Best Actress.

In February 1961 she played Sister Jeanne in John Whiting's *The Devils*, which Peter Hall had commissioned specially for this, his first London season at the Aldwych. Frank Granville-Barker called it a brilliant new play and compared it to

Peer Gynt and *King Lear*. Of Miss Tutin's performance he wrote: 'Dorothy Tutin showed in her portrayal of Sister Jeanne the utmost accomplishment and carried off the fiendishly difficult scenes of diabolic possession with almost miraculous success. I felt, however, that her playing did not reveal the full complexity of the unhappy creature's twisted soul burning within her.'

Back at Stratford in August 1961 (the group was now called the Royal Shakespeare Company) she once more played Juliet and was Desdemona to Gielgud's Othello, directed by Zeffirelli. The entire production left Caryl Brahms extremely cold, and she reported: 'Miss Dorothy Tutin played Desdemona like the girl next door off to bed with the boy next door.' Miss Tutin was with Gielgud again in December 1961 when at the Aldwych they were in *The Cherry Orchard*, with Peggy Ashcroft. Tutin played Varya. With the RSC Dorothy Tutin appeared at the Edinburgh Festival in September 1962 in *The Devils* and *Troilus and Cressida* and continued in the two productions at the Aldwych for October 1962.

In January 1963 Dorothy Tutin made her New York début with the company at the Henry Miller Theater in *The Hollow Crown*. Back at the Aldwych in July she was Polly Peachum in *The Beggar's Opera*, and in November was at the Festival Hall in a concert — *Beatrice et Benedict*. That year she also found time to marry the actor Derek Waring.

At the Bristol Old Vic in March 1965 Dorothy Tutin played Queen Victoria in an evening compiled from documentary material and letters called *Portrait of a Queen*. She transferred to London with it to the Vaudeville in May. Frank Cox reported: '... Dorothy Tutin's Queen is strong, pretty and sad, conjuring a real woman out of next to nothing, a performance which, given a script and a play, might well be great.'

In the New Year Honours for 1967, Dorothy Tutin received the CBE. She returned to the RSC for the summer to play Rosalind in *As You Like It*. Michael Billington wrote: 'Dorothy Tutin's Rosalind is naturally the centrepiece of the production and a glowing, intelligent performance it is ...' She repeated the performance at the Ahmanson Theater in Los Angeles in January 1968, and then in February went to New York where she played Queen Victoria at the Henry Miller Theater.

Dorothy Tutin then took on the lead in the musical *Ann Veronica*, and opened the pre-London tour in February 1969 at the Belgrade Theatre, Coventry. She was uncertain about her ability to succeed in such a role, and chose not to open in London. At the St Martin's Theatre in

Herbert Beerbohm Tree as Svengali in George du Maurier's play *Trilby*
(London, October 1895)

At the Criterion Theatre, Charles Wyndham
played the title role in *David Garrick*
(London, May 1896)

January 1970 she was Francine in a translation from the French, *Play On Love*, and in November she was with the RSC Theatregoround Festival at the Roundhouse playing Alice in *Arden of Faversham*. At the Aldwych in June 1971 she played Kate in Harold Pinter's *Old Times*. John Russell Taylor wrote: 'Dorothy Tutin in comparison (to Vivien Merchant's showy part as Anna) has to make her effect largely by sheer presence, by saying little and radiating a lot — which she does extraordinarily well ...' For Christmas that year at the Coliseum she flew around as Peter Pan, repeating it the following Christmas. In the meantime in March she toured as Maggie in J. M. Barrie's *What Every Woman Knows*.

For the 1974 Chichester season she played Natalya in *A Month in the Country*, and the critics agreed it was the best thing in the season. In November the same year she brought *What Every*

Woman Knows to the Albery Theatre in the West End, and Garry O'Connor wrote: 'Dorothy Tutin's Maggie is a completely endearing and moving performance, in which there is no nuance of understanding or sharpness of mind passed over. Miss Tutin has a perfect combination of toughness and pathos ...' The following November at the same theatre she played Natalya once more, and once more received the *Evening Standard* Award as Best Actress. Geoff Brown reported that she '... is breathlessly eloquent as Natalya, caught by more conflicting emotions than she knows what to do with'. Since then her performances have included Cleopatra at the Old Vic and Madame Ranevskaya and Lady Macbeth at the National. In 1985 she appeared at the Duchess in three of the one-act plays of Harold Pinter.

Dorothy Tutin lives in Barnes in London with her husband, a son and a daughter.

PETER USTINOV

Writing in the mid-1970s, the critic Alan Brien said of Ustinov: 'In his mercurial ambitions, tireless dedication to the arts, he has often appeared to be the son of Orson Welles ... But in the end he often ends up more like the nephew of Sacha Guitry.' He also wrote: 'Peter Ustinov is probably the most famous and popular middlebrow entertainer in Britain today. Equally in his plays, as in his turns, he always seems to be "on", to be there, providing a characteristic flourish, a typical ironic joke, a custom-built piece of business, as if the characters and their players were projections of himself beamed from some 3-D projector backstage.'

Peter Ustinov was born on 16 April 1921 in Swiss Cottage, London, but is always quick to point out that he was conceived in Leningrad. His father was a journalist and his mother, Nadia Benois, a painter and stage designer. He went to prep school in Sloane Street and then on to Westminster where he began writing plays, and getting into trouble because he usually did it during maths lessons. As a child he was a natural mimic, and he left Westminster at the age of 16 before taking any exams to study with Michel Saint-Denis at his London Theatre Studio. He made his first stage appearance as Waffles in *The Wood Demon* at the Barn Theatre, Shere, on 18 July 1938. He then played the lecherous Spanish Chief of Police in

Lorca's *Mariana Pineda*, and the *Times* reported: 'Peter Ustinov gave the part of Pedrosa a sinister restraint which was acceptable.' He spent two years at drama school and though Saint-Denis, not really seeing a place for him as yet on the commercial stage, urged him to stay on for another year, Ustinov left and went to the Players' Theatre, run by Leonard Sachs, which specialized in a Victorian cabaret. There he performed monologues he had written himself. He made his début there on 30 August 1939 as the Bishop of Limpopoland. He attracted good notices, and T. C. Worsley later wrote: 'Peter Ustinov first became known as a very young man who was giving very witty, if slightly cruel character monologues at the Players' Theatre. His subjects were mostly exiles from old Russia; all old decayed aristocrats, faded prima donnas, generals at their last gasp. Their gestures, intonations, tricks of speech, postures were caught with malicious exactness: they lived before us on the great podgy mobile face of the young diseur.' Ustinov then went to the Aylesbury Repertory Company, where between October and December 1939 he played in many pieces including *White Cargo*, *Rookery Nook* and *Laburnum Grove*. At Richmond in January he played the Rev. Alroy Whitingstall in *First Night*. In May he went to the Ambassadors', where he appeared in the revue *Swinging on the Gate* with Hermione Gingold.

Then, aged only 19, he married Isolde Denham, also 19, an old childhood friend.

At that time, too, he began working in films. His first was a semi-documentary, *Mein Kampf*; then he recited one of his monologues in a short film full of young starlets, called *Hello, Fame!* He played a Dutch priest in *One of Our Aircraft Is Missing*. The theatres had been closed temporarily during the bombings, but his next venture was in October 1940 when he played at Wyndham's in the daytime revue *Diversion*, with Edith Evans and Dorothy Dickson. He wrote his own material, and also that for *Diversion No. 2* which appeared in January 1941. During this time he wrote a play, *House of Regrets*, which he showed to the director of *Diversions*, Herbert Farjeon, who in turn showed it to the drama critic James Agate. This led to Agate's writing a long piece in his *Sunday Times* column heralding the arrival of a new playwright and looking forward to the play's production. Meanwhile Ustinov began his directing career in August 1941 when he did *Squaring the Circle* at the Vaudeville.

He was called into the army on 16 January 1942, to the Royal Sussex Regiment, but soon joined the Directorate of Army Psychiatry to write recruitment and propaganda films. While in the army his play *House of Regrets* was directed by Alec Clunes at the Arts Theatre and was a great success. Three further plays of his were produced while he was still in the army — a one-acter called *Beyond* at the Arts, *Blow Your Own Trumpet*, which ran only thirteen performances at the Old Vic, and *The Banbury Nose*, which met with greater success. With the Army Entertainment Unit in Salisbury he directed Edith Evans as Mrs Malaprop in *The Rivals* and played Sir Anthony Absolute himself.

Peter Ustinov returned to the West End stage in June 1946 when he played the police chief Petrovitch in Rodney Ackland's adaptation of *Crime and Punishment*, which starred John Gielgud and Edith Evans. At the St Martin's in April 1948 he was Caligula in his own adaptation of *Frenzy*, and at the Lyric, Hammersmith, in June 1949 he was Sergeant Dohda in *Love in Albania*. He also directed the production and transferred with it to the St James's in July. At this time he seemed to be everywhere both in the theatre and on film.

At Wyndham's in May 1951 Peter Ustinov played Carabosse in his own play *The Love of Four Colonels*, which was an enormous success. Writing of this fantasy, T. C. Worsley said: 'It is a most ingenious idea and one of its great merits is that it gives Mr Ustinov himself the chance of giving a very large number of his impersonations. (Indeed there are a number of parts which he doesn't play, but which if he could be in two places at once he very well might.) . . . In his own person he epitomizes in a few sharp strokes one aspect of Shakespeare, of artificial comedy, of American films and of Chekhov. The only difficulty is that as actor he steals the show from himself as playwright.' He then received the Academy Award nomination as best supporting actor for *Quo Vadis*.

At the Theatre Royal in Brighton in October 1952 he directed his own play *No Sign of the Dove*. The following year he married the actress Suzanne Cloutier. In May 1956 Peter Ustinov opened at the Piccadilly Theatre in his own play *Romanoff and Juliet*, in which he played the General. Of his performance Caryl Brahms wrote: 'Never can so many twitches, squeaks, skips, hops, winks, blinks, nods and finger flutterings have afflicted one and the same Elder Statesman, poor gentleman. Mr Ustinov has scooped all the gargoyles off Salisbury Cathedral and attached them to his bearded General in a frenzy of collage.' The play ran a year at the Piccadilly and won the *Evening Standard* Award for Best New Play. He took it to New York, where he opened at the Plymouth in October 1957. After touring the United States with it, Ustinov then made the film.

He returned to the London stage in April 1962 playing Sam Old in his own play, *Photo-Finish*, which he co-directed. Clives Barnes reported: 'For sheer hey-presto magic we have had nothing like Peter Ustinov in the British theatre since Shaw. He is the master entertainer, the complete theatrical conjurer who plants his rabbits with startling ingenuity and dashingly saws his characters in half before our eyes . . . Ustinov, as a bearded truculent of 80, shambles through with mountainous assurance.'

Ustinov directed *L'Heure Espagnole*, *Erwartung* and *Gianni Schicci* at the Royal Opera House, Covent Garden, in June 1962 and in February 1963 opened on Broadway at the Brooks Atkinson Theater in *Photo-Finish*. At the same theatre in November 1967 he directed his own play, *Halfway Up the Tree*.

He returned to England in May 1968 where at the Chichester Festival he directed and played the Archbishop in his own play, *The Unknown Soldier and His Wife*. Michael Billington reported: 'Whatever Mr Ustinov's shortcomings as a dramatist, his skill as an actor and director is undeniable. Here he offers us a marvellous gallery of moon-faced prelates, blinking myopically through owlish spectacles, muttering to themselves as they trundle off-stage or letting their pendulous upper-lip wantonly quiver.' Ustinov opened the New

London Theatre in January 1973 with this play. He returned to New York in December 1974 when he played Boris Vassilievitch in his own play, *Who's Who in Hell*. Since then he has played in London and New York in his own *Beethoven's Tenth*.

Peter Ustinov received an Oscar for his performance in the film *Topkapi* and is the winner of three Emmy Awards for his television work. He was Rector of Dundee University from 1968 to 1973 and received a CBE in the 1976 Birthday Honours. As well as his work on stage, in films and on television, Peter Ustinov has written novels, autobiography and a book of cartoons. His third wife is Hélène du Lau d'Allemans.

FREDERICK VALK

'*H*e was of somewhat more than middle height, but the head and chest were those of a giant; and the limbs seemed by comparison rather short and thick; the whole effect was immensely powerful but squat. A great head on a great barrel, round, incredibly thick, but not fat: hard, not soft. The face, like the whole figure, was broad in comparison with its length; wide-set eyes, a short thick nose, a wide mouth and very square jaw. The neck was short and immensely thick. But any impression of coarseness was immediately obliterated by the eyes, the directness of their glance, the candour and intelligence of their expression, their extraordinary and benevolent magnetism. His colouring was extremely swarthy; dark, but not black hair; a darkly sallow complexion quite unlike the ruddy colouring of a robust Briton; the eyes were a warm bright brown and, for all their brilliance, the ''white'' of the eyes was not white at all, but like dark ivory ... Valk's voice matched his physique; a warm and velvety baritone with an upper register of extraordinary brilliance and power. Probably it was due to the gigantic muscular development of the diaphragm, but I do not think I have ever heard a man's voice which had the same ringing, uninhibited power at the top.' Thus the director Tyrone Guthrie described Frederick Valk, who was born in Hamburg, Germany, on 10 June 1895.

Valk's family intended him for the business world but he had different ideas after viewing a fit-up production of *Hamlet* in the Hamburg dockland. He auditioned for the stage and made his first appearance at the Deutsches Schauspielhaus in Hamburg in November 1914. He was a conscript in the Kaiser's army during the First World War, but as he put it, 'an unhappy warrior — the best day of my military life was the day I discarded my uniform.' He was billeted in a farmhouse in northern France during the war and spent most of his time sitting under a peach tree learning the major Shakespearian roles. At the end of the war he demobilized himself and made his way home. The evening of his arrival back in Berlin he returned to the theatre, where he walked on in *The Merchant of Venice*. He was engaged at the Staatstheater in Berlin from 1924 to 1928 but it was in the small town of Lubeck, an hour from Hamburg, that he first played the major Shakespearian roles.

With the rise of Nazism, Valk went to the New Theatre in Prague, where he played Shylock, Othello, Lear and Macbeth to great acclaim. He also became a Czech citizen. During the summer of 1938 he was stricken first with scarlet fever and then diphtheria; he was just recovering when, at the time of the Munich crisis, the theatre in Prague was closed during the rehearsals for *Hamlet*, in which Valk was playing Claudius. Knowing he was high on the Nazi hit-list he managed to flee Prague before the Germans entered in March 1939, and he made his way to England. Learning English very quickly, he made his London début at Wyndham's Theatre on 5 July 1939 where he played Ottakar Brandt in *Alien Corn*. He never, however, lost his accent and was restricted to playing roles which could be interpreted as 'foreign'.

At the Globe Theatre in July 1940 he was Dr Kurtz in *Thunder Rock* and played the part again at St Martin's in February 1941. Tyrone Guthrie saw this performance and remembered: 'He played a doctor, and gave the impression, which is one of the hallmarks of top-flight acting, not of being just a particular doctor, but the Idea of Medicine; he was the archetype of Doctor.' During 1941 Frederick Valk toured with the Old Vic Company playing Nick in *The Time of Your Life*, Dr Kurtz in *Thunder Rock*, as well as Shylock and Othello. Still with the Old Vic Company, at the New Theatre in July 1942 he played Othello, with Bernard Miles as his Iago. Audrey Williamson reported: 'Emotion surges up in this actor like a tidal wave, submerging and uprooting every obstacle that lies in its path. He is monumental as an Epstein, a vast vessel of wrath in which suffering and rage contend stormily for dominion ... [but for long passages of the play he was] all but unintelligible ... The actor may have carried the imagination in his heart, but he was without the instrument through which to express it.'

He toured during 1942 playing Absolom in *The Witch* and was back at the New Theatre in February 1943 playing Shylock in *The Merchant of Venice*. Audrey Williamson said he was ' ... a Shylock of titanic dimensions ... The actor here was extraordinarily moving, but without for a moment descending to sentimentality. The performance had leonine royalty and the cruelty of the jungle, but something besides that swept the hackneyed play into magnificence.' In August of that year he was at the Phoenix playing Kutuzov in *War and Peace* and in October succeeded Anton Walbrook as Kurt Muller at the Aldwych in *Watch on the Rhine*.

At the Theatre Royal in Glasgow in February 1944, Frederick Valk played Max in *The Fifth Column* and at the Q in May was the Egyptian Doctor in *The Millionairess*. He spent from August through October with the Old Vic Company at the Playhouse in Liverpool playing the title role in *John Gabriel Borkman* and Stefan in *Point Valaine*, and returned to the Piccadilly Theatre in London in May 1945 as King George III in *The Gay Pavilion*, a play which the critic James Agate did not like but of which he reported: 'Halfway through *The Gay Pavilion* Mr Frederick Valk gave us ten minutes of the old king—a superb piece of acting which blew all the other characters off the stage and left it vacant.' The following month at the Chanticleer he was Janko Lenov in *More Than Science*. At the Phoenix in September he played Tomasino in *A Bell for Adano* and at the Lyric, Hammersmith, in February 1946 he was once again Nick in *The Time of Your Life*. He joined Donald Wolfit's company at the Winter Garden in April 1946 to play Othello once more and toured with the production. At the Lyric, Hammersmith, in June he was Karamazov in *The Brothers Karamazov*.

Frederick Valk played Halvard Solness at the Arts Theatre in January 1947 in *The Master Builder*, and Harold Hobson reported: 'Mr Frederick Valk's Solness is a magnificent struggle between this fine actor's great energy and power and his imperfect acquaintance with the trickier rhythms of English speech.' Valk then returned to touring in *Othello* and came into the Savoy with the production in April 1947.

At the Aldwych in March 1948 he was Uncle Chris in *I Remember Mama* and at the Q in

November played Karaoul in *Indictment*. He was at the Lyric in April 1949 playing Mitrich in *The Power of Darkness* and at the Winter Garden that October was Salvador di Breno in *Top Secret*.

Frederick Valk had, once more, the title role in Ibsen's *John Gabriel Borkman* in March 1950. This time it was at the Arts Theatre, and T. C. Worsley reported: 'Mr Frederick Valk as Borkman makes a fine impression of weight as we first see him with his back to us in the long room, pacing like a maimed bull. And there is a happy touch of resemblance to the playwright himself in the stocky figure, the full face, the rocky chin. Mr Valk, I have found, sometimes overdoes the noise, but not here. His restraint is admirable and it gives just the right feeling of being exercised by a constant and terrible effort of the will. This, and the deep voice with its echoes of vanished power, and the solidly planted weight add up to tell effectively in that long winding climb up through the snow in the last act. This difficult scene at least held us completely, and this is a tribute to the sensitiveness, intelligence and grasp which had gone into Mr Valk's preparation for it. It did not, as one felt it might have done in other hands, absolutely carry us away. Actors from the centre of Europe have one great advantage over ours. They can grunt and they can shout as no English actor can; but they carry the invincible handicap of foreign intonation. Mr Valk's Austrian accentuation and phrasing do have the effect of ironing out for our ears nearly all the subtleties in the quieter passages ...'

At the Bedford Theatre in Camden Town in May 1950 he played Mathias in *The Bells* and in September of that year was Chris Christopherson in *Anna Christie* at the Q. At the same theatre in October he played Schindler in *Musical Chairs*, and then was the Father in Yvonne Mitchell's *The Same Sky*. Two years of film work followed. He had made his first film, *Night Train to Munich*, in 1940, and many notable cinema performances followed, including the role of the Doctor in *I Am a Camera* and the German Commandant in *The Colditz Story*. In the spring of 1955 he played Marcus Hoff in *The Big Knife* in London, and then in the summer he went to Tyrone Guthrie's Stratford Shakespearian Festival in Ontario, where he once more played Shylock.

Back in London at the Piccadilly Theatre in May 1956 he opened in Peter Ustinov's *Romanoff and Juliet*. Caryl Brahms reported: 'Mr Valk stands for acting in the grand manner. Amid the clap-trap, he remains Sir Faithful, a Knight in Shining Armour. Truth is his breastplate. Timing is his sword thrust. And his humour is genial as sunshine on a summer's day and infinitely more reliable. Be the piece never so trivial, in his presence no one can fail to realize that here is a great actor, running through the scales and exercises of his art.'

Frederick Valk planned to make his New York début in the Broadway production of *Romanoff and Juliet* but he died on 23 July 1956 during the London run, leaving a widow and two small sons.

IRENE VANBRUGH

*I*rene Barnes was born in Exeter on 2 December 1872. Her father was the vicar of Heavitree and Prebendary of Exeter Cathedral, and her mother was the daughter of a barrister, a friend of Edmund Kean and according to her daughter a natural actress, though she never appeared on any stage. There were six children in the family and their mother insisted on a musical education at home and that they all become accomplished dancers. Irene spent a year in Switzerland in 1880 when her father's health required it, but when they were in England there were annual summer visits to the London theatre. In 1884 her elder sister Violet decided to go on the stage, and on Ellen Terry's advice adopted a stage name, choosing Vanbrugh.

After the family moved to London Irene was in a school production of *Beauty and the Beast*, and Ellen Terry declared: 'Irene, you seem to be a professional acting with amateurs.'

Irene was constantly at the Lyceum watching Irving and Terry, and spent her spare time trekking around the agents with Violet, who was looking for work. When her elder sister was hired by Sarah Thorne for a stock season at the Theatre Royal, Margate, Irene went with her and attended all the rehearsals. She then went to Paris to join another sister, Angela, who was there studying the violin, and herself studied elocution at the Conservatoire.

When in 1888 Irene decided to go on the stage she also took the name of Vanbrugh, and made her début on 20 August 1888 as Phoebe in *As You Like It* at the Theatre Royal, Margate, in Sarah Thorne's company, of which by this time Violet was the star and playing Rosalind. Also at Margate that season Irene played Titania in *A Midsummer Night's Dream*, Arrah Meelish in *Arrah-Na-Pogue* and Rose in *Leah*.

Irene made her London début at the Olympic Theatre in Wych Street when she played the White Queen in a revival of *Alice in Wonderland* at Christmas 1888. She had been recommended for the part by the author who was a friend of her father. In April 1889 she was at the Crystal Palace playing Jessica in *The Merchant of Venice* and at the Strand in June was Nina St Croix in *Faustine's Love*. She returned to Margate in August 1889 when she briefly played Juliet in *Romeo and Juliet*. That autumn she was hired by John L. Toole for a tour and returned to London with him in December, when she played Kitty Severs in *A Broken Sixpence*, Bertha in *Dot*, Mary Belton in *Uncle Dick's Darling*, Eliza in *Paul Pry*, Dora in *The Don*, Alice Marshall in *The Butler*, Lucy Garner in *Dearer than Life*, and small parts in other productions.

She went to Australasia with Toole's company in March 1890, and she played juvenile leads for a year, returning to London to Toole's Theatre where in April 1891 she played Hester in *Hester's Mystery* and Norah Doublechick in *The Upper Crust*. In May she was Thea Tesman in J. M. Barrie's burlesque, *Ibsen's Ghost*, and in June played Angeline in *Ici on (ne) parle (pas) Français*. In February 1892 she was Bell Golightly in Barrie's first full-length play, which Toole had commissioned, called *Walker, London*. She had a character part and the play was a great success, running for over a year. Also with Toole she played Miss Otis Hopkins in *Homburg*.

Although she was happy in Toole's company Irene Vanbrugh decided it was time to test her wings, and she opened at the Haymarket in Tree's company in September 1893 playing the serving maid, Lettice, in Henry Arthur Jones' *The Tempter*. Also at the Haymarket she played Mabel Seabrook in *Captain Swift*, Eugenia in *Six Persons* and Olive Darnley in *The Charlatan*.

In April 1894 Irene Vanbrugh joined George Alexander's company at the St James's Theatre, where she played Charley Wishanger in a red wig in *The Masqueraders*. She toured with the company playing Ellen in *The Second Mrs Tanqueray* and on her return to London played in that as well as being Fanny in *Guy Domville*, Kate Merryweather in *The Idler*, and creating the role of the Hon. Gwendolyn Fairfax in Oscar Wilde's *The Importance of Being Earnest*.

Violet had married the actor–manager Arthur

Bouchier, and in September 1895 they took over the management of the Royalty Theatre. Irene left Alexander's company and joined them. There in the opening production, for the first time in London, the sisters played together in *The Chili Widow*. Irene went on to play Faith in *The New Baby*, the title role in *Kitty Clive*, and Miss Grantham in *The Liar*. She went with the company to America and made her New York début at the Bijou Theater on 30 November 1896 playing Dulcie in *The Chili Widow*.

When she returned to London it was to the Theatre Royal in Kilburn, where in April 1897 she played Ellen Bracegirdle in *Our Hostess*. She then joined Charles Wyndham at the Criterion in October 1897 when she played Lady Rosamund Tatton in Henry Arthur Jones' *The Liars*. The production was a great success, but Wyndham released her in January 1898 when she went to the Court Theatre to play Rose Trelawney in the first production of Pinero's *Trelawney of the 'Wells'*. Sir William Gower was played by Dot Boucicault, whom she had met in Australia.

In June 1898 she played Stella de Gex in *His Excellency the Governor*, and in October was Mrs Millingdale in *When a Man's in Love* by Anthony Hope. The latter was not a success. She left the Court and joined John Hare's company, and at the Globe opened in April 1899 as Sophie Fullgarney in Pinero's *The Gay Lord Quex* which was an enormous success, running nearly a year in London. At the Criterion in February 1900 she played in a revival of *His Excellency the Governor* and then went with Hare to America where she played in *The Gay Lord Quex* at the Criterion in New York in November. During their six-month stay in America they played with great success in Boston, Philadelphia, Washington and Chicago.

When Irene Vanbrugh returned to England she agreed, against her mother's wishes, to marry Boucicault. They both became associated with the impresario Charles Frohman at the Duke of York's Theatre, an association which lasted thirteen years. In March 1902 she played Princess de Chalenson in Henry Arthur Jones' *The Princess' Nose* which was not a great success, so in May they quickly revived *The Gay Lord Quex*. In November she was Lady Mary Lasenby in Barrie's *The Admirable Crichton*, a production beset with difficulties that Boucicault managed to overcome. She repeated the role at the Renaissance Theatre in Paris in June 1903. Irene Vanbrugh had another enormous success when in October 1903 at the Duke of York's she played the title role in Pinero's *Letty*. In February 1904 she was Countess Lucia d'Orano in *Captain Dieppe* and in March once more played Stella in *His Excellency the Governor*. In April 1905 she played Amy Grey with Ellen Terry in Barrie's *Alice-Sit-by-the-Fire*, and Max Beerbohm reported: 'Her personality is in no way Barrieish. She looks, indeed, quite young enough for her part; but her soul is not childish enough.' That October she played Gwendolen Cobb in *The Painful Predicament of Sherlock Holmes*.

In February 1906 Irene Vanbrugh returned to the St James's to George Alexander's company to play Nina Jesson in Pinero's *His House in Order*, which was an enormous success and ran for fourteen months. She then returned to the Duke of York's where in March 1907 she played Jeanne de Briantes in *The Great Conspiracy*. At the Court in June 1907 she was the Strange Lady in Shaw's *The Man of Destiny*, and Max Beerbohm wrote: 'Miss Irene Vanbrugh plays with much humour the part of the lady who outwits Napoleon.' Napoleon was played by her husband. She had another success at the St James's in November 1907 when she played Marise in *The Thief*, adapted from *Le Voleur*. At the same theatre in November 1908 she played Dorothy Faringay in *The Builder of Bridges*. In April 1909 she was Velia Faraday in *Colonel Smith* and in September played Zoe Blundell in Pinero's *Mid-Channel*, which was not a great success. She took over from Marie Lohr at the Comedy in November playing the title role in *Smith*.

Irene Vanbrugh returned to the Duke of York's in April 1910 for a revival of *Trelawney of the 'Wells'* and in May was the Marchesa di San Servolo in *Helena's Path*. In June she played Mrs Hyphen-Brown in *A Slice of Life*, and in September was Irma Lurette in *A Bolt from the Blue*. She played Grace Insole in October in Somerset Maugham's *Grace*.

As Gerald du Maurier's leading lady, she went to Wyndham's Theatre in March 1911 where she played Margaret Summers in Haddon Chambers' *Passers-By*. In May 1911 there was a Command Performance at Drury Lane and Irene Vanbrugh played Clara Douglas in *Money*. She returned to the Duke of York's in August 1911 where she played Helen Arany in *The Concert*.

In October 1911 Irene Vanbrugh went on the music-hall stage with Barrie's *The Twelve Pound Look*, and she did little but music hall for the next four years. She also appeared in Barrie's *Half an Hour* and *Rosalind*, and *The Land of Promise*.

At the St James's in October 1914 she was in a revival of *His House in Order*, and at the Coliseum at Christmas was the Spirit of Culture in *Der Tag*. In February 1915 she was in an all-star charity production of *The School for Scandal*, playing Lady Teazle. At His Majesty's in May 1915 she was Lady Falkland in *The Right to Kill*, and at the St James's in September was Countess Ottoline de Chaumie in Pinero's *The Big Drum*.

In 1916 her husband took over the management of the New Theatre and in February Irene played the title role in Maugham's *Caroline* — a very high, high comedy. Also at the New she played Helen Lytton in *The Riddle*, Emily Ladew in *Her Husband's Wife*, and Leonora in *Seven Women*. She also spent a good deal of time organizing an all-star film of *Masks and Faces*, which was being made in aid of the Academy of Dramatic Art, at that time run by her brother Kenneth. During the 1917 air raids they revived *Trelawney of the 'Wells'*, and at His Majesty's Theatre in December 1917 in aid of the King George Pension Fund, Irene Vanbrugh played Cecilia Flinder in *The Man from Blankeleys*.

At the New Theatre in April 1918 she played the title part in A. A. Milne's *Belinda*, and toured the provinces with it the following year. She had a season at the Gaiety in Manchester in 1919 playing Agnes Ebbsmith in *The Notorious Mrs Ebbsmith* and Olivia in *Mr Pim Passes By*, which she brought to the New Theatre in January 1920 before touring with it. At the Duke of York's in February 1921 she was Nelly Daventry in *Miss Nell o' New Orleans*, and at the Palace in December for the King George Pension Fund created the part of Miss Isit in *Shall We Join the Ladies?*, which she then toured. She was at the Globe that December playing Isobel in *The Truth About Blayds* and in April 1922 played Olivia Marden in a revival of *Mr Pim Passes By*. In May she had the title role in *Eileen* and in July revived *Belinda*. She revived *Mid-Channel* at the Royalty in October. At His Majesty's in February 1923 for charity she was Lady Garson in *Half an Hour*.

Boucicault had had a serious illness and had been confined to his bed for two years, but by early 1923 he had recovered and they set out in March for Australia by way of South Africa for a tour which included a repertory of twelve plays. They returned to London in January 1926, where at the Globe, Irene played Alice in *All the King's Horses*. At the Playhouse in June she once again had the title part in *Caroline* and at the Comedy the following January she was the Baroness della Rocca in *The Desperate Lovers*. At the Coliseum in April 1927 she played Clarissa Marlow in *Miss Marlow at Play*. She and Dot Boucicault then returned to Australia for another tour, but he became ill again and the couple returned to England, where he died at their house in Hurley, Berkshire, on 25 June 1929.

Irene Vanbrugh was back on the stage in November when she played Celia Bottle in *Art and Mrs Bottle* at the Criterion with Robert Loraine. At the Court in March 1930 she was Lina Szczepanowska in *Misalliance*, and at the Haymarket in April she was Queen Gertrude in an all-star revival of *Hamlet*. At the St James's in June she played Princess Maria Dominica in *The Swan* and returned to the Haymarket in March 1931 where once again she played Gertrude. Irene Vanbrugh spent 1932 touring in *Miss Nell o' New Orleans* and *Noughts and Crosses*. She brought the latter, retitled *The Price of Wisdom*, to the Ambassadors' in June 1932, and then resumed her tour. At the Palace in January 1933 she played Millicent Jordan in *Dinner at Eight*.

At the Hippodrome in Manchester in May 1934 she played Mistress Page in *The Merry Wives of Windsor* while her sister Violet played Mrs Ford. It was the first time they had acted together since 1895. Back in London at the Whitehall in February 1935 she was the Duchess of Marlborough in *Viceroy Sarah* and at the Ambassadors' in November was Camilla Everard in *Our Own Lives*. During March 1936 she toured as Mrs Mingott in *The Old Maid*, and in June was at the Arts playing Lady Lynyates in *When the Bough Breaks*. At the St James's in February 1937 she was Lady McKenna in *The Orchard Walls* and at the Ring Theatre in Blackfriars in March was once more Mistress Page in *The Merry Wives of Windsor*, performing the part yet again at the Open Air Theatre in June. In September 1937 she set out on a tour of *Viceroy Sarah* and at His Majesty's in March 1938 had a very difficult ten-minute scene playing the Countess of Messiter in Noel Coward's *Operette*.

The golden jubilee on stage of Irene Vanbrugh was celebrated with a charity matinée in the presence of the Queen at His Majesty's Theatre on 20 June 1938. Noel Coward spoke the prologue and Irene Vanbrugh performed in an act each of *The Gay Lord Quex* and *Belinda*, and also performed the one-act play *Rosalind*.

At the Lyric Theatre in March 1939 she played Lady Shufflepenny in *The Jealous God*, and at the Playhouse in May was Lady Villiers in *Only Yesterday*. She appeared at the Malvern Festival in August 1939 in *Dead Heat* and *In Good King Charles's Golden Days*. At the Strand in December 1940 she was once again Mistress Page in *The Merry Wives of Windsor*.

Irene Vanbrugh was created a dame in the 1941 New Year Honours, and in September of that year was at the Apollo playing Lady Hermione Radshaw in *Forty-Eight Hours' Leave*. She appeared at the Opera House, Manchester, in 1942 as Lady Maulden in *The Grand Manner* before taking it on a tour, and was back in London at the Lyric in March 1943 playing the Comtesse de la Brière in *What Every Woman Knows*. At the Westminster in November 1943 she played Lady Markby in *An Ideal Husband* and then toured with it through 1944. She spent much of 1945 touring as Lady Stanhope in *She Slept Lightly* and returned to London to the Embassy in September 1945 as Lady Wimpole in *Fit for Heroes*. The production transferred to the Whitehall in December. In May 1946, back at the St James's, she was Lady

Rivers in *The Kingmaker*. At the Winter Garden in November 1948 she played in Donald Wolfit's production of Winston Clewes' *The Solitary Lover* and Harold Hobson reported: 'Dame Irene Vanbrugh's gossipy Miss Dingley is a discreet joy.'

Irene Vanbrugh began appearing in films in 1933 and made many notable ones including *Escape Me Never*, *Knight Without Armour*, *Wings of the Morning* and *I Lived in Grosvenor Square*. She died on 30 November 1949.

GWEN VERDON

Gwen Verdon, the epitome of the brash Broadway musical star with four Tony Awards to her name, remains a very private person. 'There are no stories about Gwen,' a friend said. 'People just like her.'

She was born in Culver City, Los Angeles, on 13 January 1925. Her father was an electrician and her mother a dancer. 'I was crippled when I was little,' she said, 'and I wore special black shoes. I could see people look at me and think I'm pretty but still think I'm crippled. And even after I was able to take those shoes off, I was afraid something would stick out and give me away.' When she did take those shoes off she studied dancing with her mother, and went on to study with Carmelita Marrachi and Jack Cole.

Gwen Verdon made her stage début playing the Gambling Dancer in a pre-Broadway tryout of *Bonanza Bound*, which opened at the Shubert Theater in Philadelphia on 26 December 1947 — and closed there on 3 January 1948. She became Jack Cole's assistant in September 1948 for the production of *Magdalena* at the Ziegfeld Theatre and his assistant choreographer in January 1950 when she also danced in *Alive and Kicking* at the Winter Garden. She went as assistant choreographer with him to Hollywood in 1951 where she appeared for Fox in *On the Riviera*, *David and Bathsheba* and *Meet Me After the Show*.

She returned to Broadway in May 1953 where she opened in the secondary role of Claudine at the Shubert in *Can-Can*. The part may have been secondary but she stole the show and became the proverbial overnight success. For her performance she received a Tony, two Donaldson Awards and the Theater World Award.

Her next Broadway venture was in May 1955 when at the 46th Street Theater she played Lola in

Damn Yankees. Lewis Funke, writing in the *New York Times*, reported: '... Miss Verdon is just about as alluring a she-witch as was ever bred in the nether regions. Vivacious, as sleek as a cat on the showroom floor and as nice to look at, she gives brilliance and sparkle to the evening with her exuberant dancing, her wicked, glistening eyes and her sheer delight in the foolery ...' *Damn Yankees* ran for over 1000 performances and brought Miss Verdon her second Tony.

She played Anna Christie in *New Girl in Town* at the same theatre in May 1957. This musical version of the O'Neill play won her her third Tony. Still at the 46th Street Theater in February 1959 she was Essie Whimple in *Redhead*, a musical about a Victorian waxworks. This ran for 452 performances and earned her another Tony. She toured with the production during 1960. That year she also married the choreographer and director, Bob Fosse.

At the Palace Theatre in New York in January 1966 she opened as Charity Agnes Valentine in *Sweet Charity*. The critic John Simon did not care for it and even found something wrong with Miss Verdon. 'Gwen Verdon,' he wrote, 'is appetizing and resourceful but her bag of tricks is not bottomless.' The show ran more than two years.

At the Library and Museum of the Performing Arts in December 1971 Miss Verdon gave a dance recital, and at the Ritz in March 1972 she played Helen Giles in *Children! Children!* She was at the Waldorf-Astoria in June 1973 in a revue, *Milliken's Breakfast Show*, and at the Westbury, Long Island, Music Fair in June 1974 she revived the part of Lola in *Damn Yankees*.

Back at the 46th Street Theater in June 1975 she was again in a smash hit musical, playing Roxie Hart in *Chicago*, which was directed by her husband Bob Fosse. During the production the marriage ended in divorce. As her friends pointed out, it was a very difficult time — but since then she has worked with him in various movie musicals, as well as making frequent television and stage appearances in other musicals. Most recently she appeared in the film *The Cotton Club*.

MADAME VESTRIS

*L*ucia Elizabetta Bartolozzi was born in London in January 1797. Her parents soon separated and her father went to Paris where he ran an academy for dancing and fencing and her mother, in London, supported her two daughters as a music teacher. Eliza was a well-educated child, studying at the Manor Hall in Fulham Road and learning to speak Italian and French fluently. As a child she also studied music.

When Lucia was 15 she met Armand Vestris who was 22 and an excellent dancer with little else to recommend him. Nevertheless they were married on 28 January 1813. He was already heavily in debt and the debt only increased. He was ballet master at the King's Theatre, and was determined to help finances by putting his wife on the stage. She was quite willing, and appeared first at the King's Theatre on 20 July 1815 in Peter von Winter's *Il Ratto di Proserpina*; the *Morning Post* reported: 'Madame Vestris made her début on this occasion, and her performance was such as leaves no doubt of her becoming a splendid acquisition to this theatre.' The *Theatrical Inquisitor* wrote: 'Her voice is a perfect contr'alto possessing a peculiar sweetness accompanied by a correct harmonious articulation which imparts to each note a mellowness creating delight rather than astonishment. She appears about eighteen, is elegant in her person and has a countenance expressive rather of modest loveliness than of any marked passion. There is a chasteness in her acting which seldom fails to please, yet we know no representation so little calculated for a display of an actress's powers as that of an opera, no situation so embarrassing as that of patiently awaiting the conclusion of another's song. Yet we scarcely ever remember to have seen so much ease and simplicity evinced on a first appearance.' Madame Vestris made an enormous popular success as well, on the strength of which her husband got himself even further into debt.

She opened the 1816 season with *Proserpina* and then played the name part in *Zaire*, also by Winter, and the *Morning Post* wrote: 'She looked better and sang better than we expected even from her handsome person and captivating voice.' Nevertheless her husband went bankrupt; he took her to Paris, where they separated. He went on to Naples with a friend, and she played in Paris — on stage and off, according to the gossips.

In 1820 Madame Vestris returned to London where she appeared under the management of Robert Elliston at the Drury Lane Theatre in February as Lilla in Cobb's *Siege of Belgrade*. About her performance in this play with songs inserted, the *Times* reported: 'If I must hesitate to place her in the first rank of the profession, it is because her command of its mechanical difficulties is less complete than is required, failing sometimes in brilliancy and her execution in distinction, but in all that constitutes the soul of art, in grace, pathos and just intonation, we may associate her with the greatest name of the day.'

Next she played the title role in Arne's *Artaxerxes* and the *Morning Post* reported: 'The character of Artaxerxes, though it gives its name to the opera, is a part of second-rate importance and much below the level of Madame Vestris's talent. But talents can give a prominence to parts of inferior importance.' Of her Dolly Snip in *Shakespeare versus Harlequin* Mrs Baron-Wilson wrote: 'Madame Vestris . . . evinced a spirit and a naiveté which was highly captivating, and if cultivated with zealous attention will render her one of the most pleasing actresses it has ever been our honest enjoyment to applaud.'

At the Haymarket in July 1820 Madame Vestris played the first of her male roles — Captain Macheath in *The Beggar's Opera*. One critic wrote: '. . . we are half inclined to instance the momentous efforts as the most amusing impersonation in which we have hitherto beheld her. The muses, according to Gay's ''Beggar'', pay no attention to dress . . . but Madame Vestris in her scarlet frock and blue cravat . . . her dapper appearance, high spirits and unflagging activity, were apparent in every branch of her impersonation and rendered her Captain Macheath . . . one of the prettiest rattles for overgrown children with which the stage can at present supply them.' This ran for ten consecutive nights and was wisely revived by Elliston at the Lane in the autumn. It was a role to which she returned frequently. At the Lane she was soon in another 'breeches part' playing the title role in Moncrieff's burlesque of Mozart's *Don Giovanni* called *Giovanni in London*. This caused an uproar in the press. The *Theatrical Inquisitor* reported that it 'appears to have been introduced at Drury Lane for the sole purpose of making money by the sacrifice of every feeling which ought to be devoted to the respectability of the establishment'. Needless to say the charge of immodesty led to packed houses every night from 30 May to 8 July, an unprecedented run at a time when most offerings were changed almost every night.

As well as working at Drury Lane she also sang at the King's Theatre, where she was noted for her performance in Rossini's *La Gazza Ladra*. At the Lane she played in *Lord of the Manor*, *Rob Roy* and *The Heart of Midlothian*, and had a noticeable failure with *Giovanni in Ireland*, a sequel to her great success. In 1822 she played another breeches part in *The Duenna*, and continued to sing in Italian opera at the King's while during the summer she performed at the Haymarket. In 1824 she played Rosina in *The Barber of Seville*, and one critic reported: 'Madame Vestris was the Rosina and as the arrangement of the theatre forced her into the part, we shall only compare her with herself. Everyone knows that the music requires greater power of voice and execution than she has ever aspired to, but we must do her the justice to say that if the attempt was not equal to the occasion it displayed better singing than we have ever heard or expected to hear from her lips.' During that year she had a great success at the Lane in *Philandering, or The Rose Queen*. She also played Mrs Ford in *The Merry Wives of Windsor*, Luciana in *The Comedy of Errors*, Nell in *The Devil to Pay* and Susanna in *The Marriage of Figaro*. She had another breeches part in *Alcaid*, and *London Magazine* reported: 'Madame Vestris enacted Don Felix in a good, loose, dashing, rakehelly fashion. She is the best bad young man about town, and can stamp a smart leg in white tights with the air of a fellow who has an easy heart and a good tailor.'

Her salary was constantly on the increase and her popularity undiminished. In 1826 she played Fatima in *Oberon*, Lydia Languish in *The Rivals* and resurrected Captain Macheath and Giovanni yet again. That year she was at the height of her popularity as a ballad singer, and she introduced Cherry Ripe in *Paul Pry*. She left Drury Lane, convinced — rightly — of her own drawing power, and proved it at the Tottenham Street Theatre —

the old Dust Hole — when she played in *Lord of the Manor* and *Fra Diavolo*.

As an actress Madame Vestris saw a lot wrong with the theatre of the day and she determined to change it. In 1831 she took over the management of the Olympic Theatre. She completely redecorated it, shortened the presentation by an hour (most theatres' presentations went on from six p.m. to midnight in those days) and opened on 3 January with *The Olympic Revels*. She was bored with the old faithfuls that were constantly revived, and the audience applauded her innovations. She had nine seasons at the Olympic, most of which were great popular successes; however, it was a small auditorium and as she never spared money on a production it was difficult to do more than break even at the box office, and usually she lost money. She managed to recoup some money during her summer provincial tours, but by 1837 she was in deep financial difficulty and declared bankruptcy. She married Charles James Mathews, a member of the Olympic company, in July 1838, and they immediately embarked on an American tour in the hope of becoming solvent. Madame Vestris made her American début as Gertrude in *The Loan of a Lover* at the Park Theater in New York. The critic for the *Spirit of the Times* wrote: '. . . the distinguishing feature of Madame V.'s Gertrude was the surpassing melody of her ballads; nothing we have ever heard is comparable with them, and the one commencing with "I've no money", we are confident, has never been equalled on our stage. We have since seen her in *Clarisse*, in *The Barrack Room*, a farce written expressly for her by Haynes Bailey, as Julia in *One Hour* and in *The Welsh Girl*, etc., in all of which we need not say that her general acting is worthy of that high reputation she has maintained "in mouths of wisest censure" for so many years. Was she not the beautiful woman she really is, the charms of her acting, the delicious melody of her voice, and the care and taste with which she has cultivated every gift of mind and person would of themselves render her without a rival in that range of characters she has adopted and made so emphatically her own.' The *New York Mirror* reported: 'The principal charm of her performance is in her singing. Nothing can exceed the effect of the execution of the beautiful little song, "I've No Money", in *The Loan of a Lover*. It excites the enthusiasm of the audience to the highest pitch. In *Don Giovanni*, which is rich in beautiful and popular airs, Madame Vestris is deservedly celebrated.' Nevertheless the puritanical Americans were not impressed by the reputation that preceded her and the trip was not a monetary success. The couple returned to the Olympic and reappeared there in an extravaganza entitled *Blue Beard*. After nine seasons noted for accuracy in costume and realistic scenery they ended their tenancy of the Olympic, and Vestris and Mathews took over Covent Garden Theatre. They opened it on 30 September 1839 with a production of *Love's Labour's Lost*. It was a failure and was quickly withdrawn. In November they produced Sheridan Knowles' *Love*, and a critic reported: 'Mrs Mathews as Katharine had the only part which gave relief to the play and her assumption of the knight was excellent. She looked in her male attire as young and as handsome as ever she was.' That season, which was not a moneymaker, also included *The Merry Wives of Windsor*. They had better success there with their second season, and in 1841 Vestris played Grace Harkaway in *London Assurance*, Titania in *A Midsummer Night's Dream*, and Beauty in *Beauty and the Beast*. She was also Cherubino in *The Marriage of Figaro*. Although they were drawing the audiences, so costly were the productions that they remained in great debt — even the rent was owing — so Charles Kemble took over the theatre. Vestris's final evening there was on 30 April 1842 when she presented *La Sonnambula*, *Patter v. Chatter* and *The White Cat*. The *Morning Post* carried a long piece bemoaning her· leaving 'a stage she has both refined and adorned and we will not suffer the occasion to pass without paying a valedictory tribute to her claims as a lady and an actress upon a public she has more delighted than any individual of her time ... She has banished vulgarity, coarse manners, double-entendre, and impertinence from the boards over which she presided, and in their place has evoked the benefits that flow from a dramatic interpretation of polished manners, refinement and politeness. Her green-room was the resort of the learned, the witty and the wise, a miniature picture of polite and well-bred society whence wholesome example spread itself on all within its influence ... To art she gave an impulse of no mean importance. Witness the magnificent

scenery, as appropriate as it was beautiful, which her fine taste caused to be continually brought before the public. The *mise en scène* was never perfect until Madame Vestris taught her painters how to execute and the public how to appreciate her own pictorial conceptions, and to her judgement in this way the playgoing world has been indebted for much of its theatrical enjoyment.' Nevertheless, bankruptcy and brief imprisonment followed for Mathews.

They went to Macready's Drury Lane for the 1842–43 season where they appeared in *Follies of a Night*, but a clash of temperament led to their leaving in November for the Haymarket, managed by Ben Webster. In 1845 at the Haymarket Madame Vestris played Flipante in Farquhar's *Confederacy*, and the *Age and Argus* reported that her performance was 'admirable in conception, perfect in execution — the best thing she has done for years'. They then appeared at the Princess Theatre and despite only just surviving three bankruptcies they desired once more to go into management. They completely redecorated the Lyceum and opened there on 18 October 1847 with *The Light Dragoons* and *The Pride of the Market*. They continued their theatrical innovation by abolishing the half-prices for those who came in later in the evening, and they had 'house full' signs up for a season. They managed to hang on at the Lyceum for seven seasons — seven seasons full of opulent productions — but by 1854 financial problems once again had the upper hand, and moreover Vestris's health was failing.

On 26 July 1854 she played in *Sunshine Through the Clouds* and was greatly praised, though neither she nor anyone else knew that it was to be her last performance on any stage. They had to relinquish the Lyceum in March 1855 and Charles Mathews was imprisoned for debt once more in July the following year. He was released on 1 August and was at his wife's bedside when she died on 8 August 1856.

DAVID WARNER

David Warner was born in Manchester on 29 July 1941. He went to Feldon School in Leamington Spa where, he declares, he was hopeless, failing all his exams and keeping himself off street corners by acting in amateur theatricals. He sold books for a while, and trained at RADA.

Warner made his stage début at the Royal Court in January 1962 playing Snout in *A Midsummer Night's Dream*, and then at the Belgrade in Coventry in March he was Conrade in *Much Ado About Nothing*. At the New Arts in June 1962 he was Jim in David Rudkin's *Afore Night Come*. In 1963 David Warner joined the Royal Shakespeare Company, at first for small parts — Trinculo in *The Tempest* and Cinna in *Julius Caesar* — but in July he was Henry VI in *The Wars of the Roses*. Kenneth Tynan wrote: '. . . I have seldom witnessed such a finished performance by an actor who has barely started. Mr Warner is tall, lean and gangling; he cares about his subjects, whom he addresses in a vein of embarrassed regret, as befits a man who believes in peace yet cannot enforce his will. When he is murdered by Richard of York, he accepts the blade not only with forgiveness, but with a kind of wry affection for his assassin. I have seen nothing more Christlike in modern theatre.' Peter Roberts, however, writing in *Plays and Players*, did have a few reservations: 'Henry VI, played by David Warner as a slender gangling youth, is a finely executed study but Mr Warner will have to make more of his later scenes, particularly the soliloquy on the Yorkshire battlefield, to deserve the almost hysterical praise he has received.' *The Wars of the Roses* came to London, to the Aldwych, in January 1964 and Frank Cox wrote: 'Savour his entrance at the beginning of *Edward IV* for instance when, with a suggestion of extra confidence as he ascends steps to the throne and new firmness in the voice, he establishes a whole acre of character development. A magnificent performance this, and outstanding for its being so unmistakably rooted in the modern idiom; vocally he is natural and unstrained, yet the verse is negotiated with clarity and sensitivity, while he exploits his gangling physique with a shuffling naturalism which gets right into the soul of this so human saint.' When Frank Cox viewed it for the third time, back at Stratford the following season, he referred to Warner's 'incredibly haunting performance'. At the Aldwych in February 1964 Warner also appeared in *The Rebel*, an anthology devised and directed by Patrick Garland.

As well as *The Wars of the Roses* during the RSC's 1964 Stratford season David Warner played the title role in *Richard II*. The RSC's production presented a departure from the general portrait of the King but Peter Roberts reported: 'As it happens, David Warner, who plays the King, would anyway not be ideally equipped to provide a dominating artist-monarch singing out the self-pity arias with a ravishing legato that would annihilate the rest of the play. His voice lacks the necessary richness of tone and he is too inclined to clip his final vowels, giving us "matta" for matter and "letta" for letter. But he does have a God-given instinct to speak familiar lines unfamiliarly and his elongated limbs and features — stretched like an El Greco Christ between heaven and earth — are a tremendous asset, particularly in the deposition scene where, robed in luminous white, he has Bolingbroke all but begging for the crown. The elegiac note struck here neatly captures the wry and wistful quality of this Richard whose failings are the failings of temperamental youth and of an over-impulsive imagination.' That season he was also Mouldy in *Henry IV Part 2*.

At the Aldwych in October 1964 he played Valentine Brose in Henry Livings' farce, *Eh?*, and John Holstrom wrote: 'David Warner, I insist, is not yet a complete actor, but his stage presence is so attractive and bizarre — the enormous gentle length of him, sheathed here in a cutaway brown suit which is Beatle before and Norfolk behind — that he makes an ideal Brose.'

During the RSC's 1965 Stratford season David Warner became that town's youngest Hamlet when, at the age of 24, he played the Dane. Hugh Leonard reported at length: 'Mr Warner's Prince is a gangling young swine in an Oxbridge scarf who spreads woe and disquiet around him with such a prodigality as to make Claudius seem endearingly put-upon. The Ghost's revelations are to him no more than an excuse for callow histrionics; there is a hint of sadistic glee in his treatment of Ophelia; he is never more insufferable than when he has an audience — even his soliloquies are addressed not *at* us but *to* us; and when he lectures the players it is with the happy air of a medieval Prince Philip telling somebody's grandmother how to suck eggs. Four hours is perhaps a long time to spend watching egotistical fireworks — although Mr Warner becomes inexplicably and alarmingly unaffected in the last scene; but in conception at least the approach was excitingly valid . . . this was the most exciting Hamlet I have seen. Mr Warner is a cold actor — on this viewing, at any rate — and therefore lacks the emotionalism beneath which others might conceal cheap, sloppy or muddle-headed playing. Therefore he is all the more remorselessly exposed to criticism; nevertheless, from the ''nunnery'' scene onwards his perform-ance was intelligent, honest and — sometimes — technically superb. If Mr Warner can learn, he will some day be a great actor.'

David Warner had his first film part in 1962 when he played Blifil in *Tom Jones*, but it was as Morgan in *Morgan, a Suitable Case for Treatment* that he made an enormous impact on the screen.

Still with the RSC he repeated his Hamlet in London at the Aldwych in December 1965 and Charles Marowitz reported: 'Warner is essentially a belligerent Hamlet, but because the real trouble lies inside himself rather than the Court, it becomes not a social antagonism . . . but the outward bluster of a personal hang-up. The political and the historical are swallowed up by the psychiatric. Still his last moments are genuinely touching; a manic, almost uncontrollable giggle cuts through his final speeches; a diabolical joke has been played on him by those fiendish gods who, in a monumental piece of miscasting, chose Hamlet to be a revenging hero.' In January at the Aldwych he was the Postmaster in Gogol's *The Govern-ment Inspector*, which starred Paul Scofield, and Mary Holland said: 'David Warner is . . . quiet and credible . . .'

For the RSC's 1966 season Warner once more played Hamlet, and was also Sir Andrew Aguecheek in *Twelfth Night*. Hugh Leonard said this part was 'beautifully played by David Warner as a sheep who had been overlooked at slaughter time'.

In 1968 David Warner secretly married a Scandinavian girl whom he divorced just as quietly seven years later, though she remained his secretary and he was her best man when she remarried. Warner himself later also remarried. In 1970 he fell from a Rome hotel window and smashed both feet, which laid him up for some time; he has refused ever to discuss what happened. Just before that, in January 1970 he had been at the Aldwych in Albee's incomprehensible *Tiny Alice*.

David Warner returned to the stage in February 1972 when at the Hampstead Theatre Club he played Hammett in David Hare's *The Great Exhibition*. Mary Holland reported that 'the actors in *The Great Exhibition* struggle manfully, never quite sure whether they are playing a witty farce or a piece about real people suffering all too recognizable pain. David Warner, in particular, seems lost in this dilemma, flailing between an introspective, troubled liberal and a gag-a-minute funster.' That July he was at the Queen's Theatre playing the title role in *I, Claudius*, which John Mortimer had adapted from the Robert Graves books. The critic John Crosby thought it was an impossible task and reported: 'Why so many tal-ented people got mixed up in this disaster is beyond mental comprehension . . . David Warner, a many faceted actor, uses his stammer, his limp, his flowing hands and large eyes with great skill to rivet our wandering wits on the complexities of Roman high life.'

David Warner has made many notable films including *The Bofors Gun, Little Malcolm, Galileo* and *The Omen II*. He was nominated for an Emmy for his performance as the Nazi Heydrich in television's 'Holocaust'. Although constantly in work in film and on television his theatre work seems to have come to a halt. He is no longer credited as an associate artist at the RSC. 'I was a little sad about that, getting the elbow from that company,' he said. 'But I really do not like the West End now. It's so expensive to buy tickets for a start. I honestly don't feel I'm worth the money people would have to pay.'

ETHEL WATERS

*E*thel Waters was born on 31 October 1900 in Chester, Pennsylvania. She married when she was only 14 but was divorced the following year. She was in domestic service until her natural, untrained talent took her into vaudeville, where she made her début at the Lincoln Theater in Baltimore, Maryland, in 1917. She sang and danced with the Hill Sisters Trio for ten years on the vaudeville circuit before making her Broadway début at Daly's Theater on 11 July 1927 in the revue *Africana*. At the Royale Theater in 1930 she appeared in *Lew Leslie's Blackbirds;* Brooks Atkinson, reporting in the *New York Times*, deplored the material in this revue in two acts and twenty scenes and wrote: 'Even Ethel Waters, the vocal clown of the Negro stage, has nothing more original than "Lucky to Me" to lavish her sundry blandishments on.' At the Sam H. Harris Theater in 1931 she was in the revue *Rhapsody in Black*. Her next Broadway revue, *As Thousands Cheer*, which opened at the Music Box in 1933, was not only topical but written by Irving Berlin and Moss Hart, and this time Atkinson wrote: 'Ethel Waters takes full control of the audience and the show whenever she appears. Her abandon to the ruddy tune of 'Heat Wave Hits New York', her rowdy comedy as the wife of a stage-struck "Green Pastures" actor and her pathos in a deep-toned song about lynching give some notion of the broad range she can encompass in musical shows.'

The revue *At Home Abroad*, which was written by Howard Dietz and Arthur Schwartz and staged by Vincente Minnelli, opened at the Winter Garden in 1935 and was equally successful. Atkinson reported: 'Let us also speak a few words in praise of Ethel Waters, the gleaming tower of dusky regality, who knows how to make a song stand on tip-toe. Having sufficient appreciation of her talent the authors have written for her "Hottentot Potentate" which runs a high temperature, and "The Steamboat Whistle" which hails from Jamaica. Miss Waters can sing numbers like that with enormous lurking vitality; but she can also wear costumes. Mr Minnelli has taken full advantage of that. He has set her in a jungle scene that is laden with magic, dressing her in gold bands and a star-struck gown of blue, and put her in a Jamaican set that looks like a modern painting. Miss Waters is decorative as well as magnetic.' In 1934 Miss Waters was divorced from her second husband, Clyde Edward Matthews, whom she had married in 1929. During 1938 she sang in concert at Carnegie Hall, the Roxy and the Palace.

Ethel Waters made her straight acting début at the Empire in 1938 when she played Hagar in *Mamba's Daughters*, and then scored a great success at the Martin Beck Theater in 1940 when she played Petunia Jackson in the Negro musical fantasy *Cabin in the Sky*. The *New York Times* reported: 'Ethel Waters has been essential to happiness in the theater for some time. But she has never given a performance as rich as this before. She is cast as Petunia, faithful wife of an ingratiating rascal ... Without once stepping out of character or assuming the airs of a star performer Miss Waters captures all the innocence and humor of a story-book character, investing it also with that rangy warmth of spirit that distinguishes her acting. At the present moment this theatregoer imagines that he has never heard a song better sung than "Taking a Chance on Love", music by Vernon Duke, lyrics by John Latouche and voice and acting by Ethel Waters. She stood that song on its head last evening and ought to receive a Congressional medal by way of a reward.' During her career Ethel Waters also introduced such evergreen songs as: 'Dinah', 'Am I Blue?', 'Stormy Weather' and 'St Louis Blues'.

During the Second World War Ethel Waters served with the Seventh Women's Ambulance Corps and was honorary captain of the California State Militia. She returned to the New York stage in May 1945 when she appeared in the revue *Blue Holiday* at the Belasco, and in summer stock she played in *The Voice of Strangers*.

At the Empire in 1950 she played Berenice Sadie Brown in *Member of the Wedding* by Carson McCullers, and Brooks Atkinson was once again ecstatic: 'As the Negro cook and symbol of maternity, Miss Waters gives one of those rich and eloquent performances that lay such a deep spell on any audience that sees her. Although the character has a physical base in Miss Waters' mountainous personality, it has exalted spirit and great warmth of sympathy.' She toured with the production in 1952. In 1953 she was in concert at the 48th Street Theater with *At Home with Ethel Waters* and then had an unsuccessful pre-Broadway tryout of *Gentle Folk* before going to the Congress Hall in Berlin in 1957 under the auspices of the United States State Department to play again in *Member of the Wedding*. At the Renata in New York in 1959 she was once again in concert with *An Evening with Ethel Waters*, and she repeated her role of Berenice in *Member of the Wedding* in

California in 1964 at the Pasadena Playhouse.

During the 1960s and early 1970s Ethel Waters was frequently seen appearing for Billy Graham's 'Youth for Christ' rallies. She made her first film in 1929 when she appeared in Warner Brothers' *On with the Show*. She also made the film version of *Cabin in the Sky* (1943) and was twice nominated for an Oscar — for her performance in *Pinky* (1949) and that in *Member of the Wedding* (1952).

She died on 1 September 1977, survived by her third husband, Edward Mallory.

ORSON WELLES

Georg Orson Welles was born on 6 May 1915 in Kenoska, Wisconsin. His mother was a concert pianist and his father a playboy and an inventor. Orson himself was a child prodigy — onstage aged three at the Ravinia Opera House in *Madam Butterfly*, at nine he was playing Peter Rabbit in Marshall Field's department store in Chicago. A newspaper headline the following year proclaimed, 'Cartoonist, Actor, Painter — and only Ten'. His mother, who was separated from his father and doted on Orson, died when he was still young and then he travelled extensively with his father. At the age of 10 he was finally sent to school for the first time, attending Todd School, a progressive establishment in Woodstock, Illinois. While there, in 1927 he directed *Julius Caesar*, playing the Soothsayer in the production.

After his father's death Orson, aged 16, set off with some of his legacy on a sketching trip in Europe. He got no further than Ireland, where he told the director of the famous Gate Theatre in Dublin that he was an actor from the Theater Guild in New York. Whether or not they believed him, they hired him and he made his professional début there on 13 October 1931 playing Duke Alexander in Lion Feuchtwanger's *Jew Süss*. The *Irish Press* reported: 'The Duke was played with notable success by Mr Orson Welles. He held the audience tense.' Welles remained at the Gate throughout the season, playing Ralph Bentley in *The Dead Ride Fast*, General Bazaine in *The Archduke*, the King of Persia in *Magu of the Desert*, Duke Lamberto in *Death Takes a Holiday* and the Ghost and Fortinbras in *Hamlet*. The season ended in March 1932 and Welles went to London, where he was offered employment by a number of managements; but the Government refused to give him a work permit so he returned to the United States and dragged his press cutting book unsuccessfully around the managements on Broadway. He returned to Chicago, where he worked on a Players Edition of Shakespeare published as *Everybody's Shakespeare*. He then took an extended trip to Morocco, where he sketched and wrote short stories, sending them back to the United States where they were published in pulp magazines. He went on to Spain where he briefly worked as a picador but then — money all spent — he returned to Chicago. Luckily, at a cocktail party he met Thornton Wilder who gave him a letter of introduction to the New York critic Alexander Woollcott, who in turn introduced him to Katharine Cornell who hired him for her company's United States tour. For the 1933–34 season he travelled the country playing Octavius Barrett in *The Barretts of Wimpole Street*, Marchbanks in *Candida* and Mercutio in *Romeo and Juliet*.

During summer 1934 he organized the Woodstock Drama Festival, bringing MacLiammòir and Hilton Edwards over from Dublin to perform with him. During the six-week season he staged *Trilby*, in which he played Svengali, *Hamlet*, in which he was Claudius, and *Czar Paul*, taking the role of Count Pahlen. MacLiammòir reported: 'Orson's Count Pahlen and his King in *Hamlet* were outrageously exciting. Had he kept control and given the performance he promised during rehearsal it would have been the finest Claudius I had seen, but Orson in those days was a victim of stage intoxication; the presence of an audience caused him to lose his head; his horses panicked and one was left with the impression of a man in the acute stages of delirium tremens.' Still, it was a triumphant season which Welles ended with the temperance melodrama, *The Drunkard*. Also in the company was a young actress called Virginia Nicholson, with whom Welles fell in love; they were married on Christmas Day 1934.

That same December, Orson Welles made his New York début at the Martin Beck Theater playing both the Chorus and Tybalt in Katharine Cornell's production of *Romeo and Juliet*. John Mason Brown said he was a 'passable Tybalt'. In March 1935 he played McGafferty in John Houseman's Phoenix Theater production of *Panic* at the Imperial. By this time he was earning a very satisfactory living as a radio actor; he was heard on 'The March of Time' and 'The Shadow' as well as in many individual plays.

The Federal Theater Project was launched in 1936 and John Houseman, who was in charge of Negro Theater, invited Welles to join him on the project, at the Lafayette Theater in Harlem. Welles directed an all-black *Macbeth*, changing the locale from Scotland to Haiti, and it was the sensation of the season. Also for the project he directed *Turpentine* and *Horse Eats Hat*. At the St James Theater he played André Pequot in Sydney Kingsley's anti-war play *Ten Million Ghosts*. It opened on 23 October 1936 and closed the same night. He then designed, directed and played the title role in *Dr Faustus*, which opened at the Maxine Elliott Theater in January 1937. He had cut the play to a running time of an hour and a half without an interval. Brooks Atkinson reported in the *New York Times*: 'As the learned doctor of damnation, Orson Welles gives a robust performance that is mobile and commanding and he speaks verse with a deliberation that clarifies the meaning and invigorates the sound of words.' It was an enormous popular as well as critical success, and ran for six months. By this time Welles' earnings as a radio actor were astonishing, and he raced from studio to studio in an ambulance he hired to avoid being held up at traffic lights.

In 1937, with Houseman, Orson Welles founded the Mercury Theater which they intended to be a permanent repertory on continental lines. They leased the Comedy Theatre, which they then renamed. They opened on 11 November with a modern-dress (because they could not afford costumes) version of *Julius Caesar* in which Welles played Brutus. Brooks Atkinson wrote: 'Mr Welles's mind is not only his own but it is theatrically brilliant and he is an actor of remarkable cogency ... Mr Welles's Brutus is an admirable study in the somber tones of reverie and calm introspection; it is all kindness, reluctance and remorse.' And John Mason Brown reported: 'To an extent no other director in our day and country has equalled, Mr Welles proves in his production that Shakespeare was indeed not of an age but for all time ... As Brutus Mr Welles shows once again how uncommon is his gift for speaking great words simply. His tones are conversational. His manner is quiet; far too quiet to meet the traditional needs of the part. But it is a quiet with a reason. The deliberation of Mr Welles's speech is a mark of the honesty which flames within him. His reticent Brutus is at once a foil to the staginess of the production as a whole and to the oratory of Caesar and Antony.' *Julius Caesar* was such a

success that they transferred to the larger National Theater.

Welles then directed *The Cradle Will Rock*, which opened in December 1937, and *The Shoemaker's Holiday* which opened in January 1938. Then in April he played Captain Shotover in his own production of Shaw's *Heartbreak House*. For the summer of 1938 he directed *The Importance of Being Earnest* at the Cape Playhouse in Dennis, Massachusetts, and was at the Stony Creek Summer Theater for two weeks with *Too Much Johnson*.

The Mercury Theater Group had a weekly radio series in which they presented plays, and Welles created a sensation when he broadcast H. G. Wells' *The War of the Worlds*. This famous Martian broadcast convinced thousands of Americans that they had been invaded from outer space.

The 1938–39 Mercury season opened with *Danton's Death* in which Welles played St Just. It was not a success. Welles then condensed a number of Shakespeare's plays into a history of England ranging from 1377 to 1485 which he called *Five Kings*, and in which he played Falstaff. Beset by money problems, as was usual with Welles, the production opened in Boston at the Colonial Theater in February 1939 and got no further. He then went on the RKO vaudeville circuit playing the Rajah in scenes from *The Green Goddess*.

Welles went off to Hollywood hoping to raise money for his *Five Kings*. Instead he wrote, produced, directed and starred in the astonishing *Citizen Kane*. He returned to Broadway to direct *Native Son*, which opened at the St James Theater in March 1941. Brooks Atkinson reported: 'Mr Welles is a dramatic showman; he likes big scenes, broad sweeps of color and vigorous contrast in tempo. He likes theater that tingles with life. Once or twice perhaps, the exigencies of the script drive him into a melodramatic absurdity ... But the production as a whole represents theatre that has been released from stuffy conventions.' Welles then returned to Hollywood, where he made such interesting films as *The Magnificent Ambersons*, *Journey Into Fear*, and also performed in *Jane Eyre* and *The Stranger*.

Asthma and flat feet kept Welles out of the services during the war, but he undertook lecture tours for the United States Government in Latin America and entertained the troops with magic shows. It was in one of his magic shows that he met Rita Hayworth, whom he married on 7 September 1943. It was a turbulent marriage, not helped by his casting and direction of her in his confused film *The Lady from Shanghai*, in which he cut her famous long red hair, bleached it blonde

For his first production at the Mercury Theatre, Orson Welles (left)
played Brutus in a modern-dress version of *Julius Caesar*
(New York, 1937)

Emlyn Williams as Maddoc Thomas in *The Light of Heart*
at the Globe Theatre
(London, June 1941)

and turned her into a Lana Turner lookalike. They were divorced in 1947. He campaigned for Roosevelt and in 1945 took up political writing with his column 'Orson Welles' Almanac' in the *New York Post*.

Welles returned to the stage when in 1946 he adapted, directed and played Dick Fix in Jules Verne's *Around the World in Eighty Days*. It opened at the Adelphi in May and was a disaster. It also cost a fortune and left Welles in such debt and owing so much to the taxman that he went to Europe and remained there for seven years.

At the Théâtre Edouard VII in Paris he participated in the production of his own play, *The Unthinking Lobster*, playing Jake, in June 1950. He then toured West Germany in his own adaptation of *Faust* in which he played the title part and which he had retitled *Time Runs*.

Orson Welles made his London début at the St James's on 18 October 1951, when he directed and played the title role in *Othello*. Kenneth Tynan reported: 'In last night's boldly staged *Othello* he gave a performance brave and glorious to the eye; but it was the performance of a magnificent amateur ... He was grand and gross, and wore some garish costumes superbly. His close-cropped head was starkly military, and he never looked in need of a banjo. But his voice, a musical instrument in one bass octave, lacked range; he toyed moodily with every inflexion. His face expressed wryness and strangulation, but little else. And his bodily relaxation frequently verged on sloth. Above all, he never built to a vocal climax: he positively waded through the great speeches, pausing before key words like a landing craft breasting a swell ... Welles' Othello is the lordly and mannered performance we saw in *Citizen Kane* slightly adapted to read *Citizen Coon*.' However, T. C. Worsley said: 'The great lumbering dazed bull which Mr Welles gives us for Othello may, too, have its shortcomings in detail, but the fact remains that it imposes itself on us so powerfully and terrifyingly that we hardly notice them ... This huge, goaded figure rolls onto the stage the dreadful fog of menace and horror, thickening, wave after wave, with each successive entrance ... Mr Welles ... gave off an aura of terror such as I have seen no actor before produce ... He does not depend on trickery or effect. On the contrary his own performance is an extraordinarily still one: movement is rare and slow. It is done by sheer weight of personality and an imagination that feels the climax mounting, mounting, mounting, and projects that above everything onto us.' In 1951 Welles wrote the scenario for the ballet *The Lady in the Ice* which was staged at the Stoll in September 1953. Then, in June 1955, he opened at the Duke of York's in London with his own adaptation of Melville's *Moby Dick* in which he played the Actor–Manager. Kenneth Tynan wrote: ' ... Mr Welles has fashioned a piece of pure theatrical megalomania — a sustained assault on the senses which dwarfs anything London has seen since, perhaps, the Great Fire ... In aspect he is a leviathan plus. He has a voice of bottled thunder ... The trouble is that everything he does is on such a vast scale that it quickly becomes monotonous. He is too big for the boots of any part ... though Mr Welles plays Ahab less than convincingly, there are few actors alive who could play it at all.'

At last Welles returned to New York, where in January 1956 at the City Center he directed and played the title role in *King Lear*. Brooks Atkinson wrote: 'As a theatrical conception his production is massive and resonant. Taking Shakespeare's most titanic poem more or less as it was written, Mr Welles has made full use of the huge City Center stage by mounting an enormous show. It goes straight through the evening without an intermission, from Lear's fanatical renunciation of his kingdom in the first scene to the death of the beaten old man in the last. In all his capacities, Mr Welles interprets the drama in epochal style. His baleful scenery uses space boldly. The performance is always in motion; the actors rush across the stage in groups; the vocal tones are big and full. One of Mr Welles' virtues is that he is theatrical. He likes a stirring show. Mr Welles has a genius for the theater. It is fine to have him back again.' And John McLain wrote in the *Journal American*: 'There have been more subtle Lears in our time ... but I doubt if there has ever been an equally overwhelming one. You may not go along with Welles' Lear all the way but, by Jupiter, you won't be bored.' During the production Welles broke one ankle and sprained the other, so he had a wheelchair disguised as a throne. It was also in 1956 that Orson Welles married the Italian film actress Paola Mori.

At the Gaiety Theatre in Dublin in February 1960 Welles played Falstaff in his own adaptation of *Henry IV Parts 1 and 2* and *Henry V*, called *Chimes at Midnight*. In London he designed and directed Ionesco's *Rhinoceros* at the Royal Court in April 1960, and in 1962 he took his *Moby Dick* to New York to the Ethel Barrymore Theater.

Welles made many important film appearances, including roles in *The Third Man*, *Compulsion* and *Touch of Evil*. In later life, he was seen mainly on television commercials — or merely heard as the voice behind them. He died in October 1985.
See photograph opposite page 406.

EMLYN WILLIAMS

George Emlyn Williams, one of three sons, was born on 26 November 1905 in the north-east corner of Wales, in a small village called Pen-y-ffordd where his parents ran a greengrocer's business. His strongly Welsh boyhood always made him feel a foreigner in England. He learned English when at the age of eight he attended the convent school of Talacre, run by French nuns. When he was 10 he won a scholarship to the Holywell County School, where he had the good fortune to come under the tuition of Grace Cook, who recognized great talent in the boy and encouraged him in every way possible. By the age of 15 he had already decided to be an actor. In 1923 Williams won another scholarship, this time to Christ Church, Oxford, to study French. There he joined the Oxford University French Club and played the Maître d'hôtel in a farce they mounted called *La Poudre aux yeux*. He then got into the OUDS, and in 1924 had his first part playing Anthony Dull in *Love's Labour's Lost*. In November of that year he was Yvette in a vaudeville production called *By Degrees*, which included a sketch he had written. By February 1925 he had four parts in *Peer Gynt*, and in March played Pola la Marr in *Peter Passes*. At the Presbyterian Church Hall back in his native Connah Quay in May he played Dai Williams in the Welsh *Y Bobl Fach Ddu*. That same month for the OUDS he was the Old Man in *Medea*, and for the British–Italian League at Lady Margaret's Hall played Micuccio Bonavino in the Italian *Lumie di Sicilia*. The following month for the OUDS he was the head waiter in Rostand's *The Two Pierrots* and a Notary in his *The Fantasticks*. In November the OUDS mounted Williams' own play, *Vigil*, in which he played Isaiah.

In February 1926 he played Silence and Morton in *Henry IV Part 2* for the OUDS and James Agate wrote: 'I think I can spy an actor in Mr G. E. Williams, who played the small part of Morton very well indeed.' His own *Vigil* was again produced at a university conference at the Playhouse in Cambridge in March.

Not surprisingly, considering his dramatic output in terms of acting and writing, as well as his study load, in the spring of 1926 Williams had a nervous breakdown and returned home to convalesce. Typically, though, he spent the time writing a full-length play set in Italy and called *Full Moon* which J. B. Fagan staged at the Playhouse.

Emlyn Williams made his professional stage début on 4 April 1927 playing Pelling's 'Prentice in Fagan's *And So to Bed* at the Savoy Theatre. The production transferred to the Globe Theatre the following month. Also at the Globe in June Williams walked on in Strindberg's *The Spook Sonata*, and during July and August he was at the Playhouse, Oxford, in rep playing a Workman in *Uncle Vanya*, Sir Andrew Aguecheek in *Twelfth Night*, the Burglar in *Heartbreak House* and a Footman in Maugham's *The Circle*. He spent the early autumn in a provincial tour of *And So to Bed* playing Pepys' boy, and made his New York début in the part at the Shubert Theater on 9 November 1927.

Returning to London, he played Billy Saunders and the Rev. Yorke in *The Pocket Money Husband* at the Arts Theatre in October 1928, and then in December at the Embassy was Jack in his own play *Glamour*, which he had written while he was in New York. It transferred to the Royal Court, but was not a success. Although greeted with something approaching joy by the critics, who all called him promising, and being a novelty because of his Welshness, Williams did not have an easy time. He was kept going by money sent by the ever-enthusiastic Miss Cook. During 1929 he played two special performances with J. T. Grien's French Players in Zola's *Thérèse Raquin*, Beppo in *Mafro Darling* at the Queen's, and at the same theatre Berthold in *The Mock Emperor*. In April there was one performance of Jean Sarment's *Le Pêcheur d'ombres* in which he played Réné, then in July there was one performance of *The Conspiracy and Tragedy of Charles, Duke of Byron* for the Elizabethan Stage Circle. In October he had four parts in Sean O'Casey's *The Silver Tassie* at the Apollo, which starred Charles Laughton, and in November he played three parts in Hubert Griffith's *Tunnel Trench*, which ran only a few days at the Duchess Theatre.

In January 1930 he was with Laughton once more, this time playing Jules Marnier in Reginald Berkeley's *French Leave* at the Vaudeville Theatre. That same month for the Oxford Preservation Trust he played the First Apprentice in *Savonarola Brown* at the Haymarket and at the Arts Theatre performed in German in *Das Blaue von Himmel*. In March he was acting in Italian in *La Piccola*, and then it was back to English at the Everyman Theatre in Hampstead, where he played Usher in *Fire in the Opera House*. That same month there was a special performance of Clifford

Bax's *Socrates* at the Prince of Wales for the Three Hundred Club in which Williams played Agathon and an Officer.

Then, knowing his linguistic expertise, Laughton recommended Williams to Edgar Wallace for the part of Angelo in the gangster drama *On the Spot*, which opened at Wyndham's in April 1930. While it was running, Williams continued his performances for theatrical societies, which included acting in French and German. In November he played Commissar Neufeld in Edgar Wallace's *The Mouthpiece* at Wyndham's, and then the following month he rejoined the cast of *On the Spot* which had transferred to the Cambridge Theatre.

In February 1931 at the St James's Theatre he had the title role in *Etienne*, which one critic said he performed 'with all the pathos of an imprisoned animal'. Then he had the star role (originally intended for Nigel Bruce) in Edgar Wallace's *The Case of the Frightened Lady*, which opened at Wyndham's in August. This play brought him to the attention of the public not so much as an excellent character actor but as a star. He was also accorded this recognition when he opened it on Broadway, retitled *Criminal at Large*, at the Belasco Theater in October 1932. It also launched his film career. In the meantime his play *A Murder Has Been Arranged* was staged at the St James's Theatre and he performed in his own *Port Said* at the Arts Theatre Club, and directed the production.

In March 1932 he was a Young Frenchman in *The Man I Killed* at the Apollo, and in May played Jack in *Man Overboard* at the Garrick. In May the following year he was Patrick Branwell Brontë in Clemence Dane's *Wild Decembers* at the Apollo Theatre, but more successful that same month was his own adaptation of Réné Fauchois's *Prenez garde à la peinture* which he called *The Late Christopher Bean* and which opened at the St James's starring Edith Evans.

In September 1934 Emlyn Williams opened at the Westminster Theatre playing Piers Gaveston in *Rose and Glove*, and that same month played Eugene Beauharnais in his own adaptation of Hermann Bahr's *Josephine*. Then in May 1935 at the Duchess Theatre, actor and playwright combined to make a notable success when Williams took the role of Dan in his own *Night Must Fall*. It ran for a year and Audrey Williamson reported that his was a '... cheeky, vivid and macabre portrait of the curly-haired and baby-faced murderer. This actor had the mask of a cherub but showed us the vicious twist beneath it; always his dramatic power held the stage, and, with a per-

verted charm, wrung pity from the pitiless.'

In October 1936 Williams opened *Night Must Fall* at the Ethel Barrymore Theater in New York and repeated his London success. He was not so successful with his next venture, *He Was Born Gay*, which he wrote, then co-starred and co-directed with John Gielgud. The *Times* wrote: 'What made Mr Emlyn Williams write this play or Mr Gielgud or Miss Ffrangcon-Davies appear in it is not to be understood.' It lasted twelve performances.

Emlyn Williams joined the Old Vic Company in August 1937, when he played Oswald in *Ghosts* at the Opera House in Buxton. He then played Angelo in *Measure for Measure*, and Audrey Williamson reported that he 'conveyed most vividly the man's leaping sensuality and tortured conflict of soul. One sensed here the tragic stature Angelo might have attained had Shakespeare continued with him as he began ... The facial expression was subtle and varied throughout and for an actor new to Shakespeare Williams spoke the verse with a fine clarity and rhythmic fire. Never for one moment did he cease to dominate the scene; in flesh or spirit his strange beauty haunted the play like the image of a fallen Lucifer.' Also that season with the Old Vic he was Richard III, and Audrey Williamson said: 'This was a short, swarthy Richard, deformed, unkempt and oily; there was no attempt at romanticism and the plausibility of the scene of the wooing of Anne suffered in consequence. But the figure had a darting power, enormous subtlety and humour, and the quick satiric emphasis on the line "this princely heap" flashed at the bowing courtiers, raised a laugh I have never heard equalled in the course of this play ... There were several moments when for a quivering instant one sensed the loneliness of this Richard, the isolation of his deformity that marks him out from other men. Perhaps it was the actor's strain of Welsh poetry that enabled him to reveal this in almost indefinable touches. The monster was also human, and given half a chance would have lifted the play from melodrama to tragedy.'

Emlyn Williams left Shakespeare and returned to Williams in September 1938 when he played Morgan Evans in his autobiographical *The Corn Is Green*, which he also directed. It was the story of the young Williams and the influence his teacher had on him. Williamson wrote: 'Williams' uncouth yet arresting personality had on it that glow that one must recognize as genius. His one emotional breakdown was at once perfectly timed and perfectly true in feeling; the result of that complete fusion of technique and expression that one gets on the stage only occasionally, from the actor or the dancer at the highest artistic point of interpretation.' *The Corn Is Green*, which co-starred Sybil Thorndike, transferred from the Duchess to the Piccadilly Theatre and Williams had yet another enormous success, and a two-year run.

Godfrey Tearle starred in his next play, *The Light of Heart*, but the run came to an end with the phoney war. Williams rewrote the part of Maddoc Thomas for himself and reappeared in London with it at the Globe Theatre in June 1941. At the same theatre in December he played Cliff Parrilow in his own *The Morning Star* and had yet another enormous success — though when it was played in New York with Gregory Peck in the lead it failed. During 1942 he directed two of Lillian Hellman's plays and adapted and directed Turgenev's *A Month in the Country*. Then between 1943 and the spring of 1945 he was on tour for ENSA, first in the provinces and then in the Middle East, Italy, France, Belgium and Holland.

Emlyn Williams, writer, actor and director, was back in the West End in April 1945 playing Ambrose Ellis in *The Wind of Heaven* at the St James's, and James Agate wrote: 'As the travelling showman the author himself perfectly suggests the man in spiritual travail — a beautifully thought-out piece of acting.'

In May 1946 he played Sir Robert Morton in Terence Rattigan's *The Winslow Boy* at the Lyric Theatre, and Audrey Williamson said he 'brilliantly suggested the stab of genius beneath the stiff celebrated barrister's facade'. But he was back writing and directing, as well as starring, at the Globe Theatre in July 1947 when he played Saviello in *Trespass*, a spine-chiller in which he played an Italian medium, thought not to be able to speak English; in fact, Williams remained mute through the first half of the play.

In October 1949 he went to New York, where at the Fulton Theater he was directed by Lillian Hellman in her own adaptation of Emanuel Robles' *Montserrat*, in which Williams played Izquierdo. The following September, back on home ground, he was Will Trenting in his own *Accolade* at the Aldwych Theatre, but this time he let Glen Byam Shaw direct.

Although his writing output was prodigious and his acting powers in various productions much praised, it is probably inevitable that it is as a solo performer that Emlyn Williams will be best remembered. He first performed Charles Dickens in a three-minute reading from *Bleak House* at an all-star charity at Drury Lane in February 1951. Since then he has been around the world with that author, adapting, reciting and acting out the stories. He enjoyed both long runs and one-night

stands on tour, and was still doing it in 1970 in New York when John Simon reported: '... for people who cannot or will not read, and who enjoy Williams' snappy way with a snippet (quite generous snippets too) *Charles Dickens* may be as pleasant a way of not reading a book, or of not going to the theater, as anyone could ask for.'

His other great solo performance is that of Dylan Thomas. He began reading Thomas aloud in 1954 when he appeared in *Homage to Dylan Thomas* for the Dylan Thomas Memorial Fund at the Globe Theatre. By April 1955 he was presenting a full evening, *Dylan Thomas Growing Up*, at the Connaught Theatre in Worthing. It came to London to the Globe by way of Bath in May. Richard Findlater described in detail Williams' effect: 'A chair, a screen and a spell are the only furniture at the Globe on this summer night in Shaftesbury Avenue. From the wings a stocky, white-haired sorcerer walks forward, papers under his arm, Wales in his voice, and the life of a dead poet in his head. He wears a navy blue suit, a red tie, and an air of deceptive neutrality; his trousers are, somewhat ostentatiously, supported by a belt; and he, no less conspicuously, is supported by nothing at all. Bowing sedately to the audience, he puts the papers on a chair, tests his aura, and begins to talk. It is Emlyn Williams at his wizard's work. For over two hours he is in command, alone on this bare stage, with the irresistible authority that marks the true star ... Unravelling a ladder of words, he climbs up with a knowing smile into a Welsh landscape of bawdy, lyrical fantasy and fun, and pulls the spectators up after him. It is a brilliant performance of the Cambrian Rope Trick ...'

In December 1955 at the Saville Theatre, Emlyn Williams played Hjalmar Ekdal in Ibsen's *The Wild Duck*, with Dorothy Tutin. Although the critic Caryl Brahms did not like the production she reported: 'His was a carefully considered, perfectly timed solo performance. I never expect to see a better-carpentered, more brilliantly amusing Ekdal.' Kenneth Tynan, however, did not care for it: 'Mr Williams exposes Hjalmar's paltriness with the cool competence of an accountant tabulating forged entries in the firm's books, but he does not feel for the man; nor, in consequence, can we.'

Williams went to the Shakespeare Memorial Theatre in Stratford-on-Avon, where in the 1956 season he once more played Angelo in *Measure for Measure*. He also played Iago to Harry Andrews' Othello, and Henry Alleyn reported: 'Mr Williams gives us half the spleen and none of the exuberance. His villainy is never credible because he does not believe in it enough.' That season he was also Shylock in *The Merchant of Venice* directed by

Margaret Webster, and Frank Granville-Barker wrote at length: 'Emlyn Williams has clearly made a close study of Shylock and he makes a very human figure of this hater of Christians. His interpretation is consistent, logical, and skilfully carried out. Yet his performance left me unmoved. Shylocks tend either to stimulate pity or revulsion, and I feel that Emlyn Williams is trying to make us experience both responses. With his fine dramatic technique he should have achieved this, but for me at least he did not quite do so. I was conscious, too, of his trick of isolating and emphasizing a single word in a sentence — a device which he used most tellingly in his readings from Dickens and Dylan Thomas. In these instances he was enlivening writing that was not in itself dramatic, and the result was triumphantly successful. But here the case is different; too frequent isolation of a word, however important its bearing on the play, sounds like an affectation.'

At the Piccadilly Theatre in October 1958 he wore an overcoat and a muffler and played the Author in Robert Ardrey's documentary about the Hungarian revolution, *Shadow of Heroes*, with Peggy Ashcroft. Caryl Brahms wrote: 'Mr Emlyn Williams as "the author" seemed pompous, spurious, and quite unnecessary, but then it was the part, not the actor, who was to blame.'

At the Arts Theatre in January 1961 he was in *Three*, a triple-bill comprising *Lunch Hour* by John Mortimer, *The Form* by N. F. Simpson and *A Slight Ache* by Harold Pinter. He then went to the Music Box in New York, where he played Ascolini in *Daughter of Silence* in November. In June 1962 at the ANTA in New York he took over the part of Sir Thomas More in *A Man for All Seasons*; that same month he received a CBE. Still in New York, in February 1964 he played Pope Pius XII at the Brooks Atkinson Theater in *The Deputy*. According to Howard Taubman writing in the *New York Times*, he played the Pontiff 'coldly and shrewdly'. Williams then set out on a tour of the United States, Canada, Pakistan, India and Japan with *Charles Dickens*, before bringing it back to London to the Globe in August 1965.

At the Cambridge in September 1965 he played Ignatyillyich in *A Month in the Country*, and Martin Esslin reported that 'Emlyn Williams as the doctor leads a fine supporting cast of real comedy characters'. In September 1969 he took over the part of the Headmaster from John Gielgud in *Forty Years On* at the Apollo. The following year he set off on a Dickens Centenary World Tour.

Emlyn Williams' film career has been notable, and includes such movies as *The Citadel*, *I Accuse* and *The Walking Stick*. He has written several novels and two highly praised volumes of autobiography.

See photograph opposite page 407.

NICOL WILLIAMSON

Nicol Williamson was born in Hamilton, Scotland, on 14 September 1938. His father was a manufacturer in Dundee who wanted his son to be a metallurgist but gracefully conceded to his desire to be an actor. Williamson studied drama in Birmingham where his reputation for being 'difficult' began, but he explained that he was unpopular because he believed he knew best, because he wanted to apply the discipline to himself rather than have it imposed from outside. Williamson spent two seasons at the Dundee Repertory Theatre, and in Cambridge in October 1961 at the Arts Theatre played in *That's Us*. He made his London début in that production the following month at the Royal Court. That same month he toured as Black Will in *Arden of Faversham* and was back at the Royal Court in January 1962, playing Flute in *A Midsummer Night's Dream*, directed by Tony Richardson. The critic Caryl Brahms did not like the production, saying it was '. . . badly spoken, badly acted, badly lit, badly set'; however, '. . . how grateful we are . . . for the really funny theatrical débutant Flute, the bellows mender'. The following month he was an excellent Malvolio at the same theatre in a Production without Décor of *Twelfth Night*.

In April 1962 Nicol Williamson joined the Royal Shakespeare Company at the New Arts Theatre to play Albert Meaken in Henry Livings' play about life in the modern RAF, *Nil Carborundum*. Peter Roberts said he gave a '. . . faultless performance in the regional post-Theatre Workshop manner so much in demand at the moment'. Still at the New Arts with the RSC, in May Williamson played Satin in Gorky's *The Lower Depths*, and Clive Barnes wrote: 'Nicol Williamson, as Satin (Stanislavsky's original role and the best part in the play) is as hungry and as generous as a lion, handling the final resolution of Gorky's theme with a sort of impassioned tact. The message that all men owe a duty to others could, taken out of context, seem as flatly platitudinous as a cracker motto. It was the triumph of both Williamson's performance and ultimately [Toby] Robertson's production that it carried utter conviction.' For the RSC in July he was Leantio in Middleton's *Women, Beware Women*, and Clive Barnes was once again very happy with his performance: 'Nicol Williamson's masterly portrayal of the clerk Leantio [was] full of bitterness but a bitterness obviously motivated by a sense of social inequality and injustice.'

Williamson returned to the Royal Court in April 1963 when he played the Man at the End in another Production without Décor, *Spring Awakening*, and there in June he was Kelly in Henry Livings' play about obsessive love, *Kelly's Eye*, with Sarah Miles. John Russell Taylor reported: '... the whole weight of the production falls on Nicol Williamson as Kelly, and fortunately he is superbly capable of meeting all the role's demands: elsewhere he has looked in lesser roles like one of our more interesting young actors; here he effortlessly puts himself in the front rank.'

He opened at the Ashcroft Theatre in Croydon in November 1963, as Sebastian Dangerfield in J. P. Donleavy's *The Ginger Man* and transferred with the production that same month to the Royal Court where, Simon Trussler reported, he was '... a delightful mixture of lethargy and vitality'.

It was in September 1964 at the Royal Court that Nicol Williamson first played Bill Maitland in the original production of John Osborne's *Inadmissible Evidence*. Martin Esslin wrote: 'Nicol Williamson is the anti-hero. He gives a memorable performance, eloquent, varied, full of imaginative touches. A mammoth achievement. My only quibble is that he does not, he cannot look like a credible solicitor. In fact, to me he looks much more like an actor.' The following month at the Royal Court he was Peter Wykeham in a revival of Ben Travers' *A Cuckoo in the Nest*, and John Russell Taylor reported: 'Nicol Williamson's reading of Peter Wykeham, the silly-ass hero, is much too strenuous and heavyweight, lacking entirely the well-bred vagueness that the part calls for ... The part, obviously, has to be played completely in period, and this Nicol Williamson, though he makes a game attempt, never quite manages to do.' In December at the same theatre he was Vladimir in *Waiting for Godot*. Of this performance Alan Simpson wrote in *Plays and Players*: 'Nicol Williamson has been widely praised for a number of his performances recently. But in a

slightly in-group sort of way. ''A clever actor for these clever Royal Court audiences'' has been the critical implication. His playing of Vladimir, however, is of a quality rarely seen on the London stage except during the visits of the Moscow Art Theatre. Stardom? Perhaps. Not your Cult of the Personality stardom, but the stardom of pure acting.'

Nicol Williamson returned to Bill Maitland and *Inadmissible Evidence* at Wyndham's in March 1965 and John Russell Taylor reported at length: '... his role of Bill Maitland, the fortyish solicitor whose world slowly dissolves about his ears in the course of the play, is extremely, if not quite uniquely taxing, and since most of the play is virtually a monologue by him, if he is not absolutely on top of it the whole production suffers much more than most would from an off-night of most actors. At his best, however, he is absolutely superb, and gives one of the great performances of the modern English theatre. The role is written brilliantly, but within a very narrow range of emotions — self-pity, petulance, despair, savage irony. On a good night Nicol Williamson can extract the maximum variety of light and shade from Maitland's great rhetorical excursions about, and largely against, the way we live now. On a bad night though, a certain monotony makes itself felt, but the gamble is worth taking for the possible prizes of the production when it is on form.'

In April 1965 back at the Royal Court, Williamson, in a Production without Décor, played Joe Johnson in *Miniatures*, and in June at the Globe Theatre was Sweeney in *Sweeney Agonistes* in a 'Programme of Homage to T. S. Eliot'.

Nicol Williamson made his New York début at the Belasco Theater in December 1965 where once more he played Bill Maitland in *Inadmissible Evidence*. John Simon wrote: 'Perfectly embodying Osborne's sourly scintillating humor, there sits, slouches and sidles, groans, grumbles and fulminates Nicol Williamson, an actor whose looks, sounds and movements have a heroic asymmetry, who emits a truculent lopsidedness that mauls our eyes and ears. Take his face: is it cadaverous or fleshy? It squiggles in both directions. Take his voice: is it an outrage or a joke? Mere phonemes become laden with ambivalence. Never absent from the stage throughout the play, Williamson prestidigitates more than he acts: our stock responses to Maitland are kept dextrously in abeyance.' And Martin Gottfried said: 'Nicol Williamson's performance in the bravura central role is everything the word ''virtuoso'' means — the sweating, frightened, boastful, confident, hopelessly neurotic Everyman, unwanted by a world he wants.' Williamson won the New York

Drama Critics Award for Best Actor 1965–66. Also during that production he met the American actress Jill Townsend, who played his daughter and was to become his wife in 1971.

Back in London in March 1967 he opened at the Duchess Theatre playing Alexei Ivanovitch Poprichtchine in Gogol's one-character *Diary of a Madman*. Hugh Leonard wrote: 'Gogol would have loved Nicol Williamson's performance in the production now at the Duchess Theatre. The play never for an instant compromises with the conventional demands of the theatre, or acknowledges the presence of an audience, and neither does Mr Williamson or his director Anthony Page. It is an extraordinary performance, done meticulously and without passion or sentiment. Probably nine out of ten other actors would have played against and around the lines, attempting to extract a degree of sympathy, but Mr Williamson gives us the unadorned original: he fills the dimensions of the play fully, without ever breaking through the perimeter. Gogol receives perfect justice from him but no favours. The diary extracts are read in a plummy Brummy [Birmingham] accent which reminds one of E. L. Wisty; and in the fussiness of the delivery Mr Williamson quite brilliantly suggests the man's pretensions. He is one of the best technicians in theatre today: his voice is as well-tuned as a concert grand.' He returned to New York in June 1968 where at the Plymouth Theater he took over three parts in Neil Simon's *Plaza Suite*.

At the Round House in London in March 1969, Nicol Williamson played the title role in *Hamlet*. Michael Billington analysed his performance: 'No doubt about it: Nicol Williamson's Hamlet undoubtedly leaves a lot out. The observer's eye is mercilessly there but scarcely the scholar's tongue or soldier's sword ... and yet, for its excess coarseness and over-reliance on a note of unmasked contempt, this is the most exciting Hamlet since Redgrave's 1958 Stratford performance ... it combines a relish for grandiose romantic effect with a scrupulous attention to detail and to the sheer basic sense of the lines ... This is not a complete Hamlet ... It lacks irony, delicacy, gentleness. Its virtues, however, plead trumpet-tongued on its behalf. It matches the play's questing feverishness with a bottled hysteria of its own. It informs the lines with a bristling, bruising intelligence and is constantly showing Hamlet to be testing those around him ... And it provides the rarest of all sensations: the feeling that the actor rejoices wholeheartedly in his presence on the stage ... it is refreshing to find a man-sized, ravenously hungry attack on the part. Some actors take the stage by default: Mr Williamson invariably takes it by storm.' For his performance Williamson

won the *Evening Standard* Award for Best Actor of 1969. He took the production to the Lunt-Fontanne Theater in New York in May 1969, and John Simon reported that this Hamlet seemed to '... suffer from an acute sinus condition. Williamson has a tendency to sound like an electric guitar twanged away at, with fearful symmetry, high-low, high-low. It is a maniacal singsong, so stringently nasal that the lips seem to part only for visual effect ... Even in some of his weakest moments Williamson will erupt from among some shabbily or indifferently read lines with one or two that possess marvelous shrewdness, animal vitality or insidiously ironic scorn. And there are times when the tenor of querulous fault-finding does rise to metaphysical exasperation, and the play becomes not poetry but a superb prose translation.' Williamson then toured the United States with *Hamlet* before returning to the Circle in the Square in New York in June 1973, where he played the title role in *Uncle Vanya* and also appeared in his own *Late Show*.

Back in England with the RSC in October 1973 he was a much-praised Coriolanus at the Aldwych, where in November he played in *Midwinter Spring*. The following season he played Malvolio in *Twelfth Night* and the title role in *Macbeth*. According to Williamson in an interview in the *Herald Tribune*: 'The *Macbeth* was the best and truest thing I've been involved in in seven years. Again, there was no way London would accept it. Even though the *Times* said it was the definitive *Macbeth* — I don't mean my performance, I mean the central conception — they hated it and hated us for doing it. What some people want from Shakespeare is red robes and rolled R's.' At the Other Place in 1975 he directed *Uncle Vanya* and once more played the title role.

Williamson then went back to New York, where he played Henry VIII briefly in the ill-fated Richard Rodgers musical *Rex*. As he said, 'It was a mistake — you can only find out by doing it. There is no way of predicting these things. I will never do another musical. Never again. Never!'

In 1978 Williamson was back at the Royal Court once more playing Bill Maitland in *Inadmissible Evidence*. Irving Wardle reported in the *Times*: 'Nicol Williamson's original performance was a staggering *tour de force* for a young actor. He is now the right age for the part. I have not the memory to draw any detailed contrast but, taking the added emotional maturity for granted, the really astounding factor in the new production is its technical virtuosity. Some of Osborne's asides (often delivered in telephone conversations) are distinctly top-heavy but Williamson gets through them with amazingly articulated speed; he excels also in doing emotional turns on a sixpence, passing from a moan to a snarl on a single vowel, and abruptly changing from the hollow-eyed wreck into the master of the office. Emotionally he has clearly identifiable vocal colours for dutiful conversations with his regular women, and has genially slurred approaches to virgin territory. But, of course, all these effects are a product of the inner turmoil; and the most powerful of them verge on the inarticulate, and reveal his contradictory need to drive people away while suffering panic when anybody threatens to desert him.' This revival was also seen off-Broadway.

Nicol Williamson has appeared notably in many films, including *The Seven Per Cent Solution*, *The Human Factor* and *Excalibur*. He lives in New York and Rhodes.
See photograph opposite.

PEG WOFFINGTON

*I*f she had as many lovers as reported and gossiped about, it is doubtful whether Peg Woffington could have had time to learn the more than 125 major roles she performed during her thirty years on the stage. That she was exceptionally beautiful, charming and witty and had a great number of lovers is, however, not in doubt.

Margaret Woffington was born in Dublin in about 1718. Her father was a travelling bricklayer and Peg, a bright child, attended a local Dame school. Her mother was widowed while her two daughters were still young, and to support them opened a grocery shop, but the venture failed. With the two girls in tow she took to the streets hawking fresh vegetables; when she branched out on her own Peg, thanks to her beauty and wit, became an excellent saleswoman. She was noticed by an ex-rope walker, Madame Violante, who ran a children's acting troupe in a booth at George's Lane. The group was called the Lilliputians; Peg joined them as an apprentice when she was 12. Madame Violante taught her diction and dance and her first role was that of Polly Peachum in Gay's *The Beggar's Opera*. The writer Robert Hitchcock reported: '. . . the uncommon abilities of the little performers and the great merit of the piece, attracted the notice of the town to an extraordinary degree . . .' She next played the country ale-wife and several small parts in Christopher Bullock's *The Cobbler of Preston*. In August 1732 Madame Violante took her troupe to London, where at the theatre in the Haymarket Peg performed several small roles in *The Beggar's Opera* as well as the role of Captain Macheath, the first of the 'breeches' roles for which she would become famous. During their two-week London stay she also played Columbine in *The Jealous Husband Outwitted*. As it was summer and there were not many theatregoers in the capital their stay was not successful. Madame Violante decided to stay on in London and sent her troupe back without her.

Through the intercession of the schoolmaster, poet and playwright Charles Coffey, Peg was allowed to sit in on rehearsals of Erlington's company at the Theatre Royal in Smock Alley. A new Theatre Royal was built in Aungier Street and opened in March 1734 with Farquhar's *The Recruiting Officer*, in which Peg played a country wench. That season she also played a French peasant and Miss Crotchet in the satirical opera *The Rival Theatres, or, a Playhouse to Be Lett*. She also danced between the acts and spent her spare time reading widely and studying parts so that when at the last minute an actress cast as Ophelia was taken ill, Peg stepped into the role. Hitchcock reported: 'She began to unveil those beauties and display those graces and accomplishments which for so many years afterwards charmed mankind.' At the Theatre Royal in Dublin she played Miss Lucy in Fielding's *Virgin Unmask'd*, and Phyllis in Steele's *Conscious Lovers* which was to become one of her favourite roles. She played Nell in Charles Coffey's *The Devil to Pay* and had a breeches part when she played the title role in *The Female Officer*. William Rufus Chetwood reported: 'She never displayed herself to more advantage than in character where she assumed the other sex. Her figure, which was a model of perfection, then free from restraints, appeared in its natural form.' The company toured Ireland during the summers, mostly giving fit-up productions in barns.

In November 1737 the theatres were closed for six weeks in mourning for the death of Queen Caroline and Peg went to Paris as a dancer. On her return to Dublin she played another breeches role, Silvia in *The Recruiting Officer*, which was hailed as a great success. At her own instigation she next played another male part — that of the rake

Nicol Williamson as Bill Maitland in John Osborne's *Inadmissible Evidence* at the Royal Court
(London, November 1978)

With his own Shakespearian company, Donald Wolfit staged and
played the title role in *Hamlet*
(London, August 1941)

Wildair in Farquhar's *The Constant Couple*, and Hitchcock reported: '. . . so infinitely did she surpass expectation that the applause she received was beyond any at the time ever known.' It was an enormous success and made her name. Verses were written in her honour and she was the talk of the drawing rooms. She continued most successfully until the theatres were closed during the severe winter of 1739–40. Peg retired to the country for a period with her current lover. When the theatres reopened in April she played Lappet in *The Miser*, Silvia in *The Recruiting Officer* and Polly Peachum in *The Beggar's Opera*.

Charles Coffey took her to London in May 1740 where she endeavoured to see John Rich, manager of Covent Garden. At first she was turned away — it is reported as often as nineteen times — as her reputation had not crossed the Irish Sea. Finally, however, her perseverance was rewarded and she was granted an interview. Rich, overwhelmed by her beauty, hired her immediately and she made a great success of her Covent Garden début on 6 November 1740 as Silvia in *The Recruiting Officer*. She also played in *The Double Gallant* and was Audrey in *The Country Lovers* before giving the amazed Londoners her Wildair in *The Constant Couple*. A contemporary critic reported: 'In the well-bred rake of quality, who lightly tripped across the stage, singing a blithe song, and followed by two footmen, there was no trace of the woman. The audience beheld only a young man of faultless figure, distinguished by an ease of manner, polish of address, and nonchalance that at once surprised and fascinated them.' She had an unprecedented run for that time of twenty nights.

After one season at Covent Garden Peg quarrelled with Rich over money and left for the rival theatre, Drury Lane. That season she played Nerissa in *The Merchant of Venice*, Lady Brute in *The Provok'd Wife* and Helen in *All's Well that Ends Well*. On 16 May she was Cordelia in David Garrick's *King Lear*, and then she returned to playing Silvia. In June 1742 she departed for Ireland and the Smock Alley Theatre with Garrick, where they performed, among other plays, *The Recruiting Officer*, *Richard III*, *Hamlet*, *Lear* and *The Constant Couple*; by the end of the summer she and Garrick were involved in an affair. They set up house together on their return to London and were a much-approved couple in London society, but as they were temperamentally unsuited they soon parted, though they continued their professional connection. Garrick had an argument with the management of Drury Lane and went over to Covent Garden, but Peg stayed on and played, among other roles, Isabella in *Measure for*

Measure and a breeches role in *The Humours of the Army*.

Garrick returned to Drury Lane as a partner in 1747, bringing the actress Kitty Clive with him. Enmity broke out between her and Peg who although acting with Garrick refused to resume their former relationship; he then turned against her, refusing her any good roles, and in the spring of 1748 she gave in her notice. That summer she visited Paris, where she studied 'natural' acting techniques with Madame Dumesnil.

For the 1748–49 season she returned to John Rich at Covent Garden. There she played her popular roles. However, the audiences did not respond as warmly as before; the young actress George Anne Bellamy was now their favourite, although Peg re-established herself with audiences when she played Lady Macbeth to James Quin's Macbeth and the title role in *Lady Jane Grey*. John Rich introduced other stars into Covent Garden to weigh the scales in favour of his theatre over Garrick's Drury Lane; however, it only caused rivalry within the company, particularly when Susan Cibber came along. A disagreement with John Rich over billing caused Peg to refuse to appear and the audiences blamed her, not him.

In 1751 Peg Woffington returned to Dublin to Sheridan's company at Smock Alley, where she opened the season with a gala command performance of *The Provok'd Wife*. She played a wide range of roles that season to enormous critical and financial success, and was re-engaged for the following season at more than double her salary. That 1752–53 season was to be the highlight of her career. She played Andromache, Hermione in *The Distrest Mother*, Calista in *The Fair Penitent*, Maria in *The Non-Juror*, Silvia in *The Recruiting Officer*, Wildair in *The Constant Couple*, Portia in *The Merchant of Venice*, Ophelia in *Hamlet* and Rosalind in *As You Like It*. She was once more the Queen of Dublin and presided over the Beefsteak Club, which indulged once a week in extravagantly luxurious meals, often entertaining English aristocrats. This annoyed the ordinary Irish even more than her love life.

During the 1753 season she played the Widow Lackit in *Oroonoko*, and then in February Sheridan decided to stage Voltaire's *Mahomet*, in spite of advice warning him that the play was considered politically dangerous. It was performed on 2 February 1754, with Peg playing Palmyra. That time they got away with just a vocal demonstration, but when he presented it again in March the audience rioted and smashed up the theatre. In a fit of pique Sheridan went to England, but the theatre was refurbished and reopened in March with a benefit for Peg in which she played in *All for Love* and the audiences greeted her warmly once more. She went to London for the summer, intending to return to Smock Alley for the next season; however, she was not re-engaged because the new management thought her price too high. Once more she went to Rich at Covent Garden, where she made her return playing Maria in *The*

Non-Juror. She also resumed her squabbling with George Anne Bellamy.

By 1757 her health was declining. On 17 May she played Rosalind and collapsed as she came off-stage, unable to speak her finishing lines. She never appeared again on stage. She weakened progressively and died on 26 March 1760.

DONALD WOLFIT

Donald Wolfit was born on 20 April 1902 at Newark-on-Trent, where his father worked for a brewery. When he was a child he recited and sang at concerts during the First World War, and then taught briefly in a school at Eastbourne before setting out for a career in theatre, which was his obsession. He was taken on as a student with Charles Doran's Shakespeare Company and made his stage début with the company in a walk-on role in *The Merchant of Venice* at the Theatre Royal in York on 13 September 1920. Wolfit stayed with Doran for two years and then joined the Fred Terry Company, where he remained for another two years touring in *The Scarlet Pimpernel*, *The Borderer* and *The Mask and the Face*.

In November 1924 Donald Wolfit joined Matheson Lang at the New Theatre and made his London début playing Phirous in *The Wandering Jew*. At the same theatre during February and March 1925 he was Tomasso in *Carnival* and the Swiss Soldier in *The Tyrant*. He then spent two years with the Arts League of Service playing and directing, and in 1927 joined the Sheffield Repertory Company. Back in London at the Strand in July 1928 he played Stephan in *Such Men Are Dangerous* and in January 1929 was Abdul in *The Chinese Bungalow*. At the Everyman in May 1929 Wolfit played Professor Drysell in *Smoke Persian* before joining the Old Vic Company for their 1929–30 season, during which he played Tybalt in *Romeo and Juliet*, Cassius in *Julius Caesar*, as well as Touchstone, Macduff and Claudius. At the Queen's Theatre in May 1930 he was once more Claudius in *Hamlet*, and at the Arts in July he played Jaroslav Prus in *The Macropoulos Secret*. At the New Theatre that October he was Roger de Berville in *Topaze*, and he spent from November 1930 until February 1931 at the Embassy playing Absolom in *The Witch*, Dr Carelli in *Black Coffee*, Beguildy in *Precious Bane* and Blaskovics in *Lady in Waiting*.

He then toured as Maurice Mullins in *A Murder Has Been Arranged* before returning to the Embassy in May 1931 as Paul Cortot in *Marriage by Purchase*. He joined Sir Barry Jackson's company in 1931, and toured Canada as Robert Browning in *The Barretts of Wimpole Street*, Young Marlow in *She Stoops to Conquer* and Joe Varwell in *Yellow Sands*. Back in London in September 1932 at the New Theatre he played the Doctor in Shaw's *Too True to Be Good* and then toured with the production in the role of the Burglar. In February 1933 he began a year's run as Thomas Mowbray in *Richard of Bordeaux* at the New Theatre and then in April 1933 he played the title role in *Hamlet* at the Arts Theatre Club. It was a great success and made him eager to produce Shakespeare himself. Meanwhile, at the Westminster Theatre in April 1934 he played Halvard Solness for the first time in *The Master Builder*. At His Majesty's in September 1934 he was the Orderly in *Josephine* and at the Gate the following month played André Merin in *The Sulky Fire*. At the Haymarket in November he was Darrell Blake in *The Moon in the Yellow River*, and at the Q in May 1935 played Leonard Charteris in *The Philanderer*. At the same theatre the following month he was Young Marlow in *She Stoops to Conquer* and transferred with the production to the Westminster in July. At the Arts in October he was Kenyon Mallory in *Pirate Mallory*, and back at the Q in November 1935 Wolfit played Adolphus Cusins in Shaw's *Major Barbara*. In January 1936 Donald Wolfit opened in Croydon as Lucius Catiline in *Catiline* and transferred with the production to the Royalty in February.

Donald Wolfit joined the company at the Memorial Theatre at Stratford-on-Avon for their 1936 season, during which he played Hamlet, Orsino, Cassius, Kent, Ulysses, Tranio, Gratiano and Don Pedro. Hamlet was a part he was to play many times, and Audrey Williamson later wrote:

'A fine Hamlet of the thirties, though never as physically suited as Gielgud, was that of Donald Wolfit, who when he first played the part at Stratford-on-Avon in 1936 and 1937 gave it an electric drive and force of suffering. Time later blunted the edge of that earlier spontaneity, and mannerisms crept in: the performance became mellower, more studied, but remained to the last, in passion and intellect, one of the best Hamlets of the decade. There was thought behind every gesture and line and again and again one was struck by the subtlety of detail ...'

In London at the New Theatre in October 1936 Wolfit played Antony in *Antony and Cleopatra* and at the Q in December was Sir Percy Blakeney in *The Scarlet Pimpernel*. He returned to Stratford for the 1937 season where he played Iachimo, Ford, Touchstone, Autolycus, and Bobadil in *Everyman in His Humour*. Then that September he fulfilled his dream of founding his own Shakespearian company, which he toured playing Hamlet, Macbeth, Shylock and Malvolio with Phyllis Neilson Terry as his leading lady.

At the Westminster Theatre in London in January 1938 he played the title role in *Volpone*, another role with which he would become identified, and then was back on tour as Cyrano de Bergerac. At the Malvern Festival in 1938 Wolfit played the title role in *Alexander* and Richard de Beauchamp in *Saint Joan*, and created the role of the Judge in Shaw's *Geneva*. He spent the autumn of 1938 touring in his Shakespearian company, and in January 1939 succeeded Alexander Knox and Clement McCullin at the St James's Theatre playing his original role in *Geneva*.

Donald Wolfit went to the Gaiety Theatre in Dublin in May 1939 where he appeared in a season of modern plays, and then in February 1940 he brought his Shakespeare company to London for the first time when at the Kingsway Theatre he played Hamlet, Shylock, Petruchio, Malvolio, Othello and Benedick. In September 1940 during the Blitz he remained at the Strand Theatre playing Shakespeare at lunchtime—he held on for three months and appeared as Touchstone in *As You Like It*, Falstaff in *The Merry Wives of Windsor*, Bottom in *A Midsummer Night's Dream*, Giovanni in *'Tis Pity She's a Whore* and the title role in *Richard III*. In June 1941 he set out on a tour as Sir Percy Blakeney in *The Scarlet Pimpernel*, and for most of the rest of his career was on the road, making periodic visits to London, with his company. He was at the Strand in 1942 and at the St James's in 1943; James Agate wrote of his performance as Solness in *The Master Builder*: 'Wolfit has every natural attribute of a fine Solness. Playing the architect as a bearded romantic of not-too-advanced middle age, he magnificently depicts the ruthlessness, charm and tortured restlessness of mind of a man in whom dread of the younger generation ''knocking at the door'' alternates with dreams of cloud capp'd towers, greater and greater architectural triumphs. He began the play with admirable speed and drive, but a hanging onto syllables in the last scene suggested that at this time he had not yet successfully thrown off the Shakespearian manner.' He was also at the Westminster Theatre in 1943, and the following year he was at the Scala, where Agate saw his King Lear and reported: 'Mr Wolfit had and was all the things we demand, and created the impression Lear calls for. I say deliberately that his performance on Wednesday was the greatest piece of Shakespearean acting I have seen since I have been privileged to write for the *Sunday Times*.' Of his Hamlet that season, Agate wrote: 'Mr Wolfit plays the whole of Hamlet, though this is quite a different matter from presenting Hamlet as a whole ... I have seen many Hamlets of greater elegance and charm, and I agree that to those who rate the Prince of Denmark according to his pettableness, Mr Wolfit must come very low. But this is to take the lap-dog view of Shakespeare's character ... If I must choose a caretaker to show me round [the play] I think it would be Wolfit, who puts me back into Shakespeare's day and time even if the character presented is not Hamlet but some elder, stronger-minded brother ...'

As well as touring the provinces during the war Wolfit took his company through most of the RAF stations and garrisons, and in 1944 was in Paris, Brussels and Versailles on a National Service Tour. In London in 1945 he touched down at the Winter Garden Theatre and added Macbeth to his repertoire. Agate reported: 'The fact that Mr Wolfit cannot play Macbeth is neither here nor there, since many great actors have failed in the part.' He also took his company to Cairo and Alexandria that year. During 1946 Donald Wolfit toured as Feyda in *Redemption*, and the following year he toured Canada in repertory.

He made his New York début at the Century Theater in February 1947 playing King Lear, as well as Touchstone in *As You Like It*, Shylock, Volpone and Hamlet. In April he came back to England to the Savoy, where he played the same roles in repertory with the addition of Iago in *Othello* and Malvolio in *Twelfth Night*. Of his Volpone, Harold Hobson wrote: 'I have rarely seen Mr Wolfit give a better performance ... In his representation of the miser and mountebank who pretends illness in order to squeeze presents out of his expectant heirs, there is flamboyance, a self-rejoicing, exuberant and chuckling delight, that matches the gaily corrupted eloquence of a piece which, if it resembles a catalogue of diseases, a doctor's dictionary, is nevertheless a considerable work. *Volpone* has the teeming life of worms in a rotting corpse, and Mr Wolfit plays it with all the fifty-seven kinds of relish.'

Donald Wolfit toured Canada from coast to coast in 1948, and returned to London to the Westminster in May where once more he played in *The Master Builder*. At the Winter Garden in November 1948 he directed and played Jonathan Swift in *The Solitary Lover* and Hobson reported: '... one feels that Mr Wolfit's performance as Swift, though rich in power and richer in noise, is not quite right. It is a pity, for the purpose of tragedy, that this actor's face, in its pale roundness, should so much resemble a pasty plum pudding; it is a pity, too, that Mr Wolfit fills his speeches with as many hems as if he were a ladies' dressmaker ... A more serious matter is Mr Wolfit's failure to communicate an essential element in Swift ... If the brain were divine, Swift would be a god: but his imagination was filthy ... Now for all his roaring, his flashing of eye, and his rasping of voice, and that profound knowledge of theatrical geography which tells him infallibly where the centre of the stage is to be found, Mr Wolfit does not ever manage to suggest this strangeness, which should move us to a withdrawing horror, but to pity also. Mr Wolfit does do all that doth become a man and we need both more and less.'

In 1949 Donald Wolfit leased the Bedford Theatre in Camden Town, where he remained with his Shakespeare repertory for four months. Of his Brutus in *Julius Caesar* T. C. Worsley wrote: 'Mr Wolfit has never aspired to the epithet "unselfish" but the inescapable fact is that however many qualifications one may make, or the actor himself may impose, we are on his entrance in the presence of the great tradition of acting; Brutus is not a part he does well: indeed it reveals more of his weaknesses than his gifts. Yet he stands there and he speaks, and his mere presence and the pitch of his voice swell and expand the entire emotional atmosphere, broaden it, deepen it, lengthen it — carry us, in short, into a larger and intenser mood ...' Of Wolfit's Lear the same critic wrote: 'His king is a magnificent creation, as deeply felt as thought and acted with the most detailed skill.'

For Christmas 1949 Wolfit played Long John Silver in *Treasure Island* at the Fortune, and in May 1950 he was in Richmond playing Sir Giles Overreach in *A New Way to Pay Old Debts*. That year he was awarded the CBE. He appeared with his own company at the Malvern Festival that year in a repertoire of nine classical plays, and then set off on another tour before returning to London

where, at the Middle Temple Hall in the presence of Her Majesty the Queen, he appeared with his company in a performance of *Twelfth Night*. He then took over the lead in *His Excellency* at the Piccadilly Theatre.

In September 1951 Donald Wolfit joined the Old Vic Company where, directed by Tyrone Guthrie, he played the title role in Marlowe's *Tamburlaine the Great*. T. C. Worsley reported: 'Mr Donald Wolfit is the very man for Tamburlaine. His voice has the widest range of any actor on the stage today. He has the force and power. In the first half he projects an adolescent relish in animal cruelty, and rises in the second to a kind of madness which is turned in on itself in a lust for destruction. Only the death scene where, like a great bear in shaggy fur, he stumbles to and fro across the outspread map of the world, doesn't quite come off. But this is surely Marlowe's fault.' In December with the Old Vic Company he played Lord Ogleby in *The Clandestine Marriage*, and Worsley said: 'Mr Donald Wolfit's performance as Lord Ogleby is in the very highest class ... crammed with little subtleties of surprise and ingenuities of the unexpected and yet each of these touches, once they have been added, have about them that inevitability of being exactly right. Tact, restraint, invention, style, in all these Mr Wolfit excels ...' And Kenneth Tynan reported: 'The authors envisaged Ogleby as a flimsy, dew-lapped ruin of a man; Wolfit is as staunch and four square as an Olympic wrestler, and what he achieves is a tremendous display of sheer toil, a triumph of art over nature, in which the actor tests all the resources of his paint box ... Possessing not one of the qualities, physical or temperamental, of the part ... he attacks it with the knockdown aplomb that Grimaldi, one imagines, might have brought to Coriolanus. Mr Wolfit is an actor with a comedian's face and a tragedian's soul and for this reason nearly always looks mysteriously miscast.'

Wolfit had a disagreement with the Old Vic and left the company. In April 1952 he co-presented *Lords of Creation*, in which he played Rear-Admiral Sir Benjamin McGuffie at the Vaudeville Theatre. In February 1953, with a newly re-formed company, he appeared at the King's, Hammersmith, in his usual repertoire with the addition of *Oedipus Tyrannus* and *Colonus*, *The School for Scandal*, *Henry IV Part 1* and *The Wandering Jew*. There were the usual complaints that Wolfit surrounded himself with inferior players all the better to shine through — but most critics were only saddened by this habit. Wolfit did not need to increase his stature by inferior surroundings. Of his Lear, this time round, Kenneth Tynan wrote: 'Mr Wolfit's Lear is a brilliant compound of earth, fire and flood. Only the airy element is missing.'

Wolfit took over from Roger Livesey as Marcus McLeod in *Keep in a Cool Place* at the Saville Theatre in October 1954, and that year appeared in the Royal Variety Performance at the London Palladium. At Christmas at the Scala he was Captain Hook in *Peter Pan*, and the following November he played Fr Alfonso Fernandez at the Piccadilly in *The Strong Are Lonely*, transferring with the production, which was a great success, to the Haymarket in January 1956. In February 1957 at the Lyric, Hammersmith, he directed Henri de Montherlant's *The Master of Santiago* and played the part of Don Alvaro. The play had run for more than a year in its native France, but more than one English critic found it 'unrelievedly serious and sombre'. The following month at the same theatre he co-directed *Malatesta*, a play by the same author, and played the title role. Sidney Heaven, writing in *Plays and Players*, said: 'Donald Wolfit shows us all the facets of his character: the crude murderer and the fine connoisseur whose hands tremble to touch a fine text: the schoolboy joker, the philanderer, and the sober home-keeping husband; the poisoner and the penitent; the conjurer and the simpleton. It is a performance of magnificent range and one which may still perhaps gain in subtlety.' He became Sir Donald Wolfit in the 1957 Birthday Honours List.

At the Lyceum in Edinburgh in September 1958 Donald Wolfit directed *The Broken Jug* and played Adam. In January 1959 he went on a Shakespeare recital tour which took him to Kenya, Ethiopia, Uganda and Italy. Back in London at the Prince's Theatre in April he played Pastor Manders in *Ghosts* and then set out on another tour in 1960. This time his Shakespeare recital was seen across the United States, in Canada, New Zealand, Australia, Malaya, India, the Persian Gulf and the Lebanon. At Leatherhead in December 1961 he played Cromwell in *Cromwell at Drogheda* and back in London at the Duke of York's in July 1962 he was the newspaperman Archie Pander-Brown in Alastair Dunnet's *Fit to Print*. In November he went off to South Africa with his Shakespeare recital, and returned to London to the Duchess Theatre in December 1963 playing the title role in *John Gabriel Borkman*. Hugh Leonard reported: 'Sir Donald Wolfit managed to display a superb comic talent before symbolism set in, and I intend no irony by saying that his Borkman was never more than the hollowest of men. Not once did one believe that this erstwhile tycoon had ever been a financial genius

... The rich smoked smell of charlatanism permeated Wolfit's performance ... Sir Donald's impish rendering of Borkman deserves to become the definitive version and I think Ibsen would have been highly pleased.'

At the Prince Charles Theatre in February 1964 Sir Donald appeared in *Fielding's Music Hall*, giving a monologue taken from *Oliver Twist*, and at the Royale Theater in New York the following February he played Ezra Fitton in *All in Good Time*.

At the Theatre Royal in Brighton in September 1965 he was Screwtape in *Dear Wormwood*, and for Christmas that year at the Mermaid played Long John Silver once more. His last stage appearance was at the Lyric, when in March 1966 he took over the role of Edward Moulton-Barrett in *Robert and Elizabeth*.

Donald Wolfit made some notable films, including *Trilby*, *Room at the Top* and *Lawrence of Arabia*, but his home was always the stage and in particular the Shakespearian stage. He believed firmly that Shakespeare should be taken to the people, and though touring was an expensive business he found that he could manage if he continued to nip into the West End or a film to fill the coffers. Frank Granville-Barker summed up his talent: 'What always distinguishes Wolfit's playing is his dramatic range and intensity, his splendid eloquence, and his ability to present Shakespeare's tragic heroes in truly noble colours. So many other actors play down Lear, Hamlet, Macbeth, Othello and Antony whereas Wolfit lets us see them in their full heroic stature. The wind, the sea, and the noise of battle echo in his voice; arrogance, nobility and suffering are given perfect expression in his generous yet always disciplined gestures, and his features mould themselves to show us emotions that are human but larger than those of everyday life. He is never afraid to pull out all the stops and sweep us off our feet in a torrent of theatrical excitement. This excitement, which we rarely experience in our over-refined theatre, is Wolfit's hallmark. He may lack the funds to mount his productions very lavishly, he may have a company who pale beside his own bright colour but his own performances have genuine magic, and his productions of Shakespeare reflect his love and understanding of the dramatist.'

Sir Donald Wolfit died on 17 February 1968. He had been married three times and his last wife, Rosalind Iden, the actress, was often associated with him in his work.

See photograph opposite page 415.

IRENE WORTH

*I*rene Worth was born in Nebraska on 23 June 1916. As a child she studied piano and cello, and graduated from the University of California at Los Angeles in 1937 with a degree in education before becoming a teacher.

Miss Worth made her first stage appearance when in 1942 she toured with Elisabeth Bergner in *Escape Me Never*, playing Fenella. In August the following year she made her New York début at the Booth Theater playing Cecily Harden in *The Two Mrs Carrolls*. She then went to London, where she studied acting with Elsie Fogerty; she made her London début at the Lyric, Hammersmith, in February 1946 playing Elsie in *The Time of Your Life*. At the Mercury Theatre in April she was in *This Way to the Tomb*, and at the Embassy in June played Annabelle Jones in *Love Goes to Press*, transferring with the production following month to the Duchess. She toured Britain in October 1946, playing Ilone Szabo in *The Play's the Thing*, and at the Embassy in December was Donna Pascuala in *Drake's Drum*. *The Play's the Thing* opened at the Lyric, Hammersmith, in April and transferred to the St James's in May 1947, with Irene Worth playing her original role. In October she was back on tour, this time in *Return Journey*. At the Q in December she played Olivia Brown in *Love in Idleness*, and in February at the same theatre had the title role in Pinero's *Iris*. That same month at the Bolton she played Mary Dalton in *Native Son*, and in April was *Lucrece*.

At the Lyric Theatre in July 1948 Irene Worth took over the part of Eileen Perry from Leueen McGrath in Robert Morley's *Edward My Son*, and then toured as Lady Fortrose in J. B. Priestley's *Home Is Tomorrow*. This production came to London, to the Cambridge Theatre, in November 1948, and Audrey Williamson said her performance was 'brilliant and incisive'. At the New Theatre in June 1949 Irene Worth played Olivia Raines in *Champagne for Delilah*, and Harold Hobson reported: 'Irene Worth plays the vamp with a touch most amusingly down in the mouth.'

Irene Worth created the part of Celia Coplestone in T. S. Eliot's *The Cocktail Party* at the Edinburgh Festival in August 1949, and Audrey Williamson said it was a 'superb performance played movingly and at white heat'. She took the role to New York, where she opened at the Henry Miller Theater in January 1950; Brooks Atkinson reported: 'Irene Worth finds the lonely depths of the character of the woman in a remarkably skilful, passionate and perceptive

performance.' She returned to London and took over the role from Margaret Leighton, who had been playing it at the New Theatre in July 1950.

In October 1951 Irene Worth joined the Old Vic Company and appeared at the Berlin Festival playing Desdemona in *Othello*. She played the same part at the Old Vic on the company's return to London that same month, and Audrey Williamson wrote: 'The girl who could flout convention and choose for love not colour, who ''saw Othello's visage in his mind'', and concentrated all the spiritual and physical warmth and intensity of her nature on this one figure who held her tenderness, respect and imagination, became at last fully alive on the stage, and the essential gentleness of Desdemona, and her breeding, lost nothing in the humanizing process.' That same season with the Old Vic Company she played Helena in *A Midsummer Night's Dream* and Catherine de Vausselles in *The Other Heart*. She toured South Africa with the company playing these parts, and also Lady Macbeth. Back at the Old Vic Theatre in January 1953 she played Portia in *The Merchant of Venice* and Kenneth Tynan wrote: 'Portia's lines are not unremittingly funny, but they are certainly not improved by the frills and flatness which Miss Worth hangs out on them. She repeatedly falls into the classic Old Vic error of supposing that all Elizabethans laughed aloud at their own jokes. For her first entrance she wears an ill-advised tip-tilted straw hat, such as an amusing aunt might pop on after a few sherries, and within seconds she is practically bursting an appendix with suppressed giggles. I agree that Portia must unbend with her maids, but there is no necessity to go down on all fours. This roguey-poguey style is at present all the voguey-poguey, and I call upon Miss Worth to take a stand against it.'

Irene Worth went to Stratford, Ontario, for their first Shakespeare Festival Season in 1953, playing Helena in *All's Well that Ends Well* and Queen Margaret in *Richard III*. Back in London at the Haymarket Theatre in November she played Frances Farrar in *A Day by the Sea*. Then in March 1955 with the Midland Theatre Company in Coventry she created the part of Argia in Ugo Betti's *The Queen and the Rebels*. At the Edinburgh Festival that year she played Alcestis in *A Life in the Sun*, and in October came to London to the Haymarket with *The Queen and the Rebels*. Kenneth Tynan reported: 'Up to the moment of her conversion Miss Worth presents a prostitute so noisily world-weary that it is a bore for her even to deafen us; and afterwards, when the switch to queenship has been made, she becomes full-bloodedly operatic ... Miss Worth gives the author what his lines demand, a display of technique which is grandiose, heartfelt, marvellously controlled, clear as crystal and totally unmoving. The house exploded in cheers when she had done, which was only natural. Having been roared at for two and a half hours, it restored the balance by roaring back.' Frank Granville-Barker, however, was moved: 'The task of sustaining the play falls to Irene Worth who gives a performance in which brilliance and depth are balanced to razor-edged perfection. Her transformation, from a rejected slut abjectly cowering at her lover's feet into a redemptress of regal poise, has the conviction that only an actress of rare accomplishment and integrity can ever achieve.'

At the Winter Garden in May 1956 Irene Worth played Marcelle in *Hotel Paradiso* with Alec Guinness. Caryl Brahms thought she was miscast: '... she is droll and terrifyingly expert without being right in the part ... She gives an energetic and extremely witty portrayal of an actress in a farce ...'

At the Phoenix Theater in New York in October 1957 Miss Worth played the title role in Schiller's *Mary Stuart* with Eva Le Gallienne playing Elizabeth. She then returned to London in February 1958 where at the Globe she played Sara Callifer in Graham Greene's *The Potting Shed*.

She was once again Mary Stuart, at the Edinburgh Festival, in September 1958 and the same month transferred with the production to the Old Vic Theatre. Peter Roberts reported: 'Irene Worth is an actress blessed with a rich, deep plummy voice of extraordinary range. An artist of sensitivity, imagination and fine technical accomplishment, she brilliantly suggested Mary's underlying *joie de vivre*, her sensuality, her love of beautiful things, the power and pride of a spirit fettered but not broken.'

Irene Worth returned to the Shakespeare Festival at Stratford, Ontario, in June 1959 to play Rosalind in *As You Like It*. At the Hudson Theater in New York in February 1960 she was Albertine Prine in Lillian Hellman's *Toys in the Attic*. She returned to England and joined the RSC at the Aldwych in March 1962 to play the Marquise de Merteuil in *The Art of Seduction*, John Barton's adaptation of *Les Liaisons dangereuses*, and then at Stratford-on-Avon in June she was Lady Macbeth to Eric Porter's Thane. Harold Hobson said it was a 'restrained and credible' performance, and Peter Roberts said it '... remained interesting even if it did not reach the grand scale'. In November, at Stratford she played

Goneril in *King Lear*, which starred Paul Scofield and was directed by Peter Brook. Irving Wardle reported that her '... Goneril is a creation of fierce sexuality which burns through her slightest gesture and lowest-toned utterances. With the minimum assistance from the text Miss Worth establishes the fact that Goneril's rule even over her servants is one of erotic appeal ... [it is a performance] charged with a passion which one normally regards as beyond the range of English actresses.' Irene Worth repeated the role at the Aldwych in December 1962 and the following month at the same theatre played Doktor Mathilde von Zahnd in *The Physicists*, by Dürrenmatt, again directed by Peter Brook. John Russell Taylor reported: 'Irene Worth gives a very actressy performance in a part which can hardly help being showy and the result is quite acceptable.' At the Haymarket in August of that year she played Clodia Pulcher in *The Ides of March*, and then in February 1964 returned to the RSC, playing in *King Lear* again at the Aldwych before setting off on a British Council tour of Europe, the USSR and Canada. The company also played at the opening of the New York State Theater in May 1964. At the Billy Rose Theater in New York in December she played Alice in Albee's *Tiny Alice* and won a Tony for her performance.

Back in London in April 1966 Irene Worth co-starred with Lilli Palmer and Noel Coward in Coward's *Suite in Three Keys* at the Queen's Theatre. She played Hilde Latymer in *A Song at Twilight*, Anne Hilgay in *Shadows of the Evening* and Anna-Mary Conklin in *Come into the Garden, Maud*. John Russell Taylor said she 'hits exactly the right note as the wife [in *A Song at Twilight*], a role which only just skirts the edge of caricature and could easily be pushed over by an off-key performance.' She received the *Evening Standard* Award for Best Actress in 1966.

In November 1966 she set out on a tour for the British Council which took her through South America and the United States universities in *Men and Women of Shakespeare*, and at Yale University in May 1967 she played in *Prometheus Unbound*.

Irene Worth returned to England in July 1967 when at the Chichester Festival she played Hesione Hushabye in *Heartbreak House*. Peter Roberts said: '... she proves to be an exceedingly glamorous and effortlessly commanding Mrs Hushabye. Indeed, she seems to take Shaw's dialogue on the palm of her hand and blow it out into the auditorium like a feather. It is a performance that is by turns caressing, seductive, witty, languid and good humoured.' The production transferred to the Lyric in November 1967, and the critic of *Plays* and Players wrote: 'It would be irresponsible not to point out that Irene Worth's Hesione towers regally above the rest of the cast. Although Shaw may well have thought of Hesione as irresistible, he wrote her as a tease, and Miss Worth, by some combination of acting and personality which defies analysis, has restored the irresistibility.'

She was next seen at the Old Vic in March 1967 playing Jocasta in Peter Brook's 'happening' production of *Oedipus*. At the Aldwych in January 1970 she repeated her performance as Miss Alice in *Tiny Alice*. At Stratford, Ontario, in June that year she played the title role in *Hedda Gabler*. At the Globe in London in March 1972 she was the playwright Dora Lang in Frank Marcus' *Notes on a Love Affair*. Irene Worth returned to Chichester in May 1973 to play Irina Arkadina in *The Seagull*, directed by Jonathan Miller. She played the same part at Greenwich in January 1974 and then at the same theatre was Mrs Alving in *Ghosts* and in March played Gertrude in *Hamlet*. At the Brooklyn Academy in December 1975 she played Princess Kosmonopolis in *Sweet Bird of Youth* and transferred with the production to the Harkness, winning another Tony. She has also been awarded a CBE.

In 1984 she was back on the London stage as Volumnia to the Coriolanus of Ian McKellen.

CHARLES WYNDHAM

C harles Culverwell was born in Liverpool on 18 July 1837. His father was a watchmaker at the time, but eventually became a victualler and then a hotelier. At the age of 10 Charles was sent to Sandgate School, near Folkestone, and was then educated in Germany and Paris. He went to the University of St Andrews, where he began acting in amateur productions at Sir Hugh Playfair's private theatre. He wanted to be an actor, and although his father insisted that he study medicine, Charles was not to be dissuaded. He acted in the Cabinet at King's Cross where amateurs paid to play roles, but then he went to Dublin to study at the Peter Street Anatomical School. In 1860 he married the well connected Emma Silberaad, granddaughter of Baron Silberaad of Hesse-Darmstadt, and set up as a general practitioner, but no patients appeared. On 30 November 1860 he appeared at the Royalty Theatre in Dean Street playing Captain Hawksley in a charity performance of *Still Waters Run Deep*. It was then that he took the stage name of Wyndham. He made his professional début at the old Royalty Theatre on 8 February 1862 playing Christopher Carnation in *Carnation of Carnation Cottage* under the management of Madame Albina de Rhona. He remained with the company for six months playing various roles. He was by this time rather impoverished, as patients were still not coming to his practice, and went to America where the Civil War was raging, joining the Federal army as a surgeon. During this time he also managed to have an unsuccessful season as an actor in Washington. Leaving the army, he made his New York début at the Olympic Theater on 8 October 1863 with Mrs John Wood in *Brother and Sister*. This was not a great success either.

He returned to England and made his next appearance at the Theatre Royal in Manchester in July 1865 playing Howard Ormsby in his own play *Her Ladyship's Guardian*. After other provincial appearances he returned to London in May 1866 where at the Royalty Theatre, now under the management of Patty Oliver, he played the wicked baronet Sir Arthur Lascelles in *All that Glitters Is Not Gold*. He remained at the Royalty for ten months playing various parts, including John Mildmay in Tom Taylor's *Still Waters Run Deep*, and even danced as Hatchett the Smuggler in *Black Ey'd Susan*.

In April 1867 he joined Louisa Herbert's company at the St James's Theatre, where he shared a dressing room with Henry Irving. There he played the hero in *Idalia*, and then joined Kate Terry for her farewell season at the Prince's Theatre in Manchester, playing Mercutio, Claudio and Laertes, among other roles.

Back in London in October 1867 at the Queen's in Long Acre he played Colonel Dujardin in *The Double Marriage* with Ellen Terry, next playing Captain Hawksley in *Still Waters Run Deep*. In January 1868 he had a success when he played Charley Garner in H. J. Byron's *Dearer than Life*.

At the Queen's Charles Wyndham was involved in a series of one-act plays and in burlesques, and among other roles also played Ned Clayton in *A Lancashire Lass*, Sir Lucius O'Trigger in *The Rivals*, de Neuville in *Plot and Passion*, and Walsingham Potts in *Trying It On*. While continuing to play rather colourless heroes at the Queen's he ventured into management in May 1868 when he took the Princess Theatre and revived *Nobody's Child* there, starring Kate Reynolds. At the Princess he also revived *The Wonder* and *Richelieu at Sixteen*, but it was an unsuccessful venture. He spent the summer of 1869 at the Olympic Theatre playing Rupert Danvers in *Love and Hate*, and in September went to New York where at Wallack's Theater in September he opened as Charles Surface in *The School for Scandal*. In October he was George d'Alroy in *Caste*, and that same month played Dick Dowlas in *The Heir in Law*. In November he was John Mildmay once more in *Still Waters Run Deep*. At the same theatre in May 1870 he played Victor de Courcy in *The Lancers* and Belmour in *Is He Jealous?*, and was then Otis in *Central Park*. In partnership with Louisa Moore he started his own touring company, which opened at Wall's Opera House in Washington in March 1871. The Wyndham Comedy Company toured the United States until 1873 with a repertory that included *Caste*, *The Lancers*, *The Débutante* and *Saratoga*.

On his return to England Wyndham played Stephen Fiske in *Robert Rabagas*, an adaptation from Sardou, at the St James's in February 1873. Then in May he toured the provinces as Geoffrey Delamayn in Wilkie Collins' *Man and Wife*. The tour was under the management of the Bancrofts. At the Royalty in October 1873 Charles Wyndham played Rolando, the sailor misogynist in John Tobin's verse drama *The Honeymoon*, and was Mr Wilkinson in W. S. Gilbert's *The Realm of Joy*. In November at the same theatre he was Robert Ancrum in Albery's *Married*, and then in December played Jack Rover in *Wild Oats*. Charles Wyndham was Rawdon Crosbie in January 1874 in *Ought We to Visit Her?* and the following month played Philip in *A Breach of Promise*. At the beginning of May he played Charles Surface at the Gaiety and at the end of the month scored a notable success at the Court when he played Bob Sackett in *Brighton*, an anglicized version of *Saratoga*. He was at the Olympic in August playing Captain Dudley Smooth in *Money*. On 8 September 1874 he launched his famous series of Crystal Palace matinées, which began with his playing Rover in *Wild Oats*. In his three years of matinées he produced nearly a hundred plays at the Crystal Palace. In June 1875, at the Haymarket, he played again in *Brighton*, and at the same theatre the following month he was Dufard in *The First Night*.

Charles Wyndham went to the Criterion Theatre in December 1875 where once again he played Bob Sackett in the highly successful *Brigh-*

ton. The following April he took over the management of the Criterion, and it became his only permanent home in London until the turn of the century. He began his management that month with an adaptation of a French farce called *The Great Divorce Case*, in which he played Geoffrey Gordon. That ran most successfully, and he followed it in November with another production from the French, *Hot Water*, in which he played Chauncey Pattleton. In February 1897 he produced *Pink Dominoes*, adapted from the French by his friend Albery. He played Charles Greythorne and the piece ran for 555 performances. In February 1879 he played Alfred Sterry in *Truth*, and in August produced another farce, *Betsy*, in which he did not appear. As *Betsy* was running so successfully at the Criterion he next appeared in January 1880 at the Olympic in a revival of *Brighton*.

Charles Wyndham returned to the Criterion in November 1880 when he played Sir Garroway Fawne in *Where's the Cat?*, also an Albery adaptation, but this time from the German. It ran 150 performances. In May 1881 Wyndham played Montague Leyton in *Butterfly Fever*. He had his first failure at the Criterion in December 1881 when he played Frederick Foggerty in W. S. Gilbert's *Foggerty's Fairy*, so he quickly revived *The Great Divorce Case*. In March 1882 he was back in another farce from the French playing Peregrine Porter in *Fourteen Days*.

A new ventilation system was needed for the underground Criterion, so while the theatre was closed Wyndham toured North America, where he remained for eighteen months. There he performed in New York, Cleveland, Chicago, Milwaukee, Detroit, Cincinnati, St Louis, Indianapolis, Baltimore, Washington, Philadelphia, New England, San Francisco, Salt Lake City, Denver and throughout the Deep South, as well as in Montreal and Quebec.

The Criterion reopened on 16 April 1884 with a revival of the old reliable *Brighton*. In June he was in Albery's adaptation of *Tête de linotte* called *Featherbrain*, and in November played Viscount Oldacre in *The Candidate*, another notable success which ran for 285 performances. It was also notable for the beginning of his stage partnership with Albery's wife, Mary Moore, who co-starred. By this time he had tired of farces and in May 1886 he produced *Wild Oats* at the Criterion, once more playing Jack Rover. In October he changed his name legally to Wyndham and the following month had one of his greatest successes when, co-starring with Mary Moore, he played the title role in *David Garrick*. In January 1888 they set out on a Continental tour of the play, acting in German in Berlin and Petrograd. They returned with it to the

Criterion in February, where it ran for 376 performances. In June 1888 he played Harry Jasper in *A Bachelor of Arts*, and in January 1889 revived *Still Waters Run Deep*. In March he was Jack Wyatt in a revival of *Two Roses* and in July played Sam Hedley in *The Headless Man*.

Mary Moore's husband, James Albery, died in August 1889, and in the autumn Mary Moore and Wyndham set off on a tour of the United States. They returned to the Criterion in April 1890 where Wyndham played Sangfroid in *Delicate Ground* and Walsingham Potts in *Trying It On*. He revived *She Stoops to Conquer* in May, playing Young Marlow, and in June was Harry Grahame in *Sowing and Reaping*.

In November 1890 Charles Wyndham played Dazzle in a revival of *London Assurance* and the following April was Charles Surface once more in *The School for Scandal*. He produced *Miss Decima* in July but was not in it himself. He was Charles Hartley in *The Fringe of Society* in April 1892 and in May played John Dow in *Agatha*. The following month he was Dr Power in *Mrs Hilary Regrets*. In January 1893 Charles Wyndham played Viscount Clivebrook in *The Bauble Shop* by Henry Arthur Jones; the critic Archer reported that it was the 'strongest piece of serious acting he has given us yet'. It ran for 135 performances. His next play, *An Aristocratic Alliance* by Lady Violet Greville and derived from Sardou's *Le Gendre de M. Poirier*, in which Wyndham played the Earl of Forres, ran only two months, but he had another success with Henry Arthur Jones' *Rebellious Susan*, which opened in October 1894 and ran for 164 performances. In May 1895 he was the Rt Hon. Duncan Trendel in R. C. Carton's *The Home Secretary*, and that November played Mr Kilroy in *The Squire of Dames*, an adaptation of *L'Ami des femmes* by Dumas *fils*.

By this time Wyndham had left his wife and two children, though on the best possible terms. He and Mary Moore were a couple idolized on stage and also welcomed off stage because their personal affair was always conducted with the utmost discretion. Mary was also by this time his business partner as well as his acting partner and lover.

Charles Wyndham celebrated twenty years of management of the Criterion with a marathon theatrical event on 1 May 1896. There was an afternoon matinée at the Lyceum which consisted of *A Clerical Error*, Act I of *Money* and Acts I and II of *The School for Scandal*. In the evening at the Criterion he performed *Who's to Win Him?*, *David Garrick*, and Act II of Sheridan's *The Critic*. This celebration raised an enormous sum of money for the Actors' Benevolent Fund, and after

a day and night on stage Wyndham entertained 1500 people to supper at the new Hotel Cecil in the Strand.

In May 1896 he opened as Sir Jasper Thorndyke in *Rosemary*, a romance by Louis N. Parker and Murray Carson. This ran until the summer break came in July and then returned to the Criterion in the autumn. His next play, *The Physician* by Henry Arthur Jones, was not a success; it opened in March 1897 and he played Dr Lewin Carey. Jones' next play, which Wyndham mounted at the Criterion in October, has been called a masterpiece of English social comedy. It was *The Liars*, and in it Wyndham played Sir Christopher Deering. William Archer reported: 'Mr Wyndham, as an actor, has one great fault from the critic's point of view — he is too persistently good . . . Here is a little problem for an aspiring actor: a piano is heard off stage, there is a pause in the conversation, a lady asks "Is that not Mrs Ebernoe?" and a gentleman answers "Yes" — how is the gentleman to convey in that one word "Yes" the fact that he is devotedly, chivalrously, adoringly, in love with this Mrs Ebernoe whom, be it observed, we have not seen and of whom we know nothing? Don't ask me how it is done but go to the Criterion and see Mr Wyndham do it.'

In November 1898 Wyndham played Cesare, the character with an embarrassingly long death speech in Parker and Carson's romantic costume drama, *The Jest*, and in April 1899 he was Mr Parbury in Haddon Chambers' *The Tyranny of Tears*. This was a great success and his last long run at the Criterion. He ended his twenty-three years there with a performance of *Rosemary* in aid of the Prince of Wales Hospital Fund. Although he retained the lease on the Criterion, Wyndham and Mary Moore had built themselves a new theatre in Charing Cross Road which they called Wyndham's. They opened it in November 1899 with a charity performance of *David Garrick*. They meant to run the play for two weeks, but because of public demand it carried on for four months. He then toured playing the title role in *Cyrano de Bergerac*, opening with it at Wyndham's in April 1900. Max Beerbohm said it was a part that every actor wanted to play. 'Mr Wyndham happens to be the man who ultimately got it. But as the part does not, from a critic's standpoint, exist, how am I to praise his performance of it? How, as one who revels in his acting, do ought but look devoutly forward to his next production?' The public did not care for their hero in a big nose either, but the play ran till June. In October Wyndham was back in a play by Henry Arthur Jones: he was Daniel Carteret in *Mrs Dane's Defence*, which Max Beerbohm called his best performance. It ran for

209 performances. The following October he played Lord Lumley in *The Mummy and the Humming Bird*, and in April 1902 he was Sir Edward Vulliamy in *The End of a Story*. That year he was knighted in the Coronation Honours by King Edward, only the third actor to be so honoured, and J. T. Grien wrote on the occasion: 'He is, on the stage and in life, the incarnation of what all the world has accepted as a model — a perfect gentleman. May he continue to flourish, a master of his art, a veteran in his profession, yet a juvenile in power, in spirit and in fertility.'

He and Mary were by this time building another theatre. This was the New, which although situated in St Martin's Lane backs onto Wyndham's. They opened the New Theatre on 12 March 1903 with a revival of *Rosemary*, then went back to Wyndham's in May where Charles played Captain Mowbray in Hubert Henry Davies' *Mrs Gorringe's Necklace*, which was a great success and transferred to the New in September. In February 1904 at the New he was Ralph Wigran in *My Lady of Rosedale*, a play adapted from the French by Comyns Carr. In May at the same theatre he was Thomas Bruse in *The Bride and Bridegroom*, after which he set off on another American tour. He had played *David Garrick* and *Mrs Gorringe's Necklace* three weeks each at the Lyceum in New York when he was hit by a car and dislocated a shoulder. He was in the middle of a run of *Rebellious Susan* and he could not play. His understudy was unprepared, as it was the first time Wyndham had ever been off — he was never ill. Then Mary caught bronchitis, so they cancelled the tour and went to Italy to recuperate. They returned to London in October 1905 where at the New Theatre he played Captain Drew, RN, in *Captain Drew on Leave*. In March 1906 at Wyndham's he revived *The Candidate*. Back at the Criterion in April 1907 he revived *The Liars*; although the houses were good the production lost money because of having a cast of sixteen — actors' salaries had increased greatly. His next production, however, had a cast of only four — a very daring experiment at this time. It was *The Mollusc* by Hubert Henry Davies, and Wyndham opened it in October 1907 playing Tom Kemp. H. M. Walbrook said that Wyndham had '. . . a scene of sheer farce in the first act, which he played with

all the gaiety of his Bob Sackett days; in the second and third there is comedy of the richest in his attempts to rouse his sister, and their abject failure; and just toward the end there is a love scene with the governess, a little spun-out perhaps, in its opening, but . . . beautifully acted. All through the play, in fact, we had this masterly comedian at his best and London theatregoers know what entertainment that means.' And Max Beerbohm wrote: 'It is beautiful to see Sir Charles Wyndham suiting the action to the word, subtly acting the man who is not an actor, overdoing the joyous gesture, and vacantly continuing it when its significance has had time to evaporate . . . Often as I have seen and shall see again Sir Charles Wyndham in just such a part . . . I cannot and never shall be able to weary of his perfection. The vitality as well as the subtlety of his art makes the thing ever new.'

The following October Wyndham was Lord Bellamy in Horniman's *Bellamy the Magnificent* at the New Theatre. This failed, however, as audiences did not care to see Wyndham in an unsympathetic role. This was to be his last 'new' play. For the rest of his career, although he did not plan it that way, he would appear only in revivals of his old successes. He went back to tour America with *The Mollusc*, and returned to the Criterion in June 1910 with a revival of *Rebellious Susan*. He revived *The Liars* there in October. In May 1911 he played Captain Dudley Smooth in *Money* for a Command Performance at Drury Lane, and the following month for a gala performance at His Majesty's he performed in the second act of *David Garrick*. At the New Theatre in May 1912 he once more played Daniel Carteret in a revival of *Mrs Dane's Defence*. By this time he was suffering very badly from aphasia and learning new parts was impossible; in fact, it was very difficult remembering the names of the most common artifacts of life. He did make a silent film of *David Garrick* — his only film.

Charles Wyndham's wife died in January 1916, and in March Wyndham married Mary at the Chertsey Registry Office. He went into a sharp decline in 1918 and lived mainly in the country at Sunningdale, though it was in London that he died on 12 January 1919; Mary lived until 1931.
See photograph opposite page 391.